Real-Time Data Analysis Exercises

Up-to-date macro data is a great way to engage in and understand the usefulness of macro variables and their impact on the economy. Real-Time Data Analysis exercises communicate directly with the Federal Reserve Bank of St. Louis's FRED site, so every time FRED posts new data, students see new data.

End-of-chapter exercises accompanied by the Real-Time Data Analysis icon include Real-Time Data versions in **MyEconLab**.

Select in-text figures labeled **MyEconLab** Real-Time Data update in the electronic version of the text using FRED data.

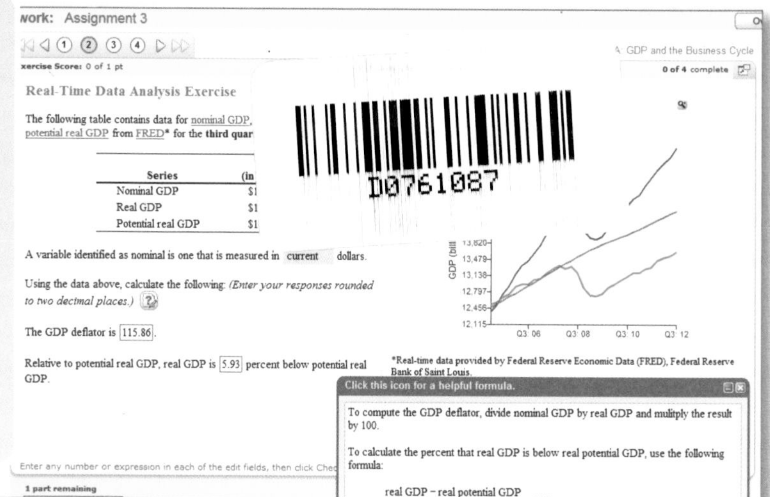

Current News Exercises

Posted weekly, we find the latest microeconomic and macroeconomic news stories, post them, and write auto-graded multi-part exercises that illustrate the economic way of thinking about the news.

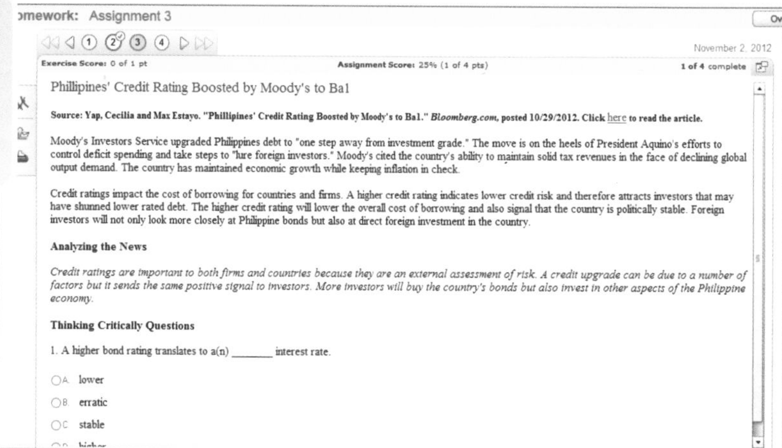

Interactive Homework Exercises

Participate in a fun and engaging activity that helps promote active learning and mastery of important economic concepts.

Pearson's experiments program is flexible and easy for instructors and students to use. For a complete list of available experiments, visit *www.myeconlab.com*.

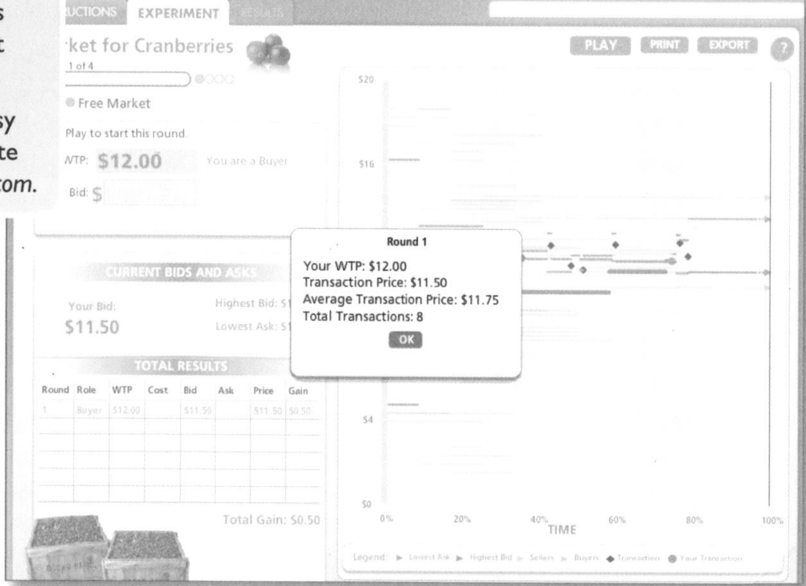

Applying the Concepts Questions and Applications

Chapter 1 Introduction: What Is Economics?

Applying the Concepts #1: How do people respond to incentives?
Application 1: *Incentives to Buy Hybrid Vehicles*

Applying the Concepts #2: What is the role of prices in allocating resources?
Application 2: *The Economic Solution to Spam*

Applying the Concepts #3: How do we compute percentage changes?
Application 3: *The Perils of Percentages*

Chapter 2 The Key Principles of Economics

Applying the Concepts #1: What is the opportunity cost of running a business?
Application 1: *Don't Forget the Costs of Time and Invested Funds*

Applying the Concepts #2: How do people think at the margin?
Application 2: *How Fast to Sail?*

Applying the Concepts #3: What is the rationale for specialization and exchange?
Application 3: *Jasper Johns and Housepainting*

Applying the Concepts #4: Do farmers experience diminishing returns?
Application 4: *Fertilizer and Crop Yields*

Applying the Concepts #5: How does inflation affect lenders and borrowers?
Application 5: *Repaying Student Loans*

Chapter 3 Exchange and Markets

Applying the Concepts #1: What is the rationale for specialization and trade?
Application 1: *Absolute Disadvantage and Comparative Advantage in Latvia*

Applying the Concepts #2: Why do markets develop?
Application 2: *The Market for Meteorites*

Applying the Concepts #3: What is the role of government in a market economy?
Application 3: *Civil Liberties and Efficiency of Government*

Chapter 4 Demand, Supply, and Market Equilibrium

Applying the Concepts #1: What is the law of demand?
Application 1: *Law of Demand and Cigarettes*

Applying the Concepts #2: What is the law of supply?
Application 2: *Law of Supply and Woolympics*

Applying the Concepts #3: What are consequences of a price above the equilibrium price?
Application 3: *Shrinking Wine Lakes*

Applying the Concepts #4: How does a change in demand affect the equilibrium price?
Application 4: *Chinese Demand and Pecan Prices*

Applying the Concepts #5: How does a change in supply affect the equilibrium price?
Application 5: *Honeybees and the Price of Ice Cream*

Applying the Concepts #6: What explains a decrease in price?
Application 6: *Why Lower Drug Prices?*

Chapter 5 Measuring a Nation's Production and Income

Applying the Concepts #1: How can we use economic analysis to compare the size of a major corporation to the size of a country?
Application 1: *Using Value Added to Measure the True Size of Wal-Mart*

Applying the Concepts #2: How long did it take to recover from the last recession?
Application 2: *Recovering from a Recession*

Applying the Concepts #3: Do increases in gross domestic product necessarily translate into improvements in the welfare of citizens?
Application 3: *The Links between Self-Reported Happiness and GDP*

Chapter 6 Unemployment and Inflation

Applying the Concepts #1: What factors account for the decline in the labor force participation rate in the last decade?
Application 1: *Declining Labor Force Participation*

Applying the Concepts #2: Does more liberal disability insurance decrease measured unemployment?
Application 2: *More Disability, Less Unemployment?*

Applying the Concepts #3: Are you less upset about being unemployed if unemployment is common in your peer group?
Application 3: *Social Norms, Unemployment, and Perceived Happiness*

Applying the Concepts #4: How large is the bias in the CPI due to not immediately incorporating new goods?
Application 4: *The Introduction of Cell Phones and the Bias in the CPI*

Chapter 7 The Economy at Full Employment

Applying the Concepts #1: How can changes in the supply of labor affect real wages?
Application 1: *The Black Death and Living Standards in Old England*

Applying the Concepts #2: What evidence is there that taxes on high-paid soccer stars in Europe affect their location decisions among countries?
Application 2: *Do European Soccer Stars Change Clubs to Reduce Their Taxes?*

Applying the Concepts #3: Can real business cycle models explain the origin and persistence of the Great Depression?
Application 3: *Can Labor Market Policies Account for the Great Depression?*

Chapter 8 Why Do Economies Grow?

Applying the Concepts #1: How may global warming affect economic growth?
Application 1: *Global Warming, Rich Countries, and Poor Countries*

Applying the Concepts #2: Is there a necessary trade-off between equality and growth?
Application 2: *Economic Equality May Sustain Economic Growth*

Applying the Concepts #3: How can we use economic analysis to understand the sources of growth in different countries?
Application 3: *Sources of Growth in China and India*

Economics

PRINCIPLES, APPLICATIONS, AND TOOLS

EIGHTH EDITION

The Pearson Series in Economics

Abel/Bernanke/Croushore
*Macroeconomics**

Bade/Parkin
*Foundations of Economics**

Berck/Helfand
The Economics of the Environment

Bierman/Fernandez
Game Theory with Economic Applications

Blanchard
*Macroeconomics**

Blau/Ferber/Winkler
The Economics of Women, Men and Work

Boardman/Greenberg/Vining/Weimer
Cost-Benefit Analysis

Boyer
Principles of Transportation Economics

Branson
Macroeconomic Theory and Policy

Brock/Adams
The Structure of American Industry

Bruce
Public Finance and the American Economy

Carlton/Perloff
Modern Industrial Organization

Case/Fair/Oster
*Principles of Economics**

Caves/Frankel/Jones
World Trade and Payments: An Introduction

Chapman
Environmental Economics: Theory, Application, and Policy

Cooter/Ulen
Law & Economics

Downs
An Economic Theory of Democracy

Ehrenberg/Smith
Modern Labor Economics

Farnham
Economics for Managers

Folland/Goodman/Stano
The Economics of Health and Health Care

Fort
Sports Economics

Froyen
Macroeconomics

Fusfeld
The Age of the Economist

Gerber
*International Economics**

González-Rivera
Forecasting for Economics and Business

Gordon
*Macroeconomics**

Greene
Econometric Analysis

Gregory
Essentials of Economics

Gregory/Stuart
Russian and Soviet Economic Performance and Structure

Hartwick/Olewiler
The Economics of Natural Resource Use

Heilbroner/Milberg
The Making of the Economic Society

Heyne/Boettke/Prychitko
The Economic Way of Thinking

Hoffman/Averett
Women and the Economy: Family, Work, and Pay

Holt
Markets, Games, and Strategic Behavior

Hubbard/O'Brien
*Economics**
*Money, Banking, and the Financial System**

Hubbard/O'Brien/Rafferty
*Macroeconomics**

Hughes/Cain
American Economic History

Husted/Melvin
International Economics

Jehle/Reny
Advanced Microeconomic Theory

Johnson-Lans
A Health Economics Primer

Keat/Young
Managerial Economics

Klein
Mathematical Methods for Economics

Krugman/Obstfeld/Melitz
*International Economics: Theory & Policy**

Laidler
The Demand for Money

Leeds/von Allmen
The Economics of Sports

Leeds/von Allmen/Schiming
*Economics**

Lipsey/Ragan/Storer
*Economics**

Lynn
Economic Development: Theory and Practice for a Divided World

Miller
*Economics Today**
Understanding Modern Economics

Miller/Benjamin
The Economics of Macro Issues

Miller/Benjamin/North
The Economics of Public Issues

Mills/Hamilton
Urban Economics

Mishkin
*The Economics of Money, Banking, and Financial Markets**
*The Economics of Money, Banking, and Financial Markets, Business School Edition**
*Macroeconomics: Policy and Practice**

Murray
Econometrics: A Modern Introduction

Nafziger
The Economics of Developing Countries

O'Sullivan/Sheffrin/Perez
*Economics: Principles, Applications, and Tools**

Parkin
*Economics**

Perloff
*Microeconomics**
*Microeconomics: Theory and Applications with Calculus**

Phelps
Health Economics

Pindyck/Rubinfeld
*Microeconomics**

Riddell/Shackelford/Stamos/Schneider
Economics: A Tool for Critically Understanding Society

Ritter/Silber/Udell
*Principles of Money, Banking, & Financial Markets**

Roberts
The Choice: A Fable of Free Trade and Protection

Rohlf
Introduction to Economic Reasoning

Ruffin/Gregory
Principles of Economics

Sargent
Rational Expectations and Inflation

Sawyer/Sprinkle
International Economics

Scherer
Industry Structure, Strategy, and Public Policy

Schiller
The Economics of Poverty and Discrimination

Sherman
Market Regulation

Silberberg
Principles of Microeconomics

Stock/Watson
Introduction to Econometrics

Studenmund
Using Econometrics: A Practical Guide

Tietenberg/Lewis
Environmental and Natural Resource Economics
Environmental Economics and Policy

Todaro/Smith
Economic Development

Waldman
Microeconomics

Waldman/Jensen
Industrial Organization: Theory and Practice

Walters/Walters/Appel/Callahan/Centanni/Maex/O'Neill
Econversations: Today's Students Discuss Today's Issues

Weil
Economic Growth

Williamson
*Macroeconomics**

* denotes MyEconLab titles

Visit www.myeconlab.com to learn more

Editor in Chief: Donna Battista
Executive Editor: David Alexander
Senior Acquisitions Editor: Noel Seibert
Digital Publisher, Economics: Denise Clinton
Senior Editorial Project Manager: Carolyn Terbush
Managing Editor: Jeff Holcomb
Senior Production Project Manager: Meredith Gertz
Director of Marketing: Maggie Moylan
Executive Marketing Manager: Lori DeShazo
Marketing Assistant: Kim Lovato
Editorial Assistant: Emily Brodeur
Art Director/Cover Designer: Jonathan Boylan
Manager, Rights and Permissions, Text: Jill Dougan
Image Manager/Image Asset Services: Rachel Youdelman
Photo Research: Integra Software Services, Ltd.
Cover Image: Shutterstock/AlexRoz
Media Director: Susan Schoenberg
Senior Media Producer: Melissa Honig
Content Leads, MyEconLab: Noel Lotz, Courtney Kamauf
Senior Manufacturing Buyer: Carol Melville
Full-Service Project Management, Composition, Text Illustrations, and Text Design: GEX Publishing Services
Printer/Binder: Courier Kendallville
Cover Printer: Lehigh, Phoenix/Hagerstown
Text Font: 10/12 Janson Text

Credits and acknowledgments borrowed from other sources and reproduced, with permission, in this textbook appear on appropriate page within text (or on page 730).

Library of Congress Cataloging-in-Publication Data
O'Sullivan, Arthur.
Economics : principles, applications, and tools / Arthur O'Sullivan, Steven M. Sheffrin, Stephen J. Perez. -- 8th ed.
p. cm.
Includes index.
ISBN-13: 978-0-13-294933-0
ISBN-10: 0-13-294933-4
1. Economics. I. Sheffrin, Steven M. II. Perez, Stephen J. III. Title.
HB171.5.O84 2014
330--dc23

2012041515

10 9 8 7 6 5 4 3 2 1

www.pearsonhighered.com

ISBN 10: 0-13-294933-4
ISBN 13: 978-0-13-294933-0

Economics

PRINCIPLES, APPLICATIONS, AND TOOLS

EIGHTH EDITION

Arthur O'Sullivan
Lewis and Clark College

Steven M. Sheffrin
Tulane University

Stephen J. Perez
California State University, Sacramento

PEARSON

Boston Columbus Indianapolis New York San Francisco Upper Saddle River
Amsterdam Cape Town Dubai London Madrid Milan Munich Paris Montréal Toronto
Delhi Mexico City São Paulo Sydney Hong Kong Seoul Singapore Taipei Tokyo

To Our Children

Conor, Maura, Meera, Kiran, Davis, and Tate

About the Authors

ARTHUR O'SULLIVAN

is a professor of economics at Lewis and Clark College in Portland, Oregon. After receiving his B.S. in economics at the University of Oregon, he spent two years in the Peace Corps, working with city planners in the Philippines. He received his Ph.D. in economics from Princeton University in 1981 and has taught at the University of California, Davis, and Oregon State University, winning teaching awards at both schools. He is the author of the best-selling textbook *Urban Economics*, currently in its eighth edition, with translations into Russian, Chinese, Korean, and Greek.

Professor O'Sullivan's research explores economic issues concerning urban land use, environmental protection, and public policy. His articles have appeared in many economics journals, including the *Journal of Urban Economics*, *Journal of Environmental Economics and Management*, *National Tax Journal*, *Journal of Public Economics*, and *Journal of Law and Economics*.

Professor O'Sullivan lives with his family in Portland, Oregon. For recreation, he enjoys hiking, kiteboarding, and squash.

STEVEN M. SHEFFRIN

is professor of economics and executive director of the Murphy Institute at Tulane University. Prior to joining Tulane in 2010, he was a faculty member at the University of California, Davis, and served as department chairman of economics and dean of social sciences. He has been a visiting professor at Princeton University, Oxford University, London School of Economics, and Nanyang Technological University, and he has served as a financial economist with the Office of Tax Analysis of the United States Department of the Treasury. He received his B.A. from Wesleyan University and his Ph.D. in economics from the Massachusetts Institute of Technology.

Professor Sheffrin is the author of 10 other books and monographs and over 100 articles in the fields of macroeconomics, public finance, and international economics. His most recent books include *Rational Expectations* (second edition) and *Property Taxes and Tax Revolts: The Legacy of Proposition 13* (with Arthur O'Sullivan and Terri Sexton).

Professor Sheffrin has taught macroeconomics and public finance at all levels, from general introduction to principles classes (enrollments of 400) to graduate classes for doctoral students. He is the recipient of the Thomas Mayer Distinguished Teaching Award in economics.

He lives with his wife Anjali (also an economist) in New Orleans, Louisiana, and has two daughters who have studied economics. In addition to a passion for current affairs and travel, he plays a tough game of tennis.

STEPHEN J. PEREZ

is a professor of economics and NCAA faculty athletics representative at California State University, Sacramento. After receiving his B.A. in economics at the University of California, San Diego, he was awarded his Ph.D. in economics from the University of California, Davis, in 1994. He taught economics at Virginia Commonwealth University and Washington State University before coming to California State University, Sacramento, in 2001. He teaches macroeconomics at all levels as well as econometrics, sports economics, labor economics, and mathematics for economists.

Professor Perez's research explores most macroeconomic topics. In particular, he is interested in evaluating the ability of econometric techniques to discover the truth, issues of causality in macroeconomics, and sports economics. His articles have appeared in many economics journals, including the *Journal of Monetary Economics*; *Econometrics Journal*; *Economics Letters*; *Journal of Economic Methodology*; *Public Finance and Management*; *Journal of Economics and Business*; *Oxford Bulletin of Economics and Statistics*; *Journal of Money, Credit, and Banking*; *Applied Economics*; and *Journal of Macroeconomics*.

Brief Contents

PART 1 Introduction and Key Principles

1 Introduction: What Is Economics? 1
2 The Key Principles of Economics 28
3 Exchange and Markets 49
4 Demand, Supply, and Market Equilibrium 67

PART 2 The Basic Concepts in Macroeconomics

5 Measuring a Nation's Production and Income 97
6 Unemployment and Inflation 120

PART 3 The Economy in the Long Run

7 The Economy at Full Employment 139
8 Why Do Economies Grow? 159

PART 4 Economic Fluctuations and Fiscal Policy

9 Aggregate Demand and Aggregate Supply 185
10 Fiscal Policy 205
11 The Income-Expenditure Model 223
12 Investment and Financial Markets 253

PART 5 Money, Banking, and Monetary Policy

13 Money and the Banking System 272
14 The Federal Reserve and Monetary Policy 291

PART 6 Inflation, Unemployment, and Economic Policy

15 Modern Macroeconomics: From the Short Run to the Long Run 311
16 The Dynamics of Inflation and Unemployment 329
17 Macroeconomic Policy Debates 347

PART 7 The International Economy

18 International Trade and Public Policy 364
19 The World of International Finance 385

PART 8 A Closer Look at Demand and Supply

20 Elasticity: A Measure of Responsiveness 409
21 Market Efficiency and Government Intervention 439
22 Consumer Choice: Utility Theory and Insights from Neuroscience 464

PART 9 Market Structures and Pricing

23 Production Technology and Cost 497
24 Perfect Competition 519
25 Monopoly and Price Discrimination 545
26 Market Entry and Monopolistic Competition 566
27 Oligopoly and Strategic Behavior 582
28 Controlling Market Power: Antitrust and Regulation 609

PART 10 Externalities and Information

29 Imperfect Information: Adverse Selection and Moral Hazard 625
30 Public Goods and Public Choice 651
31 External Costs and Environmental Policy 668

PART 11 The Labor Market and Income Distribution

32 The Labor Market and the Distribution of Income 689

Contents

Preface xxxiv

PART 1
Introduction and Key Principles

1 Introduction: What Is Economics? 1

What Is Economics 2

Positive versus Normative Analysis 3

The Three Key Economic Questions: What, How, and Who? 4

Economic Models 4

Economic Analysis and Modern Problems 5

Economic View of Traffic Congestion 5

Economic View of Poverty in Africa 5

Economic View of the Current World Recession 6

The Economic Way of Thinking 7

Use Assumptions to Simplify 7

Isolate Variables—*Ceteris Paribus* 7

Think at the Margin 8

Rational People Respond to Incentives 8

APPLICATION 1 Incentives to Buy Hybrid Vehicles 9

Example: London Addresses Its Congestion Problem 9

APPLICATION 2 The Economic Solution to Spam 10

Preview of Coming Attractions: Macroeconomics 10

Using Macroeconomics to Understand Why Economies Grow 11

Using Macroeconomics to Understand Economic Fluctuations 11

Using Macroeconomics to Make Informed Business Decisions 11

Preview of Coming Attractions: Microeconomics 12

Using Microeconomics to Understand Markets and Predict Changes 12

Using Microeconomics to Make Personal and Managerial Decisions 12

Using Microeconomics to Evaluate Public Policies 12

* SUMMARY 13 * KEY TERMS 13

* EXERCISES 13

APPENDIX: Using Graphs and Percentages 15

USING GRAPHS 15

COMPUTING PERCENTAGE CHANGES AND USING EQUATIONS 23

APPLICATION 3 The Perils of Percentages 24

2 The Key Principles of Economics 28

The Principle of Opportunity Cost 29

The Cost of College 29

The Cost of Military Spending 30

Opportunity Cost and the Production Possibilities Curve 31

APPLICATION 1 Don't Forget the Costs of Time and Invested Funds 33

The Marginal Principle 33

How Many Movie Sequels? 34

Renting College Facilities 35

Automobile Emissions Standards 35

Driving Speed and Safety 36

APPLICATION 2 How Fast to Sail? 36

The Principle of Voluntary Exchange 37

Exchange and Markets 37

Online Games and Market Exchange 38

APPLICATION 3 Jasper Johns and Housepainting 38

The Principle of Diminishing Returns 39

APPLICATION 4 Fertilizer and Crop Yields 40

The Real-Nominal Principle 40

The Design of Public Programs 41

The Value of the Minimum Wage 41

APPLICATION 5 Repaying Student Loans 42

* SUMMARY 43 * KEY TERMS 43
* EXERCISES 43

* ECONOMIC EXPERIMENT 47

3 Exchange and Markets 49

Comparative Advantage and Exchange 50

Specialization and the Gains from Trade 50

Comparative Advantage versus Absolute Advantage 52

The Division of Labor and Exchange 53

Comparative Advantage and International Trade 53

Outsourcing 54

APPLICATION 1 Absolute Disadvantage and Comparative Advantage in Latvia 55

Markets 55

Virtues of Markets 56

The Role of Entrepreneurs 58

Example of the Emergence of Markets: POW Camps 58

APPLICATION 2 The Market for Meteorites 59

Market Failure and the Role of Government 59

Government Enforces the Rules of Exchange 60

Government Can Reduce Economic Uncertainty 61

APPLICATION 3 Civil Liberties and Efficiency of Government 62

* SUMMARY 62 * KEY TERMS 63
* EXERCISES 63

4 Demand, Supply, and Market Equilibrium 67

The Demand Curve 68

The Individual Demand Curve and the Law of Demand 68

From Individual Demand to Market Demand 70

APPLICATION 1 Law of Demand and Cigarettes 71

The Supply Curve 71

The Individual Supply Curve and the Law of Supply 72

Why Is the Individual Supply Curve Positively Sloped? 73

From Individual Supply to Market Supply 74

Why Is the Market Supply Curve Positively Sloped? 75

APPLICATION 2 Law of Supply and Woolympics 76

Market Equilibrium: Bringing Demand and Supply Together 76

Excess Demand Causes the Price to Rise 76

Excess Supply Causes the Price to Drop 77

APPLICATION 3 Shrinking Wine Lakes 78

Market Effects of Changes in Demand 78

Change in Quantity Demanded versus Change in Demand 78

Increases in Demand Shift the Demand Curve 79

Decreases in Demand Shift the Demand Curve 81

A Decrease in Demand Decreases the Equilibrium Price 82

APPLICATION 4 Chinese Demand and Pecan Prices 82

Market Effects of Changes in Supply 83

Change in Quantity Supplied versus Change in Supply 83

Increases in Supply Shift the Supply Curve 83

An Increase in Supply Decreases the Equilibrium Price 85

Decreases in Supply Shift the Supply Curve 86

A Decrease in Supply Increases the Equilibrium Price 87

Simultaneous Changes in Demand and Supply 87

APPLICATION 5 Honeybees and the Price of Ice Cream 89

Predicting and Explaining Market Changes 90

APPLICATION 6 Why Lower Drug Prices? 90

* SUMMARY 91 * KEY TERMS 91
* EXERCISES 91

* ECONOMIC EXPERIMENT 96

PART 2
The Basic Concepts in Macroeconomics

5 Measuring a Nation's Production and Income 97

The "Flip" Sides of Macroeconomic Activity: Production and Income 98

The Circular Flow of Production and Income 99

APPLICATION 1 Using Value Added to Measure the True Size of Wal-Mart 100

The Production Approach: Measuring a Nation's Macroeconomic Activity Using Gross Domestic Product 100

The Components of GDP 102

Putting It All Together: The GDP Equation 105

APPLICATION 2 Recovering from a Recession 106

The Income Approach: Measuring a Nation's Macroeconomic Activity Using National Income 106

Measuring National Income 106

Measuring National Income through Value Added 107

An Expanded Circular Flow 108

APPLICATION 3 The Links between Self-Reported Happiness and GDP 109

A Closer Examination of Nominal and Real GDP 109

Measuring Real versus Nominal GDP 109

How to Use the GDP Deflator 110

Fluctuations in GDP 112

GDP as a Measure of Welfare 113

Shortcomings of GDP as a Measure of Welfare 114

* SUMMARY 115 * KEY TERMS 115
* EXERCISES 116

6 Unemployment and Inflation 120

Examining Unemployment 121

How Is Unemployment Defined and Measured? 121

Alternative Measures of Unemployment and Why They Are Important 122

Who Are the Unemployed? 123

APPLICATION 1 Declining Labor Force Participation 125

Categories of Unemployment 125

Types of Unemployment: Cyclical, Frictional, and Structural 125

The Natural Rate of Unemployment 126

APPLICATION 2 More Disability, Less Unemployment? 127

The Costs of Unemployment 128

APPLICATION 3 Social Norms, Unemployment, and Perceived Happiness 129

The Consumer Price Index and the Cost of Living 129

The CPI versus the Chain Index for GDP 130

Problems in Measuring Changes in Prices 131

APPLICATION 4 The Introduction of Cell Phones and the Bias in the CPI 132

Inflation 132

Historical U.S. Inflation Rates 132

The Perils of Deflation 133

The Costs of Inflation 134

Anticipated Inflation 134

Unanticipated Inflation 135

* SUMMARY 136 * KEY TERMS 136
* EXERCISES 136

PART 3
The Economy in the Long Run

7 The Economy at Full Employment 139

Wage and Price Flexibility and Full Employment 140

The Production Function 140

Wages and the Demand and Supply for Labor 143

Labor Market Equilibrium 144

Changes in Demand and Supply 144

APPLICATION 1 The Black Death and Living Standards in Old England 145

Labor Market Equilibrium and Full Employment 146

Using the Full-Employment Model 147

Taxes and Potential Output 147

Real Business Cycle Theory 148

APPLICATION 2 Do European Soccer Stars Change Clubs to Reduce Their Taxes? 150

APPLICATION 3 Can Labor Market Policies Account for the Great Depression? 151

Dividing Output among Competing Demands for GDP at Full Employment 151

International Comparisons 152

Crowding Out in a Closed Economy 152

Crowding Out in an Open Economy 154

Crowding In 154

* SUMMARY 155 * KEY TERMS 155
* EXERCISES 155

8 Why Do Economies Grow? 159

Economic Growth Rates 160

Measuring Economic Growth 161

Comparing the Growth Rates of Various Countries 162

Are Poor Countries Catching Up? 163

APPLICATION 1 Global Warming, Rich Countries, and Poor Countries 164

APPLICATION 2 Economic Equality May Sustain Economic Growth 165

Capital Deepening 165

Saving and Investment 166

How Do Population Growth, Government, and Trade Affect Capital Deepening? 167

The Key Role of Technological Progress 168

How Do We Measure Technological Progress? 169

Using Growth Accounting 170

APPLICATION 3 Sources of Growth in China and India 170

APPLICATION 4 Growth Accounting and Intangible Capital 171

What Causes Technological Progress? 172

Research and Development Funding 172

Monopolies That Spur Innovation 172

The Scale of the Market 173

Induced Innovations 173

Education, Human Capital, and the Accumulation of Knowledge 173

New Growth Theory 174

APPLICATION 5 The Role of Political Factors in Economic Growth 174

APPLICATION 6 Culture, Evolution, and Economic Growth 175

A Key Governmental Role: Providing the Correct Incentives and Property Rights 176

APPLICATION 7 Lack of Property Rights Hinders Growth in Peru 177

* SUMMARY 177 * KEY TERMS 178
* EXERCISES 178

APPENDIX A: A Model of Capital Deepening 180

PART 4
Economic Fluctuations and Fiscal Policy

9 Aggregate Demand and Aggregate Supply 185

Sticky Prices and Their Macroeconomic Consequences 186

Flexible and Sticky Prices 186

How Demand Determines Output in the Short Run 187

APPLICATION 1 Measuring Price Stickiness in Consumer Markets 188

Understanding Aggregate Demand 188

What Is the Aggregate Demand Curve? 188

The Components of Aggregate Demand 189

Why the Aggregate Demand Curve Slopes Downward 189

Shifts in the Aggregate Demand Curve 190

How the Multiplier Makes the Shift Bigger 192

APPLICATION 2 Two Approaches to Determining the Causes of Recessions 195

Understanding Aggregate Supply 196

The Long-Run Aggregate Supply Curve 196

The Short-Run Aggregate Supply Curve 197

APPLICATION 3 Oil Supply Disruptions, Speculation and Supply Shocks 199

Supply Shocks 199

From the Short Run to the Long Run 200

* SUMMARY 202 * KEY TERMS 202
* EXERCISES 202

10 Fiscal Policy 205

The Role of Fiscal Policy 206

Fiscal Policy and Aggregate Demand 206

The Fiscal Multiplier 207

The Limits to Stabilization Policy 208

APPLICATION 1 Increasing Life Expectancy and Aging Populations Spur Costs of Entitlement Programs 210

The Federal Budget 211

Federal Spending 211

Federal Revenues 212

The Federal Deficit and Fiscal Policy 214

Automatic Stabilizers 214

Are Deficits Bad? 215

APPLICATION 2 The Confucius Curve? 216

Fiscal Policy in U.S. History 216

The Depression Era 216

The Kennedy Administration 217

The Vietnam War Era 217

The Reagan Administration 218

The Clinton and George W. Bush Administrations 218

APPLICATION 3 A Closer Look at the 2009 Stimulus Package 219

* SUMMARY 220 * KEY TERMS 220
* EXERCISES 221

11 The Income-Expenditure Model 223

A Simple Income-Expenditure Model 224

Equilibrium Output 224

Adjusting to Equilibrium Output 226

The Consumption Function 227

Consumer Spending and Income 227

Changes in the Consumption Function 228

APPLICATION 1 Falling Home Prices, the Wealth Effect, and Decreased Consumer Spending 229

Equilibrium Output and the Consumption Function 229

Saving and Investment 230

Understanding the Multiplier 232

APPLICATION 2 Using Long-Term Macro Data to Measure Multipliers 233

Government Spending and Taxation 233

Fiscal Multipliers 234

Using Fiscal Multipliers 235

Understanding Automatic Stabilizers 237

APPLICATION 3 The Broken Window Fallacy and Keynesian Economics 238

Exports and Imports 241

APPLICATION 4 The Locomotive Effect: How Foreign Demand Affects a Country's Output 243

The Income-Expenditure Model and the Aggregate Demand Curve 243

* SUMMARY 245 * KEY TERMS 246
* EXERCISES 246

* ECONOMIC EXPERIMENT 248

APPENDIX: Formulas for Equilibrium Income and the Multiplier 249

12 Investment and Financial Markets 253

An Investment: A Plunge into the Unknown 254

APPLICATION 1 Energy Price Uncertainty Reduces Investment Spending 255

Evaluating the Future 256

Understanding Present Value 256

Real and Nominal Interest Rates 258

APPLICATION 2 The Value of an Annuity 259

Understanding Investment Decisions 260

Investment and the Stock Market 261

APPLICATION 3 Debt Forgiveness? 263

How Financial Intermediaries Facilitate Investment 263

When Financial Intermediaries Malfunction 265

APPLICATION 4 Securitization: The Good, the Bad, and the Ugly 267

* SUMMARY 268 * KEY TERMS 268
* EXERCISES 269

* ECONOMIC EXPERIMENT 270

PART 5 Money, Banking, and Monetary Policy

13 Money and the Banking System 272

What *Is* Money? 273

Three Properties of Money 273

Measuring Money in the U.S. Economy 275

APPLICATION 1 Money with the Face of Rodents 276

How Banks Create Money 277

A Bank's Balance Sheet: Where the Money Comes from and Where It Goes 277

How Banks Create Money 278

How the Money Multiplier Works 279

How the Money Multiplier Works in Reverse 280

APPLICATION 2 The Growth in Excess Reserves 280

A Banker's Bank: The Federal Reserve 281

Functions of the Federal Reserve 281

The Structure of the Federal Reserve 282

The Independence of the Federal Reserve 283

What the Federal Reserve Does during a Financial Crisis 284

APPLICATION 3 The Financial System under Stress: September 11, 2001 284

APPLICATION 4 Coping with the Financial Chaos Caused by the Mortgage Crisis 285

* SUMMARY 286 * KEY TERMS 286
* EXERCISES 286

* ECONOMIC EXPERIMENT 288

APPENDIX: Formula for Deposit Creation 290

14 The Federal Reserve and Monetary Policy 291

The Money Market 292

The Demand for Money 292

APPLICATION 1 Beyond Purchasing Treasury Securities 294

How the Federal Reserve Can Change the Money Supply 295

Open Market Operations 295

Other Tools of the Fed 296

APPLICATION 2 Did Fed Policy Cause the Commodity Boom? 297

How Interest Rates Are Determined: Combining the Demand and Supply of Money 297

Interest Rates and Bond Prices 299

APPLICATION 3 The Effectiveness of Committees 301

Interest Rates and How They Change Investment and Output (GDP) 301

Monetary Policy and International Trade 303

Monetary Policy Challenges for the Fed 305

Lags in Monetary Policy 305

Influencing Market Expectations: From the Federal Funds Rate to Interest Rates on Long-Term Bonds 306

* SUMMARY 307 * KEY TERMS 308
* EXERCISES 308

PART 6
Inflation, Unemployment, and Economic Policy

15 Modern Macroeconomics: From the Short Run to the Long Run 311

Linking the Short Run and the Long Run 312

The Difference between the Short and Long Run 312

Wages and Prices and Their Adjustment over Time 312

APPLICATION 1 How to Fight a Liquidity Trap 313

How Wage and Price Changes Move the Economy Naturally Back to Full Employment 314

Returning to Full Employment from a Recession 314

Returning to Full Employment from a Boom 315

Economic Policy and the Speed of Adjustment 316

Liquidity Traps 317

Political Business Cycles 318

APPLICATION 2 Elections, Political Parties, and Voter Expectations 318

Understanding the Economics of the Adjustment Process 319

The Long-Run Neutrality of Money 320

Crowding Out in the Long Run 322

APPLICATION 3 Increasing Health-Care Expenditures and Crowding Out 323

Classical Economics in Historical Perspective 324

Say's Law 324

Keynesian and Classical Debates 325

* SUMMARY 325 * KEY TERMS 326
* EXERCISES 326

16 The Dynamics of Inflation and Unemployment 329

Money Growth, Inflation, and Interest Rates 330

Inflation in a Steady State 330

How Changes in the Growth Rate of Money Affect the Steady State 331

APPLICATION 1 Shifts in the Natural Rate of Unemployment 332

Understanding the Expectations Phillips Curve: The Relationship between Unemployment and Inflation 333

Are the Public's Expectations about Inflation Rational? 334

U.S. Inflation and Unemployment in the 1980s 334

Shifts in the Natural Rate of Unemployment in the 1990s 336

APPLICATION 2 Increased Political Independence for the Bank of England Lowered Inflation Expectations 337

How the Credibility of a Nation's Central Bank Affects Inflation 337

APPLICATION 3 The Ends of Hyperinflations 339

Inflation and the Velocity of Money 340

Hyperinflation 341

How Budget Deficits Lead to Hyperinflation 343

* SUMMARY 344 * KEY TERMS 344
* EXERCISES 344

* ECONOMIC EXPERIMENT 346

17 Macroeconomic Policy Debates 347

Should We Balance the Federal Budget? 348

The Budget in Recent Decades 348

Five Debates about Deficits 350

APPLICATION 1 Creating the U.S. Federal Fiscal System through Debt Policy 354

Should the Fed Target Both Inflation and Employment? 355

Two Debates about Targeting 355

APPLICATION 2 Would a Policy Rule Have Prevented the Housing Boom? 357

Should We Tax Consumption Rather than Income? 358

Two Debates about Consumption Taxation 358

APPLICATION 3 Is a VAT in Our Future? 360

* SUMMARY 361 * KEY TERMS 361
* EXERCISES 361

PART 7
The International Economy

18 International Trade and Public Policy 364

Benefits from Specialization and Trade 365

Production Possibilities Curve 365

Comparative Advantage and the Terms of Trade 367

The Consumption Possibilities Curve 367

How Free Trade Affects Employment 368

Protectionist Policies 369

Import Bans 369

Quotas and Voluntary Export Restraints 370

Responses to Protectionist Policies 371

APPLICATION 1 The Impact of Tariffs on the Poor 372

What Are the Rationales for Protectionist Policies? 372

To Shield Workers from Foreign Competition 373

To Nurture Infant Industries until They Mature 373

To Help Domestic Firms Establish Monopolies in World Markets 373

APPLICATION 2 Chinese Imports and Local Economies 374

A Brief History of International Tariff and Trade Agreements 374

Recent Policy Debates and Trade Agreements 376

Are Foreign Producers Dumping Their Products? 376

APPLICATION 3 Are They Really Dumping? 376

Do Trade Laws Inhibit Environmental Protection? 377

APPLICATION 4 Trade, Consumption, and Inequality 379

Do Outsourcing and Trade Cause Income Inequality? 379

Why Do People Protest Free Trade? 380

* SUMMARY 381 * KEY TERMS 381
* EXERCISES 381

19 The World of International Finance 385

How Exchange Rates Are Determined 386

What Are Exchange Rates? 386

How Demand and Supply Determine Exchange Rates 387

Changes in Demand or Supply 388

Real Exchange Rates and Purchasing Power Parity 390

APPLICATION 1 The Chinese Yuan and Big Macs 392

The Current Account, the Financial Account, and the Capital Account 393

Rules for Calculating the Current, Financial, and Capital Accounts 394

APPLICATION 2 World Savings and U.S. Current Account Deficits 396

Fixed and Flexible Exchange Rates 397

Fixing the Exchange Rate 398

Fixed versus Flexible Exchange Rates 399

The U.S. Experience with Fixed and Flexible Exchange Rates 400

Exchange Rate Systems Today 401

APPLICATION 3 A Troubled Euro 402

Managing Financial Crises 402

APPLICATION 4 The Argentine Financial Crisis 404

* SUMMARY 405 * KEY TERMS 405
* EXERCISES 405

* ECONOMIC EXPERIMENT 408

PART 8 A Closer Look at Demand and Supply

20 Elasticity: A Measure of Responsiveness 409

The Price Elasticity of Demand 410

Computing Percentage Changes and Elasticities 411

Price Elasticity and the Demand Curve 412

Elasticity and the Availability of Substitutes 413

Other Determinants of the Price Elasticity of Demand 414

APPLICATION 1 A Closer Look at the Elasticity of Demand for Gasoline 415

Using Price Elasticity 416

Predicting Changes in Quantity 416

Price Elasticity and Total Revenue 417

Using Elasticity to Predict the Revenue Effects of Price Changes 418

APPLICATION 2 Vanity Plates and the Elasticity of Demand 419

Elasticity and Total Revenue for a Linear Demand Curve 420

Price Elasticity along a Linear Demand Curve 420

Elasticity and Total Revenue for a Linear Demand Curve 421

APPLICATION 3 Trampolines and the Lower Half of a Linear Demand Curve 422

Other Elasticities of Demand 422

Income Elasticity of Demand 422

Cross-Price Elasticity of Demand 423

APPLICATION 4 I Can Find that Elasticity in Four Clicks! 424

The Price Elasticity of Supply 424

What Determines the Price Elasticity of Supply? 425

The Role of Time: Short-Run versus Long-Run Supply Elasticity 426

Extreme Cases: Perfectly Inelastic Supply and Perfectly Elastic Supply 426

Predicting Changes in Quantity Supplied 427

APPLICATION 5 The Short-Run and Long-Run Elasticity of Supply of Milk 428

Using Elasticities to Predict Changes in Prices 428

The Price Effects of a Change in Demand 428

The Price Effects of a Change in Supply 430

APPLICATION 6 A Broken Pipeline and the Price of Gasoline 432

* SUMMARY 432 * KEY TERMS 433
* EXERCISES 433

21 Market Efficiency and Government Intervention 439

Consumer Surplus and Producer Surplus 440

The Demand Curve and Consumer Surplus 441

The Supply Curve and Producer Surplus 442

APPLICATION 1 Consumer Surplus of Internet Service 443

Market Equilibrium and Efficiency 443

Total Surplus Is Lower with a Price below the Equilibrium Price 444

Total Surplus Is Lower with a Price above the Equilibrium Price 445

Efficiency and the Invisible Hand 445

Government Intervention in Efficient Markets 445

APPLICATION 2 Rent Control and Mismatches 446

Controlling Prices—Maximum and Minimum Prices 446

Setting Maximum Prices 446

Rent Control 447

Setting Minimum Prices 448

APPLICATION 3 Price Controls and the Shrinking Candy Bar 449

Controlling Quantities—Licensing and Import Restrictions 449

Taxi Medallions 449

Licensing and Market Efficiency 450

Winners and Losers from Licensing 451

Import Restrictions 451

APPLICATION 4 The Cost of Protecting a Luggage Job 452

Who Really Pays Taxes? 453

Tax Shifting: Forward and Backward 453

Tax Shifting and the Price Elasticity of Demand 454

Cigarette Taxes and Tobacco Land 455

The Luxury Boat Tax and Boat Workers 455

Tax Burden and Deadweight Loss 455

APPLICATION 5 Response to Lower Taxes in French Restaurants 457

* SUMMARY 458 * KEY TERMS 458
* EXERCISES 458

* ECONOMIC EXPERIMENT 463

22 Consumer Choice: Utility Theory and Insights from Neuroscience 464

Traditional Consumer Choice: Utility Theory 465

Consumer Constraints: The Budget Line 465

Total and Marginal Utility 467

The Marginal Principle and the Equimarginal Rule 468

Conditions for Utility Maximization 470

APPLICATION 1 Measuring Diminishing Marginal Utility 472

The Law of Demand and the Individual Demand Curve 472

Effect of a Decrease in Price 472

Income and Substitution Effects of a Decrease in Price 474

The Individual Demand Curve 475

APPLICATION 2 A Revenue-Neutral Gasoline Tax 476

The Neuroscience of Consumer Choice 477

The Neuroscience of Benefit Valuation 477

The Neuroscience of Cost Valuation 478

The Wisdom of Gut Feelings 479

Cognition and Choice 479

Predicting Consumer Choice 480

Fuel for Cognition 480

APPLICATION 3 Stores vs. Online Retailers 481

Consumer Decisions: Insights from Neuroscience 482

Dietary Choice: Donut versus Apple 482

Present Bias: Spending versus Saving 483

Present Bias and Credit Cards 485

Present Bias and Smoking 486

Gambling as a Consumer Good 486

APPLICATION 4 Taxing Cigarettes to Offset Present Bias 488

* SUMMARY 488 * EXERCISES 489

APPENDIX to Chapter 22: Mental Shortcuts and Consumer Puzzles 493

PART 9 Market Structures and Pricing

23 Production Technology and Cost 497

Economic Cost and Economic Profit 498

APPLICATION 1 Opportunity Cost and Entrepreneurship 499

A Firm with a Fixed Production Facility: Short-Run Costs 499

Production and Marginal Product 499

Short-Run Total Cost 501

Short-Run Average Costs 502

Short-Run Marginal Cost 504

The Relationship between Marginal Cost and Average Cost 505

APPLICATION 2 Idle Capital and Short-Run Marginal Cost 506

Production and Cost in the Long Run 506

Expansion and Replication 507

Reducing Output with Indivisible Inputs 508

Scaling Down and Labor Specialization 509

Economies of Scale 509

Diseconomies of Scale 509

Actual Long-Run Average-Cost Curves 510

Short-Run versus Long-Run Average Cost 511

APPLICATION 3 Indivisible Inputs and the Cost of Fake Killer Whales 511

Examples of Production Cost 512

Scale Economies in Wind Power 512

The Average Cost of a Music Video 513

Solar versus Nuclear: The Crossover 513

* SUMMARY 514 * KEY TERMS 515
* EXERCISES 515

24 Perfect Competition 519

Preview of the Four Market Structures 520

APPLICATION 1 Wireless Women in Pakistan 522

The Firm's Short-Run Output Decision 522

The Total Approach: Computing Total Revenue and Total Cost 522

The Marginal Approach 524

Economic Profit and the Break-Even Price 525

APPLICATION 2 The Break-Even Price for Switchgrass, A Feedstock for Biofuel 526

The Firm's Shut-Down Decision 527

Total Revenue, Variable Cost, and the Shut-Down Decision 527

The Shut-Down Price 528

Fixed Costs and Sunk Costs 529

APPLICATION 3 Straddling the Zinc Cost Curve 529

Short-Run Supply Curves 530

The Firm's Short-Run Supply Curve 530

The Short-Run Market Supply Curve 530

Market Equilibrium 531

APPLICATION 4 Short-Run Supply Curve for Cargo 532

The Long-Run Supply Curve for an Increasing-Cost Industry 532

Production Cost and Industry Size 533

Drawing the Long-Run Market Supply Curve 533

Examples of Increasing-Cost Industries: Sugar and Apartments 534

APPLICATION 5 Chinese Coffee Growers Obey the Law of Supply 535

Short-Run and Long-Run Effects of Changes in Demand 535

The Short-Run Response to an Increase in Demand 535

The Long-Run Response to an Increase in Demand 536

APPLICATION 6 The Upward Jump and Downward Slide of Wine Prices 537

Long-Run Supply for a Constant-Cost Industry 537

Long-Run Supply Curve for a Constant-Cost Industry 537

Hurricane Andrew and the Price of Ice 538

APPLICATION 7 Economic Detective and the Case of Margarine Prices 539

* SUMMARY 539 * KEY TERMS 540
* EXERCISES 540

25 Monopoly and Price Discrimination 545

The Monopolist's Output Decision 546

Total Revenue and Marginal Revenue 547

A Formula for Marginal Revenue 548

Using the Marginal Principle 549

APPLICATION 1 Marginal Revenue from a Baseball Fan 551

The Social Cost of Monopoly 552

Deadweight Loss from Monopoly 552

Rent Seeking: Using Resources to Get Monopoly Power 554

APPLICATION 2 A Casino Monopoly in Creswell, Oregon? 554

Monopoly and Public Policy 555

Patents and Monopoly Power 555

Incentives for Innovation 555

Trade-Offs from Patents 555

APPLICATION 3 Bribing the Makers of Generic Drugs 556

Price Discrimination 557

Senior Discounts in Restaurants 558

Price Discrimination and the Elasticity of Demand 558

Examples: Movie Admission versus Popcorn, and Hardback versus Paperback Books 559

APPLICATION 4 Why Does Movie Popcorn Cost So Much? 560

* SUMMARY 560 * KEY TERMS 561
* EXERCISES 561

* ECONOMIC EXPERIMENT 564

26 Market Entry and Monopolistic Competition 566

The Effects of Market Entry 567

Entry Squeezes Profits from Three Sides 568

Examples of Entry: Car Stereos, Trucking, and Tires 569

APPLICATION 1 Satellite v Cable 570

Monopolistic Competition 570

When Entry Stops: Long-Run Equilibrium 571

Differentiation by Location 572

APPLICATION 2 Opening a Dunkin' Donuts Shop 573

Trade-Offs with Entry and Monopolistic Competition 573

Average Cost and Variety 574

Monopolistic Competition versus Perfect Competition 574

APPLICATION 3 Happy Hour Pricing 575

Advertising for Product Differentiation 576

APPLICATION 4 Picture of Man versus Picture of Woman 576

* SUMMARY 578 * KEY TERMS 578
* EXERCISES 578

* ECONOMIC EXPERIMENT 580

27 Oligopoly and Strategic Behavior 582

Cartel Pricing and the Duopolists' Dilemma 584

Price Fixing and the Game Tree 586

Equilibrium of the Price-Fixing Game 587

Nash Equilibrium 588

APPLICATION 1 Failure of the Salt Cartel 588

Overcoming the Duopolists' Dilemma 589

Low-Price Guarantees 589

Repeated Pricing Games with Retaliation for Underpricing 590

Price Fixing and the Law 591

Price Leadership 592

APPLICATION 2 Low-Price Guarantee Increases Tire Prices 592

Simultaneous Decision Making and the Payoff Matrix 593

Simultaneous Price-Fixing Game 593

The Prisoners' Dilemma 594

APPLICATION 3 Cheating On the Final Exam: The Cheaters' Dilemma 595

The Insecure Monopolist and Entry Deterrence 595

Entry Deterrence and Limit Pricing 596

Examples: Aluminum and Campus Bookstores 597

Entry Deterrence and Contestable Markets 598

When Is the Passive Approach Better? 598

APPLICATION 4 Microsoft as an Insecure Monopolist 599

The Advertisers' Dilemma 599

APPLICATION 5 Got Milk? 601

* SUMMARY 602 * KEY TERMS 602
* EXERCISES 602

* ECONOMIC EXPERIMENT 607

28 Controlling Market Power: Antitrust and Regulation 609

Natural Monopoly 610

Picking an Output Level 610

Will a Second Firm Enter? 612

Price Controls for a Natural Monopoly 613

APPLICATION 1 Public versus Private Waterworks 614

APPLICATION 2 Satellite Radio as a Natural Monopoly 615

Antitrust Policy 615

Breaking Up Monopolies 616

Blocking Mergers 616

Merger Remedy for Wonder Bread 618

Regulating Business Practices 619

A Brief History of U.S. Antitrust Policy 619

APPLICATION 3 Merger of Pennzoil and Quaker State 620

APPLICATION 4 FAQ about Predatory Pricing from the FTC 621

* SUMMARY 621 * KEY TERMS 622
* EXERCISES 622

PART 10 Externalities and Information

29 Imperfect Information: Adverse Selection and Moral Hazard 625

Adverse Selection for Buyers: The Lemons Problem 626

Uninformed Buyers and Knowledgeable Sellers 626

Equilibrium with All Low-Quality Goods 627

A Thin Market: Equilibrium with Some High-Quality Goods 628

APPLICATION 1 Are Baseball Pitchers Like Used Cars? 630

Evidence of the Lemons Problem 631

Responding to the Lemons Problem 631

Buyers Invest in Information 631

Consumer Satisfaction Scores from ValueStar and eBay 632

Guarantees and Lemons Laws 632

APPLICATION 2 Regulation of the California Kiwifruit Market 633

Adverse Selection for Sellers: Insurance 633

Health Insurance 633

Equilibrium with All High-Cost Consumers 635

Responding to Adverse Selection in Insurance: Group Insurance 636

The Uninsured 636

Other Types of Insurance 637

APPLICATION 3 Unisex Automobile Insurance in the European Union 637

Insurance and Moral Hazard 638

Insurance Companies and Moral Hazard 638

Deposit Insurance for Savings and Loans 639

APPLICATION 4 Car Insurance and Risky Driving 639

The Economics of Consumer Search 640

Search and the Marginal Principle 640

Reservation Prices and Searching Strategy 642

The Effects of Opportunity Cost and Product Prices on Search Effort 642

APPLICATION 5 Income and Consumer Search 644

* SUMMARY 644 * KEY TERMS 644
* EXERCISES 645

* ECONOMIC EXPERIMENT 649

30 Public Goods and Public Choice 651

External Benefits and Public Goods 654

Public Goods and the Free-Rider Problem 654

Overcoming the Free-Rider Problem 655

APPLICATION 1 Free Riders and the Three-Clock Tower 655

APPLICATION 2 Global Weather Observation 656

Private Goods with External Benefits 656

External Benefits from Education 656

External Benefits and the Marginal Principle 657

Other Private Goods That Generate External Benefits 658

APPLICATION 3 External Benefits from LoJack 658

APPLICATION 4 The Private and External Benefit of Trees 659

Public Choice and the Median Voter 659

Voting and the Median-Voter Rule 659

The Median Voter and the Median Location 661

Alternative Models of Government: Self-Interest and Special Interests 661

APPLICATION 5 The Median Voter in the NBA 663

Which Theory Is Correct? 663

* SUMMARY 663 * KEY TERMS 664
* EXERCISES 664

* ECONOMIC EXPERIMENT 667

31 External Costs and Environmental Policy 668

The Optimal Level of Pollution 669

Using the Marginal Principle 669

Example: The Optimal Level of Water Pollution 670

Coase Bargaining 671

APPLICATION 1 Reducing Methane Emissions 672

Taxing Pollution 672

A Firm's Response to a Pollution Tax 673

The Market Effects of a Pollution Tax 673

Example: A Carbon Tax 675

APPLICATION 2 Pollution Taxes in Rural and Urban Areas 676

Traditional Regulation 676

Uniform Abatement with Permits 676

Command and Control 677

Market Effects of Pollution Regulations 677

Lesson from Dear Abby: Options for Pollution Abatement 677

APPLICATION 3 Options for Reducing CO_2 Emissions from International Shipping 678

Marketable Pollution Permits 678

Voluntary Exchange and Marketable Permits 679

Supply, Demand, and the Price of Marketable Permits 680

APPLICATION 4 Weather and the Price of Pollution Permits 681

External Costs from Automobiles 681

External Costs from Pollution 681

External Costs from Congestion 683

External Costs from Collisions 683

APPLICATION 5 Young Drivers and Collisions 684

* SUMMARY 684 * KEY TERMS 685
* EXERCISES 685

* ECONOMIC EXPERIMENT 688

PART 11 The Labor Market and Income Distribution

32 The Labor Market and the Distribution of Income 689

The Demand for Labor 690

Labor Demand by an Individual Firm in the Short Run 690

Market Demand for Labor in the Short Run 693

Labor Demand in the Long Run 694

APPLICATION 1 Marginal Revenue Product in Major League Baseball 695

Short-Run versus Long-Run Demand 695

The Supply of Labor 696

The Individual Labor-Supply Decision: How Many Hours? 696

An Example of Income and Substitution Effects 697

The Market Supply Curve for Labor 697

APPLICATION 2 Cabbies Respond to an Increase in the Wage 698

Labor Market Equilibrium 699

Changes in Demand and Supply 699

The Market Effects of the Minimum Wage 700

Why Do Wages Differ across Occupations? 701

The Gender Pay Gap 702

Racial Discrimination 703

Why Do College Graduates Earn Higher Wages? 704

Labor Unions and Wages 705

APPLICATION 3 The Beauty Premium 705

The Distribution of Income 706

Income Distribution in 2007 706

Recent Changes in the Distribution of Income 708

APPLICATION 4 Trade-Offs from Immigration 709

Public Policy and the Distribution of Income 710

Effects of Tax and Transfer Policies on the Distribution of Income 710

Poverty and Public Policy 711

The Earned Income Tax Credit 713

APPLICATION 5 State Lotteries and the Distribution of Income 714

* SUMMARY 715 * KEY TERMS 715
* EXERCISES 716

Glossary 721

Photo Credits 730

Index 732

ALTERNATIVE COURSE SEQUENCE

Alternative Economics Sequence

The following chart helps you organize your syllabus based on your teaching preferences and objectives:

		Core	Policy	Optional
1	Introduction: What Is Economics?	X		
	Appendix: Using Graphs and Percentages			X
2	The Key Principles of Economics	X		
3	Exchange and Markets			X
4	Demand, Supply, and Market Equilibrium	X		
5	Measuring a Nation's Production and Income	X		
6	Unemployment and Inflation	X		
7	The Economy at Full Employment			X
8	Why Do Economies Grow?	X		
	Appendix: A Model of Capital Deepening			X
9	Aggregate Demand and Aggregate Supply	X		
10	Fiscal Policy	X		
11	The Income-Expenditure Model			X
	Appendix: Formulas for Equilibrium Income and the Multiplier			X
12	Investment and Financial Markets	X		
13	Money and the Banking System	X		
	Appendix: Formula for Deposit Creation			X
14	The Federal Reserve and Monetary Policy	X		
15	Modern Macroeconomics: From the Short Run to the Long Run	X		
16	The Dynamics of Inflation and Unemployment			X
17	Macroeconomic Policy Debates		X	
18	International Trade and Public Policy		X	
19	The World of International Finance	X		
20	Elasticity: A Measure of Responsiveness	X		
21	Market Efficiency and Government Intervention	X		
22	Consumer Choice: Utility Theory and Insights from Neuroscience			X
	Appendix: Mental Shortcuts and Consumer Puzzles			X
23	Production Technology and Cost	X		
24	Perfect Competition	X		
25	Monopoly and Price Discrimination	X		
26	Market Entry and Monopolistic Competition	X		
27	Oligopoly and Strategic Behavior	X		
28	Controlling Market Power: Antitrust and Regulation		X	
29	Imperfect Information: Adverse Selection and Moral Hazard		X	
30	Public Goods and Public Choice		X	
31	External Costs and Environmental Policy		X	
32	The Labor Market and the Distribution of Income	X		

Alternative Microeconomics Sequence

		Mix of Theory and Policy	Supply, Demand, and Policy	Supply, Demand, and Market Structure	Challenging Theory	Short Policy Course
1	Introduction: What Is Economics?	X	X	X	X	X
2	The Key Principles of Economics	X	X	X	X	X
3	Exchange and Markets	X	X	X	X	
4	Demand, Supply, and Market Equilibrium	X	X	X	X	X
5	Elasticity: A Measure of Responsiveness	X	X	X	X	X
6	Market Efficiency and Government Intervention	X	X	X	X	X
7	Consumer Choice: Utility Theory and Insights from Neuroscience				X	
8	Production Technology and Cost	X	X	X	X	
9	Perfect Competition	X	X	X	X	
10	Monopoly and Price Discrimination	X		X	X	
11	Market Entry and Monopolistic Competition	X		X	X	
12	Oligopoly and Strategic Behavior	X		X	X	
13	Controlling Market Power: Antitrust and Regulation	X		X	X	
14	Imperfect Information: Adverse Selection and Moral Hazard	X	X		X	X
15	Public Goods and Public Choice		X			X
16	External Costs and Environmental Policy		X			X
17	The Labor Market and the Distribution of Income	X	X		X	X
18	International Trade and Public Policy	X	X		X	

Alternative Macroeconomics Sequence

		Standard Course	Long-Run Focus	Short-Run Focus	Challenging Course
1	Introduction: What Is Economics?	X	X	X	X
2	The Key Principles of Economics	X	X	X	X
3	Exchange and Markets	X	X	X	X
4	Demand, Supply, and Market Equilibrium				X
5	Measuring a Nation's Production and Income	X	X	X	X
6	Unemployment and Inflation	X	X	X	X
7	The Economy at Full Employment		X		X
8	Why Do Economies Grow?	X	X	X	X
9	Aggregate Demand and Aggregate Supply	X	X	X	X
10	Fiscal Policy	X	X	X	X
11	The Income-Expenditure Model	X		X	X
12	Investment and Financial Markets	X		X	
13	Money and the Banking System	X	X	X	X
14	The Federal Reserve and Monetary Policy	X	X	X	X
15	Modern Macroeconomics: From the Short Run to the Long Run	X	X	X	X
16	The Dynamics of Inflation and Unemployment		X		X
17	Macroeconomic Policy Debates				
18	International Trade and Public Policy				X
19	The World of International Finance	X	X	X	X

Preface

In preparing this eighth edition, we had three primary goals. First, we wanted to incorporate the sweeping changes in the U.S. and world economies we have all witnessed in the last several years, and the difficulties that the world economics have experienced in recovering from the severe economic downturn. Second, we strived to update this edition to reflect the latest exciting developments in economic thinking and make these accessible to new students of economics. Finally, we wanted to stay true to the philosophy of the textbook—using basic concepts of economics to explain a wide variety of timely and interesting economic applications.

▶ WHAT'S NEW TO THIS EDITION

In addition to updating all the figures and data, we made a number of other key changes in this edition. They include the following:

- At the beginning of each chapter, we introduced a set of *Learning Objectives*. These give the students a preview of what they will learn in each section of the chapter, facilitating their learning.
- We revised and updated our discussion of fiscal policy in Chapter 10 to reflect our continuing difficulties in attempting to restore the economy to full employment and the changing views of the effectiveness of fiscal stimulus.
- We revised and updated our treatment of monetary policy in Chapter 14, as the Federal Reserve has continued to experiment with quantitative easing and other new monetary policies.
- We discuss in Chapter 15 how the thinking of Fed Chairman Ben Bernanke evolved during this past decade as he faced unprecedented challenges.
- We discuss in Chapter 5 the length of economic recoveries and the slow pace of the current recovery.
- We revised and expanded our discussion of the euro in Chapter 19, reflecting the serious challenges now facing the European Monetary Union.
- We highlight in Chapter 18 how rapid increases in imports can affect employment in local labor markets.
- We revised our presentation of consumer theory in Chapter 22 to (a) use modern tools to present traditional utility theory and (b) incorporate recent insights from neuroscience. For instructors who choose not to cover the insights from neuroscience, that part of the chapter can be skipped without loss of continuity.
- We expanded and upgraded our discussion of poverty and the distribution of income in Chapter 32, including a discussion of reasons for recent changes in the distribution of income and the effects of government policy.
- We consolidated our presentation of labor economics into a single chapter (Chapter 32).

We also incorporated a total of 61 exciting new applications into this edition, including 11 in the common chapters (Chapter 1–4), 17 in macroeconomics, and 33 in microeconomics. In addition, we incorporated a total of 19 new chapter-opening stories, including 2 in the common chapters, 10 in macroeconomics, and 7 in microeconomics. These fresh applications and chapter openers show the widespread relevance of economic analysis.

In the chapters common to macroeconomics and microeconomics, the new applications include incentives to purchase hybrid cars (Chapter 1), choosing how fast to sail a container ship (Chapter 2), the markets for meteorites (Chapter 3), and the economic forces behind the proposal to include sheep shearing as an Olympic sport (Chapter 4).

- In the macroeconomics chapters, the new applications include understanding changes in labor force participation (Chapter 6), taxes and the mobility of international soccer stars (Chapter 7), the "broken window fallacy" and Keynesian economics (Chapter 11), whether debt forgiveness for "underwater" homeowners is a good policy (Chapter 12), how hyperinflations end (Chapter 16), and how the federal government has handled the financial difficulties of the states in U.S. history (Chapter 17).
- In the microeconomics chapters, the new applications include the effects of supply disruptions on the price of gasoline (Chapter 20), the use of a large cigarette tax to overcome consumers' present bias and make current low-income smokers better off (Chapter 22), the decision of some Chinese farmers to shift from growing tea to coffee (Chapter 24), the economic logic of low prices during "happy hour", a period of relatively high demand (Chapter 26), Microsoft as an insecure monopolist (Chapter 27), gender discrimination in insurance (Chapter 29), the economics of energy-efficient buildings (Chapter 31), and state lotteries as regressive taxes (Chapter 32).

▶ APPLYING THE CONCEPTS

This is an Applications-driven textbook. We carefully selected over 120 real-world Applications that help students develop and master essential economic concepts. Here is an example of our approach from Chapter 4, "Demand, Supply, and Market Equilibrium."

application 2

LAW OF SUPPLY AND WOOLYMPICS

APPLYING THE CONCEPTS #2: What is the law of supply?

In the 1990s, the world price of wool decreased by about 30 percent, and prices have remained relatively low since then. Based on the law of supply, we would expect the quantity of wool supplied from New Zealand and other exporters to decrease, and that's what happened. Land formerly used to grow grass for wool-producing sheep has been converted into other uses, including dairy products, forestry, and the domestication of deer.

There have been several attempts to revive the wool industry by boosting the demand for wool and thus increasing its price. The United Nations General Assembly declared 2009 as the International Year of Natural Fibres, with the objective "to raise awareness and stimulate demand for natural fibres." In 2012, the Federated Farmers of New Zealand proposed that sheep shearing be added to the Commonwealth Games and Olympics as a demonstration sport. The favorites for Olympic titles are the current world record holders Ivan Scott (744 sheep in 24 hours) and Kerry-Jo Te Huia (507 sheep in 24 hours). Of course, it's not obvious that Olympic shearing would increase the demand for wool, and then there is the problem of what to do with all the sheared wool. Speed knitting? **Related to Exercises 2.6 and 2.10.**

SOURCE: Based on "Wait Wait Don't Tell Me." National Public Radio (January 21, 2012).

Each chapter includes three to five thought-provoking Applying the Concepts questions that convey important economic concepts, paired with and illustrated by an Application that discusses the concept and conveys its real-world use.

For each Application and Applying the Concepts question, we provide end-of-chapter exercises that test students' understanding of the concepts.

1.4 The market demand curve is the (horizontal/vertical) sum of the individual demand curves.

1.5 A change in price causes movement along a demand curve and a change in ________.

1.6 When several provinces in eastern Canada cut their cigarette taxes, the price of cigarettes decreased by roughly 50 percent, and the youth smoking rate increased by roughly________ (1, 17, 50, 90) percent. (Related to Application 1 on page 71.)

1.7 **Draw a Demand Curve.** Your state has decided to offer its citizens vanity license plates for their cars and wants to predict how many vanity plates it will sell at different prices. The price of the state's regular license plates is $20 per year, and the state's per-capita income is $30,000. A recent survey of other states with approximately the same population (3 million people) generated the following data on incomes, prices, and vanity plates:

State	B	C	D	E
Price of vanity plate	$ 60	$ 55	$ 50	$ 40
Price of regular plates	20	20	35	20
Income	30,000	25,000	30,000	30,000
Quantity of vanity plates	6,000	6,000	16,000	16,000

a. Use the available data to identify some points on the demand curve for vanity plates and connect the points to draw a demand curve. Don't forget *ceteris paribus*.

b. Suppose the demand curve is linear. If your state sets a price of $50, how many vanity plates would be purchased?

1.8 **Youth Smoking.** Use a demand and supply graph of the youth smoking market to show the effects of the tax cut in eastern Canada. Assume that the initial price is $6.00, the initial quantity is 100 units, and each youth smoker smokes 5 cigarettes per day. (Related to Application 1 on page 71.)

4.2 The Supply Curve

2.1 Arrow up or down: According to the law of supply, an increase in price ________ the quantity supplied.

2.2 From the following list, choose the variables that are held fixed when drawing a market supply curve:
- The price of the product
- Wages paid to workers
- The price of materials used in production
- Taxes paid by producers
- The quantity of the product purchased

2.3 The minimum supply price is the ________ price at which a product is supplied.

2.4 The market supply curve is the (horizontal/vertical) sum of the individual supply curves.

2.5 A change in price causes movement along a supply curve and a change in ________.

2.6 Arrows up or down: In the 1990s, the world price of wool ________ and the quantity of wool supplied ________. (Related to Application 2 on page 76.)

2.7 **Marginal Cost of Housing.** When the price of a standard three-bedroom house increases from $150,000 to $160,000, a building company increases its output from 20 houses per year to 21 houses per year. What does the increase in the quantity of housing reveal about the cost of producing housing?

2.8 **Imports and Market Supply.** Two nations supply sugar to the world market. Lowland has a minimum supply price of 10 cents per pound, while Highland has a minimum supply price of 24 cents per pound. For each nation, the slope of the supply curve is 1 cent per million pounds.

a. Draw the individual supply curves and the market supply curve. At what price and quantity is the supply curve kinked?

b. The market quantity supplied at a price of 15 cents is ________ million pounds. The market quantity supplied at a price of 30 cents is ________ million pounds.

2.9 **Responses to Higher Soybean Prices.** Suppose that in initial equilibrium in the soybean market, each of the 1,000 farmers produces 50 units, for a total of 50,000 units of soybeans. Suppose the price of soybeans increases, and everyone expects the price to stay at the higher level for many years.

a. Arrows up or down: Over a period of several years, we expect the quantity of soybeans supplied to ________ as the number of soybean farmers ________ and the output per farmer ________.

b. A farmer who enters the market is likely to have a (higher/lower) marginal cost of production than an original firm.

2.10 **Response to Lower Wool Price.** Use a demand and supply graph of the wool market to show the effects of the decrease in the price of wool on the quantity supplied in New Zealand. Assume that the initial price is $20 per unit and the initial quantity is 100 units. Also assume that for each 1 percent decrease in price, the quantity supplied decreases by 1 percent. (Related to Application 2 on page 76.)

92

ECONOMIC EXPERIMENT

MARKET EQUILIBRIUM

This simple experiment takes about 20 minutes. We start by dividing the class into two equal groups: consumers and producers.

- The instructor provides each consumer with a number indicating the maximum amount he or she is willing to pay (WTP) for a bushel of apples: The WTP is a number between $1 and $100. Each consumer has the opportunity to buy one bushel of apples per trading period. The consumer's score for a single trading period equals the gap between the WTP and the price actually paid for apples. For example, if the consumer's WTP is $80 and he or she pays only $30 for apples, the consumer's score is $50. Each consumer has the option of not buying apples. This will be sensible if the best price the consumer can get exceeds the WTP. If the consumer does not buy apples, his or her score will be zero.
- The instructor provides each producer with a number indicating the cost of producing a bushel of apples (a number between $1 and $100). Each producer has the opportunity to sell one bushel per trading period. The producer's score for a single trading period equals the gap between the selling prices and the cost of producing apples. So if a producer sells apples for $20, and the cost is only $15, the producer's score is $5. Producers have t option of not selling apples, which is sensible if the b price the producer can get is less than the cost. If the pr ducer does not sell apples, his or her score is zero.

Once everyone understands the rules, consumers a producers meet in a trading area to arrange transactio A consumer may announce how much he or she is willi to pay for apples and wait for a producer to agree to s apples at that price. Alternatively, a producer may announ how much he or she is willing accept for apples and w for a consumer to agree to buy apples at that price. Onc transaction has been arranged, the consumer and produ inform the instructor of the trade, record the transacti and leave the trading area.

Several trading periods are conducted, each of whi lasts a few minutes. After the end of each trading peri the instructor lists the prices at which apples sold duri the period. Then another trading period starts, providi consumers and producers another opportunity to buy or s apples. After all the trading periods have been complet each participant computes his or her score by adding t scores from the trading periods.

MyEconLab
For additional economic experiments, please visit *www.myeconlab.com*.

96

In addition, some chapters contain an Economic Experiment section that gives students the opportunity to do their own economic analysis.

▶ WHY FIVE KEY PRINCIPLES?

In Chapter 2, "The Key Principles of Economics," we introduce the following five key principles and then apply them throughout the book:

1. **The Principle of Opportunity Cost.** The opportunity cost of something is what you sacrifice to get it.
2. **The Marginal Principle.** Increase the level of an activity as long as its marginal benefit exceeds its marginal cost. Choose the level at which the marginal benefit equals the marginal cost.
3. **The Principle of Voluntary Exchange.** A voluntary exchange between two people makes both people better off.
4. **The Principle of Diminishing Returns.** If we increase one input while holding the other inputs fixed, output will increase, but at a decreasing rate.
5. **The Real-Nominal Principle.** What matters to people is the real value of money or income—its purchasing power—not the face value of money or income.

This approach of repeating five key principles gives students the big picture—the framework of economic reasoning. We make the key concepts unforgettable by using them repeatedly, illustrating them with intriguing examples, and giving students many opportunities to practice what they've learned. Throughout the text, economic concepts are connected to the five key principles when the following callout is provided for each principle:

PRINCIPLE OF OPPORTUNITY COST
The opportunity cost of something is what you sacrifice to get it.

▶ HOW IS THE BOOK ORGANIZED?

Chapter 1, "Introduction: What Is Economics?" uses three current policy issues—traffic congestion, poverty in Africa, and Japan's prolonged recession—to explain the economic way of thinking. Chapter 2, "The Key Principles of Economics," introduces the five principles we return to throughout the book. Chapter 3, "Exchange and Markets," is devoted entirely to exchange and trade. We discuss the fundamental rationale for exchange and introduce some of the institutions modern societies developed to facilitate trade.

Students need to have a solid understanding of demand and supply to be successful in the course. Many students have difficulty understanding movement along a curve versus shifts of a curve. To address this difficulty, we developed an innovative way to organize topics in Chapter 4, "Demand, Supply, and Market Equilibrium." We examine the law of demand and changes in quantity demanded, the law of supply and changes in quantity supplied, and then the notion of market equilibrium. After students have a firm grasp of equilibrium concepts, we explore the effects of changes in demand and supply on equilibrium prices and quantities. You can present either macroeconomics or microeconomics chapters first, depending on your preference. See the alternative course sequence charts on pages xxviii-xxix of this preface for organization options.

Summary of the Macroeconomics Chapters

Part 2, "The Basic Concepts of Macroeconomics" (Chapters 5 and 6), introduces students to the key concepts—GDP, inflation, unemployment—that are used throughout the text and in everyday economic discussion. The two chapters in this section provide the building blocks for the rest of the book. Part 3, "The Economy in the Long Run" (Chapters 7 and 8), analyzes how the economy operates at full employment and explores the causes and consequences of economic growth.

Next we turn to the short run. We begin the discussion of business cycles, economic fluctuations, and the role of government in Part 4, "Economic Fluctuations and Fiscal Policy" (Chapters 9 through 12). We devote an entire chapter to the structure of government spending and revenues and the role of fiscal policy. In Part 5, "Money, Banking, and Monetary Policy" (Chapters 13 and 14), we introduce the key elements of both monetary theory and policy into our economic models. Part 6, "Inflation, Unemployment, and Economic Policy" (Chapters 15 through 17), brings the important questions of the dynamics of inflation and unemployment into our analysis. Finally, the last two chapters in Part 7, "The International Economy" (Chapter 18 and 19), provide an in-depth analysis of both international trade and finance.

A Few Features of Our Macroeconomics Chapters

The following are a few features of our macroeconomics chapters:

- **Flexibility.** A key dilemma confronting economics professors has always been how much time to devote to long-run topics, such as growth and production, versus short-run topics, such as economic fluctuations and business cycles. Our book is designed to let professors choose. It works like this: To pursue a long-run approach, professors should initially concentrate on Chapters 1 through 4, followed by Chapters 5 through 8.
- To focus on economic fluctuations, start with Chapters 1 through 4, present Chapter 5, "Measuring a Nation's Production and Income," and Chapter 6, "Unemployment and Inflation," and then turn to Chapter 9, "Aggregate Demand and Aggregate Supply."
- Chapter 11, "The Income-Expenditure Model," is self-contained, so instructors can either skip it completely or cover it as a foundation for aggregate demand.
- **Long Run.** Throughout most of the 1990s, the U.S. economy performed very well—low inflation, low unemployment, and rapid economic growth. This robust performance led to economists' increasing interest in trying to understand the processes of economic growth. Our discussion of economic growth in Chapter 8, "Why Do Economies Grow?" addresses the fundamental question of how long-term living standards are determined and why some countries prosper while others do not. This is the essence of economic growth. As Nobel Laureate Robert E. Lucas, Jr., once wrote, "Once you start thinking about growth, it is hard to think of anything else."
- **Short Run.** The great economic expansion of the 1990s came to an end in 2001, as the economy started to contract. The recession beginning in 2007 was the worst downturn since World War II. Difficult economic times remind us that macroeconomics is also concerned with understanding the causes and consequences of economic fluctuations. Why do economies experience recessions and depressions, and what steps can policymakers take to stabilize the economy and ease the devastation people suffer from them? This has been a constant theme of macroeconomics throughout its entire history and is covered extensively in the text.
- **Policy.** Macroeconomics is a policy-oriented subject, and we treat economic policy in virtually every chapter. We discuss both important historical and more recent macroeconomic events in conjunction with the theory. In addition, we devote Chapter 17, "Macroeconomic Policy Debates," to three important policy topics that recur frequently in macroeconomic debates: the role of government deficits, whether the Federal Reserve should target inflation or other objectives, and whether income or consumption should be taxed.

Summary of the Microeconomics Chapters

A course in microeconomics starts with the first four chapters of the book, which provide a foundation for more detailed study of individual decision making and markets.

Part 8, "A Closer Look at Demand and Supply," (Chapters 20 through 22), provides a closer look at demand and supply, including elasticity, market efficiency, and consumer choice. Part 9, "Market Structures and Pricing" (Chapters 23 through 28), starts with a discussion of production and costs, setting the stage for an examination of alternative market structures, including the extremes of perfect competition and monopoly, as well as the middle ground of monopolistic competition and oligopoly. The last chapter in Part 9 discusses antitrust policy and deregulation. Part 10, "Externalities and Information" (Chapters 29 through 31), discusses the circumstances under which markets break down, including imperfect information, public goods, and environmental degradation.

Part 11, "The Labor Market and Income Distribution" (Chapter 32), explores the economic forces that determine wages, and also examines recent changes in the distribution of income and the effects of government programs on the income distribution.

▶ MyEconLab

Both the text and supplement package provide ways for instructors and students to assess their knowledge and progress through the course. MyEconLab, the new standard in personalized online learning, is a key part of O'Sullivan, Sheffrin, and Perez's integrated learning package for the eighth edition.

For the Instructor

MyEconLab is an online course management, testing, and tutorial resource. Instructors can choose how much or how little time to spend setting up and using MyEconLab. Each chapter contains two Sample Tests, Study Plan Exercises, and Tutorial Resources. The online Gradebook records each student's performance and time spent on the Tests and Study Plan and generates reports by student or by chapter. Instructors can assign tests, quizzes, and homework in MyEconLab using four resources:

- Preloaded Sample Test questions
- Problems similar to the end-of-chapter exercises
- Test Bank questions
- Self-authored questions using the Econ Exercise Builder

Exercises use multiple-choice, graph drawing, and free-response items, many of which are generated algorithmically so that each time a student works them, a different variation is presented. MyEconLab grades each of these problem types, even those with graphs. When working homework exercises, students receive immediate feedback with links to additional learning tools.

For the Student

MyEconLab puts students in control of their learning through a collection of tests, practice, and study tools tied to the online, interactive version of the textbook, and other media resources. Within MyEconLab's structured environment, students practice what they learn, test their understanding, and pursue a personalized Study Plan generated from their performance on Sample Tests and tests set by their instructors. At the core of MyEconLab are the following features:

- Sample Tests, two per chapter
- Personal Study Plan
- Tutorial Instruction
- Graphing Tool

Sample Tests Two Sample Tests for each chapter are preloaded in MyEconLab, enabling students to practice what they have learned, test their understanding, and identify areas in which they need further work. Students can study on their own, or they can complete assignments created by their instructor.

Personal Study Plan Based on a student's performance on tests, MyEconLab generates a personal Study Plan that shows where the student needs further study. The Study Plan consists of a series of additional practice exercises with detailed feedback and guided solutions that are keyed to other tutorial resources.

Tutorial Instruction Launched from many of the exercises in the Study Plan, MyEconLab provides tutorial instruction in the form of step-by-step solutions and other media-based explanations.

Graphing Tool A graphing tool is integrated into the Tests and Study Plan exercises to enable students to make and manipulate graphs. This feature helps students understand how concepts, numbers, and graphs connect.

Additional MyEconLab Tools MyEconLab includes the following additional features:

1. **Weekly News Update**—This feature provides weekly updates during the school year of news items with links to sources for further reading and discussion questions.
2. **eText**—While students are working in the Study Plan or completing homework assignments, part of the tutorial resources available is a direct link to the relevant page of the text so that students can review the appropriate material to help them complete the exercise.
3. **Glossary Flashcards**—Every key term is available as a flashcard, allowing students to quiz themselves on vocabulary from one or more chapters at a time.

Real-Time Data Analysis

New real-time data exercises that students can complete on MyEconLab.

Real-Time Data Analysis Exercises allow instructors to assign problems which use up-to-the-minute data. Each RTDA exercise loads the appropriate and most currently available data from FRED®, a comprehensive and up-to-date data set maintained by the Federal Reserve Bank of St. Louis. Exercises are graded based on that instance of data, and feedback is provided.

In the eText available in MyEconLab, select figures labeled MyEconLab Real-Time Data can upon student direction display a pop-up graph updated with real-time data from FRED.

MyEconLab content has been created over the years through the efforts of Charles Baum, Middle Tennessee State University; Peggy Dalton, Frostburg State University; Sarah Ghosh, University of Scranton; Russell Kellogg, University of Colorado, Denver; Bert G. Wheeler, Cedarville University; and Douglas A. Ruby, Noel Lotz, and Courtney Kamauf, Pearson Education.

▶ WHAT INSTRUCTOR'S SUPPLEMENTS DID WE DEVELOP?

A fully integrated teaching and learning package is necessary for today's classroom. Our supplement package helps you provide new and interesting real-world Applications and assess student understanding of economics. The supplements are coordinated with the main text through the numbering system of the headings in each section. The major sections of the chapters are numbered (1.1, 1.2, 1.3, and so on), and that numbering system is used consistently in the supplements to make it convenient and flexible for instructors to develop assignments.

Four Test Banks

Economics, eighth edition, is supported by a comprehensive set of four test banks.

There are two test banks for *Macroeconomics* and two test banks for *Microeconomics*. Each test bank offers multiple-choice, true/false, and short-answer questions. The questions are referenced by topic and are presented in sequential order. Each question is keyed by degree of difficulty, with questions ranging on a scale of one to three. Easy questions involve straightforward recall of information in the text. Moderate questions require some analysis on the student's part. Difficult questions usually entail more complex analysis and may require the student to go one step further than the material presented in the text. Questions are also classified as *fact*, *definition*, *conceptual*, and *analytical*. Fact questions test the student's knowledge of factual information presented in the text. Definition questions ask the student to define an economic concept. Conceptual questions test the student's understanding of a concept. Analytical questions require the student to apply an analytical procedure to answer the question.

The test banks include tables and a series of questions asking students to solve for numeric values, such as profit or equilibrium output. There are also numerous questions based on graphs: Several questions ask students to interpret data presented in a graph, draw a graph on their own, and answer related questions.

In each chapter there are several questions that support the Applications in the main book. There are also new questions to support the updated and new content in the main book.

The Association to Advance Collegiate Schools of Business (AACSB) The authors of the test banks have connected questions to the general knowledge and skill guidelines found in the AACSB assurance of learning standards.

What Is the AACSB? AACSB is a not-for-profit corporation of educational institutions, corporations, and other organizations devoted to the promotion and improvement of higher education in business administration and accounting. A collegiate institution offering degrees in business administration or accounting may volunteer for AACSB accreditation review. The AACSB makes initial accreditation decisions and conducts periodic reviews to promote continuous quality improvement in management education. Pearson Education is a proud member of the AACSB and is pleased to provide advice to help you apply AACSB assurance of learning standards.

What Are AACSB Assurance of Learning Standards? One of the criteria for AACSB accreditation is quality of the curricula. Although no specific courses are required, the AACSB expects a curriculum to include learning experiences in the following areas:

- Communication
- Ethical Reasoning
- Analytic Skills
- Use of Information Technology
- Multiculturalism and Diversity
- Reflective Thinking

Questions that test skills relevant to these guidelines are appropriately tagged. For example, a question testing the moral questions associated with externalities would receive the Ethical Reasoning tag.

How Can Instructors Use the AACSB Tags? Tagged questions help you measure whether students are grasping the course content that aligns with the AACSB guidelines noted. In addition, the tagged questions may help instructors identify potential applications of these skills. This in turn may suggest enrichment activities or other educational experiences to help students achieve these skills.

For Macroeconomics ... Test Bank 1, prepared by Randy Methenitis of Richland College, includes approximately 3,000 multiple-choice, true/false, short-answer, and graphing questions. Test Bank 2, prepared by Brian Rosario of California State University, Sacramento, contains over 3,000 multiple-choice, true/false, and short-answer questions. Both test banks are available in a computerized format using TestGen, test-generating software.

For Microeconomics ... Test Bank 1, prepared by Randy Methenitis of Richland College, includes approximately 3,000 multiple-choice, true/false, short-answer, and graphing questions. Test Bank 2, prepared by Robert Shoffner III of Central Piedmont Community College, contains over 2,000 multiple-choice, true/false, and short-answer questions. Both test banks are available in a computerized format using TestGen, test-generating software.

TestGen

Microeconomics and *Macroeconomics* test banks 1 and 2 appear in print and as computer files that may be used with TestGen test-generating software. This test-generating program permits instructors to edit, add, or delete questions from the test bank; analyze test results; and organize a database of tests and student results. This software allows for flexibility and ease of use. It provides many options for organizing and displaying tests, along with a search and sort feature.

Instructor's Resource Manuals

The instructor's resource manuals, revised by Jeff Phillips of Colby-Sawyer College, follow the textbook's organization, incorporating extra Applications questions. The manuals also provide detailed outlines (suitable for use as lecture notes) and solutions to all questions in the textbook. The instructor's resource manuals are also designed to help the instructor incorporate applicable elements of the supplement package. Each instructor's resource manual contains the following for each chapter:

- Summary: a bulleted list of key topics in the chapter
- Approaching the Material: student-friendly examples to introduce the chapter
- Chapter Outline: summary of definitions and concepts
- Teaching Tips on how to encourage class participation
- Summary and discussion points for the Applications in the main text
- New Applications and discussion questions
- Solutions to all end-of-chapter exercises

The instructor's resource manuals are also available for download from the Instructor's Resource Center.

PowerPoint® Presentations

Three sets of PowerPoint slides are available for download from the Instructor's Resource Center at **www.pearsonhighered.com/irc**.

1. A comprehensive set of PowerPoint slides that can be used by instructors for class presentations. These PowerPoints, prepared by Brock Williams of Metropolitan Community College, include all the graphs, tables, and equations in the textbook, as well as lecture notes that outline the chapter.
2. A comprehensive set of PowerPoint slides with Classroom Response Systems (CRS) questions built in so that instructors can incorporate CRS "clickers" into their classroom lectures. This presentation is also prepared by Brock Williams of Metropolitan Community College. For more information on Pearson's partnership with CRS, see the following description. Instructors may download these PowerPoint presentations from the Instructor's Resource Center (**www.pearsonhighered.com/irc**).
3. A PDF version of the PowerPoint slides is also available as PDF files from the Instructor's Resource Center. This version of the PowerPoint slides can be printed and used in class.

Instructor's Resource Center on CD-ROM

The test banks, TestGen files, instructor's resource manuals, and PowerPoint slides are also available on this CD-ROM. Faculty can pick and choose from the various supplements and export them to their hard drive.

CourseSmart

The CourseSmart eTextbook for the text is available through **www.coursesmart.com**. CourseSmart goes beyond traditional expectations, providing instant, online access to the textbooks and course materials you need at a lower cost to students. And, even as students save money, you can save time and hassle with a digital textbook that allows you to search the most relevant content at the very moment you need it. Whether it's evaluating textbooks or creating lecture notes to help students with difficult concepts, CourseSmart can make life a little easier. See how when you visit **www.coursesmart.com/instructors**.

Instructor's Resource Center Online

This password-protected site is accessible from **www.pearsonshighered.com/irc** and hosts all of the resources previously listed: test banks, TestGen files, instructor's resource manuals, and PowerPoint slides. Instructors can click on the "Help downloading Instructor Resources" link for easy-to-follow instructions on getting access or contact their sales representative for further information.

Classroom Response Systems

Classroom Response Systems (CRS) is an exciting new wireless polling technology that makes large and small classrooms even more interactive because it enables instructors to pose questions to their students, record results, and display those results instantly. Students can answer questions easily using compact remote-control transmitters. Pearson has partnerships with leading CRS providers and can show you everything you need to know about setting up and using a CRS system. We'll provide the classroom hardware, text-specific PowerPoint slides, software, and support, and we'll also show you how your students can benefit! Learn more at **www.pearsonhighered.com/elearning**.

▶ WHAT STUDENT SUPPLEMENTS DID WE DEVELOP?

To accommodate different learning styles and busy student lifestyles, we provide a variety of online supplements.

Study Guides

The study guides, created by David Eaton of Murray State University, reinforce economic concepts and Applications from the main book and help students assess their learning. Each chapter of the study guides includes the following features:

- Chapter Summary: Provides a summary of the chapter, key term definitions, and review of the Applications from the main book.
- Study Tip: Provides students with tips on understanding key concepts.
- Key Equations: Alerts students to equations they are likely to see throughout the class.
- Caution!: Alerts students to potential pitfalls and key figures or tables that deserve special attention.
- Activity: Encourages students to think creatively about an economic problem. An answer is provided so students can check their work.
- Practice Test: Includes approximately 25 multiple-choice and short-answer questions that help students test their knowledge. Select questions include a graph or table for students to analyze. Some of these questions support the Applications in the main book.
- Solutions to the practice test.

These student study guides are available as an additional resource in the MyEconLab course discussed earlier.

▶ REVIEWERS

A long road exists between the initial vision of an innovative principles text and the final product. Along our journey we participated in a structured process to reach our goal. We wish to acknowledge the assistance of the many people who participated in this process.

▶ REVIEWERS OF THE CURRENT EDITION

The guidance and recommendations from the following professors helped us develop the revision plans for this new edition:

Arizona

BASIL AL-HASHIMI, *Mesa Community College, Red Mountain*

Connecticut

STEPHEN RUBB, *Sacred Heart University*

Indiana

ROBERT B. HARRIS, *Indiana Univ. Purdue Univ. Indianapolis*

Minnesota

IHSUAN LI, *Minnesota State University, Mankato*

Mississippi

BILLY L. CARSON II, *Itawamba Community College*

Nebraska

DEBBIE GASPARD, *Southeast Community College*

BROCK WILLIAMS, *Metropolitan Community College*

North Carolina

JULIANNE TREME, *University of North Carolina, Wilmington*

Ohio

KENNETH C. FAH, *Ohio Dominican University*

Washington

CHARLES S. WASSELL, JR., *Central Washington University*

Colombia

MICHAEL JETTER, *Universidad EIFIT*

▶ REVIEWERS OF PREVIOUS EDITIONS

We benefited from the assistance of many dedicated professors who reviewed all or parts of previous editions in various stages of development:

Alabama

Jim Payne, *Calhoun Community College*

James Swofford, *University of South Alabama*

Alaska

Paul Johnson, *University of Alaska, Anchorage*

Arizona

Pete Mavrokordatos, *Tarrant County College/University of Phoenix*

Evan Tanner, *Thunderbird, The American Graduate School of International Management*

Donald Wells, *University of Arizona*

California

Antonio Avalos, *California State University, Fresno*

Collette Barr, *Santa Barbara Community College*

T. J. Bettner, *Orange Coast College*

Peter Boelman-Lopez, *Riverside Community College*

Matthew Brown, *Santa Clara University*

Jim Cobb, *Orange Coast College*

John Constantine, *Sacramento City College*

Peggy Crane, *San Diego State University*

Albert B. Culver, *California State University, Chico*

Jose L. Esteban, *Palomar College*

Gilbert Fernandez, *Santa Rosa Junior College*

E. B. Gendel, *Woodbury University*

Charles W. Haase, *San Francisco State University*

John Henry, *California State University, Sacramento*

George Jensen, *California State University, Los Angeles*

Janis Kea, *West Valley College*

Rose Kilburn, *Modesto Junior College*

Philip King, *San Francisco State University*

Anthony Lima, *California State University, Hayward*

Bret Mcmurran, *Chaffey College*

Jon J. Nadenichek, *California State University, Northridge*

Alex Obiya, *San Diego City College*

Jack W. Osman, *San Francisco State University*

Jay Patyk, *Foothill College*

Stephen Perez, *California State University, Sacramento*

Ratha Ramoo, *Diablo Valley College*

Greg Rose, *Sacramento City College*

Kurt Schwabe, *University of California, Riverside*

Terri Sexton, *California State University, Sacramento*

David Simon, *Santa Rosa Junior College*

Xiaochuan Song, *San Diego Mesa College*

Ed Sorensen, *San Francisco State University*

Susan Spencer, *Santa Rosa Junior College*

Linda Stoh, *Sacramento City College*

Rodney Swanson, *University of California, Los Angeles*

Daniel Villegas, *California Polytechnic State University*

Colorado

Steve Call, *Metropolitan State College of Denver*

Connecticut

John A. Jascot, *Capital Community Technical College*

Delaware

Lawrence Stelmach, *Delaware Valley College*

Florida

Irma de Alonso, *Florida International University*

Jay Bhattacharya, *Okaloosa-Walton Community College*

Edward Bierhanzl, *Florida A&M University*

Eric P. Chiang, *Florida Atlantic University*

Martine Duchatelet, *Barry University*

George Greenlee, *St. Petersburg College, Clearwater*

Martin Markovich, *Florida A&M University*

Thomas McCaleb, *Florida State University*

Barbara Moore, *University of Central Florida*

Stephen Morrell, *Barry University*

Carl Schmertmann, *Florida State University*

Garvin Smith, *Daytona Beach Community College*

Noel Smith, *Palm Beach Community College*

Michael Vierk, *Florida International University*

Joseph Ward, *Broward Community College, Central*

Virginia York, *Gulf Coast Community College*

Andrea Zanter, *Hillsborough Community College*

Georgia

Scott Beaulier, *Mercer College*

Ashley Harmon, *Southeastern Technical College*

Steven F. Koch, *Georgia Southern University*

L. Wayne Plumly, Jr., *Valdosta State University*

Greg Trandel, *University of Georgia*

Hawaii

Barbara Ross-Pfeiffer, *Kapiolani Community College*

Idaho

Charles Scott Benson, Jr., *Idaho State University*

Tesa Stegner, *Idaho State University*

Illinois

Diane Anstine, *North Central College*

Rosa Lea Danielson, *College of DuPage*

Sel Dibooglu, *Southern Illinois University*

Linda Ghent, *Eastern Illinois University*

Gary Langer, *Roosevelt University*

Nampeang Pingkarawat, *Chicago State University*

Dennis Shannon, *Belleville Area College*

Chuck Sicotte, *Rock Valley College*

Indiana

John L. Conant, *Indiana State University*

Mousumi Duttaray, *Indiana State University*

James T. Kyle, *Indiana State University*

Virginia Shingleton, *Valparaiso University*

Iowa

Dale Borman, *Kirkwood Community College*

Jonathan O. Ikoba, *Scott Community College*

Saul Mekies, *Kirkwood Community College, Iowa City*

Kansas

Carl Parker, *Fort Hays State University*

James Ragan, *Kansas State University*

Tracy M. Turner, *Kansas State University*

Kentucky

David Eaton, *Murray State University*

John Robertson, *University of Kentucky*

Louisiana

John Payne Bigelow, *Louisiana State University*

Sang Lee, *Southeastern Louisiana University*

Richard Stahl, *Louisiana State University*

Maine

George Schatz, *Maine Maritime Academy*

Maryland

Carey Borkoski, *Anne Arundel Community College*

Gretchen Mester, *Anne Arundel Community College*

Irvin Weintraub, *Towson State University*

Massachusetts

Hans Despain, *Nichols College*

Brian Deuriarte, *Middlesex Community College*

Dan Georgianna, *University of Massachusetts, Dartmouth*

James E. Hartley, *Mount Holyoke College*

Marlene Kim, *University of Massachusetts, Boston*

Mark Siegler, *Williams College*

Gilbert Wolfe, *Middlesex Community College*

Michigan

Christine Amsler, *Michigan State University*

Bharati Basu, *Central Michigan University*

Norman Cure, *Macomb Community College*

Susan Linz, *Michigan State University*

Scanlon Romer, *Delta College*

Robert Tansky, *St. Clair County Community College*

Wendy Wysocki, *Monroe Community College*

Minnesota

Mike McIlhon, *Augsburg College*

Richard Milani, *Hibbing Community College*

Mississippi

Arlena Sullivan, *Jones County Junior College*

Missouri

Duane Eberhardt, *Missouri Southern State College*

David Gillette, *Truman State University*

Brad Hoppes, *Southwest Missouri State University*

Denise Kummer, *St. Louis Community College*

Steven M. Schamber, *St. Louis Community College, Meramec*

Elias Shukralla, *St. Louis Community College, Meramec*

Keith Ulrich, *Valencia Community College*

George Wasson, *St. Louis Community College, Meramec*

Nebraska

Theodore Larsen, *University of Nebraska, Kearney*

Timothy R. Mittan, *Southeast Community College*

Stanley J. Peters, *Southeast Community College*

Brock Williams, *Metropolitan Community College*

Nevada

Stephen Miller, *University of Nevada, Las Vegas*

Charles Okeke, *College of Southern Nevada*

New Jersey

Len Anyanwu, *Union County College*

Richard Comerford, *Bergen Community College*

John Graham, *Rutgers University*

Paul C. Harris, Jr., *Camden County College*

Calvin Hoy, *County College of Morris*

Taghi Ramin, *William Paterson University*

Brian de Uriarte, *Middlesex County College*

New Hampshire

Jeff Phillips, *Colby-Sawyer College*

New Mexico

Carl Enomoto, *New Mexico State University*

New York

Farhad Ameen, *State University of New York, Westchester County Community College*

Karijit K. Arora, *Le Moyne College*

Alex Azarchs, *Pace University*

Kathleen K. Bromley, *Monroe Community College*

Barbara Connelly, *Westchester Community College*

George Frost, *Suffolk County Community College*

Susan Glanz, *St. John's University*

Serge S. Grushchin, *ASA College of Advanced Technology*

Robert Herman, *Nassau Community College*

Christopher Inya, *Monroe Community College*

Marie Kratochvil, *Nassau Community College*

Marianne Lowery, *Erie Community College*

Jeannette Mitchell, *Rochester Institute of Technology*

Ted Muzio, *St. John's University*

Gray Orphee, *Rockland County Community College*

Craig Rogers, *Canisius College*

Fred Tyler, *Fordham University*

Ezgi Uzel, *SUNY-Maritime*

Michael Vardanyan, *Binghamton University*

North Carolina

Katie Canty, *Cape Fear Community College*

Lee Craig, *North Carolina State University*

Hossein Gholami, *Fayetteville Technical Community College*

Michael G. Goode, *Central Piedmont Community College*

Charles M. Oldham, Jr., *Fayetteville Technical Community College*

Randall Parker, *East Carolina University*

Diane Tyndall, *Craven Community College*

Chester Waters, *Durham Technical Community College*

James Wheeler, *North Carolina State University*

North Dakota

Scott Bloom, *North Dakota State University*

Ohio

Fatma Abdel-Raouf, *Cleveland State University*

Jeff Ankrom, *Wittenberg University*

Erwin Ehrardt, *University of Cincinnati*

Ken Fah, *Ohio Dominican University*

Taghi T. Kermani, *Youngstown State University*

Dandan Liu, *Kent State University*

Oklahoma

Jeff Holt, *Tulsa Community College*

Marty Ludlum, *Oklahoma City Community College*

Dan Rickman, *Oklahoma State University*

Oregon

Tom Carroll, *Central Oregon Community College*

Jim Eden, *Portland Community College*

John Farrell, *Oregon State University*

David Figlio, *University of Oregon*

Randy R. Grant, *Linfield College*

Larry Singell, *University of Oregon*

Pennsylvania

Kevin A. Baird, *Montgomery County Community College*

Charles Beem, *Bucks County Community College*

Ed Coulson, *Pennsylvania State University*

Tahany Naggar, *West Chester University*

Abdulwahab Sraiheen, *Kutztown University*

South Carolina

Donald Balch, *University of South Carolina*

Calvin Blackwell, *College of Charleston*

Janice Boucher Breuer, *University of South Carolina*

Bill Clifford, *Trident Technical College*

Frank Garland, *Tri-County Technical College*

Charlotte Denise Hixson, *Midlands Technical College*

Woodrow W. Hughes, Jr., *Converse College*

Miren Ivankovic, *Southern Wesleyan University*

Chirinjev Peterson, *Greenville Technical College*

Gary Stone, *Winthrop University*

Denise Turnage, *Midlands Technical College*

Chad Turner, *Clemson University*

South Dakota

Joseph Santos, *South Dakota State University*

Tennessee

Cindy Alexander, *Pellissippi State University*

Nirmalendu Debnath, *Lane College*

Quenton Pulliam, *Nashville State Technical College*

Rose Rubin, *University of Memphis*

Thurston Schrader, *Southwest Tennessee Community College*

Texas

Rashid Al-Hmoud, *Texas Technical University*

Mahamudu Bawumia, *Baylor University*

Steven Beckham, *Amarillo College*

Omar Belazi, *Midland College*

Jack Bucco, *Austin Community College*

Cindy Cannon, *North Harris College*

David L. Coberly, *Southwest Texas State University*

Ed Cohn, *Del Mar College*

Dean Drainey, *St. Phillips College*

Michael I. Duke, *Blinn College*

Ghazi Duwaji, *University of Texas, Arlington*

Harry Ellis, *University of North Texas*

S. Aun Hassan, *Texas Tech University*

Thomas Jeitschko, *Texas A&M University*

Delores Linton, *Tarrant County Community College, Northwest*

Jessica McCraw, *University of Texas, Arlington*

Randy Methenitis, *Richland College*

William Neilson, *Texas A&M University*

Michael Nelson, *Texas A&M University*

Rhey Nolan, *Tyler Junior College*

Paul Okello, *University of Texas, Arlington*

Joshua Pickrell, *South Plains College*

John Pisciotta, *Baylor University*

John Rykowski, *Kalamazoo Valley Community College*

Dave Shorrow, *Richland College*

Steve Schwiff, *Texas A&M University, Commerce*

James R. VanBeek, *Blinn College*

Inske Zandvliet, *Brookhaven College*

Utah

Reed Gooch, *Utah Valley University*

Ali Hekmat, *College of Eastern Utah*

Glenn Lowell, *Utah Valley University*

Virginia

James Brumbaugh, *Lord Fairfax Community College, Middleton Campus*

Bruce Brunton, *James Madison University*

Michael G. Heslop, *North Virginia Community College*

George Hoffer, *Virginia Commonwealth University*

Melanie Marks, *Longwood College*

Thomas J. Meeks, *Virginia State University*

John Min, *Northern Virginia Community College, Alexandria*

Shannon K. Mitchell, *Virginia Commonwealth University*

Bill Reese, *Tidewater Community College, Virginia Beach*

Washing ton

William Hallagan, *Washington State University*

Mark Wylie, *Spokane Falls Community College*

Australia

Hak Youn Kim, *Monash University*

▶ CLASS TESTERS

A special acknowledgment goes to the instructors who were willing to class-test drafts of early editions in different stages of development. They provided us with instant feedback on parts that worked and parts that needed changes:

Sheryl Ball, *Virginia Polytechnic Institute and State University*

John Constantine, *University of California, Davis*

John Farrell, *Oregon State University*

James Hartley, *Mt. Holyoke College*

Kailash Khandke, *Furman College*

Peter Lindert, *University of California, Davis*

Louis Makowski, *University of California, Davis*

Barbara Ross-Pfeiffer, *Kapiolani Community College*

▶ FOCUS GROUPS

We want to thank the participants who took part in the focus groups for the first and second editions; they helped us see the manuscript from a fresh perspective:

Carlos Aquilar, *El Paso Community College*

Jim Bradley, *University of South Carolina*

Thomas Collum, *Northeastern Illinois University*

David Craig, *Westark College*

Jeff Holt, *Tulsa Junior College*

Thomas Jeitschko, *Texas A&M University*

Gary Langer, *Roosevelt University*

Mark McLeod, *Virginia Polytechnic Institute and State University*

Tom McKinnon, *University of Arkansas*

Amy Meyers, *Parkland Community College*

Hassan Mohammadi, *Illinois State University*

John Morgan, *College of Charleston*

Norm Paul, *San Jacinto Community College*

Nampeang Pingkaratwat, *Chicago State University*

Scanlan Romer, *Delta Community College*

Barbara Ross-Pfeiffer, *Kapiolani Community College*

Zahra Saderion, *Houston Community College*

Virginia Shingleton, *Valparaiso University*

Jim Swofford, *University of South Alabama*

Janet West, *University of Nebraska, Omaha*

Linda Wilson, *University of Texas, Arlington*

Michael Youngblood, *Rock Valley Community College*

▶ A WORLD OF THANKS ...

We would also like to acknowledge the team of dedicated authors who contributed to the various ancillaries that accompany this book: Jeff Phillips of Colby-Sawyer College; David Eaton of Murray State University; Randy Methenitis of Richland College; Robert L. Shoffner III of Central

Piedmont Community College; Brian Rosario of California State University, Sacramento; and Brock Williams of Metropolitan Community College.

For the eighth edition, Meredith Gertz was the senior production project manager who worked with Jacki Russell at GEX Publishing Services to turn our manuscript pages into a beautiful published book. Noel Seibert, senior acquisitions editor, and Carolyn Terbush, senior editorial project manager, guided the project and coordinated the schedules for the book and the extensive supplement package that accompanies the book. David Alexander, executive acquisitions editor, stepped in at the end to help wrap the project up and to support us and our users during the life of this edition.

From the start, Pearson provided us with first-class support and advice. Over the first seven editions, many people contributed to the project, including Leah Jewell, Rod Banister, P. J. Boardman, Marie McHale, Gladys Soto, Lisa Amato, Victoria Anderson, Cynthia Regan, Kathleen McLellan, Sharon Koch, David Theisen, Steve Deitmer, Christopher Bath, Ben Paris, Elisa Adams, Jodi Bolognese, David Alexander, Virginia Guariglia, and Lynne Breitfeller.

Last but not least, we must thank our families, who have seen us disappear, sometimes physically and other times mentally, to spend hours wrapped up in our own world of principles of economics. A project of this magnitude is very absorbing, and our families have been particularly supportive in this endeavor.

Arthur O'Sullivan

Steven Sheffrin

Stephen Perez

Introduction: What Is Economics?

CHAPTER 1

Economics is the science of choice, exploring the choices made by individuals and organizations.

Over the last few centuries, these choices have led to substantial gains in the standard of living around the globe. In the United States, the typical person today has roughly seven times the income and purchasing power of a person 100 years ago. Our prosperity is the result of choices made by all sorts of people, including inventors, workers, entrepreneurs, and the people who saved money and loaned it to others to invest in machines and other tools of production. One reason we have prospered is greater efficiency: We have discovered better ways to use our resources—raw materials, time, and energy—to produce the goods and services we value.

As an illustration of changes in the standard of living and our growing prosperity, let's compare the way people listened to music in 1891 with how we listen today. You can buy an iPod shuffle® for $49 and fill it with 500 songs at $0.99 each. If you earn a wage of $15 per hour, it would take you about 36 hours of work to purchase and then fill an iPod. Back in 1891, the latest technological marvel was Thomas Edison's cylinder phonograph, which played music recorded on 4-inch cylinders. Imagine that you lived back then and wanted to get just as much music as you could fit on an iPod. Given the wages and prices in 1891, it would take you roughly 800 hours of work to earn enough money to buy the phonograph and all the cylinders. And if you wanted to keep your music with you, you would need 14 backpacks to carry the cylinders.

Although prosperity and efficiency are widespread, they are not universal. In some parts of the world, many people live in poverty. For example, in sub-Saharan Africa 388 million people—about half the population—live on less than $1.25 per day. And in all nations of the world, inefficiencies still exist, with valuable resources being wasted. For example, each year the typical urban commuter in the United States wastes more than 47 hours and $84 worth of gasoline trapped in rush hour traffic.

LEARNING OBJECTIVES

- List the three key economic questions.
- Discuss the insights from economics for a real-world problem such as congestion.
- List the four elements of the economic way of thinking.
- List three ways to use macroeconomics.
- List three ways to use microeconomics.

MyEconLab

MyEconLab helps you master each objective and study more efficiently.

Economics provides a framework to diagnose all sorts of problems faced by society and then helps create and evaluate various proposals to solve them. Economics can help us develop strategies to replace poverty with prosperity, and to replace waste with efficiency. In this chapter, we explain what economics is and how we all can use economic analysis to think about practical problems and solutions.

1.1 What Is Economics?

scarcity
The resources we use to produce goods and services are limited.

economics
The study of choices when there is scarcity.

Economists use the word **scarcity** to convey the idea that resources—the things we use to produce goods and services—are limited, while human wants are unlimited. Therefore, we cannot produce everything that everyone wants. As the old saying goes, you can't always get what you want. **Economics** studies the choices we make when there is scarcity; it is all about trade-offs. Here are some examples of scarcity and the trade-offs associated with making choices:

- You have a limited amount of time. If you take a part-time job, each hour on the job means one fewer hour for study or play.
- A city has a limited amount of land. If the city uses an acre of land for a park, it has one fewer acre for housing, retailers, or industry.
- You have limited income this year. If you spend $17 on a music CD, that's $17 fewer you have to spend on other products or to save.

factors of production
The resources used to produce goods and services; also known as *production inputs* or *resources*.

natural resources
Resources provided by nature and used to produce goods and services.

labor
Human effort, including both physical and mental effort, used to produce goods and services.

physical capital
The stock of equipment, machines, structures, and infrastructure that is used to produce goods and services.

human capital
The knowledge and skills acquired by a worker through education and experience and used to produce goods and services.

entrepreneurship
The effort used to coordinate the factors of production—natural resources, labor, physical capital, and human capital—to produce and sell products.

People produce goods (music CDs, houses, and parks) and services (the advice of physicians and lawyers) by using one or more of the following five **factors of production**, also called *production inputs* or simply *resources*:

- **Natural resources** are provided by nature. Some examples are fertile land, mineral deposits, oil and gas deposits, and water. Some economists refer to all types of natural resources as *land*.
- **Labor** is the physical and mental effort people use to produce goods and services.
- **Physical capital** is the stock of equipment, machines, structures, and infrastructure that is used to produce goods and services. Some examples are forklifts, machine tools, computers, factories, airports, roads, and fiber-optic cables.
- **Human capital** is the knowledge and skills acquired by a worker through education and experience. Every job requires some human capital: To be a surgeon, you must learn anatomy and acquire surgical skills. To be an accountant, you must learn the rules of accounting and acquire computer skills. To be a musician, you must learn to play an instrument.
- **Entrepreneurship** is the effort used to coordinate the factors of production—natural resources, labor, physical capital, and human capital—to produce and sell products. An entrepreneur comes up with an idea for a product, decides how to produce it, and raises the funds to bring it to the market. Some examples of entrepreneurs are Bill Gates of Microsoft, Steve Jobs of Apple Computer, Howard Schultz of Starbucks, and Ray Kroc of McDonald's.

Given our limited resources, we make our choices in a variety of ways. Sometimes we make our decisions as individuals, and other times we participate in collective decision making, allowing the government and other organizations to choose for us. Many of our choices happen within *markets*, institutions or arrangements that enable us to buy and sell things. For example, most of us participate in the labor market, exchanging our time for money, and we all participate in consumer markets, exchanging money for food and clothing. But we make other choices outside markets—from our personal decisions about everyday life to our political choices about matters that concern society as a whole. What unites all these decisions is the notion of scarcity: We can't have it all; there are trade-offs.

Economists are always reminding us that there is scarcity—there are trade-offs in everything we do. Suppose that in a conversation with your economics instructor you share your enthusiasm about an upcoming launch of the space shuttle. The economist may tell you that the resources used for the shuttle could have been used instead for an unmanned mission to Mars.

By introducing the notion of scarcity into your conversation, your instructor is simply reminding you that there are trade-offs, that one thing (a Mars mission) is sacrificed for another (a shuttle mission). Talking about alternatives is the first step in a process that can help us make better choices about how to use our resources. For example, we could compare the scientific benefits of a shuttle mission to the benefits of a Mars mission and choose the mission with the greater benefit.

Positive versus Normative Analysis

Economics doesn't tell us what to choose—shuttle mission or Mars mission—but simply helps us to understand the trade-offs. President Harry S. Truman once remarked,

> All my economists say, "On the one hand, . . . ; On the other hand, ..." Give me a one-handed economist!

An economist might say, "On the one hand, we could use a shuttle mission to do more experiments in the gravity-free environment of Earth's orbit; on the other hand, we could use a Mars mission to explore the possibility of life on other planets." In using both hands, the economist is not being evasive, but simply doing economics, discussing the alternative uses of our resources. The ultimate decision about how to use our resources—shuttle mission or Mars exploration—is the responsibility of citizens or their elected officials.

Most modern economics is based on **positive analysis**, which predicts the consequences of alternative actions by answering the question "What *is*?" or "What *will be*?" A second type of economic reasoning is normative in nature. **Normative analysis** answers the question "What *ought to be*?"

positive analysis
Answers the question "What *is*?" or "What *will be*?"

normative analysis
Answers the question "What *ought to be*?"

In Table 1.1, we compare positive questions to normative questions. Normative questions lie at the heart of policy debates. Economists contribute to policy debates by conducting positive analyses of the consequences of alternative actions. For example, an economist could predict the effects of an increase in the minimum wage on the number of people employed nationwide, the income of families with minimum-wage workers, and consumer prices. Armed with the conclusions of the economist's positive analysis, citizens and policymakers could then make a

TABLE 1.1 Comparing Positive and Normative Questions

Positive Questions	Normative Questions
• If the government increases the minimum wage, how many workers will lose their jobs?	• Should the government increase the minimum wage?
• If two office-supply firms merge, will the price of office supplies increase?	• Should the government block the merger of two office-supply firms?
• How does a college education affect a person's productivity and earnings?	• Should the government subsidize a college education?
• How do consumers respond to a cut in income taxes?	• Should the government cut taxes to stimulate the economy?
• If a nation restricts shoe imports, who benefits and who bears the cost?	• Should the government restrict imports?

normative decision about whether to increase the minimum wage. Similarly, an economist could study the projects that could be funded with $1 billion in foreign aid, predicting the effects of each project on the income per person in an African country. Armed with this positive analysis, policymakers could then decide which projects to support.

Economists don't always reach the same conclusions in their positive analyses. The disagreements often concern the magnitude of a particular effect. For example, most economists agree that an increase in the minimum wage will cause unemployment, but disagree about how many people would lose their jobs. Similarly, economists agree that spending money to improve the education system in Africa will increase productivity and income, but disagree about the size of the increase in income.

The Three Key Economic Questions: What, How, and Who?

We make economic decisions at every level in society. Individuals decide what products to buy, what occupations to pursue, and how much money to save. Firms decide what goods and services to produce and how to produce them. Governments decide what projects and programs to complete and how to pay for them. The choices of individuals, firms, and governments answer three questions:

1. *What products do we produce?* Trade-offs exist: If a hospital uses its resources to perform more heart transplants, it has fewer resources to care for premature infants.
2. *How do we produce the products?* Alternative means of production are available: Power companies can produce electricity with coal, natural gas, or wind power. Professors can teach in large lecture halls or small classrooms.
3. *Who consumes the products?* We must decide how to distribute the products of society. If some people earn more money than others, should they consume more goods? How much money should the government take from the rich and give to the poor?

As we'll see later in the book, most of these decisions are made in markets, where prices play a key role in determining what products we produce, how we produce them, and who gets the products. In Chapter 3, we'll examine the role of markets in modern economies and the role of government in market-based economies.

Economic Models

Economists use *economic models* to explore the choices people make and the consequences of those choices. An economic model is a simplified representation of an economic environment, with all but the essential features of the environment eliminated. An **economic model** is an abstraction from reality that enables us to focus our attention on what really matters. As we'll see throughout the book, most economic models use graphs to represent the economic environment.

economic model
A simplified representation of an economic environment, often employing a graph.

To see the rationale for economic modeling, consider an architectural model. An architect builds a scale model of a new building and uses the model to show how the building will fit on a plot of land and blend with nearby buildings. The model shows the exterior features of the building, but not the interior features. We can ignore the interior features because they are unimportant for the task at hand—seeing how the building will fit into the local environment.

Economists build models to explore decision making by individuals, firms, and other organizations. For example, we can use a model of a profit-maximizing firm to predict how a firm will respond to increased competition. If a new car stereo store opens up in your town, will the old firms be passive and simply accept smaller market shares, or will they aggressively cut their prices to try to drive the new rival out of business? The model of the firm includes the monetary benefits and costs of doing business, and assumes that firms want to make as much money as possible. Although there may be other motives in the business world—to have fun or to help the world—the economic model ignores these other motives. The model focuses our attention on the profit motive and how it affects a firm's response to increased competition.

1.2 Economic Analysis and Modern Problems

Economic analysis provides important insights into real-world problems. To explain how we can use economic analysis in problem solving, we provide three examples. You'll see these examples again in more detail later in the book.

Economic View of Traffic Congestion

Consider first the problem of traffic congestion. According to the Texas Transportation Institute, the typical U.S. commuter wastes about 47 hours per year because of traffic congestion.[1] In some cities, the time wasted is much greater: 93 hours in Los Angeles, 72 hours in San Francisco, and 63 hours in Houston. In addition to time lost, we also waste 2.3 billion gallons of gasoline and diesel fuel each year.

To an economist, the diagnosis of the congestion problem is straightforward. When you drive onto a busy highway during rush hour, your car takes up space and decreases the distance between the vehicles on the highway. A driver's normal reaction to a shorter distance between moving cars is to slow down. So when you enter the highway, you force other commuters to slow down and thus spend more time on the highway. If each of your 900 fellow commuters spends just two extra seconds on the highway, you will increase the total travel time by 30 minutes. In deciding whether to use the highway, you will presumably ignore these costs you impose on others. Similarly, your fellow commuters ignore the cost they impose on you and others when they enter the highway. Because no single commuter pays the full cost (30 minutes), too many people use the highway, and everyone wastes time.

One possible solution to the congestion problem is to force people to pay for using the road, just as they pay for gasoline and tires. The government could impose a congestion tax of $8 per trip on rush-hour commuters and use a debit card system to collect the tax: Every time a car passes a checkpoint, a transponder would charge the commuter's card. Traffic volume during rush hours would then decrease as travelers (a) shift their travel to off-peak times, (b) switch to ride sharing and mass transit, and (c) shift their travel to less congested routes. The job for the economist is to compute the appropriate congestion tax and predict the consequences of imposing it.

Economic View of Poverty in Africa

Consider next the issue of poverty in Africa. In the final two decades of the twentieth century, the world economy grew rapidly, and the average per capita income (income per person) increased by about 35 percent. In contrast, the economies of poverty-stricken sub-Saharan Africa shrank, and per capita income *decreased* by about 6 percent. Africa is the world's second-largest continent in both area and population and accounts for more than 12 percent of the world's human population. Figure 1.1 shows a map of Africa. The countries of sub-Saharan Africa are highlighted in orange.

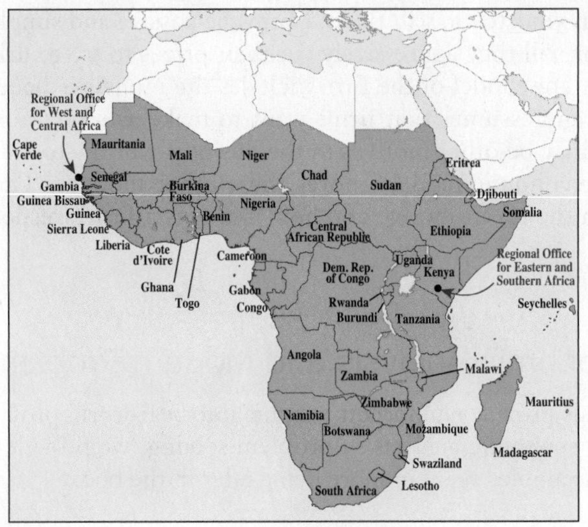

▲ **FIGURE 1.1**
Map of Africa
Africa is the world's second-largest continent in both area and population, and accounts for more than 12 percent of the world's human population. The countries of sub-Saharan Africa are highlighted in orange.
SOURCE: web.worldbank.org/WEBSITE/EXTERNAL/COUNTRIES/AFRICA

Economists have found that as a nation's economy grows, its poorest households share in the general prosperity.[2] Therefore, one way to reduce poverty in sub-Saharan Africa is to increase economic growth. Economic growth occurs when a country expands its production facilities (machinery and factories), improves its public infrastructure (highways and water systems), widens educational opportunities, and adopts new technology.

The recent experience of sub-Saharan Africa is somewhat puzzling because in the last few decades the region has expanded educational opportunities and received large amounts of foreign aid. Some recent work by economists on the sources of growth suggests that institutions such as the legal system and the regulatory environment also play key roles in economic growth.[3] In sub-Saharan Africa, a simple legal dispute about a small debt takes about 30 months to resolve, compared to 5 months in the United States. In Mozambique, it takes 174 days to complete the procedures required to set up a business, compared to just 2 days in Canada. In many cases, institutions impede rather than encourage the sort of investment and risk taking—called entrepreneurship—that causes economic growth and reduces poverty. As a consequence, economists and policymakers are exploring ways to reform the region's institutions. They are also challenged with choosing among development projects that will generate the biggest economic boost per dollar spent—the biggest bang per buck.

Economic View of the Current World Recession

Over the last several decades, the U.S. economy has performed well and has raised our standard of living. The general consensus was that our policymakers had learned to manage the economy effectively. Although the economy faltered at times, policymakers seemed to know how to restore growth and prosperity.

That is why the financial crisis and the recession that began in late 2007 has so shaken the confidence of people in the United States and around the world. The problems started innocently enough, with a booming market for homes that was fueled by easy credit from financial institutions. But we later discovered that many purchasers of homes and properties could not really afford them, and when many homeowners had trouble making their mortgage payments, the trouble spread to banks and other financial institutions. As a result, businesses found it increasingly difficult to borrow money for everyday use and investment, and economic activity around the world began to contract.

The major countries of the world have implemented aggressive policies to try to halt this downturn. Policymakers want to avoid the catastrophes that hit the global economy in the 1930s. Fortunately, they can draw on many years of experience in economic policy to guide the economy during this difficult time.

1.3 The Economic Way of Thinking

How do economists think about problems and decision making? The economic way of thinking is best summarized by British economist John Maynard Keynes (1883–1946):[4]

> The theory of economics does not furnish a body of settled conclusions immediately applicable to policy. It is a method rather than a doctrine, an apparatus of the mind, a technique of thinking which helps its possessor draw correct conclusions.

Let's look at the four elements of the economic way of thinking.

Use Assumptions to Simplify

Economists use assumptions to make things simpler and focus attention on what really matters. If you use a road map to plan a car trip from Seattle to San Francisco, you make two unrealistic assumptions to simplify your planning:

- The earth is flat: The flat road map doesn't show the curvature of the earth.
- The roads are flat: The standard road map doesn't show hills and valleys.

Instead of a map, you could use a globe that shows all the topographical features between Seattle and San Francisco, but you don't need those details to plan your trip. A map, with its unrealistic assumptions, will suffice because the curvature of the earth and the topography of the highways are irrelevant to your trip. Although your analysis is based on two unrealistic assumptions, that does not mean your analysis is invalid. Similarly, if economic analysis is based on unrealistic assumptions, that doesn't mean the analysis is faulty.

What if you decide to travel by bike instead of by automobile? Now the assumption of flat roads really matters, unless of course you are eager to pedal up and down mountains. If you use a standard map, and thus assume there are no mountains between the two cities, you may inadvertently pick a mountainous route instead of a flat one. In this case, the simplifying assumption makes a difference. The lesson is that we must think carefully about whether a simplifying assumption is truly harmless.

Isolate Variables—*Ceteris Paribus*

Economic analysis often involves *variables* and how they affect one another. A **variable** is a measure of something that can take on different values, for example, your grade point average. Economists are interested in exploring relationships between two variables—like the relationship between the price of apples and the quantity of apples consumers purchase. Of course, the quantity of apples purchased depends on many other variables, including the consumer's income. To explore the relationship between the quantity and price of apples, we must assume that the consumer's income—and anything else that influences apple purchases—doesn't change during the time period we're considering.

variable
A measure of something that can take on different values.

Alfred Marshall (1842–1924) was a British economist who refined the economic model of supply and demand and provided a label for this process.[5] He picked one variable that affected apple purchases (price) and threw the other variable (income) into what he called the "pound" (in Marshall's time, the "pound" was an enclosure for holding stray cattle; nowadays, a pound is for stray dogs). That variable waited in the pound while Marshall examined the influence of the first variable. Marshall labeled the pound ***ceteris paribus***, the Latin expression meaning that other variables are held fixed:

ceteris paribus
The Latin expression meaning that other variables are held fixed.

> . . . the existence of other tendencies is not denied, but their disturbing effect is neglected for a time. The more the issue is narrowed, the more exactly can it be handled.

This book contains many statements about the relationship between two variables. For example, the quantity of computers produced by Dell depends on the price of computers, the wage of computer workers, and the cost of microchips. When we say, "An increase in the price of computers increases the quantity of computers produced," we are assuming that the other two variables—the wage and the cost of microchips—do not change. That is, we apply the *ceteris paribus* assumption.

Think at the Margin

Economists often consider how a small change in one variable affects another variable and what impact that has on people's decision making. In other words, if circumstances change only slightly, how will people respond? A small, one-unit change in value is called a **marginal change**. The key feature of marginal change is that the first variable changes by only one unit. For example, you might ask, "If I study just one more hour, by how much will my exam score increase?" Economists call this process "thinking at the margin." Thinking at the margin is like thinking on the edge. You will encounter marginal thinking throughout this book. Here are some other marginal questions:

marginal change
A small, one-unit change in value.

- If I keep my barber shop open one more hour, by how much will my revenue increase?
- If I stay in school and earn another degree, by how much will my lifetime earnings increase?
- If a car dealer hires one more sales associate, how many more cars will the dealer sell?

As we'll see in the next chapter, economists use the answer to a marginal question as a first step in deciding whether to do more or less of something, for example, whether to keep your barber shop open one more hour.

Rational People Respond to Incentives

A key assumption of most economic analysis is that people act rationally, meaning they act in their own self-interest. Scottish philosopher Adam Smith (1723–1790), who is also considered the founder of economics, wrote that he discovered within humankind[6]

> a desire of bettering our condition, a desire which, though generally calm and dispassionate, comes with us from the womb, and never leaves us until we go to the grave.

Smith didn't say people are motivated exclusively by self-interest, but rather that self-interest is more powerful than kindness or altruism. In this book, we will assume that people act in their own self-interest. Rational people respond to incentives. When the payoff, or benefit, from doing something changes, people change their behavior to get the benefit.

application 1

INCENTIVES TO BUY HYBRID VEHICLES

APPLYING THE CONCEPTS #1: How do people respond to incentives?

Consider the incentives to buy a hybrid vehicle, which is more fuel efficient but more expensive than a gas-powered vehicle. Between 2000 and 2007, the number of hybrid vehicles increased from fewer than 10,000 vehicles to more than 340,000 vehicles. Over this period, the price of gasoline increased significantly, and the higher price of gasoline was responsible for roughly one third of the hybrid vehicles purchased in 2007. An additional factor in hybrid purchases was a federal subsidy of up to \$3,400 per hybrid vehicle. The subsidy was responsible for roughly one fifth of the hybrid vehicles purchased in 2007. The increase in the number of hybrid vehicles decreased the emission of the greenhouse gas carbon dioxide (CO_2).

How efficient is the hybrid subsidy in reducing CO_2? On average, the cost of abating one ton of CO_2 through the hybrid subsidy is \$177. There are less costly ways to reduce CO_2 emissions, including building insulation, energy-efficient lighting, reforestation, and switching to electric power systems that use fuels that generate less CO_2. For example, a switch from coal to natural gas in power plants reduces CO_2 emissions at less than one third the cost associated with the hybrid subsidy. **Related to Exercise 3.4.**

SOURCE: Based on Arie Beresteanu and Shanjun Li, "Gasoline Prices, Government Support, and the Demand for Hybrid Vehicles in the United States," *International Economic Review* 52 (2011), pp. 161–182.

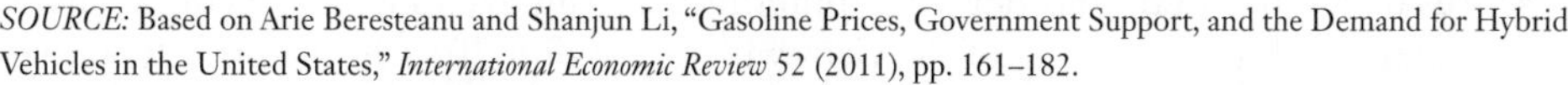

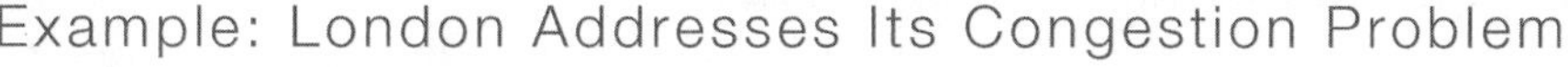

Example: London Addresses Its Congestion Problem

To illustrate the economic way of thinking, let's consider again how an economist would approach the problem of traffic congestion. Recall that each driver on the highway slows down other drivers but ignores these time costs when deciding whether to use the highway. If the government imposes a congestion tax to reduce traffic during rush hour, the economist is faced with a question: How high should the tax be?

To determine the appropriate congestion tax, an economist would assume that people respond to incentives and use the three other elements of the economic way of thinking:

- **Use assumptions to simplify.** To simplify the problem, we would assume that every car has the same effect on the travel time of other cars. Of course, this is unrealistic because people drive cars of different sizes in different ways. But the alternative—looking at the effects of each car on travel speeds—would needlessly complicate the analysis.
- **Isolate variables—use *ceteris paribus*.** To focus attention on the effects of a congestion tax on the number of cars using the highway, we would make the *ceteris paribus* assumption that everything else that affects travel behavior—the price of gasoline, bus fares, and consumer income—remains fixed.
- **Think at the margin.** To think at the margin, we would estimate the effects of adding one more car to the highway. Now consider the marginal question: If we add one more car to the highway, by how much does the total travel time for commuters increase? Once we answer this question, we can determine the cost imposed by the marginal driver. If the marginal driver forces each of

application 2

THE ECONOMIC SOLUTION TO SPAM

APPLYING THE CONCEPTS #2: What is the role of prices in allocating resources?

Spam—unwanted commercial e-mail—torments people around the world, interrupting their work and congesting their computer networks. What's more, spam is spreading to cell phones, with annoying beeps to announce its arrival and sometimes a $0.20 charge to the recipient. A spammer pays nothing to send a million e-mail messages, but earns a profit if just a few people buy an advertised product. The first response to the spam problem was a system of e-mail filters to separate spam from legitimate e-mail. When that didn't work, many states passed laws that made spam illegal. Despite these efforts, the spam problem persists.

The economic approach to spam is to establish a price for commercial e-mail. One idea is to follow the lead of snail mail and require a $0.01 electronic stamp for each commercial e-mail message. A bundle of one million e-mails would cost $10,000, so if a spammer expects just a few people to buy an advertised product, spamming won't be profitable. A second approach is to charge senders a penalty of $1 for each e-mail that is declared "unwanted" by a recipient. If each e-mail account has a credit limit of $200, the sender's internet service provider (ISP) would shut down an account once it receives 200 complaints. This actually solves the problem of viral spam because if a virus turns your grandmother's computer into a spam machine, her account will be shut down—and the spreading of the virus will stop—after 200 complaints. Of course, the ISP must be clever enough to quickly realize that grandma is not a spammer, and then reconnect her. **Related to Exercise 3.5.**

SOURCES: Based on "Make 'em Pay: The Fight against Spam," *Economist*, February 14, 2004, 58; Laura M. Holson, "Spam Moves to Cellphones and Gets More Invasive," *New York Times*, May 10, 2008.

---

the 900 commuters to spend two extra seconds on the highway, total travel time increases by 30 minutes. If the value of time is, say, $16 per hour, the appropriate congestion tax would be $8 (equal to $16 × 1/2 hour).

If the idea of charging people for using roads seems odd, consider the city of London, which for decades had experienced the worst congestion in Europe. In February 2003, the city imposed an $8 tax per day to drive in the city between 7:00 A.M. and 6:30 P.M. The tax reduced traffic volume and cut travel times for cars and buses in half. Because the tax reduced the waste and inefficiency of congestion, the city's economy thrived. Given the success of London's ongoing congestion tax, other cities, including Toronto, Singapore, and San Diego, have implemented congestion pricing.

1.4 Preview of Coming Attractions: Macroeconomics

The field of economics is divided into two categories: macroeconomics and microeconomics. **Macroeconomics** is the study of the nation's economy as a whole; it focuses on the issues of inflation (a general rise in prices), unemployment, and economic growth. These issues are regularly discussed on Web sites, in newspapers, and on television. Macroeconomics explains why economies grow and change and why economic growth is sometimes interrupted. Let's look at three ways we can use macroeconomics.

macroeconomics
The study of the nation's economy as a whole; focuses on the issues of inflation, unemployment, and economic growth.

Using Macroeconomics to Understand Why Economies Grow

As we discussed earlier in the chapter, the world economy has been growing in recent decades, with per capita income increasing by about 1.5 percent per year. Increases in income translate into a higher standard of living for consumers—better cars, houses, and clothing and more options for food, entertainment, and travel. People in a growing economy can consume more of all goods and services because the economy has more of the resources needed to produce these products. Macroeconomics explains why resources increase over time and the consequences for our standard of living. Let's look at a practical question about economic growth.

Why do some countries grow much faster than others? Between 1960 and 2001, the economic growth rate was 2.2 percent per year in the United States, compared to 2.3 percent in Mexico and 2.7 percent in France. But in some countries, the economy actually shrunk, and per capita income dropped. Among the countries with declining income were Sierra Leone and Haiti. In the fastest-growing countries, citizens save a large fraction of the money they earn. Firms can then borrow the funds saved to purchase machinery and equipment that make their workers more productive. The fastest-growing countries also have well-educated workforces, allowing firms to quickly adopt new technologies that increase worker productivity.

Using Macroeconomics to Understand Economic Fluctuations

All economies, including those that experience a general trend of rising per capita income, are subject to economic fluctuations, including periods when the economy temporarily shrinks. During an economic downturn, some of the economy's resources—natural resources, labor, physical capital, human capital, and entrepreneurship—are idle. Some workers are unemployed, and some factories and stores are closed. By contrast, sometimes the economy grows too rapidly, causing prices to rise. Macroeconomics helps us understand why these fluctuations occur—why the economy sometimes cools and sometimes overheats—and what the government can do to moderate the fluctuations. Let's look at a practical question about economic fluctuations.

Should Congress and the president do something to reduce the unemployment rate? For example, should the government cut taxes to free up income to spend on consumer goods, thus encouraging firms to hire more workers to produce more output? If unemployment is very high, the government may want to reduce it. However, it is important not to reduce the unemployment rate too much, because, as we'll see later in the book, a low unemployment rate will cause inflation.

Using Macroeconomics to Make Informed Business Decisions

A third reason for studying macroeconomics is to make informed business decisions. As we'll see later in the book, the government uses various policies to influence interest rates (the price of borrowing money) and the inflation rate. A manager who intends to borrow money for a new factory or store could use knowledge of macroeconomics to predict the effects of current public policies on interest rates and then decide whether to borrow the money now or later. Similarly, a manager must keep an eye on the inflation rate to help decide how much to charge for the firm's products and how much to pay workers. A manager who studies macroeconomics will be better equipped to understand the complexities of interest rates and inflation and how they affect the firm.

1.5 Preview of Coming Attractions: Microeconomics

microeconomics
The study of the choices made by households, firms, and government and how these choices affect the markets for goods and services.

Microeconomics is the study of the choices made by households (an individual or a group of people living together), firms, and government and how these choices affect the markets for goods and services. Let's look at three ways we can use microeconomic analysis.

Using Microeconomics to Understand Markets and Predict Changes

One reason for studying microeconomics is to better understand how markets work and to predict how various events affect the prices and quantities of products in markets. In this book, we answer many practical questions about markets and how they operate. Let's look at a practical question that can be answered with some simple economic analysis.

How would a tax on beer affect the number of highway deaths among young adults? Research has shown that the number of highway fatalities among young adults is roughly proportional to the total amount of beer consumed by that group. A tax on beer would make the product more expensive, and young adults, like other beer drinkers, would therefore consume less of it. Consequently, a tax that decreases beer consumption by 10 percent will decrease highway deaths among young adults by about 10 percent, too.

Using Microeconomics to Make Personal and Managerial Decisions

On the personal level, we use economic analysis to decide how to spend our time, what career to pursue, and how to spend and save the money we earn. Managers use economic analysis to decide how to produce goods and services, how much to produce, and how much to charge for them. Let's use some economic analysis to look at a practical question confronting someone considering starting a business.

If the existing coffee shops in your city are profitable and you have enough money to start your own shop, should you do it? If you enter this market, the competition among the shops for consumers will heat up, causing some coffee shops to drop their prices. In addition, your costs may be higher than the costs of the stores that are already established. It would be sensible to enter the market only if you expect a small drop in price and a small difference in costs. Indeed, entering what appears to be a lucrative market may turn out to be a financial disaster.

Using Microeconomics to Evaluate Public Policies

Although modern societies use markets to make most of the decisions about production and consumption, the government does fulfill several important roles. We can use economic analysis to determine how well the government performs its roles in the market economy. We can also explore the trade-offs associated with various public policies. Let's look at a practical question about public policy.

Like other innovations, prescription drugs are protected by government patents, giving the developer the exclusive right to sell a new drug for a fixed period of time. Once the patent expires, other pharmaceutical companies can legally produce and sell generic versions of the drug, which causes its price to drop. Should drug patents be shorter? Shortening the patent has trade-offs. The good news is that generic versions of the drug will be available sooner, so prices will drop sooner and more people will use the drug to improve their health. The bad news is that the financial payoff from developing new drugs will be smaller, so pharmaceutical companies won't develop as many new drugs. The question is whether the benefit of shorter patents (lower prices) exceeds the cost (fewer drugs developed).

SUMMARY

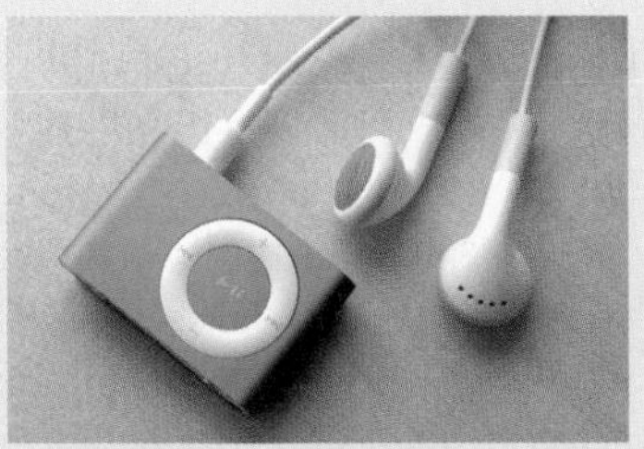

Economics is about making choices when options are limited. Options in an economy are limited because the factors of production are limited. We can use economic analysis to understand the consequences of our choices as individuals, organizations, and society as a whole. Here are the main points of the chapter:

1 Most of modern economics is based on *positive analysis*, which answers the question "What *is*?" or "What *will be*?" Economists contribute to policy debates by conducting positive analyses about the consequences of alternative actions.

2 *Normative analysis* answers the question "What *ought to be*?"

3 The choices made by individuals, firms, and governments answer three questions: What products do we produce? How do we produce the products? Who consumes the products?

4 To think like an economist, we (a) use assumptions to simplify, (b) use the notion of *ceteris paribus* to focus on the relationship between two variables, (c) think in marginal terms, and (d) assume that rational people respond to incentives.

5 We use *macroeconomics* to understand why economies grow, to understand economic fluctuations, and to make informed business decisions.

6 We use *microeconomics* to understand how markets work, to make personal and managerial decisions, and to evaluate the merits of public policies.

KEY TERMS

ceteris paribus, p. 8
economic model, p. 4
economics, p. 2
entrepreneurship, p. 2
factors of production, p. 2
human capital, p. 2
labor, p. 2
macroeconomics, p. 10
marginal change, p. 8
microeconomics, p. 12
natural resources, p. 2
normative analysis, p. 3
physical capital, p. 2
positive analysis, p. 3
scarcity, p. 2
variable, p. 7

EXERCISES

All problems are assignable in MyEconLab.

1.1 What Is Economics?

1.1 The three basic economic questions a society must answer are __________ products do we produce? __________ do we produce the products? __________ consumes the products?

1.2 List the five factors of production.

1.3 Which of the following statements is true?

a. Positive statements answer questions like "What will happen if . . .?" Normative economic statements answer questions like "What ought to happen to . . .?"

b. Normative statements answer questions like "What will happen if . . .?" Positive economic statements answer questions like "What ought to happen to . . .?"

c. Most modern economics is based on normative analysis.

1.4 Indicate whether each of the following questions is normative or positive.

a. Should your city build levees strong enough to protect the city from Category Five hurricanes?

b. How did Hurricane Katrina affect housing prices in New Orleans and Baton Rouge?

c. Who should pay for a new skate park?

d. Should a school district increase teachers' salaries by 20 percent?

e. Would an increase in teachers' salaries improve the average quality of teachers?

1.2 Economic Analysis and Modern Problems

2.1 What is the economist's solution to the congestion problem?

a. Require people to carpool.

b. Charge a toll during rush hour.

c. Require people to move closer to their jobs.

d. No economist would suggest any of the above.

2.2 Some recent work by economists on the sources of growth suggests that institutions such as the __________ and the __________ play key roles in economic growth.

1.3 The Economic Way of Thinking

3.1 A road map incorporates two unrealistic assumptions: (1) __________ and (2) __________.

3.2 The four elements of the economic way of thinking are (1) use __________ to simplify the analysis, (2) explore the relationship between two variables by __________, (3) think at the __________, and (4) rational people respond to __________.

3.3 Which of the following is the Latin expression meaning *other things being held fixed*?

a. *setiferous proboscis*

b. *ceteris paribus*

c. *e pluribus unum*

d. *tres grand fromage*

3.4 The federal subsidy for hybrid cars was responsible for roughly __________ of the hybrid cars purchased in 2007. (Related to Application 1 on page 9.)

3.5 The economic approach to spam is to follow the lead of __________ and establish a __________ for e-mail. (Related to Application 2 on page 10.)

3.6 True or False: Adam Smith suggested that people are motivated solely by self-interest.

APPENDIX

USING GRAPHS AND PERCENTAGES

Economists use several types of graphs to present data, represent relationships between variables, and explain concepts. In this appendix, we review the mechanics of graphing variables. We'll also review the basics of computing percentage changes and using percentages to compute changes in variables.

1A.1 Using Graphs

A quick flip through the book will reveal the importance of graphs in economics. Every chapter has at least several graphs, and many chapters have more. Although it is possible to do economics without graphs, it's a lot easier with them in your toolbox.

Graphing Single Variables

As we saw earlier in Chapter 1, a *variable* is a measure of something that can take on different values. Figure 1A.1 shows two types of graphs, each presenting data on a single variable. Panel A uses a pie graph to show the breakdown of U.S. music sales by type of music. The greater the sales of a type of music, the larger the pie slice. For example, the most popular type is rock music, comprising 24 percent of the market. The next largest type is country, followed by rap/hip-hop, R&B/urban, and so on. Panel B of Figure 1A.1 uses a bar graph to show the revenue from foreign sales (exports) of selected U.S. industries. The larger the revenue, the taller the bar. For example, the bar for computer software, with export sales of about $60 billion, is over three times taller than the bar for motion pictures, TV, and video, with export sales of $17 billion.

▼ **FIGURE 1A.1**
Graphs of Single Variables

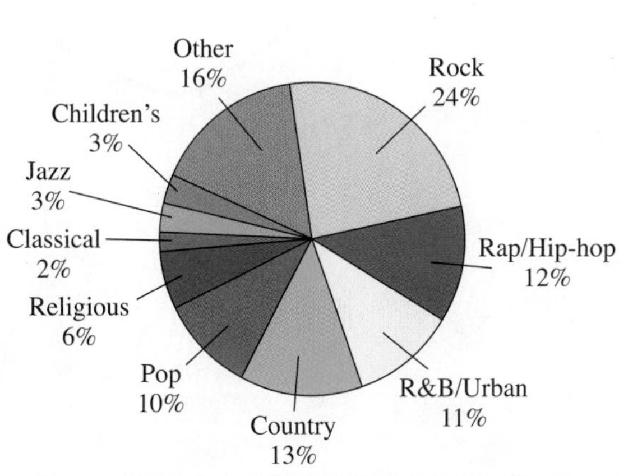

(A) Pie Graph for Types of Recorded Music Sold in the United States

SOURCE: Author's calculations based on Recording Industry Association of America, *"2004 Consumer Profile."*

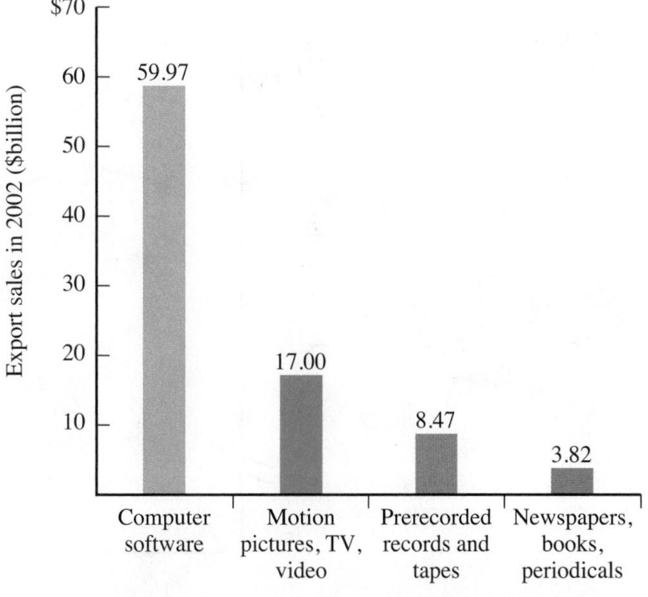

(B) Bar Graph for U.S. Export Sales of Copyrighted Products

SOURCE: Author's calculations based on International Intellectual Property Alliance, *"Copyright Industries in the U.S. Economy, 2004 Report."*

A third type of single-variable graph shows how the value of a variable changes over time. Panel A of Figure 1A.2 shows a time-series graph, with the total dollar value of a hypothetical industry for years 1 through 10. Time is measured on the horizontal axis, and sales are measured on the vertical axis. The height of the line in a particular year shows the value in that year. For example, in Year 1 the value was $12.32 billion. After reaching a peak of $14.59 billion in Year 5, the value dropped over the next several years.

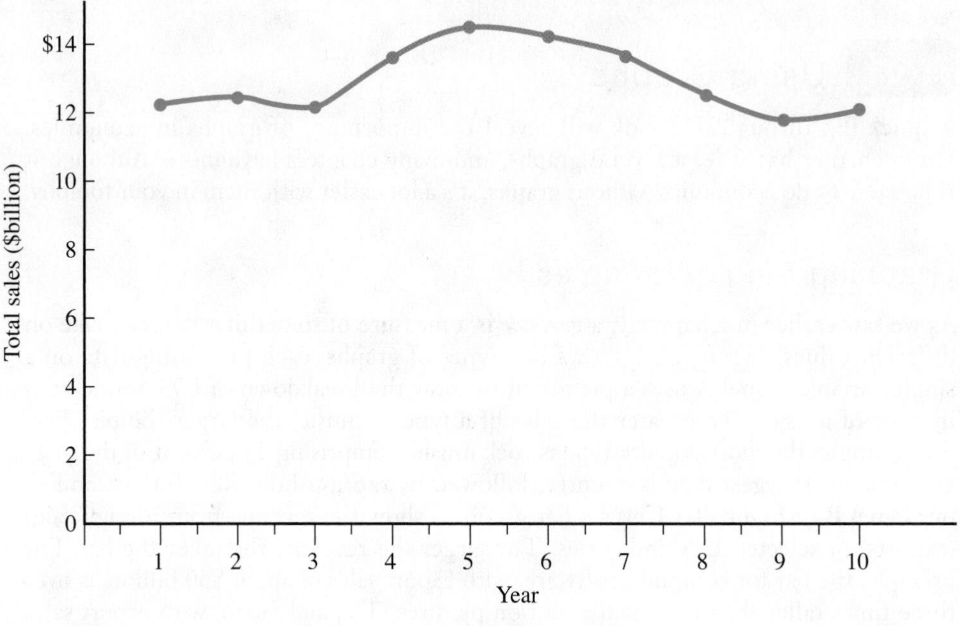

(A) Total Sales of Industry

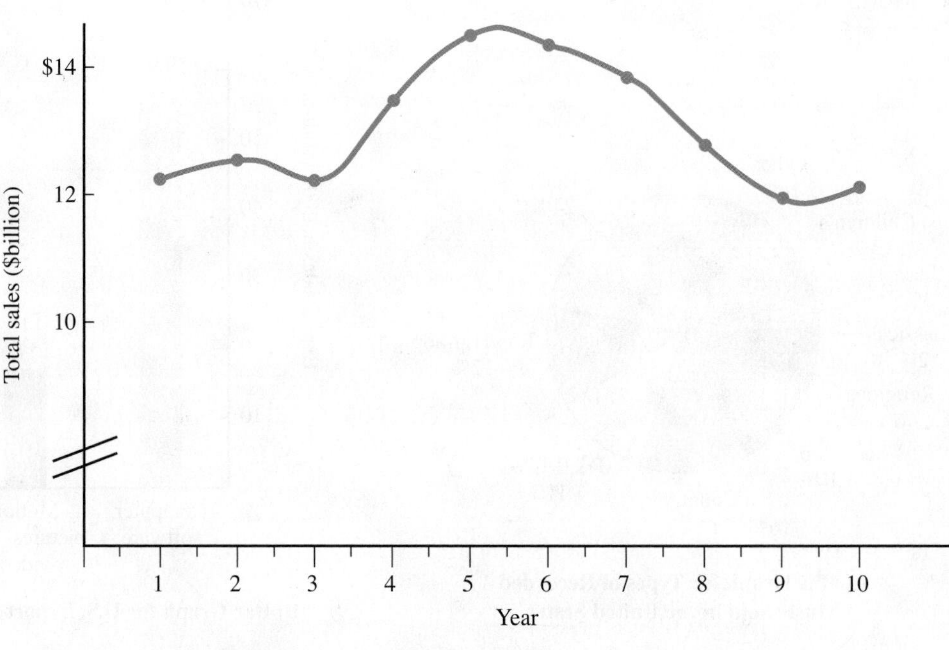

(B) Truncated Vertical Axis

▲ FIGURE 1A.2
Time-Series Graph

Panel B of Figure 1A.2 shows a truncated version of the graph in Panel A. The double hash marks in the lower part of the vertical axis indicate that the axis doesn't start from zero. This truncation of the vertical axis exaggerates the fluctuations in total sales.

Graphing Two Variables

We can also use a graph to show the relationship between two variables. Figure 1A.3 shows the basic elements of a two-variable graph. One variable is measured along the horizontal, or *x*, axis, while the other variable is measured along the vertical, or *y*, axis. The *origin* is the intersection of the two axes, where the values of both variables are zero. Dashed lines show the values of the two variables at a particular point. For example, for point *a*, the value of the horizontal, or *x*, variable is 10, and the value of the vertical, or *y*, variable is 13.

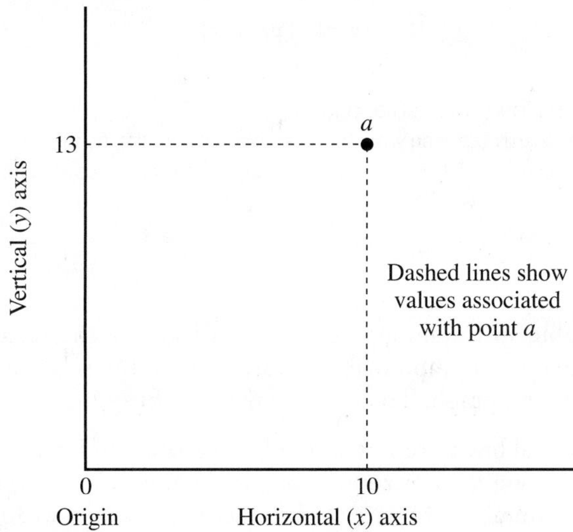

▲ FIGURE 1A.3

Basic Elements of a Two-Variable Graph

One variable is measured along the horizontal, or *x*, axis, while the other variable is measured along the vertical, or *y*, axis. The origin is defined as the intersection of the two axes, where the values of both variables are zero. The dashed lines show the values of the two variables at a particular point.

To see how to draw a two-variable graph, suppose that you have a part-time job and you are interested in the relationship between the number of hours you work and your weekly income. The relevant variables are the hours of work per week and your weekly income. In Figure 1A.4, the table shows the relationship between the hours worked and income. Let's assume that your weekly allowance from your parents is $40 and your part-time job pays $8 per hour. If you work 10 hours per week, for example, your weekly income is $120 ($40 from your parents and $80 from your job). The more you work, the higher your weekly income: If you work 20 hours, your weekly income is $200; if you work 30 hours, it is $280.

Hours Worked per Week	Income per Week	Point on the Graph
0	$ 40	*a*
10	120	*b*
20	200	*c*
30	280	*d*

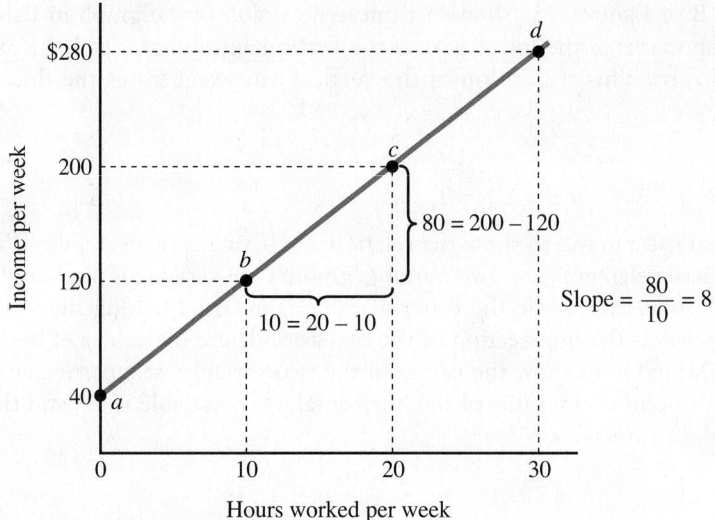

▲ FIGURE 1A.4

Relationship between Hours Worked and Income

There is a positive relationship between work hours and income, so the income curve is positively sloped. The slope of the curve is $8: Each additional hour of work increases income by $8.

Although a table with numbers is helpful in showing the relationship between work hours and income, a graph makes it easier to see the relationship. We can use data in a table to draw a graph. To do so, we perform five simple steps:

1 Draw a horizontal line to represent the first variable. In Figure 1A.4, we measure hours worked along the horizontal axis. As we move to the right along the horizontal axis, the number of hours worked increases, from 0 to 30 hours.

2 Draw a vertical line intersecting the first line to represent the second variable. In Figure 1A.4, we measure income along the vertical axis. As we move up along the vertical axis, income increases from $0 to $280.

3 Start with the first row of numbers in the table, which shows that with 0 hours worked, income is $40. The value of the variable on the horizontal axis is 0, and the value of the variable on the vertical axis is $40, so we plot point *a* on the graph. This is the *vertical intercept*—the point where the curve cuts or intersects the vertical axis.

4 Pick a combination with a positive number for hours worked. For example, in the second row of numbers, if you work 10 hours, your income is $120.

4.1 Find the point on the horizontal axis with that number of hours worked—10 hours—and draw a dashed line vertically straight up from that point.

4.2 Find the point on the vertical axis with the income corresponding to those hours worked—$120—and draw a dashed line horizontally straight to the right from that point.

4.3 The intersection of the dashed lines shows the combination of hours worked and income. Point *b* shows the combination of 10 hours worked and $120 in income.

5 Repeat step 4 for different combinations of work time and income shown in the table. Once we have a series of points on the graph (*a*, *b*, *c*, and *d*), we can connect them to draw a curve that shows the relationship between hours worked and income.

There is a **positive relationship** between two variables if they move in the same direction. As you increase your work time, your income increases, so there is a positive relationship between the two variables. In Figure 1A.4, as the number of hours worked increases, you move upward along the curve to higher income levels. Some people refer to a positive relationship as a *direct relationship*.

positive relationship
A relationship in which two variables move in the same direction.

There is a **negative relationship** between two variables if they move in opposite directions. For example, there is a negative relationship between the amount of time you work and the time you have available for other activities such as recreation, study, and sleep. Some people refer to a negative relationship as an *inverse relationship*.

negative relationship
A relationship in which two variables move in opposite directions.

Computing the Slope

How sensitive is one variable to changes in the other variable? We can use the slope of the curve to measure this sensitivity. To compute the **slope of a curve**, we pick two points and divide the vertical difference between the two points (the *rise*) by the horizontal difference (the *run*):

slope of a curve
The vertical difference between two points (the *rise*) divided by the horizontal difference (the *run*).

$$\text{Slope} = \frac{\text{Vertical difference between two points}}{\text{Horizontal difference between two points}} = \frac{\text{rise}}{\text{run}}$$

To compute the slope of a curve, we take four steps:

1. Pick two points on the curve, for example, points *b* and *c* in Figure 1A.4.
2. Compute the vertical difference between the two points (the rise). For points *b* and *c*, the vertical difference between the points is \$80 (\$200 – \$120).
3. Compute the horizontal distance between the same two points (the run). For points *b* and *c*, the horizontal distance between the points is 10 hours (20 hours – 10 hours).
4. Divide the vertical distance by the horizontal distance to get the slope. The slope between points *b* and *c* is \$8 per hour:

$$\text{Slope} = \frac{\text{Vertical difference}}{\text{Horizontal difference}} = \frac{\$200 - 120}{20 - 10} = \frac{\$80}{10} = \$8$$

In this case, a 10-hour increase in time worked increases income by \$80, so the increase in income per hour of work is \$8, which makes sense because this is the hourly wage. Because the curve is a straight line, the slope is the same at all points along the curve. You can check this yourself by computing the slope between points *c* and *d*.

We can use some shorthand to refer to the slope of a curve. The mathematical symbol Δ (delta) represents the change in a variable. So we can write the slope of the curve in Figure 1A.4 as

$$\text{Slope} = \frac{\Delta\ \text{Income}}{\Delta\ \text{Work hours}}$$

In general, if the variable on the vertical axis is y and the variable on the horizontal axis is x, we can express the slope as

$$\text{Slope} = \frac{\Delta y}{\Delta x}$$

Moving along the Curve versus Shifting the Curve

Up to this point, we've explored the effect of changes in variables that cause movement along a given curve. In Figure 1A.4, we see the relationship between hours of work (on the horizontal axis) and income (on the vertical axis). Because the total income also depends on the allowance and the wage, we can make two observations about the curve in Figure 1A.4:

1 To draw this curve, we must specify the weekly allowance ($40) and the hourly wage ($8).

2 The curve shows that an increase in time worked increases the student's income, *ceteris paribus*. In this case, we are assuming that the allowance and the wage are both fixed.

A change in the weekly allowance will shift the curve showing the relationship between work time and income. In Figure 1A.5, when the allowance increases from $40 to $90, the curve shifts upward by $50. For a given number of work hours, income increases by $50. For example, the income associated with 10 hours of work is $170 (point *f*), compared to $120 with the original allowance (point *b*). The upward shift also means that to reach a given amount of income, fewer work hours are required. In other words, the curve shifts upward and to the left.

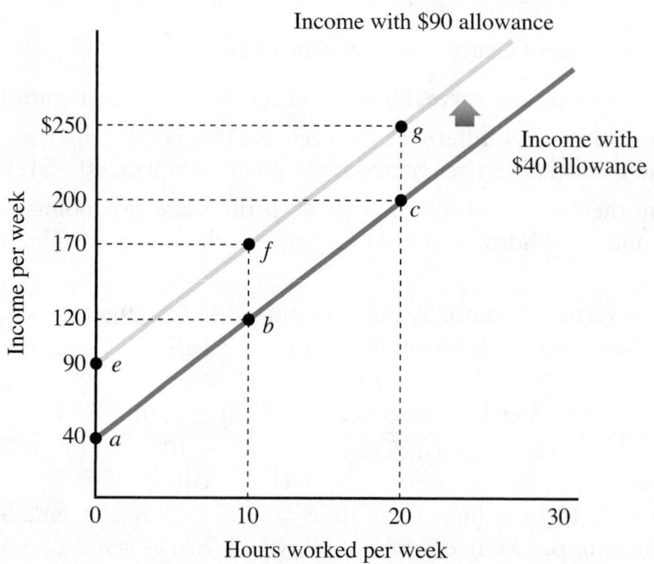

▲ **FIGURE 1A.5**

Movement Along a Curve versus Shifting the Curve

To draw a curve showing the relationship between hours worked and income, we fix the weekly allowance ($40) and the wage ($8 per hour). A change in the hours worked causes movement along the curve, for example, from point *b* to point *c*. A change in any other variable shifts the entire curve. For example, a $50 increase in the allowance (to $90) shifts the entire curve upward by $50.

We can distinguish between movement along a curve and a shift of the entire curve. In Figure 1A.5, an increase in the hours worked causes movement along a single income curve. For example, if the allowance is $40, we are operating on the lower of the two curves, and if the hours worked increases from 10 to 20, we move from point *b* to point *c*. In contrast, if something other than the hours worked changes, we shift the entire curve, as we've seen with an increase in the allowance.

This book uses dozens of two-dimensional curves, each of which shows the relationship between *only two* variables. A common error is to forget that a single curve tells only part of the story. In Figure 1A.5, we needed two curves to explore the effects of changes in three variables. Here are some simple rules to keep in mind when you use two-dimensional graphs:

- A change in one of the variables shown on the graph causes movement along the curve. In Figure 1A.5, an increase in work time causes movement along the curve from point *a* to point *b*, to point *c*, and so on.
- A change in one of the variables that is not shown on the graph—one of the variables held fixed in drawing the curve—shifts the entire curve. In Figure 1A.5, an increase in the allowance shifts the entire curve upward.

Graphing Negative Relationships

We can use a graph to show a negative relationship between two variables. Consider a consumer who has an annual budget of $360 to spend on CDs at a price of $12 per CD and downloaded music at a price of $1 per song. The table in Figure 1A.6 shows the relationship between the number of CDs and downloaded songs. A consumer who doesn't buy any CDs has $360 to spend on downloaded songs and can get 360 of them at a price of $1 each. A consumer who buys 10 CDs at $12 each has $240 left to spend

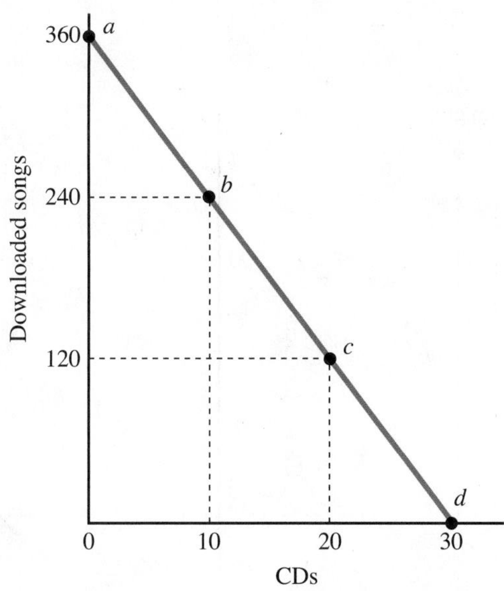

▲ **FIGURE 1A.6**

Negative Relationship between CD Purchases and Downloaded Songs

There is a negative relationship between the number of CDs and downloaded songs that a consumer can afford with a budget of $360. The slope of the curve is –$12: Each additional CD (at a price of $12 each) decreases the number of downloadable songs (at $1 each) by 12 songs.

Number of CDs Purchased	Number of Songs Downloaded	Point on the Graph
0	360	a
10	240	b
20	120	c
30	0	d

on downloaded songs (point *b*). Moving down through the table, as the number of CDs increases, the number of downloaded songs decreases.

The graph in Figure 1A.6 shows the negative relationship between the number of CDs and the number of downloaded songs. The vertical intercept (point *a*) shows that a consumer who doesn't buy any CDs can afford 360 downloaded songs. There is a negative relationship between the number of CDs and downloaded songs, so the curve is negatively sloped. We can use points *b* and *c* to compute the slope of the curve:

$$\text{Slope} = \frac{\text{Vertical difference}}{\text{Horizontal difference}} = \frac{120 - 240}{20 - 10} = \frac{-120}{10} = -12$$

The slope is 12 downloaded songs per CD: For each additional CD, the consumer sacrifices 12 downloaded songs.

Graphing Nonlinear Relationships

We can also use a graph to show a nonlinear relationship between two variables. Panel A of Figure 1A.7 shows the relationship between hours spent studying for an exam and the grade on the exam. As study time increases, the grade increases,

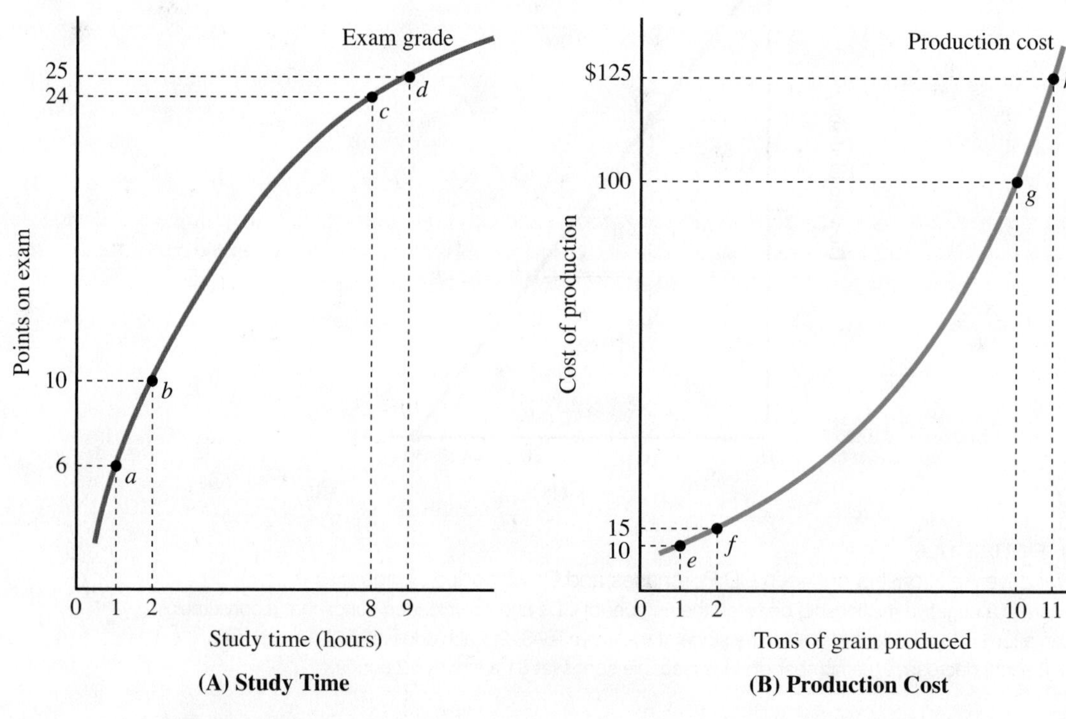

▲ FIGURE 1A.7

Nonlinear Relationships

(A) Study time There is a positive and nonlinear relationship between study time and the grade on an exam. As study time increases, the exam grade increases at a decreasing rate. For example, the second hour of study increased the grade by 4 points (from 6 points to 10 points), but the ninth hour of study increases the grade by only 1 point (from 24 points to 25 points).

(B) Production cost There is a positive and nonlinear relationship between the quantity of grain produced and total production cost. As the quantity increases, the total cost increases at an increasing rate. For example, to increase production from 1 ton to 2 tons, production cost increases by $5 (from $10 to $15) but to increase the production from 10 to 11 tons, total cost increases by $25 (from $100 to $125).

but at a decreasing rate. In other words, each additional hour increases the exam grade by a smaller and smaller amount. For example, the second hour of study increases the grade by 4 points—from 6 to 10 points—but the ninth hour of study increases the grade by only 1 point—from 24 points to 25 points. This is a nonlinear relationship: The slope of the curve changes as we move along the curve. In Figure 1A.7, the slope decreases as we move to the right along the curve: The slope is 4 points per hour between points *a* and *b* but only 1 point per hour between points *c* and *d*.

Another possibility for a nonlinear curve is that the slope increases as we move to the right along the curve. Panel B of Figure 1A.7 shows the relationship between the amount of grain produced on the horizontal axis and the total cost of production on the vertical axis. The slope of the curve increases as the amount of grain increases, meaning that production cost increases at an increasing rate. On the lower part of the curve, increasing output from 1 ton to 2 tons increases production cost by \$5, from \$10 to \$15. On the upper part of the curve, increasing output from 10 to 11 tons increases production cost by \$25, from \$100 to \$125.

1A.2 Computing Percentage Changes and Using Equations

Economists often express changes in variables in terms of percentage changes. This part of the appendix provides a brief review of the mechanics of computing percentage changes. It also reviews some simple rules for solving equations to find missing values.

Computing Percentage Changes

In many cases, the equations that economists use involve percentage changes. In this book, we use a simple approach to computing percentage changes: We divide the change in the variable by the initial value of the variable and then multiply by 100:

$$\text{Percentage change} = \frac{\text{New value} - \text{initial value}}{\text{Initial value}} \times 100$$

For example, if the price of a book increases from \$20 to \$22, the percentage change is 10 percent:

$$\text{Percentage change} = \frac{22 - 20}{20} \times 100 = \frac{2}{20} \times 100 = 10\%$$

Going in the other direction, suppose the price decreases from \$20 to \$19. In this case, the percentage change is –5 percent:

$$\text{Percentage change} = \frac{19 - 20}{20} \times 100 = -\frac{1}{20} \times 100 = -5\%$$

The alternative to this simple approach is to base the percentage change on the average value, or the midpoint, of the variable:

$$\text{Percentage change} = \frac{\text{New value} - \text{initial value}}{\text{Average value}} \times 100$$

For example, if the price of a book increases from \$20 to \$22, the computed percentage change under the midpoint approach is 9.52 percent:

$$\text{Percentage change} = \frac{22 - 20}{(20 + 22) \div 2} \times 100 = \frac{2}{42 \div 2} \times 100$$

$$= \frac{2}{21} \times 100 = 9.52\%,$$

If the change in the variable is relatively small, the extra precision associated with the midpoint approach is usually not worth the extra effort. The simple approach allows us to spend less time doing tedious arithmetic and more time doing economic analysis. In this book, we use the simple approach to compute percentage changes: If the price increases from \$20 to \$22, the price has increased by 10 percent.

If we know a percentage change, we can translate it into an absolute change. For example, if a price has increased by 10 percent and the initial price is \$20, then we add 10 percent of the initial price (\$2 is 10 percent of \$20) to the initial price (\$20), for a new price of \$22. If the price decreases by 5 percent, we subtract 5 percent

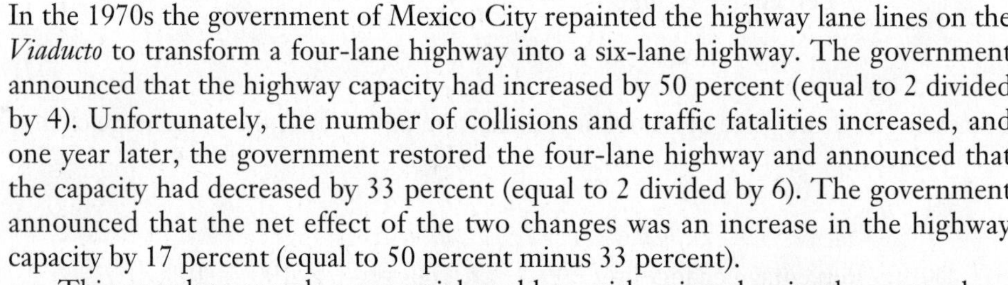

application 3

THE PERILS OF PERCENTAGES

APPLYING THE CONCEPTS #3: How do we compute percentage changes?

In the 1970s the government of Mexico City repainted the highway lane lines on the *Viaducto* to transform a four-lane highway into a six-lane highway. The government announced that the highway capacity had increased by 50 percent (equal to 2 divided by 4). Unfortunately, the number of collisions and traffic fatalities increased, and one year later, the government restored the four-lane highway and announced that the capacity had decreased by 33 percent (equal to 2 divided by 6). The government announced that the net effect of the two changes was an increase in the highway capacity by 17 percent (equal to 50 percent minus 33 percent).

This anecdote reveals a potential problem with using the simple approach to compute percentage changes. Because the initial value (the denominator) changes, the computation of percentage increases and decreases are not symmetric. In contrast, if the government had used the midpoint method, the percentage increase in capacity would be 40 percent (equal to 2 divided by 5), the same as the percentage decrease. In that case, we get the more sensible result that the net effect of the two changes is zero. **Related to Exercise A8.**

SOURCE: Based on "The Perils of Percentages," *Economist*, April 18, 1998, 70.

of the initial price ($1 is 5 percent of $20) from the initial price ($20), for a new price of $19.

Using Equations to Compute Missing Values

It will often be useful to compute the value of the numerator or the denominator of an equation. To do so, we use simple algebra to rearrange the equation to put the missing variable on the left side of the equation. For example, consider the relationship between time worked and income. The equation for the slope is

$$\text{Slope} = \frac{\Delta \text{ Income}}{\Delta \text{ Work hours}}$$

Suppose you want to compute how much income you'll earn by working more hours. We can rearrange the slope equation by multiplying both sides of the equation by the change in work hours:

$$\text{Work hours} \times \text{Slope} = \Delta \text{ Income}$$

By swapping sides of the equation, we get

$$\Delta \text{ Income} = \Delta \text{ Work hours} \times \text{Slope}$$

For example, if you work seven extra hours and the slope is $8, your income will increase by $56:

$$\Delta \text{ Income} = \Delta \text{ Work hours} \times \text{Slope} = \$7 \times \$8 = \$56$$

We can use the same process to compute the difference in work time required to achieve a target change in income. In this case, we multiply both sides of the slope equation by the change in work time and then divide both sides by the slope. The result is

$$\Delta \text{ Work hours} = \frac{\Delta \text{ Income}}{\text{Slope}}$$

For example, to increase your income by $56, you need to work seven hours:

$$\Delta \text{ Work hours} = \frac{\Delta \text{ Income}}{\text{Slope}} = \frac{\$56}{\$8} = 7$$

KEY TERMS

negative relationship, p. 19

positive relationship, p. 19

slope of a curve, p. 19

EXERCISES

All problems are assignable in MyEconLab.

A.1 Suppose you belong to a tennis club that has a monthly fee of $100 and a charge of $5 per hour to play tennis.

a. Using Figure 1A.4 on page 18 as a model, prepare a table and draw a curve to show the relationship between the hours of tennis (on the horizontal axis) and the monthly club bill (on the vertical axis). For the table and graph, use 5, 10, 15, and 20 hours of tennis.

b. The slope of the curve is ________ per ________.

c. Suppose you start with 10 hours of tennis and then decide to increase your tennis time by 3 hours. On your curve, show the initial point and the new point. By how much will your monthly bill increase?

d. Suppose you start with 10 hours and then decide to spend an additional $30 on tennis. On your curve, show the initial point and the new point. How many additional hours can you get?

A.2 The following graph shows the relationship between the number of Frisbees produced and the cost of production. The vertical intercept is $________, and the slope of the curve is $________ per Frisbee. Point *b* shows that the cost of producing ________ Frisbees is $________. The cost of producing 15 Frisbees is $________.

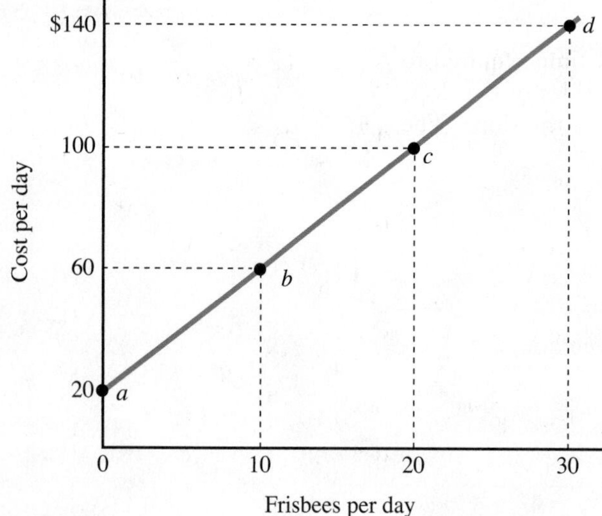

A.3 Suppose you have $120 to spend on CDs and movies. The price of a CD is $12, and the price of a movie is $6.

a. Using Figure 1A.6 on page 21 as a model, prepare a table and draw a curve to show the relationship between the number of CDs (on the horizontal axis) and movies (on the vertical axis) you can afford to buy.

b. The slope of the curve is ________ per ________.

A.4 You manage Gofer Delivery Service. You rent a truck for $50 per day, and each delivery takes an hour of labor time. The hourly wage is $8.

a. Draw a curve showing the relationship between the number of deliveries (on the horizontal axis) and your total cost (on the vertical axis). Draw the curve for between 0 and 20 deliveries.

b. The slope of the cost curve is ________ per ________.

c. To draw the curve, what variables are held fixed?

d. A change in ________ would cause a movement upward along the curve.

e. Changes in ________ would cause the entire curve to shift upward.

A.5 A change in a variable measured on an axis of a graph causes movement ________ a curve, while a change in a relevant variable that is not measured on an axis ________ the entire curve.

A.6 Compute the percentage changes for the following:

Initial Value	New Value	Percentage Change
10	11	
100	98	
50	53	

A.7 Compute the new values for the following changes:

Initial Value	Percentage Change	New Value
100	12%	
50	8	
20	15	

A.8 Suppose the price of an MP3 player decreases from $60 to $40. Using the midpoint approach, the percentage change in price is ________. Using the initial-value approach, the percentage change in price is ________. (Related to Application 3 on page 24.)

NOTES

1. Texas Transportation Institute, *2005 Urban Mobility Study*, http://mobility.tamu.edu/ums/

2. William Easterly, *The Elusive Quest for Growth* (Cambridge, MA: MIT Press, 2001), Chapter 1.

3. William Easterly, *The Elusive Quest for Growth* (Cambridge, MA: MIT Press, 2001); World Bank, *World Development Report 2000/2001: Attacking Poverty* (New York: Oxford University Press, 2000).

4. John Maynard Keynes, *The Collected Writings of John Maynard Keynes, Volume* 7, ed. Donald Moggridge (London: Macmillan, 1973), 856. Reproduced with permission of the publisher.

5. Alfred Marshall, *Principles of Economics*, 9th ed., ed. C.W. Guillebaud (1920; repr., London: Macmillan, 1961), 366. Reproduced with permission of the publisher.

6. Adam Smith, *An Inquiry into the Nature and Causes of the Wealth of Nations* (1776); Book 2, Chapter 3.

CHAPTER

2 The Key Principles of Economics

What do we sacrifice by preserving tropical rainforests rather than mining or logging the land?

Recent experiences in Guyana and other tropical countries suggest that in some places, the answer is "not much"—only \$1 per hectare per year (\$0.40 per acre per year).[1] Conservation groups have a new strategy for conserving rainforests—bidding against loggers and miners for the use of the land. When the payoff from developing tropical forest land is relatively low, conservation groups can outbid developers at a price as low as \$1 per hectare. When we add the cost of hiring locals to manage the ecosystems, the total cost of preservation is as low as \$2 per hectare per year. A conservation group based in Amherst, New Hampshire, started by leasing 81,000 hectares of pristine forest in Guyana, and since then has leased land in Peru, Sierra Leone, Papua New Guinea, Fiji, and Mexico.

LEARNING OBJECTIVES

- Apply the principle of opportunity cost.
- Apply the marginal principle.
- Apply the principle of voluntary exchange.
- Apply the principle of diminishing returns.
- Apply the real-nominal principle.

MyEconLab

MyEconLab helps you master each objective and study more efficiently.

In this chapter, we introduce five key principles that provide a foundation for economic analysis. A *principle* is a self-evident truth that most people readily understand and accept. For example, most people readily accept the principle of gravity. As you read through the book, you will see the five key principles of economics again and again as you do your own economic analysis.

2.1 The Principle of Opportunity Cost

Economics is all about making choices, and to make good choices we must compare the benefit of something to its cost. **Opportunity cost** incorporates the notion of scarcity: No matter what we do, there is always a trade-off. We must trade off one thing for another because resources are limited and can be used in different ways. By acquiring something, we use up resources that could have been used to acquire something else. The notion of opportunity cost allows us to measure this trade-off.

opportunity cost
What you sacrifice to get something.

PRINCIPLE OF OPPORTUNITY COST

The opportunity cost of something is what you sacrifice to get it.

In most decisions we choose from several alternatives. For example, if you spend an hour studying for an economics exam, you have one fewer hour to pursue other activities. To determine the opportunity cost of an activity, we look at what you consider the best of these "other" activities. For example, suppose the alternatives to studying economics are studying for a history exam or working in a job that pays $10 per hour. If you consider studying for history a better use of your time than working, then the opportunity cost of studying economics is the four extra points you could have received on a history exam if you studied history instead of economics. Alternatively, if working is the best alternative, the opportunity cost of studying economics is the $10 you could have earned instead.

We can also apply the principle of opportunity cost to decisions about how to spend money from a fixed budget. For example, suppose that you have a fixed budget to spend on music. You can buy your music either at a local music store for $15 per CD or online for $1 per song. The opportunity cost of 1 CD is 15 one-dollar online songs. A hospital with a fixed salary budget can increase the number of doctors only at the expense of nurses or physician's assistants. If a doctor costs five times as much as a nurse, the opportunity cost of a doctor is five nurses.

In some cases, a product that appears to be free actually has a cost. That's why economists are fond of saying, "There's no such thing as a free lunch." Suppose someone offers to buy you lunch if you agree to listen to a sales pitch for a timeshare condominium. Although you don't pay any money for the lunch, there is an opportunity cost because you could spend that time in another way—such as studying for your economics or history exam. The lunch isn't free because you sacrifice an hour of your time to get it.

The Cost of College

What is the opportunity cost of a college degree? Consider a student who spends a total of $40,000 for tuition and books. Instead of going to college, the student could have spent this money on a wide variety of goods, including housing, electronic devices, and world travel. Part of the opportunity cost of college is the $40,000 worth of other goods the student sacrifices to pay for tuition and books. Also, instead of going to college, the student could have worked as a bank clerk for $20,000 per year and earned $80,000 over four years. That makes the total opportunity cost of this student's college degree $120,000:

Opportunity cost of money spent on tuition and books	$ 40,000
Opportunity cost of college time (four years working for $20,000 per year)	80,000
Economic cost or total opportunity cost	$120,000

We haven't included the costs of food or housing in our computations of opportunity cost. That's because a student must eat and live somewhere even if he or she doesn't go to college. But if housing and food are more expensive in college, then we would include the extra costs of housing and food in our calculations.

There are other things to consider in a person's decision to attend college. As we'll see later, a college degree can increase a person's earning power, so there are benefits from a college degree. In addition, college offers the thrill of learning and the pleasure of meeting new people. To make an informed decision about whether to attend college, we must compare the benefits to the opportunity costs.

The Cost of Military Spending

We can use the principle of opportunity cost to explore the cost of military spending.[2] In 1992, Malaysia bought two warships. For the price of the warships, the country could have built a system to provide safe drinking water for 5 million citizens who lacked it. In other words, the opportunity cost of the warships was safe drinking water for 5 million people. The policy question is whether the benefits of the warships exceed their opportunity cost.

In the United States, economists have estimated that the cost of the war in Iraq will be at least $1 trillion. The economists' calculations go beyond the simple budgetary costs and quantify the opportunity cost of the war. For example, the resources used in the war could have been used in various government programs for children—to enroll more children in preschool programs, to hire more science and math teachers to reduce class sizes, or to immunize more children in poor countries. For example, each $100 billion spent on the war could instead support one of the following programs:

- Enroll 13 million preschool children in the Head Start program for one year.
- Hire 1.8 million additional teachers for one year.
- Immunize all the children in less-developed countries for the next 33 years.

The fact that the war has a large opportunity cost does not necessarily mean that it is unwise. The policy question is whether the benefits from the war exceed its opportunity cost. Taking another perspective, we can measure the opportunity cost of war in terms of its implications for domestic security. The resources used in the war in Iraq could have been used to improve domestic security by securing ports and cargo facilities, hiring more police officers, improving the screening of airline passengers and baggage, improving fire departments and other first responders, upgrading the Coast Guard fleet, and securing our railroad and highway systems. The cost of implementing the domestic-security recommendations of various government commissions would be about $31 billion, a small fraction of the cost of the war. The question for policymakers is whether money spent on domestic security would be more beneficial than money spent on the war.

Opportunity Cost and the Production Possibilities Curve

Just as individuals face limits, so do entire economies. As we saw in Chapter 1, the ability of an economy to produce goods and services is determined by its factors of production, including labor, natural resources, physical capital, human capital, and entrepreneurship.

Figure 2.1 shows a production possibilities graph for an economy that produces wheat and steel. The horizontal axis shows the quantity of wheat produced by the economy, and the vertical axis shows the quantity of steel produced. The shaded area shows all the possible combinations of the two goods the economy can produce. At point *a*, for example, the economy can produce 700 tons of steel and 10 tons of wheat. In contrast, at point *e*, the economy can produce 300 tons of steel and 20 tons of wheat. The set of points on the border between the shaded and unshaded area is called the **production possibilities curve** (or *production possibilities frontier*) because it separates the combinations that are attainable from those that are not. The attainable combinations are shown by the shaded area within the curve and the curve itself. The unattainable combinations are shown by the unshaded area outside the curve. The points on the curve show the combinations that are possible if the economy's resources are fully employed.

production possibilities curve
A curve that shows the possible combinations of products that an economy can produce, given that its productive resources are fully employed and efficiently used.

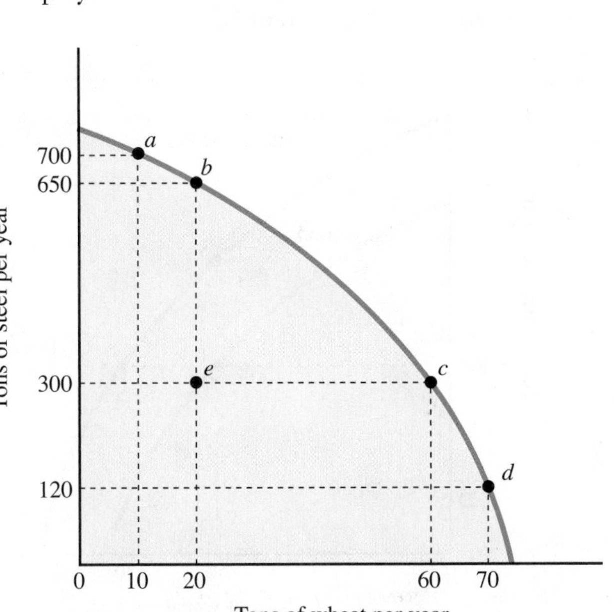

▲ FIGURE 2.1
Scarcity and the Production Possibilities Curve
The production possibilities curve illustrates the principle of opportunity cost for an entire economy. An economy has a fixed amount of resources. If these resources are fully employed, an increase in the production of wheat comes at the expense of steel.

The production possibilities curve illustrates the notion of opportunity cost. If an economy is fully utilizing its resources, it can produce more of one product only if it produces less of another product. For example, to produce more wheat, we must take resources away from steel. As we move resources out of steel, the quantity of steel produced will decrease. For example, if we move from point *a* to point *b* along the production possibilities curve in Figure 2.1, we sacrifice 50 tons of steel (700 tons – 650 tons) to get 10 more tons of wheat (20 tons – 10 tons). Further down the curve, if we move from point *c* to point *d*, we sacrifice 180 tons of steel to get the same 10-ton increase in wheat.

Why is the production possibilities curve bowed outward, with the opportunity cost of wheat increasing as we move down the curve? The reason is that resources are not perfectly adaptable for the production of both goods. Some resources are more suitable for steel production, while others are more suitable for wheat production. Starting at point *a*, the economy uses its most fertile land to produce wheat. A 10-ton increase in wheat reduces the quantity of steel by only 50 tons, because plenty of fertile land is available for conversion to wheat farming. As the economy moves downward along the production possibilities curve, farmers will be forced to use land that is progressively less fertile, so to increase wheat output by 10 tons, more and more resources must be diverted from steel production. In the move from point *c* to point *d*, the land converted to farming is so poor that increasing wheat output by 10 tons decreases steel output by 180 tons.

The production possibilities curve shows the production options for a given set of resources. As shown in Figure 2.2, an increase in the amount of resources available to the economy shifts the production possibilities outward. For example, if we start at point *f*, and the economy's resources increase, we can produce more steel (point *g*), more wheat (point *h*), or more of both goods (points between g and *h*). The curve will also shift outward as a result of technological innovations that enable us to produce more output with a given quantity of resources.

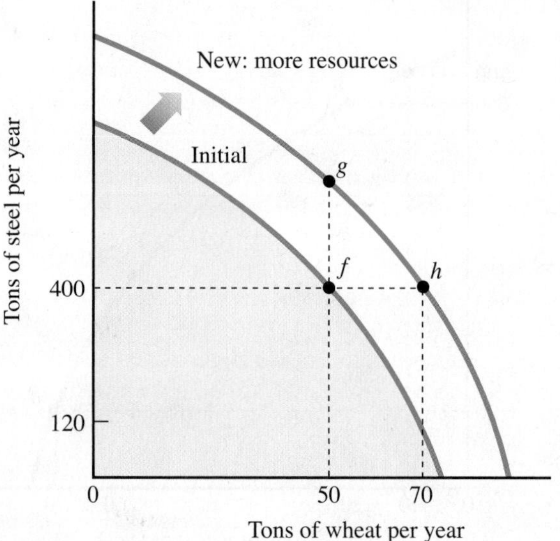

▲ FIGURE 2.2
Shifting the Production Possibilities Curve
An increase in the quantity of resources or technological innovation in an economy shifts the production possibilities curve outward. Starting from point *f*, a nation could produce more steel (point *g*), more wheat (point *h*), or more of both goods (points between *g* and *h*).

application 1

DON'T FORGET THE COSTS OF TIME AND INVESTED FUNDS

APPLYING THE CONCEPTS #1: What is the opportunity cost of running a business?

Suppose you run a lawn-cutting business and use solar-powered equipment (mower, edger, blower, truck) that you could sell tomorrow for $5,000. Instead of cutting lawns, you could work as a janitor for $300 per week. You have a savings account that pays a weekly interest rate of 0.20 percent (or $0.002 per dollar). What is your weekly cost of cutting lawns?

We can use the principle of opportunity cost to compute the cost of the lawn business. The opportunity cost of the $5,000 you have invested in the business is the $10 weekly interest you could have earned by selling the equipment and investing the $5,000 in your savings account. Adding in the opportunity cost of cutting lawns instead of earning $300 as a janitor, the weekly cost is $310. **Related to Exercise 1.7.**

2.2 The Marginal Principle

Economics is about making choices, and we rarely make all-or-nothing choices. For example, if you sit down to read a book, you don't read the entire book in a single sitting, but instead decide how many pages or chapters to read. Economists think in marginal terms, considering how a one-unit change in one variable affects the value of another variable and people's decisions. When we say *marginal*, we're looking at the effect of a small, or incremental, change.

The marginal principle is based on a comparison of the marginal benefits and marginal costs of a particular activity. The **marginal benefit** of an activity is the additional benefit resulting from a small increase in the activity. For example, the marginal benefit of keeping a bookstore open for one more hour equals the additional revenue from book sales. Similarly, the **marginal cost** is the additional cost resulting from a small increase in the activity. For example, the marginal cost of keeping a bookstore open for one more hour equals the additional expenses for workers and utilities for that hour. Applying the marginal principle, the bookstore should stay open for one more hour if the marginal benefit (the additional revenue) is at least as large as the marginal cost (the additional cost). For example, if the marginal benefit is $80 of additional revenue and the marginal cost is $30 of additional expense for workers and utilities, staying open for the additional hour increases the bookstore's profit by $50.

marginal benefit
The additional benefit resulting from a small increase in some activity.

marginal cost
The additional cost resulting from a small increase in some activity.

MARGINAL PRINCIPLE

Increase the level of an activity as long as its marginal benefit exceeds its marginal cost. Choose the level at which the marginal benefit equals the marginal cost.

Thinking at the margin enables us to fine-tune our decisions. We can use the marginal principle to determine whether a one-unit increase in a variable would make us better off. Just as a bookstore owner could decide whether to stay open for one more hour, you could decide whether to study one more hour for a psychology midterm. When we reach the level where the marginal benefit equals the marginal cost, we cannot do any better, and the fine-tuning is done.

How Many Movie Sequels?

To illustrate the marginal principle, let's consider movie sequels. When a movie is successful, its producer naturally thinks about doing another movie, continuing the story line with the same set of characters. If the first sequel is successful too, the producer thinks about producing a second sequel, then a third, and so on. We can use the marginal principle to explore the decision of how many movies to produce.

Figure 2.3 shows the marginal benefits and marginal costs for movies. On the benefit side, a movie sequel typically generates about 30 percent less revenue than the original movie, and revenue continues to drop for additional movies. In the second column of the table, the first movie generates $300 million in revenue, the second generates $210 million, and the third generates $135 million. This is shown in the graph as a negatively sloped marginal-benefit curve, with the marginal benefit decreasing from $300 for the first movie (point *a*), to $210 (point *b*), and then to $135 (point *c*). On the cost side, the typical movie in the United States costs about $50 million to produce and about $75 million to promote.[3] In the third column of the table, the cost of the first movie (the original) is $125 million. In the graph, this is shown as point *d* on the marginal-cost curve. The marginal cost increases with the number of movies because film stars typically demand

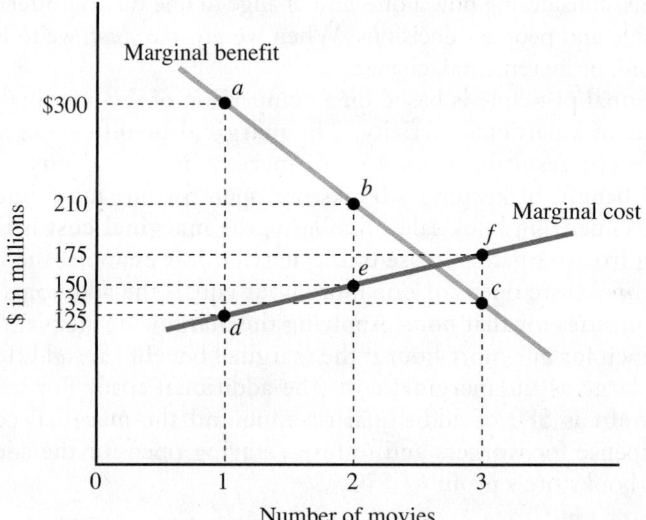

Number of Movies	Marginal Benefit ($ millions)	Marginal Cost ($ millions)
1	$300	$125
2	210	150
3	135	175

▲ **FIGURE 2.3**
The Marginal Principle and Movie Sequels
The marginal benefit of movies in a series decreases because revenue falls off with each additional movie, while the marginal cost increases because actors demand higher salaries. The marginal benefit exceeds the marginal cost for the first two movies, so it is sensible to produce two, but not three, movies.

higher salaries to appear in sequels. In the table and the graph, the marginal cost increases to $150 million for the second movie (point *e*) and to $175 million for the third (point *f*).

In this example, the first two movies are profitable, but the third is not. For the original movie, the marginal benefit ($300 million at point *a*) exceeds the marginal cost ($125 million at point *d*), generating a profit of $175 million. Although the second movie has a higher cost and a lower benefit, it is profitable because the marginal benefit still exceeds the marginal cost, so the profit on the second movie is $60 million ($210 million – $150 million). In contrast, the marginal cost of the third movie of $175 million exceeds its marginal benefit of only $135 million, so the third movie *loses* $40 million. In this example, the movie producer should stop after the second movie.

Although this example shows that only two movies are profitable, other outcomes are possible. If the revenue for the third movie were larger, making the marginal benefit greater than the marginal cost, it would be sensible to produce the third movie. Similarly, if the marginal cost of the third movie were lower—if the actors didn't demand such high salaries—the third movie could be profitable. Many movies have had multiple sequels, such as *Harry Potter and the Sorcerer's Stone* and *Star Wars*. Conversely, many profitable movies, such as *Wedding Crashers* and *Groundhog Day*, didn't result in any sequels. In these cases, the expected drop-off in revenues and run-up in costs for the second movie were large enough to make a sequel unprofitable.

Renting College Facilities

Suppose that your student film society is looking for an auditorium to use for an all-day Hitchcock film program and is willing to pay up to $200. Your college has a new auditorium that has a daily rent of $450, an amount that includes $300 to help pay for the cost of building the auditorium, $50 to help pay for insurance, and $100 to cover the extra costs of electricity and janitorial services for a one-day event. If your film society offers to pay $150 for using the auditorium, should the college accept the offer? The college could use the marginal principle to make the decision.

To decide whether to accept your group's offer, the college should determine the marginal cost of renting out the auditorium. The marginal cost equals the extra costs the college incurs by allowing the student group to use an otherwise vacant auditorium. In our example, the extra cost is $100 for additional electricity and janitorial services. It would be sensible for the college to rent the auditorium, because the marginal benefit ($150 offered by the student group) exceeds the marginal cost ($100). In fact, the college should be willing to rent the facility for any amount greater than $100. If the students and the college split the difference between the $200 the students are willing to pay and the $100 marginal cost, they would agree on a price of $150, leaving both parties better off by $50.

Most colleges do not use this sort of logic. Instead, they use complex formulas to compute the perceived cost of renting out a facility. In most cases, the perceived cost includes some costs that the university bears even if it doesn't rent out the facility for the day. In our example, the facility manager included $300 worth of construction costs and $50 worth of insurance, for a total cost of $450 instead of just $100. Because many colleges include costs that aren't affected by the use of a facility, they overestimate the actual cost of renting out their facilities, missing opportunities to serve student groups and make some money at the same time.

Automobile Emissions Standards

We can use the marginal principle to analyze emissions standards for automobiles. The U.S. government specifies how much carbon monoxide a new car is allowed to emit per mile. The marginal question is "Should the standard be stricter, with fewer units of carbon monoxide allowed?" On the benefit side, a stricter standard reduces health-care costs resulting from pollution: If the air is cleaner, people with respiratory ailments will make fewer visits to doctors and hospitals, have lower medication costs, and lose fewer work days. On the cost side, a stricter standard requires more expensive control equipment on cars and may also reduce fuel efficiency. Using the marginal principle, the government should make the emissions standard stricter as long as the marginal benefit (savings in health-care costs and work time lost) exceeds the marginal cost (the cost of additional equipment and extra fuel used).

Driving Speed and Safety

Consider the decision about how fast to drive on a highway. The marginal benefit of going one mile per hour faster is the travel time you'll save. On the cost side, an increase in speed increases your chances of colliding with another car, and also increases the severity of injuries suffered in a collision. A rational person will pick the speed at which the marginal benefit of speed equals the marginal cost.

In the 1960s and 1970s, the federal government required automakers to include a number of safety features, including seat belts and collapsible steering columns. These new regulations had two puzzling effects. Although deaths from automobile collisions decreased, the reduction was much lower than expected. In addition, more bicyclists were hit by cars and injured or killed.

We can use the marginal principle to explain why seat belts and other safety features made bicycling more hazardous. The mandated safety features decreased the marginal cost of speed: People who wear seat belts suffer less severe injuries in a collision, so every additional unit of speed is less costly. Drivers felt more secure because they were better insulated from harm in the event of a collision, and so they drove faster. As a result, the number of collisions between cars and bicycles increased, meaning that the safer environment for drivers led to a more hazardous environment for bicyclists.

application 2

HOW FAST TO SAIL?

APPLYING THE CONCEPTS #2: How do people think at the margin?

Consider the decision about how fast to sail an ocean cargo ship. As the ship's speed increases, fuel consumption increases. For example, a 70,000-ton cargo ship burns 16.5 tons of fuel per day at 11 knots, compared to 21.4 tons at 12 knots, 27.2 tons at 13 knots, and 33.9 tons at 14 knots. In other words, speed is costly. On the benefit side, an increase in speed means that the ship delivers more cargo per year. To decide the best speed, the ship operator must find the speed at which the marginal cost (the increase in fuel cost) equals the marginal benefit (the increase in revenue from delivered cargo). An increase in the price of fuel increases the marginal cost of speed, causing the shipper to slow the ship. **Related to Exercise 2.4.**

SOURCE: Based on Martin Stopard, *Maritime Economics*, 3rd edition (New York: Routledge, 2007).

2.3 The Principle of Voluntary Exchange

The principle of voluntary exchange is based on the notion that people act in their own self-interest. Self-interested people won't exchange one thing for another unless the trade makes them better off.

PRINCIPLE OF VOLUNTARY EXCHANGE

A voluntary exchange between two people makes both people better off.

Here are some examples.

- If you voluntarily exchange money for a college education, you must expect you'll be better off with a college education. The college voluntarily provides an education in exchange for your money, so the college must be better off, too.
- If you have a job, you voluntarily exchange your time for money, and your employer exchanges money for your labor services. Both you and your employer are better off as a result.

Exchange and Markets

Adam Smith stressed the importance of voluntary exchange as a distinctly human trait. He noticed[4]

> a propensity in human nature . . . to truck, barter, and exchange one thing for another . . . It is common to all men, and to be found in no other . . . animals . . . Nobody ever saw a dog make a fair and deliberate exchange of one bone for another with another dog.

As we saw in Chapter 1, a market is an institution or arrangement that enables people to exchange goods and services. If participation in a market is voluntary and people are well informed, both people in a transaction—buyer and seller—will be better off. The next time you see a market transaction, listen to what people say after money changes hands. If both people say "thank you," that's the principle of voluntary exchange in action: The double "thank you" reveals that both people are better off.

The alternative to exchange is *self-sufficiency*: Each of us could produce everything for him- or herself. As we'll see in the next chapter, it is more sensible to specialize, doing what we do best and then buying products from other people, who in turn are doing what they do best. For example, if you are good with numbers but an awful carpenter, you could specialize in accounting and buy furniture from Woody, who could specialize in making furniture and pay someone to do his bookkeeping. In general, exchange allows us to take advantage of differences in people's talents and skills.

Online Games and Market Exchange

As another illustration of the power of exchange, consider the virtual world of online games. Role-playing games such as *World of Warcraft* and *EverQuest* allow thousands of people to interact online, moving their characters through a landscape of survival challenges. Each player constructs a character—called an *avatar*—by choosing some initial traits for it. The player then navigates the avatar through the game's challenges, where it acquires skills and accumulates assets, including clothing, weapons, armor, and even magic spells.

The curious part about these role-playing games is that players use real-life auction sites, including eBay and Yahoo! Auctions, to buy products normally acquired in the game.[5] Byron, who wants a piece of armor for his avatar (say, a Rubicite girdle), can use eBay to buy one for $50 from Selma. The two players then enter the online game, and Selma's avatar transfers the armor to Byron's avatar. It is even possible to buy another player's avatar, with all its skills and assets. Given the time required to acquire various objects such as Rubicite girdles in the game and the prices paid for them on eBay, the implicit wage earned by the typical online player auctioning them off is $3.42 per hour: That's how much the player could earn by first taking the time to acquire the assets in the game and then selling them on eBay.

application 3

JASPER JOHNS AND HOUSEPAINTING

APPLYING THE CONCEPTS #3: What is the rationale for specialization and exchange?

Jasper Johns is a contemporary American artist whose painting *False Start* sold for $80 million, the largest sum paid for a painting of a living artist. According to Skate's Art Market Research, Mr. Johns is among the top 30 artists in terms of the monetary value of art produced. Mr. Johns appears as a guest star in a 1999 episode of *The Simpsons* in which Homer uses a mangled barbeque to launch a career as a contemporary artist.

Mr. Johns is a very productive painter, and his painting skills presumably translate into house painting. If Mr. Johns is ten times more productive at house painting than a professional house painter, should he paint his own house? For example, suppose Mr. Johns can paint his house in one day, compared to 10 days for a professional. Should he take a day to paint his house, or hire someone who will take 10 days to complete the same task?

We can use the principle of voluntary exchange to explain why Mr. Johns should hire the less productive house painter to paint his house. If Mr. Johns can earn $5,000 per day painting works of art, the opportunity cost of house painting is $5,000—the income he sacrifices by spending a day painting the house rather than producing works of art. If the housepainter charges $150 per day, Mr. Johns could hire him to paint the house for only $1,500. By switching one day from house painting to art production, Mr. Johns earns $5,000 and incurs a cost of only $1,500, so he is better off by $3,500. Mr. Johns specializes in what he does best, and then buys goods and services from other people. **Related to Exercise 3.5.**

2.4 The Principle of Diminishing Returns

Xena has a small copy shop, with one copying machine and one worker. When the backlog of orders piled up, she decided to hire a second worker, expecting that doubling her workforce would double the output of her copy shop from 500 pages per hour to 1,000. Xena was surprised when output increased to only 800 pages per hour. If she had known about the principle of diminishing returns, she would not have been surprised.

PRINCIPLE OF DIMINISHING RETURNS

Suppose output is produced with two or more inputs, and we increase one input while holding the other input or inputs fixed. Beyond some point—called the *point of diminishing returns*—output will increase at a decreasing rate.

Xena added a worker (one input) while holding the number of copying machines (the other input) fixed. Because the two workers must share a single copying machine, each worker spent some time waiting for the machine to be available. As a result, adding the second worker increased the number of copies, but did not double the output. With a single worker and a single copy machine, Xena has already reached the point of diminishing returns: As she increases the number of workers, output increases, but at a decreasing rate. The first worker increases output by 500 pages (from 0 to 500), but the second worker increases output by only 300 pages (from 500 to 800).

This principle of diminishing returns is relevant when we try to produce more output in an existing production facility (a factory, a store, an office, or a farm) by increasing the number of workers sharing the facility. When we add a worker to the facility, each worker becomes less productive because he or she works with a smaller piece of the facility: More workers share the same machinery, equipment, and factory space. As we pack more and more workers into the factory, total output increases, but at a decreasing rate.

It's important to emphasize that diminishing returns occurs because one of the inputs to the production process is fixed. When a firm can vary all its inputs, including the size of the production facility, the principle of diminishing returns is not relevant. For example, if a firm doubled all its inputs, building a second factory and hiring a second workforce, we would expect the total output of the firm to at least double. The principle of diminishing returns does not apply when a firm is flexible in choosing all its inputs.

application 4

FERTILIZER AND CROP YIELDS

APPLYING THE CONCEPTS #4: Do farmers experience diminishing returns?

The notion of diminishing returns applies to all inputs to the production process. For example, one of the inputs in the production of corn is nitrogen fertilizer. Suppose a farmer has a fixed amount of land (an acre) and must decide how much fertilizer to apply. The first 50-pound bag of fertilizer will increase the crop yield by a relatively large amount, but the second bag is likely to increase the yield by a smaller amount, and the third bag is likely to have an even smaller effect. Because the farmer is changing just one of the inputs, the output will increase, but at a decreasing rate. Eventually, additional fertilizer will actually decrease output as the other nutrients in the soil are overwhelmed by the fertilizer.

Table 2.1 shows the relationship between the amount of fertilizer and the corn output. The first 50-pound bag of fertilizer increases the crop yield from 85 to 120 bushels per acre, a gain of 35 bushels. The next bag of fertilizer increases the yield by only 15 bushels (from 120 to 135), followed by a gain of 9 bushels (from 135 to 144) and then a gain of only 3 bushels (from 144 to 147). The farmer experienced diminishing returns because the other inputs to the production process are fixed. **Related to Exercises 4.5 and 4.6.**

TABLE 2.1 Fertilizer and Corn Yield

Bags of Nitrogen Fertilizer	Bushels of Corn per Acre
0	85
1	120
2	135
3	144
4	147

2.5 The Real-Nominal Principle

One of the key ideas in economics is that people are interested not just in the amount of money they have but also in how much their money will buy.

REAL-NOMINAL PRINCIPLE

What matters to people is the real value of money or income—its purchasing power—not its "face" value.

To illustrate this principle, suppose you work in your college bookstore to earn extra money for movies and snacks. If your take-home pay is $10 per hour, is this a high wage or a low wage? The answer depends on the prices of the goods you buy. If a movie costs $4 and a snack costs $1, with one hour of work you could afford to see two movies and buy two snacks. The wage may seem high enough for you. But if a movie costs $8 and a snack costs $2, an hour of work would buy only one movie and one snack, and the same $10 wage doesn't seem so high. This is the real-nominal principle in action: What matters is not how many dollars you earn, but what those dollars will purchase.

Economists use special terms to express the ideas behind the real-nominal principle:

- The **nominal value** of an amount of money is simply its face value. For example, the nominal wage paid by the bookstore is $10 per hour.
- The **real value** of an amount of money is measured in terms of the quantity of goods the money can buy. For example, the real value of your bookstore wage would fall as the prices of movies and snacks increase, even though your nominal wage stayed the same.

nominal value
The face value of an amount of money.

real value
The value of an amount of money in terms of what it can buy.

The real-nominal principle can explain how people choose the amount of money to carry around with them. Suppose you typically withdraw $40 per week from an ATM to cover your normal expenses. If the prices of all the goods you purchase during the week double, you would have to withdraw $80 per week to make the same purchases. The amount of money people carry around depends on the prices of the goods and services they buy.

The Design of Public Programs

Government officials use the real-nominal principle when they design public programs. For example, Social Security payments are increased each year to ensure that the checks received by the elderly and other recipients will purchase the same amount of goods and services, even if prices have increased. The government also uses this principle when it publishes statistics about the economy. For example, its reports about changes in "real wages" in the economy over time take into account the prices of the goods workers purchase. Therefore, the real wage is stated in terms of its buying power, rather than its face value or nominal value.

The Value of the Minimum Wage

Between 1974 and 2011, the federal minimum wage increased from $2.00 to $7.25. Was the typical minimum-wage worker better or worse off in 2011? We can apply the real-nominal principle to see what's happened over time to the real value of the federal minimum wage.

As shown in the second row of Table 2.2, a full-time worker earning the minimum wage earned $80 in 1974 and $290 in 2011. The third row of Table 2.2 shows the cost of a standard basket of consumer goods, which includes a standard mix of housing, food, clothing, and transportation. In 1974, consumer prices were relatively low, and the cost of buying all the goods in the standard basket was only $47. Between 1974 and 2011, consumer prices increased, and the cost of this standard basket of goods increased to $225.

The last row in Table 2.2 shows the purchasing power of the minimum wage. In 1974, the $80 in weekly income could buy 1.70 standard baskets of goods. Between 1974 and 2011, the weekly income more than tripled, but the cost of the standard basket of goods more than quadrupled. As a result, the weekly income of $290 in 2011 could buy only 1.29 baskets of goods. Because prices increased faster than the nominal wage, the real value of the minimum wage actually decreased over this period.

TABLE 2.2 The Real Value of the Minimum Wage, 1974–2011

	1974	2011
Minimum wage per hour	$ 2.00	$ 7.25
Weekly income from minimum wage	80	290
Cost of a standard basket of goods	47	225
Number of baskets per week	1.70	1.29

application 5

REPAYING STUDENT LOANS

APPLYING THE CONCEPTS #5: How does inflation affect lenders and borrowers?

Suppose you finish college with $20,000 in student loans and start a job that pays a salary of $40,000 in the first year. In 10 years, you must repay your college loans. Which would you prefer: stable prices, rising prices, or falling prices?

We can use the real-nominal principle to compute the real cost of repaying your loans. The first row of Table 2.3 shows the cost of the loan when all prices in the economy are stable—including the price of labor, your salary. In this case, your nominal salary in 10 years is $40,000, and the real cost of repaying your loan is the half year of work you must do to earn the $20,000 you owe. However, if all prices double over the 10-year period, your nominal salary will double to $80,000, and, as shown in the second row of Table 2.3, it will take you only a quarter of a year to earn $20,000 to repay the loan. In other words, a general increase in prices lowers the real cost of your loan. In contrast, if all prices decrease and your annual salary drops to $20,000, it will take you a full year to earn the money to repay the loan. In general, people who owe money prefer inflation (a general rise in prices) to deflation (a general drop in prices). **Related to Exercises 5.6 and 5.9.**

TABLE 2.3 Effect of Inflation and Deflation on Loan Repayment

Change in Prices and Wages	Annual Salary	Years of Work to Repay $20,000 Loan
Stable	$40,000	1/2 year
Inflation: Salary doubles	80,000	1/4 year
Deflation: Salary cut in half	20,000	1 year

SUMMARY

This chapter covers five key principles of economics, the simple, self-evident truths that most people readily accept. If you understand these principles, you are ready to read the rest of the book, which will show you how to do your own economic analysis.

1 Principle of opportunity cost. The opportunity cost of something is what you sacrifice to get it.

2 Marginal principle. Increase the level of an activity as long as its marginal benefit exceeds its marginal cost. Choose the level at which the marginal benefit equals the marginal cost.

3 Principle of voluntary exchange. A voluntary exchange between two people makes both people better off.

4 Principle of diminishing returns. Suppose that output is produced with two or more inputs, and we increase one input while holding the other inputs fixed. Beyond some point—called the *point of diminishing returns*—output will increase at a decreasing rate.

5 Real-nominal principle. What matters to people is the real value of money or income—its purchasing power—not the face value of money or income.

KEY TERMS

marginal benefit, p. 33
marginal cost, p. 33
nominal value, p. 41
opportunity cost, p. 29
production possibilities curve, p. 31
real value, p. 41

EXERCISES

All problems are assignable in MyEconLab**; exercises that update with real-time data are marked with** **.**

2.1 The Principle of Opportunity Cost

1.1 Consider Figure 2.1 on page 31. Between points *c* and *d*, the opportunity cost of __________ tons of wheat is __________ tons of steel.

1.2 Arrow up or down: An increase in the wage for high-school graduates __________ the opportunity cost of college.

1.3 Arrow up or down: An increase in the market interest rate __________ the economic cost of holding a $500 collectible for a year.

1.4 You just inherited a house with a market value of $300,000, and do not expect the market value to change. Each year, you will pay $1,000 for utilities and $3,000 in taxes. You can earn 6 percent interest on money in a bank account. Your cost of living in the house for a year is $ __________.

1.5 What is the cost of a pair of warships purchased by Malaysia?

1.6 Conservationists have a new strategy for preserving rainforests: __________ loggers and other developers for the land, paying as little as $ __________ per hectare per year.

1.7 **The Cost of a Flower Business.** Jen left a job paying $40,000 per year to start her own florist shop in a building she owns. The market value of the building is $200,000. She pays $30,000 per year for flowers and other supplies, and has a bank account that pays 8 percent interest. The annual economic cost of Jen's business is __________. (Related to Application 1 on page 33.)

1.8 The Opportunity Cost of a Mission to Mars. The United States has plans to spend billions of dollars on a mission to Mars. List some of the possible opportunity costs of the mission. What resources will be used to execute the mission, and what do we sacrifice by using these resources in a mission to Mars?

1.9 Interest Rates and ATM Trips. Carlos, who lives in a country where interest rates are very high, goes to an ATM every day to get $10 of spending money. Art, who lives in a country with relatively low interest rates, goes to the ATM once a month to get $300 of spending money. Why does Carlos use the ATM more frequently?

1.10 Correct the Cost Statements. Consider the following statements about cost. For each incorrect statement, provide a correct statement about the relevant cost.

a. One year ago, I loaned a friend $100, and she just paid me back the whole $100. The loan didn't cost me anything.

b. An oil refinery bought a million barrels of oil a month ago, when the price was only $75 per barrel, compared to $120 today. The cost of using a barrel of oil to produce gasoline is $75.

c. Our new football stadium was built on land donated to the university by a wealthy alum. The cost of the stadium equals the $50 million construction cost.

d. If a commuter rides a bus to work and the bus fare is $2, the cost of commuting by bus is $2.

1.11 Production Possibilities Curve. Consider a nation that produces baseball mitts and soccer balls. The following table shows the possible combinations of the two products.

Baseball mitts (millions)	0	2	4	6	8
Soccer balls (millions)	30	24	18	10	0

a. Draw a production possibilities curve with mitts on the horizontal axis and balls on the vertical axis.

b. Suppose the technology for producing mitts improves, meaning that fewer resources are needed for each mitt. In contrast, the technology for producing soccer balls does not change. Draw a new production possibilities curve.

c. The opportunity cost of the first two million mitts is __________ million soccer balls and the opportunity cost of the last two million mitts is __________ million soccer balls.

1.12 Cost of Antique Furniture. Colleen owns antique furniture that she bought for $5,000 ten years ago. Your job is to compute Colleen's cost of owning the furniture for the next year. To compute the cost, you need two bits of information: __________ and __________.

2.2 The Marginal Principle

2.1 A taxi company currently has nine cabs in its fleet, and its total daily cost is $4,000. If the company added a tenth cab, its daily total cost would be $4,200, or $420 per cab. Adding the tenth cab will increase the daily total revenue by $300. Should the company add the tenth cab? __________ (Yes/No)

2.2 In Figure 2.3 on page 34, suppose the marginal cost of movies is constant at $125 million. Is it sensible to produce the third movie? __________ (Yes/No)

2.3 Suppose that stricter emissions standards would reduce health-care costs by $50 million but increase the costs of fuel and emissions equipment by $30 million. Is it sensible to tighten the emissions standards? __________ (Yes/No)

2.4 Arrows up or down: The decision about how fast to sail a cargo ship is based on the __________ benefit and the __________ cost. (Related to Application 2 on page 36.)

2.5 How Fast to Drive? Suppose Duke is driving to a nearby town to attend a dance party, and must decide how fast to drive. The marginal benefit of speed is the extra dance time he will get by driving faster, and the marginal cost is the additional risk of a collision. The marginal-benefit curve is negatively sloped, and the marginal-cost curve is positively sloped.

a. Draw a pair of curves that suggest Duke will drive 40 mph.

b. Suppose the normal country band is replaced by Adam Smith and the Invisible Hands, Duke's favorite punk band. Duke's utility from slam dancing is twice his utility from the two-step. Use your curves to show how Duke's chosen speed will change.

c. Suppose Duke's favorite dance partner, Daisy, is grounded for makeup violations. Use your curves to show how Duke's chosen speed will change.

d. Suppose the legal speed limit is set at 35 mph, and there is a 50 percent chance that Duke will be caught if he speeds. Use your curves to show how Duke's chosen speed will change.

2.6 Continental Airlines Goes Marginal. In the 1960s, Continental Airlines puzzled observers of the airline industry and dismayed its stockholders by running flights with up to half the seats empty. The average cost of running a flight was $4,000, a figure that includes fixed costs such as airport fees and the cost of running the reservation system. A half-full aircraft generated only $3,100 of revenue.

a. Use the marginal principle to explain why Continental ran half-empty flights.

b. It will be sensible to run a half-empty flight if the marginal __________ of flight is __________ than $ __________.

2.7 **Marginal Airlines.** Marginal Airlines runs 10 flights per day at a total cost of $50,000, including $30,000 in fixed costs for airport fees and the reservation system and $20,000 for flight crews and food service.

a. If an 11th flight would have 25 passengers, each paying $100, would it be sensible to run the flight?

b. If the 11th flight would have only 15 passengers, would it be sensible to run the flight?

2.8 **How Many Police Officers?** In your city, each police officer has a budgetary cost of $40,000 per year. The property loss from each burglary is $4,000. The first officer hired will reduce crime by 40 burglaries, and each additional officer will reduce crime by half as much as the previous one. How many officers should the city hire? Illustrate with a graph with a marginal-benefit curve and a marginal-cost curve.

2.9 **How Many Hours at the Barber Shop?** The opportunity cost of your time spent cutting hair at your barber shop is $20 per hour. Electricity costs $6 per hour, and your weekly rent is $250. You normally stay open nine hours per day.

a. What is the marginal cost of staying open for one more hour?

b. If you expect to give two haircuts in the 10th hour and you charge $15 per haircut, is it sensible to stay open for the extra hour?

2.10 **How Many Pints of Blackberries?** The pleasure you get from each pint of freshly picked blackberries is $2.00. It takes you 12 minutes to pick the first pint, and each additional pint takes an additional 2 minutes (14 minutes for the second pint, 16 minutes for the third pint, and so on). The opportunity cost of your time is $0.10 per minute.

a. How many pints of blackberries should you pick? Illustrate with a complete graph.

b. How would your answer to (a) change if your pleasure decreased by $0.20 for each additional pint ($1.80 for the second, $1.60 for the third, and so on)? Illustrate with a complete graph.

2.3 The Principle of Voluntary Exchange

3.1 When two people involved in an exchange say "thank you" afterwards, they are merely being polite. __________ (True/False)

3.2 Consider a transaction in which a consumer buys a book for $15. The value of the book to the buyer is at least $__________, and the cost of producing the book is no more than $__________.

3.3 Arrow up or down: Andy buys and eats one apple per day, and smacks his lips in appreciation as he eats it. The greater his satisfaction with the exchange of money for an apple, the larger the number of smacks. If the price of apples decreases, the number of smacks per apple will __________.

3.4 Sally sells one apple per day to Andy, and says "ca-ching" to show her satisfaction with the transaction. The greater her satisfaction with the exchange, the louder her "ca-ching." If the price of apples decreases, her "ca-ching" will become __________ (louder/softer).

3.5 **Should a Heart Surgeon Do Her Own Plumbing?** A heart surgeon is skillful at unplugging arteries and rerouting the flow of blood, and these skills also make her a very skillful plumber. She can clear a clogged drain in six minutes, about 10 times faster than the most skillful plumber in town. (Related to Application 3 on page 38.)

a. Should the surgeon clear her own clogged drains? Explain.

b. Suppose the surgeon earns $20 per minute in heart surgery, and the best plumber in town charges $50 per hour. How much does the surgeon gain by hiring the plumber to clear a clogged drain?

3.6 **Fishing versus Boat Building.** Half the members of a fishing tribe catch two fish per day and half catch eight fish per day. A group of 10 members could build a boat for another tribe in one day and receive a payment of 40 fish for the boat.

a. Suppose the boat builders are drawn at random from the tribe. From the tribe's perspective, what is the expected cost of building the boat?

b. How could the tribe decrease the cost of building the boat, thus making it worthwhile?

3.7 **Solving a Tree Cutting Problem.** Consider a hilly neighborhood where large trees provide shade but also block views. When a resident announces plans to cut down several trees to improve her view, her neighbors object and announce plans to block the tree cutting.

One week later, the trees are gone, but everyone is happy. Use the principle of voluntary exchange to explain what happened.

2.4 The Principle of Diminishing Returns

4.1 Consider the example of Xena's copy shop. Adding a second worker increased output by 300 pages. If she added a third worker, her output would increase by fewer than __________ pages.

4.2 If a firm is subject to diminishing marginal returns, an increase in the number of workers decreases the quantity produced. __________ (True/False)

4.3 Fill in the blanks with "at least" or "less than": If a firm doubles one input but holds the other inputs fixed, we normally expect output to __________ double; if a firm doubles all inputs, we expect output to __________ double.

4.4 Fill in the blanks with "flexible" or "inflexible": Diminishing returns is applicable when a firm is __________ in choosing inputs, but does not apply when a firm is __________ in choosing its inputs.

4.5 Arrows up or down: As a farmer adds more and more fertilizer to the soil, the crop yield __________, but at a __________ rate. (Related to Application 4 on page 40.)

4.6 **Feeding the World from a Flowerpot?** Comment on the following statement: "If agriculture did not experience diminishing returns, we could feed the world using the soil from a small flowerpot." (Related to Application 4 on page 40.)

4.7 **When to Use the Principle of Diminishing Returns?** You are the manager of a firm that produces memory chips for mobile phones.

a. In your decision about how much output to produce this week, would you use the principle of diminishing returns? Explain.

b. In your decision about how much output to produce two years from now, would you use the principle of diminishing returns? Explain.

4.8 **Diminishing Returns in Microbrewing?** Your microbrewery produces craft beer, using a single vat, various ingredients, and workers.

a. If you double the number of workers and ingredients, but don't add a second vat, would you expect your output (gallons per hour) to double? Explain.

b. If you double the number of workers and ingredients and add a second vat, would you expect your output (gallons per hour) to double? Explain.

4.9 **Diminishing Returns and the Marginal Principle.** Molly's Espresso Shop has become busy, and the more hours Ted works, the more espressos Molly can sell. The price of espressos is $2 and Ted's hourly wage is $11. Complete the following table:

Hours for Ted	Espressos Sold	Marginal Benefit from Additional Hour	Marginal Cost from Additional Hour
0	100	—	—
1	130	$60 = $2 × 30 additional espressos	$11 = hourly wage
2	154		
3	172		
4	184		
5	190		
6	193		

If Molly applies the marginal principle, how many hours should Ted work?

2.5 The Real-Nominal Principle

5.1 Your savings account pays 4 percent per year: Each $100 in the bank grows to $104 over a one-year period. If prices increase by 3 percent per year, by keeping $100 in the bank for a year you actually gain $__________.

5.2 You earn 5 percent interest on funds in your money-market account. If consumer prices increase by 7 percent per year, your earnings on $1,000 in the money-market account is $__________ per year.

5.3 Suppose that over a one-year period, the nominal wage increases by 2 percent and consumer prices increase by 5 percent. Fill in the blanks: The real wage __________ by __________ percent.

5.4 Suppose you currently live and work in Cleveland, earning a salary of $60,000 per year and spending $10,000 for housing. You just heard that you will be transferred to a city in California where housing is 50 percent more expensive. In negotiating a new salary, your objective is to keep your real income constant. Your new target salary is $__________.

5.5 Between 1974 and 2011, the federal minimum wage increased from $2.00 to $7.25. Was the typical minimum-wage worker better off in 2011? __________ (Yes/No)

5.6 Suppose you graduate with $20,000 in student loans and repay the loans 10 years later. Which is better for you, inflation (rising prices) or deflation (falling prices)? __________ (Related to Application 5 on page 42.)

5.7 **Changes in Welfare Payments.** Between 1970 and 1988, the average monthly welfare payment to single mothers increased from $160 to $360. Over the same period, the cost of a standard basket of consumer goods (a standard bundle of food, housing, and other goods and services) increased from $39 to $118. Fill the blanks in the following table. Did the real value of welfare payments increase or decrease over this period?

	1970	1988
Monthly welfare payment	$160	$360
Cost of a standard basket of goods	39	118
Number of baskets per week		

5.8 **Changes in Wages and Consumer Prices.** The following table shows for 1980 and 2004 the cost of a standard basket of consumer goods (a standard bundle of food, housing, and other goods and services) and the nominal average wage (hourly earnings) for workers in several sectors of the economy.

Year	Cost of Consumer Basket	Nominal Wage: Manufacturing	Nominal Wage: Professional Services	Nominal Wage: Leisure and Hospitality	Nominal Wage: Information
1980	$ 82	$ 7.52	$ 7.48	$4.05	$ 9.83
2004	189	16.34	17.69	9.01	21.70
Percent change from 1980 to 2004					

a. Complete the table by computing the percentage changes of the cost of the basket of consumer goods and the nominal wages.

b. How do the percentage changes in nominal wages compare to the percentage change in the cost of consumer goods?

c. Which sectors experienced an increase in real wages, and which sectors experienced a decrease in real wages?

5.9 **Repaying a Car Loan.** Suppose you borrow money to buy a car and must repay $20,000 in interest and principal in five years. Your current monthly salary is $4,000. (Related to Application 5 on page 42.)

a. Complete the following table.

b. Which environment has the lowest real cost of repaying the loan?

Change in Prices and Wages	Monthly Salary	Months of Work to Repay $20,000 Loan
Stable	$4,000	
Inflation: Prices rise by 25%		
Deflation: Prices drop by 50%		

5.10 **Inflation and Interest Rates.** Len buys MP3 music at $1 per tune, and prefers music now to music later. He is willing to sacrifice 10 tunes today as long as he gets at least 11 tunes in a year. When Len loans $50 to Barb for a one-year period, he cuts back his music purchases by 50 tunes.

a. To make Len indifferent about making the loan, Barb must repay him __________ tunes or $__________. The implied interest rate is __________ percent.

b. Suppose that over the one-year period of the loan, all prices (including the price of MP3 tunes) increase by 20 percent, and Len and Barb anticipate the price changes. To make Len indifferent about making the loan, Barb must repay him __________ tunes or $__________. The implied interest rate is __________ percent.

ECONOMIC EXPERIMENT

PRODUCING FOLD-ITS

Here is a simple economic experiment that takes about 15 minutes to run. The instructor places a stapler and a stack of paper on a table. Students produce "fold-its" by folding a page of paper in thirds and stapling both ends of the folded page. One student is assigned to inspect each fold-it to be sure that it is produced correctly. The experiment starts with a single student, or worker, who has one minute to produce as many fold-its as possible. After the instructor records the number of fold-its produced, the process is repeated with two students, three students, four students, and so on. How does the number of fold-its change as the number of workers increases?

MyEconLab

For additional economic experiments, please visit ***www.myeconlab.com.***

NOTES

1. "Rent a Tree," *The Economist*, March 3, 2008.

2. United Nations Development Program, *Human Development Report 1994* (New York: Oxford University Press, 1994); Linda Bilmes and Joseph Stiglitz, "The Economic Costs of the Iraq War: An Appraisal Three Years after the Beginning of the Conflict," *Faculty Research Working Papers*, Harvard University, January 2006; Center for American Progress, "The Opportunity Costs of the Iraq War," August 25, 2004; Scott Wallsten and Katrina Kosec, "The Economic Costs of the War in Iraq," AEI-Brookings Joint Center for Regulatory Studies, September 2005; Joseph Stiglitz and Linda Bilmes, *The Three Trillion Dollar War* (New York: WW Norton, 2008).

3. Colin Kennedy, "Lord of the Screens," in *Economist: The World in 2003* (London, 2003), 29.

4. Adam Smith, *An Inquiry into the Nature and Causes of the Wealth of Nations* (1776), Book 1, Chapter 2.

5. Edward Castronova, *Synthetic Worlds: The Business and Culture of Online Games* (Chicago: University of Chicago Press, 2005).

CHAPTER 3

Exchange and Markets

The nation of Latvia is located on the shore of the Baltic Sea, and since the 14th century has been a major commercial hub between west and east.

Latvia was at the center of the Hanseatic League, the world's first Free Trade Area. But in the early 1990s, after several decades of being part of the Soviet Union, Latvia suffered from low labor productivity in the production of most goods. The following table shows output per worker for Latvia and the European Community (EC, a group of six nearby European countries).

	European Community	Latvia
Saw timber	1200	200
Milk	250	15
Livestock	100	4
Grain	200	10

Latvia's prospects for trade with the EC appear to be dim: Why would a member of the EC purchase goods produced by such low-productivity workers? Why not just use more productive EC workers to produce everything?

LEARNING OBJECTIVES

- Use opportunity cost to explain the rationale for specialization and trade.
- Explain how markets allow specialization and trade.
- List the roles of government in a market economy.

MyEconLab
MyEconLab helps you master each objective and study more efficiently.

In Chapter 1, we saw that a society makes three types of economic decisions: what products to produce, how to produce them, and who gets them. In modern economies, most of these decisions are made in markets. Most of us participate in the labor market and are paid for jobs in which we produce goods and services for others. We participate in consumer markets, spending our incomes on food, clothing, housing, and other products. In this chapter, we explain why markets exist and then explore the virtues and the shortcomings of markets. We also examine the role of government in a market-based economy.

3.1 Comparative Advantage and Exchange

As we saw earlier in the book, a market is an institution or arrangement that enables people to buy and sell things. An alternative to buying and selling in markets is to be self-sufficient, with each of us producing everything we need for ourselves. Rather than going it alone, most of us specialize: We produce one or two products for others and then exchange the money we earn for the products we want to consume.

Specialization and the Gains from Trade

We can explain how people can benefit from specialization and trade with a simple example of two people and two products. Suppose that the crew of the television show *Survivor* finishes filming a season of episodes on a remote tropical island, and when the crew returns to the mainland two people miss the boat and are left behind. The two real survivors produce and consume two goods, coconuts and fish. The first row of Table 3.1 shows their production possibilities. Each day Fred can either gather 2 coconuts or catch 6 fish, while Kate can either gather 1 coconut or catch 1 fish.

TABLE 3.1 Productivity and Opportunity Costs

	Fred		Kate	
	Coconuts	*Fish*	*Coconuts*	*Fish*
Output per day	2	6	1	1
Opportunity cost	3 fish	1/3 coconut	1 fish	1 coconut

We'll show that the two survivors will be better off if each person specializes in one product and then exchanges with the other person. We can use one of the key principles of economics to explore the rationale for specialization.

PRINCIPLE OF OPPORTUNITY COST

The opportunity cost of something is what you sacrifice to get it.

Fred's opportunity cost of 1 coconut is 3 fish—that's how many fish he could catch in the time required to gather 1 coconut. Similarly, his opportunity cost of a fish is 1/3 coconut, the number of coconuts he could gather in the time required to catch 1 fish. For Kate, the opportunity cost of 1 coconut is 1 fish, and the opportunity cost of 1 fish is 1 coconut.

To demonstrate the benefits of exchange, let's imagine that both people are initially self-sufficient, with each producing enough of both goods to satisfy their own desires. Suppose they devote six days per week to finding food. If Fred initially devotes two days per week to gathering coconuts and four days per week to catching fish, he will produce and consume 4 coconuts (2 per day times two days) and 24 fish (6 per day times four days) per week. This is shown in the first column of Figure 3.1. If Kate initially devotes one day per week to coconuts and five days per week to fish, she will produce and consume 1 coconut and 5 fish per week.

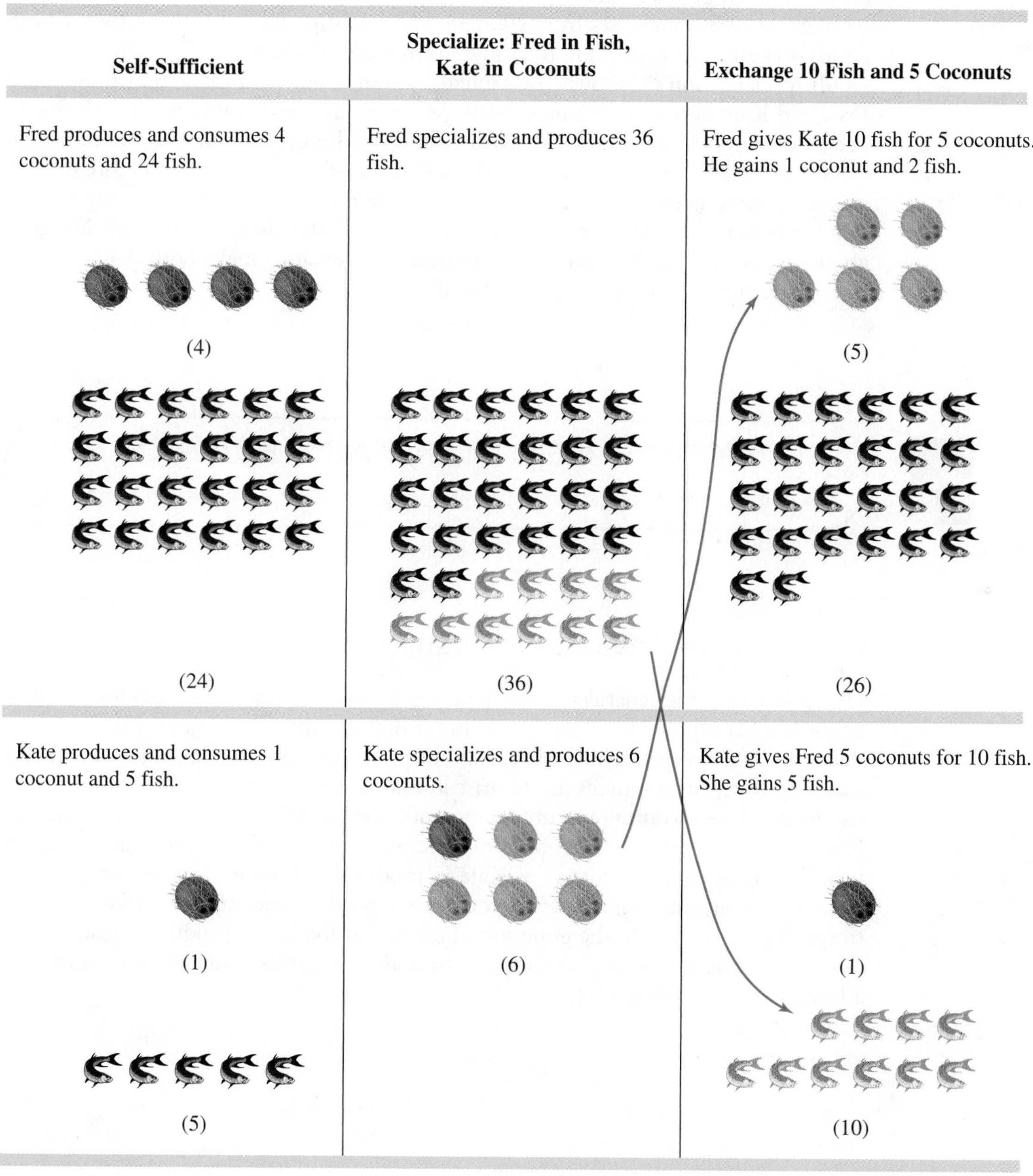

Self-Sufficient	Specialize: Fred in Fish, Kate in Coconuts	Exchange 10 Fish and 5 Coconuts
Fred produces and consumes 4 coconuts and 24 fish. (4) (24)	Fred specializes and produces 36 fish. (36)	Fred gives Kate 10 fish for 5 coconuts. He gains 1 coconut and 2 fish. (5) (26)
Kate produces and consumes 1 coconut and 5 fish. (1) (5)	Kate specializes and produces 6 coconuts. (6)	Kate gives Fred 5 coconuts for 10 fish. She gains 5 fish. (1) (10)

▲ **FIGURE 3.1**
Specialization and the Gains from Trade

Specialization will increase the total output of our little survivor economy. It is sensible for each person to specialize in the good for which he or she has a lower opportunity cost. We say that a person has a **comparative advantage** in producing a particular product if he or she has a lower opportunity cost than another person:

comparative advantage
The ability of one person or nation to produce a good at a lower opportunity cost than another person or nation.

- Fred has a comparative advantage in producing fish because his opportunity cost of fish is 1/3 coconut per fish, compared to 1 coconut per fish for Kate.
- Kate has a comparative advantage in harvesting coconuts because her opportunity cost of coconuts is 1 fish per coconut, compared to 3 fish per coconut for Fred.

The second column of Figure 3.1 shows what happens to production when the two people specialize: Fred produces 36 fish and Kate produces 6 coconuts. The total output of both goods increases: The number of coconuts increases from 5 to 6, and the number of fish increases from 29 to 36. Specialization increases the output of both goods because both people are focusing on what they do best.

If specialization is followed by exchange, both people will be better off. Suppose Fred and Kate agree to exchange 2 fish per coconut. Fred could give up 10 fish to get 5 coconuts. As shown in the third column of Figure 3.1, that leaves him with 5 coconuts and 26 fish. Compared to the self-sufficient outcome, he has more of both goods—1 more coconut and 2 more fish. If Kate gives up 5 coconuts to get 10 fish, that leaves her with 1 coconut and 10 fish, which is better than her self-sufficient outcome of 1 coconut and 5 fish. Specialization and exchange make both people better off, illustrating one of the key principles of economics:

PRINCIPLE OF VOLUNTARY EXCHANGE

A voluntary exchange between two people makes both people better off.

Comparative Advantage versus Absolute Advantage

We've seen that it is beneficial for each person to specialize in the product for which he or she has a comparative advantage—a lower opportunity cost. You may have noticed that Fred is more productive than Kate in producing both goods. Fred requires a smaller quantity of resources (in this case less labor time) to produce both goods, so he has an **absolute advantage** in producing both goods. Despite his absolute advantage, Fred gains from specialization and trade because he has a comparative advantage in fish. Fred is twice as productive as Kate in producing coconuts, but six times as productive in producing fish. By relying on Kate to produce coconuts, Fred frees up time to spend producing fish, the good for which he has the larger productivity advantage over Kate. The lesson is that specialization and exchange result from comparative advantage, not absolute advantage.

absolute advantage
The ability of one person or nation to produce a product at a lower resource cost than another person or nation.

The Division of Labor and Exchange

So far we've seen that specialization and trade exploit differences in productivity across workers and make everyone better off. We've assumed that the differences in productivity are innate, not acquired. In his 1776 book *An Inquiry into the Nature and Causes of the Wealth of Nations*, Adam Smith noted that specialization actually increased productivity through the division of labor. He used the example of the pin factory to illustrate how the division of labor increased output:[1]

> A workman . . . could scarce, perhaps with his utmost industry, make one pin a day, and certainly could not make twenty. But the way in which this business is now carried on . . . one man draws out the wire, another straightens it, a third cuts it, a fourth points it, a fifth grinds the top for receiving the head; to make the head requires two or three distinct operations. . . . The . . . making of a pin is, in this manner, divided into about eighteen distinct operations. . . . I have seen a small manufactory of this kind where ten men . . . make among them . . . upward of forty eight thousand pins in a day.

Smith listed three reasons for productivity to increase with specialization, with each worker performing a single production task:

1 *Repetition.* The more times a worker performs a particular task, the more proficient the worker becomes at that task.
2 *Continuity.* A specialized worker doesn't spend time switching from one task to another. This is especially important if switching tasks requires a change in tools or location.
3 *Innovation.* A specialized worker gains insights into a particular task that lead to better production methods. Smith believed that workers were innovators:[2]

> A great part of the machines made use of in those manufacturies in which labour is most subdivided, were originally the inventions of common workmen, who, being each of them employed in some simple operation, naturally turned their thoughts toward finding out easier and readier methods of performing it.

To summarize, specialization and exchange result from differences in productivity that lead to comparative advantage. Differences in productivity result from differences in innate skills and the benefits associated with the division of labor. Adam Smith wrote that "every man thus lives by exchanging, or becomes in some measure a merchant, and the society itself grows to be what is properly a commercial society."[3]

Comparative Advantage and International Trade

The lessons of comparative advantage and specialization apply to trade between nations. Each nation could be self-sufficient, producing all the goods it consumes, or it could specialize in products for which it has a comparative advantage. Even if one nation is more productive than a second nation in producing all goods, trade will be beneficial if the first nation has a bigger productivity advantage in one

import
A good or service produced in a foreign country and purchased by residents of the home country (for example, the United States).

export
A good or service produced in the home country (for example, the United States) and sold in another country.

product—that is, if one nation has a comparative advantage in some product. An **import** is a product produced in a foreign country and purchased by residents of the home country. An **export** is a product produced in the home country and sold in another country.

Many people are skeptical about the idea that international trade can make everyone better off. President Abraham Lincoln expressed his discomfort with importing goods:[4]

> I know if I buy a coat in America, I have a coat and America has the money—If I buy a coat in England, I have the coat and England has the money.

What President Lincoln didn't understand is that when he buys a coat in England, he sends dollars to England, but the dollars don't just sit there. Eventually they are sent back to the United States to buy goods produced by U.S. workers. In the words of economist Todd Buchholz, the author of *New Ideas from Dead Economists*,[5]

> Money may not make the world go round, but money certainly goes around the world. To stop it prevents goods from traveling from where they are produced most inexpensively to where they are desired most deeply.

Outsourcing

When a domestic firm shifts part of its production to a different country, we say the firm is *outsourcing* or *offshoring*. In the modern global economy, transportation and communication costs are relatively low, so firms can spread production across many countries. By taking advantage of the comparative advantages of different countries, a firm can produce its product at a lower cost, charge a lower price, and sell more output.

Firms shift functions such as customer service, telemarketing, document management, and medical transcription overseas to reduce production costs, allowing them to sell their products at lower prices. Some recent studies of outsourcing have reached a number of conclusions:[6]

1. The loss of domestic jobs resulting from outsourcing is a normal part of a healthy economy because technology and consumer preferences change over time. The number of jobs lost to outsourcing is a small fraction of the normal job loss experienced by a healthy economy. For example, in the first three months of 2004, a total of 239,361 workers were laid off, with 9,985 jobs moving to another location within the United States, 4,633 outsourced to another country, and the rest simply lost to the economy. This means that roughly 2 percent of reported layoffs were caused by outsourcing.
2. The jobs lost to outsourcing are at least partly offset by jobs gained through *insourcing*, jobs that are shifted from overseas to the United States.
3. The cost savings from outsourcing are substantial, leading to lower prices for consumers and more output for firms. The jobs gained from increased output at least partly offset the jobs lost to outsourcing.

application 1

ABSOLUTE DISADVANTAGE AND COMPARATIVE ADVANTAGE IN LATVIA

APPLYING THE CONCEPTS #1: What is the rationale for specialization and trade?

Recall the chapter opener about the nation of Latvia, which in the 1990s was much less productive than nations in the European Community. The question is, Why would a member of the EC, whose workers are more productive than Latvian workers in the production of all goods, buy any products from Latvia? The following table shows worker productivity and the opportunity cost of production for two products, saw timber and grain.

	EC: Saw Timber	EC: Grain	Latvia: Saw Timber	Latvia: Grain
Output	1200	200	200	10
Opportunity Cost	1/6 Grain	6 Saw timber	1/20 Grain	20 Saw timber

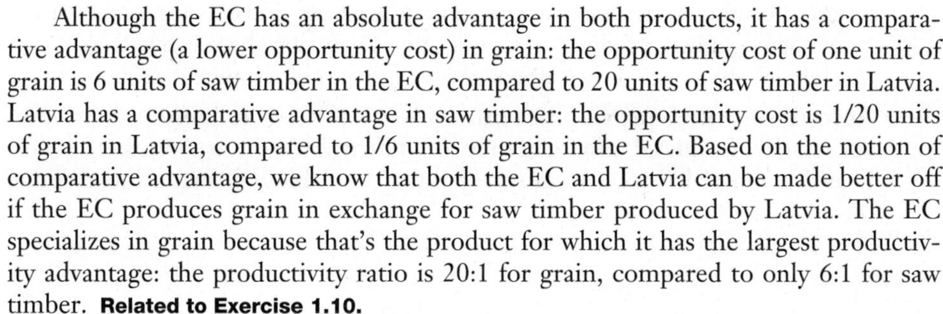

Although the EC has an absolute advantage in both products, it has a comparative advantage (a lower opportunity cost) in grain: the opportunity cost of one unit of grain is 6 units of saw timber in the EC, compared to 20 units of saw timber in Latvia. Latvia has a comparative advantage in saw timber: the opportunity cost is 1/20 units of grain in Latvia, compared to 1/6 units of grain in the EC. Based on the notion of comparative advantage, we know that both the EC and Latvia can be made better off if the EC produces grain in exchange for saw timber produced by Latvia. The EC specializes in grain because that's the product for which it has the largest productivity advantage: the productivity ratio is 20:1 for grain, compared to only 6:1 for saw timber. **Related to Exercise 1.10.**

SOURCE: Based on Aleksandrs Fedotovs, "A small nation's comparative advantage: The case of Latvia," *Business and Economic Horizons* 1 (2010), pp. 51–57.

3.2 Markets

Earlier in the chapter, we used a simple example of direct exchange to show the benefits of specialization and exchange. In a modern economy, people don't directly exchange goods like fish and coconuts, but instead rely on all sorts of markets to exchange goods and services, trading what they have for what they want. In a **market economy**, most people specialize in one productive activity by picking

market economy
An economy in which people specialize and exchange goods and services in markets.

an occupation, and use their incomes to buy most of the goods they consume. In addition to the labor and consumer markets, many of us participate in the market for financial capital: We earn interest from savings accounts and money-market accounts and pay interest on mortgages, car loans, and student loans. Friedrich Hayek, a famous twentieth-century economist, suggested that if the market system hadn't arisen naturally, it would have been proclaimed the greatest invention in human history.[7]

Although it appears that markets arose naturally, a number of social and government inventions have made them work better:

- **Contracts specify the terms of exchange, facilitating exchange between strangers.** If you have a cell phone provider, you expect to have reliable phone service as long as you pay your bill. If you operate a bookstore, you expect book wholesalers to deliver the books you've purchased. In both cases, a contract specifies the terms of exchange.
- **Insurance reduces the risk entrepreneurs face.** If you operate a bagel shop, fire insurance reduces your losses in the event of a fire.
- **Patents increase the profitability of inventions, encouraging firms to develop new products and production processes.** Pharmaceutical companies such as Bayer Pharmaceutical and Merck spend billions of dollars to create, test, and bring new products to the market. A patent prevents other companies from copying a new product, making it more likely that the revenue from a new product will be large enough to cover research and development costs.
- **Accounting rules provide potential investors with reliable information about the financial performance of a firm.** If you are thinking about investing in Apple Inc., you can use publicly available information to examine the company's financial history.

Virtues of Markets

centrally planned economy
An economy in which a government bureaucracy decides how much of each good to produce, how to produce the good, and who gets the good.

To assess the virtues of the market system, imagine an alternative—a **centrally planned economy** in which a planning authority decides what products to produce, how to produce them, and who gets them. To make these decisions, a planner must first collect a huge amount of widely dispersed information about consumption desires (what products each individual wants), production techniques (what resources are required to produce each product), and the availability of factors of production (labor, human capital, physical capital, and natural resources). Then the planner must decide how to allocate the productive resources among the alternative products. Finally, the planner must divide the output among the economy's citizens. Clearly, a central planner has a formidable task.

Under a market system, decisions are made by the millions of people who already have information about consumers' desires, production technology, and resources. These decisions are guided by prices of inputs and outputs. To illustrate, suppose you buy a wool coat. The dozens of people who contributed to the production of the coat—including the farmers who manage the sheep, the workers who transform raw wool into cloth and the cloth into a coat, the truckers who transport the inputs and the actual coat, and the merchant who sold the coat—didn't know *you* wanted a coat:

- The farmer knew that the price of wool was high enough to justify raising and shearing sheep.
- The workers knew that wages were high enough to make their efforts worthwhile.
- The merchant knew that the retail price of the coat was high enough to make it worthwhile to acquire the coat in anticipation of selling it.

In a market system, prices provide individuals the information they need to make decisions.

Prices provide signals about the relative scarcity of a product and help an economy respond to scarcity. For example, suppose wool becomes scarcer, either because a new use for wool is discovered or an old source of wool disappears. The greater scarcity will increase the price of wool, and producers and consumers will respond in ways that diminish scarcity:

- The higher price encourages fabric producers to use the available wool more efficiently and encourages farmers to produce more of it.
- The higher price also encourages consumers to switch to coats made from alternative fabrics.

These two responses help the economy accommodate an increase in scarcity. Consumers and producers don't need to know why wool is scarcer for these mechanisms to kick in—they only need to know that the price is higher.

The decisions made in markets result from the interactions of millions of people, each motivated by his or her own interest. Adam Smith used the metaphor of the "invisible hand" to explain that people acting in self-interest may actually promote the interest of society as a whole:[8]

> It is not from the benevolence of the butcher, the brewer, or the baker that we expect our dinner, but from their regard to their own interest. We address ourselves, not to their humanity but to their self-love, and never talk to them of our own necessities but of their advantages. . . [Man is] led by an invisible hand to promote an end which was no part of this intention. . . . By pursuing his own interest he frequently promotes that of the society more effectually than when he really intends to promote it. . . . Nobody but a beggar chooses to depend chiefly upon the benevolence of his fellow citizens.

The market system works by getting each person, motivated by self-interest, to produce products for other people.

The Role of Entrepreneurs

Entrepreneurs play a key role in a market economy. Prices and profits provide signals to entrepreneurs about what to produce. If a product suddenly becomes popular, competition among consumers to obtain it will increase its price and increase the profits earned by firms producing it. Entrepreneurs will enter the market and increase production to meet the higher demand, switching resources from the production of other products. As entrepreneurs enter the market, they compete for customers, driving the price back down to the level that generates just enough profit for them to remain in business. In contrast, if a product becomes less popular, the process is reversed. Producers will cut prices in order to be sure of selling the product to the smaller number of customers who want it. Entrepreneurs will leave the unprofitable market, finding other products to produce, and the price will eventually rise back to the level where profits are high enough for the remaining producers to justify staying in business.

Example of the Emergence of Markets: POW Camps

To illustrate the pervasiveness of exchange, consider the emergence of markets in prisoner of war (POW) camps during World War II.[9] During World War II, the International Red Cross gave each Allied prisoner a weekly parcel with the same mix of products—tinned milk, jam, butter, biscuits, corned beef, chocolate, sugar, and cigarettes. In addition, many prisoners received private parcels from family and friends. The prisoners used barter to exchange one good for another, and cigarettes emerged as the medium of exchange. Prisoners wandered through the camp calling out their offers of goods. For example, "cheese for seven" meant that the prisoner was willing to sell a cheese ration for 7 cigarettes. In addition to food, the prisoners bought and sold clothing (80 cigarettes per shirt), laundry services (2 cigarettes per garment), and hot cups of coffee (2 cigarettes per cup).

The prices of products reflected their scarcity. The tea-drinking British prisoners demanded little coffee. Because the British were confined to their compound, packets of coffee beans sold for just a few cigarettes. Enterprising British prisoners bribed prison guards to permit them to travel to the French compound, where they could sell coffee for dozens of cigarettes. Religious groups such as the Sikhs didn't eat beef, and the excess supply of beef in the Sikh compound led to low beef prices. One prisoner who knew the Sikh language bought beef at a low price in the Sikh compound and sold it at a higher price in other compounds. Eventually, other people entered the Sikh beef trade, and beef prices across compounds became roughly equal.

application 2

THE MARKET FOR METEORITES

APPLYING THE CONCEPTS #2: Why do markets develop?

When a meteoroid, a chunk of debris in the solar system, enters the earth's atmosphere it becomes a meteor, and if a meteor reaches the ground and survives impact, it becomes a meteorite. Meteorites are prized by private collectors and scientists, who study them for astronomical insights.

The market for meteorites is highly organized. Meteorites have been hitting the earth for millions of years, and they can still be found in many desert areas. In Morocco, people bring meteorites picked up in the desert to local dealers, who then sell them to the public through websites and eBay. And there are professional meteorite hunters, who listen for news of meteorite showers and then travel to the landfalls to gather fresh meteorites. Recently some scientists traveled to Morocco to purchase a meteorite from Mars for $17,400 ($300 per gram). The scientists will examine the meteorite to get insights into the geology of Mars. The market price of meteorites varies from a few dollars per gram for the most common types to hundreds of dollars per gram for the rarest, including objects that originated from Mars and the moon. **Related to Exercise 2.4.**

SOURCE: Based on Ira Flato, *Science Friday* January 20, 2012 (National Public Radio, 2012).

3.3 Market Failure and the Role of Government

Although markets often operate efficiently on their own, sometimes they do not. *Market failure* happens when a market doesn't generate the most efficient outcome. Later in the book, we'll explore several sources of market failure and discuss possible responses by government. Here is a preview of the topics:

- **Pollution.** For markets to work efficiently, the people making the decisions about production and consumption must bear the full costs of their decisions. In some cases, however, other people bear some of the costs. For example, people living downwind from a paper mill breathe dirty air. The people who decide how much paper to produce will ignore these other costs, so their decisions about how much paper to produce will be inefficient from the social perspective. Similarly, people with asthma suffer from the emissions of cars and

SUVs. Drivers ignore these other costs, so their decisions about how much to drive will be inefficient from the social perspective. The role of government is to ensure that polluters bear the full cost of their production and consumption decisions.

- **Public goods.** A public good is available for everyone to utilize, regardless of who pays and who doesn't. Another requirement for market efficiency is that decision makers must reap the full benefits from their decisions. In the case of a public good such as a levee, the benefits go to everyone in the area protected from flooding, not just the person who builds the levee. The role of government is to facilitate the collective decision making for public goods such as levees, national defense, parks, and space exploration.
- **Imperfect information.** For markets to operate efficiently, people must have enough information to make informed decisions about how much to produce or consume. When they don't, the role of government is to disseminate information and promote informed choices.
- **Imperfect competition.** Some markets are dominated by a few large firms, and the lack of competition leads to high prices and small quantities. For example, DeBeers dominates the diamond market. The role of government is to foster competition, which leads to lower prices and more choices.

What are the other roles of government in a market-based economy? The government enforces property rights by protecting the property and possessions of individuals and firms from theft. The government uses the legal system—police, courts, and prisons—to enforce those rights. The protection of private property guarantees that people will keep the fruits of their labor, encouraging production and exchange. The government has two additional roles to play in a market economy:

- Establishing rules for market exchange and using its police power to enforce the rules.
- Reducing economic uncertainty and providing for people who have lost a job, have poor health, or experience other unforeseen difficulties and accidents.

Government Enforces the Rules of Exchange

The market system is based on exchanges between strangers. These exchanges are covered by implicit and explicit contracts that establish the terms of trade. For example, real-estate transactions and other business dealings are sealed with explicit contracts that specify who pays what, and when. To facilitate exchange, the government helps to enforce contracts by maintaining a legal system that punishes people who violate them. This system allows people to trade with the confidence that the terms of the contracts they enter will be met.

In the case of consumer goods, the implicit contract is that the product is safe to use. The government enforces this implicit contract through product liability or tort law. If a consumer is harmed by using a particular product, the consumer can file a lawsuit against the manufacturer and seek compensation. For example, consumers who are injured in defective automobiles may be awarded settlements to cover the cost of medical care, lost work time, and pain and suffering.

The government also disseminates information about consumer products. The government requires firms to provide information about the features of their products, including warnings about potentially harmful uses of the product. For example, cigarettes have warning labels like "Quitting Smoking Now Greatly Reduces Serious Risks to Your Health." Some cold medications warn consumers to avoid driving while taking the medication.

We've already seen one of the virtues of a market system—competition among producers tends to keep prices low. As we'll see later, the government uses antitrust policy to foster competition by (a) breaking up monopolies (a single seller of a product), (b) preventing firms from colluding to fix prices, and (c) preventing firms that produce competing products from merging into a single firm. In some markets, the emergence of a single firm—a monopolist—is inevitable because the entry of a second firm would make both firms unprofitable. Some examples are cable television providers and electricity producers. Governments regulate these firms, controlling the price of the products they produce.

Government Can Reduce Economic Uncertainty

A market economy provides plenty of opportunities to people, but it has risks. Your level of success in a market economy—how much income you earn and how much wealth you accumulate—will depend on your innate intelligence as well as your efforts. But there is also an element of luck: Your fate is affected by where you were born, what occupation you choose, and your genetic makeup and health. Chance events, such as natural disasters and human accidents, also can affect your prosperity. Finally, some people lose their jobs when the national economy is in a slump and firms lay off workers. Given the uncertainty of market economies, most governments fund a "social safety net" that provides for citizens who fare poorly in markets. The safety net includes programs that redistribute income from rich to poor, from the employed to the unemployed. The idea behind having a social safety net is to guarantee a minimum income to people who suffer from job losses, poor health, or bad luck.

Of course, there are private responses to economic uncertainty. For example, we can buy our own insurance to cover losses from fire and theft, to cover our medical expenses, and to provide death benefits to our survivors in the event of an accident or disaster. Private insurance works because only a fraction of the people who buy insurance eventually file claims and receive reimbursements from insurance companies. In other words, the payments, or premiums, of many are used to pay the claims of a few. Private insurance works when enough low-risk people purchase insurance to cover the costs of reimbursing the high-risk people.

Some types of insurance are unavailable in the private insurance market. As a result, the government steps in to fill the void. For example, unemployment insurance (UI) is a government program that provides 26 weeks of compensation for people who lose their jobs. The insurance is financed by mandatory contributions from employers. Because all employers contribute to the system, the cost of the insurance stays low.

application 3

CIVIL LIBERTIES AND EFFICIENCY OF GOVERNMENT

APPLYING THE CONCEPTS #3: What is the role of government in a market economy?

One role of government is to promote civil liberties such as the freedom of expression, the freedom of religion, and the right to own personal property. Several organizations score different countries with respect to the strength of their civil liberties. For example, the Freedom House uses a checklist of 14 civil liberties to score countries on a scale of 1–7, and the Humana index scores countries on a scale of 0–100.

A recent study shows that countries with relatively strong civil liberties have relatively high rates of return on government investment projects. The World Bank funds all sorts of development projects, including roads, systems for electricity and water, and health services. If we move from a country with relatively weak civil liberties to a country with relatively strong civil liberties, the economic rate of return on World Bank projects increases by about 15 percentage points. For a less extreme comparison, if we move from a country with a Humana index of 32 to a country with a Humana index of 50, the average rate of return increases from 12 percent to 16 percent. The positive relationship between the strength of civil liberties and the economic rate of return suggests that civil liberties promote citizen participation and public accountability, increasing the efficiency of government projects. **Related to Exercise 3.5.**

SOURCE: Based on Jonathan Isham, Daniel Kaufmann, Lant Pritchett, "Civil Liberties, Democracy, and the Performance of Government Projects," *The World Bank Economic Review* 11 (1997), pp. 219–242.

SUMMARY

This chapter explored specialization and exchange and the virtues and shortcomings of markets. We also discussed the role of government in a market economy. Here are the main points of the chapter:

1. It is sensible for a person to produce the product for which he or she has a *comparative advantage*, that is, a lower opportunity cost than another person.
2. *Specialization* increases productivity through the division of labor, a result of the benefits of repetition, continuity, and innovation.
3. A system of international specialization and trade is sensible because nations have different opportunity costs of producing goods, giving rise to comparative advantages.
4. Under a *market system*, self-interested people, guided by prices, make the decisions about what products to produce, how to produce them, and who gets them.
5. Government roles in a market economy include establishing the rules for exchange, reducing economic uncertainty, and responding to market failures.

KEY TERMS

absolute advantage, p. 52
centrally planned economy, p. 56
comparative advantage, p. 52
export, p. 54
import, p. 54
market economy, p. 55

EXERCISES

All problems are assignable in MyEconLab; exercises that update with real-time data are marked with [icon].

3.1 Comparative Advantage and Exchange

1.1 Consider an accounting firm with two accountants.

a. Fill in the blanks in the following table.

	Quigley		Slokum	
	Financial Statements	*Tax Returns*	*Financial Statements*	*Tax Returns*
Output per hour	2	8	1	1
Opportunity cost				

b. Quigley has a comparative advantage in _________, while Slokum has a comparative advantage in _________.

1.2 Mike, the manager of a car wash, is more productive at washing cars than any potential workers he could hire. Should he wash all the cars himself? _________ (Yes/No)

1.3 Pat and Terry run a landscaping firm that cuts lawns and prunes trees. Pat is more productive than Terry at both tasks. Pat should cut lawns and Terry should prune trees if Pat has a _________ in cutting lawns.

1.4 Adam Smith listed three reasons for specialization to increase productivity: (1)_________; (2) _________; and (3)_________.

1.5 President Lincoln's discomfort with imports resulted from his failure to recognize that money sent to England eventually_________.

1.6 Arrows up or down: Outsourcing _________ production costs and _________ consumer prices.

1.7 In the first three months of 2004, the number of jobs moving to another state was _________ (larger/smaller) than the number of jobs moving to another country.

1.8 Approximately what percentage of job losses in the first three months of 2004 were caused by outsourcing—2, 10, or 25 percent?

1.9 Consider a bicycle producer that initially employs 200 production workers and 10 customer-service workers. When the firm outsources its customer-service operation to India, the 10 customer-service workers lose their jobs.

a. Explain why the net effect from outsourcing could be a loss of fewer than 10 jobs in the firm.

b. Under what circumstances will there be a net gain in jobs in the firm?

1.10 Although Latvia had an absolute disadvantage in most products relative to EC countries, trade was mutually beneficial because Latvia had a _________ advantage in _________. (Related to Application 1 on page 55.)

1.11 **Exchange in an Island Economy.** Robin and Terry are stranded on a deserted island and consume two products, coconuts and fish. In a day, Robin can catch 2 fish or gather 8 coconuts, and Terry can catch 1 fish or gather 1 coconut.

a. Use these numbers to prepare a table like Table 3.1 on page 50. Which person has a comparative advantage in fishing? Which person has a comparative advantage in gathering coconuts?

b. Suppose that each person is initially self-sufficient. In a six-day week, Robin produces and consumes 32 coconuts and 4 fish, and Terry produces and consumes 3 coconuts and 3 fish. Show that specialization and exchange (at a rate of 3 coconuts per fish) allows Robin to consume more coconuts and the same number of fish and allows Terry to consume more coconuts and the same number of fish. Illustrate your answer with a graph like Figure 3.1 on page 51.

1.12 **Technological Innovation and Exchange.** Recall the example of Fred and Kate shown in Table 3.1 on page 50. Suppose a technological innovation, such as a rope ladder, increases the coconut productivity of both people: Fred can now produce three coconuts per day, while Kate can now produce two coconuts per day. Their productivity for fish has not changed. Suppose they agree to trade one coconut for each fish. Will both people gain from specialization and trade?

1.13 **Comparative Advantage in Selling.** Selma is a better salesperson than Mark in both city A and city B.

	Selma	Mark
Sales per day in city A	48	24
Sales per day in city B	40	10

a. If each person handles one city and the objective is to maximize total sales, which city should each person handle?

b. Is your answer to (a) consistent with the notion of exploiting comparative advantage?

1.14 **Data on Exports and Imports.** Access the *Statistical Abstract of the United States* on the Internet and download the tables in the section entitled "Foreign Commerce and Aid." One of the tables lists U.S. exports and imports by selected Standard Industrial Trade Classification (SITC) commodity. Fill in the blanks in the following table for the most recent year listed in the table.

Commodity	Export Value ($ millions)	Import Value ($ millions)	Net Exports = Exports – Imports ($ millions)
Coffee			
Corn			
Soybeans			
Airplanes			
Footwear			
Vehicles			
Crude oil			

1.15 **Trade Balances by Country.** Access the *Statistical Abstract of the United States* on the Internet and download the tables in the section entitled "Foreign Commerce and Aid." One of the tables lists U.S. exports and imports and merchandise trade balance by country. Fill in the blanks in the following table for the most recent year listed in the table.

Country	Exports ($ millions)	General Imports ($ millions)	Merchandise Trade Balance ($ millions)
Australia			
China			
Italy			
Japan			
Mexico			
Netherlands			
Saudi Arabia			
Singapore			

3.2 Markets

2.1 Four social inventions that support markets are (1) __________, which specify the terms of exchange; (2) __________, which reduce the risk of entrepreneurs; (3) __________ , which increases the profitability of inventions; and (4) __________ rules, which provide potential investors with reliable information about the financial performance of firms.

2.2 Arrow up or down: Trade between different POW compounds __________ the difference in the price of beef across the compounds.

2.3 To explain the virtues of markets, Adam Smith used the metaphor of the invisible pancreas. __________ (True/False)

2.4 Meteorites travel from Mars to science laboratories on Earth with the help of markets that involve __________. (Related to Application 2 on page 59.)

2.5 **Coffee and Cheese Exchange in a POW Camp.** Suppose that in the British compound of a POW camp, the price of cheese is 6 cigarettes per cheese ration and the price of coffee beans is 3 cigarettes per coffee ration. In the French compound, the price of coffee beans is 24 cigarettes per ration.

a. Is there an opportunity for beneficial exchange?

b. A British prisoner could exchange his cheese ration for ________ cigarettes, then exchange the extra cigarettes for ________ coffee rations in the British compound. If he travels to the French compound, he could exchange the extra coffee for ________ cigarettes. When he returns to the British compound, he can exchange the extra cigarettes for ________ cheese rations. In other words, his net gain from trade is ________ cheese rations.

2.6 **Extending Trade outside the Camp.** Late in World War II, a German guard exchanged bread and chocolate at the rate of one loaf for one chocolate bar. Inside the Allied POW camp, the price of chocolate was 15 cigarettes per bar, and the price of bread was 40 cigarettes per loaf.

a. Is there an opportunity for beneficial exchange?

b. With the guard, a POW could exchange three chocolate bars for ________ loaves of bread. In the camp, the POW could exchange the extra loaves for ________ cigarettes, and then exchange the extra cigarettes for chocolate bars. In other words, the POW's net gain from trade is ________ chocolate bars.

3.3 Market Failure and the Role of Government

3.1 For markets to operate efficiently, the people making consumption and production decisions must bear the full ________ and reap the full ________ from their decisions.

3.2 Pollution from a paper mill is an example of market failure because people living downwind of the mill bear part of ________ of production.

3.3 Some markets are dominated by a few large firms, leading to high ________ and small ________.

3.4 By promoting competition, the government generates ________ product prices.

3.5 There is a ________ (positive/negative) relationship between the strength of civil liberties and the economic rate of return on World Bank projects, suggesting that civil liberties lead to ________ (more/less) efficient government. (Related to Application 3 on page 62.)

3.6 **Pirating Textbooks?** The government protects intellectual property rights by enforcing copyright rules on textbooks. Suppose an organization scans the pages of this and other introductory economics textbooks and makes them available for downloading at no charge.

a. As a current textbook consumer, would you be better off or worse off?

b. What are the implications for the next generation of economics students?

3.7 **Unemployment Insurance.** Each worker employed by Risky Business has a 20 percent chance of losing his or her job in the next year. Each worker employed by Safe Business has a 2 percent chance of losing his or her job. You manage an insurance company that provides a lump sum of $10,000 to each unemployed worker.

a. What is the minimum amount you would charge Risky Business for each employee covered by the unemployment policy?

b. What is the minimum amount you would charge Safe Business for each employee covered by the unemployment policy?

c. Suppose you charge the same premium to both businesses. The companies have the same number of workers and are required to purchase unemployment insurance. What is the minimum amount you would charge?

NOTES

1. Adam Smith, *An Inquiry into the Nature and Causes of the Wealth of Nations* (1776), Book 1, Chapter 1.

2. Ibid.

3. Adam Smith, *An Inquiry into the Nature and Causes of the Wealth of Nations* (1776), Book 4, Chapter 2.

4. Todd G. Buchholz, New Ideas from Dead Economists: *An Introduction to Modern Economic Thought* (New York: Penguin, 2007), 76.

5. Todd G. Buchholz, New Ideas from Dead Economists: *An Introduction to Modern Economic Thought* (New York: Penguin, 2007), 76–77.

6. U.S. Bureau of Labor Statistics, "Extended Mass Layoffs Associated with Domestic and Overseas Relocations, First Quarter 2004," June 2004.

7. Todd G. Buchholz, New Ideas from Dead Economists: *An Introduction to Modern Economic Thought* (New York: Penguin, 2007), 21.

8. Adam Smith, *An Inquiry into the Nature and Causes of the Wealth of Nations* (1776), Book 4, Chapter 2.

9. R. A. Radford, "The Economic Organization of a P.O.W. Camp," *Economica*, November 1945, 189–201.

Demand, Supply, and Market Equilibrium

CHAPTER

4

In recent years, thousands of workers have moved to North Dakota to work in the oil industry, which uses hydraulic fracturing to extract oil from the Bakken formation, a 360-million-year-old shale bed.

Between 2009 and 2012, mining employment in the state increased by about 11,000 jobs and total employment increased by over 40,000 jobs. Given the limited options for increasing the housing stock in the short run, increased demand for housing caused housing prices to rise dramatically. In the town of Williston, the rent for a two-bedroom apartment increased from $350 per month to $2,000.

The housing industry is responding to higher housing prices in a number of ways. The number of building permits for homes and apartment complexes increased to record levels, and five new hotels are being built in Williston. One innovative response is the building of "man camps," dormitory-style housing complexes that accommodate up to 1,000 men. The daily rent of $100 includes three meals per day, and in many cases is paid by employers.

LEARNING OBJECTIVES

- Describe and explain the law of demand.
- Describe and explain the law of supply.
- Explain the role of price in reaching a market equilibrium.
- Describe the effect of a change in demand on the equilibrium price.
- Describe the effect of a change in supply on the equilibrium price.
- Use information on price and quantity to determine what caused a change in price.

MyEconLab

MyEconLab helps you master each objective and study more efficiently.

Our discussion of the virtues of exchange and markets in Chapter 3 has set the stage for this chapter, where we explore the mechanics of markets. We use the model of demand and supply—the most important tool of economic analysis—to see how markets work. We'll see how the prices of goods and services are affected by all sorts of changes in the economy, including bad weather, higher income, technological innovation, bad publicity, and changes in consumer preferences. This chapter will prepare you for the applications of demand and supply you'll see in the rest of the book.

The model of demand and supply explains how a perfectly competitive market operates. A **perfectly competitive market** has many buyers and sellers of a product, so no single buyer or seller can affect the market price. The classic example of a perfectly competitive firm is a wheat farmer who produces a tiny fraction of the total supply of wheat. No matter how much wheat an individual farmer produces, the farmer can't change the market price of wheat.

perfectly competitive market
A market with many sellers and buyers of a homogeneous product and no barriers to entry.

4.1 The Demand Curve

On the demand side of a market, consumers buy products from firms. We have one main question about this side of the market: How much of a particular product are consumers willing to buy during a particular period? Notice that we define *demand* for a particular period, for example, a day, a month, or a year.

We'll start our discussion of demand with the individual consumer. A consumer who is willing to buy a particular product is willing to sacrifice enough money to purchase it. The consumer doesn't merely have a desire to buy the good, but is also willing and able to sacrifice something to get it. How much of a product is an individual willing to buy? It depends on a number of variables. Here is a list of the variables that affect an individual consumer's decision, using the pizza market as an example:

- The price of the product (for example, the price of a pizza)
- The consumer's income
- The price of substitute goods (for example, the prices of tacos or sandwiches or other goods that can be consumed instead of pizza)
- The price of complementary goods (for example, the price of lemonade or other goods consumed with pizza)
- The consumer's preferences or tastes and advertising that may influence preferences
- The consumer's expectations about future prices

Together, these variables determine how much of a particular product an individual consumer is willing and able to buy, the **quantity demanded**. We'll start our discussion of demand with the relationship between price and quantity demanded, a relationship we represented graphically by the demand curve. Later in the chapter, we will discuss the other variables that affect the individual consumer's decision about how much of a product to buy.

quantity demanded
The amount of a product that consumers are willing and able to buy.

The Individual Demand Curve and the Law of Demand

The starting point for a discussion of individual demand is a **demand schedule**, which is a table of numbers showing the relationship between the price of a particular product and the quantity that an individual consumer is willing to buy. The demand schedule shows how the quantity demanded by an individual changes with the price, *ceteris paribus* (everything else held fixed). The variables that are held fixed in the demand

demand schedule
A table that shows the relationship between the price of a product and the quantity demanded, *ceteris paribus*.

schedule are the consumer's income, the prices of substitutes and complements, the consumer's tastes, and the consumer's expectations about future prices.

The table in Figure 4.1 shows Al's demand schedule for pizza. At a price of $2, Al buys 13 pizzas per month. As the price rises, he buys fewer pizzas: 10 pizzas at a price of $4, 7 pizzas at a price of $6, and so on, down to only 1 pizza at a price of $10. Remember that in a demand schedule, any change in quantity results from a change in price alone.

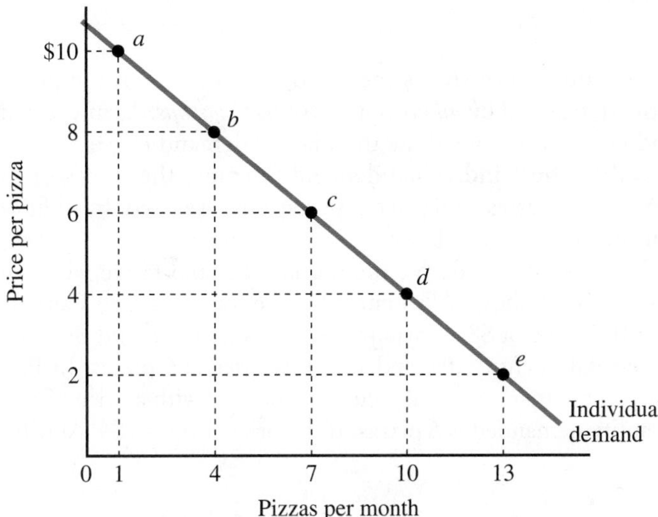

AL'S DEMAND SCHEDULE FOR PIZZAS		
Point	Price	Quantity of Pizzas per Month
a	$10	1
b	8	4
c	6	7
d	4	10
e	2	13

▲ **FIGURE 4.1**
The Individual Demand Curve
According to the law of demand, the higher the price, the smaller the quantity demanded, everything else being equal. Therefore, the demand curve is negatively sloped: When the price increases from $6 to $8, the quantity demanded decreases from seven pizzas per month (point ***c***) to four pizzas per month (point ***b***).

The **individual demand curve** is a graphical representation of the demand schedule. By plotting the numbers in Al's demand schedule—various combinations of price and quantity—we can draw his demand curve for pizza. The demand curve shows the relationship between the price and the quantity demanded by an individual consumer, *ceteris paribus*. To get the data for a single demand curve, we change only the price of pizza and observe how a consumer responds to the price change. In Figure 4.1, Al's demand curve shows the quantity of pizzas he is willing to buy at each price.

individual demand curve
A curve that shows the relationship between the price of a good and quantity demanded by an individual consumer, *ceteris paribus*.

Notice that Al's demand curve is negatively sloped, reflecting the **law of demand.** This law applies to all consumers:

law of demand
There is a negative relationship between price and quantity demanded, *ceteris paribus*.

> There is a negative relationship between price and quantity demanded, *ceteris paribus*.

The words *ceteris paribus* remind us that in order to isolate the relationship between price and quantity demanded, we *must* assume that income, the prices of related goods such as substitutes and complements, and tastes are unchanged. As the price of pizza increases and nothing else changes, Al moves upward along his demand curve and buys a smaller quantity of pizza. For example, if the price increases from $8 to $10, Al moves upward along his demand curve from point *b* to point *a*, and buys only one pizza per month, down from four pizzas at the lower price. A movement along a single demand curve is called a **change in quantity demanded**, a change in the quantity a consumer is willing to buy when the price changes.

change in quantity demanded
A change in the quantity consumers are willing and able to buy when the price changes; represented graphically by movement along the demand curve.

From Individual Demand to Market Demand

market demand curve
A curve showing the relationship between price and quantity demanded by all consumers, *ceteris paribus*.

The **market demand curve** shows the relationship between the price of the good and the quantity demanded by *all* consumers, *ceteris paribus*. As in the case of the individual demand curve, when we draw the market demand curve we assume that the other variables that affect individual demand (income, the prices of substitute and complementary goods, tastes, and price expectations) are fixed. In addition, we assume the number of consumers is fixed.

Figure 4.2 shows how to derive the market demand curve when there are only two consumers. Panel A shows Al's demand curve for pizza, and Panel B shows Bea's demand curve. At a price of $8, Al will buy 4 pizzas (point *a*) and Bea will buy 2 pizzas (point *b*), so the total quantity demanded at this price is 6 pizzas. In Panel C, point *c* shows the point on the market demand curve associated with a price of $8. At this price, the market quantity demanded is 6 pizzas. If the price drops to $4, Al will buy 10 pizzas

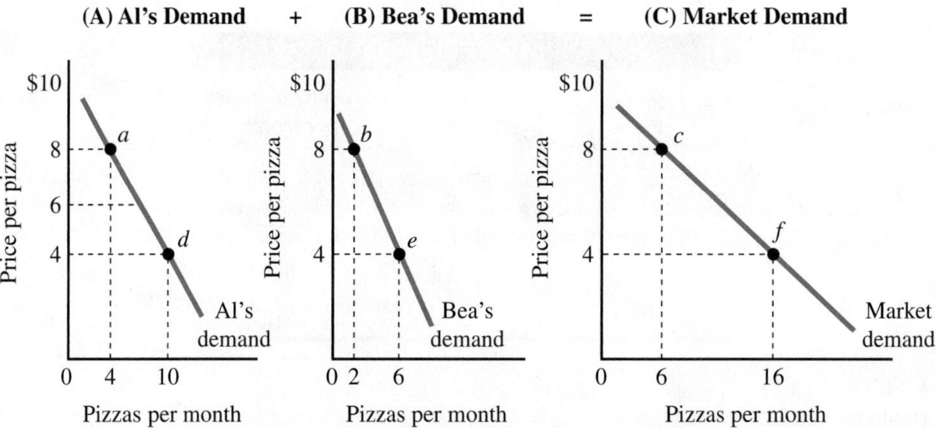

QUANTITY OF PIZZA DEMANDED			
Price	Al +	Bea =	Market Demand
$8	4	2	6
6	7	4	11
4	10	6	16
2	13	8	21

▲ FIGURE 4.2
From Individual to Market Demand
The market demand equals the sum of the demands of all consumers. In this case, there are only two consumers, so at each price the market quantity demanded equals the quantity demanded by Al plus the quantity demanded by Bea. At a price of $8, Al's quantity is four pizzas (point *a*) and Bea's quantity is two pizzas (point *b*), so the market quantity demanded is six pizzas (point *c*). Each consumer obeys the law of demand, so the market demand curve is negatively sloped.

application 1

LAW OF DEMAND AND CIGARETTES

APPLYING THE CONCEPTS #1: What is the law of demand?

As price decreases and we move downward along the market demand for cigarettes, the quantity of cigarettes demanded increases for two reasons. First, people who smoked cigarettes at the original price respond to the lower price by smoking more. Second, some people start smoking.

A change in cigarette taxes in Canada illustrates the second effect, the new-smoker effect. In 1994, several provinces in eastern Canada cut their cigarette taxes in response to the smuggling of cigarettes from the U.S. (where taxes are lower), and the price of cigarettes in the provinces decreased by roughly 50 percent. Researchers tracked the choices of 591 youths from the Waterloo Smoking Prevention Program, and concluded that the lower price increased the smoking rate by roughly 17 percent. **Related to Exercises 1.6 and 1.8.**

SOURCE: Based on Anindya Sen and Tony Wirjanto, "Estimating the impacts of cigarette taxes on youth smoking participation, initiation, and persistence: empirical evidence from Canada," *Health Economics* 19 (2010), pp. 1264–1280.

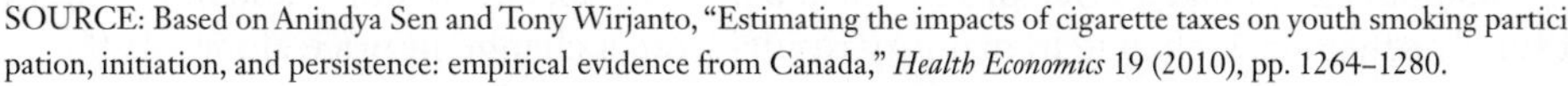

(point *d*) and Bea will buy 6 pizzas (point *e*), for a total of 16 pizzas (shown by point *f* on the market demand curve). The market demand curve is the horizontal sum of the individual demand curves.

The market demand is negatively sloped, reflecting the law of demand. This is sensible, because if each consumer obeys the law of demand, consumers as a group will too. When the price increases from $4 to $8, there is a change in quantity demanded as we move along the demand curve from point *f* to point *c*. The movement along the demand curve occurs if the price of pizza is the only variable that has changed.

4.2 The Supply Curve

On the supply side of a market, firms sell their products to consumers. Suppose you ask the manager of a firm, "How much of your product are you willing to produce and sell?" The answer is likely to be "it depends." The manager's decision about how much to produce depends on many variables, including the following, using pizza as an example:

- The price of the product (for example, the price per pizza)
- The wage paid to workers
- The price of materials (for example, the price of dough and cheese)
- The cost of capital (for example, the cost of a pizza oven)
- The state of production technology (for example, the knowledge used in making pizza)
- Producers' expectations about future prices
- Taxes paid to the government or *subsidies* (payments from the government to firms to produce a product)

Together, these variables determine how much of a product firms are willing to produce and sell, the **quantity supplied**. We'll start our discussion of market supply

quantity supplied
The amount of a product that firms are willing and able to sell.

with the relationship between the price of a good and the quantity of that good supplied, a relationship we represent graphically by the supply curve. Later in the chapter we will discuss the other variables that affect the individual firm's decision about how much of a product to produce and sell.

The Individual Supply Curve and the Law of Supply

supply schedule
A table that shows the relationship between the price of a product and quantity supplied, *ceteris paribus*.

Consider the decision of an individual producer. The starting point for a discussion of individual supply is a **supply schedule**, a table that shows the relationship between the price of a particular product and the quantity that an individual producer is willing to sell. The supply schedule shows how the quantity supplied by an individual producer changes with the price, *ceteris paribus*. The variables we hold fixed in the supply schedule are input costs, technology, price expectations, and government taxes or subsidies.

The table in Figure 4.3 shows the supply schedule for pizza at Lola's Pizza Shop. At a price of $2, Lola doesn't produce any pizzas, indicating that a $2 price is not high enough to cover her cost of producing a pizza. In contrast, at a price of $4 she supplies 100 pizzas. In this example, each $2 increase in price increases the quantity supplied by 100 pizzas to 200 at a price of $6, 300 at a price of $8, and so on. Remember that in a supply schedule, a change in quantity results from a change in price alone.

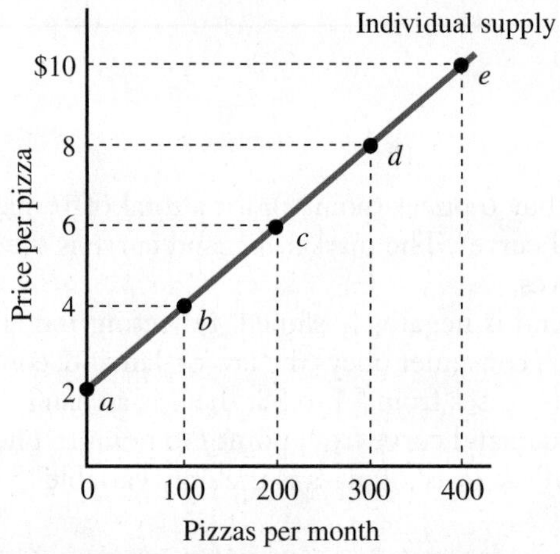

INDIVIDUAL SUPPLY SCHEDULE FOR PIZZA		
Point	Price	Quantity of Pizzas per Month
a	$2	0
b	4	100
c	6	200
d	8	300
e	10	400

▲ FIGURE 4.3
The Individual Supply Curve
The supply curve of an individual supplier is positively sloped, reflecting the law of supply. As shown by point ***a***, the quantity supplied is zero at a price of $2, indicating that the minimum supply price is just above $2. An increase in price increases the quantity supplied to 100 pizzas at a price of $4, 200 pizzas at a price of $6, and so on.

individual supply curve
A curve showing the relationship between price and quantity supplied by a single firm, *ceteris paribus*.

The **individual supply curve** is a graphical representation of the supply schedule. By plotting the numbers in Lola's supply schedule—different combinations of price and quantity—we can draw her supply curve for pizza. The individual supply curve shows the relationship between the price of a product and the quantity supplied by a single firm, *ceteris paribus*. To get the data for a supply curve, we change only the price of pizza and observe how a producer responds to the price change.

Figure 4.3 shows Lola's supply curve for pizza, which shows the quantity of pizzas she is willing to sell at each price. The individual supply curve is positively sloped, reflecting the **law of supply**, a pattern of behavior that we observe in producers:

law of supply
There is a positive relationship between price and quantity supplied, *ceteris paribus*.

There is a positive relationship between price and quantity supplied, *ceteris paribus*.

The words *ceteris paribus* remind us that to isolate the relationship between price and quantity supplied we assume the other factors that influence producers are unchanged. As the price of pizza increases and nothing else changes, Lola moves upward along her individual supply curve and produces a larger quantity of pizza. For example, if the price increases from \$6 to \$8, Lola moves upward along her supply curve from point *c* to point *d*, and the quantity supplied increases from 200 to 300. A movement along a single supply curve is called a **change in quantity supplied**, a change in the quantity a producer is willing and able to sell when the price changes.

change in quantity supplied
A change in the quantity firms are willing and able to sell when the price changes; represented graphically by movement along the supply curve.

The **minimum supply price** is the lowest price at which a product is supplied. A firm won't produce a product unless the price is high enough to cover the marginal cost of producing it. As shown in Figure 4.3, a price of \$2 is not high enough to cover the cost of producing the first pizza, so Lola's quantity supplied is zero (point *a*). But when the price rises above \$2, she produces some pizzas, indicating that her minimum supply price is just above \$2.

minimum supply price
The lowest price at which a product will be supplied.

Why Is the Individual Supply Curve Positively Sloped?

The individual supply curve is positively sloped, consistent with the law of supply. To explain the positive slope, consider how Lola responds to an increase in price. A higher price encourages a firm to increase its output by purchasing more materials and hiring more workers. To increase her workforce, Lola might be forced to pay overtime or hire workers who are more costly or less productive than the original workers. But the higher price of pizza makes it worthwhile to incur these higher costs.

The supply curve shows the marginal cost of production for different quantities produced. We can use the marginal principle to explain this.

MARGINAL PRINCIPLE

Increase the level of an activity as long as its marginal benefit exceeds its marginal cost. Choose the level at which the marginal benefit equals the marginal cost.

For Lola, the marginal benefit of producing a pizza is the price she gets for it. When the price is only \$2.00, she doesn't produce any pizza, which tells us that the marginal cost of the first pizza must be greater than \$2.00; otherwise, she would have produced it. But when the price rises to \$2.01, she produces the first pizza because now the marginal benefit (the \$2.01 price) exceeds the marginal cost. This tells us that the marginal cost of the first pizza is less than \$2.01; otherwise, she wouldn't produce it at a price of \$2.01. To summarize, the marginal cost of the first pizza is between \$2.00 and \$2.01, or just over \$2.00. Similarly, point *b* on the supply curve in Figure 4.3 shows that Lola won't produce her 100th pizza at a price of \$3.99, but will produce at a price of \$4.00, indicating that her marginal cost of producing that pizza is between \$3.99 and \$4.00, or just under \$4.00. In general, the supply curve shows the marginal cost of production.

From Individual Supply to Market Supply

market supply curve
A curve showing the relationship between the market price and quantity supplied by all firms, *ceteris paribus*.

The **market supply curve** for a particular good shows the relationship between the price of the good and the quantity that all producers together are willing to sell, *ceteris paribus*. To draw the market supply curve, we assume the other variables that affect individual supply are fixed. The market quantity supplied is simply the sum of the quantities supplied by all the firms in the market. To show how to draw the market supply curve, we'll assume there are only two firms in the market. Of course, a perfectly competitive market has a large number of firms, but the lessons from the two-firm case generalize to a case of many firms.

Figure 4.4 shows how to derive a market supply curve from individual supply curves. In Panel A, Lola has relatively low production costs, as reflected in her relatively low minimum supply price ($2 at point *a*). In Panel B, Hiram has higher production costs, so he has a higher minimum price ($6 at point *f*). As a result, his supply curve lies above Lola's. To draw the market supply curve, we add the individual supply curves horizontally. This gives us two segments for the market supply curve:

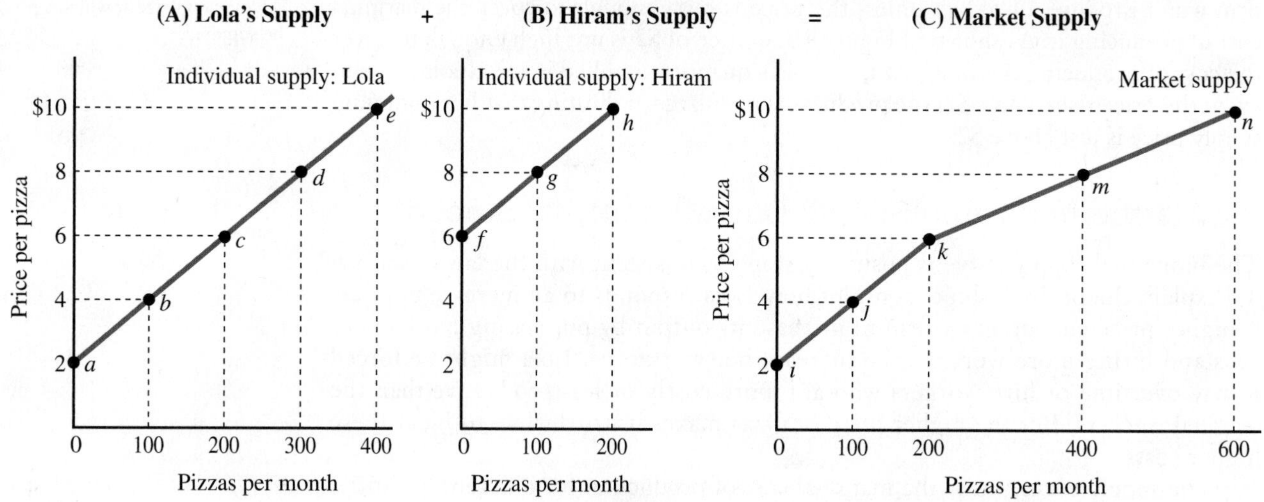

QUANTITY OF PIZZA SUPPLIED			
Price	Lola +	Hiram =	Market Supply
2	0	0	0
4	100	0	100
6	200	0	200
8	300	100	400
10	400	200	600

▲ **FIGURE 4.4**
From Individual to Market Supply
The market supply is the sum of the supplies of all firms. In Panel A, Lola is a low-cost producer who produces the first pizza once the price rises above $2 (shown by point *a*). In Panel B, Hiram is a high-cost producer who doesn't produce pizza until the price rises above $6 (shown by point *f*). To draw the market supply curve, we sum the individual supply curves horizontally. At a price of $8, market supply is 400 pizzas (point *m*), equal to 300 from Lola (point *d*) plus 100 from Hiram (point *g*).

- **Prices between $2 and $6:** Segment connecting points *i* and *k*. Hiram's high-cost firm doesn't supply any output, so the market supply is the same as the individual supply from Lola. For example, at a price of $4 Lola supplies 100 pizzas (point *b*) and Hiram does not produce any, so the market supply is 100 pizzas (point *j*).

- **Prices above $6:** Segment above point *k*. At higher prices, the high-cost firm produces some output, and the market supply is the sum of the quantities supplied by the two firms. For example, at a price of $8 Lola produces 300 pizzas (point *d*) and Hiram produces 100 pizzas (point *g*), so the market quantity supplied is 400 pizzas (point *m*).

A perfectly competitive market has hundreds of firms rather than just two, but the process of going from individual supply curves to the market supply curve is the same. We add the individual supply curves horizontally by picking a price and adding up the quantities supplied by all the firms in the market. In the more realistic case of many firms, the supply curve will be smooth rather than kinked. This smooth line is shown in Figure 4.5. In this case, we assume that there are 100 firms identical to Lola's firm. The minimum supply price is $2, and for each $2 increase in price, the quantity supplied increases by 10,000 pizzas.

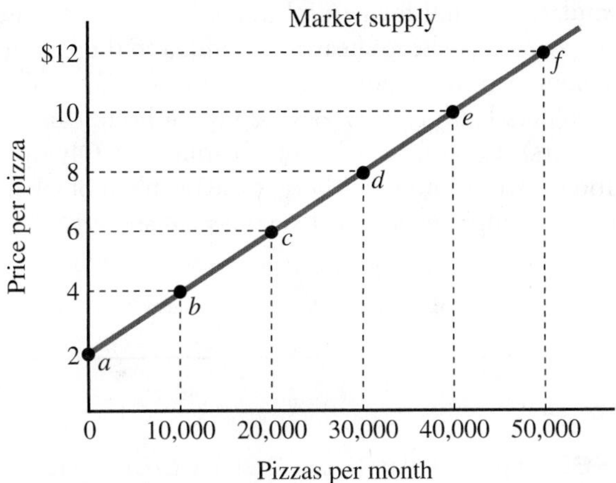

▲ FIGURE 4.5
The Market Supply Curve with Many Firms
The market supply is the sum of the supplies of all firms. The minimum supply price is $2 (point *a*), and the quantity supplied increases by 10,000 for each $2 increase in price to 10,000 at a price of $4 (point *b*), 20,000 at a price of $6 (point *c*), and so on.

Why Is the Market Supply Curve Positively Sloped?

The market supply curve is positively sloped, consistent with the law of supply. To explain the positive slope, consider the two responses by firms to an increase in price:

- **Individual firm.** As we saw earlier, a higher price encourages a firm to increase its output by purchasing more materials and hiring more workers.
- **New firms.** In the long run, new firms can enter the market and existing firms can expand their production facilities to produce more output. The new firms may have higher production costs than the original firms, but the higher output price makes it worthwhile to enter the market, even with higher costs.

Like the individual supply curve, the market supply curve shows the marginal cost of production for different quantities produced. In Figure 4.5, the marginal cost of the first pizza is the minimum supply price for the firm with the lowest cost (just over $2.00). Similarly, point *d* on the supply curve shows that the 30,000th pizza won't be produced at a price of $7.99, but will be produced at a price of $8.00. This indicates that the marginal cost of producing the 30,000th pizza is just under $8.00. Like the individual supply curve, the market supply curve shows the marginal cost of production.

application 2

LAW OF SUPPLY AND WOOLYMPICS

APPLYING THE CONCEPTS #2: What is the law of supply?

In the 1990s, the world price of wool decreased by about 30 percent, and prices have remained relatively low since then. Based on the law of supply, we would expect the quantity of wool supplied from New Zealand and other exporters to decrease, and that's what happened. Land formerly used to grow grass for wool-producing sheep has been converted into other uses, including dairy products, forestry, and the domestication of deer.

There have been several attempts to revive the wool industry by boosting the demand for wool and thus increasing its price. The United Nations General Assembly declared 2009 as the International Year of Natural Fibres, with the objective "to raise awareness and stimulate demand for natural fibres." In 2012, the Federated Farmers of New Zealand proposed that sheep shearing be added to the Commonwealth Games and Olympics as a demonstration sport. The favorites for Olympic titles are the current world record holders Ivan Scott (744 sheep in 24 hours) and Kerry-Jo Te Huia (507 sheep in 24 hours). Of course, it's not obvious that Olympic shearing would increase the demand for wool, and then there is the problem of what to do with all the sheared wool. Speed knitting? **Related to Exercises 2.6 and 2.10.**

SOURCE: Based on "Wait Wait Don't Tell Me." National Public Radio (January 21, 2012).

4.3 Market Equilibrium: Bringing Demand and Supply Together

In Chapter 3 we saw that a market is an arrangement that brings buyers and sellers together. So far in this chapter we've seen how the two sides of a market—demand and supply—work. Now we bring the two sides of the market together to show how prices and quantities are determined.

market equilibrium
A situation in which the quantity demanded equals the quantity supplied at the prevailing market price.

When the quantity of a product demanded equals the quantity supplied at the prevailing market price, we have reached a **market equilibrium**. When a market reaches an equilibrium, there is no pressure to change the price. If pizza firms produce exactly the quantity of pizza that consumers are willing to buy, each consumer will get a pizza at the prevailing price, and each producer will sell all its pizza. In Figure 4.6, the equilibrium price is shown by the intersection of the demand and supply curves. At a price of $8, the supply curve shows that firms will produce 30,000 pizzas, which is exactly the quantity that consumers are willing to buy at that price.

Excess Demand Causes the Price to Rise

excess demand
A situation in which, at the prevailing price, the quantity demanded exceeds the quantity supplied.

If the price is below the equilibrium price, there will be excess demand for the product. **Excess demand** (sometimes called a *shortage*) occurs when, at the prevailing market price, the quantity demanded exceeds the quantity supplied, meaning that consumers are willing to buy more than producers are willing to sell. In Figure 4.6, at a price of $6, there is an excess demand equal to 16,000 pizzas: Consumers are willing to buy 36,000 pizzas (point *c*), but producers are willing to sell only 20,000 pizzas (point *b*) because the price is less than the marginal cost of producing pizza number 20,001 and beyond. This mismatch between demand and supply will cause the price of pizza to rise. Firms will increase the price they charge for their limited supply of pizza, and anxious consumers will pay the higher price to get one of the few pizzas available.

An increase in price eliminates excess demand by changing both the quantity demanded and quantity supplied. As the price increases, the excess demand shrinks for two reasons:

- The market moves upward along the demand curve (from point *c* toward point *a*), decreasing the quantity demanded.
- The market moves upward along the supply curve (from point *b* toward point *a*), increasing the quantity supplied.

Because the quantity demanded decreases while the quantity supplied increases, the gap between the quantity demanded and the quantity supplied narrows. The price will continue to rise until excess demand is eliminated. In Figure 4.6, at a price of $8 the quantity supplied equals the quantity demanded, as shown by point *a*.

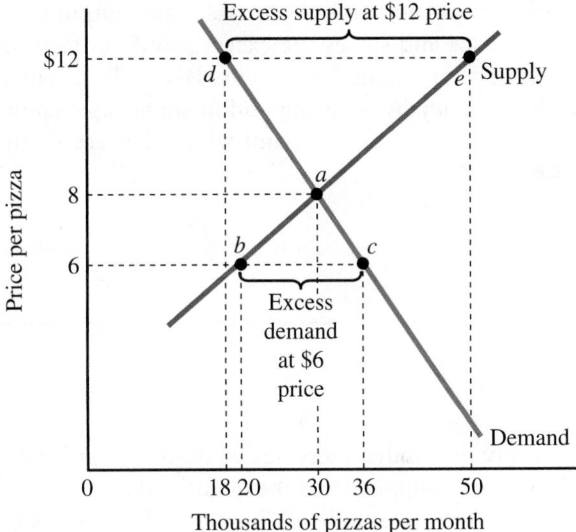

▲ **FIGURE 4.6**
Market Equilibrium
At the market equilibrium (point *a*, with price = $8 and quantity = 30,000), the quantity supplied equals the quantity demanded. At a price below the equilibrium price ($6), there is excess demand—the quantity demanded at point *c* exceeds the quantity supplied at point *b*. At a price above the equilibrium price ($12), there is excess supply—the quantity supplied at point *e* exceeds the quantity demanded at point *d*.

In some cases, government creates an excess demand for a good by setting a maximum price (sometimes called a *price ceiling*). If the government sets a maximum price that is less than the equilibrium price, the result is a permanent excess demand for the good. Later in the book we will explore the market effects of such policies.

Excess Supply Causes the Price to Drop

What happens if the price is *above* the equilibrium price? **Excess supply** (sometimes called a *surplus*) occurs when the quantity supplied exceeds the quantity demanded, meaning that producers are willing to sell more than consumers are willing to buy. This is shown by points *d* and *e* in Figure 4.6. At a price of $12, the excess supply is 32,000 pizzas: Producers are willing to sell 50,000 pizzas (point *e*), but consumers are willing to buy only 18,000 (point *d*). This mismatch will cause the price of pizzas to fall as firms cut the price to sell them. As the price drops, the excess supply will shrink for two reasons:

excess supply
A situation in which the quantity supplied exceeds the quantity demanded at the prevailing price.

- The market moves downward along the demand curve from point *d* toward point *a*, increasing the quantity demanded.
- The market moves downward along the supply curve from point *e* toward point *a*, decreasing the quantity supplied.

application 3

SHRINKING WINE LAKES

APPLYING THE CONCEPTS #3: What are consequences of a price above the equilibrium price?

Under the Common Agricultural Policy (CAP) the European Union uses a number of policies to support the agricultural sectors of member countries. Under a minimum-price policy the government sets a price above the market-equilibrium price. The EU guarantees farmers minimum prices for products such as grain, dairy products, and wine. This policy causes artificial excess supply: if the minimum price exceeds the market-equilibrium price, the quantity supplied will exceed the quantity demanded. To support the minimum prices, the EU purchases any output that a farmer cannot sell at the guaranteed price and stores the excess supply in facilities labeled by the European press as "butter mountains" and "wine lakes." In recent years the EU has reformed its agriculture policy by reducing and in some cases eliminating minimum prices. As a result, the butter mountains and wine lakes are shrinking. **Related to Exercises 3.6 and 3.8.**

SOURCE: Europa, "Reform of the Common Agricultural Policy," *Summaries of EU Legislation* (europa.eu/legislation_summaries).

Because the quantity demanded increases while the quantity supplied decreases, the gap between the quantity supplied and the quantity demanded narrows. The price will continue to drop until excess supply is eliminated. In Figure 4.6, at a price of $8, the quantity supplied equals the quantity demanded, as shown by point *a*.

The government sometimes creates an excess supply of a good by setting a minimum price (sometimes called a *price floor*). If the government sets a minimum price that is greater than the equilibrium price, the result is a permanent excess supply. We'll discuss the market effects of minimum prices later in the book.

4.4 Market Effects of Changes in Demand

We've seen that market equilibrium occurs when the quantity supplied equals the quantity demanded, shown graphically by the intersection of the supply curve and the demand curve. In this part of the chapter, we'll see how changes on the demand side of the market affect the equilibrium price and equilibrium quantity.

Change in Quantity Demanded versus Change in Demand

Earlier in the chapter we listed the variables that determine how much of a particular product consumers are willing to buy. The first variable is the price of the product. The demand curve shows the negative relationship between price and quantity demanded, *ceteris paribus*. In Panel A of Figure 4.7, when the price decreases from $8 to $6, we move downward along the demand curve from point *a* to point *b*, and the quantity demanded increases. As noted earlier in the chapter, this is called a *change in quantity demanded*. Now we're ready to take a closer look at the other variables that affect demand besides price—income, the prices of related goods, tastes, advertising, and the number of consumers—and see how changes in these variables affect the demand for the product and the market equilibrium.

If any of these other variables change, the relationship between the product's price and quantity—shown numerically in the demand schedule and graphically in the demand curve—will change. That means we will have an entirely different demand schedule and an entirely different demand curve. In Panel B of Figure 4.7, we show this result as a *shift* of the entire demand curve from D_1 to D_2. This particular shift means that at any price consumers are willing to buy a larger quantity of the product. For example, at a price of $8 consumers are willing to buy 46,000 pizzas (point *c*), up from 30,000 with the initial demand curve. To convey the idea that changes in these other variables change the demand schedule and the demand curve, we say that a change in any of these variables causes a **change in demand.**

change in demand
A shift of the demand curve caused by a change in a variable other than the price of the product.

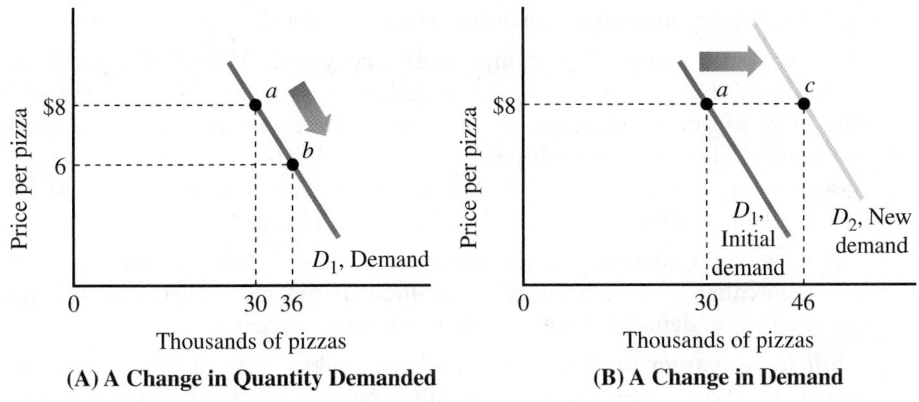

▲ FIGURE 4.7
Change in Quantity Demanded versus Change in Demand
(A) A change in price causes a change in quantity demanded, a movement along a single demand curve. For example, a decrease in price causes a move from point *a* to point *b*, increasing the quantity demanded.
(B) A change in demand caused by changes in a variable other than the price of the good shifts the entire demand curve. For example, an increase in demand shifts the demand curve from D_1 to D_2.

Increases in Demand Shift the Demand Curve

What types of changes will increase the demand and shift the demand curve to the right, as shown in Figure 4.7? An increase in demand like the one represented in Figure 4.7 can occur for several reasons, listed in Table 4.1:

TABLE 4.1 Increases in Demand Shift the Demand Curve to the Right

When this variable ...	increases or decreases ...	the demand curve shifts in this direction ...
Income, with normal good	↑	Price Quantity D_1, Initial demand D_2, New demand
Income, with inferior good	↓	
Price of a substitute good	↑	
Price of complementary good	↓	
Population	↑	
Consumer preferences for good	↑	
Expected future price	↑	

- **Increase in income.** Consumers use their income to buy products, and the more money they have, the more money they spend. For a **normal good**, there is a positive relationship between consumer income and the quantity consumed. When income increases, a consumer buys a larger quantity of a normal good. Most goods fall into this category—including new clothes, movies, and pizza.

normal good
A good for which an increase in income increases demand.

inferior good
A good for which an increase in income decreases demand.

- **Decrease in income.** An **inferior good** is the opposite of a normal good. Consumers buy larger quantities of inferior goods when their income *decreases*. For example, if you lose your job you might make your own coffee instead of buying it in a coffee shop, rent DVDs instead of going to the theater, and eat more macaroni and cheese. In this case, homemade coffee, DVDs, and macaroni and cheese are examples of inferior goods.

substitutes
Two goods for which an increase in the price of one good increases the demand for the other good.

- **Increase in price of a substitute good.** When two goods are **substitutes**, an increase in the price of the first good causes some consumers to switch to the second good. Tacos and pizzas are substitutes, so an increase in the price of tacos increases the demand for pizzas as some consumers substitute pizza for tacos, which are now more expensive relative to pizza.

complements
Two goods for which a decrease in the price of one good increases the demand for the other good.

- **Decrease in price of a complementary good.** When two goods are **complements**, they are consumed together as a package, and a decrease in the price of one good decreases the cost of the entire package. As a result, consumers buy more of both goods. Pizza and lemonade are complementary goods, so a decrease in the price of lemonade decreases the total cost of a lemonade-and-pizza meal, increasing the demand for pizza.
- **Increase in population.** An increase in the number of people means there are more potential pizza consumers—more individual demand curves to add up to get the market demand curve—so market demand increases.
- **Shift in consumer preferences.** Consumers' preferences or tastes can change over time. If consumers' preferences shift in favor of pizza, the demand for pizza increases. One purpose of advertising is to change consumers' preferences, and a successful pizza advertising campaign will increase demand.
- **Expectations of higher future prices.** If consumers think next month's pizza price will be higher than they had initially expected, they may buy a larger quantity today and a smaller quantity next month. That means the demand for pizza today will increase.

We can use Figure 4.8 to show how an increase in demand affects the equilibrium price and equilibrium quantity. An increase in the demand for pizza resulting from

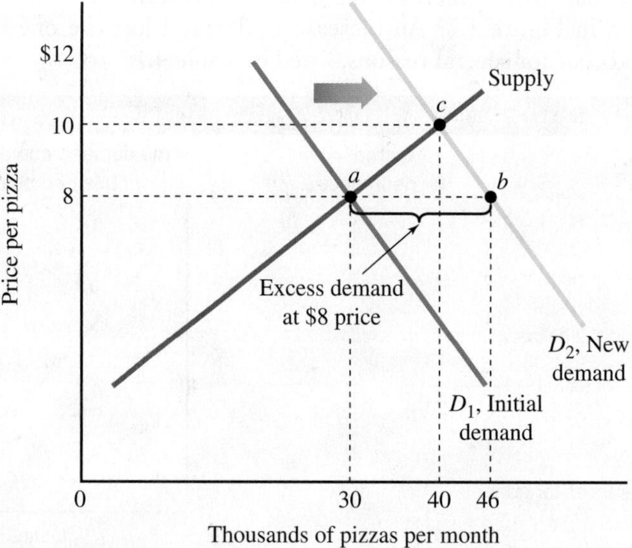

▲ FIGURE 4.8
An Increase in Demand Increases the Equilibrium Price
An increase in demand shifts the demand curve to the right: At each price, the quantity demanded increases. At the initial price ($8), there is excess demand, with the quantity demanded (point *b*) exceeding the quantity supplied (point *a*). The excess demand causes the price to rise, and equilibrium is restored at point *c*. To summarize, the increase in demand increases the equilibrium price to $10 and increases the equilibrium quantity to 40,000 pizzas.

one or more of the factors listed in Table 4.1 shifts the demand curve to the right, from D_1 to D_2. At the initial price of $8, there will be excess demand, as indicated by points *a* and *b*: Consumers are willing to buy 46,000 pizzas (point *b*), but producers are willing to sell only 30,000 (point *a*). Consumers want to buy 16,000 more pizzas than producers are willing to supply, and the excess demand causes upward pressure on the price. As the price rises, the excess demand shrinks because the quantity demanded decreases while the quantity supplied increases. The supply curve intersects the new demand curve at point *c*, so the new equilibrium price is $10 (up from $8), and the new equilibrium quantity is 40,000 pizzas (up from 30,000).

Decreases in Demand Shift the Demand Curve

What types of changes in the pizza market will decrease the demand for pizza? A decrease in demand means that at each price consumers are willing to buy a smaller quantity. In Figure 4.9, a decrease in demand shifts the market demand curve from D_1 to D_0. At the initial price of $8, the quantity demanded decreases from 30,000 pizzas (point *a*) to 14,000 pizzas (point *b*). A decrease in demand like the one represented in Figure 4.9 can occur for several reasons, listed in Table 4.2:

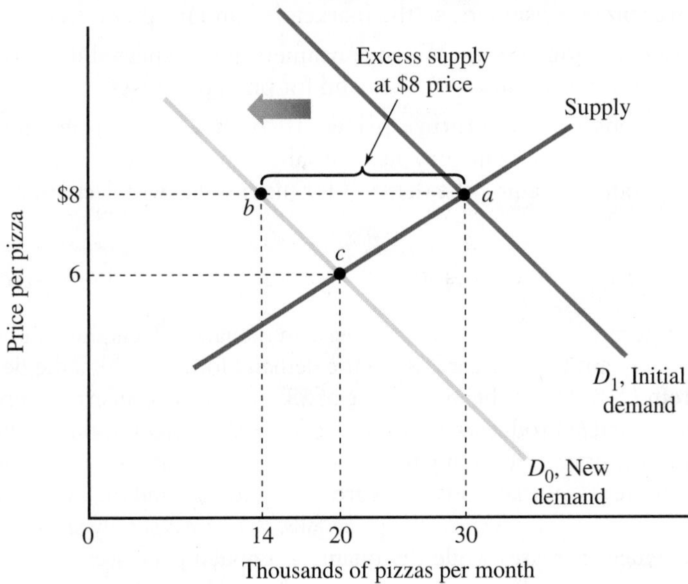

▲ FIGURE 4.9
A Decrease in Demand Decreases the Equilibrium Price
A decrease in demand shifts the demand curve to the left: At each price, the quantity demanded decreases. At the initial price ($8), there is excess supply, with the quantity supplied (point *a*) exceeding the quantity demanded (point *b*). The excess supply causes the price to drop, and equilibrium is restored at point *c*. To summarize, the decrease in demand decreases the equilibrium price to $6 and decreases the equilibrium quantity to 20,000 pizzas.

- **Decrease in income.** A decrease in income means that consumers have less to spend, so they buy a smaller quantity of each normal good.
- **Increase in income.** Consumers buy smaller quantities of an inferior good when their income increases.
- **Decrease in the price of a substitute good.** A decrease in the price of a substitute good such as tacos makes pizza more expensive relative to tacos, causing consumers to demand less pizza.
- **Increase in the price of a complementary good.** An increase in the price of a complementary good such as lemonade increases the cost of a lemonade-and-pizza meal, decreasing the demand for pizza.

TABLE 4.2 Decreases in Demand Shift the Demand Curve to the Left

When this variable ...	increases or decreases ...	the demand curve shifts in this direction ...
Income, with normal good	↓	
Income, with inferior good	↑	
Price of a substitute good	↓	
Price of complementary good	↑	
Population	↓	
Consumer preferences for good	↓	
Expected future price	↓	

- **Decrease in population.** A decrease in the number of people means that there are fewer pizza consumers, so the market demand for pizza decreases.
- **Shift in consumer tastes.** When consumers' preferences shift away from pizza in favor of other products, the demand for pizza decreases.
- **Expectations of lower future prices.** If consumers think next month's pizza price will be lower than they had initially expected, they may buy a smaller quantity today, meaning the demand for pizza today will decrease.

A Decrease in Demand Decreases the Equilibrium Price

We can use Figure 4.9 to show how a decrease in demand affects the equilibrium price and equilibrium quantity. The decrease in the demand for pizza shifts the demand curve to the left, from D_1 to D_0. At the initial price of $8, there will be an excess supply, as indicated by points *a* and *b*: Producers are willing to sell 30,000 pizzas (point *a*), but given the lower demand consumers are willing to buy only 14,000 pizzas (point *b*). Producers want to sell 16,000 more pizzas than consumers are willing to buy, and the excess supply causes downward pressure on the price. As the price falls, the excess supply shrinks because the quantity demanded increases while the quantity supplied decreases. The supply curve intersects the new demand curve at point *c*, so the new equilibrium price is $6 (down from $8), and the new equilibrium quantity is 20,000 pizzas (down from 30,000).

application 4

CHINESE DEMAND AND PECAN PRICES

APPLYING THE CONCEPTS #4: How does a change in demand affect the equilibrium price?

Between 2006 and 2009, Chinese imports of U.S. pecans increased from 9 million pounds per year to 88 million pounds. The increase in demand from China is roughly 30 percent of the total annual crop. The increase in demand was caused in part by widespread reports in the Chinese media that pecans promote brain and cardiovascular health. As a result of the increase in demand, the equilibrium price of pecans increased by about 50 percent, increasing the price of pecan pie, a holiday favorite. **Related to Exercises 4.6 and 4.10.**

4.5 Market Effects of Changes in Supply

We've seen that changes in demand shift the demand curve and change the equilibrium price and quantity. In this part of the chapter, we'll see how changes on the supply side of the market affect the equilibrium price and equilibrium quantity.

Change in Quantity Supplied versus Change in Supply

Earlier in the chapter we listed the variables that determine how much of a product firms are willing to sell. Of course, one of these variables is the price of the product. The supply curve shows the positive relationship between price and quantity, *ceteris paribus*. In Panel A of Figure 4.10, when the price increases from $6 to $8 we move along the supply curve from point *a* to point *b*, and the quantity of the product supplied increases. As noted earlier in the chapter, this is called a *change in quantity supplied*. Now we're ready to take a closer look at the other variables that affect supply—including wages, material prices, and technology—and see how changes in these variables affect the supply curve and the market equilibrium.

If any of these other variables change, the relationship between price and quantity—shown numerically in the supply schedule and graphically in the supply curve—will change. That means that we will have an entirely different supply schedule and a different supply curve. In Panel B of Figure 4.10, this is shown as a shift of the entire supply curve from S_1 to S_2. In this case, the supply curve shifts downward and to the right:

- The shift to the right means that at any given price (for example, $6), a larger quantity is produced (25,000 pizzas at point *c*, up from 20,000 at point *a*).
- The shift downward means that the price required to generate a particular quantity of output is lower. For example, the new minimum supply price is just over $1 (point *f*), down from just over $2 (point *e*). Similarly, the price required to generate 20,000 pizzas is $5 (point *d*), down from $6 (point *a*).

To convey the idea that changes in these other variables change the supply curve, we say that a change in any of these variables causes a **change in supply**.

change in supply
A shift of the supply curve caused by a change in a variable other than the price of the product.

Increases in Supply Shift the Supply Curve

What types of changes increase the supply of a product, shifting the supply curve downward and to the right? Consider first the effect of a decrease in the wage paid to pizza workers. A decrease in the wage will decrease the cost of producing pizza and shift the supply curve:

- **Downward shift.** When the cost of production decreases, the price required to generate any given quantity of pizza will decrease. In general, a lower wage means a lower marginal cost of production, so each firm needs a lower price to cover its production cost. In other words, the supply curve shifts downward.
- **Rightward shift.** The decrease in production costs makes pizza production more profitable at a given price, so producers will supply more at each price. In other words, the supply curve shifts to the right.

A decrease in the wage is just one example of a decrease in production costs that shifts the supply curve downward and to the right. These supply shifters are listed in Table 4.3. A reduction in the costs of materials (dough, cheese) or capital (pizza oven) decreases production costs, decreasing the price required to generate any particular quantity (downward shift) and increasing the quantity supplied at any particular price (rightward shift). An improvement in technology that allows the firm to economize on labor or material inputs cuts production costs and shifts the supply curve in a similar fashion. The technological improvement could be a new machine or a new way of doing business—a new layout for a factory or store, or a more efficient system of ordering inputs and

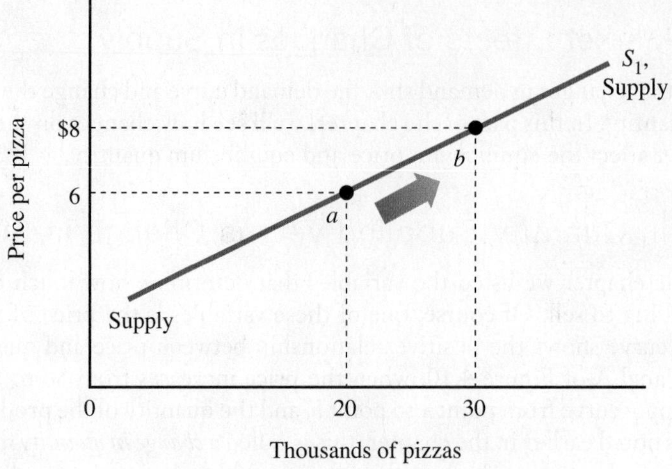

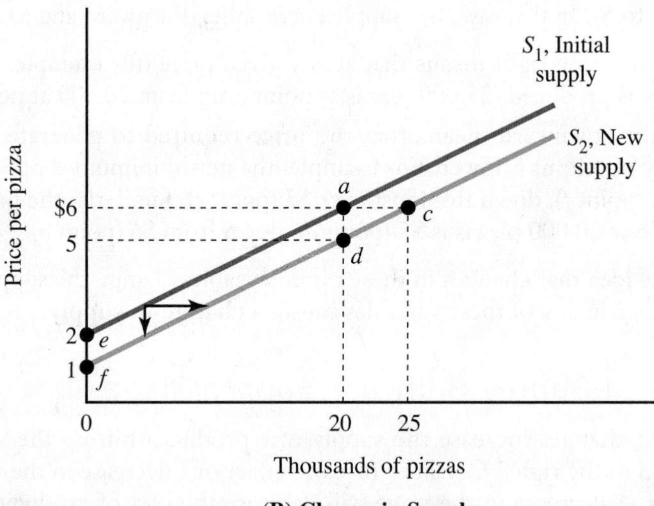

▲ **FIGURE 4.10**
Change in Quantity Supplied versus Change in Supply
(A) A change in price causes a change in quantity supplied, a movement along a single supply curve. For example, an increase in price causes a move from point *a* to point *b*. **(B)** A change in supply (caused by a change in something other than the price of the product) shifts the entire supply curve. For example, an increase in supply shifts the supply curve from S_1 to S_2. For any given price (for example, $6), a larger quantity is supplied (25,000 pizzas at point *c* instead of 20,000 at point *a*). The price required to generate any given quantity decreases. For example, the price required to generate 20,000 pizzas drops from $6 (point *a*) to $5 (point *d*).

distributing output. Finally, if a government subsidizes production by paying the firm some amount for each unit produced, the net cost to the firm is lowered by the amount of the subsidy, and the supply curve shifts downward and to the right.

Two other possible sources of increases in supply are listed in Table 4.3. First, if firms believe that next month's price will be lower than they had initially expected, they may try to sell more output now at this month's relatively high price, increasing supply this month. Second, because the market supply is the sum of the quantities supplied by all producers, an increase in the number of producers will increase market supply.

TABLE 4.3 Changes in Supply Shift the Supply Curve Downward and to the Right		
When this variable ...	**increases or decreases ...**	**the supply curve shifts in this direction ...**
Wage	↓	S_1, Initial supply; S_2, New supply; Price; Quantity
Price of materials or capital	↓	
Technological advance	↑	
Government subsidy	↑	
Expected future price	↓	
Number of producers	↑	

As summarized in Table 4.3, the language of shifting supply is a bit tricky. An increase in supply is represented graphically by a shift to the right (a larger quantity supplied at each price) and down (a lower price required to generate a particular quantity). The best way to remember this is to recognize that the *increase* in "increase in supply" refers to the increase in quantity supplied at a particular price—the horizontal shift of the supply curve to the right.

An Increase in Supply Decreases the Equilibrium Price

We can use Figure 4.11 to show the effects of an increase in supply on the equilibrium price and equilibrium quantity. An increase in the supply of pizza shifts the supply curve to the right, from S_1 to S_2. At the initial price of \$8, the quantity supplied increases from 30,000 pizzas (point *a*) to 46,000 (point *b*).

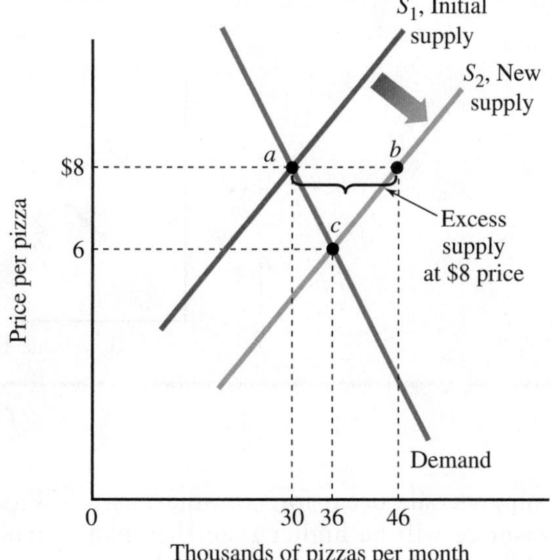

▲ **FIGURE 4.11**

An Increase in Supply Decreases the Equilibrium Price

An increase in supply shifts the supply curve to the right: At each price, the quantity supplied increases. At the initial price (\$8), there is excess supply, with the quantity supplied (point *b*) exceeding the quantity demanded (point *a*). The excess supply causes the price to drop, and equilibrium is restored at point *c*. To summarize, the increase in supply decreases the equilibrium price to \$6 and increases the equilibrium quantity to 36,000 pizzas.

The shift of the supply curve causes excess supply that eventually decreases the equilibrium price. At the initial price of $8 (the equilibrium price with the initial supply curve), there will be an excess supply, as indicated by points *a* and *b*: Producers are willing to sell 46,000 pizzas (point *b*), but consumers are willing to buy only 30,000 (point *a*). Producers want to sell 16,000 more pizzas than consumers are willing to buy, and the excess supply causes pressure to decrease the price. As the price decreases, the excess supply shrinks, because the quantity supplied decreases while the quantity demanded increases. The new supply curve intersects the demand curve at point *c*, so the new equilibrium price is $6 (down from $8) and the new equilibrium quantity is 36,000 pizzas (up from 30,000).

Decreases in Supply Shift the Supply Curve

Consider next the changes that cause a decrease in supply. As shown in Table 4.4, anything that increases a firm's production costs will decrease supply. An increase in production cost increases the price required to generate a particular quantity (an upward shift of the supply curve) and decreases the quantity supplied at each price (a leftward shift). Production costs will increase as a result of an increase in the wage, an increase in the price of materials or capital, or a tax on each unit produced. As we saw earlier, the language linking changes in supply and the shifts of the supply curve is tricky. In the case of a decrease in supply, the *decrease* refers to the change in quantity at a particular price—the horizontal shift of the supply curve to the left.

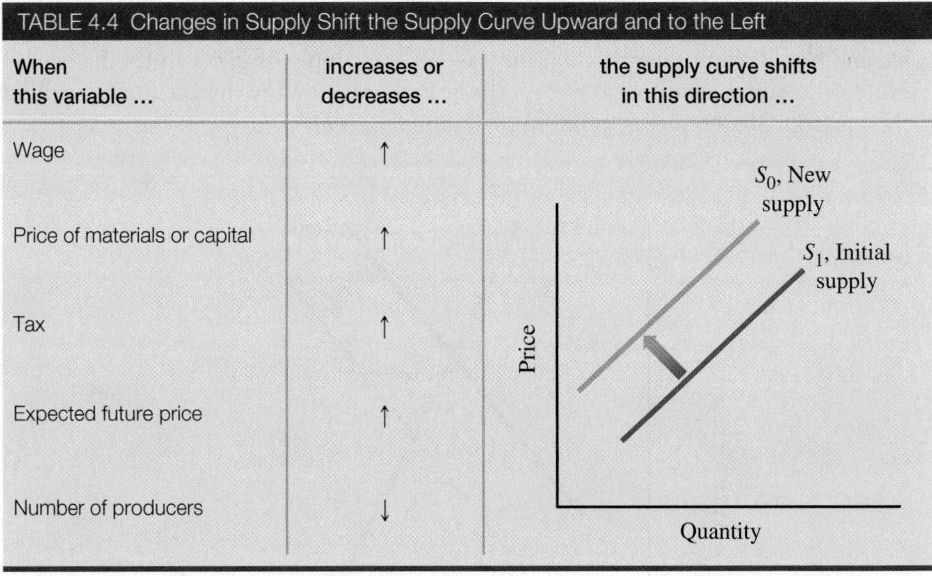

TABLE 4.4 Changes in Supply Shift the Supply Curve Upward and to the Left

When this variable ...	increases or decreases ...	the supply curve shifts in this direction ...
Wage	↑	
Price of materials or capital	↑	
Tax	↑	
Expected future price	↑	
Number of producers	↓	

A decrease in supply could occur for two other reasons. First, if firms believe next month's pizza price will be higher than they had initially expected, they may be willing to sell a smaller quantity today and a larger quantity next month. That means that the supply of pizza today will decrease. Second, because the market supply is the sum of the quantities supplied by all producers, a decrease in the number of producers will decrease market supply, shifting the supply curve to the left.

A Decrease in Supply Increases the Equilibrium Price

We can use Figure 4.12 to show the effects of a decrease in supply on the equilibrium price and equilibrium quantity. A decrease in the supply of pizza shifts the supply curve to the left, from S_1 to S_0. At the initial price of $8 (the equilibrium price with the initial supply curve), there will be an excess demand, as indicated by points *a* and *b*: Consumers are willing to buy 30,000 pizzas (point *a*), but producers are willing to sell only 14,000 pizzas (point *b*). Consumers want to buy 16,000 more pizzas than producers are willing to sell, and the excess demand causes upward pressure on the price. As the price increases, the excess demand shrinks because the quantity demanded decreases while the quantity supplied increases. The new supply curve intersects the demand curve at point *c*, so the new equilibrium price is $10 (up from $8), and the new equilibrium quantity is 24,000 pizzas (down from 30,000).

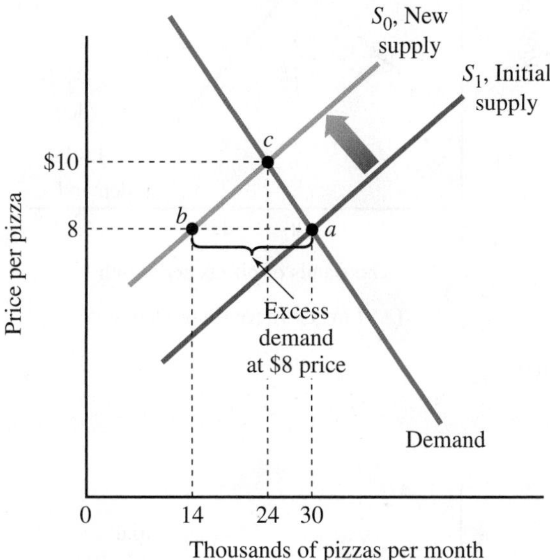

▲ **FIGURE 4.12**
A Decrease in Supply Increases the Equilibrium Price
A decrease in supply shifts the supply curve to the left. At each price, the quantity supplied decreases. At the initial price ($8), there is excess demand, with the quantity demanded (point *a*) exceeding the quantity supplied (point *b*). The excess demand causes the price to rise, and equilibrium is restored at point *c*. To summarize, the decrease in supply increases the equilibrium price to $10 and decreases the equilibrium quantity to 24,000 pizzas.

Simultaneous Changes in Demand and Supply

What happens to the equilibrium price and quantity when both demand and supply increase? It depends on which change is larger. In Panel A of Figure 4.13, the increase in demand is larger than the increase in supply, meaning the demand curve shifts by a larger amount than the supply curve. The market equilibrium moves from point *a* to point *b*, and the equilibrium price increases from $8 to $9. This is sensible because an increase in demand tends to pull the price up, while an increase in supply tends to push the price down. If demand increases by a larger amount, the upward pull will be stronger than the downward push, and the price will rise.

We can be certain that when demand and supply both increase, the equilibrium quantity will increase. That's because both changes tend to increase the equilibrium quantity. In Panel A of Figure 4.13, the equilibrium quantity increases from 30,000 to 44,000 pizzas.

Panel B of Figure 4.13 shows what happens when the increase in supply is larger than the increase in demand. The equilibrium moves from point *a* to point *c*, meaning that the price falls from $8 to $7. This is sensible because the downward pull on the price resulting from the increase in supply is stronger than the upward pull from the increase in demand. As expected, the equilibrium quantity rises from 30,000 to 45,000 pizzas.

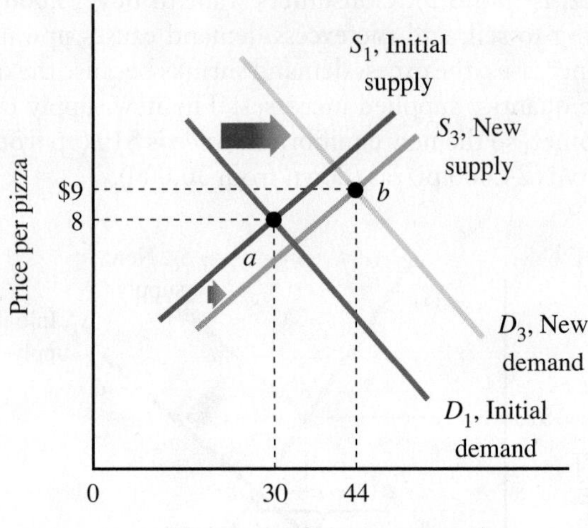

(A) Larger Increase in Demand

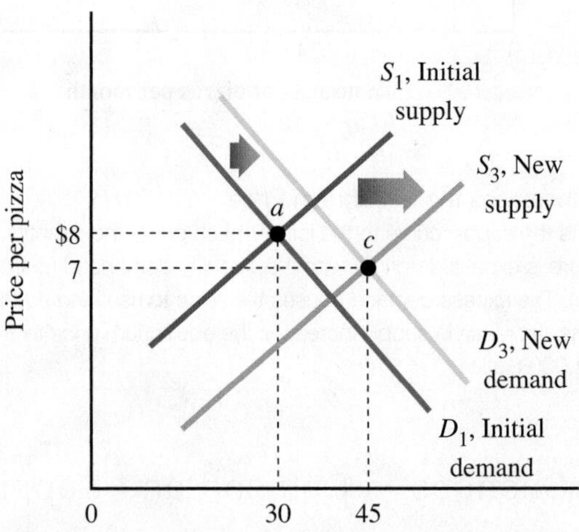

(B) Larger Increase in Supply

▲ FIGURE 4.13

Market Effects of Simultaneous Changes in Demand and Supply

(A) Larger increase in demand. If the increase in demand is larger than the increase in supply (if the shift of the demand curve is larger than the shift of the supply curve), both the equilibrium price and the equilibrium quantity will increase. **(B)** Larger increase in supply. If the increase in supply is larger than the increase in demand (if the shift of the supply curve is larger than the shift of the demand curve), the equilibrium price will decrease and the equilibrium quantity will increase.

What about simultaneous *decreases* in demand and supply? In this case, the equilibrium quantity will certainly fall because both changes tend to decrease the equilibrium quantity. The effect on the equilibrium price depends on which change is larger, the decrease in demand, which pushes the price downward, or the decrease in supply, which pulls the price upward. If the decrease in demand is larger, the price will fall because the force pushing the price down will be stronger than the force pulling it up. In contrast, if the decrease in supply is larger, the price will rise because the force pulling the price up will be stronger than the force pushing it down.

application 5

HONEYBEES AND THE PRICE OF ICE CREAM

APPLYING THE CONCEPTS #5: How does a change in supply affect the equilibrium price?

In the last few years thousands of honeybee colonies have vanished, a result of bee colony collapse disorder (CCD). Roughly one-third of the U.S. food supply—including a wide variety of fruits, vegetables, and nuts—depends on pollination from bees. The decline of honeybees threatens $15 billion worth of crops in the United States. The decrease in pollination by bees has decreased the supply of strawberries, raspberries, and almonds, leading to higher prices. The higher prices for berries and nuts have increased the cost of producing food products such as ice cream, increasing their prices as well.

The collapsing of bee colonies is a mystery. The ice cream maker Haagen-Dazs donated money to Pennsylvania State University and the University of California, Davis to support research exploring the causes of CCD and possible solutions. To increase consumer awareness of the problem, Haagen-Dazs launched a new flavor, Vanilla Honey Bee. **Related to Exercises 5.8 and 5.15.**

SOURCE: Based on Parija Kavilanz, "Disappearing Bees Threaten Ice Cream Sellers," CNNMoney.com, February 20, 2008.

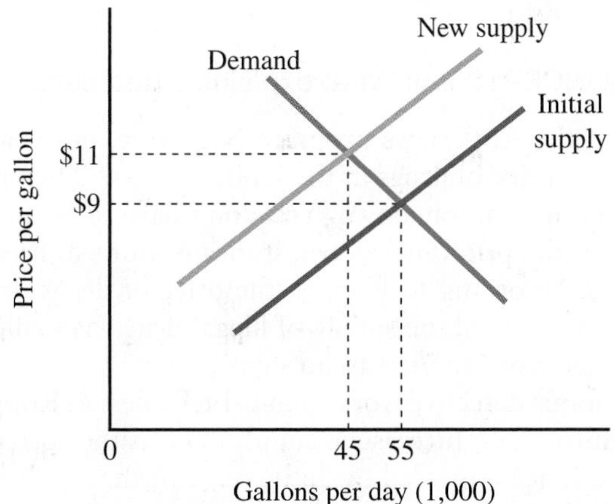

▲ FIGURE 4.14
Honeybees and the Price of Ice Cream
A decrease in pollination by bees decreases the output of fruit and nuts, increasing the prices of some ingredients for ice cream. The resulting increase in the cost of producing ice cream shifts the supply curve upward, increasing the equilibrium price and decreasing the equilibrium quantity.

4.6 Predicting and Explaining Market Changes

We've used the model of demand and supply to show how equilibrium prices are determined and how changes in demand and supply affect equilibrium prices and quantities. Table 4.5 summarizes what we've learned about how changes in demand and supply affect equilibrium prices and quantities:

- When demand changes and the demand curve shifts, price and quantity change in the *same* direction: When demand increases, both price and quantity increase; when demand decreases, both price and quantity decrease.
- When supply changes and the supply curve shifts, price and quantity change in *opposite* directions: When supply increases, the price decreases but the quantity increases; when supply decreases, the price increases but the quantity decreases.

TABLE 4.5 Market Effects of Changes in Demand or Supply

Change in Demand or Supply	How does the equilibrium price change?	How does the equilibrium quantity change?
Increase in demand	↑	↑
Decrease in demand	↓	↓
Increase in supply	↓	↑
Decrease in supply	↑	↓

We can use these lessons about demand and supply to predict the effects of various events on the equilibrium price and equilibrium quantity of a product.

We can also use the lessons listed in Table 4.5 to explain the reasons for changes in prices or quantities. Suppose we observe changes in the equilibrium price and quantity of a particular good, but we don't know what caused these changes. Perhaps it was a change

application 6

WHY LOWER DRUG PRICES?

APPLYING THE CONCEPTS # 6: What explains a decrease in price?

Ted Koppel, host of the ABC news program Nightline, once said, "Do you know what's happened to the price of drugs in the United States? The price of cocaine, way down, the price of marijuana, way down. You don't have to be an expert in economics to know that when the price goes down, it means more stuff is coming in. That's supply and demand." According to Koppel, the price of drugs dropped because the government's efforts to control the supply of illegal drugs had failed. In other words, the lower price resulted from an increase in supply.

Is Koppel's economic detective work sound? In Table 4.5, Koppel's explanation of lower prices is the third case—Increase in supply. This is the correct explanation only if a decrease in price is accompanied by an increase in the equilibrium quantity. But according to the U.S. Department of Justice, the quantity of drugs consumed actually decreased during the period of dropping prices. Therefore, the correct explanation of lower prices is the second case—Decrease in demand. In this case, lower demand—not a failure of the government's drug policy—was responsible for the decrease in drug prices. **Related to Exercises 6.5 and 6.13.**

SOURCES: Kenneth R. Clark, "Legalize Drugs. A Case for Koppel," *Chicago Tribune*, August 30, 1988, sec. 5, p. 8; U.S. Department of Justice, "Drugs, Crime, and the Justice System" (Washington, DC: U.S. Government Printing Office, 1992), p. 30.

in demand, or maybe it was a change in supply. We can use the information in Table 4.5 to work backward, using what we've observed about changes in prices and quantities to determine which side of the market—demand or supply—caused the changes:

- If the equilibrium price and quantity move in the same direction, the changes were caused by a change in demand.
- If the equilibrium price and quantity move in opposite directions, the changes were caused by a change in supply.

SUMMARY

In this chapter, we've seen how demand and supply determine prices. We also learned how to predict the effects of changes in demand or supply on prices and quantities. Here are the main points of the chapter:

1 A *market demand curve* shows the relationship between the quantity demanded and price, *ceteris paribus*.

2 A *market supply curve* shows the relationship between the quantity supplied and price, *ceteris paribus*.

3 *Equilibrium* in a market is shown by the intersection of the demand curve and the supply curve. When a market reaches equilibrium, there is no pressure to change the price.

4 A *change in demand* changes price and quantity in the same direction: An increase in demand increases the equilibrium price and quantity; a decrease in demand decreases the equilibrium price and quantity.

5 A *change in supply* changes price and quantity in opposite directions: An increase in supply decreases price and increases quantity; a decrease in supply increases price and decreases quantity.

KEY TERMS

change in demand, p. 79
change in quantity demanded, p. 70
change in quantity supplied, p. 73
change in supply, p. 83
complements, p. 80
demand schedule, p. 68
excess demand (shortage), p. 76
excess supply (surplus), p. 77
individual demand curve, p. 69
individual supply curve, p. 72
inferior good, p. 80
law of demand, p. 69
law of supply, p. 73
market demand curve, p. 70
market equilibrium, p. 76
market supply curve, p. 74
minimum supply price, p. 73
normal good, p. 79
perfectly competitive market, p. 68
quantity demanded, p. 68
quantity supplied, p. 71
substitutes, p. 80
supply schedule, p. 72

EXERCISES

All problems are assignable in MyEconLab.

4.1 The Demand Curve

1.1 Arrow up or down: According to the law of demand, an increase in price __________ the quantity demanded.

1.2 From the following list, choose the variables that are held fixed in drawing a market demand curve:
- The price of the product
- Consumer income
- The price of other related goods
- Consumer expectations about future prices
- The quantity of the product purchased

1.3 From the following list, choose the variables that change as we draw a market demand curve:
- The price of the product
- Consumer income
- The price of other related goods
- Consumer expectations about future prices
- The quantity of the product purchased

1.4 The market demand curve is the (horizontal/vertical) sum of the individual demand curves.

1.5 A change in price causes movement along a demand curve and a change in ________.

1.6 When several provinces in eastern Canada cut their cigarette taxes, the price of cigarettes decreased by roughly 50 percent, and the youth smoking rate increased by roughly________ (1, 17, 50, 90) percent. (Related to Application 1 on page 71.)

1.7 **Draw a Demand Curve.** Your state has decided to offer its citizens vanity license plates for their cars and wants to predict how many vanity plates it will sell at different prices. The price of the state's regular license plates is $20 per year, and the state's per-capita income is $30,000. A recent survey of other states with approximately the same population (3 million people) generated the following data on incomes, prices, and vanity plates:

State	B	C	D	E
Price of vanity plate	$ 60	$ 55	$ 50	$ 40
Price of regular plates	20	20	35	20
Income	30,000	25,000	30,000	30,000
Quantity of vanity plates	6,000	6,000	16,000	16,000

a. Use the available data to identify some points on the demand curve for vanity plates and connect the points to draw a demand curve. Don't forget *ceteris paribus*.

b. Suppose the demand curve is linear. If your state sets a price of $50, how many vanity plates would be purchased?

1.8 **Youth Smoking.** Use a demand and supply graph of the youth smoking market to show the effects of the tax cut in eastern Canada. Assume that the initial price is $6.00, the initial quantity is 100 units, and each youth smoker smokes 5 cigarettes per day. (Related to Application 1 on page 71.)

4.2 The Supply Curve

2.1 Arrow up or down: According to the law of supply, an increase in price ________ the quantity supplied.

2.2 From the following list, choose the variables that are held fixed when drawing a market supply curve:

- The price of the product
- Wages paid to workers
- The price of materials used in production
- Taxes paid by producers
- The quantity of the product purchased

2.3 The minimum supply price is the ________ price at which a product is supplied.

2.4 The market supply curve is the (horizontal/vertical) sum of the individual supply curves.

2.5 A change in price causes movement along a supply curve and a change in ________.

2.6 Arrows up or down: In the 1990s, the world price of wool ________ and the quantity of wool supplied ________. (Related to Application 2 on page 76.)

2.7 **Marginal Cost of Housing.** When the price of a standard three-bedroom house increases from $150,000 to $160,000, a building company increases its output from 20 houses per year to 21 houses per year. What does the increase in the quantity of housing reveal about the cost of producing housing?

2.8 **Imports and Market Supply.** Two nations supply sugar to the world market. Lowland has a minimum supply price of 10 cents per pound, while Highland has a minimum supply price of 24 cents per pound. For each nation, the slope of the supply curve is 1 cent per million pounds.

a. Draw the individual supply curves and the market supply curve. At what price and quantity is the supply curve kinked?

b. The market quantity supplied at a price of 15 cents is ________ million pounds. The market quantity supplied at a price of 30 cents is ________ million pounds.

2.9 **Responses to Higher Soybean Prices.** Suppose that in initial equilibrium in the soybean market, each of the 1,000 farmers produces 50 units, for a total of 50,000 units of soybeans. Suppose the price of soybeans increases, and everyone expects the price to stay at the higher level for many years.

a. Arrows up or down: Over a period of several years, we expect the quantity of soybeans supplied to ________ as the number of soybean farmers ________ and the output per farmer ________.

b. A farmer who enters the market is likely to have a (higher/lower) marginal cost of production than an original firm.

2.10 **Response to Lower Wool Price.** Use a demand and supply graph of the wool market to show the effects of the decrease in the price of wool on the quantity supplied in New Zealand. Assume that the initial price is $20 per unit and the initial quantity is 100 units. Also assume that for each 1 percent decrease in price, the quantity supplied decreases by 1 percent. (Related to Application 2 on page 76.)

4.3 Market Equilibrium: Bringing Demand and Supply Together

3.1 The market equilibrium is shown by the intersection of the __________ curve and the __________ curve.

3.2 Excess demand occurs when the price is (less/greater) than the equilibrium price; excess supply occurs when the price is (less/greater) than the equilibrium price.

3.3 Arrow up or down: An excess demand for a product will cause the price to __________. As a consequence of the price change, the quantity demanded will __________ and the quantity supplied will __________.

3.4 Arrow up or down: An excess supply of a product will cause the price to __________. As a consequence of the price change, the quantity demanded will __________, and the quantity supplied will __________.

3.5 A minimum price above the equilibrium price generates excess __________ (supply/demand). (Related to Application 3 on page 78.)

3.6 **Interpreting the Graph.** The following graph shows the demand and supply curves for CD players. Complete the following statements.

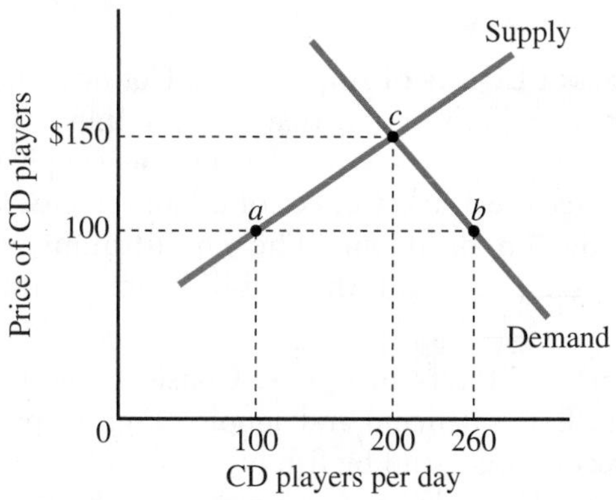

a. At the market equilibrium (shown by point __________), the price of CD players is __________ and the quantity of CD players is __________.

b. At a price of $100, there would be excess __________, so we would expect the price to __________.

c. At a price exceeding the equilibrium price, there would be excess __________, so we would expect the price to __________.

3.7 **Draw and Find the Equilibrium.** The following table shows the quantities of corn supplied and demanded at different prices.

Price per Ton	Quantity Supplied	Quantity Demanded
$ 80	600	1,200
90	800	1,100
100	1,000	1,000
110	1,200	900

a. Draw the demand curve and the supply curve.

b. The equilibrium price of corn is __________, and the equilibrium quantity is __________.

c. At a price of $110, there is excess (supply/demand) equal to __________.

3.8 **Relax Price Control.** Use a demand and supply graph to illustrate the effects of relaxing a minimum-price policy by allowing the price to decrease and narrow the gap between the controlled price and the equilibrium price. (Related to Application 3 on page 78.)

4.4 Market Effects of Changes in Demand

4.1 A change in demand causes a (movement along/shift of) the demand curve. A change in quantity demanded causes a (movement along/shift of) the demand curve.

4.2 Circle the variables that change as we move along the demand curve for pencils and cross out those that are assumed to be fixed.

- Quantity of pencils demanded
- Number of consumers
- Price of pencils
- Price of pens
- Consumer income

4.3 Consider the effects of online distribution of movies. A decrease in the price of online movies shifts the demand for DVD movies to the (left, right). A decrease in downloading time shifts the demand for DVD movies to the (left, right).

4.4 Arrow up or down: The market demand curve for a product will shift to the right when the price of a substitute good __________, the price of a complementary good __________, consumer income __________, and the population __________.

4.5 Arrow up or down: An increase in demand for a product __________ the equilibrium price and __________ the equilibrium quantity.

4.6 Between 2006 and 2009 the equilibrium price of pecans increased by roughly __________ (15, 50, 70) percent, a result of increased __________ (demand, supply) from China. (Related to Application 4 on page 82.)

4.7 **Market Effects of Increased Income.** Consider the market for restaurant meals. Use a demand and supply graph to predict the market effects of an increase in consumer income. Arrow up or down: The equilibrium price of restaurant meals will __________, and the equilibrium quantity of restaurant meals will __________.

4.8 **Public versus Private Colleges.** Consider the market for private college education. Use a demand and supply graph to predict the market effects of an increase in the tuition charged by public colleges. Arrow up or down: The equilibrium price of a private college education will __________, and the equilibrium quantity will __________.

4.9 **Gas Prices and New Gas Guzzlers.** Use a demand and supply graph to predict the implications for the market for new full-size SUVs. Arrow up or down: The equilibrium price of a full-size SUV will __________, and the equilibrium quantity will __________.

4.10 **Pecan Prices.** Use a demand and supply graph to illustrate the effects of the increase in the demand for pecans from Chinese consumers. Assume that the initial equilibrium price is $6 per unit. (Related to Application 4 on page 82.)

4.5 Market Effects of Changes in Supply

5.1 A change in supply causes a (movement along/shift of) the supply curve. A change in quantity supplied causes a (movement along/shift of) the supply curve.

5.2 Circle the variables that change as we move along the supply curve for pencils and cross out those that are assumed to be fixed:

- Quantity of pencils supplied
- Price of wood
- Price of pencils
- Production technology

5.3 Arrow up or down: An increase in the price of wood shifts the supply curve for pencils __________; an improvement in pencil-production technology shifts the supply curve for pencils __________; a tax on pencil production shifts the supply curve for pencils __________.

5.4 Arrow up or down: An increase in the supply of a product __________ the equilibrium price and __________ the equilibrium quantity.

5.5 If both demand and supply increase simultaneously, the equilibrium price will increase if the change in __________ is relatively large.

5.6 Arrow up or down: If supply increases while demand decreases, the equilibrium price will __________.

5.7 If supply increases while demand decreases, the equilibrium quantity will decrease if the change in (supply/demand) is relatively large.

5.8 Arrows up or down: The decrease in the number of bee colonies __________ the supply of fruits and berries, __________ the cost of producing ice cream, and __________ the equilibrium price of ice cream. (Related to Application 5 on page 89.)

5.9 **Effect of Weather on Prices.** Suppose a freeze in Florida wipes out 20 percent of the orange crop. How will this affect the equilibrium price and quantity of Florida oranges? Illustrate your answer with a graph.

5.10 **Immigration Control and Prices.** Consider the market for raspberries. Suppose a new law outlaws the use of foreign farm workers on raspberry farms, and the wages paid to farm workers increase as a result. Use a demand and supply graph to predict the effects of the higher wage on the equilibrium price and quantity of raspberries. Arrow up or down: The equilibrium price of raspberries will __________, and the equilibrium quantity of raspberries will __________.

5.11 **Market Effects of Import Ban.** Consider the market for shoes in a nation that initially imports half the shoes it consumes. Use a demand and supply graph to predict the market effect of a ban on shoe imports. Arrow up or down: The equilibrium price will __________, and the equilibrium quantity will __________.

5.12 **Market Effects of a Tax.** Consider the market for fish. Use a demand and supply graph to predict the effect of a tax paid by fish producers of $1 per pound of fish. Use a demand and supply graph to predict the market effect of the tax. Arrow up or down: The equilibrium price will __________, and the equilibrium quantity will __________.

5.13 **Innovation and the Price of Mobile Phones.** Suppose that the initial price of a mobile phone is $100 and that the initial quantity demanded is 500 phones per day. Use a graph to show the effects of a technological innovation that decreases the cost of producing mobile phones. Label the starting point with "*a*" and the new equilibrium with "*b*."

5.14 **Used Cars: Gas Guzzlers versus Gas Sippers.** Consider the market for used cars. In 2008, the price of gas rose while the price of used full-size SUVs dropped and the price of used compact cars increased.

   a. Use a supply–demand graph to show the effects of a higher gasoline price on the market for used full-size SUVs.

   b. Use a supply–demand graph to show the effects of a higher gasoline price on the market for used compact cars.

5.15 **Honeybees and Ice Cream.** Suppose the decline of bee colonies increases the prices of some ingredients used to produce ice cream. Consider two flavors of ice cream, strawberry and vanilla. The cost of producing strawberry ice cream increases by 20 percent, while the cost of producing vanilla ice cream increases by only 5 percent. Use a supply–demand graph to show the implications for the equilibrium prices and quantities of the two flavors of ice cream. (Related to Application 5 on page 89.)

4.6 Predicting and Explaining Market Changes

6.1 Fill in the blanks in the following table. Note that the ordering of the first column has been scrambled.

Change in Demand or Supply	How does the equilibrium price change?	How does the equilibrium quantity change?
Increase in supply		
Decrease in demand		
Decrease in supply		
Increase in demand		

6.2 When (supply/demand) changes, the equilibrium price and the equilibrium quantity change in the same direction. When (supply/demand) changes, the equilibrium price and the equilibrium quantity change in opposite directions.

6.3 Suppose the equilibrium price of accordions recently increased while the equilibrium quantity decreased. These changes were caused by a(n) (increase/decrease) in (supply/demand).

6.4 Suppose the equilibrium price of housing recently increased, and the equilibrium quantity increased as well. These changes were caused by a(n) (increase/decrease) in (supply/demand).

6.5 If a decrease in the price of drugs is accompanied by a decrease in quantity, the decrease in price was caused by a change in ________ (supply, demand). (Related to Application 6 on page 90.)

6.6 **What Caused the Higher Gasoline Price?** In the last month, the price of gasoline increased by 20 percent. Your job is to determine what caused the increase in price: a change in demand or a change in supply. Ms. Info has all the numbers associated with the gasoline market, and she can answer a single factual question. (She cannot answer the question "Was the higher price caused by a change in demand or a change in supply?")

   a. What single question would you ask?

   b. Provide an answer to your question that implies that the higher price was caused by a change in demand. Illustrate with a complete graph.

   c. Provide an answer to your question that implies that the higher price was caused by a change in supply. Illustrate with a complete graph.

6.7 **Rising Price of Milk.** In 2007, the price of milk increased by roughly 10 percent while the quantity consumed decreased. Use a supply–demand graph to explain the changes in price and quantity.

6.8 **Rising Price of Used Organs.** Over the last few years, the price of transplantable human organs (livers, kidneys, hearts) has increased dramatically. Why? What additional information about the market for used organs would allow you to prove that your explanation is the correct one?

6.9 **The Price of Summer Cabins.** As summer approaches, the equilibrium price of rental cabins increases and the equilibrium quantity of cabins rented increases. Draw a demand and supply graph that explains these changes.

6.10 **Simplest Possible Graph.** Consider the market for juice oranges. Draw the simplest possible demand and supply graph consistent with the following observations. You should be able to draw a graph with no more than four curves. Label each of your curves as "supply" or "demand" and indicate the year (1, 2, or 3).

Year	1	2	3
Price	$5	$7	$4
Quantity	100	80	110

6.11 **Zero Price for Used Newspapers.** In 1987 you could sell a ton of used newspaper for $60. Five years later, you couldn't sell them at any price. In other words, the price of used newspapers dropped from $60 to zero in just five years. Over this period, the quantity of used newspapers bought and sold increased. What caused the drop in price? Illustrate your answer with a complete graph.

6.12 **Koppel and Drug Prices.** Use a demand and supply graph to show that Ted Koppel's proposed explanation of a decrease in drug prices is incorrect. (Related to Application 6 on page 90.)

ECONOMIC EXPERIMENT

MARKET EQUILIBRIUM

This simple experiment takes about 20 minutes. We start by dividing the class into two equal groups: consumers and producers.

- The instructor provides each consumer with a number indicating the maximum amount he or she is willing to pay (WTP) for a bushel of apples: The WTP is a number between $1 and $100. Each consumer has the opportunity to buy one bushel of apples per trading period. The consumer's score for a single trading period equals the gap between the WTP and the price actually paid for apples. For example, if the consumer's WTP is $80 and he or she pays only $30 for apples, the consumer's score is $50. Each consumer has the option of not buying apples. This will be sensible if the best price the consumer can get exceeds the WTP. If the consumer does not buy apples, his or her score will be zero.
- The instructor provides each producer with a number indicating the cost of producing a bushel of apples (a number between $1 and $100). Each producer has the opportunity to sell one bushel per trading period. The producer's score for a single trading period equals the gap between the selling prices and the cost of producing apples. So if a producer sells apples for $20, and the cost is only $15, the producer's score is $5. Producers have the option of not selling apples, which is sensible if the best price the producer can get is less than the cost. If the producer does not sell apples, his or her score is zero.

Once everyone understands the rules, consumers and producers meet in a trading area to arrange transactions. A consumer may announce how much he or she is willing to pay for apples and wait for a producer to agree to sell apples at that price. Alternatively, a producer may announce how much he or she is willing accept for apples and wait for a consumer to agree to buy apples at that price. Once a transaction has been arranged, the consumer and producer inform the instructor of the trade, record the transaction, and leave the trading area.

Several trading periods are conducted, each of which lasts a few minutes. After the end of each trading period, the instructor lists the prices at which apples sold during the period. Then another trading period starts, providing consumers and producers another opportunity to buy or sell apples. After all the trading periods have been completed, each participant computes his or her score by adding the scores from the trading periods.

MyEconLab

For additional economic experiments, please visit *www.myeconlab.com*.

Measuring a Nation's Production and Income

CHAPTER 5

During the recent deep economic downturn, economists, business writers, and politicians anxiously awaited the news from the government about the latest economic developments.

They pored over the data to determine if the economy was beginning to recover from its doldrums and when more robust economic activity would resume.

At the same time, a distinguished group of economists, led by Nobel Laureates Joseph Stiglitz and Amartya Sen and French economist Jean-Paul Fitoussi, issued a report calling for major revision in the way we measure economic performance. They suggested that our government statisticians focus more on how much we consume and how much leisure we enjoy, and not solely on what we produce. They also suggested that we should be more concerned about whether our current activities are sustainable over the long run, perhaps recognizing environmental constraints.

But perhaps their most radical suggestion was that we switch our focus away from economic production to measuring people's economic well-being. This could include examining the diets and living conditions of the poorest people. For residents of developed countries, this might involve analyzing surveys of people's reported happiness with their own lives.

These changes, however, may be far in the future. Economists and businesses will still rely for some time on the traditional measures of economic activity that we study in this chapter.

LEARNING OBJECTIVES

- Explain the circular flow.
- Identify the components of GDP
- Describe the steps from GDP to income
- Calculate real and nominal GDP
- List the phases of the business cycle
- Discuss the relationship of GDP to welfare.

MyEconLab
MyEconLab helps you master each objective and study more efficiently.

macroeconomics
The study of the nation's economy as a whole; focuses on the issues of inflation, unemployment, and economic growth.

This chapter begins your study of **macroeconomics**: the branch of economics that deals with a nation's economy as a whole. Macroeconomics focuses on the economic issues—unemployment, inflation, growth, trade, and the gross domestic product—that are most often discussed in newspapers, on the radio and television, and on the Internet.

Macroeconomic issues lie at the heart of political debates. In fact, all presidential candidates learn a quick lesson in macroeconomics. Namely, their prospects for reelection will depend on how well the economy performs during their term in office. If voters believe the economy has performed well, the president will be reelected. Democrat Jimmy Carter as well as Republican George H. W. Bush failed in their bids for reelection in 1980 and 1992, respectively, partly because of voters' macroeconomic concerns. Both Republican Ronald Reagan in 1984 and Democrat Bill Clinton in 1996 won reelection easily because voters believed the economy was performing well in their first terms. Public opinion polling shows that presidential popularity rises and falls with the performance of the economy.

Macroeconomic events profoundly affect our everyday lives. For example, if the economy fails to create enough jobs, workers will become unemployed throughout the country, and millions of lives will be disrupted. Similarly, slow economic growth means that living standards will not increase rapidly. If prices for goods begin rising rapidly, some people will find it difficult to maintain their lifestyles.

This chapter and the next will introduce you to the concepts you need to understand what macroeconomics is all about. In this chapter, we'll focus on a nation's production and income. We'll learn how economists measure the income and production for an entire country and how they use these measures. In the next chapter, we'll look carefully at unemployment and inflation. Both chapters will explain the terms the media often uses when reporting economic information.

Macroeconomics focuses on two basic issues: long-run economic growth and economic fluctuations. We need to understand what happens during the long run to understand the factors behind the rise in living standards in modern economies. Today, living standards are much higher in the United States than they were for our grandparents. Living standards are also much higher than those of millions of people throughout the globe. Although living standards have improved over time, the economy has not always grown smoothly. Economic performance has fluctuated over time. During periods of slow economic growth, not enough jobs are created, and large numbers of workers become unemployed. Both the public and policymakers become concerned about the lack of jobs and the increase in unemployment.

At other times, unemployment may not be a problem, but we become concerned that the prices of everything that we buy seem to increase rapidly. Sustained increases in prices are called **inflation**. We'll explore inflation in the next chapter.

inflation
Sustained increases in the average prices of all goods and services.

5.1 The "Flip" Sides of Macroeconomic Activity: Production and Income

Before we can study growth and fluctuations, we need to have a basic vocabulary and understanding of some key concepts. We begin with the terms *production* and *income* because these are the "flip" sides of the macroeconomic "coin," so to speak. Every day, men and women go off to work, where they produce or sell merchandise or provide services. At the end of the week or month, they return home with their paychecks or "income." They spend some of that money on other products and services, which are produced by other people. In other words, production leads to income, and income leads to production.

But this chapter really isn't about production and income of individuals in markets. That's what a microeconomist studies. On the contrary, this chapter is about the production and income of the economy *as a whole*. From a "big picture" perspective, we will look at certain measures that will tell us how much the economy is producing and how well it is growing. We will also be able to measure the total income generated in the economy and how this income flows back to workers and investors. These two measures—a country's production and income—are critical to a nation's economic health. Macroeconomists collect and analyze production and income data to understand how many people will find jobs and whether their living standards are rising or falling. Government officials use the data and analysis to develop economic policies.

The Circular Flow of Production and Income

Let's begin with a simple diagram known as the *circular flow*, shown in Figure 5.1 We'll start with a very simple economy that does not have a government or a foreign sector. Households and firms make transactions in two markets known as *factor markets* and *product markets*. In factor, or input, markets, households supply labor to firms. Households are also the ultimate owners of firms, as well as of all the resources firms use in their production, which we call *capital*. Consequently, we can think of households as providing capital to firms—land, buildings, and equipment—to produce output. Product, or output, markets are markets in which firms sell goods and services to consumers.

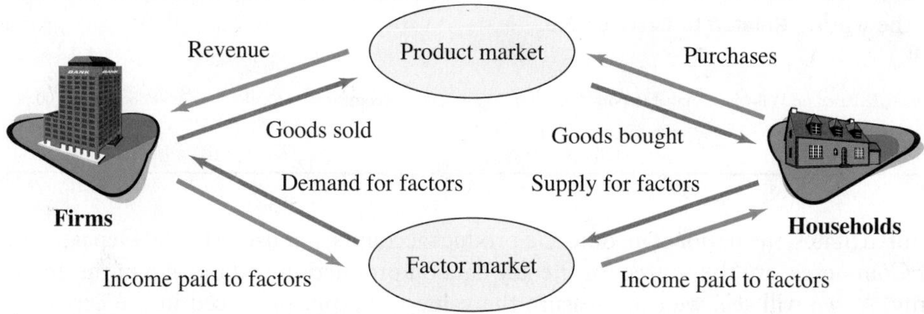

▲ FIGURE 5.1
The Circular Flow of Production and Income
The circular flow shows how the production of goods and services generates income for households and how households purchase goods and services produced by firms.

The point of the circular flow diagram is simple and fundamental: Production generates income. In factor markets, when households supply labor and capital to firms they are compensated by the firms. They earn wages for their work, and they earn interest, dividends, and rents on the capital they supply to the firms. The households then use their income to purchase goods and services in the product markets. The firm uses the revenues it receives from the sale of its products to pay for the factors of production (land, labor, and capital).

When goods and services are produced, income flows throughout the economy. For example, consider a manufacturer of computers. At the same time the computer manufacturer produces and sells new computers, it also generates income through its production. The computer manufacturer pays wages to workers, perhaps pays rent on offices and factory buildings, and pays interest on money it borrowed from a bank. Whatever is left over after paying for the cost of production is the firm's profit, which is income to the owners of the firm. Wages, rents, interest, and profits are all different forms of income.

In an example with a government, your taxes pay for a school district to hire principals, teachers, and other staff to provide educational services to the students in your community. These educational services are an important part of production in our modern economy that produces both goods and services. At the same time, the principals, teachers, and staff all earn income through their employment with the school district. The school district may also rent buildings where classes are held and pay interest on borrowed funds.

Our goal is to understand both sides of this macroeconomic "coin"—the production in the economy and the generation of income in the economy. In the

application 1

USING VALUE ADDED TO MEASURE THE TRUE SIZE OF WAL-MART

APPLYING THE CONCEPTS #1: How can we use economic analysis to compare the size of a major corporation to the size of a country?

During 2008, Wal-Mart's sales were approximately $374 billion, nearly 2.6 percent of U.S. GDP. Some social commentators might want to measure the impact of Wal-Mart just through its sales. But to produce those sales, Wal-Mart had to buy goods from many other companies. Wal-Mart's value added was substantially less than its total sales. Based on Wal-Mart's annual reports, its cost of sales was $286 billion, leaving approximately $88 billion in value added. This is a very large number, as might be expected from the world's largest retailer, but it is much smaller than its total sales. If we used Wal-Mart's sales to compare it to a country, it would have a GDP similar to that of Belgium, which is ranked 28th in the world. However, using the more appropriate measure of value added, Wal-Mart's size is closer to Bulgaria, ranked 56th in the world. **Related to Exercise 3.9.**

SOURCE: Based on Wal-Mart Annual Report, 2008, http://walmartstores.com/sites/AnnualReport/2008/docs/finrep_00.pdf (accessed July, 2008).

United States, the national income and product accounts, published by the Department of Commerce, are the source for the key data on production and income in the economy. As we will see, we can measure the value of output produced in the economy by looking at either the production or income side of the economy. Let's begin by learning how to measure the production for the entire economy.

5.2 The Production Approach: Measuring a Nation's Macroeconomic Activity Using Gross Domestic Product

gross domestic product (GDP)
The total market value of final goods and services produced within an economy in a given year.

To measure the production of the entire economy, we need to combine an enormous array of goods and services—everything from new computers to NBA and WNBA basketball games. We can actually add computers to basketball games, as we could add apples and oranges if we were trying to determine the total monetary value of a fruit harvest. Our goal is to summarize the total production of an entire economy into a single number, which we call the **gross domestic product (GDP)**. Gross domestic product is the total market value of all the final goods and services produced within an economy in a given year. GDP is also the most common measure of an economy's total output. All the words in the GDP definition are important, so let's analyze them.

"Total market value" means we take the quantity of goods produced, multiply them by their respective prices, and then add up the totals. If an economy produced two cars at $25,000 per car and three computers at $2,000 per computer, the total value of these goods will be

$$\begin{aligned} 2 \text{ cars} \times \$25{,}000 \text{ per car} &= \$50{,}000 \\ &+ \\ 3 \text{ computers} \times \$2{,}000 \text{ per computer} &= \$6{,}000 \\ &= \$56{,}000 \end{aligned}$$

The reason we multiply the goods by their prices is that we cannot simply add together the number of cars and the number of computers. Using prices allows us to express the value of everything in a common unit of measurement—in this case, dollars. (In countries other than the United States, we express the value in terms of the local currency.) We add apples and oranges together by finding out the value of both the apples and the oranges, as measured by what you would pay for them, and adding them up in terms of their prices.

"Final goods and services" in the definition of GDP means those goods and services that are sold to ultimate, or final, purchasers. For example, the two cars that were produced would be final goods if they were sold to households or to a business. However, to produce the cars the automobile manufacturer bought steel that went into the body of the cars, and we do not count this steel as a final good or service in GDP. Steel is an example of an **intermediate good**, one that is used in the production process. An intermediate good is not considered a final good or service.

intermediate goods
Goods used in the production process that are not final goods and services.

The reason we do not count intermediate goods as final goods is to avoid double-counting. The price of the car already reflects the price of the steel contained in it. We do not want to count the steel twice. Similarly, the large volumes of paper a commercial printing firm uses also are intermediate goods, because the paper becomes part of the final product delivered by the printing firm to its clients.

The final words in our definition of GDP are "in a given year." GDP is expressed as a rate of production, that is, as "X" amount of dollars per year. In 2010, for example, GDP in the United States was $14,526 billion. Goods produced in prior years, such as cars or houses, are not included in GDP for a given year, even if one consumer sells a house or car to another in that year. Only *newly produced* products are included in GDP.

Because we measure GDP using the current prices for goods and services, GDP will increase if prices increase, even if the physical amount of goods that are produced remains the same. Suppose that next year the economy again produces two cars and three computers, but all the prices in the economy double: The price of cars is $50,000, and the price of computers is $4,000. GDP will also be twice as high, or $112,000, even though the quantity produced is the same as during the prior year:

$$\begin{aligned} 2 \text{ cars} \times \$50{,}000 \text{ per car} &= \$100{,}000 \\ &+ \\ 3 \text{ computers} \times \$4{,}000 \text{ per computer} &= \$12{,}000 \\ &= \$112{,}000 \end{aligned}$$

But to say that GDP has doubled would be misleading, because exactly the same goods were produced. To avoid this problem, let's apply the real-nominal principle, one of our five basic principles of economics.

REAL-NOMINAL PRINCIPLE

What matters to people is the real value of money or income—its purchasing power—not the face value of money or income.

What we need is another measure of total output that doesn't increase just because prices increase. For this reason, economists have developed the concept of **real GDP**, a measure that controls for changes in prices. Later in this chapter, we explain how real GDP is calculated. The basic idea is simple. When we use current prices to measure GDP, we are using **nominal GDP**. Nominal GDP can increase for one of two reasons: Either the production of goods and services has increased, or the prices of those goods and services have increased.

real GDP
A measure of GDP that controls for changes in prices.

nominal GDP
The value of GDP in current dollars.

To explain the concept of real GDP, we first need to look at a simple example. Suppose an economy produces a single good: computers. In year 1, 10 computers were produced, and each sold for $2,000. In year 2, 12 computers were produced, and each sold for $2,100. Nominal GDP is $20,000 in year 1 and $25,200 in year 2; it has increased by a factor of 1.26 or 26 percent. However, we can also measure real

GDP by using year 1 prices as a measure of what was produced in year 1 *and* what was produced in year 2. In year 1, real GDP is

$$10 \text{ computers} \times \$2{,}000 \text{ per computer} = \$20{,}000$$

In year 2, real GDP (in year 1 terms) is

$$12 \text{ computers} \times \$2{,}000 \text{ per computer} = \$24{,}000$$

Real GDP in year 2 is still greater than real GDP in year 1, now by a factor of 1.2, or 20 percent. The key idea is that we construct a measure using the same prices for both years and thereby take price changes into account.

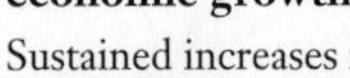

economic growth
Sustained increases in the real GDP of an economy over a long period of time.

Figure 5.2 plots real GDP for the U.S. economy for the years 1930 through 2011. The graph shows that real GDP has grown substantially over this period. This is what economists call **economic growth**—sustained increases in the real GDP of an economy over a long period of time. In Chapter 8, we'll study economic growth in detail. Later in this chapter, we'll look carefully at the behavior of real GDP over shorter periods, during which time it can rise and fall. Decreases in real GDP disrupt the economy greatly and lead to unemployment.

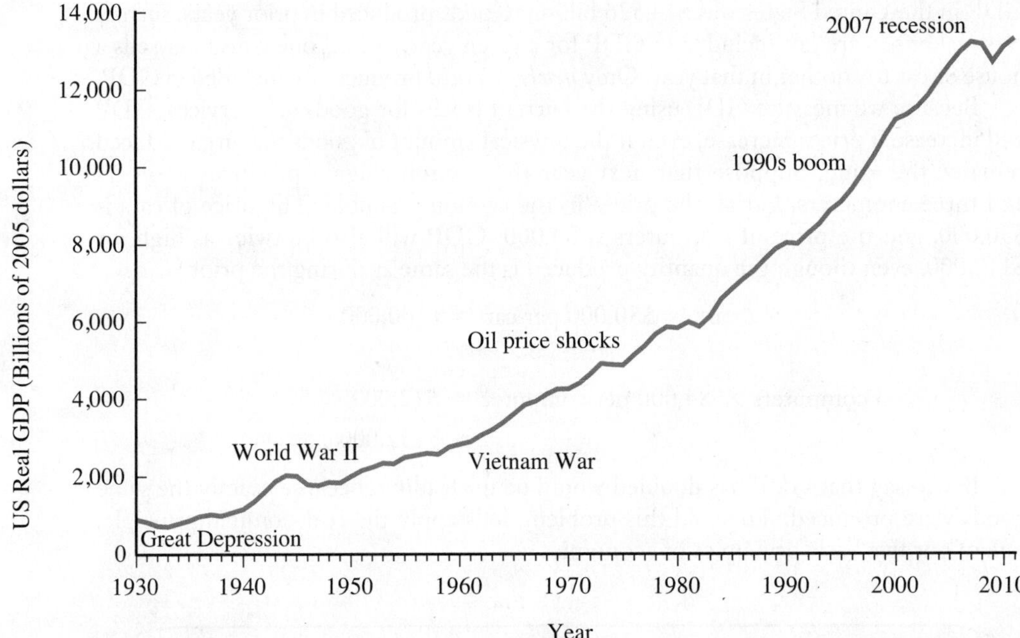

▲ FIGURE 5.2
U.S. Real GDP, 1930–2011
During the Great Depression in the 1930s, GDP initially fell and then was relatively flat. The economy was not growing much. However, the economy began growing rapidly in the 1940s during World War II and has grown substantially since then.
SOURCE: U.S. Department of Commerce.

MyEconLab Real-time data

The Components of GDP

Economists divide GDP into four broad categories, each corresponding to different types of purchases represented in GDP:

1 *Consumption expenditures:* purchases by consumers
2 *Private investment expenditures:* purchases by firms
3 *Government purchases:* purchases by federal, state, and local governments
4 *Net exports:* net purchases by the foreign sector (domestic exports minus domestic imports)

Before discussing these categories, let's look at some data for the U.S. economy to get a sense of the size of each of these four components. Table 5.1 shows the figures for GDP for the third quarter of 2011. (A quarter is a three-month period; the first quarter runs from January through March, while the third quarter runs from July through September. Quarterly GDP expressed at annual rates is GDP for a year if the entire year were the same as the measured quarter.) In the third quarter of 2011, GDP was $ 15,176 billion, or approximately $15.2 trillion. To get a sense of the magnitude, consider that the U.S. population is approximately 300 million people, making GDP per person approximately $50,586. (This does not mean every man, woman, and child actually spends $50,586, but it is a useful indicator of the productive strength of the economy.)

TABLE 5.1 Composition of U.S. GDP, Third Quarter 2011 (Billions of Dollars Expressed at Annual Rates)

GDP	Consumption Expenditures	Private Investment Expenditures	Government Purchases	Net Exports
$15,176	$10,784	$1,906	$3,047	–$562

SOURCE: U.S. Department of Commerce.

MyEconLab Real-time data

CONSUMPTION EXPENDITURES **Consumption expenditures** are purchases by consumers of currently produced goods and services, either domestic or foreign. These purchases include flat-screen TVs, smart phones, automobiles, clothing, hair-styling services, jewelry, movie or basketball tickets, food, and all other consumer items. We can break down consumption into durable goods, nondurable goods, and services. *Durable goods*, such as automobiles or refrigerators, last for a long time. *Nondurable goods*, such as food, last for a short time. *Services* are work in which people play a prominent role in delivery (such as a dentist filling a cavity). They range from haircutting to health care and are the fastest-growing component of consumption in the United States. Overall, consumption spending is the most important component of GDP, constituting about 71 percent of total purchases.

consumption expenditures
Purchases of newly produced goods and services by households.

PRIVATE INVESTMENT EXPENDITURES **Private investment expenditures** in GDP consist of three components:

private investment expenditures
Purchases of newly produced goods and services by firms.

1 First, there is spending on new plants and equipment during the year. If a firm builds a new factory or purchases a new machine, the new factory or new machine is included in the year's GDP. Purchasing an existing building or buying a used machine does not count in GDP, because the goods were not produced during the current year.
2 Second, newly produced housing is included in investment spending. The sale of an existing home to a new owner is not counted, because the house was not built in the current year.
3 Finally, if firms add to their stock of inventories, the increase in inventories during the current year is included in GDP. If a hardware store had $1,000 worth of nuts and bolts on its shelves at the beginning of the year and $1,100 at the year's end, its inventory investment is $100 ($1,100 – $1,000). This $100 increase in inventory investment is included in GDP.

We call the total of new investment expenditures **gross investment**. During the year, some of the existing plant, equipment, and housing will deteriorate or wear out. This wear and tear is called **depreciation**, or sometimes a *capital consumption allowance*. If we subtract depreciation from gross investment, we obtain **net investment**.

Make sure you understand this distinction between gross investment and net investment. Consider the $1,906 billion in total investment spending for the third quarter of 2011, a period in which there was $1,607 billion in depreciation in the

gross investment
Total new investment expenditures.

depreciation
Reduction in the value of capital goods over a one-year period due to physical wear and tear and also to obsolescence; also called *capital consumption allowance*.

net investment
Gross investment minus depreciation.

private sector. That means there was only $299 billion ($1,906 – $1,607) in net investment by firms in that year; 84 percent of gross investment went to make up for depreciation of existing capital.

When we discuss measuring production in the GDP accounts, we use *investment* in a different way than that with which you may be accustomed. For an economist, investment in the GDP accounts means purchases of new final goods and services by firms. In everyday conversation, we may talk about investing in the stock market or investing in gold. Buying stock for $1,800 on the stock market is a purchase of an existing financial asset; it is not the purchase of new goods and services by firms. Therefore, that $1,800 does not appear anywhere in GDP. The same is true of purchasing a gold bar. In GDP accounting, *investment* denotes the purchase of new capital. Be careful not to confuse the common usage of *investment* with the definition of *investment* as we use it in the GDP accounts.

government purchases
Purchases of newly produced goods and services by local, state, and federal governments.

GOVERNMENT PURCHASES **Government purchases** are the purchases of newly produced goods and services by federal, state, and local governments. They include any goods that the government purchases plus the wages and benefits of all government workers (paid when the government purchases their services as employees). Investment spending by government is also included. The majority of spending in this category comes from state and local governments: $1,798 billion of the total $3,047 billion in 2011. Government purchases affect our lives very directly. For example, all salaries of U.S. postal employees and federal airport security personnel are counted as government purchases.

transfer payments
Payments from governments to individuals that do not correspond to the production of goods and services.

This category does not include all spending by governments. It excludes **transfer payments**, payments to individuals that are not associated with the production of goods and services. For example, payments for Social Security, welfare, and interest on government debt are all considered transfer payments and thus are not included in government purchases in GDP. Nothing is being produced by the recipients in return for money being paid, or "transferred," to them. But wage payments to the police, postal workers, and the staff of the Internal Revenue Service are all included, because they do correspond to services these workers are currently producing.

Because transfer payments are excluded from GDP, a vast portion of the budget of the federal government is not part of GDP. In 2010, the federal government spent approximately $3,703 billion, of which only $1,222 billion (about 33 percent) was counted as federal government purchases. Transfer payments are important, however, because they affect both the income of individuals and their consumption and savings behavior. Transfer payments also affect the size of the federal budget deficit, which we will study in a later chapter. At this point, keep in mind the distinction between government purchases—which are included in GDP—and total government spending or expenditure—which may *not* be included.

import
A good or service produced in a foreign country and purchased by residents of the home country (for example, the United States).

export
A good or service produced in the home country (for example, the United States) and sold in another country.

net exports
Exports minus imports.

NET EXPORTS To understand the role of the foreign sector, we first need to define three terms. **Imports** are goods and services we buy from other countries. **Exports** are goods and services made here and sold to other countries. **Net exports** are total exports minus total imports. In Table 5.1, we see that net exports in the third quarter of 2011 were –$562 billion. Net exports were negative because our imports exceeded our exports.

Consumption, investment, and government purchases include all purchases by consumers, firms, and the government, whether or not the goods were produced in the United States. However, GDP is supposed to measure the goods produced in the United States. Consequently, we subtract purchases of foreign goods by consumers, firms, or the government when we calculate GDP, because these goods were not produced in the United States. At the same time, we add to GDP any goods produced here and sold abroad, for example, airplanes made in the United States and sold in Europe. By including net exports as a component of GDP, we correctly measure U.S. production by adding exports and subtracting imports.

Suppose someone in the United States buys a $25,000 car made in Japan. If we look at final purchases, we will see that consumption spending rose by $25,000 because a consumer made a purchase of a consumption good. Net exports fell by \$25,000, however, because we subtracted the value of the import (the car) from total exports. Notice that total GDP did not change with the purchase of the car. This is exactly what we want in this case, because the car wasn't produced in the United States.

Now suppose the United States sells a car for \$22,000 to a resident of Spain. In this case, net exports increase by \$22,000 because the car was a U.S. export. GDP will also be a corresponding \$22,000 higher because this sale represents U.S. production.

Recall that for the United States in the third quarter of 2011 net exports were –\$562 billion dollars. In other words, in that quarter the United States bought \$562 billion more goods from abroad than it sold abroad. When we buy more goods from abroad than we sell, we have a **trade deficit**. A **trade surplus** occurs when our exports exceed our imports. Figure 5.3 shows the U.S. trade surplus as a share of GDP from 1960 to 2011. Although at times the United States has had a small trade surplus, it has generally run a trade deficit. In recent years, the trade deficit has increased and has fluctuated between 3 and 6 percent of GDP. In later chapters, we study how trade deficits can affect a country's GDP.

trade deficit
The excess of imports over exports.

trade surplus
The excess of exports over imports.

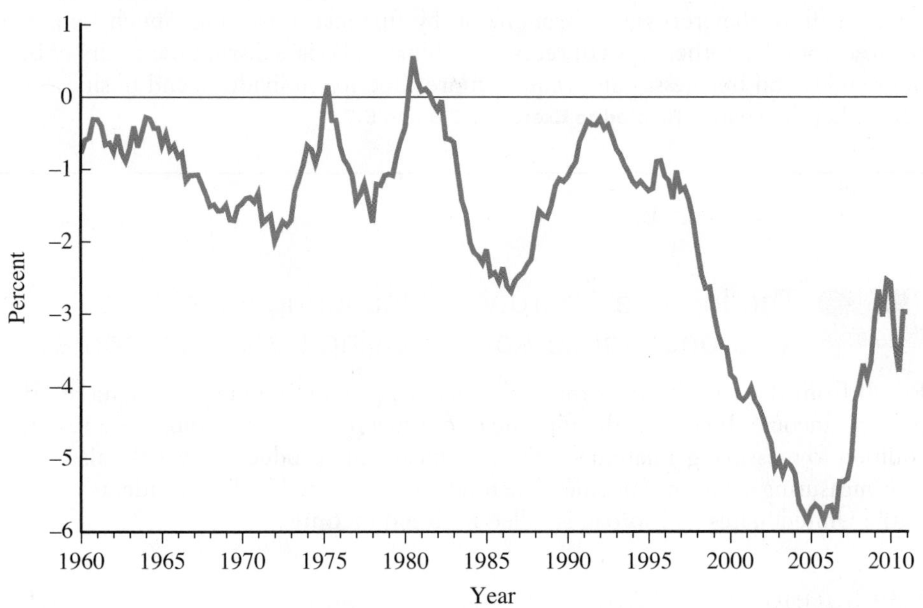

◀ FIGURE 5.3
U.S. Trade Balance as a Share of GDP, 1960–2011
In the early 1980s, the United States ran a trade surplus (when the line on the graph is above zero, this indicates a surplus). However, in other years the United States has run a trade deficit. In 2004 through 2006, the trade deficit exceeded 5 percent of GDP, although it most recently is near 3 percent of GDP.
SOURCE: Department of Commerce.
MyEconLab Real-time data

Putting It All Together: The GDP Equation

We can summarize our discussion of who purchases GDP with a simple equation that combines the four components of GDP:

$$Y = C + I + G + NX$$

where

$$Y = \text{GDP}$$
$$C = \text{Consumption}$$
$$I = \text{Investment}$$
$$G = \text{Government purchases}$$
$$NX = \text{Net exports}$$

In other words,

GDP = consumption + investment + government purchases + net exports

This equation is an *identity*, which means it is always true no matter what the values of the variables are. In any economy, GDP consists of the sum of its four components.

application 2

RECOVERING FROM A RECESSION

APPLYING THE CONCEPTS #2: How long did it take to recover from the last recession?

The most recent recession was not only deep and severe, it took a long time for the U.S. economy to recover from it. How can we measure how long it takes to recover from a recession? Recall that a recession begins when real GDP starts to fall from its peak. One useful measure would be to ask how long it takes for real GDP to finally return to the level of the peak before the recession started.

The last recession started in the fourth quarter of 2007. Real GDP then started to fall. It did not return to its peak until the second quarter of 2011—3.5 years later! This truly was a deep recession and a very slow and protracted recovery. Most recessions do not have as prolonged a recovery period. For example, the severe recession that began in the fourth quarter of 1973 only took two years to recover to its previous peak.

Why was the economy so slow to recover from this last recession? Some economists believe that recessions brought on by financial crises take much longer to recover from than other types of recessions. Financial crises disrupt the affairs of both households and businesses and require more time for individuals and businesses to adjust their behavior. **Related to Exercises 5.6 and 5.7.**

5.3 The Income Approach: Measuring a Nation's Macroeconomic Activity Using National Income

Recall from the circular flow that one person's production ends up being another person's income. Income is the flip side of our macroeconomic "coin." As a result, in addition to measuring a nation's activity by measuring production, we can also gauge it by measuring a nation's income. The total income earned by U.S. residents working in the United States and abroad is called **national income**.

national income
The total income earned by a nation's residents both domestically and abroad in the production of goods and services.

Measuring National Income

To measure national income, economists first make two primary adjustments to GDP.

First, we add to GDP the net income earned by U.S. firms and residents abroad. To make this calculation, we add to GDP any income earned abroad by U.S. firms or residents and subtract any income earned in the United States by foreign firms or residents. For example, we add the profits earned by U.S. multinational corporations that are sent back to the United States but subtract the profits from multinational corporations operating in the United States that are sent back to their home countries. The profits Wal-Mart sends back to the United States from its stores in Mexico are added to GDP. The profits Toyota earns in the United States that it sends back to Japan are subtracted from GDP. The result of these adjustments is the total income earned worldwide by U.S. firms and residents. This is the **gross national product (GNP)**.

gross national product
GDP plus net income earned abroad.

The distinction between what they produce within their borders, GDP, and what their citizens earn, GNP, is not that important to most countries. For the United States, the difference between GDP and GNP is typically just 1 percent. In some countries, however, the differences are much larger. The country of Kuwait, for example, earned vast amounts of income from its oil riches, which it invested abroad in stocks, bonds, and other types of investments. These earnings comprised approximately 9 percent of Kuwait's 2006 GNP. Foreigners have traditionally made large investments in Australia. As they sent their profits back to their home countries, Australia's net income from abroad was negative in 2006, and Australian GDP in that year exceeded Australian GNP by 4.1 percent.

The second adjustment we make when calculating national income is to subtract depreciation from GNP. Recall that depreciation is the wear and tear on plant and equipment that occurred during the year. In a sense, our income is reduced because our buildings and machines are wearing out. When we subtract depreciation from GNP, we reach *net national product (NNP)*, where *net* means "after depreciation."

After making these adjustments and taking into account statistical discrepancies, we reach *national income*. (Statistical discrepancies arise when government statisticians make their calculations using different sources of the same data.) Table 5.2 shows the effects of these adjustments for the third quarter of 2011.

TABLE 5.2 From GDP to National Income, Third Quarter 2011 (Billions of Dollars)

Gross domestic product	$15,176
Gross national product	15,443
Net national product	13,480
National income	13,431

In turn, national income is divided among six basic categories: compensation of employees (wages and benefits), corporate profits, rental income, proprietors' income (income of unincorporated business), net interest (interest payments received by households from business and from abroad), and other items. Approximately 62 percent of all national income goes to workers in the form of wages and benefits. For most of the countries in the world, wages and benefits are the largest part of national income.

In addition to national income, which measures the income earned in a given year by the entire private sector, we are sometimes interested in determining the total payments that flow directly into households, a concept known as **personal income**. To calculate personal income, we begin with national income and subtract any corporate profits that are retained by the corporation and not paid out as dividends to households. We also subtract all taxes on production and imports and social insurance taxes, which are payments for Social Security and Medicare. We then add any personal interest income received from the government and consumers and all transfer payments. The result is the total income available to households, or personal income. The amount of personal income that households retain after paying income taxes is called **personal disposable income**.

personal income
Income, including transfer payments, received by households.

personal disposable income
Personal income that households retain after paying income taxes.

Measuring National Income through Value Added

Another way to measure national income is to look at the **value added** of each firm in the economy. For a firm, we can measure its value added by the dollar value of the firm's sales minus the dollar value of the goods and services purchased from other firms. What remains is the sum of all the income—wages, profits, rents, and interest—that the firm generates. By adding up the value added for all the firms in the economy (plus nonprofit and governmental organizations), we can calculate national income. Let's consider a simple example illustrated in Table 5.3.

value added
The sum of all the income—wages, interest, profits, and rent—generated by an organization. For a firm, we can measure value added by the dollar value of the firm's sales minus the dollar value of the goods and services purchased from other firms.

TABLE 5.3 Calculating Value Added in a Simple Economy

	Automobile Firm	Steel Firm	Total Economy
Total sales	$16,000	$6,000	$22,000
Less purchases from other firms	6,000	0	6,000
Equals value added: the sum of all wages, interest, profits, and rents	10,000	6,000	16,000

Suppose an economy consists of two firms: an automobile firm that sells its cars to consumers and a steel firm that sells only to the automobile firm. If the automobile company sells a car for $16,000 to consumers and purchases $6,000 worth of steel from the steel firm, the auto firm has $10,000 remaining—its value added—which it can then distribute as wages, rents, interest, and profits. If the steel firm sells $6,000 worth of steel but does not purchase any inputs from other firms, its value added is $6,000, which it pays out in the form of wages, rents, interest, and profits. Total value added in the economy from both firms is $16,000 ($10,000 + $6,000), which is the sum of wages, rents, interest, and profits for the entire economy (consisting of these two firms).

As this example illustrates, we measure the value added for a typical firm by starting with the value of its total sales and subtracting the value of any inputs it purchases from other firms. The amount of income that remains is the firm's value added, which is then distributed as wages, rents, interest, and profits. In calculating national income, we need to include all the firms in the economy, even the firms that produce intermediate goods.

An Expanded Circular Flow

Now that we have examined both production and income, including both the government and the foreign sector, let's take another look at a slightly more realistic circular flow. Figure 5.4 depicts a circular flow that includes both the government and the foreign sector. Both households and firms pay taxes to the government. The government, in turn, supplies goods and services in the product market and also purchases inputs—labor and capital—in the factor markets, just like private-sector firms do. Net exports, which can be positive or negative, are shown entering or leaving the product market.

In summary, we can look at GDP from two sides: We can ask who buys the output that is produced, or we can ask how the income that is created through the production process is divided between workers and investors. From the spending side, we saw that nearly 70 percent of GDP consists of consumer expenditures. From the income side, we saw that nearly 65 percent of national income is paid in wages and

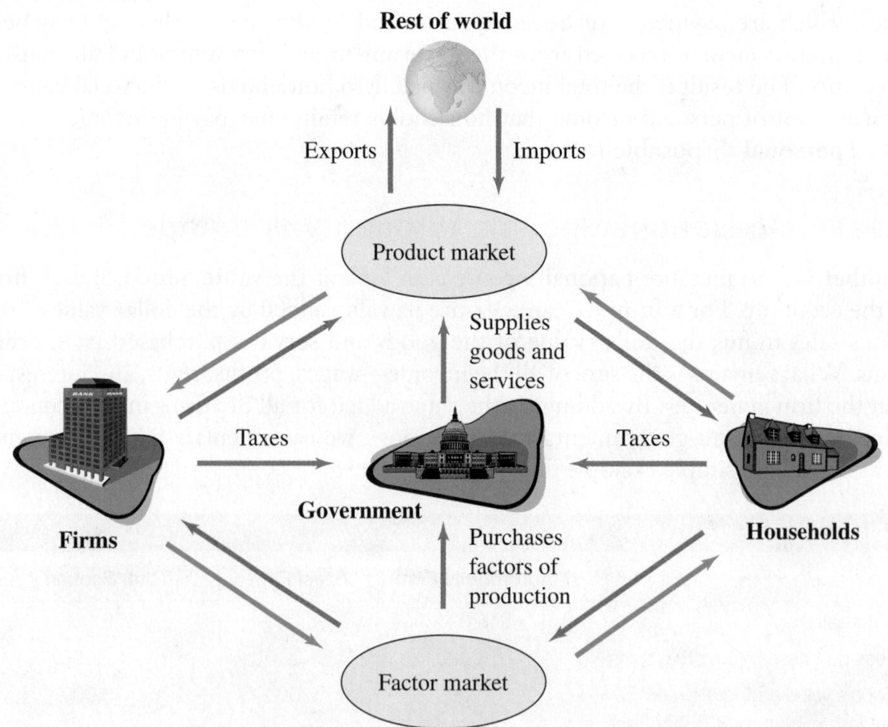

▶ FIGURE 5.4
The Circular Flow with Government and the Foreign Sector
The new linkages (in blue) demonstrate the roles that the government and the foreign sector (imports and exports) play in the circular flow.

application 3

THE LINKS BETWEEN SELF-REPORTED HAPPINESS AND GDP

APPLYING THE CONCEPTS #3: Do increases in gross domestic product necessarily translate into improvements in the welfare of citizens?

Two economists, David Blanchflower of Dartmouth College and Andrew Oswald of Warwick University in the United Kingdom, have systematically analyzed surveys over a nearly 30-year period that ask individuals to describe themselves as "happy, pretty happy, or not too happy." The results of their work are provocative. Over the last 30 years, reported levels of happiness have declined slightly in the United States and remained relatively flat in the United Kingdom despite very large increases in per capita income in both countries. Could it be the increased stress of everyday life has taken its toll on our happiness despite the increase in income?

At any point in time, however, money does appear to buy happiness. Holding other factors constant, individuals with higher incomes do report higher levels of personal satisfaction. But these "other factors" are quite important. Unemployment and divorce lead to sharply lower levels of satisfaction. Blanchflower and Oswald calculate that a stable marriage is worth $100,000 per year in terms of equivalent reported satisfaction.

Perhaps most interesting are their findings about trends in the relative happiness of different groups in our society. While whites report higher levels of happiness than African Americans, the gap has decreased over the last 30 years, as the happiness of African Americans has risen faster than that of whites. Men's happiness has risen relative to that of women over the last 30 years.

Finally, in recent work Blanchflower and Oswald looked at how happiness varies over the life cycle. Controlling for income, education, and other personal factors, they found that in the United States, happiness among men and women reaches a minimum at the ages of 49 and 45, respectively. Since these are also the years in which earnings are usually the highest, it does suggest that work takes its toll on happiness. **Related to Exercises 6.2 and 6.9.**

SOURCE: David Blanchflower and Andrew Oswald, "Well-Being Over Time in Britain and the USA," (working paper 7847, National Bureau of Economic Research, January 2000) and "Is Well-being U-Shaped over the Life Cycle," (working paper 12935, February 2007).

benefits. Macroeconomists may use data based either on the production that occurs in the economy or on its flip side, the income that is generated, depending on whether they are more focused on current production or on current income.

5.4 A Closer Examination of Nominal and Real GDP

We have discussed different ways to measure the production of an economy, looking at both who purchases goods and services and the income it generates. Of all the measures we have discussed, GDP is the one most commonly used both by the public and by economists. Let's take a closer look at it.

Measuring Real versus Nominal GDP

Output in the economy can increase from one year to the next. And prices can rise from one year to the next. Recall that we defined nominal GDP as GDP measured in current prices, and we defined real GDP as GDP adjusted for price changes.

Now we take a closer look at how real GDP is measured in modern economies. Let's start with a simple economy in which there are only two goods—cars and computers—produced in the years 2011 and 2012. The data for this economy—the prices and quantities produced for each year—are shown in Table 5.4. The production of cars and the production of computers increased, but the production of computers increased more rapidly. The price of cars rose, while the price of computers remained the same.

TABLE 5.4 GDP Data for a Simple Economy

	Quantity Produced		Price	
Year	*Cars*	*Computers*	*Cars*	*Computers*
2011	4	1	$10,000	$5,000
2012	5	3	12,000	5,000

Let's first calculate nominal GDP for this economy in each year. Nominal GDP is the total market value of goods and services produced in each year. Using the data in the table, we can see that nominal GDP for the year 2011 is

$$(4 \text{ cars} \times \$10{,}000) + (1 \text{ computer} \times \$5{,}000) = \$45{,}000$$

Similarly, nominal GDP for the year 2012 is

$$(5 \text{ cars} \times \$12{,}000) + (3 \text{ computers} \times \$5{,}000) = \$75{,}000$$

Now we'll find real GDP. To compute real GDP, we calculate GDP using constant prices. What prices should we use? For the moment, let's use the prices for the year 2011. Because we are using 2011 prices, real GDP and nominal GDP for 2011 are both equal to $45,000. But for 2012, they are different. In 2012, real GDP is

$$(5 \text{ cars} \times \$10{,}000) + (3 \text{ computers} \times \$5{,}000) = \$65{,}000$$

Note that real GDP for 2012, which is $65,000, is less than nominal GDP for 2012, which is $75,000. The reason real GDP is less than nominal GDP here is that prices of cars rose by $2,000 between 2011 and 2012, and we are measuring GDP using 2011 prices. We can measure real GDP for any other year simply by calculating GDP using constant prices.

We now calculate the growth in real GDP for this economy between 2011 and 2012. Because real GDP was $45,000 in 2011 and $65,000 in 2012, real GDP grew by $20,000. In percentage terms, this is a $20,000 increase from the initial level of $45,000 or

$$\text{Percentage growth in real GDP} = \frac{\$20{,}000}{\$45{,}000} = .444$$

which equals 44.4 percent. This percentage is an average of the growth rates for both goods—cars and computers.

Figure 5.5 depicts real and nominal GDP for the United States from 1950 to 2011. Real GDP is measured in 2005 dollars, so the curves cross in 2005. Before 2005, nominal GDP is less than real GDP because prices in earlier years were lower than they were in 2005. After 2005, nominal GDP exceeds real GDP because prices in later years were higher than they were in 2005.

How to Use the GDP Deflator

GDP deflator
An index that measures how the prices of goods and services included in GDP change over time.

We can also use the data in Table 5.4 to measure the changes in prices for this economy of cars and computers. The basic idea is that the differences between nominal GDP and real GDP for any year arise only because of changes in prices. So by comparing real GDP and nominal GDP, we can measure the changes in prices for the economy. In practice, we do this by creating an index, called the **GDP deflator**, that measures how prices of goods and services change over time. Because we are calculating real GDP using year 2011 prices, we will set the value of this index equal to 100 in the

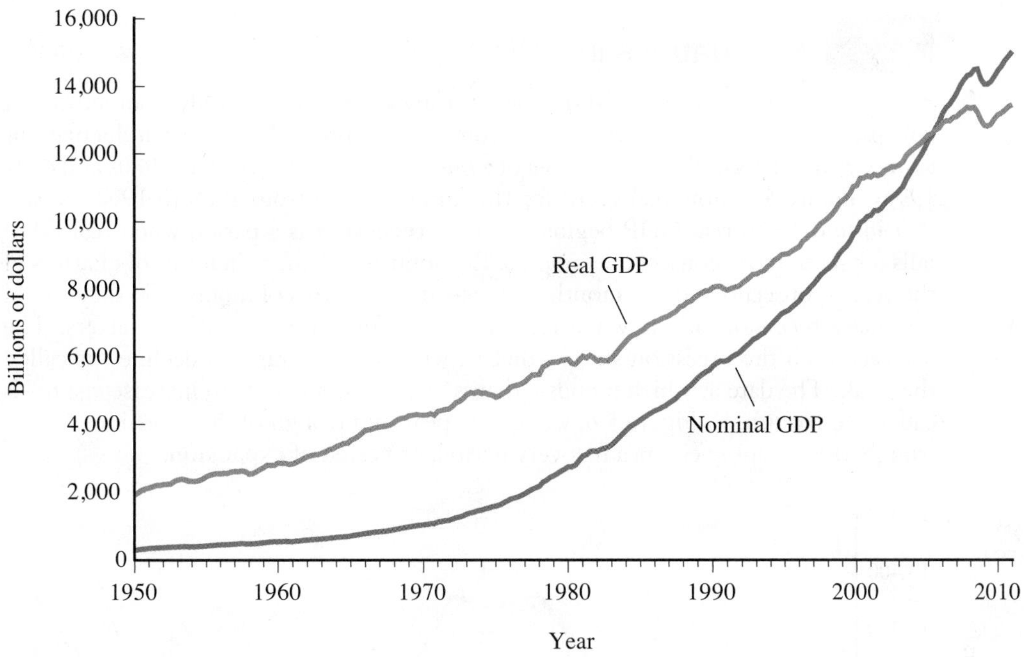

▲ FIGURE 5.5
U.S. Nominal and Real GDP, 1950–2011
This figure plots both real and nominal GDP for the United States in billions of dollars. Real GDP is measured in 2005 dollars.
MyEconLab Real-time data

year 2011, which we call the base year. To find the value of the GDP deflator for the year 2012 (or other years), we use the following formula:

$$\text{GDP Deflator} = \frac{\text{Nominal GDP}}{\text{Real GDP}} \times 100$$

Using this formula, we find that the value of the GDP deflator for 2012 is

$$\frac{\$75{,}000}{\$65{,}000} \times 100 = 1.15 \times 100 = 115$$

Because the value of the GDP deflator is 115 in 2012 and was 100 in the base year of 2011, this means prices rose by 15 percent between the two years:

$$\frac{115 - 100}{100} = \frac{15}{100} = 0.15$$

Note that this 15 percent is a weighted average of the price changes for the two goods—cars and computers.

Until 1996, the Commerce Department, which produces the GDP figures, used these formulas to calculate real GDP and measure changes in prices. Economists at the department chose a base year and measured real GDP by using the prices in that base year. They also calculated the GDP deflator, just as we did, by taking the ratio of nominal GDP to real GDP. Today, the Commerce Department calculates real GDP and the price index for real GDP using a more complicated method. In our example, we measured real GDP using 2011 prices. But we could have also measured real GDP using prices from 2012. If we did, we would have come up with slightly different numbers both for the increase in prices between the two years and for the increase in real GDP. To avoid this problem, the Commerce Department now uses a **chain-weighted index**, which is a method for calculating price changes that takes an average of price changes using base years from consecutive years (that is, 2011 and 2012 in our example). If you look online or at the data produced by the Commerce Department, you will see real GDP measured in chained dollars and a chain-type price index for GDP.

chain-weighted index
A method for calculating changes in prices that uses an average of base years from neighboring years.

5.5 Fluctuations in GDP

recession
Commonly defined as six consecutive months of declining real GDP.

peak
The date at which a recession starts.

trough
The date at which output stops falling in a recession.

expansion
The period after a trough in the business cycle during which the economy recovers.

As we have discussed, real GDP does not always grow smoothly—sometimes it collapses suddenly, and the result is an economic downturn. We call such fluctuations *business cycles*. Let's look at an example of a business cycle from the late 1980s and early 1990s. Figure 5.6 plots real GDP for the United States from 1988 to 1992. Notice that in mid-1990, real GDP begins to fall. A **recession** is a period when real GDP falls for six or more consecutive months. Economists talk more in terms of quarters of the year—consecutive three-month periods—than in terms of months. So they would say that a recession occurs when real GDP falls for two consecutive quarters. The date at which the recession starts—that is, when output starts to decline—is called the **peak**. The date at which it ends—that is, when output starts to increase again—is called the **trough**. In Figure 5.6, we see the peak and trough of the recession. After a trough, the economy enters a recovery period, or period of **expansion**.

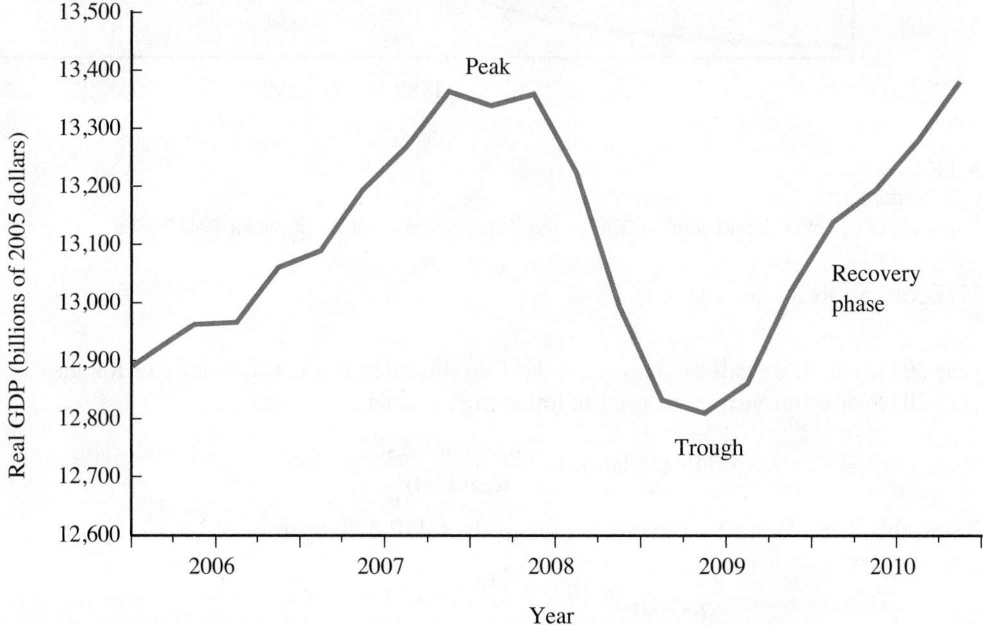

▲ **FIGURE 5.6**
The 2007–2009 Recession
Recessions can be illustrated by peaks, troughs, and an expansion phase. The date at which the recession starts and output begins to fall is called the peak. The date at which the recession ends and output begins to rise is called the trough. The expansion phase begins after the trough. The 2007–2009 recession began in December 2007 and ended in June 2009.
SOURCE: U.S. Department of Commerce.

From World War II through 2010, the United States experienced 11 recessions. Table 5.5 contains the dates of the peaks and troughs of each recession, the percent decline in real GDP from each peak to each trough, and the length of the recessions in months. The recession from 1973 to 1975, which started as a result of a sharp rise in world oil prices, was very severe. The recession from 2007 to 2009 was perhaps the worst downturn since World War II.

In the last three decades, there have been four recessions, three of them starting near the beginning of each of the decades: 1981, 1990, and 2001. In the 2001 recession, employment began to fall in March 2001, before the terrorist attack on the United States on September 11, 2001. The attack further disrupted economic activity and damaged producer and consumer confidence, and the economy tumbled through a recession. The recession that began in December 2007 followed a sharp decline in

TABLE 5.5 Eleven Postwar Recessions

Peak	Trough	Percent Decline in Real GDP	Length of Recession (months)
November 1948	October 1949	−1.5	11
July 1953	May 1954	−3.2	10
August 1957	April 1958	−3.3	8
April 1960	February 1961	−1.2	10
December 1969	November 1970	−1.0	11
November 1973	March 1975	−4.1	16
January 1980	July 1980	−2.5	6
July 1981	November 1982	−3.0	16
July 1990	March 1991	−1.4	8
March 2001	November 2001	−0.6	8
December 2007	June 2009	−4.1	18

SOURCE: National Bureau of Economic Research, "Business Cycle Expansions and Contractions," http://www.dev.nber.org/cycles/cyclesmain.html.

the housing sector and the financial difficulties associated with this decline. It deepened during the financial crisis that hit in September and October of 2008. As credit became less available to both businesses and consumers, the effects of the financial crisis began to show up in reduced consumer spending for durable goods such as automobiles and reduced business investment.

Throughout the broader sweep of U.S. history, other downturns have occurred—20 of them from 1860 up to World War II. Not all were particularly severe, and in some unemployment hardly changed. However, some economic downturns, such as those in 1893 and 1929, were severe.

Although we used the common definition of a recession as a period when real GDP falls for six months, in practice, a committee of economists at the National Bureau of Economics Research (NBER), a private research group in Cambridge, Massachusetts, of primarily academic economists, officially proclaims the beginning and end of recessions in the United States using a broader set of criteria than just GDP. The NBER's formal definition is "a significant decline in economic activity, spread across the economy, lasting more than a few months, normally visible in production, employment, real income, and other indicators." As you can see, it uses a wide variety of indicators to determine whether a recession has occurred and its length.

Depression is the common term for a severe recession. In the United States, the Great Depression refers to the years 1929 through 1933, the period when real GDP fell by over 33 percent. This drop in GDP created the most severe disruptions to ordinary economic life in the United States during the twentieth century. Throughout the country and in much of the world, banks closed, businesses failed, and many people lost their jobs and their life savings. Unemployment rose sharply. In 1933, over 25 percent of people who were looking for work failed to find jobs.

depression
The common name for a severe recession.

Although the United States has not experienced a depression since that time, other countries have. In the last 20 years, several Asian countries (for example, Thailand) and Latin American countries (for example, Argentina) suffered severe economic disruptions that were true depressions.

5.6 GDP as a Measure of Welfare

GDP is our best measure of the value of output produced by an economy. As we have seen, we can use GDP and related indicators to measure economic growth within a country. We can also use GDP to compare the value of output across countries as well. Economists use GDP and related measures to determine if an economy has fallen into a recession or has entered into a depression. But while GDP is a very valuable measure of the health of an economy, it is not a perfect measure.

Shortcomings of GDP as a Measure of Welfare

There are several recognized flaws in the construction of GDP. We should thus be cautious in interpreting GDP as a measure of our economic well-being, because it does not take into account housework and childcare, leisure, the underground economy, or pollution.

HOUSEWORK AND CHILDCARE First, GDP ignores transactions that do not take place in organized markets. The most important example is services, such as cleaning, cooking, and providing free childcare, that people do for themselves in their own homes. Because these services are not transferred through markets, GDP statisticians cannot measure them. If we included household production in GDP, measured GDP would be considerably higher than currently reported.

LEISURE Second, leisure time is not included in GDP because GDP is designed to be a measure of the production that occurs in the economy. To the extent that households value leisure, increases in leisure time will lead to higher social welfare, but not to higher GDP.

UNDERGROUND ECONOMY Third, GDP ignores the underground economy, where transactions are not reported to official authorities. These transactions can be legal, but people don't report the income they have generated because they want to avoid paying taxes on it. For example, wait staff may not report all their tips and owners of flea markets may make under-the-table cash transactions with their customers. Illegal transactions, such as profits from the illegal drug trade, also result in unreported income. In the United States in 2005, the Internal Revenue Service estimated (based on tax returns from 2001) that about $310 billion in federal income taxes from the underground economy was not collected each year. If the federal income tax rate that applies to income evaded from taxes was about 20 percent, approximately $1.5 trillion ($310/0.20) in income from the underground economy escaped the GDP accountants that year, or about 15 percent of GDP at the time.

Economists have used a variety of methods to estimate the extent of the underground economy throughout the world. They typically find that the size of the underground economy is much larger in developing countries than in developed countries. For example, in the highly developed countries, estimates of the underground economy are between 15 and 20 percent of reported or official GDP. However, in developing countries, estimates are closer to 40 percent of reported GDP. Table 5.6 contains estimates of the underground economy as a percent of reported GDP for different regions of the world.

TABLE 5.6 The World Underground Economy, 2002–2003

Region of the World	Underground Economy as Percent of Reported GDP
Africa	41%
Central and South America	41
Asia	30
Transition Economies	38
Europe, United States, and Japan	17
Unweighted Average over 145 Countries	35

SOURCE: Based on estimates by Friedrich Schneider in "The Size of Shadow Economies in 145 Countries from 1999 to 2003," unpublished paper, 2005.

POLLUTION Fourth, GDP does not value changes in the environment that occur in the production of output. Suppose a factory produces $1,000 of output but pollutes a river and lowers its value by $2,000. Instead of recording a loss to society of $1,000, GDP will show a $1,000 increase. This is an important limitation of GDP accounting as a measure of our economic well-being, because changes in the environment affect our daily lives. Previous attempts by the Commerce Department to measure the effects of changes in environment by adding positive or subtracting negative changes to the environment from national income did not yield major results. But they were limited and looked only at a very select part of the environment. Has our environment improved or deteriorated as we experienced economic growth? Finding the answer to this question will pose a real challenge for the next generation of economic statisticians.

Most of us would prefer to live in a country with a high standard of living, and few of us would want to experience poverty up close. But does a higher level of GDP really lead to more satisfaction?

SUMMARY

In this chapter, we learned how economists and government statisticians measure the income and production for an entire country and what these measures are used for. Developing meaningful statistics for an entire economy is difficult. As we have seen, statistics can convey useful information—if they are used with care. Here are some of the main points to remember in this chapter:

1 The circular flow diagram shows how the production of goods and services generates income for households and how households purchase goods and services by firms. The expanded circular flow diagram includes government and the foreign sector.

2 *Gross domestic product* (GDP) is the market value of all final goods and services produced in a given year.

3 GDP consists of four components: consumption, investment, government purchases, and net exports. The following equation combines these components:

$$Y = C + I + G + NX$$

The *GDP deflator* is an index that measures how the prices of goods and services included in GDP change over time. The following equation helps us find the GDP deflator:

$$\text{GDP Deflator} = \frac{\text{Nominal GDP}}{\text{Real GDP}} \times 100$$

4 *National income* is obtained from GDP by adding the net income U.S. individuals and firms earn from abroad, then subtracting depreciation.

5 *Real GDP* is calculated by using constant prices. The Commerce Department now uses methods that take an average using base years from neighboring years.

6 *A recession* is commonly defined as a six-month consecutive period of negative growth. However, in the United States, the National Bureau of Economic Research uses a broader definition.

7 GDP does not include nonmarket transactions, leisure time, the underground economy, or changes to the environment.

KEY TERMS

chain-weighted index, p. 111
consumption expenditures, p. 103
depreciation, p. 103
depression, p. 113
economic growth, p. 102
expansion, p. 112
export, p. 104
GDP deflator, p. 110
government purchases, p. 104
gross domestic product (GDP), p. 100
gross investment, p. 103
gross national product (GNP), p. 106
import, p. 104
inflation, p. 98
intermediate good, p. 101
macroeconomics, p. 98
national income, p. 106
net exports, p. 104
net investment, p. 103
nominal GDP, p. 101
peak, p. 112
personal disposable income, p. 107
personal income, p. 107
private investment expenditures, p. 103
real GDP, p. 101

recession, p. 112
trade deficit, p. 105
trade surplus, p. 105
transfer payments, p. 104
trough, p. 112
value added, p. 107

EXERCISES

All problems are assignable in MyEconLab; exercises that update with real-time data are marked with **.**

5.1 The "Flip" Sides of Macroeconomic Activity: Production and Income

1.1 The circular flow describes the process by which GDP generates ________, which is spent on goods and services.

1.2 Goods and services are exchanged in ________ markets.

1.3 Which government department produces the National Income and Product Accounts?

a. The Department of Education

b. The Department of Commerce

c. The Congressional Budget Office

d. The Council of Economic Advisors

1.4 The provision of educational services is not counted as output in modern economies. ________ (True/False)

1.5 **Understanding the Circular Flow Diagram.** In the circular flow diagram, why do the arrows corresponding to the flow of dollars and the arrows corresponding to the flow of goods go in the opposite direction?

1.6 **Types of Income.** Sometimes economists distinguish between wages on the one hand, and rents, interest, and profits on the other. What is the basis of that distinction?

5.2 The Production Approach: Measuring a Nation's Macroeconomic Activity Using Gross Domestic Product

2.1 Which of the following is not a component of GDP?

a. Consumption

b. Investment

c. Producer Price Index

d. Government purchases

e. Net exports

2.2 What part of government spending is excluded from GDP because it does not correspond to goods and services currently being produced?

a. National defense

b. Transfer payments

c. Education

d. Purchases of police cars

2.3 If depreciation exceeds gross investment, net investment will be ________.

2.4 A trade surplus occurs when ________ exceeds ________.

2.5 **GDP Statistics and Unemployed Workers.** In Economy A, the government puts workers on the payroll who cannot find jobs for long periods, but these "employees" do no work. In Economy B, the government does not hire any long-term unemployed workers but gives them cash grants. Comparing the GDP statistics between the two otherwise identical economies, what can you determine about measured GDP and the actual level of output in each economy?

2.6 **Child Care Subsidies.** If the federal government provides subsidies for individuals to buy child care, is this included in the federal budget? Is it included in GDP?

2.7 **The Upside and Downside of Trade Deficits.** A student once said, "Trade deficits are bad because we are buying goods from abroad and not making them here." What is an upside to trade deficits?

2.8 **Depreciation and Consumer Durables.** Consumer durables depreciate just like investment goods. Suppose you purchase a refrigerator for $1000 and, at the same time, four new designer dresses worth $1,000. After one year, has the refrigerator or the designer dresses depreciated more? Why?

2.9 **Investment Spending versus Intermediate Goods.** A publisher buys paper, ink, and computers to produce textbooks. Which of these purchases is included in investment spending? Which are intermediate goods?

5.3 The Income Approach: Measuring a Nation's Macroeconomic Activity Using National Income

3.1 What do we add to GDP to reach GNP?

a. Net income earned abroad by U.S. households

b. Personal income

c. Depreciation

d. Net exports

3.2 What is the largest component of national income?

a. Compensation of employees (wages and benefits)

b. Corporate profits

c. Rental income

d. Proprietors' income (income of unincorporated business)

e. Net interest

3.3 Personal income and personal disposable income refer to payments ultimately flowing to ________ (households/firms).

3.4 The difference between gross national product and net national product is ________.

3.5 **Measuring Value Added for a Think Tank.** The Brookings Institution is a nonprofit think tank and does not typically sell its products. Explain one way you could measure its value added.

3.6 **Understanding Why GNP and GDP May Differ.** If a country discovered vast amounts of oil, sold it abroad, and invested the proceeds throughout the world, how would its GDP and GNP compare?

3.7 **Transfer Payments, National Income, and Personal Income.** Taking into account the role of transfer payments, explain why national income could fall more than personal income during a recession.

3.8 **Philippine Immigrants Abroad.** Every year, the Philippines sends many workers abroad including nurses, health professionals, and oil workers. How do you think GNP and GDP in the Philippines compare?

3.9 **Sales versus Value Added.** Explain carefully why value added may be a better measure than total sales in comparing a country to a corporation. Hint: If we measured total sales in a country, would this exceed GDP? (Related to Application 1 on page 100.)

5.4 A Closer Examination of Nominal and Real GDP

4.1 The GDP deflator is calculated for any given year by dividing nominal GDP by ________ GDP and multiplying by 100.

4.2 If the base year is 2010, then real and nominal GDP in 2010 will be equal. ________ (True/False)

4.3 Measured price changes do not depend on the particular base year chosen when calculating

a. the traditional GDP deflator.

b. the chain-weighted GDP deflator.

c. real GDP.

4.4 To compute nominal GDP, it is important to use an accurate price index. ________ (True/False)

4.5 **Calculating Real GDP, Price Indices, and Inflation.** Using data from the following table, answer the following questions:

a. Calculate real GDP using prices from 2011. By what percent did real GDP grow?

b. Calculate the value of the price index for GDP for 2012 using 2011 as the base year. By what percent did prices increase?

	Quantities Produced		Prices	
	CDs	*Tennis Rackets*	*Price per CD*	*Price per Tennis Racket*
2011	100	200	$20	$110
2012	120	210	22	120

4.6 **Using a New Base Year to Calculate Real GDP and Inflation.** Repeat Exercise 4.5 but use prices from 2012.

4.7 **Understanding the Relationship between Real and Nominal GDP in a Figure.** In Figure 5.5 the base year is 2005. Explain why the line for nominal GDP lies below the line for real GDP in the years prior to 2005. If the base year was 2000, where would the two lines cross?

4.8 **Using U.S. Economic Data to Measure the Economy.** Go to the Web site for the Federal Reserve Bank of St. Louis (www.research.stlouisfed.org/fred2). Find the data for nominal GDP, real GDP in chained dollars, and the chain price index for GDP.

a. Calculate the percentage growth for nominal GDP since 2000 until the most recent year.

b. Calculate the percentage growth in real GDP since 2000 until the most recent year.

c. Finally, calculate the percentage growth in the chain price index for GDP over this same period and compare it to the difference between your answers to (a) and (b).

5.5 Fluctuations in GDP

5.1 The date that a recession begins is called the __________.

5.2 Since World War II, the United States has experienced seven recessions. __________ (True/False)

5.3 The __________ marks the date that ends a recession and output starts to increase again.

5.4 The organization that officially dates recessions in the United States is the

a. Congressional Budget Office.

b. Department of Commerce.

c. National Bureau of Economic Research.

d. Council of Economic Advisors.

5.5 **Counting Recessions.** Consider the data for the fictitious economy of Euronet:

Year and Quarter	2003: 1	2003: 2	2003: 3	2003: 4	2004: 1	2004: 2	2004: 3
Real GDP	195	193	195	196	195	194	198

How many recessions occurred in the economy over the time indicated?

5.6 **Long Recoveries.** Explain why the time it takes the economy to recover to the level where it originally was when the recession started is longer than the time from peak to trough. (Related to Application 2 on p. 106.)

5.7 **Most Severe Recession?** Using the data in Table 5.5, identify the two most severe recessions since World War II in terms of the fall from peak to trough. What other information might you want to know about these and other recessionary periods to judge their severity? (Related to Application 2 on page 106.)

5.6 GDP as a Measure of Welfare

6.1 Which of the following are not included in GDP?

a. Leisure time

b. Sales of new cars

c. Strawberries sold in a grocery store

d. Economics textbooks sold in the bookstore

6.2 Men's reported happiness has increased relative to women's reported happiness in the last several decades. __________ (True/False) (Related to Application 3 on page 109.)

6.3 The approximate percentage of GDP in the United States that goes unreported because of the underground economy is __________.

6.4 Illegal activities are not computed as part of measured GDP because they are not

a. legal.

b. production.

c. reported.

d. big enough to worry about.

6.5 **Does Spending Measure Welfare?** Suppose a community spends $1 million on salaries and equipment for its police department. Because it believes that citizens are now more law abiding, the community decides to cut back on the number of police it employs. As a result, the community now spends $800,000 less on the police officers. The crime rate remains the same.

a. What happens to measured GDP?

b. Does GDP accurately reflect welfare in this case? Discuss the underlying issue that this example poses.

6.6 **Disappearing Trees and National Income.** Suppose you were worried that national income does not adequately take into account the extraction of trees that provide shade and help stem global warming. How would you advise the Commerce Department to include this factor in its calculations?

6.7 **Fracking and Natural Gas.** In the last several years, there have been considerable increases in the production of natural gas in the United States through a technique known as "fracking" where fluids are injected into wells. While fracking has generally been very successful, on occasion there was contamination of the water supplies. How should you properly measure the contributions from fracking in this case?

6.8 **Comparing Welfare across Countries.** Suppose Country A and Country B have exactly the same measured real GDP, but in Country A, the average worker spends more time at home, either doing housework or on vacation. Which country has a higher level of welfare and why?

6.9 Does Money Buy Happiness? Although people with high incomes appear to be happier than those with low incomes, people in the United States in general have become less happy over the last 30 years even though real GDP has risen. What are some of the reasons why the increase in real GDP does not always imply greater happiness? (Related to Application 3 on page 109.)

6.10 Measuring Happiness across States. Suppose statisticians find from survey data that the residents of California and Louisiana report that they are equally happy. However, incomes in California are higher, on average, than those in Louisiana. Could you make a case that living in Louisiana actually makes you happier than living in California?

CHAPTER 6

Unemployment and Inflation

Do governments care about their reported inflation statistics? Argentina certainly does, but not in the right way.

After an economic crisis in 2002, the Argentine government took a number of actions to try to resuscitate an ailing economy. While the economy began to recover from its doldrums, eventually inflation began to re-emerge. The government did not wish to draw domestic or international attention to the emerging inflation, so they took a series of steps to "cook the books" and pretend that inflation was not as high as it truly was.

The government of President Cristina Kirchner replaced the head of the agency charged with developing price statistics by her own political appointee, who quickly ordered changes in statistical methods in order to produce artificially lower inflation numbers. The government also took the dramatic step of stopping independent private economic analysts within Argentina from publishing their own numbers. External estimates of the inflation rate produced outside of Argentina were typically double the official rate.

While the Argentine government's efforts may have produced lower official numbers, it did not fool many people. The World Bank noted the problems with the data in its 2011 report and *The Economist* magazine stopped using official Argentine statistics in its own tables and reporting. Even the Argentine unions used external estimates of inflation in their negotiations with the government!

Source: Based in part on *The Economist*, February 25, 2012.

LEARNING OBJECTIVES

- Define these concepts: the labor force, the labor force participation rate, and the unemployment rate.
- Distinguish between cyclical, structural, and frictional unemployment.
- Describe the costs of unemployment.
- Discuss how the Consumer Price Index is calculated.
- Explain the difference between inflation and the price level.
- Summarize the costs of anticipated and unanticipated inflation.

MyEconLab

MyEconLab helps you master each objective and study more efficiently.

In this chapter, we look at unemployment and inflation, two key phenomena in macroeconomics. Losing a job is one of the most stressful experiences a person can suffer. For the elderly, the fear that the purchasing power of their wealth will evaporate with inflation is also a source of deep concern.

We will examine how economists define unemployment and inflation and the problems in measuring them. We also will explore the various costs that unemployment and inflation impose on society. Once we have a basic understanding of what unemployment and inflation are, we will be able to investigate their causes further.

6.1 Examining Unemployment

When an economy performs poorly, it imposes costs on individuals and society. Recall from the last chapter that one of the key issues for macroeconomics is understanding fluctuations—the ups and downs of the economy. During periods of poor economic performance and slow economic growth, unemployment rises sharply and becomes a cause of public concern. During times of good economic performance and rapid economic growth, unemployment falls, but does not disappear. Our first task is to understand how economists and government statisticians measure unemployment and then learn to interpret what they measure.

How Is Unemployment Defined and Measured?

Let's begin with some definitions. The *unemployed* are those individuals who do not currently have a job but who are actively looking for work. The phrase *actively looking* is critical. Individuals who looked for work in the past but who are not looking currently are not counted as unemployed. The *employed* are individuals who currently have jobs. Together, the unemployed and employed comprise the **labor force**:

$$\text{labor force} = \text{employed} + \text{unemployed}$$

labor force
The total number of workers, both the employed and the unemployed.

The **unemployment rate** is the number of unemployed divided by the total labor force. This rate represents the percentage of the labor force unemployed and looking for work:

unemployment rate
The percentage of the labor force that is unemployed.

$$\text{unemployment rate} = \frac{\text{unemployed}}{\text{labor force}} \times 100$$

Finally, we need to understand what is meant by the **labor force participation rate**, which is the labor force divided by the population 16 years of age and older. This rate represents the percentage of the population 16 years of age and older that is in the labor force:

labor force participation rate
The percentage of the population over 16 years of age that is in the labor force.

$$\text{labor force participation rate} = \frac{\text{labor force}}{\text{population 16 years and older}} \times 100$$

To illustrate these concepts, suppose an economy consists of 200,000 individuals 16 years of age and older. Of all these people, 122,000 are employed and 8,000 are unemployed. This means that 130,000 (122,000 + 8,000) people are in the labor force. The labor force participation rate is 0.65, or 65 percent (130,000/200,000), and the unemployment rate is 0.0615, or 6.15 percent (8,000/130,000).

Figure 6.1 helps to put these measurements into perspective for the U.S. economy. The total civilian population 16 years of age and older in March 2012 was 242,604,000 individuals. We divide this population into two groups: those in the labor force (the employed plus the unemployed, totaling 154,707,000) and those outside the labor force 87,897,000. For this year, the labor force participation rate was 64 percent (154,707,000/242,604,000). As you can see, approximately two-thirds of the U.S. population participates in the labor force. Within the labor force, 142,034,000 were employed and 12,673,000 were unemployed. The unemployment rate was

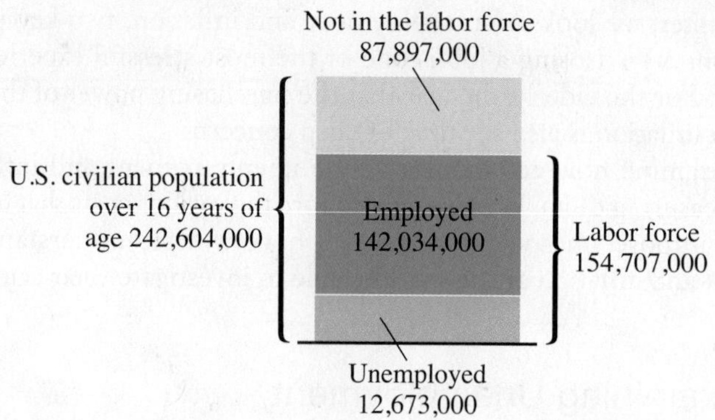

▶ **FIGURE 6.1**
Unemployment Data, March 2012
Approximately 64 percent of the civilian population is in the labor force. The unemployment rate in March 2012 was 8.2 percent.
SOURCE: Bureau of Labor Statistics, U.S. Department of Labor, 2012.

8.2 percent (12,673,000/154,707,000). Military personnel and prisoners are excluded from these measures.

One of the most important trends in the last 50 years has been the increase in the participation of women in the labor force. In 1948, the labor force participation rate for women 20 years and older was 32 percent. By 1970, it had grown to 43 percent, and by 1997 it had reached 60 percent. This trend reflected remarkable changes in our economy and society as women dramatically increased their presence in the workforce. Since 1997, the figure has remained virtually constant at 60 percent.

Figure 6.2 contains international data on unemployment for 2012 for developed countries. Despite the fact these countries all have modern, industrial economies, notice the sharp differences in unemployment. For example, Italy had a 9.3 percent unemployment rate, whereas Japan had an unemployment rate of 4.5 percent. These sharp differences reflect a number of factors, including how much government support is provided to unemployed workers. In countries in which support is the most generous, there is less incentive to work and unemployment will tend to be higher.

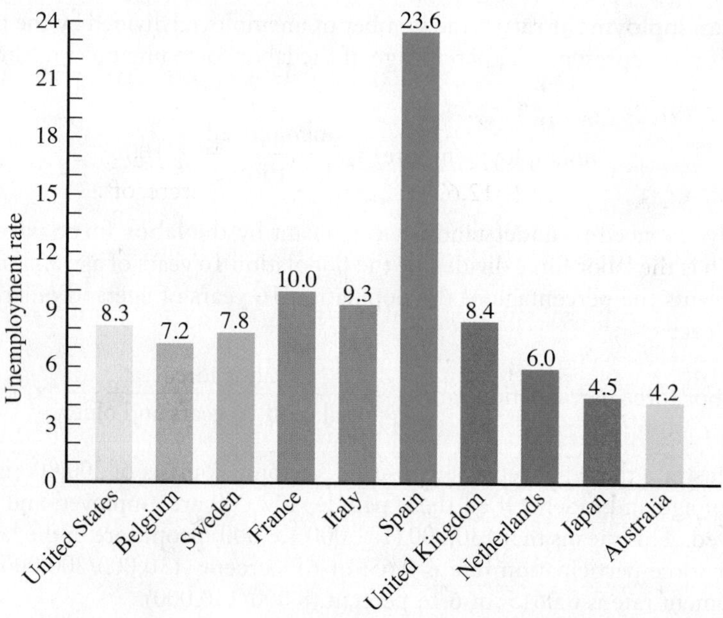

▶ **FIGURE 6.2**
Unemployment Rates in Developed Countries
Among the developed countries, unemployment rates vary substantially.
SOURCE: The Economist, April 7, 2012.
MyEconLab Real-time data

Alternative Measures of Unemployment and Why They Are Important

We defined the unemployed as those people who are looking for work but who do not currently have jobs. With that in mind, let's take a closer look at our measures of unemployment.

It is relatively straightforward in principle to determine who is employed: Just count the people who are working. What is more difficult is to distinguish between those who are unemployed and those who are not in the labor force. How are these two groups distinguished? The BLS, which is part of the Department of Labor, interviews a large sample of households each month. The BLS asks about the employment situation of all household members 16 years of age and older. If someone in a household is not working, the interviewer asks whether the person is actively looking for work. If the answer is "yes," he or she is classified as unemployed. If the answer is "no"—he or she is not actively looking for work—that person is classified as not being in the labor force.

The BLS measure of unemployment, however, does not capture all the employment experiences individuals face. Consider the cases of three individuals who want full-time jobs but do not have them: a steelworker who stopped looking for work because he felt there were no jobs, a young woman who did not seek work because she had no transportation to the workplace, and a computer programmer who worked only part time but sought full-time employment. None of them would be counted as unemployed in the official statistics—the first two are not included in the labor force and the third is counted as employed. Because of these limitations, in 1994 the BLS began to publish alternative statistics that reflect these circumstances.

Individuals who want to work and have searched for work in the prior year, but are not currently looking for work because they believe they won't be able to find a job are called **discouraged workers**. Note that these individuals are not included in the official statistics because they are not currently looking for work.

discouraged workers
Workers who left the labor force because they could not find jobs.

In addition to discouraged workers, there are individuals who would like to work and have searched for work in the recent past, but have stopped looking for work for a variety of reasons. These individuals are known as *marginally attached workers*. Marginally attached workers consist of two groups: discouraged workers (who left the labor force because they could not find jobs) and workers who are not looking for jobs for other reasons, including lack of transportation or childcare.

Finally, there are those workers who would like to be employed full-time but hold part-time jobs. These individuals are counted as employed in the BLS statistics because they have a job. However, they would like to be working more hours. They are known as *individuals working part time for economic reasons*. We do not include in this category individuals who prefer part-time employment.

How important are these alternative measures? Figure 6.3 puts them into perspective. In March 2012, 12.67 million individuals were officially classified as unemployed. The number of discouraged workers was .86 million. Including the discouraged workers, there were 2.35 million marginally attached workers. If we add the marginally attached individuals to those who were involuntarily working part time, the total is 10.02 million. Thus, depending on the statistic you want to emphasize, there were anywhere between 12.67 million unemployed (the official number) and 22.69 million unemployed (the official number plus all those seeking full-time employment who did not have it). If we count those 22.69 million as unemployed, the unemployment rate in 2012 would be 14.4 percent—substantially higher than the official rate of 8.2 percent. As we have seen, the official statistics for unemployment do not include the full range of individuals who would like to participate fully in the labor market.

Who Are the Unemployed?

Another fact about unemployment is that different groups of people suffer more unemployment than others. Figure 6.4 contains some unemployment statistics for selected groups for March 2012. Adults have substantially lower unemployment rates than teenagers. Minorities have higher unemployment rates. African-American teenagers have extremely high unemployment rates. On average, men and women have similar unemployment rates, but the unemployment rates for married men and married women are lower than unemployment rates of women who maintain families alone.

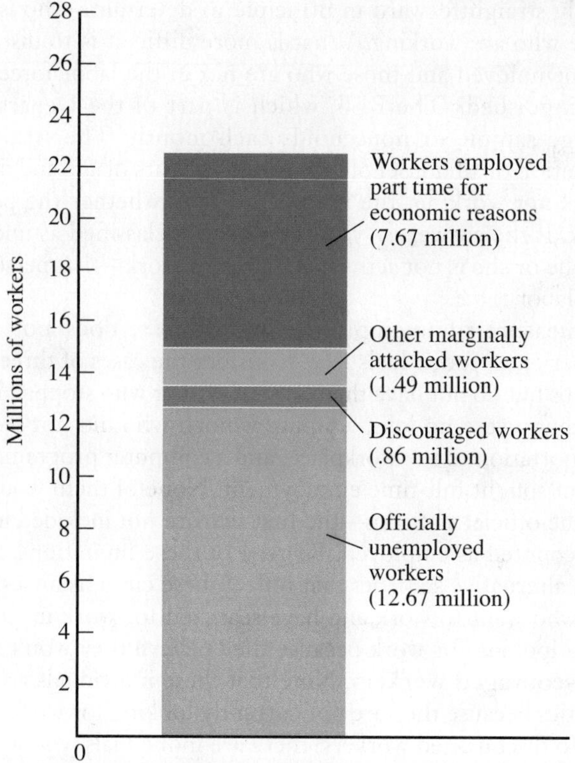

▶ **FIGURE 6.3**
Alternative Measures of Unemployment, March 2012
Including discouraged workers, marginally attached workers, and individuals working part time for economic reasons substantially increases measured unemployment in 2012 from 12.67 million to 22.69 million.
SOURCE: Bureau of Labor Statistics, U.S. Department of Labor, 2012.

These differentials do vary somewhat as GDP rises and falls. Teenage and minority unemployment rates often rise very sharply during poor economic times, as was the case in the most recent recession. In better times, a reduction of unemployment for all groups typically occurs. Nonetheless, teenage and minority unemployment remains relatively high at all times.

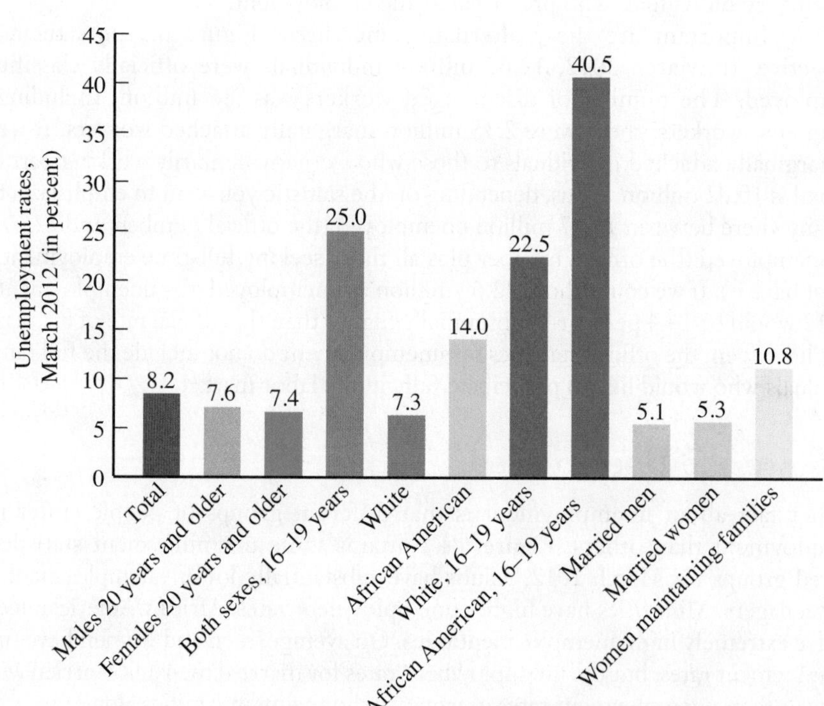

▶ **FIGURE 6.4**
Selected U.S. Unemployment Statistics, Unemployment Rates for March 2012
The incidence of unemployment differs sharply among demographic groups.
SOURCE: Bureau of Labor Statistics, U.S. Department of Labor, 2012.
MyEconLab Real-time data

application 1

DECLINING LABOR FORCE PARTICIPATION

APPLYING THE CONCEPTS #1: What factors account for the decline in the labor force participation rate in the last decade?

Since reaching a peak of 67.3 percent in 1999, the labor force participation rate has fallen to 64.0 percent by end of 2011. What can account for this decline?

Two factors have been prominently discussed by economists. The past decade experienced two recessions and low economic growth by historical standards. Perhaps a large number of individuals just decided that job prospects were too poor and left the labor force during this decade. An alternative explanation focuses on the baby boomers—the generation born after 1946. As this large generation ages, a significant number of the baby boomers will naturally retire and leave the labor force.

A recent study by the Federal Bank of Chicago suggested both factors were operative. Based on some statistical models, they estimated that about one-half of the decline in labor force participation was due to a longer run trend of increased retirements from the baby boomers. The rest could be explained by other factors, including sluggish economic growth. Of course, sluggish growth might prompt even more baby boomers to retire, so these factors might not be fully independent. **Related to Exercise 1.8.**

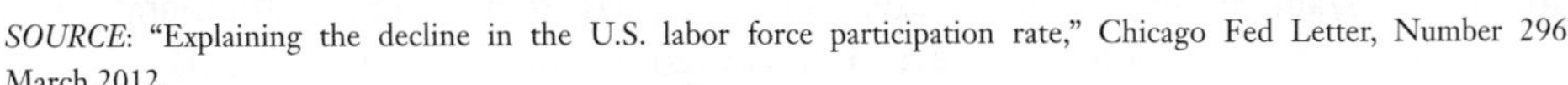

SOURCE: "Explaining the decline in the U.S. labor force participation rate," Chicago Fed Letter, Number 296, March 2012.

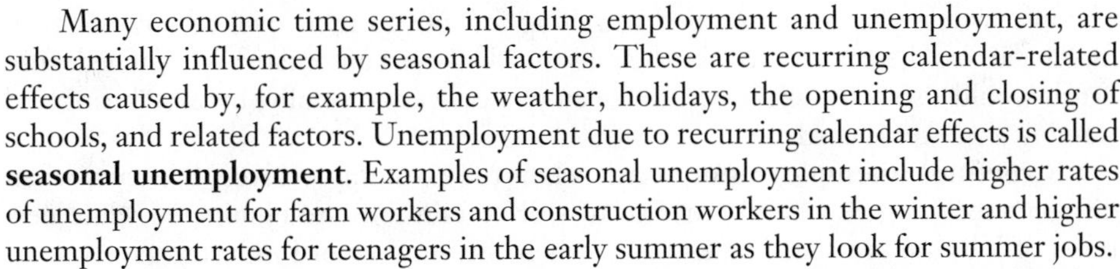

Many economic time series, including employment and unemployment, are substantially influenced by seasonal factors. These are recurring calendar-related effects caused by, for example, the weather, holidays, the opening and closing of schools, and related factors. Unemployment due to recurring calendar effects is called **seasonal unemployment**. Examples of seasonal unemployment include higher rates of unemployment for farm workers and construction workers in the winter and higher unemployment rates for teenagers in the early summer as they look for summer jobs.

seasonal unemployment
The component of unemployment attributed to seasonal factors.

The BLS uses statistical procedures to remove these seasonal factors—that is, it seasonally adjusts the statistics—so that users of the data can more accurately interpret underlying trends in the economy. The seasonally adjusted unemployment rates control for these predictable patterns, so those patterns aren't reflected in the overall unemployment numbers.

6.2 Categories of Unemployment

To better understand the labor market, economists have found it very useful to break unemployment into a variety of categories. As we shall see, it is valuable to distinguish among the several different types of unemployment.

Types of Unemployment: Cyclical, Frictional, and Structural

After seasonally adjusting the unemployment statistics, we can divide unemployment into three other basic types: cyclical, frictional, and structural. By studying each type separately, we can gain insight into some of the causes of each type of unemployment.

The unemployment rate is closely tied to the overall fortunes of the economy. Unemployment rises sharply during periods when real GDP falls and decreases when real GDP grows rapidly. During periods of falling GDP, firms will not want to employ as many workers as they do in good times because they are not producing as many goods and services. Firms will lay off or fire some current workers and will be more reluctant to add new workers to their payrolls. The result will be fewer workers with jobs and rising unemployment. Economists call the unemployment that occurs during fluctuations in real GDP **cyclical unemployment**. Cyclical unemployment rises during periods when real GDP falls or grows at a slower-than-normal rate and decreases when the economy improves.

cyclical unemployment
Unemployment that occurs during fluctuations in real GDP.

However, unemployment still exists even when the economy is growing. For example, the unemployment rate in the United States has not fallen below 3.9 percent of the labor force since 1970. Unemployment that is not associated with economic fluctuations is either frictional unemployment or structural unemployment.

frictional unemployment
Unemployment that occurs with the normal workings of the economy, such as workers taking time to search for suitable jobs and firms taking time to search for qualified employees.

Frictional unemployment is the unemployment that occurs naturally during the normal workings of an economy. It occurs because it simply takes time for people to find the right jobs and for employers to find the right people to hire. This happens when people change jobs, move across the country, get laid off from their current jobs and search for new opportunities, or take their time after they enter the labor force to find an appropriate job. Suppose that when you graduate from college, you take six months to find a job you like. During the six months in which you are looking for a good job, you are among those unemployed who make up frictional unemployment. Searching for a job, however, makes good sense. It would not be wise to take the first job you were offered if it had low wages, poor benefits, and no future. Likewise, employers are wise to interview multiple applicants for jobs to find the best employees, even if it takes some time.

Could we eliminate unemployment by posting all job vacancies on the Internet along with the résumés of job seekers and automatically match them up with one another? It's possible that such an automated system could shorten the duration of frictional unemployment, but it wouldn't eliminate it entirely. Some workers, for example, would prefer to continue searching for jobs in their own area rather than moving across the country to take the jobs they had been automatically matched with. Firms would also still want to scrutinize employees very carefully, because hiring and training a worker is costly.

structural unemployment
Unemployment that occurs when there is a mismatch of skills and jobs.

Structural unemployment occurs when the economy evolves. It occurs when different sectors give way to other sectors or certain jobs are eliminated while new types of jobs are created. For example, when the vinyl record industry gave way to the CD music industry in the 1980s, some workers found themselves structurally unemployed, which meant they had to take the time to train themselves for jobs in different industries. Structural unemployment is more of a "permanent condition" than frictional unemployment.

The line between frictional unemployment and structural unemployment is sometimes hard to draw. Suppose a highly skilled software engineer is laid off because his company shuts down its headquarters in his area and moves his job overseas. The worker would like to find a comparable job, but only lower-wage work is available in his immediate geographic location. Jobs are available, but not his kind of job, and this high-tech company will never return to the area. Is this person's unemployment frictional or structural? There really is no correct answer. You might think of the software engineer as experiencing either frictional or structural unemployment. For all practical purposes, however, it does not matter which it is. The former software engineer is still unemployed.

The Natural Rate of Unemployment

natural rate of unemployment
The level of unemployment at which there is no cyclical unemployment. It consists of only frictional and structural unemployment.

Total unemployment in an economy is composed of all three types of unemployment: cyclical, frictional, and structural. The level of unemployment at which there is no cyclical unemployment is called the **natural rate of unemployment**. The natural rate of unemployment consists of only frictional unemployment and structural unemployment. The natural rate of unemployment is the economist's notion of what the rate of unemployment should be when there is **full employment**. It may seem strange to think that workers can be unemployed when the economy is at full employment. However, the economy actually needs some frictional unemployment to operate efficiently: Frictional unemployment exists so that workers and firms find the right employment matches. An economy that lacks frictional unemployment will become stagnant.

full employment
The level of unemployment that occurs when the unemployment rate is at the natural rate.

In the United States today, economists estimate that the natural rate of unemployment is between 5.0 and 6.5 percent. The natural rate of unemployment varies over time and differs across countries. In Europe, for example, estimates of the natural rate of unemployment place it between 7 and 10 percent. In a later chapter, we explore why the natural rate of unemployment is higher in Europe than in the United States and why the natural rate of unemployment can vary over time in the same country.

The actual unemployment rate can be higher or lower than the natural rate of unemployment. During a period in which the real GDP fails to grow at its normal rate, there will be positive cyclical unemployment, and actual unemployment can far exceed the natural rate of unemployment. For example, in the United States in 2012 unemployment was over 8 percent of the labor force. As we pointed out in the previous chapter, a more extreme example occurred in 1933 during the Great Depression, when the unemployment rate reached 25 percent. When the economy grows very rapidly for a long period, actual unemployment can fall below the natural rate of unemployment. With sustained rapid economic growth, employers will be aggressive in hiring workers. During the late 1960s, unemployment rates fell below 4 percent, and the natural rate of unemployment was estimated to be over 5 percent. In this case, cyclical unemployment was negative.

Unemployment also fell to 4 percent in 2000. In this case, many economists believed that the natural rate of unemployment had fallen to close to 5 percent, so that cyclical unemployment in that year was negative.

Just as a car will overheat if the engine is overworked, so will the economy overheat if economic growth is too rapid. At low unemployment rates, firms will find it difficult

application 2

MORE DISABILITY, LESS UNEMPLOYMENT?

APPLYING THE CONCEPTS #2: Does more liberal disability insurance decrease measured unemployment?

The federal Disability Insurance program provides income to nonelderly workers who are deemed unable to engage in substantial employment. It also provides health care to these individuals. After 1984, the guidelines were changed to make it easier for individuals to enter the program. From 1984 to 2001, the number of nonelderly adults receiving payments from this program rose by 60 percent to 5.3 million.

Economists David Autor and Mark Duggan studied the impact of this program on labor force participation. They found that the changes in the rules administering the program, the increased generosity of the benefits of the program for low-skilled workers, and the increase in the value of health-care services all contributed to an increase in participation in this program. They estimated that the combination of these factors led to a decrease in the labor force participation for high school dropouts and other low-skilled workers. Since these workers, a portion of whom would have been unemployed, were no longer in the labor force, the economists estimated that the effect of the Disability Insurance program was to lower the measured unemployment rate by 0.5 percent, a very large effect. **Related to Exercises 1.4 and 1.9.**

SOURCE: Based on David H. Autor and Mark G. Duggan, "The Rise in Disability Rolls and the Decline in Unemployment," *Quarterly Journal of Economics* (February 2003): 157–206.

to recruit workers, and competition among firms will lead to increases in wages. As wages increase, increases in prices soon follow. The sign of this overheating will be a general rise in prices for the entire economy, which we commonly call *inflation*. As we discuss in later chapters, when the actual unemployment rate falls below the natural rate of unemployment, inflation will increase.

6.3 The Costs of Unemployment

When there is excess unemployment—actual unemployment above the natural rate of unemployment—both society and individuals suffer economic loss. From a social point of view, excess unemployment means that the economy is no longer producing at its potential. The resulting loss of output can be very large. For example, in 1983, when the unemployment rate averaged 9.6 percent, typical estimates of the shortfall of GDP from potential were near 6 percent. Simply put, this meant that society was wasting 6 percent of the total resources at its disposal.

unemployment insurance
Payments unemployed people receive from the government.

To families with fixed obligations such as mortgage payments, the loss in income can bring immediate hardships. **Unemployment insurance**, payments received from the government upon becoming unemployed, can cushion the blow to some degree, but unemployment insurance is typically only temporary and does not replace a worker's full earnings.

The effects of unemployment can also linger into the future. Workers who suffer from a prolonged period of unemployment are likely to lose some of their skills. For example, an unemployed stockbroker might be unaware of the latest developments and trends in financial markets. This lack of knowledge will make it more difficult for that person to find a job in the future. Economists who have studied the high rates of unemployment among young people in Europe point to the loss of both skills and good work habits (such as coming to work on time) as key factors leading to long-term unemployment.

The costs of unemployment are not simply financial. In our society, a person's status and position are largely associated with the type of job the person holds. Losing a job can impose severe psychological costs. Some studies have found, for example, that increased crime, divorce, and suicide rates are associated with increased unemployment.

Not all unemployment lasts a long period of time for individuals. Some unemployment is very short term. Table 6.1 shows the percent of unemployed by the duration or length of unemployment. In March 2012, approximately 20.6 percent of unemployed workers had been out of work less than 5 weeks. At the other end, 42.5 percent were unemployed 27 weeks or longer. During better economic times with lower overall unemployment, the percentage of short-term spells of unemployment increases and percentage of long-term spells decrease. In the United States, unemployment is a mixture of both short- and long-term unemployment.

TABLE 6.1 The Duration of Unemployment, March 2012

Weeks of Unemployment	Percent of the Unemployed
Fewer than 5 weeks	20.6
5 to 14 weeks	22.0
15 to 26 weeks	14.9
27 weeks or longer	42.5

SOURCE: Bureau of Labor Statistics, U.S. Department of Labor, 2012.

Although unemployment insurance can temporarily offset some of the financial costs of job loss, the presence of unemployment insurance also tends to increase the length of time that unemployed workers remain unemployed. The extra financial

application 3

SOCIAL NORMS, UNEMPLOYMENT, AND PERCEIVED HAPPINESS

APPLYING THE CONCEPTS #3: Are you less upset about being unemployed if unemployment is common in your peer group?

We know that individuals do not like to become unemployed. But how do feelings about becoming unemployed depend on the experiences of those around one? Economist Andrew E. Clark carefully examined the perceptions and the behavior of the unemployed in Great Britain over a seven-year period. He looked at the responses to survey questions by those individuals who became unemployed and constructed an index of their general happiness or well-being.

He found, as expected, that people's perceived well-being declined as they became unemployed, and also that employed people become less happy if others around them became unemployed. But his interesting and somewhat surprising finding was that, for men, becoming unemployed caused *less* of a decrease in perceived well-being if those in their peer group—family, household, or region—were also unemployed. In other words, misery loved company. It was better (or less worse) to be unemployed if others in their peer group were also unemployed.

Why did this matter? Clark also found that the more unhappy an individual was, the more aggressive he or she would be to try to find a new job. So, if your peer group is also unemployed, you may not be as aggressive in searching for work. Unemployment, therefore, may last longer for individuals in these circumstances. **Related to Exercise 3.5.**

SOURCE: Based on Andrew E. Clark, "Unemployment as a Social Norm: Psychological Evidence from Panel Data," *Journal of Labor Economics* 21, no. 2 (2003): 323–351.

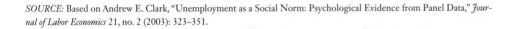

cushion that unemployment insurance provides allows workers to remain unemployed a bit longer before obtaining another job. In other words, unemployment insurance actually leads to additional time spent unemployed.

6.4 The Consumer Price Index and the Cost of Living

Suppose you were reading a book written in 1964 in which the main character received a starting salary of $5,000. Was that a high or low salary back then? To answer that, we need to know what $5,000 could purchase. Or, to put it another way, we need to know the *value* of the dollar—what a dollar would actually buy—in 1964. Only then could we begin to know whether this was a high or low salary.

Or take another example. In 1976, a new starting professor in economics received a salary of $15,000. In 2010, at the same university, a new starting professor received $90,000. Prices, of course, had risen in these 30 years along with salaries. Which starting professor had the better deal?

These examples are illustrations of one of our five principles of economics, the real-nominal principle.

REAL-NOMINAL PRINCIPLE

What matters to people is the real value of money or income—its purchasing power—not the face value of money or income.

Consumer Price Index
A price index that measures the cost of a fixed basket of goods chosen to represent the consumption pattern of a typical consumer.

Economists have developed a number of different measures to track the cost of living over time. The best known of these measures is the **Consumer Price Index (CPI)**.

The CPI is widely used to measure changes in the prices consumers face. It measures changes in prices of a fixed *basket of goods*—a collection of items chosen to represent the purchasing pattern of a typical consumer. We first find out how much this basket of goods costs in a given year. This is called the *base year* (it serves a similar purpose as the base year we designated for the GDP deflator). We then ask how much it costs in other years and measure changes in the cost of living relative to this base year. The CPI index for a given year, say year K, is defined as

$$\text{CPI in year } K = \frac{\text{cost of basket in year } K}{\text{cost of basket in base year}} \times 100$$

Suppose a basket of goods costs $200 in 1992, which we'll define as the base year. In 2004, the same basket of goods is $250. First, the value for the CPI in 1992 (the base year) is

$$\text{CPI in 1992} = \frac{200}{200} \times 100 = 100$$

That is, the CPI for 1992 is 100. Note that the base year for the CPI will always equal 100. Now let's calculate the value of the CPI for 2004:

$$\text{CPI in 2004} = \frac{250}{200} \times 100 = 125$$

The CPI in 2004 is 125. The CPI rose from 100 in 1992 to 125 in 2004 in this example, a 25 percent increase in average prices over this 12-year period.

Here is how you would use this information. Suppose you had $300 in 1992. How much money would you need to be able to have the same standard of living in 2004? Find the answer by multiplying the $300 by the ratio of the CPI in 2004 to the CPI in 1992:

$$\$300 \times \frac{125}{100} = 375$$

You need $375 in 2004 just to maintain what was your standard of living in 1992. This is the type of calculation that economists do to evaluate changes in living standards over time.

How do we actually calculate the CPI in practice? Each month, the BLS sends its employees out to sample prices for over 90,000 specific items around the entire country. This is how they construct their representative basket of goods. Figure 6.5 shows the broad categories the BLS uses in the CPI and the importance of each category in household budgets. Rent and food and beverages account for 44 percent of total spending by households.

The CPI versus the Chain Index for GDP

In the last chapter, we discussed measuring nominal GDP and real GDP. We also mentioned that since 1996 the Commerce Department has used a chain-weighted index (replacing the GDP deflator) to measure changes in prices for goods and services included in GDP. The chain-weighted index for GDP and the CPI are both measures of average prices for the economy, yet they differ in several ways.

First, the CPI measures the costs of a typical basket of goods for consumers. It includes goods produced in prior years (such as older cars) as well as imported goods. The chain-weighted price index for GDP does not measure price changes from either used goods or imports. The reason is that it is based on the calculation of GDP, which, as we've seen, measures only goods and services produced in the United States in the current year.

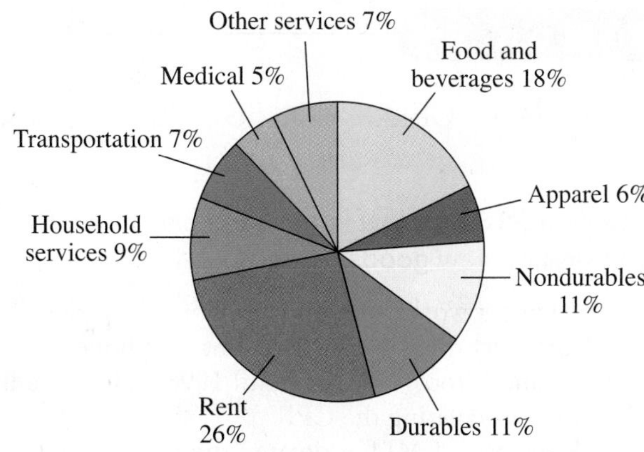

▲ FIGURE 6.5
Components of the Consumer Price Index (CPI)
Rent and food and beverages make up 44 percent of the CPI basket. The remainder consists of other goods and services.
SOURCE: Bureau of Labor Statistics, U.S. Department of Labor, 2006.

Second, unlike the chain-weighted price index for GDP, the CPI asks how much a *fixed* basket of goods costs in the current year compared to the cost of those same goods in a base year. Because consumers tend to buy less of goods whose prices rise, the CPI will tend to overstate true changes in the cost of living. For example, if the price of steak rises, consumers may switch to chicken and spend less on steak. But if the current basket of goods and services in the CPI includes steak, the CPI thinks the amount of higher-priced steak in the basket is the same as the amount of steak before its price increase. It does not allow the amount of steak in the index to decrease. Another measurement problem occurs when new products are introduced into the marketplace, again because the CPI measures a fixed basket of goods. The BLS will eventually adjust its "basket" to account for successful new products, but it takes some time.

Problems in Measuring Changes in Prices

Most economists believe that in reality all the indexes, including the chain-weighted index for GDP and the CPI, overstate actual changes in prices. In other words, the increase in prices is probably less than the reported indexes tell us. The principal reason for this overstatement is that we have a difficult time measuring quality improvements. Suppose the new computers sold to consumers become more powerful and more efficient each year. Suppose further that the dollar price of a new computer remains the same each year. Even though the price remains the same, the computers in later years are of much higher quality. If we looked simply at the price and did not take into account the change in quality, we would say there was no price change for computers. But in later years we are getting more computer power for the same price. If we failed to take the quality change into account, we would not see that the price of computer power has fallen.

Government statisticians do try to adjust for quality when they can. But quality changes are so common in our economy and products evolve so rapidly that it is impossible to keep up with all that is occurring. As a result, most economists believe we overestimate the inflation rate by between 0.5 and 1.5 percent each year. This overstatement has important consequences. Some government programs, such as Social Security, automatically increase payments when the CPI goes up. Some union contracts also have **cost-of-living adjustments (COLAs)**, automatic wage changes based on the CPI. If the CPI overstates increases in the cost of living, the government and employers might be overpaying Social Security recipients and workers for changes in the cost of living.

cost-of-living adjustments (COLAs) Automatic increases in wages or other payments that are tied to the CPI.

application 4

THE INTRODUCTION OF CELL PHONES AND THE BIAS IN THE CPI

APPLYING THE CONCEPTS #4: How large is the bias in the CPI due to not immediately incorporating new goods?

Today, it is hard to imagine a world without cell phones. Every college student and most high school students carry them everywhere. But cell phones were not introduced to the public until 1983, and it took 15 years, until 1998, before the Bureau of Labor Statistics included them in calculating the CPI!

Economist Jerry Hausman of MIT estimated the bias in the CPI caused by the failure to include cell phones in a timely manner. He calculated that because of this delay, the telecommunication component of the price index was biased upwards by between 0.8 and 1.9 percent per year. In other words, instead of rising by 1.1 percent per year, telecommunication prices should have been falling by 0.8 percent per year. This is a significant bias.

But cell phones are not the only examples of the slow introduction of goods into the CPI. The BLS also took 15 years to recognize room air conditioners in the CPI. Since new products are constantly invented and introduced, the bias in the CPI can be large. **Related to Exercise 4.9.**

SOURCE: Based on Jerry Hausman, "Cellular Telephone, New Products, and the CPI," *Journal of Business & Economic Statistics* 17, no. 2 (1999): 186–194.

6.5 Inflation

inflation rate
The percentage rate of change in the price level.

We have now looked at two different price indexes: the chain-weighted price index used for calculating real GDP and the Consumer Price Index. Using either price index, we can calculate the percentage rate of change of the index. The percentage rate of change of a price index is the **inflation rate**:

$$\text{inflation rate} = \text{percentage rate of change of a price index}$$

Here is an example. Suppose a price index in a country was 200 in 1998 and 210 in 1999. Then the inflation rate between 1998 and 1999 was

$$\text{inflation rate} = \frac{210 - 200}{200} = 0.05 = 5\%$$

In other words, the country experienced a 5 percent inflation rate.

It is important to distinguish between the price level and the inflation rate. In everyday language, people sometimes confuse the level of prices with inflation. You might hear someone say inflation is high in San Francisco because rents for apartments are high, but this is not a correct use of the term *inflation*. Inflation refers not to the level of prices, whether they are high or low, but to their *percentage change*. If rents were high in San Francisco but remained constant over two years, there would be no inflation in rents there during that time.

Historical U.S. Inflation Rates

To gain some historical perspective, Figure 6.6 plots a price index for GDP from 1875 to 2009 for the United States. As you can see from the figure, from 1875 to the period just before World War I, there was virtually no change in the price level. The price level rose during World War I, fell after the war ended, and also fell sharply during the early 1930s. However, the most pronounced feature of the figure is the sustained rise in prices beginning around the 1940s. Unlike the earlier periods, in which the price level did not have a trend, after 1940 the price level increased sharply. By 2010, the price level had increased by a factor of 14 over its value in 1940. Table 6.2 contains the prices of a few selected goods from the 1940s and in 2010. Wouldn't you like to buy a postage stamp today for $0.03?

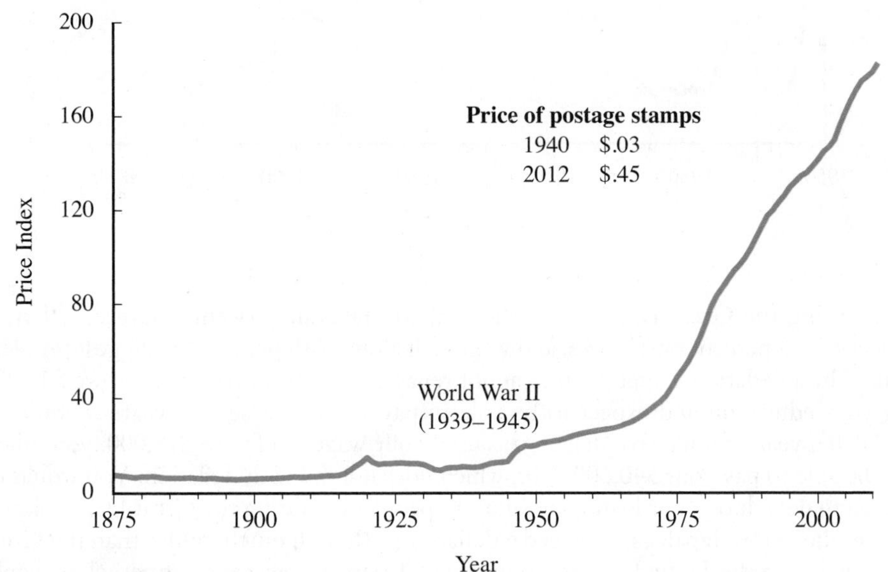

◀ **FIGURE 6.6**
Price Index for U.S. GDP, 1875–2012

After remaining relatively flat for 60 years, the price level began to steadily increase after World War II. The price of a postage stamp in 1940 and 2012 illustrates the change in the overall price level that occurred.

SOURCES: R. J. Gordon, *Macroeconomics* (New York: Harper Collins, 1993) and U.S. Department of Commerce, 2010.

MyEconLab Real-time data

TABLE 6.2 Prices of Selected Goods, 1940s and 2012

Item	1940s Price	2012 Price
Gallon of gasoline	$0.18	$3.65
Loaf of bread	0.08	3.59
Gallon of milk	0.34	3.49
Postage stamp	0.03	0.45
House	6,550	350,000
Car	800	22,000
Haircut in New York City	0.50	50
Movie tickets in New York City	0.25	12.00
Men's tweed sports jacket in New York City	15	189
Snake tattoo on arm	0.25	80.00

SOURCES: Scott Derks, *The Value of a Dollar 1860–1989* (Farmington Hills, MI: Gale Group, 1993) and author's research and estimates.

Taking a closer look at the period following World War II, Figure 6.7 plots the inflation rate, the percentage change in the price index, from 1950 to 2009. In the 1950s and 1960s, the inflation rate was frequently less than 2 percent a year. The inflation rate was a lot higher in the 1970s, reaching nearly 10 percent per year. In those years, the economy suffered from several increases in the world price of oil. In recent years, the inflation rate has subsided and has been between 2 and 3 percent.

The Perils of Deflation

Prices rarely fall today, but they have actually fallen at times in world history. You might think it would be great if prices fell and we had what economists term a **deflation**. It may surprise you, however, that we think you should hope deflation never occurs.

deflation
Negative inflation or falling prices of goods and services.

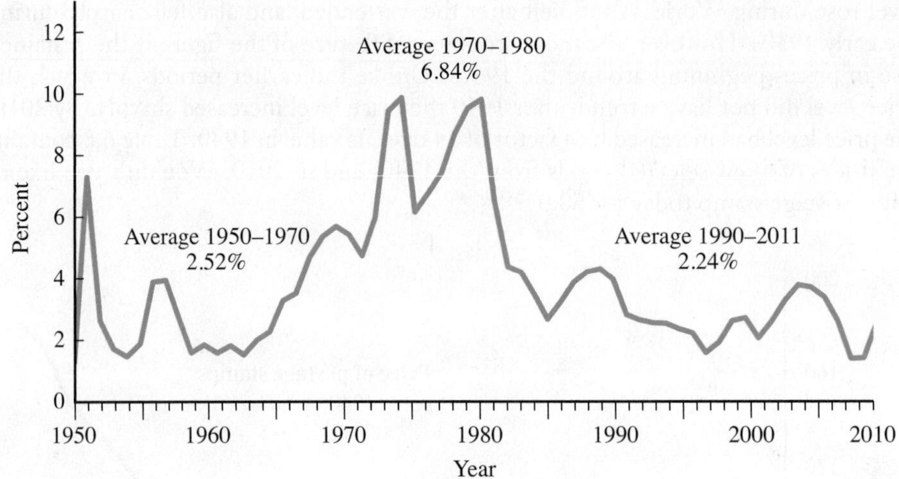

▶ **FIGURE 6.7**
U.S. Inflation Rate, 1950–2011, Based on Chain-Weighted Price Index
Inflation reached its highest peaks in the postwar era during the decade of the 1970s when the economy was hit with several increases in oil prices. In recent years, the inflation rate has been relatively low.
SOURCE: U.S. Department of Commerce, 2012.

MyEconLab Real-time data

During the Great Depression, the United States underwent a severe deflation. Prices fell 33 percent on average, and wages fell along with prices. The biggest problem caused by a deflation is that people cannot repay their debts. Imagine you owe $40,000 for your education and expect to be able to pay it off over several years if you earn $27,000 a year. If a massive deflation caused your wages to fall to $18,000, you might not be able to pay your $40,000 debt, which does not fall with deflation. You would be forced to default on your loan, as millions of people did during the Great Depression.

In the 1990s, Japan experienced a deflation, although much milder than the Great Depression in the United States—only about 1 percent per year. Nonetheless, banks in Japan faced rocky economic times as borrowers, including large corporations, defaulted on their loans. With its banks in difficult shape, Japan's economy has suffered. Its experience in the 1990s mirrored the experience of other countries throughout the world in the 1930s during the period of deflation.

6.6 The Costs of Inflation

anticipated inflation
Inflation that is expected.

unanticipated inflation
Inflation that is not expected.

Economists typically separate the costs of inflation into two categories. One includes costs associated with fully expected or **anticipated inflation**. The other includes the costs associated with unexpected or **unanticipated inflation**. Although inflation causes both types of costs, it is convenient to discuss each case separately.

Anticipated Inflation

Let's consider the costs of anticipated inflation first. Suppose the economy had been experiencing 5 percent annual inflation for many years and everyone was fully adjusted to it.

menu costs
The costs associated with changing prices and printing new price lists when there is inflation.

Even in this case, inflation still has some costs. First, there are the actual physical costs of changing prices, which economists call **menu costs**. Restaurant owners, catalog producers, and any other business that must post prices will have to incur costs to physically change their prices because of inflation. For example, they will need to pay to reprint their menus or billboards. Economists believe these costs are relatively small for the economy.

shoe-leather costs
Costs of inflation that arise from trying to reduce holdings of cash.

Second, inflation will erode the value of the cash people hold. They will respond by holding less cash at any one time. If they hold less cash, they must visit the bank or their ATM more frequently because they will run out of cash sooner. Economists use the term **shoe-leather costs** to refer to the additional costs people incur to hold less cash. Economists who have estimated these costs find that they can be large, as much as 1 percent of GDP.

In practice, our tax and financial systems do not fully adjust even to anticipated inflation. It is difficult for the government and businesses to change their normal rules of operation every time inflation changes. As an example, consider the tax system. Our tax system is typically based on nominal income, not real income. Suppose you own a stock in a corporation and its value increases by 5 percent during the year. If the inflation rate is also 5 percent a year, your stock did not increase in real terms—it just kept up with inflation. Nonetheless, if you sold your stock at the end of the year, you would be taxed on the full 5 percent gain, despite the fact that the real value of your stock did not increase. Inflation distorts the operation of our tax and financial system.

Unanticipated Inflation

What if inflation is unexpected? The cost of unexpected inflation is arbitrary redistributions of income. Suppose you expected the inflation rate would be 5 percent and you negotiated a salary based on that expectation. On the one hand, if you miscalculate and the inflation rate turns out to be higher, the purchasing power of your wages will be less than you anticipated. Your employer will have gained at your expense. On the other hand, if the inflation rate turned out to be less than 5 percent, the purchasing power of your wage would be higher than you had anticipated. In this case, you would gain at the expense of the company. As long as the inflation rate differs from what is expected, there will be winners and losers.

These redistributions eventually impose real costs on the economy. Consider an analogy. Suppose you live in a very safe neighborhood where no one locks the doors. If a rash of burglaries (transfers between you and crooks) starts to occur, people will invest in locks, alarms, and more police. You and your community will incur real costs to prevent these arbitrary redistributions.

The same is true for unanticipated inflation. If a society experiences unanticipated inflation, individuals and institutions will change their behavior. For example, potential homeowners will not be able to borrow from banks at fixed rates of interest, but will be required to accept loans whose rates can be adjusted as inflation rates change. Banks do not want to lend money at a fixed interest rate if there is a strong likelihood that inflation will erode the real value of the income stream they expected. However, if banks become reluctant to make loans with fixed interest rates, this imposes more risk on homeowners.

What about the loans made prior to the unanticipated inflation? In this case, debtors will gain at the expense of creditors. Creditors, on the one hand, will lose because inflation will erode the amount of money they planned to earn on the loans. But since the loans have already been made, there's nothing they can do about it. Debtors, on the other hand, will get a deal. It will be easier for them to repay their loans with inflated dollars.

If unanticipated inflation becomes extreme, individuals will spend more of their time trying to profit from inflation rather than working at productive jobs. As inflation became more volatile in the late 1970s in the United States, many people devoted their time to speculation in real estate and commodity markets to try to beat inflation, and the economy became less efficient. Latin American countries that have experienced high and variable inflation rates know all too well these costs from inflation. Indeed, when inflation rates exceed 50 percent per month, we have what is called **hyperinflation**. Think about what an inflation rate of 50 percent a month means: If a can of soda costs $1.25 at the beginning of the year, it would cost $162.00 at the end of year! In a later chapter, we'll study the causes of hyperinflation, but you can readily see that inflation of this magnitude would seriously disrupt normal commerce.

hyperinflation
An inflation rate exceeding 50 percent per month.

Even in less extreme cases, the costs of inflation are compounded as inflation rises. At high inflation rates, these costs grow rapidly, and at some point policy-makers are forced to take actions to reduce inflation. As we mentioned earlier, when unemployment falls below the natural rate, inflation increases. Similarly, in later chapters we'll see that stopping inflation may require unemployment to exceed its natural rate and even plunge an economy into a recession. Although unemployment and recessions are quite costly to society, they sometimes become necessary in the face of high inflation.

SUMMARY

In this chapter, we continued our introduction to the basic concepts of macroeconomics and explored the nature of both unemployment and inflation. We also looked at the complex issues involved in measuring unemployment and inflation as well as the costs of both to society. Here are the key points to remember:

1 The unemployed are individuals who do not have jobs but who are actively seeking employment. The *labor force* comprises both the employed and the unemployed. The *unemployment rate* is the percentage of the labor force that is unemployed:

$$\text{unemployment rate} = \frac{\text{unemployed}}{\text{labor force}} \times 100$$

2 Economists distinguish among different types of unemployment. Seasonal patterns of economic activity lead to *seasonal unemployment*. There are three other types of unemployment. *Frictional unemployment* occurs through the normal dynamics of the economy as workers change jobs and industries expand and contract. *Structural unemployment* arises because of a mismatch of workers' skills with job opportunities. *Cyclical unemployment* occurs with the fluctuations in economic activity.

3 Unemployment rates vary across demographic groups. Alternative measures of unemployment take into account individuals who would like to work full time, but who are no longer in the labor force or are holding part-time jobs.

4 Economists measure changes in the cost of living through the *Consumer Price Index (CPI)*, which is based on the cost of purchasing a standard basket of goods and services. The CPI is used to measure changes in average prices over different periods of time. The CPI index for a given year, say year *K*, is defined as

$$\text{CPI in year } K = \frac{\text{cost of basket in year } K}{\text{cost of basket in base year}} \times 100$$

5 We measure *inflation* as the percentage change in the price level.

6 Economists believe that most price indexes, including the CPI and the chain-weighted index for GDP, overstate true inflation because they fail to capture quality improvements in goods and services.

7 Unemployment imposes both financial and psychological costs on workers.

8 Both *anticipated* and *unanticipated* inflation impose costs on society.

KEY TERMS

anticipated inflation, p. 134
Consumer Price Index (CPI), p. 130
cost-of-living adjustments (COLAs), p. 131
cyclical unemployment, p. 126
deflation, p. 133
discouraged workers, p. 123
frictional unemployment, p. 126
full employment, p. 127
hyperinflation, p. 135
inflation rate, p. 132
labor force, p. 121
labor force participation rate, p. 121
menu costs, p. 134
natural rate of unemployment, p. 126
seasonal unemployment, p. 125
shoe-leather costs, p. 134
structural unemployment, p. 126
unanticipated inflation, p. 134
unemployment insurance, p. 128
unemployment rate, p. 121

EXERCISES

All problems are assignable in MyEconLab; exercises that update with real-time data are marked with **.**

6.1 Examining Unemployment

1.1 Which of the following is not included in the labor force?
a. People who are employed.
b. People who do not have a job, but who are actively searching for one.
c. People who do not have jobs and do not want one.
d. The entire population is included in the labor force.

1.2 Individuals who are working part time for economic reasons and would like to work full time are counted as unemployed in the traditional unemployment statistics. ________ (True/False)

1.3 The labor force participation rate shows the percentage of the
a. labor force that has a job.
b. labor force that is unemployed.
c. relevant population that is employed.
d. relevant population that is in the labor force.

1.4 What would happen to the measured unemployment rate if unemployed individuals left the labor force to enter a disability program? (Related to Application 2 on page 127.)

1.5 **New Government Employment and True Unemployment.** Suppose the U.S. government hires workers who are currently unemployed but does not give them any work to do. What will happen to the measured U.S. unemployment rate? Under these circumstances, do changes in the measured U.S. unemployment rate accurately reflect changes in the underlying economic situation and production?

1.6 **Part-Time Work.** Paul and Karen are married. Karen works as a stockbroker while Paul works part time to take care of their kids at home. He is happy with this arrangement. Is Paul unemployed? Would he be counted as working part time for economic reasons?

1.7 **Calculating Data for the U.S. Economy.** Here are some data for the U.S. economy in January 2010:

236.8 million individuals 16 years of age and older

138.3 million employed

14.8 million unemployed

Calculate the labor force, the labor force participation rate, and the unemployment rate for the U.S. economy.

1.8 **Baby Boomers and Labor Force Participation.** Robert is 62 and lost his job in an engineering firm. Pamela is 53 and also lost her job. What options do you think Robert has that Pamela does not? How might this affect labor force participation rates? (Related to Application 1 on page 125.)

1.9 **Disability and Low-Skilled Workers.** Disability payments replace a higher fraction of the wages of low-wage workers than of high-wage workers. Overall, average disability payments rise with the average wage. Suppose wages of low-skilled workers fell sharply relative to high-wage workers. How would this affect the incentives to enter disability for low-wage workers? (Related to Application 2 on page 127.)

1.10 **Unemployment Rates in June.** Raw, unadjusted data show virtually every year that the number of unemployed rise in June. Why? Would this show up in seasonally adjusted data?

1.11 **Alternative Unemployment Measures.** An economy has 100,000,000 people employed, 8,000,000 unemployed, and 4,000,000 marginally attached workers. What is the conventional measure of the unemployment rate? What would be the best alternative measure that takes into account marginally attached workers?

1.12 **Discouraged Workers in Japan and the United States.** Japan was concerned about a group of workers called "NEETs," which meant "not in education, employment, or training." In the United States, we also have young, discouraged workers. Discuss the types of young, discouraged workers you would most likely find in the United States.

6.2 Categories of Unemployment

2.1 The three key types of unemployment are cyclical, structural, and __________.

2.2 The natural rate of unemployment consists solely of __________ and __________ unemployment.

2.3 When the economy is at full employment, there is only cyclical unemployment. __________ (True/False)

2.4 When iPods and MP3 players came on to the scene, replacing CDs, what type or types of unemployment were created?

a. Structural and frictional

b. Structural and cyclical

c. Frictional and cyclical

d. Discouraged and cyclical

2.5 **Understanding Unemployment Differences across Countries.** A student looking at Figure 6.2 on page 122 argues that Spain must have very high cyclical unemployment compared to Japan because the Spanish unemployment rate is so high. Explain why the student could be right or could be wrong.

2.6 **Apartment Vacancies and Unemployment.** In a major city, the vacancy rate for apartments was approximately 5 percent, yet substantial numbers of individuals were searching for new apartments. Explain why this occurs. Relate this phenomenon to unemployment.

2.7 **Unemployment Rates in Large African Cities.** In many African countries, the government and international corporations pay high wages for jobs in the major cities, and many people migrate to the cities from farms where earnings are low. Unemployment rates in the city, therefore, are large. Can this be explained in terms of frictional unemployment? Why or why not?

2.8 **Rising Oil Prices and Frictional Unemployment.** Explain how rising oil prices, which benefit some industries more than others, can affect frictional unemployment.

6.3 The Costs of Unemployment

3.1 Virtually all unemployment has a duration of less than five weeks. __________ (True/False)

3.2 Most states do not replace the entire wages of individuals on unemployment insurance; instead, they replace about __________ percent.

3.3 The effects of unemployment today may carry over into the future because

a. discouraged workers are not measured in the unemployment rate.

b. those that experience prolonged unemployment lose job skills that are difficult to recover.

c. a person must be actively seeking work to be counted as unemployed.

d. None of the above

3.4 In 2012, over 40 percent of the unemployed had been unemployed __________ weeks or more.

3.5 **Understanding Peer Effects of Unemployment.** You might think it would be worse if other people are unemployed at the same time as you were because it would be harder to find a job. But the psychological evidence shows the opposite. Give a few reasons why unemployment may seem less painful to individuals if their peers are also unemployed. (Related to Application 3 on page 129.)

3.6 **Long-Term Effects of Unemployment.** Why might you expect individuals who were unemployed in their 20s to have lower wages at the age of 40 than individuals with identical educational backgrounds but who were not unemployed?

3.7 **Recessions and the Duration of Unemployment.** During a recession, what do you think happens to the fraction of workers with spells of unemployment less than five weeks? Can you find data to support your theory?

6.4 The Consumer Price Index and the Cost of Living

4.1 The value of a price index in the base year is equal to __________.

4.2 Economists believe that the CPI tends to overestimate the increase in the cost of living over time. __________. (True/False)

4.3 Unlike the CPI, the chain-weighted price index for GDP does not include used goods or __________ goods.

4.4 The single largest component of the basket of goods that comprises the CPI is the category for __________.

4.5 **Which Professor Is Better Off?** The starting salary for a new assistant economics professor was $15,000 in 1976 and $90,000 in 2010. The value of the CPI for 2010 was 216.3, compared to 56.9 in 1976. In which year did a newly hired professor earn more in real terms?

4.6 **What Are Comparable Real Salaries?** A job paid $53,000 in 2002. The CPI in 1960 was 29.6, compared to 179.9 in 2002. In 1960, what salary would be comparable to 2002's $53,000 in real terms?

4.7 **High Prices and Inflation.** Critically evaluate the following statement: "Tokyo is an expensive place to live. There must be a high inflation rate in Japan."

4.8 **What Does It Cost?** The Bureau of Labor Statistics now makes price data available on its Web site at http://data.bls.gov/PDQ/outside.jsp?survey=ap. Use this search engine to see how the price of spaghetti and macaroni has increased.

4.9 **New Goods and the CPI Bias.** Many "cell phones" today are more than cell phones—they are mini-computers on which you check your e-mail and surf the Web. Suppose the BLS treated them as old-fashioned cell phones. How would this cause a bias in the CPI? (Related to Application 4 on page 132.)

6.5 Inflation

5.1 If a price index is 50 in 1998 and 60 in 1999, the rate of inflation between the two years is __________.

5.2 Inflation in the United States was higher from 1990 to 2009 than it was from 1970 to 1980. __________ (True/False)

5.3 Which of the following countries experienced a deflation in the 1990s?

a. United States

b. Japan

c. Canada

5.4 If the price of gasoline in 1940 was $0.18 a gallon and $3.00 a gallon in 2009, the percentage rate of change for gasoline over this period was __________ percent.

5.5 **Calculating an Inflation Rate.** A country reports a price index of 55 in 2005 and 60 in 2006. What is the inflation rate between 2005 and 2006?

5.6 **Price Indexes for the Elderly.** Use the Web to find articles that discuss price indexes that are most appropriate for elderly Americans. Why might the inflation rate for the elderly differ from the nonelderly? How would a finding that the elderly face a different inflation rate affect the debates on Social Security?

6.6 The Costs of Inflation

6.1 Inflation that is not expected is known as __________ inflation.

6.2 Shoe-leather costs typically increase with rate of inflation. __________ (True/False)

6.3 Creditors gain from unanticipated inflation. __________ (True/False)

6.4 Hyperinflation occurs when the inflation rate exceeds __________ percent per month.

6.5 **Online Shopping and Menu Costs.** How do you think the Internet and online shopping would affect the menu costs of inflation?

6.6 **Taxes on Stock Gains and Inflation.** Suppose you bought a stock for $100 and its value stayed constant in real terms. Over 20 years, the price of the stock in dollar terms has doubled. If you sold the stock after 20 years and your tax rate was 15%, how much tax would you owe? How much do you think you should owe?

6.7 **Inflation and ATM Withdrawals.** As the inflation rate increases, would you take more or less money out per each ATM visit? If you walked to the ATM, would that increase or decrease the wear and tear on your shoes?

The Economy at Full Employment

CHAPTER 7

Gross domestic product per capita is higher in the United States than in France. The primary reason for this is that the French (and other Europeans) work one-third fewer hours than do U.S. workers. You might be tempted to attribute this difference to Europeans' taste for leisure or vacations. However, in the early 1970s Europeans actually worked slightly more hours than did U.S. workers. What explains this dramatic turnaround in the space of just 20 years?

Some economists have said the differences can be explained by taxes. In France, taxes are substantially higher than in the United States as France provides more public services and a larger fraction of health care is supplied by the government. Since 1970, there has been a substantial increase in taxes in France relative to the United States.

But can taxes really explain these differences? If so, how do taxes affect employment? And what lessons might this have for the United States?

LEARNING OBJECTIVES

- Identify the key assumption of classical models in macroeconomics.
- Explain the concept of diminishing returns to labor.
- Analyze how shifts in demand and supply affect wages and employment.
- Explain how full employment is determined in a classical model.
- Describe how changes in taxes can affect full employment.
- Compare crowding out in a closed and open economy.

MyEconLab
MyEconLab helps you master each objective and study more efficiently.

In this chapter we will explain how the amount of capital and labor helps determine GDP when the economy is operating at full employment. Although the economy experiences booms and busts, in the long run it returns to full employment. This makes full employment an important benchmark, or barometer, of real GDP.

We will see how full employment is determined at any point in time when wages and prices adjust freely and quickly to changes in demand and supply. It is this flexibility in wages and prices that allows the economy to operate at full employment. In the next chapter we will study economic growth when the amount of capital and technology evolves over time.

We will develop the model of full employment and use it to examine important macroeconomic issues and debates, such as the extent to which taxes may depress economic activity and lower the level of GDP. We will also learn about real business cycle theory, a school of thought that can help us understand why booms and busts occur.

7.1 Wage and Price Flexibility and Full Employment

classical models
Economic models that assume wages and prices adjust freely to changes in demand and supply.

The economic model of the economy at full employment that we develop in this chapter assumes wages and prices adjust freely and quickly to changes in demand and supply. Models that make this assumption are called **classical models**. The term *classical* refers to a school of economics that believed that over a relatively short period of time wages and prices would adjust quickly and naturally to bring the economy back to full employment. The classical school of thought dominated economics until about the mid-1930s.

Following the Great Depression in the 1930s, though, economists began to change their minds about the classical school. During the Great Depression, unemployment was rampant—nearly 25 percent of the labor force was unemployed—and economists began to develop models that explained persistent unemployment. In these models, wages and prices don't always adjust quickly to changes in demand and supply—which is why booms and busts occur.

Economists today, however, believe that even though wages and prices may be slow to adjust in the short run, they will respond eventually and restore the economy to full employment. That's why it is important to study the full-employment model. We can use this model to analyze the long-term issues we address in this chapter, such as the role taxes play in determining the level of GDP and how immigration affects wages and GDP.

An economy at full employment doesn't mean that there are no unemployed workers. Recall the distinctions among frictional, structural, and cyclical unemployment. Frictional unemployment occurs naturally in the labor market as workers search for jobs. Structural unemployment arises from a mismatch of skills and jobs. Cyclical unemployment is the part of unemployment that rises and falls with economic fluctuations. Cyclical unemployment can be positive, when unemployment exceeds the natural rate during a recession, or negative, when unemployment is less than the natural rate during a boom. Full employment means an economy has frictional and structural unemployment but no cyclical unemployment. In other words, at full employment the economy is experiencing neither a boom nor a bust.

7.2 The Production Function

Recall that a critical part of the circular flow of economic activity is the production of total goods and services from the factors of production. The factors of production include the labor, natural resources, physical capital, human capital, and entrepreneurship that are the inputs to a technologically based production process. We'll discuss more of these aspects in the next chapter. In this chapter, however, we develop the idea of a **production function** to study how this production actually occurs. The production function explains how the total level of output or GDP in the economy is generated from the factors of production.

production function
The relationship between the level of output of a good and the factors of production that are inputs to production.

To simplify our discussion of the economy's production function, let's first assume there are only two factors of production: capital and labor. The **stock of capital** is all the machines, equipment, and buildings in the entire economy. **Labor** consists of the efforts, both physical and mental, of all the workers in the economy used to produce goods and services. The production function is written as follows:

stock of capital
The total of all machines, equipment, and buildings in an entire economy.

labor
Human effort, including both physical and mental effort, used to produce goods and services.

$$Y = F(K, L)$$

where Y is total output, or GDP; K is the stock of capital; and L is the labor force. (F represents the relationship between the factors of production and output.) What the math says in words is that we produce total output from both capital and labor. The production function, $F(K, L)$, is a model that tells us how much output we produce from the inputs to production, K and L: More inputs of either capital or labor in an economy lead to increased output.

The stock of capital a society has at any point in time is determined by investments it has made in new buildings, machines, and equipment in the past. Investments made today will have little or no immediate effect on the total stock of buildings, machines, and equipment used in production today, because today's level of investment is typically just a small fraction of all past investments. Therefore, it takes time for investment to change the stock of capital. In this chapter, we will assume for most of our discussion that the stock of capital is fixed at a constant level, which we call K. But we will stray from that assumption a few times to consider what happens when the stock of capital changes. (We promise to let you know where we are straying from the assumption of fixed capital.)

With the stock of capital fixed at the constant level K, only variations in the amount of labor can change the level of output in the economy. Figure 7.1 plots the relationship between the amount of labor used in an economy and the total level of output with a fixed stock of capital. Although the stock of capital is fixed, we do vary the amount of labor employed in production.

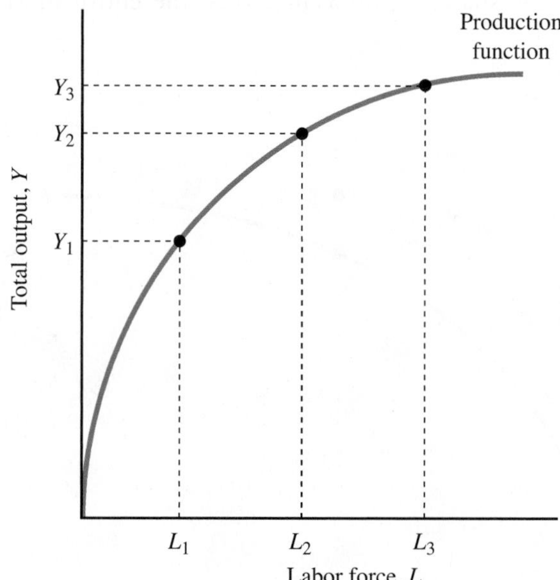

◄ FIGURE 7.1
The Relationship between Labor and Output with Fixed Capital
With capital fixed, output increases with labor input, but at a decreasing rate.

Figure 7.1 shows that as we increase labor from L_1 to L_2, output increases sharply from Y_1 to Y_2. However, as more labor is put into production to get us to L_3 and Y_3, output does not rise as sharply. With capital fixed, the relationship between output and labor shown here reflects the principle of diminishing returns.

PRINCIPLE OF DIMINISHING RETURNS

Suppose we produce output with two or more inputs and we increase one input while holding the other inputs fixed. Beyond some point—called the *point of diminishing returns*—output will increase at a decreasing rate.

To explain what diminishing marginal returns means, look at the data in Table 7.1 from a typical production function. The table shows the amount of output we can produce from different amounts of labor inputs while we hold the stock of capital constant at some amount. (We don't care what amount, as long as it is constant.) First, notice that as the amount of labor increases, so does the amount of output we produce. Second, as output increases, it increases at a diminishing rate. For example, as labor input increases from 300 to 400 labor units, output increases by 500 output units—from 1,000 to 1,500 output units. But as labor input increases from 400 to 500 labor units, output increases by only 400 output units—from 1,500 to 1,900 output units. The rate of output dropped from 500 output units per additional unit of labor to 400 output units per additional unit of labor input. That's diminishing returns at work.

TABLE 7.1 Output and Labor Input

Y (Output)	*L* (Labor Input)
1,000	300
1,500	400
1,900	500
2,200	600

What happens if the stock of capital increases, say, from K_1 to K_2? Figure 7.2 shows that when the stock of capital increases, the entire short-run production

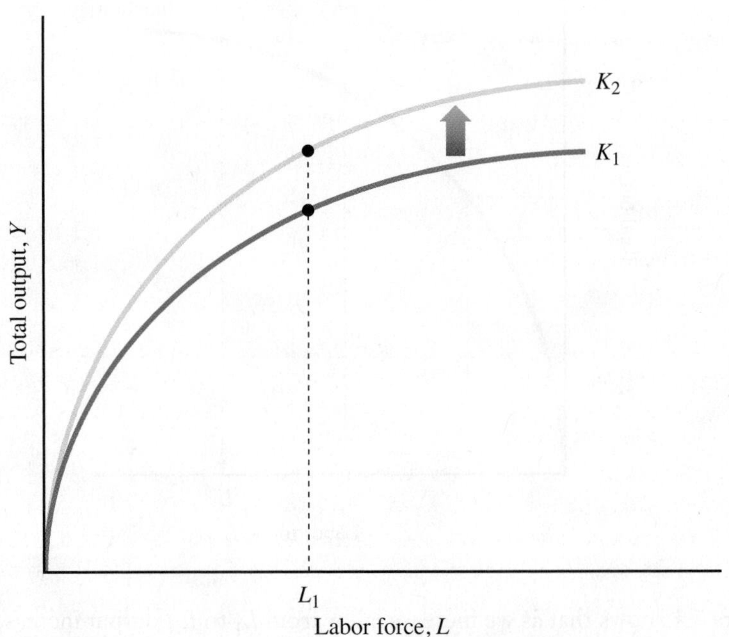

▶ **FIGURE 7.2**

An Increase in the Stock of Capital

When the capital increases from K_1 to K_2, the production function shifts up. At any level of labor input, the level of output increases.

function shifts upward. At any level of labor input, we can produce more output than before we increased the stock of capital. As we add more capital, workers become more productive and can produce more output. That's why the production function curve is higher for more capital. For example, suppose an office has five staff members who must share one copier. They will inevitably waste some time waiting to use it. Adding a copier will enable the staff to be more productive.

Capital is one of the key factors of production. As we have seen, the benefits of additional capital are a higher level of output from any level of labor input. Throughout the world, countries have increased their level of output by adding to their stock of capital.

7.3 Wages and the Demand and Supply for Labor

We've just learned from the production function that with the amount of capital fixed, the level of output in the economy will be determined exclusively by the amount of labor employed. Now we'll see how the amount of employment in an economy is determined by the demand and supply for labor.

On the basis of what you already know about demand and supply from Chapter 4, you should be able to see what Figure 7.3 represents when it comes to wages and the demand and supply for labor for the entire economy. The amount of labor firms in the economy will hire depends on the **real wage**: the wage rate paid to employees adjusted for changes in the price level. The real wage tells us what goods and services workers are able to purchase from their labor and also what it costs, in real terms, for employers to pay their workers for their services.

real wage
The wage rate paid to employees adjusted for changes in the price level.

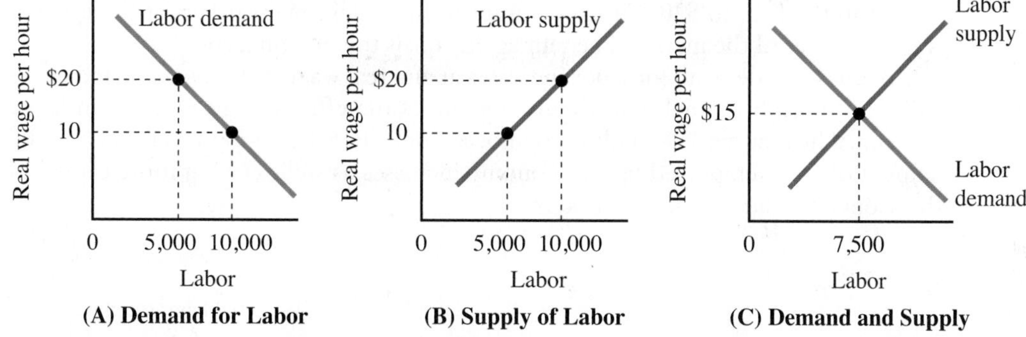

▲ FIGURE 7.3
The Demand and Supply of Labor
Together, the demand and supply for labor determine the level of employment and the real wage.

As the real-wage rate falls, firms will hire more labor. That is, consistent with the law of demand, the labor demand curve in Figure 7.3 is downward sloping. In Panel A we see that as the real wage falls from $20 to $10 per hour, the firm will increase the amount of its labor from 5,000 to 10,000 workers.

While the labor-demand curve is based on the decisions by firms, the labor-supply curve is based on the decisions of workers. They must decide how many hours they want to work and how much leisure they want to enjoy. Although many complex factors enter into the decision to supply labor, in this chapter we will typically assume an increase in the real wage will lead to an increase in the quantity of labor supplied in the market. In Panel B of Figure 7.3 we see that 5,000 people would like to work at $10 per hour, but $20 per hour motivates 10,000 people to want to work.

Labor Market Equilibrium

Panel C of Figure 7.3 puts the demand and supply curves together. At a wage of $15 per hour, the amount of labor firms want to hire—7,500 workers—will be equal to the number of people who want to work—7,500 workers. This is the labor market equilibrium: The quantity demanded for labor equals the quantity supplied. Together, the demand and supply curves determine the level of employment in the economy and the level of real wages. Now that we have a model of labor market equilibrium, we can analyze changes in demand and supply for labor.

Changes in Demand and Supply

In deciding how many workers to hire, a firm will compare the marginal benefit from hiring a worker to the marginal cost. This is an example of the marginal principle.

MARGINAL PRINCIPLE

Increase the level of an activity as long as its marginal benefit exceeds its marginal cost. Choose the level at which the marginal benefit equals the marginal cost.

Now let's apply this principle to understanding how a change in the capital stock affects the demand for labor. When firms increase their capital stock, they find that each worker becomes more productive with the additional capital. For example, suppose the marginal benefit to the firm of an additional hour of work is initially $15, and the wage rate is also $15. An increase in the supply of capital raises the marginal benefit to the firm to $20. Firms will want to hire additional workers at the existing wage of $15 until the marginal benefit again equals the marginal cost.

Because the demand for labor increases at any real wage, the labor-demand curve shifts to the right. Panel A of Figure 7.4 shows the effects of an increase in labor demand. The new market equilibrium moves from *a* to *b*. Real wages increase, and the amount of labor employed in the economy increases as well. Having more capital in the economy is beneficial for workers.

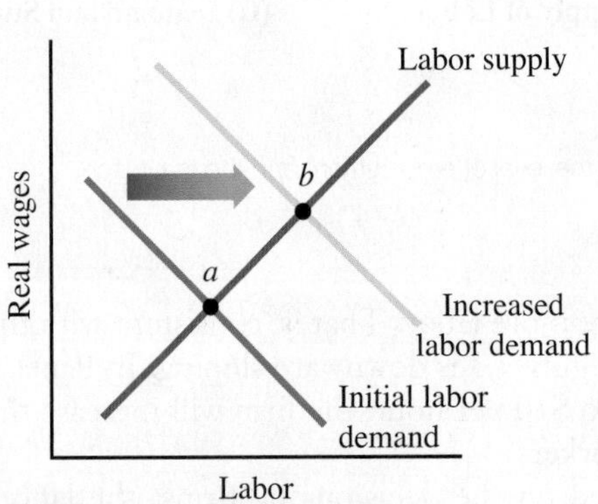

(A) If the demand for labor increases, real wages rise and the amount of labor employed increases.

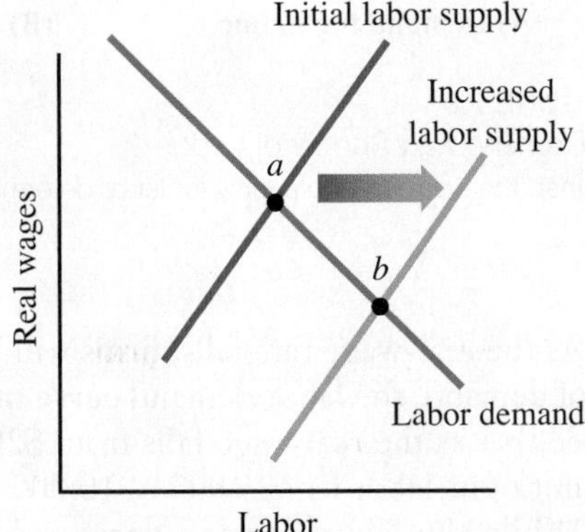

(B) If the supply of labor increases, real wages fall and the amount of labor employed increases.

▲ FIGURE 7.4
Shifts in Labor Demand and Supply
Shifts to demand and supply will change both real wages and employment.

We also can analyze the effect of an increase in the supply of labor that might come, for example, from immigration. If the population increases, we would expect more people would want to work at any given wage. This means the labor-supply curve would shift to the right. Panel B of Figure 7.4 shows that with an increase in the supply of labor, the labor market equilibrium moves from *a* to *b*. Real wages have fallen, and the amount of labor employed has increased. Workers who were employed before the increase in labor supply suffer because real wages have fallen—all wages, including theirs.

Our demand and supply of labor model helps us see why currently employed workers might be reluctant to favor increased immigration—their wages fall. However, there's a flip side to this. Wages are an input price that firms use in determining the price of the goods and services they produce. Lower input prices—such as wages—eventually lead to lower prices for the products workers buy. In other words, there are trade-offs from immigration for society. Our model also explains why workers would like to see increases in the supply of machines and equipment as long as full employment can be maintained. The increased supply of capital (which increases labor productivity) increases labor demand and leads to higher real wages.

Demand and supply for labor can often change at the same time, but by looking at wages and employment we can determine which effect dominates. Here is an example: Suppose you were told that in a small European country both wages and employment increased substantially over a five-year period. As you try to determine what happened, would you look primarily at factors that increased labor demand or that increased labor supply?

To answer this question, we would want to examine some factors, such as the increase in the stock of capital or a change in technology, that would increase labor demand and both wages and employment. These factors could account for why wages and employment increased in the small European country. Increases in the supply of labor (more people in the workforce) would account for the increase in employment, but not for the increase in wages.

application 1

THE BLACK DEATH AND LIVING STANDARDS IN OLD ENGLAND

APPLYING THE CONCEPTS #1: How can changes in the supply of labor affect real wages?

According to the research of Professor Gregory Clark of the University of California, Davis, the level of real wages for laborers in England was nearly the same in 1200 as it was in 1800. Yet, during the period from 1350 to 1550, wages were considerably higher—nearly 75 percent higher in 1450, for instance, than they were in 1200. Why were real wages temporarily so high during this period?

The simple answer was the bubonic plague—also known as the Black Death—that arrived from Asia in 1348 and caused a long decline in total population through the 1450s. With fewer workers, there was less labor supplied to the market. The result was higher real wages, although less total output.

In the era before consistent and rapid technological advance, changes in population were the primary factor controlling living standards. As the economist Thomas Malthus (1766–1834) observed, social maladies such as the Black Death would temporarily raise living standards until higher living standards led to increased population. **Related to Exercises 3.8 and 3.9.**

SOURCE: Based on Gregory Clark, *A Farewell to Alms* (Princeton University Press, 2007).

7.4 Labor Market Equilibrium and Full Employment

We can now join the production function and the demand and supply for labor. Together, they will give us a model that helps us determine how much output the economy can produce when it is operating at full employment and also help us understand how taxes on employers affect the level of output.

Figure 7.5 brings the model of the labor market together with the short-run production function. Panel B depicts equilibrium in the labor market, which we saw in Figure 7.3. The demand and supply for labor determine the real-wage rate W and identify the level of employment L. Panel A plots the short-run production function. With the level of employment determined at L in Panel B, we move upward to Panel A and use that level of employment to determine that the level of production is Y. **Full-employment output** is the level of output produced when the labor market is in equilibrium and the economy is producing at full employment. It is also known as *potential output*.

full-employment output
The level of output that results when the labor market is in equilibrium and the economy is producing at full employment.

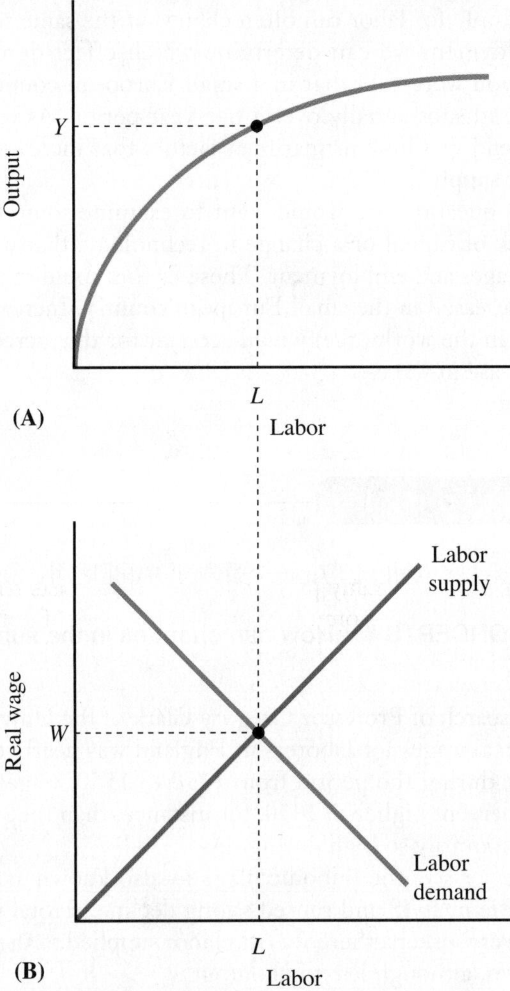

▶ FIGURE 7.5
Determining Full-Employment Output
Panel B determines the equilibrium level of employment at L and the real wage rate of W. Full-employment output in Panel A is Y.

Note that full-employment output is based on the idea that the labor market is in equilibrium, with the quantity of labor supplied equal to the quantity of labor demanded at the equilibrium wage. Potential output is not the absolute maximum level of output an economy can produce—an economy could produce more with higher levels of labor input—but potential output reflects the level of labor input that workers wish to supply.

How do economists typically measure the level of full-employment output, or potential output? They start with an estimate of what the unemployment rate would be if cyclical unemployment were zero—that is, if the only unemployment were due to frictional or structural factors. In the United States, estimates of the natural rate in recent years have varied between 5.0 and 6.5 percent. Economists then estimate how many workers will be employed and use the production function to determine potential output.

Let's look at some real numbers. In 1996, the unemployment rate was 5.6 percent, very close to the natural rate of unemployment. The labor force in that year was approximately 133.9 million, and 126.7 million individuals were employed. Real GDP in that year was $7.8 trillion, measured in 1996 dollars. This level of GDP was produced with the labor of the 126.7 million employed workers and the existing stock of capital and technology. Because the unemployment rate in 1996 was close to the natural rate, the level of real GDP was also very close to the level of potential output in that year.

The level of potential output in an economy increases as the supply of labor increases or the stock of capital increases. An increase in the supply of labor, perhaps from more liberal immigration, would shift the labor-supply curve to the right and lead to a higher level of employment in the economy. With a higher level of employment, the level of full-employment output will increase. An increase in the stock of capital will increase the demand for labor. As labor demand increases, the result will be higher wages and increased employment. Higher employment will again raise the level of full-employment output.

Potential output depends on both capital and labor. Consequently, differences in the quantity of labor supplied to the market will affect the level of potential output in a country. Countries do differ in the amount of labor their workers supply to the market. Apart from national holidays, workers in the United States take an average of 12 days of vacation, compared to 28 days in the United Kingdom, 35 days in Germany, and an amazing 42 days (over eight work weeks) in Italy. These differences in labor supply are important. Per capita output is higher in the United States than in Germany but, other things being equal, this difference would disappear if German workers toiled as much as their U.S. counterparts.

7.5 Using the Full-Employment Model

We use the full-employment model extensively in macroeconomics to analyze a wide range of issues. For example, many politicians and economists have argued that high tax rates have hurt the U.S. economy and reduced the level of output and production. We can use the full-employment model to explore the logic of these claims. We will also see how to use the model to explain booms and recessions—fluctuations in output. This will allow us to understand the fundamental idea of an influential school of economic thought known as real business cycle theory.

Taxes and Potential Output

We use the full-employment model in Figure 7.6 to study the effects of taxes employers pay for hiring labor, such as the taxes they pay for their portion of workers' Social Security. (Economists use similar arguments to study a variety of taxes, including personal and corporate income taxes.) A tax on labor will make labor more expensive and raise the marginal cost of hiring workers. For example, let's say there is no tax on labor and suddenly a tax of 10 percent is imposed. An employer who had been paying $10 an hour for workers will now find that labor costs $11 an hour. Because the marginal cost of hiring workers has gone up but the marginal benefit to the firm has not changed, employers will respond by hiring fewer workers at any given wage. In Panel A of Figure 7.6, the labor-demand curve shifts to the left, reflecting the change in demand due to the tax. As the demand curve shifts to the left, the market equilibrium moves from *a* to *b*. The result is lower real wages and lower employment.

▶ FIGURE 7.6
How Employment Taxes Affect Labor Demand and Supply
In Panel A, a tax burden on labor shifts the labor demand curve to the left and leads to lower wages and reduced employment. In Panel B, the supply curve for labor is vertical, which means that wages fall but employment does not change.

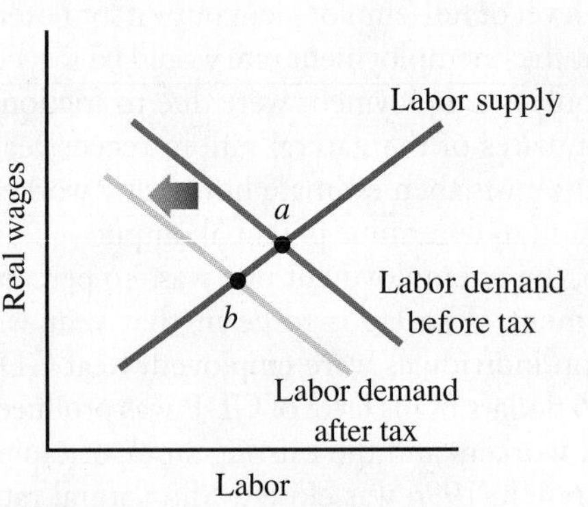

(A) A tax on labor shifts the labor demand curve to the left and leads to lower wages and reduced employment.

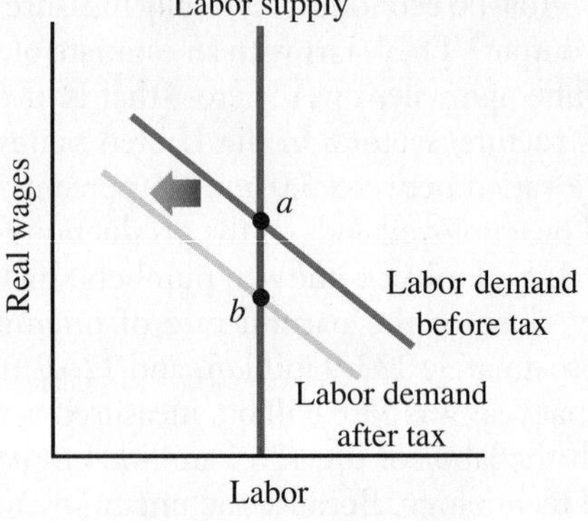

(B) If the supply curve for labor is vertical, wages fall but employment does not change.

As we have just seen, higher taxes lead to less employment. With reduced employment, potential output in the economy will be reduced as the economy moves to a lower level of output on the short-run production function. Higher taxes therefore lead to lower output. The size of the reduction in output depends critically on the slope of the labor-supply curve. The slope of the labor-supply curve indicates how sensitive labor supply is to changes in real wages.

Panel B in Figure 7.6 shows the effect of the same tax with a vertical labor-supply curve. A vertical labor-supply curve means workers will supply the same amount of labor regardless of the wage. For example, a single parent might work a full 40 hours a week regardless of the wage, so the supply curve will be vertical. If, say, other workers in the economy also put in the same hours regardless of the wage, the supply curve for labor in the entire economy will be vertical. In Panel B, we see that with a vertical supply curve, the change in demand will move the market equilibrium from *a* to *b*. The tax will reduce wages but have no effect on employment and therefore no effect on output.

This example illustrates that taxes can affect wages and output. In both cases, either output or wages were lowered when the tax was imposed. However, the extent of the decline in output depends on the slope of the labor-supply curve. To understand the effects of taxes on output, we need information about the slope of the labor-supply curve.

Labor supply has been the focus of many studies. The evidence is strong that part-time workers or second earners in a family are very sensitive to changes in wages and do vary their labor supply when wages change. There is less of a consensus about the behavior of primary earners in the family. For many years, economists believed their labor supply was not very sensitive to changes in compensation. However, recent research has shown that taxes do matter, even for primary earners, especially high earners.

The entire area of taxation and economics is an active branch of economics research. Economists such as Martin Feldstein of Harvard University have studied how many different types of taxes affect employment, saving, and production. Economists use models to try to measure these effects, just as we did for the employment tax.

Real Business Cycle Theory

Fluctuations in economic activity can result from a variety of causes. Here are some examples: A developing country that is highly dependent on agriculture can lose its cash crop because of a prolonged drought. According to economic historian Stanley Lebergott, the nineteenth-century U.S. agricultural-based economy was devastated by grasshopper invasions in North Dakota from 1874 to 1876 and by the boll-weevil migration from Mexico to Texas in 1892.[1] Sharp increases in the price of oil can hurt economies that use oil in production, as was the case throughout the world in both 1973 and 1979. Wars can devastate entire regions of the world, and natural disasters, such as earthquakes or floods, can cause sharp reductions in GDP.

Major shifts in technology, which we'll discuss more in the next chapter, can also cause economic fluctuations. Consider some economic developments, starting with the early nineteenth century. There were large investments in textile mills and steam power. The birth of the steel industry and railroads dominated the last half of the century. At the end of the nineteenth century, new industries arose that were based on chemical manufacturing, electricity, and the automobile. It is inconceivable that the vast changes in technology that led to the creation of these new industries would not have profound effects on the economy. For example, the invention of the automobile sounded the death knell for makers of horse-drawn buggies, buggy whips, and a host of other industries.

Economic fluctuations can also occur because a number of small shocks all hit the economy at the same time. For example, a case of mad cow disease could cause consumer preferences to change from beef to pork. Or a series of small improvements in breeding technology could cause output to rise among worldwide producers of cattle.

One school of economic thought, known as **real business cycle theory**, emphasizes that shocks to technology can be a major cause of economic fluctuations. Led by Nobel Laureate economist Edward Prescott, real business cycle economists have developed newer models that integrate shocks to technology into the full-employment model we have been discussing.

real business cycle theory
The economic theory that emphasizes how shocks to technology can cause fluctuations in economic activity.

The idea behind real business cycle theory is simple: Changes in technology will usually change the level of full employment or potential output. A significant technological improvement will enable the economy to increase the level of both actual and potential output. For example, the advances in technology that allowed computer users to transfer data-intensive images easily across the Internet created many new opportunities for businesses to grow and flourish. Adverse technological developments (or adverse shocks to the economy) will cause output and potential output to fall. For example, the Internet crashing would bring business communication systems and ordering systems to a halt.

Figure 7.7 gives a simple example of how the real business cycle theory works. Suppose an adverse technological shock occurred, decreasing the demand for labor. The demand curve for labor would shift to the left, and the labor market equilibrium would move from *a* to *b*. The result would be a lower level of employment and lower real wages. Total GDP would fall because employment is low and because the economy is less productive than before.

Conversely, a positive technological shock would increase labor demand and result in both higher wages and higher employment. Total GDP would rise because employment is high and because the economy is more productive than before.

An economy buffeted by positive and negative technological shocks would experience economic fluctuations even though it would always be at full-employment output. The key lesson from real business cycle theory is that potential output itself will vary over time.

The real business cycle school of thought has been influential with some academic economists, but in its most extreme form it has been viewed as controversial. Critics find it difficult to understand how many of the post–World War II recessions can be explained by adverse changes in technology. In addition, the real business cycle model does not provide an explanation of unemployment. In the model the labor market is in equilibrium, and the quantity demanded for labor equals the quantity supplied. At the equilibrium wage, the quantity of labor demanded equals the quantity of labor supplied, and everyone who seeks employment finds employment.

Proponents of the real business cycle model counter that other types of economic models can explain unemployment and that the real business cycle can still explain fluctuations in employment. Real business cycle theory is an active area of research, and both its methods and approach, grounded in firm economic reasoning, have had

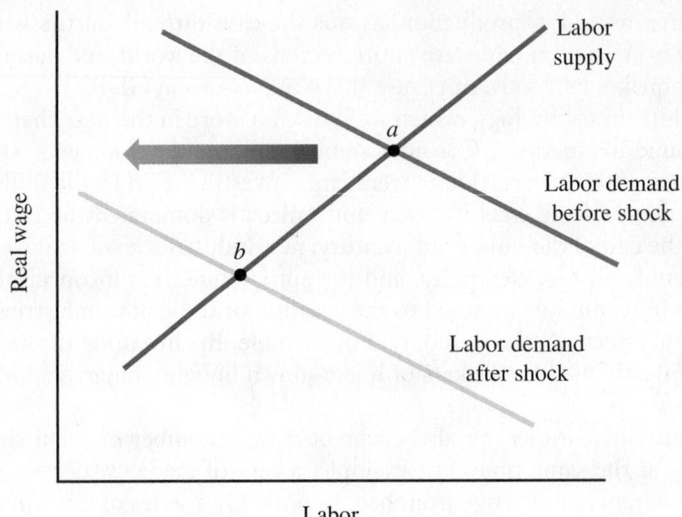

▶ **FIGURE 7.7**
How an Adverse Technology Shock Affects Labor Demand and Supply
An adverse shock to technology will decrease the demand for labor. As a result, both real wages and employment fall as the market equilibrium moves from *a* to *b*.

a major influence on professional research today. Scholars working in this tradition have begun to offer modifications of the basic model that can potentially explain major economic events.

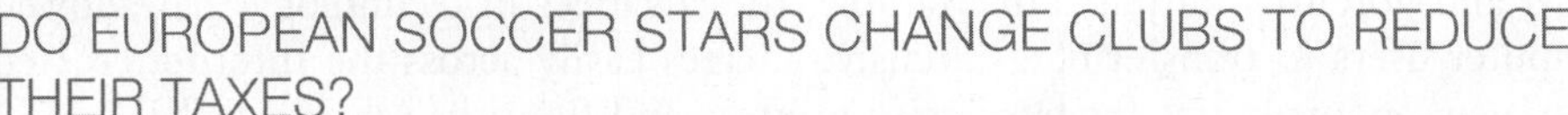

DO EUROPEAN SOCCER STARS CHANGE CLUBS TO REDUCE THEIR TAXES?

APPLYING THE CONCEPTS #2: What evidence is there that taxes on high-paid soccer stars in Europe affect their location decisions among countries?

In 2009, the Portuguese soccer star Cristiano Ronaldo moved from Manchester United in the United Kingdom to Real Madrid in Spain. At the time, many speculated that the reason he moved was to avoid a top United Kingdom tax rate of 50 percent in favor of a flat 24 percent rate (with no deductions) created to entice foreigners to locate in Spain. While this is an interesting anecdote, is there any other evidence that the very top earners will move to countries with lower tax rates?

In an interesting study, economists Henrik Jacobsen Kleven, Camille Landais, and Emmanuel Saez used changes in the market for international soccer stars to test for the effects of tax rates. Prior to 1995, the top European soccer clubs had limits on the number of foreign players on any one team. The European Court of Justice, however, ruled that these limits violated the treaty of the European community. After 1995, the rules limiting foreign players were relaxed. The economists found that, prior to 1995, taxes on high earners did not have much effect on mobility of soccer stars, but after 1995, top tax rates did matter. They also found that specific tax breaks offered by countries also influenced the players' decisions on where to locate.

This type of evidence suggests that countries may not only be in competition for top athletes, but also for other highly paid individuals—from tennis players to corporate executives. Many economists believe that the increase in "globalization" in the last 30 years has limited the ability of countries to levy taxes at rates that differ substantially from other countries. **Related to Exercises 5.4 and 5.5.**

SOURCE: Based on Henrik Jacobsen Kleven, Camille Landais, and Emmanuel Saez, "Taxation and the International Mobility of Superstars; Evidence from the European Football Market," November 2010, National Bureau of Economic Research Working Paper, No. 16545.

application 3

CAN LABOR MARKET POLICIES ACCOUNT FOR THE GREAT DEPRESSION?

APPLYING THE CONCEPTS #3: Can real business cycle models explain the origin and persistence of the Great Depression?

Early critics of real business cycle models claimed that these models could not explain major events like the Great Depression, and, indeed, there appears to be a puzzle about the Great Depression. If negative technology shocks were responsible for the origin and decade-long persistence of the Great Depression, we would expect that the fall in output would be accompanied by a decline in the real wage, just as in Figure 7.7. However, real wages actually rose substantially during the 1930s.

Economists Harold L. Cole and Lee E. Ohanian of the University of California, Los Angeles, extended the standard real business cycle model to include other important factors, in particular government interventions that affected the labor market. For example, President Franklin Roosevelt's New Deal featured the National Industrial Recovery Act, which allowed firms to collude with one another and avoid competition as long as they recognized unions and raised wages. Prior to the onset of the Great Depression, President Herbert Hoover also promoted policies that led firms to raise wages. Ohanian and Cole show that incorporating these factors into a standard real business cycle model can explain both the origin and severity of the Great Depression.

Of course, as we will see in later chapters, many other factors could have added to the severity of the Great Depression. Banks failed both in the United States and worldwide, and international trade—which had been very vibrant in the 1930s—ground to a halt. Nonetheless, the work of Ohanian and Cole demonstrates that a modified version of real business cycle models can add to our understanding of this important episode. **Related to Exercise 5.8.**

SOURCE: Based on Harold L. Cole and Lee E. Ohanian, "New Deal Policies and the Persistence of the Great Depression: A General Equilibrium Analysis," *Journal of Political Economy* 112, no. 4 (2004): 779–816 and Lee E. Ohanian, "What—or Who—Started the Great Depression," *Journal of Economic Theory* 144 (2009): 2310–2335.

7.6 Dividing Output among Competing Demands for GDP at Full Employment

Our model of full employment is based entirely on the supply of factors of production and the state of technology. The demand for and supply of labor determine the real wage and total employment in the economy. Together, labor and the supply of capital determine the level of output through the production function. And that means that in a full-employment economy, total GDP is determined by the supply of factors of production.

Because society faces scarce resources, it must divide full-employment GDP among competing demands. From Chapters 5 and 6, you know that GDP is composed of consumption, investment, government purchases, and net exports, which we denote as $C + I + G + NX$. In this section, we see how societies divide total spending among these four components. Because governments, for many different reasons, increase their level of spending, we would like to know how increased government spending affects private spending. We will see how increases in government spending must reduce other types of expenditures when the economy is operating at full employment.

International Comparisons

Countries divide GDP among its four components in very different ways. Table 7.2 presents data on the percent of GDP in alternative uses for five countries in 2010. Recall that consumption (*C*), investment (*I*), and government purchases (*G*) refer to total spending by residents of that country. Net exports (*NX*) is the difference between exports (sales of goods to foreign residents) and imports (purchases of goods abroad). If a country has positive net exports—for example, Hong Kong, China, and Germany—it is selling more goods in other countries than it is buying from other countries. If a country has negative net exports—such as the United States and France—it is buying more goods than it is selling to other countries.

TABLE 7.2 Shares of Spending in GDP, Assorted Countries, 2010

	C	I	G	NX
Hong Kong	62	23	10	5
United States	71	16	16	–3
France	58	19	25	–2
China	36	47	12	5
Germany	57	17	20	6

SOURCE: *International Monetary Statistics*, International Monetary Fund, 2012.

Let's make one more point: These data are from the International Financial Statistics, which is published by the International Monetary Fund. In these statistics, government purchases include only government consumption, such as military spending or wages for government employees. Government investment, such as spending on bridges or roads, is included in the investment category (*I*).

Table 7.2 reveals considerable diversity among countries. The United States consumes 71 percent of its GDP, a higher fraction than all the other countries. As far as investment goes, Germany and the United States invest a smaller share of GDP than the other countries in the table. China invests the most by far—47 percent. Countries also differ greatly when it comes to government consumption. France has the highest rate of government consumption, while Hong Kong has the lowest. Finally, the countries also differ in the size of net exports relative to GDP.

This wide diversity challenges economists to explain these differences. Some economists have suggested that China's high savings rate (low share of consumption) can be explained by its one-child-per-family policy. They argue that this leads workers to save more for retirement because they cannot depend on their children to support them. Other economists attribute the high savings rate to the fact that China provides very little government-sponsored retirement benefits. In general, differences across countries are hard to explain. For example, there are no obvious, purely economic reasons why the United States, France, and Germany should exhibit such different behavior.

Crowding Out in a Closed Economy

We know government spending is part of GDP. Let's say GDP is fixed and the government increases its spending. What happens in a country that increases its government purchases within a fixed GDP? Because the level of full-employment output is given by the supply of factors in the economy, an increase in government spending must come at the expense of other uses of GDP. Or, stated another way, increased government spending crowds out other demands for GDP. This is called **crowding out**. Crowding out illustrates the principle of opportunity cost:

crowding out
The reduction in investment (or other component of GDP) caused by an increase in government spending.

PRINCIPLE OF OPPORTUNITY COST
The opportunity cost of something is what you sacrifice to get it.

At full employment, the opportunity cost of increased government spending is some other component of GDP.

To understand crowding out, let's first consider what will happen when government spending increases in an economy without international trade, called a **closed economy**. In a closed economy, full-employment output is divided among just three different demands: consumption, investment, and government purchases. We can write this as

closed economy
An economy without international trade.

output = consumption + investment + government purchases

$$Y = C + I + G$$

Because we are considering an economy at full employment, the supply of output (Y) is fixed. Increases in government spending must reduce—that is, crowd out—either consumption or investment. In general, both are affected. On the investment side, the government will be in increased competition with businesses trying to borrow funds from the public to finance its investment plans. This increased competition from the government will make it more difficult and costly for businesses to make those investments. As a result, business investment spending will decrease. In other words, government crowds out investment.

Crowding out occurred in the United States during World War II as the share of government spending as a part of GDP rose sharply. Figures 7.8 and 7.9 show that at the same time the share of government spending increased, the shares of consumption and investment spending in GDP decreased.

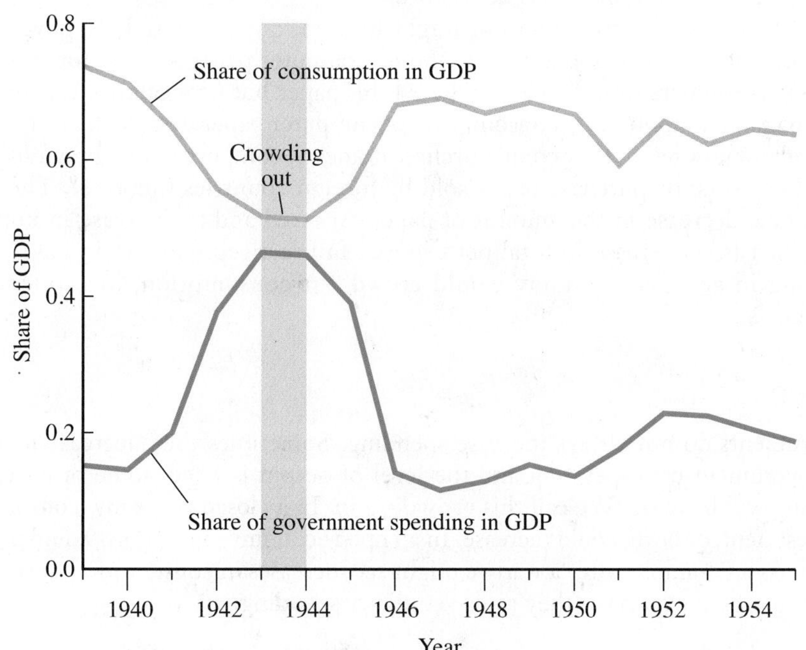

◄ FIGURE 7.8
U.S. Consumption and Government Spending during World War II
Increased government spending crowds out consumption by consumers. The vertical bar highlights the time period during which crowding out occurred.
SOURCE: U.S. Department of Commerce.

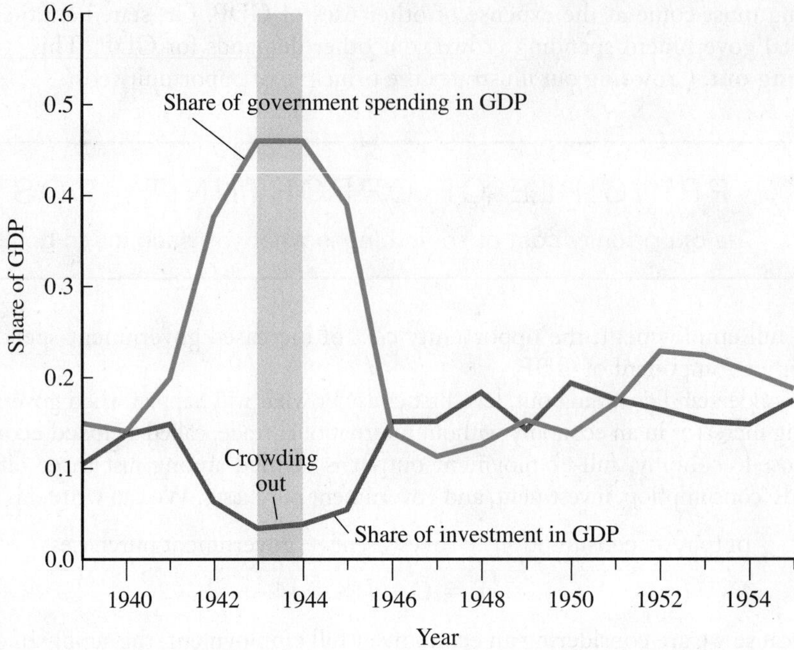

▶ **FIGURE 7.9**
U.S. Investment and Government Spending during World War II
Increased government spending also crowds out private investment spending. The vertical bar highlights the time period during which crowding out occurred.
SOURCE: U.S. Department of Commerce.

Crowding Out in an Open Economy

open economy
An economy with international trade.

An economy with international trade is called an **open economy**. In an open economy, full-employment output is divided among four uses: consumption, investment, government purchases, and net exports (exports – imports):

$$Y = C + I + G + NX$$

Increased government spending need not crowd out either consumption or investment. It could lead to reduced exports and increased imports. Therefore, what could get crowded out instead is net exports.

Here is how this crowding out might happen: Suppose the U.S. government began buying domestic goods—for example, computer paper—to use for its offices. Let's say consumers would have purchased this paper but now cannot. If consumers want to maintain their same consumption of computer paper despite the fact that the government now has it, they could purchase domestic computer paper previously sold abroad (exports) or purchase paper sold by foreign countries (imports). The result would be a decrease in the amount of paper exported and an increase in imported paper, that is, a decrease in total net exports. In practice, increases in government spending in an open economy would crowd out consumption, investment, and net exports.

Crowding In

crowding in
The increase of investment (or other component of GDP) caused by a decrease in government spending.

Governments do not always increase spending. Sometimes they decrease it. When the government cuts spending and the level of output is fixed, some other type of spending will increase. We call this **crowding in**. In a closed economy, consumption or investment, or both, could increase. In an open economy, net exports could increase as well. As an example, after a war we might see increases in consumption, investment spending, or net exports as they replace military spending.

The nature of changes in government spending will have some effect on the type of spending that is crowded in (or crowded out). If the government spent less on mail service—leading to longer delays in the mail—businesses and households would most likely want to spend more on private mail or delivery services. If the government built more public swimming pools, households would most likely cut back their own spending on backyard pools.

SUMMARY

In this chapter, we studied the economy at full employment. In the model we developed, the level of GDP is determined by the supply of the factors of production—labor, natural resources, physical capital, human capital, and entrepreneurship. We focused on how the economy operates when it is at full employment. In later chapters, we consider economic fluctuations. Here are the main points from this chapter:

1 Models that assume wages and prices adjust freely to changes in demand and supply are called *classical models*. They are useful to understand how the economy operates at full employment.

2 *Full-employment output*, or potential output, is the level of GDP produced from a given supply of capital when the labor market is in equilibrium. Potential output is fully determined by the supply of factors of production in the economy.

3 Increases in the *stock of capital* raise the level of full-employment output and real wages.

4 Increases in the supply of labor will raise the level of full-employment output but lower the level of real wages.

5 The full-employment model has many applications. Many economists use it to study the effects of taxes on potential output. Others have found the model useful in understanding economic fluctuations in models of *real business cycles*.

6 At full employment, increases in government spending must come at the expense of other components of GDP. In a closed economy, either consumption or investment must be crowded out. In an open economy, net exports can be crowded out as well. Decreases in government spending will crowd in other types of spending.

KEY TERMS

classical models, p. 140
closed economy, p. 153
crowding in, p. 154
crowding out, p. 153
full-employment output, p. 146
labor, p. 141
open economy, p. 154
production function, p. 141
real business cycle theory, p. 149
real wage, p. 143
stock of capital, p. 141

EXERCISES

All problems are assignable in MyEconLab.

7.1 Wage and Price Flexibility and Full Employment

1.1 Economic models that assume that wages and prices adjust freely to changes in demand and supply are known as __________ models.

1.2 At full employment, there are only structural and __________ unemployment.

1.3 The classical school of thought came to its fruition during the Great Depression. __________ (True/False)

1.4 There is no __________ unemployment at full employment.

7.2 The Production Function

2.1 The production function illustrates the relationship between __________ and __________.

2.2 With the stock of capital fixed, output increases with labor input, but at a rate that __________ (increases/decreases).

2.3 A decrease in the stock of capital shifts the production function __________ (upward/downward). Show this with a graph.

2.4 A decrease in human capital is likely to shift the production function __________ (upward/downward).

2.5 **The Production Function and the Effects of War on the Stock of Capital.** During World War II, France lost 30 percent of its capital stock. Draw a graph that illustrates how the production function shifted.

2.6 **The Production Function and the Effects of War on the Labor Force.** France lost 550,000 people of 42 million in World War II. Show how this affected output using the graph from Exercise 2.5.

2.7 **Diminishing Returns?** An economy increased employment first from 10,000 to 20,000 and then from 20,000 to 30,000. The corresponding increases in output were 15,000 and 20,000, respectively. Nothing else changed during this period. Did this economy exhibit diminishing returns?

7.3 Wages and the Demand and Supply for Labor

3.1 Labor market equilibrium occurs at a real wage at which the quantity demanded for labor equals the quantity __________ of labor.

3.2 An increase in the amount of capital in the economy will shift the demand for labor curve to the __________ (right/left), leading to higher real wages and employment.

3.3 An increase in labor force participation is likely to lead to a shift in the labor-supply curve to the __________ (right/left).

3.4 If wages and employment both rise, this is likely caused by an increase in the supply for labor. __________ (True/False)

3.5 **Historical Immigration Patterns and Real Wages.** Between 1870 and 1910, 60 million Europeans left Europe to go to the United States, Canada, Australia, and Argentina. This immigration sharply increased the labor force in these countries, but decreased it in Europe.

a. Draw demand and supply graphs to show what happened to wages in Europe.

b. Draw demand and supply graphs to show what happened to wages in other countries.

3.6 **Immigration and the Wage Gap between High-School Graduates and College Graduates.** Some economists have argued that while immigration does not have a major effect on the overall level of wages, it does increase the wage gap between high-school graduates and college graduates. Can you explain this effect of immigration on the wage gap?

3.7 **Philippines and Emigration.** Roughly 10 percent of the population of the Philippines works overseas. Suppose overseas Philippine workers returned to their home country. Using Figure 7.4 on page 144, illustrate the effects of this reverse flow of people on wages and employment.

3.8 **Malthus and Subsistence Wages.** Thomas Malthus wrote that if wages exceeded subsistence levels the population would increase, which in turn would drive real wages back down to subsistence. Suppose there were an increase in the demand for labor, which raised real wages. Under Malthus's theory, show how the supply curve for labor would shift. (Related to Application 1 on page 145.)

3.9 **Malthus, Population Size, and Technology.** Malthus believed the population would always adjust to bring real wages back to a fixed subsistence level. Using a demand and supply for labor diagram, show that an improvement in technology will lead to a higher level of population. (Related to Application 1 on page 145.)

7.4 Labor Market Equilibrium and Full Employment

4.1 Suppose the supply of labor increases. Draw a graph to show how potential output and wages change.

4.2 Draw a graph to show how potential output and wages change when the stock of capital decreases.

4.3 The typical European works more hours per year than the typical U.S. worker. __________ (True/False)

4.4 Another term for potential output is __________.

4.5 **Estimates of the Natural Rate and Full Employment.** Two economists differ on their estimates of the natural rate. One economist believes it is 6 percent, while the other believes it is 5 percent. All else being equal, which economist will estimate a higher value for potential output?

4.6 **Germany and the United States.** Per-capita output is higher in the United States than in Germany. According to recent studies, what is the main cause of this difference?

4.7 **Technology and Potential Output.** Suppose that technology improves: for any level of the capital stock, the short-run production function shifts up. What happens to potential output?

7.5 Using the Full-Employment Model

5.1 On a graph of the labor market, show the effects of an increase in the payroll tax.

5.2 On a graph of the labor market, show the effects of a negative shock to technology on wages and employment.

5.3 Two examples of major technological innovations that could have caused major economic fluctuations are __________ and __________.

5.4 Explain why the very top athletes or entertainers would be more likely to change countries to reduce their taxes as compared to ordinary middle-class workers. (Related to Application 2 on page 150.)

5.5 **Payroll Tax for a Health Program.** To finance a universal health-care program, the government decides to place a 10-percent payroll tax on all labor hired. (Related to Application 2 on page 150.)

a. Draw a graph to show how this shifts the demand for labor.

b. If the labor-supply curve is vertical, what are the effects on real wages, output, and employment? Explain why economists say labor bears the full burden of the tax in this case.

c. If the labor-supply curve were horizontal, what would be the effects on wages, output, and employment?

d. Can your answer to part (c) explain Edward Prescott's claim about the causes of the changes in hours of work in Europe compared to Japan and the United States?

5.6 **Analyzing the Effects of Tax Rate Changes for Families with Different Incomes.** The Tax Reform Act of 1986 cut the tax rates sharply for high-income earners. Consider the families in the top 1 percent of all families ranked in terms of income. Before the law was passed, a woman in this group faced a marginal tax rate (the tax rate applied to the last dollar she earned) of 52 percent on average. After the law was passed, the rate fell to 38 percent. The decreases in tax rates were much less, however, for families with lower levels of income. According to a study by Professor Nada Eissa,[2] after the decrease in taxes took effect, the labor supply of women in the highest income group increased more than that of women in other income groups. Use a labor demand and supply model to illustrate the differences between the high-income group and the other groups.

5.7 **Tax Revenue and Labor Supply.** Tax revenue collected from a payroll tax equals the tax rate times the earnings of individuals subject to the payroll tax. Let's say the labor-supply curve is close to vertical. Explain why, in this case, raising payroll tax rates will increase the total revenue the government receives from the payroll tax.

5.8 **Explaining a Depression Using Real Business Cycle Theory.** Real business cycle theorists look at economic fluctuations in a particular way.

a. Draw a graph to show how a real business cycle economist would explain an economic depression.

b. According to real business cycle theory, how do real wages behave during depressions?

c. How did actual real wages behave during the Great Depression?

d. According to Professor Ohanian, what other factors may have caused wages to behave this way? (Related to Application 3 on page 151.)

5.9 **Could Raising Capital Gains Taxes Reduce Revenues?** The U.S. government currently taxes increases in the value of stocks when they are sold. This is called the capital gains tax. Explain why, if the government increased the tax rate on capital gains, it could actually receive less total revenue. In your answer, carefully distinguish between the tax rate and tax revenues.

5.10 **Researching Studies on Taxation, Economic Behavior, and Revenue Collection.** Go to the Web site for the Congressional Budget Office (www.cbo.gov) and find a study that explores the effects of taxation on economic behavior and on total tax revenue. Draw a graph that shows how an increase in tax rates can increase tax revenue.

7.6 Dividing Output among Competing Demands for GDP at Full Employment

6.1 When the economy operates at full employment, an increase in government spending must crowd out consumption. __________ (True/False)

6.2 A(n) __________ economy is open to trade, whereas a closed economy is not.

6.3 In an open economy, increases in government spending can crowd out consumption, investment, or __________.

6.4 Compared to other countries, China has a relatively __________ share of consumption spending in GDP.

6.5 A Consumption Binge in an Open Economy. Suppose consumers decide they want to spend more on all types of goods. Investment and government purchases remain the same. In an open economy, what must happen to allow the increase in consumption?

6.6 Consumption or Investment Crowding Out? Suppose local governments in suburban communities around the country started building large community swimming pools. Explain what type of spending this might crowd out. Compare this to the effect of government spending on exploration of Mars.

6.7 Marital Gifts and Savings. In Japan, it is a custom for the bride's family to give a gift having very large monetary value to the family of the groom. How might this affect the savings rate in Japan?

NOTES

1. Stanley Lebergott, *The Americans* (W.W. Norton: New York and London, 1984), chap. 30.

2. Nada Eissa, "Taxation and the Labor Supply of Married Women: The Tax Reform Act of 1986 as a Natural Experiment," (working paper 5023, National Bureau of Economic Research, 1995).

Why Do Economies Grow?

CHAPTER **8**

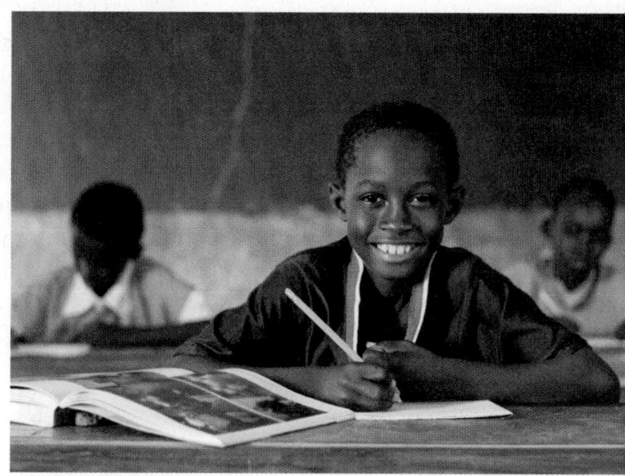

For many people, the thought of poverty conjures up poor, African children.

Indeed, Africa is a poor continent, but as economists Xavier Sala-i-Martin and Maxim Pinkovskiy have recently shown, prospects are improving.

Since 1995, poverty rates in Africa have been falling steadily. Indeed, if this trend continues, the rate of poverty could meet ambitious goals set by the United Nations for poverty reduction by 2015. Economic growth in Africa has not come at the expense of the poor. The current income distribution in Africa is less unequal than it was in 1995, indicating that the growth of income has been shared across the population. The decline poverty has been widespread across the continent. It has fallen in landlocked as well as coastal countries, mineral-rich and mineral-poor countries, and in countries with varying degrees of agriculture.

Their results even apply to countries that were particularly disadvantaged by slavery. The message of these economists is optimistic: Even countries hindered by geography or history can still reduce poverty through economic growth.[1]

LEARNING OBJECTIVES

- Calculate economic growth rates.
- Explain the role of capital in economic growth.
- Apply growth accounting to measure technological progress.
- Discuss the sources of technological progress.
- Assess the role of government in assisting economic growth.

MyEconLab

MyEconLab helps you master each objective and study more efficiently.

Our living standards are dramatically different today because of the remarkable growth in GDP per person. Growth in GDP is perhaps the most critical aspect of a country's economic performance. Over long periods, it is the only way to raise the standard of living in an economy.

This chapter begins by looking at some data from both rich and poor countries over the last several decades. We will see how GDP per capita (meaning per person—every man, woman, and child) compares over this period. We'll then look at how growth occurs. Economists believe two basic mechanisms increase GDP per capita over the long term. One is **capital deepening**, or increases in an economy's stock of capital (such as buildings and equipment) relative to its workforce. **Technological progress** is the other; to economists this means an economy operates more efficiently, producing more output, but without using any more inputs such as capital or labor. We'll examine different theories of the origins of technological progress and discuss how to measure its overall importance for the economy. We'll also discuss in detail the role of education, experience, and investments in human beings, which are called **human capital**.

capital deepening
Increases in the stock of capital per worker.

technological progress
More efficient ways of organizing economic affairs that allow an economy to increase output without increasing inputs.

human capital
The knowledge and skills acquired by a worker through education and experience and used to produce goods and services.

The appendix to this chapter contains a simple model of capital deepening known as the Solow model. It shows how increases in capital per worker lead to economic growth. The model will also allow us to better understand the role of technological progress in sustaining economic growth.

8.1 Economic Growth Rates

Throughout the world there are vast differences in standards of living and in rates of economic growth. To understand these differences, we first need to look at the concepts and the tools economists use to study economic growth.

But before we learn how to measure growth, let's take a broad overview of what we mean by *economic growth*. We can understand economic growth by using one of the tools we developed in Chapter 2: the production possibilities curve. The production possibilities curve shows the set of feasible production options for an economy at a given point of time. In Figure 8.1 we show an economy's trade-off when it comes to producing consumer goods versus military goods. As the economy grows, the entire production possibilities curve shifts outward. This means the economy can produce

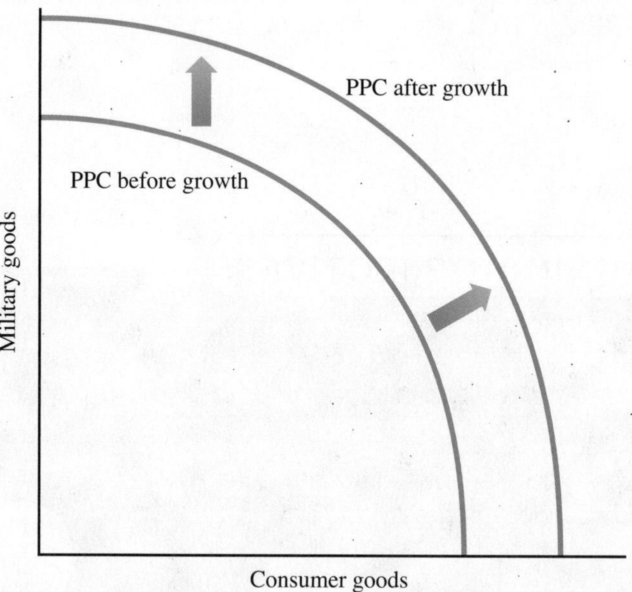

▲ **FIGURE 8.1**
What Is Economic Growth?
Economic growth means an expanded production possibilities curve (PPC).

more of both goods—that is what we mean by economic growth. Growth also expands the amount of goods available for people to consume. Just think about your own family. A typical family 40 years ago had only one car, whereas today many families have two or three. As our chapter-opening story highlights, the economic growth we take for granted is recent and does not apply evenly across all societies.

Measuring Economic Growth

From earlier chapters we know that real gross domestic product (GDP) measures in constant prices the total value of final goods and services in a country. Because countries differ in the size of their populations, we want to know a country's real GDP per person, or its **real GDP per capita.**

Real GDP per capita typically grows over time. A convenient way to describe the changes in real GDP per capita is with growth rates. The **growth rate** of a variable is the percentage change in that variable from one period to another. For example, to calculate the growth rate of real GDP from year 1 to year 2, suppose real GDP was 100 in year 1 and 104 in year 2. In this case, the growth rate of real GDP is

real GDP per capita
Gross domestic product per person adjusted for changes in prices. It is the usual measure of living standards across time and among countries.

growth rate
The percentage rate of change of a variable from one period to another.

$$\text{growth rate} = \frac{(\text{GDP in year 2} - \text{GDP in year 1})}{(\text{GDP in year 1})}$$

$$= \frac{(104 - 100)}{100}$$

$$= \frac{4}{100}$$

$$= 4\% \text{ per year}$$

In other words, real GDP grew by 4 percent from year 1 to year 2. This also means that GDP in year 2 was $(1 + 0.04)$ times GDP in the year 1.

Economies can grow at different rates from one year to the next. But it often is useful to consider what happens when an economy grows at a constant rate, say g, for a number of years. Let's start simply. Suppose real GDP for an economy was 100 and the economy grew at a rate g for two years. How large would the real GDP be two years later? After one year, GDP would be $(1 + g)$ 100. In the second year, it would grow by $(1 + g)$ again, or

$$\text{GDP [2 years later]} = (1 + g)^2\,(100)$$

We can generalize this to consider the case where the economy grows a constant rate g for n years. How large would GDP be after n years? A simple formula gives the answer:

$$\text{GDP [}n\text{ years later]} = (1 + g)^n\,(100)$$

Example: If the economy starts at 100 and grows at a rate of 4 percent a year for 10 years, output (after 10 years) will be

$$\text{GDP [10 year later]} = (1 + 0.04)^{10}\,(100) = (1.48)(100) = 148$$

which is nearly 50 percent higher than in the first year.

Here's a rule of thumb to help you understand the power of growth rates. Suppose you know the growth rate of real GDP, and it is constant, but you want to know how many years it will take until the level of real GDP doubles. The answer is given by the **rule of 70**:

rule of 70
A rule of thumb that says output will double in $70/x$ years, where x is the percentage rate of growth.

$$\text{years to double} = \frac{70}{(\text{percentage growth rate})}$$

Example: For an economy that grew at 5 percent a year, it would take

$$\frac{70}{5} = 14 \text{ years}$$

for real GDP to double. (In case you are curious, the rule of 70 is derived by using the mathematics of logarithms.)

Comparing the Growth Rates of Various Countries

Making comparisons of real GDP or GNP across countries is difficult. Not only do countries have their own currencies, but patterns of consumption and prices can differ sharply among countries. Two examples can illustrate this point. First, because land is scarce in Japan, people live in smaller spaces than do residents of the United States, so the price of housing is higher (relative to other goods) than in the United States. Second, developing countries (such as India or Pakistan) have very different price structures than developed countries. In particular, in developing countries goods that are not traded—such as household services or land—are relatively cheaper than goods that are traded in world markets. In other words, while all residents of the world may pay the same price for gold jewelry, hiring a cook or household helper is considerably less expensive in India or Pakistan than in the United States.

It is important to take these differences into account. Fortunately, a team of economists led by Robert Summers and Alan Heston of the University of Pennsylvania has devoted decades to developing methods for measuring real GNP across countries. The team's procedures are based on gathering extensive data on prices of comparable goods in each country and making adjustments for differences in relative prices and consumption patterns. These methods are now used by the World Bank and the International Monetary Fund, two prominent international organizations.

According to these methods, the country with the highest level of income in 2011 was Qatar; its income per capita was $102,943; Luxemborg was second at $80,119, Singapore was third at $59,711 while Norway, with its oil wealth, was fourth at $53,471. The United States was sixth (behind Brunei and Hong Kong) at $48,347.

Table 8.1 lists real Gross National Income (GNI) per capita for 2008 and the average annual growth rate of GNI per capita between 1960 and 2008 for 11 countries. (Gross National Income is most commonly used in international comparisons and a fully consistent series from 1960 to 2008 is available for these countries.) The United Kingdom, with a GNI per capita of $36,130, follows the United States. Not far behind are Japan, France, and Italy. More representative of typical countries are Mexico and Costa Rica,

TABLE 8.1 Gross National Income Per Capita and Economic Growth

Country	Gross National Income Per Capita in 2008 Dollars	Per Capita Growth Rate 1960–2008
United States	$46,970	2.38%
United Kingdom	36,130	2.54
Japan	35,220	4.09
France	34,400	2.91
Italy	30,250	2.92
Mexico	14,270	2.95
Costa Rica	10,950	2.35
India	2,960	2.05
Pakistan	2,770	1.53
Nigeria	1,940	1.11
Zambia	1,230	–0.60

SOURCES: World Bank Development Indicators (2010) and Alan Heston, Robert Summers, and Bettina Aten, *Penn World Table* Version 6.3, Center for International Comparisons at the University of Pennsylvania (CICUP), October 2010.

with GNIs per capita in 2008 of $14,270 and $10,950, respectively. Costa Rica's GNI per capita is less than 25 percent of per capita GNI in the United States. Very poor countries have extremely low GNI per capita. Pakistan, for example, had a GNI per capita of $2,770—less than 6 percent of the GNI per capita of the United States.

In the third column of Table 8.1, notice the differences in growth rates. Consider Japan. In 1960, Japan had a GNI per capita that was only one-half that of France and one-fourth that of the United States. But notice from the third column that Japan's GNI per capita grew on average 4.09 percent per year during the period, compared to 2.38 percent for the United States and 2.91 percent for France. To place Japan's growth rate for this period into perspective, recall the rule of 70. If an economy grows at an average annual rate of x percent a year, it takes $70/x$ years for output to double. In Japan's case, per capita output was doubling every 70/4.09 years, or approximately every 17 years. At this rate, from the time someone was born to the time he or she reached the age of 34, living standards would have increased by a factor of four—an extraordinary rate of growth. The rule of 70 reinforces the importance of small differences in economic growth rates. A per capita GDP growth rate of 5 percent per year means that the living standard doubles in 14 years. With only 1 percent growth, doubling would take 70 years.

The differences in per capita incomes between the developed and developing countries are very large and are also reflected in many different aspects of society. Take, for example, child labor. In the developed world, we disapprove of child labor and wonder how we can work toward its elimination. Economic research has shown that as countries grow they are less likely to use child labor.

Are Poor Countries Catching Up?

One question economists ask is whether poorer countries can close the gap between their level of GDP per capita and the GDP per capita of richer countries. Closing this gap is called **convergence**. To converge, poorer countries have to grow at more rapid rates than richer countries. Since 1960, Japan, Italy, and France all have grown more rapidly than the United States and have narrowed the gap in per capita incomes.

convergence
The process by which poorer countries close the gap with richer countries in terms of real GDP per capita.

Let's look at some evidence provided by two distinguished international economists, Maurice Obstfeld of the University of California, Berkeley, and Kenneth Rogoff of Harvard University. Figure 8.2 plots the average growth rate for 16 currently developed

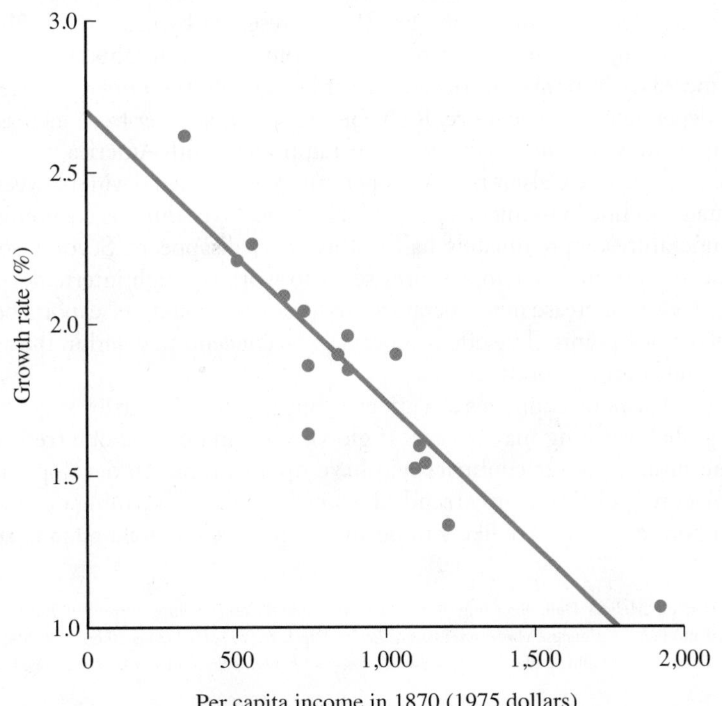

◄ FIGURE 8.2
Growth Rates versus Per Capita Income, 1870–1979
Each point on the graph represents a different currently developed country. Notice that the countries with the lowest per capita incomes in 1870 (shown along the horizontal axis) are plotted higher on the graph. In other words, the tendency was for countries with lower levels of initial income to grow faster.
SOURCE: M. Obstfeld and K. Rogoff, Foundations of International Macroeconomics (Cambridge, MA: MIT Press, 1996), Table 7.1.

countries from 1870 to 1979 against the level of per capita income in 1870. Each point represents a different country. Notice that the countries with the lowest initial per capita incomes are plotted higher on the graph. That is, they had higher growth rates than the countries with more income per capita. The downward-sloping line plotted through the points indicates that the countries with higher levels of per capita income in 1870 grew more slowly than countries with lower levels. In other words, the tendency was for countries with lower levels of initial income to grow faster and catch up. The graph shows that among the currently developed countries—for example, the United States, France, and the United Kingdom—there was a tendency for convergence over the last century.

Now let's compare the countries that are currently less developed to the advanced industrial countries using the data in Table 8.1. Here, the picture is not so clear in recent times. While Mexico grew at a faster rate than the United States, Pakistan grew only 1.53 percent per year and fell farther behind advanced economies. In Africa, Zambian GNI per capita grew only slightly more than 1 percent. In general, economists who have studied the process of economic growth in detail find weak evidence that poorer countries are currently closing the gap in per capita income with richer countries.

Indeed, in the last 20 years there has been little convergence. Economist Stanley Fischer, governor of the Bank of Israel and formerly with the IMF and the Massachusetts Institute of Technology, found that, on average, countries with higher GDP per capita in 1980 grew slightly faster from 1980 to 2000 than countries with lower GDP per capita.[2] African countries, which were among the poorest, grew most slowly. However, there were some important exceptions: The two most populous countries, China and India, grew very rapidly. Because these countries contain approximately 35 percent of the world's population, the good news is that living conditions for many people around the globe have therefore improved substantially in the last 20 years.

application 1

GLOBAL WARMING, RICH COUNTRIES, AND POOR COUNTRIES

APPLYING THE CONCEPTS #1: How may global warming affect economic growth?

Many people believe that global warming will hurt economic development, but research shows that the effects are more complex. Recent research by economists Melissa Dell, Benjamin Jones, and Benjamin Olken provides some useful insights. First, the adverse effects of increases in temperature seem to afflict mainly the poor countries, most of whom are dependent on agriculture. Rich countries do not suffer from increases in temperature. In a study of municipalities within Latin and South America, the economists found that a one-degree Celsius rise in temperature was associated with between a 1.2 and 1.9 percentage decline in municipal per capita income. Over time, as economies adapt to higher temperatures approximately half of this effect disappears. Second, some of the adverse effects from higher temperatures seem to work through international trade. A one-degree Celsius increase in temperatures reduces poor countries' exports between 2.0 and 5.7 percentage points. The effect appears to be concentrated within the agricultural and light manufacturing goods sectors.

The fact that poor countries are affected but not rich countries suggests that the timing of global warming may matter. If global warming can be deferred sufficiently far into the future, poorer countries will have opportunities to develop and perhaps be less subject to global warming trends. However, if global warming occurs relatively soon, then poor countries are likely to be adversely affected. **Related to Exercise 1.9.**

SOURCES: Based on Melissa Dell, Benjamin Jones, and Benjamin Olken, "Temperature and Income: Reconciling Cross-Sectional and Panel Estimates," *American Economic Review Papers & Proceedings* (May 2009): 199–204, and Benjamin Jones and Benjamin Olken, "Climate Shocks and Exports," *American Economic Review Papers & Proceedings* (May 2010).

application 2

ECONOMIC EQUALITY MAY SUSTAIN ECONOMIC GROWTH

APPLYING THE CONCEPTS #2: Is there a necessary trade-off between equality and growth?

What is the connection between inequality and economic growth? Is there a trade-off such that higher growth can only occur if there is increased inequality? Perhaps surprisingly, some recent research suggests that this may not be the case—equality may be beneficial to economic growth.

Andrew Beg and Jonathan Ostry explored the factors that determined why some countries had longer spells of sustained growth than others. Almost all countries can begin to grow, but it is more difficult to sustain growth. What they found was that when there was more equality, spells of growth within a country tended to last longer. Other important factors appeared to be the quality of political institution and an economy's openness to trade.

Why might equality have a beneficial effect? The authors speculate that, when there is more equality, governments may be able to have enough power and authority to make the tough choices to sustain growth. Growth and equality could, however, possibly be caused by some common factor. For example, well-functioning markets for credit and loans may lead to both more growth and more equality. The good news is that it does not appear necessary to create inequality in order to promote growth. **Related to Exercise 1.10.**

SOURCE: Based on Andrew G. Berg and Jonathan D. Ostry, "Equality and Efficiency," *Finance & Development*, September 2011, Vol. 48, No. 3.

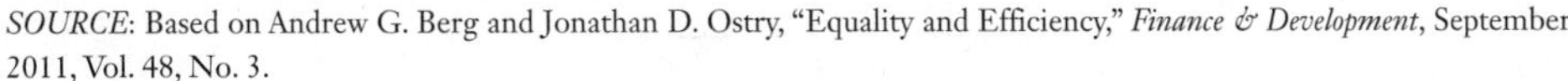

Other commentators are less sanguine. Professor Brad DeLong at UC Berkeley wrote, "Those nations and economies that were relatively rich at the start of the twentieth century have by and large seen their material wealth and prosperity explode. Those nations and economies that were relatively poor have grown richer, but for the most part slowly. And the relative gulf between rich and poor economies has grown steadily. Today this relative gulf is larger than at any time in humanity's previous experience, or at least larger than at any time since there were some tribes that had discovered how to use fire and other tribes that had not."[3]

What about the distribution of income *within* countries as they develop? Many economists thought that as countries developed, inequality would increase among their populations. But recent research challenges this finding.

8.2 Capital Deepening

One of the most important mechanisms of economic growth economists have identified is increases in the amount of capital per worker due to capital deepening.

In Chapter 7, We studied the effects of an increase in capital in a full-employment economy. Figure 8.3 shows the effects on output and real wages. For simplicity, we assume the supply of labor is not affected by real wages and therefore draw a vertical line (see Panel B). In Panel A, an increase in capital shifts the production function upward because more output can be produced from the same amount of labor. In addition, firms increase their demand for labor because the marginal benefit from employing labor will increase. Panel B shows how the increase in capital raises the demand for labor and increases real wages. That is, as firms increase their demand and compete for a fixed supply of labor, they will bid up real wages in the economy.

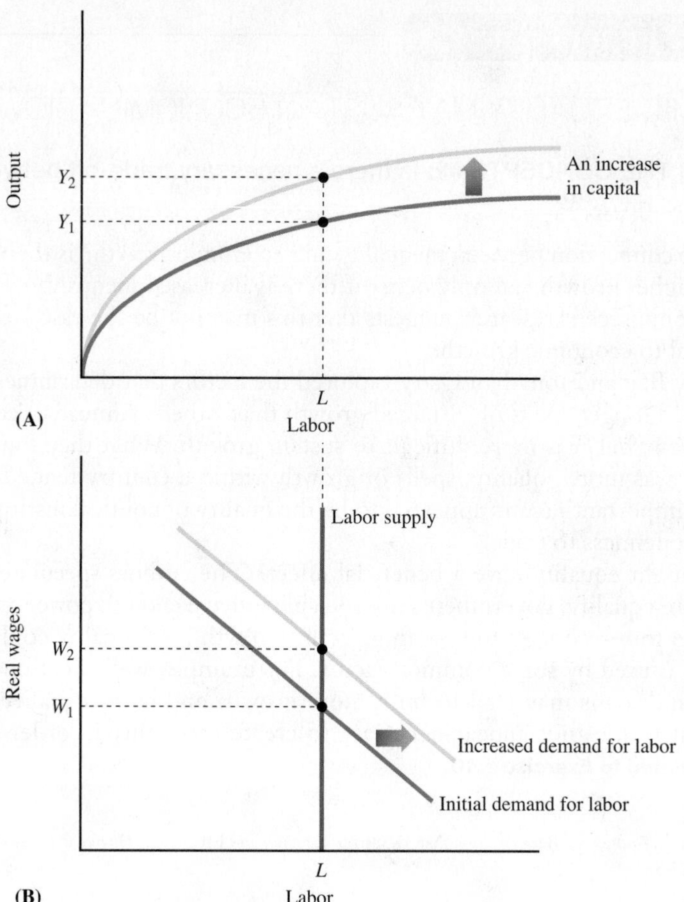

▸ FIGURE 8.3
Increase in the Supply of Capital
An increase in the supply of capital will shift the production function upward, as shown in Panel A, and increase the demand for labor, as shown in Panel B. Real wages will increase from W_1 to W_2, and potential output will increase from Y_1 to Y_2.

An economy is better off with an increase in the stock of capital. With additions to the stock of capital, workers will enjoy higher wages, and total GDP in the economy will increase. Workers are more productive because each worker has more capital at his or her disposal. But how does an economy increase its stock of capital per worker? The answer is with saving and investment, which we'll discuss next.

Saving and Investment

Let's begin with the simplest case: an economy with a constant population, producing at full employment. This particular economy has no government or foreign sector. Its output can be purchased only by consumers or by firms. In other words, output consists solely of consumption (C) and investment (I). At the same time, output generates an amount of income equivalent to the amount of output. That is, output (Y) equals income. Any income that is not consumed we call **saving**.

saving
Income that is not consumed.

In this economy, saving must equal investment. Here's why: By definition, consumption plus saving equals income:

$$C + S = Y$$

but at the same time income—which is equivalent to output—also equals consumption plus investment:

$$C + I = Y$$

Thus, saving must equal investment:

$$S = I$$

This means that whatever consumers decide to save goes directly into investment. Here is a simple way to remember this idea: A farmer produces corn (Y) and can either consume it directly (C) or set it aside as "seed corn" (I) for next year. The part the farmer sets aside and does not consume is also the farmer's saving (S).

Next, we need to link the level of investment in the economy to the stock of capital in the economy. The stock of capital depends on two factors: investment and depreciation. The stock of capital increases with any gross investment spending but decreases with depreciation. Why does depreciation decrease the stock of capital? The answer is simple: As capital stock items such as buildings and equipment get older (depreciate), they wear out and become less productive. New investment is needed to replace the buildings and equipment that become obsolete.

Suppose, for example, the stock of capital at the beginning of the year is $10,000. During the year, if there were $1,000 in gross investment and $400 in depreciation, the capital stock at the end of the year would be $10,600 (= $10,000 + $1000 − $400).

It may be helpful to picture a bathtub. The level of water in the bathtub (the stock of capital) depends on the flow of water into the bathtub through the input faucet (gross investment) minus the flow of water out of the bathtub down the drain (depreciation). As long as the flow in exceeds the flow out, the water level in the bathtub (the stock of capital) will increase.

Higher saving, which leads to higher gross investment, will therefore tend to increase the stock of capital available for production. As the stock of capital grows, however, there typically will be more depreciation, because there is more capital (building and equipment) to depreciate. It is the difference between gross investment and depreciation—*net investment*—that ultimately determines the change in the stock of capital for the economy, the level of real wages, and output. In our example, net investment is $1,000 − $400 = $600.

How Do Population Growth, Government, and Trade Affect Capital Deepening?

So far, we've considered the simplest economy. Let's consider a more realistic economy that includes population growth, a government, and trade.

First, consider the effects of population growth: A larger labor force will allow the economy to produce more total output. However, with a fixed amount of capital and an increasing labor force, the amount of capital per worker will be less. With less capital per worker, output per worker will also be less, because each worker has fewer machines to use. This is an illustration of the principle of diminishing returns.

PRINCIPLE OF DIMINISHING RETURNS

Suppose that output is produced with two or more inputs and that we increase one input while holding the other inputs fixed. Beyond some point—called the *point of diminishing returns*—output will increase at a decreasing rate.

Consider India, the world's second most populous country, with over a billion people. Although India has a large labor force, its amount of capital per worker is low. With sharp diminishing returns to labor, per capita output in India is low, only $2,960 per person.

The government can affect the process of capital deepening in several ways through its policies of spending and taxation. Suppose the government taxed its citizens so that it could fight a war, pay its legislators higher salaries, or give foreign aid to needy countries—in other words, to engage in government consumption spending. The higher taxes will reduce total income. If consumers save a fixed fraction of their income, total private savings (savings from the nongovernmental sector) will fall. This taxation drains the private sector of savings that would have been used for capital deepening.

Now suppose the government took all the extra tax revenues and invested them in valuable infrastructure, such as roads, buildings, and airports. These infrastructure investments add to the capital stock. We illustrate this idea in Figure 8.4. If consumers were saving 20 percent of their incomes and the government collected $100 in taxes from each taxpayer, private saving and investment would fall by $20 per taxpayer, but government investment in the infrastructure would increase by a full $100 per taxpayer. In other words, the government "forces" consumers (by taxing them) to invest an additional $80 in infrastructure that they otherwise wouldn't invest. The net result is an increase in total social investment (private plus government) of $80 per taxpayer.

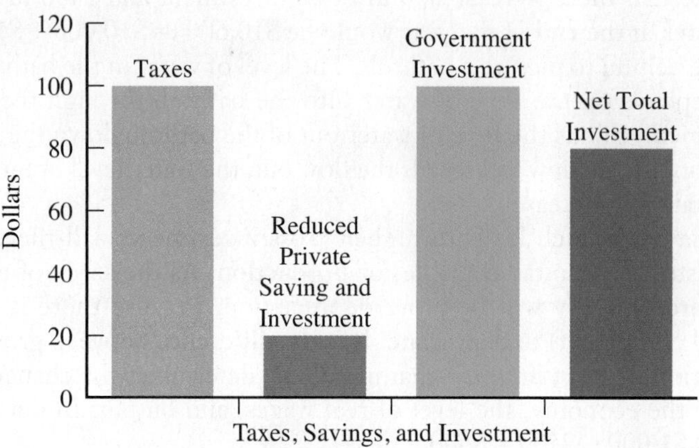

► **FIGURE 8.4**
Taxes and Government Investment
If the government raises taxes by $100 and the people tend to save 20 percent of changes in income, then private savings and investment will fall by $20. However, if the government invests the funds, total investment—private and public—will increase by $80.

Finally, the foreign sector can affect capital deepening. The United States, Canada, and Australia built their vast railroad systems in the nineteenth century by running *trade deficits*—selling fewer goods and services to the rest of the world than they were buying—and financing this gap by borrowing. This enabled them to purchase the large amount of capital needed to build their rail networks and grow at more rapid rates by deepening capital. Eventually, these economies had to pay back the funds they had borrowed from abroad by running *trade surpluses*—selling more goods and services to the rest of the world than they were buying from abroad. But because economic growth had increased their GDP and wealth, the three countries were able to afford to pay back the borrowed funds. Therefore, this approach to financing deepening capital was a reasonable strategy for them to pursue.

Not all trade deficits promote capital deepening, however. Suppose a country runs a trade deficit because it wants to buy more consumer goods. The country would be borrowing from abroad, but there would be no additional capital deepening—just additional consumption spending. When the country is forced to pay back the funds, there will be no additional GDP to help foot the bill. In order to fund current consumption, the country will be poorer in the future.

8.3 The Key Role of Technological Progress

The other mechanism affecting economic growth is technological progress. Economists use the term *technological progress* in a very specific way: It means an economy operates more efficiently by producing more output without using any more inputs.

In practice, technological progress can take many forms. The invention of the light bulb made it possible to read and work indoors at night, the invention of the thermometer assisted doctors and nurses in their diagnoses, and the invention of disposable diapers made life easier at home. All these examples—and you could provide many more—enable society to produce more output without more labor or more capital. With higher output per person, we enjoy a higher standard of living.

We can think of technological progress as the birth of new ideas. These new ideas enable us to rearrange our economic affairs and become more productive. Not all technological innovations are necessarily major scientific breakthroughs; some are much more basic. An employee of a soft-drink company who discovers a new and popular flavor for a soft drink is engaged in technological progress, just like scientists and engineers. Even simple, commonsense ideas from workers or managers can help a business use its capital and labor more efficiently to deliver a better product to consumers at a lower price. For example, a store manager may decide that rearranging the layout of merchandise and location of cash registers helps customers find products and pay for them more quickly and easily. This change is also technological progress. As long as there are new ideas, inventions, and new ways of doing things, the economy can become more productive and per capita output can increase.

How Do We Measure Technological Progress?

If someone asked you how much of the increase in your standard of living was due to technological progress, how would you answer? Robert Solow, a Nobel Laureate in economics from the Massachusetts Institute of Technology, developed a method for measuring technological progress in an economy. Like most good ideas, his theory was simple. It was based on the idea of a production function.

You know from Chapter 7 that the production function links inputs to outputs:

$$Y = F(K, L)$$

where output (Y) is produced from capital (K) and labor (L), which are linked through the production function (F). What Solow did was include in the production function some measure of technological progress, A:

$$Y = F(K, L, A)$$

Increases in A represent technological progress. Higher values of A mean that more output is produced from the same level of inputs K and L. If we could find some way to measure A, we could estimate how much technological progress affects output.

Solow noted that over any period we can observe increases in capital, labor and output. Using these we can measure technological progress indirectly. We first ask how much of the change in output can be explained by contributions from increases in the amount of capital and labor used. Whatever growth we cannot explain in this way must therefore be caused by technological progress. The method Solow developed to measure the contributions to economic growth from capital, labor, and technological progress is called **growth accounting**.

growth accounting
A method to determine the contribution to economic growth from increased capital, labor, and technological progress.

Figure 8.5 illustrates the relative contributions of these growth sources for the U.S. economy from 1929 to 1982 using growth accounting, based on a classic study by the economist Edward Denison. During this period, total output grew at a rate of nearly 3 percent. Because capital and labor growth are measured at 0.56 and 1.34 percent per year, respectively, the remaining portion of output growth, 1.02 percent per year, must be due to technological progress. That means approximately 35 percent of output growth came directly from technological progress.

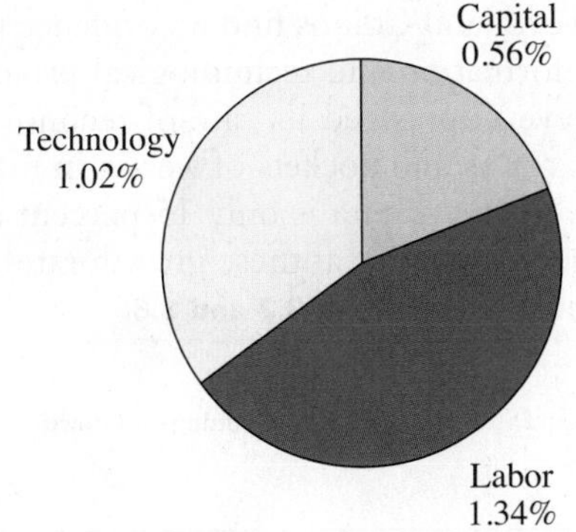

◀ **FIGURE 8.5**
Contributions to Real GDP Growth, 1929–1982 (average annual percentage rates)
SOURCE: Edward F. Denison, Trends in American Economic Growth 1929–1982 *(Washington, D.C.: The Brookings Institution, 1985).*

Other recent estimates give a similar picture of the contribution of technological progress to economic growth. For example, the Bureau of Labor Statistics estimates that between 1987 and 2007 technological progress accounted for 1.0 percentage points of economic growth in the private nonfarm business sector, very similar to Denison's estimates.

Using Growth Accounting

Growth accounting is a useful tool for understanding different aspects of economic growth. As an example, economic growth slowed throughout the entire world during the 1970s. Using growth accounting methods, economists typically found the slowdown could not be attributed to changes in the quality or quantity of labor inputs or to capital deepening. Either a slowdown in technological progress or other factors not directly included in the analysis, such as higher worldwide energy prices, must have been responsible. This led economists to suspect that higher energy prices were the primary explanation for the reduction in economic growth.

Review the two other applications of how economists use growth accounting. The first compares growth in China and India, the second explores how growth accounting can be used when capital is hard to measure.

application 3

SOURCES OF GROWTH IN CHINA AND INDIA

APPLYING THE CONCEPTS #3: How can we use economic analysis to understand the sources of growth in different countries?

China and India are the two most populous countries in the world and have also grown very rapidly in recent years. From 1978 to 2004, GDP in China grew at the astounding rate of 9.3 percent per year while India's GDP grew at a lower but still robust rate of 5.4 percent per year. What were the sources of this growth? Economists Barry Bosworth from the Brookings Institution and Susan Collins from the University of Michigan used growth accounting to answer this question.

Employment in China and India both grew at 2 percent per year over the period, so the remaining differences must be attributed to capital deepening and technological progress. Bosworth and Collins in turn broke capital deepening into two parts: increases in physical capital (buildings, machines, and equipment) and increases in human capital (the knowledge of workers, as measured by their educational attainment). Their analysis revealed that China's more rapid growth was primarily caused by more rapid accumulation of physical capital and more rapid technological progress. The contributions from human capital for each country were similar. Why did China grow faster than India over this 26-year period? Simply put, China invested much more than India in physical capital and was able to increase its technological progress at a more rapid rate.

Looking ahead, Bosworth and Collins find no evidence that growth in China and India is slowing. Capital formation and technological progress is still rapid in both countries and India has even improved its rate of technological advance in recent years. Despite this rapid growth and pockets of wealth in major cities, both countries are still poor: Chinese GNP per capita is only 15 percent and India's GDP is only 8 percent of U.S. GNP per capita. But at these growth rates, the gap will diminish in the coming decades. **Related to Exercises 3.3 and 3.6.**

SOURCE: Based on Barry Bosworth and Susan M. Collins, "Accounting for Growth: Comparing China and India," *Journal of Economic Perspectives* (Winter 2008): 45–66.

Before we complete our discussion of growth accounting, we will introduce one more term. In analyses of the sources of economic growth, a common statistic reported about the U.S. economy is **labor productivity**. Defined as output per hour of work, labor productivity is a simple measure of how much a typical worker can produce given the amount of capital in the economy and the state of technological progress.

labor productivity
Output produced per hour of work.

Figure 8.6 shows U.S. productivity growth for different periods since 1947. From 1947 to the worldwide oil crisis in 1973, labor productivity grew rapidly. Productivity growth fell in the remainder of the 1970s and slowly increased over the next two decades. Since 2007, productivity growth has also slowed from recent trends, partly due to the recession. Economists have used growth accounting to help explain these trends in productivity growth in the United States. Economic research suggests that the oil shocks in the 1970s reduced technological progress but the information revolution in the 1980s and 1990s led to a resurgence of technological progress.

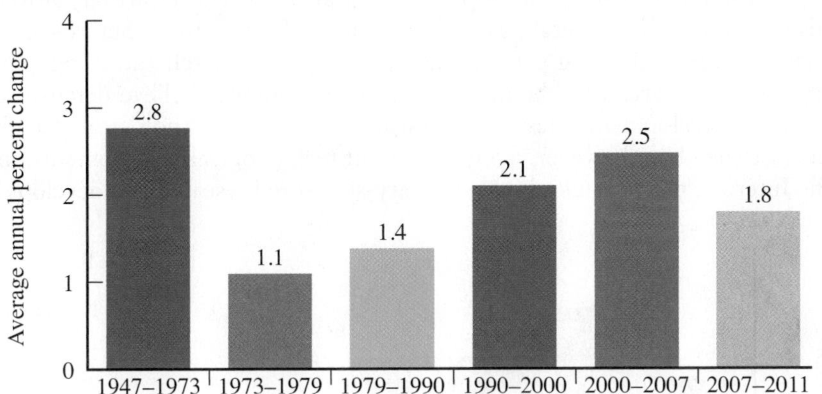

◄ **FIGURE 8.6**
U.S. Annual Productivity Growth, 1947–2011
Productivity growth was very high in the United States until the first oil shock in 1973. It slowly began to increase over the next several decades.
SOURCE: Bureau of Labor Statistics, 2012.

application 4

GROWTH ACCOUNTING AND INTANGIBLE CAPITAL

APPLYING THE CONCEPTS #4: How do you measure the technological revolution?

Traditional growth theory focused on easily measured items, such as hours of work or the amount of physical capital. But as our economy advances, we all recognize that the factors that contribute to production are harder to measure. For example, why has Google had such a big impact on our economy? They do not produce machines or cars—they mostly produce ideas and information-related products. Can we still use growth accounting in this new world?

A number of economists have thought long and hard about this problem and have made considerable progress in adapting growth accounting to this new environment. The idea they use is to create a measure of "intangible" capital based on expenditures on research and development, marketing, design, and customer support. Once they have this measure of intangible capital, they can use it along with conventional measures of capital and labor to understand the sources of economic growth.

Estimates by economists Carol Corrado and Charles Hulten suggest that intangible capital is an important source of economic growth. They found that in recent years, the contribution from intangible capital actually exceeded the contribution from traditional or tangible capital. Together, the two capital measures also contributed more to economic growth than technological progress. **Related to Exercises 3.7 and 3.8.**

SOURCES: Based on Carol A. Corrado and Charles R. Hulten, "How Do You Measure a 'Technological Revolution'?" *American Economic Review, Papers and Proceedings*, May 2010, pp. 99–104.

8.4 What Causes Technological Progress?

Because technological progress is an important source of growth, we want to know how it occurs and what government policies can do to promote it. Economists have identified a variety of factors that may influence the pace of technological progress in an economy.

Research and Development Funding

One way for a country to induce more technological progress in its economy is to pay for it. If the government or large firms employ workers and scientists to advance the frontiers of knowledge in basic sciences, their work can lead to technological progress in the long run. Figure 8.7 presents data on the spending on research and development as a percent of GDP for seven major countries for 1999. The United States has the highest number of scientists and engineers in the world. However, although it spends the most money overall, as a percent of GDP the United States spends less than Japan. Moreover, a big part of U.S. spending on research and development is in defense-related areas, unlike in Japan. Some economists believe defense-related research and development is less likely to lead to long-run technological change than nondefense spending; however, many important technological developments, including the Internet, partly resulted from military-sponsored research and development.

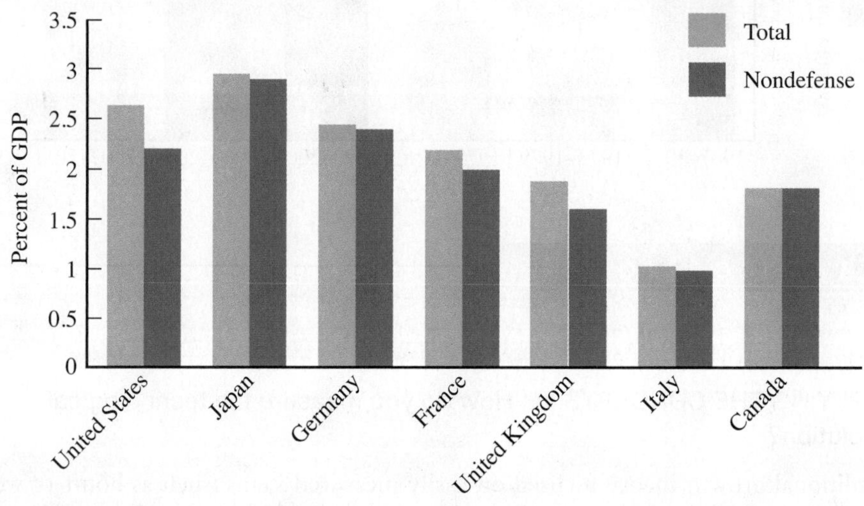

► **FIGURE 8.7**
Research and Development as a Percent of GDP, 1999
The United States spends more total money than any other country on research and development. However, when the spending is measured as a percentage of each nation's GDP, Japan spends more. A big part of U.S. spending on research and development is in defense-related areas.
SOURCE: National Science Foundation, National Patterns of R&D Resources, *2002, Washington D.C.*

Monopolies That Spur Innovation

The radical notion that monopolies spur innovation was put forth by economist Joseph Schumpeter. In Schumpeter's view, a firm will try to innovate—that is, come up with new products and more efficient ways to produce existing products—only if it reaps a reward. The reward a firm seeks from its innovations is high profit, and it can obtain a high profit if it is the sole seller, or monopolist, for the product. Other firms will try to break the firm's monopoly through more innovation, a process Schumpeter called **creative destruction.** Schumpeter believed that by allowing firms to compete to become monopolies, society benefits from increased innovation.

creative destruction
The view that a firm will try to come up with new products and more efficient ways to produce products to earn monopoly profits.

Governments do allow temporary monopolies for new ideas by issuing patents. A *patent* allows the inventor of a product to have a monopoly until the term of the patent expires, which in the United States is now 20 years. With a patent, we tolerate some monopoly power (the power to raise prices that comes with limited competition) in the hope of spurring innovation.

An idea related to patents that is becoming increasingly important is the need to protect intellectual property rights. Information technology has made possible the free flow of products and ideas around the world. Publishers of both books and computer software face problems of unauthorized copying, particularly in some developing countries. While residents of those countries clearly benefit from inexpensively copied books or software, producers in the developed countries then face reduced incentives to enter the market. Even in the United States, pirated music and movies pose a threat to the viability of the entertainment industry. Large and profitable firms may continue to produce despite unauthorized copying, but other firms may be discouraged. The United States has put piracy and unauthorized reproduction among its top agenda items in recent trade talks with several countries.

The Scale of the Market

Adam Smith stressed that the size of a market was important for economic development. In larger markets, firms have more incentives to come up with new products and new methods of production. Just as Schumpeter suggested, the lure of profits guides the activities of firms, and larger markets provide firms the opportunity to make larger profits. This supplies another rationale for free trade. With free trade, markets are larger, and there is more incentive to engage in technological progress.

Induced Innovations

Some economists have emphasized that innovations come about through inventive activity designed specifically to reduce costs. This is known as *induced innovation*. For example, during the nineteenth century in the United States, the largest single cost in agriculture was wages. Ingenious farmers and inventors came up with many different machines and methods to cut back on the amount of labor required.

Education, Human Capital, and the Accumulation of Knowledge

Education can contribute to economic growth in two ways. First, the increased knowledge and skills of people complement our current investments in physical capital. Second, education can enable the workforce in an economy to use its skills to develop new ideas or to copy ideas or import them from abroad. Consider a developing country today. In principle, it has at its disposal the vast accumulated knowledge of the developed economies. But using this knowledge probably requires a skilled workforce—one reason why many developing countries send their best students to educational institutions in developed countries.

Increasing knowledge and skills are part of human capital—an investment in human beings. Human capital is as important, maybe even more important, than physical capital. Many economists, including Nobel Laureate Gary Becker of the University of Chicago, have studied human capital in detail.

A classic example of human capital is the investment a student makes to attend college. The costs of attending college consist of the direct out-of-pocket costs (tuition and fees) plus the opportunity costs of forgone earnings while at school. The benefits of attending college are the higher wages and more interesting jobs offered to college graduates compared to high-school graduates. Individuals decide to attend college when these benefits exceed the costs, and it is a rational economic decision. A similar calculation faces a newly graduated doctor who must decide whether to pursue a specialty. Will the forgone earnings of a general physician (which are quite substantial) be worth the time spent learning a specialty that will eventually result in extra income? We can analyze investments in health and nutrition within the same framework. The benefits of regular exercise and watching your weight are a healthier lifestyle and higher energy level.

Human capital theory has two implications for understanding economic growth. First, not all labor is equal. When economists measure the labor input in a country, they must adjust for differing levels of education. These levels of education reflect past investments in education and skills; individuals with higher educational levels will, on average, be more productive. Second, health and fitness also affect productivity. In developing countries, economists have found a strong correlation between the height of individuals (reflecting their health) and the wages they can earn in the farming sector.

Human capital theory can also serve as a basis for important public policy decisions. Should a developing country invest in capital (either public or private) or in education? The poorest developing countries lack good sanitation systems, effective transportation, and capital investment for agriculture and industry. However, the best use of investment funds may not be for bridges, sewer systems, and roads, but for human capital and education. Studies demonstrate that the returns from investing in education are extremely high in developing countries. The gains from elementary and secondary education, in particular, often exceed the gains from more conventional investments. In developing countries, an extra year in school can often raise individuals' wages by 15 to 20 percent a year.

New Growth Theory

For many years, economists who studied technological progress typically did so independently of economists who studied models of economic growth. But starting in the mid-1980s, several economists, including Nobel Laureate Robert E. Lucas of the University of Chicago and Paul Romer of Stanford University, began to develop models of growth that contained technological progress as essential features. Their work helped to initiate what is known as **new growth theory**, which accounts for technological progress within a model of economic growth.

new growth theory
Modern theories of growth that try to explain the origins of technological progress.

In this field, economists study, for example, how incentives for research and development, new product development, or international trade interact with the accumulation of physical capital. New growth theory enables economists to address policy issues, such as whether subsidies for research and development are socially justified and whether policies that place fewer taxes on income earned from investment will spur economic growth or increase economic welfare. Current research in economic growth now takes place within a broad framework that includes explanations of technological progress. As an example, new growth theory suggests that investment in

application 5

THE ROLE OF POLITICAL FACTORS IN ECONOMIC GROWTH

APPLYING THE CONCEPTS #5: How do varying political institutions affect economic growth?

Economist Daron Acemoglu of the Massachusetts Institute of Technology has written extensively about the role of political institutions and economic growth. Acemoglu distinguishes broadly between two types of political institutions: *authoritarian* institutions, such as monarchies, dictatorships, or tightly controlled oligarchies, and *participatory* institutions, such as constitutionally limited monarchies and democracies. History has witnessed growth under both types of regimes. At various points in time, China, Spain, Turkey, and ancient Greece and Rome all exhibited technological innovation and economic growth.

But transformative economic growth, such as the world witnessed with the Industrial Revolution that began in western Europe in the late 1700s, typically requires more participatory institutions. The key reason is that sustained technological progress is disruptive and authoritarian regimes have difficulty coping with all the subsequent changes. Acemoglu highlights the fall in the old, authoritarian regimes in Europe and the rise of constitutional or limited monarchies that set the preconditions for the birth of the Industrial Revolution.

Acemoglu's theory does raise important questions for today. Can China, with its authoritarian political culture, continue to grow without eventual political transformation? If that does eventually come, can it be absorbed peacefully within the society? **Related to Exercise 4.6.**

SOURCE: Based on Daron Acemoglu, epilogue to *Introduction to Modern Economic Growth* (University Press, 2009).

comprehensive education in a developing country will lead to permanent increases in the rate of technological progress as the workforce will be better able to incorporate new ideas and technologies into the workplace.

Some researchers also suggest the type of education might also matter for technological innovation. Philippe Aghion of Harvard University and Peter Howitt of Brown University make the case that when a country is far behind the world's technological frontier, it is best for that country to invest in relatively basic education so that the workforce can essentially copy the changes that are occurring in the more advanced economies. But once an economy reaches the world's technological frontier, investment in the most advanced higher education might be most advantageous.[4]

New growth theory suggests that any social factor influencing the willingness of individuals to pursue technological advancement will be a key to understanding economic growth. Can cultural factors also play a role? The historical sociologist Max Weber argued that changes in religious beliefs could help us understand growth, as he emphasized how the rise of Protestantism, with its emphasis on the individual, set the stage for the Industrial Revolution in Europe. This thesis has always been controversial because the links between changes in religious beliefs and changes in economic or other behaviors are not well understood. More recently, Professor Gregory Clark has emphasized how the growth of middle-class values in England could possibly explain why the Industrial Revolution began there.

application 6

CULTURE, EVOLUTION, AND ECONOMIC GROWTH

APPLYING THE CONCEPT #6: Did culture or evolution spark the Industrial Revolution?

In studying the economic history of England before the Industrial Revolution, Professor Gregory Clark discovered an interesting fact. Examining archival data on wills and estates, he found that children of the more affluent members of English society were more likely to survive than those of the less affluent. Coupled with the slow growth of population over several centuries, this differential survival of the wealthy had the effect of creating downward mobility for the rich, as their sons and daughters increasingly populated the society.

According to Professor Clark, this change had profound effects on English society. The cultural habits of the rich filtered through the entire society. Social virtues such as thrift, prudence, and hard work became more commonplace, while impulsive and violent behaviors were reduced. Eventually, these changes in culture became sufficiently pronounced that a qualitative change took place in society. Individuals now were able to take advantage of new developments in science and technology and embrace new technologies and social change.

Economists Oded Galor and Omer Moav suggest that development can be viewed in more traditional evolutionary terms. They argue that at some point during the human evolutionary process, families that had fewer children but invested more in them gained a competitive advantage in the evolutionary cycle. The offspring of these families had more human capital and more easily adapted to technological progress and the other changes that were taking place in societies. Human genetic evolution, in their view, set the stage for the Industrial Revolution. Both views share some similarities. According to Clark, the evolution was primarily cultural, whereas for Galor and Moav it was genetic. In both cases, however, humans transformed themselves as the Industrial Revolution began. **Related to Exercise 4.10.**

SOURCES: Based on Gregory Clark, *A Farewell to Alms* (Princeton: Princeton University Press, 2007) and Oded Galor and Omer Moav, "Natural Selection and the Origin of Economic Growth," *Quarterly Journal of Economics* (November 2002): 1133–1191.

8.5 A Key Governmental Role: Providing the Correct Incentives and Property Rights

As we discussed in Chapter 3, governments play a critical role in a market economy. They must enforce the rules of the market economy, using police powers to ensure that contracts are upheld, individual property rights are enforced, and firms can enter safely into economic transactions. Although we may take these features of our economy for granted, not all countries enjoy the benefits of clear enforcement of property rights.

What is the connection between property rights and economic growth? Without clear property rights, there are no proper incentives to invest in the future—the essence of economic growth. Suppose, for example, that you lived on land that needed costly improvements in order to be made valuable. You might be willing to make the investment in these improvements if you were sure you would gain the economic benefits from making them. But suppose there was a risk someone else would reap the benefits—in that case, you would not have incentive to invest.

Clear property rights are, unfortunately, lacking in many developing countries throughout the world. As many economists have argued, their absence has severely impeded the growth of these economies.

Governments also have a broader role in designing the institutions in which individuals and firms work, save, and invest. Economists have increasingly recognized the importance of these institutions in determining economic growth. For example, the residents of Hong Kong link their rapid economic growth to free and open institutions that provide the right incentives for technological innovations. They wanted to preserve these institutions after they officially became part of China in 1997 and have indeed been successful in maintaining an open society.

But for many countries, growth has been more elusive. For many years, international organizations such as the World Bank—a consortium of countries created to promote development—have tried a variety of diverse methods to assist developing countries. These have included increases in foreign aid, infusions of new machinery, promotion of universal education, and efforts to stem population growth. Despite these efforts, some areas of the world, such as sub-Saharan Africa, have failed to grow at all.

William Easterly, a former World Bank economist, believes the World Bank and other international organizations have failed to take into account one of the basic laws of economics: Individuals and firms respond to incentives. According to Easterly, governments in developing countries have failed to provide the proper economic environment that would motivate individuals and firms to take actions that promote economic development.[5] As an example, providing free schooling is not enough—individuals need to know their investments in education will pay off in the future in terms of higher incomes or better jobs. Without the prospect that it will lead to an improvement in their lives, individuals will not make the effort to obtain an education.

What else can go wrong? Governments in developing countries often adopt policies that effectively tax exports, pursue policies that lead to rampant inflation, and enforce laws that inhibit the growth of the banking and financial sectors. The results are predictable: fewer exports, an uncertain financial environment, and reduced saving and investment. All these outcomes can cripple an economy's growth prospects. Sometimes they are based on bad economic advice. Other times, racial or ethnic groups in polarized societies use the economic system to take advantage of their rivals.

What can be done? In Easterly's view, the World Bank and other international organizations need to stop searching for the magic bullet for development. Instead, they should hold governments responsible for creating the proper economic environment. With the right incentives, Easterly believes individuals and firms in developing countries will take actions that promote economic growth.

application 7

LACK OF PROPERTY RIGHTS HINDERS GROWTH IN PERU

APPLYING THE CONCEPTS #7: Why are clear property rights important for economic growth in developing countries?

On the hills surrounding Lima, Peru, and many other South American cities, large numbers of residents live in urban slums, many having taken over these lands through "urban invasions." Many families have resided in these dwellings for a long time, and most have basic water, sewage, and electricity. But what they don't have is clear titles to their properties.

Hernando DeSoto, a Peruvian economist and author of *The Mystery of Capital*, has studied the consequences of "informal ownership" in detail. He argues that throughout the developing world, property is often held without clear title. Without this evidence of ownership, people are not willing to make long-term investments to improve their lives. But there are other important consequences as well.

Economists recognize that strong credit systems—the ability to borrow and lend easily—are critical to the health of developing economies. But without clear title, people cannot use property as collateral (or security) for loans. As a consequence, the poor may in fact be living on very valuable land, but are unable to borrow against that land to start a new business. Also, the types of investments made will depend on the availability of credit. DeSoto observed that producing palm oil in Peru is very profitable, but it takes time and depends upon the ability to borrow funds. Production of coca paste—an ingredient of cocaine—does not take as much time and does not depend on finance. It is also a plague on the developed world. Switching farmers away from production of coca paste to palm oil requires improvements in finance, which are very difficult without clear property rights. **Related to Exercise 5.7.**

SOURCE: Based on Hernando DeSoto, *The Mystery of Capital: Why Capitalism Triumphs in the West and Fails Everywhere Else* (New York: Basic Books, 2000).

SUMMARY

In this chapter, we explored the mechanisms of economic growth. Although economists do not have a complete understanding of what leads to growth, they regard increases in capital per worker, technological progress, human capital, and governmental institutions as key factors. Here are the main points to remember:

1 *Per capita GDP* varies greatly throughout the world. There is debate about whether poorer countries in the world are converging in per capita incomes to richer countries.

2 Economies grow through two basic mechanisms: *capital deepening* and *technological progress*. Capital deepening is an increase in capital per worker. Technological progress is an increase in output with no additional increases in inputs.

3 Ongoing technological progress will lead to sustained economic growth.

4 Various theories try to explain the origins of technological progress and determine how we can promote it. They include spending on research and development, *creative destruction*, the scale of the market, induced inventions, and education and the accumulation of knowledge, including investments in human capital.

5 Governments can play a key role in designing institutions that promote economic growth, including providing secure property rights.

KEY TERMS

capital deepening, p. 160
convergence, p. 163
creative destruction, p. 172
growth accounting, p. 169
growth rate, p. 161
human capital, p. 160
labor productivity, p. 171
new growth theory, p. 174
real GDP per capita, p. 161
rule of 70, p. 161
saving, p. 166
technological progress, p. 160

EXERCISES

All problems are assignable in MyEconLab; exercises that update with real-time data are marked with **.**

8.1 Economic Growth Rates

1.1 To gauge living standards across countries with populations of different sizes, economists use ________.

1.2 In poor countries, the relative prices for nontraded goods (such as household services) to traded goods (such as jewelry) are ________ than in rich countries.

1.3 Economists who have studied economic growth find strong evidence for convergence among countries between 1980 and 2000. ________ (True/False)

1.4 At a 2 percent annual growth rate in GDP per capita, it will take ________ years for GDP per capita to double.

1.5 **Learning to Look Up Data.** Go to the Website for World Economic Outlook Database of the International Monetary Fund at http://www.imf.org/external/pubs/ft/weo/2012/01/weodata/index.aspx and create a table for 10 countries of your choosing showing GDP per capita adjusted for purchasing power parity in current international dollars for 2010 and 2011. Start by clicking on the "By Countries" link and then make your choices and prepare your report.

1.6 **Will the Poorer Country Catch Up?** Suppose one country has a GDP that is one-eighth the GDP of its richer neighbor. But the poorer country grows at 10 percent a year, while the richer country grows at 2 percent a year. In 35 years, which country will have a higher GDP? (Hint: Use the rule of 70.)

1.7 **Understanding Convergence in a Figure.** Suppose the line in Figure 8.2 was horizontal. What would that tell us about economic convergence?

1.8 **Growth in Per Capita GDP.** The growth rate of real GDP per capita equals the growth rate of real GDP minus the growth rate of the population. If the growth rate of the population is 1 percent per year, how fast must real GDP grow for real GDP per capita to double in 14 years?

1.9 **Economic Growth and Global Warning.** Basing your answer on the research reported in the text, is it likely that India is more vulnerable now to increases in temperatures than it will be in 20 years? (Related to Application 1 on page 164.)

1.10 **Equality and Growth: Reverse Causation?** Can you think of reasons why a sustained period of economic growth leads to more equality? In this case, sustained growth would cause equality. (Related to Application 2 on page 165.)

1.11 **Comparing Economic Performance Using International GDP Data.** The Web site for the Penn World Tables (http://pwt.econ.upenn.edu) contains historical economic data. Using this link, compare the relative growth performance for real GDP per capita of France and Japan from 1950 to 2000. Do the data support the theory of convergence for these two countries?

8.2 Capital Deepening

2.1 In an economy with no government sector or foreign sector, saving must equal investment because
- **a.** total demand is equal to consumption and investment.
- **b.** total income is equal to consumption and saving.
- **c.** total income is equal to total demand.
- **d.** All of the above
- **e.** None of the above

2.2 If everything else is held equal, an increase in the size of the population will ________ total output and ________ per capita output.

2.3 If the private sector saves 10 percent of its income and the government raises taxes by $200 to finance public investments, total investment—private and public investment—will increase by ________.

2.4 If a country runs a trade surplus to finance increased current consumption, it will have to reduce consumption in the future to pay back its borrowings. ________ (True/False)

2.5 **Policies That Promote Capital Deepening.** Which of the following will promote economic growth through capital deepening?
- **a.** Higher taxes used to finance universal health care

b. Increased imports to purchase new DVD players for consumers

c. Increased imports to purchase supercomputers for industry

2.6 **Diminishing Returns to Capital and Real Wages.** Explain why this statement is wrong: "Since capital is subject to diminishing returns, an increase in the supply of capital will reduce real wages."

2.7 **Government Spending, Taxes, and Investment.** Suppose a government places a 10 percent tax on incomes and spends half the money from taxes on investment and half on public consumption goods, such as military parades. Individuals save 20 percent of their income and consume the rest. Does total investment (public and private) increase or decrease in this case?

2.8 **Trade Deficits: Capital Deepening or Consumption?** Suppose a country that had balanced trade began to run a trade deficit. At the same time, consumption as a share of GDP increased but the investment share did not. Do you think there was an increase in capital deepening?

8.3 The Key Role of Technological Progress

3.1 Robert Solow added __________ to the conventional production function to account for technological change.

3.2 Once we account for changes in the labor force, __________ is the next biggest source of the growth of GDP in the United States.

3.3 China has a higher rate of technological progress than India. __________ (True/False) (Related to Application 3 on page 170.)

3.4 Labor productivity growth was higher from 2007–2011 compared to recent years. (True/False)

3.5 **Technological Progress in Banking.** Computers have revolutionized banking for consumers through the growth of ATMs and electronic bill paying capabilities. Why might not all of these improvements for consumers be counted as technological progress?

3.6 **Foreign Investment and Technological Progress.** Many economists believe countries that open themselves to foreign investment of plant and equipment will benefit in terms of increased technological change because local companies will learn from the foreign companies. In the last several decades, China has been more open to foreign investment than India. Explain how this is consistent with the two countries' patterns of economic growth. (Related to Application 3 on page 170.)

3.7 **Coke and Pepsi.** Soft-drink companies spend a considerable amount of money on marketing. Explain why these expenditures could be considered a form of capital. (Related to Application 4 on page 171.)

3.8 **Trends in Intangible Capital.** The authors of the study in Application 4 found that intangible capital became more important relative to conventional capital in terms of accounting for economic growth in recent years. Can you explain their finding? (Related to Application 4 on page 171.)

3.9 **Health Insurance, Wages, and Compensation.** In recent years, total compensation of employees—including benefits—has grown, but wages, not including benefits, have not. Explain why this may have occurred, taking into account that many employers provide health insurance to their employees and health-care costs have grown more rapidly than GDP. Is health insurance "free" to employees?

8.4 What Causes Technological Progress?

4.1 Who developed the theory of scale of the market?

a. Joseph Schumpeter

b. Milton Friedman

c. Adam Smith

d. John Maynard Keynes

4.2 Investment in human capital includes purchases of computers used by professors. __________ (True/False)

4.3 Which of the following may influence technological progress?

a. The scale of the market

b. Monopolies

c. Research and development spending

d. All of the above

4.4 A policy of not enforcing patents or copyrights would __________ the incentive to be innovative.

4.5 **Cutting the Length of Patents.** Suppose a group of consumer activists claims drug companies earn excessive profits because of the patents they have on drugs. The activists advocate cutting the length of time that a drug company can hold a patent to five years. They argue that this will lead to lower prices for drugs because competitors will enter the market after the five-year period. Do you see any drawbacks to this proposal?

4.6 **Dictatorships and Economic Growth.** Discuss this quote: "With a strong economy, dictators could raise more money for armies and police to help keep themselves in power. Therefore, dictators should welcome rapid economic growth." (Related to Application 5 on page 174.)

4.7 **Green Energy and Induced Innovations** Suppose a country reduced imports of oil in order to raise the price of oil within the country. How would this affect the incentive to develop green energy technologies?

4.8 **Height and Weight during Rapid Industrialization.** Economic historians have found that the average height of individuals in both the United States and the United Kingdom fell during the mid-nineteenth century before rising again. This was a period of rapid industrialization as well as migration into urban areas. What factors do you think might account for this fall in height and how would it affect your evaluation of economic welfare during the period?

4.9 **Going to Medical School at the Age of 50.** Although we might admire someone who decides to attend medical school at the age of 50, explain using human capital theory why this is so rare.

4.10 **Timing and Cultural Explanations of Economic Growth.** Some critics of cultural theories of economic growth note that some societies can suddenly start to grow very rapidly with no obvious accompanying cultural changes. How well does Professor Gregory Clark's theory fit the rapid growth in some East Asian economies in recent years? (Related to Application 6 on page 175.)

8.5 A Key Governmental Role: Providing the Correct Incentives and Property Rights

5.1 Clear property rights reduce growth in an economy because producers are not able to freely use innovations. __________ (True/False)

5.2 Which of the following methods has the World Bank not tried to assist developing countries?

a. Increases in foreign aid

b. Infusions of new machinery

c. Promotion of universal education

d. Promotion of population growth

5.3 The return from education in developing countries is often higher than in developed countries. __________ (True/False)

5.4 New growth theory suggests that consumption spending will lead to permanent increases in the rate of technological progress. __________ (True/False)

5.5 **Diversity and Economic Growth.** Some economists and political scientists have suggested that when communities are more racially or ethnically diverse, they invest less in education and spend more on private goods. Assuming this theory is true, what are the consequences for economic growth?

5.6 **The "Brain Drain" and Incentives for Education.** Some economists are concerned about the "brain drain," the phenomenon in which highly educated workers leave developing countries to work in developed countries. Other economists have argued that "brain drain" could create incentives for others in the country to secure increased education, and many of the newly educated might not emigrate. Explain why the "brain drain" could lead to increased education among the remaining residents. How would you test this theory?

5.7 **Secure Property Rights and Work outside the Home.** With secure land titles, parents can work outside the home (rather than guarding their property) and earn higher incomes. Explain why this might reduce child labor. (Related to Application 7 on page 177.)

APPENDIX A

A MODEL OF CAPITAL DEEPENING

Here's a simple model showing the links among saving, depreciation, and capital deepening. Developed by Nobel Laureate Robert Solow of the Massachusetts Institute of Technology, the Solow model will help us understand more fully the critical role technological progress must play in economic growth. We rely on one of our basic principles of economics to help explain the model as well as make a few simplifying assumptions. We assume constant population and no government or foreign sector. In the chapter, we discussed the qualitative effects of population growth, government, and the foreign sector on capital deepening. Here we focus solely on the relationships among saving, depreciation, and capital deepening. Figure 8A.1 plots the relationship in the economy between output and the stock of capital, holding the labor force constant. Notice that output increases as the stock of capital increases, but at a decreasing rate. This is an illustration of the principle of diminishing returns.

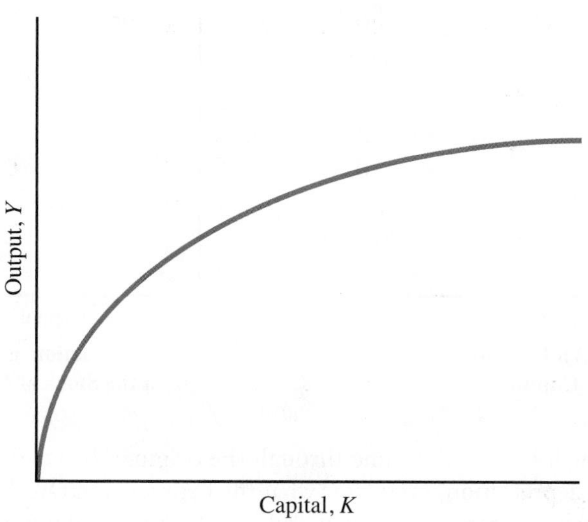

▲ **FIGURE 8A.1**
Diminishing Returns to Capital
Holding labor constant, increases in the stock of capital increase output, but at a decreasing rate.

PRINCIPLE OF DIMINISHING RETURNS

Suppose output is produced with two or more inputs and we increase one input while holding the other inputs fixed. Beyond some point—called the *point of diminishing returns*—output will increase at a decreasing rate.

Increasing the stock of capital while holding the labor force constant will increase output, but at a decreasing rate.

As Figure 8A.1 indicates, output increases with the stock of capital. But what causes the stock of capital to increase? The capital stock will increase as long as gross investment exceeds depreciation. Therefore, we need to determine the level of gross investment and the level of depreciation to see how the capital stock changes over time.

Recall that without government or a foreign sector, saving equals gross investment. Thus, to determine the level of investment, we need to specify how much of output is saved and how much is consumed. We will assume that a fraction s of total output (Y) is saved. For example, if $s = 0.20$, then 20 percent of GDP would be saved and 80 percent would be consumed. Total saving will be sY, the product of the saving rate and total output.

In Panel A of Figure 8A.2, the top curve is total output as a function of the stock of capital. The curve below it represents saving as a function of the stock of capital. Because saving is a fixed fraction of total output, the saving curve is a constant fraction of the output curve. If the saving rate is 0.2, saving will always be 20 percent of output for any level of the capital stock. Total saving increases in the economy with the stock of capital, but at a decreasing rate.

To complete our model, we need to determine depreciation. Let's say the capital stock depreciates at a constant rate of d per year. If $d = 0.03$, the capital stock would depreciate at 3 percent per year. If the capital stock were 100 at the beginning of the year, depreciation would equal 3. Total depreciation can be written as dK, where K is the stock of capital.

Panel B of Figure 8A.2 plots total depreciation as a function of the stock of capital. The larger the stock of capital, the more total depreciation there will be. Because the depreciation rate is assumed to be constant, total depreciation as a function of the

▸ FIGURE 8A.2
Saving and Depreciation as Functions of the Stock of Capital

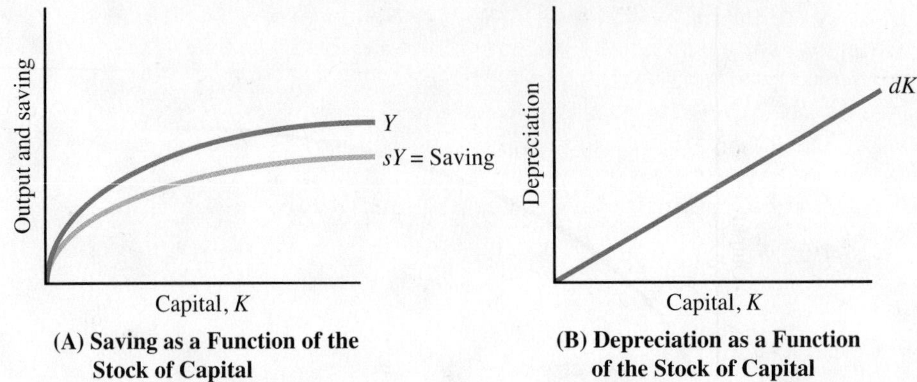

(A) Saving as a Function of the Stock of Capital

(B) Depreciation as a Function of the Stock of Capital

stock of capital will be a straight line through the origin. Then if there is no capital, there will be no depreciation, no matter what the depreciation rate.

If the depreciation rate is 3 percent and the stock of capital is 100, depreciation will be 3; if the stock of capital is 200, the depreciation rate will be 6. Plotting these points will give a straight line through the origin.

We are now ready to see how the stock of capital changes:

$$\text{change in the stock of capital} = \text{saving} - \text{depreciation} = sY - dK$$

The stock of capital will increase—the change will be positive—as long as total saving in the economy exceeds depreciation.

Figure 8A.3 shows how the Solow model works by plotting output, saving, and depreciation all on one graph. Suppose the economy starts with a capital stock K_0. Then total saving will be given by point *a* on the saving schedule. Depreciation at the capital stock K_0 is given by point *b*. Because *a* lies above *b*, total saving exceeds depreciation, and the capital stock will increase. As the capital stock increases, there will be economic growth through capital deepening. With more capital per worker in the economy, output is higher and real wages increase. The economy benefits from the additional stock of capital.

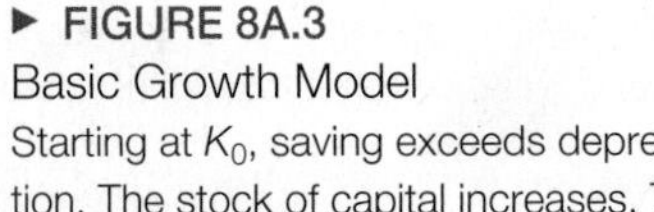
▸ FIGURE 8A.3
Basic Growth Model
Starting at K_0, saving exceeds depreciation. The stock of capital increases. This process continues until the stock of capital reaches its long-run equilibrium at K^*.

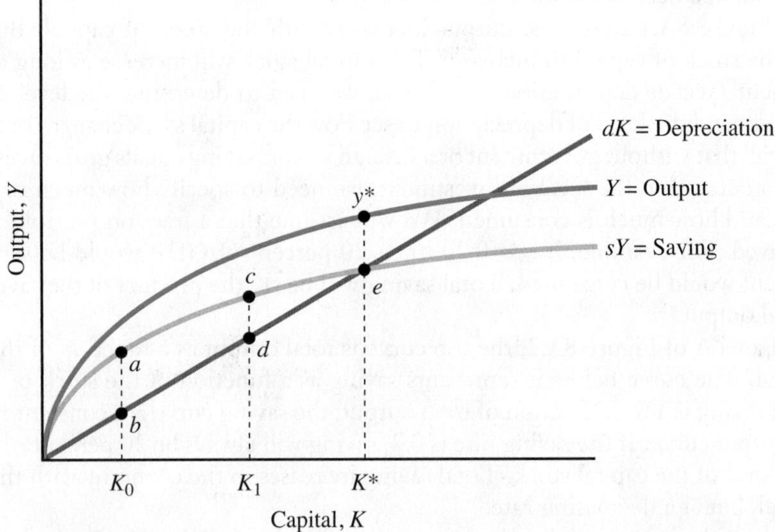

Using the graph, we can trace the future for this economy. As the stock of capital increases, we move to the right. When the economy reaches K_1, total saving is at point *c* and total depreciation is at point *d*. Because *c* is still higher than *d*, saving exceeds depreciation and the capital stock continues to increase. Economic growth continues. Eventually, after many years, the economy reaches capital stock K^*. The level of output in the economy now is Y^*, and the saving and depreciation schedules intersect at point e. Because total saving equals depreciation, the stock of capital no longer increases. The process of economic growth through capital deepening has stopped.

In this simple model, the process of capital deepening must eventually come to an end. As the stock of capital increases, output increases, but at a decreasing rate because of diminishing returns. Because saving is a fixed fraction of output, it will also increase but at a diminishing rate. On the other hand, total depreciation is proportional to the stock of capital. As the stock of capital increases, depreciation will always catch up with total saving in the economy. It may take decades for the process of capital deepening to come to an end. But as long as total saving exceeds depreciation, the process of economic growth through capital deepening will continue.

What would happen if a society saved a higher fraction of its output? Figure 8A.4 shows the consequences of a higher saving rate. Suppose the economy were originally saving at a rate s_1. Eventually, the economy would reach e_1, where saving and depreciation meet. If the economy had started to save at the higher rate s_2, saving would exceed depreciation at K_1, and the capital stock would increase until the economy reached K_2. At K_2, the saving line again crosses the line representing depreciation. Output is higher than it was initially, but the process of capital deepening stops at this higher level of output.

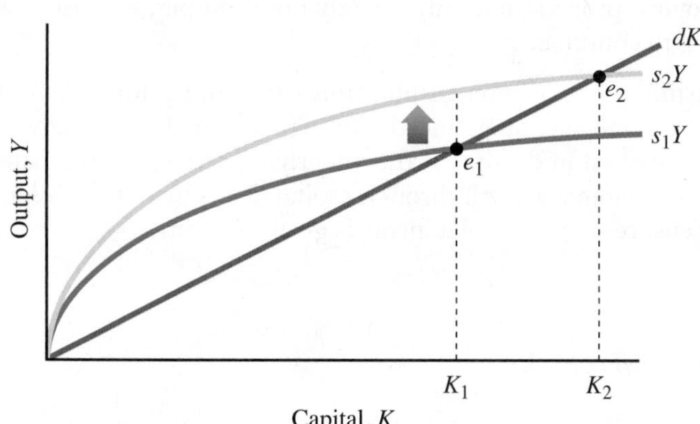

◄ **FIGURE 8A.4**
Increase in the Saving Rate
A higher saving rate will lead to a higher stock of capital in the long run. Starting from an initial capital stock of K_1, the increase in the saving rate leads the economy to K_2.

If there is ongoing technological progress, economic growth can continue. If technological progress raises GDP, saving will increase as well, because saving increases with GDP. This will lead to a higher stock of capital. In Figure 8A.5, technological progress is depicted as an upward shift of the saving function. The saving

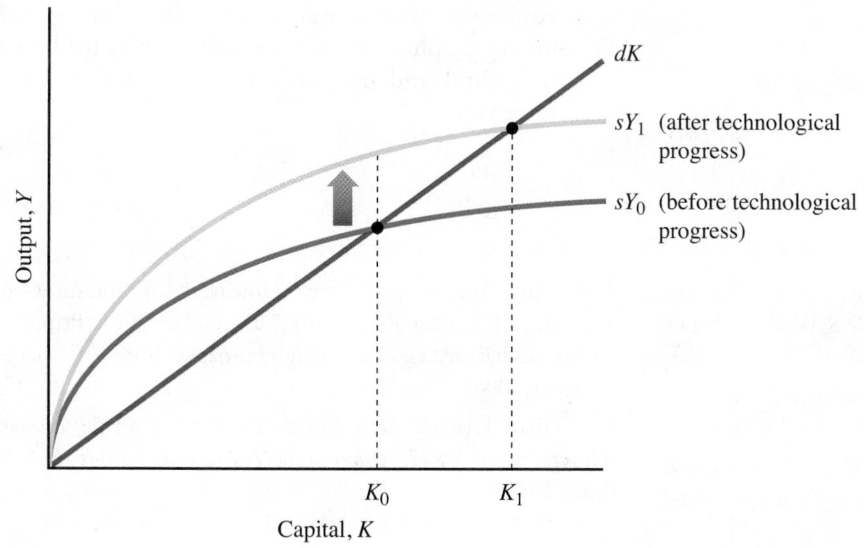

◄ **FIGURE 8A.5**
Technological Progress and Growth
Technological progress shifts up the saving function and promotes capital deepening.

function shifts up because saving is a fixed fraction of output, and we have assumed that technological progress has raised the level of output.

With a higher level of saving, the stock of capital will increase. If the stock of capital were originally at K_0, the upward shift in the saving schedule will lead to increases in the stock of capital to K_1. If there is further technological progress, capital deepening will continue.

Technological progress conveys a double benefit to a society. Not only does the increased efficiency directly raise per capita output, it also leads to additional capital deepening. Therefore, output increases for two reasons.

Let's summarize the basic points of the Solow model:

1 Capital deepening, an increase in the stock of capital per worker, will occur as long as total saving exceeds depreciation. As capital deepening occurs, there will be economic growth and increased real wages.

2 Eventually, the process of capital deepening will come to a halt as depreciation catches up with total saving.

3 A higher saving rate will promote capital deepening. If a country saves more, it will have a higher output. But eventually, the process of economic growth through capital deepening alone comes to an end, even though this may take decades to occur.

4 Technological progress not only directly raises output, but also it allows capital deepening to continue.

It is possible to relax our assumptions and allow for population growth, government taxes and spending, and the foreign sector. In more advanced courses, these issues are treated in detail, but the underlying message is the same. There is a natural limit to economic growth through capital deepening. Technological progress is required to ensure that per capita incomes grow over time.

EXERCISES

All problems are assignable in MyEconLab.

A.1. __________ and __________ are the two factors that determine how the stock of capital changes over time.

A.2. Which of the following causes capital deepening to come to an end?

a. The marginal principle

b. The principle of diminishing returns

c. The principle of opportunity cost

d. The reality principle

A.3. A higher saving rate leads to a permanently higher rate of growth. __________ (True/False)

A.4. Germany and Japan after World War II. Much of the stock of capital in the economies of Japan and Germany was destroyed during World War II. Use the Solow model graph to show and explain why growth in these economies after the war was higher than that in the United States.

A.5. Faster Depreciation. Suppose a society switches to equipment that depreciates rapidly. Use the Solow model graph to show what will happen to the stock of capital and output if the rate of depreciation increases.

NOTES

1. Xavier Sala-i-Martin and Maxim Pinkovskiy, "African Poverty is Falling: Much Faster Than You Think," NBER Working Paper Series, Working Paper No. 15775, February 2010.

2. Stanley Fischer, "Globalization and Its Challenges," *American Economic Review Papers and Proceedings* 93, no. 2 (May 2003): 1–32.

3. Bradford DeLong, "Slouching Toward Utopia," http://www.j-bradford-delong.net/TCEH/Slouch_divergence5.html (accessed June 27, 2008).

4. Phillipe Aghion and Peter Howitt, "Appropriate Growth Theory: A Unifying Framework," December 2005, http://www.economics.harvard.edu/faculty/aghion/papers.html (accessed February 2006).

5. William Easterly, *The Elusive Quest for Growth: Economists' Adventures and Misadventures in the Tropics* (Cambridge, MA: MIT Press, 2002).

Aggregate Demand and Aggregate Supply

CHAPTER 9

As we explained in previous chapters, recessions occur when output fails to grow and unemployment rises.

But *why* do recessions occur? And how do economies recover from these recessions?

In a sense, recessions are massive failures in economic coordination. For example, during the Great Depression in the 1930s, nearly one-fourth of the U.S. labor force was unemployed. Unemployed workers could not afford to buy goods and services. Factories that manufactured those goods and services had to be shut down because there was little or no demand. As these factories closed, even more workers became unemployed, fueling additional factory shutdowns. This vicious cycle caused the U.S. economy to spiral downward. This failure of coordination is not just a historical phenomenon. In December 2007 the economy also entered a very steep downturn—although not nearly as severe as the Great Depression. How could the destructive chain of events have been halted?

Equally important is how economies can recover from recessions. The U.S. economy was very slow to recover from the Great Depression and did not truly reach full employment until World War II. And, despite active government intervention, the recovery from the 2007 recession was also painfully slow.

LEARNING OBJECTIVES

- Explain the role sticky wages and prices play in economic fluctuations.
- List the determinants of aggregate demand.
- Distinguish between the short-run and long-run aggregate supply curves.
- Describe the adjustment process back to full employment.

MyEconLab
MyEconLab helps you master each objective and study more efficiently.

Economies do not always operate at full employment, nor do they always grow smoothly. At times, real GDP grows below its potential or falls steeply, as it did in the Great Depression. Recessions and excess unemployment occur when real GDP falls. At other times, GDP grows too rapidly, and unemployment falls below its natural rate.

"Too slow" or "too fast" real GDP growth are examples of *economic fluctuations*—movements of GDP away from potential output. We now turn our attention to understanding these economic fluctuations, which are also called *business cycles*.

During the Great Depression, there was a failure in coordination. Factories would have produced more output and hired more workers if there had been more demand for their products. In his 1936 book, *The General Theory of Employment, Interest, and Money*, British economist John Maynard Keynes explained that insufficient demand for goods and services was a key problem of the Great Depression. Following the publication of Keynes's work, economists began to distinguish between real GDP in the long run, when prices have time to fully adjust to changes in demand, and real GDP in the short run, when prices don't yet have time to fully adjust to changes in demand. During the short run, economic coordination problems are most pronounced. In the long run, however, economists believe the economy will return to full employment, although economic policy may assist it in getting there more quickly.

In the previous two chapters, we analyzed the economy at full employment and studied economic growth. Those chapters provided the framework for analyzing the behavior of the economy in the long run, but not in the short run, when there can be sharp fluctuations in output. We therefore need to develop an additional set of tools to analyze both short- and long-run changes and the relationship between the two.

9.1 Sticky Prices and Their Macroeconomic Consequences

Why do recessions occur? We previously discussed how real adverse shocks to the economy could cause economic downturns. We also outlined the theory of real business cycles, which focuses on how shocks to technology cause economic fluctuations. Now we examine another approach to understanding economic fluctuations.

Led by Keynes, many economists have focused attention on economic coordination problems. Normally, the price system efficiently coordinates what goes on in an economy—even in a complex economy. The price system provides signals to firms as to who buys what, how much to produce, what resources to use, and from whom to buy. For example, if consumers decide to buy fresh fruit rather than chocolate, the price of fresh fruit will rise and the price of chocolate will fall. More fresh fruit and less chocolate will be produced on the basis of these price signals. On a day-to-day basis, the price system works silently in the background, matching the desires of consumers with the output from producers.

Flexible and Sticky Prices

But the price system does not always work instantaneously. If prices are slow to adjust, then they do not give the proper signals to producers and consumers quickly enough to bring them together. Demands and supplies will not be brought immediately into equilibrium, and coordination can break down. In modern economies, some prices are very flexible, whereas others are not. In the 1970s, U.S. economist Arthur Okun distinguished between *auction prices*, prices that adjust on a nearly daily basis, and *custom prices*, prices that adjust slowly. Prices for fresh fish, vegetables, and other food products are examples of auction prices—they typically are very flexible and adjust rapidly. Prices for industrial commodities, such as steel rods or machine tools, are custom prices and tend to adjust slowly to changes in demand. As shorthand, economists often refer to slowly adjusting prices as "sticky prices" (just like a door that won't open immediately but sometimes gets stuck).

Steel rods and machine tools are input prices. Like other input prices, the price of labor also adjusts very slowly. Workers often have long-term contracts that do not allow employers to change wages at all during a given year. Union workers, university professors, high-school teachers, and employees of state and local governments are all groups whose wages adjust very slowly. As a general rule, there are very few workers in the economy whose wages change quickly. Perhaps movie stars, athletes, and rock stars are the exceptions, because their wages rise and fall with their popularity. But they are far from the typical worker in the economy. Even unskilled, low-wage workers are often protected from a decrease in their wages by minimum-wage laws.

For most firms, the biggest cost of doing business is wages. If wages are sticky, firms' overall costs will be sticky as well. This means that firms' product prices will remain sticky, too. Sticky wages cause sticky prices and hamper the economy's ability to bring demand and supply into balance in the short run.

How Demand Determines Output in the Short Run

Typically, firms that supply intermediate goods such as steel rods or other inputs let demand—not price—determine the level of output in the short run. To understand this idea, consider an automobile firm that buys material from a steelmaker on a regular basis. Because the auto firm and the steel producer have been in business with one another for a long time and have an ongoing relationship, they have negotiated a contract that keeps steel prices fixed in the short run.

But suppose the automobile company's cars suddenly become very popular. The firm needs to expand production, so it needs more steel. Under the agreement made earlier by the two firms, the steel company would meet this higher demand and sell more steel—without raising its price—to the automobile company. As a result, the production of steel is totally determined in the short run by the demand from automobile producers, not by price.

But what if the firm discovered that it had produced an unpopular car and needed to cut back on its planned production? The firm would require less steel. Under the agreement, the steelmaker would supply less steel but not reduce its price. Again, demand—not price—determines steel production in the short run.

Similar agreements between firms, both formal and informal, exist throughout the economy. Typically, in the short run, firms will meet changes in the demand for their products by adjusting production with only small changes in the prices they charge their customers.

What we have just illustrated for an input such as steel applies to workers, too, who are also "inputs" to production. Suppose the automobile firm hires union workers under a contract that fixes their wages for a specific period. If the economy suddenly thrives at some point during that period, the automobile company will employ all the workers and perhaps require some to work overtime. If the economy stagnates at some point during that period, the firm will lay off some workers, using only part of the union labor force. In either case, wages are sticky—they will not change during the period of the contract.

Retail prices to consumers, like input prices to producers, are also subject to some "stickiness." Economists have used information from mail-order catalogues to document this stickiness. Retail price stickiness is further evidence that many prices in the economy are simply slow to adjust.

Over longer periods of time, prices do change. Suppose the automobile company's car remains popular for a long time. The steel company and the automobile company will adjust the price of steel on their contract to reflect this increased demand. These price adjustments occur only over long periods. In the short run, demand, not prices, determines output, and prices are slow to adjust.

To summarize, the **short run in macroeconomics** is the period in which prices do not change or do not change very much. In the macroeconomic short run, both formal and informal contracts between firms mean that changes in demand will be reflected primarily in changes in output, not prices.

short run in macroeconomics
The period of time in which prices do not change or do not change very much.

application 1

MEASURING PRICE STICKINESS IN CONSUMER MARKETS

APPLYING THE CONCEPTS #1: What does the behavior of prices in consumer markets demonstrate about how quickly prices adjust in the U.S. economy?

Economists have taken a number of different approaches to analyze the behavior of retail prices. Anil Kashyap of the University of Chicago examined prices in consumer catalogs. In particular, he looked at the prices of 12 selected goods from L.L. Bean, Recreational Equipment, Inc. (REI), and The Orvis Company, Inc. Kashyap tracked several goods over time, including several varieties of shoes, blankets, chamois shirts, binoculars, and a fishing rod and fly. He found considerable price stickiness. Prices of the goods he tracked were typically fixed for a year or more (even though the catalogs came out every six months). When prices did eventually change, Kashyap observed a mixture of both large and small changes. During periods of high inflation, prices tended to change more frequently, as we might expect.

Mark Bils of the University of Rochester and Peter Klenow of Stanford University examined the frequency of price changes for 350 categories of goods and services covering about 70 percent of consumer spending, based on unpublished data from the BLS for 1995 to 1997. Compared with previous studies they found more frequent price changes, with half of goods' prices lasting less than 4.3 months. Some categories of prices changed much more frequently. Price changes for tomatoes occurred about every three weeks. And some, like coin-operated laundries, changed prices on average only every $6\frac{1}{2}$ years or so. **Related to Exercises 1.5, 1.7, and 1.8.**

SOURCES: Based on Anil Kashyap, "Sticky Prices: New Evidence from Retail Catalogs," *Quarterly Journal of Economics* 110, no. 1 (1995): 245–274, and Mark Bils and Peter Klenow, "Some Evidence on the Importance of Sticky Prices," *Journal of Political Economy* 112, no. 5 (2004): 987–985.

9.2 Understanding Aggregate Demand

In this section, we develop a graphical tool known as the *aggregate demand curve*. Later in the chapter, we will develop the *aggregate supply curve*. Together the aggregate demand and aggregate supply curves form an economic model that will enable us to study how output and prices are determined in both the short run and the long run. This economic model will also provide a framework in which we can study the role the government can play in stabilizing the economy through its spending, tax, and money-creation policies.

What Is the Aggregate Demand Curve?

Aggregate demand is the total demand for goods and services in an entire economy. In other words, it is the demand for currently produced GDP by consumers, firms, the government, and the foreign sector. Aggregate demand is a macroeconomic concept, because it refers to the economy as a whole, not to individual goods or markets.

aggregate demand curve (AD)
A curve that shows the relationship between the level of prices and the quantity of real GDP demanded.

The **aggregate demand curve (AD)** shows the relationship between the level of prices and the quantity of real GDP demanded. An aggregate demand curve, AD, is shown in Figure 9.1. It plots the total demand for GDP as a function of the price level. (Recall that the price level is the average level of prices in the economy, as measured by a price index.) At each price level, shown on the *y* axis, we ask what the total quantity demanded will be for all goods and services in the economy, shown on the *x* axis.

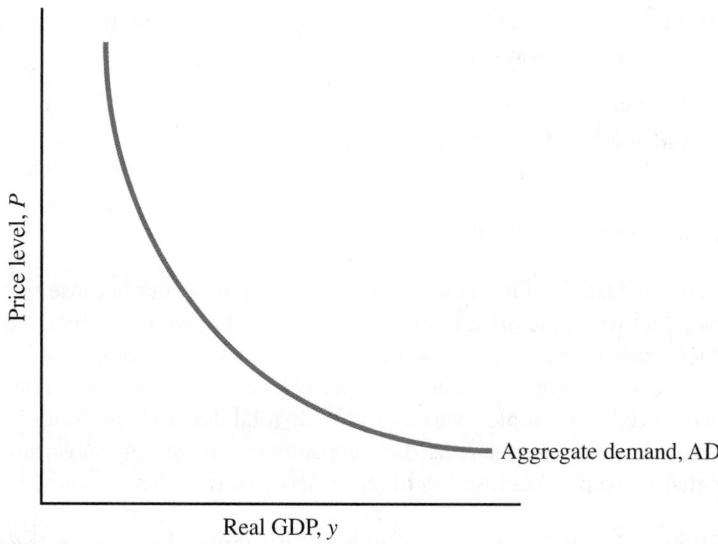

▲ **FIGURE 9.1**
Aggregate Demand
The aggregate demand curve plots the total demand for real GDP as a function of the price level. The aggregate demand curve slopes downward, indicating that the quantity of aggregate demand increases as the price level in the economy falls.

In Figure 9.1, the aggregate demand curve is downward sloping. As the price level falls, the total quantity demanded for goods and services increases. To understand what the aggregate demand curve represents, we must first learn the components of aggregate demand, why the aggregate demand curve slopes downward, and the factors that can shift the curve.

The Components of Aggregate Demand

In our study of GDP accounting, we divided GDP into four components: consumption spending (*C*), investment spending (*I*), government purchases (*G*), and net exports (*NX*). These four components are also the four parts of aggregate demand because the aggregate demand curve really just describes the demand for total GDP at different price levels. As we will see, changes in demand coming from any of these four sources—*C*, *I*, *G*, or *NX*—will shift the aggregate demand curve.

Why the Aggregate Demand Curve Slopes Downward

To understand the slope of the aggregate demand curve, we need to consider the effects of a change in the overall price level in the economy. First, let's consider the supply of money in the economy. We discuss the supply of money in detail in later chapters, but for now, just think of the supply of money as being the total amount of currency (cash plus coins) held by the public and the value of all deposits in savings and checking accounts. As the price level or average level of prices in the economy changes, so does the purchasing power of your money. This is an example of the real-nominal principle.

REAL-NOMINAL PRINCIPLE

What matters to people is the real value or purchasing power of money or income, not the face value of money or income.

As the purchasing power of money changes, the aggregate demand curve is affected in three different ways:

- The wealth effect
- The interest rate effect
- The international trade effect

Let's take a closer look at each.

wealth effect
The increase in spending that occurs because the real value of money increases when the price level falls.

THE WEALTH EFFECT The increase in spending that occurs because the real value of money increases when the price level falls is known as the **wealth effect**. Lower prices lead to higher levels of wealth, and higher levels of wealth increase spending on total goods and services. Conversely, when the price level rises, the real value of money decreases, which reduces people's wealth and their total demand for goods and services in the economy. When the price level rises, consumers can't simply substitute one good for another that's cheaper, because at a higher price level *everything* is more expensive.

THE INTEREST RATE EFFECT With a given supply of money in the economy, a lower price level will lead to lower interest rates. With lower interest rates, both consumers and firms will find it cheaper to borrow money to make purchases. As a consequence, the demand for goods in the economy (consumer durables purchased by households and investment goods purchased by firms) will increase. (We'll explain the effects of interest rates in more detail in later chapters.)

THE INTERNATIONAL TRADE EFFECT In an open economy, a lower price level will mean that domestic goods (goods produced in the home country) become cheaper relative to foreign goods, so the demand for domestic goods will increase. For example, if the price level in the United States falls, it will make U.S. goods cheaper relative to foreign goods. If U.S. goods become cheaper than foreign goods, exports from the United States will increase and imports will decrease. Thus, net exports—a component of aggregate demand—will increase.

Shifts in the Aggregate Demand Curve

A fall in price causes the aggregate demand curve to slope downward because of three factors: the wealth effect, the interest rate effect, and the international trade effect. What happens to the aggregate demand curve if a variable *other* than the price level changes? An increase in aggregate demand means that total demand for all the goods and services contained in real GDP has increased—even though the price level hasn't changed. In other words, increases in aggregate demand shift the curve to the right. Conversely, factors that decrease aggregate demand shift the curve to the left—even though the price level hasn't changed.

Let's look at the key factors that cause these shifts. We will discuss each factor in detail in later chapters:

- Changes in the supply of money
- Changes in taxes
- Changes in government spending
- All other changes in demand

CHANGES IN THE SUPPLY OF MONEY An increase in the supply of money in the economy will increase aggregate demand and shift the aggregate demand curve to the right. We know that an increase in the supply of money will lead to higher demand by both consumers and firms. At any given price level, a higher supply of money will mean more consumer wealth and an increased demand for goods and services. A decrease in the supply of money will decrease aggregate demand and shift the aggregate demand curve to the left.

CHANGES IN TAXES A decrease in taxes will increase aggregate demand and shift the aggregate demand curve to the right. Lower taxes will increase the income available to households and increase their spending on goods and services—even though the price level in the economy hasn't changed. An increase in taxes will decrease aggregate demand and shift the aggregate demand curve to the left. Higher taxes will decrease the income available to households and decrease their spending.

CHANGES IN GOVERNMENT SPENDING At any given price level, an increase in government spending will increase aggregate demand and shift the aggregate demand curve to the right. For example, the government could spend more on national defense or on interstate highways. Because the government is a source of demand for goods and services, higher government spending naturally leads to an increase in total demand for goods and services. Similarly, decreases in government spending will decrease aggregate demand and shift the curve to the left.

ALL OTHER CHANGES IN DEMAND Any change in demand from households, firms, or the foreign sector will also change aggregate demand. For example, if the Chinese economy expands very rapidly and Chinese citizens buy more U.S. goods, U.S. aggregate demand will increase. Or, if U.S. households decide they want to spend more, consumption will increase and aggregate demand will increase. Expectations about the future also matter. For example, if firms become optimistic about the future and increase their investment spending, aggregate demand will also increase. However, if firms become pessimistic, they will cut their investment spending and aggregate demand will fall.

When we discuss factors that shift aggregate demand, we must *not* include any changes in the demand for goods and services that arise from movements in the price level. Changes in aggregate demand that accompany changes in the price level are already included in the curve and do not shift the curve. The increase in consumer spending that occurs when the price level falls from the wealth effect, the interest rate effect, and the international trade effect is already *in* the curve and does not shift it.

Figure 9.2 and Table 9.1 summarize our discussion. Decreases in taxes, increases in government spending, and increases in the supply of money all shift the aggregate demand curve to the right. Increases in taxes, decreases in government spending, and decreases in the supply of money shift it to the left. In general, any increase in demand

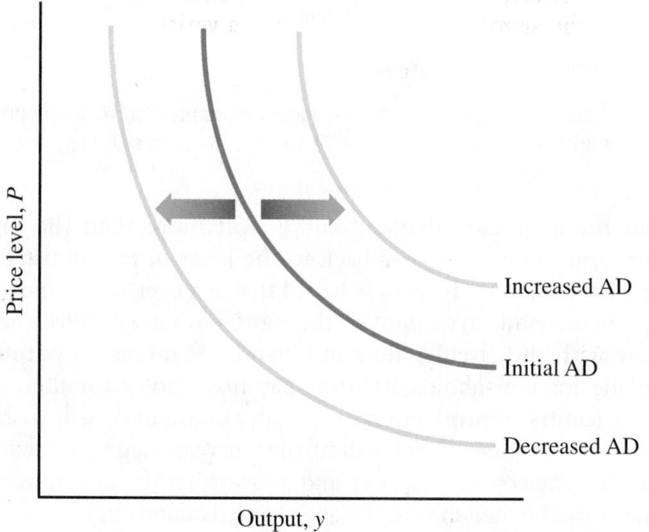

▲ **FIGURE 9.2**
Shifting Aggregate Demand
Decreases in taxes, increases in government spending, and an increase in the supply of money all shift the aggregate demand curve to the right. Higher taxes, lower government spending, and a lower supply of money shift the curve to the left.

TABLE 9.1 Factors That Shift Aggregate Demand

Factors That Increase Aggregate Demand	Factors That Decrease Aggregate Demand
Decrease in taxes	Increase in taxes
Increase in government spending	Decrease in government spending
Increase in the money supply	Decrease in the money supply

(not brought about by a change in the price level) will shift the curve to the right. Decreases in demand shift the curve to the left.

How the Multiplier Makes the Shift Bigger

Let's take a closer look at the shift in the aggregate demand curve and see how far changes really make the curve shift. Suppose the government increases its spending on goods and services by $10 billion. You might think the aggregate demand curve would shift to the right by $10 billion, reflecting the increase in demand for these goods and services. Initially, the shift will be precisely $10 billion. In Figure 9.3, this is depicted by the shift (at a given price level) from *a* to *b*. But after a brief period of time, total aggregate demand will increase by *more* than $10 billion. In Figure 9.3, the total shift in the aggregate demand curve is shown by the larger movement from *a* to *c*. The ratio of the total shift in aggregate demand to the initial shift in aggregate demand is known as the **multiplier**.

multiplier
The ratio of the total shift in aggregate demand to the initial shift in aggregate demand.

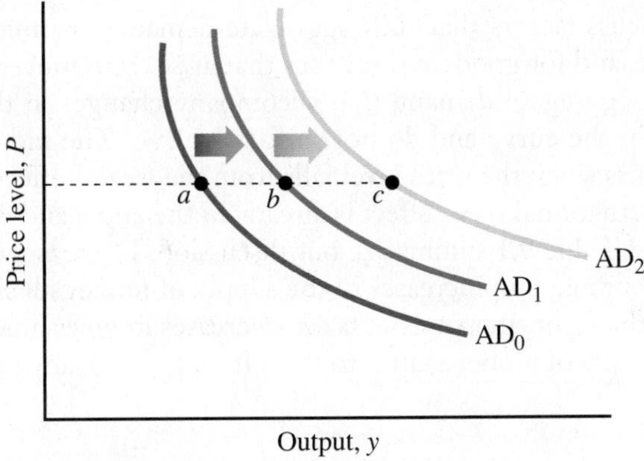

▲ FIGURE 9.3
The Multiplier
Initially, an increase in desired spending will shift the aggregate demand curve horizontally to the right from *a* to *b*. The total shift from *a* to *c* will be larger. The ratio of the total shift to the initial shift is known as the multiplier.

Why does the aggregate demand curve shift more than the initial increase in desired spending? The logic goes back to the ideas of economist John Maynard Keynes. Here's how it works: Keynes believed that as government spending increases and the aggregate demand curve shifts to the right, output will subsequently increase, too. As we saw with the circular flow in Chapter 5, increased output also means increased income for households, as firms pay households for their labor and for supplying other factors of production. Typically, households will wish to spend, or consume, part of that income, which will further increase aggregate demand. It is this additional spending by consumers, over and above what the government has already spent, that causes the further shift in the aggregate demand curve.

The basic idea of how the multiplier works in an economy is simple. Let's say the government invests $10 million to renovate a federal court building. Initially, total spending in the economy increases by this $10 million paid to a private construction firm. The construction workers and owners are paid $10 million for their work. Suppose the owners and workers spend $6 million of their income on new cars (although, as we will see, it does not really matter what they spend it on). To meet the increased demand for new cars, automobile producers will expand their production and earn an additional \$6 million in wages and profits. They, in turn, will spend part of this additional income—let's say, \$3.6 million—on televisions. The workers and owners who produce televisions will then spend part of the \$3.6 million they earn, and so on.

To take a closer look at this process, we first need to look more carefully at the behavior of consumers and how their behavior helps to determine the level of aggregate demand. Economists have found that consumer spending depends on the level of income in the economy. When consumers have more income, they want to purchase more goods and services. The relationship between the level of income and consumer spending is known as the **consumption function**:

$$C = C_a + by$$

where consumption spending, C, has two parts. The first part, C_a, is a constant and is independent of income. Economists call this **autonomous consumption spending**.

consumption function
The relationship between consumption spending and the level of income.

autonomous consumption spending
The part of consumption spending that does not depend on income.

Autonomous spending is spending that does not depend on the level of income. For example, all consumers, regardless of their current income, will have to purchase some food. The second part, by, represents the part of consumption that is dependent on income. It is the product of a fraction, b, called the **marginal propensity to consume (MPC)**, and the level of income, or y, in the economy. The MPC (or b in our formula) tells us how much consumption spending will increase for every dollar that income increases. For example, if b is 0.6, then for every \$1.00 that income increases, consumption increases by \$0.60.

marginal propensity to consume (MPC)
The fraction of additional income that is spent.

Here is another way to think of the MPC: If a household receives some additional income, it will increase its consumption by some additional amount. The MPC is defined as the ratio of additional consumption to additional income, or

$$\text{MPC} = \frac{\text{additional consumption}}{\text{additional income}}$$

For example, if the household receives an additional \$100 and consumes an additional \$70, the MPC will be

$$\frac{\$70}{\$100} = 0.7$$

You may wonder what happens to the other \$30. Whatever the household does not spend out of income, it saves. Therefore, the **marginal propensity to save (MPS)** is defined as the ratio of additional savings to additional income

marginal propensity to save (MPS)
The fraction of additional income that is saved.

$$\text{MPS} = \frac{\text{additional savings}}{\text{additional income}}$$

The sum of the MPC and the MPS always equals one. By definition, additional income is either spent or saved.

Now we are in a better position to understand the multiplier. Suppose the government increases its purchases of goods and services by \$10 million. This will initially raise aggregate demand and income by \$10 million. But because income has risen by \$10 million, consumers will now wish to increase their spending by an amount equal to the marginal propensity to consume multiplied by the \$10 million. (Remember that the MPC tells us how much consumption spending will increase for every dollar that income increases.) If the MPC were 0.6, then consumer spending would increase by \$6 million when the government spends \$10 million. Thus, the aggregate demand curve would continue to shift to the right by another \$6 million in addition to the original \$10 million, for a total of \$16 million.

But the process does not end there. As aggregate demand increases by \$6 million, income will also increase by \$6 million. Consumers will then wish to increase their spending by the MPC × \$6 million or, in our example, by \$3.6 million (0.6 × \$6 million). The aggregate demand curve will continue to shift to the right, now by *another* \$3.6 million. Adding \$3.6 million to \$16 million gives us a new aggregate demand total of \$19.6 million. As you can see, this process will continue, as consumers now have an additional \$3.6 million in income, part of which they will spend again. Where will it end?

Table 9.2 shows how the multiplier works in detail. In the first round, there is an initial increase in government spending of \$10 million. This additional demand leads to an initial increase in GDP and income of \$10 million. Assuming that the MPC is 0.6, the \$10 million of additional income will increase consumer spending by \$6 million. The second round begins with this \$6 million increase in consumer spending. Because of this increase in demand, GDP and income increase by \$6 million. At the end of the second round, consumers will have an additional \$6 million; with an MPC of 0.6, consumer spending will therefore increase by 0.6 × \$6 million, or \$3.6 million. The process continues in the third round with an increase in consumer spending of \$2.16 million. It continues, in diminishing amounts, through subsequent rounds. If we add up the spending in all the (infinite) rounds, we will find that the initial \$10 million of spending leads to a \$25 million increase in GDP and income. That's 2.5 times what the government initially spent. So in this case, the multiplier is 2.5.

TABLE 9.2 THE MULTIPLIER IN ACTION
The initial \$10 million increase in aggregate demand will, through all the rounds of spending, eventually lead to a \$25 million increase.

Round of Spending	Increase in Aggregate Demand (millions)	Increase in GDP and Income (millions)	Increase in Consumption (millions)
1	\$10.00	\$10.00	\$6.00
2	6.00	6.00	3.60
3	3.60	3.60	2.16
4	2.16	2.16	1.30
.	.	.	.
Total	**\$25.00**	**\$25.00**	**\$15.00**

Instead of calculating spending round by round, we can use a simple formula to figure out what the multiplier is:

$$\text{multiplier} = \frac{1}{(1 - \text{MPC})}$$

Thus, in the preceding example, when the MPC is 0.6, the multiplier would be

$$\frac{1}{(1 - 0.6)} = 2.5$$

Now you should clearly understand why the total shift in the aggregate demand curve from *a* to *c* in Figure 9.3 is greater than the initial shift in the curve from *a* to *b*. This is the multiplier in action. The multiplier is important because it means that relatively small changes in spending could lead to relatively large changes in output. For example, if firms cut back on their investment spending, the effects on output would be "multiplied," and this decrease in spending could have a large, adverse impact on the economy.

In practice, once we take into account other realistic factors such as taxes and indirect effects through financial markets, the multipliers are smaller than our previous examples, typically near 1.5 for the U.S economy. This means that a \$10 million increase in one component of spending will shift the U.S. aggregate demand curve by approximately \$15 million. Some economists believe the multiplier is even closer to one. Knowing the value of the multiplier is important for two reasons. First, it tells us how much shocks to aggregate demand are "amplified." Second, to design effective economic policies to shift the aggregate demand curve, we need to know the value of the multiplier to measure the proper "dose" for policy. In the next chapter, we present a more detailed model of aggregate demand and see how policymakers use the real-world multipliers.

application 2

TWO APPROACHES TO DETERMINING THE CAUSES OF RECESSIONS

APPLYING THE CONCEPTS #2: How can we determine what factors cause recessions?

Economists have used the basic framework of aggregate demand and supply analysis to explain recessions. Recessions can occur either when there is a sharp decrease in aggregate demand—a leftward shift in the aggregate demand curve—or a decrease in aggregate supply—an upward shift in the short-run aggregate supply curve. But this just puts the question back one level: During particular historical episodes, what actually shifted the curves?

Figuring out what caused a recession in any particular episode is very challenging. Here is one complication. Policymakers typically respond to shocks that hit the economy. So, for example, when worldwide oil prices rose in 1973 causing U.S. prices to increase, policymakers also reduced aggregate demand to prevent further price increases. Was the recession that resulted due to (1) the increase in oil prices that shifted the short-run aggregate supply curve or (2) the decrease in aggregate demand engineered by policymakers? It is very difficult to know.

One approach is to use economic models to address this question. Economists James Fackler and Douglas McMillin built a small model of the economy to address this issue. To distinguish between demand and supply shocks, they used an idea that we discuss in this chapter. Shocks to aggregate demand only affect prices in the long run but do not affect output. On the other hand, shocks to aggregate supply can affect potential output in the long run. Using this approach, they find that a mixture of demand and supply shocks were responsible for fluctuations in output in the United States.

Using more traditional historical methods, economic historian Peter Temin looked back at all recessionary episodes from 1893 to 1990 in the United States to try to determine their ultimate causes. According to his analysis, recessions were caused by many different factors. Sometimes, as in 1929, they were caused by shifts in aggregate demand from the private sector, as consumers cut back their spending. Other times, as in 1981, the government cut back on aggregate demand to reduce inflation. Supply shocks were the cause of the recessions in 1973 and 1979.

Based on both economic models and traditional economic history, it does appear that both supply and demand shocks have been important in understanding recessions. **Related to Exercises 3.6 and 3.9.**

SOURCE: Based on Peter Temin, "The Causes of American Business Cycles: An Essay in Economic Historiography," in Federal Reserve Bank of Boston Conference Series 42, *Beyond Shocks: What Causes Business Cycles*, http://www.bos.frb.org/economic/conf/conf42 (accessed April 12, 2010), and James Fackler and Douglas McMillin, "Historical Decomposition of Aggregate Demand and Supply Shocks in a Small Macro Model," *Southern Economic Journal* 64, no. 3 (1998): 648–684.

9.3 Understanding Aggregate Supply

aggregate supply curve (AS)
A curve that shows the relationship between the level of prices and the quantity of output supplied.

Now we turn to the supply side of our model. The **aggregate supply curve (AS)** shows the relationship between the level of prices and the total quantity of final goods and output that firms are willing and able to supply. The aggregate supply curve will complete our macroeconomic picture, uniting the economy's demand for real output with firms' willingness to supply output. To determine both the price level and real GDP, we need to combine *both* aggregate demand and aggregate supply. One slight complication is that because prices are "sticky" in the short run, we need to develop two different aggregate supply curves, one corresponding to the long run and one to the short run.

The Long-Run Aggregate Supply Curve

long-run aggregate supply curve
A vertical aggregate supply curve that reflects the idea that in the long run, output is determined solely by the factors of production and technology.

First we'll consider the aggregate supply curve for the long run, that is, when the economy is at full employment. This curve is also called the **long-run aggregate supply curve**. In previous chapters, we saw that the level of full-employment output, y_p (the "p" stands for potential), depends solely on the supply of factors—capital, labor—and the state of technology. These are the fundamental factors that determine output in the long run, that is, when the economy operates at full employment.

In the long run, the economy operates at full employment and changes in the price level do not affect employment. To illustrate why this is so, imagine that the price level in the economy increases by 50 percent. That means firms' prices, on average, will also increase by 50 percent. However, so will their input costs. Their profits will be the same and, consequently, so will their output. Because the level of full-employment output does not depend on the price level, we can plot the long-run aggregate supply curve as a vertical line (unaffected by the price level), as shown in Figure 9.4.

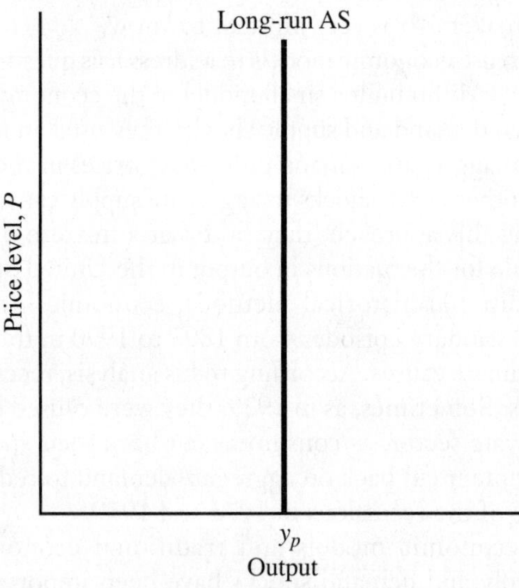

▶ FIGURE 9.4
Long-Run Aggregate Supply
In the long run, the level of output, y_p, is independent of the price level.

DETERMINING OUTPUT AND THE PRICE LEVEL We combine the aggregate demand curve and the long-run aggregate supply curve in Figure 9.5. Together, the curves show us the price level and output in the long run when the economy returns to full employment. Combining the two curves will enable us to understand how changes in aggregate demand affect prices in the long run.

The intersection of an aggregate demand curve and an aggregate supply curve determines the price level and equilibrium level of output. At that intersection point, the total amount of output demanded will just equal the total amount supplied by producers—the economy will be in macroeconomic equilibrium. The exact position

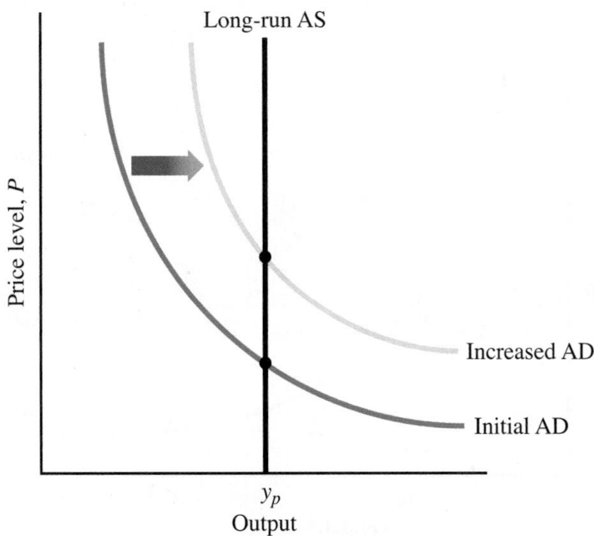

▲ FIGURE 9.5
Aggregate Demand and the Long-Run Aggregate Supply
Output and prices are determined at the intersection of AD and AS. An increase in aggregate demand leads to a higher price level.

of the aggregate demand curve will depend on the level of taxes, government spending, and the supply of money, although it will always slope downward. The level of full-employment output determines the long-run aggregate supply curve.

An increase in aggregate demand (perhaps brought about by a tax cut or an increase in the supply of money) will shift the aggregate demand curve to the right, as shown in Figure 9.5. In the long run, the increase in aggregate demand will raise prices but leave the level of output unchanged. In general, shifts in the aggregate demand curve in the long run do not change the level of output in the economy, but only change the level of prices. Here is an important example to illustrate this idea: If the money supply is increased by 5 percent a year, the aggregate demand curve will also shift by 5 percent a year. In the long run, this means that prices will increase by 5 percent a year—that is, there will be 5 percent inflation. An important lesson: In the long run, increases in the supply of money do not increase real GDP—they only lead to inflation.

This is the key point about the long run: In the long run, output is determined solely by the supply of human and physical capital and the supply of labor, not the price level. As our model of the aggregate demand curve with the long-run aggregate supply curve indicates, changes in demand will affect only prices, not the level of output.

The Short-Run Aggregate Supply Curve

In the short run, prices are sticky (slow to adjust) and output is determined primarily by demand. This is what Keynes thought happened during the Great Depression. We can use the aggregate demand curve combined with a **short-run aggregate supply curve** to illustrate this idea. Figure 9.6 shows a relatively flat short-run aggregate supply curve (AS). The short-run aggregate supply curve shows the short-run relationship between the price level and the willingness of firms to supply output to the economy. Let's look first at its slope and then the factors that shift the curve.

short-run aggregate supply curve
A relatively flat aggregate supply curve that represents the idea that prices do not change very much in the short run and that firms adjust production to meet demand.

The short-run aggregate supply curve has a relatively flat slope because we assume that in the short run firms supply all the output demanded, with small changes in prices. We've said that with formal and informal contracts firms will supply all the output demanded with only relatively small changes in prices. The short-run aggregate supply curve has a small upward slope. As firms supply more output, they may have to increase prices somewhat if, for example, they have to pay higher wages to obtain more overtime from workers or pay a premium to obtain some raw materials. Our description of the short-run aggregate supply curve is consistent with evidence about

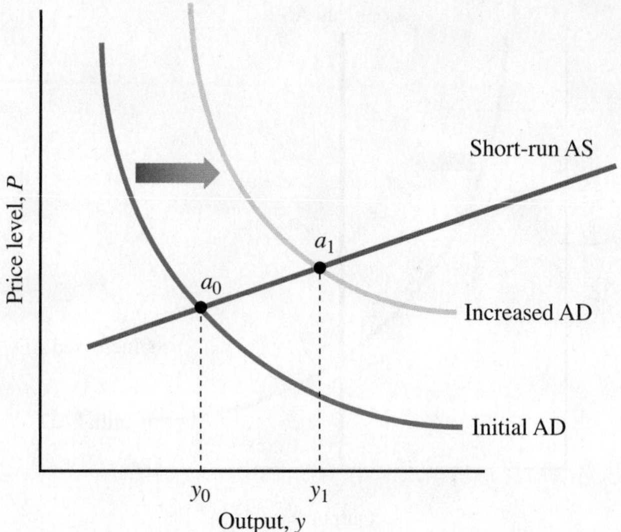

▲ **FIGURE 9.6**
Aggregate Demand and Short-Run Aggregate Supply
With a short-run aggregate supply curve, shifts in aggregate demand lead to large changes in output but small changes in price.

the behavior of prices in the economy. Most studies find that changes in demand have relatively little effect on prices within a few quarters. Thus, we can think of the aggregate supply curve as relatively flat over a limited time.

The position of the short-run supply curve will be determined by the costs of production that firms face. Higher costs will shift up the short-run aggregate supply curve, while lower costs will shift it down. Higher costs will shift up the curve because, faced with higher costs, firms will need to raise their prices to continue to make a profit. What factors determine the costs firms must incur to produce output? The key factors are

- input prices (wages and materials),
- the state of technology, and
- taxes, subsidies, or economic regulations.

Increases in input prices (for example, from higher wages or oil prices) will increase firms' costs. This will shift up the short-run aggregate supply curve. Improvement in technology will shift the curve down. Higher taxes or more onerous regulations raise costs and shift the curve up, while subsidies to production shift the curve down. As we shall see later in this chapter, when the economy is not at full employment, wages and other costs will change. These changes in costs will shift the entire short-run supply curve upward or downward as costs rise or fall.

The intersection of the AD and AS curves at point a_0 determines the price level and the level of output. Because the aggregate supply curve is flat, aggregate demand primarily determines the level of output. In Figure 9.6, as aggregate demand increases, the new equilibrium will be at a slightly higher price, and output will increase from y_0 to y_1.

If the aggregate demand curve moved to the left, output would decrease. If the leftward shift in aggregate demand were sufficiently large, it could push the economy into a recession. Sudden decreases in aggregate demand have been important causes of recessions in the United States. However, the precise factors that shift the aggregate demand curve in each recession will typically differ.

Note that the level of output where the aggregate demand curve intersects the short-run aggregate supply curve need not correspond to full-employment output. Firms will produce whatever is demanded. If demand is very high and the economy is "overheated," output may exceed full-employment output. If demand is very low and the economy is in a slump, output will fall short of full-employment output. Because prices do not adjust fully over short periods of time, the economy need not always remain at

application 3

OIL SUPPLY DISRUPTIONS, SPECULATION AND SUPPLY SHOCKS

APPLYING THE CONCEPTS #3: Are oil price increases caused by true shocks to supply?

Economists have long believed that disruptions to oil supplies were the cause of supply shocks for the U.S economy. If this were the case, supply disruptions would be true external "shocks" to the economy. But not all changes in oil prices are necessarily caused by supply disruptions. Oil price increases may be caused by increases in world demand or due to the activities of speculators in the oil market.

How important are actual supply disruptions to oil market for the U.S. economy? Economist Lutz Kilian carefully examined this issue by constructing measures of supply disruptions in oil producing countries, based on a detailed examination of prior trends in demand and specifications in oil contracts. While Kilian did find evidence of some supply disruptions, these only explained a small fraction of the variability of oil prices. In his view, other factors dominated the price movements for oil, even during the time periods that are conventionally associated with supply disruptions.

Speculation in oil markets may be one such factor. Speculators can be countries, firms, or individuals. If speculators believe prices are going to rise in the future, they will buy oil now or, if they own it, sell less into the market. Either action increases the current price of oil. Note that if speculators are on average correct in their assessments, they will smooth out the price of oil over time—raising it now and lowering it later. This can actually benefit the economy. While politicians often complain about speculators, in many cases they may be helping the economy. Of course, speculators can be wrong and make fluctuations in prices worse, but in this case at least some of them will lose money. **Related to Exercises 3.4 and 3.7.**

SOURCE: In part based on Lutz Kilian, "Exogenous Oil Supply Shocks: How Big Are They and How Much Do They Matter for the U.S. Economy?" *Review of Economics and Statistics*, May 2008, Vol. 90, No. 2, pp. 216–240.

---

full employment or potential output. With sticky prices, changes in demand in the short run will lead to economic fluctuations and over- and underemployment. Only in the long run, when prices fully adjust, will the economy operate at full employment.

Supply Shocks

Up to this point, we have been exploring how changes in aggregate demand affect output and prices in the short run and in the long run. However, even in the short run, it is possible for external disturbances to hit the economy and cause the short-run aggregate supply curve to move. **Supply shocks** are external events that shift the aggregate supply curve.

supply shocks
External events that shift the aggregate supply curve.

The most notable supply shocks for the world economy occurred in 1973 and again in 1979 when oil prices increased sharply. Oil is a vital input for many companies because it is used to both manufacture and transport their products to warehouses and stores around the country. The higher oil prices raised firms' costs and reduced their profits. To maintain their profit levels, firms raised their product prices. As we have seen, increases in firms' costs will shift up the short-run aggregate supply curve—increases in oil prices are a good example.

Figure 9.7 illustrates a supply shock that raises prices. The short-run aggregate supply curve shifts up with the supply shock because, as their costs rise, firms will supply their output only at a higher price. The AS curve shifts up, raising the price level and lowering the level of output from y_0 to y_1. Adverse supply shocks can therefore cause a recession (a fall in real output) with increasing prices. This phenomenon is known as

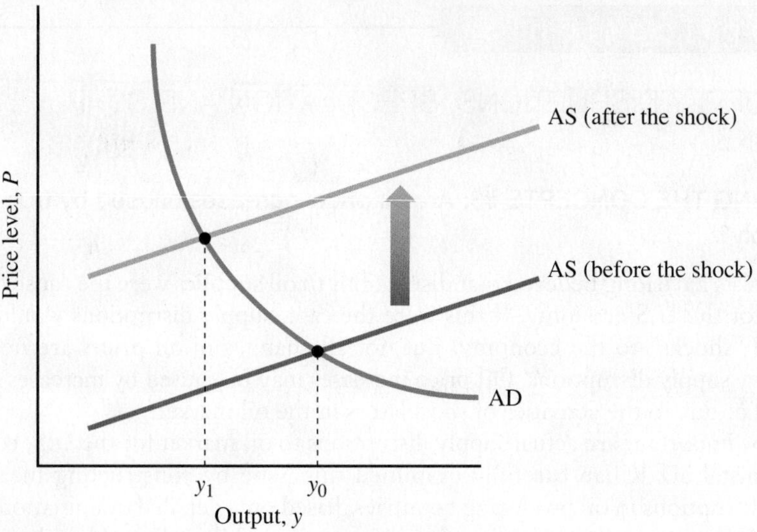

▲ FIGURE 9.7
Supply Shock
An adverse supply shock, such as an increase in the price of oil, will cause the AS curve to shift upward. The result will be higher prices and a lower level of output.

stagflation
A decrease in real output with increasing prices.

stagflation, and it is precisely what happened in 1973 and 1979. The U.S. economy suffered on two grounds: rising prices and falling output. Favorable supply shocks, such as falling prices, are also possible, and changes in oil prices can affect aggregate demand.

9.4 From the Short Run to the Long Run

Up to this point, we have examined how aggregate demand and aggregate supply determine output and prices both in the short run and in the long run. You may be wondering how long it takes before the short run becomes the long run. Here is a preview of how the short run and the long run are connected.

In Figure 9.8, we show the aggregate demand curve intersecting the short-run aggregate supply curve at a_0 at an output level y_0. We also depict the long-run aggregate supply curve in this figure. The level of output in the economy, y_0, exceeds the level of potential output, y_p. In other words, this is a boom economy: Output exceeds potential.

► FIGURE 9.8
The Economy in the Short Run
In the short run, the economy produces at y_0, which exceeds potential output y_p.

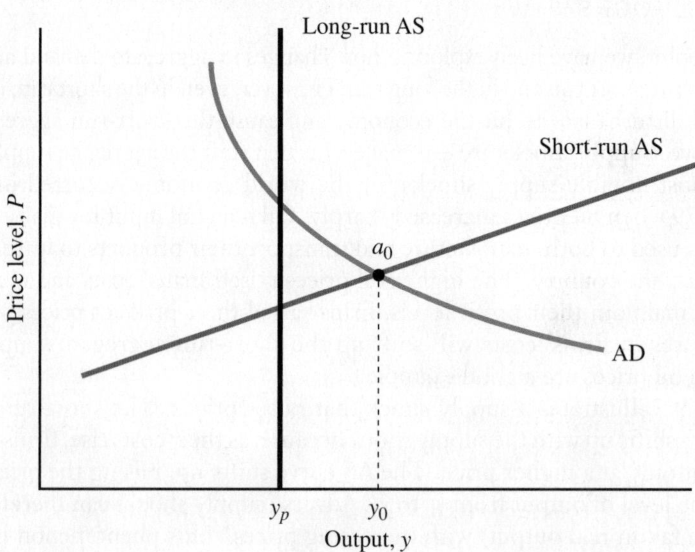

What happens during a boom? Because the economy is producing at a level beyond its long-run potential, the level of unemployment will be very low. This will make it difficult for firms to recruit and retain workers. Firms will also find it more difficult to purchase needed raw materials and other inputs for production. As firms compete for labor and raw materials, the tendency will be for both wages and prices to increase over time.

Increasing wages and prices will shift the short-run aggregate supply curve upward as the costs of inputs rise in the economy. Figure 9.9 shows how the short-run aggregate supply curve shifts upward over time. As long as the economy is producing at a level of output that exceeds potential output, there will be continuing competition for labor and raw materials that will lead to continuing increases in wages and prices. In the long run, the short-run aggregate supply curve will keep rising until it intersects the aggregate demand curve at a_1. At this point, the economy reaches the long-run equilibrium—precisely the point where the aggregate demand curve intersects the long-run aggregate supply curve.

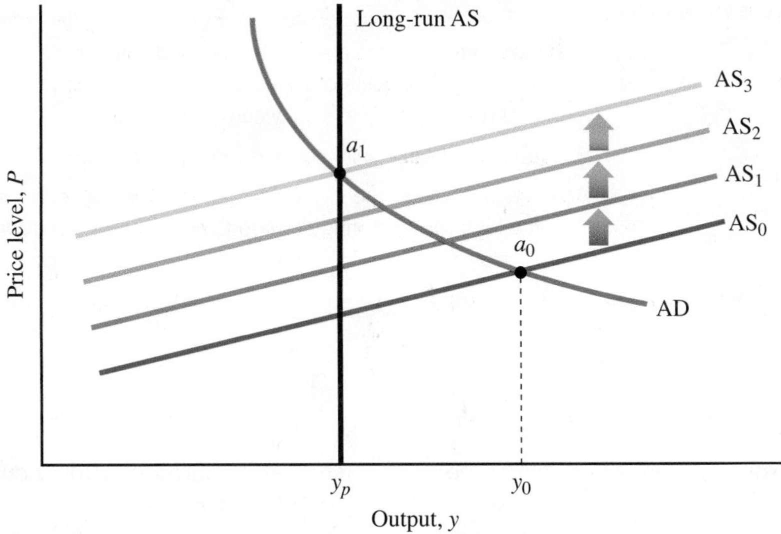

▲ FIGURE 9.9
Adjusting to the Long Run
With output exceeding potential, the short-run AS curve shifts upward over time. The economy adjusts to the long-run equilibrium at a_1.

When the economy is producing below full employment or potential output, the process works in reverse. Unemployment will exceed the natural rate, and there will be excess unemployment. Firms will find it easy to hire and retain workers, and they will offer workers less wages. As firms cut wages, the average wage level in the economy falls. Because wages are the largest component of costs and costs are decreasing, the short-run aggregate supply curve shifts down, causing prices to fall as well.

The lesson here is that adjustments in wages and prices take the economy from the short-run equilibrium to the long-run equilibrium. In later chapters, we will explain in detail how this adjustment occurs, and we will show how changes in wages and prices can steer the economy back to full employment in the long run.

The aggregate demand and aggregate supply model in this chapter provides an overview of how demand affects output and prices in both the short run and the long run. We will expand our discussion of aggregate demand to see in detail how such realistic and important factors as spending by consumers and firms, government policies on taxation and spending, and foreign trade affect the demand for goods and services. We will also study the critical role that the financial system and monetary policy play in determining demand. Finally, we will study in more depth how the aggregate supply curve shifts over time, enabling the economy to recover both from recessions and the inflationary pressures generated by economic booms.

SUMMARY

In this chapter we discussed how sticky prices—or lack of full-wage and price flexibility—cause output to be determined by demand in the short run. We developed a model of aggregate demand and supply to help us analyze what is happening or has happened in the economy. Here are the main points in this chapter:

1 Because prices are sticky in the short run, economists think of GDP as being determined primarily by demand factors in the short run.
2 The *aggregate demand curve* depicts the relationship between the price level and total demand for real output in the economy. The aggregate demand curve is downward sloping because of the wealth effect, the interest rate effect, and the international trade effect.
3 Decreases in taxes, increases in government spending, and increases in the supply of money all increase aggregate demand and shift the aggregate demand curve to the right. Increases in taxes, decreases in government spending, and decreases in the supply of money all decrease aggregate demand and shift the aggregate demand curve to the left. In general, anything (other than price movements) that increases the demand for total goods and services will increase aggregate demand.
4 The total shift in the aggregate demand curve is greater than the initial shift. The ratio of the total shift in aggregate demand to the initial shift in aggregate demand is known as the *multiplier*.
5 The *aggregate supply curve* depicts the relationship between the price level and the level of output that firms supply in the economy. Output and prices are determined at the intersection of the aggregate demand and aggregate supply curves.
6 The *long-run aggregate supply curve* is vertical because, in the long run, output is determined by the supply of factors of production. The *short-run aggregate supply curve* is fairly flat because, in the short run, prices are largely fixed, and output is determined by demand. The costs of production determine the position of the short-run aggregate supply curve.
7 *Supply shocks* can shift the short-run aggregate supply curve.
8 As costs change, the short-run aggregate supply curve shifts in the long run, restoring the economy to the full-employment equilibrium.

KEY TERMS

aggregate demand curve (AD), p. 188
aggregate supply curve (AS), p. 196
autonomous consumption spending, p. 193
consumption function, p. 193
long-run aggregate supply curve, p. 196
marginal propensity to consume (MPC), p. 193
marginal propensity to save (MPS), p. 193
multiplier, p. 192
short run in macroeconomics, p. 187
short-run aggregate supply curve, p. 197
stagflation, p. 200
supply shocks, p. 199
wealth effect, p. 190

EXERCISES

All problems are assignable in MyEconLab; exercises that update with real-time data are marked with **.**

9.1 Sticky Prices and Their Macroeconomic Consequences

1.1 Arthur Okun distinguished between auction prices, which changed rapidly, and ________ prices, which are slow to change.

1.2 For most firms, the biggest cost of doing business is ________.

1.3 The price system always coordinates economic activity, even when prices are slow to adjust to changes in demand and supply. ________ (True/False)

1.4 Determine whether the wages of each of the following adjust slowly or quickly to changes in demand and supply.
a. Union workers
b. Internationally known movie stars or rock stars
c. University professors
d. Athletes

1.5 **The Internet and Price Flexibility.** The Internet enables consumers to search for the lowest prices of various goods, such as books, music CDs, and airline tickets. Prices for these goods are likely to become more flexible as consumers shop around quickly and easily on the Internet. What types of goods and services do you think may not become more flexible because of the Internet? Give an example of a good or service for which you have searched the Internet for price information and one for which you have not. (Related to Application 1 on page 188.)

1.6 **Airlines and Stable Fuel Prices.** Southwest Airlines made it a company policy to engage in complex financial transactions to keep the cost of fuel constant. Why would the airline want to have stable fuel prices?

1.7 **Supermarket Prices.** In a supermarket, prices for tomatoes change quickly, but prices for mops tend to not change as rapidly. Can you offer an explanation why? (Related to Application 1 on page 188.)

1.8 **Retail Price Stickiness in Catalogs.** During periods of high inflation, retail prices in catalogs changed more frequently. Explain why this occurred. (Related to Application 1 on page 188.)

9.2 Understanding Aggregate Demand

2.1 Which of the following is *not* a component of aggregate demand?

a. Consumption

b. Investment

c. Government expenditures

d. The supply of money

e. Net exports

2.2 In the Great Depression, prices in the United States fell by 33 percent. *Ceteris paribus*, this led to an increase in aggregate demand through three channels: the __________ effect, the interest rate effect, and the international trade effect.

2.3 President Barack Obama lowered taxes in 2009. He also increased government spending. *Ceteris paribus*, these actions shifted the aggregate demand curve to the __________.

2.4 If the MPC is 0.8, the simple multiplier will be __________.

2.5 Because of other economic factors, such as taxes, the multiplier in the United States is __________ (larger/smaller) than 2.5.

2.6 **Opening Export Markets.** Suppose a foreign country, which originally prevented the United States from exporting to it, opens its market and U.S. firms start to make a considerable volume of sales. What happens to the aggregate demand curve?

2.7 **Calculating the MPS and MPC.** In one year, a consumer's income increases by $200 and her savings increases by $40. What is her marginal propensity to *save*. What is her marginal propensity to *consume*?

2.8 **Saving Behavior and Multipliers in Two Countries.** Consumers in Country A have an MPS of 0.5 while consumers in Country B have an MPS of 0.4. Which country has the higher value for the multiplier?

2.9 **State and Local Governments during Recessions.** During recessions, state governments often will have to raise taxes and cut spending in order to keep their own budgets balanced. If a large number of states do this, what will happen to the aggregate demand curve at the national level?

9.3 Understanding Aggregate Supply

3.1 The long-run aggregate supply curve is __________ (vertical/horizontal).

3.2 A decrease in material costs will shift the short-run aggregate supply __________.

3.3 Using the long-run aggregate supply curve, a decrease in aggregate demand will __________ prices and output.

3.4 A negative supply shock, such as higher oil prices, will __________ output and __________ prices in the short run. (Related to Application 3 on page 199.)

3.5 **Higher Gas Prices, Frugal Consumers, and Economic Fluctuations.** Suppose gasoline prices increased sharply and consumers became fearful of owning too many expensive cars. As a consequence, they cut back on their purchases of new cars and decided to increase their savings. How would this behavior shift the aggregate demand curve? Using the short-run aggregate supply curve, what will happen to prices and output in the short run?

3.6 **What Caused This Recession?** Suppose the economy goes into a recession. The political party in power blames it on an increase in the price of world oil and food. Opposing politicians blame a tax increase that the party in power had enacted. On the basis of aggregate demand and aggregate supply analysis, what evidence should you look at to try to determine what, or who, caused the recession? (*Hint*: look at the behavior of both prices and output in each case.) (Related to Application 2 on page 195.)

3.7 **The Role of Expectations and Supply Shocks.** Suppose an oil producing country believed that political instability was likely in the future in other parts of the world and prices would rise in the next year. Do you think they would sell more or less today? What will happen to today's price? Will this affect either aggregate demand or supply? (Related to Application 3 on page 199.)

3.8 **China Comes Roaring Back.** In the 2008 recession, China was one of the first economies to recover and its GDP growth quickly returned to its pre-recession levels. How did China's actions affect aggregate demand in the rest of the world?

3.9 **Long-Run Effects of a Shock to Demand.** Suppose consumption spending rose quickly and then fell back to its normal level. What do you think would be the long-run effect on real GDP of this temporary shock? (Related to Application 2 on page 195.)

9.4 From the Short Run to the Long Run

4.1 Suppose the supply of money increases, causing output to exceed full employment. Prices will ________ and real GDP will ________ in the short run, and prices will ________ and real GDP will ________ in the long run.

4.2 Consider a decrease in the supply of money that causes output to fall short of full employment. Prices will ________ and real GDP will ________ in the short run, and prices will ________ and real GDP will ________ in the long run.

4.3 In a recession, real GDP is ________ potential GDP. This implies that unemployment is ________ the natural rate, driving wages ________. This results in a(n) shift of the short-run aggregate supply curve.

4.4 A negative supply shock temporarily lowers output below full employment and raises prices. After the negative supply shock, real GDP is ________ potential GDP. This implies that unemployment is ________ the natural rate, driving up wages. This results in a(n) ________ shift of the short-run aggregate supply curve.

4.5 **The Internet Crashes.** Suppose that computer hackers managed to crash the Internet in the United States for a week and no one had computer access. Explain why this might be considered a negative supply shock.

4.6 **Shifts in Aggregate Demand and Cost-Push Inflation.** When wages rise and the short-run aggregate supply curve shifts up, the result is "cost-push" inflation. If the economy was initially at full-employment and the aggregate demand curve was shifted to the right, explain how "cost-push" inflation would result as the economy adjusts back to full employment.

4.7 **Exports and Real GDP.** Are increases in exports associated with increases in real GDP? A good place to start to find out is the Web site of the Federal Reserve Bank of St. Louis (http://research.stlouisfed.org/fred2).

Fiscal Policy

CHAPTER

10

Economists generally believe that permanent tax cuts will stimulate the economy and lead to higher output, but disagree about why this happens.

Some advocates for tax cuts stress how they lead to increases in spending and aggregate demand. Others suggest that the main effect comes from changes in incentives and aggregate supply.

Can we tell which view is correct by looking back at U.S. fiscal history? The tax cuts proposed by President John F. Kennedy and enacted after his death are typically viewed as triumphs of the aggregate demand view. Kennedy's economic advisers believed that tax cuts worked through changing aggregate demand. On the other hand, President Ronald Reagan is famously known for his "supply side" economics. His economic advisers placed great emphasis on how cutting tax rates would create a better economic climate through improved economic incentives.

But the economic policy world is not that simple. Kennedy's tax cuts included incentives to increase aggregate supply, including cutting the top income tax rate and providing specific tax incentives for business investments. While Reagan's tax cuts lowered tax rates for everyone, they also directly increased household incomes, which led to more spending. A careful look at actual policies suggests that tax cuts are always a mixture of demand and supply elements.

Today, proponents of permanent tax cuts typically cite *both* the Kennedy and Reagan administrations as evidence that tax cuts work, regardless of their own view. By associating themselves with past successes, proponents of tax cuts hope to benefit from the favorable glow of history.

LEARNING OBJECTIVES

- Explain how fiscal policy works using aggregate demand and aggregate supply.
- Identify the main elements of spending and revenue for the U.S. federal government.
- Discuss the key episodes of active fiscal policy in the U.S. since World War II.

MyEconLab

MyEconLab helps you master each objective and study more efficiently.

When the U.S. economy began to slow in late 2007 and early 2008, it was not long before policymakers and politicians from both major parties were calling for government action to combat the downturn. Common prescriptions included increasing government spending or reducing taxes, although specific recommendations differed sharply among those making them. Even after the recession ended and the slow recovery began, there were still some calls for additional action to stimulate the economy.

fiscal policy
Changes in government taxes and spending that affect the level of GDP.

In this chapter, we study how governments can use **fiscal policy**—changes in taxes and spending that affect the level of GDP—to stabilize the economy. We explore the logic of fiscal policy and explain why changes in government spending and taxation can, in principle, stabilize the economy. However, stabilizing the economy is much easier in theory than in actual practice, as we will see.

The chapter also provides an overview of spending and taxation by the federal government. These are essentially the tools the government uses to implement its fiscal policies. We will examine the federal deficit and begin to explore the controversies surrounding deficit spending.

One of the best ways to really understand fiscal policy is to see it in action. In the last part of the chapter, we trace the history of U.S. fiscal policy from the Great Depression in the 1930s to the present. As you will see, the public's attitude toward government fiscal policy has not been constant but has instead changed over time.

10.1 The Role of Fiscal Policy

In the last chapter, we discussed how output and prices are determined where the aggregate demand curve intersects the short-run aggregate supply curve. In this section, we will explore how the government can shift the aggregate demand curve.

Fiscal Policy and Aggregate Demand

As we discussed in the last chapter, government spending and taxes can affect the level of aggregate demand. Increases in government spending or decreases in taxes will increase aggregate demand and shift the aggregate demand curve to the right. Decreases in government spending or increases in taxes will decrease aggregate demand and shift the aggregate demand curve to the left.

Why do changes in government spending or taxes shift the aggregate demand curve? Recall from our discussion in the last chapter that aggregate demand consists of four components: consumption spending, investment spending, government purchases, and net exports. These four components are the four parts of aggregate demand. Thus, increases in government purchases directly increase aggregate demand because they are a component of aggregate demand. Decreases in government purchases directly decrease aggregate demand.

Changes in taxes affect aggregate demand indirectly. For example, if the government lowers taxes consumers pay, consumers will have more income at their disposal and will increase their consumption spending. Because consumption spending is a component of aggregate demand, aggregate demand will increase as well. Increases in taxes will have the opposite effect. Consumers will have less income at their disposal and will decrease their consumption spending. As a result, aggregate demand will decrease. Changes in taxes can also affect businesses and lead to changes in investment spending. Suppose, for example, that the government cuts taxes in such a way as to provide incentives for new investment spending by businesses. Because investment spending is a component of aggregate demand, the increase in investment spending will increase aggregate demand.

In Panel A of Figure 10.1 we show a simple example of fiscal policy in action. The economy is initially operating at a level of GDP, y_0, where the aggregate demand curve AD_0 intersects the short-run aggregate supply curve AS. This level of output

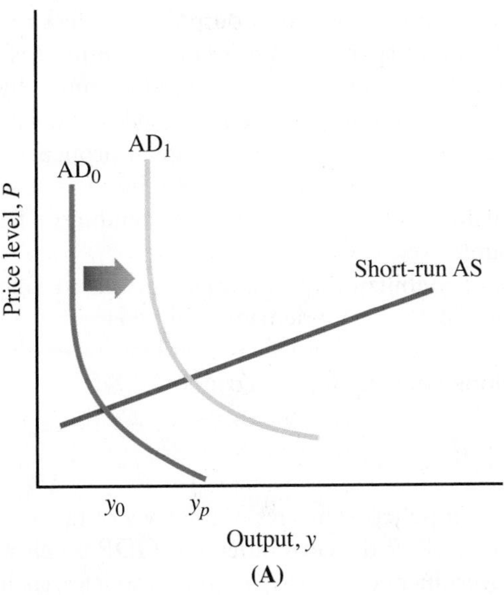

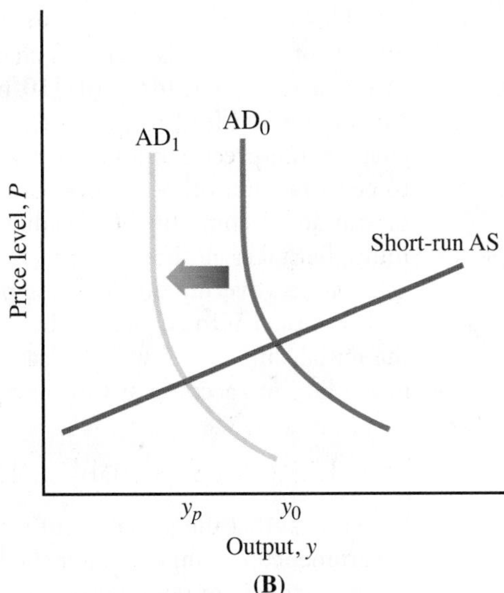

▲ **FIGURE 10.1**
Fiscal Policy in Action
Panel A shows that an increase in government spending shifts the aggregate demand curve from AD_0 to AD_1, restoring the economy to full employment. This is an example of expansionary policy. Panel B shows that an increase in taxes shifts the aggregate demand curve to the left, from AD_0 to AD_1, restoring the economy to full employment. This is an example of contractionary policy.

is below the level of full employment or potential output, y_p. To increase the level of output, the government can increase government spending—say, on military goods—which will shift the aggregate demand curve to the right, to AD_1. Now the new aggregate demand curve intersects the aggregate supply curve at the full-employment level of output. Alternatively, instead of increasing its spending, the government could reduce taxes on consumers and businesses. This would also shift the aggregate demand curve to the right. Government policies that increase aggregate demand are called **expansionary policies**. Increasing government spending and cutting taxes are examples of expansionary policies.

expansionary policies
Government policy actions that lead to increases in aggregate demand.

The government can also use fiscal policy to decrease GDP if the economy is operating at too high a level of output, which would lead to an overheating economy and rising prices. In Panel B of Figure 10.1, the economy is initially operating at a level of output, y_0, that exceeds full-employment output, y_p. An increase in taxes can shift the aggregate demand curve from AD_0 to AD_1. This shift will bring the economy back to full employment.

Alternatively, the government could cut its spending to move the aggregate demand curve to the left. Government policies that decrease aggregate demand are called **contractionary policies**. Decreasing government spending and increasing taxes are examples of contractionary policies.

contractionary policies
Government policy actions that lead to decreases in aggregate demand.

Both examples illustrate how policymakers use fiscal policy to stabilize the economy. In these two simple examples, fiscal policy seems very straightforward. But as we will soon see, in practice it is more difficult to implement effective policy.

The Fiscal Multiplier

Let's recall the multiplier we developed in the last chapter. The basic idea is that the final shift in the aggregate demand curve will be larger than the initial increase. For example, if government purchases increased by $10 billion, that would initially shift the aggregate demand curve to the right by $10 billion. However, the total shift in the aggregate demand curve will be larger, say, $15 billion. Conversely, a decrease in purchases by $10 billion may cause a total shift of the aggregate demand curve to the left by $15 billion.

This multiplier effect occurs because an initial change in output will affect the income of households and thus change consumer spending. For example, an increase in government spending of $10 billion will initially raise household incomes by $10 billion and lead to increases in consumer spending. As we discussed in the last chapter, the precise amount of the increase will depend on the marginal propensity to consume and other factors. In turn, the increase in consumer spending will raise output and income further, leading to further increases in consumer spending. The multiplier takes all these effects into account.

As the government develops policies to stabilize the economy, it needs to take the multiplier into account. The total shift in aggregate demand will be larger than the initial shift. As we will see later in this chapter, U.S. policymakers have taken the multiplier into account as they have developed policies for the economy.

The Limits to Stabilization Policy

We've seen that the government can use fiscal policy—changes in the level of taxes or government spending—to alter the level of GDP. If the current level of GDP is below full employment or potential output, the government can use expansionary policies, such as tax cuts and increased spending, to raise the level of GDP and reduce unemployment.

stabilization policies
Policy actions taken to move the economy closer to full employment or potential output.

Both expansionary and contractionary policies are examples of **stabilization policies**, actions to move the economy closer to full employment or potential output.

It is very difficult to implement stabilization policies for two big reasons. First, there are lags, or delays, in stabilization policy. Lags arise because decision makers are often slow to recognize and respond to changes in the economy, and fiscal policies and other stabilization policies take time to operate. Second, economists simply do not know enough about all aspects of the economy to be completely accurate in all their forecasts. Although economists have made great progress in understanding the economy, the difficulties of forecasting the precise behavior of human beings, who can change their minds or sometimes act irrationally, place limits on our forecasting ability.

LAGS Poorly timed policies can magnify economic fluctuations. Suppose that (1) GDP is currently below full employment but will return to full employment on its own within one year, and that (2) stabilization policies take a full year to become effective. If policymakers tried to expand the economy today, their actions would not take effect until a year from now. One year from now, the economy would normally be back at full employment by itself. But if stabilization policies were enacted, one year from now the economy would be stimulated unnecessarily, and output would exceed full employment.

Figure 10.2 illustrates the problem caused by lags. Panel A shows an example of successful stabilization policy. The solid line represents the behavior of GDP in the absence of policies. Successful stabilization policies can dampen, that is, reduce in magnitude, economic fluctuations, lowering output when it exceeds full employment and raising output when it falls below full employment. This would be easy to accomplish if there were no lags in policy. The dashed curve shows how successful policies can reduce economic fluctuations.

Panel B shows the consequences of ill-timed policies. Again, assume that policies take a year before they are effective. At the start of year 0, the economy is below potential. If policymakers engaged in expansionary policies at the start of year 1, the change would not take effect until the end of year 1. This would raise output even higher above full employment. Ill-timed stabilization policies can magnify economic fluctuations.

inside lags
The time it takes to formulate a policy.

outside lags
The time it takes for the policy to actually work.

Where do the lags in policy come from? Economists recognize two broad classes of lags: *inside lags* and *outside lags*. **Inside lags** refer to the time it takes to formulate a policy. **Outside lags** refer to the time it takes for the policy to actually work. To help you understand inside and outside lags, imagine that you are steering a large ocean liner and you are looking out for possible collisions with hidden icebergs. The time it takes you to spot an iceberg, communicate this information to the crew, and initiate the process of changing course is the inside lag. Because ocean liners are large and

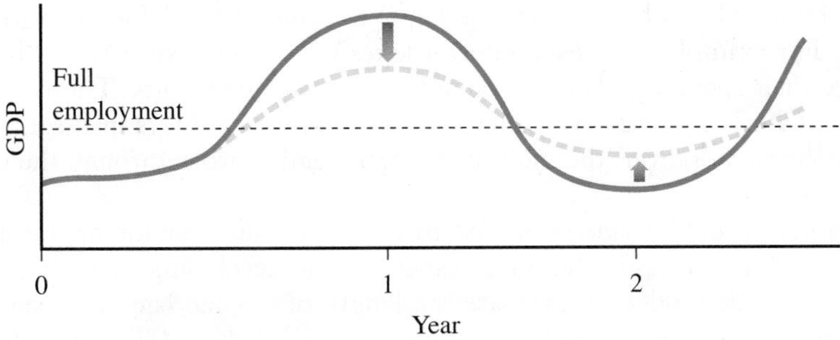

(A) Successful stabilization policy can dampen fluctuations.

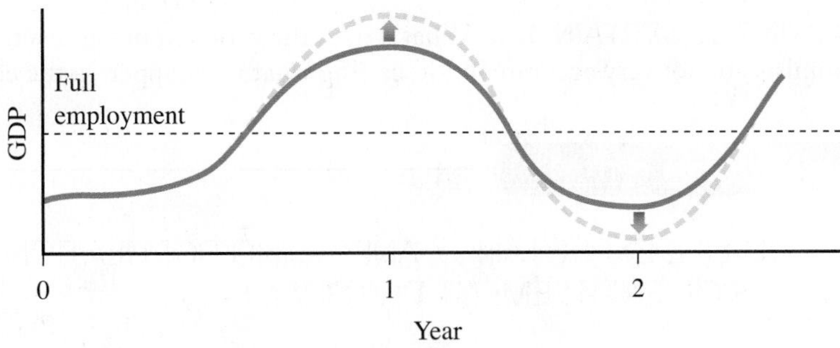

(B) Ill-timed policies can magnify fluctuations.

▲ FIGURE 10.2
Possible Pitfalls in Stabilization Policy
Panel A shows an example of successful stabilization policy. The solid line represents the behavior of GDP in the absence of policies. The dashed line shows the behavior of GDP when policies are in place. Successfully timed policies help smooth out economic fluctuations. Panel B shows the consequences of ill-timed policies. Again, the solid line shows GDP in the absence of policies and the dashed line shows GDP with policies in place. Notice how ill-timed policies make economic fluctuations greater.

have lots of momentum, it will take a long time before your ocean liner begins to turn; this time is the outside lag.

Inside lags occur for two basic reasons. One is that it takes time to identify and recognize a problem. For example, the data available to policymakers may be poor and conflicting. Some economic indicators may look fine, but others may cause concern. It often takes several months to a year before it is clear that there is a serious problem with the economy.

A good example of an inside lag occurred at the beginning of the Great Depression. Although the stock market crashed in October 1929, we know from newspaper and magazine accounts that business leaders were not particularly worried about the economy for some time. Not until late in 1930 did the public begin to recognize the severity of the depression.

The other reason for inside lags is that once a problem has been diagnosed, it still takes time before the government can take action. This delay is most severe for fiscal policy because any changes in taxes or spending must be approved by both houses of Congress and by the president. In recent years, political opponents have been preoccupied with disagreements about the size of the government and the role it should play in the economy, making it difficult to reach a consensus on action in a timely manner.

For example, soon after he was inaugurated in 1993, President Bill Clinton proposed an expansionary stimulus package as part of his overall budget plan. The package contained a variety of spending programs designed to increase the level of GDP and avert a recession. However, the plan was attacked as wasteful and unnecessary, and it did not survive. As it turned out, the stimulus package was not necessary—the economy grew rapidly in the next several years. Nonetheless, this episode illustrates how difficult it is to develop expansionary fiscal policies in time to have the effect we want them to.

Policies are also subject to outside lags—the time it takes for them to become effective. For example, if taxes are cut, it takes time for individuals and businesses to change their spending plans to take advantage of the tax cuts. Therefore, it will be a while before increases in spending raise GDP. Outside lags in fiscal policy are relatively short. Moreover, the multiplier effects tend to work through the economy rather quickly.

Economists use *econometric models* to replicate the behavior of the economy mathematically and statistically, and to assist them in developing economic forecasts. They can also use models to estimate the length of outside lags. One such model predicts that an increase in government spending will increase GDP by its maximum effect after just six months.

FORECASTING UNCERTAINTIES What makes the problem of lags even worse is that economists are not very accurate in forecasting what will happen in the economy.

application 1

INCREASING LIFE EXPECTANCY AND AGING POPULATIONS SPUR COSTS OF ENTITLEMENT PROGRAMS

APPLYING THE CONCEPTS #1: Why are the United States and many other countries facing dramatically increasing costs for their government programs?

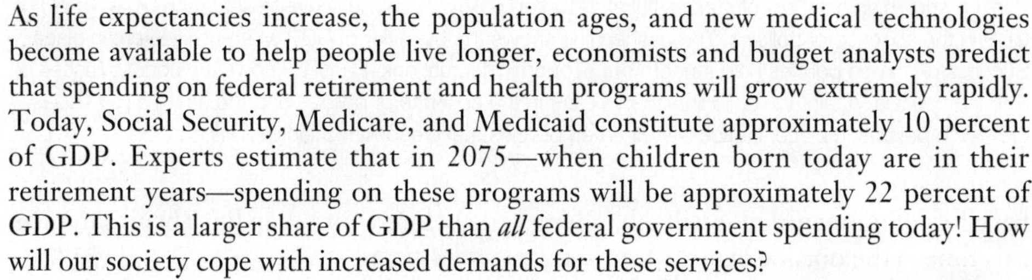

As life expectancies increase, the population ages, and new medical technologies become available to help people live longer, economists and budget analysts predict that spending on federal retirement and health programs will grow extremely rapidly. Today, Social Security, Medicare, and Medicaid constitute approximately 10 percent of GDP. Experts estimate that in 2075—when children born today are in their retirement years—spending on these programs will be approximately 22 percent of GDP. This is a larger share of GDP than *all* federal government spending today! How will our society cope with increased demands for these services?

One possibility is to leave the existing programs in place and just raise taxes to pay for them. This strategy would have two implications. First, if we maintained the federal share of GDP of all other programs, it would mean a large expansion of federal government spending, from our traditional average of 21 percent of GDP to 32 percent of GDP. Second, it would mean a very large increase in the tax burden on future workers and businesses.

Some economists suggest the government should save and invest now to increase GDP in the future, reducing the burden on future generations. However, the saving and investment would increase GDP, and entitlement payments would grow right along with it. As a result, the relative burden of taking care of the elderly would not change dramatically.

Another strategy is to try to reform the entitlement systems, placing more responsibility on individuals and families for their retirement and well-being. For example, we could increase the age at which retirement benefits begin to be paid, and thereby encourage individuals to spend more years in the labor force. Or we could try to reform the health-care system to encourage more competition to reduce health-care expenditures.

All these changes would be very difficult to make, however. Other countries, including Japan and many nations in Europe, which have even older populations and low birth rates, will face more severe challenges and face them earlier than the United States will. Perhaps we can learn from them. Nonetheless, pressures on the federal budget will begin to escalate in the next decade, and policymakers will need to take steps soon to cope with the challenge. **Related to Exercise 2.8.**

For example, a classic problem policymakers face when the economy appears to be slowing down is knowing whether the slowdown is temporary or will persist. Unfortunately, stabilization policy cannot be effective without accurate forecasting. If economic forecasters predict an overheated economy and the government adopts a contractionary policy, the result could be disastrous if the economy weakened before the policy took effect. Today, most economic policymakers understand these limitations and are cautious in using activist policies.

10.2 The Federal Budget

The federal budget—the document that describes what the federal government spends and how it pays for that spending—provides the framework for fiscal policy. In this section, we will take a closer look at federal spending and taxation and what happens when one exceeds the other. The federal budget is extremely large, and the programs that the federal government supports are very complex. To give you a sense of the magnitude of the budget, in 2011 total federal spending was approximately 24.1 percent of GDP, or $3.59 trillion. Federal taxes were 15.4 percent of GDP. With a U.S. population of about 300 million, total federal spending amounted to approximately $12,000 per person.

Probably the best way to begin to grasp the scope and complexities of the U.S. federal budget is to look at recent data to see where we spend money and how we raise it. As we explore the budgetary data, keep in mind that the government runs its budget on a *fiscal-year basis*, not a calendar-year basis. Fiscal year 2011, for example, began on October 1, 2010, and ended on September 30, 2011.

States and local governments also provide government services and collect taxes. Some important services (for example, education) are primarily funded by state and local governments, and others, such as welfare and health care for the poor, are funded jointly by the federal government and state governments. However, because our focus in this chapter is on federal fiscal policy, we will concentrate our discussion on federal spending and taxation.

Federal Spending

Federal spending, spending by the U.S. government, consists of two broad components: federal government purchases of goods and services and transfer payments. As you should recall from our discussion of GDP accounting, only federal government purchases of goods and services are included in GDP. Transfer payments, although an important part of the federal budget, are not a component of GDP because they do not represent any currently produced goods or services.

To study the components of federal spending, we will look at the final data from fiscal year 2011 provided by the Congressional Budget Office, a nonpartisan agency of Congress that provides both budgetary forecasts and historical data on the budget. Table 10.1 provides key data on federal expenditures for fiscal year 2011, both in absolute dollar terms and as a percent of GDP.

Let's begin with the broad categories of the budget. Total spending, or outlays, in fiscal year 2011 were $3,598 billion or approximately 24.1 percent of GDP. Three components of the budget comprise this total: discretionary spending, entitlements and mandatory spending, and net interest.

Discretionary spending constitutes all the programs that Congress authorizes on an annual basis that are not automatically funded by prior laws. It includes defense spending and all nondefense domestic spending. When people commonly discuss federal spending, they often focus on this category, which includes the Defense Department, the Environmental Protection Agency, the State Department, the Interior Department, and other agencies. However, discretionary spending is less than 40 percent of total federal spending. Total nondefense spending is about 4.3 percent of GDP.

discretionary spending
The spending programs that Congress authorizes on an annual basis.

TABLE 10.1 Federal Spending for Fiscal Year 2011

Category	Outlays (billions)	Percent of GDP
Total outlays	$3,598	24.1%
Discretionary spending	1346	9.0
Defense	700	4.7
Nondefense	646	4.3
Entitlements and mandatory spending	2,025	13.5
Social Security	725	4.8
Medicare and Medicaid	835	5.5
Other programs and offsetting receipts	466	3.1
Net interest	227	1.5

SOURCE: Congressional Budget Office, January 2012.

Congress and the president can use discretionary funds directly for activist fiscal policy. To stimulate the economy, they can authorize additional spending by government agencies, or they can urge agencies to accelerate their current spending plans. However, it does take time for bureaucracies to act, and just because Congress authorizes new spending does not mean the agencies will spend the funds immediately.

entitlement and mandatory spending
Spending that Congress has authorized by prior law, primarily providing support for individuals.

Entitlement and mandatory spending constitutes all spending that Congress has authorized by prior law. These expenditures must be made by the federal government unless Congress changes the laws. The terms *entitlement* and *mandatory* spending are not totally accurate, however. Individuals are "entitled" to benefits only to the extent they meet the requirements passed by Congress. Congress can always change the rules. Similarly, this category of spending is "mandatory" only to the extent Congress maintains the current programs in place.

Social Security
A federal government program to provide retirement support and a host of other benefits.

Medicare
A federal government health program for the elderly.

Medicaid
A federal and state government health program for the poor.

Entitlements and mandatory spending are the single largest component of the federal budget. One of the most familiar programs is **Social Security**, which provides retirement payments to retirees as well as a host of other benefits to widows and families of disabled workers. **Medicare** provides health care to all individuals once they reach the age of 65. **Medicaid** provides health care to the poor, in conjunction with the states. Spending on these two health programs by the federal government now exceeds spending on Social Security. The government provides a range of other programs as well, including additional retirement and disability programs (aside from Social Security) and farm price supports to provide income to farmers. Some of these programs are *means tested*. That is, the amount of benefit is partly based on the income of the recipient. Medicaid, for example, is a means-tested program.

Net interest is the interest the government pays on the government debt held by the public, for example, U.S. Treasury bonds, bills, and U.S. savings bonds. We will discuss how the government borrows money later in the chapter. In fiscal year 2011, total net interest payments to the public were $227 billion, or approximately 1.5 percent of GDP. Total expenditures on net interest are directly related to the total government debt held by the public and the level of interest rates. Increased government debt and higher interest rates will lead to higher net interest payments by the government.

As the population ages, entitlements and net interest are becoming the fastest-growing component of the federal budget.

Federal Revenues

The federal government receives its revenue from taxes levied on both individuals and businesses. Table 10.2 shows the revenues the federal government received in fiscal year 2011 in both dollar terms and as a percent of GDP.

Let's review the categories that comprise total federal revenue. The single largest component of federal revenue is the familiar *individual income tax*. Tax returns

TABLE 10.2 Sources of Federal Government Revenue, Fiscal Year 2011

Category	Receipts (billions)	Percent of GDP
Total revenue	$2,302	15.4%
Individual income taxes	1091	7.3
Social insurance taxes	819	5.5
Corporate taxes	181	1.2
Estate, excise, and others	211	1.4

SOURCE: Congressional Budget Office, January 2012.

calculating the tax individuals or couples owed during the prior year must be filed by April 15 of every year. During the year, the federal government collects in advance some of the taxes due by *withholding* a portion of workers' paychecks. Taxpayers not subject to withholding or who earn income through investments must make estimated tax payments each quarter, so the tax due the federal government is paid evenly over the year in which it is earned.

The second-largest component of federal revenue is *social insurance taxes*, which are taxes levied on earnings to pay for Social Security and Medicare. Today, social insurance taxes are almost as large as individual income taxes, and together they comprise over 80 percent of total federal revenue. Unlike individual income taxes, social insurance taxes are paid only on wages and not on income from investments.

Other taxes paid directly by individuals and families include *estate and gift taxes*, *excise taxes*, and *custom duties*. Estate and gift taxes, sometimes known as the "death tax," are levied on the estates and previous gifts of individuals when they pass away. In 2012 estates were taxed only if they exceeded a threshold of $5.0 million—so small estates did not pay this tax. There is considerable uncertainty as to the future level for the estate tax. The estate and gift tax typically raises little revenue but generates a great deal of controversy. Opponents of the tax argue that it destroys family-held businesses, such as family farms passed down from one generation to the next. Proponents claim the tax is necessary to prevent what they see as unfair accumulation of wealth across generations.

The corporate tax is a tax levied on the earnings of corporations. This tax raised less than 8 percent of total federal revenues during fiscal year 2011. The tax was a more important source of revenue in past decades but has declined to today's relatively low level. This decline has been attributed to many factors, including falling corporate profits as a share of GDP, the growth of opportunities for tax shelters, incentives provided by Congress to stimulate business investment and research and development, and complex rules for taxing multinational corporations that operate on a global basis. The other sources of government revenue are relatively minor. *Federal excise taxes* are taxes levied on the sale of certain products, for example, gasoline, tires, firearms, alcohol, and tobacco. *Custom duties* are taxes levied on goods imported to the United States, such as foreign cars or wines.

SUPPLY-SIDE ECONOMICS AND THE LAFFER CURVE Is it possible for a government to cut tax rates yet still raise more revenue? That's a politician's dream. People would face lower tax rates, yet there would be more money for politicians to spend. Economist Arthur Laffer argued in the late 1970s that there was a strong possibility we could do this in the U.S. economy. Laffer's views influenced many politicians at the time and became the basis for supply-side economics. **Supply-side economics** is a school of thought that emphasizes the role taxes play in the supply of output in the economy. Supply-side economists look at the effects of taxes not just on aggregate demand, as we did earlier in this chapter, but also on aggregate supply. A decrease in tax rates will typically tend to increase labor supply and output. Thus, changes in taxes can also shift the aggregate supply curve.

supply-side economics
A school of thought that emphasizes the role that taxes play in the supply of output in the economy.

Laffer curve
A relationship between the tax rates and tax revenues that illustrates that high tax rates could lead to lower tax revenues if economic activity is severely discouraged.

Laffer also developed a model known today as the **Laffer curve**. Suppose a government imposed extremely high tariffs (taxes) on imported goods—tariffs so high that no one could afford to import any goods whatsoever. If this were the case, the government would not collect any revenue from the tariffs. But if the government cut the rates and individuals began to buy imported goods, the government would start to collect at least some tariff revenue. This was Laffer's point: Lower taxes (tariffs) could actually lead to higher government revenues.

Virtually all economists today believe Laffer's tax revenue idea won't work when it comes to broad-based income taxes or payroll taxes. For these types of taxes, cutting rates from their current levels would simply reduce the revenues the government collects, because most economists believe the supply of labor is not as sensitive to changes in tax rates as Laffer believed it was. But there are some taxes, such as tariffs or taxes on the gains investors earn by holding stocks and bonds, for which Laffer's claim is plausible.

The Federal Deficit and Fiscal Policy

budget deficit
The amount by which government spending exceeds revenues in a given year.

The federal government runs a **budget deficit** when it spends more than it receives in tax revenues in a given year. Here is how it works. Suppose a government wishes to spend $100 billion but receives only $95 billion in tax revenue. To actually spend the $100 billion, the government must obtain funds from some source. Facing a $5 billion shortfall, it will borrow that money from the public by selling the public government bonds. A *government bond* is an IOU in which the government promises to later pay back the money lent to it, with interest. Thus, when the public purchases $5 billion of these bonds, it transfers $5 billion to the government. Later the public will receive its $5 billion back with interest.

budget surplus
The amount by which government revenues exceed government expenditures in a given year.

If the government collects more in taxes than it wishes to spend in a given year, it is running a **budget surplus**. In this case, the government has excess funds and can buy back bonds it previously sold to the public, eliminating some of its debt.

Many political and economic considerations enter into the decisions to change government spending or taxes or raise or lower deficits. In the last part of this chapter we will see how fiscal policy has been used historically in the United States. In later chapters, we will look in more depth at other political considerations that influence fiscal policy.

Automatic Stabilizers

Both government spending and tax revenues are very sensitive to the state of the economy. Because tax collections are based largely on individual and corporate income, tax revenues will fall sharply during a recession as national income falls. At the same time, government transfer payments for programs such as unemployment insurance and food stamps will also tend to increase during a recession. The result is higher government spending and lower tax collections and the increased likelihood that the government will run a budget deficit. Similarly, when the economy grows rapidly, tax collections increase and government expenditures on transfer payments decrease, and the likelihood of the federal government running a surplus is greater.

Now suppose an economy had a balanced federal budget—neither deficit nor surplus. An external shock (such as a dramatic increase in oil prices or drought) then plunged the economy into a recession. Tax revenues fall and expenditures on transfer payments increase, resulting in a budget deficit. Believe it or not, the deficit actually serves a valuable role in stabilizing the economy. It works through three channels:

1 Increased transfer payments such as unemployment insurance, food stamps, and other welfare payments increase the income of some households, partly offsetting the fall in household income.

2 Other households whose incomes are falling pay less in taxes, which partly offsets the decline in their household income. Because incomes do not fall as much as they would have in the absence of the deficit, consumption spending does not decline as much.

3 Because the corporation tax depends on corporate profits and profits fall in a recession, taxes on businesses also fall. Lower corporate taxes help to prevent businesses from cutting spending as much as they would otherwise during a recession.

The government deficit itself, in effect, offsets part of the adverse effect of the recession and thus helps stabilize the economy.

Similarly, during an economic boom, transfer payments fall and tax revenues increase. This dampens the increase in household income and also the increase in consumption and investment spending that would accompany higher household income and higher corporate profits. Taxes and transfer payments that stabilize GDP without requiring explicit actions by policymakers are called **automatic stabilizers.**

automatic stabilizers
Taxes and transfer payments that stabilize GDP without requiring policymakers to take explicit action.

The great virtue of automatic stabilizers is that they do not require explicit action from the president and Congress to change the law. Given the long inside lags caused by ideological battles in Washington, D.C., over spending, taxes, and the deficit, it is fortunate that we have mechanisms in place to dampen economic fluctuations without requiring explicit and deliberative action.

Are Deficits Bad?

Let's take a closer look at fiscal policy designed to stabilize the economy. If the budget were initially balanced and the economy plunged into a recession, a budget deficit would emerge as tax revenues fell and expenditures increased. To combat the recession, policymakers could then either increase government spending or cut taxes. Both actions, however, would increase the deficit—an important point to remember.

Despite concerns about increasing the deficit, this is precisely the right policy. If policymakers tried to avoid running a deficit by raising taxes or cutting spending, that would actually make the recession worse. The key lesson here is that during a recession, we should focus on what our fiscal policy actions do to the economy, not what they do to the deficit.

Does that mean concerns about the federal budget deficit are misplaced? No, because in the long run, large budget deficits can have an adverse effect on the economy. We explore these issues in more detail in a later chapter, but we can easily understand the basic problem. We have seen that when an economy is operating at full employment, output must be divided between consumption, investment, government spending, and net exports. Suppose, then, the government cuts taxes for households and runs a deficit. The reduced taxes will tend to increase consumer spending. Consumers may save some of the tax cut but will consume the rest. However, because output is fixed at full employment, some other component of output must be reduced, or crowded out. Crowding out is an example of the principle of opportunity cost.

PRINCIPLE OF OPPORTUNITY COST

The opportunity cost of something is what you sacrifice to get it.

In this case, we normally expect that the increased consumption spending will come at the sacrifice of reduced investment spending. As we have seen, with reduced investment spending the economy will grow more slowly in the future. Thus, the budget deficit will increase current consumption but slow the growth of the economy in the future. This is the real concern with prolonged budget deficits.

Another way to understand the concern about long-run deficits is to think of what happens in the financial markets when the government runs large deficits. As the government runs large deficits, it will have to borrow increasing amounts of money from the public by selling U.S. government bonds. In the financial markets, the government will be in increased competition with businesses that are trying to

application 2

THE CONFUCIUS CURVE?

APPLYING THE CONCEPTS #2: How are tax rates and tax revenues related?

While the idea that cutting tax rates might actually increase tax revenue is often attributed to economist Arthur Laffer, in fact, it is actually a much older idea than that. Yu Juo, one of the 12 wise men who succeeded Confucius in ancient China, had a very similar idea.

He was asked by Duke Ai, "It has been a year of famine and there are not enough revenues to run the state. What should I do?"

Juo said, "Why can't you use a 10 percent tax?"

The Duke answered, "I can't even get by on a 20 percent tax; how am I going to do it on 10 percent?"

Juo said, "If the people have enough what prince can be in want? If the people are in want how can the Prince be satisfied?"

Clearly, Yu Juo was skeptical that raising rates would raise revenues and advocated for lower tax rates.

Today, revenue estimators in Washington, D.C., do not share entirely in Yu Juo's wisdom. But they do recognize that cutting tax rates will stimulate economic activity, which will offset some of the loss in potential revenues to the government. **Related to Exercise 2.9.**

SOURCE: Based on author's rendition of The Analects of Confucius, 12.9, http://www.iub.edu/~p374/Analects_of_Confucius_(Eno-2010).pdf (accessed April 23, 2012).

---

raise funds from the public to finance their investment plans, too. This increased competition from the government will make it more difficult and costly for businesses to raise funds and, as a result, investment spending will decrease.

10.3 Fiscal Policy in U.S. History

The fiscal policies that Congress and the president use have evolved over many years. In this section, we review the historical events that helped create today's U.S. fiscal policies.

The Depression Era

The basic principles of fiscal policy—using government spending and taxation to stabilize the economy—have been known for many years and, indeed, were discussed in the 1920s. However, it took a long time before economic policy decisions were based on these principles. Many people associate active fiscal policy in the United States with actions taken by President Franklin Roosevelt during the Great Depression of the 1930s. But this view is misleading, according to E. Cary Brown, a former economics professor at the Massachusetts Institute of Technology.[1]

During the 1930s, politicians did not believe in modern fiscal policy, largely because they feared the consequences of government budget deficits. According to Brown, fiscal policy was expansionary only during two years of the Great Depression, 1931 and 1936. In those years, Congress voted for substantial payments to veterans, over objections of presidents Herbert Hoover and Franklin Roosevelt. Although government spending increased during the 1930s, taxes increased sufficiently during that same period, with the result that there was no net fiscal expansion.

The Kennedy Administration

Although modern fiscal policy was not deliberately used during the 1930s, the growth in military spending at the onset of World War II in 1941 increased total demand in the economy and helped pull the economy out of its long decade of poor performance. But to see fiscal policy in action, we need to turn to the 1960s. It was not until the presidency of John F. Kennedy during the early 1960s that modern fiscal policy came to be accepted.

Walter Heller, the chairman of the president's Council of Economic Advisers under John F. Kennedy, was a forceful advocate of active fiscal policy. From his perspective, the economy was operating far below its potential, and a tax cut was the perfect medicine to bring it back to full employment. When Kennedy entered office, the unemployment rate was 6.7 percent. Heller believed the unemployment rate at full employment—the "natural rate" of unemployment, that is—was really only about 4 percent. He convinced Kennedy of the need for a tax cut to stimulate the economy, and Kennedy put forth an economic program based largely on modern fiscal policy principles.

Two other factors led the Kennedy administration to support the tax cut. First, tax rates were extremely high at the time. The top individual tax rate was 91 percent, compared to about 40 percent today. The corporate tax rate was 52 percent, compared to 35 percent today. Second, Heller convinced Kennedy that even if a tax cut led to a federal budget deficit, it was not a problem. In 1961, the federal deficit was less than 1 percent of GDP, and future projections indicated it would disappear as the economy grew because of higher tax revenues.

The tax cuts were enacted in February 1964, after Lyndon Johnson became president following Kennedy's assassination. They included permanent cuts in rates for both individuals and corporations. Estimating the actual effects these tax cuts had on the economy is difficult. To make a valid comparison, we need to estimate how the economy would have behaved without them. What we do know is that the economy grew at a rapid rate following the tax cuts. From 1963 to 1966, both real GDP and consumption grew at rates exceeding 4 percent per year. We cannot rule out the possibility that the economy could have grown just as rapidly without the tax cuts. Nonetheless, the rapid growth during this period suggests the tax cuts had the effect, predicted by Heller's theory, of stimulating economic growth.

The Vietnam War Era

The next major use of modern fiscal policy occurred in 1968. As the Vietnam War began and military spending increased, unemployment fell to very low levels. From 1966 to 1969, the overall unemployment rate fell below 4 percent. Policymakers became concerned that the economy was overheating and this would lead to a higher inflation rate. In 1968, a temporary tax surcharge of 10 percent was enacted to reduce total demand for goods and services. The 10 percent surcharge was a "tax on a tax," so it raised the taxes paid by households by 10 percent. Essentially, the surcharge was specifically designed to be temporary and expired within a year.

The surcharge did not decrease consumer spending as much as economists had initially estimated, however. Part of the reason was that it was temporary. Economists who have studied consumption behavior have noticed that consumers often base their spending on an estimate of their long-run average income, or **permanent income**, not on their current income.

permanent income
An estimate of a household's long-run average level of income.

For example, consider a salesperson who usually earns $50,000 a year, although her income in any single year might be slightly higher or lower. Knowing her permanent income is $50,000, she consumes $45,000. If her income in one year is higher than average, say $55,000, she is still likely to consume $45,000 (as if she earned just her normal $50,000) and save the rest.

The one-year tax surcharge during the Vietnam War had a similar effect. Because consumers knew the surcharge was not permanent, they didn't alter their spending habits very much. The surtax reduced households' savings, not their consumption. The result was a smaller decrease in demand for goods and services than economists anticipated.

During the 1970s, there were many changes in taxes and spending but no major changes in overall fiscal policy. A recession in 1973 led to a tax rebate and other incentives in 1975, but, by and large, changes to fiscal policy were mild.

The Reagan Administration

The tax cuts enacted during 1981 at the beginning of the first term of President Ronald Reagan were significant. However, they were not proposed to increase aggregate demand. Instead, the tax cuts were justified on the basis of improving economic incentives and increasing the supply of output. In other words, they were supply-side motivated. Taxes can have important effects on the supply of labor, saving, and economic growth. Proponents of the 1981 tax cuts emphasized the effects of supply and not increases in aggregate demand. Nonetheless, the tax cuts did appear to increase consumer demand and helped the economy recover from the back-to-back recessions in the early 1980s.

By the mid-1980s, large government budget deficits began to emerge, and policymakers became concerned. As the deficits grew and became the focus of attention, interest in using fiscal policy to manage the economy waned because policymakers placed primary concern on deficit reduction, not stabilization policy. Although there were government spending and tax changes in the 1980s and 1990s, few were justified solely as policies to change aggregate demand.

The Clinton and George W. Bush Administrations

At the beginning of his administration, President Bill Clinton proposed a "stimulus package" that would increase aggregate demand, but it was defeated in Congress. Clinton later successfully passed a major tax increase that brought the budget into balance. A Republican-controlled Congress that had different priorities than the Clinton administration limited government spending. By 1998, the federal budget actually began to show surpluses rather than deficits, setting the stage for tax cuts.

During his first year in office in 2001, President George W. Bush passed a 10-year tax cut plan that decreased tax rates, in part to eliminate the government surpluses and return revenues to households, but also to stimulate the economy that was slowing down as the high-tech investment boom was ending.

The first year of the tax cut featured tax rebates or refunds of up to $600 per married couple. The refunds were intended to increase aggregate demand.

After the September 11, 2001, terrorist attacks, President Bush and Congress became less concerned with balancing the federal budget and authorized new spending programs to provide relief to victims and to stimulate the economy, which had entered into a recession prior to September 11.

In May 2003, President Bush signed another tax bill to stimulate the sluggish economy and, in particular, to increase investment spending. This bill had many distinct features, including moving up some of the previously scheduled cuts in tax rates that were part of the 2001 tax bill, increasing the child tax credit, and lowering taxes on dividends and capital gains.

In 2008, a slowing economy led President Bush and Congress to adopt tax rebates and some investment incentives in early 2008. The tax cuts were relatively large, approximately 1 percent of GDP, and the rebates, some as large as $1,800, were designed to reach 128 million households. In February 2009, President Obama and Congress enacted the largest stimulus package in United States history. The stimulus package proved to be controversial both in its size and composition. While many economists believe it helped the economy recover, others have been more skeptical.

The combination of the 2001 and 2007 recessions, the financial crisis of 2008 and its aftermath, the various tax cuts, the large stimulus package of 2009, and the increased expenses associated with the wars in Afghanistan and Iraq sharply changed the fiscal landscape from the beginning of the decade. Although the deficit temporarily became smaller in 2006 and 2007, the situation changed radically. By fiscal year 2011 the deficit was 8.7 percent of GDP, far above usual historical levels. Future projections indicated that the deficit would likely fall, but still remain high for future years.

Figure 10.3 plots the course of spending, taxes, and the deficit since 1996 and shows the recent reemergence of deficits from the surpluses of the late 1990s and the deficits in 2011. The prospect of future deficits may limit the ability of the U.S. government to conduct expansionary fiscal policy in the near future and will set the background for the political debates in Washington, D.C., for many years to come.

application 3

A CLOSER LOOK AT THE 2009 STIMULUS PACKAGE

APPLYING THE CONCEPTS #3: Was the fiscal stimulus in 2009 successful?

In 2009, President Obama signed into law the American Recovery and Reinvestment Act, the largest fiscal stimulus in United States history. Although the recovery of the economy from the 2007 recession was still sluggish, many economists—including those at the Congressional Budget Office—believe that the stimulus did have a significant impact on the economy.

But not all economists share this belief. John B. Taylor, at Stanford University, looked carefully at the three key elements of the stimulus package: temporary tax cuts, increases in federal government purchases of goods and services, and aid to state and local governments. Based on his analysis, Taylor believes the stimulus was ineffective.

Taylor first examined whether the temporary tax cuts stimulated consumption spending. Consistent with much prior research on this topic, he found little evidence that the temporary tax cuts stimulated consumption; they were essentially saved. With respect to government purchases, this turned out to be a relatively small part of the stimulus package. Regardless of one's view about the government spending multiplier, there was simply not enough to matter.

Analyzing the effects of grants to state and local governments was more complex. Taylor found that state and local governments increased their spending on transfer programs (welfare and Medicaid) but cut back on their spending on goods and services. Taylor argues that, on balance, state and local governments simply saved the money they received from the federal government and used it to reduce their borrowing. Other economists disagree and have suggested that without the aid to state and local governments, there would have been substantially more cuts in spending and the provision of state and local services.

Even President Obama admitted it was hard to find "shovel ready" projects to build new infrastructure in a timely manner. While the federal government can provide stimulus funds to individuals, businesses, and state and local governments, getting them to increase their spending is much more difficult. **Related to Exercise 3.7.**

SOURCE: Based on John B. Taylor, "An Empirical Analysis of the Revival of Fiscal Activism in the 2000s," *Journal of Economic Literature*, 2011, v. 49,3, pp. 686–702.

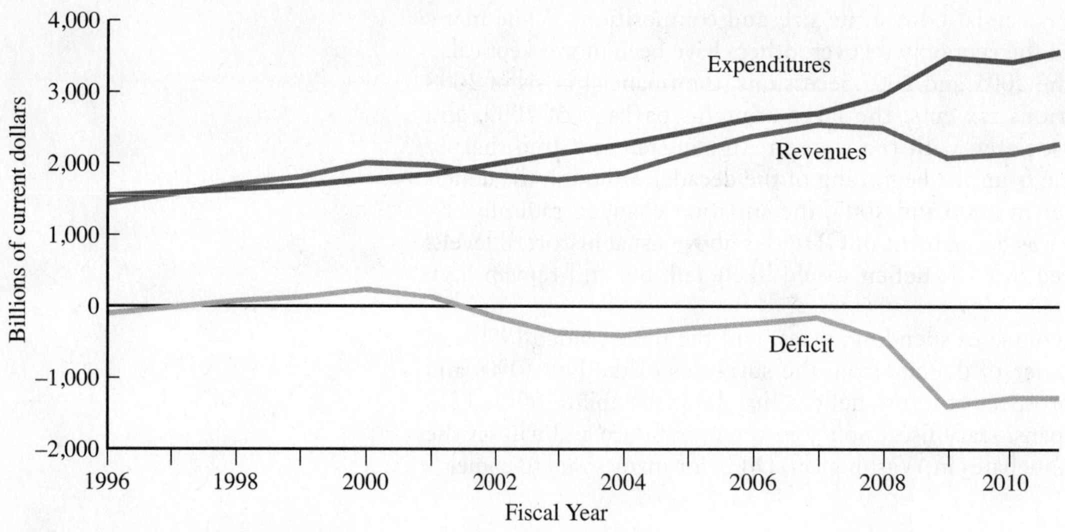

▲ **FIGURE 10.3**
Federal Taxes, Spending, and Deficits, Fiscal Years 1996–2011
SOURCE: Congressional Budget Office, January 2012.

MyEconLab Real-time data

SUMMARY

This chapter explored the role of government fiscal policy. Using the AD-AS model, we showed how fiscal policy can stabilize the economy. We also discussed the multiplier and the limits to stabilization policy. In addition, the chapter gave us an overview of the federal budget, including spending, revenues, deficits, and surpluses. Finally, we explored how fiscal policy in the United States has changed over time. Here are the key points:

1 Increases in government spending or decreases in taxes will increase aggregate demand.

2 Decreases in government spending or increases in taxes will decrease aggregate demand.

3 Because of the multiplier, the total shift in the aggregate demand curve will be larger than the initial shift. Policymakers need to take the multiplier into account as they formulate policy.

4 Both *inside lags* (the time it takes to formulate policy) and *outside lags* (the time it takes the policy to work) limit the effectiveness of active fiscal policy.

5 The largest component of federal spending is *entitlements and mandatory programs*.

6 The largest components of federal revenues are income taxes and social insurance taxes collected from individuals.

7 Government deficits act as an *automatic stabilizer* that helps to stabilize the economy in the short run.

8 In the short run, fiscal policy actions taken to combat a recession will increase the deficit; in the long run, deficits are a concern because they may lead to the crowding out of investment spending.

9 Active fiscal policy has been periodically used in the United States to stimulate the economy; at other times, concerns about deficits have limited the use of fiscal policy.

KEY TERMS

automatic stabilizers, p. 215
budget deficit, p. 214
budget surplus, p. 214
contractionary policies, p. 207
discretionary spending, p. 211
entitlement and mandatory spending, p. 212
expansionary policies, p. 207
fiscal policy, p. 206
inside lags, p. 208
Laffer curve, p. 213
Medicaid, p. 212
Medicare, p. 212
outside lags, p. 208
permanent income, p. 217
Social Security, p. 212
stabilization policies, p. 208
supply-side economics, p. 213

EXERCISES

All problems are assignable in MyEconLab.

10.1 The Role of Fiscal Policy

1.1 To decrease aggregate demand, a government can either decrease spending or __________ taxes.

1.2 Contractionary fiscal policy shifts the aggregate demand curve to the __________, __________ prices, and __________ real GDP.

1.3 If the multiplier for taxation is –1.50, then a $150 billion increase in taxes will ultimately shift the demand curve by __________.

1.4 __________ lags refer to the time it takes for policymakers to recognize an economic problem and take appropriate actions.

1.5 **A Chinese Experiment.** In 2000 the Chinese government mandated three one-week holidays throughout the year to stimulate consumer spending. The idea was that these extended vacations would induce the Chinese to spend more of their earnings while on vacation.

   a. Using the AD–AS framework, show the mechanism through which the Chinese government believed that the mandated holidays would stimulate the economy.

   b. Although consumption spending rose during the vacation period, the data show that consumption fell before and after the vacation. Did the policy work?

1.6 **Time-Dated Debit Cards as a Fiscal Stimulus.** Here is one unusual fiscal policy: The government would issue time-dated debit cards to each person that had to be spent on goods and services produced *only* by U.S. firms within a fixed period (say, three months) or become worthless. Suppose the government was considering whether to issue $400 in time-dated debit cards to each household or give each household $400 in cash instead.

   a. Which plan would lead to the greatest economic stimulus?

   b. Which plan do you think the government would find easier to administer?

   c. Suppose a household had large credit card debt, which it wished to reduce. Which of the two plans would that household prefer?

1.7 **Political Systems and the Inside Lag for Fiscal Policy.** Under a parliamentary system like in Britain, there are fewer checks and balances on the government than in the United States. In a parliamentary system, the party that controls the legislature also runs the executive branch. How do you think the inside lag for fiscal policy in England compares to that in the United States?

1.8 **Looking Backward.** Some critics of stabilization policy say that policymakers are always looking backward—through a rear view mirror at past data—and thus cannot conduct stabilization policy. Can you give a defense for policymakers despite the fact that they must look at past data?

1.9 **Shorter Business Cycles and Lags.** Suppose the typical business cycle as shown in Figure 10.2 becomes shorter. Does this make the conduct of active fiscal policy easier or harder? Explain.

10.2 The Federal Budget

2.1 Fiscal year 2012 began on October 1, __________.

2.2 Discretionary spending is the largest component of federal spending. __________ (True/False)

2.3 Two examples of entitlement spending are __________ and __________.

2.4 The two primary sources of federal government revenue are __________ and __________.

2.5 **The States and Balanced Budgets.** Unlike the U.S. federal government, virtually all states have requirements that they must either plan for or maintain a balanced budget.

   a. Suppose the national economy experiences a recession. How will this affect the budgets of the states?

   b. What actions must the states then take to balance the budget?

   c. Graphically show how these actions, taken together, may destabilize the national economy.

2.6 **Automatic Stabilizers and Fluctuations in Output.** Because of automatic stabilizers, states with more generous unemployment insurance programs will experience __________ fluctuations in output.

2.7 **Partnerships and Corporate Tax Revenues.** In recent years, many large organizations—such as global accounting firms—have been structured as partnerships for tax purposes rather than corporations. This means that they do not have to pay the corporate tax. How would the growth of partnerships as a form of business organization explain some of the historical trends with the corporate tax?

2.8 **Mandatory Spending and Entitlements.** Is "mandatory spending" really mandatory? __________ (yes/no) Explain how mandatory spending differs from discretionary spending. In the face of the coming crisis in entitlement spending, do you believe that mandatory spending will be harder to change than discretionary spending? (Related to Application 1 on page 210.)

2.9 **High Tax Rates and Summer Employment.** Suppose you were considering taking a summer job to earn additional spending money for school. The job pays $12 an hour but you have to pay both income and social insurance taxes on your earnings. If you faced a 50 percent rate of taxation on your earnings (so you could keep only $6), would you keep working? How about a 70 percent rate? (Related to Application 2 on page 216.)

10.3 Fiscal Policy in U.S. History

3.1 __________ was the first president to consciously use fiscal policy to stabilize the economy.

3.2 Walter Heller was President Lyndon Johnson's chief economic adviser. __________ (True/False)

3.3 The U.S. economy witnessed federal budget surpluses in __________.

3.4 Long-run average income is known as __________ income.

3.5 **Tax Refunds and Consumer Spending.** In 1999, the Internal Revenue Service began to mail out refund checks because of changes in the tax law in 1998. Economic forecasters predicted that consumption and GDP would increase because of higher refunds on income taxes. Using each of the following assumptions, do you think the forecasters were correct? Answer yes or no.

a. Taxpayers were not aware they would receive refunds until they had completed their income tax statements.

b. Taxpayers did know they would receive refunds but, as consumers, based their spending decisions solely on their current levels of income.

c. Taxpayers did know they would receive refunds and, as consumers, based their consumption decisions on their permanent incomes.

3.6 **The Rise and Fall of Fiscal Surpluses.** What factors led the United States from federal surpluses at the end of the 1990s to deficits in the first decade of the twenty-first century? What factors led to the demise of surpluses?

3.7 **Personal Debt and Tax Cuts.** Suppose you had a large unpaid balance on your credit card and were paying a high rate of interest. You then received a one-time tax rebate from the government and decided to pay down the balance on your credit card. If there were many others like you in the economy, would the tax cut be an effective stimulus? (Related to Application 3 on page 219.)

3.8 **College Students and Tax Rebates.** If a college student with a low credit card limit received a tax rebate, do you think he or she would be more likely to save it or spend it? How about a middle-aged married man who does not have a low credit card limit? Explain your reasoning.

3.9 **A Dramatic Drop in the Corporate Tax.** Go to the Web site for the Congressional Budget Office (www.cbo.gov) and find the data for corporate tax revenue between 2007 and 2009. What was the decrease and how can you explain it?

3.10 **Long-Run Deficit Projections.** The Congressional Budget Office makes long-run deficit budget projections, extending far into the twenty-first century. What are the main causes of the long-run deficits projected by the CBO?

NOTES

1. E. Cary Brown, "Fiscal Policy in the 1930s: A Reappraisal," *American Economic Review* 46 (December 1956): 857–879.

The Income-Expenditure Model

CHAPTER

11

Heading into the global recession in 2007, the Chinese economy was growing at the extraordinary rate of 11 percent per year.

As Chinese policymakers began to see the severity of the oncoming global recession, they became concerned that real GDP growth would fall below the 7 percent level they needed to incorporate the influx of new entrants into the labor force. As a consequence, they embarked on a massive stimulus package, more in the spirit of Keynes than Mao.

In late 2008 the Chinese government announced it was undertaking a stimulus plan equivalent to $586 billion in U.S. dollars. This was a massive program, approximately 13 percent of GDP. Public infrastructure was the largest single component of the plan, with investments for new railways, roads, irrigation, and transportation. Another major component of the plan was funds to restore the damage caused by the severe earthquakes that had hit Sichuan province earlier in the year. Additional funds in the package were allocated for housing, social programs, and human capital.

Since China was already embarking on a state-run, large-scale investment program, it was able to put these programs into effect rather quickly. That was in sharp contrast to the United States, which needed to gear up new programs to spend funds on infrastructure. As a result, China managed to avoid the worst of the global recession, with real GDP growth around 9 percent for both 2008 and 2009 and continued strong growth through 2011. A robust Chinese economy also helped the other economies in the world to recover as well.[1]

LEARNING OBJECTIVES

- Discuss the income-expenditure model.
- Identify the two key components of the consumption function.
- Calculate equilibrium income in a simple model.
- Explain how government spending and taxes affect equilibrium income.
- Discuss the role of exports and imports in determining equilibrium income.
- Explain how the aggregate demand curve is related to the income-expenditure model.

Newspaper and television stories about the economy tend to focus on what causes changes in short-term real GDP. For example, we often read about how changes in economic conditions in Europe or Asia or changes in government spending or taxation will affect near-term economic growth. To understand these stories, we need to understand the behavior of the economy in the short run.

As we have seen, in the short run changes in aggregate demand play the key role in determining the level of output. In the short run, prices are slow to change, and therefore fluctuations in aggregate demand translate directly into fluctuations in GDP and income. In this chapter, we take a more detailed look at short-run fluctuations in GDP.

The model we develop in this chapter is called the *income-expenditure model*, sometimes referred to as the *Keynesian cross*. The model was developed by the economist John Maynard Keynes in the 1930s and later extended and refined by many economists. When Keynes developed his approach to macroeconomics, the world economy was in the midst of a severe depression. Unlike many other economists at the time, Keynes did not believe the economy would return to full employment by itself. An economy could get "trapped" in a depression and not recover.

Keynes provided both a diagnosis of an economic depression and a cure. He argued that the fundamental problem causing the world depression was insufficient demand for goods and services. Here was the problem: Firms would not increase their production and put the unemployed back to work unless there was sufficient demand for the goods and services they produced. But consumers and firms would not demand enough goods and services unless the economy improved and their incomes were higher. Keynes argued that active fiscal policy—increasing government spending or cutting taxes—could increase total demand for goods and services and bring the economy back to full employment. This income-expenditure model is based on the idea that higher *expenditures* were necessary to generate higher levels of *income* in the economy.

The income-expenditure model focuses on changes in the level of output or real GDP. However, it does not take into account changes in prices. The model is thus very useful for understanding economic fluctuations in the short run when prices do not change very much. It is less useful in the intermediate or longer run, when prices do adjust to economic conditions. For intermediate or longer-run analysis, we need to use the aggregate demand and aggregate supply curves to understand movements in both output and prices.

In this chapter, we focus on the short run. In the last part of this chapter, we show how Keynes's income-expenditure model also provides an important building block for our model of aggregate demand. In later chapters, we will incorporate financial markets into our discussion of aggregate demand.

This chapter will primarily use graphical tools to explain the income-expenditure model. An appendix to the chapter provides an algebraic treatment of the model and shows how some of the key formulas are derived.

11.1 A Simple Income-Expenditure Model

First, we will develop a very simple income-expenditure model to illustrate the ideas of Keynes. Later in the chapter, we will expand the income-expenditure model to make it more realistic.

Equilibrium Output

Let's begin with the simplest income-expenditure model. It uses a graph like Figure 11.1, with total expenditures for goods and services represented on the vertical axis, output (y) represented on the horizontal axis, and a 45° line. The 45° line marks all the points on the graph at which the value of the variable measured on the horizontal axis (output) equals the value of the variable measured on the vertical axis (total expenditures). In our most basic model, we temporarily omit the government and the foreign sector. Only consumers and firms can demand output: Consumers demand consumption goods, and firms demand investment goods. We make things even simpler by assuming that consumers and firms each demand a fixed amount of goods. Let consumption demand be an amount C, and let investment demand be an amount I. Total demand will be $C + I$. Total demand for goods and services is also called **planned expenditures**. Thus, planned expenditures in this simple economy are equal to $C + I$.

planned expenditures
Another term for total demand for goods and services.

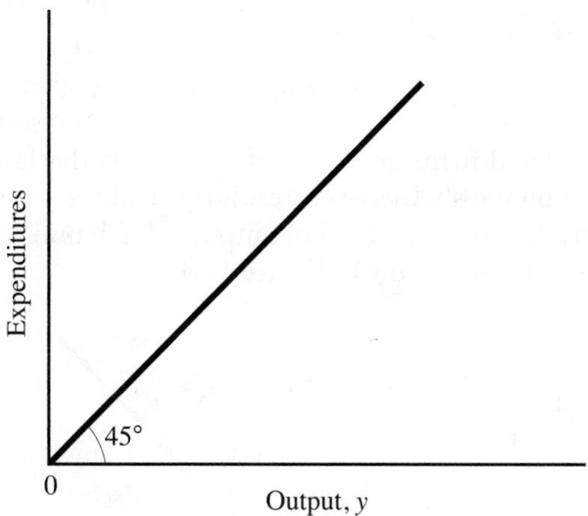

◄ FIGURE 11.1
The 45° Line
At any point on the 45° line, the distance to the horizontal axis is the same as the distance to the vertical axis.

In the income-expenditure model, we assume firms supply all the output that is demanded. This means the short-run aggregate supply curve is flat, so firms will produce whatever is demanded without changing their prices. This assumption is reasonable in the short run.

Because firms are willing to supply whatever is demanded, demand is the key factor in determining the level of output, or GDP. In the income-expenditure model, the level of output will adjust to equal the level of planned expenditures. We call the level of output the **equilibrium output**.

equilibrium output
The level of GDP at which planned expenditure equals the amount that is produced.

Let's denote the level of equilibrium output as y^*. Then the level of equilibrium output will be

$$\text{equilibrium output} = y^* = C + I = \text{planned expenditures}$$

At equilibrium output, planned expenditures for goods and services equal the level of output or GDP.

Figure 11.2 can help us understand how the level of equilibrium output, or GDP, in the economy is determined. On the expenditure-output graph, we superimpose the line representing planned expenditures, $C + I$, which is a horizontal line because both

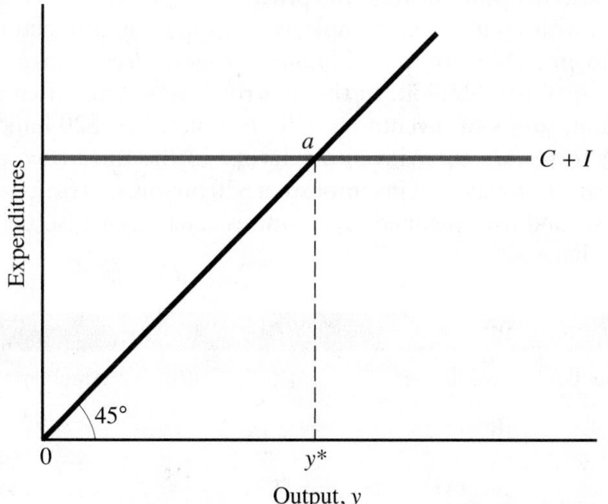

◄ FIGURE 11.2
Determining Equilibrium Output
At equilibrium output y^*, total expenditures demand y^* equals output y^*.

C and I are fixed amounts. Because planned expenditures are fixed at $C + I$, they do not depend on the level of output. Equilibrium output is at y^*, the level of output at which the planned expenditure line crosses the 45° line. The two lines cross at point a, where output measured on the horizontal axis equals planned expenditures by consumers and firms measured on the vertical axis. Recall that on a 45° line the value on the horizontal axis equals the value on the vertical axis.

Adjusting to Equilibrium Output

What would happen if the economy were producing at a higher level of output, such as y_1 in Figure 11.3? At that level of output, more goods and services are being produced than consumers and firms are demanding. Goods that are produced but not purchased will pile up on the shelves of stores. Firms will react to these piles of goods by cutting back on production. The level of output will fall until the economy reaches y^*, as indicated by the leftward arrow in Figure 11.3.

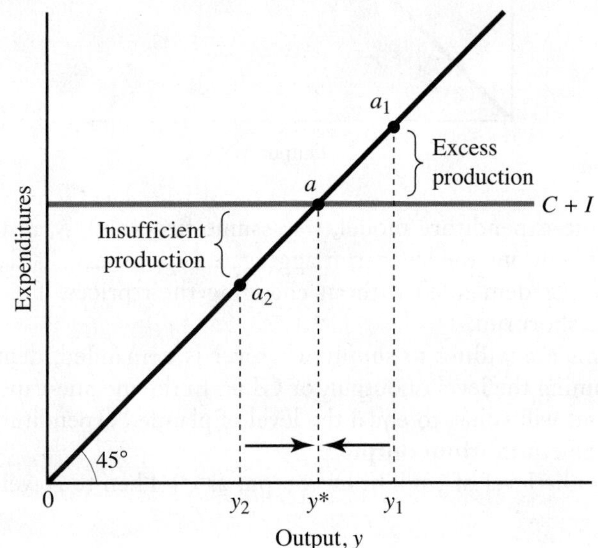

► **FIGURE 11.3**
Equilibrium Output
Equilibrium output (y^*) is determined at a, where demand intersects the 45° line. If output were higher (y_1), it would exceed demand and production would fall. If output were lower (y_2), it would fall short of demand and production would rise.

If the economy were producing at a lower level of output, y_2, planned expenditures would exceed total output. Firms would find that the demand for consumption and investment goods is greater than their current production. Inventories now disappear from the shelves of stores, and firms face increasing backlogs of orders for their products. They respond by stepping up production, so GDP increases back to y^*, as indicated by the rightward arrow in Figure 11.3.

Table 11.1 also helps to illustrate the process that determines equilibrium output. The table shows, with a numerical example, what happens to production when planned expenditures do not equal output. Planned expenditures, consumption (C) plus investment (I), equal \$100 billion. In the first row, we see that if current production is only \$80 billion, stocks of inventories will be depleted by \$20 billion, so firms will increase output to restore their inventory levels. In the third row, production is at \$120 billion, creating an excess of inventories of \$20 billion, and firms will cut back production. In the second row, planned expenditures equal output, so neither inventories nor production changes.

TABLE 11.1 Adjustments to Equilibrium Output (in Billions of Dollars)

C + I	Production	Inventories	Direction of Output
\$100	\$ 80	Depletion of inventories of \$20	Output increases
100	100	No change	Output stays constant
100	120	Excess of inventories of \$20	Output decreases

Be sure you remember that the equilibrium level of output occurs where planned expenditures equal production. If the economy were not producing at that level, we would find either that the demand for goods was too great relative to production, or that there was insufficient demand relative to production. In either case, the economy would rapidly adjust to reach the equilibrium level of output.

11.2 The Consumption Function

To make the income-expenditure model more realistic, we will need to introduce other components of demand, including the government and the foreign sector. But first we need to recognize that consumers' planned expenditures will depend on their level of income.

Consumer Spending and Income

Let's begin by reviewing the **consumption function** we first introduced in Chapter 9. The consumption function describes the relationship between desired spending by consumers and the level of income. When consumers have more income, they will want to purchase more goods and services.

consumption function
The relationship between consumption spending and the level of income.

As we have seen, a simple consumption function can be described by the equation

$$C = C_a + by$$

in which total consumption spending, C, has two parts. The first part, C_a, is called **autonomous consumption**, and it does not directly depend on the level of income. The second part, by, represents the part of consumption that does depend on income. It is the product of the fraction b, called the **marginal propensity to consume (MPC)**, and level of income in the economy, y. The MPC, which has a value of b in our formula, tells us how much consumption spending will increase for every dollar that income increases. If b equals 0.7, then for every \$1 that income increases, consumption would increase by $0.7 \times \$1$, or \$0.70.

autonomous consumption
The part of consumption that does not depend on income.

marginal propensity to consume (MPC)
The fraction of additional income that is spent.

In our simple income-expenditure model, *output is also equal to the income that flows to households*. As firms produce output, they pay households income in the form of wages, interest, profits, and rents. We can therefore use y to represent both output and income.

We plot a consumption function in Figure 11.4. The consumption function is a line that intersects the vertical axis at C_a, the level of autonomous consumption spending, which is typically greater than zero (therefore, it has a positive intercept). The slope of the consumption function equals b, the marginal propensity to consume. Although output is plotted on the horizontal axis, remember that it is also equal to income, so income rises dollar for dollar with output. That is why we can plot the consumption function, which depends on income, on the same graph that determines output.

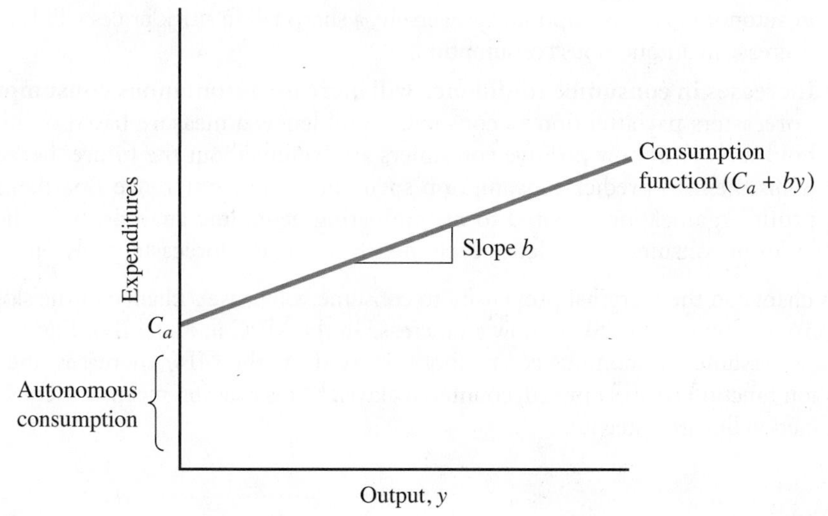

◄ FIGURE 11.4
Consumption Function
The consumption function relates desired consumer spending to the level of income.

Changes in the Consumption Function

The consumption function is determined by the level of autonomous consumption and by the MPC. The level of autonomous consumption can change, and so can the MPC. Changes in either shift the consumption function to another position on the graph. A higher level of autonomous consumption but no change in MPC will shift the entire consumption function upward and parallel to its original position. More consumption occurs at every level of income. We show an increase in autonomous consumption in Panel A of Figure 11.5.

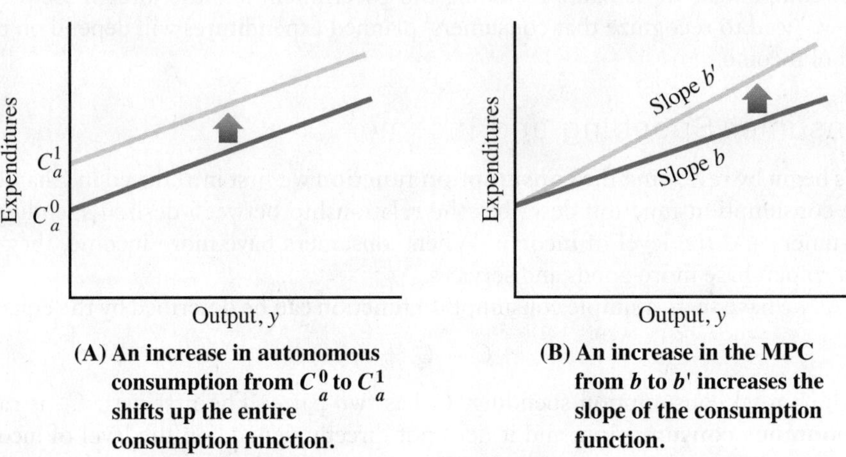
Expenditures
C_a^1
C_a^0
Output, y
(A) An increase in autonomous consumption from C_a^0 to C_a^1 shifts up the entire consumption function.
Expenditures
Slope b'
Slope b
Output, y
(B) An increase in the MPC from b to b' increases the slope of the consumption function.

▲ FIGURE 11.5

Movements of the Consumption Function

Panel A shows that an increase in autonomous consumption from C_a^0 to C_a^1 shifts the entire consumption function upward. Panel B shows that an increase in the MPC from b to b' increases the slope of the consumption function.

A number of factors can cause autonomous consumption to change. Here are two:

- **Increases in consumer wealth will cause an increase in autonomous consumption.** Wealth consists of the value of stocks, bonds, and consumer durables (consumer goods that last a long time, such as automobiles and refrigerators). Note that a person's wealth is not the same as income. *Income* is the amount of money someone earns during a period, such as in a given year, whereas *wealth* represents the person's total net worth. Nobel Laureate Franco Modigliani found that increases in stock prices, which raise consumer wealth, will lead to increases in autonomous consumption. Conversely, a sharp fall in stock prices will lead to a decrease in autonomous consumption.
- **Increases in consumer confidence will increase autonomous consumption.** Forecasters pay attention to consumer confidence, a measure based on household surveys of how positive consumers are feeling about the future, because it helps them to predict consumption spending. The Conference Board, a nonprofit organization devoted to disseminating economic analysis, publishes an index of consumer confidence each month that many forecasters rely on.

A change in the marginal propensity to consume will cause a change in the slope of the consumption function. We show an increase in the MPC in Panel B of Figure 11.5, where we assume autonomous consumption is fixed. As the MPC increases, the consumption function rotates upward, counterclockwise. This rotation means the consumption function line gets steeper.

application 1

FALLING HOME PRICES, THE WEALTH EFFECT, AND DECREASED CONSUMER SPENDING

APPLYING THE CONCEPTS #1: How do changes in the value of homes affect consumer spending?

The value of homes in excess of what people borrow with a mortgage is known as their home equity. Home equity is the single largest component of net wealth for most families in the United States. Compared to wealth holdings in the stock market, which tend to be concentrated in the highest income brackets, home-equity wealth is more widely dispersed across the income spectrum. Changes in the value of home equity—like other forms of wealth—affect consumer spending.

The period from 1997 to mid-2006 was paradise for consumers. Housing prices rose nationally by approximately 90 percent and consumer wealth grew by $6.5 trillion dollars over that period. The party ended in the summer of 2006 as housing prices began to fall. In some regions of the country, where housing prices had risen most sharply, they fell from their peak by about 30 percent. No longer were households refinancing their mortgages and pulling out money to buy new cars, boats, or other consumer durables. Instead, many recent home purchasers actually owed more than their homes were worth—and, as a result, some defaulted on their loans and turned their property over to lenders. How do these changes affect consumer spending?

In its review of the literature, the Congressional Budget Office found most studies estimated a decrease of consumer wealth of $1 would lower consumption spending by somewhere between $0.02 and $0.07. Based on forecasts for housing prices, the Congressional Budget Office estimated the declines in housing prices would reduce consumer wealth and ultimately consumer spending between $21 and $72 billion or subtract 0.1 to 0.5 percentage points from economic growth during 2007. This partly explains the reduced rate of economic growth that occurred during that year. **Related to Exercises 2.5 and 2.7.**

SOURCE: Based on Congressional Budget Office, *Housing Wealth and Consumer Spending*, January 2007, http://www.cbo.gov/publication/18279 (accessed April 24, 2012).

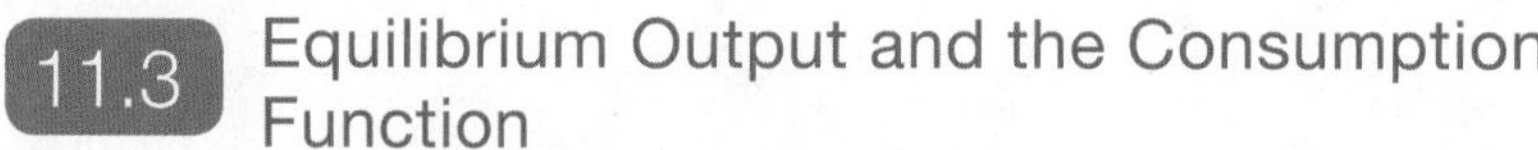

11.3 Equilibrium Output and the Consumption Function

Using the consumption function, we can now begin to look at more complex versions of the income-expenditure model. We continue to assume investment spending, I, does not depend on the level of income. The only difference between what we did in the preceding section and what we are about to do here is that we now recognize consumption increases with the level of income. Figure 11.6 shows how GDP is determined. We first plot the consumption function, C, as before: A sloping line graphically representing that consumption spending is a function of income. Because we are assuming investment is constant at all levels of income, to get the $C + I$ line, we can simply vertically add the constant level of investment I to the consumption function. Adding vertically gives us the $C + I$ line, which represents total planned expenditures in the economy. This line is upward sloping because consumption spending increases with income. At any level of income, we now know the level of total planned expenditures, $C + I$.

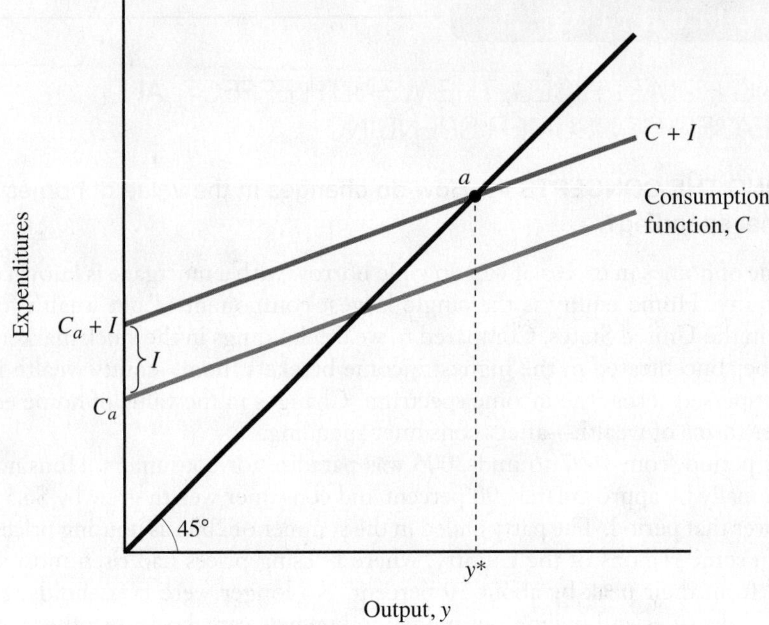

▶ **FIGURE 11.6**
Equilibrium Output and the Consumption Function
Equilibrium output is determined where the $C + I$ line intersects the 45° line. At that level of output, y^*, desired spending equals output.

The level of equilibrium output, y^*, occurs where the planned expenditure line $C + I$ crosses the 45° line. At this level of output, planned expenditures equal output. At any other level of production, planned expenditures will not equal output, and the economy will adjust back to y^* for the same reasons and in the same way as in the corresponding example in the preceding section.

In the appendix to this chapter, we show that the equilibrium output in this simple economy is

$$\text{equilibrium output} = \frac{(\text{autonomous consumption} + \text{investment})}{(1 - \text{MPC})}$$

or, in the mathematical terms representing those words,

$$y^* = \frac{(C_a + I)}{(1 - b)}$$

From this relationship and the numerical values for C_a, b, and I, we can calculate equilibrium output. Suppose

$$C_a = 100$$

$$b = 0.6$$

$$I = 40$$

This means the consumption function is $C = 100 + 0.6y$. Then, using our formula for equilibrium output, we have

$$y^* = \frac{100 + 40}{1 - 0.6} = \frac{140}{0.40} = 350$$

Saving and Investment

We can determine equilibrium output another way, which highlights the relationship between saving and investment. To understand this relationship, recall that in an economy without taxation or government, the value of output, or production (y), equals the value of income. Households receive this income and either consume it (C), save it (S), or a combination of both. We can therefore say that saving equals output minus consumption or, in mathematical terms,

$$S = y - C$$

In our simple economy, output is determined by planned expenditures, $C + I$, or

$$y = C + I$$

If we subtract consumption from both sides of this equation, we have

$$y - C = I$$

But we just saw that the left side, $y - C$, equals saving, S, so we have

$$S = I$$

Thus, equilibrium output is determined at the level of income where savings equal investment.

However, the level of savings in the economy is not fixed. A **savings function** describes the relationship between savings and the level of income. Total savings will increase with the level of GDP. Recall from Chapter 9 the concept of the marginal propensity to save (MPS): It is the ratio of additional savings to additional income. Since households will increase their total savings as their income increases, total savings will increase with GDP.

savings function The relationship between the level of saving and the level of income.

Figure 11.7 illustrates how equilibrium income is determined where savings equals investment. The horizontal line is a fixed level of investment in the economy. The upward-sloping line is the savings function. The two lines intersect at the equilibrium level of output, y^*.

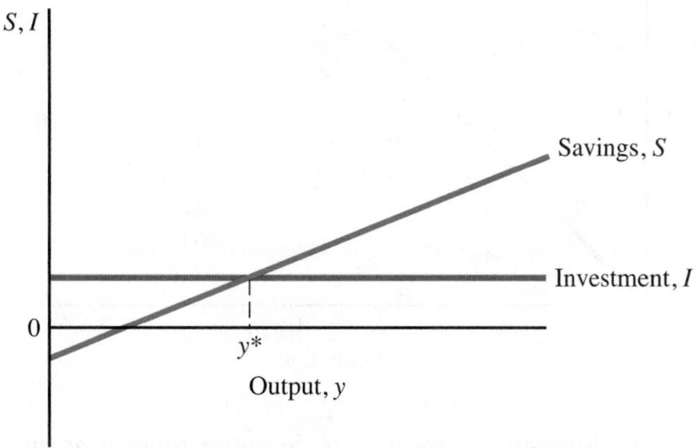

◄ FIGURE 11.7
Savings, Investment, and Equilibrium Output
Equilibrium output is determined at the level of output, y^*, where savings equals investment.

To illustrate these ideas with a numerical example, let's return to the previous case in which the consumption function is $C = 100 + 0.6y$. Because $S = y - C$, saving is

$$S = y - (100 + 0.6y)$$
$$S = -100 + 0.4y$$

This equation is the savings function for this example. The marginal propensity to save (MPS) is 0.4. That means that for every dollar y increases, saving increases by \$0.40. Notice the slope of the savings function is the MPS.

In our previous example, investment was 40 and equilibrium output was 350. Let's check that saving does equal that level of investment. Plugging in the value of equilibrium output, or income, into the savings function, we get

$$S = -100 + 0.4(350)$$
$$S = -100 + 140$$
$$S = 40$$

So saving equals investment at the level of equilibrium output.

Understanding the Multiplier

In all economies, investment spending fluctuates. We can use the model we developed that determines output in the short run, the income-expenditure model, to see what happens if there are changes in investment spending. Suppose investment spending originally was I_0 and increased to I_1—an increase we will call ΔI (the symbol Δ, the Greek capital letter delta, is universally used to represent change). What happens to equilibrium output?

Figure 11.8 shows how equilibrium output is determined at the original level of investment and at the new level of investment. The increase in investment spending shifts the $C + I$ curve upward by ΔI. The intersection of the $C + I$ curve with the 45° line shifts from a_0 to a_1. GDP increases from y_0 to y_1 by the amount Δy. The figure shows that the increase in GDP—that is, the amount Δy—is greater than the increase in investment—the amount ΔI—or $\Delta y > \Delta I$. This is a general result: The increase in output always exceeds the increase in investment because of the multiplier effect we discussed in the last chapter.

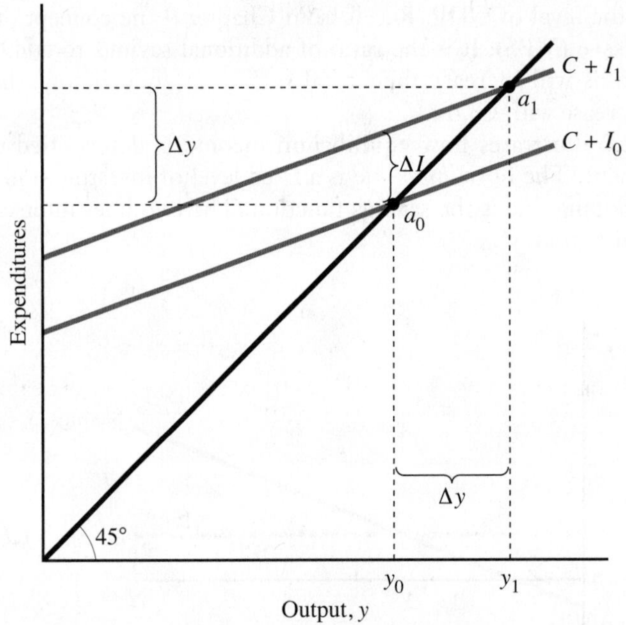

► **FIGURE 11.8**
The Multiplier
When investment increases from I_0 to I_1, equilibrium output increases from y_0 to y_1. The change in output (Δy) is greater than the change in investment (ΔI).

Let's review the logic of the multiplier. Suppose there is an initial increase of investment spending by \$20 million. This additional demand will initially increase output, income, and aggregate demand by \$20 million. Assuming the MPC is 0.8, the \$20 million in additional income will lead to \$16 million in increased consumer spending (the MPC of 0.8 × \$20 million). With an increase in consumer demand of \$16 million, output, income, and aggregate demand will therefore increase by another \$16 million. In turn, this will increase consumer spending by another \$12.8 million (the MPC of 0.8 × \$16 million). This increased demand will therefore increase output, income, and aggregate demand by \$12.8 million, generating further increases in consumer spending of \$10.24 million. As this process continues over time, total spending will continue to increase, but in diminishing amounts. If we add up all the spending in the (infinite) rounds, we find the initial increase in investment spending will generate a total increase in equilibrium income of \$100 million, far more than the initial \$20 million with which we began. In this case, the multiplier is 5 (5 × \$20 million = \$100 million).

We show how to derive the formula for a simple multiplier in the appendix to this chapter:

$$\text{multiplier} = \frac{1}{(1 - \text{MPC})}$$

application 2

USING LONG-TERM MACRO DATA TO MEASURE MULTIPLIERS

APPLYING THE CONCEPTS #2: What evidence does the long historical record provide about multipliers?

One of the difficulties in estimating multipliers is that during normal times, government spending and taxes do not change too much so it is difficult to isolate their effects on the economy. Economists Robert Barro and Charles Redlick went back in the historical record to look at times when government expenditures and taxes did change substantially: during the buildups and aftermaths of major wars.

In their work, they typically found much smaller multipliers for defense expenditures, typically less than one. This means that increases in government spending did increase the economy, but less than the amount of government spending itself. It also implies that there must have been crowding out of other components of spending. They found that multipliers were larger when there was more unemployment in the economy. Barro and Redlick also suggest that other researchers found larger associations between government spending and GDP because they had the causality backward—nondefense spending often rises when GDP grows rapidly. Untangling these issues is a difficult task for social scientists. **Related to Exercise 3.9.**

SOURCE: Based on Robert J. Barro and Charles Redlick, "Stimulus Spending Doesn't Work," *Wall Street Journal*, October 1, 2009.

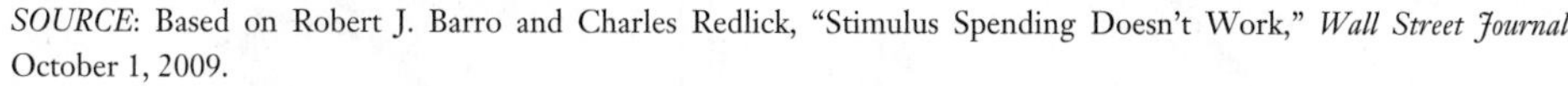

Suppose the MPC equals 0.8. Then the multiplier would be

$$\text{multiplier} = \frac{1}{(1 - 0.8)} = 5$$

Notice that the multiplier increases as the MPC increases. If MPC equals 0.4, the multiplier is 1.67; if the MPC equals 0.6, the multiplier is 2.5. To see why the multiplier increases as the marginal propensity to consume increases, think back to our examples of the multiplier. The multiplier occurs because the initial increase in investment spending increases income, which leads to higher consumer spending. With a higher MPC, the increase in consumer spending will be greater, because consumers will spend a higher fraction of the additional income they receive as the multiplier increases. For example, if the MPC is 0.8, they will spend an additional $0.80, whereas if the multiplier was 0.6, they would spend only an additional $0.60. With a higher MPC, the eventual increase in output will be greater, and therefore so will the multiplier.

One implication of the multiplier is that the effect of any change in investment "multiplies" throughout the economy. This explains why economies can often recover quickly after natural disasters.

11.4 Government Spending and Taxation

We now make our income-expenditure model more realistic by bringing in government spending and taxation, which makes the model useful for understanding economic policy debates. In those debates, we often hear recommendations for either increasing government spending or cutting taxes to increase GDP. As we will explain, both the level of government spending and the level of taxation, through their influence on the demand for goods and services, affect the level of GDP in the short run.

Using taxes and spending to influence the level of GDP in the short run is known as *Keynesian fiscal policy*. As we discussed in Chapter 7, changes in taxes can also affect the supply of output in the long run through the way taxes can change incentives to work or invest. However, in this chapter we concentrate on the role of taxes and spending in determining demand for goods and services, and therefore output, in the short run.

Fiscal Multipliers

Let's look first at the role government spending plays in determining GDP. Government purchases of goods and services are a component of total spending:

$$\text{planned expenditures including government} = C + I + G$$

Increases in government purchases, G, shift the $C + I + G$ line upward, just as increases in investment, I, or autonomous consumption do. If government spending increases by \$1, the $C + I + G$ line will shift upward by \$1.

Panel A of Figure 11.9 shows how increases in government spending affect GDP. The increase in government spending from G_0 to G_1 shifts the $C + I + G$ line upward and increases the level of GDP from y_0 to y_1.

► **FIGURE 11.9**
Government Spending, Taxes, and GDP
Panel A shows that an increase in government spending leads to an increase in output. Panel B shows that an increase in taxes leads to a decrease in output.

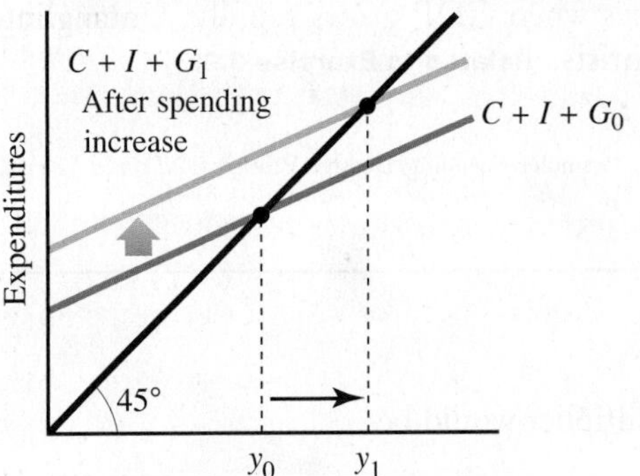

(A) An increase in government spending leads to an increase in output.

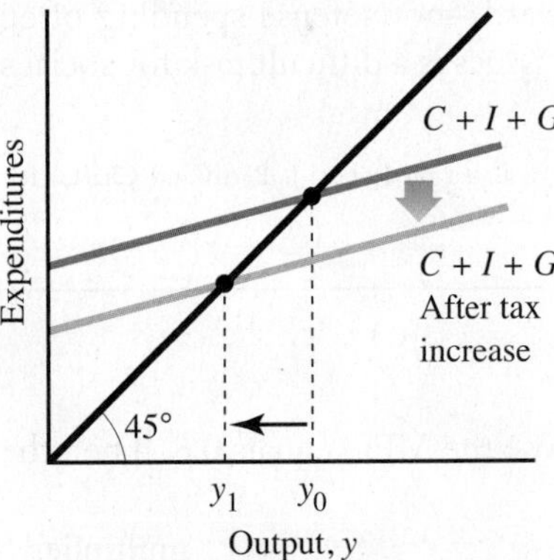

(B) An increase in taxes leads to a decrease in output.

As you can see, changes in government purchases have exactly the same effects as changes in investment or changes in autonomous consumption. The multiplier for government spending is also the same as for changes in investment or autonomous consumption:

$$\text{multiplier for government spending} = \frac{1}{(1 - \text{MPC})}$$

For example, if the MPC is 0.6, the multiplier is 2.5:

$$\frac{1}{(1 - 0.6)} = 2.5$$

Therefore, a \$10 billion increase in government spending will increase GDP by \$25 billion. The multiplier for government spending works just like the multiplier for investment or consumption. An initial increase in government spending raises GDP and income. The increase in income, however, generates further increases in demand as consumers increase their spending.

Now let's consider taxes. We need to take into account that government programs affect households' disposable personal income—income that ultimately flows back to households (and thus consumption) after subtraction from their income of any taxes paid and after addition to their income of any transfer payments they receive, such as Social Security, unemployment insurance, or welfare. If the government takes \$10 net of every \$100 you make, your income after taxes and transfer payments is only \$90.

Here's how we include taxes and transfers into the model: We make consumption spending depend on income after taxes and transfers, or $y - T$, where T is net taxes (taxes paid to government minus transfers received by households). For simplicity, we'll just refer to T as taxes, but remember that it is taxes less transfer payments. The consumption function with taxes is

$$C = C_a + b(y - T)$$

If taxes increase by \$1, after-tax income will decrease by \$1. Because the marginal propensity to consume is b, this means consumption will fall by $b \times \$1$, and the $C + I + G$ line will shift downward by $b \times \$1$. For example, if b is 0.6, a \$1 increase in taxes will mean that consumers will have a dollar less of income and will therefore decrease consumption spending by \$0.60.

Panel B of Figure 11.9 shows how an increase in taxes will decrease the level of GDP. As the level of taxes increases, the demand line will shift downward by b (the increase in taxes). Equilibrium income will fall from y_0 to y_1. The multiplier for taxes is slightly different than the multiplier for government spending. If we cut government spending by \$1, the $C + I + G$ line will shift downward by \$1. However, if we increase taxes by \$1, consumers will cut back their consumption by only $b \times \$1$. Thus, the $C + I + G$ line will shift downward by slightly less than \$1, or $b \times \$1$. For example, if b is 0.6, the demand line would shift down vertically by \$0.60.

Because the demand line does not shift by the same amount with taxes as it does with government spending, the formula for the tax multiplier is slightly different. Here's the formula for the tax multiplier; we show how to derive it in the appendix:

$$\text{tax multiplier} = \frac{-\text{MPC}}{(1 - \text{MPC})}$$

The tax multiplier is negative because increases in taxes decrease disposable personal income and lead to a reduction in consumption spending. If the MPC is 0.6, the tax multiplier will be

$$\frac{-0.6}{(1 - 0.6)} = -1.5$$

Notice that the tax multiplier is smaller (in absolute value) than the government spending multiplier, which for the same MPC is 2.5. The reason the tax multiplier is smaller is that an increase in taxes first reduces income of households by the amount of the tax. However, because the MPC is less than one (0.6), the decrease in consumer spending is less than the increase in taxes.

Finally, you may wonder what would happen if we increased both government spending and taxes by an equal amount at the same time. Because the multiplier for government spending is larger than the multiplier for taxes, equal increases in both government spending and taxes will increase GDP. Economists call the multiplier for equal increases in government spending and taxes the *balanced-budget multiplier* because equal changes in government spending and taxes will not unbalance the budget. In the appendix we show that the balanced-budget multiplier in our simple model is always equal to one. For example, if spending and taxes are both increased by \$10 billion, then GDP will also increase by \$10 billion.

Using Fiscal Multipliers

Let's look at several examples of how we can use fiscal policy, altering taxes, and government spending to affect GDP. In all these examples, suppose GDP is

$6,000 billion and the marginal propensity to consume is 0.6. The government-spending multiplier is

$$\frac{1}{(1 - 0.6)} = 2.5$$

The tax multiplier is

$$\frac{-0.6}{(1 - 0.6)} = -1.5$$

1 *Suppose policymakers want to increase GDP by 1 percent, or $60 billion.* By how much do policymakers have to increase government spending to meet this target? Because the multiplier for government spending is 2.5, we need to increase government spending by only $24 billion. With a multiplier of 2.5, the $24 billion increase in government spending leads to an increase in GDP of $60 billion ($24 billion × 2.5 = $60 billion).

2 *Suppose policymakers wanted to use tax cuts rather than government-spending increases to increase GDP by $60 billion.* How large a tax cut would be necessary? Because the tax multiplier is −1.5, we need to cut taxes by $40 billion. The $40 billion tax cut times the multiplier will lead to the objective, a $60 billion increase in GDP (−$40 billion × (−1.5) = $60 billion).

3 *If policymakers wanted to change taxes and government spending by equal amounts, so as to not affect the federal budget, how large a change would be needed to increase GDP by $60 billion?* Because the balanced-budget multiplier is one, both government spending and taxes must be increased by $60 billion.

The models we are using are very simple and leave out important factors. Nonetheless, the same basic principles apply in real situations. Here are five examples of activist Keynesian fiscal policy from recent times:

1 In 1993, the three members of the President's Council of Economic Advisers wrote a letter to President Clinton stating they thought the cuts in government spending being proposed at the time were $20 billion too large. The economic model the council members used had a multiplier for government spending of approximately 1.5. With this multiplier, the decrease in GDP from the $20 billion spending cut would be $30 billion ($20 billion × 1.5). This was approximately 0.5 percent of GDP. If GDP was expected to grow at 3 percent a year without the cuts, the president's advisers estimated that with the cuts, GDP would grow at only 2.5 percent a year. However, their advice came too late to influence the policy decisions.

2 During 1994, the U.S. government urged the Japanese to increase public spending and cut taxes to stimulate their economy. The Japanese came up with a plan and presented it to U.S. policymakers, who evaluated it using multiplier analysis. They thought the plan did not provide enough fiscal stimulus and urged the Japanese to take more aggressive actions. Several years later, the Japanese did adopt a more aggressive plan. Unfortunately the Japanese government raised taxes in 1997, actually sending the country further into a recession.

3 During the late 1990s, the Chinese economy came under pressure from the economic downturn in Asia and its own attempts to reform and restructure its economy. To prevent a severe economic slowdown, the Chinese successively engaged in active fiscal policy, increasing spending on domestic infrastructure, including roads, rails, and urban facilities.

4 After the September 11, 2001, terrorist attack on the United States, the government increased spending for disaster relief in New York and provided subsidies and loan guarantees to the airlines. In addition, President Bush and Congress immediately began to work on additional spending programs and tax-relief programs to stimulate the economy.

5 President Obama's economic advisors used multiplier analysis to gauge the size of their stimulus package. The multipliers they used ranged between 1 and 2 for different components of spending. Although some observers suggested the stimulus package should be even larger than $800 billion, or 5.5 percent of GDP, the economic advisors argued that this size stimulus would be sufficient to offset the worst of the recession.

Though it is very simple, our income-expenditure model illustrates some important lessons:

- An increase in government spending will increase total planned expenditures for goods and services.
- Cutting taxes will increase the after-tax income of consumers and will also lead to an increase in planned expenditures for goods and services.
- Policymakers need to take into account the multipliers for government spending and taxes as they develop policies.

The idea that governments should use active fiscal policy to combat recessions was argued forcibly by John Maynard Keynes in the 1930s. His book *The General Theory of Employment, Interest, and Money* provided the intellectual foundation for the income-expenditure model in this chapter and explained why economies could become mired in recessions and fail to recover on their own. As a consequence, Keynes strongly advocated aggressive fiscal policymaking as the best option policymakers have for bringing economies out of recessions. Keynes was a very public figure and took a major role in policy debates throughout his life.

One of Keynes's controversial ideas was that governments could stimulate the economy even if they spent money on wasteful projects. In the *General Theory*, he even remarked (tongue-in-cheek) how lucky the Egyptians were, because the death of the pharaohs would lead to new pyramids being built. Pyramids do not add to the stock of capital to produce regular goods and services. But Keynes's point was that building pyramids (or antisatellite missiles today) does add to planned expenditures and stimulates GDP in the short run.

In the long run, of course, we are better off if government spends the money wisely, such as on needed infrastructure like roads and bridges. This is an example of the principle of opportunity cost.

PRINCIPLE OF OPPORTUNITY COST

The opportunity cost of something is what you sacrifice to get it.

But even here, we can carry things too far. Japan is notorious for its excessive public spending on infrastructure, driven in part by the central government's doing favors for local politicians by creating jobs in their districts. Economists have even compared spending on bridges and roads in Japan to Keynes's famous pyramids.

Understanding Automatic Stabilizers

With a slight addition to our basic model, we can explain one of the important facts in U.S. economic history. Figure 11.10 plots the rate of growth of U.S. real GDP from 1871 to 2009. It is apparent from the graph that the U.S. economy has been much more stable after World War II than before. A major reason is that government taxes and transfer payments, such as unemployment insurance and welfare payments, grew sharply after the war. These taxes and transfer payments can automatically reduce fluctuations in real GDP and thereby stabilize the economy. As we saw in the last chapter, taxes and transfers act as automatic stabilizers for the economy.

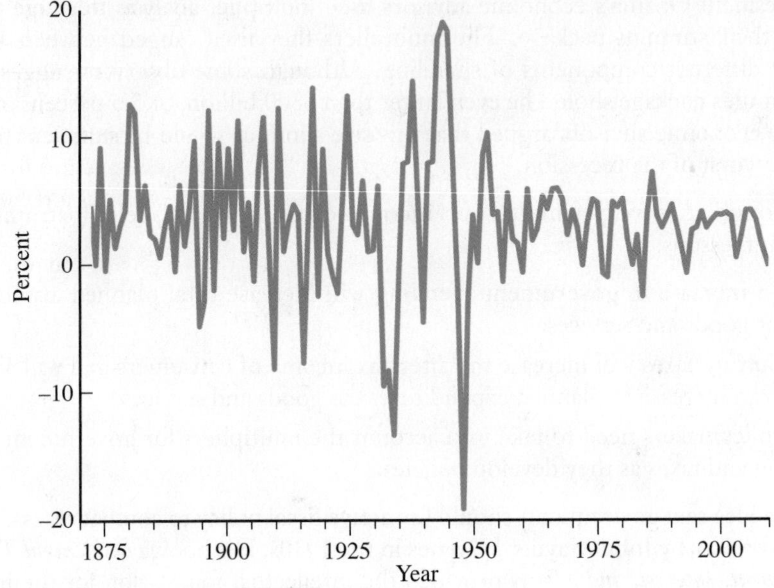

▶ **FIGURE 11.10**
Growth Rates of U.S. GDP, 1871–2011
After World War II, fluctuations in GDP growth became considerably smaller.
SOURCE: Angus Maddison, *Dynamic Forces in Capitalist Development* (New York: Oxford University Press, 1991); U.S. Department of Commerce.

MyEconLab Real-time data

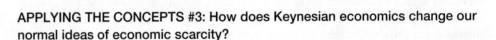

application 3

THE BROKEN WINDOW FALLACY AND KEYNESIAN ECONOMICS

APPLYING THE CONCEPTS #3: How does Keynesian economics change our normal ideas of economic scarcity?

The Austrian economist, Henry Hazlitt, popularized the "Broken Windows" fallacy in economics. Imagine that a hoodlum threw a brick through a store window. While at first this seems to be a tragedy, the store owner has to hire a firm to fix the window. That generates business for the window repair firm and, through a multiplier, additional business throughout the community. Was the broken window good for society?

The fallacy here is that the money that the store owner paid to have the window repaired would have been spent elsewhere in the economy, say on clothing. While the window repair business profited, the clothing store lost business. In other words, there was an opportunity cost from the funds spent to repair the broken window.

Hazlitt applies a similar argument to public spending financed by taxes. A government spending program may appear to increase business, but the taxes needed to finance the spending—either paid now or in the future—will mean less business for other firms. Government spending and the taxes necessary to finance it will just crowd out other production of goods and services in the economy.

Hazlitt's argument works in the classical world when the economy is operating at full employment. But in the Keynesian world, where resources are underemployed, the story is quite different. Here the increase in spending—even financed by taxes—will bring resources that are not being utilized into the economy. As long as there is excess capacity in the economy, the extra spending will increase output and not crowd out other goods and services. In the Keynesian world, the logic of opportunity costs is temporarily suspended. Once the economy is restored to full employment, however, we return to the world where opportunity costs matter. **Related to Exercises 3.8 and 4.6.**

SOURCE: Henry Hazlitt, *Economics in One Lesson*, New Rochelle, New York: Arlington House, 1979, Chapters 2–4.

Again, here is how the automatic stabilizers work. On the one hand, when income is high the government collects more taxes and pays out less in transfer payments. Because the government is taking funds out of the hands of consumers, there will be reduced consumer spending. On the other hand, when output is low (such as during recessions), the government collects less in taxes and pays out more in transfer payments, increasing consumer spending because the government is putting funds into the hands of consumers. The automatic stabilizers prevent consumption from falling as much in bad times and from rising as much in good times. This stabilizes the economy without any need for decisions from Congress or the White House.

To see how automatic stabilizers work in our model, we must take into account that the government levies income taxes by applying a tax rate to the level of income. To simplify, suppose there is a single tax rate of 0.2 (or 20 percent) and income is \$100. The government would then collect \$20 in taxes (0.2 × \$100).

If consumption depends on after-tax income, we have the following consumption function:

$$C = C_a + b(1 - t)y$$

This is the consumption function with income taxes. The only difference between the consumption function with income taxes and the consumption function without income taxes is that the marginal propensity to consume is adjusted for taxes, and so

$$\text{adjusted MPC} = b(1 - t)$$

The reason for this adjustment is that consumers keep only a fraction $(1 - t)$ of their income; the rest, t, goes to the government. When income increases by \$1, consumers' after-tax incomes increase by only \$1 × $(1 - t)$, and of that \$$(1 - t)$ they spend a fraction, b.

Raising the tax rate therefore lowers the MPC adjusted for taxes. Figure 11.11 shows the consequences of raising tax rates. With a higher tax rate, the government takes a higher fraction of income, and less is left over for consumers. Recall that the slope of the $C + I + G$ line is the marginal propensity to consume. Raising the tax rate lowers the adjusted MPC and reduces the slope of this line. The $C + I + G$ line with taxes intersects the 45° line at a lower level of income. Output falls from y_0 to y_1.

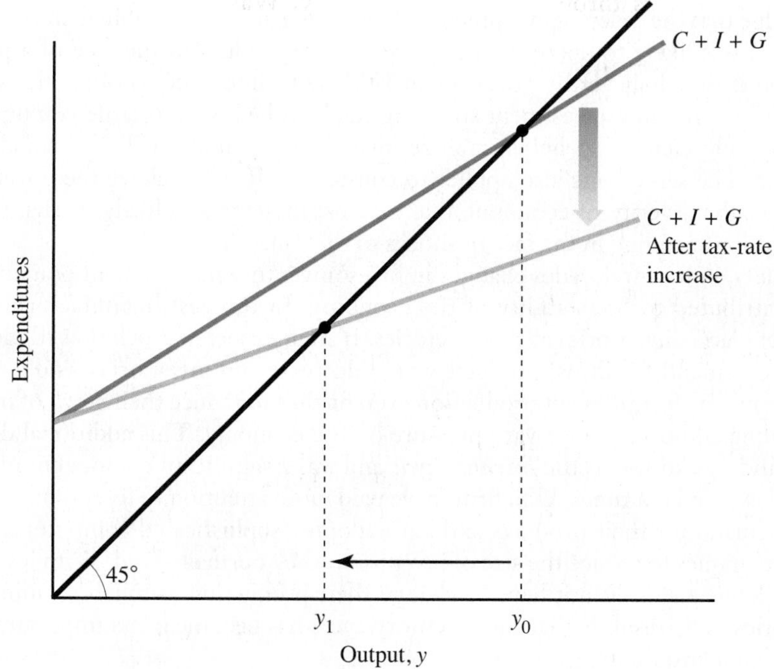

◄ **FIGURE 11.11**
Increase in Tax Rates
An increase in tax rates decreases the slope of the $C + I + G$ line. This lowers output and reduces the multiplier.

Note that as we raise tax rates, the $C + I + G$ schedule rotates and does not just move down vertically as in our previous examples. The reason for this difference is that as we change the tax rate, we change the adjusted MPC, and thus the slope of the line.

Remember that a smaller marginal propensity to consume also leads to a lower value for the multiplier. As tax rates increase and the adjusted MPC falls, the multiplier will decrease. A smaller multiplier means that any shocks, such as shocks to investment, will have less of an impact on the economy.

Now that we have introduced income taxes into our model, we can see how automatic stabilizers work. Since World War II, taxes and transfer payments in the United States have increased sharply. As we have seen, higher tax rates will lower the multiplier and make the economy less susceptible to shocks. With higher taxes and transfer payments, the link between fluctuations in disposable personal income and fluctuations in GDP is much looser. Because disposable personal income is more stable, consumption spending is also more stable. Thus, the multiplier is smaller, and the economy is more stable.

As we have said, automatic stabilizers work silently in the background, doing their job without requiring explicit action by policymakers. Total tax collections rise and fall with GDP without requiring that policymakers change tax rates. The fact that the automatic stabilizers work without any laws being enacted is particularly important at times when it is difficult to obtain a political consensus for taking any action, and policymakers are reluctant to use Keynesian fiscal policy as a deliberate policy tool.

Other factors contribute to the stability of the economy as depicted in Figure 11.10. As we explained in the last chapter, many consumers base their spending decisions in part on their long-run average income or permanent income, not just their current level of income. If households base their consumption on their long-run income, they will not be very sensitive to changes in their current income. For example, if their income temporarily rises, they are likely to save, not spend, the additional income. Similarly, if their income temporarily falls, they are likely to maintain their consumption and reduce their current savings. In effect, when consumers base their consumption on their long-run average income, their MPC out of current income (which could be higher or lower than their long-run income) will be small. And because the MPC out of current income is small, the multiplier will be small as well.

Another important factor in promoting the stability of the economy is firms' knowledge that the federal government will be taking actions to stabilize the economy. Firms are less likely to decrease their investment spending in the face of a possible recession if they believe the government is likely to intervene to offset the severity of recessions. Because investment spending tends to be a very volatile component of spending, any factor that helps stabilize investment spending will also stabilize the economy. The same logic also applies to consumers. If they believe the government will offset the severity of economic fluctuations, they are less likely to change their consumption spending in the face of shocks to their income.

Finally, in recent decades changes in firms' inventory management practices have also contributed to the stability of the economy. In the past, manufacturing firms often kept large inventories at their factories. If an unexpected shock slowed the economy, the demand for firms' products would decrease and inventories would pile up. Firms would be forced to cut production even further to reduce their stock of inventories, adding additional downward pressure on the economy. This additional decrease in demand was known as the *inventory cycle* and was a significant component of earlier recessions. In recent times, U.S. firms have paid more attention to forecasting changes in the demand for their products and have adopted sophisticated computer management techniques to reduce the size of inventories they normally hold. With less inventory on hand, firms do not have to change their production as much to adjust their inventories. The result is that the inventory cycle has become a less important factor for economic instability.

11.5 Exports and Imports

With international trade becoming increasingly important economically and politically, it is critical to understand how exports and imports affect the level of GDP. Two simple modifications of our income-expenditure model will enable us to understand how exports and imports affect GDP in the short run.

Exports affect GDP through their influence on how other countries demand goods and services produced in the United States. An increase in exports means there's an increase in the demand for goods produced in the United States. An increase in imports means there's an increase in foreign goods purchased by U.S. residents. Importing goods rather than purchasing them from our domestic producers reduces the demand for U.S. goods. For example, if we in the United States spend a total of $10 billion on all automobiles but we import $3 billion of them, then we've spent only $7 billion on U.S. automobiles.

To get a clearer picture of the effects on GDP from exports and imports, let's for the moment ignore government spending and taxes. In the appendix, we present a complete model with both a domestic government and foreign countries to whom we sell our exports and from whom we buy our imports. To modify our model to include the effects of world spending on exports and U.S. spending on imports, we need to take two steps:

1 Add exports, X, as another source of demand for U.S. goods and services.
2 Subtract imports, M, from total spending by U.S. residents. We will assume that imports, like consumption, increase with the level of income.

Consumers will import more goods as their income rises. We can write this as

$$M = my$$

where m is a fraction known as the **marginal propensity to import**. We subtract this fraction from b, the overall marginal propensity to consume, to obtain the MPC for spending on domestic goods, $b - m$. For example, if b is 0.8 and m is 0.2, then for every $1 that GDP increases, total consumption increases by $0.80, but spending on domestic goods increases by only $0.60 because $0.20 is spent on imports. The MPC in this example, adjusted for imports, is 0.8 – 0.2, or 0.6.

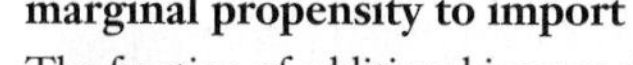

marginal propensity to import
The fraction of additional income that is spent on imports.

Figure 11.12 shows how equilibrium output is determined in an open economy, that is, an economy that engages in trade with the rest of the world. We plot planned expenditures for U.S. goods and services on our graph and find the level of equilibrium

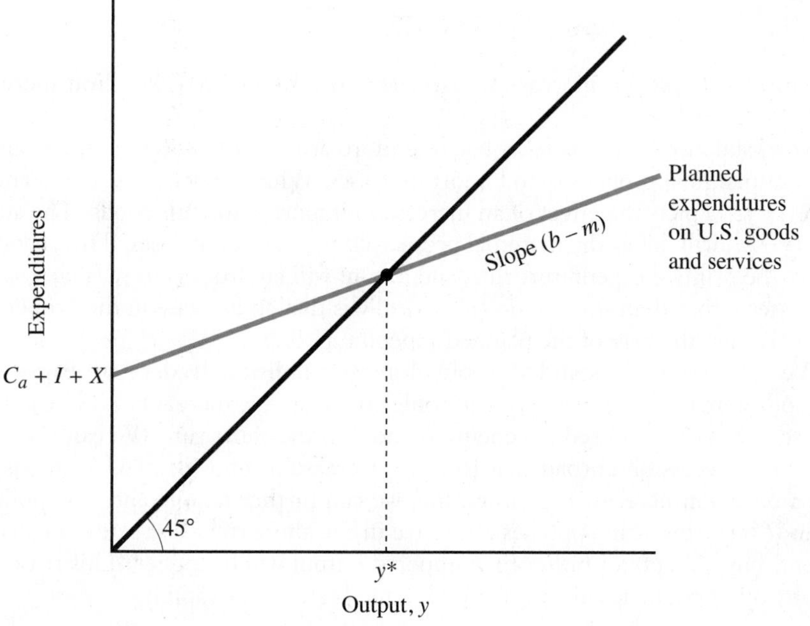

◄ FIGURE 11.12
U.S. Equilibrium Output in an Open Economy
Output is determined when the demand for domestic goods equals output.

income where it intersects the 45° line. The planned expenditure line has an intercept on the vertical axis of $C_a + I + X$, which is the sum of autonomous consumption, investment, and exports. The slope of the line is $b - m$, which is the MPC adjusted for imports. Equilibrium output is the value of output where planned expenditures for U.S. goods cross the 45° line.

Let's examine an application of the model we just developed. Suppose Japan decides to buy another \$5 billion worth of goods from the United States. What will happen to U.S. domestic output? Panel A of Figure 11.13 shows the effect of an increase in exports. The demand line will shift vertically upward by the increase in exports (ΔX). This will increase equilibrium income from y_0 to y_1.

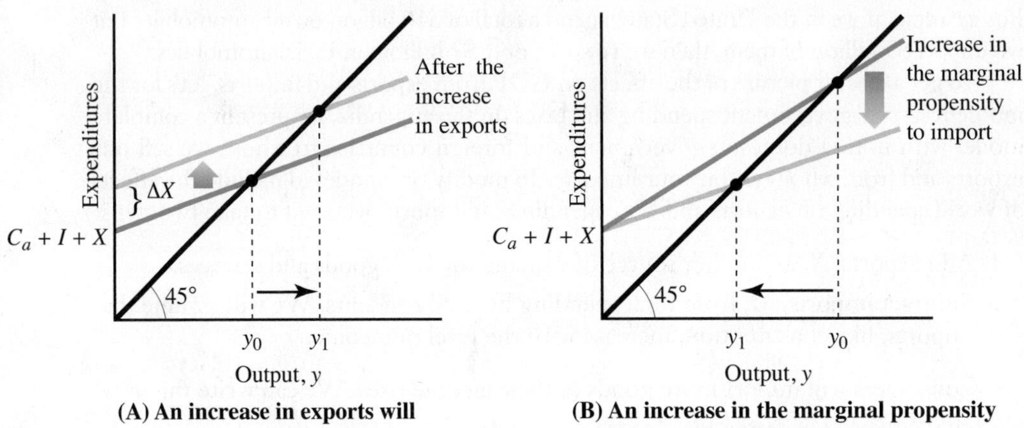

(A) An increase in exports will increase the level of GDP.

(B) An increase in the marginal propensity to import will decrease the level of GDP.

▲ FIGURE 11.13
How Increases in Exports and Imports Affect U.S. GDP
Panel A shows that an increase in exports will increase the level of GDP. Panel B shows that an increase in the marginal propensity to import will decrease the level of GDP.

The increase in income will be larger than the increase in exports because of the multiplier effect. This multiplier is based on the MPC adjusted for trade. For example, if b is 0.8 and m is 0.2, the adjusted MPC $(b - m)$ is 0.6, and the multiplier will be

$$\frac{1}{(1 - 0.6)} = 2.5$$

Therefore, a \$5 billion increase in exports will lead to a \$12.5 billion increase in GDP.

Now, suppose U.S. residents become more attracted to foreign goods, and as a result our marginal propensity to import increases. What happens to GDP? Panel B of Figure 11.13 depicts the effect of an increase in imported foreign goods. The adjusted MPC $(b - m)$ will fall as the marginal propensity to import increases. This reduces the slope of the planned expenditure line, and output will fall from y_0 to y_1. The reason the line rotates rather than shifting down vertically is that an increase in the propensity to import changes the *slope* of the planned expenditure line.

We can now understand why our domestic political leaders are eager to sell our goods abroad. Whether it is electronics or weapons, increased U.S. exports will increase U.S. GDP and reduce unemployment in the short run. We can also understand how a recession abroad that led to a decrease in imports of U.S. goods could cause a recession here. At the same time, we can further understand why politicians will find "buy American" policies attractive in the short run. To the extent that U.S. residents buy U.S. goods rather than imports, output will be higher. This reasoning is also why other countries like to see the United States grow rapidly.

application 4

THE LOCOMOTIVE EFFECT: HOW FOREIGN DEMAND AFFECTS A COUNTRY'S OUTPUT

APPLYING THE CONCEPTS #4: How do countries benefit from growth in their trading partners?

From the early 1990s until quite recently, the United States was what economists term the "locomotive" for global growth, growing faster than the rest of the world and increasing its demand for foreign products. As a share of the world economy, the United States grew from approximately 26 percent in 1992 to over 32 percent in 2001. Imports increase as an economy grows, and U.S. imports also increased along with output during this period. Because the U.S. economy is such an important part of the world economy, its demands for foreign goods—U.S. imports—fueled exports in foreign countries and promoted their growth. Studies have shown that the increase in demand for foreign goods was actually more pronounced for developing countries than for developed countries. The United States was truly a locomotive, pulling the developing countries along.

When the U.S. economy began to slow in 2007 because of our housing and financial difficulties, growth in other parts of the world, including China and India, was still robust. Their demand for U.S. goods spurred our exports and helped prevent U.S. GDP from falling any further. In this case, foreign countries were the true locomotives. As our chapter opening story describes, China remained a locomotive during the downturn. **Related to Exercise 5.7.**

SOURCE: Based on William R. Cline, *The United States as a Debtor Nation* (Washington, D.C.: Institute for International Economics, 2005), Chap. 6.

11.6 The Income-Expenditure Model and the Aggregate Demand Curve

We used the income-expenditure model in this chapter to understand more fully short-term economic fluctuations. The income-expenditure model is based on the assumption that prices do not change. In Figure 11.14, we see how the model provides the foundation for the aggregate demand curve, which will enable us to analyze changes both in output and prices.

Suppose the price level in the economy is P_0 and, at that level of prices, planned expenditures are $C_0 + I_0$. At the top of the figure, we show how equilibrium output is determined at level of output, y_0. In the bottom part of the figure, we plot the price level, P_0, and corresponding level of output, y_0. In the graph, this is point *a*.

Now let's lower the price level to P_1. Recall from our discussion in Chapter 9 that a lower price level will increase the demand for goods and services through wealth effects, the interest rate effect, and the international trade effect. (You may want to go back and review this discussion.) As a consequence of the increased demand for goods and services arising from a lower price level, we show a higher level of planned expenditure, $C_1 + I_1$, and a higher level of equilibrium output, y_1, in the top part of the figure. In the bottom part, we again plot the price level, P_1, and the corresponding level of output, y_1. In the graph, this is point *b*.

Both point *a* and point *b* are on the aggregate demand curve. By the same logic, we can create all the other points on the aggregate demand curve by either raising or lowering the aggregate price level. For any price level, the income-expenditure

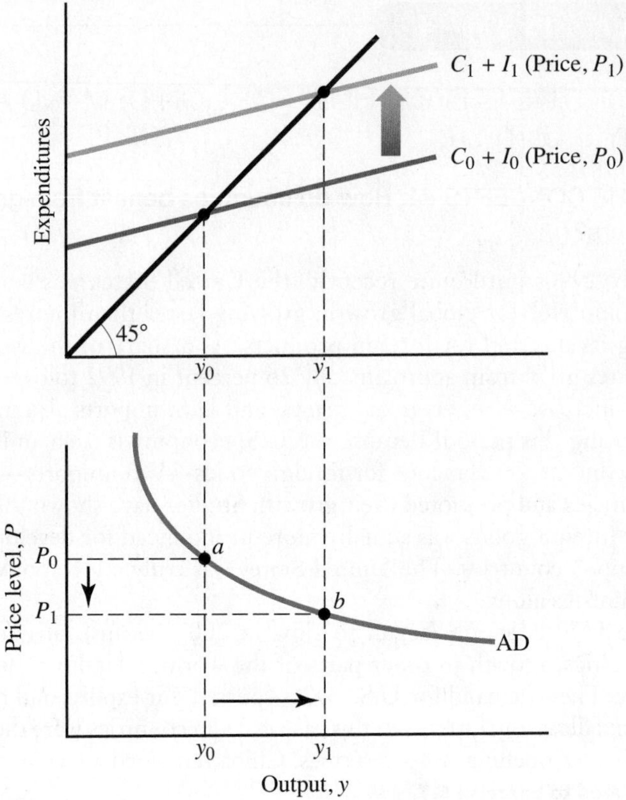

▲ FIGURE 11.14
Deriving the Aggregate Demand Curve
As the price level falls from P_0 to P_1, planned expenditures increase, which increases the level of output from y_0 to y_1. The aggregate demand curve shows the combination of prices and equilibrium output.

model can be used to determine the level of output and the corresponding point on the aggregate demand curve. Thus, the income-expenditure model provides the basic foundation for the aggregate demand curve.

At any price level, the income-expenditure model determines the level of equilibrium output and the corresponding point on the aggregate demand curve. What would happen if we kept the price level at P_0 but increased planned expenditures, let's say through an increase in government expenditures from G_0 to G_1? We depict this case in Figure 11.15. The increase in government expenditure will raise the equilibrium output, from y_0 to y_1. Because the price level has not changed, we have a higher level of output at the same level of price. This means the aggregate demand curve would shift to the right, from AD_0 to AD_1. In general, increases in planned expenditures that are not directly caused by changes in prices will shift the aggregate demand curve to the right; decreases in planned expenditures will shift the curve to the left.

In the remaining chapters, we will use the aggregate demand and supply curves to analyze economic fluctuations. This will enable us to understand movements in both prices and output in the intermediate and longer runs. But, as we have seen, the income-expenditure model developed in this chapter provides the underlying foundation for the aggregate demand curve.

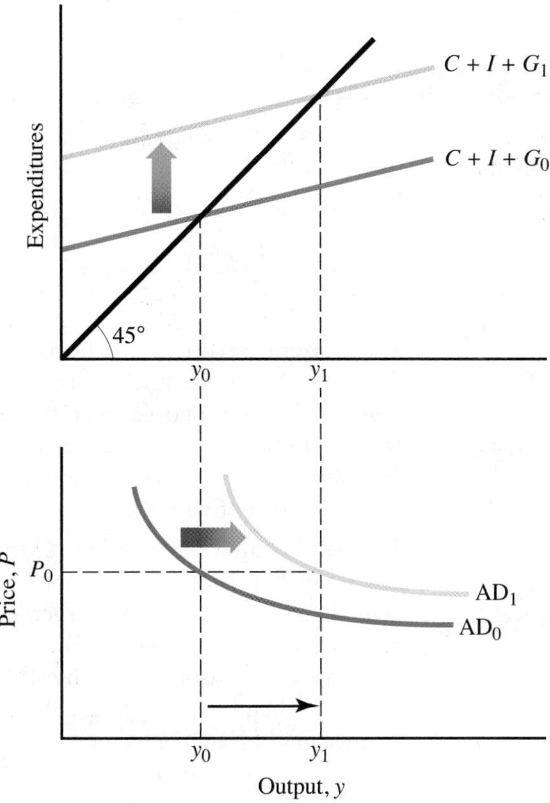

▲ **FIGURE 11.15**
Shifts in Aggregate Demand
As government spending increases from G_0 to G_1, planned expenditures increase, which raises output from y_0 to y_1. At the price level P_0, this shifts the aggregate demand curve to the right, from AD_0 to AD_1.

SUMMARY

This chapter developed the income-expenditure model, which is useful for understanding short-run fluctuations. We developed the graphical and algebraic tools to study the effects of consumer behavior, government spending and taxation, and exports and imports in determining GDP in the short run. Here are the chapter's main points:

1 In the *income-expenditure model*, the level of output in the economy will adjust to equal the level of planned expenditures. This level of output is called *equilibrium output.*

2 Consumption spending consists of two parts. One part is independent of income, but it can be influenced by changes in wealth or consumer sentiment. The other part depends on the level of income.

3 Increases in planned expenditures by households, the government, or the foreign sector lead to increases in equilibrium output.

4 Because of the multiplier, the final increase in equilibrium output is larger than the initial increase. The formula for the simple multiplier is

$$\text{multiplier} = \frac{1}{(1 - \text{MPC})}$$

5 Policymakers can use *multipliers* to calculate the appropriate size of economic policies.

6 Higher tax rates, by reducing the multiplier, can reduce fluctuations in GDP.

7 Increases in exports lead to increases in equilibrium output; increases in imports lead to decreases in equilibrium output.

8 The income-expenditure model can be used to derive the aggregate demand curve.

KEY TERMS

autonomous consumption, p. 227
consumption function, p. 227
equilibrium output, p. 225
marginal propensity to consume (MPC), p. 227
marginal propensity to import, p. 241
planned expenditures, p. 225
savings function, p. 231

EXERCISES

All problems are assignable in MyEconLab.

11.1 A Simple Income-Expenditure Model

1.1 The income-expenditure model is most appropriate for long-run analysis. __________ (True/False)

1.2 Equilibrium output occurs when real output equals planned expenditures. __________ (True/False)

1.3 If output is currently lower than planned expenditures, inventories are __________ (increasing/decreasing).

1.4 At any point on the 45° line, planned expenditures equal __________.

1.5 **Understanding Inventory Behavior.** Use the simple income-expenditure model to analyze the following scenarios.

a. Suppose clothing stores anticipate a good fashion season and add substantially to inventories in their stores. What will happen to GDP?

b. Suppose economists see inventories suddenly increasing. Does this necessarily mean that there are increases in demand for final goods and services?

1.6 **Understanding the 45° Line.** Use the simple income-expenditure diagram depicted in Figure 11.3 on page 226 to answer the following questions.

a. If output equals y_1, what is the level of expenditures?

b. At output equal to y_1, does the level of expenditures fall above, below, or on the 45° line?

c. What does this say about the relationship between output and expenditures?

11.2 The Consumption Function

2.1 The intercept of the consumption function is called __________.

2.2 A decrease in consumer confidence will shift the consumption function __________ (upward/downward).

2.3 If housing prices fall, you would expect the consumption function to shift __________ (upward/downward).

2.4 If the MPC increases, the slope of the consumption function will __________ (increase/decrease).

2.5 **Housing Price Increases and Falling Savings.** Explain why some economists believed the increase in housing prices after 2002 was related to the fall in household savings that was also observed during that period. (Related to Application 1 on page 229.)

2.6 **Retirement Savings and the Decline in the Stock Market.** When the stock market fell sharply in 2007 and 2008, many people near retirement found that their savings for retirement were dramatically reduced. What would be their logical response in this situation? Is this consistent with the wealth effect?

2.7 **Is the Wealth Effect on Consumption from Housing Symmetrical?** When housing prices rose, some households took out a larger loan on their homes and used the additional funds they borrowed to finance purchases of consumer durables. This option is not available when housing prices fall. Explain how this difference might lead to a larger wealth effect for increases in housing prices than decreases in prices. (Related to Application 1 on page 229.)

11.3 Equilibrium Output and the Consumption Function

3.1 In our simple model, if $C = 100 + 0.8y$, and $I = 50$, equilibrium output will be __________.

3.2 If in Exercise 3.1 I increases to 100,

a. the equilibrium income will be __________.

b. the multiplier is __________.

3.3 If the marginal propensity to save is 0.3, the MPC must be __________.

3.4 If the MPC decreases, the multiplier will __________.

3.5 **Estimating Changes in Aggregate Demand.**

a. Suppose $C = C_a + 0.6y$ and that a shock decreases C_a by $10 billion. By how much will equilibrium income decrease?

b. An economy has an MPC of 0.6. By how much will a $10 billion increase in government purchases increase equilibrium income? By how much will a $10 billion increase in taxes decrease equilibrium income?

3.6 **The Paradox of Thrift.** The United States has instituted many policies to attempt to increase savings rates in the United States. One such policy was the creation of individual retirement accounts and other incentives for savvings. An implication of the income-expenditure model is that an increase in the desire of consumers to save will not necessarily lead to higher savings. In fact, total savings will either remain the same or perhaps fall. This is known as the paradox of thrift. Let's see why this is true with an example.

a. Suppose I equals 40 and the savings function is $S = -100 + 0.4y$. Equilibrium income, y, in the economy is 350. Now suppose consumers wish to increase their savings; the new savings function becomes $S = -80 + 0.4y$. Calculate the new level of equilibrium output and savings after the change in the savings function.

b. Explain why equilibrium savings are unchanged.

c. Now suppose that with a decline in equilibrium income, investment also falls. What would be the effect on equilibrium output and total savings if households now wished to increase their desired savings?

d. What does this suggest about the ability of policymakers to increase aggregate savings by affecting citizens' savings rates?

3.7 **Solving a Simple Model.** Consider an economy in which $C = 200 + 0.5y$ and $I = 200$.

a. Determine the equilibrium income algebraically.

b. What is the multiplier for investment spending for this economy?

c. What is the savings function?

d. Draw the savings function on a graph with the investment level and indicate how equilibrium income is determined.

e. What is the level of saving at the level of equilibrium income? Show it is equal to investment.

3.8 **Hurricanes and Subsequent GDP Growth.** Devastating hurricanes, such as those that afflicted the Gulf Coast during the first decade of the 2000s are terrible events. Yet, economists believe that GDP typically rises after them. Explain why this happens and whether that means that hurricanes are really "good things." (Related to Application 3 on page 238.)

3.9 **A Difficulty in Estimating Government Spending Multipliers.** Tax revenues typically rise along with GDP. Governments may typically spend some of this additional revenue on discretionary items in the budget. Assuming this is true, how does this complicate the work of analysts trying to determine the multiplier effects of discretionary spending on GDP? (Related to Application 2 on page 233.)

11.4 Government Spending and Taxation

4.1 The multiplier for taxes is greater than the multiplier for government spending. __________ (True/False)

4.2 A decrease in the tax rate will __________ the government spending multiplier.

4.3 Economic fluctuations have __________ since World War II.

4.4 An increase in both government spending and taxes by the same amount __________ GDP.

4.5 **Using Fiscal Multipliers.** Suppose that during a recession a country wishes to increase its GDP by 100. The MPC is 0.8.

a. Using the government spending multiplier, by how much should government spending be increased?

b. Using the tax multiplier, by how much should taxes be decreased?

4.6 **Seen and Not Seen.** Another way to describe the broken windows fallacy is to say that we often concentrate on what we see and not on what we do not see. How does this way of expressing the fallacy relate to government public works in a classical world? (Related to Application 3 on page 238 .)

4.7 **President Ford's Theory.** During the 1970s, President Gerald Ford proposed that taxes be decreased but that, to avoid increasing the government budget deficit, government spending should be decreased by the same amount.

a. What happens to GDP if taxes and government spending are both decreased by the same amount?

b. Should President Ford have been worried about his tax-reduction plan? Why or why not?

4.8 **Inventory Policies and Economic Stability.** In recent years, many companies have adopted Japanese-style "just-in-time" inventory management. For example, when your cashier at Walmart records your purchase of a new toaster, it automatically triggers a process to re-order a toaster for the store. In the past, store managers had to forecast their inventory needs. Why might this method of inventory management lead to more economic stability?

4.9 **Keynes's Other Contributions.** Although John Maynard Keynes is best known today for his book *The General Theory of Employment, Interest, and Money*, he made other important contributions as well. Search the Web to find out (1) Keynes's main criticism of the Treaty of Versailles, which ended World War I and (2) his contribution to the post–World War II monetary system.

11.5 Exports and Imports

5.1 An increase in the marginal propensity to import will __________ the multiplier for investment spending.

5.2 An increase in exports will lead to a(n) __________ in GDP.

5.3 Use the income-expenditure graph to illustrate how an increase in exports will affect GDP.

5.4 As a country's income increases, imports will also increase. __________ (True/False)

5.5 **Trade Wars.** During the 1930s, many countries in the world—including the United States—tried to help their own economies by restricting imported goods. But because one country's imports are another country's exports, such actions cause international repercussions. Let's look at the worldwide consequences of such policies using the income-expenditure model.

a. Suppose the United States adopted policies to reduce imports from Europe. This means European exports to the United States would be reduced. What would happen to European equilibrium income?

b. Suppose, in response to U.S. policies, Europe decides to restrict imports from the United States. What then happens to U.S equilibrium income?

c. What do you think happened to the volume of world trade during the 1930s?

5.6 **Using Open-Economy Multipliers.** In an open economy, the marginal propensity to consume is 0.9, and the marginal propensity to import is 0.3. How much of an increase in investment would be necessary to raise GDP by 200? What would be your answer if this was a closed economy?

5.7 **U.S. Export Growth.** In 2007, several components of GDP grew much more slowly than in prior years but exports increased sharply. The rest of the world was growing rapidly during this period. Based on this information, what is the most natural explanation for the growth in U.S. exports? (Related to Application 4 on page 243.)

11.6 The Income-Expenditure Model and the Aggregate Demand Curve

6.1 An increase in the price level will __________ GDP and thereby move the economy __________ the aggregate demand curve.

6.2 At any price level, the income-expenditure model determines the level of equilibrium output and the corresponding point on the __________ curve.

6.3 An increase in the price level will not shift the aggregate demand curve. __________ (True/False)

6.4 A rightward shift in the aggregate demand curve corresponds to a(n) __________ in equilibrium income.

6.5 **Using Multipliers to Determine the Shift of the Aggregate Demand Curve.**

a. Suppose the MPC is equal to 0.8. Government spending increases by $20 billion. How far does the aggregate demand curve shift to the right?

b. Now suppose that the MPC is 0.8 and the marginal propensity to import is 0.2. How far to the right will the $20 billion in government spending shift the aggregate demand curve?

6.6 **Increasing Exports and Aggregate Demand.** Suppose foreign countries grow more rapidly than anticipated and U.S. exports also grow.

a. Using the income-expenditure model, first show how the increase in exports will increase U.S. GDP.

b. Using your results in part (a), explain how the aggregate demand curve shifts with the increase in exports.

6.7 **The Size of the Wealth Effect and the Slope of the Aggregate Demand Curve.** Suppose the wealth effect is very small; that is, a large fall in prices will not increase consumption by very much. Explain carefully why this will imply that the aggregate demand curve will have a steep slope.

ECONOMIC EXPERIMENT

ESTIMATING THE MARGINAL PROPENSITY TO CONSUME

For this experiment, each class member is asked to fill out the following table. Given a certain monthly income, how would you spend it and how much would you save? The top row of each column gives you the monthly disposable income. How would you allocate it each month among the various categories of spending in the table and savings? Complete each column in the table. The sum of your entries should equal your disposable income at the top of each column. After you have filled out the chart, compute the changes in your savings and total consumption as your income goes up. What is your marginal propensity to save (MPS)? What is your marginal propensity to consume (MPC) over your total expenditures? Graph your consumption function.

Monthly Disposable Income	$1,250	$1,500	$1,750	$2,000
Expenditures and Savings				
Food				
Housing				
Transportation				
Medical				
Entertainment				
Other expenses				
Savings				

MyEconLab

For additional economic experiments, please visit ***www.myeconlab.com*****.**

APPENDIX

FORMULAS FOR EQUILIBRIUM INCOME AND THE MULTIPLIER

In the chapter, we developed the logic of the income-expenditure model and generally relied on graphical analysis. However, we also referred to a few formulas. In this appendix, we explain where these formulas, both for equilibrium income and the multiplier, come from.

Specifically, in this appendix, we do three things:

- Derive a simple formula for calculating equilibrium output for the simplest economy in which there is no government spending or taxes.
- Derive the multipliers for the economy with the government.
- Derive equilibrium output with both government and the foreign sector.

To derive the formula for equilibrium output, we use simple algebra in the following steps:

1 We know that equilibrium output occurs where output equals planned expenditures, and we know that planned expenditures equal $C + I$; therefore,

$$\text{output} = \text{planned expenditures} = C + I$$
$$\text{output} = C + I$$

2 Next, we substitute the symbol y for output; more importantly, we substitute for the consumption function, $C = (C_a + by)$:

$$y = (C_a + by) + I$$

3 Collect all terms in y on the left side of the equation:

$$y - by = C_a + I$$

4 Factor the left side:

$$y(1 - b) = C_a + I$$

5 Divide both sides by $(1 - b)$:

$$y^* = \frac{(C_a + I)}{(1 - b)}$$

where y^* means the equilibrium level of output. This is the formula for equilibrium output in the text.

Now let's find the multiplier for investment in this simple economy. To do that, we use the formula we just derived and calculate the equilibrium income at one level of investment, which we call the *original level*, and then calculate the equilibrium income at some other level of investment, which we call the *new level*. (We will "calculate" in general terms, not in specific numerical quantities.) What we will get is a formula for the change in output that results from the changes in investment.

For the original level of investment at I_0, we have

$$y_0 = \frac{(C_a + I_0)}{(1 - b)}$$

For a new level of investment at I_1, we have

$$y_1 = \frac{(C_a + I_1)}{(1 - b)}$$

The change in output, Δy, is the difference between the two levels of output that occur at each level of investment:

$$\Delta y = y_1 - y_0$$

Substituting for the levels of output, we have

$$\Delta y = \frac{(C_a + I_1)}{(1 - b)} - \frac{(C_a + I_0)}{(1 - b)}$$

Because the denominator in both expressions is the same $(1 - b)$, we can put the numerators over that common denominator:

$$\Delta y = \frac{(C_a + I_1) - (C_a + I_0)}{(1 - b)}$$

$$\Delta y = \frac{(I_1 - I_0)}{(1 - b)}$$

Finally, because $(I_1 - I_0)$ is the change in investment, ΔI, we can write

$$\Delta y = \frac{\Delta I}{(1 - b)}$$

or

$$\frac{\Delta y}{\Delta I} = \frac{1}{(1 - b)}$$

Therefore, because the multiplier is the ratio of the change in income to the change in investment spending, we have

$$\text{the multiplier} = \frac{\Delta y}{\Delta I} = \frac{1}{(1 - b)}$$

Here is another way to derive the formula for the multiplier. This way helps to illustrate its underlying logic. Suppose investment spending increases by \$1. Because spending determines output, output will rise by \$1. However, because consumption depends on income, consumption will increase by the marginal propensity to consume times the change in income. This means that as output rises by \$1, consumption will increase by $(b \times \$1)$. Because spending determines output, this additional increase in consumer demand will cause output to rise further $(b \times \$1)$. But again, as output and income increase, consumption will increase by MPC times the change in income, which in this case will be $b \times (b \times \$1)$ or $b^2 \times \$1$. As we allow this process to continue, the total change in output will be

$$\Delta y = \$1 + (\$1 \times b) + (\$1 \times b^2) + (\$1 \times b^3)\ldots$$

or

$$\Delta y = \$1 \times (1 + b + b^2 + b^3 + \ldots)$$

The term in parentheses is an infinite series whose value is equal to

$$\frac{1}{(1 - b)}$$

Substituting this value for the infinite series, we have the expression for the multiplier:

$$\Delta y = \$1 \times \frac{1}{(1 - b)}$$

Now we introduce government spending and taxes. Government spending is another determinant of planned expenditures, and consumption spending depends on after-tax income, so consumption equals $C_a + b(y - T)$. Following the same steps we used for equilibrium output without government, we do the same, but now with government:

$$\text{output} = \text{planned expenditures} = (C + I + G)$$
$$y = C_a + b(y - T) + I + G$$

We first collect all terms in y on the left and leave the other terms on the right:

$$y - by = C_a - bT + I + G$$

We then factor the left side:

$$y(1 - b) = C_a - bT + I + G$$

We then divide both sides by $(1 - b)$:

$$y^* = \frac{(C_a - bT + I + G)}{(1 - b)}$$

Using this formula and the method just outlined, we can find the multiplier for changes in government spending and the multiplier for changes in taxes:

$$\text{government spending multiplier} = \frac{1}{(1 - b)}$$

$$\text{tax multiplier} = \frac{-b}{(1 - b)}$$

The multiplier for an increase in government spending is larger than the tax multiplier for a reduction in taxes in the same amount as an increase in government spending. Government spending increases total demand directly. Reductions in taxes first affect consumer's incomes. Because consumers will save a part of their income increase from the tax cut, not all of the tax cut is spent. Therefore, the tax multiplier is smaller (in absolute value) than the government spending multiplier.

As we explained in the text, because government spending has a larger multiplier than taxes, equal increases in government spending and taxes, called balanced-budget increases, will increase total output. For equal dollar increases in both taxes and government spending, the positive effects from the spending increase will outweigh the negative effects from the tax increase. To find the balanced-budget multiplier, just add the government spending and tax multipliers:

$$\begin{aligned}\text{balanced-budget multiplier} &= \text{government spending multiplier} + \text{tax multiplier} \\ &= \frac{1}{(1 - b)} + \frac{-b}{(1 - b)} \\ &= \frac{(1 - b)}{(1 - b)} \\ &= 1\end{aligned}$$

The balanced-budget multiplier equals 1; a \$10 billion increase in both taxes and government spending will increase GDP by \$10 billion.

Finally, we derive equilibrium output with government spending, taxes, and the foreign sector. First, recall that equilibrium output occurs where output equals demand. We now must include planned expenditures from both the government sector and the foreign sector. Planned expenditures from the foreign sector are exports minus imports:

$$\text{output} = \text{planned expenditures} = (C + I + G + X - M)$$

Consumption depends on disposable income:

$$C = C_a + b(y - T)$$

and imports depend on the level of output:

$$M = my$$

Substitute the equations for consumption and imports into the equation where output equals demand:

$$y = C_a + b(y - T) + I + G + X - my$$

Collect all terms in y on the left and leave the other terms on the right:

$$y - (b - m)y = C_a - bT + I + G + X$$

Factor the left side:

$$y[1 - (b - m)] = C_a - bT + I + G + X$$

Divide both sides by $[1 - (b \quad m)]$:

$$y^* = \frac{(C_a - bT + I + G + X)}{[1 - (b - m)]}$$

This is the expression for equilibrium income with government in an open economy. It can be used, following the method we outlined, to calculate multipliers in the open economy.

EXERCISES

All problems are assignable in MyEconLab.

A.1 Find the Multiplier. An economy has a marginal propensity to consume (b) of 0.6 and a marginal propensity to import (m) of 0.2. What is the multiplier for government spending for this economy?

A.2 The Effects of Taxes and Spending. Suppose the economy has a marginal propensity to consume (b) of 0.6 and a marginal propensity to import (m) of 0.2. The government increases its spending by $2 billion and raises taxes by $1 billion. What happens to equilibrium income?

A.3 Savings and Taxes. When there are taxes, savings is defined as disposable income minus consumption, or $S = (y - T) - C$. In an economy with government but no foreign sector—a closed economy—equilibrium income is determined where output equals demand, or $y = C + I + G$. Show that we can also determine equilibrium income using the relationship $S + T = I + G$.

A.4 Working with a Model. An economy has the following dimensions:

$$C = 100 + 0.5(y - T)$$
$$I = 50$$
$$G = 50$$
$$T = 20$$

a. Draw the income-expenditure graph for this economy.

b. Find the equilibrium income and plot it on the graph.

c. What is the multiplier for government spending?

d. Find the savings function.

e. What is the level of savings when the economy is in equilibrium?

f. Show that at equilibrium $S + T = I + G$.

NOTES

1. "GDP Growth in China 1952–2011," Chinability, http://www.chinability.com/GDP.htm

Investment and Financial Markets

CHAPTER 12

The housing market is a perfect example of the close links between investment and finance.

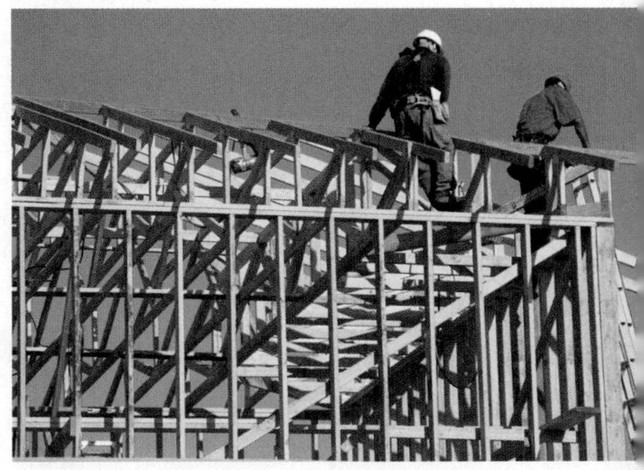

With the stock market falling sharply in 2000, housing looked like an alternative and attractive investment. Interest rates were low and homeowners and potential investors found that it was easy to borrow money to purchase new or larger homes. Wall Street and government agencies developed ever more complex ways to pour money into the housing market, and banks and finance companies did not seem to be asking too many questions about their borrowers. As housing prices continued to rise, the building industry responded to the general euphoria. Investment in residential housing increased 40 percent in real terms from 2000 to 2006.

It was too good to last. With all the new construction, the increased supply of housing stopped the rise in prices. Some buyers made foolish decisions and took on loans that were too large for their incomes. As financial markets became nervous, lenders became more cautious and sharply cut back on funds available to the market. With increased supply and reduced demand, housing prices began to fall. The building industry recognized it had too many new houses in the pipeline and began to cut back. From its peak in the first quarter of 2006 to the fourth quarter of 2009, new housing construction fell by 53 percent. The fall in residential housing alone brought down real GDP by 3 percent and devastated many state economies. The lingering effects of the housing crisis prevented a fast recovery from the recession.

LEARNING OBJECTIVES

- Explain why investment spending is a volatile component of GDP.
- Discuss the concept of present value.
- Describe the role of interest rates in making investment decisions.
- List the ways that financial intermediation can facilitate investment.

MyEconLab

MyEconLab helps you master each objective and study more efficiently.

Investment spending plays a number of critical roles in the economy. As we have seen, economic growth depends on whether the stock of capital—plant and equipment—increases in the economy. Moreover, investment is also a key component of aggregate demand, so fluctuations in investment spending can cause recessions and booms. In this chapter, we will study the factors that determine investment spending by firms. We also will examine the role that institutions such as banks, savings and loans, and other new and evolving financial institutions play in facilitating that investment.

An *investment*, broadly defined, is an action that creates a cost today but provides benefits in the future. A firm builds a new plant today to earn more revenue in the future. College students pay money to attend school now so they can earn higher salaries later. A government spends money today to construct a dam that will provide hydroelectric power for years to come. These are examples of investments. Notice that we're using the term *investment* in a broader sense than we did in Chapter 5 when we discussed GDP. In that chapter when we talked about investment, we were talking about expenditures by firms on currently produced goods and services. In this chapter, we broaden the definition to include actions taken by anyone—individuals, firms, and governments—to improve well-being later.

12.1 An Investment: A Plunge into the Unknown

When individuals, firms, or governments make an investment, they incur costs today in the hope of future gains. The phrase "hope of" is an important aspect of investment decisions. That simply means that payoffs occurring in the future cannot be known with certainty. Investments are a plunge into the unknown.

Firms and individuals frequently revise their outlook on the future precisely because it is uncertain. These revisions can occur suddenly and lead to sharp swings in investment spending. Sometimes investors are optimistic and decide to increase their investment spending; at other times, they may quickly become pessimistic and cut back on their investment spending. To estimate future events, firms pay careful attention to the current pace of the economy. If economic growth is sluggish, they are likely to forecast that it will be sluggish in the future and cut back on investment spending. If economic growth is strong, they are likely to forecast that it will remain so and increase their investment spending. In other words, investment spending tends to be closely related to the current pace of economic growth.

accelerator theory
The theory of investment that says that current investment spending depends positively on the expected future growth of real GDP.

This phenomenon is known as the **accelerator theory** of investment spending. It postulates that when real GDP growth is expected to be high, firms anticipate that investing in plants and equipment will pay off later, so they increase their total investment spending. However, John Maynard Keynes had another theory. Keynes said the sharp swings in optimism and pessimism related to investment spending were often irrational, reflecting, perhaps, our most basic, primal instincts. He often referred to them as "the animal spirits" of investors. It was, in part, animal spirits that led to the rise and fall in residential investment that we discussed in the chapter-opening story.

It is likely that *both* projections for the future *and* Keynes's animal spirits are closely associated with current investment. If this is the case, we would expect investment spending to be a very volatile component of GDP. As Figure 12.1 indicates, this is indeed the case.

Figure 12.1 plots total investment spending as a share of U.S. GDP from 1970 to 2011. Notice two things about Figure 12.1:

- From 1970 to 2011, the share of investment as a component of GDP ranged from a low of about 10 percent in 1975 to a high of over 18 percent in 2000—a dramatic 8-percentage-point difference.
- Swings in investment spending often occurred over short periods of time. For example, during recessions (noted by the shaded areas in the figure), investment spending fell sharply. During booms, investment spending rose sharply. In other words, investment spending is highly **procyclical**; it increases during booms and falls during recessions.

procyclical
Moving in the same direction as real GDP.

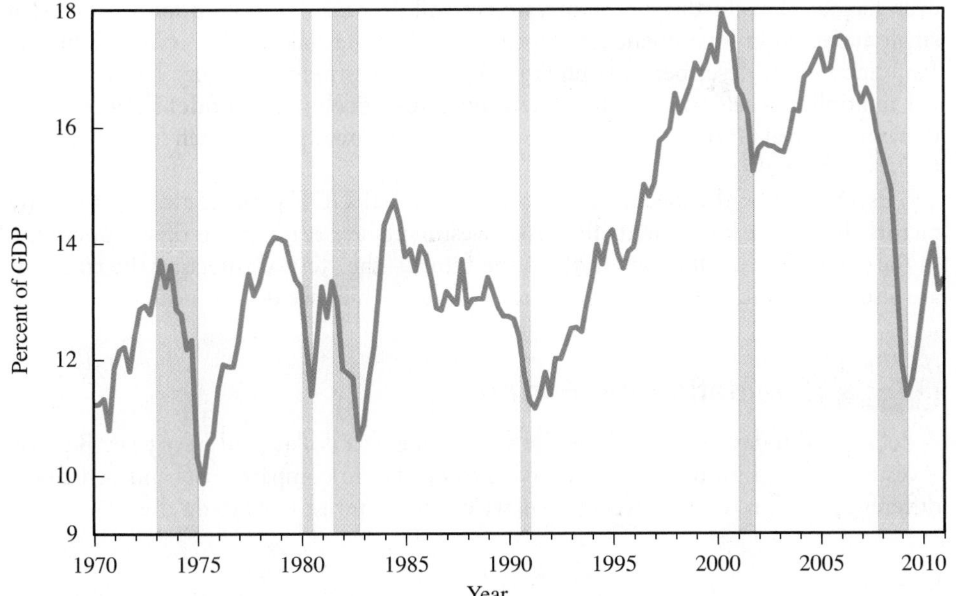

◄ **FIGURE 12.1**
Investment Spending as a Share of U.S. GDP, 1970–2011
The share of investment as a component of GDP ranged from a low of about 10 percent in 1975 to a high of over 18 percent in 2000. The shaded areas represent U.S. recessions.

MyEconLab Real-time data

Many different factors can contribute to uncertainty in the economy. Volatile energy prices are one. In general, when the future is uncertain, firms become cautious in their behavior and may postpone making investment decisions.

Although investment spending is a much smaller component of GDP than consumption (approximately 70 versus 16 percent), it is much more volatile than consumption. Recall that changes in the components of GDP—*C*, *I*, *G*, or *NX*—are amplified by the multiplier. For example, if the multiplier is 1.5, and investment spending initially falls by 1 percent of GDP, then GDP will fall by 1.5 percent. However, if the fall in GDP makes firms more pessimistic, they may cut investment

application 1

ENERGY PRICE UNCERTAINTY REDUCES INVESTMENT SPENDING

APPLYING THE CONCEPTS #1: How Do Fluctuations in Energy Prices Affect Investment Decisions by Firms?

As we have seen in previous chapters, increases in oil prices can lead to a drop in GDP. However, uncertainty about oil prices is also an important factor. Economists Hui Guo and Kevin Kliesen found evidence that volatility in oil prices adversely affects GDP growth.

One important way volatility of oil prices can hurt the economy is by creating uncertainty for firms making investment decisions. For example, consider whether a firm should invest in an energy-saving technology for a new plant. If energy prices remain high, it may be profitable to invest in energy-saving technology, but if energy prices fall, these investments would be unwise. If firms are faced with an increasingly uncertain future, they will delay their investment decisions until the uncertainty is resolved. In 2008, oil prices reached $145 a barrel, but later in the year fell below $50. On what number should firms base their investment decisions? **Related to Exercise 1.8.**

SOURCE: Based on Hui Guo and Kevin Kliesen, "Oil Price Volatility and Macroeconomic Activity," *Federal Reserve Bank of St. Louis Review* (November–December 2005): 669–684.

even further. This further cut in investment will decrease GDP even more. That is, a small initial fall in investment can trigger a much larger fall in GDP. Nobel Laureate Paul Samuelson described this phenomenon of investment volatility by developing the multiplier-accelerator model. The **multiplier-accelerator model** showed that a downturn in real GDP leads to an even sharper fall in investment, which further reduces GDP via the multiplier.

multiplier-accelerator model
A model in which a downturn in real GDP leads to a sharp fall in investment, which triggers further reductions in GDP through the multiplier.

Psychology and expectations about future real GDP growth are not the only factors that affect investment. Because investments are really trade-offs—something in the present traded for something in the future—the "terms" affecting the trade-off are also important. These terms are interest rates, which we discuss next.

12.2 Evaluating the Future

A dollar paid today does not have the same value as a dollar paid next year. Because investments yield future payoffs, we need to be able to compare costs and benefits at different points in time. As we will see, we can use interest rates to do this.

Understanding Present Value

Suppose a good friend comes to you and says, "I need some cash, badly. If you give me $100 today, I can give you back $105 next year. Do we have a deal?" How would you decide whether to accept this deal? Somehow, you need a tool to be able to compare dollars today with dollars received in the future. That tool is present value. The **present value** of a payment to be received in the future is the maximum amount a person is willing to pay today to receive the future payment. Recall the principle of opportunity cost.

present value
The maximum amount a person is willing to pay today to receive a payment in the future.

PRINCIPLE OF OPPORTUNITY COST
The opportunity cost of something is what you sacrifice to get it.

Let's think about how much you are willing to pay for the right to receive $105 in one year. Suppose you can earn 5 percent per year in a savings account or money market account. A moment of thought will show you that you would be willing to lend your friend $100. Here is why: If you kept your $100 in the bank at 5 percent interest, you would have $105 at the end of the year—just the amount your friend would repay you. While you would have sacrificed $5 in interest, you would have earned $5 on the loan ($105 – $100).

However, you would not want to lend your friend more than $100. If you lent more—say $102—then your loss in interest of $5.10 (5 percent of $102) would be greater than your $3 gain on the loan ($105 – $102). In this case, the amount you sacrifice will be greater than what you get in return.

Of course, you would like to lend your friend less than $100 and make even more profit. But the *maximum amount* you would be willing to pay today to receive $105 next year, when the interest rate is 5 percent, is $100. Thus, the present value of $105 in this example is $100.

PRESENT VALUE AND INTEREST RATES Here is another useful way to think of present value. Suppose you want to buy a new car in five years for $20,000. You want to know how much you need to have in your bank account today, so that after five years you have the $20,000 to make the payment for the car. A simple formula can answer this and similar questions. If K is an amount of money at some point in the future; t is the amount of time, or years, in the future until you need the money; and i is the interest rate you earn on your account, then the amount you need today is just the present value of the K dollars, which is

$$\text{present value} = \frac{K}{(1 + i)^t}$$

In the example of your friend, her payment (K) is \$105, the interval of time (t) in which she's going to pay it is one year, and the interest rate (i) is 0.05. Using the present value formula, the present value of \$105 in one year is \$100:

$$\text{present value} = \frac{\$105}{(1 + 0.05)^1} = \$100$$

This is the maximum amount you are willing to lend her today to receive \$105 from her in one year.

Let's consider another example. Suppose the interest rate were 10 percent and you were offered \$1,000 to be paid to you in 20 years. How much is that \$1,000 worth today? That is, how much of your money today would you be willing to "tie up" (loan out) to get \$1,000 in 20 years? At an interest rate of 10 percent, this is how much:

$$\text{present value} = \frac{\$1{,}000}{(1 + 0.10)^{20}} = \$148.64$$

You would be willing to pay only \$148.64 today to receive \$1,000 in 20 years. The reason you would be willing to pay so much less than \$1,000 is that money earning interest grows over time. At a 10 percent interest rate, after 20 years you would have received exactly \$1,000 by initially investing just \$148.64.

Returning to our original example with your friend, what happens if the interest rate is 10 percent instead of 5 percent? If your friend still promises you \$105 after one year but the interest rate is double, how much would you be willing to loan her today? Using the formula, you would loan only \$95.45 today:

$$\text{present value} = \frac{\$105}{(1 + 0.10)^1} = \$95.45$$

What this means is that if the interest rate is higher, you will be willing to pay *less* for the same payment in the future. This is an important result. *The present value of a given payment in the future decreases as the interest rate increases.* Here is why: With a higher interest rate, the opportunity cost of lending out your money is higher. Because you can earn more on your money with a higher rate, you will not be willing to pay as much now to get the same \$105 dollars in the future. Similarly, *when interest rates fall, the present value of a given payment in the future increases.* For example, if interest rates fell to 2 percent, the present value (the value today) of \$105 in one year would be higher—\$102.94:

$$\text{present value} = \frac{\$105}{(1 + 0.02)^1} = \$102.94$$

With a lower interest rate, the opportunity cost of keeping your money in the bank or loaning it to a friend is less. That means you will be willing to pay more money now for the same \$105 payment in the future.

Let's summarize our discussion of present value:

1 The present value—the value today—of a given payment in the future is the maximum amount a person is willing to pay today for that payment.

2 As the interest rate increases, the opportunity cost of your funds also increases, so the present value of a given payment in the future falls. In other words, you need *less* money today to get to your future "money goal."

3 As the interest rate decreases, the opportunity cost of your funds also decreases, so the present value of a given payment in the future rises. In other words, you need *more* money today to get to your money goal.

Individuals, firms, and the government all use interest rates to make decisions that involve the future. For example, individuals take interest rates into account when they decide how much to save for the future or even when to retire. And, as we will see, firms and the government use interest rates to decide whether to undertake important investments.

Real and Nominal Interest Rates

Even if you deposit $100 in a bank account and get $105 at the end of the year, if the economy's annual rate of inflation amounts to 5 percent or more, your purchasing power would not have increased at all. In other words, the 5 percent inflation will eat up all your 5 percent earnings. This is an example of the real-nominal principle.

REAL-NOMINAL PRINCIPLE

What matters to people is the real value of money or income—the purchasing power—not the face value of money.

nominal interest rate
Interest rate quoted in the market.

real interest rate
The nominal interest rate minus the inflation rate.

When there is inflation, economists make a distinction between the interest rate quoted in the market, which is called the **nominal interest rate**, and the **real interest rate**, which is what you actually earn after taking account of inflation. The real interest rate is defined as the nominal interest rate minus the inflation rate:

$$\text{real rate} = \text{nominal rate} - \text{inflation rate}$$

If the nominal rate of interest is 6 percent per year and the inflation rate is 4 percent during the year, the real rate of interest is 2 percent (6 – 4).

To understand what the real rate of interest means, suppose you have $100 and annual inflation is 4 percent. It's not hard to figure out that next year you will need $104 to have the same purchasing power you do today. Let's say you deposit today $100 at a 6 percent annual interest rate. At the end of the year, you will have $106 ($100 × 1.06).

Now let's calculate your real gain. After one year, you will have increased your holdings by $6, but taking into account the $4 you needed to keep up with inflation, your gain is only $2. The real rate of interest you earned, the nominal rate adjusted for inflation, is 2 percent, or $2.

Let's see what happens when you borrow money. Suppose you borrow $100 at a 10 percent annual interest rate, but inflation is 6 percent during the year. At the end of the year, you must pay back $110 ($100 × 1.10). But with an inflation rate of 6 percent, the lender would need 6 of the 10 dollars you paid in interest just to keep up with inflation. That means the lender would effectively get just a $4 gain ($10 – $6), instead of the full $10 gain. Thus, when corrected for the effects of inflation, the real rate of interest you will have to pay is just 4 percent, or $4, on the original $100 loan.

As an example, in 2002 if seniors invested their money in three-month U.S. government Treasury bills, they would have earned an average interest rate of 1.6 percent. However, inflation, as measured by the Consumer Price Index, was 2.4 percent. In real terms, these seniors would have actually lost money during the year, earning a negative real rate of interest of –0.8 percent.

expected real interest rate
The nominal interest rate minus the expected inflation rate.

We defined the real interest rate as the nominal interest rate minus the actual inflation rate. When firms or individuals borrow or lend money, they do not know what the rate of inflation will actually be in the future. Instead, they must form an expectation—an estimate—of what they believe the inflation rate will be in the future. For a given nominal interest rate, we can define the **expected real interest rate** as the nominal interest rate minus the expected inflation rate. The expected real interest rate is the rate at which borrowers or lenders *expect* to make transactions.

It is difficult to precisely determine expected real rates of interest because we never know exactly what inflation rates people really anticipate. One approach is to rely on the judgments of professional forecasters. Here is an example. In April 2010, the nominal interest rate on three-month U.S. government securities was 0.22 percent. The nominal rate was very low, but positive. However, inflation forecasts for the remainder of that year were about 2 percent. This meant that the expected real rate was –1.78 percent. To determine real returns, we need to know both the nominal rate of interest and forecasts for inflation.

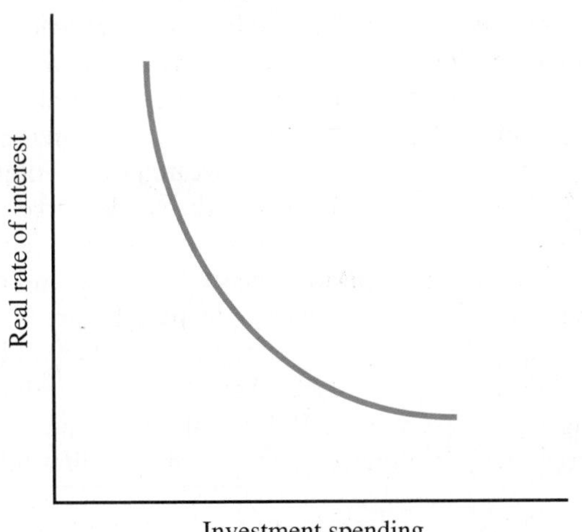

◄ FIGURE 12.3
The Relationship between Real Interest Rates and Investment Spending
As the real interest rate declines, investment spending in the economy increases.

In practice, firms need to take into account other factors besides interest rates in making their investment decisions. In the **neoclassical theory of investment**, pioneered by Dale Jorgenson of Harvard University, taxes along with real interest rates play a key role in determining investment spending. Jorgenson used his theory to analyze how investors respond to a variety of tax incentives, including investment tax credits.

neoclassical theory of investment
A theory of investment that says both real interest rates and taxes are important determinants of investment.

Should we use a real or nominal interest rate to determine whether to invest? The answer is that it doesn't really matter, as long as we are consistent. If the future benefits of the project are not adjusted for inflation, then we should use the nominal interest rate because it takes into account overall inflation—inflation is built into the nominal rate, so to speak. But if we first express the future benefits of the investment in current dollars—that is, if we reduce their nominal value by the amount that prices in the economy are expected to increase—then we should use the real rate of interest in our calculations.

Keep this distinction between real and nominal interest rates in mind. If nominal interest rates are 10 percent but inflation is 9 percent, the real rate of interest is only 1 percent. A firm makes its investment decisions by comparing its expected real net return from investment projects to the real rate of interest. Just because nominal interest rates are high does not mean the real interest rate is also high.

During the 1970s, homeowners in California understood this. They purchased homes in record numbers, even though it meant borrowing money at interest rates exceeding 10 percent. Buyers were willing to borrow at such high rates because housing prices in California had been rising by more than 10 percent annually, and they believed the trend would continue. They realized, for example, that if housing prices rose by 12 percent per year, they were essentially earning a 2 percent annual return because their mortgage loans were just 10 percent. (They would earn the returns only when they sold their homes.) That would make the real interest rate of the money borrowed –2 percent. This caused a housing boom in California that lasted until housing prices stopped rising at such high rates.

Investment and the Stock Market

Economists have long noticed a correlation between the stock market and investment spending. All other things being equal, when the level of the stock market is high, investment spending also tends to be high. It makes sense that the two are related. Consider a firm's options when it wants to finance a new project. The firm really has three choices: First, it can rely on its **retained earnings**—the earnings the firm hasn't paid out in dividends to its owners. Second, it can borrow funds from a bank or sell **corporate bonds** to the public. Third, it can issue and sell new shares, or stock. When a firm's stock price is high, it can issue shares at a premium and use the proceeds from

retained earnings
Corporate earnings that are not paid out as dividends to their owners.

corporate bond
A bond sold by a corporation to the public in order to borrow money.

their sale to finance new investments. The higher the share price, the fewer shares the firm needs to sell to raise capital. This means, essentially, that the cost of the project the firm wants to undertake falls as the company's stock price climbs. In other words, high stock prices lead to high investment. This is known as the **Q-theory of investment**, and it was originally developed by the late Nobel Laureate James Tobin of Yale University. In the boom of the late 1990s when the level of the stock market was high along with share prices, many firms financed large investments by selling their shares.

Q-theory of investment
The theory of investment that links investment spending to stock prices.

During roughly this same time period, the stock market and investment spending appeared to be even more tightly linked than in the past. Figure 12.4 plots the Standard and Poor's index of stock prices on the same graph as the share of investment spending as a component of GDP from 1997 to 2003. As you can see, both the stock market and investment spending rose sharply from 1997, peaking in mid-2000. They then both fell sharply—the stock market plunged, investment spending fell, and the economy entered a recession.

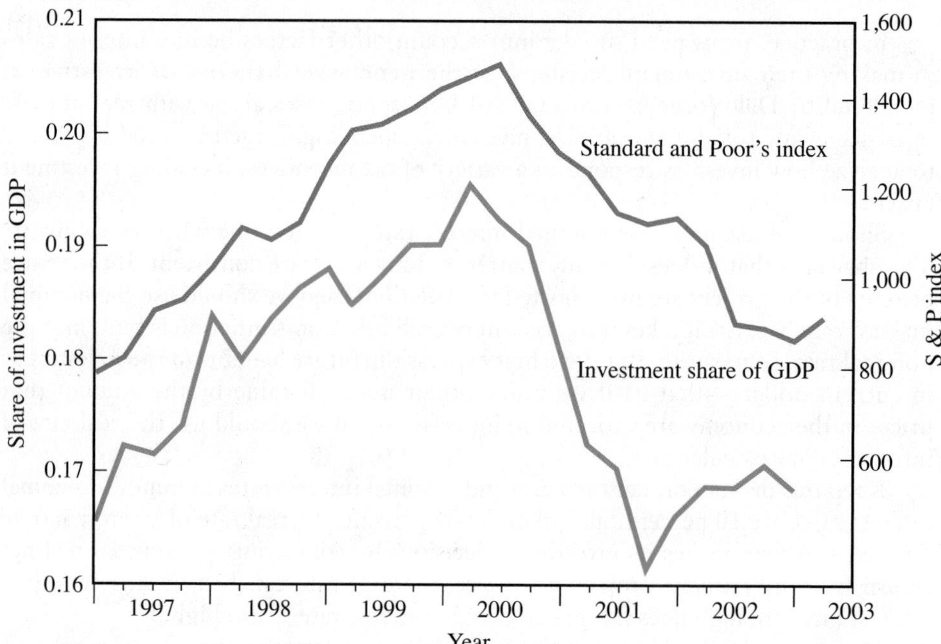

▲ **FIGURE 12.4**
The Stock Market and Investment Levels, 1997–2003
Both the stock market and investment spending rose sharply from 1997, peaking in mid-2000.

The reason the two were so tightly linked was that investors were overly optimistic about the future. They believed that, driven by new technology, the newfound economic prosperity would last forever (or at least certainly longer than it did). With optimistic expectations about the future, stock prices should have been high because stock prices are based on the present value of the dividends people expect firms to pay in the future:

$$\text{price of a stock} = \text{present value of expected future dividend payments}$$

Because investors' expectations about future dividends were high, stock prices were high. Firms, like individual investors, rushed to make massive, long-term investments, particularly in the fiber-optics and telecommunications industries. Some observers questioned whether the expectations were rational. Still, there were enough optimistic investors to sufficiently drive up prices.

As we saw in Figure 12.1 on page 255, investment spending during this period in the United States reached new highs. In many cases, stock prices for companies that had never turned a profit nonetheless soared to astronomical heights. Unfortunately,

application 3

DEBT FORGIVENESS?

APPLYING THE CONCEPTS #3: Is reducing the debt owed on home mortgages a good policy to deal with an ailing housing market?

During the housing boom, many homeowners borrowed money to purchase their property but then saw the value of their homes fall sharply. As a consequence, in 2012 approximately 12 million U.S. homeowners owed more on their home mortgages than their home was actually worth. These homeowners are commonly known as being "underwater." While the majority of underwater homeowners were making their mortgage payments on time, a significant minority were delinquent on their payments and on a path to defaulting on their mortgages.

To assist these homeowners who are behind on their payments and may eventually lose their homes to foreclosure, many in Congress have advocated for reduction on the amount of money they actually owe—or principal reduction. The hope is that with a reduction in the amount they owed they would start making timely payments on their mortgages and avoid a messy default.

This idea, however, has proven to be extremely controversial for several reasons. First, the holders of the mortgage may not want to reduce the principal because they believe they will be eventually repaid. Second, what about those underwater homeowners who are meeting their mortgage payments? Would they stop making payments in order to obtain some principal relief? Rather than actual principal reduction, some lenders have allowed borrowers to postpone payments or make other arrangements. **Related to Exercise 4.5.**

---

both investors and firms may have been subject to what former Federal Reserve chairman Alan Greenspan famously dubbed "irrational exuberance"—something similar to Keynes's "animal spirits." Although the economy had performed very well in the late 1990s, it could not grow at those rates forever. Many investors and firms believed it could, though. When they began to realize it couldn't, the stock market plunged and investment plans were curtailed. What linked the stock market and investment in both their rise and their fall were first optimistic and then pessimistic expectations about the economy. Rather than causing the rise and fall of investment spending, the stock market mirrored expectations about the economy held by firms and individual investors.

12.4 How Financial Intermediaries Facilitate Investment

Households save and invest their funds for different reasons than firms. A typical couple might be saving money for their retirement or for their children's education, and they generally won't like the idea of their savings being subject to risk. They do, however, want their savings to be readily accessible and convertible to money—what economists call **liquid**—in case they have a financial emergency. Funds deposited in a bank account, for example, provide a source of liquidity for households because they can be withdrawn at any time.

liquid
Easily convertible into money on short notice.

Unlike households, firms and business managers are typically risk-takers. They are gambling that their vision of the future will come true and make them vast profits. These investors need funds they can tie up for long periods of time. For example, an entrepreneur who wants to build a skyscraper or casino may need financing for several years before beginning construction and for years afterward until the business begins to produce profits.

Suppose individual entrepreneurs had to obtain funds directly from individual savers. First, they would have to negotiate with thousands of people to obtain sufficient funds. This would take a lot of time and be costly. Second, the savers would face extraordinarily high risks if they loaned all their money to a single entrepreneur who had a risky project to undertake. Not only would all their funds be tied up in a single project, it would not be easy to monitor the investor's decisions. How could they be certain the entrepreneur wouldn't run off with their money? Additionally, their investments would not be liquid. To compensate these savers for the risk they would be taking and the lack of liquidity they would face, entrepreneurs would have to pay them extremely high interest rates, but higher interest rates would make it harder, perhaps impossible, for the entrepreneur to make a profit. No prospect of profits would mean no one would invest in the project in the first place. In other words, society would not be able to turn its savings into profitable investment projects. Figure 12.5 depicts this dilemma. How can the problem be solved?

► FIGURE 12.5
Savers and Investors

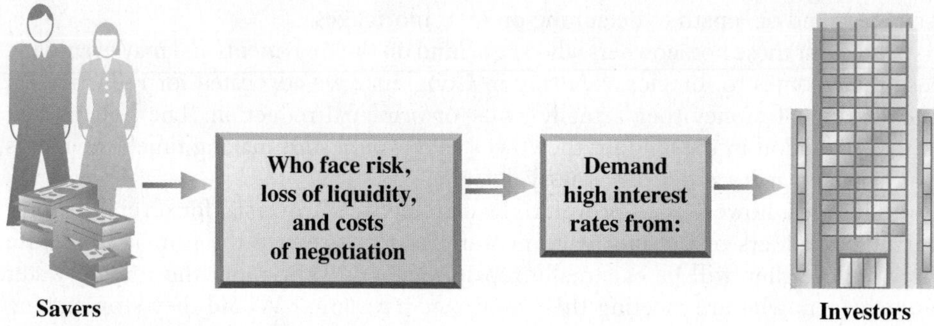

financial intermediaries Organizations that receive funds from savers and channel them to investors.

The answer is through financial intermediaries. **Financial intermediaries** include banks, savings and loans, insurance companies, brokerage firms, companies that run mutual funds, and other types of financial institutions. These institutions accept funds from savers and make loans to businesses and individuals. For example, a local bank accepts deposits from savers and uses the funds to make loans to local businesses. Savings and loan institutions will accept deposits in savings accounts and use these funds to make loans, often for housing. Insurance companies accept premium payments from individuals in exchange for the protection provided by the insurance payments. Then insurance companies lend the premiums received to earn returns from investments so they can pay off the insurance claims of individuals. Figure 12.6 shows how financial intermediaries create a valuable link between savers and investors. Pooling the funds of savers to make loans to individual borrowers reduces the costs of negotiation. Financial institutions also have more expertise to evaluate and monitor investments than most individual investors.

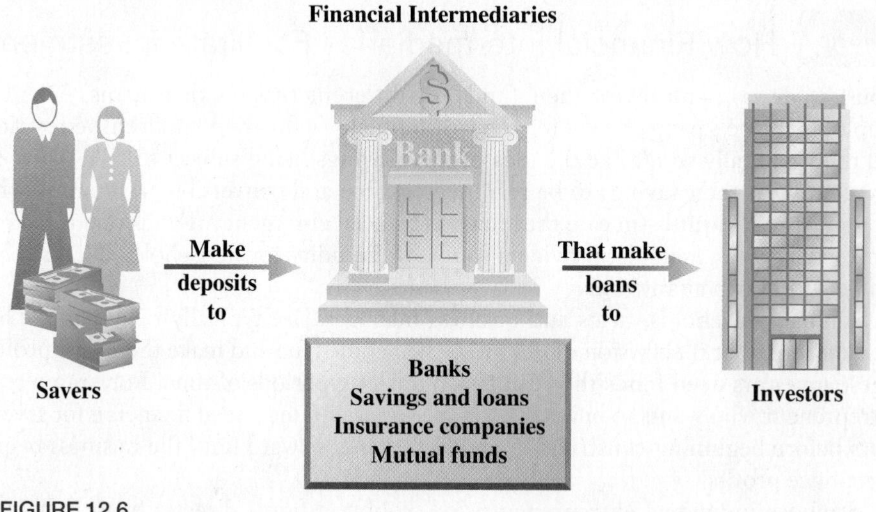

▲ FIGURE 12.6
Financial Intermediaries

To some degree, these financial intermediaries also provide liquidity. In normal circumstances, not all households withdraw their money at the same time, so financial intermediaries can lend out most of the money and still have enough on hand to meet withdrawals by depositors.

But how do financial intermediaries reduce risk? They do this by diversifying investors' assets—by not putting "all the eggs in one basket," so to speak. Intermediaries invest (that is, make loans) in a large number of projects whose returns, although uncertain, are independent of one another. By *independent*, we mean the return from one investment is unrelated to the return on another investment. Consider a bank investing in a large number of projects that all together produce an average return of 8 percent annually. Each project alone is risky and could pay a return either higher or lower than 8 percent. However, as long as the returns on all these projects are independent of one another, those with higher returns will likely offset those with lower returns. By investing in a large number of projects, the bank increases the odds that as a group the projects will earn 8 percent.

Other financial intermediaries reduce risks in related ways. A fire insurance company accepts premiums from many individuals in communities throughout the country and uses the funds to make investments. Because not all houses will burn down in the same year, the insurance company knows it will have a stable source of funds for its investments. Insurance diversification works well only when companies insure events that are independent of one another, however. Some situations are not independent and therefore can't easily be insured by the same company. For example, an insurance company would be unwise to provide earthquake insurance for just the Los Angeles area. If an earthquake did occur, the firm would be faced with making payments to many clients who suffered loss without anyone else's payments to offset them. In somewhat the same way, even bank loans are not fully independent. During a recession, many more firms will experience financial difficulties and have trouble meeting their loan obligations to their banks.

In recent years, we have seen an innovation in financial intermediation. In the past, if a savings and loan company made a loan to a home purchaser, it would hold onto the loan until it was paid off. That meant the savings and loan could make new loans or mortgages only if it was able to attract new deposits to provide the funds.

Two large government-sponsored financial intermediaries, Fannie Mae and Freddie Mac, changed the way mortgage markets operated. They purchased mortgages from savings and loans and banks throughout the country, packaged them, and sold them to investors in the financial market. This enabled savings and loans to offer additional mortgages with the funds they received from Fannie Mae or Freddie Mac, and it allowed investors to own a part of a diversified collection of mortgages from around the country. The private sector quickly adopted these practices as well.

The practice of purchasing loans, re-packaging them, and selling them to the financial markets is known as **securitization**. Although it started with home mortgages, securitization now applies to other types of financial obligations, such as credit card and consumer debt. Financial intermediaries will often borrow money from financial markets to purchase loans in order to re-package and sell them. Using borrowed funds to purchase assets is known as **leverage**. Increases in leverage increase the risk that financial intermediaries undertake because they are obligated to pay off the funds they have borrowed, regardless of the actual performance of the assets they have purchased.

securitization
The practice of purchasing loans, re-packaging them, and selling them to the financial markets.

leverage
Using borrowed funds to purchase assets.

When Financial Intermediaries Malfunction

Financial intermediation can sometimes go wrong. When it does, the economy suffers. Important examples of the failure of financial intermediation include commercial bank failures during the Great Depression, the U.S. savings and loan crisis of the 1980s, a similar crisis in Japan in the 1990s, and the U.S. housing credit and securitization crisis of 2007 and 2008.

In the early days of the Great Depression, many banks in the United States, particularly in rural areas, provided farmers and local businesses with loans that turned out to be unprofitable. This worried depositors, and rumors circulated that banks would fail. Depositors panicked, and many tried to withdraw their money simultaneously in what is called a **bank run**. During the Great Depression, bank runs occurred throughout the world. In 1931, a panic broke out after the collapse of Creditanstalt, Austria's largest bank. Banking panics occurred throughout other countries in Europe, including Belgium, France, Germany, Italy, and Poland.

bank run
Panicky investors simultaneously trying to withdraw their funds from a bank they believe may fail.

Few banks, profitable or unprofitable, can survive a run, because not all deposits are kept on hand. The result of the bank runs was that thousands of healthy U.S. banks shut down, leaving large parts of the United States without a banking system. Many farms and businesses could no longer find a source of loans, and the severity of the Great Depression worsened. Studies have shown that the countries with the most severe banking panics were hardest hit by the Depression.

To prevent banking panics from happening again, in 1933 the U.S. government began providing **deposit insurance** on money placed in banks and savings and loans. Today deposit insurance guarantees the government will reimburse depositors for amounts up to $250,000 in each account at each bank should their banks fail. Because everyone knows their deposits are secure, bank runs no longer regularly occur. Today, most countries have some form of deposit insurance intended to prevent panics.

deposit insurance
Federal government insurance on deposits in banks and savings and loans.

Ironically, deposit insurance indirectly led to the U.S. savings and loan crisis, which occurred during the 1980s. In the early 1970s, savings and loan institutions (S&Ls) made mortgage loans to households at low interest rates. However, later in the decade nominal interest rates rose sharply as inflation increased. The savings and loans were in trouble: They had to pay high interest rates to attract deposits, but they were earning interest at low rates from the money they had loaned out previously. Many of the S&Ls failed.

The government tried to assist the savings and loan industry by broadening the range of investments the industry could make. Some S&Ls soon began aggressively investing in speculative real estate and other risky projects to earn higher returns. Depositors weren't worried, though, because they knew their savings were insured by the government. Unfortunately, many of these risky projects failed, and the government was forced to bail out the S&Ls at a cost of nearly $100 billion to taxpayers. Because depositors' savings were insured, most people didn't suffer directly from the collapse of their savings and loan institutions. As taxpayers they suffered, though, because they had to foot the bill.

Japan suffered similar problems in the 1990s. By 1995, seven of the eight largest Japanese mortgage lenders had gone bankrupt following a crash in real estate prices. Like the U.S. government, the Japanese government also used taxpayers' funds to bail these lenders out.

The decline in housing prices that we described in the chapter-opening story triggered a severe crisis in the newly developed securitization markets. Although the actual details are complex, the basic story is simple. Lenders had made loans to borrowers who had limited ability to repay, and when borrowers began to miss payments or default on their loans, it caused major disruptions in the market for securitized loans, which, in turn, disrupted credit to other sectors in the economy, causing a massive disruption to financial markets. Even Fannie Mae and Freddie Mac fell victim to the housing decline and were placed under direct government control in September 2008.

As the housing-generated financial crisis spread to the rest of the financial markets, the credit markets essentially "froze" and banks worldwide would no longer lend to each other. Customers scrambled to withdraw their funds in financial institutions that they perceived were weak, leading to a "run" on these institutions. As a result, financial institutions such as Bear Stearns and Lehman Brothers were forced to close and institutions such as Merrill Lynch and Wachovia Bank were taken over by other financial institutions. When the financial institution Lehman Brothers failed, it set off a panic in the markets that spread to other international banks and financial institutions. The stock market plunged dramatically worldwide, reflecting the severity of the crisis and fear that it would lead to a total worldwide financial collapse. As credit became unavailable, businesses began to suffer as well, as they were not able to borrow funds to run their enterprises on a day-to-day basis. State and local government also found it nearly impossible to borrow at the height of the crisis.

Governments around the world took a number of steps to alleviate this crisis. Central banks, whose activities during the crisis are described in more detail in the next chapter, provided loans and credit through a wide variety of channels. After considerable turmoil, the U.S. Congress passed a bailout package, called the Troubled Asset Relief Program, or TARP, that enabled the Treasury to use up to $700 billion to shore up the financial system. Following the lead of Great Britain, the U.S. Treasury used some of these proceeds to provide funds to large banks in order to restore confidence in the financial system and took limited ownership in these banks. As previously noted, the government took control of Fannie Mae and Freddie Mac and also provided funding to some large financial firms, such as the American International Group (AIG), which provided financial insurance to other firms and was deemed essential to keep afloat during the crisis. The United States and other countries around the world also increased the limits on the amounts eligible for deposit insurance to bolster consumer confidence in banking institutions. The goals of all these actions were to restore confidence in a system of financial intermediation that was under considerable stress.

application 4

SECURITIZATION: THE GOOD, THE BAD, AND THE UGLY

APPLYING THE CONCEPTS #4: How have recent financial innovations created new risks for the economy?

As securitization developed, it allowed financial intermediaries to provide new funds for borrowers to enter the housing market. This led to a rise in the rate of homeownership and was hailed as a positive development. But there was a dark side to this process as well.

As the housing boom began in 2002, lenders and home purchasers began to take increasing risks. Lenders made "subprime" loans to borrowers with limited ability to actually repay their mortgages and did not exercise full diligence in making loans. Some households were willing to take on considerable debt because they were confident they could make money in a rising housing market. Lenders securitized the subprime loans and financial firms offered exotic investment securities to investors based on these loans. Many financial institutions purchased these securities without really knowing what was inside them. Because the securities were so new, the agencies that traditionally evaluated the riskiness of these investments did not post sufficient warning.

When the housing boom stopped and borrowers stopped making payments on subprime loans, it created panic in the financial market. Not only did investors and financial firms now realize their investments were extremely risky, they began to worry about the creditworthiness of banks and other financial intermediaries that held these securities as assets. Many were highly leveraged and exposed to great risk. Effectively, through securitization the damage from the subprime loans spread to the entire financial market, causing a major crisis. **Related to Exercise 4.7.**

From these examples you can see why financial intermediation does not always work. There is a continual debate on the role government should play in investment decisions for the economy and its role in regulating financial intermediaries. Today, some economists and policymakers are carefully reassessing the risks in our complex financial markets.

SUMMARY

In this chapter we discussed investment spending, present value, interest rates, and financial intermediaries. We saw that investment spending is volatile, rising and falling sharply with real GDP, and depends on expectations about the future. By developing the concept of present value, we saw how firms can make investment decisions when the costs and benefits of an investment occur at different times. We also explained why investment spending also depends inversely on real interest rates and explained the distinction between real and nominal interest rates. Finally, we examined how financial intermediaries channel funds from savers to investors, reduce interest rates, and promote investment—and sometimes malfunction. Here are the main points to keep in mind:

1 Investments incur costs today but provide benefits in the future.

2 Investment spending is a volatile component of GDP because expectations about the future are uncertain and ever changing.

3 We use the concept of *present value* to compare the costs and benefits of investments that occur at different points in time. The present value of a payment K, t years in the future, at an interest rate of i is

$$\text{present value} = \frac{K}{(1 + i)^t}$$

4 The *real interest rate* equals the *nominal interest rate* minus inflation.

5 Investment spending depends inversely on real interest rates.

6 *Financial intermediaries* reduce the risk and costs of making investments by pooling the funds of savers and monitoring the projects of borrowers. Financial intermediaries can package loans for sale to the broader financial markets through *securitization*.

7 While financial intermediaries do make the economy more efficient, they can break down at times, causing severe economic disruptions.

KEY TERMS

accelerator theory, p. 254
bank run, p. 266
corporate bond, p. 261
deposit insurance, p. 266
expected real interest rate, p. 258
financial intermediaries, p. 264
leverage, p. 265
liquid, p. 263
multiplier-accelerator model, p. 256
neoclassical theory of investment, p. 261
nominal interest rate, p. 258
present value, p. 256
procyclical, p. 254
Q-theory of investment, p. 262
real interest rate, p. 258
retained earnings, p. 261
securitization, p. 265

EXERCISES

All problems are assignable in MyEconLab.

12.1 An Investment: A Plunge into the Unknown

1.1 Investment is a larger component of GDP than consumption, but it is much more volatile. __________ (True/False)

1.2 Investment spending is very __________, since it moves in conjunction with GDP.

1.3 The economist who coined the phrase "animal spirits" to refer to investment spending by firms was __________.

1.4 Since investment spending rises and falls with GDP, it is __________.

1.5 **Accelerator Theory of Investment.** Explain how in the accelerator theory of investment that future expectation of high GDP growth will cause GDP to increase in the current period.

1.6 **Index of Consumer Confidence and Investment in Durable Goods.** Using the ideas of "animal spirits," explain why changes in measures of consumer confidence would be correlated to consumer spending on durable goods.

1.7 **Residential Housing Investment, the 1990 Recession, and the Most Recent Downturn.** Use the Web site for the Federal Reserve Bank of St. Louis (www.research.stlouisfed.org/fred2) to find out how investment in residential housing behaved over the 1990–1991 recession and compare it to the period from 2006 to 2011.

1.8 **Oil Price Floor and Investment Spending.** Suppose the government said that it would not let the U.S. price for a barrel of oil fall below $50. It could do this by raising taxes on oil if the price fell below $50. What incentives do you think this would provide for investment in energy-saving technologies? (Related to Application 1 on page 255.)

12.2 Evaluating the Future

2.1 If the interest rate is 10 percent, the present value of $200 paid one year from now equals __________.

2.2 If the interest rate is 5 percent, the present value of $200 paid one year from now equals __________. If the $200 is received in two years, the present value will equal __________.

2.3 If interest rates increase, the present value of a fixed payment in the future __________.

2.4 The present value of lottery winnings paid over a 20-year period will __________ (rise/fall) with a rise in interest rates.

2.5 **Investments in Solar Energy.** Proponents of solar energy point to the vast savings that come in the long run from using a free source of energy (the sun) rather than paying high prices for electricity. Unfortunately, solar energy systems typically have large up-front expenses to install the system. Use the concept of present value to show that solar energy systems are more likely to be profitable when interest rates are low.

2.6 **Annuity Payments and Interest Rates.** Suppose you have $500,000 to purchase an annuity. Currently the annuity payments are $35,000 per year as long as you live. What do you think would happen to the annuity payments if interest rates increased? Explain carefully. (Related to Application 2 on page 259.)

2.7 **Present Value of Lottery Payments.** A lottery pays a winner $1 million a year for 20 years (starting in year 1). What is the present value of this sum at an interest rate of 8 percent? You can do this by hand (not recommended) or in an Excel spreadsheet. Here is how: Enter "1" in cells A1 through A20. In cell C3, enter @NPV(.08, A1:A20) and press enter. This will give you the result. What happens to the present value of the lottery if the interest rate falls to 5 percent?

2.8 **Pension Funds and Interest Rates.** Many firms have pension funds that have fixed dollar obligations to their retirees. For financial purposes, firms must estimate the present value of these obligations to determine how much they truly owe their retirees. What happens to the value of these obligations as interest rates fall? Why?

12.3 Understanding Investment Decisions

3.1 If a project costs $100 and pays $107 next year, the maximum interest rate at which the present value of the investment exceeds its cost is __________.

3.2 As real interest rates rise, investment spending in the economy __________.

3.3 Corporate bonds, retained earnings, and tax deductions are the three sources of funds that firms have for investments. __________ (True/False)

3.4 The Q-theory of investment was developed by __________.

3.5 The price of a stock can be thought of as the present value of future __________.

3.6 **Low Interest Rates but No Takers.** In 2010, interest rates on home mortgages were in the neighborhood of 5 percent—very low by historical standards—but many individuals did not wish to buy homes. Using the concept of the real interest rate, can you explain why low interest rates did not entice new buyers?

3.7 **Stock Prices, Investment, and Causation.** Figure 12.4 shows that from 1997 through 2003, that investment spending followed the same trends as stock prices. Does this mean that movements in stock prices cause movements in investment spending?

3.8 **Hydroelectric Dams.** Hydroelectric dams are very costly to build and construct, but there are considerable savings in operating costs compared to other energy alternatives. Explain why hydroelectric dams are more likely to be profitable when interest rates are low.

3.9 **Stock Prices, Interest Rates, and Corporate Earnings.** Holding other factors constant, explain why stock prices tend to rise when

a. interest rates fall.

b. expected corporate earnings rise.

12.4 How Financial Intermediaries Facilitate Investment

4.1 An illiquid financial asset is one that can easily be used to buy goods and services. __________ (True/False)

4.2 Creation of __________ following the Great Depression has greatly reduced the likelihood of runs on banks today.

4.3 Financial intermediaries reduce the risk of assets through __________.

4.4 If a financial intermediary buys loans from a mortgage company and then packages them to sell in the financial markets, this is known as __________.

4.5 **Banks and Debt Forgiveness.** Can you think of any circumstances in which a bank would reduce (or forgive) part of the loan amount it made to a customer? How might this voluntary decision made by a bank differ from a government program that required loan forgiveness? (Related to Application 3 on p. 270.)

4.6 **A Leverage Example.** Suppose you purchased an asset for \$1000. The asset is risky and can either increase in value to \$1,200 or fall in value to \$900. Let's look at the effects of leverage on your returns to this investment.

a. Suppose you did not borrow any money, but put in your own \$1000 to purchase the asset. What percent gain would you make if the asset increased and what percent loss would you experience if the asset fell in value?

b. Now, suppose you borrowed \$950 to purchase the asset. What is your percentage gain or loss on your investment now?

4.7 **"Ninja" Loans.** During the housing boom, overeager lenders were said to have made "ninja" loans—that is, loans to individuals with "no income, job, or assets." How did ninja loans contribute to the securitization crisis in financial markets in 2007 and 2008? (Related to Application 4 on page 267.)

4.8 **Savings and Loans and Risk.** Traditionally, savings and loan institutions made loans only for home mortgages and held on to those mortgages. At one point, this was viewed as a safe way of doing business. However, it became a risky way of doing business for U.S. savings and loans in the 1970s. Explain why making loans only for housing and holding on to the mortgages may be very risky. Why does this risk provide a rationale for securitization?

4.9 **Mutual Funds.** Why does it make sense for individual investors to invest in mutual funds (which invest in a wide range of stocks), rather than in just a few individual companies?

ECONOMIC EXPERIMENT

DIVERSIFICATION

This classroom exercise illustrates the power of diversification. Your instructor will describe the game and how to participate. To take part in this exercise, you need to recall a simple lesson from basic statistics: If you flip a coin many times, the fraction of heads that results approaches one-half as you increase the number of flips. You are offered a chance to play this game in which you receive a payoff according to the following formula:

$$\text{Payoff} = \$10 + \$100\ [(\text{number of heads}/\text{number of tosses}) - 0.5]$$

In this game, you first get \$10, but you win or lose additional funds, depending on whether the fraction of heads that comes up exceeds one-half. To help you understand what's going on in this game, suppose you toss the coin only once. Here, the outcome depends only on whether the coin comes up either heads or tails:

$$\text{Heads: } \$10 + \$100(1/1 - 0.5) = \$60$$

$$\text{Tails: } \$10 + \$100(0/1 - 0.5) = -\$40$$

The game does have a positive expected payoff. The expected or average payoff for this game is the probability of getting a head (one-half) times \$60 plus the probability of getting a tail (one-half) times –\$40. This is

$$\text{Expected payoff} = (0.5)\$60 + (0.5)(-\$40) = \$10$$

On average, if you toss the coin many times, this game would pay \$10. But this game is risky if you are allowed to toss the coin only once. Now that you understand the game, answer the following question: Would you play this game if limited to only one toss? Now suppose you were free to toss the coin 1,000 times and received 450 heads. If that happened, your payoff would be

$$\$10 + \$100(450/1000 - 0.5) = \$5$$

Would you play if you could toss the coin 1,000 times?

QUESTIONS FOR DISCUSSION

1. Did a higher percentage of the class agree to play the game with 1,000 tosses? How does this illustrate the principle of diversification?
2. If you toss the coin 1,000 times, what is the expected payoff?
3. If you toss the coin 1,000 times and receive heads fewer than 400 times, you will lose money. What do you think is the probability of this occurring?

CHAPTER 13

Money and the Banking System

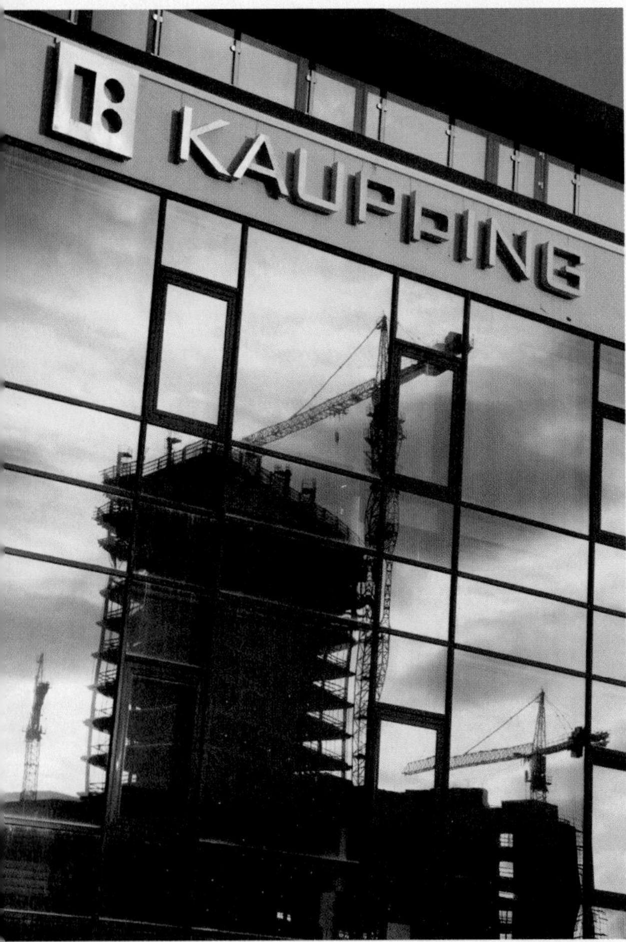

Normally we expect governments to prevent the wholesale failures of banks.

But during the recent financial crisis, the country of Iceland took the opposite approach and let the major banks in the country simply collapse.

Beginning in 2003, the three major banks in Iceland changed their business model to become aggressive international banking institutions, attracting deposits from foreign countries and vastly expanding their portfolio of loans. The result was five years of incredible prosperity for the country and its bank. Unfortunately, when the world financial crisis hit in 2008, this financing model no longer was sustainable. Funds quickly disappeared from the banks and the government and the people of Iceland faced a stark choice: bail out the banks by using public funds or let the banks go bankrupt and let those who invested in the banks take losses.

Eventually, Iceland decided on the bankruptcy route, much to the dismay of investors abroad. Unlike Ireland, which faced a similar situation, the government and the people of Iceland were willing to let the banks fail. Although this caused a severe recession for Iceland, the longer run prospects for the economy are sound and Iceland has actually recovered faster than many of the countries that bailed out its banks.

LEARNING OBJECTIVES

- Identify the components of money in the U.S. economy.
- Explain the process of multiple expansion and contraction of deposits.
- Describe the structure of the Federal Reserve.
- Discuss examples of how the Federal Reserve acts during financial crises.

MyEconLab

MyEconLab helps you master each objective and study more efficiently.

The term *money* has a special meaning for economists, so in this chapter we'll look carefully at how money is defined and the role it plays in the economy. The overall level of money affects the performance of an economy. In a prior chapter, we learned that increases in the money supply increase aggregate demand. In the short run, when prices are largely fixed, this increase will raise total demand and output. But in the long run, continuing money growth leads to inflation.

Our nation's central bank, the Federal Reserve (commonly called the "Fed"), is responsible for controlling the money supply. In this chapter, we'll see how the Federal Reserve is structured, how it operates, and why it's so powerful.

13.1 What *Is* Money?

Economists define **money** as any items that are regularly used in economic transactions or exchanges and accepted by buyers and sellers. Let's consider some examples of money used in that way.

money
Any items that are regularly used in economic transactions or exchanges and accepted by buyers and sellers.

We use money regularly every day. In a coffee shop, we hand the person behind the counter some dollar bills and coins, and we receive a cup of coffee. This is an example of an economic exchange: One party hands over currency—the dollar bills and the coins—and the other party hands over goods and services—the coffee. Why do the owners of coffee shops accept dollar bills and coins in payment for coffee? The reason is that they will be making other economic exchanges with the dollar bills and coins they accept. Suppose a cup of coffee costs $1.50 and 100 cups are sold in a day. The seller then has $150 in currency. If the coffee costs the seller $100, the seller pays $100 of the currency received and keeps $50 for other expenses and profits. Money makes that possible.

In the real world, transactions are somewhat more complicated. The coffee shop owners take the currency they receive each day, deposit it in bank accounts, and then pay suppliers with checks drawn on those accounts. Clearly, currency is money because it is used to purchase coffee. Checks also function as money because they are used to pay suppliers. In some ancient cultures, precious stones were used in exchanges. In more recent times, gold bars have served as money. During World War II, prisoners of war did not have currency, but they did have rations of cigarettes, so they used them like money, trading them for what they wanted.

Three Properties of Money

Regardless of what money is used in a particular society, it serves several functions, all related to making economic exchanges easier. Here we discuss three key properties of money.

MONEY SERVES AS A MEDIUM OF EXCHANGE As our examples illustrate, money is given by buyers to sellers in economic exchanges; therefore, it serves as a **medium of exchange**. Suppose you had a car you wanted to sell in order to buy a boat and money did not exist. You could look for a person who had a boat and wanted to buy a car and then trade your car directly for a boat. This is an example of **barter**: the exchange of one good or service for another.

medium of exchange
Any item that buyers give to sellers when they purchase goods and services.

barter
The exchange of one good or service for another.

But there are obvious problems with barter. Suppose local boat owners were interested in selling boats but not interested in buying your car. Unless there were a **double coincidence of wants**—that is, unless you wanted to trade a car for a boat, and the boat owner wanted to trade a boat for your car—this economic exchange wouldn't occur. The probability of a double coincidence of wants occurring is very, very tiny. Even if a boat owner wanted a car, he or she might want a different type of car than yours.

double coincidence of wants
The problem in a system of barter that one person may not have what the other desires.

By serving as a medium of exchange, money solves this bartering problem. The car owner can sell the car to anyone who wants it and receive money in return. With that money, the car owner can then find someone who owns a boat and purchase the boat for money. The boat owner can use the money in any way he or she pleases. With money, there is no need for a double coincidence of wants. This is why money exists in all societies: It makes economic transactions much easier.

Here is another way to think about this. One of our key principles of economics is that individuals are better off through voluntary exchange.

PRINCIPLE OF VOLUNTARY EXCHANGE

A voluntary exchange between two people makes both people better off.

Money allows individuals to actually *make* these exchanges. Without money, we would be left with a barter system, and most transactions that make both people better off would not be possible.

MONEY SERVES AS A UNIT OF ACCOUNT Money also provides a convenient measuring rod when prices for all goods are quoted in money terms. A boat may be listed for sale at $5,000 in money terms, a car at $10,000, and a movie ticket at $5. We could, in principle, quote everything in terms of movie tickets. The boat would be worth 1,000 tickets, and the car would be worth 2,000 tickets. But because we are using money and not movie tickets as a medium of exchange, it is much easier to express all prices in terms of money. A **unit of account** is a standard unit in which we can state prices and compare the value of goods and services. In our economy, money is the unit of account because we quote all prices in terms of money. It is convenient to use the medium of exchange as the unit of account, so we can quote prices for all goods and services in terms of the same units we use in transactions—in our case, money.

unit of account
A standard unit in which prices can be stated and the value of goods and services can be compared.

MONEY SERVES AS A STORE OF VALUE If you sell your car to purchase a boat, you may not be able to purchase the boat immediately. In the meantime, you will be holding the money you received from the sale. Ideally, during that period, the value of the money will not fall. What we are referring to here is the function of money as a **store of value**.

store of value
The property of money that holds that money preserves value until it is used in an exchange.

Money is actually a somewhat imperfect store of value because of inflation. Suppose inflation is 10 percent a year, which means average prices rise 10 percent each year. Let's say you sold a tennis racket for $100 in order to buy 10 CDs worth $100, but you waited a year to buy them. Unfortunately, because of inflation, at the end of the year the 10 CDs cost $110 (%100 × 1.10), or $11 each. With your $100, you can now buy only 9 CDs and get $1 in change. Your money has lost some of its stored value.

As long as inflation is low and you do not hold the money for a long time, the loss in its purchasing power won't be a big problem. But as inflation rates increase, money becomes less useful as a store of value.

DIFFERENT TYPES OF MONETARY SYSTEMS Through history, the world has witnessed different types of monetary systems. In one system a commodity serves as money, such as gold or silver in bars or coins. This is an example of **commodity money**. At some point, governments began issuing paper money. However, the paper money was backed by an underlying commodity, for example, so many ounces of gold per unit of paper currency. Under a traditional **gold standard**, an individual could present paper money to the government and receive its stated value in gold. In other words, paper money could be exchanged for gold. Until 1933 in the United States, individuals could exchange their dollars for gold. However, President Franklin Roosevelt banned private possession of gold in 1933, although foreign governments could still exchange dollars for gold until 1971. The next step in the evolution of monetary systems was to break the tie between paper money and gold and create a system of *fiat money*. **Fiat money** has no intrinsic value like gold or silver—it is simply created by a government decree and becomes the official legal tender of the society.

commodity money
A monetary system in which the actual money is a commodity, such as gold or silver.

gold standard
A monetary system in which gold backs up paper money.

fiat money
A monetary system in which money has no intrinsic value but is backed by the government.

In the United States today, if you take a $100 bill to the government you will not receive any gold or silver—just another $100 bill in return.

You may wonder what gives money value under a fiat system if it has no intrinsic value. The answer is that the government controls the value of fiat money by controlling its supply in the economy. That is why it is important to prevent counterfeiting. In the next chapter, we will see precisely how the government controls the supply of money.

Measuring Money in the U.S. Economy

In the United States and other modern economies, people can carry out economic transactions in several different ways. In practice, this leads to different measures of money. The most basic measure of money in the United States is called **M1**. It is the sum of currency in the hands of the public, demand deposits, other checkable deposits, and traveler's checks. M1 totaled $2,220 billion in March 2012. Table 13.1 contains the components of M1 and their size; Figure 13.1 shows their relative percentages.

M1
The sum of currency in the hands of the public, demand deposits, other checkable deposits, and traveler's checks.

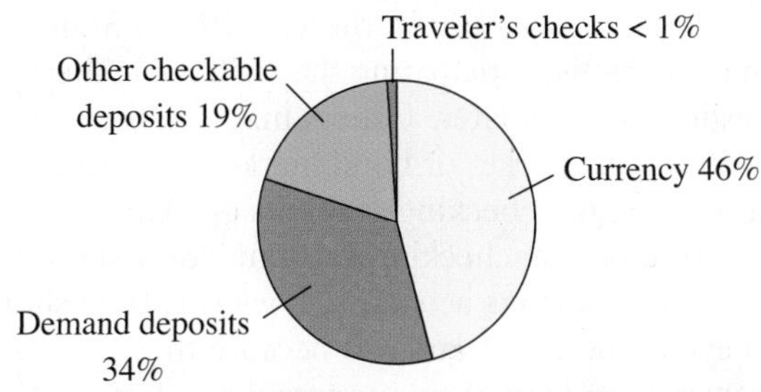

◄ FIGURE 13.1
Components of M1 for the United States
Currency is the largest component of M1, the most basic measure of money. Demand and other checkable deposits are the next largest components.
SOURCE: Board of Governors of the Federal Reserve.

MyEconLab Real-time data

TABLE 13.1 Components of M1, March 2012

Currency held by the public	$ 1,028 billion
Demand deposits	763 billion
Other checkable deposits	424 billion
Traveler's checks	4 billion
Total of M1	2,220 billion

SOURCE: Board of Governors of the Federal Reserve. MyEconLab Real-time data

The first part of M1 is currency held by the public, that is, all currency held outside bank vaults. The second component is deposits in checking accounts, called *demand deposits*. Until the 1980s, checking accounts did not pay interest. The third component, other checkable deposits, was introduced in the early 1980s and did pay interest. Today, the distinction between the two types of deposit accounts is not as meaningful as it used to be because many checking accounts earn interest if the balances are sufficiently high. Finally, traveler's checks are included in M1 because they are regularly used in economic exchanges.

Let's take a closer look at the amount of currency in the economy. Because there are approximately 300 million people in the United States, the $1.028 billion of currency amounts to over $3,427 in currency for every man, woman, and child in the United States. Do you and your friends each have $3,427 of currency?

Most of the currency in the official statistics is not used in ordinary commerce in the United States. Who is using and holding this currency? Some is used in illegal transactions such as the drug trade. Few drug dealers open bank accounts to deposit currency. In addition, a substantial fraction of U.S. currency is held abroad.

M1 does not include all the assets we use to make economic exchanges. **M2** is a somewhat broader definition of money that includes M1 plus deposits in saving accounts, deposits in retail money market mutual funds, and time deposits of less than $100,000. These investment-type assets often can't readily be used for exchanges

M2
M1 plus other assets, including deposits in savings and loans accounts and money market mutual funds.

without first being converted to M1. In March 2012 M2 totaled $ 9,798 billion. That's about 4.5 times the total of M1. Figure 13.2 shows the relative sizes of the components of M2.

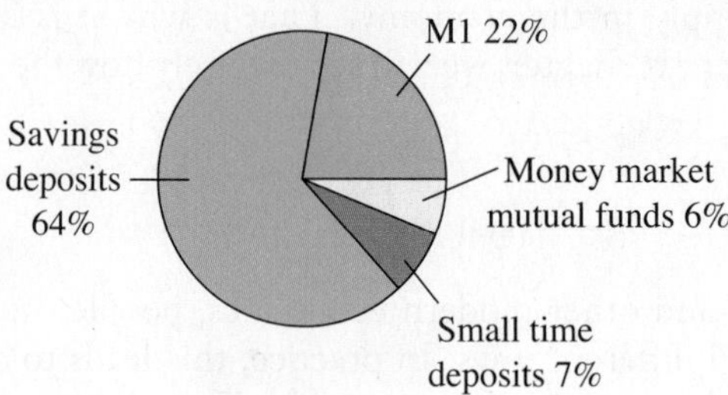

► **FIGURE 13.2**
Components of M2 in the United States
Savings deposits are the largest component of M2, followed by M1, small time deposits, and money market mutual funds.
SOURCE: Board of Governors of Federal Reserve.

MyEconLab Real-time data

Economists use different definitions of money because it is not always clear which assets are used primarily as money—that is, which assets are used for economic exchanges and which are used primarily for saving and investing. Money market mutual funds came into existence only in the late 1970s. Some people temporarily "park" their assets in these funds, anticipating they will move them into riskier, higher-earning stock market investments later. Others may use them to earn interest while avoiding the risks of the stock market or bond market. Sometimes, people use money market mutual funds like regular checking accounts or like savings accounts. If money market mutual funds are used like checking accounts, they should be considered part of M1. If they are used like savings accounts, however, they should be part of M2. Economists keep an eye on both M1 and M2 because they don't know precisely how people are using all these money market accounts.

Although consumers commonly use credit cards to make transactions in our economy, they are not part of the money supply. Here's why: Suppose you have a credit card from the First Union Bank and purchase a new television from an electronics store. As you use your credit card, you are effectively borrowing the amount you charge from the First Union Bank, which, in turn, will pay the electronics store on your behalf. When you receive your credit card bill from the bank, you must begin to

application 1

MONEY WITH THE FACE OF RODENTS

APPLYING THE CONCEPTS #1: How do small Brazilian towns use currency to encourage local commerce?

In order to entice local residents to spend their money on stores in town, the small city of Silva Jardim in Brazil, hatched a plan for its own currency. The currency is called the *capivari* and features a picture of a local rodent on the bills. The capivaris are issued by a local bank, which holds one unit of official Brazilian currency for each capivari issued. Local merchants, however, give discounts for paying in capivaris so that local residents are therefore encouraged to make local purchases.

The capivaris circulate like money and have all the functions of money even though they are backed by official Brazilian currency. In many ways, the capivaris are like discount coupons for local purchases. The capivaris are issued in small denominations so they circulate and are not simply hoarded. This idea has caught on in 63 other towns in Brazil that have each issued their own type of money. **Related to Exercise 1.9.**

SOURCE: Based on Paulo Prada, "In Pockets of Booming Brazil, a Mint Idea Gains Currency," *Wall Street Journal*, September 21, 2011, online edition, A-Hed column.

pay off the loan. Credit cards enable you to purchase goods now but pay for them at a later date. Unlike money, a credit card is not a medium of exchange, a unit of account, or a store of value. Credit cards do make it easier to conduct business, but they are not an official part of the money supply.

What about debit cards? If you own a debit card, you can use it to access the funds you have in your checking account when you make the transaction. When you use your debit card to make a purchase—say at a supermarket—it is exactly the same thing as writing a check. Thus, a debit card is not an independent source of money. The money supply consists of the balances in checking accounts plus currency held by the public.

13.2 How Banks Create Money

In this section, we will learn the role that banks play in the creation of money in a modern economy. To understand this role, we first have to look more carefully at the behavior of banks.

A Bank's Balance Sheet: Where the Money Comes from and Where It Goes

A typical commercial bank accepts funds from savers in the form of deposits, for example, in checking accounts. The bank does not leave all these funds idle, because if it did it would never make a profit. Instead, the bank turns the money around and loans it out to borrowers. It will be easier to understand how banks create money if we first look at a simplified **balance sheet** for a commercial bank. The balance sheet will show us how the bank raises money and what it does with it.

Balance sheets have two sides: one for assets and one for liabilities. **Liabilities** are the source of funds for the bank. If you open a checking account and deposit your funds in it, the bank is liable for returning the funds to you when you want them. The bank must also pay you interest on the account if you keep enough money in it. Your deposits are therefore the bank's liabilities. **Assets**, in contrast, generate income for the bank. Loans made by the bank are examples of its assets, because borrowers must pay interest on the loans the bank collects.

When a bank is initially opened, its owners must place their own funds into it so it has some startup funds. We call these funds **owners' equity**. If the bank subsequently makes a profit, owners' equity increases; if it loses money, owners' equity decreases.

In Figure 13.3, we show the assets and liabilities of a hypothetical bank. On the liability side, the bank has $2,000 of deposits, and owners' equity is $200. Owners' equity is entered on the liability side of the balance sheet because it is a source of the bank's funds. The total source of funds is therefore $2,200—the deposits in the bank plus owners' equity.

balance sheet
An account statement for a bank that shows the sources of its funds (liabilities) as well as the uses of its funds (assets).

liabilities
The sources of funds for a bank, including deposits and owners' equity.

assets
The uses of the funds of a bank, including loans and reserves.

owners' equity
The funds provided to a bank by its owners.

Assets	Liabilities
$ 200 Reserves	$2,000 Deposits
$2,000 Loans	$ 200 Owners' equity
Total: $2,200	Total: $2,200

▲ **FIGURE 13.3**
A Balance Sheet for a Bank
The figure shows a hypothetical balance sheet for a bank holding 10 percent in required reserves, $200. Banks don't earn interest on their reserves, so they will usually want to loan out any excess of the amounts they are required to hold. This bank has loaned out all of its excess reserves, $2,000.

reserves
The portion of banks' deposits set aside in either vault cash or as deposits at the Federal Reserve.

required reserves
The specific fraction of their deposits that banks are required by law to hold as reserves.

excess reserves
Any additional reserves that a bank holds above required reserves.

On the asset side, the bank holds $200 in **reserves**. These are assets that are not lent out. Reserves can be either cash kept in a bank's vaults or deposits in the nation's central bank, the Federal Reserve. Banks are required by law to hold a specific fraction of their deposits as reserves, called **required reserves**. If a bank chooses to hold additional reserves beyond what is required, these are called **excess reserves**. A bank's reserves are the sum of its required and excess reserves.

In our example, the bank is holding 10 percent of its deposits, or $200, as reserves. The remainder of the bank's assets, $2,000, consists of the loans it has made. By construction, total assets will always equal liabilities, including owners' equity. Balance sheets must therefore always balance.

How Banks Create Money

To understand the role banks play in determining the supply of money, let's suppose someone walks into the First Bank of Hollywood and deposits $1,000 in cash to open a checking account. Because currency held by the public and checking deposits are both included in the supply of money, the total money supply has not changed with this transaction. The cash deposited into the checking account reduced the currency held by the public by precisely the amount the checking account increased it.

reserve ratio
The ratio of reserves to deposits.

Now let's assume banks keep 10 percent of their deposits as reserves. That means the **reserve ratio**—the ratio of reserves to deposits—will be 0.1. The First Bank of Hollywood will keep $100 in reserves and make loans totaling $900. The top panel in Figure 13.4 shows the change in the First Bank of Hollywood's balance sheet after it has made its loan.

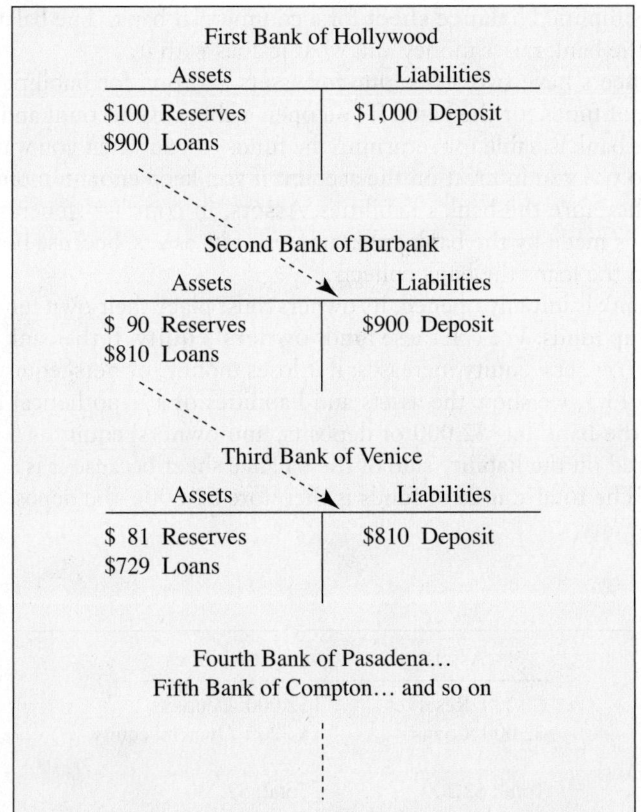

First Bank of Hollywood
Assets
Liabilities
$100 Reserves
$900 Loans
$1,000 Deposit
Second Bank of Burbank
Assets
Liabilities
$ 90 Reserves
$810 Loans
$900 Deposit
Third Bank of Venice
Assets
Liabilities
$ 81 Reserves
$729 Loans
$810 Deposit
Fourth Bank of Pasadena…
Fifth Bank of Compton… and so on

▶ FIGURE 13.4
Process of Deposit Creation: Changes in Balance Sheets
The figure shows how an initial deposit of $1,000 can expand the money supply. The first three banks in the figure loaned out all their excess reserves and the borrowers deposited the full sum of their loans. In the real world, though, people hold part of their loans as cash and banks don't necessarily loan out all their excess reserves. Consequently, a smaller amount of money will be created than what's shown here.

Suppose the First Bank of Hollywood loans the funds to an aspiring movie producer. The producer opens a checking account at the First Bank of Hollywood with the $900 he borrowed. He then buys film equipment from a supplier, who accepts his $900 check and deposits it in the Second Bank of Burbank. The next panel in Figure 13.4 shows what happens to the balance sheet of the Second Bank of Burbank.

Liabilities increase by the deposit of $900. The bank holds $90 in reserves (10 percent of the $900 deposit) and can lend out $810.

Suppose the Second Bank of Burbank lends the $810 to the owner of a coffeehouse and she opens a checking account there with the $810 as her balance. She then purchases $810 worth of coffee with a check made out to a coffee supplier, who deposits it into the Third Bank of Venice.

The Third Bank of Venice receives a deposit of $810. It keeps $81 in reserves and can lend out $729. This process continues throughout the Los Angeles area with new loans and deposits. The Fourth Bank of Pasadena will receive a deposit of $729, hold $72.90 in reserves, and lend out $656.10. The Fifth Bank of Compton will receive a deposit of $656.10, and the process goes on.

How the Money Multiplier Works

The original $1,000 cash deposit has created checking account balances throughout Los Angeles. What's the total amount? Adding up the new accounts in all the banks (even the ones we have not named), we have

$$\$1{,}000 + \$900 + \$810 + \$729 + 656.10 + \ldots = \$10{,}000$$

How did we come up with this sum? It's from the following simple formula, which we derive in the appendix to this chapter:

$$\text{total increase in checking account balance throughout all banks}$$

$$= (\text{initial cash deposit}) \times \frac{1}{(\text{reserve ratio})}$$

In our example, the reserve ratio is 0.1, so the increase in checking account balances is 1/0.1, or 10 times the initial cash deposit. The initial $1,000 deposit led to a total increase in checking account balances of $10,000 throughout all of the banks.

Recall that the money supply, M1, is the sum of deposits at commercial banks plus currency held by the public. Therefore, the change in the money supply, M1, will be the change in deposits in checking accounts plus the change in currency held by the public. Notice that we referred to "change," meaning an increase or decrease. Here's why: In our example, the public, represented by the person who initially made the $1,000 deposit at the First Bank of Hollywood, holds $1,000 less in currency. However, deposits increased by $10,000. Therefore, the money supply, M1, increased by $9,000 ($10,000 – $1,000). No single bank lent out more than it had in deposits. Yet for the banking system as a whole, the money supply expanded by a multiple of the initial cash deposit.

The term 1/reserve ratio in the formula is called the **money multiplier**. It tells us what the total increase in checking account deposits would be for any initial cash deposit. Recall the multiplier for government spending in our demand-side models: An increase in government spending led to larger increases in output through the multiplier. The government-spending multiplier arose because additional rounds of consumption spending were triggered by an initial increase in government spending. In the banking system, an initial cash deposit triggers additional rounds of deposits and lending by banks. This leads to a multiple expansion of deposits.

money multiplier
The ratio of the increase in total checking account deposits to an initial cash deposit.

As of 2012 in the United States, banks were required to hold 3 percent in reserves against checkable deposits between $11.5 million and $71.0 million and 10 percent on all checkable deposits exceeding $71.0 million. Because large banks would face a 10 percent reserve requirement on any new deposits, you might think, on the basis of our formula, that the money multiplier would be approximately 10.

However, the money multiplier for the United States has typically been between two and three—much smaller than the value of 10 implied by our simple formula. There are two reasons for this. First, our formula assumed all loans made their way directly into checking accounts. In reality, people hold part of their loans as cash.

That cash is not available for the banking system to lend out. The more money people hold in cash, the less they have on deposit that can be loaned out again. This decreases the money multiplier. Second, the money multiplier will also be less if banks held excess reserves. Until recently, this was not an important factor, but a recent change to pay interest on excess reserves has sharply increased their levels. We can represent these factors in a money multiplier ratio, but it will not be as simple as the one we introduced here.

How the Money Multiplier Works in Reverse

The money-creation process also works in reverse. Suppose you go to your bank and ask for $1,000 in cash from your checking account. The bank must pay you the $1,000. The bank's liabilities fall by $1,000, but its assets must also fall by $1,000. Withdrawing your $1,000 means two things at the bank. First, if the reserve ratio is 0.1, the bank will reduce its reserves by $100. Second, your $1,000 withdrawal minus the $100 reduction in reserves means the bank has $900 less to lend out. The bank

application 2

THE GROWTH IN EXCESS RESERVES

APPLYING THE CONCEPTS #2: Why have banks recently started to hold vast amounts of excess reserves?

During the height of the financial crisis in September 2008, the Fed injected large amounts of reserves into banks, and in the next month, it started paying interest to banks on these reserves. Prior to this time, banks earned no interest on either required or excess reserves. This created an incentive for banks to keep minimal excess reserves and lend any extra funds they had. However, once banks began to earn interest on excess reserves, they did not have to lend their funds out to earn interest. If lending opportunities were not very attractive, the bank could safely keep their funds on hand.

As Figure 13.5 indicates, banks have responded to the new incentives. Prior to the change in law, banks held few excess reserves. After the change in the law, excess reserves increased sharply and total reserves now far exceed required reserves. In the long run, the Federal Reserve will need to make sure that banks do not lend out too many reserves or the result will be higher inflation. **Related to Exercises 2.2 and 2.10.**

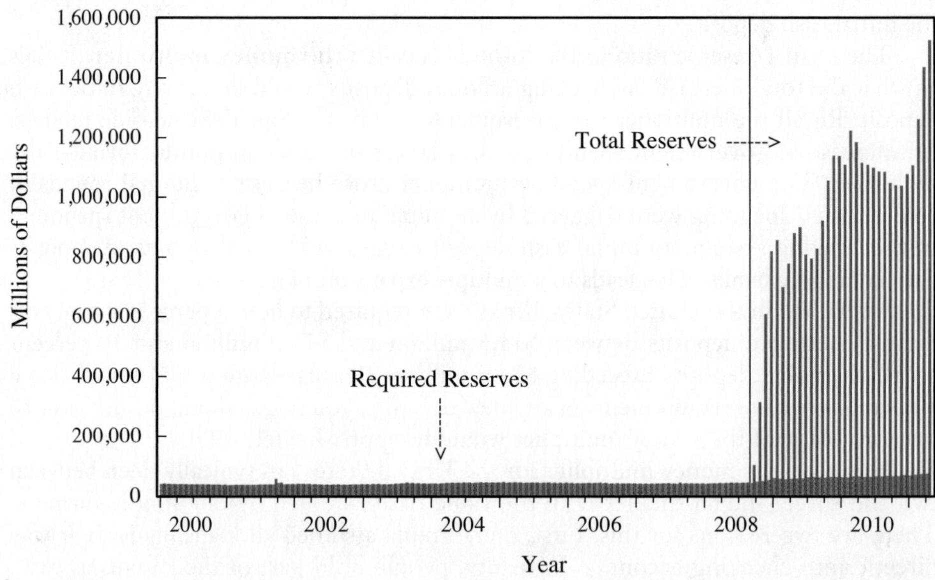

▸ **FIGURE 13.5**
Required and Total Reserves of Banks
Until September of 2008, banks held few excess reserves so total reserves (in red) were very close to required reserves (in purple). In response to the financial crisis of 2008, the Fed injected large amounts of reserves into the system and began paying interest on reserves in October. As a result, excess reserves rose and total reserves now exceed excess reserves.

will therefore reduce its loans by $900. With fewer loans, there will be fewer deposits in other banks. The money multiplier working in reverse decreases the money supply.

You may wonder how a bank goes about reducing its outstanding loans. If you had borrowed from a bank to invest in a project for your business, you would not want the bank phoning you to ask for its funds, which are not lying idle but are invested in your business. Banks do not typically call in outstanding loans from borrowers. Instead, if banks cannot tap into their excess reserves when their customers want to withdraw cash, they have to make fewer new loans. In these circumstances, a new potential borrower would find it harder to obtain a loan from the bank.

Up to this point, our examples have always started with an initial cash deposit. However, suppose Paul receives a check from Freda and deposits it into his bank. Paul's bank will eventually receive payment from Freda's bank. When it does, it will initially have an increase in both deposits and reserves—just as if a cash deposit were made. Because Paul's bank has to hold only a fraction of the deposits as reserves, it will be able to make loans with the remainder.

However, there is one crucial difference between this example, in which one individual writes a check to another, and our earlier example, in which an individual makes a cash deposit: When Paul receives the check from Freda, the money supply will not be changed in the long run. Here's why: When Freda's check is deposited in Paul's bank, the money supply will begin to expand, but when Freda's bank loses its deposit, the money supply will start to contract. The expansions and contractions offset each other when private citizens and firms write checks to one another.

In the next chapter, we will see how the Federal Reserve can *change* the money supply to stabilize the economy. In the remainder of this chapter, we'll look at the structure of the Federal Reserve and the critical role that it plays as a central bank stabilizing the financial system.

13.3 A Banker's Bank: The Federal Reserve

The Federal Reserve System was created in 1913 after a series of financial panics in the United States. Financial panics can occur when there is bad news about the economy or the stability of financial institutions. During these panics, numerous bank runs occurred, depleting the funds on hand that banks could loan out. Severe economic downturns followed.

Congress created the Federal Reserve System to be a **central bank**, or "a banker's bank." One of the Fed's primary jobs is thus to serve as a **lender of last resort**. When banks need to borrow money during a financial crisis, they can turn to the central bank as "a last resort" for these funds. If a bank experienced a run, the Federal Reserve could lend it the funds it needed.

central bank
A banker's bank: an official bank that controls the supply of money in a country.

lender of last resort
A central bank is the lender of last resort, the last place, all others having failed, from which banks in emergency situations can obtain loans.

Functions of the Federal Reserve

The Federal Reserve has several key functions. Let's briefly describe them.

THE FED SUPPLIES CURRENCY TO THE ECONOMY Working through the banking system, the Federal Reserve is responsible for supplying currency to the economy. Although currency is only one component of the money supply, if individuals prefer to hold currency rather than demand deposits, the Federal Reserve and the banking system will facilitate the public's preferences.

THE FED PROVIDES A SYSTEM OF CHECK COLLECTION AND CLEARING The Federal Reserve is responsible for making our system of complex financial transactions "work." This means that when Paul writes Freda a check, the Federal Reserve oversees the banks to ensure Freda's bank receives the funds from Paul's bank. This is known as *check clearing*. As our economy moves to more electronic transactions, the Federal Reserve provides oversight over these transactions as well.

THE FED HOLDS RESERVES FROM BANKS AND OTHER DEPOSITORY INSTITUTIONS AND REGULATES BANKS As we have seen, banks are required to hold reserves with the Federal Reserve System. The Federal Reserve also serves as a regulator to banks to ensure they are complying with rules and regulations. Ultimately, the Federal Reserve wants to ensure the financial system is safe.

THE FED CONDUCTS MONETARY POLICY One of the important responsibilities of the Federal Reserve is to conduct **monetary policy**, the range of actions that influence the level of real GDP or inflation.

monetary policy
The range of actions taken by the Federal Reserve to influence the level of GDP or inflation.

Virtually all countries have central banks. The Indian central bank is known as the Reserve Bank of India. In the United Kingdom, the central bank is the Bank of England. Central banks serve as lenders of last resort to the banks in their countries and also help to control the level of economic activity. If the economy is operating at a level that's "too hot" or "too cold," they can manipulate the money supply to fend off economic problems. We'll see how central banks use monetary policy to influence real GDP or inflation and fend off economic problems in the next chapter.

The Structure of the Federal Reserve

When members of Congress created the Federal Reserve System, they were aware the institution would be very powerful. Consequently, they deliberately created a structure that attempted to disperse the power, moving it away from major U.S. financial centers (such as New York) to other parts of the country. They divided the United States into 12 Federal Reserve districts, each of which has a **Federal Reserve Bank**. These district banks provide advice on monetary policy, take part in decision making on monetary policy, and act as a liaison between the Fed and the banks in their districts.

Federal Reserve Bank
One of 12 regional banks that are an official part of the Federal Reserve System.

Figure 13.6 shows where each of the 12 Federal Reserve Banks is located. At the time the Fed was created, economic and financial power in the United States was concentrated in the East and the Midwest. Although this is no longer the case, the locations of the Federal Reserve Banks still reflect the Fed's historical roots. Which major western city does not have a Federal Reserve Bank? It is, of course, Los Angeles.

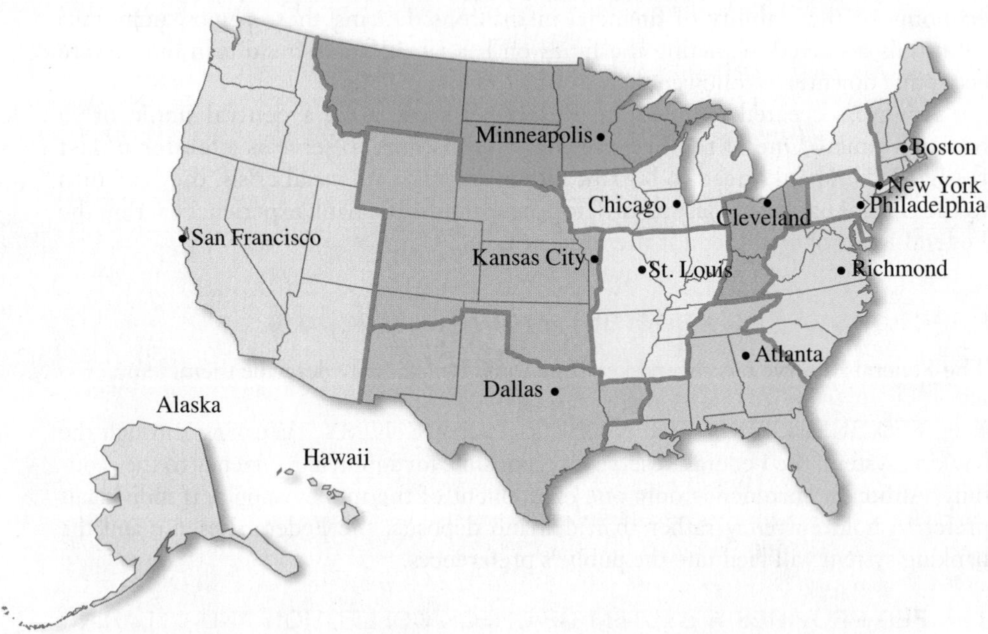

▲ **FIGURE 13.6**
Locations of the 12 Federal Reserve Banks
The 12 Federal Reserve Banks are scattered across the United States. These district banks serve as a liaison between the Fed and the banks in their districts. Hawaii and Alaska are in the 12th district, which is headquartered in San Francisco.

There are two other subgroups of the Fed in addition to the Federal Reserve Banks. The **Board of Governors of the Federal Reserve** is the true seat of power in the Federal Reserve System. Headquartered in Washington, D.C., the seven members of the board are appointed for 14-year terms by the president and confirmed by the Senate. The chairperson serves a 4-year term as the principal spokesperson for monetary policy in the United States. Financial markets throughout the world anticipate and carefully observe what the chairperson says.

Board of Governors of the Federal Reserve
The seven-person governing body of the Federal Reserve System in Washington, D.C.

The third subgroup of the Fed is the **Federal Open Market Committee (FOMC)**, which makes decisions about monetary policy. The FOMC is a 12-person board consisting of the 7 members of the Board of Governors, the president of the New York Federal Reserve Bank, and the presidents of four other regional Federal Reserve Banks. (The presidents of the regional banks other than New York serve on a rotating basis; the 7 nonvoting bank presidents attend the meetings and offer their opinions.) The chairperson of the Board of Governors also serves as the chairperson of the FOMC. The FOMC makes the actual decisions on changes in the money supply. Its members are assisted by vast teams of professionals at the Board of Governors and at the regional Federal Reserve Banks. The structure of the Federal Reserve System is depicted in Figure 13.7.

Federal Open Market Committee (FOMC)
The group that decides on monetary policy: It consists of the 7 members of the Board of Governors plus 5 of 12 regional bank presidents on a rotating basis.

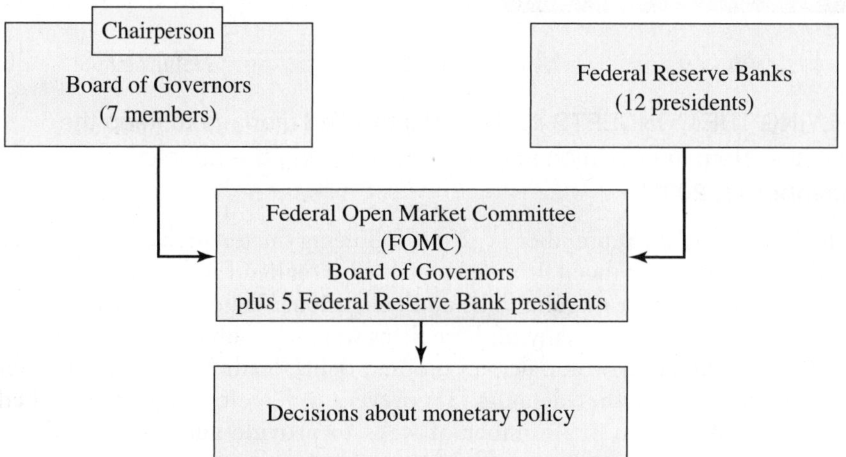

◄ **FIGURE 13.7**
The Structure of the Federal Reserve System
The Federal Reserve System in the United States consists of the Federal Reserve Banks, the Board of Governors, and the Federal Open Market Committee (FOMC). The FOMC is responsible for making monetary policy decisions.

On paper, monetary policymaking power appears to be spread throughout the government and the country. In practice, however, the Board of Governors, and especially the chairperson, has the real control. The Board of Governors operates with considerable independence. Presidents and members of Congress can bring political pressures on the Board of Governors, but their 14-year terms tend to insulate the members from external pressures. The current chairman of the Federal Reserve is Ben S. Bernanke, who began his term on February 1, 2006.

The Independence of the Federal Reserve

Countries differ in the degree to which their central banks are independent of political authorities. In the United States, the chairperson of the Board of Governors is required to report to Congress on a regular basis, but in practice the Fed makes its own decisions and later informs Congress what it did. The Fed chairperson also often meets with members of the executive branch to discuss economic affairs. Following the Fed's interventions during the financial crisis, there is increasing interest in Congress to make the Fed disclose additional information.

The central banks in both the United States and the United Kingdom currently operate with considerable independence of elected officials. In other countries, the central bank is part of the treasury department of the government and is potentially subject to more direct political control. There has been a lively debate among economists and political scientists as to whether countries with more independent central banks (banks with less external political pressure) experience less inflation. Central banks that are not independent will always be under pressure to help finance their country's government deficits by creating money. When central banks succumb to this pressure, the result is inflation. Independence, on the other hand, typically means less inflation.

13.4 What the Federal Reserve Does during a Financial Crisis

As the lender of last resort, the Fed can quell disturbances in the financial markets. Let's look at historical examples and the Fed's action in 2001 and in the midst of the 2008 financial crisis.

application 3

THE FINANCIAL SYSTEM UNDER STRESS: SEPTEMBER 11, 2001

APPLYING THE CONCEPTS #3: How did the Fed manage to keep the financial system in operation immediately following the attacks on September 11, 2001?

The Fed was tested on September 11, 2001, following the terrorist attacks against the United States. Many financial firms keep little cash on hand and expect to borrow on a daily basis to pay their ongoing bills and obligations. When the financial markets closed after September 11, many of these firms were in trouble. Unless some actions were taken quickly, they would default on their debts, leading to payment problems for other firms and further defaults. To prevent a default avalanche, the Federal Reserve immediately took a number of steps to provide additional funds to the financial system.

The first tool the Federal Reserve used was to allow banks to borrow more. Ordinarily the volume of these direct loans from the Federal Reserve is not very large. On Wednesday, September 12, total lending to banks rose to $45.5 *billion*, up from just $99 million the week before.

The Federal Reserve System also serves as a clearinghouse for checks. A bank will bring checks it receives from customers to the Federal Reserve and receive immediate credit on its accounts. The Federal Reserve then debits the account of the bank upon which the check was written. The difference between the credits and the debits extended by the Federal Reserve is called the "Federal Reserve float." Immediately following September 11, the Federal Reserve allowed this float to increase sharply from $2.9 billion to $22.9 billion. These actions effectively put an additional $20 billion into the banking system.

The Federal Reserve also purchased government securities in the marketplace and as a result put $30 billion into the hands of private citizens and their banks. It arranged to provide dollars to foreign central banks such as the Bank of England so they could meet their needs and the needs of their banks to facilitate any dollar transactions they had during the crisis. Taken together, these actions increased the credit extended by the Federal Reserve by over $90 billion. This massive response prevented a financial panic that could have had devastating effects on the world economy. **Related to Exercises 4.3 and 4.7.**

application 4

COPING WITH THE FINANCIAL CHAOS CAUSED BY THE MORTGAGE CRISIS

APPLYING THE CONCEPTS #4: How did the Fed successfully respond to the collapse of major financial institutions in 2008?

Sunday, March 16, 2008, was not a peaceful day for the Board of Governors. Over the prior week, one of Wall Street's most famous investment houses, Bear Stearns, had gone into full collapse. Although Bear Stearns had roughly $17 billion in readily available assets, it appeared this was not enough to satisfy the market. Other investment firms believed Bear Stearns had made so many poor investments that it was not financially viable. They rapidly began pulling out their funds from the firm.

The Fed feared that a complete collapse of Bear Stearns would devastate the financial system and cause a global panic as investors would want to pull out their funds from all financial institutions, effectively causing a "run" in the financial markets. During the week, the Fed began to search for ways to deal with this crisis. One solution was to try to convince another financial institution to take over Bear Stearns and keep the financial markets open. The problem, however, was that no one had a clear idea precisely what quality of assets Bear Stearns had on its balance sheet, and thus no firm wanted to be exposed to the risk of purchasing them. Finally, the Fed convinced the investment firm JPMorgan Chase & Co. to buy Bear Stearns—but only after the Fed agreed to loan Chase $30 billion. The Fed had successfully averted a major financial crisis but had put U.S. taxpayers at risk by lending such a large amount to a private investment house.

Unfortunately, Bear Stearns was only an early symptom of a problem that increased in severity over the coming months. As we discussed in Chapter 12, by September and October of 2008 the mortgage crisis had effectively spilled over into the world's financial markets. Banks and other financial institutions were afraid to lend to one another because they were not sure whether or not their loans would be repaid. The world's financial markets were freezing up, stock markets were in sharp decline, and there was growing panic.

The panic was brought to a head when the Fed and Treasury decided not to arrange a bailout for Lehman Brothers, another major financial institution, as they had done for Bear Stearns. The markets worldwide reacted adversely to this decision. The Fed and Treasury quickly changed tactics, however, and authorized an $85 billion loan to the American International Group (AIG) and took an 80 percent ownership stake in the company. The Fed had thought that the failure of AIG would trigger massive failures of other institutions whose assets were insured by AIG. As the crisis continued, the Fed continued to develop new programs, such as purchasing the short-term debt of corporations—commercial paper—so that it effectively spread its lender of last resort function beyond financial institutions. It also began a program to extend loans to money market funds, some of which had come under financial pressure, and it started to make purchases of securities backed by mortgages in order to keep funds flowing to the housing sector. Finally, it began to pay interest on deposits held at the Fed, a move designed to induce banks to hold more reserves and increase the Fed's own ability to make critical loans.

Taken together, these were sweeping changes to the Fed's role in the financial system. The Fed has now abandoned its efforts to support the commercial paper market and money market funds, but has maintained the other programs. Only time will tell whether the remaining changes, adopted during a two-month period, will become permanent tools of the Fed or will fade away when the economy eventually recovers. **Related to Exercises 4.1, 4.6, and 4.8.**

SUMMARY

We began this chapter by examining the role money plays in the economy and how economists define money. We then looked at the flow of money in and out of banks and saw how banks can create money with deposits and loans. Finally, we examined the structure of the Federal Reserve and the key roles that central banks can play during financial crises. Here are the main points you should remember from this chapter:

1 *Money* consists of anything we regularly use to make exchanges. In modern economies, money consists primarily of currency and deposits in checking accounts.

2 Banks are financial intermediaries that earn profits by accepting deposits and making loans. Deposits, which are liabilities of banks, are included in the money supply.

3 Banks are required by law to hold a fraction of their deposits as reserves, either in cash or in deposits with the Federal Reserve. Total reserves consist of *required reserves* plus *excess reserves*.

4 If there is an increase in reserves in the banking system, the supply of money will expand by a multiple of the initial deposit. This multiple is known as the *money multiplier*.

5 Decisions about the supply of money are made at the *Federal Open Market Committee* (FOMC), which includes the 7 members on the Board of Governors and the president of the New York Federal Reserve Bank, as well as 4 of the 11 other regional bank presidents, who serve on a rotating basis.

6 In a financial crisis like those that occurred in 2001 and 2008, the Fed can help stabilize the economy. Current and recent Fed chairmen have been powerful figures in the national economy.

KEY TERMS

assets, p. 277
balance sheet, p. 277
barter, p. 273
Board of Governors of the Federal Reserve, p. 283
central bank, p. 281
commodity money, p. 274
double coincidence of wants, p. 273
excess reserves, p. 278
Federal Open Market Committee (FOMC), p. 283
Federal Reserve Bank, p. 282
fiat money, p. 274
gold standard, p. 274
lender of last resort, p. 281
liabilities, p. 277
M1, p. 275
M2, p. 275
medium of exchange, p. 273
monetary policy, p. 282
money, p. 273
money multiplier, p. 279
owners' equity, p. 277
required reserves, p. 278
reserve ratio, p. 278
reserves, p. 278
store of value, p. 274
unit of account, p. 274

EXERCISES

All problems are assignable in MyEconLab.

13.1 What *Is* Money?

1.1 Money solves the problem of double coincidence of wants that would regularly occur under a system of ________.

1.2 Gold is a good example of commodity money. ________ (True/False)

1.3 Deposits in checking accounts are included in the definition of money because they are a very liquid asset. ________ (True/False)

1.4 The largest component of M2 is deposits in ________.

1.5 Money market mutual funds are hard to classify in a definition of money because they are only held to facilitate transactions. ________ (True/False)

1.6 So much U.S. currency is in global circulation because it is a safe asset compared to assets denominated in foreign currency. ________ (True/False)

1.7 **Debit Cards.** In recent years, debit cards have become popular. Debit cards allow the holder of the card to pay a merchant for goods and services directly from a checking account. How do you think the introduction of debit cards affected the amount of currency in the economy? How about the amount of checking account deposits?

1.8 **Gift Cards.** Gift cards have grown in popularity as a mechanism to give gifts. Cards are available for popular bookstores and for coffee shops. Should these gift cards be considered part of the money supply? How do they differ from traveler's checks?

1.9 **Brazilian Local Money** "The capavaris issued in Brazil can be viewed as a type of gift card for purchases made locally." Explain this quote. (Related to Application 1 on page 276.)

1.10 **Credit Cards.** Why aren't traditional credit cards part of the money supply?

1.11 **Inflation and Currency Held Abroad.** Suppose inflation in the United States rose to around 7 percent a year. How do you think this would affect the demand for U.S. currency by foreigners?

1.12 **Currency and Underground Economy.** Search the Web for articles on "currency and the underground economy." How have various authors used estimates of currency to measure the underground economy?

13.2 How Banks Create Money

2.1 Banks are required by law to keep a fraction of their deposits as __________.

2.2 When reserves do not pay interest, banks prefer to keep reserves rather than make loans. __________ (True/False) (Related to Application 2 on page 280.)

2.3 If the reserve ratio is 0.2 and a deposit of $100 is made into a bank, the bank can lend out __________.

2.4 If the reserve ratio is 0.2, the simplified money multiplier will be __________.

2.5 **A Bad Trade at a Bank.** In 2012, the bank JPMorgan Chase lost over $2 billion in a bad trade in the market. What happened to owners' equity after the trade?

2.6 **Banks versus Insurance Companies.** Both insurance companies and banks are financial intermediaries. Why do macroeconomists study banks more intensively than insurance companies?

2.7 **Understanding M1 and M2.** If you write a check from your checking account to your money market account, what happens to M1 and M2?

2.8 **Cash Withdrawals and Changes in the Money Supply.** If a customer withdrew $2,000 in cash from a bank and the reserve ratio was 0.2, by how much could the supply of money eventually be reduced?

2.9 **Money Market Mutual Funds, Banks, and Reserves.** Money market mutual funds typically invest in government securities and other financial instruments that can be easily bought and sold. They are not subject to reserve requirements and, in fact, hold minimal reserves. Banks, on the other hand, make loans to businesses for investment purposes. If there were no reserve requirements for banks, how do you think their reserve holdings would compare to money market mutual funds?

2.10 **Setting the Interest Rate on Reserves.** What would be the danger if the Fed set an interest rate on reserves close to the market interest rate on loans? (Related to Application 2 on page 280.)

13.3 A Banker's Bank: The Federal Reserve

3.1 The Federal Reserve is the "__________ of last resort."

3.2 The San Francisco Federal Reserve Bank is the only one in the West because San Francisco outbid Los Angeles to be its host. __________ (True/False)

3.3 The __________ votes on monetary policy.

3.4 __________-year terms help ensure the political independence of the Board of Governors.

3.5 The Fed provides a system of check collection and __________.

3.6 **The Treasury Secretary and the Fed.** Occasionally, some economists or politicians suggest that the secretary of the Treasury become a member of the Federal Open Market Committee. How do you think this would affect the operation of the Federal Reserve?

3.7 **Where Should Regional Banks Be Located Today?** Given the changes in the location of economic activity that have occurred since the founding of the Federal Reserve, how would the location of the regional banks change if they were allocated by economic activity?

3.8 **The President of the New York Federal Reserve Bank.** The president of the New York Federal Reserve Bank is always a voting member of the Federal Open Market Committee. Given your understanding of the conduct of monetary policy, why is this true?

3.9 **Additional Congressional Oversight?** A presidential candidate in 2012, Ron Paul, has strongly argued for more accountability and auditing of the Federal Reserve. What are the pros and cons of more Congressional oversight of the Fed?

13.4 What the Federal Reserve Does during a Financial Crisis

4.1 The Federal Reserve arranged for JPMorgan Chase & Co. to __________ Bear Stearns during the financial crisis in 2008. (Related to Application 4 on page 285.)

4.2 The "float" in the banking system is the difference between the Federal Reserve's __________ and __________ when clearing checks.

4.3 Two actions the Fed took after September 11, 2001, to ensure the financial system operated smoothly were __________ and __________. (Related to Application 3 on page 284.)

4.4 **Required Reserves during the Great Depression.** During the Great Depression, banks held excess reserves because they were concerned depositors might be more inclined to withdraw funds from their accounts. At one point, the Fed became concerned that excess reserves were too high and raised the reserve requirements for banks.

   a. Assuming banks were holding excess reserves for precautionary purposes, do you think they would continue to want to hold them even after reserve requirements were raised? Explain.

   b. What do you think happened to the money supply after the Fed raised reserve requirements?

4.5 **Crisis in the Short-Term Credit Market.** In 1973, several major companies went bankrupt and were not going to be able to pay interest on their short-term loans. This caused a crisis in the market. There was concern that the short-term credit market would collapse, and that even healthy corporations would not be able to borrow. How do you think the Fed should have handled that situation?

4.6 **The Federal Reserve Loan to JPMorgan Chase & Co.** When the Federal Reserve makes a loan to a bank or financial institution, it requires the institution to specify certain assets the Federal Reserve can take possession of if the loan is not repaid. These assets are known as collateral. When the Federal Reserve made its $30 billion loan to JPMorgan, it allowed JPMorgan to use some of the assets of Bear Stearns as collateral. Why was this risky for the Federal Reserve and a good deal for JPMorgan? (Related to Application 4 on page 285.)

4.7 **Check Clearing and September 11.** How did the Federal Reserve manipulate the check-clearing process to increase liquidity in response to the potential financial crisis following the terrorist attacks of September 11, 2001? (Related to Application 3 on page 284.)

4.8 **Bailouts?** Some critics of the Fed's actions with AIG and Bear Stearns said that the government was just bailing out failing financial firms that should have been allowed to fail. It is true that owners of both firms did benefit from these actions. Nonetheless, can you defend the Fed? (Related to Application 4 on page 285.)

ECONOMIC EXPERIMENT

MONEY CREATION

This experiment demonstrates the money-creation process. Students act like bankers and investors. Bankers loan money to investors, who then buy machines that produce output. The experiment is divided into several separate days. On each day, all loans are executed in the morning, all deposits happen over the lunch hour, and all machines are purchased in the afternoon. Each bank can receive only one deposit and issue only one loan. The interest rate paid to depositors and the interest rate paid by borrowers are negotiable. The experiment starts when the instructor deposits $625 from the sale of a government bond into a bank.

BANK ACTIONS

The sequence of possible bank actions on a given day is as follows:

1. Early morning: Count money. Check for excess reserves, including deposits from the previous noon.
2. Middle morning: Loan out any excess reserves in a single loan to a borrower and negotiate an interest rate for the loan. The loan is executed by writing a bank check to the borrower.
3. Noon: Receive a deposit (bank check deposited into a checking account).
4. Afternoon: Relax, golf.

RULES FOR BANKS

The rules for banks are as follows:

1. For each $1 deposited, you must hold $0.20 in reserve.
2. If you don't issue a loan, you can earn 3 percent by investing overseas.

INVESTOR ACTIONS

The sequence of possible investor actions on a given day is as follows:

1. Early morning: Sleep in while bankers count their money.
2. Middle morning: Borrow money from a bank and negotiate an interest rate for the loan.
3. Noon: Deposit the loan at the bank of your choice and negotiate an interest rate for the deposit.
4. Afternoon: Buy machines from Machine, Inc., paying with a personal check.

INVESTOR PAYOFFS

Each machine costs $1, generates $1.10 worth of output, and then expires. As the students play, the instructor keeps track of the model economy on a tally sheet, which shows the money-creation process in action, round by round. What role do the return on overseas investment (3 percent) and the return from owning a machine ($1.10 on a $1.00 investment) play in this experiment?

Money-Creation Experiment: Tally Sheet Bank Receiving Deposit	Amount Deposited	Interest Rate on Deposit	Amount Loaned	Interest Rate on Loan	Amount Added to Reserves	Change in Money Supply

APPENDIX

FORMULA FOR DEPOSIT CREATION

To show how to derive the formula for deposit creation, let's use the example in the text. We showed that with 10 percent held as reserves, a \$1,000 deposit led to total deposits of

$$\$1{,}000 + \$900 + \$810 + \$729 + \$656.10 + \ldots$$

Let's find the total sum of all these deposits. Because each bank successively had to hold 10 percent in its reserves, each successive bank received only 0.9 of the deposits of the prior bank. Therefore, we can write the total for the deposits in all the banks as

$$\$1{,}000 \times (1 + 0.9 + 0.9^2 + 0.9^3 + 0.9^4 + \ldots)$$

We need to find the sum of the terms in parentheses. Using a formula for an infinite sum,

$$1 + b + b^2 + b^3 + b^4 + \ldots = \frac{1}{(1 - b)}$$

the expression becomes

$$1 + 0.9 + 0.9^2 + 0.9^3 + 0.9^4 + \ldots = \frac{1}{(1 - 0.9)} = 10$$

Therefore, the total increase in deposits will be

$$\$1{,}000 \times 10 = \$10{,}000$$

To derive the general formula, note that if the reserve ratio is r, the bank will lend out $(1 - r)$ per dollar of deposits. Following the steps we just outlined, we find the infinite sum will be $1/[1 - (1 - r)] = 1/r$, or 1/reserve ratio. Therefore, in general, we have the formula

$$\text{Increase in checking account balances} = (\text{initial deposit}) \times \frac{1}{\text{reserve ratio}}$$

The Federal Reserve and Monetary Policy

CHAPTER 14

Little did Ben S. Bernanke know when he took over the reins as chairman of the Federal Reserve on February 1, 2006, that he would face a novel and complex crisis brought on by the fall in housing prices and its reverberations throughout the entire financial system in 2007 and 2008.

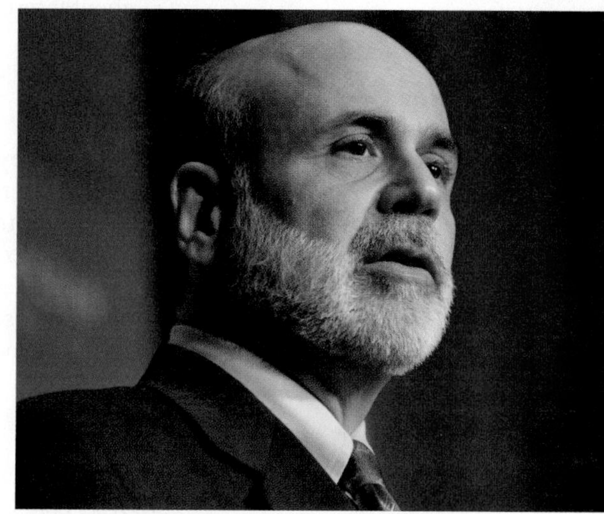

Unlike his immediate predecessors, Alan Greenspan and Paul Volcker, who had gained their experience and expertise working on Wall Street and in banking, Bernanke had primarily an academic career. As a former chairman of the Economics Department at Princeton University, he was known for his scholarly work focused on the Great Depression and the role of monetary policy in promoting economic growth and controlling inflation. Although he had little direct experience in financial markets, he did have some experience in economic policy and monetary policy in Washington.

Bernanke used his academic and policy experience to his advantage in meeting the challenges of the financial crisis. He convened brainstorming sessions with the president of the New York Federal Reserve Bank and leading financiers on Wall Street to further develop his own understanding of rapidly changing financial structures and the risks the mortgage crisis posed to them. As a scholar of the Great Depression, he also understood that the Federal Reserve had to take bold action to avert major crises. This background helped him to devise new and daring strategies for the Fed to deal with an unforeseen financial crisis. Later, when the economic recovery proved to be painfully slow, he used his earlier scholarship to consider other methods the Fed could use to stimulate the economy. His prior career in academia suited him well and gave him the perspective to face new and unforeseen economic events.

LEARNING OBJECTIVES

- Explain the role of demand and supply in the money market.
- List the tools that the Fed can use to change short-term interest rates.
- Demonstrate using supply and demand curves how the Fed can determine short-term interest rates.
- Describe both the domestic and international channels through which monetary policy can affect real GDP.
- Assess the challenges the Fed faces in implementing monetary policy.

MyEconLab

MyEconLab helps you master each objective and study more efficiently.

In this chapter, we will learn why everyone is so interested in what the Federal Reserve is about to do. In the short run, when prices don't have enough time to change and we consider them temporarily fixed, the Federal Reserve can influence interest rate levels in the economy. When the Federal Reserve lowers interest rates, investment spending and GDP increase because the cost of funds is cheaper. Conversely, when the Fed increases interest rates, investment spending and GDP decrease because the cost of funds is higher. It is this power of the Fed to affect interest rates in the short run that will influence firms' decisions to invest. Individuals who want to invest in or purchase homes also want to know what the Fed will do about interest rates in the near future.

14.1 The Money Market

money market
The market for money in which the amount supplied and the amount demanded meet to determine the nominal interest rate.

The **money market** is the market for money where the amount supplied and the amount demanded meet to determine the nominal interest rate. Recall that the nominal interest rate is the stated or quoted interest rate before adjusting for inflation. We begin by learning the factors that determine the public's demand for money. Once we understand what affects the demand for money, we can see how the actions of the Federal Reserve determine the supply of money. Then we'll see how the demand and supply of money together determine interest rates.

The Demand for Money

Let's think of money as simply one part of wealth. Suppose your total wealth is valued at $1,000. In what form will you hold your wealth? Should you put all your wealth into the stock market? Or perhaps into the bond market? Or should you hold some of your wealth in money, that is, currency and deposits in checking accounts?

INTEREST RATES AFFECT MONEY DEMAND If you invest in assets such as stocks or bonds, you will generally earn income on them. *Stocks* are shares in the ownership of a corporation. There are two sources of income from stocks: dividends paid to their owners out of the profits of the corporation, and the typical increase in their value over time. *Bonds* are loans that are repaid with interest. Thus, both stocks and bonds provide returns to investors. If you hold your wealth in currency or in a checking account, however, you will receive either no interest or very low interest. And if inflation rises sharply, you might even lose money. Holding your wealth as money in currency or a checking account means you sacrifice some potential income.

Money does, however, provide a valuable service. It facilitates transactions. If you go to a grocery store to purchase cereal, the store will accept currency or a check, but you won't be able to pay for cereal with your stocks and bonds. People hold money primarily for this basic reason: Money makes it easier to conduct everyday transactions. Economists call this reason for holding money the **transaction demand for money**.

transaction demand for money
The demand for money based on the desire to facilitate transactions.

To understand the demand for money, we rely on the principle of opportunity cost.

PRINCIPLE OF OPPORTUNITY COST
The opportunity cost of something is what you sacrifice to get it.

The opportunity cost of holding money is the return you could have earned by holding your wealth in other assets. We measure the opportunity cost of holding money by the interest rate. Suppose the interest rate available to you on a long-term bond is 6 percent per year. If you hold $100 of your wealth in the form of this bond, you'll earn \$6 a year. If you hold currency instead, you'll earn no interest. So the opportunity cost of holding \$100 in currency is \$6 per year, or 6 percent per year.

As interest rates increase in the economy, the opportunity cost of holding money also increases. Economists have found that as the opportunity cost of holding money increases, the public demands less money. The quantity demanded of money will decrease with an increase in interest rates.

In Figure 14.1, we draw a demand for money curve, M^d, as a function of the interest rate. At higher interest rates, individuals will want to hold less money than they will at lower interest rates because the opportunity cost of holding money is higher. As interest rates rise from r_0 to r_1, the quantity of money demanded falls from M_0 to M_1.

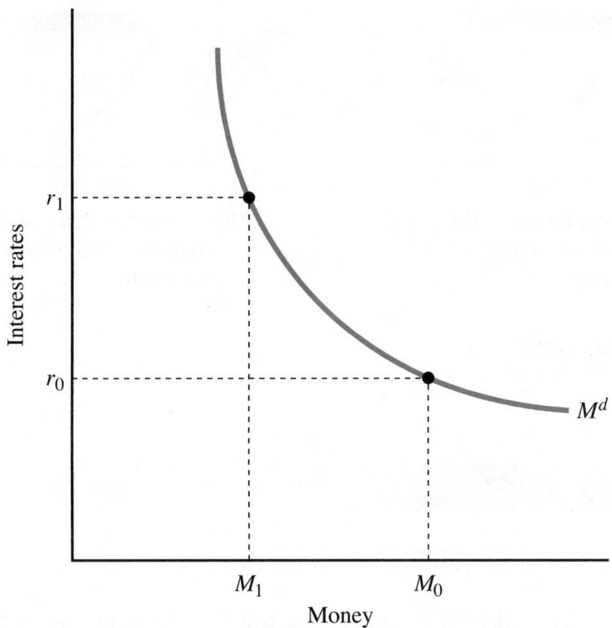

▲ **FIGURE 14.1**
Demand for Money
As interest rates increase from r_0 to r_1, the quantity of money demanded falls from M_0 to M_1.

THE PRICE LEVEL AND GDP AFFECT MONEY DEMAND The demand for money also depends on two other factors. One is the overall price level in the economy. The demand for money will increase as the level of prices increases. If prices for your groceries are twice as high, you will need twice as much money to purchase them. The amount of money people typically hold during any time period will be closely related to the dollar value of the transactions they make. This is an example of the real-nominal principle in action.

REAL-NOMINAL PRINCIPLE

What matters to people is the real value of money or income—its purchasing power—not the face value of money or income.

The other factor that influences the demand for money is the level of real GDP or real income. It seems obvious that as income increases, individuals and businesses will make more purchases. Similarly, as real GDP increases, individuals and businesses will make more transactions. To facilitate these transactions, they will want to hold more money.

Figure 14.2 shows how changes in prices and GDP affect the demand for money. Panel A shows how the demand for money shifts to the right as the price level increases. At any interest rate, people will want to hold more money as prices increase. Panel B shows how the demand for money shifts to the right as real GDP increases. At any interest rate, people will want to hold more money as real GDP increases. These graphs both show the same result. An increase in prices or an increase in real GDP will increase money demand.

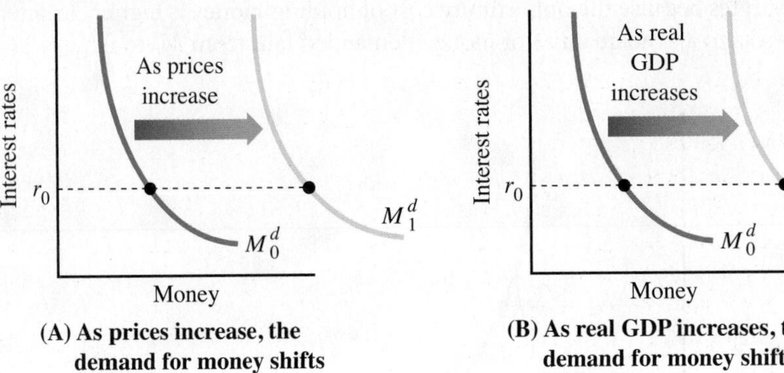

(A) As prices increase, the demand for money shifts to the right.

(B) As real GDP increases, the demand for money shifts to the right.

▲ FIGURE 14.2
Shifting the Demand for Money
Changes in prices and real GDP shift the demand for money.

application 1

BEYOND PURCHASING TREASURY SECURITIES

APPLYING THE CONCEPTS #1: How has the Fed recently expanded its role in financial markets?

Traditionally, to conduct monetary policy and to expand the money supply, the Fed purchased—either outright or on a temporary basis—Treasury securities. When it purchased these securities for the public, it credited the reserve accounts in banks and the amount of these reserves in banks would, in part, determine the amount of money and credit in the economy. The Fed did not intervene directly in particular security or credit markets, instead leaving those decisions to be made by the private market.

After the financial crisis of 2008, the Fed sharply changed its policies. It greatly expanded its involvement in the economy both in size and scope. The first way to see this is to note that the Fed's total assets increased during 2008 from less than $1 trillion to over $2 trillion. The second way is to note the change in composition of its assets. Prior to the financial crisis, the Fed primarily held Treasury securities as its assets. By 2010 the Fed held over $1 trillion in mortgage-backed securities. During the financial crisis, the Fed designed a wide variety of new programs to channel funds to particular credit markets.

The Fed's support of the mortgage market and other specific credit markets was designed to make these markets work more smoothly and prevent disruptions during the crisis. Critics of the Fed's policies suggest that through its support of specific markets, the Fed crossed a political threshold that may pose risks to its long-term independence. During 2009 the Fed did wind down its investments in many specific markets, but increased the size of its mortgage-backed securities. Through these financial holdings, the Fed is still playing a direct role in the housing market. **Related to Exercise 2.7.**

OTHER COMPONENTS OF MONEY DEMAND Traditionally, economists have identified other motives besides transactions for individuals or firms to hold money. If you hold your wealth in the form of property, such as a house or a boat, it is costly to sell it on short notice if you need to obtain funds. These forms of wealth are **illiquid**, meaning that they are not easily transferable into money. If you hold your wealth in currency or checking accounts, you do not have this problem. Economists recognize that people have a **liquidity demand for money**; they want to hold money so they can make transactions on quick notice.

illiquid
Not easily transferable to money.

liquidity demand for money
The demand for money that represents the needs and desires individuals and firms have to make transactions on short notice without incurring excessive costs.

During periods of economic volatility, investors might not want to hold stocks and bonds because their prices might fall. Instead, they might convert them into holdings that fall into the M2 category, such as savings accounts and money market funds. These investments earn lower interest rates on average, but are less risky than stocks and bonds, whose prices can fluctuate. This demand for safer assets is called the **speculative demand for money**. For example, after the stock market began to fall in 2000, individuals became very uncertain about the future and shifted their funds from the stock market to money market mutual funds. This shift of assets from stocks to money temporarily increased M2. When the market started to recover, some investors shifted funds back into the stock market.

speculative demand for money
The demand for money that arises because holding money over short periods is less risky than holding stocks or bonds.

In summary, individuals hold money for three motives: to facilitate transactions, to provide liquidity, and to reduce risk. The amount of money they want to hold will depend on interest rates, the level of real GDP, and the price level.

14.2 How the Federal Reserve Can Change the Money Supply

As we discussed in the last chapter, the banking system as a whole can expand the money supply only if new reserves come into the system. As we saw, when private citizens and firms write checks to one another, there will be no net change in the supply of money. Because the total amount of reserves in the system is unchanged, the money supply cannot expand. There is one organization, however, that has the power to change the total amount of reserves in the banking system: the Federal Reserve.

Open Market Operations

The Fed can increase or decrease the total amount of reserves in the banking system through **open market operations**, which are the purchase or sale of U.S. government securities by the Fed. There are two types of open market operations:

- In **open market purchases**, the Fed buys government bonds from the private sector.
- In **open market sales**, the Fed sells government bonds to the private sector.

open market operations
The purchase or sale of U.S. government securities by the Fed.

open market purchases
The Fed's purchase of government bonds from the private sector.

open market sales
The Fed's sale of government bonds to the private sector.

To understand how the Fed can increase the supply of money, let's trace what happens after an open market purchase. Suppose the Federal Reserve purchases $1 million worth of government bonds currently owned by the private sector. The Fed writes a check for $1 million and presents it to the party who sold the bonds. The Federal Reserve now owns those bonds. The party who sold the bonds then deposits the $1 million in its bank.

Here is the key to how the supply of money increases when the Fed purchases government bonds: As we explained in the last chapter, each bank must keep an account with the Fed containing both its required and excess reserves. The check written against the Federal Reserve increases the bank's total reserves, essentially giving it more money to loan out. In this case, the bank's account balance increases by $1 million. If the reserve requirement is 10 percent, the bank must keep $100,000 in reserves, but it can now loan out $900,000 from its excess reserves. Basically, when the Fed buys bonds, the proceeds go out into the economy. Open market purchases of bonds therefore increase the money supply.

The Federal Reserve has powers that ordinary citizens and even banks do not have. The Fed can write checks against itself to purchase government bonds without having any explicit "funds" in its account for the purchase. Banks accept these checks because they count as part of their total reserves.

As you might expect, open market sales will, conversely, decrease the supply of money. Suppose the Federal Reserve sells $1 million worth of government bonds to a Wall Street firm. The firm will pay for the bonds with a check for $1 million drawn on its bank and give this check to the Federal Reserve. The bank must either hand over $1 million in cash or, more likely, reduce its total reserves with the Federal Reserve by $1 million. When the Fed sells bonds, it is basically taking the money exchanged for them out of the hands of the public. Open market sales therefore decrease the money freely available in the economy.

In summary, if the Federal Reserve wishes to increase the money supply to stimulate the economy (perhaps it is operating too sluggishly), it buys government bonds from the private sector in open market purchases. If the Fed wishes to decrease the money supply to slow the economy down (perhaps it is growing too quickly and inflation is occurring), it sells government bonds to the private sector in open market sales.

Other Tools of the Fed

Open market operations are by far the most important way in which the Federal Reserve changes the supply of money. There are three other ways in which the Fed can change the supply of money, which we'll discuss next.

CHANGING RESERVE REQUIREMENTS Another way the Fed can change the money supply is by changing the reserve requirements for banks. If the Fed wishes to increase the supply of money, it can reduce banks' reserve requirements so they have more money to loan out. This would expand the money supply. To decrease the supply of money, the Federal Reserve can raise reserve requirements.

Changing reserve requirements is a powerful tool, but the Federal Reserve doesn't use it very often, because it disrupts the banking system. Suppose a bank is required to hold exactly 10 percent of its deposits as reserves and has loaned the other 90 percent out. If the Federal Reserve suddenly increases its reserve requirement to 20 percent, the bank would be forced to call in or cancel many of its loans. Its customers would not like this! Today, the Fed doesn't make sharp changes in reserve requirements. It did in the past, including during the Great Depression, because it mistakenly believed that the banks were holding too much in excess reserves. Banks, however, were holding additional reserves because they wanted to protect themselves from bank runs. As a result, after the increase in required reserves, banks increased their reserves even more, further reducing the supply of money to the economy.

discount rate
The interest rate at which banks can borrow from the Fed.

federal funds market
The market in which banks borrow and lend reserves to and from one another.

federal funds rate
The interest rate on reserves that banks lend each other.

CHANGING THE DISCOUNT RATE Another way the Fed can change the money supply is by changing the *discount rate*. The **discount rate** is the interest rate at which banks can borrow directly from the Fed. Suppose a major customer asks for a large loan from a bank that has no excess reserves. Unless the bank can find an additional source of funds, it will not be able to make the loan. Banks are reluctant to turn away major customers. They first try to borrow reserves from other banks through the **federal funds market**, a market in which banks borrow and lend reserves to and from one another. If the rate—called the **federal funds rate**—seems too high to the bank, it could borrow directly from the Federal Reserve at the discount rate. By changing the discount rate, the Federal Reserve can influence the amount of borrowing by banks. If the Fed raises the discount rate, banks will be discouraged from borrowing reserves because it has become more costly. Lowering the discount rate will induce banks to borrow additional reserves. Recently, the Fed has developed new methods to allow banks and other institutions to borrow from it.

application 2

DID FED POLICY CAUSE THE COMMODITY BOOM?

APPLYING THE CONCEPTS #2: What is the link between a dollar depreciation and increases in commodity prices?

Starting in the summer of 2010, there was a rise in prices of commodities such as oil and food worldwide. These increases in prices helped some economies—producers of these commodities—but hurt others. Some economists suggested that monetary policy in the United States was the cause of the worldwide commodity boom. They noticed that commodity prices rose when the U.S. dollar depreciated. And they noticed that the U.S. dollar fell largely because monetary policy in the U.S. had driven interest rates down very low because the Fed was using quantitative easing to further stimulate the economy.

Federal Reserve officials did not believe that their actions were causing the worldwide increase in commodity prices. Vice-Chair of the Board of Governors, Janet L. Yellen, gave her own perspective in a speech in April 2011 to the Economic Club of New York. She noted that the sharp rise in commodity prices was many times larger than the dollar depreciation. Moreover, she pointed to increases in worldwide demand and shortages of supply that were the primary cause of these price increases. The Fed's action played a very minor role, if any, in causing the price increases.

Yellin did note that when the U.S. lowered interest rates, other countries also followed for fear that too much capital would flow into their countries if their interest rates were higher than those in the U.S. Although the Fed might not be directly responsible, the combination of low interest rates worldwide could potentially have led to the commodity price increases. **Related to Exercise 4.7.**

SOURCE: Janet L. Yellen, "Commodity Prices, the Economic Outlook, and Monetary Policy," speech delivered at the Economic Club of New York, April 11, 2011, available at: http://www.federalreserve.gov/newsevents/speech/yellen20110411a.htm

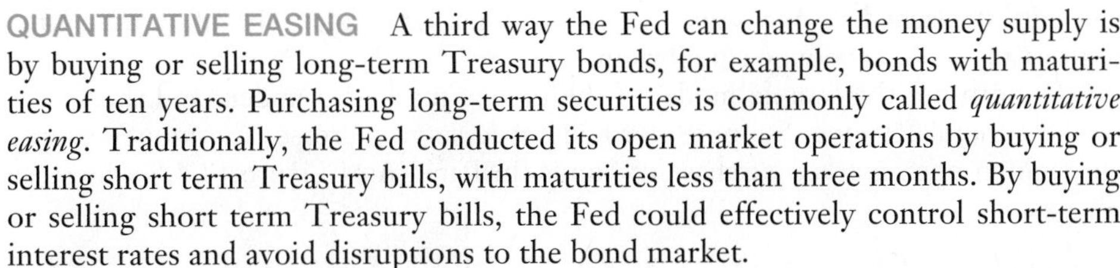

QUANTITATIVE EASING A third way the Fed can change the money supply is by buying or selling long-term Treasury bonds, for example, bonds with maturities of ten years. Purchasing long-term securities is commonly called *quantitative easing*. Traditionally, the Fed conducted its open market operations by buying or selling short term Treasury bills, with maturities less than three months. By buying or selling short term Treasury bills, the Fed could effectively control short-term interest rates and avoid disruptions to the bond market.

However, sometimes the Fed will want to affect long-term interest rates directly. By engaging in a policy of quantitative easing, the Fed can potentially lower long-term interest rates directly at the same time it injects more money in the economy. The Fed began engaging in these policies in 2010 to stimulate the economy and promote a faster recovery.

14.3 How Interest Rates Are Determined: Combining the Demand and Supply of Money

Combining the demand for money, determined by the public, with the supply of money, determined by the Fed, we can see how interest rates are determined in the short run in a demand-and-supply model of the money market.

Figure 14.3 depicts a model of the money market. The supply of money is determined by the Federal Reserve, and we assume for simplicity that it is independent of interest rates. We represent this independence by a vertical supply curve for money,

M^s. In the same graph, we draw the demand for money M^d. Market equilibrium occurs where the demand for money equals the supply of money, at an interest rate of r^*.

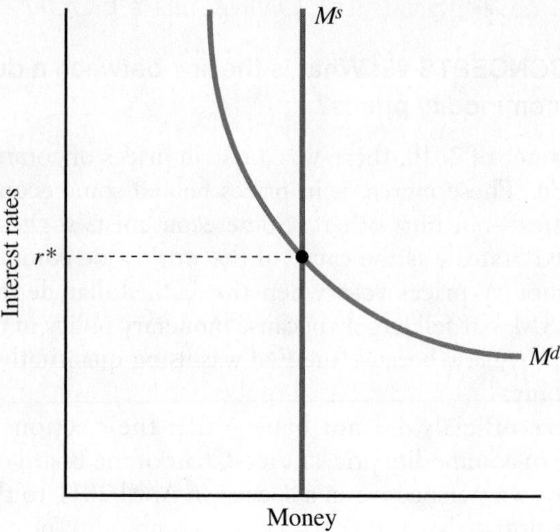

▲ FIGURE 14.3
Equilibrium in the Money Market
Equilibrium in the money market occurs at an interest rate of r^*, at which the quantity of money demanded equals the quantity of money supplied.

At this equilibrium interest rate r^*, the quantity of money demanded by the private sector equals the quantity of money supplied by the Federal Reserve. What happens if the interest rate is higher than r^*? At a higher interest rate, the quantity of money demanded will be less than the fixed quantity supplied, so there will be an excess supply of money. In other markets, excess supplies cause the price to fall. The same result happens here. The "price of money" in the market for money is the interest rate. If the interest rate were below r^*, the demand for money would exceed the fixed supply: There would be an excess demand for money. As in other markets when there are excess demands, the price rises. Here, the price of money or the interest rate would rise until it reached r^*. As you can see, money-market equilibrium follows the same logic as any other economic equilibrium.

We can use this simple model of the money market to understand the power of the Federal Reserve. Suppose the Federal Reserve increases the money supply through an open market purchase of bonds. In Panel A of Figure 14.4, an increase

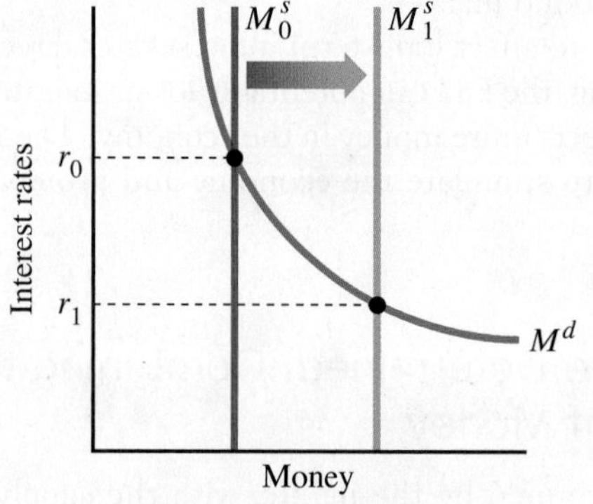

(A) An open market purchase shifts the supply of money to the right and leads to lower interest rates.

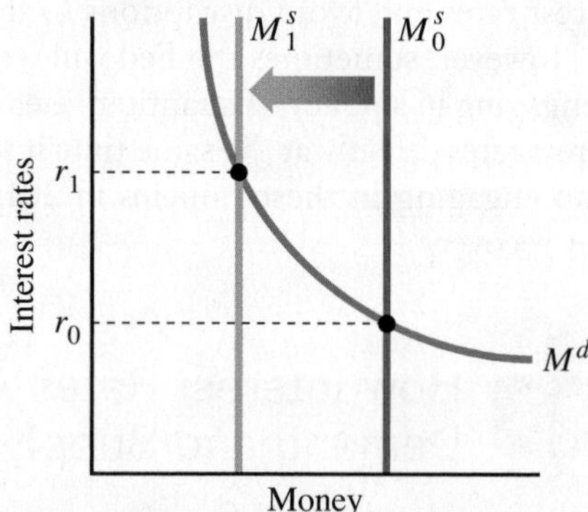

(B) An open market sale shifts the supply of money to the left and leads to higher interest rates.

▲ FIGURE 14.4
Federal Reserve and Interest Rates
Changes in the supply of money will change interest rates.

in the supply of money shifts the money supply curve to the right, leading to lower interest rates. A decrease in the money supply through the Fed's open market sale of bonds, as depicted in Panel B of Figure 14.4, decreases the supply of money, shifting the money supply curve to the left and increasing interest rates.

We can also think of the process from the perspective of banks. Recall our discussion of money creation through the banking system. After the Fed's open market purchase of bonds, some of the money the Fed paid for the bonds gets deposited into banks. Banks will want to make loans to consumers and businesses with that money, because holding it in their reserves with the Fed earns them no interest. To entice people to borrow, banks will lower the interest rates they charge on their loans. After an open market purchase of bonds by the Fed, interest rates will fall throughout the entire economy.

Now we understand why businesspeople and politicians all want to know what the Federal Reserve is likely to do in the near future. The Fed exerts direct control over interest rates in the short run. If the Fed decides interest rates should be lower, it buys bonds in the open market to increase the supply of money. If the Fed wants higher interest rates, it sells bonds in the open market to decrease the money supply.

Interest Rates and Bond Prices

Sometimes you see in the financial section of the newspaper a statement like, "Today, interest rates rose as bond prices fell." You may wonder whether these two actions are connected. Indeed they are. When the Fed raises interest rates, bond prices fall.

To see why, recall that bonds represent a promise to pay money in the future. If you own a bond, you are entitled to receive payments on it at a later time. But why do the prices of bonds move in the opposite direction of interest rates?

Because a bond payment occurs in the future, we need to use the concept of present value from Chapter 12 to determine the value of this payment today. The price of a bond is simply the present value of its future payments. Consider a bond that makes a payment one period in the future. The price of the bond—the present value of the payment—is equal to

$$\text{price of bond} = \frac{\text{promised payment}}{(1 + \text{interest rate})}$$

That is, the price of a bond is the payment promised, divided by one plus the interest rate.

Suppose the promised payment next year is \$106 and the interest rate is 6 percent per year. The price of the bond will be

$$\text{price of bond} = \frac{\$106}{1.06} = \$100$$

In this case, the bond would cost \$100 if it were issued today. But what happens if interest rates in the economy change later? What if rates rise higher than 6 percent or fall lower than 6 percent? What will the bond you are holding be worth then, if you decided, for example, you needed the money and had to sell it to someone else? This is an important question because most of the bonds for sale on the market are not newly issued bonds—they are bonds that have already been issued with specific promised payments that people are buying and selling from one another.

Let's consider two examples:

- Suppose the promised payment is still \$106, but the interest rate falls from 6 to 4 percent per year. Using the formula, the price of the bond will rise to

$106/1.04, or $101.92—$1.92 more than it was with an interest rate of 6 percent. The price of the bond rose because, at the lower interest rate of 4 percent, a buyer will need more money—$101.92 versus $100—to get the same $106 the bond will pay next year. In other words, at a lower interest rate the value today of a future payment (its present value) is higher.

- Now suppose interest rates rise from 6 to 8 percent per year. In this case, the price you could sell your bond for will fall to $106/1.08, or $98.15. The reason the price falls is that a buyer would need only $98.15 to get the $106 next year. As interest rates rose, the price of the bond fell. In other words, at a higher interest rate, the value today of a future payment (its present value) is lower.

In financial markets, many types of complex bonds pay different sums of money at different times in the future. However, all bonds, no matter how complex or simple, promise to pay some money in the future. The same logic that applies to simple one-period bonds, like the one just described, applies to more complex bonds. As interest rates rise, investors need less money to meet the promised payments in the future, so the price of all these bonds falls. As interest rates fall, investors need more money to meet the promised payments. Therefore, as the Fed changes interest rates, bond prices will move in the opposite direction of interest rates.

HOW OPEN MARKET OPERATIONS DIRECTLY AFFECT BOND PRICES There is another way to understand why when bond prices change in one direction, interest rates will change in the opposite direction. We know that when the Federal Reserve buys bonds in the open market, interest rates fall. But think about what the Federal Reserve is doing when it conducts the open-market purchase. The Federal Reserve is buying bonds from the public. As the Fed buys bonds, it increases the demand for bonds and raises their price. This is another reason bond prices rise as interest rates fall.

Similarly, interest rates rise following an open market sale of bonds by the Fed. When the Fed conducts an open-market sale, it is selling bonds, increasing the supply of bonds in the market. With an increase in the supply of bonds, the price of bonds will fall.

Because the Federal Reserve can change interest rates with open market purchases and sales and thereby affect the price of bonds, you can now see why Wall Street firms typically hire Fed watchers (often former officials of the Federal Reserve) to try to predict what the Fed will do. If a Wall Street firm correctly predicts the Fed will surprise the market and lower interest rates, the firm could buy millions of dollars of bonds for itself or its clients prior to the Fed's announcement and make vast profits as the prices of the bonds inevitably rise.

GOOD NEWS FOR THE ECONOMY IS BAD NEWS FOR BOND PRICES You may have heard on television or read in the newspaper that prices in the bond market often fall in the face of good economic news, such as an increase in real output. Are the markets perverse? Why is good news for the economy bad news for the bond market?

We can understand the behavior of the bond market by thinking about the demand for money. When real GDP increases, the demand for money will increase. As the demand for money increases, the money demand curve will shift to the right. From our model of the money market, we know that increased money demand will increase interest rates. Bond prices move in the opposite direction from interest rates. Therefore, good news for the economy is bad for the bond market.

application 3

THE EFFECTIVENESS OF COMMITTEES

APPLYING THE CONCEPTS #3: Is it better for decisions about monetary policy to be made by a single individual or by a committee?

When Professor Alan Blinder returned to teaching after serving as vice-chairman of the Federal Reserve from 1994 to 1996, he was convinced that committees were not effective for making decisions about monetary policy. With another researcher, Blinder developed an experiment to determine whether individuals or groups make better decisions.

The experiment Blinder and his colleague developed was designed to explore how quickly individuals and groups could distinguish between changes in underlying trends and random events. For example, if unemployment were to rise in one month, it could be a temporary aberration or it could be the beginning of a recession. Changing monetary policy would be a mistake if the rise were temporary, but waiting too long to change policy would be costly if the change were permanent. Who is better at making these sorts of determinations?

The results of the experiment showed that committees make decisions as quickly as, and more accurately than, individuals making decisions by themselves. Moreover, it was not the performance of the individual committee members that contributed to the superiority of committee decisions—the actual *process* of having meetings and discussions appears to have improved the group's overall performance.

In later research, Blinder also found that it did not really matter whether the committee had a strong leader. His findings suggest it is the wisdom of the group, not its leader, that really matters. Also, to the extent the leader has too much power—and the committee functions more like an individual than a group—monetary policy will actually be worse! **Related to Exercise 5.9.**

SOURCES: Based on Alan Krueger, "Economic Scene: A Study Shows Committees Can Be More Than the Sum of Their Members," *New York Times*, December 7, 2000, and Alan Blinder and John Morgan, "Leadership in Groups: A Monetary Experiment," (working paper no. 13391, National Bureau of Economic Research, September 2007).

14.4 Interest Rates and How They Change Investment and Output (GDP)

Higher or lower interest rates are just a means to an end, though, for the Fed. The Fed's ultimate goal is to change output—either to slow or speed the economy by influencing aggregate demand.

To show how the Fed affects the interest rate, which in turn affects investment (a component of GDP), and finally GDP itself, we combine our demand and supply for money with the curve that shows how investment spending is related to interest rates. This appears in Figure 14.5. Panel A in Figure 14.5 shows how interest rates are determined by the demand and supply for money. It is identical to Figure 14.3 on page 303, which we studied earlier. The graph shows us the equilibrium interest rate for money. Now let's move to Panel B in Figure 14.5. We can see that at the equilibrium interest rate r^* the level of investment in the economy will be given by I^*.

We should note that consumption as well as investment can depend on interest rates. That is, spending on consumer durables, such as automobiles and refrigerators, will also depend negatively on the rate of interest. Consumer durables are really

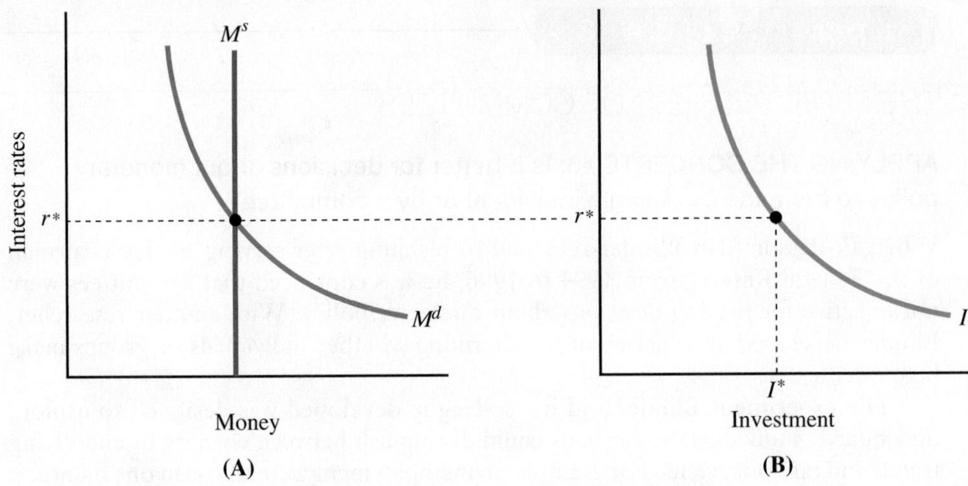

▲ **FIGURE 14.5**
The Money Market and Investment Spending
The equilibrium interest rate r^* is determined in the money market. At that interest rate, investment spending is given by I^*.

investment goods for the household: If you buy an automobile, you incur the cost today and receive benefits, such as the ability to use the car, in the future. As interest rates rise, the opportunity costs of investing in an automobile will rise. Consumers will respond to the increase in opportunity cost by purchasing fewer cars. In this chapter, we discuss how changes in interest rates affect investment, but keep in mind that the purchases of consumer durables are affected too.

In Figure 14.6, we show the effects of an increase in the money supply using our money market and investment graphs. As the supply of money increases, interest rates fall from r_0 to r_1. With lower interest rates, investment spending will increase from I_0 to I_1. This increase in investment spending will then increase aggregate demand—the total demand for goods and services in the economy—and shift the aggregate demand curve to the right.

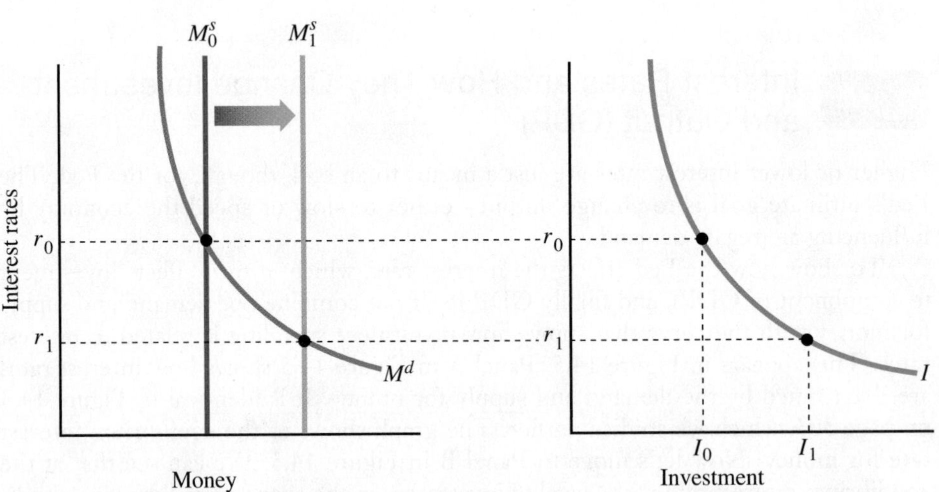

▲ **FIGURE 14.6**
Monetary Policy and Interest Rates
As the money supply increases, interest rates fall from r_0 to r_1. Investment spending increases from I_0 to I_1.

We show the shift of the aggregate demand curve in Figure 14.7. With the increase in aggregate demand, both output (y) and the price level (P) in the economy as a whole will increase in the short run. Thus, by reducing interest rates, the Fed affects output and prices in the economy.

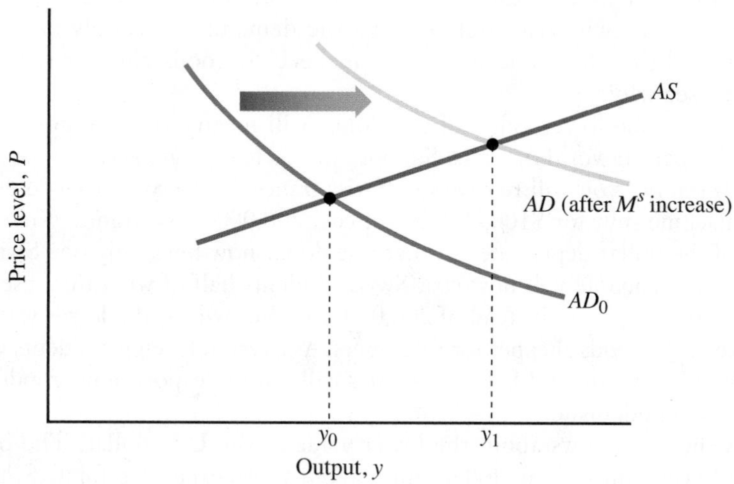

▲ FIGURE 14.7
Money Supply and Aggregate Demand
When the money supply is increased, investment spending increases, shifting the *AD* curve to the right. Output increases and prices increase in the short run.

In summary, when the Fed increases the money supply, it leads to lower interest rates and increased investment spending. In turn, a higher level of investment spending will ultimately lead to a higher level of GDP.

open market bond purchases	→	increase in money supply	→	fall in interest rates	→	rise in investment spending	→	increase in GDP

The Fed can also use its influence to increase interest rates, which will have the exact opposite effect. Investment spending will fall, along with aggregate demand. The aggregate demand curve will shift to the left, and the price level and output in the economy will fall, too. We can again represent this entire sequence of events:

open market bond sale	→	decrease in money supply	→	rise in interest rates	→	fall in investment spending	→	decrease in GDP

Monetary Policy and International Trade

We have been discussing monetary policy without taking into account international trade or international movements of financial funds across countries. Once we bring in these considerations, we will see that monetary policy operates through an additional route.

Suppose the Federal Reserve lowers U.S. interest rates through an open-market purchase of bonds. As a result, investors in the United States will be earning lower interest rates and will seek to invest some of their funds abroad. To invest abroad, they will need to sell their U.S. dollars and buy the foreign currency of the country where they intend to invest. This will affect the **exchange rate**—the rate at which one currency trades for another currency in the market. As more investors sell their dollars to buy foreign currency, the exchange rate will fall. A fall in the exchange rate or a decrease in the value of a currency is called **depreciation of a currency**. Lower U.S. interest rates brought on by the Fed will cause the dollar to depreciate. This will ultimately change the demand and supply of goods and services around the globe because it will make U.S. goods cheaper than foreign goods. Let's see why.

exchange rate
The price at which currencies trade for one another in the market.

depreciation of a currency
A decrease in the value of a currency.

In this case, the lower value of the dollar will mean that U.S. goods become relatively cheaper on world markets. Suppose the exchange rate is two Swiss francs to the dollar, meaning you will receive two Swiss francs for every dollar you exchange. If a U.S. machine sells for $100,000, it will cost 200,000 Swiss francs. Now suppose the value of the dollar depreciates so that one dollar now buys only one Swiss franc. The same U.S. machine will now cost Swiss residents half of what they used to pay for it—just 100,000 francs instead of 200,000. In other words, the lower value of the dollar makes U.S. goods cheaper for foreigners. As a result, foreign residents will want to buy more U.S. goods, and U.S. companies will want to export more goods to meet the higher foreign demand.

That's the good news about the lower value of the U.S. dollar. The bad news is that the lower value of the dollar will make it more expensive for U.S. residents to buy foreign goods. If the exchange rate were still two Swiss francs to the dollar as it originally was at the outset of our example, Swiss chemicals with a price tag of 60,000 francs would cost a U.S. resident $30,000. If the exchange rate of the dollar depreciates to one franc per dollar, however, the same chemicals will cost twice as much—$60,000. As the dollar depreciates, imports become more expensive, and U.S. residents tend to import fewer of them.

Let's recap this: As the exchange rate for the U.S. dollar falls, U.S. goods become cheaper and foreign goods become more expensive. The United States then exports more goods and imports fewer goods. *Net* exports increase, in other words. This increase in net exports increases the demand for U.S. goods and increases GDP. Remember that this all began with an open market purchase of bonds by the Fed that increased the money supply. Here is the sequence of events:

open market bond purchase	→	increase in money supply	→	fall in interest rates	→	fall in exchange rate	→	increase in net exports	→	increase in GDP

The three new links in the sequence are from interest rates to exchange rates, from exchange rates to net exports, and from net exports to GDP.

This sequence also works in reverse. If the Fed conducts an open market sale of bonds, U.S. interest rates rise. As a result, foreign investors earning lower interest rates elsewhere will want to move their money to the United States where they can earn a higher return. As they buy more U.S. dollars, the exchange rate for the dollar will increase, and the dollar will increase in value. An increase in the value of a currency is called **appreciation of a currency**. The appreciation of the dollar will make U.S. goods more expensive for foreigners and imports cheaper for U.S. residents. Suppose the U.S. dollar appreciates, and each dollar can now be exchanged for three Swiss francs instead of two. The same machine the Swiss had to pay 200,000 francs for when the exchange rate was one dollar to two francs now costs 300,000 francs. The Swiss chemicals U.S. residents bought for $30,000 will now cost them less—just $20,000.

appreciation of a currency
An increase in the value of a currency.

When U.S. interest rates rise as a result of an open market sale by the Fed, we expect exports to decrease and imports to increase, decreasing net exports. The decrease in net exports will reduce the demand for U.S. goods and lead to a fall in output. Here is the sequence of events:

open market bond sale	→	decrease in money supply	→	rise in interest rates	→	rise in exchange rate	→	decrease in net exports	→	decrease in GDP

To summarize, an increase in interest rates will reduce both investment spending (including consumer durables) and net exports. A decrease in interest rates will increase investment spending and net exports. As you can see, monetary policy in an open economy is even more powerful than monetary policy used in a closed economy.

The Fed and other central banks are well aware of the power they have to influence exchange rates and international trade. Countries that depend extensively on international trade—such as Canada and Switzerland—find that the effects of monetary policy on exchange rates are critical to their economic well-being.

14.5 Monetary Policy Challenges for the Fed

Now that we have seen how changes in the money supply affect aggregate demand, we can see that the government has two different types of tools to change the level of GDP in the short run: The government can use either fiscal policy—changes in the level of taxes or government spending—or monetary policy—changes in the supply of money and interest rates—to alter the level of GDP.

If the current level of GDP is below full employment or potential output, the government can use expansionary policies such as tax cuts, increased spending, or increases in the money supply to raise the level of GDP and reduce unemployment. If the current level of GDP exceeds full employment or potential output, the economy will overheat, and the rate of inflation will increase. To avoid this overheating, the government can use contractionary policies to reduce the level of GDP back to full employment or potential output.

Earlier, we explored some of the limitations of stabilization policy. We saw that fiscal policy is subject to lags and fraught with complications because political parties have different ideas about what the government should or should not do, and it takes them time to reach agreement. Monetary policy also has its complications.

Lags in Monetary Policy

Recall that there are two types of lags in policy. *Inside lags* are the time it takes for policymakers to recognize and implement policy changes. *Outside lags* are the time it takes for policy to actually work.

The inside lags for monetary policy are relatively short compared to those for fiscal policy. The FOMC meets eight times a year and can decide on major policy changes at any time and very quickly. It can even give the chairperson of the Board of Governors some discretion to make changes between meetings.

Of course, it does take time for the people working at the Fed to recognize that problems are beginning to occur in the economy. A good example is the 1990 recession. In 1990, Iraq invaded Kuwait. After the invasion, there was some concern that higher oil prices and the uncertainty of the political situation in Kuwait would trigger a recession in the United States, which, of course, is heavily dependent on oil. However, Alan Greenspan, then chairman of the Federal Reserve, testified before Congress as late as October 1990 that the economy had not yet slipped into a recession. Not until December did Greenspan declare that the economy had entered into a recession. Yet, looking back, we now know the recession had actually started five months earlier, in July.

The outside lags related to monetary policy, however, are quite long. Most econometric models predict it will take at least two years for most of the effects of an interest rate cut to be felt. This delay means that for the Fed to conduct successful monetary policy, it must be able to accurately forecast two years in the future! However, the Fed has difficulty predicting when recessions are about to occur. As an example, in May 2000 the Fed—fearing a rise in inflation—raised the federal funds rate from 6.00 to 6.50 percent. Yet, on January 3, 2001, the Fed reversed itself and restored the rate to 6.00 percent, because it feared a recession. It was too little—and too late—to prevent the 2001 recession. And the Fed also failed to predict our latest severe recession and did not believe the problems in the housing market would spill over to the financial sector.

Because of the lags for monetary policy and the difficulties of forecasting the economy, many economists believe the Fed should not take a very active role in trying to stabilize the economy. Instead, they recommend the Fed concentrate on keeping the inflation rate low and stable.

Decisions about monetary policy are made by a committee. How does this affect the effectiveness of monetary policy?

Influencing Market Expectations: From the Federal Funds Rate to Interest Rates on Long-Term Bonds

It is important to recognize that through its traditional open-market policies, the Fed directly controls only very short-term interest rates in the economy, not long-term interest rates. In fact, when the Fed makes its decisions on monetary policy, it really decides what the rate should be in the federal funds market—the market in which banks trade reserves *overnight*. Once the Fed decides what rate it wants in the market, it conducts open market operations—buying and selling short-term government bonds—to achieve this rate. Thus, when the Federal Reserve decides the course of monetary policy, it is really just setting a very short-term interest rate for the economy.

However, when a firm is deciding on a long-term investment or a household is deciding whether to purchase a new home, it will base its decisions on the interest rate at which it can borrow money, and this will typically be a long-term interest rate—not a short-term rate. For example, a household might take out a 30-year mortgage to purchase a home. If the rate is too high, it might not take out the loan. So for the Fed to control investment spending it must also somehow influence long-term rates. It can do this indirectly by influencing short-term rates. Here's how.

Long-term interest rates can be thought of as averages of current and expected future short-term interest rates. To see why future short-term interest rates are important, consider putting $100 of your money in the bank for two years. If the interest rate is 5 percent for the first year, you would have $105 at the end of that year. If the interest rate for the following year were 10 percent, you would then have $115.50 ($105 × 1.10) at the end of the second year. *Both* the current short-term interest rate (5 percent) and next year's short-term interest rate (10 percent) would determine the value of your bank account. Similarly, both the current short-term interest rate and future short-term rates determine the present value of payments in the future on a bond or loan. Long-term interest rates are an average of the current short-term interest rate and expected future short-term rates.

The Fed can directly control the federal funds rate and other short-term interest rates. Its actions also provide information to the market about the likely course for future short-term rates. If the Fed wishes to stimulate long-term investment by cutting the short-term interest rate, it must also convince the public that it will keep future short-term rates low as well in order to reduce long-term interest rates. Influencing expectations of the financial markets is an important part of the Fed's job.

The Fed does try to communicate its general intentions for future policy actions to the public to help make those policies more effective. However, the public ultimately must form its own expectations of what the Fed is going to do. Coping with financial market expectations complicates the Fed's task in developing monetary policy. The Fed itself has debated how best to communicate with the financial markets.

To further complicate matters, the Fed can also monitor the public's expectations of its future policies in the financial markets. There are now "futures" markets for the federal funds rates in which market participants essentially place bets on future federal funds rates. Thus, before the Fed takes any actions on interest rates or even makes any statements about its future intentions, it can see what the market is thinking. The Fed has to decide whether to take actions consistent with market expectations of Fed actions or to surprise the market in some way.

In recent years, the Fed has taken several steps to better control expectations about long-term interest rates. The first step was to purchase and sell long-term bonds directly, the policy known as quantitative easing. By intervening directly in the long-term bond market, the Fed hoped to gain more control over long-term interest rates.

The other step the Fed has taken was to ask the members of the FOMC for their predictions of short-term interest rates in the future and to make those public. While the members can always vote different interest rates in the future, making their predictions public at least lets the markets know what the current members of the FOMC believe will be the future course of monetary policy.

SUMMARY

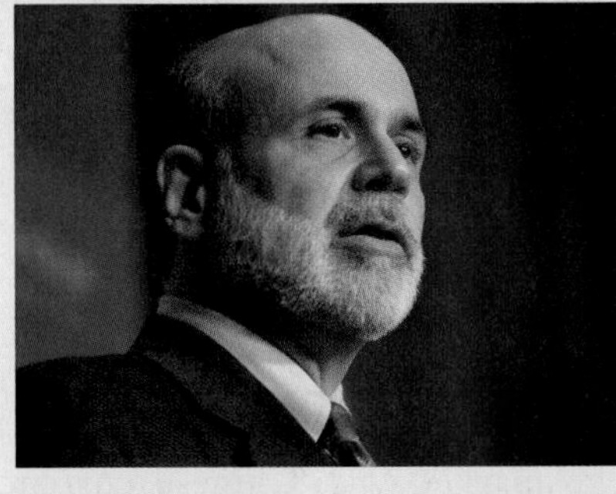

This chapter showed how monetary policy affects aggregate demand and the economy in the short run. Together, the demand for money by the public and the supply of money determined by the Federal Reserve determine interest rates. Changes in interest rates will in turn affect investment and output. In the international economy, interest rates also affect exchange rates and net exports. Still, there are limits to what effective monetary policies can do. Here are the main points of the chapter:

1 The demand for money depends negatively on the interest rate and positively on the level of prices and real GDP.

2 The Fed can determine the supply of money through *open-market purchases and sales*, changing reserve requirements, changing the discount rate, or increasing lending to banks and other institutions. Open-market operations are the primary tool the Fed uses to implement monetary policy.

3 The level of interest rates is determined in the *money market* by the demand for money and the supply of money.

4 To increase the level of GDP, the Federal Reserve buys bonds on the open market. To decrease the level of GDP, the Federal Reserve sells bonds on the open market.

5 An increase in the money supply will decrease interest rates, increase investment spending, and increase output. A decrease in the money supply will increase interest rates, decrease investment spending, and decrease output.

6 In an open economy, a decrease in interest rates will depreciate the local currency and lead to an increase in net exports. Conversely, an increase in interest rates will appreciate the local currency and lead to a decrease in net exports.

7 Both lags in economic policies and the need to influence market expectations make successful monetary policy difficult in practice.

KEY TERMS

appreciation of a currency, p. 304
depreciation of a currency, p. 304
discount rate, p. 296
exchange rate, p. 304
federal funds market, p. 296
federal funds rate, p. 296
illiquid, p. 295
liquidity demand for money, p. 295
money market, p. 292
open market operations, p. 295
open market purchases, p. 295
open market sales, p. 295
speculative demand for money, p. 295
transaction demand for money, p. 292

EXERCISES

All problems are assignable in MyEconLab.

14.1 The Money Market

1.1 We measure the opportunity cost of holding money with ________.

1.2 Money demand will ________ (increase/decrease) as prices rise.

1.3 The principle of ________ suggests that the demand for money should increase as prices increase.

1.4 The ________ demand for money arises because individuals and businesses use money in ordinary business.

1.5 **Checking Account Interest Rates.** During the 1980s, banks started to pay interest (at low rates) on checking accounts for the first time. Given what you know about opportunity costs, how would interest paid on checking affect the demand for money?

1.6 **Pegging Interest Rates.** Suppose the Federal Reserve wanted to fix, or "peg," the level of interest rates at 6 percent per year. Using a simple demand-and-supply graph, show how increases in money demand would change the supply of money if the Federal Reserve pursued the policy of this fixed interest rate. Use your answer to explain this statement: "If the Federal Reserve pegs interest rates, it loses control of the money supply."

1.7 **An ATM Next to Your Apartment Building.** Suppose an ATM connected to your own bank is installed right next to your apartment building.

a. How will this affect the average amount of currency you carry around with you?

b. If you withdraw funds at your ATM only from your checking account, will your action have any effect on total money demand?

1.8 **Flea Markets and the Demand for Money.** People often like to visit flea markets to look for unexpected opportunities. Flea markets also typically use cash. Explain why this is an example of the liquidity demand for money.

14.2 How the Federal Reserve Can Change the Money Supply

2.1 To increase the supply of money, the Fed should ________ bonds.

2.2 Increasing reserve requirements ________ the supply of money.

2.3 Banks trade reserves with one another in the ________ market.

2.4 Banks borrow from the Fed at the ________ rate.

2.5 **Purchasing Long-Term Government Bonds.** What would happen to the supply of money if a central bank purchased long-term government bonds held by the public?

2.6 **China's Increase in Reserve Requirements.** The Chinese government purchased U.S. dollars in the foreign exchange market with Chinese currency. During the same period, the Chinese sharply raised the reserve requirement on banks because they wanted to prevent the money supply from expanding too rapidly. Explain carefully how these two actions, taken together, could keep the supply of money in China from increasing.

2.7 **Other Channels of Monetary Policy.** Consider this quote: "Monetary policy does not work simply through lowering interest rates. Sometimes it can directly affect particular credit markets in the economy." Can you give an example of actions that the Fed has taken that fit this quotation? (Related to Application 1 on page 299.)

14.3 How Interest Rates Are Determined: Combining the Demand and Supply of Money

3.1 Interest rates typically fall in a recession because the demand for money depends __________ on changes in real income.

3.2 If interest rates are 9 percent per year, the price of a bond that promises to pay $109 next year will be equal to __________.

3.3 Through its effect on money demand, an increase in prices will __________ interest rates.

3.4 Open market purchases lead to rising bond prices and __________ interest rates.

3.5 **Pricing a Bond.** If a bond promises to pay $110 next year and the interest rate is 5 percent per year:

a. What will the price of the bond be?

b. What will the new price of the bond be if the interest rate falls to 3 percent?

3.6 **Buy or Sell Bonds?** If you strongly believed the Federal Reserve was going to surprise the markets and raise interest rates, would you want to buy bonds or sell bonds?

3.7 **Recessions and Interest Rates.** The economy starts to head into a recession. Using a graph of the money market, show what happens to interest rates. What happens to bond prices?

3.8 **A Decrease in the Riskiness of the Stock Market.** If investors began to think the stock market is becoming less risky, how will this belief affect the demand for money? Would this more likely affect M1 or M2?

3.9 **Quantitative Easing** How does a policy of quantitative easing differ from conventional open-market purchases?

14.4 Interest Rates and How They Change Investment and Output (GDP)

4.1 When the Federal Reserve sells bonds on the open market, it leads to __________ (higher/lower) levels of investment and output in the economy.

4.2 To decrease the level of output, the Fed should conduct an open-market __________ (sale/purchase) of bonds.

4.3 An open-market purchase __________ the supply of money, which __________ interest rates, which __________ investment, and finally results in a(n) __________ in output.

4.4 An increase in the supply of money will __________ (appreciate/depreciate) a country's currency.

4.5 **Interest Rates, Durable Goods, and Nondurable Goods.** Refrigerators and clothing are to some extent durable. Explain why the decision to purchase a refrigerator is likely to be more sensitive to interest rates than the decision to buy clothing.

4.6 **Where Is Monetary Policy Stronger?** In an open economy, changes in monetary policy affect both interest rates and exchange rates. Comparing the United States and Switzerland, in which country would monetary policy have a more significant effect on GDP through changes in exchange rates?

4.7 **Commodity Prices, the Dollar, and Monetary Policy.** Suppose the U.S. is a major source of demand for world commodities and supplies of commodities are limited. Describe how an expansionary monetary policy could affect commodity prices, both through a domestic and international channel. What would be the relationship one would observe between the value of the dollar and commodity prices following a monetary expansion? (Related to Application 2 on page 302.)

14.5 Monetary Policy Challenges for the Fed

5.1 __________ (Inside/Outside) lags are shorter for the Fed.

5.2 Experimental evidence shows us that individuals perform __________ than committees in making monetary policy decisions.

5.3 Long-term interest rates can be thought of as __________ of short-term rates.

5.4 The Fed directly controls long-term interest rates. __________ (True/False)

5.5 **Open Economies and Outside Lags in Monetary Policy.** Research suggests that the effects of monetary policy through interest rates, exchange rates, and net exports are more rapid than the effects of monetary policy on investment. As an economy becomes more open, how will this change affect the outside lag in monetary policy?

5.6 **Asset Prices as a Guide to Monetary Policy?** Some central bankers have looked at asset prices, such as prices of stocks, to guide monetary policy. The idea is that if stock prices begin to rise, it might signal future inflation or an overheated economy. Are there any dangers to using the stock market as a guide to monetary policy?

5.7 **Rates on Two-Year Bonds and One-Year Bonds.** Suppose the interest rate on a two-year bond was higher than the interest rate on a one-year bond. What does the market believe will happen next year to one-year interest rates?

5.8 **International Influences on Fed Policy.** As international trade becomes more important, monetary policy becomes more heavily influenced by developments in the foreign exchange markets. Go to the Web page of the Federal Reserve (www.federalreserve.gov) and read some recent speeches given by Fed officials. Do international considerations seem to affect policymakers in the United States today?

5.9 **Are Federal Reserve Chairmen Too Powerful?** Economic research has shown that the chairman of the Federal Reserve is more powerful, relative to other committee members, than the head of the central bank in other countries. Fed chairpersons have much more influence over actual decisions than other members. Recall Professor Blinder's findings that committees make better decisions than individuals and that leaders of groups, per se, do not matter for the quality of decision making. Make an argument that the tradition of a strong chairman in the United States reduces the effectiveness of monetary policy. (Related to Application 3 on page 306.)

5.10 **Making Future Predictions Explicit** Recently the members of the FOMC have been asked to make predictions for future interest rates and then these have been made public. What is the rationale for this policy?

Modern Macroeconomics: From the Short Run to the Long Run

CHAPTER 15

The recovery from the 2007 recession has been painfully slow. Four years after the peak of the recession, unemployment exceeded 8 percent and GDP growth was not sufficient to return the economy even close to full employment.

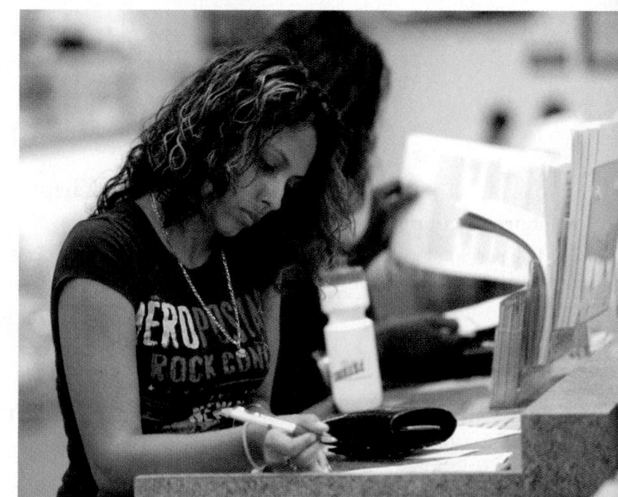

Nearly half of the official unemployed had been out of work longer than a year. Official forecasts by the Federal Reserve suggest the recovery will continue to be slow.

This slow recovery raises a number of questions for economic theory. How strong are the forces that return the economy to full employment? Do recessions brought on by financial crisis, as was the recent recession, require a longer recovery period than other types of recessions? Can monetary policy be sufficient to promote recovery or is fiscal policy also necessary?

These are not new questions. They were tackled by economists as diverse as John Maynard Keynes in the 1930s and Milton Friedman in the 1960s and 1970s. Some economists advocate aggressive government action today—others believe that aggressive action simply impedes the recovery. The debate continues.

LEARNING OBJECTIVES

- Describe the key difference between the short run and long run in macroeconomics.
- Demonstrate graphically how the economy can return to full employment.
- Analyze monetary neutrality and crowding out using graphs.
- Assess how classical economic doctrines relate to modern macroeconomics.

MyEconLab
MyEconLab helps you master each objective and study more efficiently.

One of the great debates surrounding macroeconomic policymaking centers on the short run versus the long run. Up to this point in the book, we have discussed the short and long run separately. Now, however, we'll explain how the economy evolves *from* the short run *to* the long run. The relationship between the two is one of the most important dimensions of modern macroeconomics, which carefully distinguishes between them.

15.1 Linking the Short Run and the Long Run

To begin to understand how the short run and the long run are related, let's return to what we mean by each in macroeconomics.

The Difference between the Short and Long Run

short run in macroeconomics
The period of time in which prices do not change or do not change very much.

long run in macroeconomics
The period of time in which prices have fully adjusted to any economic changes.

In Chapter 9, we explained how in the short run, wages and prices are sticky and do not change immediately in response to changes in demand. The **short run in macroeconomics** is the period of time over which prices do not change or do not change very much. Over time, though, wages and prices adjust, and the economy reaches its long-run equilibrium. Short-run analysis applies to the period when wages and prices do not change—at least not substantially. Long-run, full-employment economics applies after wages and prices have largely adjusted to changes in demand. The **long run in macroeconomics** is the period of time in which prices have fully adjusted to any economic changes.

In the short run, GDP is determined by the current demand for goods and services in the economy, so fiscal policy—such as tax cuts or increased government spending—and monetary policy—such as adjusting the money supply—can affect demand and GDP. However, in the long run, GDP is determined by the supply of labor, the stock of capital, and technological progress—in other words, the willingness of people to work and the overall resources the economy has to work with. Full employment is another characteristic of the long run. Because the economy is operating at full employment in the long run, output can't be increased in response to changes in demand. So, for example, an increase in government spending won't increase GDP in the long run because spending on one good or service has to come at the expense of another good or service. Similarly, increasing the supply of money won't increase GDP in the long run either. It will only cause the price level in the economy to rise.

Should economic policy be guided by what we expect to happen in the short run or what we expect to happen in the long run? To answer this question, we need to know two things:

1 How does what happens in the short run determine what happens in the long run?
2 How long is the short run?

Wages and Prices and Their Adjustment over Time

Wages and prices change every day. If the demand for scooters rises at the same time that demand for tennis rackets falls, we would expect to see a rise in the price of scooters and a fall in the price of tennis rackets. Wages in the scooter industry would tend to increase, and wages in the tennis racket industry would tend to fall.

Sometimes, we see wages and prices in all industries rising or falling together. For example, prices for steel, automobiles, food, and fuel may all rise together. Why? Wages and prices will all tend to increase together during booms when GDP exceeds its full-employment level or potential output. Wages and prices will fall together during periods of recessions when GDP falls below full employment or potential output.

If the economy is producing at a level above full employment, firms will find it increasingly difficult to hire and retain workers, and unemployment will be below its natural rate. Workers will find it easy to get and change jobs. To attract workers and prevent them from leaving, firms will raise their wages. As one firm raises its wage, other firms will have to raise their wages even higher to attract the workers that remain.

Wages are the largest cost of production for most firms. Consequently, as labor costs increase, firms have no choice but to increase the prices of their products. However, as prices rise, workers need higher nominal wages to maintain their real wages. This is an illustration of the real-nominal principle.

REAL-NOMINAL PRINCIPLE

What matters to people is the real value of money or income—its purchasing power—not the face value of money or income.

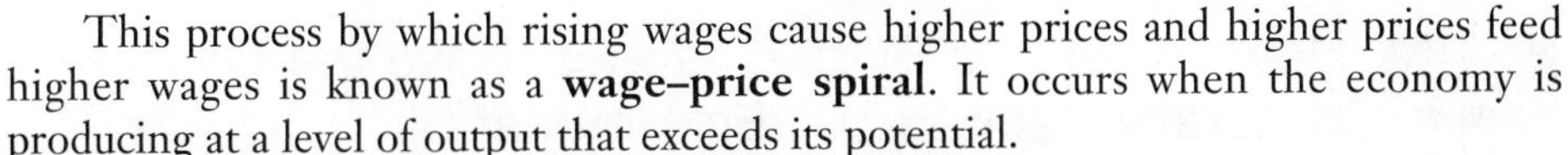

This process by which rising wages cause higher prices and higher prices feed higher wages is known as a **wage–price spiral**. It occurs when the economy is producing at a level of output that exceeds its potential.

wage–price spiral
The process by which changes in wages and prices cause further changes in wages and prices.

When the economy is producing below full employment or potential output, the process works in reverse. Unemployment will exceed the natural rate. Firms will find it easy to hire and retain workers, and they can offer workers less. As all firms cut wages, the average level of wages in the economy falls. As we have said, wages are the largest component of firms' costs. So, when wages fall, prices start to fall, too. In this case, the wage–price spiral works in reverse.

Table 15.1 summarizes our discussion of unemployment, output, and changes in wages. Let's emphasize one point: In addition to the changes in wages and prices that occur when the economy is producing at more or less than full employment, there is

application 1

HOW TO FIGHT A LIQUIDITY TRAP

APPLYING THE CONCEPTS #1: Why did Chairman Bernanke change his views on how to fight a liquidity trap?

Before he became Chairman of the Federal Reserve, Ben Bernanke was a highly regarded macroeconomist. In that role, he wrote a strong piece criticizing the Bank of Japan for not taking strong enough action when their interest rates fell close to zero. Bernanke argued that the Bank of Japan should have made substantial purchases of long term bonds and also publically commit to creating inflation. The reason for creating inflation was to make the real rate of interest negative and spur investment. Even if nominal interest rates are close to zero, if inflation is expected to be high, the result will be negative real interest rates.

After he became Chairman of the Federal Reserve, Bernanke did support a policy of purchasing long-term government bonds. But, as economist Larry Ball of Johns Hopkins University documents, Bernanke changed his mind about the virtues of creating expectations of inflation after hearing a presentation from the staff at the Fed. Ball attributes Bernanke's change of heart to "group think" and an unwillingness to dissent from a group consensus. Perhaps a more generous interpretation is that Bernanke himself realized that creating expectations of inflation has dangerous long-run consequences and the "inflation genie" cannot easily be put back into the bottle. **Related to Exercises 2.7 and 2.8.**

SOURCE: Larry Ball, "Ben Bernanke and the Zero Bound," NBER Working Paper #17836, February 2012.

also typically ongoing inflation in the economy. For example, suppose an economy that has been operating at full employment has been experiencing 4 percent annual inflation. If output later exceeds full employment, prices will begin to rise at a rate faster than 4 percent. Conversely, if output falls to a level less than full employment, prices will then rise at a slower rate than 4 percent.

TABLE 15.1 Unemployment, Output, and Wage and Price Changes

When unemployment is below the natural rate ...	When unemployment is above the natural rate ...
• output is above potential. • wages and prices rise.	• output is below potential. • wages and prices fall.

In summary, when output exceeds potential output, wages and prices throughout the economy will rise above previous inflation rates. If output is less than potential output, wages and prices will fall relative to previous inflation rates.

15.2 How Wage and Price Changes Move the Economy Naturally Back to Full Employment

The transition between the short run and the long run is easy to understand. If GDP is higher than potential output, the economy starts to overheat and wages and prices increase. This increase in wages and prices will then push the economy back to full employment.

Using aggregate demand and aggregate supply, we can illustrate graphically how changing prices and wages help move the economy from the short to the long run. First, let's review the graphical representations of aggregate demand and aggregate supply:

aggregate demand curve
A curve that shows the relationship between the level of prices and the quantity of real GDP demanded.

short-run aggregate supply curve
A relatively flat aggregate supply curve that represents the idea that prices do not change very much in the short run and that firms adjust production to meet demand.

long-run aggregate supply curve
A vertical aggregate supply curve that reflects the idea that in the long run, output is determined solely by the factors of production and technology.

1 *Aggregate demand.* Recall that the **aggregate demand curve** shows the relationship between the level of prices and the quantity of real GDP demanded.
2 *Aggregate supply.* Also recall that there are two aggregate supply curves: one for the short run and one for the long run. The **short-run aggregate supply curve** is represented as a relatively flat curve. The shape of the curve reflects the idea that prices do not change very much in the short run and that firms adjust production to meet demand. The **long-run aggregate supply curve**, however, is represented by a perfectly vertical line. The vertical line means that at any given price level, firms in the long run are producing all that they can, given the amount of labor, capital, and technology available to them in the economy. The line represents what firms can supply in the long run at a state of full employment or potential output.

Returning to Full Employment from a Recession

In an earlier chapter, we looked at the adjustment process for an economy producing at a level of output exceeding full employment or potential output. Now let's look at what happens if the economy is in a slump, producing below full employment or potential output. Panel A of Figure 15.1 shows an aggregate demand curve and the two aggregate supply curves. In the short run, output and prices are determined where the aggregate demand curve intersects the short-run aggregate supply curve—point *a*. This point corresponds to the level of output y_0 and a price level P_0. Notice that y_0 is a level less than full employment or potential output, y_p. In the long run, the level of prices and output is given by the intersection of the aggregate demand curve and the long-run aggregate supply curve—point *c*. Output is at full employment, y_p, and prices are at P_F. How does the economy move from point *a* in the short run to point *c* in the long run? Panel B shows us how.

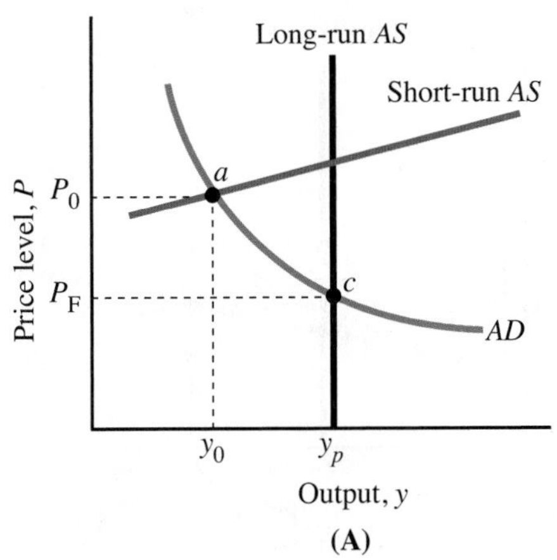

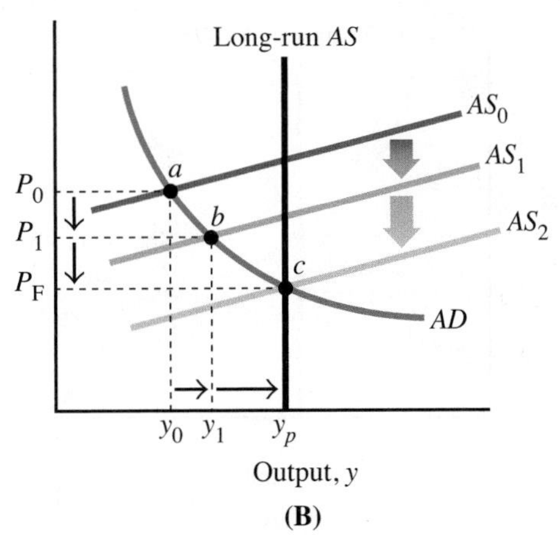

◀ **FIGURE 15.1**
How the Economy Recovers from a Downturn
If the economy is operating below full employment, as shown in Panel A, prices will fall, shifting down the short-run aggregate supply curve, as shown in Panel B. This will return output to its full-employment level.

At point *a*, the current level of output, y_0, falls short of the full-employment level of output, y_p. With output less than full employment, the unemployment rate is above the natural rate. Firms find it relatively easy to hire and retain workers, and wages and then prices begin to fall. As the level of prices decreases, the short-run aggregate supply curve shifts downward over time, as shown in Panel B. This downward shift occurs because decreases in wages lower costs for firms. Competition between firms will lead to lower prices for their products.

As shown in Panel B, this shift in the short-run aggregate supply curve will bring the economy to long-run equilibrium. The economy initially starts at point *a*, where output falls short of full employment. As prices fall from P_0 to P_1, the aggregate supply curve shifts downward from AS_0 to AS_1. The aggregate demand curve and the new aggregate supply curve intersect at point *b*. This point corresponds to a lower level of prices and a higher level of real output. However, the higher level of output still is less than full employment. Wages and prices will continue to fall, shifting the short-run aggregate supply curve downward.

Eventually, the aggregate supply curve will shift to AS_2, and the economy will reach point *c*, the intersection of the aggregate demand curve and the long-run aggregate supply curve. At this point, the adjustment stops because the economy is at full employment and the unemployment rate is at the natural rate. With unemployment at the natural rate, the downward wage–price spiral ends. The economy has made the transition to the long run. Prices are lower and output returns to full employment. This is how an economy recovers from a recession or a downturn.

Returning to Full Employment from a Boom

But what if the economy is "too hot" instead of sluggish? What will then happen is the process we just described, only in reverse, as we show in Figure 15.2. When output exceeds potential, unemployment will be below the natural rate. As firms bid for labor, the wage–price spiral will begin, but this time in an upward direction instead of downward as in Panel B. The short-run aggregate supply curve will shift upward until the economy returns to full employment. That is, wages and prices will rise to return the economy to its long-run equilibrium at full employment.

In summary:

- If output is less than full employment, prices will fall as the economy returns to full employment, as shown in Figure 15.1.
- If output exceeds full employment, prices will rise and output will fall back to full employment, as shown in Figure 15.2.

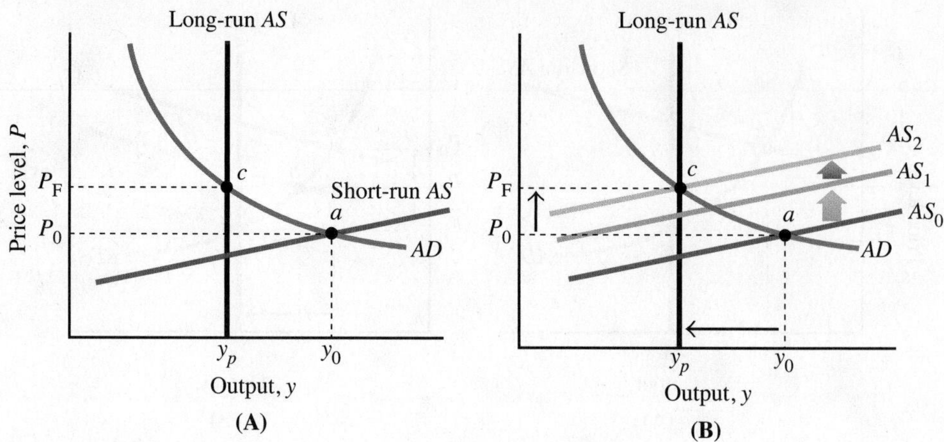

▲ **FIGURE 15.2**
How the Economy Returns from a Boom
If the economy is operating above full employment, as shown in Panel A, prices will rise, shifting the short-run aggregate supply curve upward, as shown in Panel B. This will return output to its full-employment level.

Economic Policy and the Speed of Adjustment

How long does it take to move from the short run to the long run? Economists disagree on the answer. Some economists estimate it takes the U.S. economy two years or less, some say six years, and others say somewhere in between. Because the adjustment process is slow, there is room, in principle, for policymakers to step in and guide the economy back to full employment.

Suppose the economy is operating below full employment at point *a* in Figure 15.3. One alternative for policymakers is to do nothing, allowing the economy to adjust itself with falling wages and prices until it returns by itself to full employment, point *b*. This may take several years. During that time, the economy will experience excess unemployment and a level of real output below potential.

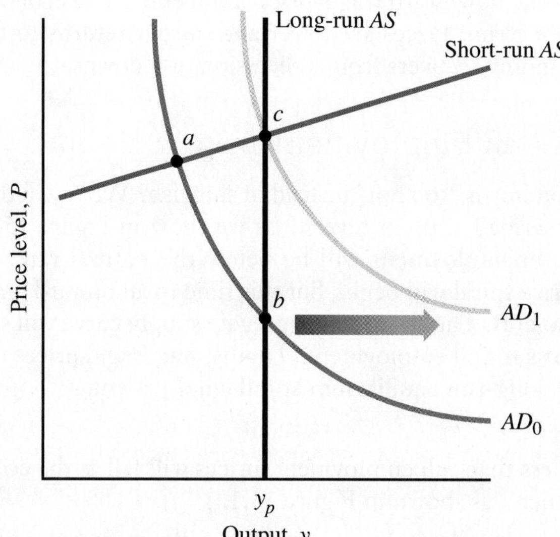

► **FIGURE 15.3**
Using Economic Policy to Fight a Recession
Rather than letting the economy naturally return to full employment at point *b*, economic policies could be implemented to increase aggregate demand from AD_0 to AD_1 to bring the economy to full employment at point *c*. The price level within the economy, however, would be higher.

Another alternative is to use expansionary policies, such as open market purchases by the Fed or increases in government spending and tax cuts, to shift the aggregate demand curve to the right. In Figure 15.3, we show how expansionary policies could shift the aggregate demand curve from AD_0 to AD_1 and move the economy to full employment, point *c*. Notice here that the price level is higher at point *c* than it would be at point *b*.

Demand policies can also prevent a wage–price spiral from emerging if the economy is producing at a level of output above full employment. Rather than letting an increase in wages and prices bring the economy back to full employment, we can reduce aggregate demand. Either contractionary monetary policy—open-market sales—or contractionary fiscal policy—cuts in government spending or tax increases—can be used to reduce aggregate demand and the level of GDP until it reaches potential output.

Expansionary policies and demand policies are stabilization policies, which look simple on paper or on graphs. In practice, the lags and uncertainties we discussed for both fiscal and monetary policy make economic stabilization difficult to achieve. For example, suppose we are in a recession and the Fed decides to increase aggregate demand using expansionary monetary policy. There will be a lag in the time it takes for the aggregate demand curve to shift to the right. In the meantime, the adjustment that occurs during a recession—falling wages and prices—has begun to shift the short-run aggregate supply curve downward. It is conceivable that if the adjustment were fast enough, the economy would be restored to full employment before the effects of the expansionary monetary policy were actually felt. When the expansionary monetary policy kicks in and the aggregate demand curve finally shifts to the right, the additional aggregate demand would increase the level of output so it exceeded the full-employment level, leading to a wage–price spiral. In this case, monetary policy would have destabilized the economy.

Active economic policies are more likely to destabilize the economy if the adjustment is quick enough. Economists like Milton Friedman of the University of Chicago (1912–2006) believed the economy adjusts rapidly to full employment and generally opposed using monetary or fiscal policy to try to stabilize the economy. Economists like John Maynard Keynes believed that the economy adjusted slowly and were more sympathetic to using monetary or fiscal policy to stabilize the economy.

It is possible that the speed of adjustment can vary over time, making decisions about policy even more difficult. As an example, economic advisers for President George H. W. Bush had to decide whether the economy needed any additional stimulus after the recession of 1990. Based on the view that the economy would recover quickly on its own, they took only some minor steps. The economy did largely recover by the very end of the Bush administration, but too late for his reelection prospects.

Liquidity Traps

Up to this point, we have assumed the economy could always recover from a recession without active policy, although it may take a long time. As our chapter-opening story mentioned, Keynes expressed doubts about whether a country could recover from a major recession without active policy. He had two distinct reasons for these doubts. First, as we will discuss later in the chapter, the adjustment process requires interest rates to fall and thereby increase investment spending. But suppose nominal interest rates become so low that they could not fall any further. Keynes called this situation a **liquidity trap**. When the economy is experiencing a liquidity trap, the adjustment process no longer works. Second, Keynes feared falling prices could hurt businesses. Japan seems to have suffered from both these problems in the 1990s and the United States faced similar issues during the first decade of this century.

liquidity trap
A situation in which nominal interest rates are so low, they can no longer fall.

Political Business Cycles

Up to now, we have assumed policymakers are motivated to use policy to try to improve the economy. But suppose they are more interested in promoting their personal well-being and the fortunes of their political parties? Using monetary or fiscal policy in the short run to improve a politician's reelection prospects may generate what is known as a **political business cycle**.

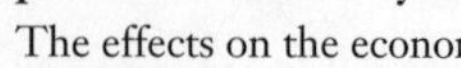

political business cycle
The effects on the economy of using monetary or fiscal policy to stimulate the economy before an election to improve reelection prospects.

Here is how a political business cycle might work. About a year or so before an election, a politician might use expansionary monetary policy or fiscal policy to stimulate the economy and lower unemployment. If voters respond favorably to lower unemployment, the incumbent politician may be reelected. After reelection, the politician faces the prospect of higher prices or crowding out. To avoid this, the politician may engage in contractionary policies. The result is a classic political business cycle: Because of actions taken by politicians for reelection, the economy booms before an election but contracts afterwards. Good news comes before the election, and bad news comes later.

It is clear the classic political business cycle does not always occur; however, a number of episodes fit the scenario. President Nixon used expansionary policies during a reelection campaign in 1972, which resulted in inflation. However, counterexamples also exist, such as President Carter's deliberate attempt to reduce inflation with contractionary policies just before his reelection bid in the late 1970s. Although the evidence on the classic political business cycle is mixed, there may be links between elections and economic outcomes. More recent research has investigated the systematic differences that may exist between political parties and economic outcomes. All this research takes into account both the short- and long-run effects of economic policies.

application 2

ELECTIONS, POLITICAL PARTIES, AND VOTER EXPECTATIONS

APPLYING THE CONCEPTS #2: What are the links between presidential elections and macroeconomic performance?

The original political business cycle theories focused on incumbent presidents trying to manipulate the economy in their favor to gain reelection. Subsequent research began to incorporate other, more realistic factors.

The first innovation was to recognize that political parties could have different goals or preferences. In particular, in the United States, Republicans historically have been more concerned about fighting inflation, whereas Democrats have placed more weight on reducing unemployment. Economists and political scientists began to incorporate these *partisan* effects into their analyses.

The second major innovation was to recognize that the public would anticipate that politicians will try to manipulate the economy. Suppose that, if elected, Republicans will contract the economy to fight inflation, whereas Democrats will stimulate the economy to lower unemployment. If the public is not sure who will win the election, the outcome will be a surprise to them—a contractionary surprise if Republicans win and an expansionary surprise if Democrats win. As Professor Alberto Alesina of Harvard University first pointed out, this suggests that economic growth should be less if Republicans win and greater if Democrats win. The postwar U.S. evidence is generally supportive of this theory. **Related to Exercise 2.9.**

SOURCE: Based on Steven M. Sheffrin, *The Making of Economic Policy* (New York: Basil Blackwell, 1989), chap. 6.

15.3 Understanding the Economics of the Adjustment Process

Earlier in the chapter we explained that changes in wages and prices restore the economy to full employment in the long run, and that the government and the Fed can get it there more quickly with fiscal and monetary policy. But what is happening behind the scenes? What do changes in wages and the price level mean for the economy in terms of money demand, interest rates, and investment spending? Let's go back and take a closer look at the adjustment process in terms of these factors so we can better understand how the adjustment process actually works.

First, recall that when an economy is producing below full employment, the tendency will be for wages and prices to fall. Similarly, when an economy is producing at a level exceeding full employment or potential output, the tendency will be for wages and prices to rise.

The adjustment process first begins to work as changes in prices affect the demand for money. Recall the real-nominal principle.

REAL-NOMINAL PRINCIPLE

What matters to people is the real value of money or income—its purchasing power—not the face value of money or income.

According to this principle, the amount of money people want to hold depends on the price level in the economy. If prices are cut in half, you need to hold only half as much money to purchase the same goods and services. Decreases in the price level will cause the money demand curve to shift to the left; increases in the price level will shift it to the right. Now let's put this idea to use.

Suppose the economy is initially in a recession. With output below full employment, actual unemployment will exceed the natural rate of unemployment, so there will be excess unemployment. Wages and prices will start to fall. Figure 15.4 shows how the fall in the price level can restore the economy to full employment via money demand, interest rates, and investment without active fiscal or monetary policy. First, we show with the *AD–AS* diagram in Panel A of Figure 15.4 how prices fall

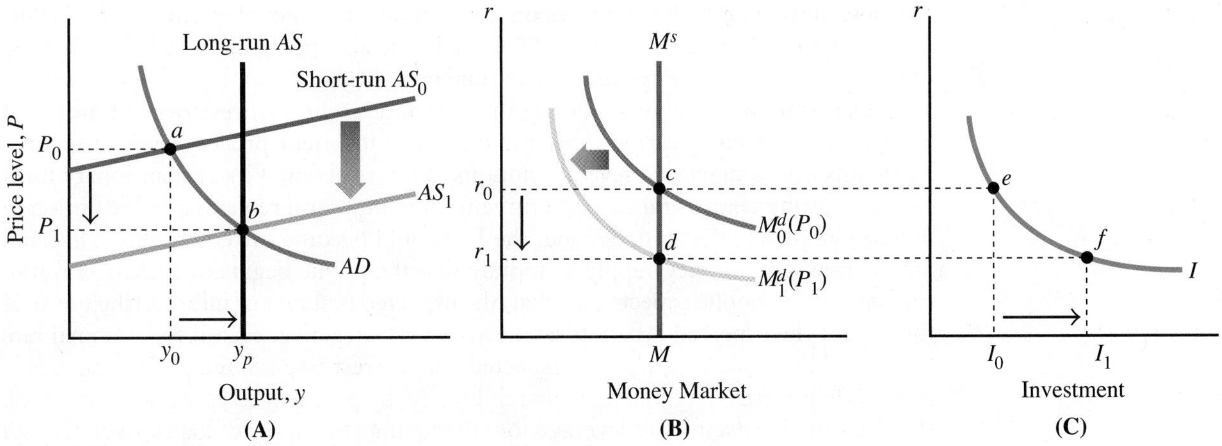

▲ **FIGURE 15.4**
How the Changing Price Level Restores the Economy to Full Employment
With the economy initially below full employment, the price level falls, as shown in Panel A, stimulating output. In Panel B, the lower price level decreases the demand for money and leads to lower interest rates at point *d*. In Panel C, lower interest rates lead to higher investment spending at point *f*. As the economy moves down the aggregate demand curve from point *a* toward full employment at point *b* in Panel A, investment spending increases along the aggregate demand curve.

when the economy is operating below full employment. Second, in Panel B, the fall in the price level decreases the demand for holding money. As the price level decreases from P_0 to P_1, the demand for money shifts to the left from M_0^d to M_1^d. Interest rates fall from r_0 to r_1, and the falling interest rates increase investment spending from I_0 to I_1. As the level of investment spending in the economy increases, total demand for goods and services also increases, and the economy moves down along the aggregate demand curve as it returns to full employment.

Now you can also understand why the aggregate demand curve is downward-sloping through the interest rate effect. As we move down the aggregate demand curve, lower prices lead to lower interest rates, higher investment spending, and a higher level of aggregate demand. Thus, aggregate demand increases as the price level falls, which explains why the curve slopes downward.

What we have just described continues until the economy reaches full employment. As long as actual output is below the economy's full-employment level, prices will continue to fall. A fall in the price level reduces money demand and interest rates.

Lower interest rates stimulate investment spending and push the economy back toward full employment. All this works in reverse if output exceeds the economy's potential output. In this case, the economy is overheating and wages and prices rise. A higher price level will increase the demand for money and raise interest rates. Higher interest rates will decrease investment spending and reduce the level of output. The process continues until the economy "cools off" and returns to full employment.

Now you should understand why changes in wages and prices restore the economy to full employment. The key is that (1) changes in wages and prices change the demand for money, and (2) this changes interest rates, which then affect aggregate demand for goods and services and ultimately GDP.

We can also use the model we just developed to understand the liquidity trap. If an economy is in a recession, interest rates will fall, restoring the economy to full employment. But at some point, interest rates may become so low they equal zero. Nominal interest rates cannot go far below zero, because investors would rather hold money (which pays a zero rate) than hold a bond that promises a negative return. Suppose, however, that as interest rates approach zero, the economy is still in a slump. The adjustment process then has nowhere to go. This appears to be what happened in Japan in the 1990s. Interest rates on government bonds were zero, but prices continued to fall. At this point, the fall in prices by itself could not restore the economy to full employment. Policymakers in the United States also became concerned by this possibility. When interest rates on three-month U.S. government bills fell below 1 percent from June 2003 to May 2004, Fed officials openly discussed their limited options if further monetary stimulus became necessary.

What can policymakers do if an economy is in a recession but nominal rates become so close to zero that the natural adjustment process ceases to work? Economists have suggested several solutions to this problem. First, expansionary fiscal policy—cutting taxes or raising government spending—still remains a viable option to increase aggregate demand. Second, the Fed could become extremely aggressive and try to expand the money supply so rapidly that the public begins to anticipate future inflation. If the public expects inflation, the expected real rate of interest (the nominal rate minus the expected inflation rate) can become negative, even if the nominal rate cannot fall below zero. A negative expected real interest rate will tempt firms to invest, and this will increase aggregate demand. Finally, by paying interest on bank reserves, the Fed can give itself more leverage for controlling the supply of loans. Even though a liquidity trap may make it more difficult for an economy to recover on its own, there is still room for proper economic policy to have an impact.

The Long-Run Neutrality of Money

An increase in the money supply has a different effect on the economy in the short run than it does in the long run. In Figure 15.5, we show the effects of expansionary monetary policy in both the short run and the long run. In the short run, as the supply

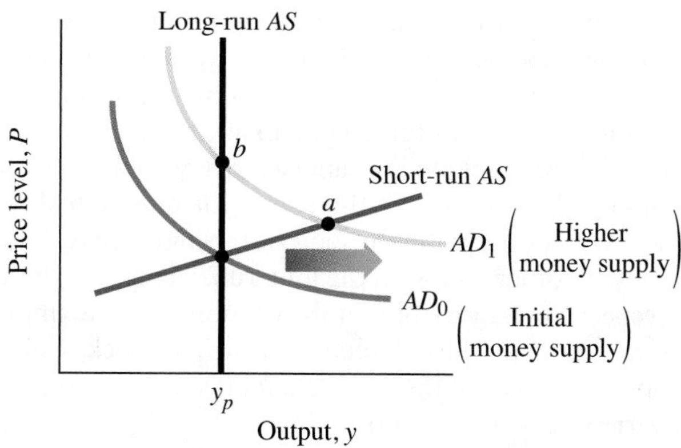

▲ FIGURE 15.5
Monetary Policy in the Short Run and the Long Run
As the Fed increases the supply of money, the aggregate demand curve shifts from AD_0 to AD_1 and the economy moves to point *a*. In the long run, the economy moves to point *b*.

of money increases, the economy moves from the original equilibrium to point *a*, with output above potential. But in the long run, the economy returns to point *b* at full employment, but at a higher price level than at the original equilibrium. How can the Federal Reserve change the level of output in the short run but affect prices only in the long run? Why is the short run different from the long run? We can use our model of the demand for money and investment to understand this issue.

Assume the economy starts at full employment. In Figure 15.6, interest rates are at r_F, and investment spending is at I_F. Now, suppose the Federal Reserve increases the money supply from M_0^s to M_1^s. We show this as a rightward movement in the money-supply curve. In the short run, the increase in the supply of money will reduce interest rates to r_0, and the level of investment spending will increase to I_0. Increased investment will stimulate the economy and increase output above full employment. All this occurs in the short run. The red arrows show the movements in interest rates and investment in the short run.

However, once output exceeds full employment, wages and prices will start to increase. As the price level increases, the demand for money will increase. This will shift the money-demand curve upward and will start to increase interest rates. Investment will start to fall as interest rates increase, leading to a fall in output. The blue arrows in Figure 15.6 show the transition as prices increase. As long as output exceeds full employment, prices will continue to rise, money demand will continue to increase, and interest rates will continue to rise. Where does this process end? It ends only when

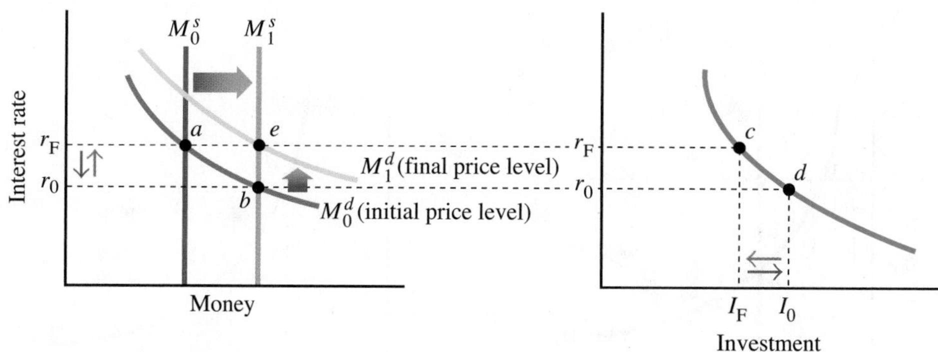

▲ FIGURE 15.6
The Neutrality of Money
Starting at full employment, an increase in the supply of money from M_0^s to M_1^s will initially reduce interest rates from r_F to r_0 (from point *a* to point *b*) and raise investment spending from I_F to I_0 (point *c* to point *d*). We show these changes with the red arrows. The blue arrows show that as the price level increases, the demand for money increases, restoring interest rates and investment to their prior levels—r_F and I_F, respectively. Both money supplied and money demanded will remain at a higher level, though, at point *e*.

interest rates return to their original level of r_F. At an interest rate of r_F, investment spending will have returned to I_F. This is the level of investment that meets the total level of demand for goods and services and keeps the economy at full employment.

When the economy returns to full employment, the levels of real interest rates, investment, and output are precisely the same as they were before the Fed increased the supply of money. The increase in the supply of money had no effect on real interest rates, investment, or output in the long run. Economists call this the **long-run neutrality of money**. In other words, in the long run, changes in the supply of money are neutral with respect to real variables in the economy. For example, if the price of everything in the economy doubles, including your paycheck, you are no better or worse off than you were before. In the long run, increases in the supply of money have no effect on real variables, only on prices.

long-run neutrality of money
A change in the supply of money has no effect on real interest rates, investment, or output in the long run.

This example points out how, in the long run, it really does not matter how much money is in circulation, because prices will adjust to the amount of nominal money available. In the short run, however, money is not neutral. In the short run, changes in the supply of money do affect interest rates, investment spending, and output. The Fed does have strong powers over real GDP, but those powers are ultimately temporary. In the long run, all the Fed can do is determine the level of prices in the economy.

Now we can understand why the job of the Federal Reserve has been described by William McChesney Martin, Jr., a former Federal Reserve chairman, as "taking the punch bowl away at the party." The punch bowl is money: If the Fed sets out the punch bowl, this will temporarily increase output or give the economy a brief high. But if the Federal Reserve is worried about increases in prices in the long run, it must take the punch bowl away and everyone must sober up. If not, the result will be continuing increases in prices, or inflation.

Crowding Out in the Long Run

Some economists are strong proponents of increasing government spending on defense or other programs to stimulate the economy. Critics, however, say increases in spending provide only temporary relief and ultimately harm the economy because government spending "crowds out" investment spending. In an earlier chapter, we discussed the idea of *crowding out*. We can now understand the idea in more detail.

Suppose the economy starts out at full employment and then the government increases its spending. This will shift the aggregate demand curve to the right, causing output to increase beyond full employment. As we have seen, the result of this boom will be that wages and prices increase.

Now let's turn to our model of money demand and investment. Figure 15.7 shows that as prices increase, the demand for money shifts upward in Panel A, raising interest

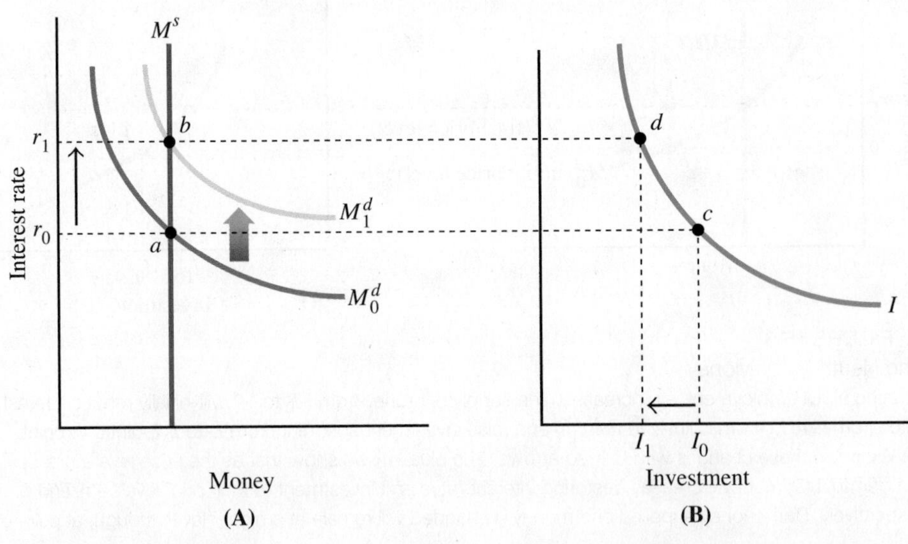

▶ **FIGURE 15.7**
Crowding Out in the Long Run
Starting at full employment, an increase in government spending raises output above full employment. As wages and prices increase, the demand for money increases, as shown in Panel A, raising interest rates from r_0 to r_1 (point *a* to point *b*) and reducing investment from I_0 to I_1 (point *c* to point *d*). The economy returns to full employment, but at a higher level of interest rates and a lower level of investment spending.

rates from r_0 to r_1 and reducing investment from I_0 to I_1, as shown in Panel B. Higher interest rates are the mechanism through which crowding out of public investment occurs. As investment spending by the public then falls (gets crowded out), we know that aggregate demand decreases. This process will continue until the economy returns to full employment. Once the economy returns to full employment, the decrease in investment spending by the public will exactly match the increase in government spending. However, when the economy does return to full employment, it will be at a higher interest rate level and lower level of investment spending by the public.

Thus, the increase in government spending has no long-run effect on the level of output—just on the interest rate. Instead, the increase in government spending displaced, or crowded out, private investment spending. If the government spending went toward government investment projects—such as bridges or roads—then it will have just replaced an equivalent amount of private investment. If the increased government spending did not go toward providing investment but, for example, went for military spending, then the reduction in private investment will have reduced total investment in the economy, private and public. This decrease in total investment would have further negative effects on the economy over time. As we saw in earlier chapters, a reduction in investment spending reduces capital deepening and leads to lower levels of real income and wages in the future.

Economists make similar arguments when it comes to tax cuts. Tax cuts initially will increase consumer spending and lead to a higher level of GDP. In the long run, however, adjustments in wages and prices restore the economy to full employment.

application 3

INCREASING HEALTH-CARE EXPENDITURES AND CROWDING OUT

APPLYING THE CONCEPTS #3: Will increases in health-care expenditures crowd out consumption or investment spending?

In 1950 health-care expenditures in the United States were 5.2 percent of GDP; by 2000 this share had risen to 15.4 percent. Driving these increases were several factors: increasing relative prices of health care compared to other goods, a larger population of the elderly, and increased longevity. Since 1950 the average life span has increased by 1.7 years per decade.

Many observers think these trends will continue. Health-care costs have continued to rise rapidly in recent years. Two economists, Charles I. Jones and Robert E. Hall, go further and suggest normal increases in economic growth will propel health-care expenditures to approximately 30 percent of GDP by mid-century. Their argument is that as societies grow wealthier, individuals face the tradeoff of buying more goods (automobiles or cars) to enjoy their current life span or spending more on health care to extend their lives. At some point, the extra years of life become more valuable than consumer durables, with the result that spending on health care rises rapidly.

Assuming this argument is correct and health-care expenditures increase, what other component of GDP will fall? If investment is crowded out, living standards would fall in the long run, reducing the ability to consume both health and nonhealth goods. Perhaps it is more likely that other types of consumption spending will fall. Spending on health would then come at the expense of spending on consumer durables or larger houses. That would be the preferred outcome. **Related to Exercise 3.7.**

SOURCE: Based on Robert E. Hall and Charles I. Jones, "The Value of Life and the Rise in Health Spending," *Quarterly Journal of Economics* (February 2007): 39–72.

However, interest rates will rise during the adjustment process and this increase in interest rates will crowd out private investment. In the long run, the increase in consumption spending will come at the expense of lower investment spending, decreased capital deepening, and lower levels of real income and wages in the future.

Crowding out can occur from sources other than the government. Expected increases in U.S. health-care expenditures will pose similar challenges to crowding out in the coming decades as well.

What about decreases in government spending or increases in taxes? Decreases in government spending, such as cuts in military spending, will lead to increases in investment in the long run, which we call *crowding in*. Initially, a decrease in government spending will cause a decrease in real GDP. But as prices fall, the demand for money will decrease, and interest rates will fall. Lower interest rates will crowd in investment as the economy returns to full employment. In the longer run, the higher investment spending will raise living standards through capital deepening. Increased taxes, to the extent they reduce consumption spending, will crowd in investment through precisely the same mechanism.

15.4 Classical Economics in Historical Perspective

The term *classical economics* refers to the work of the originators of modern economic thought. Adam Smith was the first so-called classical economist. Other classical economists—Jean-Baptiste Say, David Ricardo, John Stuart Mill, and Thomas Malthus—developed their work during the late eighteenth and nineteenth centuries. Keynes first used the term *classical model* in the 1930s to contrast it with his Keynesian model, which emphasized the difficulties the economy could face in the short run. The ideas developed in this chapter can shed some light on a historical debate in economics about the role of full employment in modern Keynesian and classical thought.

Say's Law

Classical economics is often associated with *Say's law*, the doctrine that "supply creates its own demand." To understand Say's law, recall from our discussion of GDP accounting in Chapter 5 that production in an economy creates an equivalent amount of income. For example, if GDP is $10 trillion, then production is $10 trillion, and $10 trillion in income is generated. The classical economists argued that the $10 trillion of production also created $10 trillion in demand for current goods and services. This meant there could never be a shortage of demand for total goods and services in the economy, nor any excess.

But suppose consumers, who earned the income, decided to save rather than spend it. Wouldn't this increase in saving lead to a shortfall in the total demand for goods and services? Wouldn't, say, inventories of goods pile up in warehouses? Classical economists argued no, that the increase in savings would *eventually* find its way to an equivalent increase in investment spending by firms, because the savings by households would eventually get channeled to firms via financial markets. As a result spending on consumption and investment together would be sufficient so that all the goods and services produced in the economy would be purchased.

Keynes, on the other hand, argued that there could be situations in which total demand fell short of total production in the economy for extended periods of time. In particular, if consumers increased their savings, there was no guarantee that investment spending would rise to offset the decrease in consumption. And if total spending did fall short of total demand, goods and services would go unsold. When producers could not sell their goods, they would cut back on production, and output in the economy would consequently fall, leading to a recession or depression.

Keynesian and Classical Debates

The debates between Keynesian and classical economists continued for several decades after Keynes developed his theories. In the 1940s, Professor Don Patinkin and Nobel Laureate Franco Modigliani clarified the conditions for which the classical model would hold true. In particular, they studied the conditions under which there would be sufficient demand for goods and services when the economy was at full employment. Both economists emphasized that one of the necessary conditions for the classical model to work was that wages and prices must be fully flexible—that is, they must adjust rapidly to changes in demand and supply.

If wages and prices are not fully flexible, then Keynes's view that demand could fall short of production is more likely to hold true. We've seen that over short periods of time, wages and prices, indeed, are not fully flexible, so Keynes's insights are important. However, over longer periods of time, wages and prices do adjust and the insights of the classical model are restored.

To help clarify the conditions under which the economy will return to full employment in the long run on its own, Patinkin and Modigliani developed the adjustment-process model we used in this chapter. They highlighted many of the key points we emphasized, including the speed of the adjustment process and possible pitfalls, such as liquidity traps.

In the chapter-opening story, we noted that some economists advocate aggressive government action during recessions, while others feel that such actions may impede recovery. We now have a better understanding of why economists differ on these issues. Economists who feel the adjustment process is slow typically recommend activist policies, while those who believe that adjustment is more rapid will tend to be skeptical of activist policies. In addition, economists will differ in their judgments about the ability of the government to act quickly and make effective decisions. That will also determine whether they believe policy will make the economy perform better or worse.

SUMMARY

This chapter explained how the economy makes the transition from the short run to the long run. It also highlighted why monetary and fiscal policies have different effects in the short run and in the long run. Understanding the distinction between the short run and the long run is critical to evaluating economic policy. Here are the main points to remember from this chapter:

1. *The short run in macroeconomics* refers to the period of time in which prices do not change very much. The *long run in macroeconomics* is the period over which prices have time to change in response to economic changes.
2. When output exceeds full employment, wages and prices rise faster than their past trends. If output is less than full employment, wages and prices fall relative to past trends.
3. The price changes that occur when the economy is away from full employment push the economy back to full employment. Economists disagree on the length of time this adjustment process takes; estimates range from less than two years to six years.
4. Economic policies are most effective when the adjustment process is slow. However, to improve their chances of being reelected, politicians can take advantage of the difference between the short-run and long-run effects of economic policies.
5. If the economy is operating below full employment, falling wages and prices will reduce money demand and lower interest rates. The fall in interest rates will stimulate investment and lead the economy back to full employment.
6. The reverse occurs when output exceeds full employment. Increases in wages and prices will increase money demand and interest rates. As investment spending falls, the economy returns to full employment.
7. In the long run, increases in the supply of money are neutral. That is, increases in the money supply do not affect real interest rates, investment, or output. This characteristic is known as the *long-run neutrality of money*.
8. Increases in government spending will raise real interest rates and *crowd out* investment in the long run. Decreases in government spending will lower real interest rates and crowd in investment in the long run.
9. The adjustment model in this chapter helps us to understand the debate between Keynes and the classical economists.

KEY TERMS

aggregate demand curve, p. 314
liquidity trap, p. 317
long-run aggregate supply curve, p. 314
long run in macroeconomics, p. 312
long-run neutrality of money, p. 322
political business cycle, p. 318
short-run aggregate supply curve, p. 314
short run in macroeconomics, p. 312
wage–price spiral, p. 313

EXERCISES

All problems are assignable in MyEconLab.

15.1 Linking the Short Run and the Long Run

1.1 Wages and prices will increase when actual output exceeds potential. __________ (True/False)

1.2 The short run in macroeconomics is the time period over which __________ do not adjust to economic conditions.

1.3 According to the logic of the wage–price spiral, an increase in wages leads to a(n) __________ in __________, which in turn leads to a(n) __________ in __________.

1.4 In the long run, the level of GDP is determined by supply factors. __________ (True/False)

1.5 **Cost of Living Adjustments and the Wage–Price Spiral.** Suppose organized labor has successfully bargained for cost of living increases for its workers. That is, when prices rise—as measured by the CPI—wages are automatically adjusted by the same percentage. Would this make the economy more or less likely to experience a wage–price spiral?

1.6 **Unemployment and Wage Price Changes.** If the natural rate of unemployment is 6 percent and the actual rate of unemployment is 7 percent, how will wages and prices change? Suppose the natural rate was 7 percent?

15.2 How Wage and Price Changes Move the Economy Naturally Back to Full Employment

2.1 The short-run aggregate supply curve will move __________ if the economy's actual output is above full-employment output.

2.2 If the adjustment process works slowly, then economic policy is less necessary. __________ (True/False)

2.3 A political business cycle may occur because policymakers are willing to trade off a current reduction in unemployment for future increases in inflation. __________ (True/False)

2.4 **Supply Shocks and Policy Choices.** Recall that supply shocks are sudden increases in the prices of commodities such as oil or food. These shocks shift the short-run aggregate supply curve. For example, the increase in oil prices in 2006 will shift the short-run aggregate supply curve upward, because firms' costs have risen and firms must charge higher prices to avoid losing money.

a. Suppose the economy is operating at full employment and foreign countries raise the world price of oil. Assuming policymakers do not take any action, describe what will happen to prices and output in the short run and in the long run. Show these situations graphically.

b. Suppose the Federal Reserve decided it wanted to offset any adverse effects on output due to a supply shock. What actions could it take? What would happen to the price level if the Fed used monetary policy to fight unemployment in this situation?

c. Economists say supply shocks create a dilemma for the Federal Reserve that shocks to demand (for example, from sudden increases in investment spending by optimistic firms) do not create. Using your answer to part (b) and the aggregate demand and aggregate supply graph, explain why economists say this.

2.5 **Foreign Firms Close Their Markets: Short-Run and Long-Run Effects.** Suppose the economy is at full employment and foreign firms close their markets and U.S. firms start to produce more for export. Everything else remains the same.

a. In the short run, what happens to GDP?

b. Assuming that exchange rates do not change, what happens to U.S. prices in the long run? How might this affect the export market?

2.6 **Stabilization Policy and the Speed of Adjustment.** Economists who believe the transition from the short run to the long run occurs rapidly do not generally favor using active stabilization policy. Use the aggregate demand and aggregate supply graphs to illustrate how active policy, with a rapid adjustment process, could destabilize the economy.

2.7 **Understanding the Liquidity Trap.** The adjustment process can run into problems during a liquidity trap when interest rates are driven close to zero and the economy remains below full employment. Both Japan in the 1990s and the United States during the 1930s and the first decade of this century are possible examples of liquidity traps. (Related to Application 1 on page 318.)

   a. Draw a money-demand curve and an investment schedule to illustrate this possibility.

   b. During the Great Depression in the United States, some interest rates dropped close to zero. Search the historical database at the Web site of the National Bureau of Economic Research (www.nber.org) to find out how low interest rates actually dropped and when they were at their lowest.

   c. Use the Web to find data on a variety of Japanese interest rates from 1985 through 2006. Over what period do you think low interest rates may have become a policy problem? You might wish to start with the Economagic Web site (http://www.economagic.com/bjap.htm).

2.8 **Changing Views of Liquidity Traps.** After he became Federal Reserve Chairman, Ben Bernanke no longer advocated a policy of increasing expectations of inflation in order to escape from a liquidity trap. What factors do you think might influence the Chairman of the Federal Reserve to disavow an inflationist policy? (Related to Application 1 on page 318.)

2.9 **Investigating Political Business Cycles.** Use the Web site for the Federal Reserve Bank of St. Louis (www.research.stlouisfed.org/fred2) to find historical data on unemployment rates. Use these data to explore whether unemployment behaves differently in the first two years of a presidential term than in the final two years. Are there any systematic differences in unemployment between Democratic and Republican presidencies? (Related to Application 2 on page 323.)

15.3 Understanding the Economics of the Adjustment Process

3.1 As the price level increases, the demand for money __________ and interest rates __________.

3.2 If output is above below employment, we expect wages and prices to rise, money demand to increase, and interest rates to fall. __________ (True/False)

3.3 An increase in the money supply will have no effect on the real rate of interest in the long run. (True/False)

3.4 A decrease in government spending will __________ interest rates in the long run.

3.5 **Understanding Japanese Fiscal Policy.** Japan's finance ministry agreed to income tax cuts to combat a decade-long recession in the 1990s—but only if national sales taxes were increased several years later.

   a. What would you expect to be the short-run effect of the income tax cuts? Draw a graph to show this effect.

   b. What would you expect to be the long-run effect of the income tax cuts? Draw a graph to show this effect.

   c. Why did the Finance Ministry require an increase in sales taxes several years later?

   d. What was the Finance Ministry trying to prevent?

3.6 **Can Monetary Policy Prevent Crowding Out?** Explain what is wrong with this quote: "In the long run, we do not have to worry about increased government spending causing crowding out, because the Fed can always increase the money supply to lower interest rates to prevent this."

3.7 **Increasing Health Spending and Economic Growth.** Analyze how the following factors associated with increased spending on health care might affect economic growth. (Related to Application 3 on page 328.)

   a. With increased longevity, workers will need to postpone their retirement in order to save more for old age.

   b. Households may cut down on purchases of consumer durables to spend more on health.

   c. Households may reduce their savings in order to spend more on health care.

   d. New and expensive technologies allow people to live longer.

3.8 **Real Rates, Nominal Rates, and Inflation.** Milton Friedman emphasized that, in the long run, increases in the money growth rate (which cause higher inflation) would raise interest rates, not lower them. Explain why this is true in the long run, when the economy returns to full employment. Why might this not be true in the short run? Use the concepts of real and nominal rates in your answers.

3.9 **Elderly Relying on Income from Their Past Savings.** Explain why elderly people relying on income from their investments might want to have an increase in long run government spending for its effects on financial markets.

3.10 **Tax Increases and Crowding In.** Using an aggregate demand and aggregate supply graph, show how tax increases for consumers today will eventually lead to lower interest rates and crowd in investment spending in the long run.

15.4 Classical Economics in Historical Perspective

4.1 Professors Don __________ and Franco __________ developed the adjustment-process model used in this chapter.

4.2 Keynes's objection to Say's law was that it is possible for demand to create its own supply. __________ (True/False)

4.3 Today, some economists might claim that Say's law holds in the __________ run, but not the __________ run.

4.4 David Ricardo and John Stuart Mill are known as __________ economists.

4.5 **Milton Friedman and the Great Depression.** Economist Milton Friedman was an opponent to activist stabilization policy. His views on economic policy were greatly influenced by his interpretation of the Great Depression. Search the Web for discussions of Friedman's views on the Great Depression and discuss how they may have affected his attitudes toward stabilization policy. You may want to start with the entry at http://www.econlib.org/library/Enc/bios/Friedman.html (accessed April 21, 2010).

CHAPTER 16

The Dynamics of Inflation and Unemployment

As the financial crisis spread in 2008, central banks around the world increased the supply of money and liquidity, and governments borrowed extensively and incurred increasing amounts of government debt.

Increases in the supply of money and debt are often precursors for inflation. Although a slack economy limited any inflationary pressures and, in some cases, led to mild deflation, there were concerns by some that inflation would inevitably follow in the not-too-distant future.

One traditional indicator of a fear of inflation was the price of gold. From 2005 to 2012, the price of an ounce of gold rose from approximately $400 to $1600, an increase by a factor of three! This was precisely during the same period when stock markets worldwide first rose and then sharply fell. Commercials for investing in gold products appeared on cable television and radio stations throughout the country.

Gold, however, is a very risky investment and not suitable for most people. An alternative strategy some investors use is to buy Treasury Inflation Protected Securities—or TIPS. These securities provide investors with guaranteed purchasing power, but typically with a lower return. Buying insurance against inflation is costly—it is much better if central banks do not let inflation develop in the first place.

LEARNING OBJECTIVES

- Describe how an economy at full employment with inflation differs from one without inflation.
- Explain the relationship between inflation and unemployment in the short run and long run.
- Discuss why increasing the credibility of a central bank can reduce inflation.
- Define the velocity of money.
- Identify the origins and causes of hyperinflation.

MyEconLab

MyEconLab helps you master each objective and study more efficiently.

In this chapter, we integrate two themes we've been stressing separately:

- In the short run, changes in money growth affect real output and real GDP.
- In the long run, the rate of money growth determines the rate of inflation, not real GDP.

Economic policy debates often concern inflation and unemployment because they affect us all so directly. We will look at the relationships between inflation and unemployment, examining macroeconomic developments in the United States in the last several decades. We also explore why heads of central banks typically appear to be strong enemies of inflation.

Although the United States had serious difficulties fighting inflation in the 1970s and 1980s, other countries have, at times, had much more severe problems with inflation. In this chapter, we'll study the origins of extremely high inflationary periods and their links to government budget deficits.

16.1 Money Growth, Inflation, and Interest Rates

An economy can, in principle, produce at full employment with any inflation rate. No "magic" inflation rate is necessary to sustain full employment. To understand this point, consider the long run when the economy operates at full employment. As we have seen, in the long run, money is neutral. If the Federal Reserve increases the money supply at 5 percent a year, annual inflation will be 5 percent. That is, prices in the economy will rise by 5 percent a year.

Inflation in a Steady State

nominal wages
Wages expressed in current dollars.

real wage
The wage rate paid to employees adjusted for changes in the price level.

money illusion
Confusion of real and nominal magnitudes.

expectations of inflation
The beliefs held by the public about the likely path of inflation in the future.

Let's think about how this economy looks in this "steady state" of constant inflation. The **nominal wages**—wages in dollars—of workers are all rising at 5 percent a year. However, because prices are also rising at 5 percent a year, **real wages**—wages adjusted for changes in purchasing power—remain constant.

Some workers may feel cheated by the inflation. They might believe that without inflation, they would experience real-wage increases, because their nominal wages are rising 5 percent a year. Unfortunately, these workers are wrong. They suffer from what economists call **money illusion**, a confusion of real and nominal magnitudes. Here's the source of the illusion: Because real wages are constant, the only reason nominal wages are rising by 5 percent a year is the general 5 percent inflation. If there were no inflation, nominal wages would not increase at all.

After a time, everyone in the economy would begin to expect the 5 percent annual inflation that had occurred in the past to continue in the future. Economists call this belief **expectations of inflation**. People's expectations of inflation affect all aspects of economic life. For example, in the steady-state economy we just described, automobile producers will expect to increase the price of their products by 5 percent every year. They will also expect their costs—of labor and steel, for example—to increase by 5 percent a year. Workers will begin to believe the 5 percent increase in their wages will be matched by a 5 percent increase in the prices of the goods they buy. Continued inflation becomes the normal state of affairs, and people build it into their daily decision making. For example, they expect the price of a car to be 5 percent higher next year and will take that into consideration when they go shopping for a new car.

INFLATION EXPECTATIONS AND INTEREST RATES When the public expects inflation, real and nominal rates of interest will differ because we need to account for inflation in calculating the real return from lending and borrowing. Recall that the nominal interest rate—the rate quoted in the market—is equal to the real rate of interest plus the expected inflation rate. If the real rate of interest is 2 percent and inflation is 5 percent a year, the nominal interest rate will be 7 percent. Although lenders receive 7 percent a year on their loans, their real return after inflation is just 2 percent.

In an earlier chapter you saw that in the long run, the *real* rate of interest does not depend on monetary policy because money is neutral. That is, even though the money supply may be higher or lower, the price level will be higher or lower. However, *nominal* rates of interest do depend on monetary policy, because whether the Fed expands or contracts the money supply affects the rate of inflation, which in the long run is determined by the growth of the money supply. As Nobel Laureate Milton Friedman pointed out, countries with higher money growth typically have higher nominal interest rates than countries with lower money growth rates because they have higher inflation. If Country A and Country B have the same real rate of interest, but Country A has a higher inflation rate, Country A will also have a higher nominal interest rate.

INFLATION EXPECTATIONS AND MONEY DEMAND Money demand—the amount of money people want to hold—will also be affected by expectations about inflation. If people expect 5 percent inflation a year, then their demand for money will also increase by 5 percent a year. The reason, of course, is that people know everything will cost 5 percent more, so they'll need more money in their pockets to pay for the same goods and services. This is an example of the real-nominal principle.

REAL-NOMINAL PRINCIPLE

What matters to people is the real value of money or income—its purchasing power—not the face value of money or income.

As long as the Fed allows the supply of money to increase by 5 percent—the same amount as inflation—the demand for money and its supply will both grow at the same rate. Because money demand and supply are both growing at the same rate, real interest rates and nominal interest rates will not change.

How Changes in the Growth Rate of Money Affect the Steady State

If the growth rate of money changes, however, there will be short-run effects on real interest rates. To continue with our example, suppose the public expects 5 percent annual inflation and both the money supply and money demand grow at 5 percent a year. Now suppose the Fed suddenly decreases the annual growth rate of money to 4 percent, while the public continues to expect 5 percent annual inflation. Because money demand grows at 5 percent but the money supply grows at only 4 percent, growth in the demand for money will exceed growth in the supply of money. The result will be an increase in both real interest rates and nominal interest rates.

We have seen that higher real rates of interest will reduce investment spending by firms and reduce consumer durable goods spending by households. With reduced firm and consumer demand for goods and services, real GDP will fall and unemployment will rise. The reduction in the growth rate of the money supply is contractionary. In the long run, however, output will return to full employment through the adjustment process described in prior chapters. The economy will eventually adjust to the lower rate of money growth, and inflation will eventually fall from 5 percent to 4 percent per year to match it. In the long run, the *real* rate of interest will eventually fall and return to its previous value. *Nominal* interest rates, which reflect expectations of ongoing inflation, will be 1 percent lower, because inflation has fallen from 5 percent to 4 percent per year. Table 16.1 depicts the long-run relationships between money growth, inflation, increases in money demand, and real and nominal interest rates in this example.

TABLE 16.1 Money, Inflation, and Interest Rates in a Steady-State Economy

Money Growth Rate	Inflation	Growth in Money Demand	Real Interest Rate	Nominal Interest
4%	4%	4%	2%	6%
5%	5%	5%	2%	7%

This basic pattern fits U.S. history in the late 1970s and early 1980s. At that time, the Federal Reserve sharply decreased the growth rate of the money supply, so interest rates rose temporarily. By 1981, interest rates on three-month Treasury bills rose to over 14 percent from 7 percent in 1978. The economy went into a severe recession, with unemployment exceeding 10 percent. By the mid-1980s, however, the economy returned to full employment with lower interest rates and lower inflation rates. By 1986, Treasury bill rates were below 6 percent.

This is another example in which the long-run effects of policy actions differ from their short-run effects. In the short run, a policy of tight money leads to slower money growth, higher interest rates, and lower output. In the long run, reduced money growth results in lower interest rates, lower inflation, and no effect on the level of output.

application 1

SHIFTS IN THE NATURAL RATE OF UNEMPLOYMENT

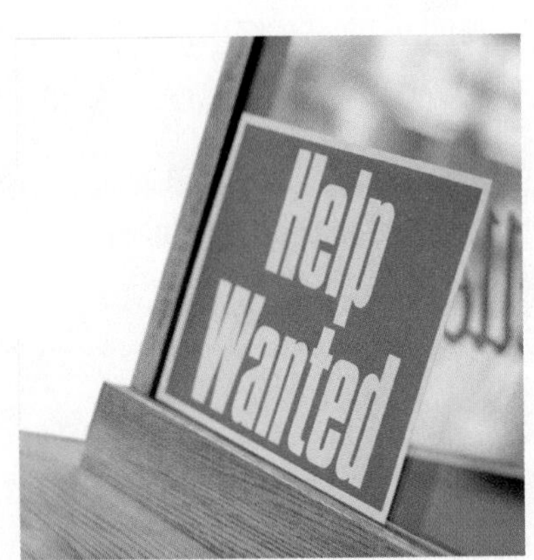

APPLYING THE CONCEPTS #1: How can data on vacancies and unemployment be used to measure shifts in the natural rate?

Economists believe that the natural rate of unemployment changes over time, although they often have difficulty pinning down an exact estimate. Policymakers need to have an accurate assessment of the natural rate to avoid any unnecessary unemployment or prevent inflation from emerging. But how can we estimate changes in the natural rate?

One way to estimate the shifts in the natural rate of unemployment is to look at the relationships between job vacancies and unemployment. Normally, the higher the unemployment rate, the fewer job vacancies there will be. This relationship is known as the Beveridge curve. But if the labor market matches individuals with jobs more efficiently, resulting in a decline in the natural rate of unemployment—for example, through the use of Internet searches or new technology—there will be fewer job vacancies corresponding to any level of unemployment. Using a variety of vacancy measures, economist William Dickens found that shifts in the relationship between vacancies and unemployment allowed him to make new estimates of the natural rate. He found that the natural rate was approximately 5 percent in the mid-1960s, but then rose in the late 1960s and peaked near 7 percent in the late 1970s and early 1980s. The natural rate began to drift down in the late 1980s and through the 1990s, again reaching the 5 percent level in 2000. It has since remained at this level. **Related to Exercise 2.8.**

SOURCE: Based on William Dickens, "A New Approach to Estimating the Natural Rate of Unemployment," July 2009, paper available at http://www.brookings.edu/papers/2009/07_unemployment_dickens.aspx (Accessed June 2012).

 16.2 Understanding the Expectations Phillips Curve: The Relationship between Unemployment and Inflation

In the late 1950s, A. W. Phillips was studying British economic data and noticed that lower unemployment was associated with higher inflation. That is, the inflation rate rises when economic activity booms and unemployment is low. Phillips also noticed that the inflation rate falls when the economy is in a recession and unemployment is high. This inverse relationship between unemployment and inflation became known as the *Phillips curve*.

In the early 1960s, Nobel Laureates Paul Samuelson and Robert Solow found a similar relationship between unemployment and the inflation rate in the United States. However, these early studies examined periods when there was no significant underlying inflation, and they did not take into account people's expectations of inflation. The relationship between unemployment and inflation when we take into account expectations of inflation is known as the **expectations Phillips curve**.

expectations Phillips curve
The relationship between unemployment and inflation when taking into account expectations of inflation.

The expectations Phillips curve was introduced into the economics profession in the late 1960s by Edmund Phelps of Columbia University and Milton Friedman, then at the University of Chicago. The expectations Phillips curve included the notion that unemployment varies with *unanticipated inflation*. Friedman argued, for example, that when the inflation rate suddenly increases, it is likely that workers did not fully anticipate some of this sudden increase. Actual inflation will then exceed expected inflation. Workers will see their nominal wages increase, but because they do not fully expect this sudden inflation, they will think their real wages have risen. With higher perceived real wages being offered, potential workers will be inclined to accept the jobs firms offer them. As a result, unemployment will fall below the natural rate. That's why we often see an association between increases in the inflation rate and a decrease in the unemployment rate.

After workers recognize that the inflation rate is higher, though, they will incorporate this higher inflation rate into their expectations of inflation. They will no longer confuse the higher nominal wages firms offer with higher real wages. Unemployment will then return to its natural rate. So there is no permanent relationship between the level of unemployment and the level of inflation.

Similarly, if the inflation rate falls, workers may not expect some of this fall. Because inflation is less than expected, workers will believe their real wages aren't rising as fast as they actually are. With lower perceived real wages being offered, potential workers will be less inclined to accept the jobs firms offer them. The unemployment rate will increase as a result. However, once they recognize that inflation is lower than they realized, and that the wages firms offered them really aren't that low, workers will be more inclined to accept work. Unemployment will then again return to the natural rate. So a decrease in the inflation rate is likely to be associated with temporary increases in unemployment.

Later in this chapter we'll see an example of this relationship between inflation and unemployment in the late 1980s and early 1990s. A "disconnect" between what people expect and what ultimately occurs can adversely affect the economy, as we'll see next. Table 16.2 summarizes the key points about the expectations Phillips curve.

TABLE 16.2 Expectations and Business Fluctuations

When the economy experiences a ...	Unemployment is ...	Inflation is ...
boom	below the natural rate.	higher than expected.
recession	above the natural rate.	lower than expected.

Are the Public's Expectations about Inflation Rational?

As we just saw, expectations about inflation affect actual inflation because workers and firms build their inflation forecasts into their wage- and price-setting decisions. Mistakes in predicting inflation therefore have consequences. But *how* do workers and firms form inflation expectations in the first place? And, second, *when* do they form their inflation expectations?

Two broad classes of theories attempt to explain how the public forms its expectations of inflation. Some economists and psychologists, including Nobel Laureate Herbert Simon, believe the public uses simple *rules of thumb* to predict future inflation. One such rule of thumb might be to assume next year's inflation rate will be the same as this year's. According to this view, it is unreasonable to expect too much sophistication from the public because of the complexity of the economy and the difficulty of forecasting it.

In the 1970s, a group of economists led by Nobel Laureate Robert E. Lucas, Jr., from the University of Chicago developed an alternative view, called the theory of **rational expectations**. The rational expectations theory portrayed workers and firms as much more sophisticated, basing their expectations on all the information available to them. According to the theory, the public, on average, anticipates the future correctly. Although the public may make mistakes in specific instances, on average, people's expectations are rational or correct.

rational expectations
The economic theory that analyzes how the public forms expectations in such a manner that, on average, it forecasts the future correctly.

The two approaches—rules of thumb versus rational expectations—tend to deliver similar predictions when the economy is very stable and there are no major policy changes. However, when there are major policy changes—for example, when the government introduces new policies to fight inflation or reduce federal deficits—the two approaches predict different outcomes. The rational expectations theory predicts the public will anticipate the consequences of these policies and change its expectations about inflation accordingly; the rule-of-thumb theory says it won't. Which view is correct? The truth lies somewhere in the middle. On the one hand, sophisticated firms, such as Microsoft and Walmart, do appear to take advantage of available information. On the other hand, a considerable amount of inertia and nonrationality appears to enter into the general public's decision-making process. And sometimes the public may be rational about small signals but miss the big picture. For example, during the stock-market boom in the late 1990s, investors may have had an accurate assessment of *which* tech stocks were relatively more promising but failed to recognize that *all* tech stocks were overvalued.

The other major issue is the question of *when* inflation expectations are formed. As we discussed in Chapter 9, both workers and firms often make explicit long-term contracts or enter into implicit long-term agreements. With long-term contracts, workers and firms must make forecasts far into the future. For example, if a union is negotiating wages for three years, it will need to forecast inflation three years into the future and negotiate current and future wages today based on that forecast. Making decisions this far in advance is clearly very difficult, so it is understandable that mistakes can occur. Indeed, workers and firms can be quite rational but still make mistakes when predicting inflation simply because of the long time frames involved. Wage contracts set in the early 1980s, for example, would have "rationally" anticipated continued high inflation, although changes in monetary policy brought inflation below what was predicted.

U.S. Inflation and Unemployment in the 1980s

We can use the expectations Phillips curve to help understand the patterns of inflation and unemployment that occurred in the 1980s. For the sake of this discussion, we will assume workers and firms follow relatively simple rules of thumb and that sudden increases in inflation are partly unanticipated and thus accompanied by lower unemployment. Conversely, sudden decreases in inflation are accompanied by temporarily higher unemployment.

When President Jimmy Carter took office at the beginning of 1977, the inflation rate was approximately 6.5 percent per year and unemployment exceeded 7 percent of the labor force. By 1980, inflation had risen to 9.4 percent. There were two reasons for this increase. First, utilizing expansionary policy, the Carter administration had steadily reduced unemployment to under 6 percent by 1979. Because the natural rate of unemployment was close to 6 percent of the labor force at that time, reducing unemployment below this rate led to an increase in the annual inflation rate. Second, there was an oil shock in 1979, which also contributed to higher inflation.

Fears of even higher inflation led President Carter to appoint a well-known inflation fighter, Paul Volcker, as chairman of the Federal Reserve. Volcker immediately began to institute a tight money policy, and interest rates rose sharply by 1980. When President Ronald Reagan took office, he supported Volcker's policy. Eventually, high real-interest rates took their toll, and unemployment rose to over 10 percent by 1983. As actual unemployment exceeded the natural rate of unemployment, the inflation rate fell, just as the expectations Phillips curve predicted. By 1986, the inflation rate fell to approximately 2.7 percent per year with unemployment at 7 percent of the labor force. The severe recession had done its job in reducing the inflation rate.

However, as we can see in Figure 16.1, after 1986 the unemployment rate began to fall again, from about 7 percent to a little over 6 percent in 1987. Notice that as actual unemployment fell below the natural rate (which, at that time, was about 6.5 percent), inflation began to rise, increasing from about 2.75 to 3 percent. By 1989, as unemployment continued to fall, annual inflation had risen to 4.5 percent, and the Fed then raised interest rates to combat it. The Fed's action reduced output and increased unemployment to over 7 percent. Notice that by 1992, inflation had fallen dramatically because unemployment exceeded the natural rate.

By the time President George H. W. Bush took office in 1989, actual unemployment was below the natural rate of unemployment, inflation had been rising, and the Fed started slowing down the economy. The rate of inflation was eventually reduced, but the recovery back to full employment in 1992–1993 came too late in Bush's term for the voters to fully appreciate, and he lost his bid for reelection.

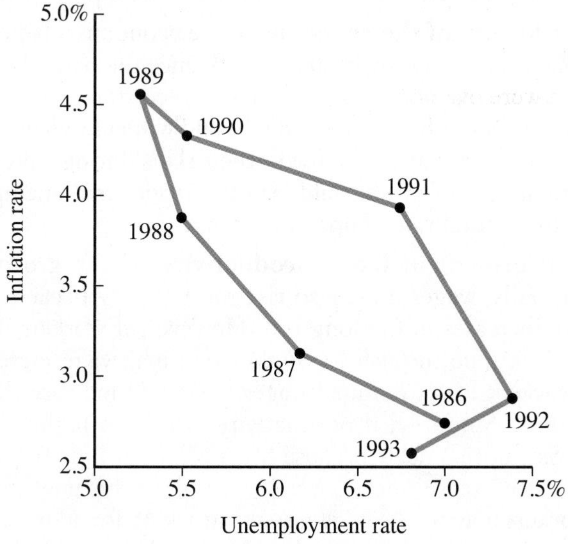

▲ FIGURE 16.1

The Dynamics of Inflation and Unemployment, 1986–1993

Inflation rose and the unemployment rate fell below the natural rate. Inflation later fell as unemployment exceeded the natural rate.

SOURCE: Economic Report of the President (Washington, D.C.: U.S. Government Printing Office, yearly).

Shifts in the Natural Rate of Unemployment in the 1990s

Up to this point, our analysis assumes that the natural rate of unemployment is a constant—say, for example, 5 percent of the labor force. If actual unemployment falls below this constant rate (the economy is hot, in other words), inflation will tend to increase. Similarly, if the actual unemployment exceeds 5 percent (the economy is sluggish), inflation will fall.

But the natural rate of unemployment can shift over time. At the beginning of the 1980s in the United States, most economists believed that the natural rate of unemployment was between 6 or 7 percent. By the late 1990s, many economists had begun to believe the natural rate of unemployment had fallen to about 5 percent. What can shift the natural rate of unemployment? Economists have identified a number of factors:

- **Demographics.** The composition of the workforce can change, decreasing the natural rate. For example, we know teenagers have higher unemployment rates than adults. If changes in population lead to a lower percentage of teenagers in the labor force, we would expect the natural rate of unemployment to decrease. In the 1990s, the share of teenagers in the labor force fell. This change in demographics appears to have been what caused the natural rate of unemployment to decline in the United States.
- **Institutional changes.** Changes in laws, regulations, and economic institutions can influence the natural rate of unemployment. Suppose the government shortens the length of time unemployed workers can collect benefits. We would then expect the unemployed to return to work more rapidly and the natural rate of unemployment to fall. Some economists have argued that the rise of temporary employment agencies in the United States during the 1990s made the labor market more efficient. Workers were matched more quickly with jobs, and this contributed to the decline of the natural rate. In Europe, a very different set of institutional factors had the opposite result: Generous benefits for the unemployed increased the time they spent unemployed. Restrictions on employers making it difficult to fire workers led them to hire fewer people in the first place. Both these factors raised the natural rate of employment.
- **The recent history of the economy.** Some economists believe the economic performance of the economy itself may influence the natural rate of unemployment. Suppose the economy goes into a long recession. During that time, many young people may not be able to find jobs and will fail to develop a strong work ethic. Other workers may lose some of their skills during a prolonged period of unemployment. Both factors could lead to longer-term unemployment and an increase in the natural rate of unemployment.
- **Changes in growth of labor productivity.** If the growth rate in labor productivity falls, wages must also rise more slowly because they are tied to productivity increases in the long run. However, if workers don't realize this, they might continue to push for higher nominal wage increases and be less inclined to accept lower nominal wages. This will increase the natural rate of unemployment. Similarly, if productivity growth is higher than anticipated, wages will rise more quickly because firms will be willing to pay more to retain their workers and recruit new ones. As a result of this unexpected productivity growth, workers may not be as aggressive in asking for additional nominal wage increases because they are pleased with what they are already getting. They will be more inclined to accept these wages, and this will effectively lower the natural rate of unemployment. Some economists believe this in fact happened in the late 1990s when productivity growth soared and the natural rate of unemployment temporarily fell. Actual unemployment fell to near 4 percent without any visible signs of increasing inflation. Of course, once workers in the economy understand that a shift in productivity growth has occurred, the natural rate will return to its original value, closer to, say, 5 percent.

application 2

INCREASED POLITICAL INDEPENDENCE FOR THE BANK OF ENGLAND LOWERED INFLATION EXPECTATIONS

APPLYING THE CONCEPTS #2: Can changes in the way central banks are governed affect inflation expectations?

On May 6, 1997, the then-chancellor of the exchequer in Great Britain, Gordon Brown, announced a major change in monetary policy. From that time forward, the Bank of England would be more independent from the government. Although the government would still retain the authority to set the overall goals for policy, the Bank of England would be free to pursue its policy goals without direct political control.

Mark Spiegel, an economist with the Federal Reserve Bank of San Francisco, studied how the British bond market reacted to the policy change. He compared the interest rate changes on two types of long-term bonds: British bonds that are automatically adjusted (or indexed) for inflation (such as TIPS in the United States) and bonds that are not. The difference between the two interest rates primarily reflects expectations of inflation. Thus, if the gap narrowed following the policy announcement, this would be evidence that the new policy reduced expectations of inflation. If it did not, the announced policy would have had no effect on inflation expectations.

After the announcement, the gap narrowed, and Spiegel concluded the announcement did, indeed, cause expectations about inflation to fall by about half a percentage. **Related to Exercise 3.5.**

SOURCE: Based on "British Central Bank Independence and Inflation Expectations," *Federal Reserve Bank of San Francisco Economic Letter*, November 28, 1997.

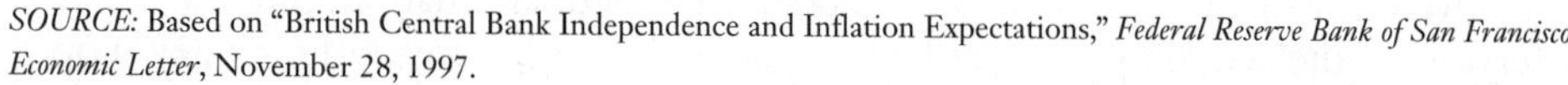

16.3 How the Credibility of a Nation's Central Bank Affects Inflation

Why are the heads of central banks, such as the chair of the Federal Reserve Board of Governors, typically very conservative and constantly warning about the dangers of inflation? The basic reason is that these monetary policymakers can influence expectations of inflation, and expectations of inflation will influence actual behavior of workers and firms. For example, when workers anticipate inflation, they will push for higher nominal wages. When firms anticipate inflation, they will set their prices accordingly. If policymakers are not careful in the way they respond to expectations of inflation, they can actually make it difficult for a society to fight inflation.

Consider an example. A large union is negotiating wages for workers in the auto and steel industries. If the union negotiates a very high nominal wage, other unions will likely follow, negotiating for and winning higher wages. Prices of autos and steel will inevitably rise as a result, and the Fed will begin to see higher inflation emerge. Suppose the Fed has been keeping the money supply constant. What are its options?

We depict the Fed's dilemma in Figure 16.2. By setting a higher nominal wage, the union shifts the aggregate supply curve from AS_0 to AS_1. The Fed then has a choice:

- Keep the money supply and aggregate demand at AD_0. The economy will initially fall into a recession.
- Increase the money supply and raise aggregate demand from AD_0 to AD_1. This will keep the economy at full employment but lead to higher prices.

The actions of the union will depend on what its leaders expect the Fed to do. On the one hand, if they believe the Fed will not increase aggregate demand, their actions will trigger a recession. Union leaders know this and might be reluctant to negotiate a high

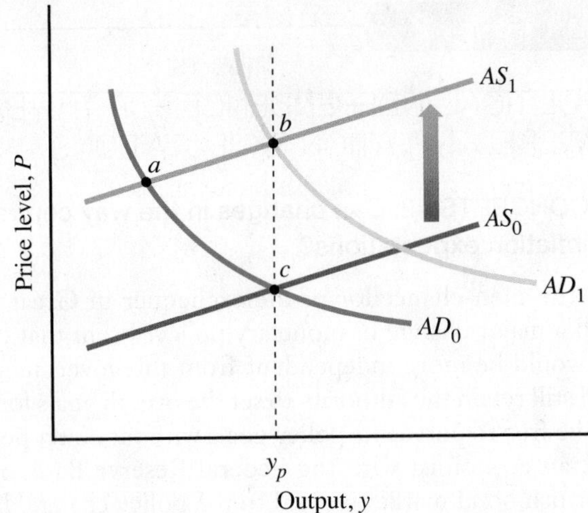

▶ **FIGURE 16.2**
Choices of the Fed: Recession or Inflation
If workers push up their nominal wages, the aggregate supply curve will shift from AS_0 to AS_1. If the Fed keeps aggregate demand constant at AD_0, a recession will occur at point *a*, and the economy will eventually return to full employment at point *c*. If the Fed increases aggregate demand, the economy remains at full employment at *b*, but with a higher price level.

wage because of it. If they don't negotiate an increase in nominal wages, the economy will remain at full employment and there will be no increase in prices. On the other hand, if union leaders believe the Fed will increase aggregate demand, they have nothing to lose and will push for higher nominal wages. The result will be higher prices in the economy.

As this example illustrates, expectations about the Fed's determination to fight inflation will affect behavior in the private sector. If the Fed is credible in its desire to fight inflation, it can deter the private sector from taking aggressive actions that drive up prices. This is the reason the heads of central banks are conservative, preferring to risk increasing unemployment rather than inflation. For example, having a conservative chair of the Fed, someone who strongly detests inflation, sends a signal to everyone in the economy that the Fed will be unlikely to increase the money supply, regardless of what actions are taken in the private sector.

After experiencing relatively high average inflation from 1955 to 1988, New Zealand took a different approach to ensure the credibility of its central bank. Since 1989, the central bank has been operating under a law that specifies its only goal is to attempt to maintain stable prices, which, in practice, requires it to keep inflation between 0 and 2 percent a year. This policy sharply limits the central bank's ability to stabilize real GDP, but it does signal to the private sector that the central bank will not be increasing the money supply, regardless of the actions taken by wage setters or unions.

Our example suggests that with a credible central bank, a country can have lower inflation without experiencing extra unemployment. Some political scientists and economists have suggested that central banks that have true independence from the rest of the government, and are therefore less subject to political influence, will be more credible in their commitment to fighting inflation.

There is evidence to support this conjecture. Figure 16.3 plots an index of central bank independence against average inflation rates from 1980 to 1989 for 10 countries. The points appear to lie along a downward-sloping line, meaning more independence is associated with lower inflation. Germany had the highest index of central bank independence and the lowest inflation rate in this group. Another piece of evidence that credible banks can lower inflation safely is provided by the changes that occurred in the United Kingdom in the late 1990s.

As our discussion illustrates, how a central bank influences expectations is important for understanding the behavior of prices and output in an economy. Understanding how the private sector forms its inflation expectations in the first place is also important. Economists have used the theory of rational expectations we discussed earlier to explain the credibility of central banks. In our example, the theory of rational expectations implies the union will, on average, anticipate whether the Fed will expand the money supply in the face of wage increases. A credible Fed will tend to deter wage increases by not expanding the money supply. Many economists believed Fed Chairman Alan Greenspan was very credible in his determination to fight inflation. This in itself helped reduce inflation during the 1990s. People expected that Greenspan would refuse to set out the "punch bowl" of money (see Chapter 15), and they were right.

But suppose someone does *not* believe the central bank will control inflation. Does that person have any recourse? In the United States and some other countries, he or she does. As we mentioned in the chapter-opening story, the U.S. government now sells bonds—TIPS—that protect an investor from inflation. Investors can protect themselves from unexpected inflation by buying TIPS.

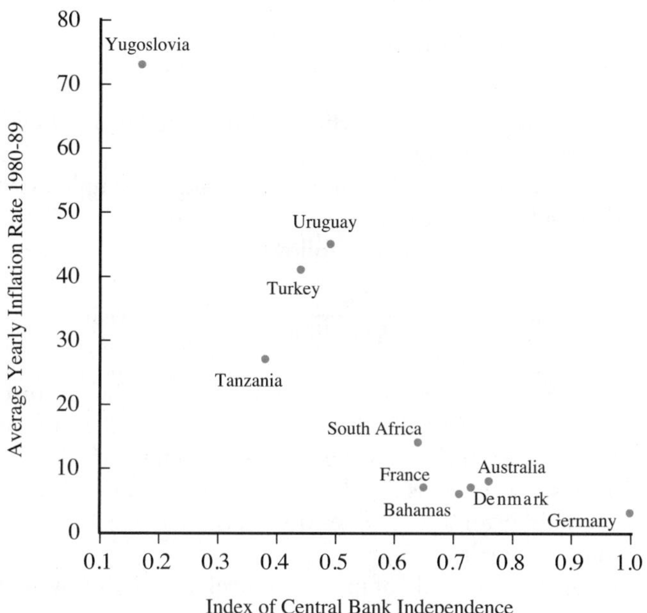

◄ **FIGURE 16.3**
How Central Bank Independence Affects Inflation
Countries in which central banks are more independent from the rest of the government have, on average, lower inflation rates.
SOURCE: Based on selected data in Table 5 of "Measuring the Independence of Central Banks and Its Effect on Policy Outcomes," Alex Cukierman, Steven Webb, and Bilin Neyapti, *The World Bank Economic Review*, 6:3, 353–398.

application 3

THE ENDS OF HYPERINFLATIONS

APPLYING THE CONCEPTS #3: Why do hyperinflations end suddenly?

In a classic study of four major hyperinflations, Nobel Laureate Thomas J. Sargent noticed that they ended rather quickly and the ends all followed similar patterns. Sargent studied the hyperinflations after World War I in Germany, Austria, Hungary, and Poland, some of the most dramatic in world history. In each case, the hyperinflation ended with the creation of a central bank and change in the way that governments were financed. No longer would the country rely on its central bank to finance its debt. Instead, debt was sold to private parties who would value the debt based on the ability of the government to meet interest and principal payments from taxes. Once the governments made these reforms, there was an abrupt end to the hyperinflations and an actual increase in the demand for money in real terms by the private sector.

Sargent used these historical episodes to emphasize how hyperinflations were ultimately caused by fiscal policy that was financed by money creation and not taxes. He also suggested that inflation could be tamed rather easily once fiscal reforms were made. While most economists agree with Sargent's views on the ends of hyperinflation, there is less agreement that moderate inflations can be ended simply by changing fiscal regimes and not enduring a recession. **Related to Exercises 5.5 and 5.6.**

SOURCE:. Thomas J. Sargent, "The Ends of Four Big Inflations," in *Inflation: Causes and Effects*, Robert E. Hall (ed.), Chicago: U of Chicago Press, 1982, pp. 41–98. Available at: http://www.nber.org/chapters/c1452.

16.4 Inflation and the Velocity of Money

Countries sometimes experience stunning inflation rates. For example, in 15 months from August 1922 to November 1923, the price level in Germany rose by a factor of 10 billion! To explain these extremely high inflation rates and their relationship to money growth, we now introduce a concept that is closely related to money demand: the *velocity of money*. The **velocity of money** is defined as the ratio of nominal GDP to the money supply:

velocity of money
The rate at which money turns over during the year. It is calculated as nominal GDP divided by the money supply.

$$\text{velocity of money} = \frac{\text{nominal GDP}}{\text{money supply}}$$

One useful way to think of velocity is that it is the number of times money must change hands, or turn over, in economic transactions during a given year for an economy to reach its GDP level. To understand this, consider a simple example. Suppose nominal GDP is $5 trillion per year and the money supply is $1 trillion. The velocity of money in this economy will then be as follows:

$$\text{velocity} = \frac{\$5 \text{ trillion per year}}{\$1 \text{ trillion}} = 5 \text{ per year}$$

In this economy, the $1 trillion money supply has to change hands, or turn over, five times a year to purchase the $5 trillion of nominal GDP. If the money supply turns over five times in one year, this means people are holding each dollar of money for 365 days/5, or 73 days. If velocity is very high, people turn money over very quickly on average and do not hold it for a long time. If velocity is low, people turn over money slowly and hold onto it longer.

To further understand the role of money and velocity, let's rewrite the definition of velocity as

$$\text{money supply} \times \text{velocity} = \text{nominal GDP}$$

or

$$M \times V = P \times y$$

where M is the money supply, V is the velocity of money, P is a price index for GDP, and y is real GDP. This equation is known as the equation of exchange, or the **quantity equation**. On the right side, $P \times y$ is nominal GDP. It is the product of the price index and real GDP. It also represents total nominal spending. On the left side, the money supply, M, is multiplied by V, the velocity, or turnover rate, of money.

quantity equation
The equation that links money, velocity, prices, and real output. In symbols, we have $M \times V = P \times y$.

As you can see, the quantity equation links the money supply and velocity to nominal GDP. If velocity is predictable, we can use the quantity equation and the supply of money to predict nominal GDP. But it's not quite that easy; the velocity of money does vary over time. Figure 16.4 plots the velocity of M2 (the measure of the money supply that includes currency, demand deposits, savings accounts, time deposits, and deposits in money market mutual funds) in the United States between 1959 and 2011. During this period, velocity reached a low of around 1.6 in the 1960s and a high of 2.1 in the late 1990s. In other words, the total amount of M2 held by the public turned over between 1.6 and 2.1 times a year for the U.S. economy to reach nominal GDP.

We can use the basic quantity equation to derive a closely related formula for understanding inflation in the long run:

$$\text{growth rate of money} + \text{growth rate of velocity}$$
$$= \text{growth rate of prices} + \text{growth rate of real output}$$

growth version of the quantity equation
An equation that links the growth rates of money, velocity, prices, and real output.

We will call this the **growth version of the quantity equation**. Here is how to use this formula: Suppose money growth is 10 percent a year, the growth of real

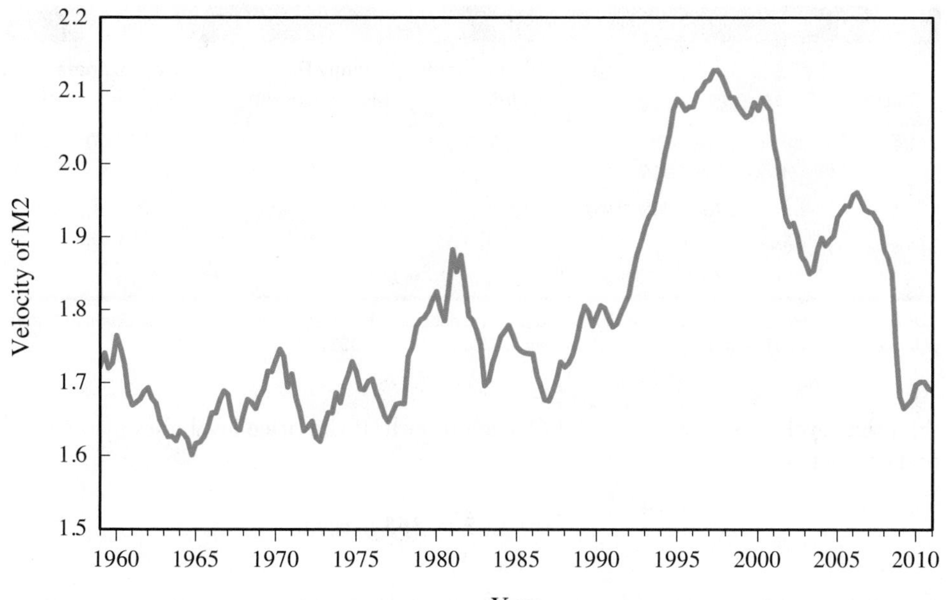

◄ FIGURE 16.4
The Velocity of M2, 1959–2011
SOURCE: Federal Reserve Bank of St. Louis.

MyEconLab Real-time data

output is 3 percent a year, and velocity has zero growth (it is constant). Then the rate of growth of prices—the inflation rate, in other words—is

$$10 \text{ percent} + 0 \text{ percent} = \text{growth rate of prices} + 3 \text{ percent}$$

$$7 \text{ percent} = \text{growth rate of prices (inflation)}$$

Inflation will be 7 percent a year. The formula allows for real economic growth and for growth in velocity. For example, if velocity grew during this period at the rate of 1 percent a year instead of zero, the annual inflation rate would be 8 percent $(10+1-3)$. Economists use this formula to provide quick estimates of the inflation rate.

As we've learned, there is a definite link between increases in the growth of money and the rate of inflation. Inflation was lowest in the 1950s, when money growth was lowest. It was also highest in the 1970s, when money growth was highest. The link is not perfect, because real GDP and velocity grew at different rates during these two decades. However, years of economic research have revealed that sustained increases in money growth will, indeed, lead to inflation.

The links between money growth and inflation are particularly dramatic when money growth is extremely high. But what leads countries to vast increases in their money supply? We'll explore that next.

16.5 Hyperinflation

The inflation rates observed in the United States in the last 40 years are insignificant compared to some of the inflation rates around the world throughout history. Economists call very high inflation rates—over 50 percent per month, which is approximately 13,000 percent per year—**hyperinflation**. One of the first hyperinflation studies was conducted by Phillip Cagan of Columbia University in the 1950s. Table 16.3 presents selected data from his study.

hyperinflation
An inflation rate exceeding 50 percent per month.

Greece, Hungary, and Russia are three countries that have experienced hyperinflation. According to the data in Table 16.3, for a period of one year, Greece had a monthly inflation rate of 365 percent. A monthly inflation rate of 365 percent means

TABLE 16.3 Hyperinflations and Velocity

Country	Dates	Monthly Rate of Inflation	Monthly Rate of Money Growth	Approximate Increase in Velocity
Greece	November 1943 to November 1944	365%	220%	14.00
Hungary	August 1945 to July 1946	19,800%	12,200%	333.00
Russia	December 1921 to January 1924	57%	49%	3.70

SOURCE: Adapted from Phillip Cagan, "The Monetary Dynamics of Hyperinflation," in *Studies in the Quantity Theory of Money*, ed. Milton Friedman (Chicago: University of Chicago Press, 1956), 26.

the price level rises by a factor of 4.65 each month. If the price level rises by 4.65, its percent increase is

$$\frac{4.65 - 1}{1} = 3.65 = 365 \text{ percent}$$

To get a sense of what a 365 percent inflation rate means, suppose we had inflation of this magnitude in the United States. At the beginning of the month, $1 could buy a large order of French fries. Because prices are rising by a factor of 4.65 each month, by the end of the month it would take $4.65 to buy the same order of French fries, and $1 by the end of the month would be worth only 21.5 cents (1/4.65 = 0.215, or 21.5 cents). After two months, a dollar would be worth only 4.6 cents (0.215 × 0.215 = 0.046). Suppose this inflation continues month after month. After one year, a dollar bill would be worth only 1 millionth of 1 cent! In hyperinflations, money doesn't hold its value very long.

In Hungary after World War II prices rose by 19,800 percent each month. The hyperinflation in Russia in the early 1920s seems moderate by comparison: Prices there rose by only 57 percent per month. However, hyperinflations have also occurred in recent times. Table 16.4 presents data on three hyperinflations during the 1980s—in Bolivia, Argentina, and Nicaragua, all averaging about 100 percent per month.

TABLE 16.4 Hyperinflations in the 1980s

Country	Year	Yearly Rate of Inflation	Monthly Rate of Inflation	Monthly Money Growth Rate
Bolivia	1985	1,152,200%	118%	91%
Argentina	1989	302,200	95	93
Nicaragua	1988	975,500	115	66

SOURCE: International Financial Statistics, International Monetary Fund.

On the basis of the quantity theory, we suspect these hyperinflations must have all been caused by money growth. You can see this in the data. For example, in Greece, the monthly inflation of 365 percent was accompanied by money growth of 220 percent. In Hungary, the monthly inflation of 19,800 percent was accompanied by money growth of 12,200 percent.

The value of money deteriorates sharply during hyperinflations and no longer serves as a good store of value. In these extreme circumstances, we would expect people wouldn't want to hold money very long but would immediately try to spend it. In other words, the velocity of money should increase sharply during hyperinflations. This is precisely what happens. The last column of Table 16.3 shows how velocity increases during hyperinflations. In the hyperinflation in Greece, velocity increased by a factor of 14. In the hyperinflation in Hungary, velocity increased by a factor of 333.

During hyperinflations, money doesn't facilitate exchange well. Because prices are changing so fast and unpredictably, there is typically massive confusion about the true value of commodities. Different stores may be raising prices at different rates, so the same commodities may sell for radically different prices. People spend all their time hunting for bargains and the lowest prices, a process that becomes very costly in human terms. Hyperinflation also means people have less time to produce goods and services. No country can easily live very long with a hyperinflation. The government must take swift measures to end a hyperinflation before it completely destroys the economy.

How Budget Deficits Lead to Hyperinflation

If the cause of hyperinflations is excessive money growth, why do governments allow the money supply to grow so fast, risking economic catastrophe? The answer lies in the way some governments finance their deficits—the gap between government spending and revenues.

A government must cover its deficit in some way. If a government wants to spend \$1,000 but is collecting only \$800 in taxes, where can it get the needed \$200? One option is to borrow the \$200 by selling government bonds—IOUs—to the public. In the future, the government will have to repay the \$200 in bonds plus the interest the public earns on them. Another alternative is to create \$200 of new money. All governments have the ability to run the printing presses and come up with \$200 in new currency. The revenue raised from money creation is called **seignorage**. In principle, governments can do a combination of both—selling bonds and printing money—as long as the deficit is covered:

seignorage
Revenue raised from money creation.

$$\text{government deficit} = \text{new borrowing from the public} + \text{new money created}$$

Now we are in a position to understand how hyperinflations originate. Consider Hungary after World War II. The country's economy was destroyed by the war, and its citizens were demanding government services. The government had limited ability to collect taxes because of the poor state of the economy, but it gave in to the demands from its citizens for spending at levels that far exceeded what it could collect. The result was a large deficit. Then the government faced a problem: How would it finance this large deficit? No individuals or governments wanted to buy bonds or IOUs from Hungary (lend it money) because the country's economy was in such bad shape that prospects for repayment in the near future were grim. Unable to borrow, Hungary resorted to printing money at a massive rate. The result was hyperinflation.

A more recent example of a devastating hyperinflation occurred in Zimbabwe, beginning in 2007. What were the causes of this hyperinflation?

To end hyperinflation, governments must eliminate their budget deficits by either increasing taxes, cutting spending, or both. This, of course, will cause some economic pain, but there is no other remedy. Once the deficit has been cut and the government stops printing money, the hyperinflation will end. Without money growth to feed it, hyperinflation will quickly die of starvation.

Economists who emphasize the role the supply of money plays in determining nominal income and inflation are called **monetarists**. The most famous monetarist was Milton Friedman, who studied complex versions of the quantity equation and explored the role of money in all aspects of economic life. Friedman had many influential students, such as Phillip Cagan, who is best known for his work on hyperinflations (see Table 16.3). Friedman and Cagan, along with other monetarist economists, pioneered research on the link between money, nominal income, and inflation. During the 1960s, little attention was being paid to the role of money in determining aggregate demand. The work of Friedman and other monetarists was extremely influential in changing the opinions of economic thinkers at that time. Moreover, the monetarists were also insistent that, in the long run, inflation was a monetary problem. Today, most economists agree with them that, in the long run, inflation is caused by growth in the money supply.

monetarists
Economists who emphasize the role that the supply of money plays in determining nominal income and inflation.

SUMMARY

In this chapter, we explored the role expectations of inflation play in the economy and how societies deal with inflation. Interest rates, as well as changes in wages and prices, both reflect expectations of inflation. These expectations depend on the past history of inflation and on expectations about central bank behavior. To reduce inflation, policymakers must increase actual unemployment above the natural rate of unemployment. We also looked at the ultimate causes of hyperinflations. Here are the key points to remember from this chapter:

1 In the long run, higher money growth leads to higher inflation and higher nominal interest rates.

2 A decrease in the growth rate of money will initially lead to higher real-interest rates and higher nominal-interest rates. In the long run, real rates return to their original level; nominal rates are permanently lower because of reduced inflation.

3 The rate of inflation increases when actual unemployment falls below the natural rate of unemployment; the rate of inflation decreases when actual unemployment exceeds the natural rate of unemployment. Economists explain this relationship using the *expectations Phillips curve*.

4 How the public forms expectations of inflation and the time frame in which it must form them are important factors in understanding the behavior of inflation and unemployment. Sometimes the public uses rules of thumb to form expectations; other times it may use *rational expectations*.

5 Monetary policymakers need to be cautious about the statements and pronouncements they make because what they say can influence inflation expectations. Conservative central bankers can dampen expectations of inflation.

6 The *quantity equation* and the *growth version of the quantity equation* show how money, velocity, and nominal income are related. The simple quantity equation is

$$M \times V = P \times y$$

7 Governments sometimes create new money to finance large portions of their budget deficits. Raising funds through printing money is known as *seignorage*. When governments do this excessively, the result is *hyperinflation*. Stopping hyperinflation requires closing the government deficit and reducing money creation.

KEY TERMS

expectations of inflation, p. 330
expectations Phillips curve, p. 333
growth version of the quantity equation, p. 340
hyperinflation, p. 341
monetarists, p. 343
money illusion, p. 330
nominal wages, p. 330
quantity equation, p. 340
rational expectations, p. 334
real wages, p. 330
seignorage, p. 343
velocity of money, p. 340

EXERCISES

All problems are assignable in MyEconLab; exercises that update with real-time data are marked with **.**

16.1 Money Growth, Inflation, and Interest Rates

1.1 The expected real rate of interest is the nominal interest rate plus the expected inflation rate. ________ (True/False)

1.2 Countries with higher rates of money growth have ________ interest rates.

1.3 If the growth rate of money increases from 3 to 5 percent, initially interest rates will ________.

1.4 A firm that expects higher profits from higher prices but does not recognize its costs are increasing is suffering from ________.

1.5 **Nominal and Real Interest Rates.** In Japan in the 1990s interest rates were near zero on government bonds. Some economists said that it was still possible to stimulate investment by creating negative real interest rates. If nominal rates could not fall below zero, explain how real interest rates could be made negative? (Hint: think about inflation.)

1.6 **Money Neutrality, Long Run Inflation, and the Natural Rate.** Explain carefully the relationship between the concept of monetary neutrality and the idea that the natural rate is independent of the long run inflation rate.

1.7 **Taxes, Inflation, and Interest Rates.** If a business borrows funds at 10 percent per year, the business has a 40 percent tax rate, and the annual inflation rate is 5 percent, what are the real after-tax costs of funds to the business? Similarly, if an investor receives a nominal return of 8 percent on a savings deposit, the tax rate is 30 percent, and the inflation rate is 6 percent, what is the after-tax rate of return?

1.8 **Examples of Money Illusion.** What do the following two quotes have in common?

a. "My wages are going up 5 percent a year. If only inflation weren't 5 percent a year, I would be rich."

b. "My bank is paying 10 percent a year, but the 8 percent inflation rate is just eating up all my real investment gains."

16.2 Understanding the Expectations Phillips Curve: The Relationship between Unemployment and Inflation

2.1 If inflation increases less than expected, the actual unemployment rate will be __________ (above/below) the natural rate.

2.2 Robert E. Lucas, Jr., explained business cycles with rational expectations. __________ (True/False)

2.3 The increase in the fraction of young people in the labor force that occurred when the baby-boom generation came of working age tended to __________ (raise/lower) the natural rate of unemployment.

2.4 In the late 1980s, as unemployment fell below the natural rate, inflation __________.

2.5 **Targeting the Natural Rate?** Because the natural rate of unemployment is the economists' notion of what constitutes "full employment," it might seem logical for the Fed to use monetary policy to move unemployment toward its natural rate. However, many economists believe such a policy would be unwise because the natural rate may shift over time and policymakers may misjudge the correct rate. What would happen if the Fed targeted a 5 percent unemployment rate but the true natural rate were 6 percent?

2.6 **Explaining a Movement in the Inflation Rate.** In Figure 16.1 you can see that inflation rose between 1988 and 1989 with little change in the unemployment rate. Can you explain why?

2.7 **Hysteresis and the Natural Rate of Unemployment.** In economics the term "hysteresis" means that the history of the economy has a lingering effect on current economic performance. During the U.S. recession starting in 2007, the number of long-term unemployed grew rapidly and remained high even during the recovery. Why is this a real social problem for the unemployed and everyone else as well?

2.8 **Oil Price Changes, Vacancies, and the Natural Rate.** During the mid-1970s, changes in oil prices required products to be produced by different types of firms in different locations. This raised the number of vacancies relative to the unemployment rate. According to the theory of William Dickens, how did this affect the natural rate of unemployment? (Related to Application 1 on page 337.)

16.3 How the Credibility of a Nation's Central Bank Affects Inflation

3.1 An aggressive union will shift the aggregate supply curve __________, causing prices to and real GDP to __________.

3.2 In the face of an upward shift in the aggregate supply curve, the Fed can increase the supply of money. This will prevent a recession, but will cause an increase in __________.

3.3 The evidence shows that lower inflation rates are associated with central bank __________.

3.4 When the Bank of England became independent, inflation expectations __________.

3.5 **Public Pronouncements and Fed Officials.** In addition to political and institutional factors, public pronouncements also affect the credibility of the Fed. When Alan Blinder, a Princeton University professor of economics, was appointed vice-chair of the Federal Reserve in 1994, he gave a speech to a group of central bankers and monetary policy specialists. In that speech, he repeated one of the lessons in this chapter: In the long run, the rate of inflation is independent of unemployment and depends only on money growth; in the short run, lower unemployment can raise the inflation rate. Blinder's speech caused an uproar in the financial press. Some commentators attacked him as not being sufficiently vigilant against inflation. Use the idea of credibility to explain why an apparently innocent speech would create such a reaction. (Related to Application 2 on page 342.)

3.6 **Pay Incentives for Fed Officials?** In the private sector, the pay of executives is typically tied to the performance of their company. Could this work in the public sector as well? Suppose pay for the chairman of the Federal Reserve is tied to the price of long-term bonds. That is, if bond prices rise, the chairman receives a bonus, but if they fall, the chairman's salary will decrease. Would this provide a credible incentive for the chairman to keep inflation low? (*Hint*: Think of the links between inflation, interest rates, and bond prices.) Do you see any disadvantages to this proposal?

3.7 **Buying Gold to Protect against Inflation.** Consider the following statement: "Since gold is a commodity and prices of commodities by definition increase with inflation, buying gold will protect me from any inflationary increases." Can you point out a possible problem with buying gold to protect yourself against inflation?

16.4 Inflation and the Velocity of Money

4.1 The velocity of money is defined as __________ income divided by the supply of money.

4.2 The quantity equation links money, velocity, real income, and __________.

4.3 If we know the growth of velocity, income, and the money supply, we can explain the __________ rate.

4.4 If the growth of the money supply is 4 percent a year, velocity decreases by 1 percent, and there is no growth in real output, the inflation rate equals __________.

4.5 **Interest Rates and the Velocity of Money.** When interest rates are high, people hold less money. How would this affect the velocity of money?

4.6 **Using the Quantity Equation.** If the growth rate of money is 10 percent per year, annual inflation is 7 percent, and the growth rate of velocity is 1 percent per year, what is the growth rate of real output?

4.7 **Velocity of Money in the United States.** Using the Federal Reserve Bank of St. Louis Web site (www.research.stlouisfed.org/fred2), calculate the velocity of M1 and M2 in 1960 and 2000. How have they changed?

16.5 Hyperinflation

5.1 To finance a budget deficit, a government can either borrow from the public or create __________.

5.2 During hyperinflations the velocity of money tends to __________ sharply.

5.3 Economists call inflation "hyperinflation" when the inflation rate exceeds __________ percent per month.

5.4 Hyperinflations cannot occur unless the growth rate of __________ is very high.

5.5 **Ending Hyperinflations and the Independence of Central Banks.** Why is it important to create an independent central bank, one that is not subservient to the rest of the government, in order to stop a hyperinflation. (Related to Application 3 on page 344.)

5.6 **Hyperinflation and Barter.** Some economists and journalists noticed that during the recent hyperinflation in Zimbabwe that the economy was turning to a barter economy. Why do you think this would occur? (Related to Application 3 on page 344.)

5.7 **Unprofitable Government Enterprises and Inflation.** In some developing countries, governments are forced to support large enterprises that persistently lose substantial sums of money. Why might this cause inflation?

ECONOMIC EXPERIMENT

MONEY ILLUSION

Economists say that people suffer from money illusion if their behavior is influenced by nominal changes that are also not real changes. Consider the following scenarios and be prepared to discuss them in class.

a. Erin bought an antique clock for $100. Two years later, Betsy bought an identical clock for $121. Meanwhile, there had been inflation each year of 10 percent. Both Erin and Betsy sold their clocks to other collectors. Erin sold hers for $130, and Betsy sold hers for $133. Who profited more from her transaction?

b. Bob and Pete are traders in classic comic books. A year ago, Bob and Pete each bought the same comic book for $10. Bob sold his a couple of days later for $20. Pete waited a year and sold his for $21. If inflation last year was 6 percent, who made the better deal?

CHAPTER 17

Macroeconomic Policy Debates

We all know that our nations are faced with great economic challenges.

As birth rates decline, the population ages, and the young are called on to provide more resources for the elderly. Regardless of the exact nature of the health system, health costs are soaring throughout the world. In part, this is due to increased longevity as well as important technological advances in medical science. And, finally, global competition has reached new heights, providing a wider range of goods and services but creating uncertainties for individual businesses and citizens.

Sound economic policy is needed to address these issues but political systems throughout the world at times seem incapable of responding to them. Virtually all countries are racked by debates over the size and role of government, the appropriate level and structure of taxation, and the role that the state should play in our lives. Sometimes these debates become rancorous and counterproductive. How can we calmly and sensibly debate these important economic issues?

LEARNING OBJECTIVES

- List the benefits and the costs for a country of running a deficit.
- Summarize the arguments in favor of inflation targeting.
- Describe the key differences between income and consumption taxes.

MyEconLab

MyEconLab helps you master each objective and study more efficiently.

As a student and citizen, you are inevitably drawn into economic debates. In most cases, the debates are complex because they involve a mixture of facts, theories, and opinions. Value judgments play a large role in economic debates. Your views on the proper role of tax policy, for example, will depend on whether you believe low-income earners should receive a higher share of national income. Your views on the size of government will depend on whether you believe individuals or the government should play a larger role in economic affairs.

In previous chapters, you learned the basic vocabulary of economics and studied different theories of the economy. Now you are ready to examine some of the key policy issues in macroeconomics. In this chapter, we will focus on three macroeconomics issues that are the subject of much debate:

- Should we balance the federal budget?
- Should the Fed target both inflation and employment?
- Should we tax consumption rather than income?

17.1 Should We Balance the Federal Budget?

Before we begin to consider answers to the question "Should we balance the federal budget?" let's review some terms from earlier chapters: *Government expenditures* include goods and services purchased by the government and transfer payments, such as Social Security and welfare, made to citizens. A *surplus* occurs when the government's revenues exceed its expenditures in a given year. The government runs a *deficit* when it spends more than it receives in revenues from either taxes or fees in a given year.

The *government debt* is the *total* of all its yearly deficits. For example, if a government initially had a debt of $100 billion and then ran deficits of $20 billion the next year, $30 billion the year after that, and $50 billion during the third year, its total debt at the end of the third year would be $200 billion: the initial $100 billion debt plus the successive yearly deficits of $20 billion, $30 billion, and $50 billion. If a government ran a surplus, it would decrease its total debt. For example, suppose the debt were $100 billion and the government ran a surplus of $10 billion. With the surplus, the government would buy back $10 billion of debt from the private sector, thereby reducing the remaining debt to $90 billion.

In this chapter, we focus on the government debt held by the public, not the total federal debt, which includes debt held by other governmental agencies. Sometimes popular accounts in the press or on the Web highlight the total federal debt. However, the debt held by the public is the best measure to assess the burden the federal debt can have on the economy.

The Budget in Recent Decades

The fiscal picture for the United States has changed substantially over the last 30 years. Beginning in the 1980s and through most of the 1990s, the federal budget ran large deficits—"deficits as far as the eye can see," as David Stockman, the director of the Office of Management and Budget in President Reagan's administration, put it. What Stockman could not see at that point, however, was what would occur in the late 1990s. In fiscal year 1998, during President Clinton's administration, the federal government ran a budget surplus of $69 billion—its first surplus in 30 years. It continued to run surpluses for the next 3 fiscal years as well.

The surplus emerged for two key reasons. First, economic growth was very rapid and tax revenues—including tax revenues from the sales of stocks and bonds—grew more quickly than anticipated. Second, federal budget rules were in place that limited total spending.

When President George W. Bush took office in January 2001, the large surplus led him to propose substantial tax cuts. Bush and Congress then passed a 10-year tax cut amounting to $1.35 trillion over the course of the decade. Although the tax cuts were large, the Congressional Budget Office (CBO) estimated at that time that the federal government would nonetheless continue to run surpluses through 2010.

The CBO noted that, as a result of these federal government surpluses, the outstanding stock of federal debt held by the public would be reduced. Because GDP would be growing over this period, the stock of debt relative to GDP, which is the standard way to measure the effect of debt in an economy, would also decline. The CBO estimated that in 2011, the ratio of debt to GDP would fall despite Bush's tax cuts, in part because the tax cuts were set to expire in 2010. Figure 17.1 depicts the debt/GDP ratio from 1791 to 2011. As you can see, except for a period in the 1980s, typically the ratio rises sharply during wars and the Great Depression and falls during peacetime. With neither a war nor a recession looming on the horizon in early 2001, the CBO predicted that the debt/GDP ratio would be relatively low by the end of the decade.

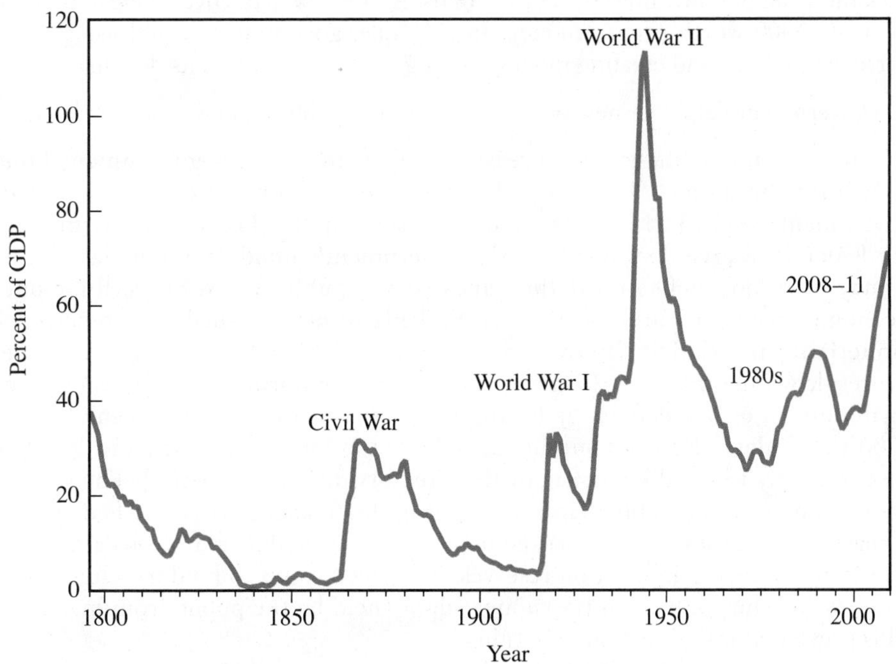

▲ **FIGURE 17.1**

Debt as a Percent of GDP, 1791–2011

The nation's debt/GDP ratio tends to rise sharply during wars because more spending is needed to finance them. However, the ratio also can rise during peacetime, as it did during the Reagan presidency in the 1980s and since 2008.

SOURCES: Congressional Budget Office, "The Long-Term Budget Outlook," December 2003, and yearly updates.

MyEconLab Real-time data

Unfortunately, a series of events intervened to bring deficits back into the picture and prevent the debt/GDP ratio from falling. The fight against terrorism led to higher spending on homeland security and military spending as wars were launched in Afghanistan and Iraq. The Bush tax cuts, the collapse of the stock market twice during the decade, the recessions that began in 2001 and 2007, and the slow recovery all sharply reduced tax revenues. President Obama's stimulus package in 2009 added new tax cuts and additional spending, which fueled the deficit. The federal government ran a budget deficit of approximately $1.3 trillion in fiscal year 2011, a far cry from the surpluses in the late 1990s. You can see from the last few years of Figure 17.1 that the debt-to-GDP ratio has recently risen. The debt-to-GDP ratio in 2011 was 67.7 percent. Alas, the CBO forecast from 2001 was far off the mark.

Five Debates about Deficits

As we have seen, federal budgets are affected by a wide range of factors, including wars, demographic pressures, recessions, and the choices our politicians make on spending and taxes. But what principles should guide policymakers? Should they cut spending and raise taxes to reduce the national debt over time? Or does the level of the national debt really matter? Let's take a look at the debates over the national debt.

DEBATE 1: DO DEFICITS LEAD TO INFLATION? If a government is spending $2,000 but collecting only $1,600 in taxes, where does it get the $400 needed to fill the gap? One option is to borrow $400 from the public in return for government bonds, which are, in effect, IOUs. In the future the government would have to pay back the $400 plus any interest on the bonds. Another way to cover the gap is simply to create $400 worth of new money. In principle, governments could use a mix of borrowing money and creating money, as long as the total covers its deficits:

government deficit = new borrowing from the public + new money created

In the United States, the Treasury Department issues government bonds to finance the deficit. The Federal Reserve has the option of buying existing government bonds, including those newly issued by the Treasury Department. If the Federal Reserve does purchase the government's bonds, the purchase creates money by taking debt out of the hands of the public in exchange for money. Economists call the purchase by a central bank of newly issued government debt **monetizing the deficit**. If governments finance deficits by creating new money, the result will be inflation. In the United States, we normally finance only a very small portion of our deficits by creating money. For example, between 2005 and 2006 the Federal Reserve purchased only $34 billion in government bonds of approximately $330 billion issued by the Treasury during that period. The Fed sold the remainder to the public. However, during the financial crisis, the Fed engaged in massive purchases in securities, adding over a trillion dollars to its balance sheet. However, by paying interest on reserves, it induced banks to hold matching excess reserves and thus prevented the money supply held by the public from increasing. This prevented inflation from emerging.

monetizing the deficit Purchases by a central bank of newly issued government bonds.

If a country has no options other than creating money to finance its deficits—in other words, if the public is unwilling to buy its bonds, as was the case in Hungary following World War II—those deficits will inevitably cause inflation. As we discussed in Chapter 16, hyperinflations occur when economies run large deficits and monetize them. Germany and Russia after World War I, Bolivia and Argentina in the 1980s, Russia in the 1990s, and most recently Zimbabwe are just some of the countries that, in addition to Hungary, have endured massive inflations because they monetized their deficits. However, large, stable countries like the United Kingdom, the United States, and Japan don't monetize much of their debt because they are able to borrow from the public. In these countries, deficits do not lead inevitably to inflation.

DEBATE 2: IS GOVERNMENT DEBT A BURDEN ON FUTURE GENERATIONS? The national debt, another commonly used term for total government debt, can impose two different burdens on society, both of which fall on the shoulders of future generations. First, a large debt can reduce the amount of capital in the economy and thereby reduce future income and real wages for its citizens. Here's how.

The savings of individuals and institutions flow into capital formation and increase an economy's capital stock. For example, when savers purchase new stocks and bonds, the companies issuing them use the proceeds to invest in plants and equipment.

When the government runs a deficit and increases its national debt, it also finances its spending by selling bonds to these same savers, who might hold both types of assets in, say, their retirement portfolios. Further, let's say that the total amount that the public can save is fixed at $1,000. If the government needs to finance a $200 deficit and does so by selling new bonds, then only $800 in savings is available to invest in private companies. The selling of $200 in government bonds to finance the deficit therefore "crowds out" $200 that could have been raised by private companies.

The result of government deficits is that less savings are available to firms for investment. This illustrates one of our basic principles in economics.

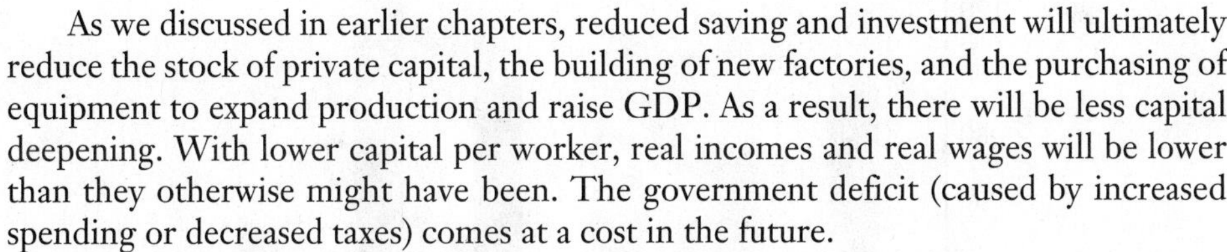

PRINCIPLE OF OPPORTUNITY COST
The opportunity cost of something is what you sacrifice to get it.

As we discussed in earlier chapters, reduced saving and investment will ultimately reduce the stock of private capital, the building of new factories, and the purchasing of equipment to expand production and raise GDP. As a result, there will be less capital deepening. With lower capital per worker, real incomes and real wages will be lower than they otherwise might have been. The government deficit (caused by increased spending or decreased taxes) comes at a cost in the future.

Governments can spend the proceeds of borrowing on investments, such as productive infrastructure—in this case, future real wages and incomes will not be adversely affected. With productive investment, government deficits will not be a burden on society.

Second, a large national debt will mean that higher taxes will be imposed on future generations to pay the interest that accumulates on the debt. Just like your college loans, the bill eventually comes due—even for the national debt.

Sometimes you hear that these interest payments are not a real burden because "we owe the national debt to ourselves." This is a misleading argument for several reasons. First, we don't owe the interest payments only to ourselves. In 2009, approximately 52 percent of U.S. public debt was held by foreigners. Second, a high proportion of the debt is held by older, wealthy individuals or by institutions, but the taxes levied to service it will be paid by everyone in the United States.

Some economists do not believe that government deficits, resulting in government debt, impose a burden on a society. These economists believe in **Ricardian equivalence**, the proposition that it does not matter whether government expenditure is financed by taxes or financed by issuing debt. This idea is named after David Ricardo, a nineteenth-century classical economist. To understand the case for Ricardian equivalence, consider the following example. A government initially has a balanced budget. It then cuts taxes and issues new debt to finance the deficit left by the reduction in taxes. Everyone understands the government will have to raise taxes in the future to service the debt, so everyone increases savings to pay for the taxes that will be increased in the future. If saving rises sufficiently, the public—everyone—will be able to purchase the new debt without reducing the funds they invest in the private sector. Because net investment doesn't decline, there will be no debt burden.

Ricardian equivalence
The proposition that it does not matter whether government expenditure is financed by taxes or debt.

As you can see, Ricardian equivalence requires that savings by the private sector increase when the deficit increases. Do savers behave this way? It is actually difficult to provide a definite answer, because we must take many other factors into account in any empirical studies of savings. It appears, however, that during the early 1980s, savings decreased somewhat when government deficits increased. This is precisely the opposite of what Ricardian equivalence predicts. As long as Ricardian equivalence does not fully hold true, it's reasonable to assume the government debt imposes a burden on society. Nonetheless, many economists believe using the deficit as the sole measure of a society's future burdens doesn't tell the whole story. These economists believe we should look at broader measures that take into account long run promises of the federal government.

From an international perspective, the United States does not have the largest government debt measured relative to GDP. Figure 17.2 depicts the percentage of debt to GDP for several developed countries. By this measure, Japan has the most serious public debt problem.

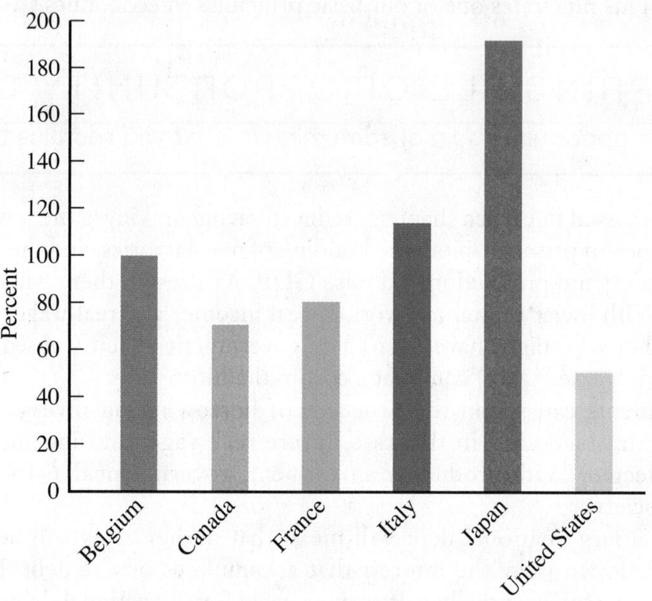

▲ **FIGURE 17.2**

International Comparisons of Government Debt as Percentage of GDP, 2009

Among developed countries, the United States has a relatively small percentage of debt to GDP. Japan has the highest percentage of debt of the countries depicted.

SOURCE: Central Intelligence Agency, *The World Factbook,* https://www.cia.gov/library/publications/the-world-factbook/index.html (accessed November 19, 2012).

DEBATE 3: HOW DO DEFICITS AFFECT THE SIZE OF GOVERNMENT? Nobel Laureate James Buchanan has argued that people are less aware of government deficits than of the taxes they're forced to pay. Therefore, financing government expenditures through deficits, rather than through higher taxes, will inevitably lead to higher government spending and bigger government. Although this argument may seem plausible, it presents two problems. First, in recent U.S. history, spending by state and local governments has grown much faster than federal spending. However, state and local governments face many more restrictions when it comes to borrowing money than the federal government faces. For example, many states require legislators to run a balanced budget. Deficit spending isn't allowed. Second, if politicians trying to get reelected really prefer higher government spending and deficits to higher taxes and surpluses, why did the federal government run surpluses in the late 1990s?

Some research suggests politicians can use deficits strategically to actually reduce the growth of government. During the 1980s, for example, the government ran large deficits caused by a combination of a deep recession and major tax cuts. The deficits subsequently made it difficult for other politicians to propose new spending programs.

Proponents of smaller government, therefore, may wish to cut taxes to reduce surpluses or increase deficits in order to make it more difficult for other politicians to increase government spending. These deficit proponents want to create deficits to prevent Congress from having too much money to be able to spend. Some congressmen supported President Bush's tax cut in 2001, which reduced the surplus over a 10-year period, precisely for this reason.

DEBATE 4: CAN DEFICITS BE GOOD FOR AN ECONOMY? Recall from our fiscal policy discussion that, during a downturn, running a deficit helps stimulate private-sector spending. Consequently, the government may deliberately run a deficit to pull the economy out of a recession. The deficit the government creates puts additional income into the hands of the public. With more money, people don't have to drastically cut their consumption spending. Because total spending in the economy does not fall as much, the severity of the recession is lessened.

Deficits automatically emerge during recessions, which also stabilize the economy. Recall how automatic stabilizers work. As incomes fall during a recession, so do tax payments. Moreover, transfer payments such as welfare and food stamps rise. Because government spending increases while tax revenues fall, the deficit must, of course, rise. However, a rising deficit may be what it takes to steer the economy back to full employment. Automatic stabilizers were clearly in evidence in the recession that began in late 2007, as tax revenues fell sharply for the next several years.

The existence of automatic stabilizers and the use of expansionary fiscal policy during recessions suggest that we should not worry about short-run government deficits. Over short time periods, deficits can help the economy to cope with shocks, such as oil price increases or a collapse in the stock market. They give the government some room to maneuver out of a recession. Most economists believe automatic stabilizers reduced economic fluctuations during the twentieth century.

Deficits can also play a role in tax smoothing. Suppose there is a large, temporary increase in government spending, as might occur during a war. The government could either finance the war by running a deficit and issuing debt or by increasing tax rates to keep the budget in balance. Professor Robert Barro of Harvard University has argued that it is more efficient to keep tax rates relatively constant than to raise them sharply and then lower them later. Temporarily raising tax rates to very high levels could cause distortions in economic behavior that we would like to avoid. Thus, by running deficits and only gradually raising taxes later to service the debt, we avoid creating excess distortions in the economy.

DEBATE 5: WOULD A BALANCED-BUDGET AMENDMENT REALLY WORK? For many years, there were strong efforts to enact a Constitutional amendment to balance the federal budget. As recently as 1995, Congress came very close to passing a balanced-budget amendment, sending it back to the states for ratification. The amendment passed in the House of Representatives but failed by a single vote in the Senate. How would a balanced-budget amendment actually work?

Many different budgetary constitutional amendments have been proposed. They all require that, after a phase-in period, Congress propose in each fiscal year a budget in which total revenues (excluding borrowing) cover total expenditures. The amendments also have various escape clauses—for example, to allow borrowing during wartime. Some amendments also allow Congress to suspend the requirement to balance the budget for other reasons, such as during a recession when deficits naturally emerge. Finally, some versions would limit the rate of spending increases to the rate at which GDP is growing.

Proponents of the balanced-budget amendment say it will finally exert discipline on the federal government, preventing large deficits in peacetime, such as those that occurred in the 1980s. With a balanced budget we could be sure to avoid the negative effects of deficits: reduced capital formation and tax burdens that are shifted onto future generations.

Critics of a balanced-budget amendment point to many different problems, such as the following:

- A balanced budget may not allow enough flexibility, or room, for the government to effectively deal with recessions. Under some versions of the amendment, unless three-fifths of Congress votes to suspend requirements, the government would have to cut expenditures or raise taxes during a recession. This would make the recession worse and limit the ability of the government to use fiscal policy to stabilize the economy.
- The Constitution is not the right mechanism to try to enforce complicated budget rules. As various interested parties challenge the actions of Congress, the courts would become heavily engaged in federal budget matters.
- Congress could devise special budgets to get around the requirement, for example, by taking some types of spending "off budget," which means simply not counting them as part of the official budget.
- Congress could also find non-budgetary ways to carry out the policies that it desires. For example, it could issue more regulations or impose mandates or requirements on businesses or other governments to carry out its will. These regulations or mandates could be even more costly to the economy than added deficits.

application 1

CREATING THE U.S. FEDERAL FISCAL SYSTEM THROUGH DEBT POLICY

APPLYING THE CONCEPTS #1: Why did the early U.S. federal government take over the debts of the thirteen colonies?

When the United States enacted its new Constitution in 1789, it replaced the Continental Congress and centralized power in the federal government. As part of the grand political bargain for this new structure, the federal government became the sole power to be able to raise revenue through tariffs on imported goods, but also assumed the debts of the state governments and the Continental Congress that had been incurred during the Revolutionary War. Alexander Hamilton, who conceived and promoted this new arrangement, saw it as a way to strengthen the federal government so that it could borrow externally as needed for wars or other needs. The states were willing to give the tariff power to the federal government in exchange being absolved of their debts.

Nobel Laureate Thomas J. Sargent noted, however, that when the states again got into fiscal difficulties in the 1840s through overly ambitious infrastructure investment, the federal government did not bail out the states. This time, the federal government did not want to enhance its power and control over the states, which were forced to impose new rules and fiscal discipline on themselves to avoid future fiscal disruptions. Together, these two episodes helped define the fiscal structure of the United States: a strong central government and independent but fiscally responsible states. **Related to Exercise 1.7.**

SOURCE: Based on Thomas J. Sargent, "An American History Lesson for Europe," *Wall Street Journal*, February 3, 2012, p. A17.

17.2 Should the Fed Target Both Inflation and Employment?

In previous chapters we looked at the various roles that the Federal Reserve can play. Monetary policy can be used to stabilize the real economy, preventing unemployment from exceeding the natural rate or falling too far below the natural rate. As we also have seen, the Fed also plays a critical role as a lender of last resort and a unique resource to combat financial crises.

The Congress generally has expected the Fed along with other agencies in government to play multiple roles. In the Employment Act of 1946, the federal government was broadly charged to pursue "maximum employment, production, and purchasing power." In 1978, Congress passed the Humphrey–Hawkins legislation which calls for the nation to seek full employment, price stability as well as balances in the trade and budget.

But what should the Fed actually do? We have learned that, in the long run, money is neutral and monetary policy cannot affect the real level of output or unemployment. We also saw that the natural rate can shift over time, making it difficult to target the appropriate unemployment rate. In these circumstances, what should the Fed do? Should it just focus on inflation or try to follow some other rule or procedure to balance concerns of inflation and unemployment?

In the early years of the first decade of the twenty-first century, the rate of inflation had fallen to between 1 and 2 percent. Some economists thought the time was right for the Fed to concentrate on simply keeping the inflation rate low and stable. In other words, they thought the Fed should use monetary policy to "target" an appropriate inflation rate and make its primary objective keeping inflation in check. Following the expansion of the Fed's activities during the financial crisis of 2008 and its aftermath, there is continuing concern about long-run inflation.

In recent years, various inflation-targeting methods have been adopted in a number of developed countries, including Canada, the United Kingdom, New Zealand, Sweden, Australia, and Spain. In addition, many developing countries have found that inflation targeting increased the autonomy of their central banks, helping them fight inflation.

Two Debates about Targeting

Inflation targeting has had many strong proponents. Let's take a close look at two key debates about this topic.

DEBATE 1: SHOULD THE FED FOCUS ON ONLY INFLATION? We have learned that in the long run monetary policy can influence only the level of prices, not the level of employment. Proponents of inflation targeting argue that the Fed should have only one primary goal: controlling inflation. Having it worry about other factors—unemployment or the exchange rate—will, they say, distract it from its mission and lead to long-run inflationary pressures building in the economy. Moreover, if the Fed were committed to the single goal of controlling inflation, its credibility would be enhanced. As we have seen, if the Fed is credible, the private sector will become more responsive to changes in monetary policy. For example, long-term interest rates will become more responsive to changes in short-term rates if the public understands what the Fed's motives are and what it is doing. And credible policies may actually decrease the need for active monetary policies. Having a single goal would also help to keep the Fed free of political pressures. Such political pressures might include attempts by one political party or the other to stimulate the economy or give financial markets a temporary boost before an election.

Other proponents of inflation targeting hold a somewhat less rigid view. Although they believe fighting inflation should be the primary objective of the Fed, or of a central bank, they believe an inflation-targeting regimen could be designed to give the central bank some flexibility. For example, the central bank could be required to target a broader range of inflation—say, between 1 and 3 percent—and meet the target several years in the future. Under either of these alternatives, central banks would have some room to meet employment or other policy objectives besides just inflation. In practice, many countries do allow some "wiggle room" in their inflation targeting regimens by using broad inflation bands or distant targets.

Before he took over as chairman of the Federal Reserve in 2006, Ben Bernanke was an advocate for inflation targeting. While he was a member of the Board of Governors in 2003, Bernanke gave a speech outlining his own views on the merits of inflation targeting. For Bernanke, inflation targeting increased the effectiveness of monetary policy because it provided a long-term anchor for inflation expectations. As long as the private sector—individuals and firms—understood the Fed was holding firm to long-run inflation targets, it would have added flexibility to use aggressive monetary policy in the short run to offset adverse shocks to the economy—without upsetting long-run inflation expectations. Bernanke called inflation targeting a policy of *constrained discretion*. Under inflation targeting, the Fed could take actions to offset shocks to real output or to the financial system, but it had to keep its long-run inflation targets in clear view. After the financial crisis of 2008, Bernanke stopped speaking about inflation targeting and devoted his speeches to explaining the Fed's actions during the crisis and designing an "exit strategy" for the Fed's massive interventions.

Even prior to the recent recession, many economists disagreed with the idea of inflation targeting because they strongly objected to the Fed concentrating solely on controlling inflation. In the United States, Congress and the president are frequently incapable of quickly agreeing on a fiscal policy to stave off or end a recession. Of course, automatic fiscal stabilizers exist, but they are often not sufficient to cushion the economy when a shock hits. Practically speaking, only monetary policy is available to stabilize output and prevent deep recessions from emerging. If monetary policy is geared solely toward controlling inflation, as inflation-targeting proponents would like, and if fiscal policies are difficult for Congress and the president to pass, that leaves the government no other tools to fight a recession.

Economists also debate the level for an inflation target. Suppose there were general agreement that the ultimate goal should be total price stability—that is, zero inflation. There would still be legitimate questions about what constitutes "stable" prices. It is very difficult to measure changes in prices accurately when there is a great deal of technological change occurring in the economy, because technological improvements change the quality of goods so rapidly that government statisticians can't easily catch up with them. If, as many economists believe, our price indexes overstate the true inflation rate, annual inflation of 2 percent may in reality be true price stability. Indeed, many proponents of inflation targeting agree with this point and recommend a 2 percent inflation rate as "price stability."

Critics of stabilization policy, of course, believe that not using monetary policy to try to stabilize the economy would actually improve our economic performance. In their view, attempts to stabilize the economy have done more harm than good over the years by making fluctuations worse. In previous chapters, we discussed the difficulties in conducting stabilization policy. These include lags, uncertainties about the strength and timing of policies, and difficulties in estimating the natural rate of unemployment. If you believe these difficulties are insurmountable, you will likely think the Fed should target just inflation. If you think they can be overcome, you will likely believe the Fed should be allowed to stabilize output and employment, too.

Some economists like the idea of the Fed having to meet targets, but they have suggested alternatives to inflation targeting. One approach that has wide appeal was developed by economist John Taylor of Stanford University. Taylor suggested that the Fed follow a rule that keeps a long-run inflation target but allows the Fed to raise or lower interest rates depending on whether output is above or below potential. His own analysis suggests that the performance of the Fed would be superior if it followed a rule of this type, rather than making ad hoc decisions. The advantage of a rule of this nature is that it allows the Fed to offset shocks to the economy, but requires the Fed to meet long-run inflation targets.

application 2

WOULD A POLICY RULE HAVE PREVENTED THE HOUSING BOOM?

APPLYING THE CONCEPTS #2: Did the Federal Reserve cause the housing boom through excessively loose monetary policy?

John Taylor from Stanford University has argued that the Fed's "easy money" policy from mid-2001 through 2004 was largely responsible for the housing boom in the decade that ultimately caused so much financial damage. Taylor used his own model of monetary policy—the "Taylor rule"—to analyze the Fed's behavior. In his prior work, he demonstrated that the Fed's behavior could be closely described by a model that allowed for some monetary policy tightening and easing in response to output movements. Applying this model to the decade of 2000, however, Taylor found that, compared to past experience, the Fed was much too aggressive in lowering interest rates. Interest rates fell from 2 percent in mid-2001 to 1 percent by 2004. Past experience, however, would have suggested that the Fed would have raised interest rates to 4 percent by 2004—a very significant deviation.

Taylor then showed that housing starts—which are very sensitive to interest rates—would have been much lower if the Fed had not followed its easy money policy. The boom and bust would have been avoided. Finally, as an additional piece of evidence, Taylor looked at the experiences of European countries. There the same phenomenon occurred. Countries that deviated most from the Taylor rule—for example, Spain—experienced the worst boom and bust cycles for housing. **Related to Exercise 2.7.**

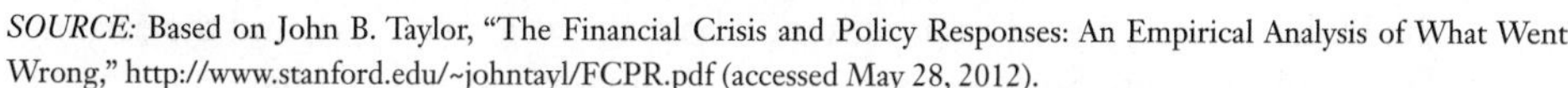

SOURCE: Based on John B. Taylor, "The Financial Crisis and Policy Responses: An Empirical Analysis of What Went Wrong," http://www.stanford.edu/~johntayl/FCPR.pdf (accessed May 28, 2012).

Another approach that has been recently been discussed is *price-level targeting*. The idea would be that the Fed would target the price level, which would grow, for example, at the targeted inflation rate of 2 percent per year. How does price-level targeting differ from inflation targeting? Suppose that inflation was lower than its target for a period of time—for example, inflation was 1 percent for several years rather than 2 percent targeted rate. This would necessarily mean that the price level grew less than 2 percent and was also below its trend. Under price-level targeting, the Fed would be required to temporarily raise inflation above 2 percent to reach its price-level target. For example, it could be required to cause inflation to reach 3–4 percent until the economy reached its earlier price-level target. On the other hand, under inflation targeting, the Fed would simply be required to raise its inflation rate back to its 2 percent target and not go any higher.

Proponents of price-level targeting, including some members of the FOMC, believe it will more properly balance the goals of employment and price stability. On the other hand, critics believe that is dangerous for the Fed to allow inflation to exceed its target, as it may prove difficult to reduce inflation at a later time.

DEBATE 2: IF THERE WERE AN INFLATION TARGET, WHO WOULD SET IT? Even if the United States decided to adopt inflation targeting as a policy, several important questions would remain. Perhaps the most important is "Who would set the target?"

In the United Kingdom, which adopted targeting in 1992, the elected government decides on the inflation target for the central bank. These elected officials typically specify a range for the inflation rate that the bank must meet. The central bank participates in the discussions and has an opportunity to present its views to the public through its publications and published minutes of its meetings. But ultimately it is the elected government that makes the final decision.

In other countries, the central bank has even more influence in setting the inflation target. In New Zealand, for example, the central bank has the responsibility of "achieving and maintaining stability in the general level of prices" without any competing goals, such as stabilizing employment or output. The law also requires the head of the central bank and the finance minister to negotiate inflation goals and make them public.

What would be an appropriate arrangement for the United States? Under current law, the Fed chairman reports regularly to Congress, but the Fed has considerable power to use monetary policy to stabilize output as well as to fight inflation as it pleases. Would our Congress and president be willing to cede power to the Fed and allow it to focus only on fighting inflation? And, if they did, would Congress or the president want to determine the target range for inflation and instruct the Fed how quickly to meet these targets?

As you can see, changing our current system would require major decisions about who has authority and control over our economic system. Currently, the Fed has considerable power and autonomy. Although inflation targeting might make the Fed more independent, another phenomenon could occur, too: Congress and the president might end up with more power over monetary policy. And that might lead to more inflation, not less.

17.3 Should We Tax Consumption Rather than Income?

As we discussed in earlier chapters, the United States is a country with a low saving rate. This hurts our long-run growth prospects because our investment spending is determined by our own savings and savings from abroad. Many factors—not purely economic ones—contribute to our low saving rate. For example, colleges generally give less financial aid to students whose families have saved for their education. Many of our welfare programs cut the benefits of families who have saved in the past and still have some funds left in their accounts. The U.S. tax system also discourages savings. Here's how.

In the United States, you must pay taxes on both the wages you earn and the earnings you make on your savings. Suppose you earn $100 at your job and you have a tax rate of 20 percent. That means you keep $80 after taxes. Now suppose you save $50 of that money and invest it at 10 percent. At the end of one year, you will have earned an additional $5 on the $50 you saved (10% × $50), but you will get to keep only $4 of it because the government will take $1 in taxes (20% × $5). So, you will have to pay the government $21 in total: $20 on the $100 you earned in wages, plus $1 on the $5 you earned on your savings. If you did not save at all, you would pay only $20 in taxes, not $21.

Not all tax systems work this way. Tax systems based on consumption do not penalize individuals who save. Sales taxes in the United States and value-added taxes abroad are familiar examples of **consumption taxes**. It is also possible to create a consumption tax from an income tax by not taxing the earnings on savings—just as we do with tax-exempt bonds issued by state and municipal governments. Or, as an alternative, the government could allow savings to be deducted from gross income before the calculation for total taxes owed is made. The key feature of consumption taxation is that you do not face any additional taxes if you decide to save more of your income.

consumption taxes
Taxes based on the consumption, not the income, of individuals.

There are, however, ways in the United States to save money and still limit your taxes. In addition to buying tax-exempt bonds, you can invest in an IRA (individual retirement account) or 401(k), 403(b), and Keogh plans, which are also types of retirement accounts. The money in pension funds is treated similarly. It isn't taxed until the person who contributed it retires and withdraws it. During retirement, most people earn less money than when they were working, so the tax rate they pay on the money they withdraw from these accounts is lower than when they saved it. Also, the money accumulates more quickly because it grows tax-free while it's in these accounts. In practice, the U.S. tax system is a hybrid system, part way between an income tax and a consumption tax.

Two Debates about Consumption Taxation

Proponents claim that taxes based on consumption will increase total savings and may even be more equitable. Let's explore these claims.

DEBATE 1: WILL CONSUMPTION TAXES LEAD TO MORE SAVINGS? There is no question that taxing consumption instead of savings creates an incentive to save. However, there's no guarantee the incentive will actually result in more money saved in the economy. Suppose the tax burden is shifted to consumption by reducing the tax rate on savings. People will want to take advantage of this incentive and reduce their consumption and increase their saving. On the other hand, people will also want to spend more because, with the tax cut, they are wealthier.

Although there has been much research done on how a consumption tax would affect savings, the results are far from conclusive. It is true that individuals will allocate their savings to tax-favored investments over investments that are not favored. For example, they will put money into their IRAs. What is not clear is whether the funds they will put there are literally new savings—meaning reduced consumption—or merely transfers from other accounts, such as conventional savings accounts, which do not have the same tax advantages. Untangling these effects is a difficult issue, and it remains an active area of ongoing research.

The tax system imposed on corporations in the United States also creates disincentives to save and invest. Suppose you purchase a share of stock in a corporation. When the corporation earns a profit, it pays taxes on the profit at the corporate tax rate. When the corporation pays you a dividend on the stock out of the profits it earns, you must pay taxes on the dividend income that you receive. Corporate income is taxed twice, in other words—first when it is earned by the corporation and again when it is paid out to shareholders.

Some economists have argued that the corporate taxes lead to less-efficient investment because they result in capital flowing into other sectors of the economy (into real estate, for example) that do not suffer from double taxation. For this reason, in 2003 Congress passed a bill introduced by President Bush that lowered—but did not eliminate—taxes on corporate dividends.

DEBATE 2: ARE CONSUMPTION TAXES FAIR? The basic idea behind a consumption tax seems fair. Individuals should be taxed on what they take away from the economy's total production—that is, what they consume—not on what they actually produce. If an individual produces a lot but does not consume the proceeds from what was produced and instead plows it back into the economy for investment, that individual is contributing to the growth of total output and should be rewarded, not punished. Individual A earns $50 and consumes it all; individual B earns $100 but consumes only $40. Who should pay more?

In practice, moving to a consumption-tax system could have a major impact on the distribution of income in the economy. Suppose we simply exempted the returns from savings from the income tax. This exception would clearly favor wealthy and high-income individuals who save the most and earn a lot of income in interest, dividends, rents, and capital gains. Table 17.1 shows estimates based on the capital gains received by different income classes for the year 2009 and dividends paid by

TABLE 17.1 Distribution of Capital Gains and Dividends by Income Class, 2009

Cash Income Level	Share of Capital Gains and Dividends
Less than $40,000	0%
$40,000 to $50,000	0.1
$50,000 to $75,000	0.9
$75,000 to $100,000	1.4
$100,000 to $200,000	8.2
$200,000 to $500,000	19.5
$500,000 to $1,000,000	13.8
Greater than $1,000,000	55.9

SOURCE: Estimates from the Urban-Brookings Tax Policy Center Microsimulation Model, http://www.taxpolicycenter.org/index.cfm (Accessed May 28, 2012).

capital gains
Profits investors earn when they sell stocks, bonds, real estate, or other assets.

corporations. **Capital gains** are the profits investors earn when they sell stocks, bonds, real estate, or other assets. As you can see, taxpayers with annual incomes exceeding $1,000,000 earned over half of the economy's capital gains over this period. Obviously, capital assets are highly concentrated among the wealthy.

If capital gains and other types of capital income were not taxed, total tax revenue would fall, and the government would have to raise tax rates on everyone to maintain the same level of spending. Excluding capital income from taxation does have its costs.

Some economists believe it is important that high-income individuals continue to pay a significant share of total taxes. In the last several decades, the distribution of income has become more unequal, as superstar athletes, famous actors and musicians, CEOs, and successful entrepreneurs and investors have all earned large fortunes. The tax system is one way we have to at least partially reduce inequalities in income. Critics of consumption taxes worry that moving our tax system in that direction will take away this important tool for social equality. However, other economists believe that high-income individuals already shoulder a very high share of the total tax burden and that we need to focus on designing an efficient system to promote economic growth.

Proponents of consumption taxes have tried to meet the challenge of fairness in different ways. The "flat tax" designed by Robert E. Hall of Stanford University and Alvin Rabushka of the Hoover Institute brings the personal income tax and corporate income tax into a single, unified tax system. Under the flat tax, one low, single tax rate applies to both businesses and individuals. Businesses deduct their wage payments before they pay taxes. In addition, they can deduct any investment spending they make from their income before the tax is calculated. Recall that in a simple economy, without government or the foreign sector, saving equals investment, $S = I$. Allowing a deduction for investment has generally the same effect as allowing a deduction for savings. So this flat tax is a type of consumption tax.

This version of the flat tax has an important feature that ensures that wealthy individuals (and other owners of corporations) still pay taxes. Suppose the corporation or business makes an extraordinary return on its investment. Consider, for example, the tremendous profit generated by Apple's iPad. As of April 2012, over 67 million iPads have been sold. If the profit for each iPad were $100, Apple's total profit from

application 3

IS A VAT IN OUR FUTURE?

APPLYING THE CONCEPTS #3: Can the United States adopt a European-style value-added tax?

Virtually all developed countries and many developing countries have a value-added tax, commonly known as a VAT. The United States is a prominent exception. The VAT is essentially a sales tax that is levied on each stage of production. Firms pay the VAT on their sales and then receive a credit for VAT paid on their purchases. Unlike a sales tax, the VAT is embedded in the price of goods. It is rebated when goods are exported but imports are required to pay the VAT. Rates on the VAT can be high—for example, the basic rate in the United Kingdom is 17.5 percent.

The VAT has some important advantages. It is relatively easy to collect and, as a consumption tax, does not penalize savings. There are some potential difficulties. Since U.S. states already levy retail sales taxes, incorporating a VAT at the state level could be difficult and be seen to impinge on state taxing authority. In addition, some conservatives worry that it is too efficient and consumers will not notice all the taxes they pay. Liberals worry that the VAT, like all consumption taxes, could be regressive. An old joke goes that the time will come for the VAT when liberals recognize it is a money machine and conservatives recognize it is regressive. **Related to Exercise 3.7.**

iPads would be $6.7 billion. Under this version of the flat tax, these extraordinary gains would be taxed in full. Owners of a corporation or business may earn extraordinary gains, but if they do, they will pay taxes on them.

The projected federal deficit has led many policymakers to consider whether a European-style value-added tax (VAT) would make sense for the United States. Grafting a VAT on to the U.S. fiscal system would pose many challenges.

SUMMARY

In this chapter we explored three topics that are the center of macroeconomic policy debates today. Here are the key points to remember:

1 A *deficit* is the difference between the government's current expenditures and revenue. The government debt is the sum of all past yearly deficits.

2 Deficits can be financed through either borrowing or money creation. Financing deficits through money creation is called *monetizing the deficit*. It leads to inflation.

3 Deficits can be good for the country. Automatic stabilizers and expansionary fiscal policy both work through the creation of deficits.

4 The national debt incurs two burdens on citizens: It can reduce the amount of capital in an economy, leading to lower levels of income; it can also result in higher taxes that future generations will have to pay.

5 A number of developed countries have recently changed their monetary policy to emphasize targeting the inflation rate or a range for the inflation rate.

6 Although targeting inflation can increase the credibility of a central bank, it does limit the tools left for active stabilization policy.

7 A *consumption tax* would increase the incentives for private saving. However, it is not clear that total savings would necessarily increase, and there would be concerns about the fairness of this form of taxation.

KEY TERMS

capital gains, p. 360

consumption taxes, p. 358

monetizing the deficit, p. 350

Ricardian equivalence, p. 351

EXERCISES

All problems are assignable in MyEconLab.

17.1 Should We Balance the Federal Budget?

1.1 If a government runs a deficit, it will __________ its outstanding debt.

1.2 Proponents of Ricardian equivalence believe that deficits do not really matter as long as taxes are raised in the future. __________ (True/False)

1.3 When a central bank purchases new government bonds, it is __________ the deficit.

1.4 Historically, debt/GDP ratios increase during periods of __________.

1.5 **Debt and Deficits in Belgium.** Here are some data for Belgium in 1989:

GDP: 6,160 billion Belgian francs
Debt: 6,500 billion Belgian francs
Deficit: 380 billion Belgian francs
Interest Rate on Bonds: 8.5 percent

Use the data to answer the following questions:

a. What are the deficit/GDP ratio and debt/GDP ratio? How do these ratios compare to the same ratios in the United States today? To what period in U.S. history does the debt/GDP ratio in Belgium correspond?

b. Approximately how much of the budget in Belgium is devoted to interest payments on its debt? If Belgium could wipe out its debt overnight, what would happen to its current budget deficit?

1.6 Interest Rates, Primary Surpluses, and Government Debt. The gap between taxes and spending, *excluding* interest on the debt, is known as the *primary surplus*. Suppose there is $100 million of outstanding public debt. Show that a primary surplus of $10 million with an interest rate of 10 percent has the same consequence for next year's debt level as a primary surplus of $5 million and an interest rate of 5 percent.

1.7 Fiscally Troubled States Today. A number of major states, for example California, have been experiencing fiscal problems. Although no states have defaulted on their debts in recent years, a number of cities have. Should the federal government "bail out" the states and help them meet their debts? Give one argument in favor and one argument against this policy based on U.S history. (Related to Application 1 on page 354.)

1.8 Tax Smoothing or Strategic Tax Policy? Assume the pressures of an aging population and increases in health-care costs will increase total federal spending in the future significantly.

a. Under the theory of tax smoothing, what should happen to the current level of taxes if future spending is scheduled to rise?

b. Now suppose future spending increases are not inevitable and that, as a practical matter, you believe Congress will spend whatever revenue it collects. Would you still recommend tax smoothing?

1.9 Policy Options for the Federal Budget. The Web site for the Congressional Budget Office (www.cbo.gov) contains its projections for future budget surpluses and deficits as well as options for increasing the surplus. Using this site, find some options you think are desirable and that would have a significant effect on increasing the budget surplus.

17.2 Should the Fed Target Inflation or Pursue Other Objectives?

2.1 Proponents of inflation targeting argue that it would make central banks more __________ if they were committed to a long-run inflation target.

2.2 In __________, inflation targeting was adopted in 1992, and elected officials determine the precise inflation targets that the central bank must meet.

2.3 Economist __________ developed a rule for monetary policy that maintains a low rate of inflation but allows the Fed to adjust interest rates when output deviates from potential.

2.4 Price-level targeting is the same as inflation targeting. __________ (True/False)

2.5 Targeting the Price Level with Supply Shocks. Suppose the Fed has brought the inflation rate down to zero to stabilize the price level. An adverse supply shock (such as an increase in the world price of oil) now hits the economy.

a. Using the aggregate demand-and-supply model, show how targeting the price level would make the fall in output from the shock greater as compared to no policy at all.

b. Some proponents of price-level or inflation targeting recommend that the Fed target "core inflation," which is based on a price index that excludes supply shocks. What is their rationale?

2.6 What Rate for Inflation Targeting? An economist suggests that what matters for financial markets is a stable inflation rate, not a zero inflation rate. As long as inflation is stable, all individuals can take this into account in their actions.

a. What are the costs associated with a stable inflation rate of 2 percent?

b. Is it easier or more difficult to stabilize inflation at 2 percent rather than at zero?

2.7 The Fed on Autopilot. Some economists believe that the Federal Reserve should follow strict rules for the conduct of monetary policy. These rules would require the Fed to make adjustments to interest rates based on information that is fully available to the public, information such as the current unemployment rate and the current inflation rate. Essentially, they would put the Fed on autopilot and remove its discretion. What are the pros and cons of such an approach? Would it work in a financial crisis? (Related to Application 2 on page 357.)

2.8 Targeting Gold? Some observers have suggested that the Fed use gold as an indicator of inflation and tighten monetary policy when gold prices rise. What are the pros and cons of this policy?

17.3 Should We Tax Consumption Rather than Income?

3.1 Suppose there is a consumption tax of 20 percent. An individual earns $100 and saves $30. Her tax will be equal to __________.

3.2 A sales tax that is levied at all stages of production is known as a(n)__________ tax.

3.3 Most capital gains accrue to low-income individuals because there are more of them. __________ (True/False)

3.4 Under our current corporate tax system, earnings from corporations that are paid out as dividends are taxed __________ times.

3.5 Traditional and Roth IRAs. With a traditional IRA, you get to deduct the amount you contribute from your current taxable income, invest the funds free from tax, but then pay taxes on the full amount you withdraw when you retire. Suppose your tax rate is 50 percent and you initially deposit $2,000 in an IRA. The proceeds double in seven years to $4,000. You then retire and pay taxes on the $4,000 at your 50 percent rate.

a. Taking into account your tax deduction for the IRA, how much did your investment in the IRA really cost you? What is your return after seven years?

b. With a Roth IRA, you do not get a deduction for your savings but the interest you earn is tax free. Is the outcome for a Roth IRA the same as for the traditional IRA if you invest $1,000 for seven years and double your initial investment?

c. Suppose you believed that in seven years tax rates would be higher. Are the traditional and Roth IRAs still equivalent? If not, which would you prefer?

3.6 **Tax Policy and National Savings.** Suppose the government launches a new program that allows individuals to place funds of up to $2,000 in a tax-free account. Do you believe that this will have a significant effect on national savings? (Recall that federal deficits reduce national savings.) What are the arguments on both sides of this debate?

3.7 **Why Has the United States Not Instituted a VAT?** The United States differs from virtually all developed countries in that it does not have a VAT. What important aspect of the U.S. political system might account for this difference with other countries? (Related to Application 3 on page 360.)

CHAPTER

18 International Trade and Public Policy

Countries always want to have foreign markets open for their exporters.

But if a country limits access to its own markets, foreign countries may take action to limit access to their own markets. The United States, despite an overall strong record in trade, is no exception. Here are a few examples.

As part of the North American Free Trade Agreement, the United States was required to open its borders to trucks from Mexico, although it resisted allowing this. As a result, in 2009 Mexico imposed tariffs on over $2 billion of U.S. goods, reducing employment in U.S. export industries.

In 2010 the United States accused China of selling aluminum products below their fair market value and imposed sanctions on the Chinese. In turn, China decided that the United States was doing precisely the same thing with nylon products and imposed its own tariffs on these products.

Two years later, the United States again charged China with selling solar cells below costs and unfairly providing subsidies to its producers. It imposed steep tariffs on Chinese imports. The Chinese did not look upon this favorably and began investigating other U.S. products on which to impose their own sanctions.

Trade agreements can help lower barriers to international commerce, but countries still have to believe that other countries are "playing fair." Otherwise, two can tango.

LEARNING OBJECTIVES

- Explain carefully the terms *comparative advantage* and *terms of trade*.
- List the common protectionist policies.
- Describe the rationales that have been offered for protectionist policies.
- Summarize the history of international trade agreements.
- Analyze one recent controversy in trade policy.

MyEconLab
MyEconLab helps you master each objective and study more efficiently.

As the world economy grows, U.S. policies toward international trade become ever more important. Many people view trade as a "zero-sum game." They believe that if one country gains from international trade, another must lose. Based on this belief, they advocate restricting trade with other countries. The United States does restrict trade to protect U.S. jobs in many sectors, such as those in the apparel and steel industries. One lesson from this chapter is that free trade could make all countries better off. The challenge for government officials is to create policies that accomplish, or come close to accomplishing, this goal.

In this chapter, we discuss the benefits of international trade and the effects of policies that restrict trade.

18.1 Benefits from Specialization and Trade

What if you lived in a nation that could produce everything it consumed and didn't depend on any other country for its economic livelihood? If you were put in charge of your nation, would you pursue a policy of national self-sufficiency? Although self-sufficiency might sound appealing, it would actually be better for your country to specialize in the production of some products and then trade some of those products to other countries. You saw in Chapter 3 that specialization and exchange can make both parties better off. In this chapter, we use a simple example to explain the benefits of specialization and international trade between two nations.

Let's say there are two nations, Shirtland and Chipland. Each nation produces computer chips and shirts, and each consumes computer chips and shirts. Table 18.1 shows the daily output of the two goods for the two nations. In a single day, Shirtland can produce a maximum of either 108 shirts or 36 computer chips, whereas Chipland can produce a maximum of either 120 shirts or 120 computer chips. The last two rows of the table show the opportunity costs of the two goods. Recall the principle of opportunity cost.

TABLE 18.1 Output and Opportunity Cost

	Quantity Produced Per Day	Opportunity Cost of Shirts	Opportunity Cost of Chips
Shirtland	108 shirts 36 chips	1/3 chip	3 shirts
Chipland	120 shirts 120 chips	1 chip	1 shirt

PRINCIPLE OF OPPORTUNITY COST

The opportunity cost of something is what you sacrifice to get it.

In Chipland, the trade-off between shirts and chips is one to one: The opportunity cost of one shirt is one chip, and the opportunity cost of one chip is one shirt. In Shirtland, people can produce three times as many shirts as chips in a given amount of time: The opportunity cost of one chip is three shirts. Conversely, the opportunity cost of one shirt is one-third of a chip.

Production Possibilities Curve

Let's start by seeing what happens if Shirtland and Chipland are each self-sufficient. Each nation can use its resources (labor, land, buildings, machinery, and equipment) to produce its own shirts and chips. The *production possibilities curve* shows all the possible combinations of products that an economy can produce, given that its productive resources are fully employed and efficiently used. This curve, which we discussed in Chapter 2, provides a menu of production options. To keep things simple, we assume the curve is a straight line, indicating a constant trade-off between the two goods. As shown by Shirtland's production possibilities curve in Figure 18.1, the following combinations of chips and shirts are possible:

1 *All shirts and no chips*: point *a*. If Shirtland uses all its resources to produce shirts, it will produce 108 shirts per day.
2 *All chips and no shirts*: point *d*. If Shirtland uses all its resources to produce chips, it will produce 36 chips per day.
3 *Equal division of resources*: point *b*. Shirtland could divide its resources between shirts and chips to produce 54 shirts and 18 chips each day.

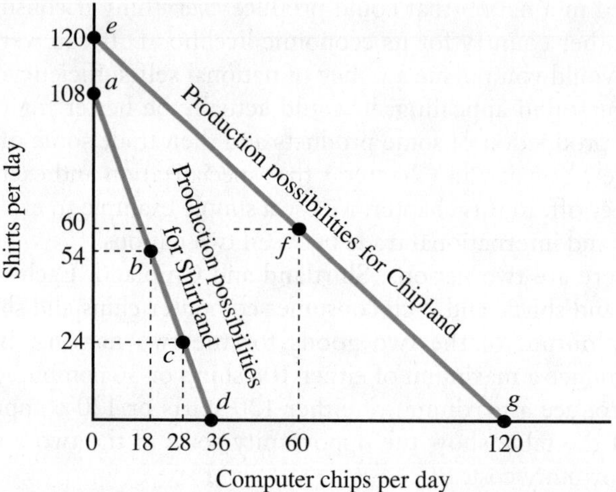

Shirtland Possibilities

Point	Shirts	Chips
a	108	0
b	54	18
c	24	28
d	0	36

Chipland Possibilities

Point	Shirts	Chips
e	120	0
f	60	60
g	0	120

▲ **FIGURE 18.1**
Production Possibilities Curve
The production possibilities curve shows the combination of two goods that can be produced with a nation's resources. For Chipland, the trade-off between the two goods is one to one. For Shirtland, the trade-off is 3 shirts for every computer chip. In the absence of trade, Shirtland can pick point *c*—28 chips and 24 shirts—and Chipland can pick point *f*—60 chips and 60 shirts.

All the other points on the line connecting points *a* and *d* are also feasible. One option is point *c*, with 28 chips and 24 shirts. The steepness of the curve's slope—negative 3.0—shows the opportunity cost of computer chips: 1 chip per 3 shirts. Figure 18.1 also shows the production possibilities curve for Chipland. Chipland can daily produce 120 shirts and no chips (point *e*), 120 chips and no shirts (point *g*), or any combination of chips and shirts between these two points. In Chipland, the trade-off is 1 shirt per computer chip: The opportunity cost of 1 chip is 1 shirt, so the slope of the production possibilities curve is negative 1.0.

Each nation could decide to be self-sufficient, picking a point on its production possibilities curve and producing everything it wants to consume. For example,

Shirtland could pick point *c*, daily producing 28 chips and 24 shirts, and Chipland could pick point *f*, daily producing 60 chips and 60 shirts. In the language of international trade, this is a case of *autarky*, or self-sufficiency (in Greek, *aut* means "self" and *arke* means "to suffice").

Comparative Advantage and the Terms of Trade

Would the two nations be better off if each specialized in the production of one good and traded with the other nation? To decide which nation should produce a particular good, we need to look at each good and figure out which nation has the lower opportunity cost of producing it. As you saw in Chapter 3, the nation with the lower opportunity cost has a *comparative advantage* in producing that good. As we emphasized in Chapter 3, it is comparative advantage that matters for trade—not *absolute advantage*, the ability of a nation to produce a particular good at a lower absolute cost than that of another nation. Let's see how it works.

1 *Chips produced in Chipland.* The opportunity cost of one chip is one shirt in Chipland, and the opportunity cost of one chip is three shirts in Shirtland. Chipland has a comparative advantage in the production of chips. Because Chipland sacrifices fewer shirts to produce one chip, Chipland should produce chips.
2 *Shirts produced in Shirtland.* The opportunity cost of one shirt is one chip in Chipland, and the opportunity cost of one shirt is one-third of a chip in Shirtland. When it comes to producing shirts, Shirtland has a comparative advantage because it sacrifices fewer chips to produce one shirt. Shirtland should therefore produce shirts.

Trade will make it possible for people in each specialized nation to consume both goods. At what rate will the two nations exchange shirts and chips? To determine the **terms of trade**, the rate at which units of one product can be exchanged for units of another product, let's look at how much Shirtland is willing to pay to get one chip and how much Chipland is willing to accept to give up one chip.

terms of trade
The rate at which units of one product can be exchanged for units of another product.

1 To get one chip, Shirtland is willing to pay up to three shirts. That's how many shirts it would sacrifice if it produced its own chip. For example, if the nations agree to exchange two shirts per chip, Shirtland could rearrange its production, producing one fewer chip but three more shirts. After exchanging two of the newly produced shirts for one chip, Shirtland will have the same number of chips but one additional shirt.
2 To give up one chip, Chipland is willing to accept any amount greater than one shirt. For example, if the nations agree to exchange two shirts per chip, Chipland could rearrange its production, producing one more chip and one fewer shirt. After it exchanges the newly produced chip for two shirts, Chipland will have the same number of chips but one additional shirt.

The potential for mutually beneficial trade between the two countries is possible because the willingness to pay—three shirts by Shirtland—exceeds the willingness to accept—one shirt by Chipland. It's possible for Shirtland and Chipland to split the difference between the willingness to pay and the willingness to accept, exchanging two shirts per chip. This will actually make both countries better off in terms of the total amount of goods they can consume. We'll see why next.

The Consumption Possibilities Curve

A nation that decides to specialize and trade is no longer limited to the options shown by its own production possibilities curve. The **consumption possibilities curve** shows the combinations of two goods (computer chips and shirts in our example) that a nation can consume when it specializes in one good and trades with another nation.

consumption possibilities curve
A curve showing the combinations of two goods that can be consumed when a nation specializes in a particular good and trades with another nation.

Figure 18.2 shows the consumption possibilities curve for our two nations, assuming that they exchange two shirts per chip:

- In Panel A, Chipland specializes in chip production, the good for which it has a comparative advantage. It produces 120 chips and no shirts (point *g*). Given the terms of trade, Chipland can exchange 40 of its 120 chips for 80 shirts, leading to point *h*. At point *h*, Chipland can consume 80 chips and 80 shirts.
- In Panel B, Shirtland specializes in shirt production. It produces 108 shirts and no chips (point *a*). Given the terms of trade, it can exchange 80 of its 108 shirts for 40 chips, leading to point *k* on its consumption possibilities curve. Shirtland can consume 28 shirts and 40 chips.

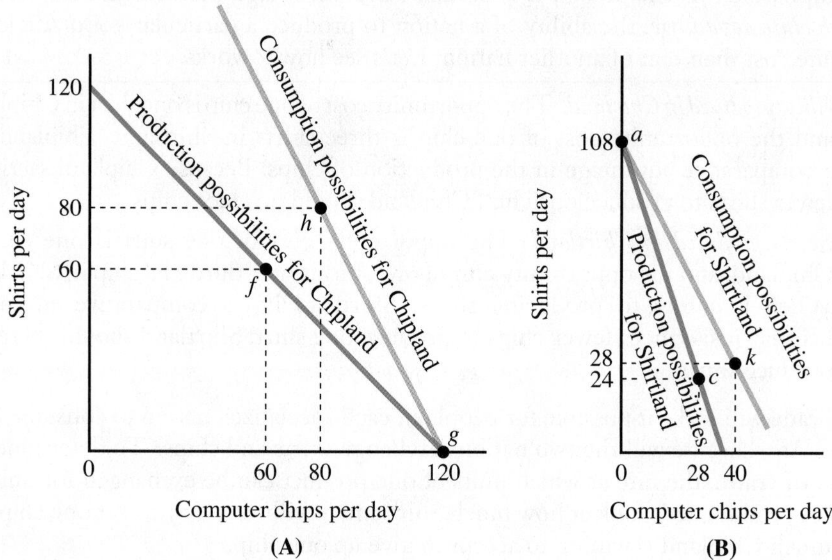

▲ **FIGURE 18.2**
Consumption Possibilities Curve
The consumption possibilities curve shows the combinations of computer chips and shirts that can be consumed if each country specializes and trades. In Panel A, Chipland produces 120 chips and trades 40 of these chips to Shirtland for 80 shirts. In Panel B, Shirtland produces 108 shirts and trades 80 of these shirts to Chipland for 40 chips. The trade allows each nation to consume more.

How do the outcomes with specialization and trade compare to the autarky outcomes? Chipland moves from point *f* (autarky) to point *h*, so trade increases the consumption of each good by 20 units. Shirtland moves from point *c* to point *k*, so this nation consumes 12 additional chips and 4 additional shirts.

In Figure 18.2, each consumption possibilities curve lies above the nation's production possibilities curves, meaning each nation has more options about how much to consume under specialization and trade. In most cases, a nation picks a point on the consumption possibilities curve that provides more of each good. Of course, this is a very simple example. In the actual world market, many countries produce and trade many goods. The marketplace determines what the terms of those trades will be, depending upon supply, demand, and pricing.

How Free Trade Affects Employment

You've now seen that trade allows each nation to consume more of each good. But we haven't yet discussed the effects of trade on employment. Under free trade, each nation will begin to specialize in a single good, causing considerable changes in the country's employment in different industries. In Chipland, the chip industry doubles in size—output increases from 60 to 120 chips per day—while the shirt industry disappears. Workers and other resources will leave the shirt industry and move to the chip industry. In Shirtland, the flow is in the opposite direction: Workers and other resources move from the chip industry to the shirt industry.

Is free trade good for everyone? Switching from self-sufficiency to specialization and trade increases consumption in both nations, so on average, people in each nation benefit from free trade. But some people in both nations will be harmed by free trade. In Chipland, for example, people in the shirt industry will lose their jobs when the shirt industry disappears. Some workers can easily move into the expanding computer chip industry. For these workers, free trade is likely to be beneficial. However, other shirt workers will be unable to make the move to the chip industry and will be forced to accept lower-paying jobs or face unemployment. Free trade is likely to make these displaced workers worse off. There is a saying, "Where you stand on an issue depends on where you sit." In our example, a worker sitting at a sewing machine in Chipland is likely to oppose free trade because that worker is likely to lose a job. A worker sitting at a workstation in a computer chip fabrication facility is likely to support free trade because the resulting increase in computer chip exports will generate more employment opportunities in that industry.

18.2 Protectionist Policies

Now that you know the basic rationale for specialization and trade, we can explore the effects of public policies that restrict it. All the restrictions we explore limit the gains from specialization and trade. We will consider four common import-restriction policies: an outright ban on imports, an import quota, voluntary export restraints, and a tariff.

Import Bans

To show how an import ban affects the market, let's start with an unrestricted market—no import ban. Figure 18.3 shows the market for shirts in Chipland, a nation with a comparative advantage in producing computer chips, not shirts. The domestic

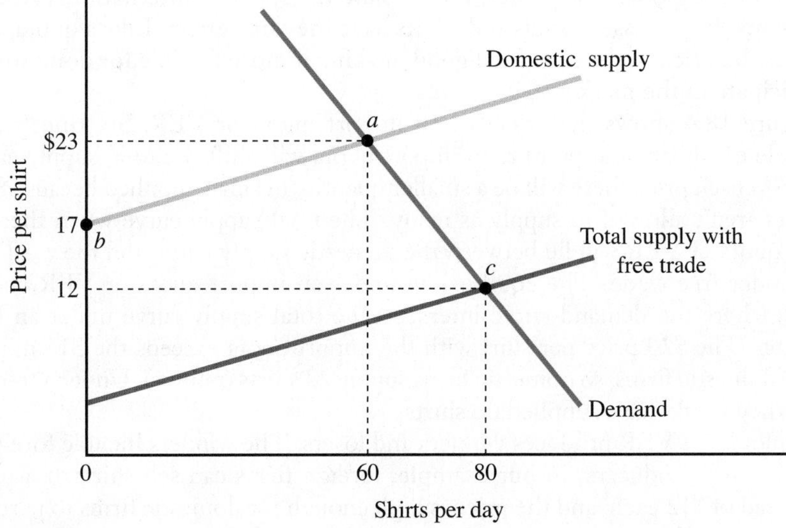

▲ **FIGURE 18.3**
Effects of an Import Ban
In the free-trade equilibrium, demand intersects the total supply curve at point *c*, with a price of $12 and a quantity of 80 shirts. If shirt imports are banned, the equilibrium is shown by the intersection of the demand curve and the domestic supply curve (point *a*). The price increases to $23.

supply curve shows the quantity of shirts supplied by firms in Chipland. Looking at point *b*, we see that Chipland firms will not supply any shirts unless the price is at least $17 per shirt. The total supply curve for shirts, which shows the quantity supplied by both domestic firms and foreign firms (in Shirtland), lies to the right of the domestic supply curve. At each price, the total supply of shirts exceeds the domestic supply because foreign firms supply shirts, too. Point *c* shows the free-trade equilibrium. The demand curve from domestic residents intersects the total supply curve at a price of $12 per shirt and a quantity of 80 shirts. Because this price is below the minimum price for domestic firms, domestic firms produce no shirts, and all the shirts in Chipland are imported from Shirtland.

What will happen if Chipland bans imported shirts? Foreign suppliers will disappear from the shirt market, so the total supply of shirts will be the domestic supply. In Figure 18.3, point *a* shows the equilibrium when Chipland bans imported shirts: The domestic demand curve intersects the domestic supply curve at a price of $23 per shirt and a quantity of 60 shirts. In other words, the decrease in supply resulting from the import ban increases the price consumers have to pay for shirts and decreases the quantity available for them to buy.

Quotas and Voluntary Export Restraints

import quota
A government-imposed limit on the quantity of a good that can be imported.

An alternative to an import ban is an **import quota**—a government-imposed limit on the quantity of a good that can be imported. An import quota is a restrictive policy that falls between free trade and an outright ban: Imports are cut, but not eliminated. For example, if a quota were put on shirts, the price consumers would have to pay would fall somewhere between the price they would pay with free trade ($12 per shirt, as in our example) and the price they would pay if imported shirts were banned ($23 per shirt). Where exactly the price would fall would depend on how high or low the quotas are.

voluntary export restraint (VER)
A scheme under which an exporting country voluntarily decreases its exports.

Import quotas are illegal under international trading rules. To get around these rules, an exporting country will sometimes agree to a **voluntary export restraint (VER)**. VERs are similar to import bans. When an exporting nation adopts a VER, it decreases its exports to avoid having to face even more restrictive trade policies importing countries might be tempted to impose on them. Although VERs are legal under global-trade rules, they violate the spirit of international free-trade agreements. In any case, quotas and VERs have the same effect. Like a quota, a VER increases the price of the restricted good, making it more feasible for domestic firms to participate in the market.

Figure 18.4 shows the effect of an import quota or VER. Starting from the free-trade equilibrium at point *c*, an import quota will shift the total supply curve to the left: At each price there will be a smaller quantity of shirts supplied because foreign suppliers aren't allowed to supply as many. The total supply curve when there is an import quota or VER will lie between the domestic supply curve and the total supply curve under free trade. The equilibrium under an import quota or VER occurs at point *d*, where the demand curve intersects the total supply curve under an import limitation. The $20 price per shirt with the import quota exceeds the $17 minimum price of domestic firms, so domestic firms supply 22 shirts (point *e*). Under a free-trade policy, they would have supplied no shirts.

import licenses
Rights, issued by a government, to import goods.

A quota or a VER produces winners and losers. The winners include foreign and domestic shirt producers. In our example, foreign firms can sell shirts at a price of $20 instead of $12 each, and the price is high enough for domestic firms to participate in the market. This generates benefits for the firms and their workers. The losers are consumers, who pay a higher price for shirts. In some cases, the government issues **import licenses** to some citizens, who can then buy shirts from foreign firms at a low price, such as $12, and sell the shirts at the higher domestic price, $20. Because import licenses provide profits to the holder, they are often awarded to politically powerful

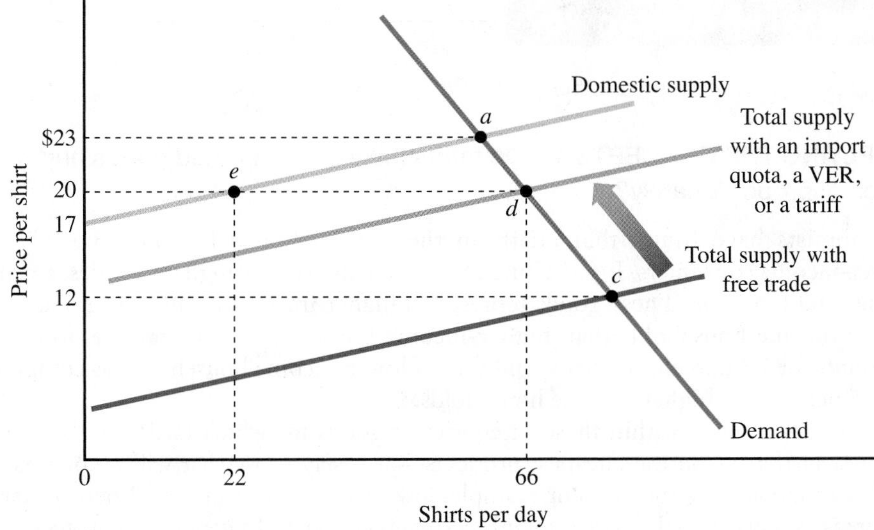

▲ FIGURE 18.4
Market Effects of a Quota, a VER, or a Tariff
An import quota shifts the supply curve to the left. The market moves upward along the demand curve to point *d*, which is between point *c* (free trade) and *a* (an import ban). We can reach the same point with a tariff that shifts the total supply curve to the same position.

firms or individuals. Moreover, because they are so valuable, some people may bribe government officials to obtain them.

We know consumers pay higher prices for goods that are subject to protectionist policies, but how much more? Here is one example. In the United States, voluntary export restraints on Japanese automobiles in 1984 increased the price of a Japanese car by about $1,300 and the price of a domestic car by about $660.[1]

An alternative to a quota or a VER is an import **tariff**, which is a tax on an imported good. Tariffs have the same effect as quotas and VERs. We know from our earlier discussions that a tax shifts the supply curve to the left and increases the equilibrium price. In Figure 18.4, suppose the tariff shifts the total supply curve with free trade so that it intersects the domestic demand curve at point *d*. In other words, we reach the same point we reached with the quota: Consumers pay the same $20 price per shirt, and domestic firms produce the same quantity (22 shirts).

tariff
A tax on imported goods.

There is one fundamental difference between a quota and a tariff. An import quota allows importers to buy shirts from foreign suppliers at a low price—say, $12 per shirt—and sell them for $20 each, the artificially high price. In other words, importers make money from the quota. Under a tariff, the government gets the money, collecting $8 per shirt from foreign suppliers. Citizens in Chipland will prefer the tariff to the quota because the government can use the revenue from the tariff to cut other taxes or expand public programs.

In the real world, tariffs can have major effects. One trade expert estimated that cutting industrial tariffs by 50 percent would increase the output of the world's economy by $270 billion per year. Similar easing of tariffs on agricultural products would cut the world's food bill by $100 billion.[2]

Tariffs also appear to disproportionately affect the poor.

Responses to Protectionist Policies

A restriction on imports is likely to lead to further restrictions on trade. For example, if Chipland bans shirt imports, Shirtland might retaliate by banning computer chips from Chipland. A trade war of this sort could escalate to the point where the two nations return to self-sufficiency. If this happens, the two countries would be forced

application 1

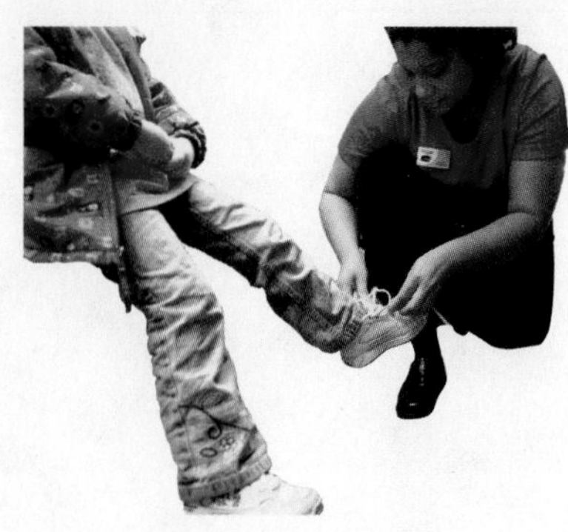

THE IMPACT OF TARIFFS ON THE POOR

APPLYING THE CONCEPTS #1: Do tariffs (taxes) on imported goods hurt the poor disproportionately?

Economists have found that tariffs in the United States fall most heavily on lower-income consumers. In the United States, tariffs are very high on textiles, apparel items, and footwear. These goods represent a higher fraction of the consumption of lower-income households than higher-income households. For example, footwear accounts for 1.3 percent of the expenditure of lower-income households, as compared to 0.5 percent for higher-income households.

Moreover, even within these categories of goods for which tariffs are high, the highest tariffs fall on the cheapest products—precisely those that will be purchased by lower-income consumers. For example, low-price sneakers face a 32 percent tariff whereas expensive track shoes face only a 20 percent tariff. In general, to protect U.S. industries, tariffs are highest on labor-intensive goods; goods that use relatively more labor than capital. But these goods tend to be lower priced. That is why tariffs do fall disproportionately on the poor. **Related to Exercise 2.7.**

SOURCE: Based on *Economic Report of the President 2006*, February 2006 (Washington, D.C.: Government Printing Office), chap. 7.

to scale back their consumption. We can see that by looking back at Figure 18.2: Chipland will move from point *h* to point *f*, and Shirtland will move from point *k* to point *c*. This sort of retaliatory response is common. Because it is, we know that protecting one industry in a nation is likely to harm that nation's other exports. Chipland's shirt industry, if protected from imports, may grow, but it will be at the expense of its computer-chip industry.

Many import restrictions have led to retaliatory policies and substantially lessened trade. The most famous was the Smoot–Hawley Tariff Act of 1930. When the United States increased its average tariff on imports to 59 percent, its trading partners retaliated with higher tariffs on U.S. products. The resulting trade war reduced international trade and deepened the worldwide depression of the 1930s.

The threat of retaliatory policies may persuade a nation to loosen its protectionist policies. For example, in 1995 the United States announced it would impose 100 percent tariffs on Japanese luxury cars if Japan didn't ease its restrictions on imported auto parts. Just hours before the tariffs were to take effect, the two nations reached an agreement that was expected to increase the sales of U.S. auto parts to Japanese firms. In 2002, President Bush imposed tariffs on steel. However, when faced with the threat of retaliatory policies in Europe, he ended the sanctions in 2003.

Import restrictions also create an incentive to smuggle goods. The restrictions create a gap between the cost of purchasing the restricted goods abroad and the price goods can be sold for in the protected economy, so there is a profit to be made.

18.3 What Are the Rationales for Protectionist Policies?

Why would a government impose protectionist policies such as an import ban, quota, VER, or tariff? We'll look at three possible reasons:

1 To shield workers from foreign competition

2 To nurture infant industries until they mature
3 To help domestic firms establish monopolies in world markets

To Shield Workers from Foreign Competition

One of the most basic arguments for protectionism is that it shields workers in industries that would be hurt by trade. Suppose, relative to the United States, nations in the Far East have a comparative advantage in producing textiles. If the United States were to reduce existing tariffs on textiles, domestic manufacturers could not compete. They would have to close their factories and lay off workers. In an ideal world, the laid-off workers would take new jobs in other sectors of the economy. In practice, this is difficult. Many workers don't immediately have the skills to go to work in other sectors, and obtaining those skills takes time. Moreover, the textile industry is heavily concentrated in the southeastern part of the United States. Politicians from that region will try to keep tariffs in place to prevent temporary unemployment and changes in employment patterns in their areas—they have an incentive to protect their own constituents, even though it may cause major economic losses for the economy. The result of this protection will be less-efficient production, higher prices, and lower consumption for the United States. How much does it cost to protect a job?

To Nurture Infant Industries until They Mature

During World War II the United States built hundreds of boats, called Liberty ships, for the navy. As more and more of these ships were built, each required fewer hours to complete because workers acquired knowledge during the production process and got better at it. Engineers and economists call this phenomenon **learning by doing**. To learn a new game, such as Ping-Pong, you learn by doing. At first, you may find it difficult to play, but your skills improve as you go along.

learning by doing
Knowledge and skills workers gain during production that increase productivity and lower cost.

infant industries
Industries that are at an early stage of development.

Tariffs and other protectionist policies are often defended on the grounds that they protect new or **infant industries** that are in the early stages of development and can benefit from learning by doing. A tariff shields a young industry from the competition of its more mature rivals. After the infant industry "grows up," the tariff can eventually be eliminated because the industry is able to compete. In practice, infant industries rarely become competitive with their foreign rivals. During the 1950s and 1960s, many Latin American countries used tariffs and other policies to protect their young manufacturing industries from foreign competition. Unfortunately, the domestic industries never became as efficient as foreign suppliers, and the Latin American countries that tried this policy suffered. Another problem with protecting an infant industry is that once a government gives an industry tariff protection, it is difficult to take that protection away. More generally, even some established companies also complain about "unfair competition," but this concept does not always make sense.

To Help Domestic Firms Establish Monopolies in World Markets

If the production of a particular good requires extremely large economies of scale, the world market will support only a few, or perhaps just one, firm. In this case, a nation might be tempted to adopt policies to ensure a company within its borders will end up being the world monopolist. Suppose the commercial aircraft industry can support only one large firm. If two firms enter the industry, both will lose money. A nation could agree to provide financial support to a domestic firm to guarantee the firm will make a profit. With such a guarantee, the domestic firm will enter the industry. Knowing this, a foreign firm will be reluctant to enter, so the domestic firm will capture the monopoly profit. The country where the successful firm is located will benefit from higher production and more jobs for its citizens.

application 2

CHINESE IMPORTS AND LOCAL ECONOMIES

APPLYING THE CONCEPTS #2: What have been the local effects of Chinese imports?

Do imports from China really make a difference in U.S. labor markets? Economists David Autor, David Dorn, and Gordon Hanson examined detailed data on Chinese imports into local communities. Some local communities are more heavily impacted by Chinese imports than others depending on the mix of products produced locally. The authors found that the pace of Chinese import growth was so rapid from 1990 to 2007 that it often had a strong and negative effect on local economies. Those communities that were more exposed to imports had larger increases in workers receiving unemployment insurance, food stamps, and disability payments.

These findings do not mean that trade with China was ultimately beneficial. Displaced workers can find new jobs and import competition lowers prices for all consumers. But it does mean that the burden of adjustment to imports varies by region. Some regions will have a more difficult time adjusting than others to a sudden influx of imports. The study also does not measure the indirect benefits from trade with China. As the Chinese economy expanded during this period, it created more export opportunities for producers in the United States. Those benefits were not measured in this study. **Related to Exercise 3.7.**

SOURCE: Based on David H. Autor, David Dorn, and Gordon H. Hanson, "The China Syndrome: Local Labor Market Effects of Import Competition in the United States," MIT Working Paper, May 2012, Available at: http://economics.mit.edu/faculty/dautor/papers/inequality (Accessed May 28, 2012).

One famous example is Airbus, an airplane-manufacturing consortium in Europe that competes with the U.S. firm Boeing. Several European countries provided large subsidies for the firms producing the Airbus line of planes. These subsidies allowed the consortium firms to underprice their rivals in the United States, and at least one U.S. manufacturer of commercial airplanes was forced out of business.

What could go wrong with these monopoly creation policies? First, if both nations subsidize their domestic firms, both firms will enter the market and lose money. The taxpayers in both countries will then have to pay for the subsidies. Second, a nation may pick the wrong industry to subsidize. Together, the British and French subsidized an airplane known as the Concorde, which flew at supersonic speeds, rapidly shuttling passengers between Europe and the United States. Although the Concorde captured the market, the market was not worth capturing. The venture lost money because the Concorde was very costly to develop and fly, and few people were willing to pay a large premium for supersonic travel. The Concorde stopped flying in 2003. Finally, the subsidized firm may not perform well. As an example, in 2006, Airbus was facing severe problems with its planes and losing business to its competitor, Boeing.

18.4 A Brief History of International Tariff and Trade Agreements

Today, the average U.S. tariff is 4.6 percent of the value of imported goods, a rate close to the average tariffs in Japan and most European nations but very low by historical standards. When the Smoot–Hawley tariffs were implemented in the

1930s, the average U.S. tariff was a whopping 59 percent of a product's price. Tariffs are lower today because several international agreements subsequently reduced them.

The first major international trade agreement following World War II was the **General Agreement on Tariffs and Trade (GATT)**. This agreement was initiated in 1947 by the United States and 23 other nations and now has over 149 members. Nine rounds of GATT negotiations over tariffs and trade regulations have taken place, resulting in progressively lower tariffs for the member nations. The last completed set of negotiations, the Uruguay round (1994), decreased tariffs by about one-third of the previous level. In 1995, the **World Trade Organization (WTO)** was formed to enforce GATT and other international trade agreements. Under GATT's "most favored nation" provision, a country that reduces tariffs for one nation must do so for all members of GATT. This provision helps reduce tariffs throughout the world.

General Agreement on Tariffs and Trade (GATT)
An international agreement established in 1947 that has lowered trade barriers between the United States and other nations.

World Trade Organization (WTO)
An organization established in 1995 that oversees GATT and other international trade agreements, resolves trade disputes, and holds forums for further rounds of trade negotiations.

The most recent round of trade negotiations began in Doha, Qatar, in 2001 but major negotiations collapsed in 2008, although the negotiations still continue on a smaller scale. This round was billed as an attempt to benefit developing countries that exported agricultural goods. The idea was that reductions in subsidies and tariffs on agriculture goods in developed countries would promote exports of agriculture goods for developing countries. In turn, developed countries wanted lower tariffs for industrial goods in developing countries. Why did the negotiations fail? One reason was that China and India, rapidly growing countries each with populations over a billion, were more interested in promoting their industrial bases than their agricultural exports. Perhaps a second reason was that previous trade negotiations had been successful, leaving less room for "grand bargains" that would motivate all countries to embrace new agreements.

If global negotiations do not work, what alternatives are there? In addition to the large group of nations in the WTO, other groups of nations have formed trade associations to lower trade barriers and promote international trade. Here are some of the best-known agreements:

- The North American Free Trade Agreement (NAFTA) took effect in 1994 and was implemented over a 15-year period. It eliminates all tariffs and other trade barriers between Canada, Mexico, and the United States.
- The European Union (EU) was designed to remove all trade barriers within Europe and create a single market. Initially, the EU consisted of just six countries: Belgium, Germany, France, Italy, Luxembourg, and the Netherlands. Denmark, Ireland, and the United Kingdom joined in 1973; Greece in 1981; Spain and Portugal in 1986; and Austria, Finland, and Sweden in 1995. In 2004, the biggest ever enlargement took place with 10 new countries joining the EU.
- The leaders of 18 Asian nations have formed an organization called Asian Pacific Economic Cooperation (APEC). In 1994, APEC signed a nonbinding agreement to reduce trade barriers among these nations.
- The Dominican Republic–Central America Free Trade Agreement (DR-CAFTA) promotes trade liberalization between the United States, the Dominican Republic, and five Central American countries: Costa Rica, El Salvador, Guatemala, Honduras, and Nicaragua. DR-CAFTA is modeled after NAFTA.

Some economists are concerned that these regional trade agreements may stand in the way of broader international trade agreements under GATT. Although regional agreements may lead to reduced tariffs for neighboring or member countries, they do little to promote efficiency across the globe. For example, a Belgian firm may find it easier to sell goods in France than does a firm from South America that has a lower cost of production.

18.5 Recent Policy Debates and Trade Agreements

We're now ready to discuss three recent policy debates concerning international trade:

1. Are foreign producers dumping their products?
2. Do trade laws inhibit environmental protection?
3. Do outsourcing and trade cause income inequality?

Are Foreign Producers Dumping Their Products?

dumping
A situation in which the price a firm charges in a foreign market is lower than either the price it charges in its home markets or the production cost.

Although tariff rates have been reduced in recent years, a number of controversies surrounding free trade remain. One of these relates to *dumping*. A firm is **dumping** when the price it charges in a foreign market is either lower than the price it charges in its home market or lower than its production cost. Dumping is illegal under international trade agreements. Hundreds of cases of alleged dumping are presented to WTO authorities each year. Here are some cases in which the WTO concluded that dumping had indeed occurred: Hong Kong VCRs sold in Europe; Chinese bicycles sold in the United States; Asian TV sets sold in Europe; steel from Brazil, India, Japan, and Spain sold in the United States; U.S. beef sold in Mexico; and Chinese computer disks sold in Japan and the United States. Under the current provisions of the WTO,

application 3

ARE THEY REALLY DUMPING?

APPLYING THE CONCEPTS #3: How does the Commerce Department try to determine whether countries are dumping their products?

Dumping is selling a product in a foreign market at a lower price than a firm's own domestic market. You might think that this would require a comparison of *actual* prices charged in home markets compared to foreign markets. But that is rarely the case in the United States. For example, from 1995 to 1998, only 4 out of 141 cases of dumping used actual prices.

Instead, the U.S. Department of Commerce typically uses a "constructed value" method where it makes its own estimates of what prices in countries' own markets *would be* based on available data on production costs, transportation, and other expenses and also a margin for profit and administration. In many cases, these are very crude and dated estimates. In other cases, they rely solely on the information provided by the parties who filed the complaint, who clearly have a vested interest in the outcome.

Perhaps this is why the Commerce Department virtually always finds that foreign countries are in fact guilty of dumping their products. Chinese companies have been accused of dumping for a wide array of products including crawfish, paint brushes, sodium nitrate, and plastic shopping bags. Critics of dumping believe that "constructed values" calculations overstate prices in domestic markets and inevitably lead to the conclusion that firms are in fact guilty of dumping their products. **Related to Exercise 5.7.**

SOURCE: Based on Douglas A. Irwin, *Free Trade under Fire* (Princeton, New Jersey: Princeton University Press, 2009), chap. 5.

a nation can impose antidumping duties, a tax, on products that are being dumped within its borders.

Why would a firm dump—charge a low price in the foreign market? The first reason is price discrimination. **Price discrimination** occurs when a firm charges a different price to different customers buying the same product. If a firm has a monopoly in its home market but faces strong competition in a foreign market, it will naturally charge a higher price in the home market. What the firm is doing is using its monopoly power to charge higher prices to consumers at home and charge lower prices to consumers abroad where it faces competition. This strategy maximizes the firm's profits.

price discrimination
The practice of selling a good at different prices to different consumers.

To illustrate how international price discrimination works, let's look at the case of Korean VCRs.[3]

In the 1980s there were only three firms, all Korean, selling VCRs in Korea, but there were dozens of firms selling VCRs in Europe. The lack of competition in Korea generated very high prices for Korean consumers, who paid much more than European consumers paid for identical Korean VCRs and VCRs produced by firms in other countries. Essentially, Korean firms used their market power to discriminate against consumers in their own country. When international trade authorities concluded these companies were, indeed, dumping VCRs in Europe, the Korean firms responded by cutting prices in their home market. However, they didn't increase their prices in Europe—much to the delight of European consumers and the dismay of European producers, who had sought relief from the dumping in the first place.

The Korean VCR example brings up a second reason for dumping: **predatory pricing**—cutting prices in an attempt to drive rival firms out of business. The predatory firm sets its price below its production cost, low enough that both the predator and its prey (a firm in the foreign market) lose money. After the prey goes out of business, the predator increases its price to earn a monopoly profit.

predatory pricing
A firm sells a product at a price below its production cost to drive a rival out of business and then increases the price.

Although the rationale for antidumping laws is to prevent predatory pricing, it is difficult to determine whether low prices are the result of this or price discrimination. Many economists are skeptical about how frequently predatory pricing actually occurs, as opposed to price discrimination. They suspect many nations use their antidumping laws as protectionist policies in disguise. Because WTO rules limit tariffs and quotas, some nations may be tempted to substitute antidumping duties for these protectionist policies.

Until the 1990s, antidumping cases were brought almost exclusively by Australia, New Zealand, Europe, Canada, and the United States. However, starting in the 1990s, the number of antidumping cases alleged by developing countries began to rise. Today, approximately half the cases are brought by developing countries. Professor Thomas Prusa of Rutgers University has studied antidumping and has found it is a potent weapon for protecting domestic industries. If an antidumping case is settled and a tariff is imposed as a result, imports typically fall by 50 to 70 percent during the first three years of the protection period. Even if a country loses a claim, imports still fall by 15 to 20 percent.[4]

Do Trade Laws Inhibit Environmental Protection?

In recent trade negotiations, a new player—environmental groups—appeared on the scene. Starting in the early 1990s, environmentalists began to question whether policies that liberalized trade could harm the environment. They were concerned that increased trade would lead to worldwide environmental degradation. An important issue that attracted their attention was the killing of dolphins by tuna fishers.

Anyone who catches tuna with a large net will also catch the dolphins that swim with the tuna, and most of the dolphins will die. In 1972, the United States outlawed the use of tuna nets by U.S. ships. However, ships from other nations, including Mexico, were still catching tuna with nets and selling that tuna in the United States. The United States responded with a ban of Mexican tuna caught with nets. The Mexican government complained to an international trade authority that the tuna boycott was an unfair trade barrier. The trade authority agreed with Mexico and forced the United States to remove the boycott.

Under current WTO rules, a country can adopt any environmental standard it chooses, as long as it does not discriminate against foreign producers. For example, the United States can limit the exhaust emissions of all cars that operate in the United States. As long as emissions rules apply equally to all cars, domestic and imports, the rules are legal according to the WTO. An international panel upheld U.S. fuel efficiency rules for automobiles on this principle.

The tuna boycott was a violation of WTO rules because killing dolphins does not harm the U.S. environment directly. For the same reason, the United States cannot ban imported goods produced by factories that generate air or water pollution in other countries. It is easy to understand why WTO rules do not allow countries to restrict trade on the basis of the methods that are used to produce goods and services. Countries differ in the value they place on the environment. For example, a poor nation may be willing to tolerate more pollution if it means attaining a higher standard of living for its citizens.

If trade restrictions cannot be used to protect the dolphins and deal with other global environmental problems, what else can we do? Shouldn't we have the right to protect dolphins? International agreements have been used for a variety of different environmental goals, from limiting the harvest of whales to reducing the chemicals that deplete the ozone layer. These agreements are difficult to reach, however, so some nations will be tempted to use trade restrictions to pursue environmental goals. If they do, they will encounter resistance because WTO rules mean that a nation can pursue its environmental goals only within its own borders. In recent years, environmentalists have lobbied Congress not to approve bilateral trade deals unless sufficient environmental standards are in place. This trend is likely to continue.

Trade disputes about environmental issues are part of a larger phenomenon that occurs when trade issues and national regulations collide. At one time, most trade disputes were simply matters of protecting domestic industries from foreign competition. Agriculture, textile, and steel industries around the world frequently benefited from various forms of protection. But in recent years, a new breed of trade disputes has erupted revolving around social problems and the role that government regulation should play in solving them.

The EU, for example, has banned imports of hormone-treated beef. The United States and Canada successfully challenged this ban with the WTO. They argued there was no scientific evidence that hormone-treated beef adversely affected human health. The EU refused to rescind the ban and, as a consequence, the United States and Canada were permitted to impose retaliatory tariffs on a wide range of European products that affected many EU industries.

The EU's ban on hormone-treated beef was intended to protect European farmers from imports, but it also reflected Europeans' nervousness about technology. After all, Europe banned all hormone-treated beef, not just imported beef. Shouldn't a country have a right to pursue this policy, even if it is not based on the best science of the day? Although the costs of the policy are straightforward in terms of higher beef prices, the benefits, in terms of potential safety and peace of mind, are much more difficult to assess. Similar issues have arisen as genetically modified crops have become more commonplace. As a world trading community, we will have to decide at what point we allow national policy concerns to override principles of free trade.

application 4

TRADE, CONSUMPTION, AND INEQUALITY

APPLYING THE CONCEPTS #4: Why might international trade reduce measured inequality in the United States?

While it is conventional wisdom now that inequality in the United States has increased in the last several decades, until recently no one had taken a careful look at the actual living standards of different income groups, taking into account the goods they purchase. Two economists from the University of Chicago, Christian Broda and John Romalis, discovered that the prices low-income groups paid for goods and services increased substantially less than for high-income groups. As a result, living standards have not become more unequal.

The key to understanding this result is that consumption patterns of the rich and poor differ. The poor consume a higher ratio of nondurable goods (such as cosmetics, toys, and sporting goods) to services than the rich, while prices for nondurable goods have risen less than prices for services. Prices for the nondurable goods purchased by the poor, which are typically sold in grocery, drug, and mass merchandise stores, also increased less than the prices of nondurable goods purchased by the rich. And the poor typically consume a higher fraction of new goods, whose prices have often fallen.

Trade with China is an important part of this story. About one-third of the change in relative prices that has helped the poor can be accounted for by an increase in imports from China. These are the goods that stock the shelves of Walmart and other lower-end stores where the poor shop. Sam Walton and his successors effectively ran their own antipoverty program.

The moral of the story: Trade does not just affect employment patterns—it also changes prices. We must take both factors into account to understand how living standards have changed for the rich and poor. **Related to Exercise 5.9.**

SOURCE: Based on Christian Broda and John Romalis, "Inequality and Prices: Does China Benefit the Poor in America?" March 26, 2008, http://siteresources.worldbank.org/INTMACRO/Resources/June5&62008MGConferencePAPERBRODA.pdf (accessed May 29, 2012).

Do Outsourcing and Trade Cause Income Inequality?

Inequality in wages has been growing in the United States since 1973. The wages of skilled workers have risen faster than the wages of unskilled workers. World trade has also boomed since 1973. Could there be a connection between the two?

Trade theory suggests a link between increased trade and increased wage inequality. Here is how they might be linked. Suppose the United States produces two types of goods: one using skilled labor (say, airplanes) and one using unskilled labor (say, textiles). The United States is likely to have a comparative advantage in products that use skilled labor, and developing countries are likely to have a comparative advantage in products that use unskilled labor. An increase in world trade will increase both exports and imports. An increase in U.S. exports means we'll need to produce more goods requiring skilled labor, so the domestic demand for skilled labor will increase, and so will the wages of these workers. At the same time, an increase in U.S. imports means we'll be buying more goods produced by unskilled laborers abroad, so the demand for unskilled workers here will decrease, and these people's wages will fall. As a result, the gap between the wages of the two types of workers in the United States will grow.

outsourcing
Firms producing components of their goods and services in other countries.

In addition, U.S. firms will produce some components of their goods and services overseas, which is known as **outsourcing**. If a firm outsources products that use unskilled labor, the demand for unskilled labor in the United States will decline, and this will also increase the gap between wages for the skilled and the unskilled.

Economists have tried to determine how much trade has contributed to growing wage inequality in the United States. As usual, other factors make such a determination difficult. It is difficult, for example, to distinguish between the effects of trade and the effects of technical progress. Technical change, such as the rapid introduction and use of computers, will also tend to increase the demand for skilled workers and decrease the demand for unskilled workers. Economists have noted, however, that the exports of goods using skilled labor and the imports of goods using unskilled labor have both increased, just as the theory predicts. Nonetheless, at least some of the increased wage inequality is caused by international trade. Trade, however, may also reduce the prices of goods and services purchased by consumers in different income classes. We must take this factor into account in assessing trade and inequality.

One response to this undesirable side effect of trade is to use trade restrictions to protect industries that use unskilled workers. Another approach is to make the transition to an economy with more skilled than unskilled jobs less traumatic. In the long run, of course, workers will move to industries that require skilled labor, and they will eventually earn higher wages. However, in the short run the government could facilitate the transition by providing assistance for the education and training of unskilled workers.

More recently, there has been another concern. In recent years, jobs in call centers for airlines and credit card companies, customer service and technical support for computers, and the work of writing computer code have been relocated overseas. Some of these jobs require considerable skill, and therefore not all jobs that are outsourced will be low-skilled jobs. Nor can all services be outsourced, particularly those that are less routine. In the coming years, we will gain better insights into how international trade and outsourcing affect the wages of skilled workers.

Why Do People Protest Free Trade?

We have seen some of the important policy issues surrounding trade. Under current international trade rules, a country cannot dictate the terms under which another country actually produces the goods and services it sells—even if production harms the environment. It is also possible that free trade can contribute to inequality within the United States, although lower prices for goods consumed partially offset this effect. But do these reasons explain the passion we sometimes see in protests against free trade, such as the riots in 1999 in Seattle at a WTO meeting or the protestors dressed in death masks gathering at world trade meetings? Possibly, but protestors are more likely driven by something very basic. As we have seen in this chapter, trade and specialization provide important opportunities to raise living standards throughout the globe. But they also mean individuals and nations surrender some of their independence and sovereignty. By not producing precisely what we consume, we become dependent on others to trade with us. By cooperating with other nations, we need to develop agreed-upon rules that, at times, limit our own actions.

The protestors may simply not understand the principles of trade, but they also may fear loss of cultural identity and independence. In today's world, "no man is an island." Nations have become increasingly dependent on one another. Multinational corporations are the ultimate symbol of this interdependence, producing and distributing goods on a global scale. Thus companies such as McDonald's, Starbucks, or Nike can come under attack by protestors. The benefits of trade, however, are so vast that countries will need to find ways to address issues of sovereignty and control while retaining an open and prosperous trading system.

SUMMARY

In this chapter, we discussed the benefits of specialization and trade, and we explored the trade-offs associated with protectionist policies. There is a basic conflict between consumers who prefer free trade because free trade decreases prices and workers in the protected industries who want to keep their jobs. Here are the main points of the chapter:

1 If one country has a *comparative advantage* vis-à-vis another country in producing a particular good (a lower opportunity cost), specialization and trade will benefit both countries.

2 An import ban or an *import quota* increases prices, protecting domestic industries, but domestic consumers pay the price.

3 Because the victims of protectionist policies often retaliate, the protection of a domestic industry can harm an exporting industry.

4 A *tariff*, a tax on imports, generates revenue for the government, whereas an *import quota*—a limit on imports—generates revenue for foreigners or importers.

5 In principle, the laws against *dumping* are designed to prevent *predatory pricing*. In practice, predatory pricing laws are often used to shield domestic industries from competition. Allegations of it are hard to prove.

6 Under *World Trade Organization (WTO)* rules, each country may pursue its environmental goals only within its own borders.

7 International trade has contributed to the widening gap between the wages of low-skilled and high-skilled labor. However, it also has reduced the relative prices facing the poor, offsetting some of the effects on inequality.

KEY TERMS

consumption possibilities curve, p. 367
dumping, p. 376
General Agreement on Tariffs and Trade (GATT), p. 375
import licenses, p. 370
import quota, p. 370
infant industries, p. 373
learning by doing, p. 373
outsourcing, p. 380
predatory pricing, p. 377
price discrimination, p. 377
tariff, p. 371
terms of trade, p. 367
voluntary export restraint (VER), p. 370
World Trade Organization (WTO), p. 375

EXERCISES

All problems are assignable in MyEconLab.

18.1 Benefits from Specialization and Trade

1.1 A country has a comparative advantage if it has a lower __________ cost of producing a good.

1.2 The terms of trade is the rate at which two goods can be __________ for one another.

1.3 Suppose a country has a comparative advantage in shirts but not computer chips. Workers in the chip industry will be __________ with trade.

1.4 Countries will always export the goods in which they have absolute advantage. __________ (True/False)

1.5 **Finding Comparative Advantage.** In one minute, Country B can produce either 1,000 TVs and no computers or 500 computers and no TVs. Similarly, in one minute Country C can produce either 2,400 TVs or 600 computers.

a. Compute the opportunity costs of TVs and computers for each country. Which country has a comparative advantage in producing TVs? Which country has a comparative advantage in producing computers?

b. Draw the production possibilities curves for the two countries.

1.6 **Benefits from Trade.** In Country U, the opportunity cost of a computer is 10 pairs of shoes. In Country C, the opportunity cost of a computer is 100 pairs of shoes.

a. Suppose the two countries split the difference between the willingness to pay for computers and the willingness to accept computers. Compute the terms of trade, that is, the rate at which the two countries will exchange computers and shoes.

b. Suppose the two countries exchange one computer for the number of shoes dictated by the terms of trade you computed in part (a). Compute the net benefit from trade for each country.

1.7 **Measuring the Gains from Trade.** Consider two countries, Tableland and Chairland, each capable of producing tables and chairs. Chairland can produce the following combinations of chairs and tables:

All chairs and no tables: 36 chairs per day

All tables and no chairs: 18 tables per day

Tableland can produce the following combinations of chairs and tables:

All chairs and no tables: 40 chairs per day

All tables and no chairs: 40 tables per day

In each country, there is a fixed trade-off of tables for chairs.

a. Draw the two production possibilities curves, with chairs on the vertical axis and tables on the horizontal axis.

b. Suppose each country is initially self-sufficient and divides its resources equally between the two goods. How much does each country produce and consume?

c. Which country has a comparative advantage in producing tables? Which country has a comparative advantage in producing chairs?

d. If the two countries split the difference between the buyer's willingness to pay for chairs and the seller's willingness to accept, in terms of chairs per table, what are the terms of trade?

e. Draw the consumption possibilities curves.

f. Suppose each country specializes in the good for which it has a comparative advantage, and it exchanges 14 tables for some quantity of chairs. Compute the consumption bundles—*bundles* mean the consumption of tables and chairs—for each country.

1.8 **Who Benefits in the Short Run?** Suppose a country is about to open its markets for trade. In the short run, would you rather be employed in an industry with a comparative advantage or a comparative disadvantage? What about in the long run?

18.2 Protectionist Policies

2.1 If a country bans the importation of a particular good, the market equilibrium is shown by the intersection of the __________ curve and the __________ curve.

2.2 The equilibrium price under an import quota is __________ (above/below) the price that occurs with an import ban and __________ (above/below) the price that occurs with free trade.

2.3 From the perspective of the government, a __________ (tariff/quota) is better.

2.4 Threatening to impose a tariff on a country's exports if it doesn't open up its markets to trade is an example of a __________ policy.

2.5 **Incentives for Smuggling.** If a country bans imports, smugglers may try to penetrate its markets. Suppose Chipland bans shirt imports, causing some importers to bribe customs officials who "look the other way" as smugglers bring shirts into the country. Your job is to combat shirt smuggling. Use the information in Figure 18.3 on page 369 to answer the following questions:

a. Suppose importers can sell their shirts on the world market at a price of $12 per shirt. How much is an importer willing to pay to get customs officials to look the other way?

b. What sort of change in trade policy would make your job easier?

2.6 **Tariffs on Computer Chips.** Suppose a country imposed tariffs on computer chips to protect its chip-making industries. What other types of firms in that economy might object to this policy?

2.7 **Tariffs and the Poor.** Historically, apparel and textiles were subject to high tariffs. Explain why this might hurt low-income consumers more than high-income consumers. (Related to Application 1 on page 372.)

2.8 **Auctioning Import Licenses.** In the text we explained that tariffs can be set to have the same effects as import quotas. However, if the government gives import licenses to producers, it will not collect any revenues. Suppose the government auctions the import licenses to the highest bidders. How will the revenue from the auction compare to the revenue raised by tariffs?

18.3 What Are the Rationales for Protectionist Policies?

3.1 The __________ industry argument is often given to provide a rationale for tariffs for new firms.

3.2 Knowledge gained during production is known as __________ by doing.

3.3 If only one firm can exist in a market, a government may try to subsidize the firm so that the country can share in the __________ profits.

3.4 In the 1950s and 1960s, countries in __________ used tariffs and other policies to nurture domestic industries.

3.5 **Learning by Doing?** An industry has been operating for 10 years under protection. The government wants to remove the trade protection, but the industry claims that it needs the protection because of learning by doing. Evaluate its claim. Can you think of a circumstance where it could be true?

3.6 **Two Countries Fighting over Airplane Production.** Suppose there are monopoly profits in the production of airplanes, but two countries are each determined to capture the industry. When one country subsidizes its domestic firm, the other country matches the tactic. As a result, both firms stay in business. Who gains and who loses? Consider the effects on the firms, consumers, and taxpayers.

3.7 **Why the Pace of Imports May Matter.** If it rains very hard during a major storm, the drains in the streets may not be able to handle all the water and flooding will temporarily occur. Use this analogy to explain why the pace of imports into a community may be important in the short run for economic adjustment. (Related to Application 2 on page 374).

3.8 **Protection for Candle Makers.** In a famous tale, the French economist Frédéric Bastiat (1801–1850) wrote a fake petition for relief from trade for the candle makers. They were complaining that the sun was hurting their business. What lesson do you draw from this tale?

18.4 A Brief History of International Tariff and Trade Agreements

4.1 The latest trade round is called the __________ round.

4.2 The __________ was formed in 1995 to oversee GATT.

4.3 NAFTA is a free-trade agreement between the United States, Mexico, and __________.

4.4 The average tariff rate in the United States is roughly __________ percent.

4.5 **A Major Change in U.S. Trade Policy?** In Chapter 7 of the 2006 *Economic Report of the President* (www.gpoaccess.gov/eop/download.html), the authors of the report discuss the important changes that occurred in 1934 under the Reciprocal Trade Agreements Act. They contend that it began to move the United States to a policy of more open trade after the Smoot–Hawley tariffs. Identify the key changes enacted in 1934.

4.6 **Expansion in the European Union.** When the EU originated, member countries generally had similar standards of living. However, with the most recent expansion of the EU, countries that were less developed joined the developed countries. What implications might the entry of the new countries have for wage inequality within the more established European countries?

4.7 **Trade in Intellectual Property.** Trade in international property (for example, patents, licenses, royalty agreements) has been particularly controversial. Go to the intellectual property section of the WTO's Web site (http://www.wto.org/english/tratop_e/trips_e/trips_e.htm) and explore some of its case studies. Do developing countries, as well as developed countries, have an interest in protecting intellectual property?

18.5 Recent Policy Debates and Trade Agreements

5.1 Pricing below production cost or selling at prices in foreign markets less than those in domestic markets is known as __________.

5.2 Under global trade rules, the United States was allowed to ban Mexican tuna because Mexico used fishing nets that killed dolphins. __________ (True/False)

5.3 Suppose the United States has a comparative advantage in goods that use skilled labor. If we trade with a country that has a comparative advantage in goods using unskilled labor, the wage differences between skilled and unskilled labor in the United States will __________.

5.4 Under a scheme of __________ pricing, a firm cuts its price to drive out rivals and then raises its price later.

5.5 **Trade in Genetically Modified Crops.** Suppose the residents of a country become fearful of using genetically modified crops in their food supply. Consider the following two possible scenarios:

   a. Aware of consumer sentiment, the largest supermarket chains in the country vow they will not purchase food products that use genetically modified crops.

   b. The government, aware of voter sentiment during an election year, bans the import of the food products that use genetically modified crops.

   In both cases, no genetically modified crops enter the country. Does either of these cases run afoul of WTO policies?

5.6 **Blinder versus Bhagwati on Outsourcing of Services.** In an essay in the journal *Foreign Affairs*, Princeton economist Alan Blinder warned that the United States potentially faces great dangers from outsourcing of services. Columbia economist Jagdish Bhagwati was highly skeptical of this argument. Read both articles and come to your own assessment. The Blinder article, "Offshoring: The Next Industrial Revolution," *Foreign Affairs*, March/April 2006, is available at http://www.foreignaffairs.com/articles/61514/alan-s-blinder/offshoring-the-next-industrial-revolution (Accessed October 29, 2012). The Bhagwati article, "Don't Cry for Free Trade," New York: Council of Foreign Relations, October 15, 2007, is available at http://www.cfr.org/trade/dont-cry-free-trade/p14526 (Accessed October 29, 2012).

5.7 A Dumping Calculation. To produce 100 units of a good, a firm needs $40,000 in labor, $60,000 in material and capital cost, and requires a 10 percent profit rate. What would be the hypothetical price calculated for this firm? Suppose the profit rate was 20 percent—how would the price change? (Related to Application 3 on page 376.)

5.8 To Whom Should China Be Compared? Under U.S. dumping rules, China is classified as a non-market economy so other market economies are used to calculate prices for dumping. Until recently, China was compared to India, but now it is compared to Thailand. Using Thailand rather than India as a comparison country was one of the key reasons that China was found to be dumping solar panels. Why does the choice of country matter?

5.9 What Do the Poor and the Rich Buy? In Application 4, we highlighted research showing that the nondurable goods the poor buy have gone up in price less than those purchased by the rich and that the poor buy a higher percentage of newer goods than the rich. Can you give some examples of these price differences from your experience at normal and upscale supermarkets? Visit a couple of same-industry stores such as Walmart and Whole Foods to collect data if necessary. (Related to Application 4 on page 379.)

NOTES

1. *A Review of Recent Developments in the U.S. Automobile Industry, Including an Assessment of the Japanese Voluntary Restraint Agreements* (Washington, D.C.: U.S. International Trade Commission, February 1985).

2. Gary C. Hufbauer, "The Benefits of Open Markets and the Costs of Trade Protection and Economic Sanction," ACCF Center for Policy Research, www.accf.org/publications/reports/sr-benefits-openmarkets1997.html (accessed June 2006).

3. Taeho Bark, "The Korean Consumer Electronics Industry: Reaction to Antidumping Actions," in *Antidumping: How It Works and Who Gets Hurt*, ed. J. Michael Finger (Ann Arbor, MI: University of Michigan Press, 1993), chap. 7.

4. Virginia Postrel, "Curb Demonstrates Faults of Courting Special Interests," *New York Times*, June 14, 2001.

The World of International Finance

CHAPTER 19

When Mario Draghi took over as President of the European Central Bank in 2011, he inherited one of the most difficult financial positions the world had to offer.

He was thrust into the center of the crisis in the euro that threatened the financial viability of the largest institutions in Europe. He had to work with countries that wanted more liberal and expansive monetary policies and other countries that feared inflation, debt, and monetary excess.

Draghi came well-prepared for this job. He received his Ph.D. in Economics at the Massachusetts Institute of Technology, overlapping with fellow student Fed Chairman Ben Bernanke. There he studied with Nobel Laureates Franco Modigliani and Robert Solow, as well as Stanley Fischer, currently the Governor of the Bank of Israel. His career included time at the World Bank, Goldman Sachs, director of the Italian treasury, and Governor of the Bank of Italy.

As one of his early acts, he took the aggressive step of making low interest, long-term loans to European banks, effectively providing them with a financial cushion to meet the oncoming economic difficulties. But the question remained whether, despite Draghi's skills, the entire European financial system could continue without fundamental changes.

LEARNING OBJECTIVES

- Discuss how the price of foreign exchange is determined by demand and supply.
- Distinguish between the nominal exchange rate and the real exchange rate.
- Explain how the current account, financial account, and capital account are all related to one another.
- List the benefits and costs of a system of fixed exchange rates compared to a system of flexible exchange rates.
- Discuss how international financial crisis can emerge.

MyEconLab

MyEconLab helps you master each objective and study more efficiently.

All currencies are traded 24 hours a day. The value of every currency depends on news and late-breaking developments throughout the world. Rising gas prices, a new terrorist attack, or a change in the leadership of a foreign government can easily affect the price at which currencies trade with one another. If the U.S. Secretary of the Treasury utters a casual remark about the dollar or the value of the Chinese currency, it reverberates instantly throughout the world. Modern communications—e-mail, instant messaging, smart phones, videoconferencing, and satellite transmissions—accelerate the process.

How do changes in the value of currencies affect the U.S. economy? In prior chapters, we explored the role of monetary policy in an open economy and its effects on exchange rates. In this chapter, we take a more comprehensive and in-depth look at exchange rates as well as other aspects of the international financial system. Understanding our international financial system will help you to interpret the often complex financial news from abroad. For example, if the value of the dollar starts to fall against the Japanese yen, what does it mean? Is this good news or bad news?

19.1 How Exchange Rates Are Determined

In this section, we examine how the value of a currency is determined in world markets. We then look at the factors that can change the value of a currency.

What Are Exchange Rates?

exchange rate
The price at which currencies trade for one another in the market.

To conduct international transactions between countries with different currencies, it is necessary to exchange one currency for another. The **exchange rate** is defined as the price at which we can exchange one currency for another.

Suppose a U.S. songwriter sells the rights of a hit song to a Japanese producer. The U.S. songwriter agrees to accept $50,000. If the exchange rate between the U.S. dollar and Japanese yen is 100 yen per dollar, it will cost the Japanese producer 5,000,000 yen to purchase the rights to the song. Because international trade occurs between nations with different currencies, the exchange rate—the price at which one currency trades for another currency—is a crucial determinant of trade. Fluctuations in the exchange rate can have a huge impact on what goods countries import or export and the overall trade balance.

euro
The common currency in Europe.

Throughout this chapter, we will measure the exchange rate in units of foreign currency per U.S. dollar, that is, as 100 Japanese yen per dollar or 0.8 euro per dollar. The **euro** is the common currency in Europe. With these exchange rates, you would receive 100 yen for each dollar, but only 0.8 euro for each dollar.

We can think of the exchange rate as the price of dollars in terms of foreign currency. Recall from Chapter 14 that an increase in the value of a currency relative to the currency of another nation is called an *appreciation of a currency*. If the exchange rate between the dollar and the yen increases from 100 yen per dollar to 110 yen per dollar, one dollar will purchase more yen. Say, for instance, you've taken a trip to Japan for spring break. Because the dollar has appreciated, your dollar will exchange for more yen. You will now have more yen to spend on Japanese goods—say, MP3 players, DVD players, or entertainment—than you had before the dollar appreciated. The dollar has become more expensive in terms of yen. Its price has risen, in other words. Because the dollar has increased in value, we say the dollar has appreciated against the yen.

A *depreciation of a currency* is a decrease in the value of a currency relative to the currency of another nation. If the exchange rate falls from 100 to 90 yen per dollar, you'll get fewer yen for each dollar you exchange. Japanese goods—whose prices remain the same in Japanese yen—will become more expensive to U.S. residents. You'll have to use more dollars to obtain the yen to purchase the same MP3 and DVD players. The price of dollars in terms of yen has fallen, in other words, so we say the dollar has depreciated against the yen.

Be sure you understand that if one currency appreciates, the other must depreciate. If the dollar appreciates against the yen, for example, the yen must depreciate against the dollar. You'll get more yen in exchange for the dollar, but now when you trade your yen back, you'll get fewer dollars. For example, if the dollar appreciates from 100 to 110 yen per dollar, when you trade 100 yen back into U.S. currency, no longer will you get $1.00—you'll get just $0.91. Conversely, if the dollar depreciates against the yen, the yen must appreciate against the dollar. If the dollar depreciates from 100 yen to 90 yen per dollar, when you trade back 100 yen, you'll get $1.11, rather than just $1.00.

The exchange rate enables us to convert prices in one country to values in another country. A simple example illustrates how an exchange rate works. If you want to buy a watch from France, you need to know what it would cost. You e-mail the store in France and are told the watch sells for 240 euros. The store owners live in France and want to be paid in euros. To figure out what it will cost you in dollars, you need to know the exchange rate between euros and dollars. If the exchange rate is 0.8 euro per dollar, the watch will cost you $300:

$$\frac{240 \text{ euros}}{0.8 \text{ euro per dollar}} = \$300$$

If the exchange rate is one euro per dollar, the watch will cost only $240. As you can see, changes in the exchange rate will affect the prices of goods purchased on world markets and partly determine the pattern of imports and exports throughout the world.

How Demand and Supply Determine Exchange Rates

How are exchange rates determined? The exchange rate between U.S. dollars and euros is determined in the foreign-exchange market, the market in which dollars trade for euros. To understand this market, we can use demand and supply. In Figure 19.1, we plot the demand and supply curves for dollars in exchange for euros.

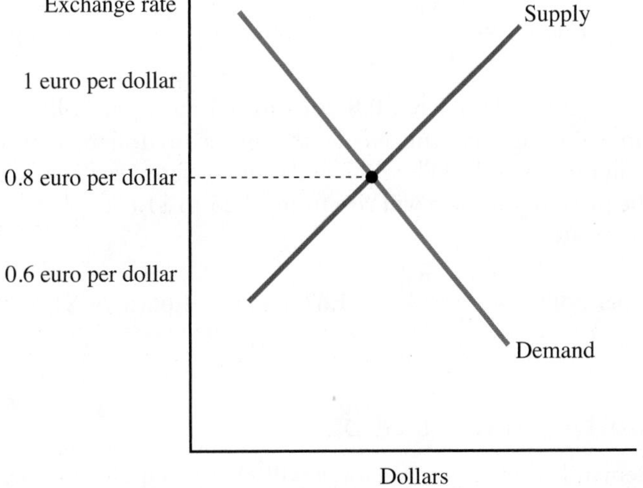

▲ **FIGURE 19.1**
The Demand for and Supply of U.S. Dollars
Market equilibrium occurs where the demand for U.S. dollars equals the supply.

The supply curve is the quantity supplied of dollars in exchange for euros. Individuals or firms that want to buy European goods or assets will need to exchange dollars for euros. The supply curve is drawn under the assumption that as euros become cheaper, total spending on European goods and assets will increase. Therefore, the supply curve slopes upward: As the value of the dollar increases, more dollars will be supplied to the currency market in exchange for euros.

The demand curve represents the quantity demanded of dollars in exchange for euros. Individuals or firms in Europe that want to buy U.S. goods or assets must trade euros for dollars. For example, to visit Disney World in Florida, a German or French family must exchange euros for dollars. As the exchange rate for the U.S. dollar falls, dollars become cheaper in terms of euros. This makes U.S. goods and assets less expensive for European residents, because each euro buys more U.S. dollars. As U.S. goods and assets become cheaper, we assume more European residents will want to trade euros for dollars. Therefore, the demand curve for dollars in exchange for euros slopes downward: Total demand for dollars will increase as the price of the dollar falls, or depreciates, against the euro.

Equilibrium in the market for foreign exchange occurs where the demand curve intersects the supply curve. In Figure 19.1, equilibrium occurs at an exchange rate of 0.8 euro per dollar. At this price, the willingness to trade dollars for euros just matches the willingness to trade euros for dollars. The foreign exchange market is in balance, and the price of euros in terms of a dollar is $1.25.

Price of euros per dollar in equilibrium:

$$0.8 \text{ euro per dollar} = \frac{1 \text{ dollar}}{0.8 \text{ euro}} = 1.25 \text{ dollars per euro, or } \$1.25 \text{ per euro}$$

Now, however, suppose the demand and supply forces between dollars and euros change. If the exchange rate, *e*, increases, the dollar buys *more* euros—the price of dollars in terms of euros increases, in other words. For example, if *e* increases from 0.8 euro per dollar to 1 euro per dollar, the dollar has become more valuable—meaning it has appreciated against the euro. Be sure you see both sides of the same exchange coin: If the dollar appreciates against the euro, then the euro must depreciate against the dollar. So, if the exchange rate increases from 0.8 to 1 euro per dollar, what will the price of a single euro be now?

When the dollar appreciates, each euro is worth less. In this case, the price of the euro will fall from $1.25 per euro to $1.00 per euro.

Dollar appreciates:

$$1.0 \text{ euro per dollar} = \frac{1 \text{ dollar}}{1 \text{ euro}} = 1.0 \text{ dollar per euro, or } \$1.00 \text{ per euro}$$

If the exchange rate falls from 0.8 euro to 0.6 euro per dollar, the dollar has depreciated in value against the euro—the price of dollars in terms of euros has decreased, in other words. When the dollar depreciates, each euro is worth more. In this case, the price of the euro will rise from $1.25 to $1.67.

Dollar depreciates:

$$0.6 \text{ euro per dollar} = \frac{1 \text{ dollar}}{0.6 \text{ euro}} = 1.67 \text{ dollars per euro, or } \$1.67 \text{ per euro}$$

Changes in Demand or Supply

Changes in demand or changes in supply will change equilibrium exchange rates. In Figure 19.2, we show how an increase in demand, a shift of the demand curve to the right, will increase, or appreciate, the exchange rate. U.S. dollars will become more expensive relative to euros as the price of U.S. dollars in terms of euros increases.

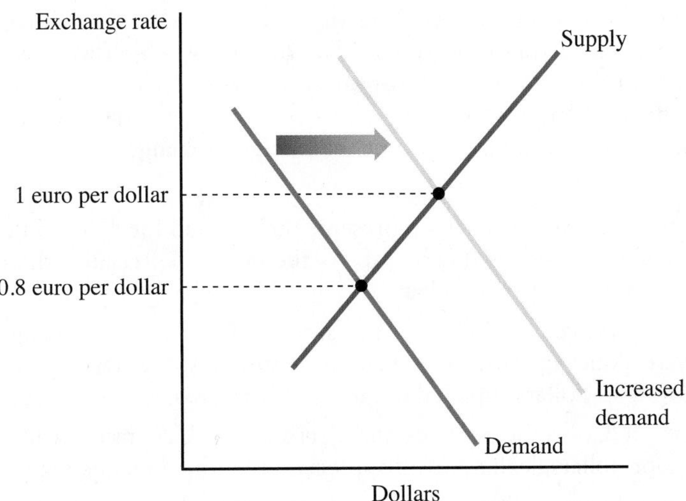

▲ **FIGURE 19.2**
Shifts in the Demand for U.S. Dollars
An increase in the demand for dollars will increase (appreciate) the dollar's exchange rate. Higher U.S. interest rates or lower U.S. prices will increase the demand for dollars.

Two factors are the main causes of shifts of the demand curve for dollars: First, higher U.S. interest rates will lead to an increased demand for dollars. With higher returns in U.S. markets, investors throughout the world will want to buy dollars to invest in U.S. assets. The other factor, lower U.S. prices, will also lead to an increased demand for dollars. For example, if prices at Disney World fell, there would be an overall increase in the demand for dollars, because more tourists would want to visit Disney World.

Figure 19.3 shows the effects of an increase in the supply of dollars, a shift in the supply curve to the right. An increase in the supply of dollars will lead to a fall, or depreciation, of the value of the dollar against the euro. What are the main causes of an increase in the supply of dollars? Again, the same two factors: interest rates and prices. Higher European interest rates will lead U.S. investors to purchase

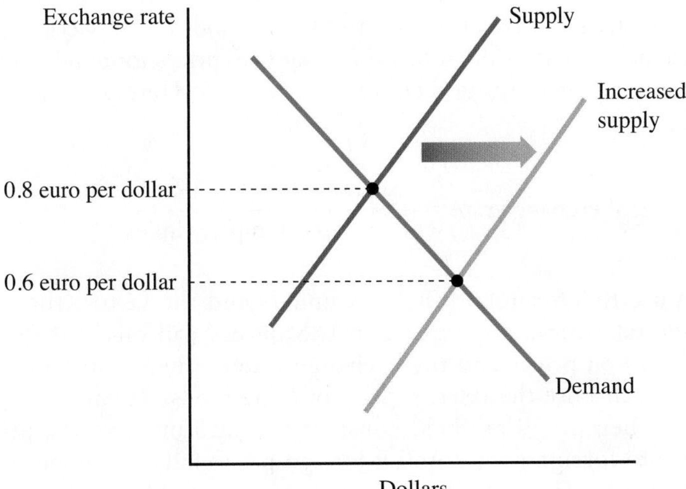

▲ **FIGURE 19.3**
Shifts in the Supply of U.S. Dollars
An increase in the supply of dollars will decrease (depreciate) the dollar exchange rate. Higher European interest rates or lower European prices will increase the supply of dollars.

European bonds or other interest-paying assets. Purchasing European bonds will require U.S. investors to supply dollars for euros, which will drive down the exchange rate for dollars. Lower European prices will also lead to an increase in the supply of dollars for euros.

Let's summarize the key facts about the foreign exchange market, using euros as our example:

1 The demand curve for dollars represents the demand for dollars in exchange for euros. The curve slopes downward. As the dollar depreciates, there will be an increase in the quantity of dollars demanded in exchange for euros.
2 The supply curve for dollars is the supply of dollars in exchange for euros. The curve slopes upward. As the dollar appreciates, there will be an increase in the quantity of dollars supplied in exchange for euros.
3 Increases in U.S. interest rates and decreases in U.S. prices will increase the demand for dollars, leading to an appreciation of the dollar.
4 Increases in European interest rates and decreases in European prices will increase the supply of dollars in exchange for euros, leading to a depreciation of the dollar.

19.2 Real Exchange Rates and Purchasing Power Parity

As our examples of Disney World and watches from France indicate, changes in market exchange rates can affect the demand for a country's goods and services. However, we have been assuming that the prices of watches and trips to Disney World do not change. In general, prices do change over time, so we need to adjust the exchange rate determined in the foreign exchange market to take into account changes in prices. This adjustment is an application of the real-nominal principle.

REAL-NOMINAL PRINCIPLE

What matters to people is the real value of money or income—its purchasing power—not the face value of money or income.

real exchange rate
The price of U.S. goods and services relative to foreign goods and services, expressed in a common currency.

Economists have developed a concept called the *real exchange rate* that adjusts the market exchange rates for changes in prices. The **real exchange rate** is defined as the price of U.S. goods and services relative to foreign goods and services, expressed in a common currency. We measure it by expressing U.S. prices for goods and services in foreign currency and comparing them to foreign prices. Here is the formula for the real exchange rate:

$$\text{real exchange rate} = \frac{\text{exchange rate} \times \text{U.S. price index}}{\text{foreign price index}}$$

We can use this formula to help us understand the factors that change the real exchange rate. First, an increase in U.S. prices will raise the real exchange rate. When foreign prices and the exchange rate are held constant, an increase in U.S. prices will raise the relative price of U.S. goods. Second, an appreciation of the dollar when prices are held constant will also increase the price of U.S. goods relative to foreign goods. And if foreign prices fall, U.S. goods will become relatively more expensive as well.

Notice that the real exchange rate takes into account changes in a country's prices over time because of inflation. Suppose Country A had an inflation rate of 20 percent, and Country B had no inflation. Suppose, too, the exchange rate of Country A's currency depreciated 20 percent against the currency of Country B. In this case, there would be no change in the real exchange rate between the two countries. Although prices in Country A would have increased by 20 percent, its currency would be 20 percent cheaper. From the point of view of residents of Country B, nothing has changed at all—they pay the same price in their currency to buy goods in Country A.

Economists have found that a country's net exports (exports minus its imports) will fall when its real exchange rate increases. For example, if the U.S. real exchange rate increases, the prices of U.S. goods will increase relative to foreign goods. This will reduce U.S. exports because our goods will have become more expensive; it will also increase imports to the United States because foreign goods will have become cheaper. As a result of the decrease in U.S. exports and the increase in U.S. imports, net exports will decline.

Figure 19.4 plots an index of the real exchange rate for the United States against net exports as a share of GDP from 1980 to 2011, a period in which there were large changes in the real exchange rate and net exports. The index, called a *multilateral real exchange rate*, is based on an average of real exchange rates with all U.S. trading partners. Notice that when the multilateral real exchange rate increased, U.S. net exports fell. As you can see in the figure, starting in both 1983 and 1996 the real exchange rate increased sharply. Subsequently, net exports as a share of GDP fell. A decrease in the real exchange rate increases net exports. For example, in 1986 and 2005, the real exchange rate began to decrease and net exports subsequently increased. The relationship between the real exchange rate and net exports is not perfect, however—other factors, such as the growth of GDP, also affect net exports.

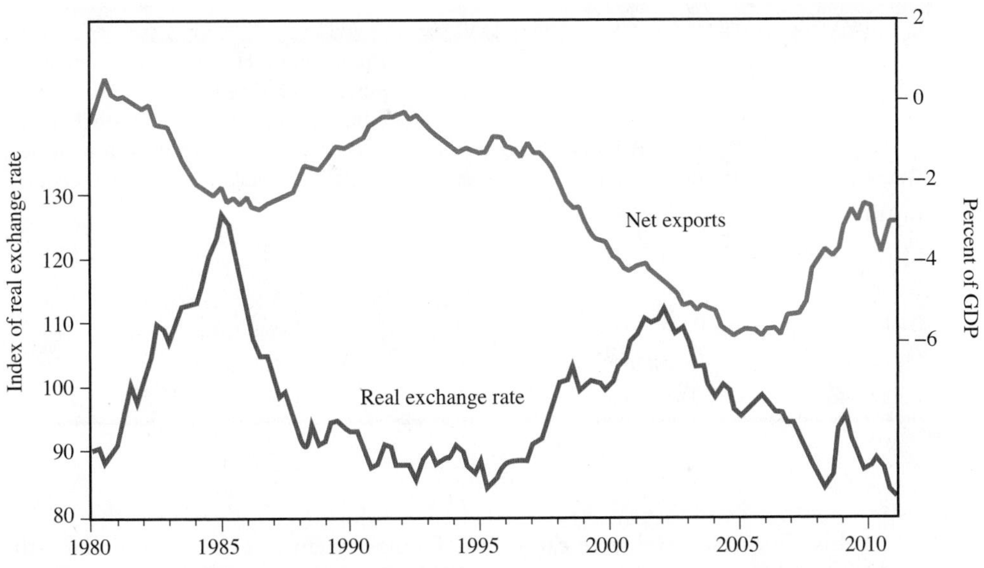

▲ **FIGURE 19.4**

Real Exchange Rate and Net Exports as Percent of GDP, 1980–2011

The figure shows the real exchange rate for the United States compared to its net exports as a share of GDP. Notice that, in general, when the real (multilateral) exchange rate increased, U.S. net exports fell.

SOURCE: U.S. Department of Commerce and the Federal Reserve.

MyEconLab Real-time data

application 1

THE CHINESE YUAN AND BIG MACS

APPLYING THE CONCEPTS #1: How can the price of a Big Mac in China shed light on the U.S.–Chinese currency tensions?

In recent years, the U.S. and Chinese governments have been at odds about the appropriate value of the exchange rate between the Chinese yuan and the U.S. dollar. The United States believes that the Chinese government is holding the yuan below its true value. Can the price of a Big Mac in China shed light on this controversy?

For a number of years, the magazine the *Economist* measured the price of a Big Mac throughout the world and used these prices to explore whether currency values were too high or too low compared to the law of one price. Table 19.1 contains the results for selected countries, including China.

Big Macs sell for widely different prices around the globe, as measured in dollars compared to the $4.20 price in the United States in January 2012. They are a bargain in China at $2.44, but very expensive in Switzerland at $6.81. Table 19.1 also contains the market-exchange rate predicted by the theory of purchasing power parity. To obtain this exchange rate, divide the price of Big Macs in the foreign country by the dollar price. For example, for China the purchasing power exchange rate is

$$\frac{\text{15.4 Chinese yuan (the price of a Big Mac in China)}}{\text{\$4.20 (the price of a Big Mac in the United States)}}$$

$$= \text{3.67 Chinese yuan per U.S. dollar}$$

TABLE 19.1 Big Mac Pricing around the World Versus Actual Exchange Rates

Country	Price of a Big Mac in Local Currency	Price of a Big Mac in Dollars	Predicted Purchasing Power Exchange Rate Based on Big Mac Pricing (Foreign Currency per U.S. Dollar)	Actual Exchange Rate (Foreign Currency per U.S. Dollar)
United States	4.20 dollars	$ 4.20	—	—
United Kingdom	2.49 pounds	3.82	0.59	0.65
China	15.4 yuan	2.44	3.67	6.32
Switzerland	6.50 Swiss francs	6.81	1.55	0.96
Mexico	37.0 pesos	2.70	8.82	13.68
Euro Area	3.44 euros	4.43	1.20	1.27

At this "Big Mac" exchange rate—3.67 Chinese yuan to every U.S. dollar—the Big Mac in China would cost the same as in the United States. However, the actual exchange rate for the Chinese yuan in January 2012 when these prices were computed was 6.32 Chinese yuan per U.S. dollar, so the Big Mac was actually cheaper in China. Relative to the exchange rate implied by the law of one price, the Chinese yuan was 42 percent undervalued. This is large difference, although smaller than in prior years. This calculation gives a hint as to the Chinese–U.S. exchange rate controversy. **Related to Exercises 2.6 and 2.7.**

SOURCE: Based on the data on from the *Economist* for January 12, 2012.

Real exchange rates vary over time, as shown in Figure 19.4. But for goods traded easily across countries (such as gold bars), we would expect the price to be the same when expressed in a common currency. For example, the price of gold bars sold in France should be nearly identical to the price of gold bars sold in New York. If the price were higher in France, demand would shift to New York, raising the price in New York and lowering the price in France until the prices were equal. The tendency for easily tradable goods to sell at the same price when expressed in a common currency is known as the **law of one price**. Metals, agricultural commodities, computer chips, and other tradable goods follow the law of one price.

law of one price
The theory that goods easily tradable across countries should sell at the same price expressed in a common currency.

If all goods were easily tradable and the law of one price held exactly, exchange rates would reflect no more than the differences in the way the price levels are expressed in the two countries. For example, if a basket of goods in Europe costs 3,000 euros and the identical basket costs \$3,750 in the United States, an exchange rate of 0.8 euros to one dollar would make the costs the same in either currency (\$3,750 × 0.8 euros/dollar = 3,000 euros).

According to one theory of how market exchange rates are determined, they simply reflect differences in the overall price levels between countries. According to the theory of **purchasing power parity**, a unit of any given currency should be able to buy the same quantity of goods in all countries. In our European–U.S. example, the theory of purchasing power parity predicts a market exchange rate of 0.8 euro per dollar. At that exchange rate, European and U.S. goods would sell for the same price if their products were expressed in a common currency. Research has shown that purchasing power parity does not hold precisely.

purchasing power parity
A theory of exchange rates whereby a unit of any given currency should be able to buy the same quantity of goods in all countries.

Many systematic studies have confirmed that purchasing power parity does not give fully accurate predictions for exchange rates. The reason is that many goods, such as housing and services like haircuts, are not traded across countries. The law of one price does not hold for nontraded goods, which make up approximately 50 percent of the value of production in an economy. There is some truth to purchasing power parity, because exchange rates do reflect differences in the price level between countries. But, as the example with the Big Mac shows, purchasing power parity can provide a clue to exchange rates in some circumstances.

19.3 The Current Account, the Financial Account, and the Capital Account

In this section, we examine international transactions in more detail. A useful framework for understanding international transactions is the **balance of payments**, a system of accounts that measures transactions of goods, services, income, and financial assets between domestic households, businesses, and governments and residents of the rest of the world during a specific time period.

balance of payments
A system of accounts that measures transactions of goods, services, income, and financial assets between domestic households, businesses, and governments and residents of the rest of the world during a specific time period.

Economists find it useful to divide international transactions in the balance of payments into three types: the current account, the financial account, and the capital account. These measures provide the most comprehensive picture of a country's balance of trade with the rest of the world and the consequences of that trade for a country's ownership of assets, such as stocks, bonds, and real estate. A country's **current account** is the sum of its

current account
The sum of net exports (exports minus imports) plus net income received from abroad plus net transfers from abroad.

- net exports (exports minus imports),
- net income received from investments abroad, and
- net transfer payments from abroad (such as foreign aid).

If a country has a positive current account, we say that its current account is in surplus. If a country has a negative current account, we say that its current account is in deficit. If the income from investments abroad and net transfer payments is negligible, the current account becomes equivalent to a country's net exports.

financial account
The value of a country's net sales (sales minus purchases) of assets.

A country's **financial account** transactions include all the purchases and sales of existing financial and produced assets (stocks, bonds, real estate) by the private sector and the government. The financial account is defined as the value of the country's net sales (sales minus purchases) of assets. If the United States sold $100 billion net in assets, its financial account would be $100 billion. If the value on the financial account is positive, we say the country has a surplus on the financial account. Similarly, if the value on the financial account is negative, we say it has a deficit on the financial account.

capital account
The value of capital transfer and transaction in nonproduced, nonfinancial assets in the international accounts.

A country's **capital account** transactions consist of two components. First, they include the purchase or sale of nonproduced, nonfinancial assets, such as patents, copyrights, trademarks, and leases. Second, they also include transfers of capital, such as debt forgiveness or migrants' transfers (goods or financial assets accompanying migrants as they leave or enter the country). Capital account transactions are much smaller in magnitude than transactions on the current or financial account.

Rules for Calculating the Current, Financial, and Capital Accounts

Here is a simple rule for understanding transactions on the current, financial, and capital accounts: Any action that gives rise to a demand for foreign currency is a deficit item. Any action that gives rise to a supply of foreign currency is a surplus item.

Let's apply this rule to the current account and the financial account, taking the point of view of the United States (a similar logic applies to the capital account):

1 *Current account.* Items imported into the United States show up as a deficit (negative) on the current account because we have to trade U.S. currency for foreign currency to buy them. Items exported from the United States show up as a surplus (positive) in the current account because foreigners have to trade their currency for U.S. dollars to buy those products. Income from investments abroad and net transfers received are treated like exports because they result in a supply of foreign currency for dollars. Summarizing, we have

$$\text{U.S. current account surplus} = \text{U.S. exports} - \text{U.S. imports} \\ + \text{net income from foreign investments} + \text{net transfers from abroad}$$

2 *Financial account.* The purchase of a foreign asset by a U.S. resident leads to a deficit (negative) item on the financial account because it requires a demand for foreign currency. (You can think of the purchase of a foreign asset as just another import.) A purchase of a U.S. asset by a foreign resident leads to a supply of foreign currency and a surplus (positive) item on the financial account. (Think of this as an export.) Summarizing, we have

$$\text{U.S. financial account surplus} = \text{foreign purchases of U.S. assets} \\ - \text{U.S. purchases of foreign assets}$$

The current, financial, and capital accounts of a country are linked by a very important relationship:

$$\text{current account} + \text{financial account} + \text{capital account} = 0$$

The current account plus the financial account, plus the capital account must sum to zero. Why?

To keep things simple, let's ignore the relatively minor capital account transactions. In that case, the current plus financial accounts must sum to zero, because any excess demand for foreign currency that arises from transactions in goods and services—that means we're looking at the current account—must be met by an excess supply of foreign currency arising from asset transactions—the financial account. Suppose the United States has a current account deficit of \$50 billion, which means it is importing more than it is exporting. This excess demand of foreign currency by people in the United States can be met only by an excess supply of foreign currency that arises from the financial account—where foreign residents are purchasing \$50 billion more in U.S. assets than U.S. residents are purchasing of foreign assets. In other words, the current account deficit is offset by the financial account surplus.

Let's look at this from a slightly different angle. Consider again the case in which the United States is running a current account deficit because imports from abroad exceed exports. (For simplicity, transfers and income earned from investments abroad are both zero.) The current account deficit means that, on net, foreign residents and their governments are the recipients of dollars because they have sold more goods to the United States than they have purchased.

What do foreign residents do with these dollars? They can either hold the dollars or use them to purchase U.S. assets. In either case, foreign residents and their governments have acquired U.S. assets, either dollars or other U.S. assets, such as U.S. Treasury bills. The value of these assets is the U.S. current account deficit. Because a sale of a U.S. asset to a foreign resident is a surplus item on the U.S. financial account, the value of the financial account will be equal to the negative of the value of the current account. So, from this perspective also, the current account and the financial account must sum to zero.

If a country runs a current account surplus—it is exporting more than importing, in other words—the country acquires foreign exchange. The country can either keep the foreign exchange or use it to buy foreign assets. In either case, its purchases of net foreign assets will equal its current account surplus. Because the financial account is the negative of the purchases of net foreign assets, the current account and financial account will again sum to zero.

Table 19.2 shows the balance of payments for the United States for 2008: the current account, the financial account, and the capital account. The current account is made up of the balance in goods, services, net investment income, and net transfers. In 2008, the United States had a negative balance on the goods account and net transfer, but a positive balance on the services and net income category. However,

TABLE 19.2 U.S. Balance of Payments: Current, Financial, and Capital Accounts, 2010 (Billions)

Current Account		**Financial Account**	
Goods	−646	Increases in U.S. holdings abroad	−1005
Services	146	Increases in foreign holding in United States	1246
Net Transfers	−136	Total on Financial Account (including other minor items)	254
Net Investment Income	165	**Capital Account**	−1
Total on Current Account	−471	**Statistical Discrepancy**	217
		Sum of Current, Financial, Capital Accounts and Statistical Discrepancy	0

SOURCE: Economic Report of the President (Washington, D.C.: U.S. Government Printing Office, 2012).

the large negative balance on the goods account made the overall current account balance negative. The financial account includes net increases in U.S. holdings abroad (negative entries in the financial account) and foreign holdings of U.S. assets (positive entries in the financial account). Because the government collects the current account, financial account, and capital account data from separate sources, a statistical discrepancy occurs. (In 2008, this was exceptionally large because of the difficulty of understanding all the transactions involved with the financial crisis.) Once we include this statistical discrepancy, the current account, the financial account, and the capital account sum to zero.

Since 1982, the United States has run a current account deficit every year. This means the United States has run a financial plus capital account surplus of equal value for these years as well. Because a financial account surplus means foreign nations acquire a country's assets, the United States has reduced its net holding of foreign assets. In 1986, the U.S. Department of Commerce estimated the United States had a **net international investment position** of $136 billion, meaning U.S. holdings of foreign assets exceeded foreign holdings of U.S. assets by $136 billion.

net international investment position
Domestic holding of foreign assets minus foreign holdings of domestic assets.

Because of its current account deficits, the U.S. net international investment position fell every year. By 2010 the U.S. net international investment position was negative $2.5 trillion, meaning foreign residents owned $2.5 trillion more U.S. assets than

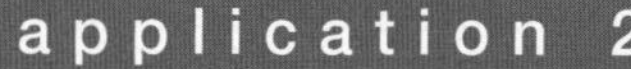

WORLD SAVINGS AND U.S. CURRENT ACCOUNT DEFICITS

APPLYING THE CONCEPTS #2: What factors may allow the United States to continue running large trade deficits with the rest of the world?

The *2006 Economic Report of the President* directly addressed whether the United States can continue to run large current account deficits and, of course, financial account surpluses. In the report, the government recognized that the current account deficits would eventually be reduced. However, it also highlighted a number of factors suggesting the deficits could continue for a long period of time.

The report explains that the U.S. current account deficit needs to be placed in a global context. For the United States to continue to run a current account deficit, other countries in the world need to continue to purchase U.S. assets. In essence, they must have total savings in excess of their own investment desires. As long as there are countries in this situation, the United States could continue to run a trade deficit.

In recent years, four major countries experienced circumstances that encouraged them to save by purchasing assets from abroad. Both Japan and Germany had high savings rates, but low rates of domestic investment. Slow economic growth in both countries led firms to be very cautious about making domestic investment. With limited domestic investment opportunities, savers in Japan and Germany thus placed their funds abroad. Russia has large reserves of oil and gas, and increasing energy prices in the last several years provided Russians with substantial new revenue. They decided to use this revenue to invest abroad. Finally, China had high investment rates but even higher savings rates. As a result, China as a whole invested abroad. For the United States to continue to run trade deficits in the future, these or other countries must want to continue to save more than they want to invest domestically. **Related to Exercise 3.7.**

SOURCE: Based on *Economic Report of the President* (Washington, D.C.: United States Government Printing Office, 2006), chap. 6.

U.S. residents owned foreign assets. You may have heard the United States referred to as a *net debtor*. This is just another way of saying the U.S. net international investment position is negative. As a consequence of the United States being a net debtor, earnings from international assets flow out of the United States to foreign countries. In the future, part of the incomes earned in the United States will be paid to foreigners abroad. This is a natural consequence of the United States being a net debtor.

What are the consequences of the large U.S. trade deficits?

When the United States runs a trade deficit, U.S. residents are spending more on goods and services than they are currently producing. Although the United States does sell many goods and services abroad (such as supercomputers, movies, DVDs, and accounting services), it buys even more goods and services from abroad (such as clothes, electronics, and machine tools).

A trade deficit forces the United States to sell some of its assets to individuals or governments in foreign countries. Here is how it works: When U.S. residents buy more goods abroad than they sell, they give up more dollars for imports than they receive in dollars from the sale of exports. These dollars given up to purchase imports end up in the hands of foreigners, who can then use them to purchase U.S. assets such as stocks, government bonds, or even real estate. In recent years, Asian investors, including foreign governments, have bought a variety of assets in the United States, including U.S. Treasury bonds and even stakes in investment banking firms. Foreign governments have accumulated considerable assets and invested them in private markets abroad through **sovereign investment funds**. Current estimates place the value of assets in these funds at $4.8 trillion.

sovereign investment fund
Assets accumulated by foreign governments that are invested abroad.

The purchase of U.S. assets by foreign investors should not be surprising, because we have been running large trade deficits with many Asian economies, especially China. These countries were willing to sell us more goods than we were selling to them, and therefore they accumulated U.S. dollars with which they could purchase U.S. assets. There is considerable debate about whether the very large U.S. current account deficits can continue.

19.4 Fixed and Flexible Exchange Rates

To set the stage for understanding exchange rate systems, let's recall what happens when a country's exchange rate appreciates—increases in value. There are two distinct effects:

1 The increased value of the exchange rate makes imports less expensive for the residents of the country where the exchange rate appreciated. For example, if the U.S. dollar appreciates against the euro, European watches will become less expensive for U.S. consumers. U.S. consumers would like an appreciated dollar, because it would lower their cost of living.

2 The increased value of the exchange rate makes U.S. goods more expensive on world markets. A U.S. exchange appreciation will increase imports, such as European watches, but decrease exports, such as California wine.

Because exports fall and imports rise, net exports (exports minus imports) will decrease. Similarly, when a country's exchange rate depreciates, there are two distinct effects:

1 For example, if the U.S. dollar depreciates against the Japanese yen, Japanese imports will become more expensive in the United States, thereby raising the cost of living in the United States.

2 At the same time, U.S. goods will become cheaper in world markets. U.S. exports will rise and imports will fall, so net U.S. exports will increase.

Fixing the Exchange Rate

Sometimes countries do not want their exchange rate to change. They may want to avoid sharp rises in the cost of living for their citizens when their currency depreciates, or they may want to keep net exports from falling when their currency appreciates. To prevent the value of the currency from changing, governments can enter the foreign exchange market to try to influence the price of foreign exchange. Economists call these efforts to influence the exchange rate **foreign exchange market intervention**.

foreign exchange market intervention
The purchase or sale of currencies by the government to influence the market exchange rate.

In the United States, the Treasury Department has the official responsibility for foreign exchange intervention, though it operates in conjunction with the Federal Reserve. In other countries, governments also intervene in the foreign exchange market. To influence the price at which one currency trades for another, governments have to affect the demand or supply for their currency. To increase the value of its currency, a government must increase the currency's demand. To decrease the value of its currency, the government must increase its supply.

In Figure 19.5, we show how governments can fix, or *peg*, the price of a currency. Suppose the U.S. and European governments want the exchange rate to be 0.8 euro per dollar. The price at which demand and supply are currently equal, however, is only 0.6 euro per dollar. To increase the price of the U.S. dollar, the governments will need to increase the dollar's demand. To do this, either government—the United States or European central banks—or both, can sell euros for dollars in the foreign exchange market. This will shift the demand curve for dollars to the right until the price of dollars rises to 0.8 euro per dollar.

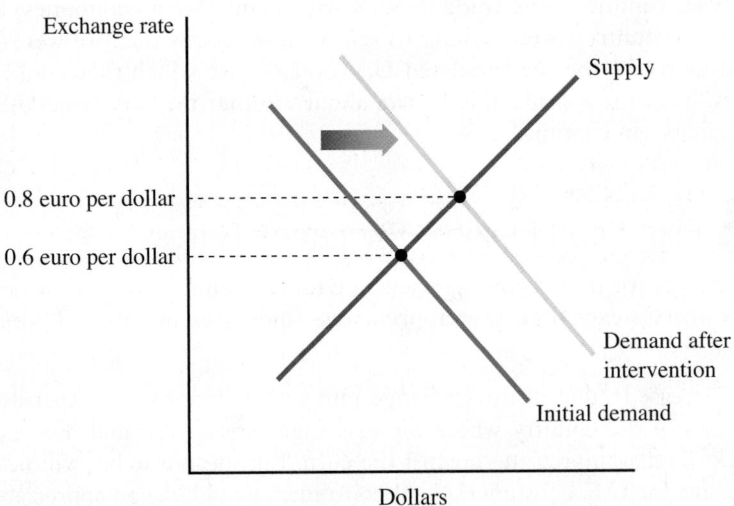

▲ FIGURE 19.5
Government Intervention to Raise the Price of the Dollar
To increase the price of dollars, the U.S. government sells euros in exchange for dollars. This shifts the demand curve for dollars to the right.

Conversely, if the governments want to lower the price of the dollar relative to euros, they will buy euros in exchange for dollars. By selling dollars for euros, they increase the supply of dollars. The price of the dollar therefore falls while the price of the euro increases. Note that to affect the price of the euro against the dollar, the U.S. government must exchange euros for dollars. The government will acquire and accumulate euros any time it tries to raise their price. To raise the price of the dollar, which lowers the value of the euro, the U.S. government must sell some of the euros it has accumulated. But what would happen if the United States had no euros to sell? The United States could borrow euros from European governments or persuade them to sell euros for dollars.

Fixed versus Flexible Exchange Rates

Next, we discuss two different types of exchange rate systems. Then we take a brief look at historical U.S exchange rate policy and developments in exchange rates in the world today.

FLEXIBLE EXCHANGE RATE SYSTEM If exchange rates are determined in free markets, we have a **flexible exchange rate system**. Under a pure flexible exchange rate system, the price of a currency will rise if the demand increases more than supply and will fall if supply increases more than demand. As we have seen, a variety of factors can determine exchange rates, including foreign and domestic interest rates as well as foreign and domestic prices. Other factors, including market psychology, can also affect the value of a nation's currency. Whatever its source, an increase in the demand for currency will raise its price. We have also seen that governments may intervene to prevent currency from changing its value. In the most extreme case, there would be no change in the value of a currency.

flexible exchange rate system A currency system in which exchange rates are determined by free markets.

FIXED EXCHANGE RATES Whether you are in California, New York, or Indiana, all prices are quoted in dollars. No one asks whether your dollar came from San Francisco or Miami. Within the United States, a dollar is a dollar. Suppose, though, that every state had its own currency. There might be a California dollar (with a picture of the Golden Gate Bridge), an Oregon dollar (showing pictures of tall trees), and a Florida dollar (showing Disney World, of course). In principle, these dollars might trade at different rates, depending on the demand and supply of one state's dollar relative to the supply and demand for another state's dollar. For example, the Texas dollar might be worth more than the Michigan dollar, trading for 1.2 Michigan dollars.

Think how much more complicated it would be to do business. To buy goods from a mail-order company in Maine, you would have to find out the exchange rate between your state's dollar and the Maine dollar. Any large business operating in all 50 states would be overwhelmed trying to keep track of all the exchange rate movements across the states. The economy would become less efficient because individuals and businesses would have to focus a lot of their attention on exchange rates.

These same ideas apply across nations. Wouldn't it be nice if all countries either used the same currency or fixed their exchange rates against one another so that no one would have to worry about exchange rate movements? Currency systems in which governments try to keep constant the values of their currencies against one another are called **fixed exchange rate systems**. After World War II, the countries of the world operated under a fixed exchange system known as Bretton Woods. The Bretton Woods system was named after the town in New Hampshire where representatives of each nation met in 1944 and agreed to adopt this system. The system centered on the United States: All countries fixed or pegged their currencies against the U.S. dollar.

fixed exchange rate system A system in which governments peg exchange rates to prevent their currencies from fluctuating.

In a typical fixed exchange rate system, every country that pegs its rate to a central country's exchange rate must intervene in the foreign exchange market when necessary to keep its exchange rate constant. For example, a government would have to intervene if, at the fixed exchange rate, the private demand and supply for its currency were unequal.

BALANCE OF PAYMENTS DEFICITS AND SURPLUSES Suppose the supply of a country's currency exceeds the demand at the fixed exchange rate. An excess supply of a country's currency at the fixed exchange rate is known as a balance of payments deficit. A **balance of payments deficit** will occur whenever there is a deficit on the current account that is not matched by net sales of assets to foreigners by the private sector. For example, a current account deficit of $100 billion with net sales of assets to foreigners of only $80 billion would mean that there is an excess supply of $20 billion. With an excess supply of a country's currency in the currency market, that currency would fall in value without any intervention. To prevent the currency from depreciating in value and to maintain the fixed exchange rate, the government would have to sell foreign currency and buy its own currency. As you saw from our foreign exchange intervention discussion, if a country sells foreign exchange, its holdings of foreign exchange will fall. So you can see that when a country runs a balance of payments deficit, it has decreased its holdings of foreign exchange.

balance of payments deficit
Under a fixed exchange rate system, a situation in which the supply of a country's currency exceeds the demand for the currency at the current exchange rate.

It's also very possible that the demand for a country's currency will exceed its supply at the fixed exchange rate. An excess demand for a country's currency at the fixed exchange rate is known as a **balance of payments surplus**. A balance of payments surplus arises when there is a current account surplus that is not matched by net purchases of foreign assets by the private sector. With an excess demand for a country's currency, it will rise in value without any intervention. To prevent its currency from appreciating—to maintain the fixed exchange rate, in other words—the government will have to buy foreign currency and sell its own. Because it is buying foreign exchange, its holdings of foreign exchange will increase. From this discussion, you should be able to see that when a country runs a balance of payments surplus, it has increased its holding of foreign exchange.

balance of payments surplus
Under a fixed exchange rate system, a situation in which the demand of a country's currency exceeds the supply for the currency at the current exchange rate.

Under a fixed exchange rate system, countries that run persistent balance of payments deficits or balance of payments surpluses must take corrective actions. If domestic policy actions, such as changing taxes, government spending, or the money supply, do not cure the problem, a country will eventually have to change the level at which the exchange rate is fixed. A country that faces a balance of payments deficit can lower the value at which the currency is pegged to increase its net exports, a process called **devaluation**. Conversely, a country that faces a balance of payments surplus can increase the value at which its currency is pegged and reduce its net exports, a process called **revaluation**.

devaluation
A decrease in the exchange rate to which a currency is pegged under a fixed exchange rate system.

revaluation
An increase in the exchange rate to which a currency is pegged under a fixed exchange rate system.

The U.S. Experience with Fixed and Flexible Exchange Rates

As we discussed earlier, after World War II the countries of the world adopted the Bretton Woods fixed exchange rate system. In the 1970s, the Bretton Woods system was replaced by the current system—a flexible exchange rate system—in which supply and demand primarily determine exchange rates.

If a fixed exchange rate system makes it easier to trade, why did it break down in the early 1970s? Fixed exchange rate systems provide benefits, but they require countries to maintain similar economic policies—especially to maintain similar inflation rates and interest rates. To understand this, suppose the exchange rate between the United States and Germany were fixed, but the United States has an annual inflation rate of 6 percent compared to 0 percent in Germany. Because prices in the United States would be rising by 6 percent per year, the U.S. real exchange rate against Germany would also be increasing at 6 percent per year. This difference in their real exchange rates over time would cause a trade deficit to emerge in the United States as U.S. goods became more expensive on world markets—including in Germany. As long as the differences in inflation continued and the exchange rate remained fixed, the U.S. real exchange rate would continue to appreciate, and the U.S. trade deficit would grow even worse. Clearly, this course of events would have to be halted under an agreed-upon fixed exchange rate system.

In the late 1960s, inflation in the United States began to exceed inflation in other countries, and a U.S. balance of payments deficit emerged—just as in our example. In 1971, President Nixon surprised the world and devalued the U.S. dollar against the currencies of all the other countries. This was a sharp departure from the rules underlying Bretton Woods. Nixon hoped that a one-time devaluation of the dollar would alleviate the U.S. balance of payments deficit and maintain the underlying system of fixed exchange rates.

However, the U.S. devaluation did not stop the U.S. balance of payments deficit. Germany tried to maintain the mark's fixed exchange rate with the U.S. dollar by purchasing U.S. dollars in the foreign exchange market. What Germany was doing was importing inflation from the United States. With the U.S. balance of payments deficit continuing, Germany was required to buy U.S. dollars to keep the mark from appreciating. Germany bought U.S. dollars with German marks. Those German marks were then put into circulation. The German supply of marks in Germany therefore increased, and this increase in marks raised the inflation rate in Germany.

Private-sector investors knew that Germany did not wish to run persistent trade surpluses and import U.S. inflation. They bet that Germany would revalue the mark against the dollar—that is, raise the value of the mark against the dollar. They bought massive amounts of German assets, trading their dollars for marks to purchase them because they thought the mark's value would eventually sharply increase. Their actions forced the German government to buy even *more* dollars to force the price of the mark upward and keep it pegged to the dollar. The resulting flow of financial capital into Germany was so massive that the German government eventually gave up all attempts to keep its exchange rate fixed to the dollar. Instead, it let the exchange rate be determined in the free market. This was the end of the Bretton Woods system.

Exchange Rate Systems Today

The flexible exchange rate system has worked well enough since the breakdown of Bretton Woods. World trade has grown at a rapid rate. Moreover, the flexible exchange rate system has seamlessly managed many diverse situations, including two major oil shocks in the 1970s, large U.S. budget deficits in the 1980s, and large Japanese and Chinese current account surpluses in the last two decades.

During the Bretton Woods period, many countries placed restrictions on the flows of financial capital by, for example, not allowing their residents to purchase foreign assets or by limiting foreigners' purchases of domestic assets. By the 1970s, these restrictions began to be eliminated, and private-sector transactions in assets grew rapidly. With massive amounts of funds being traded in financial markets, it becomes very difficult to fix, or peg, an exchange rate.

Nonetheless, countries whose economies are closely tied together might want the advantages of fixed exchange rates. One way to avoid some of the difficulties of fixing exchange rates between countries is to abolish individual currencies and establish a single currency. This is precisely what a group of European countries decided to do. They adopted a single currency, the euro, throughout Europe and a single central bank to control the supply of the currency. With a single currency, European countries hoped to capture the benefits of serving a large market like the United States does with its single currency. Unfortunately, this has turned out to be much more complicated to administer than the founders of the euro envisioned. The United Kingdom, Denmark, and Sweden decided to remain outside the European single currency system. Their currencies, like the U.S. dollar and the Japanese yen, now float against each of the other currencies and the euro. Many other countries have tied their exchange rate to either the dollar or the yen. Some economists believe that the world will eventually settle into three large currency blocs: the euro, the dollar, and the yen.

application 3

A TROUBLED EURO

APPLYING THE CONCEPTS #3: What are the fundamental causes for the problems with the euro?

When the euro was launched in 1999, the vision of its founders was to use the monetary union to further unify Europe economically and politically. They envisioned a large economic market, comparable to the United States with integrated goods and financial markets. They believed that by moving to a single currency with agreements on a number of fiscal rules that they could achieve economic stability and growth.

Unfortunately, this vision proved to be naïve. Under the umbrella of the euro, financial investors throughout the world poured funds into Spain and Ireland fueling an unsustainable housing boom and also lent excessive amounts to the governments of Greece, Italy, and Portugal that faced severe budget challenges. When the housing boom collapsed and the worldwide recession of 2007 increased budgetary pressures, it became clear that the banks and governments of these countries could not easily pay their debts. Moreover, with a single currency for the euro area, countries could not make adjustments through depreciation of their currency. The options facing Europe were bleak: either large-scale financial transfers from Germany and other successful countries, or sharp cutbacks in budgets and prolonged unemployment to reduce wage levels.

What became apparent was that the United States did not just have a single currency; it also had a unified fiscal system that provided transfers to states and regions in economic distress. Monetary union without a corresponding fiscal system cannot be easily sustained. **Related to Exercises 4.4 and 4.8.**

19.5 Managing Financial Crises

Hardly a year goes by without some international financial crisis. In 1994 Mexico experienced a severe financial crisis. In 1997 the Asian economic crisis began. The Argentinean economy collapsed in 2002. How do these crises originate? What policies can be followed to prevent or alleviate them?

Let's first consider the Mexican case. During the late 1980s and early 1990s, Mexico decided to fix, or peg, its exchange to the U.S. dollar. Mexico's goal was to signal to investors throughout the world that it was serious about controlling inflation and would take the steps needed to keep its inflation rates in line with that of the United States. Mexico also opened up its markets to let in foreign investors. The country seemed to be on a solid path to development.

However, in some sense, the policies proved to be too successful in encouraging foreign investment. As funds poured into the country, the demand for goods increased, and prices started to rise. This rise in prices caused an increase in Mexico's real exchange rate, and the rise in the real exchange rate caused a large trade deficit to emerge.

Initially, the trade deficit did not cause any difficulties for the Mexican government. Because foreign investors were willingly trading foreign currencies for Mexican pesos to buy Mexican securities, the government in Mexico did not have any problem maintaining its pegged exchange rate with the United States. Although the Mexicans were importing more than they were exporting, at this point they could still obtain the dollars they needed to finance the trade imbalance from foreign investors who were purchasing Mexican securities. The government did not have to intervene in the foreign exchange market to keep the price of the peso constant against the dollar. In other words, Mexico did not have a balance of payments deficit.

But then internal political difficulties ensued. Following an assassination of a political candidate and a rural uprising, foreign investors started to pull their funds out of Mexico. At this point, the Mexican government made a crucial mistake. Instead of trying to reduce its trade deficit by taking steps to reduce prices, it allowed the trade deficit to continue. Moreover, both the government and the private sector began to find that they had to borrow in dollars because foreign investors thought Mexico might be forced to devalue the peso. If a devaluation were to occur, any lender of pesos would suffer a loss because the debt would be repaid at a lower exchange rate. Consequently, Mexican borrowers were forced to borrow in loans denominated in dollars.

Eventually, more political turmoil caused investors to pull out their funds, selling pesos for dollars. The Mexican central bank spent nearly $50 billion buying these pesos in an effort to keep the exchange rate constant. The $50 billion was not enough. Mexico ran out of dollars. Because it could no longer buy pesos to maintain the exchange rate, Mexico had to devalue, putting the peso more in line with its market value. The devaluation created even more turmoil because the government and the private sector had borrowed billions in dollars. When the peso was devalued against the dollar, the burden of these debts measured in pesos increased sharply, so more pesos were needed to pay the dollar-denominated debts. Mexico faced the prospect of massive bankruptcies and the potential collapse of its economy.

To prevent a financial collapse that could easily have spread to many other developing countries, the U.S. government (along with other international financial institutions) arranged for Mexico to borrow dollars with an extended period for repayment. This allowed Mexican banks and corporations to avoid bankruptcies and prevented a major disaster. In 1996, the Mexican government was able to pay off nearly three-fourths of the loan from the United States.

The Asian crisis had a similar flavor. Economic growth had been remarkable in Asia for over 20 years, improving to a great extent the standard of living of millions of people. In the early 1990s, several Asian countries began to open up their capital markets to foreign investors and borrow extensively from abroad. Billions of dollars poured into Asia. In many cases, there was little financial supervision, and many of the investments proved to be unwise. Companies in both Thailand and South Korea began to lose money. Domestic investors and world investors suddenly became pessimistic and pulled their funds out of South Korea and Thailand, among other Asian countries. The withdrawal of funds forced currencies throughout Asia to be devalued. Because many businesses had borrowed in dollars, the devaluations raised the burden of the debt and further deepened the crisis, taking its toll on other countries, including Indonesia, Malaysia, and Hong Kong. The International Monetary Fund attempted to help restore the health of these economies' financial systems, but in many cases, its policies were ineffective. Some economists, such as Nobel Laureate Joseph Stiglitz, believe the entire Asian crisis was an example of market overreaction and could have been avoided by bolder action from world organizations and developed countries.

Even when a country takes strong, institutional steps to peg its currency, a collapse is still possible. This was the case with Argentina.

These examples highlight some of the many factors that can bring about financial crises. In vast global capital markets, funds can move quickly from country to country, and economic policies sometimes do not keep pace with changing political and economic developments. It can be extremely difficult to maintain a fixed exchange rate in this environment. The flow of funds, moreover, is often so large that financial failures can rock trade and commerce.

The countries of the world are searching for a reliable set of rules and institutional mechanisms that can avoid and limit the spread of financial crises. Historically, the International Monetary Fund has played a key role in assisting countries that run into financial difficulties. However, in Mexico, the sums were so large that the United States was forced to take the lead in resolving the situation. In Asia, the International Monetary Fund did not have backing from the United States, so the efforts to alleviate the crisis were less successful. In Argentina, rigid adherence to a fixed exchange rate and a government that could not control spending both contributed to a collapse. As world capital markets continue to grow, governments throughout the world will almost surely be tested by new and often unpredictable financial crises, such as they experienced in 2008. They will need to anticipate and react to rapid changes in the economic and political environment to maintain a stable financial environment for world trade.

application 4

THE ARGENTINE FINANCIAL CRISIS

APPLYING THE CONCEPTS #4: What are the causes of financial collapses that occur throughout the globe?

During the late 1980s, Argentina suffered from hyperinflation. As part of its financial reforms, it pegged its currency to the U.S. dollar, making pesos "convertible" into dollars. To issue pesos, the central bank had to have an equal amount of dollars, or its equivalent in other hard currencies, on hand. Some economists believed this reform would bring stability to the financial system. Unfortunately, they were proved wrong.

The financial and other institutional reforms worked well in the early 1990s, but then several problems developed. As the dollar appreciated sharply on world markets after 1995, Argentina began to suffer from a large trade deficit because its currency was pegged to the dollar. Essentially, the United States' rising currency became Argentina's problem. Wage increases also pushed up the real exchange rate, exacerbating the trade deficit. The Argentinean government—including its provincial governments—found it difficult to control spending and had to borrow extensively from abroad in dollar-denominated loans. Then in 1999, Brazil devalued its currency, putting additional pressure on neighboring Argentina. As investors saw the persistent trade and government deficits that were occurring in Argentina, they became doubtful that the country could repay its debts and feared its currency would be devalued. Local citizens also became fearful of a devaluation and tried to convert their pesos into dollars, further deepening the problem.

Eventually, Argentina was forced to default on its international debt in 2002 and freeze bank accounts. Middle-class Argentineans who still had funds in their banks suffered a sharp decrease in their wealth. A severe economic downturn ensued. The hopes of the reforms in the early 1990s had become a bitter memory. However, the Argentinean economy proved resilient and began a recovery over the next several years. **Related to Exercise 5.5.**

SUMMARY

In this chapter, we examined the world of international finance. You saw how exchange rates are determined in markets and how governments can influence these markets. You also learned how the real exchange rate affects the trade deficit. Behind the complex world of international financial transactions are these few simple ideas:

1. *Exchange rates* are generally determined in *foreign exchange markets* by supply and demand.
2. The *real exchange rate* is the price of U.S. goods and services relative to foreign goods and services, expressed in a common currency. The equation for the real exchange rate is

$$\text{real exchange rate} = \frac{\text{exchange rate} \times \text{U.S. price index}}{\text{foreign price index}}$$

3. The *balance of payments* consists of three types of international transactions:
   - The *current account* is equal to net exports plus net income from existing investments abroad and net transfers from abroad.
   - The *financial account* is the value of a country's sales less purchases of assets.
   - The *capital account* is the net value of a country's capital transfers and the purchase and sale of nonproduced, nonfinancial assets.

   The sum of the current account, plus the financial account, plus the capital account is zero.
4. Governments can attempt to change the value of currencies by buying or selling currencies in the foreign exchange market. Purchasing a currency will raise its value; selling a currency will decrease its value.
5. A system of *fixed exchange rates* can provide a better environment for business but requires that countries keep their inflation rates and interest rates within narrow limits.

KEY TERMS

balance of payments, p. 393
balance of payments deficit, p. 400
balance of payments surplus, p. 400
capital account, p. 394
current account, p. 393
devaluation, p. 400
euro, p. 386
exchange rate, p. 386
financial account, p. 394
fixed exchange rate system, p. 399
flexible exchange rate system, p. 399
foreign exchange market intervention, p. 398
law of one price, p. 393
net international investment position, p. 396
purchasing power parity, p. 393
real exchange rate, p. 390
revaluation, p. 400
sovereign investment funds, p. 397

EXERCISES

All problems are assignable in MyEconLab; exercises that update with real-time data are marked with [real-time data icon].

19.1 How Exchange Rates Are Determined

1.1 The dollar __________ against the euro when the European central bank raises interest rates.

1.2 If the dollar appreciates against the euro, then the euro also __________ against the dollar.

1.3 The dollar __________ against the euro when the inflation rate in the United States increases.

1.4 A shift in the demand for euros and away from dollars will __________ the dollar against the euro.

1.5 **Using Demand and Supply Analysis.** Draw a demand and supply graph for British pounds to determine the effects of the following on the exchange rate between the British pound and the Japanese yen. (The vertical axis will be yen per pound.)

a. An increase in Japanese interest rates
b. An increase in the price of British goods
c. An increase in British interest rates

1.6 The Effects of Policy Changes in Japan. Until the early 1980s, Japan required its large insurance companies to invest all of their vast holdings in Japanese securities. At the prompting of the United States, Japan relaxed the restrictions and allowed the companies to invest anywhere in the world. What effect do you think this had on the yen/dollar exchange rate and the trade balance between the two countries?

1.7 Exchange Rates and Rumors of Default on Government Debt. Suppose there are rumors that a country undergoing financial difficulties is planning to default on its debt. Explain what you think will happen to that country's exchange rate.

19.2 Real Exchange Rates and Purchasing Power Parity

2.1 When the U.S. price level increases but the nominal exchange rate remains the same, the real exchange rate will ________.

2.2 When the U.S. and foreign price levels remain the same but the dollar appreciates, the real exchange rate will ________.

2.3 The law of one price provides accurate predictions of current exchange rates. ________ (True/False)

2.4 The theory of ________ states that the exchange rate between two countries should be determined by the price levels in those two countries.

2.5 The Real Exchange Rate between Germany and the United States. Consider the following data for the United States and Germany:

Year	German GDP Price Deflator	U.S. GDP Price Deflator	Market Exchange Rate
1980	85.7	76.0	2.49 marks per dollar
1990	113.4	119.6	2.12 marks per dollar

a. By what percent did the dollar depreciate against the mark over this period?

b. Using the formula for the real exchange rate,

$$\text{real exchange rate} = \frac{(\text{exchange rate} \times \text{U.S. price index})}{\text{foreign price index}}$$

compute the real exchange rate for 1980 and for 1990.

c. By how much did the real exchange rate change over this period?

d. Compare your answer for part (c) to your answer to part (a).

2.6 Tall Lattés and the Real Exchange Rate between the Euro and the Dollar. According to the *Economist*, in early 2004 the average price of a tall latté in Starbucks in the United States was $2.80. In the countries that use the euro, the average price was 2.93 euros. Because the exchange rate at this time was 0.79 euro per dollar, the dollar price of lattés in the euro area was $3.70. (Related to Application 1 on page 392.)

a. At what exchange rate between the dollar and the euro would a latté cost the same in the euro area as it did in the United States?

b. Does this calculation suggest that the euro is "too high" or "too low" relative to the dollar?

2.7 Mexican Peso and the U.S Dollar. Based on the data in the table in Application 1, is the Mexican peso under- or overvalued with respect to the dollar? Explain your answer. (Related to Application 1 on page 392.)

2.8 Energizer Batteries around the World. According to the *Wall Street Journal* on August 5, 2008, a pack of four AA batteries sold for $2.33 in Hong Kong, $6.05 in New York, and $8.24 in Paris (prices converted to dollars). At that time, 7.80 Hong Kong dollars were equal to 1 U.S. dollar and the euro (used in Paris) cost $1.54.

a. At what exchange rates would the batteries sell in New York, Hong Kong, and Paris for the same dollar price?

b. Are the actual exchange rates "too high" or "too low" relative to these calculations?

c. The price of the batteries in Brussels was $10.57 and in Rome $6.99. Yet these cities, along with Paris, are in the euro zone. What does this suggest about the "Big Mac" method for calculating ideal exchange rates?

19.3 The Current Account, the Financial Account, and the Capital Account

3.1 Net transfers from abroad are a(n) ________ entry on the current account.

3.2 The current, financial, and capital accounts must sum to ________.

3.3 According to latest data on the U.S. international investment position, the United States is a net ________.

3.4 The United States has a large ________ on the current account but a large ________ on the financial account.

3.5 Calculating the Capital and Current Account. During the year, a country (including its government), acquires an additional $100 billion of foreign assets. At the same time, foreign residents acquire $200 billion of this country's assets. Ignoring minor items, what is the balance on the capital account for this country? What about its current account?

3.6 Understanding Sovereign Investment Funds. China, Kuwait, and other countries that have had large current account surpluses are now investing some of their funds abroad in the private sector through sovereign investment funds. These funds have raised concerns. After reading a report from the Congressional Research Service, "Sovereign Wealth Funds: Background and Policy Issues for Congress," outline what you think are the key issues. This report is available at https://opencrs.com/document/RL34336/ (accessed May 31, 2012).

3.7 A Debt Puzzle for the United States. As we discussed in the chapter, the United States is a net international debtor—that is, U.S. ownership of foreign assets is less than foreign ownership of U.S. assets. Yet, in 2006, net income from abroad was positive. Why is this a puzzle? Can you think of any possible explanations for this puzzle? (*Hint:* Some economists think it has to do with the types of assets that the United States holds abroad versus the types of U.S. assets that foreigners hold.) (Related to Application 2 on page 396.)

19.4 Fixed and Flexible Exchange Rates

4.1 The government __________ foreign currency for dollars if it wants to peg the exchange rate at a higher rate than would normally prevail in the market.

4.2 If there is an excess supply of a country's currency at the fixed exchange rate, there is a balance of payments __________.

4.3 The Bretton Woods agreement broke down during the decade of the __________.

4.4 When European countries joined together to create the euro, they created a strong, central fiscal authority to unify the finances of its members. __________ (True/False) (Related to Application 3 on page 402.)

4.5 Expectations of Depreciation and Investing. Individuals wishing to invest in Turkey in 2006 had two choices. They could invest in bonds that would pay returns in 2007 in Turkish lira and earn 14.7 percent, or they could invest in Turkish bonds that would pay returns in U.S. dollars but earn only 5.2 percent. From this data, what do you think the market believes is the expected rate of depreciation of the Turkish lira against the U.S. dollar? Explain.

4.6 Dollarization. Some countries have simply decided to let the U.S. dollar or another foreign currency serve as their local currency. This is called "dollarization." Why would a country decide to abandon its own currency and use a foreign currency?

4.7 Uncovering U.S. Exchange Rate Policy. Suppose the United States reported that the U.S. Treasury had increased its holdings of foreign currencies from last year. What does this tell you about the foreign exchange policies of the United States during the last year?

4.8 Spain and the Euro Crisis. Unlike Greece, Spain's government did not engage in excess spending. But as capital flowed into Spain during its housing boom, it raised the level of wages and prices. Discuss how this created a balance of payments problem for Spain. (Related to Application 3 on page 402.)

19.5 Managing Financial Crises

5.1 When prices rose in Mexico faster than in the United States and the nominal exchange rate remained constant, the real exchange rate __________.

5.2 If a country borrows in dollars, a depreciation of its own currency against the dollar will __________ the burden of its debt.

5.3 Joseph Stiglitz is the economist who believed that the Asian financial crisis was an example of market overreaction that could have been avoided by bolder actions from world organizations. __________ (True/False)

5.4 In the 1990s, Argentina pegged its currency to the dollar. As the dollar appreciated in world markets, this caused an increase in Argentina's trade __________.

5.5 Argentina after the Crisis. Use the Web to find data on economic growth and well-being for Argentina today. (Try searching for "Argentina and recovery.") How has Argentina fared after its financial crisis in 2002? (Related to Application 4 on page 404.)

5.6 The Dollar and the Financial Crisis. It is generally recognized that the worldwide financial crisis in 2008 originated in the United States, as its financial institutions were most active in fueling the housing boom. However, investors throughout the world had bought U.S. mortgage-related securities and this spread the global crisis. When the crisis hit, the value of the U.S. dollar rose sharply against many other currencies. What might have caused this appreciation?

ECONOMIC EXPERIMENT

DETERMINING EXCHANGE RATES

In this experiment, you will see how exchange rates are determined. The class is divided into two groups. One group will be buying a fixed number of Swiss francs. The other group will be selling a fixed number of Swiss francs. Each buyer will have a maximum price that he or she is willing to pay. Each seller will have a minimum price that he or she is willing to accept. Trade will take place in several rounds. In each round, buyers and sellers will meet individually and either negotiate a trade or not. If a trade results, the results will be reported to the instructor and then announced to the class. After each round, the instructor announces the prices at which Swiss francs were traded. After several rounds, what happens to the prices?

MyEconLab

For additional economic experiments, please visit ***www.myeconlab.com*.**

Elasticity: A Measure of Responsiveness

CHAPTER 20

The city of Phoenix, Arizona gets its gasoline from two pipelines, one running from Texas and the other from the West Coast.

In summer of 2003, the Texas pipeline broke, cutting off 30 percent of the city's gasoline supply.

A reliable study of gasoline suggests that a 5 percent increase in price decreases the quantity demanded by 1 percent. Based on this study, it appears that to counteract the 30 percent decrease, the price would have to rise by 150 percent (5 times 30). But in fact the price increased by only 40 percent. What explains the relatively small increase in price?

LEARNING OBJECTIVES

- List the determinants of the price elasticity of demand.
- Use price elasticity of demand to predict changes in quantity and total revenue.
- Explain how the price elasticity of demand varies along a linear demand curve.
- Define the income elasticity and cross-price elasticity of demand.
- List the determinants of the price elasticity of supply.
- Use demand and supply elasticities to predict changes in equilibrium prices.

MyEconLab

MyEconLab helps you master each objective and study more efficiently.

In Chapter 4 we discussed the law of demand, which states that an increase in price decreases the quantity demanded, *ceteris paribus*. The law of demand is useful, but sometimes we need to know the numbers behind the law of demand. That is, we need to know exactly how much less will be demanded at a higher price. In this chapter, we will quantify the law of demand, exploring the responsiveness of consumers to changes in price. Suppose your student film society has decided to increase the price for its tickets from \$10 to \$11. You know from the law of demand that you'll sell fewer tickets, but the question is "How many fewer tickets?" As we'll see, you can use the concept of elasticity to predict how many tickets you'll sell and how much money you'll collect in total.

Switching to the supply side of the market, the law of supply tells us that an increase in price increases the quantity supplied, *ceteris paribus*. Sometimes the question is "By how much?" We'll quantify the law of supply, showing how to predict just how much more of a product will be supplied at a higher price. For example, if the world price of oil increases from \$70 to \$80 per barrel, we know from the law of supply that domestic producers will supply more oil, but the question is "How much more?" We can use the concept of elasticity to predict how much more domestic oil will be supplied at the higher price.

20.1 The Price Elasticity of Demand

price elasticity of demand (E_d)
A measure of the responsiveness of the quantity demanded to changes in price; equal to the absolute value of the percentage change in quantity demanded divided by the percentage change in price.

The **price elasticity of demand (E_d)** measures the responsiveness of the quantity demanded to changes in price. To compute the price elasticity of demand, we divide the percentage change in the quantity demanded by the percentage change in price, and then take the absolute value of the ratio:

$$E_d = \left| \frac{\text{percentage change in quantity demanded}}{\text{percentage change in price}} \right|$$

The vertical bars indicate that we take the absolute value of the ratio, so the price elasticity is always a positive number. For example, suppose the price of milk *increases* by 10 percent and the quantity demanded *decreases* by 15 percent. The price elasticity of demand is 1.5:

$$E_d = \left| \frac{\text{percentage change in quantity demanded}}{\text{percentage change in price}} = \frac{-15\%}{10\%} = 1.50 \right|$$

The law of demand tells us that price and quantity demanded move in opposite directions. Therefore, the percentage change in quantity will always have the opposite sign of the percentage change in price. In our example, a positive 10 percent change in price results in a negative 15 percent change in quantity. The ratio of the percentage changes is –1.50, and taking the absolute value of this ratio, the elasticity is 1.50. Although it is conventional to use the absolute value to compute the price elasticity, the practice is not universal. So you may encounter a negative price elasticity, which means that the elasticity is reported as its numerical value rather than its absolute value.

When the price elasticity is listed as a positive number, the interpretation of the elasticity is straightforward. If the elasticity number is large, it means that the demand for the product is very elastic, or very responsive to changes in price. In contrast, a small number indicates that the demand for a product is very inelastic.

Computing Percentage Changes and Elasticities

As we saw in the appendix to Chapter 1, we can compute a percentage change in two ways. Using the initial-value method, we divide the change in the value of a variable by its initial value. For example, if a price increases from \$20 to \$22, the percentage change is \$2 divided by \$20, or 10 percent:

$$\text{percent change with initial value} = \frac{22 - 20}{20} \times 100 = \frac{2}{20} \times 100 = 10\%$$

Alternatively, we could use the midpoint method. We divide the change in the variable by its average value, that is, the midpoint of the two values. For example, if the price increases from \$20 to \$22, the average or midpoint value is \$21 and the percentage change is \$2 divided by \$21, or 9.52 percent:

$$\text{percent change with midpoint value} = \frac{2}{\frac{20 + 22}{2}} \times 100 = \frac{2}{21} \times 100 = 9.52\%$$

The advantage of the midpoint approach is that it generates the same absolute percentage change whether the variable has increased or decreased. The reason is that the denominator is the same in both cases. In contrast, the initial-value computation is based on the initial value, so our answer there depends on the direction of the change—which of the two values is the initial value.

Table 20.1 shows the calculation of the price elasticity of demand with the two approaches. When the price increases from \$20 to \$22, the quantity demanded decreases from 100 to 80 units. Using the initial-value method, we get an elasticity of 2.0, equal to the 20 percent change in quantity divided by the 10 percent change in price. As shown in the lower part of the table, the midpoint method generates an elasticity of 2.33.

TABLE 20.1 Computing Price Elasticity with Initial Values and Midpoints

		Price	Quantity
Data	Initial	\$20	100
	New	22	80
		Price	**Quantity**
Computation with initial-value method	Percentage change	$10\% = \frac{\$2}{\$20} \times 100$	$-20\% = -\frac{20}{100} \times 100$
	Price elasticity of demand	$2.0 = \left\|\frac{-20\%}{10\%}\right\|$	
		Price	**Quantity**
Computation with midpoint method	Percentage change	$9.52\% = \frac{\$2}{\$21} \times 100$	$-22.22\% = -\frac{20}{90} \times 100$
	Price elasticity of demand	$2.33 = \left\|\frac{-22.22\%}{9.52\%}\right\|$	

Why do the two approaches generate different elasticity numbers? The midpoint approach measures the percentage changes more precisely, so we get a more precise measure of price elasticity. In this case, the percentage changes are relatively small, so the two elasticity numbers are close to one another. If the percentage changes were larger, however, the elasticity numbers generated by the two approaches would be quite different, and it would be wise to use the midpoint approach. In this book, we use the initial-value approach because it generates nice round numbers and allows us to focus on economics rather than arithmetic. But any time you want to be more precise, you can use the midpoint formula.

Price Elasticity and the Demand Curve

Figure 20.1 shows five different demand curves, each with a different elasticity. We can divide products into five types, depending on their price elasticities of demand.

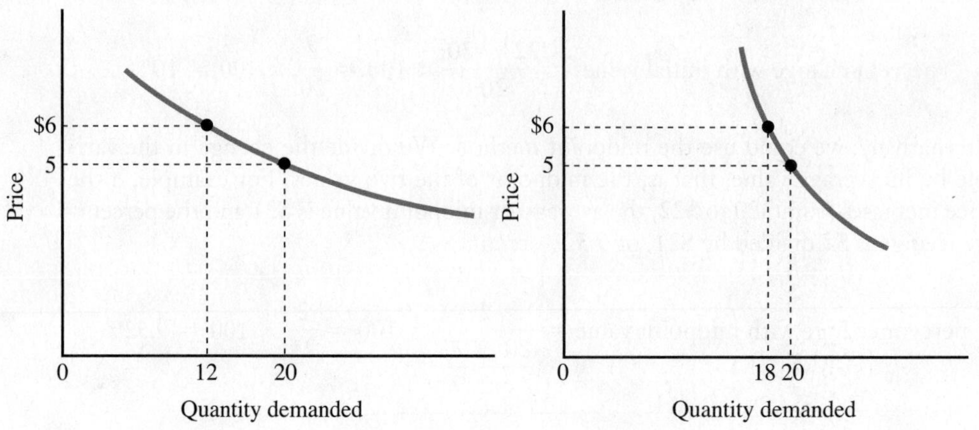

(A) Elastic Demand: $E_d = \left| \frac{-40\%}{20\%} \right| = 2.0 > 1$ (B) Inelastic Demand: $E_d = \left| \frac{-10\%}{20\%} \right| = 0.50 < 1$

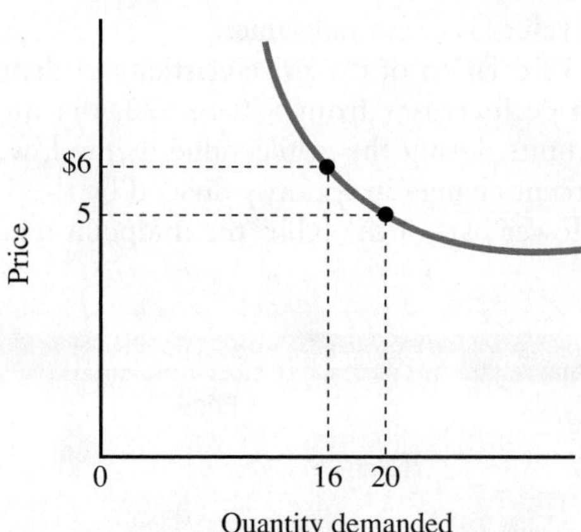

(C) Unit Elastic Demand: $E_d = \left| \frac{-20\%}{20\%} \right| = 1$

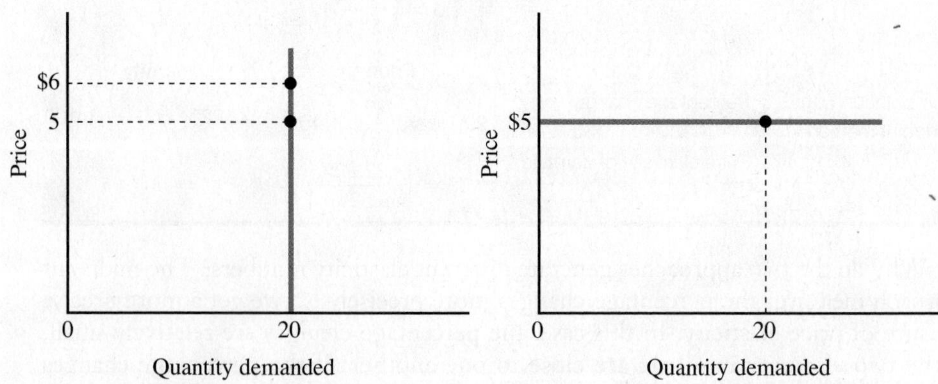

(D) Perfectly Inelastic Demand: $E_d = \left| \frac{0\%}{20\%} \right| = 0$ (E) Perfectly Elastic Demand: $E_d = \infty$

▲ FIGURE 20.1
Elasticity and Demand Curves

- **Elastic demand** (Panel A). In this case, a 20 percent increase in price (from $5 to $6) decreases the quantity demanded by 40 percent (from 20 to 12), so the price elasticity of demand is 2.0. When the price elasticity is greater than 1.0, we say that demand is *elastic*, or highly responsive to changes in price. Some examples of goods with elastic demand are restaurant meals, air travel, and movies.

elastic demand
The price elasticity of demand is greater than one, so the percentage change in quantity exceeds the percentage change in price.

- **Inelastic demand** (Panel B). The same 20 percent increase in price decreases the quantity demanded by only 10 percent (from 20 to 18), so the price elasticity of demand is 0.50. When the elasticity is less than 1.0, we say that demand is *inelastic*, or not very responsive to changes in price. Some examples of goods with inelastic demand are salt, eggs, coffee, and cigarettes.

inelastic demand
The price elasticity of demand is less than one, so the percentage change in quantity is less than the percentage change in price.

- **Unit elastic demand** (Panel C). A 20 percent increase in price decreases the quantity demanded by exactly 20 percent, so the price elasticity of demand is 1.0. Some examples of goods with *unit elasticity* are housing and fruit juice.

unit elastic demand
The price elasticity of demand is one, so the percentage change in quantity equals the percentage change in price.

- **Perfectly inelastic demand** (Panel D). When demand is *perfectly inelastic*, the quantity doesn't change as the price changes, so the demand curve is vertical at the fixed quantity. The price elasticity of demand is zero. This extreme case is rare because for most products, consumers can either switch to a substitute good or do without. For example, although there are no direct substitutes for household water, as the price of water rises, people install low-flow showerheads and water their lawns and clean their cars less frequently. The rare cases of perfectly inelastic demand are medicines—such as insulin for diabetics—that have no substitutes.

perfectly inelastic demand
The price elasticity of demand is zero.

- **Perfectly elastic demand** (Panel E). In the case of *perfect elasticity*, the price elasticity is infinite and the demand curve is horizontal, meaning that only one price is possible. At that price, the quantity demanded could be any quantity, from one unit to millions of units. If the price were to increase even a penny, the quantity demanded would drop to zero. As we'll see later in the book, firms in a perfectly competitive market face this sort of demand curve. For example, each wheat farmer can sell as much as he or she wants at the market price but would sell nothing at any price above the market price.

perfectly elastic demand
The price elasticity of demand is infinite.

Elasticity and the Availability of Substitutes

The key factor in determining the price elasticity for a particular product is the availability of substitute products. Consider the substitution possibilities for insulin and cornflakes. There are no good substitutes for insulin, so diabetics are not very responsive to changes in price. When the price of insulin increases, they cannot switch to another medicine, so the demand for insulin is inelastic. In contrast, there are many substitutes for cornflakes, including different types of corn cereals, as well as cereals made from wheat, rice, and oats. Faced with an increase in the price of cornflakes, consumers can easily switch to substitute products, so the demand for cornflakes is relatively elastic.

Table 20.2 on page 414 shows the price elasticities of demand for various products. The different elasticities illustrate the importance of substitutes in determining the price elasticity of demand. Because there are no good substitutes for water and salt, it is not surprising that the elasticities are small. For example, the price elasticity of demand for water is 0.20, meaning that a 10 percent increase in price decreases the quantity demanded by 2 percent. The demand for coffee is inelastic (0.30), because although there are alternative beverages and caffeine-delivery systems (tea, infused soft drinks, sports drinks, and pills), coffee provides a unique combination of taste and caffeine. Although there is an artificial substitute for eggs (for people concerned about dietary cholesterol), there are no natural substitutes, so the demand for eggs is relatively inelastic (0.30).

TABLE 20.2 Price Elasticities of Demand for Selected Products[1]

	Product	Price Elasticity of Demand
Inelastic	Salt	0.1
	Food (wealthy countries)	0.15
	Weekend canoe trips	0.19
	Water	0.2
	Coffee	0.3
	Physician visits	0.25
	Sport fishing	0.28
	Gasoline (short run)	0.25
	Eggs	0.3
	Cigarettes	0.3
	Food (poor countries)	0.34
	Shoes and footwear	0.7
	Gasoline (long run)	0.6
Unit elastic	Housing	1.0
	Fruit juice	1.0
Elastic	Automobiles	1.2
	Foreign travel	1.8
	Motorboats	2.2
	Restaurant meals	2.3
	Air travel	2.4
	Movies	3.7
	Specific brands of coffee	5.6

Alternative brands of a product are good substitutes for one another, so the demand for a specific brand of a product is typically elastic. For example, the elasticity of demand for a specific brand of coffee is 5.6, compared to an overall elasticity for coffee of 0.30. This means that a 10 percent increase in the price of coffee in general (all brands) will decrease the quantity of coffee sold by 3 percent, but a 10 percent increase in the price of a specific brand will decrease the quantity of that brand sold by 56 percent. Each brand of coffee is a substitute for all the other brands, so consumers are very responsive to a change in the price of a specific brand. Similarly, the demand for specific brands of tires is more elastic than the demand for tires in general.

The availability of substitutes increases over time, so the longer the time consumers have to respond to a price change, the more elastic the demand. Because it often takes time for consumers to respond to price changes, the short-run price elasticity of demand is typically smaller than the long-run elasticity. For example, when the price of gasoline increases, consumers can immediately drive fewer miles in their existing cars or switch to public transportation. As shown in Table 20.2, the short-run price elasticity of demand for gasoline is 0.25. In the long run, consumers can buy more fuel-efficient cars and move closer to workplaces. As time passes, consumers have more options to cut gasoline consumption—more substitution possibilities—so demand becomes more elastic. In Table 20.2, the long-run price elasticity of demand for gasoline is 0.60, over twice as large as the short-run elasticity.

Other Determinants of the Price Elasticity of Demand

Two other factors help determine the price elasticity of demand for a product. First, the elasticity is generally larger for goods that take a relatively large part of a consumer's budget. If a good represents a small part of the budget of the typical consumer, demand is relatively inelastic. For example, suppose the price of pencils is 20 cents and then increases by 10 percent, or 2 cents. Because the price change is tiny compared to the income of the typical consumer, we would expect a relatively small decrease in the quantity of pencils demanded. In contrast, if the price of a car is $20,000 and then increases 10 percent ($2,000), we would expect a bigger response because the change in price is large relative to the income of the typical consumer.

International comparisons of the price elasticity of demand for food suggest that demand is more price elastic when the good represents a large part of the consumer's budget. As shown in Table 20.2, in wealthy countries the price elasticity of demand for food is around 0.15. In poor countries, people spend a larger fraction of their budget on food, so they are more responsive to changes in food prices. In these poor countries, the price elasticity of demand is around 0.34.

Another factor in determining the elasticity of demand is whether the product is a necessity or a luxury good. As shown in Table 20.2, the demand for food, a necessity, is relatively low in both wealthy and poor countries. Similarly, the demand for physician visits is inelastic (elasticity = 0.25). In contrast, the elasticity of demand for luxury goods such as restaurant meals, foreign travel, and motorboats is relatively elastic. Of course, not all goods that are considered luxuries have elastic demand. For example, the price elasticity of demand for weekend canoe trips is 0.19, and the demand elasticity for sport fishing is 0.28. These elasticities suggest that one person's luxury is another person's necessity.

Table 20.3 summarizes our discussion of the determinants of the price elasticity of demand. Demand is relatively elastic if there are many good substitutes, if we allow consumers a long time to respond, if spending on the product is a large part of the consumer's budget, and if the product is a luxury as opposed to a necessity.

TABLE 20.3 Determinants of Elasticity

Factor	Demand is relatively elastic if ...	Demand is relatively inelastic if ...
Availability of substitutes	there are many substitutes.	there are few substitutes.
Passage of time	a long time passes.	a short time passes.
Fraction of consumer budget	is large.	is small.
Necessity	the product is a luxury.	the product is a necessity.

application 1

A CLOSER LOOK AT THE ELASTICITY OF DEMAND FOR GASOLINE

APPLYING THE CONCEPTS #1: How does the price elasticity of demand vary over time?

We've seen that the demand for gasoline is more elastic in the long run, when consumers have more opportunity to respond to changes in price. A recent study explores two sorts of responses to higher gasoline prices. First, when the price increases, people drive fewer miles, so there are fewer cars on the road. As shown in the following table, the elasticity of traffic volume is 0.10 in the short run (within one year) and 0.30 in the long run (after five years). In other words, a 10 percent increase in the price of gasoline decreases the number of cars on the road by 1 percent in the short run and 3 percent in the long run. A second response to higher prices is to switch to more fuel-efficient cars. As shown in the table, the elasticity of fuel efficiency is 0.15 in the short run and 0.40 in the long run. **Related to Exercises 1.6 and 1.7.**

TABLE 20.4 Gasoline Prices, Traffic Volume, and Fuel Efficiency

Elasticity of	Short Run (1 year)	Long Run (5 years)
Traffic Volume	0.10	0.30
Fuel Efficiency	0.15	0.40

SOURCE: Based on Phil Goodwin, Joyce Dargay, and Mark Hanly, "Elasticities of Road Traffic and Fuel Consumption with Respect to Price and Income: A Review," *Transport Review* 24, no. 3 (2004): 275–292.

20.2 Using Price Elasticity

The price elasticity of demand is a very useful tool for economic analysis. If we know the price elasticity of demand for a particular good, we can quantify the law of demand, predicting the change in quantity resulting from a change in price. In addition, we can use an estimate of the price elasticity of demand to predict how a change in price affects a firm's total revenue.

Predicting Changes in Quantity

If we have values for two of the three variables in the elasticity formula, we can compute the value of the third. The three variables are (1) the price elasticity of demand itself, (2) the percentage change in quantity, and (3) the percentage change in price. So if we know the values for the price elasticity and the percentage change in price, we can compute the value for the percentage change in quantity. Specifically, we can rearrange the elasticity formula:

$$\text{percentage change in quantity demanded} = \text{percentage change in price} \times E_d$$

For example, suppose you run a campus film series and you've decided to increase your admission price by 15 percent. If you know the elasticity of demand for your movies, you could use it to predict how many fewer tickets you'll sell at the higher price. If the elasticity of demand is 2.0 and you increase the price by 15 percent, we would predict a 30 percent decrease in the quantity of tickets demanded:

$$\begin{aligned}\text{percentage change in quantity demanded} &= \text{percentage change in price} \times E_d \\ &= 15\% \times 2.0 = 30\%\end{aligned}$$

We can use the concept of price elasticity to predict the effects of a change in the price of beer on drinking and highway deaths among young adults. The price elasticity of demand for beer among young adults is about 1.30.[2] If a state imposes a beer tax that increases the price of beer by 10 percent, we would predict that beer consumption will decrease by 13 percent:

$$\begin{aligned}\text{percentage change in quantity demanded} &= \text{percentage change in price} \times E_d \\ &= 10\% \times 1.30 = 13\%\end{aligned}$$

The number of highway deaths among young adults is roughly proportional to their beer consumption, so the number of deaths will also decrease by 13 percent. According to a recent study, a doubling of the beer tax from $0.16 to $0.32 per six-pack would decrease highway deaths among 18- to 20-year-olds by about 12 percent. Raising the beer tax back to where it was in 1951 would cut highway deaths by 32 percent.

Another ongoing policy objective is to reduce smoking by teenagers. Under the 1997 federal tobacco settlement, cigarette prices increased by about 62 cents per pack, a percentage increase of about 25 percent. The demand for cigarettes by teenagers is elastic, with an elasticity of 1.3.[3] Therefore, a 25 percent price hike will reduce teen smoking by 32.5 percent:

$$\text{percentage change in quantity demanded} = 25\% \times 1.30 = 32.5\%$$

About half the decrease in consumption occurs because fewer teenagers will become smokers, and the other half occurs because each teenage smoker will smoke fewer cigarettes.

Price Elasticity and Total Revenue

Firms use the concept of price elasticity to predict the effects of changing their prices. A firm produces products to sell, and a firm's **total revenue** equals the money it generates from selling products. If a firm sells its product for the same price to every consumer, total revenue equals the price per unit times the quantity sold:

total revenue
The money a firm generates from selling its product.

$$\text{total revenue} = \text{price per unit} \times \text{quantity sold}$$

Suppose a firm increases the price of its product. Will its total sales revenue increase or decrease? The answer depends on the price elasticity of demand for the product. If you know the price elasticity, you can determine whether a price hike will increase or decrease the firm's total revenue.

Let's return to the example of the campus film series. Suppose you are thinking about increasing the price of tickets by 10 percent, from $10 to $11. An increase in the ticket price brings good news and bad news:

- Good news: You get more money for each ticket sold.
- Bad news: You sell fewer tickets.

Your total revenue will decrease if the bad news (fewer tickets sold) dominates the good news (more money per ticket). The elasticity of demand tells us how bad the bad news is. The more elastic the demand, the larger the reduction in the quantity sold—the worse the bad news.

The upper part of Table 20.5 shows an example of the effects of a price hike when the demand for a product is elastic. In this case, the price elasticity of demand is 2.0, so a 10 percent increase in price decreases the quantity demanded by 20 percent, from 100 to 80 tickets. Because the percentage decrease in quantity (the bad news) exceeds the percentage increase in price (the good news), total revenue decreases, from $1,000 to $880. In general, an elastic demand means that the percentage change in quantity (the bad news from a price hike) will exceed the percentage change in price (the good news), so an increase in price will decrease total revenue.

TABLE 20.5 Price and Total Revenue with Different Elasticities of Demand

Elastic Demand: $E_d = 2.0$		
Price	**Quantity Sold**	**Total Revenue**
$10	100	$1,000
11	80	880
Inelastic Demand: $E_d = 0.50$		
Price	**Quantity Sold**	**Total Revenue**
100	10	$1,000
120	9	1,080

We get the opposite result if the demand for the good is inelastic: An increase in price increases total revenue. The lower part of Table 20.5 shows an example of the effects of a price hike when demand is inelastic (equal to 0.50). Suppose that your campus bookstore starts with a textbook price of \$100 and sells 10 books per minute. If the bookstore increases its price by 20 percent (from \$100 to \$120 per book), the quantity of textbooks sold will decrease by only 10 percent (from 10 to 9 per minute). Therefore, the store's total revenue will increase from \$1,000 per minute (\$100 × 10 books) to \$1,080 per minute (\$120 × 9 books). In general, an inelastic demand means that the percentage change in quantity will be smaller than the percentage change in price, so an increase in price will increase total revenue.

Table 20.6 shows, for different types of goods, the effects of changes in price on total revenue.

TABLE 20.6 Price Elasticity and Total Revenue

Elastic Demand: $E_d > 1.0$		
If price ...	**Total revenue ...**	**Because the percentage change in quantity is ...**
↑	↓	Larger than the percentage change in price.
↓	↑	Larger than the percentage change in price.
Inelastic Demand: $E_d < 1.0$		
If price ...	**Total revenue ...**	**Because the percentage change in quantity is ...**
↑	↑	Smaller than the percentage change in price.
↓	↓	Smaller than the percentage change in price.

- *Elastic demand.* The relationship between price and total revenue is negative: An increase in price decreases total revenue; a decrease in price increases total revenue.
- *Inelastic demand.* The relationship between price and total revenue is positive: An increase in price increases total revenue; a decrease in price decreases total revenue.
- *Unit elastic demand.* Total revenue does not vary with price.

We can use the relationships summarized in Table 20.6 to work backward. If we observe the relationship between the price of a product and total sales revenue of the product, we can determine whether the demand for the product is elastic or inelastic. Suppose that when a music store increases the price of its CDs, its total revenue from CDs drops. The negative relationship between price and total revenue means that demand for the store's CDs is elastic: Total revenue decreases because consumers are very responsive to an increase in price, buying a much smaller quantity. In contrast, suppose that when a city increases the price it charges for water, the total revenue from water sales increases. The positive relationship between price and total revenue suggests that the demand for the city's water is inelastic: Total revenue increases because consumers are not very responsive to an increase in price.

Using Elasticity to Predict the Revenue Effects of Price Changes

If we know whether the demand for a product is elastic or inelastic, we can predict the effect of a change in price on total revenue. Here are four illustrations of the revenue consequences of changes in price.

1 **Market versus Brand Elasticity:** The demand for a specific brand of a product is more elastic than the demand for the product. Although the demand for coffee is inelastic (price elasticity of demand = 0.30), the demand for a specific brand of

coffee is elastic (price elasticity = 3.0). Therefore, a price cut on a specific brand of coffee will increase a firm's total revenue.

2 **Bus Fares and Deficits:** In every large city in the United States, the public bus system runs a deficit: Operating costs exceed revenues from passenger fares. The price elasticity of demand for bus ridership in the typical city is inelastic, about 0.33.[4] Therefore, the good news associated with a fare hike (more revenue per rider) will dominate the bad news (fewer riders), and total fare revenue will increase, reducing the bus deficit.

3 **A Bumper Crop Is Bad News for Farmers:** A bumper crop of soybeans (an unusually large harvest) brings good news and bad news for farmers. The good news is that they will sell more bushels of soybeans. The bad news is that the increase in supply will decrease the equilibrium price of soybeans, so farmers will get less money per bushel. Unfortunately for farmers, the demand for soybeans and many other agricultural products is inelastic, meaning that to sell the extra output, the price must fall by a relatively large amount. The bad news dominates the good news, so a bumper crop means less total revenue for farmers.

4 **Antidrug Policies and Property Crime:** What is the connection between antidrug policies and property crimes such as robbery, burglary, and auto theft? The government uses various policies to restrict the supply of illegal drugs, and the decrease in supply increases the equilibrium price. Because the demand for illegal drugs is inelastic, the increase in price will increase total spending on illegal drugs.[5] A drug addict who supports his or her habit by stealing personal property will commit more property crimes to pay for the pricier drugs. In other words, there is a trade-off: A policy that increases drug prices will reduce drug consumption, but will also increase the amount of property crime committed by addicts who continue to abuse drugs.

application 2

VANITY PLATES AND THE ELASTICITY OF DEMAND

APPLYING THE CONCEPTS #2: How does an increase in price affect total expenditures?

The radio quiz show *Wait Wait ... Don't Tell Me!* recently asked the following question: Which state has the highest number of vanity license plates? The correct answer is Virginia, where over 10 percent of cars have vanity license plates such as 10SNE1 and GLBLWRMR. An economist might have extended the question to ask why there are so many vanity plates in Virginia. Although Virginians may be unusually vain, a more plausible explanation is that the price of vanity plates is only $10, or about one-third of the average price in the United States.

Is the low price in Virginia rational from the state's perspective? Suppose the state's objective is to maximize the revenue from vanity plates. According to a recent study, the demand for vanity plates in Virginia is inelastic, with a price elasticity of demand equal to 0.26. Therefore, if the state increased the price, the total revenue from vanity plates would increase. **Related to Exercises 2.4 and 2.14.**

SOURCE: Based on Erik Craft, "The Demand for Vanity (Plates): Elasticities, Net Revenue Maximization, and Deadweight Loss." *Contemporary Economic Policy* 20 (2002): 133–144.

20.3 Elasticity and Total Revenue for a Linear Demand Curve

It is often useful to represent the demand for a product with a linear demand curve. A linear demand curve—a straight line—has a constant slope, but that does not mean that it has a constant elasticity of demand. In fact, the price elasticity of demand decreases as we move downward along a linear demand curve. On the upper half of a linear demand curve, demand is elastic; on the lower half of the curve, demand is inelastic. At the midpoint of a linear demand curve, demand is unit elastic.

Price Elasticity along a Linear Demand Curve

We can use Panel A of Figure 20.2 to show how price elasticity varies along a linear demand curve. The slope of the demand curve is –\$2 per unit quantity. We see this by picking any two points and computing the slope as the vertical difference between the two points (the "rise") divided by the horizontal difference between the two points (the "run"). For example, between points *e* and *u*, the vertical difference is –\$30 and the horizontal difference is 15, so the slope is –\$30/15 = –\$2. That means a \$2 decrease in price increases the quantity demanded by one unit.

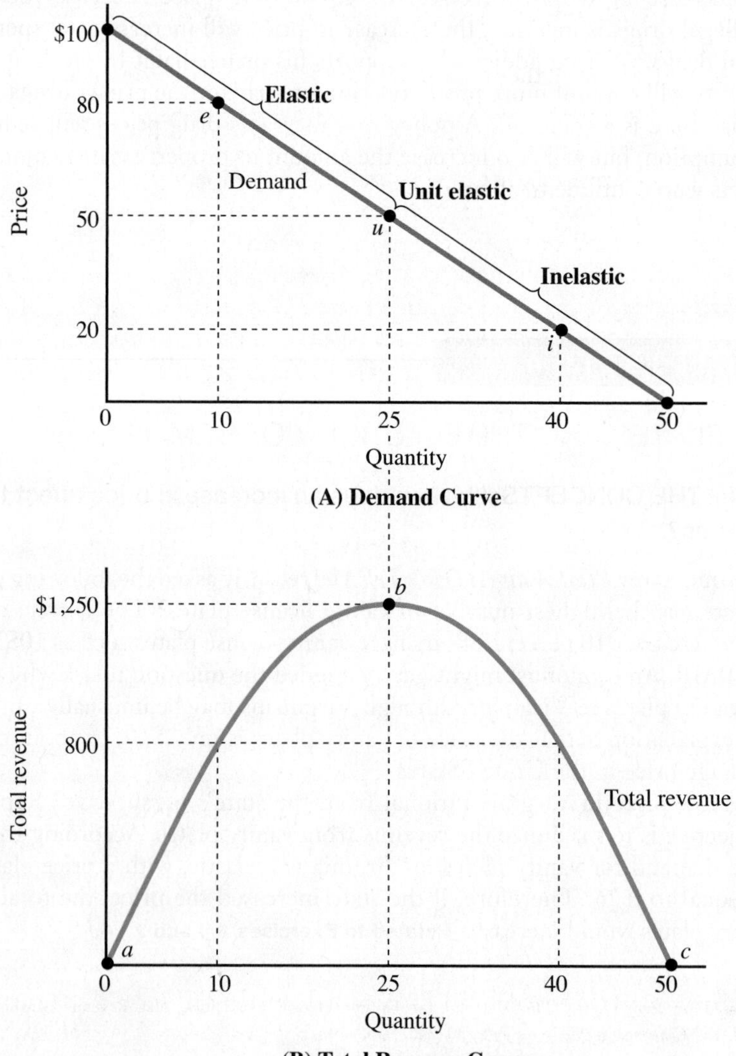

▶ **FIGURE 20.2**
Elasticity and Total Revenue along a Linear Demand Curve
Demand is elastic along the upper half of a linear demand curve, so an increase in quantity from a decrease in price increases total revenue (between points *a* and *b* on the total-revenue curve). Demand is inelastic along the lower half of a linear demand curve, so an increase in quantity from a decrease in price decreases total revenue (between points *b* and *c*). Total revenue is maximized at the midpoint of a linear demand curve (point *u*), where demand is unit elastic.

Table 20.7 shows how to compute the price elasticity of demand with three starting points: *e* (for elastic demand), *u* (for unit elastic), and *i* (for inelastic). As shown in columns B and D, a $2 reduction in price increases the quantity demanded by one unit.

TABLE 20.7 Elasticity of Demand along a Linear Demand Curve

A	B	C	D	E	F
Starting Point	Change in Price	Percentage Change in Price	Change in Quantity	Percentage Change in Quantity	Elasticity of Demand
e: Elastic	–$2	$\frac{-\$2}{\$80} = -2.5\%$	+1	$\frac{1}{10} = 10\%$	$\left\lvert\frac{10\%}{-2.5\%}\right\rvert = 4$
u: Unit elastic	–$2	$\frac{-\$2}{\$50} = -4\%$	+1	$\frac{1}{25} = 4\%$	$\left\lvert\frac{4\%}{-4\%}\right\rvert = 1$
i: Inelastic	–$2	$\frac{-\$2}{\$20} = -10\%$	+1	$\frac{1}{40} = 2.5\%$	$\left\lvert\frac{2.5\%}{-10\%}\right\rvert = 0.25$

- *Column C: Percentage change in price.* Starting from point *e*, we cut $2 off an $80 price, resulting in a 2.5 percent price cut. The same $2 price cut is larger in percentage terms farther down the demand curve, where the price is lower. For point *u*, the percentage change in price is –4 percent (equal to –$2/$50), and for point *i* the percentage change in price is –10 percent (equal to –$2/$20).
- *Column E: Percentage change in quantity.* At point *e*, we start with 10 units, so a one-unit increase in quantity is a 10 percent increase. Moving down the column, the same one-unit increase in quantity is smaller in percentage terms as we move down the demand curve, where the quantity is larger. For point *u*, the percentage change in price is 4 percent (equal to 1/25), and for point *i* the percentage change in quantity is 2.5 percent (equal to 1/40).
- *Column F: Price elasticity of demand.* Starting from point *e*, the price elasticity is large (4.0) because the percentage change in quantity (10 percent) is four times the percentage change in price (2.5 percent). Starting at point *u*, demand is unit elastic because the percentage change in quantity equals the percentage change in price. Starting from point *i*, demand is inelastic (0.25), because the percentage change in quantity is one-fourth the percentage change in price.

Why does the price elasticity vary along a linear demand curve? It's tempting to think the elasticity will be constant because a straight line has a constant slope. But that's incorrect, because we measure elasticity by percentage changes, not absolute changes. As we move downward along the demand curve, we're moving in the direction of larger quantities, so the same absolute change in quantity (one unit) becomes a smaller *percentage* change in quantity. At the same time, as we move downward along the curve, we are moving to lower prices, so a $2 price reduction leads to a larger *percentage* change in price. As a result, the elasticity (the ratio of the percentage changes) decreases as we move downward along the demand curve.

Elasticity and Total Revenue for a Linear Demand Curve

Panel B of Figure 20.2 shows the relationship between total revenue and the quantity sold for the linear demand curve. Demand is elastic along the upper half of a linear demand curve, which means that a decrease in price will increase the quantity sold by a larger percentage amount. As a result, total revenue will increase, as shown by the positively sloped total-revenue curve between points *a* and *b*. In contrast, demand is inelastic along the lower half of a linear demand curve, which means that a decrease in

application 3

TRAMPOLINES AND THE LOWER HALF OF A LINEAR DEMAND CURVE

APPLYING THE CONCEPTS #3: Will a firm choose a point on the lower half of a linear demand curve?

Suppose a firm that produces trampolines has a linear demand curve for its product, with a vertical intercept of $800. The firm currently charges a price of $300. Do you have any advice for the firm?

Your advice should be to increase the price. The price of $300 is certainly too low because it is less than the $400 price at the midpoint of the demand curve (half of $800). At a price of $300, the firm is below the midpoint of the demand curve, so the demand for its product is price-inelastic. If the firm increases its price from $300 to $400, its total revenue would increase because demand is inelastic (the percentage decrease in quantity is less than the percentage increase in price). At the same time, an increase in price would decrease the quantity of trampolines demanded (the law of demand), so the firm would produce fewer trampolines at a lower total cost. Because an increase in price increases total revenue and decreases total cost, the firm's profit would increase. The same logic applies to any price below the midpoint price of $400.

How much higher (how much above $400) should the price go? As we'll see later in the book, it depends on the cost of producing the product. Although we don't have the relevant cost information to pick the best price, we know for certain that it will be no less than $400 because a firm will never operate below the midpoint of a linear demand curve. **Related to Exercises 3.5 and 3.9.**

---

price will increase the quantity sold by a smaller percentage amount. As a result, total revenue will decrease, as shown by the negatively sloped total-revenue curve between points *b* and *c*. The total-revenue curve reaches its maximum at the midpoint of the linear demand curve, where demand is unit elastic. In Figure 20.2, demand is unit elastic at point *u* on the demand curve, so total revenue reaches its maximum at $1,250 at point *b* on the total-revenue curve.

20.4 Other Elasticities of Demand

We've seen that the price elasticity of demand measures the responsiveness of consumers to changes in the price of a particular good. Of course, the demand for a particular product also depends on other variables such as consumer income and the prices of related goods—substitutes and complements. We can use two other elasticities to measure the responsiveness of consumers to changes in these other variables that affect demand: income elasticity of demand and cross-price elasticity of demand.

Income Elasticity of Demand

income elasticity of demand
A measure of the responsiveness of demand to changes in consumer income; equal to the percentage change in the quantity demanded divided by the percentage change in income.

We saw in Chapter 4 that the demand for a particular product depends in part on the consumer's income. The **income elasticity of demand** measures the responsiveness of demand to changes in income, indicating how much more or less of a particular product is purchased as income changes. The income elasticity of demand is defined as the percentage change in quantity demanded divided by the percentage change in income:

$$E_I = \frac{\text{percentage change in quantity demanded}}{\text{percentage change in income}}$$

For example, if a 10 percent increase in income increases the quantity of books demanded by 15 percent, the income elasticity of demand for books is 1.50 (equal to 15% divided by 10%).

We can use the income elasticities of demand for various products to classify the products. Recall from Chapter 4 that when a consumer's income increases, he or she buys more of a "normal" good. If the income elasticity is positive—indicating a positive relationship between income and demand—we say that the good is normal. New cars and new clothes are products that have positive income elasticities and are thus considered normal goods. In contrast, if the income elasticity is negative—indicating a negative relationship between income and demand—we say the good is "inferior." Some examples of inferior goods are intercity bus travel, used clothing, and used cars.

Cross-Price Elasticity of Demand

We saw in Chapter 4 that the demand for a particular product also depends in part on the prices of related goods—substitutes and complements. The **cross-price elasticity of demand** measures the responsiveness of demand to changes in the prices of other goods, indicating how much more or less of a particular product is purchased as other prices change. The cross-price elasticity is defined as the percentage change in quantity demanded of one good (*X*) divided by the percentage change in the price of another good (*Y*):

cross-price elasticity of demand
A measure of the responsiveness of demand to changes in the price of another good; equal to the percentage change in the quantity demanded of one good (*X*) divided by the percentage change in the price of another good (*Y*).

$$E_{xy} = \frac{\text{percentage change in quantity of } X \text{ demanded}}{\text{percentage change in price of } Y}$$

As we saw in Chapter 4, two goods are considered substitutes if there is a positive relationship between the quantity demanded of one good and the price of the other good. For example, an increase in the price of bananas increases the demand for apples as consumers substitute apples for the now relatively expensive bananas. For substitute goods, the cross-price elasticity is positive. In contrast, two goods are considered complements if there is a negative relationship between the quantity demanded of one good and the price of the other. For example, an increase in the price of ice cream increases the cost of apple pie with ice cream, causing consumers to demand fewer apples. For complementary goods, the cross-price elasticity is negative. Table 20.8 summarizes the signs (positive or negative) for different types of goods.

TABLE 20.8 Income and Cross-Price Elasticities for Different Types of Goods

This elasticity	Is Positive for ...	Is Negative for ...
Income elasticity	Normal goods	Inferior goods
Cross-price elasticity	Substitute goods	Complementary goods

Estimates of cross-price elasticity of demand are useful to retailers in their pricing decisions. For example, when a grocery store cuts the price of peanut butter by 10 percent, the store will sell more peanut butter but will also sell more complementary goods such as jelly and bread. If the cross-price elasticity of demand for jelly is 0.5, a 10 percent decrease in the price of peanut butter will increase the demand for jelly by 5 percent. Retailers use coupons for one product to promote sales of that good as well as sales of complementary goods. Armed with the relevant cross elasticities, retailers can predict just how much more of a complementary good consumers will buy.

application 4

I CAN FIND THAT ELASTICITY IN FOUR CLICKS!

APPLYING THE CONCEPTS #4: Where do I find estimates of elasticities of demand?

Suppose you want to find estimates of the elasticities of demand (own price, income, cross-price) for orange juice. The U.S. Department of Agriculture has a Web site that provides estimates of demand elasticities for hundreds of food products (from apples to yogurt) for dozens of countries (from Albania to Zimbabwe). Starting from (http:// www.ers.usda.gov/Data/Elasticities/), you are four clicks away from the following estimates of demand elasticities for orange juice in the United States: income elasticity = 2.212; own price elasticity = –1.391; cross-price elasticity for apple juice = 0.908. Here are the clicks: (1) Demand Elasticities from Literature; (2) Choose Country; Choose Commodity; (3) Cross Commodity; (4) Submit.

It's important to note two things about the reported elasticities. First, the regular price elasticity is reported as a negative number and labeled "own price elasticity" for "Marshallian Demand." Second, the reported "expenditure elasticity" is similar to the income elasticity, with the denominator of the elasticity equal to the percentage change in total consumer expenditure (versus percentage change in income). **Related to Exercise 4.9.**

20.5 The Price Elasticity of Supply

price elasticity of supply
A measure of the responsiveness of the quantity supplied to changes in price; equal to the percentage change in quantity supplied divided by the percentage change in price.

We've used the concept of elasticity to measure the responsiveness of consumers to changes in prices. We now look at elasticity on the supply side of the market. The **price elasticity of supply** measures the responsiveness of the quantity supplied to changes in price. We compute this elasticity by dividing the percentage change in quantity supplied by the percentage change in price:

$$E_s = \frac{\text{percentage change in quantity supplied}}{\text{percentage change in price}}$$

We can use some of the numbers in Figure 20.3 to compute the price elasticity of supply of milk. Consider Panel A, with a relatively steep supply curve. When the price of milk increases from \$1.00 to \$1.20, the quantity supplied increases from 100 million gallons (point *a*) to 102 million gallons (point *b*). The percentage change in quantity is the change (2) divided by the initial value (100), or 2 percent:

$$\text{percentage change in quantity supplied} = \frac{2}{100} = 2\%$$

The percentage change in price is the change (\$0.20) divided by the initial value (\$1.00), or 20 percent:

$$\text{percentage change in price} = \frac{\$0.20}{\$1.00} = 20\%$$

Dividing the percentage change in quantity supplied by the percentage change in price, the price elasticity of supply is 0.10:

$$E_s = \frac{\text{percentage change in quantity supplied}}{\text{percentage change in price}} = \frac{2\%}{20\%} = 0.10$$

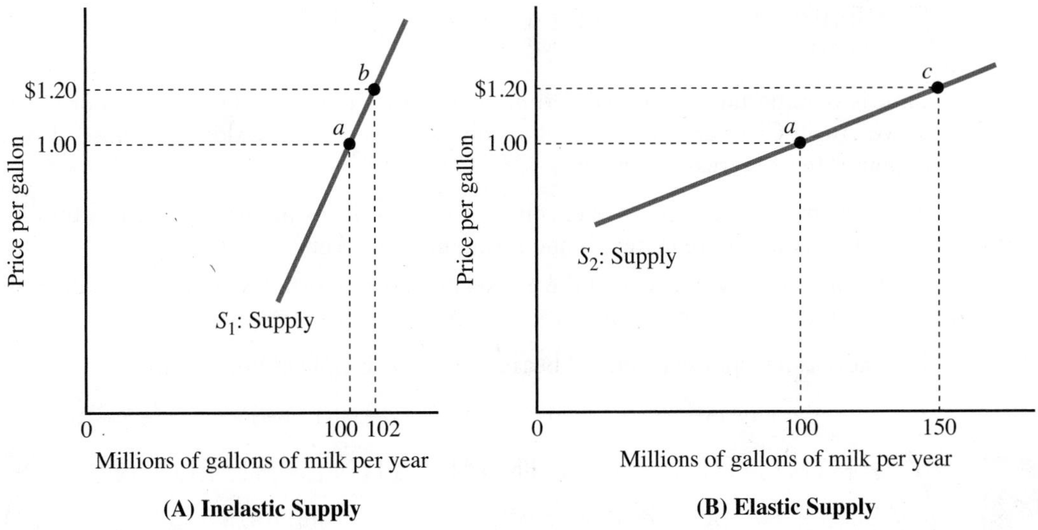

▲ FIGURE 20.3
The Slope of the Supply Curve and Supply Elasticity
(*A*) The supply curve is relatively steep. A 20 percent increase in price increases the quantity supplied by 2 percent, implying a supply elasticity of 0.10. (*B*) The supply curve is relatively flat. A 20 percent increase in price increases the quantity supplied by 50 percent, implying a supply elasticity of 2.5.

What Determines the Price Elasticity of Supply?

What's the connection between the slope of the supply curve and the price elasticity of supply? With a steep curve, a given increase in price (in the denominator of the elasticity formula) generates a small increase in quantity supplied (in the numerator of the elasticity formula). In Panel A of Figure 20.3, an increase in price from $1.00 to $1.20 increases the quantity supplied from 100 to 102, so the price elasticity of supply is 0.10 (equal to 2% divided by 10%). In contrast, with a relatively flat supply curve the same increase in price generates a larger increase in quantity supplied, so the supply elasticity is relatively large. In Panel B of Figure 20.3, an increase in price from $1.00 to $1.20 increases the quantity supplied from 100 to 150, so the price elasticity of supply is 2.50 (equal to 50% divided by 20%).

Why is the market supply curve positively sloped? As we saw in Chapter 4, the market supply curve shows the marginal cost of production. A positively sloped supply curve tells us that the marginal cost of production increases as the total output of the industry increases. In other words, if we want to get more output out of an industry, the price must rise to cover the higher production costs associated with a larger industry. For example, as the total output of the gasoline industry increases, the worldwide demand for crude oil increases, pushing up its price. So to get more gasoline, the price of gasoline must increase to cover the higher cost of crude oil. The more rapidly crude-oil prices rise, the larger the increase in the gasoline price required to get more gasoline—and the steeper the gasoline supply curve.

The price elasticity of supply is determined by how rapidly production costs increase as the total output of the industry increases. If the marginal cost increases rapidly, the supply curve is relatively steep and the price elasticity is relatively low. For example, if crude-oil prices increase rapidly as the total amount of gasoline increases, the supply curve for gasoline will be relatively steep and the price elasticity of supply of gasoline will be relatively low. In contrast, the output of the pencil industry increases the prices of wood and other inputs used to produce pencils are unlikely to increase by much, so the supply curve will be relatively flat and the price elasticity of supply will be relatively large.

The Role of Time: Short-Run versus Long-Run Supply Elasticity

Time is an important factor in determining the price elasticity of supply for a product. As we saw in Chapter 4, the market supply curve is positively sloped because of two responses to an increase in price:

- *Short run.* A higher price encourages existing firms to increase their output by purchasing more materials and hiring more workers.
- *Long run.* New firms enter the market and existing firms expand their production facilities to produce more output.

The short-run response is limited because of the principle of diminishing returns.

PRINCIPLE OF DIMINISHING RETURNS

Suppose output is produced with two or more inputs, and we increase one input while holding the other input or inputs fixed. Beyond some point—called the *point of diminishing returns*—output will increase at a decreasing rate.

In the short run, the fixed input is the firm's production facility. Although a higher price will induce firms to produce more, the response is limited by the fixed capacity of the firms' production facilities. As a result, the short-run supply curve is relatively steep and the short-run supply elasticity is relatively small. This case is illustrated by Panel A of Figure 20.4.

The long-run supply response to an increase in price is not limited by diminishing returns because production facilities are not fixed. Over time, new firms enter the market with new production facilities and old firms build new facilities. As a result, a given increase in price generates a larger increase in quantity supplied. The long-run supply curve will be relatively flat and the elasticity of supply will be relatively large. This case is illustrated by Panel B of Figure 20.4.

Extreme Cases: Perfectly Inelastic Supply and Perfectly Elastic Supply

Figure 20.4 shows the extreme cases of supply elasticity. The supply curve in Panel A is a vertical line, indicating that regardless of price, the quantity supplied is 50 units. This is the case of **perfectly inelastic supply**, with a price elasticity of supply equal to zero. The numerator in the elasticity expression (the percentage change in quantity supplied) is zero, regardless of the percentage change in the price of the good. Land is an example of a product that has a perfectly inelastic supply. In the words of American humorist and author Will Rogers, "The trouble with land is that they're not making it any more."

perfectly inelastic supply
The price elasticity of supply equals zero.

The supply curve in Panel B of Figure 20.4 is a horizontal line, indicating that the quantity supplied is infinitely responsive to any change in price. This is the case of **perfectly elastic supply**, with a price elasticity of supply equal to infinity. The numerator in the elasticity expression (the percentage change in quantity supplied)

perfectly elastic supply
The price elasticity of supply is equal to infinity.

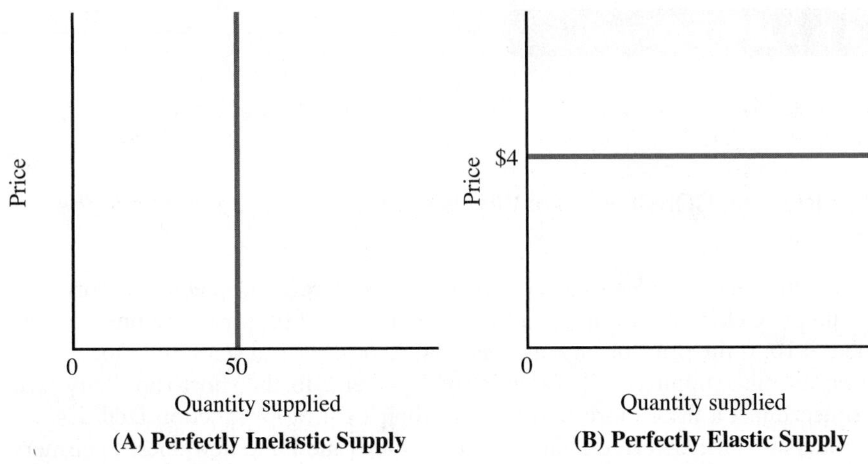

▲ FIGURE 20.4
Perfectly Inelastic Supply and Perfectly Elastic Supply
In Panel A, the quantity supplied is the same at every price, so the price elasticity of supply is zero. In Panel B, the quantity supplied is infinitely responsive to changes in price, so the price elasticity of supply is infinite.

is infinite, regardless of the percentage change in the price. One implication of this supply curve is that if the price were to drop below $4, the quantity supplied would fall to zero.

What is the economic logic behind a horizontal supply curve? Recall that the supply curve shows the marginal cost of production. A horizontal supply curve indicates that the marginal cost of production doesn't change as the total output of the industry increases. For example, if the production cost per pencil is $0.20 no matter how many pencils the industry produces, the supply curve will be horizontal at $0.20.

Predicting Changes in Quantity Supplied

We can use the price elasticity of supply to predict the effect of price changes on the quantity supplied. For example, suppose that the elasticity of supply is 0.80 and the price increases by 5 percent. Rearranging the elasticity formula, we would predict a 4 percent increase in the quantity supplied:

$$\begin{aligned}\text{percentage change in quantity supplied} &= E_s \times \text{percentage change in price}\\ &= 0.80 \times 5\% = 4\%\end{aligned}$$

As we saw in Chapter 4, many governments establish minimum prices for agricultural products. The higher the minimum price, the larger the quantity supplied, consistent with the law of supply. If we know the price elasticity of supply, we can predict just how much more will be supplied at a higher minimum price. For example, if the minimum price of cheese increases by 10 percent and the price elasticity is 0.60, the quantity of cheese supplied will rise by 6 percent:

$$\begin{aligned}\text{percentage change in quantity supplied} &= E_s \times \text{percentage change in price}\\ &= 0.60 \times 10\% = 6\%\end{aligned}$$

application 5

THE SHORT-RUN AND LONG-RUN ELASTICITY OF SUPPLY OF MILK

APPLYING THE CONCEPTS #5: Why is supply more price-elastic in the long run?

The milk industry provides a good example of the difference between the short-run and long-run price elasticity of supply. The price elasticity of supply over a one-year period is about 0.10: If the price of milk increases by 20 percent and stays there for a year, the quantity of milk supplied will rise by only 2 percent. In the short run, dairy farmers can squeeze just a little more output from their existing production facilities. In the long run, dairy farmers can expand existing facilities and build new ones, so farmers are more responsive to a higher price—the supply curve is flatter and the supply elasticity is larger. The price elasticity of supply is 2.5, so the same 20 percent rise in price increases the quantity supplied by 50 percent. **Related to Exercises 5.5 and 5.6.**

SOURCE: Based on Richard Klemme and Jean-Paul Chavas, "The Effects of Changing Milk Price on Milk Supply and National Dairy Herd Size," *Economic Issues* 92 (June 1985).

20.6 Using Elasticities to Predict Changes in Prices

When demand or supply changes—that is, when the demand curve or the supply curve shifts—we can draw a demand and supply graph to predict whether the equilibrium price will increase or decrease. In many cases, the simple graph will show all we need to know about the effects of a change in supply or demand. But what if we want to predict *how much* a price will increase or decrease? We can use a simple formula to predict the change in the equilibrium price resulting from a change in demand or a change in supply.

The Price Effects of a Change in Demand

In Figure 20.5, an increase in demand shifts the demand curve to the right and increases the equilibrium price. We explained in Chapter 4 that a demand curve shifts as a result of a change in something other than the price of the product—for example, a change in income, tastes, or the price of a related good. When demand increases, the immediate effect is excess demand: At the original price ($1.00), the quantity demanded exceeds the quantity supplied by 35 million gallons (135 million – 100 million). As the price increases, both consumers and producers help to eliminate the excess demand: Consumers buy less (the law of demand), and firms produce more (the law of supply).

Under what conditions will an increase in demand cause a relatively small increase in price?

- *Small increase in demand.* If the shift of the demand curve is relatively small, the gap between the new demand and the old supply will be relatively small, and the small excess demand can be eliminated with a relatively small increase in price.
- *Highly elastic demand.* If consumers are very responsive to changes in price, the increase in price caused by excess demand will cause a large reduction in the quantity demanded. As a result, the excess demand will be eliminated with a relatively small increase in price.

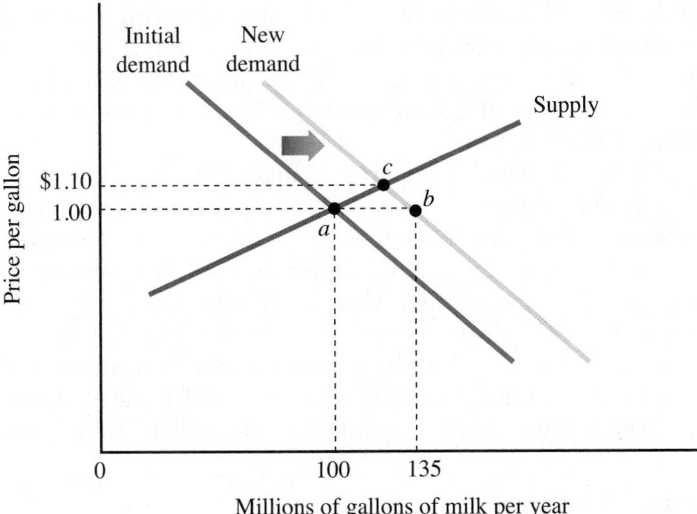

▲ **FIGURE 20.5**
An Increase in Demand Increases the Equilibrium Price
An increase in demand shifts the demand curve to the right, increasing the equilibrium price. In this case, a 35 percent increase in demand increases the equilibrium price by 10 percent. Using the price-change formula, 10% = 35% / (2.5 + 1.0).

- *Highly elastic supply.* If producers are very responsive to changes in price, the increase in price caused by excess demand will cause a large increase in the quantity supplied. As a result, the excess demand will be eliminated with a relatively small increase in price.

We can use the following *price-change formula* to predict the change in the equilibrium price resulting from a change in demand. We divide the percentage change in demand by the sum of the price elasticities of supply and demand:

$$\text{percentage change in equilibrium price} = \frac{\text{percentage change in demand}}{E_s + E_d}$$

The numerator is the rightward shift of the demand curve in percentage terms. In Figure 20.5, the initial quantity demanded at a price of $1.00 is 100 million gallons (shown by the initial demand curve), and the new quantity demanded at the same price is 135 million gallons (shown by the new demand curve). The change in demand is 35 percent (35/100). The change in demand is in the numerator of the price-change formula, indicating that the larger the increase in demand (the larger the rightward shift of the demand curve), the larger the increase in the equilibrium price. The two price elasticities appear in the denominator. This is sensible because if consumers and producers are very responsive to changes in price (the elasticities are large numbers), excess demand will be eliminated with a relatively small increase in price.

We can illustrate the price-change formula with a simple example. Suppose that demand increases by 35 percent (the demand curve shifts to the right by 35 percent). If the supply elasticity is 2.5 and the demand elasticity is 1.0, the predicted change in the equilibrium price is 10 percent:

$$\text{percentage change in equilibrium price} = \frac{35\%}{2.5 + 1.0} = \frac{35\%}{3.5} = 10\%$$

In Figure 20.5, the equilibrium price increases by 10 percent, from $1.00 to $1.10. If either demand or supply were less elastic (if either of the elasticity numbers were smaller), the predicted change in price would be larger. For example, if the supply elasticity were 0.75 instead of 2.5, we would predict a 20 percent increase in price (35% divided by 1.75).

What about the direction of the price change? We know from Chapter 4 that an increase in demand increases the equilibrium price, and a decrease in demand decreases the equilibrium price. Therefore, the percentage change in price is positive when the change in demand is positive (when demand increases and the demand curve shifts to the right), and negative when the change in demand is negative (when demand decreases and the demand curve shifts to the left). For example, suppose the demand for a product decreases by 12 percent (the demand curve shifts to the left by 12 percent). If the supply elasticity is 1.6 and the demand elasticity is 0.40, the price-change formula shows that the equilibrium price will decrease by 6 percent:

$$\text{percentage change in equilibrium price} = \frac{-12\%}{1.6 + 0.4} = \frac{-12\%}{2.0} = -6\%$$

To illustrate the practical use of the price-change formula, consider the effect of population growth on housing prices. The Portland metropolitan area is expected to grow by 12 percent in the next decade. Suppose planners want to predict the effects of population growth on the equilibrium price of housing. At the metropolitan level, the price elasticity of supply is about 5.0 and the price elasticity of demand is 1.0. If the demand for housing is proportional to population, a 12 percent increase in population will increase the equilibrium price of housing by 2 percent:

$$\text{percentage change in equilibrium price} = \frac{12\%}{5.0 + 1.0} = \frac{12\%}{6.0} = 2\%$$

The Price Effects of a Change in Supply

Consider next the effects of a change in supply on the equilibrium price. In Figure 20.6, a decrease in supply shifts the supply curve to the left and increases the equilibrium price. We explained in Chapter 4 that a change in supply results from changes in something other than the price of the product—for example, a change in the cost of labor or raw materials, a change in production technology, or a change in the number of firms. The immediate effect of a decrease in supply is excess demand: At the original price, the quantity demanded exceeds the quantity supplied. In response to the excess demand, the price increases. Consumers respond to the higher price by purchasing less, and producers respond by producing more, so the gap between the quantity demanded and the quantity supplied narrows.

Under what conditions will a decrease in supply cause a relatively small increase in price?

- *Small decrease in supply.* If the shift of the supply curve is relatively small, the gap between the new supply and the old demand will be relatively small, and the small excess demand can be eliminated with a relatively small increase in price.
- *Highly elastic demand.* If consumers are very responsive to changes in price, the increase in price caused by excess demand will cause a large reduction in the quantity demanded. As a result, the excess demand will be eliminated with a relatively small increase in price.

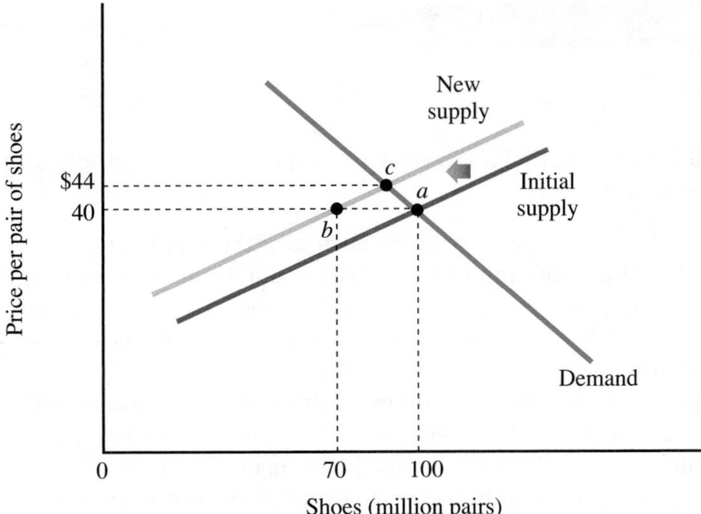

▲ FIGURE 20.6
A Decrease in Supply Increases the Equilibrium Price
An import restriction on shoes decreases the supply of shoes, shifting the market supply curve to the left and increasing the equilibrium price from $40 to $44. In this case, a 30 percent reduction in supply increases the equilibrium price by 10 percent. Using the price-change formula, 10% = –(–30% / (2.3 + 0.70)).

- *Highly elastic supply.* If producers are very responsive to changes in price, the increase in price caused by excess demand will cause a large increase in the quantity supplied. As a result, the excess demand will be eliminated with a relatively small increase in price.

We can use a variation on the price-change formula to predict the price effects of a change in supply. We modify the numerator of the formula by substituting the percentage change in supply for the percentage change in demand and then add a minus sign. The minus sign indicates a negative relationship between supply and the equilibrium price: When supply decreases (when the supply curve shifts to the left), the price increases; when supply increases, the price decreases:

$$\text{percentage change in equilibrium price} = -\frac{\text{percentage change in supply}}{E_s + E_d}$$

To illustrate the practical use of the price-change formula, consider the effects of import restrictions on equilibrium prices. Suppose that import restrictions decrease the supply of shoes by 30 percent. As shown in Figure 20.6, the policy shifts the supply curve to the left by 30 percent: At the original price of $40, the quantity supplied decreases from 100 million pairs (point *a*) to 70 million pairs (point *b*). The decrease in supply increases the equilibrium price, and the price-change formula tells us just how much the price will increase.

To use the price-change formula, we need the price elasticities of supply and demand. Suppose the supply elasticity is 2.3 and, as shown in Table 20.2, the demand elasticity is 0.70. Plugging these numbers into the price-change formula, we predict a 10 percent increase in price:

$$\text{percentage change in equilibrium price} = -\frac{-30\%}{2.3 + 0.70} = \frac{30\%}{3.0} = 10\%$$

In Figure 20.6, the price rises by 10 percent, from $40 to $44 per pair.

application 6

A BROKEN PIPELINE AND THE PRICE OF GASOLINE

APPLYING THE CONCEPTS #6: How does a decrease in supply affect the equilibrium price?

In the chapter opener, a pipeline break decreased the supply of gasoline to the city of Phoenix by 30 percent and increased the equilibrium price by only 40 percent. Given a short-run price elasticity of demand for gasoline of 0.20, a price increase of 150 percent would be required to decrease the quantity demanded by 30 percent. Why did the price increase by only 40 percent?

To predict a change in the equilibrium price, we must look at both sides of the market, demand and supply. When the Texas pipeline broke, gasoline sellers in Phoenix switched to the West Coast pipeline. The increase in the Phoenix retail price allowed Phoenix sellers to outbid sellers in other cities for gasoline produced by West Coast refineries. This is the law of supply in action: the increase in the Phoenix price diverted gasoline from other cities, reducing the impact of the pipeline break. As a result, the equilibrium price increased by only 40 percent, not the 150 percent that would have occurred in the absence of the supply boost from West Coast refineries.

We can use the price-change formula to illustrate this case. Suppose the price elasticity of supply is 0.55 and the price elasticity of demand is 0.20. In this case, a 30 percent decrease in supply generates a 40 percent increase in the equilibrium price:

$$\text{percentage change in equilibrium price} = -\frac{-30\%}{0.55 + 0.20} = \frac{30\%}{0.75} = 40\%$$

Related to Exercises 6.5 and 6.9.

SOURCE: Based on Federal Trade Commission, Gasoline Price Changes: The Dynamic of Supply, Demand, and Competition (Washington, DC: 2005).

SUMMARY

This chapter explored the numbers behind the laws of demand and supply. The law of demand tells us that an increase in price decreases the quantity demanded, *ceteris paribus*. If we know the price elasticity of demand for a particular product, we can determine just how much less of it will be purchased at the higher price. Similarly, if we know the price elasticity of supply for a product, we can determine just how much more of it will be supplied at a higher price. Here are the main points of the chapter:

1 The *price elasticity of demand*—defined as the percentage change in quantity demanded divided by the percentage change in price—measures the responsiveness of consumers to changes in price.

2 Demand is relatively elastic if there are good substitutes.

3 If demand is *elastic*, the relationship between price and total revenue is negative. If demand is *inelastic*, the relationship between price and total revenue is positive.

4 The *price elasticity of supply*—defined as the percentage change in quantity supplied divided by the percentage change in price—measures the responsiveness of producers to changes in price.

5 If we know the elasticities of demand and supply, we can predict the percentage change in price resulting from a change in demand or supply.

KEY TERMS

cross-price elasticity of demand, p. 423
elastic demand, p. 413
income elasticity of demand, p. 422
inelastic demand, p. 413
perfectly elastic demand, p. 413
perfectly elastic supply, p. 426
perfectly inelastic demand, p. 413
perfectly inelastic supply, p. 426
price elasticity of demand (E_d), p. 410
price elasticity of supply, p. 424
total revenue, p. 417
unit elastic demand, p. 413

EXERCISES

All problems are assignable in MyEconLab.

20.1 The Price Elasticity of Demand

1.1 To compute the price elasticity of demand, we divide the percentage change in ________ by the percentage change in ________ and then take the value of the ratio.

1.2 If a 10 percent increase in price decreases the quantity demanded by 12 percent, the price elasticity of demand is ________.

1.3 When the price of CDs increased from $10 to $11, the quantity of CDs demanded decreased from 100 to 80. The price elasticity of demand for CDs is ________, and demand is ________ (elastic/inelastic).

1.4 If demand is elastic, the percentage change in ________ exceeds the percentage change in ________.

1.5 As the number of substitutes for a particular product increases, the price elasticity of demand for the product ________ (increases/decreases).

1.6 Over time, the price elasticity of demand for gasoline ________ (increases/decreases). (Related to Application 1 on page 415.)

1.7 In the long run, a 20 percent increase in the price of gasoline will decrease traffic volume by ________ percent and increase fuel efficiency by ________ percent. (Related to Application 1 on page 415.)

1.8 Demand is relatively elastic if the product has ________ (many/few) substitutes, a ________ (long/short) time passes, and the consumer spends a ________ (large/small) fraction of his or her budget on the product.

20.2 Using Price Elasticity

2.1 Recall the example "Beer Prices and Highway Deaths" from the chapter. A doubling of the tax on beer will reduce the number of highway deaths among young adults by ________ percent.

2.2 Recall the example "Cigarette Prices and Teenagers" from the chapter. A 20 percent increase in the price of cigarettes will reduce the quantity of cigarettes demanded by teenagers by ________ percent.

2.3 If the price elasticity of demand is 0.60, a 10 percent increase in price will ________ the quantity demanded by ________ percent.

2.4 In the state of Virginia, the demand for vanity license plates is ________ (elastic/inelastic), so an increase in price would ________ (increase/decrease) total revenue from vanity plates. (Related to Application 2 on page 419.)

2.5 A policy that limits the supply of illegal drugs increases the number of burglaries and robberies because ________ is ________.

2.6 If demand is elastic, an increase in price (increases/decreases) total revenue; if demand is inelastic, an increase in price ________ (increases/decreases) total revenue.

2.7 Suppose that at the current price the price elasticity of demand for a campus film series is 2.0. If the price is cut, total revenue will ________ (increase/decrease).

2.8 **MADD Beer Tax.** Recall the example "Beer Prices and Highway Deaths" from the chapter. The organization Mothers Against Drunk Driving (MADD) has a goal of reducing the number of highway deaths among young adults by 39 percent. Assume that the number of highway deaths for young adults is proportional to their beer consumption. By what percentage must the price of beer increase to meet the MADD target?

2.9 **Meeting the Teenage Smoking Target.** Recall the example "Cigarette Prices and Teenagers" from the chapter. One of the stated objectives of the federal Tobacco Agreement of 1997 was to reduce teenage smoking by 60 percent. The price must increase by ________ percent to achieve this target.

2.10 **Use the Correct Elasticity.** Your company currently sells 50 units of salt per year and has decided to increase its price from $1.00 to $1.20. In a meeting, one person says, "As shown in Table 20.2 on page 414, the price elasticity of demand for salt is 0.10, so if we increase the price of salt by 20 percent, the quantity demanded will decrease by 2 percent." What's wrong with this statement?

2.11 Projecting Transit Ridership. As a transit planner, your job is to predict ridership and total fare revenue. Suppose the short-run elasticity of demand for commuter rail (over a one-month period) is 0.60, and the long-run elasticity (over a two-year period) is 1.60. The current ridership is 100,000 people per day. Suppose the transit authority decides to increase its fares from $2.00 to $2.20.

a. Predict the changes in train ridership over a one-month period (the short run) and a two-year period (the long run).

b. Over the one-month period, will total fare revenue increase or decrease? What about the two-year period?

2.12 Income and the Price Elasticity of Demand for Medical Care. Like many other developing nations, Peru subsidizes medical care, charging consumers a small fraction of the cost of providing services such as visits to medical clinics. The price elasticity of demand for medical care is 0.67 for poor households but only 0.03 for wealthy households. Suppose the government reduced its subsidies for medical care, and the price to consumers increased by 10 percent. Predict the changes in the quantity of medical care demanded (for example, the number of visits to clinics) for poor households and wealthy households.

2.13 Revenue Effects of a Bumper Crop. Your job is to predict the total revenue generated by the nation's corn crop. Last year's crop was 100 million bushels, and the price was $5 per bushel. This year's weather was favorable throughout the country, and this year's crop will be 110 million bushels, or 10 percent larger than last year's. The price elasticity of demand for corn is 0.50.

a. Predict the effect of the bumper crop on the price of corn. Assume that the entire crop is sold this year, meaning that the price elasticity of supply is zero. Illustrate with a complete graph.

b. Predict the total revenue from this year's corn crop.

c. Did the favorable weather increase or decrease the total revenue from corn? Why?

2.14 Elasticity and Vanity Plates. Suppose the price elasticity of demand for vanity plates in your state is 0.60. The initial price is $20 and the initial quantity is 1,000 plates per week. Suppose the state increases the price by 10 percent. (Related to Application 2 on page 419.)

a. Predict the new quantity per week and total revenue per week.

b. The increase in price __________ (increases, decreases) total revenue because __________ is __________.

2.15 The Price of Heroin and Property Crime. The price elasticity of demand for heroin is 0.27. Suppose that half of heroin users support their habits with property crime, so the loss from property crimes committed by heroin users equals half the total spending (total revenue) on the drug. Suppose the government reduces the supply of heroin, increasing the equilibrium price by 20 percent. Fill in the blanks in the following table.

Price	Quantity of Heroin	Total Spending (Total Revenue)	Property Crime
$10	1,000	$10,000	$5,000
12	------------	--------------	-------------

2.16 Revenue from Mobile Phones. Consider the demand for mobile phones. Suppose the price elasticity of demand for the market as a whole is 0.80.

a. If all mobile-phone companies simultaneously increased their prices, will total revenue in the industry increase or decrease?

b. If a single mobile-phone company increased its price, would you expect the company's total revenue to increase or decrease? Explain.

2.17 Price Hikes and Cable TV Revenue. Four years ago the cable company in your city increased its price by 20 percent, and its total revenue increased. Last year, a new company started providing TV service with satellite dishes. This year, the cable company increased its price by 20 percent, but its total revenue decreased. Provide an explanation for the different revenue consequences of the cable company's price hikes.

20.3 Elasticity and Total Revenue for a Linear Demand Curve

3.1 Demand is ________ on the upper portion of a linear demand curve and ________ on the lower portion of a linear demand curve.

3.2 Suppose we are on the upper portion of a linear demand curve. If the price increases by 10 percent, the quantity demanded will decrease by ________ (more/less) than 10 percent and total revenue will ________ (increase/decrease).

3.3 At the midpoint of a linear demand curve, the price elasticity of demand is ________.

3.4 If we are on the lower part of a linear demand curve, a decrease in price ________ (increases/decreases) total revenue.

3.5 A firm will never operate ________ (above, below) the midpoint of a linear demand curve, where demand is ______ (elastic, inelastic). (Related to Application 3 on page 422.)

3.6 **Maximizing Revenue from Wilderness Passes.** Your state issues wilderness passes to people who hike, bike, and ski in wilderness areas. Its objective is to maximize the total revenue from the passes. The current price is $30. The demand for wilderness passes is linear, and a price of $90 would drive the quantity demanded to zero. What is the appropriate price? Illustrate with a complete graph.

3.7 **Where on the Demand Curve?** The demand curve for your firm's product is linear. Based on recent sales data, you have determined that at the current price, the price elasticity of demand is 0.80.

a. Is the current price on the upper or lower portion of the demand curve?

b. If you want to increase your total revenue, should you increase or decrease your price?

c. Will you move upward or downward along the demand curve?

3.8 **Win-Win.** According to an economic consultant, "For your firm, an increase in price is a win-win situation. Your total revenue will increase and your total cost will decrease. Therefore, you'll earn more profit (equal to Total Revenue – Total Cost)."

a. Concerning the revenue effect of a price hike, what is the consultant assuming about your firm and its customers?

b. Concerning the cost effect of a price hike, what is the consultant assuming about your firm and its customers?

3.9 **Advice to Firm.** Suppose a firm that produces clown wigs has a linear demand for its product, with a vertical intercept of $6. If the firm currently charges a price of $1, what's your advice? (Related to Application 3 on page 422.)

20.4 Other Elasticities of Demand

4.1 The income elasticity of demand is ________ (positive/negative) for normal goods and ________ (positive/negative) for inferior goods.

4.2 If a 20 percent increase in income increases the quantity of iPods demanded by 30 percent, the income elasticity of demand is ________.

4.3 The cross-price elasticity of demand is ________ (positive/negative) for substitute goods and ________ (positive/negative) for complementary goods.

4.4 If a 10 percent increase in the price of natural gas increases the quantity of residential electricity demanded by 18 percent, the cross-price elasticity of demand is ________.

4.5 If a 10 percent increase in the price of tennis rackets decreases the quantity of tennis balls demanded by 15 percent, the cross-price elasticity of demand is ________.

4.6 **Income and Starbucks Coffee Shops.** Starbucks just hired you to determine whether your city could support a new Starbucks coffee shop. There are currently four Starbucks coffee shops in the city, and each has just enough customers to survive. The average household income in the city is expected to increase by 10 percent per year for the next few years. Suppose the income elasticity of demand for Starbucks' coffee products is 1.25. The population of the city is constant.

a. By what percentage will the demand for coffee increase each year?

b. How soon will the area have enough demand to support a fifth Starbucks?

4.7 **Gas Prices and Public Transit Ridership.** Consider the effect of higher gasoline prices on public transit ridership. The initial price of public transit is $2.00 per ride and the initial ridership is 100,000 people per day. Suppose the elasticity of transit ridership with respect to the price of gasoline is +0.667 (or 2/3) and the price of gasoline increases by 30 percent.

a. Assume the price of public transit remains at $2. Use a graph to show the effect of the increase in the gas price on transit ridership.

b. Suppose the transit authority matches the increase in the price of gasoline, increasing the transit fare by 30 percent. The price elasticity of demand for transit ridership is 0.333 (or 1/3). Use your graph to show the combined effect of the gas tax and higher transit fare.

c. Explain why the net change in transit ridership is positive or negative.

4.8 iPods and iTunes. You have been hired to predict the effects of increasing the price of iTunes songs by 10 percent, from \$0.99 to \$1.09. You are interested in the effects of the price hike on the number of songs downloaded legally from iTunes, the number of songs downloaded legally from other online music stores, the number of iPod players sold, and the number of CDs sold in stores. Given the hypothetical elasticities in the following table, fill in the blanks. Recall that conventional practice for the price elasticity of demand of a product uses the absolute value of the elasticity.

Product	Price Elasticity or Cross-Price Elasticity	Predicted Percentage Change in Quantity Demanded
iTunes songs	1.50 (absolute value)	
Songs from other online stores	+2.00	
iPod players	−0.70	
CDs in stores	+1.80	

4.9 Find the following elasticities from the USDA Web site. (Related to Application 4 on page 424.)

a. Organic broccoli in the United States: own price elasticity = __________; expenditure (similar to income) = __________; cross-price of conventional broccoli = __________. If improved production techniques decreased the equilibrium price of organic broccoli by 10 percent, the quantity of organic broccoli would increase by __________ percent and the quantity of conventional broccoli would decrease by __________ percent.

b. Soft drinks in the United States: own price (Marshallian is regular demand) = __________. If a tax on soft drinks increased the equilibrium price by 10 percent, the quantity of soft drinks would decrease by __________ percent.

c. Fish in Tanzania. Own price = __________; income = __________. If the price of fish increases by 8.37 percent, the quantity demanded would decrease by __________ percent. If per-capita income increases by 20 percent, the quantity of fish demanded would increase by about __________ percent.

20.5 The Price Elasticity of Supply

5.1 When the price of paper increases from \$100 to \$104 per ton, the quantity supplied increases from 200 to 220 tons per day. The price elasticity of supply is __________.

5.2 Suppose the price elasticity of a supply of cheese is 0.80. If the price of cheese rises by 20 percent, the quantity of cheese supplied will increase by __________ percent.

5.3 Because the principle of diminishing returns is applicable only in the __________ (short/long) run, the __________ elasticity of supply is __________ (smaller/larger) than the __________ elasticity of supply.

5.4 As the supply curve becomes flatter, the price elasticity of supply __________ (increases/decreases).

5.5 The price elasticity of supply of milk is __________ (0.10, 0.70, 1.0, 2.5) over a one-year period, compared to __________ (0.10, 0.70, 1.0, 2.5) over a 10-year period. (Related to Application 5 on page 428.)

5.6 Short Run vs. Long Run in the Pear Market. Suppose in the production of pears, the short-run supply elasticity is 0.20, while the long-run supply elasticity is 3.5. Predict the effects of a 15% increase in price on the quantity of pears supplied in the short run and the long run. (Related to Application 5 on page 428.)

20.6 Using Elasticities to Predict Changes in Equilibrium Price

6.1 Assume that the elasticity of demand for chewing tobacco is 0.70 and the elasticity of supply is 2.30. Suppose an antichewing campaign decreases the demand for chewing tobacco by 18 percent. The equilibrium price of chewing tobacco will __________ (decrease/increase) by __________ percent.

6.2 Suppose the elasticity of demand for motel rooms is 1.0 and the elasticity of supply is 0.50. If the demand for motel rooms increases by 15 percent, the equilibrium price of motel rooms will __________ (decrease/increase) by __________ percent.

6.3 Suppose the price elasticity of demand for tomatoes is 0.70 and the supply elasticity is 3.30. If publicity about an outbreak of salmonella decreases demand by 12 percent, the equilibrium price will __________ (decrease/increase) by __________ percent.

6.4 Suppose the price elasticity of demand for accordions is 2.0 and the supply elasticity is 3.0. If a subsidy on accordions increases supply by 20 percent, the equilibrium price will __________ (decrease/increase) by __________ percent.

6.5 In the case of the broken gasoline pipeline, the decrease in supply and the resulting increase in price caused a decrease in __________ and an increase in __________. (Related to Application 6 on page 432.)

6.6 **College Enrollment and Apartment Prices.** Consider a college town where the initial price of rental apartments is $400 and the initial quantity is 1,000 apartments. The price elasticity of demand for apartments is 1.0, and the price elasticity of supply of apartments is 0.50. (Related to Application 4 on page 424.)

a. Use demand and supply curves to show the initial equilibrium, and label the equilibrium point *a*.

b. Suppose that an increase in college enrollment is expected to increase the demand for apartments in a college town by 15 percent. Use your graph to show the effects of the increase in demand on the apartment market. Label the new equilibrium point *b*.

c. Predict the effect of the increase in demand on the equilibrium price of apartments.

6.7 **Regulations and the Price of Housing.** Suppose local building regulations increase the cost of building new houses, decreasing supply by 12 percent. The initial price of new housing is $200,000, the price elasticity of demand is 1.0, and the price elasticity of supply is 3.0. Predict the effect of the regulations on the equilibrium price of new housing. Illustrate your answer with a graph that shows the initial point (*a*) and the new equilibrium (*b*). (Related to Application 4 on page 424.)

6.8 **Import Restrictions and the Price of Steel.** Suppose import restrictions on steel decrease the supply of steel by 24 percent. The initial price of steel is $100 per unit, the elasticity of demand is 0.70, and the elasticity of supply is 2.3. Predict the effect of the import restrictions on the equilibrium price of steel. Illustrate your answer with a graph that shows the initial point (*a*) and the new equilibrium (*b*).

6.9 **Price Effects of a Pipeline Break.** Consider a city that gets its natural gas from two pipelines, with each pipeline supplying half the city's natural gas. Suppose the price elasticity of supply is 0.70 and the price elasticity of demand is 0.55. If one pipeline breaks, by how much will the price of natural gas increase? (Related to Application 6 on page 432.)

NOTES

1. Frank Chaloupka, "Rational Addictive Behavior and Cigarette Smoking," *Journal of Political Economy* (August 1991): 722–742; Gregory Chow, *Demand for Automobiles in the United States* (Amsterdam: North-Holland, 1957); David Ellwood and Mitchell Polinski, "An Empirical Reconciliation of Micro and Grouped Estimates of the Demand for Housing," *Review of Economics and Statistics* 61 (1979): 199–205; H. F. Houthakker and Lester B. Taylor, *Consumer Demand in the United States: Analysis and Projections*, 2nd ed. (Cambridge, MA: Harvard University Press, 1970); John R. Nevin, "Laboratory Experiments for Estimating Consumer Demand: A Validation Study," *Journal of Marketing Research* 11 (August 1974): 261–268; Herbert Scarf and John Shoven, *Applied General Equilibrium Analysis* (New York: Cambridge University Press, 1984); Phil Goodwin, "Review of New Demand Elasticities with Special Reference to Short and Long Run Effects of Price Changes," *Journal of Transport Economics* 26 (1992): 155–171; Chin-Fun Cling and James Peale, Jr., "Income and Price Elasticities," in *Advances in Econometrics Supplement*, ed. Henri Theil (Greenwich, CT: JAI Press, 1989); R. L. Adams, R. C. Lewis, and B. H. Drake, "Estimated Price Elasticity of Demand for Selected Outdoor Recreation Activities, United States," *Recreation Economic Decisions*, 2nd ed., ed. J. B. Loomis and R. G. Walsh (State College, PA: Venture Publishing, Inc., 1973), 20; U.S. Army Corps of Engineers, Walla Walla District, "Sport Fishery Use and Value on the Lower Snake River Reservoirs," May 1999; Rand Health, "The Elasticity of Demand for Health Care: A Review of the Literature and Its Application to the Military Health System" (Santa Monica, CA, 2001).
2. Henry Saffer and Michael Grossman, "Beer Taxes, the Legal Drinking Age, and Youth Motor Vehicle Fatalities," *Journal of Legal Studies* 16 (June 1987): 351–374; Frank Chaloupka, Henry Saffer, and Michael Grossman, "Alcohol Control Policies and Motor Vehicle Fatalities," *Journal of Legal Studies* 22 (January 1993): 161–183.
3. Michael M. Phillips and Suein L. Hwang, "Why Tobacco Pact Won't Hurt Industry," *Wall Street Journal*, September 12, 1997; Frank J. Chaloupka and Michael Grossman, "Price, Tobacco Control Policies, and Smoking Among Young Adults," *Journal of Health Economics* 16 (1997): 359–373.
4. Kenneth A. Small, *Urban Transportation Economics* (Philadelphia, PA: Harwood Academic Publishers, 1992).
5. L. P. Silverman and N. L. Sprull, "Urban Crime and the Price of Heroin," *Journal of Urban Economics* 4 (1977): 80–103.

Market Efficiency and Government Intervention

CHAPTER 21

The housing market in New York City is highly regulated.

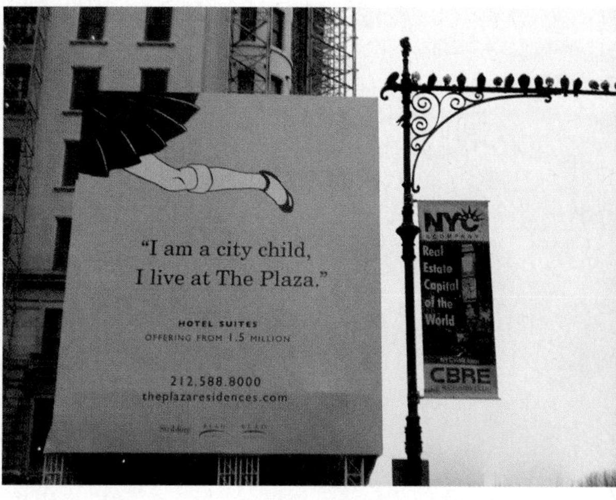

The city issues a relatively small number of permits for new condominium buildings, and rapid growth in the demand for condominiums has resulted in soaring condominium prices. To measure the effects of the city's supply restrictions on housing prices, we can compare the construction cost of a standard condominium to its market price. This is a sensible approach because in a competitive industry like housing, the equilibrium price in an unregulated market would equal the cost of construction. The construction cost for a Manhattan condominium is about \$300 per square foot, while the market price is roughly \$600 per square foot.[1] In other words, the city's supply restrictions double the price of the typical Manhattan condominium.

Other cities restrict the supply of housing and increase prices to varying degrees. The price effects are relatively large in highly restrictive cities such as San Francisco (53% gap between the market price and construction cost), Los Angeles (34%), Washington, DC (22%), and Boston (19%), and relatively small in less restrictive cities such as Chicago (6%) and Baltimore (2%). Many cities do not restrict the supply of housing, and housing prices in these cities (Houston, Minneapolis, Rochester, Tampa, Cincinnati, and Pittsburgh) match the construction cost of housing.

LEARNING OBJECTIVES

- Use demand and supply curves to compute the value of markets.
- Explain why the market equilibrium maximizes the value of a market.
- Describe the market effects of price controls.
- Describe the market effects of quantity controls.
- Explain how a tax is shifted to consumers and input suppliers.

MyEconLab

MyEconLab helps you master each objective and study more efficiently.

efficiency
A situation in which people do the best they can, given their limited resources.

When making choices, people strive for **efficiency**, trying to do the best they can, given their limited resources. The notion of efficiency applies to all sorts of decisions. A household decides how much to spend on consumer goods, how much to save, and how much to spend on a college education. The household tries to do the best it can, given its limited income. A Frisbee producer decides how many workers to hire and tries to make as much profit as possible, given the limitations of its factory. A government chooses between shuttle trips and Mars missions and tries to generate as much scientific information as possible, given its space exploration budget. As we'll see, economics provides a framework to guide us from inefficient choices to efficient ones.

In Chapter 3 we discussed the exchange principle, which conveys the simple idea that transactions make both the buyer and the seller better off.

PRINCIPLE OF VOLUNTARY EXCHANGE

A voluntary exchange between two people makes both people better off.

In this chapter, we will take a closer look at the benefits of exchange, examining the experiences of both buyers and sellers. We will see how to compute the surplus or net benefit from a market and see why the market equilibrium—where the quantity demanded equals the quantity supplied—*may* generate the largest possible surplus. We'll explore the logic behind Adam Smith's metaphor of the invisible hand—the idea that individual buyers and sellers, each acting in his or her own self-interest, *may* promote the social interest.

You'll notice that we use the word "may" in noting the virtues of markets and the invisible hand. A market equilibrium will generate the largest possible surplus when four conditions are met:

- *No external benefits:* The benefits of a product (a good or service) are confined to the person who pays for it.
- *No external costs:* The cost of producing a product is confined to the person who sells it.
- *Perfect information:* Buyers and sellers know enough about the product to make informed decisions about whether to buy or sell it.
- *Perfect competition:* Each firm produces such a small quantity that the firm cannot affect the price.

In this chapter, we discuss markets that meet these four conditions. As we'll see later in the book, when these conditions are not satisfied, free markets don't generate the largest possible surplus. A market that generates the largest possible surplus is efficient. A situation is *efficient* if we are doing the best we can, given our limited resources. In the case of a market, doing the best we can means getting the largest possible surplus. When that happens, we say that the market is efficient. Governments around the world intervene in markets, sometimes promoting efficiency, and other times preventing it. We'll see that when the four efficiency conditions are met, government intervention is inefficient in the sense that it decreases the total surplus of the market.

21.1 Consumer Surplus and Producer Surplus

We'll begin our discussion of market efficiency by showing how to measure the benefits experienced by consumers and producers. We'll start with consumers and then look at producers.

The Demand Curve and Consumer Surplus

If you said "thank you" the last time you purchased a book, did you mean it? If you were willing to pay more for the book than the price you actually paid, you probably really *did* mean it when you said "thank you," because you got what you considered to be a good deal. Your **willingness to pay** for a product (a good or a service) is the maximum amount you are willing to pay for the product. Your **consumer surplus** is equal to your willingness to pay minus the price you actually pay. For example, if you are willing to pay $21 for a book that you buy for $10, your consumer surplus is $11.

willingness to pay
The maximum amount a consumer is willing to pay for a product.

consumer surplus
The amount a consumer is willing to pay for a product minus the price the consumer actually pays.

The market demand curve shows consumers' willingness to pay for a product. Consider the demand for lawn cutting in a small town; the market demand curve is shown in Figure 21.1. The demand curve shows that at a price of $25, no one will pay to have the lawn cut (point *t*), but if the price drops to $22, the first consumer (Juan) will pay for a lawn cut. This suggests that Juan is willing to pay up to $22 to have his lawn cut, but no more. Moving down the demand curve, the second consumer (Tupak) will pay for a lawn cutting when the price drops to $19, meaning that his willingness to pay is $19. As we continue to move downward along the demand curve, the price drops below the willingness to pay for more and more consumers, so more people have their lawns cut.

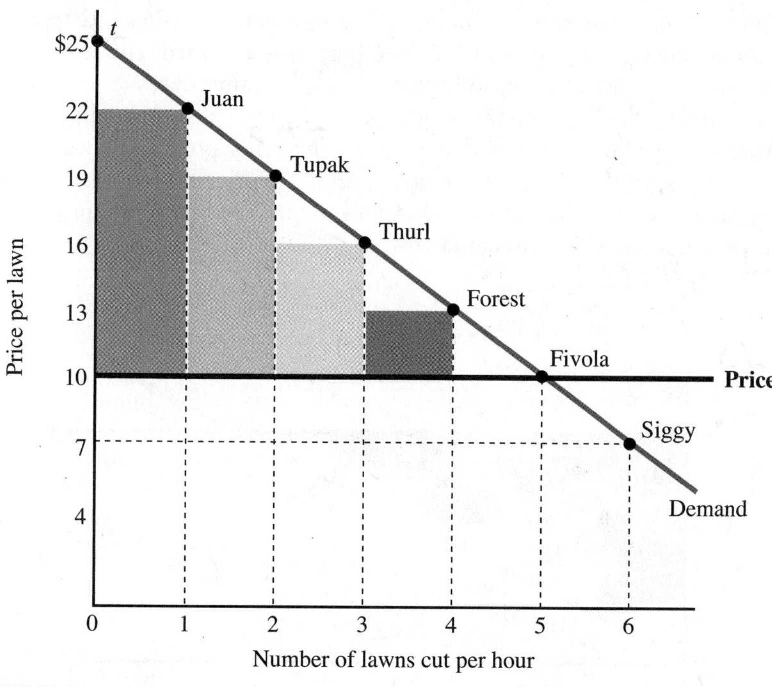

▲ FIGURE 21.1
The Demand Curve and Consumer Surplus
Consumer surplus equals the maximum amount a consumer is willing to pay (shown by the demand curve) minus the price paid. Juan is willing to pay $22, so if the price is $10, his consumer surplus is $12. The market consumer surplus equals the sum of the surpluses earned by all consumers in the market. In this case, the market consumer surplus is $30 = $12 + $9 + $6 + $3 + $0.

We can use the demand curve to measure just how much of a net benefit or surplus consumers get. Suppose that the price of a lawn cut is $10, and everyone in town pays this price. Juan's consumer surplus is $12, equal to his willingness to pay ($22) minus the price. Similarly, Tupak's consumer surplus is $9, equal to the difference between his willingness to pay ($19) and the market price. To compute the total consumer surplus in the lawn-cutting market, we simply add up the surpluses for each of the five consumers who buy lawn cutting at a price of $10. In this example, the market consumer surplus is $30, which is the sum of $12 (Juan) + $9 (Tupak) + $6 (Thurl) + $3 (Forest) + $0 (Fivola).

The fifth consumer (Fivola) gets no consumer surplus, because the price equals her willingness to pay. The sixth person (Siggy) doesn't have his lawn cut because the amount he is willing to pay is less than the price.

The Supply Curve and Producer Surplus

willingness to accept
The minimum amount a producer is willing to accept as payment for a product; equal to the marginal cost of production.

producer surplus
The price a producer receives for a product minus the marginal cost of production.

Like consumers, the people who produce goods and services say "thank you" when they sell their products. This suggests that they receive a net benefit or surplus from voluntary transactions. A seller's **willingness to accept** is the minimum amount he or she is willing to accept as payment for a product, and is equal to the marginal cost of production. For example, if your marginal cost of cutting a lawn is \$4, you will be willing to accept any amount greater than or equal to \$4. Of course, you'd prefer \$10 to \$4, but you'll accept as little as \$4, because the lower amount covers all your costs, including the opportunity cost of your time. **Producer surplus** equals the price a producer receives for a product minus the marginal cost of production. For example, if your marginal cost for cutting a lawn is \$4 and you do it for \$10, your producer surplus is \$6.

Figure 21.2 shows the market supply curve for lawn cutting in our small town. Let's imagine that up to six people are willing to cut lawns if the price is right, and each person can cut one lawn per hour. Each person incurs the same cost for renting a lawn mower but has a different opportunity cost for his or her time. The first producer (Abe) incurs a cost of \$2, so he is willing to accept as little as \$2 to cut a lawn. On the supply curve, if the price is \$2, one person—Abe—will cut lawns. Bea has a higher opportunity cost of time, so her cost is \$4, meaning that she won't cut a lawn unless she is paid at least \$4. So if the price is \$4, two people—Abe and Bea—will cut lawns. Moving upward along the supply curve, the other potential lawn cutters have even higher costs, so they don't start cutting until the price reaches their higher willingness to accept: \$6 for Cecil, \$8 for Dee, and so on. The higher the price, the larger the number of people willing to cut lawns.

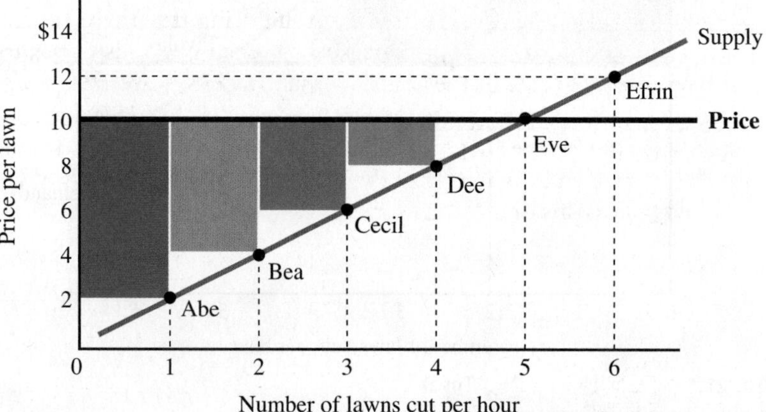

▲ FIGURE 21.2
The Supply Curve and Producer Surplus
Producer surplus equals the market price minus the producer's willingness to accept, or marginal cost (shown by the supply curve). Abe's marginal cost is \$2, so if the price is \$10, his producer surplus is \$8. The market producer surplus equals the sum of the surpluses earned by all producers in the market. In this case, the market producer surplus is \$20 = \$8 + \$6 + \$4 + \$2 + \$0.

We can use the supply curve to measure just how much of a net benefit or surplus producers get. If the price of lawn cutting is \$10, Abe's producer surplus for cutting the lawn is \$8, the price he receives minus his cost (\$2). Similarly, Bea's producer surplus is \$6, equal to the difference between the price and her cost (\$4). To compute the total producer surplus in the lawn-cutting market, we simply add up the surpluses for each of the five producers who cut lawns at a price of \$10. In this example, the market

application 1

CONSUMER SURPLUS OF INTERNET SERVICE

APPLYING THE CONCEPTS #1: How do we compute consumer surplus?

What is the consumer surplus from Internet service? Two recent studies compute consumers' willingness to pay for Internet service. For Japanese consumers, the average willingness to pay for Internet service (email and web browsing delivered over personal computers) is ¥5,623 per month, compared to an average price of broadband Internet service of ¥4,000. In other words, the average consumer surplus is ¥1,623, or about 40 percent of the price. For US consumers, the average willingness to pay for Internet service is $85 per month, and with an average monthly price of $40, the consumer surplus is $45 per month. **Related to Exercises 1.8 and 1.9.**

SOURCE: Based on (1) Gregory Rosston, Scott Savage, Donal Waldman, "Household Demand for Broadband Internet Service," Final Report to the Broadband.gov Task Force of the Federal Communications Commission, February 2010; (2) Masanori Kondo, Akihiro Nakamura, Hitoshi Mitomo, "Quantifying the Benefits of the Internet and Its Applications," *Keio Communication Review* 31 (2009), pp. 37–50.

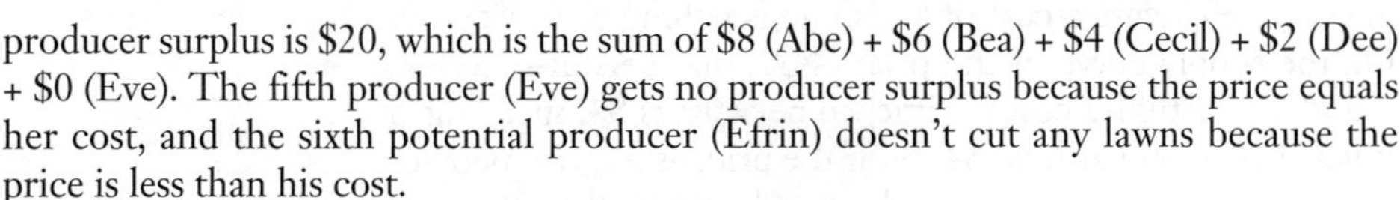

producer surplus is $20, which is the sum of $8 (Abe) + $6 (Bea) + $4 (Cecil) + $2 (Dee) + $0 (Eve). The fifth producer (Eve) gets no producer surplus because the price equals her cost, and the sixth potential producer (Efrin) doesn't cut any lawns because the price is less than his cost.

21.2 Market Equilibrium and Efficiency

Figure 21.3 puts the demand and supply curves together to show the equilibrium in the market for lawn cutting. The demand curve intersects the supply curve at a price of $10 per lawn. At this price, five lawns are cut, meaning that there are five buyers and five sellers. The **total surplus** of a market is the sum of consumer surplus and producer surplus. In Figure 21.3, the consumer surplus is $30 and the producer surplus is $20, so the total surplus of the market—shown by the shaded areas—is $50. As we'll see in this part of the chapter, the market equilibrium generates the highest possible total surplus. That's why we say that the market equilibrium is efficient: We can't do any better in terms of the total surplus.

total surplus
The sum of consumer surplus and producer surplus.

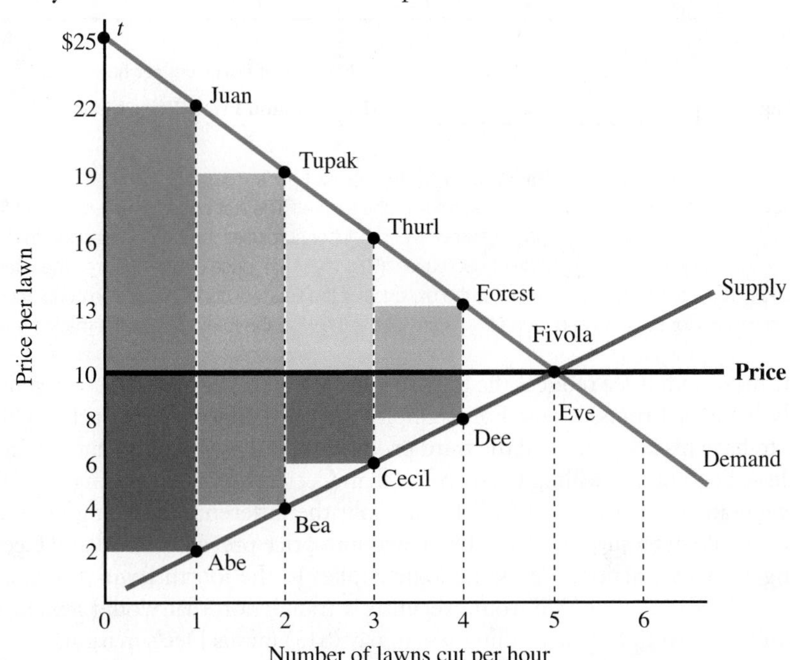

◄ **FIGURE 21.3**
Market Equilibrium and the Total Market Surplus
The total surplus of the market equals consumer surplus (the lightly shaded areas) plus producer surplus (the darkly shaded areas). The market equilibrium generates the highest possible total market value, equal to $50 = $30 (consumer surplus) + $20 (producer surplus).

Total Surplus Is Lower with a Price below the Equilibrium Price

price ceiling
A maximum price set by the government.

To see why the market equilibrium maximizes the total surplus of the market, let's look at the total surplus of the market when the price is less than the equilibrium price. The government could set a maximum price, also known as a **price ceiling**.

Suppose the government imposes a maximum price of $4 on lawn cutting. As shown in Panel A of Figure 21.4, at this price only two people cut lawns—Abe and Bea. Abe's producer surplus is shown by the darkly shaded area between the price line and the supply curve. For Bea, the price equals her willingness to accept, so she participates in the market but gets no producer surplus, receiving a price just high enough to keep her in the market. Consumers can buy only as much as producers are willing to sell, so the market consumer surplus equals the surpluses of just the first two consumers—Juan and Tupak. This is shown as the lightly shaded areas between the price line and the demand curve. By comparing Panel A in Figure 21.4 to Figure 21.3, we see that the maximum price reduces the total surplus of the market. For the first two lawns, consumers simply gain at the expense of producers. The maximum price also eliminates the surpluses from the third and fourth lawns because these transactions don't happen. Therefore, the total surplus decreases.

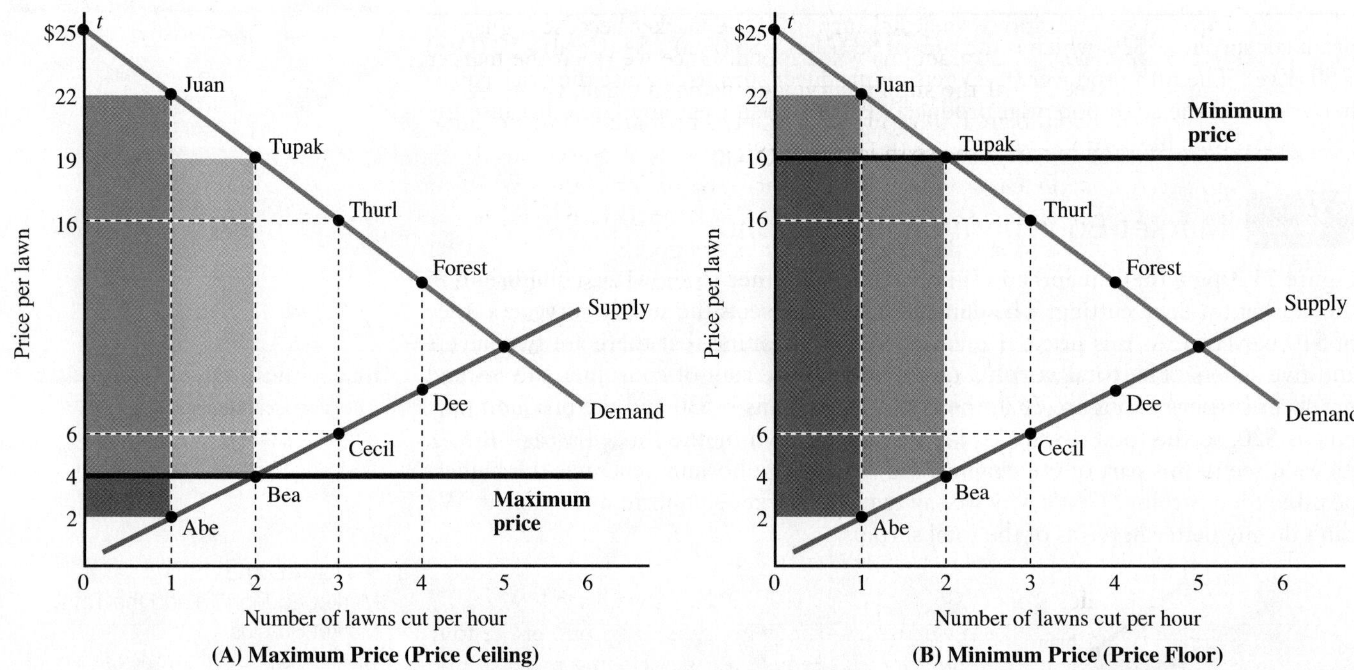

▲ FIGURE 21.4
Price Controls Decrease the Total Surplus of the Market
(A) A maximum price of $4 reduces the total surplus of the market. The first two consumers gain at the expense of the first two producers. The consumer and producer surpluses for the third and fourth lawns are lost entirely, so the total value of the market decreases. (B) A minimum price of $19 reduces the total surplus of the market. The first two producers gain at the expense of the first two consumers. The consumer and producer surpluses for the third and fourth lawns are lost entirely, so the total value of the market decreases.

The maximum price reduces the total surplus of the market because it prevents some mutually beneficial transactions. For example, the third consumer, Thurl, is willing to pay $16 to have his lawn cut, and the third producer, Cecil, is willing to cut a lawn if he is paid at least $6. Thurl is willing to pay more than Cecil requires, so cutting Thurl's lawn would generate a net benefit of $10. If they split the difference, agreeing on a price of $11, each would get a surplus of $5. The maximum price prevents Thurl and Cecil from executing their transaction. The same logic applies to the fourth lawn: The maximum price prevents Forest and Dee from executing a transaction that would generate a net benefit of $5, equal to Forest's willingness to pay ($13) minus Dee's marginal cost ($8).

Total Surplus Is Lower with a Price above the Equilibrium Price

To reinforce the notion that the market equilibrium maximizes the total surplus of the market, let's look at the total surplus of the market when the price exceeds the equilibrium price. The government could set a minimum price, also known as a **price floor**. Suppose the government sets a minimum price for lawn cutting at $19. As shown in Panel B of Figure 21.4, the demand curve indicates that at a price of $19, only two consumers, Juan and Tupak, will have their lawns cut. The total surplus of the market is the sum of consumer and producer surplus for these first two lawns, the same as it was under the maximum price. Again, this is lower than the total surplus that the consumer and producer could have gained, as shown by Figure 21.3.

price floor
A minimum price set by the government.

What's the difference between the two pricing policies? Under a maximum price, the first two consumers gain at the expense of the first two producers, whereas under the minimum price, the first two producers gain at the expense of the first two consumers. Like the maximum price, the minimum price prevents mutually beneficial transactions for the third, fourth, and fifth lawns.

Efficiency and the Invisible Hand

The market equilibrium maximizes the total surplus of the market because it guarantees that all mutually beneficial transactions will happen. Once we reach the market equilibrium at the intersection of the supply curve and demand curve, there are no more transactions that would benefit a buyer and a seller. The market demand curve tells us that the potential buyer of the sixth lawn cut (Siggy) is willing to pay only $7 for a lawn cut, and the supply curve tells us that the potential seller of the sixth lawn cut (Efrin) has a marginal cost of $12. This transaction doesn't happen because the potential buyer is not willing to pay the cost of producing the good.

Our example of the market for lawn cutting illustrates a general lesson about markets. The typical market has thousands of buyers and thousands of sellers, each acting in his or her own self-interest. The market reaches the quantity that maximizes the total surplus of the market and is therefore efficient. Instead of using a bureaucrat to coordinate the actions of everyone in the market, we can rely on the actions of individual consumers and individual producers, each guided only by self-interest. This is Adam Smith's invisible hand in action.

Government Intervention in Efficient Markets

In most modern economies, governments take an active role. As we'll see later in the book, government action can be justified on efficiency grounds when one of the four efficiency conditions listed at the beginning of the chapter is not being met. But for a market that meets the four efficiency conditions, the market equilibrium generates the largest possible total surplus, so government intervention can only decrease the surplus and cause inefficiency. A government motivated exclusively by efficiency would not intervene in such a market, but instead would permit the invisible hand to guide consumers and producers to the market equilibrium.

So why would a government intervene in an efficient market? Sometimes the government's objective is not to promote efficiency—to maximize the size of the pie—but instead to slice the pie in favor of one group or another. For example, a government that restricts shoe imports prevents some domestic workers from losing their shoemaking jobs. Of course, limiting imports will decrease the supply of shoes, and consumers will pay higher prices. As we'll see, when the government intervenes in an efficient market to slice the pie in favor of one group, the pie shrinks, so there is a trade-off between efficiency (maximizing the size of the pie) and distributional concerns (slicing the pie).

What is the role of economic analysis in exploring government intervention in efficient markets? We will focus our attention on the inefficiencies of government intervention, looking at how much the pie shrinks. We will briefly discuss some of the distributional consequences of intervention—how the slices change. The decision about whether intervention in an efficient market is worthwhile—whether the changes in the slices are worth losing part of the pie—is made in the political sphere. Economic analysis shows the trade-offs associated with public policies.

Under some circumstances, groups of people who fare poorly in the market economy deserve special consideration. If a society decides that a particular group merits special treatment—for example, workers who lose their jobs because of imports—a more direct form of assistance is generally superior than intervention in efficient markets by the government. One alternative would be for the government to provide money for workers to get training for new jobs.

application 2

RENT CONTROL AND MISMATCHES

APPLYING THE CONCEPTS: Why does the market equilibrium maximize the value of a market?

Under rent control, the government sets a maximum price for housing, decreasing the quantity supplied and the total value of the market. Rent control and other maximum prices cause inefficiency of another sort. Consider a consumer living in a rent-controlled apartment who experiences a change in circumstances that would normally cause the consumer to a move to a different apartment. For example, when a single person renting a tiny apartment gets married, he or she is likely to move to a larger place. But a consumer in a rent-controlled apartment may stay in the tiny but inexpensive apartment, generating a housing mismatch. A recent study suggests that in New York City, about 20 percent of rent-controlled apartments are mismatched.

The most famous case of a mismatched tenant is former Mayor Koch of New York. When he was elected mayor and moved into the mayor's official residence, he held onto his rent-controlled apartment, presumably anticipating his post-mayor life in an apartment at a controlled rent that was roughly one-third the market rent. **Related to Exercise 2.7.**

SOURCE: Based on Edward Glaeser and Erzo Luttmer, "The Misallocation of Housing under Rent Control," *American Economic Review* 93 (2003), pp. 1027–1046.

21.3 Controlling Prices—Maximum and Minimum Prices

We'll start our discussion of government intervention with policies that control product prices. The government could set a maximum price or a minimum price. In both cases, if the market meets the four efficiency conditions listed at the beginning of the chapter, government intervention reduces the total surplus of the market and causes inefficiency.

Setting Maximum Prices

We've already seen two different effects of a maximum price or price ceiling. In Chapter 4 we saw that when the government sets a maximum price that is less than the equilibrium price, the result is permanent excess demand for the product. The maximum price encourages firms to supply *less* and encourages consumers to buy *more*. So at the maximum price there is excess demand because consumers want to buy more than producers want to sell. In this chapter, we saw from Panel A in Figure 21.4 that a maximum price decreases the total surplus of the market: Some consumers gain at the expense of producers, and the total surplus decreases. Here are some examples of goods that have been subject to maximum prices or may be subject to maximum prices in the near future:

- *Rental housing.* During World War II, the federal government instituted a national system of rent controls. Although only New York City continued rent control after the war, during the 1970s rent control spread to dozens of cities.
- *Gasoline.* In response to sharp increases in the price of gasoline in the 1970s, the national government set a maximum price on gasoline.
- *Medical goods and services.* Some proposals to control medical costs include price controls for prescription drugs.

In all three cases, a maximum price will cause excess demand and reduce the total surplus of the market.

Rent Control

Figure 21.5 shows the effects of rent control on consumer and producer surplus. Panel A shows the market equilibrium, with a price (monthly rent) of $400 per apartment and a quantity of 1,000 apartments. The total surplus is the sum of the consumer surplus and producer surplus, shown as the area between the demand curve and the supply curve. Panel B shows the effect of a maximum price of $300 per apartment. The decrease in price causes movement downward along the supply curve to point *b*, and the quantity of apartments supplied decreases to 700. Because the policy decreases the number of apartments from 1,000 to 700, the total surplus of the market decreases. For the first 700 apartments, consumers gain at the expense of producers, paying $300 per apartment rather than $400. Apartments 701 through 1,000 disappear from the market, so the surpluses associated with these apartments are lost entirely. The decrease in total surplus means that the market is inefficient.

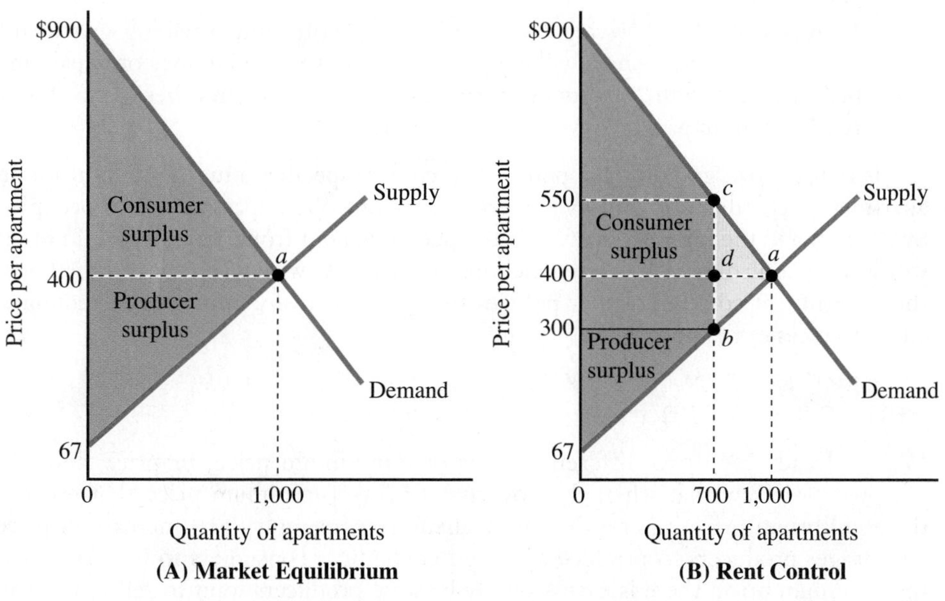

◄ **FIGURE 21.5**
Rent Control Decreases Total Surplus
(A) In the market equilibrium, with a price of $400 and 1,000 apartments, the total surplus is the area between the demand curve and the supply curve. (B) Rent control, with a maximum price of $300, reduces the quantity to 700 apartments and decreases the total surplus.

Because rent control decreases the total surplus of the market, the policy generates a **deadweight loss**. In Figure 21.5, the deadweight loss is shown by the yellow triangle *abc*, the decrease in the total surplus of the market. This is a deadweight loss in the sense that it is not offset by a gain to anyone else. The consumers and producers

deadweight loss
The decrease in the total surplus of the market that results from a policy such as rent control.

who are excluded from the market by rent control lose the surpluses they could have received in the market. The loss of consumer surplus is shown by triangle *cad*, and the loss of producer surplus is shown by triangle *dab*. Adding these together, we get the deadweight loss shown by triangle *abc*.

Another way to see the inefficiency of rent control is to apply the principle of voluntary exchange.

PRINCIPLE OF VOLUNTARY EXCHANGE

A voluntary exchange between two people makes both people better off.

As shown by the points between *c* and *a* on the demand curve, 300 consumers are willing to pay between \$400 and \$550 for an apartment. As shown by the points between points *b* and *a* on the supply curve, there are 300 producers who are willing to rent out an apartment for amounts between \$300 and \$400. Although the 300 excluded consumers are willing to pay more than these suppliers require to provide an apartment, the transactions are illegal under rent control. Because rent control outlaws transactions that would make both parties better off, it causes inefficiency.

Three more subtle effects associated with rent control add to its inefficiency:

- *Search costs.* At the artificially low maximum price, the number of people seeking apartments exceeds the number of apartments available. Consumers will spend more time searching for apartments, so an additional cost of rent control is the opportunity cost of the extra time spent searching for apartments.
- *Cheating.* Because rent control outlaws mutually beneficial transactions, many people violate the spirit and the letter of the law by cheating. In some rent-control cities, consumers pay extra money to property owners to outbid other consumers. These extra payments are often disguised as "nonrefundable security deposits" or as "key money"—thousands of dollars to get the keys to an apartment.
- *Decrease in quality of housing.* Given the lower payoff from providing apartments for rent, property owners will have less incentive to spend money on repair and maintenance, so the quality of apartments will decrease. In other words, lower rent is offset in part by lower housing quality.

Is rent control good for the poor? Rent control specifies a maximum rent for an apartment, regardless of who lives there. Rent-controlled apartments are occupied by the rich and the poor, so many wealthy people benefit from rent control. In other words, rent control is ineffective in helping the poor. As we explain later in the book, the government could use other policies to more effectively improve the economic circumstances of the poor.

Setting Minimum Prices

We've already seen two different effects of a minimum price, or price floor. In Chapter 4 we saw that when the government sets a minimum price that exceeds the equilibrium price, the result is permanent excess supply. The increase in price encourages producers to produce *more* and encourages consumers to buy *less*. So at the minimum price, there is excess supply because producers want to sell more than consumers want to buy. In this chapter, we saw from Panel A in Figure 21.4 that a minimum price decreases the total surplus of the market: Some producers gain at the expense of consumers, and the total surplus decreases.

Governments around the world establish minimum prices for agricultural goods. Under a price-support program, a government sets a minimum price for an agricultural product and then buys any resulting surpluses at that price.

application 3

PRICE CONTROLS AND THE SHRINKING CANDY BAR

APPLYING THE CONCEPTS #3: How do price controls affect the market?

During World War II, the U.S. government used a system of price controls to set maximum prices on all sorts of products, including candy bars. *Consumer Reports* compared the weights of candy bars in 1943 to their weights in 1939, before the maximum prices were imposed. In 19 of 20 cases, the candy bars had shrunk, causing the price per ounce to increase by an average of 23 percent. In other words, producers reacted to maximum prices by shrinking candy bars to match the relatively low maximum price. In the words of *Consumer Reports*, the shrinkage of candy bars is an example of "hidden price increases." **Related to Exercise 3.6.**

SOURCE: Based on foodtimeline.org, "Food Timeline FAQ: Historic Food Prices," (foodtimeline.org, accessed February 20, 2012).

21.4 Controlling Quantities—Licensing and Import Restrictions

What happens when the government controls the quantity of a particular product instead of its price? We'll consider two policies that control quantities. In the domestic economy, many state and local governments limit the number of firms in particular markets by limiting the number of business licenses to operate in those markets. Many national governments restrict imports, using import bans or quotas on the quantity of a product—for example, shoes or cheese—that can be imported.

The licensing of business by state and local government is extensive. For example, many cities and states limit the number of taxicabs, dry cleaners, tobacco farms, liquor stores, bars, and even dog groomers. Some people defend licensing programs on the grounds that they protect consumers from low-quality products and poor service. But studies have shown that most licensing programs increase prices without improving the quality of products and service.[2]

Another motive for cities to issue licenses is to limit the number of establishments that could be considered nuisances to some citizens, for example, bars, convenience stores, and gas stations.

Taxi Medallions

We can use the licensing of taxis to explain how the practice affects the market for taxi service and other markets in which licenses are common. Panel A of Figure 21.6 shows the market equilibrium in the taxi market. The demand curve intersects the supply curve at point *a*. The industry provides 10,000 miles of taxi service per day at a price of $3 per mile. Each taxi is capable of producing a maximum of 100 miles of service per day, and there are 100 taxicabs in the market. The total surplus of the market equals the sum of consumer surplus and producer surplus, shown by the area between the demand curve and the supply curve.

Now suppose that the city passes a law requiring each taxicab to have a license—also known as a taxi "medallion"—and limits the number of medallions to 80. The city then gives taxi medallions to the first 80 people who show up at city hall. In Panel B of Figure 21.6, the vertical line at 8,000 miles of service shows that this policy fixes the quantity of taxi service at 8,000 miles per day (80 taxis times 100 miles per taxi per

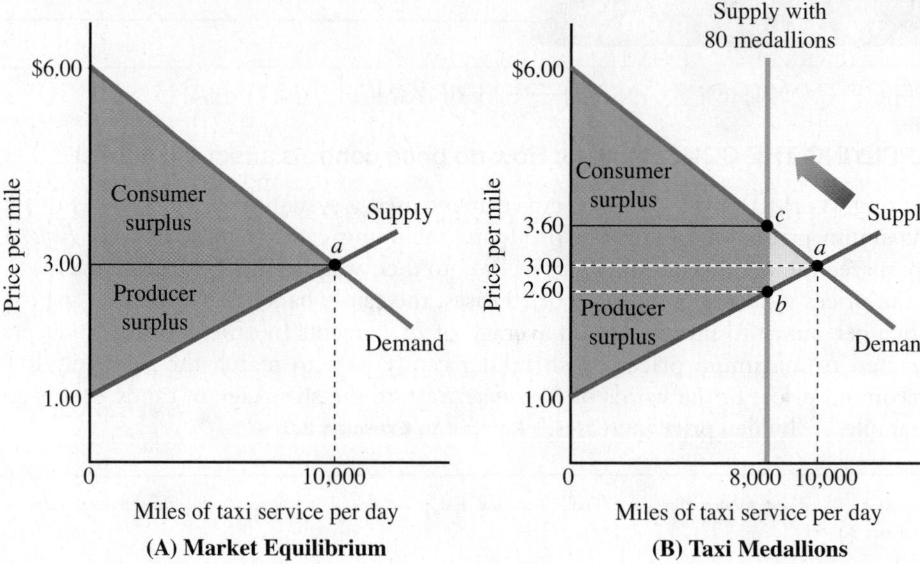

▶ **FIGURE 21.6**
The Market Effects of Taxi Medallions
(A) The market equilibrium is shown by point *a*, with a price of $3.00 and a quantity of 10,000 miles of service per day (100 taxis and 100 miles per taxi). The total surplus is the area between the demand and supply curves. (B) A medallion policy reduces the quantity of taxi service to 8,000 miles per day (80 taxis and 100 miles per taxi) and increases the price to $3.60 (point *c*). The producers of the first 8,000 miles gain at the expense of consumers, but the surpluses for between 8,000 and 10,000 miles are lost entirely. Therefore, the total surplus decreases.

day). The medallion policy creates an excess demand for taxi service: At the original price ($3.00), the quantity demanded is 10,000 miles, but the city's 80 taxicabs provide only 8,000 miles of service. As a result, the market moves upward along the demand curve to point *c*, where the price is $3.60 per mile of service. The medallion policy increases the price and decreases the quantity of taxi services.

Licensing and Market Efficiency

The medallion policy decreases the total surplus of the taxi market. In Figure 21.6, we see that the total surplus in Panel B is less than the total surplus in Panel A. The medallion policy decreases consumer surplus, a result of the higher price and the smaller quantity supplied. Producer surplus could increase or decrease, depending on the shapes of the market supply and market demand curves. In this example, the producer surplus of taxi drivers with medallions actually increases by a small amount. As in the cases of a maximum price or a minimum price, the medallion policy decreases the quantity of goods sold, decreasing the total surplus of the market. The producers of the first 8,000 miles of service gain at the expense of consumers, but the surpluses that could have been gained between 8,000 and 10,000 miles are lost entirely, so the total surplus of the market decreases. The deadweight loss is shown by the area of yellow triangle *abc*.

Another way to see the inefficiency of taxi medallions is to look at just the consumers and producers who are excluded from the market and what they lose. Some of the excluded consumers would gladly pay the cost of providing taxi service. As shown by the points between points *c* and *a* on the demand curve, many consumers are willing to pay between $3.00 and $3.60 per mile for taxi service. Although there are plenty of drivers who would be willing to provide taxi service at these prices, they can't do so without a medallion. Because the medallion policy prevents these riders and drivers from executing mutually beneficial transactions, the policy causes inefficiency.

Our analysis of taxi medallions applies to any market subject to quantity controls. State and city governments use licensing to limit many types of small businesses. When an establishment such as a convenience store or dry cleaner would cause a nuisance to its neighbors, the inefficiency of the sort shown in Figure 21.6 may be offset at least partly by the benefit of controlling nuisances. Of course, the alternative policy is to control the nuisance directly by restricting the location of the establishment rather than simply limiting the number of establishments. In general, a policy that limits entry into a market increases price, decreases quantity, and causes inefficiency in the market. In evaluating such a policy, we must compare the possible benefits from controlling nuisances to the losses of consumer and producer surplus.

Winners and Losers from Licensing

Who benefits and who loses from licensing programs such as a taxi medallion policy? The losers are consumers, who pay more for taxi rides. The winners are the people who receive a free medallion and the right to charge an artificially high price for taxi service.

In some cities, people buy and sell taxi medallions. The market value of a medallion reflects the profits it can earn its owner. For example, the market price of a medallion is over $150,000 in New York City, $140,000 in Boston, and $100,000 in Toronto.[3] In cities such as Chicago, where medallions are more plentiful, the market price is much lower.

Why don't governments simply eliminate the taxi medallion system and allow free entry into the taxi market? Because doing so would decrease the price of taxi service and reduce the market value of medallions to zero. Some city governments are reluctant to eliminate medallions because owners use their political power to keep the system (and the value of their medallions) in place.

Import Restrictions

We've seen that the government can control the quantity of a good produced by issuing a limited number of business licenses to producers. Another way to control quantity is to limit the imports of a particular good. Like a licensing policy, an import restriction increases the market price and decreases the total surplus of the market.

To show the market effects of import restrictions, let's start with an unrestricted market. Panel A of Figure 21.7 shows the market equilibrium in the sugar market when there is free trade. The domestic supply curve shows the quantity supplied by domestic (U.S.) firms at different prices. Looking at point *m*, we see that U.S. firms

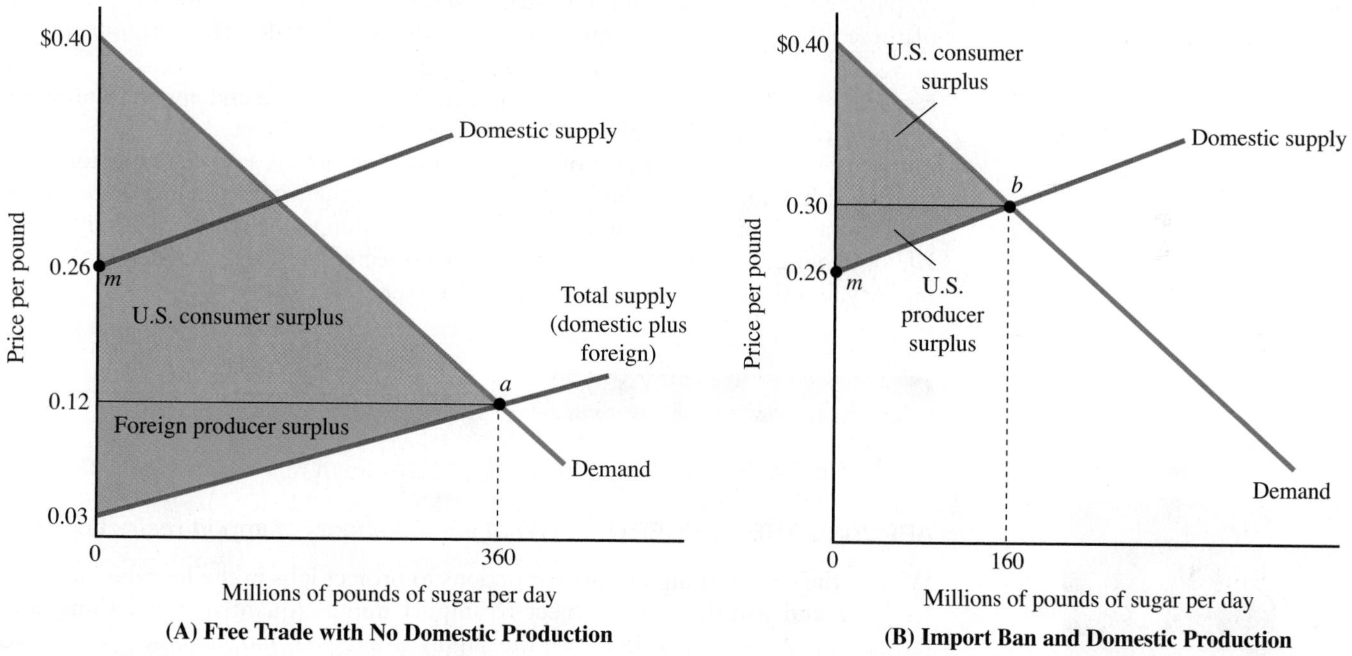

▲ FIGURE 21.7
The Effects of an Import Ban on U.S. Prices and Consumer and Producer Surplus
(A) With free trade, the demand intersects the total supply curve at point *a* with a price of $0.12 and a quantity of 360 million pounds. This price is below the minimum price of domestic suppliers ($0.26, as shown by point *m*), so domestic firms do not participate in the market. The total surplus is shown by the shaded areas (U.S. consumer surplus and foreign producer surplus). (B) If sugar imports are banned, the equilibrium is shown by the intersection of the demand curve and the domestic (U.S.) supply curve (point *b*). The price increases to $0.30. Although the ban generates a producer surplus for domestic producers, their gain is less than the loss of domestic consumers.

will not supply any sugar unless the price is at least $0.26 per pound. The total supply curve, which shows the quantity supplied by both domestic and foreign firms, lies to the right of the domestic curve. At each price, the total supply exceeds the domestic supply because foreign firms also supply sugar. Point *a* shows the free-trade equilibrium: The domestic demand curve (which shows the demand by U.S. consumers) intersects the total supply curve at a price of $0.12 per pound and a quantity of 360 million pounds per day. Because this price is below the minimum price for domestic firms, domestic firms do not supply any sugar to the U.S. market.

What would happen if the United States banned sugar imports? Foreign suppliers would disappear from the market, so the total supply of sugar would consist of only the domestic supply. In Panel B of Figure 21.7, the new equilibrium would be shown by point *b*: The demand curve would intersect the domestic supply curve at a price of $0.30 per pound and a quantity of 160 million pounds. The decrease in supply resulting from the import ban would increase the price and decrease the quantity. As a result, domestic firms would produce all the sugar for the domestic market.

The import ban would ultimately decrease the total surplus in the sugar market. The shaded areas in the two graphs show the consumer and producer surpluses that would result with and without free trade. The import ban decreases the U.S. consumer surplus, as shown by the two blue triangles in the two graphs. The ban would also eliminate the producer surplus of foreign suppliers (shown by the red triangle in Panel A of Figure 21.7) and generate a producer surplus for domestic suppliers (shown by the red triangle in Panel B of Figure 21.7). Therefore, the import ban would cause domestic producers to gain at the expense of domestic consumers. Because consumers would lose more than domestic producers would gain, the import ban would cause a net loss for people in the United States.

Import restrictions are often defended on the grounds that they increase employment in the "protected" industries, such as apparel and steel. But the protection of these jobs increases consumer prices, so there is a trade-off: more jobs in the protected industry, but higher prices for consumers.[4] According to one study, import restrictions in 1993 protected 56,464 jobs in the U.S. textile and apparel industries at a cost to consumers of about $178,000 per job and protected 3,419 jobs in the motor vehicle industry at a cost of about $271,000 per job. A study commissioned by the Swedish Ministry for Foreign Affairs concluded that import quotas imposed by the European Union (EU) increased the cost of clothing for the typical family in the EU by about 270 euros per year. The quotas protected jobs in the domestic clothing industry, but the cost per job saved was about 41,000 euros per year.

application 4

THE COST OF PROTECTING A LUGGAGE JOB

APPLYING THE CONCEPTS #4: What are the effects of import restrictions?

What is the cost of using import restrictions to protect jobs in the luggage industry? Luggage and handbags are subject to import quotas (quantity restrictions) and tariffs (import taxes) that decrease the supply of luggage and increase the price to consumers by 13 percent. These policies protect about 226 jobs in the industry and reduce consumer surplus by $290 million, so the cost per job protected is roughly $1.29 million per year. Similar calculations show that the cost per job protected is $826,000 for the sugar industry, $685,000 for the dairy industry, and $199,000 for the apparel industry. **Related to Exercise 4.5.**

SOURCE: Based on (1) Federal Reserve Bank of Dallas, The Fruits of Free Trade (2002); (2) United States International Trade Commission, The Economic Effects of Significant U.S. Import Restraints (2002).

21.5 Who Really Pays Taxes?

In this part of the chapter, we'll look at the market effects of taxes and answer two important questions. First, who really bears the burden of a tax? As we'll see, it is not necessarily the person who actually pays the tax to the government. Second, is the total burden of a tax equal to the revenue collected by the government? As we'll see, a tax changes people's behavior, so the total burden actually exceeds the revenue collected.

Tax Shifting: Forward and Backward

We can use supply and demand curves to look at the market effects of taxes. Suppose that your city imposes a tax of $100 per apartment and collects the tax from housing firms—the firms that own apartment buildings and rent out the apartments. You may think the burden of the tax falls exclusively on the housing firm, because that's who mails the check to the government. But some simple supply and demand analysis will show why this is incorrect. The housing firm will charge more for apartments and pay less for its inputs, such as labor and land, so the tax will actually be paid by consumers and input suppliers.

Figure 21.8 shows the market effects of a $100 tax on apartments. As we saw earlier in the chapter, the market supply curve tells us how high the price must be to get producers to supply a particular quantity of output. The price must be high enough to cover all the costs of production. A unit tax increases the cost of production, so we need a higher price to get firms to produce any given quantity. In other words, the supply curve shifts upward by the amount of the tax. A unit tax of $100 per apartment increases a property owner's cost per apartment by $100, so the supply curve shifts upward by $100.

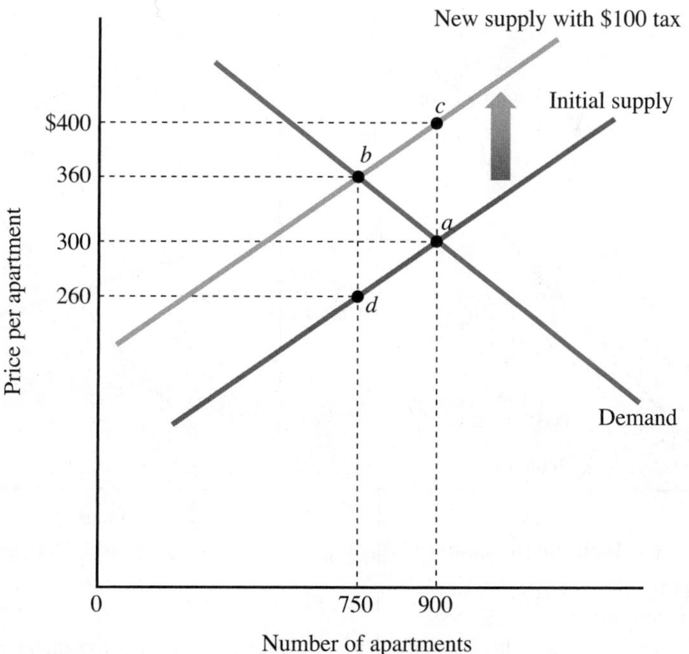

▲ **FIGURE 21.8**
The Market Effects of an Apartment Tax
A tax of $100 per apartment shifts the supply curve upward by the $100 tax, moving the market equilibrium from point *a* to point *b*. The equilibrium price increases from $300 to $360, and the equilibrium quantity decreases from 900 to 750 apartments.

The shift of the supply curve increases the equilibrium price of apartments. At the $300 price, there will be an excess demand for apartments, and the price will increase to eliminate the excess demand. In Figure 21.8, the market moves from point *a* to point *b*: The demand curve intersects the new supply curve at a price of $360, compared to $300 before the tax. In other words, housing firms shift part of the tax forward onto consumers, who pay $60 of the $100 tax. Although housing firms pay the entire $100 tax in a legal sense, they get some of the money to pay the tax by charging consumers $60 more for apartments.

The apartment tax also affects the people who supply inputs such as land and labor to the housing industry. The tax decreases the output of the industry, so the industry needs smaller quantities of the inputs used to produce apartments. The resulting excess supply of inputs like labor and land will decrease land and labor prices, decreasing the cost of producing apartments. As a result, part of the $100 tax gets shifted backward onto input suppliers. Although housing firms pay the apartment tax in a legal sense, they get some of the money to pay the tax by paying less to workers and landowners.

Tax Shifting and the Price Elasticity of Demand

The amount of the tax shifted forward to consumers depends on the price elasticity of demand for the taxed good. If the demand for a taxed good is inelastic—meaning that consumers are not very responsive to price changes—we need a large price hike to eliminate the excess demand caused by the tax. Therefore, consumers will be hit by a large increase in price, and so they will pay the bulk of the tax. This is shown in Panel A of Figure 21.9. Demand is inelastic—that is, the demand curve is steep—so a $5 tax increases the equilibrium price by $4 (from $10 to $14). In other words, consumers pay four-fifths of the tax. In Panel B of Figure 21.9, demand is elastic—that is, the demand curve is relatively flat—so consumers pay just a small part of the tax. A $5 tax increases the equilibrium price by only $1 (from $10 to $11). In this case, consumers pay only one-fifth of the tax.

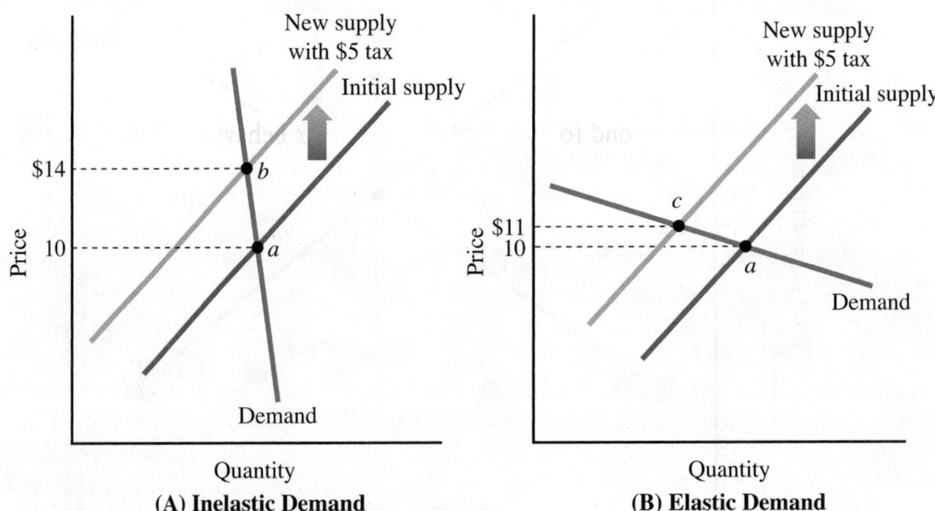

▲ **FIGURE 21.9**
Elasticities of Demand and Tax Effects
If demand is inelastic (Panel A), a tax will increase the market price by a large amount, so consumers will bear a large share of the tax. If demand is elastic (Panel B), the price will increase by a small amount and consumers will bear a small share of the tax.

Why should we care about tax shifting? We've seen that a tax increases consumer prices and decreases input prices, so to determine who actually pays a tax, we must look beyond the actual taxpayer. As shown in the following application, the subtleties of tax shifting are often revealed by the objections of people who don't actually pay a tax in a legal sense.

Cigarette Taxes and Tobacco Land

In 1994, President Clinton proposed an immediate $0.75 per pack increase in the cigarette tax. The tax had two purposes: to generate revenue for Clinton's health-care reform plan and to decrease medical costs by discouraging smoking. Based on our discussion of the market effects of a tax, we would predict that the tax would be shared by consumers, who would pay higher prices, and the owners of land where tobacco is grown. It appears tobacco farmers and landowners understand the economics of cigarette taxes. Led by a group of representatives and senators from tobacco-growing areas in North Carolina, Kentucky, and Virginia, Congress scaled back Clinton's proposed tax hike from $0.75 to $0.05. Although the government would have collected the tax from cigarette manufacturers, savvy tobacco farmers realized the tax would decrease the price of their tobacco-growing land.

The Luxury Boat Tax and Boat Workers

A lesson on backward shifting occurred when Congress passed a steep luxury tax on boats and other luxury goods in 1990. Under the new tax, a person buying a $300,000 boat paid an additional $20,000 in taxes. The burden of the tax was actually shared by consumers and input suppliers, including people who worked in boat factories and boatyards. The tax increased the price of boats, and consumers bought fewer boats. The boat industry produced fewer boats, and the resulting decrease in the demand for boat workers led to layoffs and lower wages for those who managed to keep their jobs. Although the idea behind the luxury tax was to "soak the rich," the tax actually harmed low-income workers in the boat industry. The tax was repealed a few years later.

Tax Burden and Deadweight Loss

We've seen that people respond to a tax by changing their behavior. As a result, the total burden of a tax will exceed the total amount of money the government actually collects from the tax. To see why, suppose the government imposes a tax on no. 3 pencils, and the tax is large enough that everyone who initially used no. 3 pencils switches to other types of pencils or other writing implements. If no one purchases no. 3 pencils, the tax won't raise any revenue for the government, but the tax still generates a burden because some people who would prefer to use no. 3 pencils have switched to other writing implements.

We'll use the fish market to explore the total burden of a tax. To simplify matters, let's assume that the supply curve for fish is horizontal, as shown in Figure 21.10. As we'll see later in the book, a supply curve will be horizontal if the prices of the inputs used in the industry don't change as the total output of the industry changes. For the fish market, this means that wages and the prices of bait and fuel don't change as the total fish harvest changes. The demand curve intersects the initial supply curve at point *a*, so the price is $2 per pound and the quantity is 60,000 pounds of fish per day.

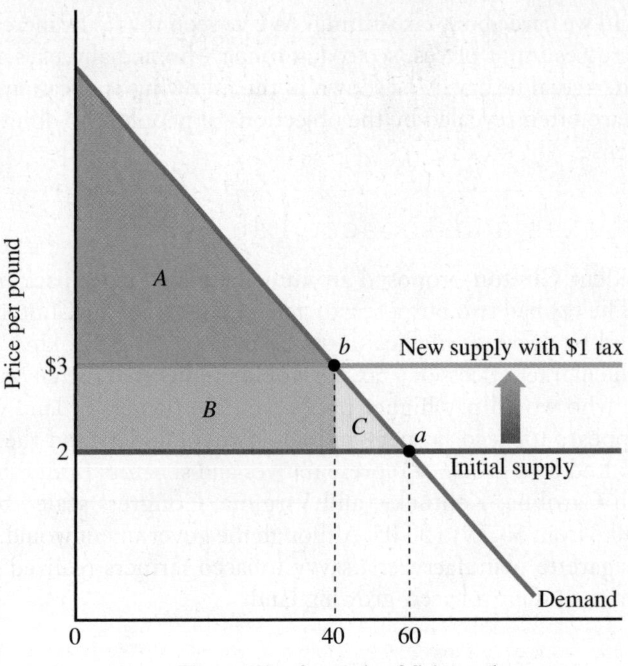

▲ **FIGURE 21.10**
The Deadweight Loss or Excess Burden of a Tax
When the supply curve is horizontal, a tax increases the equilibrium price by the tax ($1 per pound in this example). Consumer surplus decreases by the areas *B* and *C*. Total tax revenue collected is shown by rectangle *B*, so the total burden exceeds tax revenue by triangle *C*. Triangle *C* is sometimes known as the deadweight loss or excess burden of the tax.

Suppose the government imposes a tax of $1 per pound of fish, and the tax is paid in legal terms by producers. As we saw earlier, a unit tax shifts the market supply upward by the amount of the tax. As shown in Figure 21.10, a $1 tax on fish producers shifts the supply curve up by $1: Each firm now needs $3, not $2, to cover all of its costs, including the tax.

In Figure 21.10 the fish tax increases the equilibrium price of fish from $2 to $3. Why does the price increase by an amount equal to the tax? The supply curve is horizontal because input prices are fixed, regardless of how much output is produced. There is no opportunity to shift the tax backward onto input suppliers, so consumers bear the full cost of the tax.

We can use the concept of consumer surplus to determine just how much consumers lose as a result of the tax. Before the fish tax, the consumer surplus is shown by the area between the initial price line (and horizontal supply curve) and the demand curve, or areas *A*, *B*, and *C*. When the price increases to $3, the consumer surplus shrinks to the area of triangle *A*, so the loss of consumer surplus (the total burden of the tax) is shown by rectangle *B* and yellow triangle *C*. Let's take a closer look at these two areas.

- Rectangle *B* shows the extra money consumers must pay for the 40,000 pounds of fish they purchase. The tax increases the price by $1 per pound, so consumers pay an extra $40,000.

- Triangle *C* shows the loss of consumer surplus on the fish that are not consumed because of the tax. Consumers obey the law of demand, so when the price rises, they cut their purchases, buying 20,000 fewer pounds of fish. As a result, they give up the consumer surplus they would have received on these 20,000 pounds of fish.

How does the total burden of the tax compare to the tax revenue raised by the government? The total tax revenue is the tax per pound ($1) times the quantity consumed (40,000 pounds), or $40,000. This is shown by rectangle *B*: Part of the loss experienced by consumers is the revenue gain for government. But in addition to losing rectangle *B*, consumers also lose triangle *C*, so the consumer's total burden of the tax exceeds the tax revenue. Triangle *C* is sometimes known as the **deadweight loss from taxation** or the **excess burden of a tax.**

deadweight loss from taxation The difference between the total burden of a tax and the amount of revenue collected by the government.

excess burden of a tax Another name for deadweight loss.

In the example shown in Figure 21.10, we used a horizontal supply curve to simplify matters and make the analysis of deadweight loss transparent. In a market with a positively sloped supply curve, a tax generates a deadweight loss, but the analysis is a bit more complex. For students interested in a challenge, one of the problems at the end of the chapter deals with deadweight loss for the apartment market, a market with a positively sloped supply curve.

application 5

RESPONSE TO LOWER TAXES IN FRENCH RESTAURANTS

APPLYING THE CONCEPTS #5: How does a tax cut affect prices?

In France, regular restaurants pay a 20 percent value-added tax (VAT) on sit-down meals, while fast-food restaurants pay just a 5 percent tax on take-away meals. A group of large restaurant owners made the following pledge. If the nation were to cut its VAT rate on restaurant meals to 5 percent, the owners would

- cut the prices of restaurant meals by 5 percent, and
- increase the wages paid to waiters and dishwashers by 10 percent.

The owners predicted that these changes would increase the quantity of restaurant meals sold by 14 percent and increase restaurant employment by 40,000 workers.

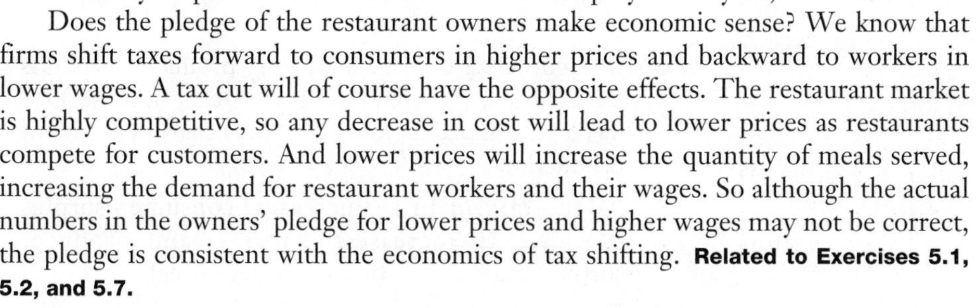

Does the pledge of the restaurant owners make economic sense? We know that firms shift taxes forward to consumers in higher prices and backward to workers in lower wages. A tax cut will of course have the opposite effects. The restaurant market is highly competitive, so any decrease in cost will lead to lower prices as restaurants compete for customers. And lower prices will increase the quantity of meals served, increasing the demand for restaurant workers and their wages. So although the actual numbers in the owners' pledge for lower prices and higher wages may not be correct, the pledge is consistent with the economics of tax shifting. **Related to Exercises 5.1, 5.2, and 5.7.**

SOURCE: Based on "Better Value, Lower Tax: French Restaurants," *Economist*, January 25, 2003.

SUMMARY

In this chapter, we discussed the efficiency of markets and the consequences of government intervention in perfectly competitive markets. In a market without external benefits or costs, government intervention prevents consumers and producers from executing beneficial transactions and thus decreases the total surplus of the market. We also saw that taxes affect the prices of consumer goods and inputs. To determine who actually bears the cost of a tax, we must look beyond the taxpayer. Here are the main points of the chapter:

1 The *total surplus* of a market equals the sum of consumer surplus and producer surplus.

2 In a market that meets the four efficiency conditions (no external cost, no external benefit, perfect information, perfect competition), the market equilibrium maximizes the total surplus and is therefore efficient.

3 Price controls reduce the total surplus of a market because they prevent mutually beneficial transactions.

4 Quantity controls (such as licensing and import restrictions) decrease consumer surplus and the total surplus of the market.

5 A tax on a good may be shifted forward onto consumers and backward onto input suppliers.

6 Because a tax causes people to change their behavior, the total burden of the tax exceeds the revenue generated by the tax.

KEY TERMS

consumer surplus, p. 441
deadweight loss, p. 447
deadweight loss from taxation, p. 457
efficiency, p. 440
excess burden of a tax, p. 457
price ceiling, p. 444
price floor, p. 445
producer surplus, p. 442
total surplus, p. 443
willingness to accept, p. 442
willingness to pay, p. 441

EXERCISES

All problems are assignable in MyEconLab.

21.1 Consumer Surplus and Producer Surplus

1.1 Consumer surplus equals ________ minus ________.

1.2 Producer surplus equals ________ minus ________.

1.3 In Figure 21.1 on page 441, Tupak's consumer surplus is ________, compared to ________ for Thurl.

1.4 In Figure 21.1 on page 441, Tupak's consumer surplus is ________ (greater/less) than Thurl's because Tupak has a ________ (lower, higher) willingness to pay.

1.5 In Figure 21.2 on page 442, Bea's producer surplus is ________ (greater/less) than Dee's because Dee has a ________ (lower, higher) marginal cost of production.

1.6 As the market price increases, consumer surplus ________ (increases/decreases) and producer surplus ________ (increases/decreases).

1.7 For a given market price, a consumer who is on the high end of the demand curve has a ________ consumer surplus than a consumer on the low end of the demand curve.

1.8 For U.S. consumers, the average consumer surplus for Internet service is $________ (10, 45, 80, 100) per month. (Related to Application 1 on page 443.)

1.9 Consider the demand for Internet service in the U.S. Assume that the demand curve is linear, the monthly price is \$40, and the equilibrium number of consumers is 50 million. For the average consumer, show willingness to pay and the consumer surplus. (Related to Application 1 on page 443.)

21.2 Market Equilibrium and Efficiency

2.1 You are willing to pay \$2,000 to have your house painted, and Pablo's marginal cost of painting a house is \$1,400. If you agree to split the difference, the price is ________, your consumer surplus is ________, and Pablo's producer surplus is ________.

2.2 In Figure 21.3 on page 443, Forest is willing to pay ________ for the fourth cut lawn, and Dee's marginal cost is ________. If they split the difference, the price would be ________ and each would get a surplus of ________.

2.3 In Figure 21.4 on page 444, a maximum price of \$4 prevents mutually beneficial transactions between Thurl and ________ and between Forest and ________.

2.4 Fill in the blanks with "consumers" or "producers": A maximum price below the equilibrium price generates benefits for some ________ and imposes costs on some ________ and some ________.

2.5 Fill in the blanks with "consumers" or "producers": A minimum price above the equilibrium price generates benefits for some ________ and imposes costs on some ________ and some ________.

2.6 In Figure 21.3 on page 443, the sixth lawn is not cut because the ________ of the sixth consumer (Siggy, in Figure 21.1) is ________ the ________ of the sixth producer (Efrin, in Figure 21.2).

2.7 A recent study suggests that in New York City, rent control causes roughly ________ percent of rent-controlled apartments are mismatched. (Related to Application 2 on page 446.)

2.8 **Identify the Surpluses.** The following graph shows a supply curve and a demand curve and several areas between the curves. Identify the areas on the figure that represent the following:

a. Consumer surplus in the market equilibrium
b. Producer surplus in the market equilibrium
c. Total surplus in the market equilibrium
d. Consumer surplus under a maximum price of \$10
e. Producer surplus under a maximum price of \$10
f. Total surplus under a maximum price of \$10
g. Consumer surplus under a maximum quantity of 70
h. Producer surplus under a maximum quantity of 70
i. Total surplus under a maximum quantity of 70

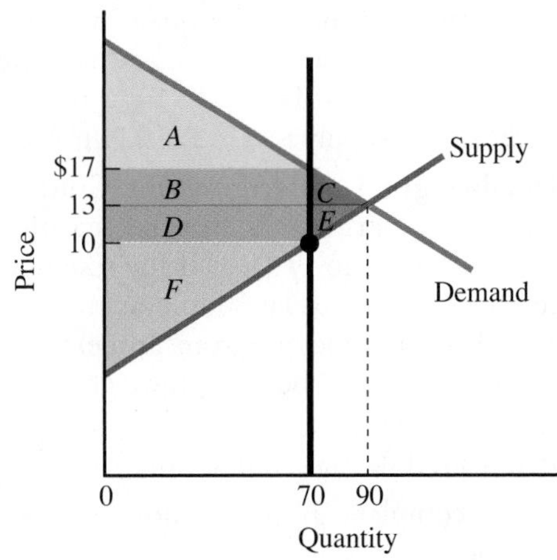

21.3 Controlling Prices—Maximum and Minimum Prices

3.1 Arrow up or down: In Figure 21.5 on page 447, rent control ________ the quantity of apartments, ________ producer surplus, ________ consumer surplus, and ________ the total market surplus.

3.2 In Figure 21.5 on page 447, rent control prevents a total of ________ mutually beneficial transactions for consumers on the demand curve between points and producers on the supply curve between points ________ and ________.

3.3 In Figure 21.5 on page 447, suppose rent control is partly relaxed, with the maximum price rising from \$300 to \$350. The quantity of apartments on the market will increase from ________ to ________.

3.4 In Figure 21.5 on page 447, a consumer who is on the demand curve halfway between points *c* and *a* would be willing to pay \$________ above the controlled price to get an apartment. A producer who is on the supply curve halfway between points *b* and *a* would be willing to supply an apartment at a price of \$________, or ________ above the maximum price.

3.5 The deadweight loss from rent control is shown by the area between the ________ curve and the ________ curve from the quantity ________ to the quantity ________.

3.6 During World War II, candy producers responded to maximum prices by ________, leading to ________ prices per ounce. (Related to Application 3 on page 449.)

3.7 **Excess Supply from a Minimum Milk Price.** In the equilibrium in the powdered milk market, the quantity is 100 million units and the price is \$9.00 per unit. The price elasticity of demand is 0.80 and the price elasticity of supply is 2.50. Suppose the government imposes a minimum price of \$9.90.

a. Draw a graph to show the market effects of the minimum price.

b. At the minimum price, the quantity of powdered milk supplied is __________ million units, the quantity demanded is __________ million units, and the excess supply is __________ million units.

3.8 **No Deadweight Loss from Rent Control?** Like other fruit flies, Frudo has an expected life span of 37 days. According to Frudo, "If my assumptions are correct, a rent-control law implemented today will simply redistribute income from property owners to consumers. There will be no deadweight loss, at least not in my lifetime."

a. What is Frudo's key assumption?

b. Draw a complete graph to show his assumption and logic.

c. The typical elephant has an expected life span of 60 years. How would its analysis of rent control differ from Frudo's? Illustrate with a complete graph.

3.9 **Price Controls for Medical Care.** Consider a town where the equilibrium price of a doctor's visit is $60 and the equilibrium quantity supplied is 90 patient visits per hour. For suppliers (doctors), each $1 increase in price increases the quantity supplied by two visits. For consumers, each $1 increase in price decreases the quantity demanded by one visit. Suppose that in an attempt to control the rising costs of medical care the government imposes price controls, setting a maximum price of $50 per visit.

a. Use a completely labeled graph to show the effects of the maximum price on (a) the quantity of visits to doctors and (b) the total surplus of the market.

b. What sort of inefficiencies does the price control cause?

c. Would you expect patients and doctors to find ways around the maximum price?

3.10 **Gasoline Price Controls.** The equilibrium price of gasoline is $3, and the equilibrium quantity is 100 million gallons per day. Suppose the government sets a maximum price of $2.90. For producers, each $0.01 increase in price increases the quantity supplied by 3 million gallons.

a. Draw a graph to show the effects of the maximum price on the gasoline market. Label the initial equilibrium point as *a* and the point that shows the quantity supplied under the maximum price as *b*.

b. How does the maximum price affect the quantity of gasoline sold?

3.11 **Maximum Rent on Land.** Consider a state where all land is occupied by mobile-home parks, and each household rents one padacre (a standard pad for a mobile home). In the market equilibrium, the rent is $200 per padacre. Suppose the government sets a maximum rent of $150 per padacre, regardless of how the land is used. Recall the old saying "The trouble with land is that they're not making it anymore."

a. Use a supply-demand graph to depict the market with the maximum rent.

b. Does the rent maximum affect the equilibrium quantity of land?

c. Does the rent maximum generate a deadweight loss? If not, why not?

3.12 **Supply Elasticity and Deadweight Loss.** Consider the following statement: As the price elasticity of supply increases, the deadweight loss from a maximum price changes.

a. Draw two sets of supply-demand curves, one with a more elastic supply curve.

b. In the case of more elastic supply, is the deadweight loss larger or smaller?

21.4 Controlling Quantities—Licensing and Import Restrictions

4.1 In Figure 21.6 on page 450, the taxi medallion policy prevents mutually beneficial transactions for consumers on the demand curve between points __________ and __________ and producers on the supply curve between points __________ and __________.

4.2 In Figure 21.6 on page 450, a consumer who is on the demand curve halfway between points *c* and *a* would be willing to pay $__________ for a mile of taxi service, while a supplier who is halfway between points *b* and *a* on the supply curve would be willing to supply a mile of taxi service at a price of $__________.

4.3 In Figure 21.7 on page 451, domestic firms will produce __________ tons of sugar at a price of $0.15, __________ tons at a price of $0.30, and __________ tons at a price of $0.28.

4.4 Arrow up or down: An import ban __________ the price of sugar, __________ the total (market) quantity of sugar, and __________ the quantity of sugar produced by domestic firms.

4.5 Import restrictions for luggage increase __________ and decrease __________, and the cost per protected job is roughly $__________ (10,000, 50,000, 1,290,000). (Related to Application 4 on page 452.)

4.6 **Compute the Changes.** Consider the example of taxi medallions shown in Figure 21.6 on page 450.

a. The policy changes consumer surplus from $__________ to $__________.

b. The policy changes producer surplus from $__________ to $__________.

c. The policy changes the total surplus of the market from $__________ to $__________.

d. The deadweight loss is shown by the area of triangle __________, which equals $__________.

4.7 Effects of Relaxing the Medallion Policy. Consider the example of taxi medallions shown in Figure 21.6 on page 450. Suppose the government relaxes the policy, increasing the number of medallions from 80 to 90.

a. The price of taxi service will change from $______ to $______.

b. The miles of taxi service will change from ______ miles to ______ miles.

c. At the margin an excluded consumer would be willing to pay up to $______ for a mile of taxi service, while an excluded supplier would be willing to supply a mile of taxi service at a price as low as $______.

4.8 Equilibrium and Surplus in a Liver Market. The following table shows different points on the linear supply curve and linear demand curve for livers for transplant.

Price	Quantity Supplied	Quantity Demanded
$ 0	50	200
2,000	70	160
5,000	100	100
7,000	120	60
10,000	150	0

a. Draw the two curves and show the market equilibrium. The equilibrium price is $______, and the equilibrium quantity is ______ livers.

b. On your graph, show the total surplus of the liver market—the sum of consumer and producer surplus.

c. Suppose the government bans the buying and selling of livers. On your graph, show the new equilibrium quantity of livers and the resulting loss in the total value of the market.

4.9 Barber Licensing. Consider the market for haircuts in a city. In the market equilibrium, the price per haircut is $6 and the quantity is 240 haircuts per day. For consumers, each $1 increase in price decreases the quantity demanded by 20 haircuts. For producers, each $1 increase in price increases the quantity supplied by 60 haircuts. In the market equilibrium, there are 24 barbers, each of whom produces 10 haircuts per day. Suppose the city passes a law requiring all barbers to have a license and then issues only 18 barber licenses. Each licensed barber continues to provide 10 haircuts per day. Use a completely labeled graph to show the effects of licensing on (a) the price of haircuts and (b) the total surplus in the haircut market.

4.10 Bidding for a Boston Taxi Medallion. In 1997, there were 1,500 taxi medallions in the city of Boston, and each medallion generated a profit of about $14,000 per year. In 1998, the city announced that it would issue 300 new taxi medallions, auctioning the new medallions to the highest bidders.[5] Even with the new medallions, the number of taxis in the city would still be less than the number that would occur in an unregulated market. Your job is to predict the annual profit from a medallion after the new medallions were issued. To predict the new annual profit, assume the following:

- The cost of providing taxi service is constant at $2.00 per mile of service.
- The initial price of taxi service (with 1,500 medallions issued) is $2.14 per mile.
- Each taxi (or medallion) provides 100,000 miles of service per year, so issuing the 300 new medallions increases the total quantity of taxi service from 150 million miles to 180 million miles.
- The slope of the demand curve is –$0.001 per million miles: For each $0.001 decrease in the price of taxi service, the quantity demanded increases by one million miles.

a. Compute the new price of taxi service.

b. Compute the new profit per medallion.

4.11 Eliminate the Mango Market? Draw a supply-demand graph depicting a situation in which banning mango imports drives the quantity of mangos sold to zero.

4.12 Import Ban for Kiwi Fruit. Initially, there are no restrictions on importing kiwi fruit. The minimum supply price of domestic producers is $0.26, while the minimum supply price of foreign suppliers is $0.08. Each supply curve is linear, with a slope of $0.01 per million pounds. In the initial equilibrium, the price is $0.18 and the quantity is 10 million pounds. The demand curve has a vertical intercept of $0.38 and a slope of –$0.02 per million pounds.

a. Draw a graph showing the initial equilibrium.

b. Suppose imports are banned, raising the price to $0.30. Draw a graph to show the new equilibrium and identify the new equilibrium quantity.

c. Compute the consumer surplus before the import ban and after the ban.

d. Suppose the import ban protects 10 jobs in the kiwi fruit industry. What is the cost to consumers for each job protected?

21.5 Who Really Pays Taxes?

5.1 The lobby group of French restaurant owners pledged that if the VAT tax on restaurant meals was cut, they would increase ________ and decrease ________. (Related to Application 5 on page 457.)

5.2 According to the numbers provided by the lobby group of French restaurant owners, the price elasticity of demand for restaurant meals is ________. (Related to Application 5 on page 457.)

5.3 A tax paid in legal terms by producers will be partly shifted forward onto ________ and partly shifted backward onto ________.

5.4 Arrow up or down: As the price elasticity of demand increases, the size of the price increase resulting from a tax ________ and the share of the tax borne by consumers ________.

5.5 The demand for coffee is relatively inelastic. Therefore, we would expect ________ to pay a relatively large share of a tax on coffee.

5.6 **The Employment and Wage Effects of a Luxury Boat Tax.** Suppose the luxury boat industry initially employs 1,000 workers and produces 100 boats per month. Suppose a tax on luxury boats increases the equilibrium price from $300,000 to $345,000. The price elasticity of demand for luxury boats is 2.0.

a. The luxury tax increases the equilibrium price of boats by ________ percent, so it decreases the quantity of boats demanded from 100 to ________. If builders continue to employ 10 workers for each boat, the number of boat workers decreases from 1,000 to ________.

b. Suppose the workers in the industry respond to the luxury boat tax by agreeing to take a wage cut that decreases the cost of producing boats by 5 percent. In addition, suppose firms pass on the savings in labor costs to boat consumers. The wage reduction decreases the price of boats by ________ percent and increases the quantity of boats demanded from ________ to ________. If builders continue to employ 10 workers for each boat, the number of boat workers is ________.

5.7 **Cutting the Hotel Tax.** Suppose your city initially has a $20-per-night tax on hotel rooms, paid in a legal sense by the hotel. Under the tax, the equilibrium price of hotel rooms is $80 per night. (Related to Application 5 on page 457.)

a. Draw a supply-demand graph to show the effects of eliminating the tax.

b. How does the elimination of the tax affect the equilibrium price of hotel rooms?

c. How does the elimination of the tax affect the wages of hotel workers?

d. Is the change in the price greater than, less than, or equal to $20? Why?

5.8 **Shifting a Housecleaning Tax.** Consider a city where poor people clean the houses of rich people. Initially, housecleaning firms charge their customers $10 per hour, keep $1 per hour for administrative costs, and pay their workers $9 per hour. Like many luxury goods, the demand for housecleaning service is very elastic. Housecleaning workers are not very responsive to changes in the wage.

a. Use supply and demand curves to show the initial equilibrium in the market for cleaning services (price = $10 per hour; quantity = 1,000 hours of cleaning per week), and label the equilibrium as point *a*.

b. Suppose the city imposes a tax of $3 per hour on cleaning services, and one-third of the tax is shifted forward to consumers. Use your graph to show the effects of the tax on the housecleaning market. Label the new equilibrium as point *b*. What is the new price?

c. Is it reasonable that only one-third of the tax is shifted forward? Explain.

d. Suppose that firms continue to keep $1 per hour for administrative costs. Predict the new wage.

e. Who bears the bulk of the housecleaning tax, wealthy households or poor ones?

5.9 **Effects of a Higher Fish Tax.** In Figure 21.10 on page 456, suppose the fish tax is $2 per pound of fish instead of $1. Draw a graph to show the effect of the $2 tax. In the new equilibrium, the price is $________, the quantity is ________, and the deadweight loss from the tax is $________.

5.10 **Tax Eliminates a Market?** Use a supply and demand graph to show a situation in which a tax on no. 3 pencils reduces the equilibrium quantity of no. 3 pencils to zero.

ECONOMIC EXPERIMENT

GOVERNMENT INTERVENTION

Recall the market equilibrium experiment from Chapter 4. We can modify that experiment to show the various forms of government intervention in the market. After several trading periods without any government intervention, you can change the rules as follows:

- The instructor sets a maximum price for apples.
- The instructor sets a minimum price for apples.
- The instructor issues licenses to a few lucky producers.
- The instructor divides producers into domestic producers and foreign producers, and some of the foreign producers are excluded from the market.

NOTES

1. Edward L. Glaeser, Joseph Gyourko, Raven Saks, "Why is Manhattan So Expensive? Regulations and the Rise in Housing Prices," *Journal of Law and Economics* 48 (2005), pp. 331–369.

2. J. K. Smith, "An Analysis of State Regulations Governing Liquor Store Licensees," *Journal of Law and Economics* (October 1982): 301–319; David Kirp and Eileen Soffer, "Taking Californians to the Cleaners," *Regulation* (September–October 1985): 24–26.

3. D. W. Taylor, "The Economic Effects of Direct Regulation of Taxicabs in Metropolitan Toronto," *Logistics and Transportation Review* (June 1989): 169–182; Laura Brown, "Hub Cabbie Hopefuls Cry: The Russians Are Coming!" *Boston Herald*, December 16, 1998.

4. *The Economic Effects of Significant U.S. Import Restraints* (Washington, D.C.: U.S. International Trade Commission), initial report in 1993, update in 1996; Joseph F. François, Hans-Hinrich Glismann, Dean Spinanger, "The Cost of EU Trade Protection in Textiles and Clothing," Kiel Institute for the World Economy, March 2000, 49.

5. Laura Brown, "Hub Cabbie Hopefuls Cry: The Russians Are Coming!" *Boston Herald*, December 16, 1998.

CHAPTER

22

Consumer Choice: Utility Theory and Insights from Neuroscience

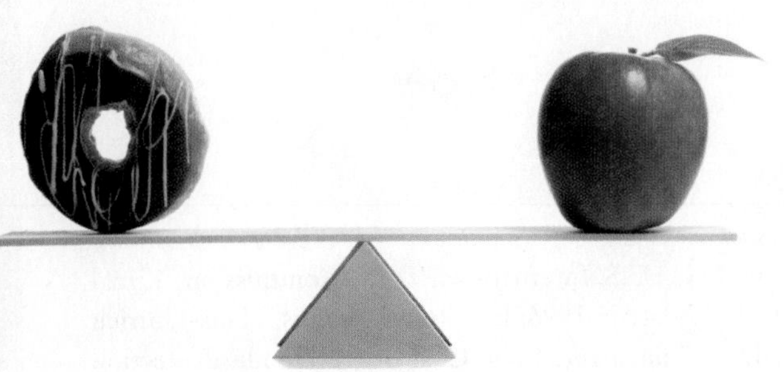

Consumer choice often involves a battle between instant and delayed gratification. For example, a consumer might choose between a donut, with its immediate taste and sugar sensations, and an apple, with its contribution to future health.

In fact, the very act of consumption involves a choice of spending money now rather than saving for the future. The outcome of the battle between instant and delayed gratification is determined by a person's self-control.

Scientists have been exploring the mental processes involved in self-control. One line of inquiry led to the following question: *Why do societies have curse words that everyone knows but no one is supposed to use?* One possibility is that suppressing the urge to use a curse word strengthens our self-control systems in the same way that calisthenics like jumping jacks strengthen our muscles. Calisthenics are not useful by themselves, but they build up our muscles for tasks that really matter. Perhaps resisting the urge to curse builds up our willpower to help resist the urge to eat unhealthy food, smoke tobacco, and go into debt.

A number of experiments have shown that seemingly trivial exercises improve self-control. In one experiment, subjects were told to improve their posture, sitting up straight rather than slouching. After two weeks of resisting the urge to slouch, the subjects performed much better on tasks that required self-control. By overriding their habit of slouching, the subjects boosted their willpower and stamina in tasks that had nothing to do with posture. Similar improvements in self-control occurred for right-handed subjects who switched to the left hand to perform everyday tasks.[1]

LEARNING OBJECTIVES

- Explain the equimarginal principle and apply it to consumer choice.
- Describe the income and substitution effects of a price change.
- Describe the general process involved in the valuation of the benefits and costs of a consumer good.
- Apply the insights from neuroscience to consumer decisions about nutrition and saving.

MyEconLab

MyEconLab helps you master each objective and study more efficiently.

In Chapter 4, we introduced the law of demand, which is shown graphically by a negatively sloped demand curve. In this chapter, we'll use the theory of consumer choice to provide the economic logic behind the law of demand. The theory is based on the notion that consumers maximize their level of satisfaction, or utility, given the constraints dictated by their income and the prices of consumer goods. As we'll see, every point on a demand curve represents the best affordable choice for a consumer at a particular price.

The first two parts of this chapter use traditional utility theory to explore consumer decision-making. Under the utilitarian framework developed by Jeremy Bentham and John Stuart Mill in the eighteenth century, every action generates a benefit ("pleasure" to the utilitarians) and a cost ("pain" to the utilitarians), and taking an action is sensible if the benefit exceeds the cost. Applying the marginal principle to the consumer choice problem, a consumer will buy a product if the marginal benefit exceeds the marginal cost. We will use this utilitarian logic to explain the law of demand and the negatively sloped demand curve.

The first two parts of the chapter provide a self-contained treatment of traditional consumer choice and demand theory. So it is possible to stop at the end of Part 2 and still get a thorough understanding of consumer decision making and the law of demand. In other words, the third and fourth parts of the chapter can be skipped without loss of continuity.

The third part of the chapter introduces recent advances in neuroscience that are relevant to consumer decision-making. In the last few decades, neuroscientists have explored the brain activity associated with making decisions, and can now map and measure the neural activity involved in consumer choice. Specifically, neuroscientists observe neural activity representing both the benefit and the cost of consuming a product. Based on the observed neural activity, neuroscientists can predict consumer choice: if the benefit activity is stronger than the cost activity, a consumer is likely to buy the product. In other words, the utilitarians got it right: consumers base their decisions on the benefits and costs of a particular product. And the utilitarians were correct in imagining that some day it would be possible to actually measure the utility associated with consuming a product.

The fourth part of the chapter integrates some insights from neuroscience into our model of consumer choice. We can use the integrated model to address the following questions.

- Why do consumers eat unhealthy food? Why so many donuts and so few apples?
- Why do people save so little money for the future?
- Why do most people who want to quit smoking fail in their efforts to quit?
- Why do people play lotteries when the typical player pays \$10 to get an average payoff of about \$5?

The lessons from neuroscience help explain puzzling consumer behavior. In addition, we can use the insights from neuroscience to identify strategies to change consumer behavior—to eat fewer donuts, to save more money, and to quit smoking.

22.1 Traditional Consumer Choice: Utility Theory

Consider a consumer who has a fixed budget to spend on movies (m) and books (b). The consumer's objective is to maximize its level of utility (satisfaction), subject to its budget constraint. In other words, the consumer wants to find the best affordable bundle of movies and books.

Consumer Constraints: The Budget Line

A consumer's ability to purchase movies and other goods is limited by her income and the prices of movies and other products. Suppose the consumer has a fixed income of \$27 per month, which she spends entirely on movies and books. The price of movies is \$3 and the price of books is \$1.

A consumer's budget line shows all the combinations of two goods that exhaust the budget. In Figure 22.1, if the consumer spends her entire $27 budget on books, she gets 27 books and no movies (point *r*). At the other extreme, she can spend her entire budget on movies, getting 9 movies at a price of $3 per movie (point *v*). The points between these two extremes are possible too. For example, she could reach point *s* (1 movie and 24 books) by spending $3 on movies and $24 on books, or point *u* (6 movies and 9 books) by spending $18 on movies and $9 on books.

The slope of the budget line is the opportunity cost of a movie in terms of books. Mathematically, the slope is the ratio of the price of the good shown on the horizontal axis (movies, with a price of $3), to the price of the good shown on the vertical axis (books, with a price of $1). In this example, the slope is 3 books per movie: a movie is three times as expensive as a book, so the opportunity cost of a movie is the three books that could be purchased instead.

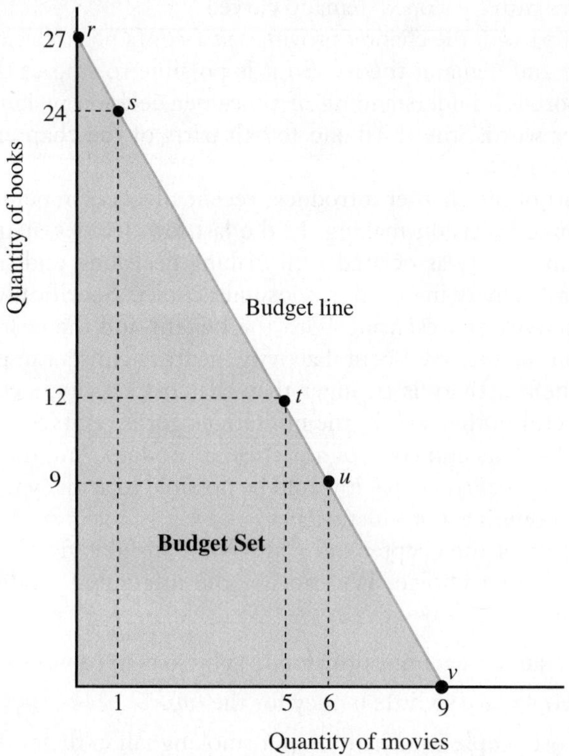

▲ **FIGURE 22.1**
Budget Set and Budget Line
The budget set (the shaded triangle) shows all the affordable combinations of books and movies, and the budget line (with endpoints *r* and *v*) shows the combinations that exhaust the budget.

A consumer's budget set is the set of affordable combinations of two goods. The budget set includes the budget line—combinations that exhaust the budget—as well as combinations that cost less than the consumer has to spend, leaving the consumer with leftover money. In Figure 22.1, the consumer's budget set is shown as a shaded triangle. She can afford any combination on or below the budget line, but cannot afford combinations above it.

It's important to distinguish the budget line from a demand curve. Although the budget line may look similar to a consumer's demand curve, they are very different graphical tools. The budget line shows the different combinations of two goods that a consumer can buy. In contrast, the demand curve shows the quantity of a single good that a consumer is willing to buy at different prices.

Total and Marginal Utility

The consumer's objective is to maximize its utility. The upper panel of Figure 22.2 shows the relationship between the number of movies watched and the total utility from movies. As the number of movies increases, total utility increases. The utility from 5 movies (point *a*) is 225 utils and the utility from 6 movies (point *b*) is 261 utils, so the marginal utility of the sixth movie is 36 utils (261 – 225). This is shown in the lower panel of Figure 22.1 by point *e*, where the marginal utility of the sixth movie is 36 utils. As the number of movies increases, utility increases, but at a decreasing rate. The utility from 9 movies (point *d*, 351 utils) is 27 utils greater than the utility from 8 movies (point *c*, 324 utils). This is shown in the lower panel by point *f*, where the marginal utility of the ninth movie is 27 utils. As the number of movies increases, utility will continue to increase, but at a decreasing rate.

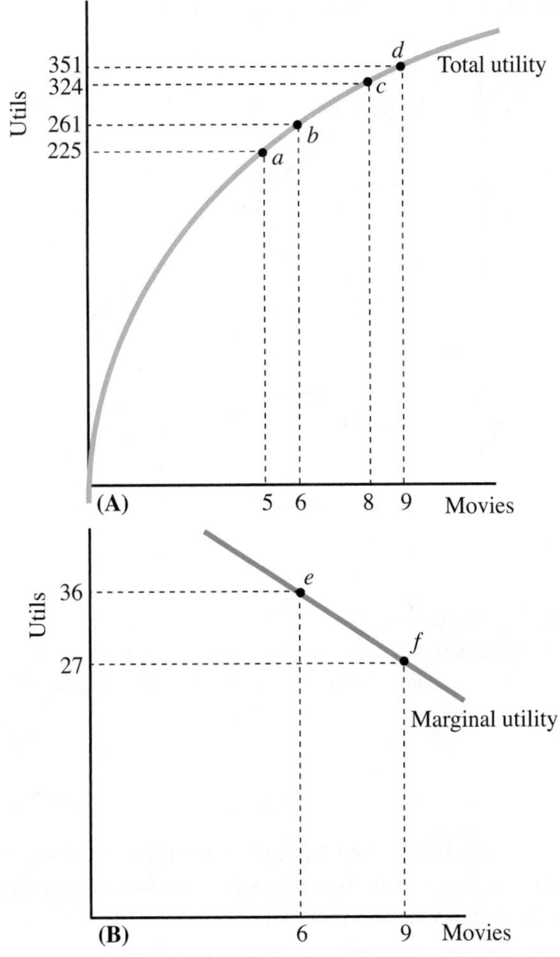

▲ FIGURE 22.2
Total Utility and Marginal Utility
A: The total utility or satisfaction from movies increases with the number of movies, but at a decreasing rate. B: The marginal utility from movies decreases as the number of movies increases.

The shapes of the utility curves reflect the law of diminishing marginal utility. The basic idea is that the first unit of a product generates more additional satisfaction or utility than the second unit, which generates more additional utility than the third, and so on. In graphical terms, this means that as the number of movies increases, the total utility curve becomes progressively flatter: the slope of the total utility curve decreases. The marginal utility curve shows the slope of the total utility curve, so by the law of diminishing marginal utility, it is negatively sloped.

It will be useful to derive one more utility curve. In Figure 22.3, the upper curve is the familiar marginal-utility curve, with a marginal utility of 36 utils for the 6th movie, compared to 27 utils for the 9th movie. The lower curve shows the marginal utility per dollar on movies, assuming that the price of movies is \$3. For the 6th movie, the marginal utility per dollar spent on movies is 12 utils (36 utils/\$3). At the margin, each dollar spent on movies (each dollar spent on the 6th movie) increases the consumer's utility by 12 utils. In popular language, this is the marginal bang per buck spent on movies: the increase in consumer utility (bang) per dollar (buck). As shown by point *d*, the marginal utility per dollar spent on the 9th movie is 9 utils (27 utils/\$3). The marginal bang per buck decreases from 12 utils for the 6th movie to 9 utils for the 9th movie, reflecting the law of diminishing marginal utility.

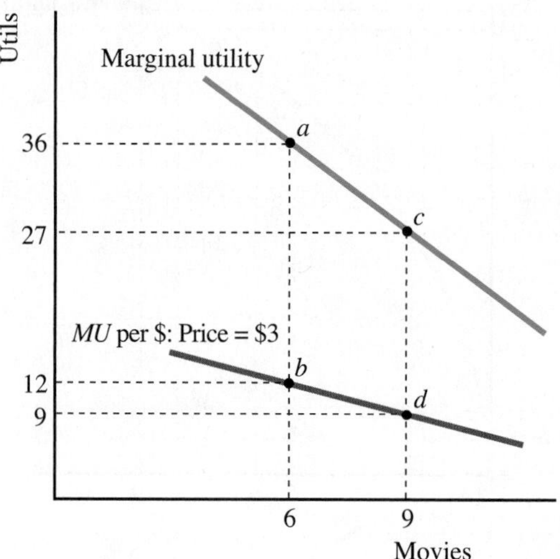

▲ **FIGURE 22.3**
Marginal Utility and Marginal Utility per Dollar
The marginal utility of movies decreases as the number of movies increases, reflecting the assumption of diminishing marginal utility. The marginal utility per dollar equals the marginal utility divided by the price of movies.

The Marginal Principle and the Equimarginal Rule

Consider a consumer who has a fixed budget to spend on movies (*m*) and books (*b*). We can use the marginal principle to model the consumer's decision about how to allocate the budget between the two products.

MARGINAL PRINCIPLE

Increase the level of an activity as long as its marginal benefit exceeds its marginal cost. Choose the level at which the marginal benefit equals the marginal cost.

To maximize utility, a consumer picks the quantity of a product at which the marginal benefit of the product equals its marginal cost. For a movie, the benefit is the utility generated by the movie, so the marginal benefit is simply the marginal utility of a movie.

$$\text{MB(movie)} - MU_m$$

The law of diminishing returns tells us that the marginal benefit decreases as the number of movies increases.

Consider next the cost associated with consuming a product. To compute the marginal cost of a movie, we use the principle of opportunity cost.

THE PRINCIPLE OF OPPORTUNITY COST

The opportunity cost of something is what you sacrifice to get it.

For a consumer who buys movies and books, the opportunity cost of a movie is the utility sacrificed by getting one movie rather than some number of books. The number of books sacrificed per movie is determined by the prices of the two goods. The number of books sacrificed per movie equals the price of movies divided by the price of books:

$$\text{Books per Movie} - \frac{p_m}{p_b}$$

For example, if $p_m = 3$ and $p_b = 1$, movies are three times as expensive as books, so the consumer sacrifices three books per movie. In utility terms, the marginal cost of a movie (the utility lost from getting one movie rather than some number of books) equals the number of books sacrificed times the marginal utility of books (the utility lost per book):

$$\text{MC(movie)} - \frac{p_m}{p_b} MU_b$$

For example, if the price ratio is 3 and the marginal utility of a book is 12 utils, the marginal cost of a movie is 3 books sacrificed per movie times the 12 utils lost per book not purchased, or 36 utils.

To satisfy the marginal principle, the marginal benefit of movies equals the marginal cost. Using the expressions for the marginal benefit and the marginal cost of movies, the marginal benefit equals the marginal cost if

$$MU_m - \frac{p_m}{p_b} MU_b$$

We can rewrite this in a more convenient way. If we divide both sides of the equation by p_m we get

$$\frac{MU_m}{p_m} - \frac{MU_b}{p_b}$$

To satisfy the marginal principle, a consumer chooses the quantities of movies and books such that the marginal utility per dollar spent on movies equals the marginal utility per dollar spent on books. This is the equimarginal rule:

EQUIMARGINAL RULE

Pick the combination of two activities where the marginal benefit per dollar for the first activity equals the marginal benefit per dollar for the second activity.

In other words, the consumer chooses the quantities of movies and books such that the two products have the marginal bang per buck (the same marginal utility per dollar).

Conditions for Utility Maximization

The consumer's objective is to maximize the utility generated by a fixed budget. Utility is maximized when the chosen bundle of goods satisfies two conditions.

1 *Equimarginal rule.* The equimarginal rule is satisfied: the marginal utility per dollar on movies equals the marginal utility per dollar on books.
2 *Affordability.* The money spent on the two goods adds up to the fixed budget for the two goods: the chosen bundle is just affordable, meaning that it is on the budget line.

To summarize, the consumer chooses the affordable bundle that satisfies the equimarginal rule.

Figure 22.4 illustrates utility maximization for a consumer with a budget of $27 for movies and books. The left panel shows the marginal utility per dollar on movies, assuming a movie price of $3. The right panel shows the marginal utility per dollar on books, assuming a book price of $1. Points *a* and *b* show the utility-maximizing bundle of 6 movies and 9 books.

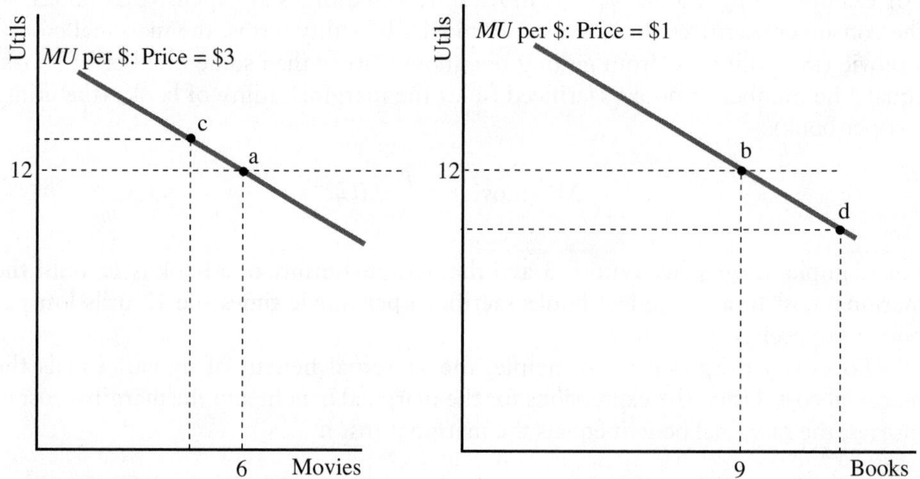

▲ FIGURE 22.4
The Equimarginal Rule: Equalize the Marginal Benefit per Dollar
The consumer picks the affordable bundle at which the marginal utility per dollar on movies equals the marginal utility per dollar on books. This is shown by point *a* (6 movies) and point *b* (9 books). Starting from any other affordable combination, the consumer can do better by reallocating the budget in favor of the good with the larger marginal utility per dollar. For example, starting from points *c* and *d*, movies have a larger marginal utility per dollar, so the consumer can increase utility by choosing more movies and fewer books.

1 *Equimarginal rule.* For each good, the marginal utility per dollar is 12 utils.
2 *Affordability.* The consumer spends $18 on movies ($3 × 6 movies) and $9 on books ($1 × 9 books), for a total of $27. This corresponds to point *u* in Figure 22.1.

The bundle is affordable and satisfies the equimarginal rule, so it generates the highest affordable utility level.

We can illustrate the logic of the equimarginal rule by showing what happens when it is violated. Consider another bundle, the one shown by points *c* (fewer than 6 movies), and *d* (more than 9 books). This bundle does not satisfy the equimarginal rule: the marginal utility per dollar for movies (greater than 12 utils per dollar) exceeds the marginal utility per dollar for books (less than 12 utils per dollar). For one dollar switched from books to movies, the gain in movie utility (the marginal utility per dollar of movies) exceeds the loss in book utility (the marginal utility per dollar of books), so the consumer's utility increases. Starting from points *c* and *d*, a consumer can do better by spending more on movies, the product with the larger marginal bang per buck. In general, whenever the equimarginal rule is violated—whenever the marginal utility per dollar of one good exceeds the marginal utility per dollar on a second good—the consumer can increase utility by shifting the budget in favor of the good with the larger marginal bang per buck.

Table 22.1 provides a detailed view of the utility-maximization process. The first two columns show the affordable bundles of movies and books, that is, the bundles on the consumer's budget line shown in Figure 22.1. Columns 3 and 4 show the marginal utility numbers for movies and books. Moving down through the table, the number of movies increases, and, consistent with the law of diminishing marginal utility, the marginal utility of movies decreases, from 51 utils for the first movie to 48 utils for the second movie, and so on. As we move down through the table, the number of affordable books decreases, so the marginal utility of books increases, from 2 utils for the 24th book, to 4 utils for the 21st book, and so on. Columns 5 and 6 show the numbers for the marginal utility per dollar for movies and books, assuming a movie price of $3 and a book price of $1. As we move down through the table, the marginal bang per buck of movies decreases, from 17 utils to 16 utils, and so on, while the marginal bang per buck of books increases, from 2 utils to 4 utils, and so on.

TABLE 22.1 Utility Maximization

Movies	Books	Marginal Utility: Movies	Marginal Utility: Books	Marginal Utility per $: Movies	Marginal Utility per $: Books	Utility from Movies	Utility from Books	Total Utility
1	24	51	2	17	2	51	216	267
2	21	48	4	16	4	99	210	309
3	18	45	6	15	6	144	198	342
4	15	42	8	14	8	186	180	366
5	12	39	10	13	10	225	156	381
6	**9**	**36**	**12**	**12**	**12**	**261**	**126**	**387**
7	6	33	14	11	14	294	90	384
8	3	30	16	10	16	324	48	372

The last three columns of Table 22.1 show that utility is maximized when the equimarginal rule is satisfied. In column 7, the utility from movies increases from 51 utils for one movie to 99 utils for two movies (51 from the first movie + 48 from the second movies), to 144 for three movies (51 + 48 + 45), and so on. To compute

application 1

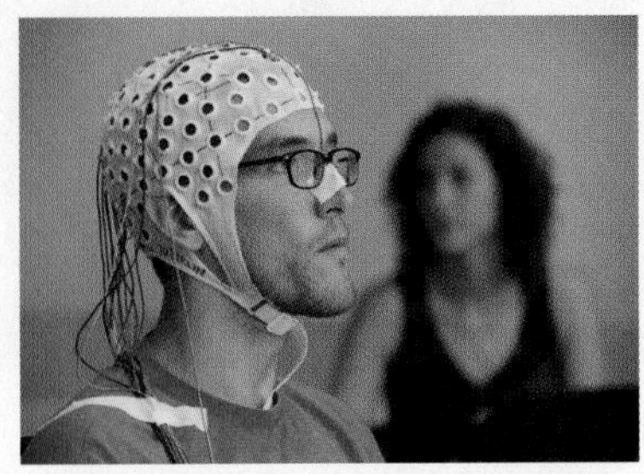

MEASURING DIMINISHING MARGINAL UTILITY

APPLYING THE CONCEPTS #1: How does marginal utility change with the quantity consumed?

Neuroscientists have used brain imaging techniques to provide some insights into the law of diminishing marginal utility. The scientists offered subjects in an experiment varying monetary rewards, and observed the neural activity in a subject's striatum, the region of the brain responsible for the valuation of rewards. As the monetary reward increased, the subjective benefit (the utility value, as measured in neuron activity) increased, but at a decreasing rate. In other words, the larger the reward, the lower the marginal utility of the reward money. For example, starting with a $15 reward, the marginal utility was 1 util per dollar, but starting with a $150 reward, the marginal utility was only 0.25 utils per dollar. Although this experiment does not provide a direct demonstration of the law of diminishing marginal utility for a particular product, it does show that general rewards are subject to diminishing marginal utility. **Related to Exercise 1.10.**

the numbers in Column 8, we work from the bottom up. From the bottom of Column 2, for the first three books, the marginal utility per book is 16 utils, so the utility from the first 3 books is 48 utils. Working upward, the additional utility from the next trio of books is 42 (equal to 14 utils per book times 3 books), so the utility from 6 books is 90 utils (48 + 42). Continuing to move upward in Column 8, the utility from books increases to 126 utils for 9 books, 156 for 12 books, and so on. Column 9 shows total utility, the sum of utility from movies and books. Moving down through the column, total utility increases from 267 (equal to 51 + 216), to 309, and so on until we reach a total of 387 utils with the bundle of 6 movies and 9 books. Beyond that point, total utility decreases. As shown by the bold numbers in the row associated with 6 movies and 9 books, utility is maximized when the equimarginal rule is satisfied: the marginal utility per dollar of movies (12 utils = 36 utils/$3) equals the marginal utility per dollar of books (12 utils = 12 utils/$1).

22.2 The Law of Demand and the Individual Demand Curve

We can use our model of consumer choice to demonstrate the law of demand and derive an individual demand curve. In addition, we can decompose the effect of a change in price into two effects: the substitution effect and the income effect.

Effect of a Decrease in Price

Suppose the price of movies decreases from $3 to $2. In the left panel of Figure 22.5, the curve shifts upward: a decrease in price increases the marginal utility per dollar of movies. In other words, the lower the price of movies, the larger the marginal bang per buck for movies. For the original choice of 6 movies, the marginal bang per buck increases from 12 utils (36 utils/$3, shown by point *a*) to 18 utils (36 utils/$2, shown by point *c*).

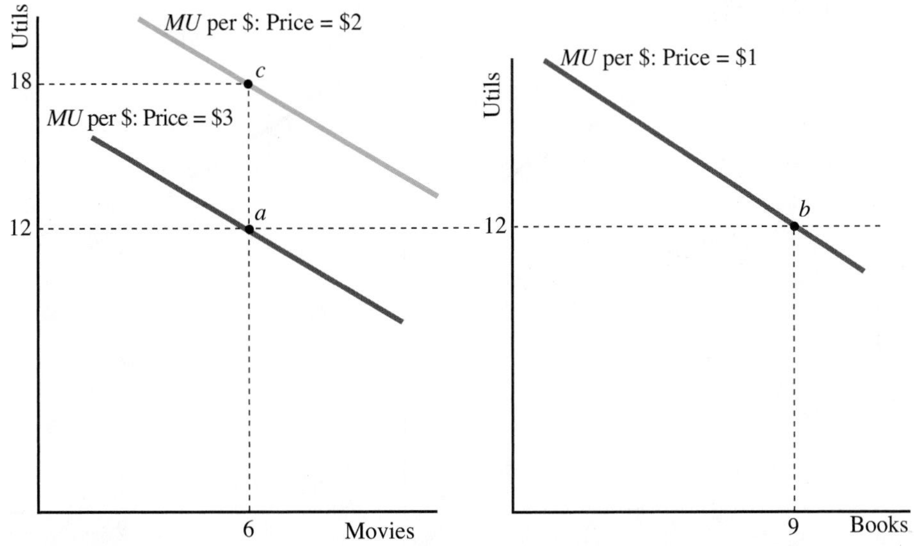

▲ FIGURE 22.5
A Decrease in the Price of Movies Increases the Utility-Maximizing Number of Movies
A decrease in the price of movies shifts the movie benefit curve (MU per $ of movies) upward. At the original bundle (6 movies and 9 books), the MU per $ of movies (18 utils at point *c*) exceeds the MU per $ of books (12 utils at point *b*), so the consumer increases the number of movies.

The decrease in the price of movies means that the original bundle violates the equimarginal rule. As shown by points *c* and *b*, the marginal utility per dollar on movies (18 utils) now exceeds the marginal utility per dollar on books (12 utils). Given the larger marginal bang per buck for movies, the rational consumer will reallocate the budget in favor of movies. In other words, a decrease in the price of movies increases the quantity of movies demanded: the consumer obeys the law of demand.

How far will the consumer go in response to a decrease in the price of movies? In Figure 22.6, the consumer chooses points *d* and *e*, with 10 movies and 7 books. This bundle satisfies the two conditions for utility maximization.

1 *Equimarginal rule.* For each good, the marginal utility per dollar is 14 utils.
2 *Affordability.* The consumer spends $20 on movies ($2 × 10 movies) and $7 on books, for a total of $27.

In this case, a decrease in the movie price from $3 to $2 increases the quantity of movies demanded from 6 to 10, consistent with the law of demand.

The same logic applies, in reverse, to an increase in the price of movies. An increase in price decreases the marginal utility per dollar on movies, shifting the marginal-bang-per-buck curve downward. At the original bundle of 6 movies and 9 books, the marginal bang per buck of movies will be less than the marginal bang per buck of books (12 utils). The consumer will respond by reallocating the budget away from movies, consistent with the law of demand: An increase in price decreases the quantity of movies demanded.

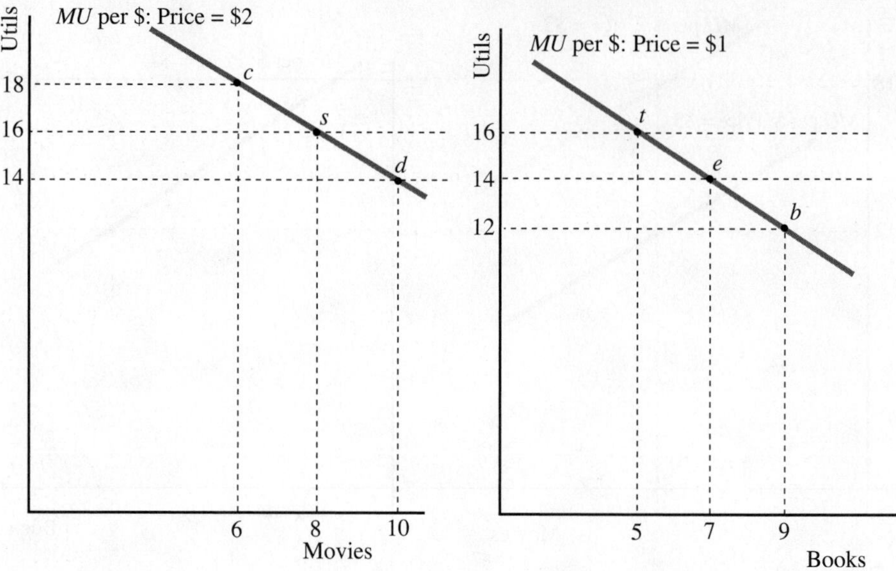

▲ **FIGURE 22.6**

Income and Substitution Effects of a Decrease in Price

For a price of movies of $2, utility is maximized at points *d* and *e*, with 10 movies and 7 books. The move from point *c* to point *s* is the substitution effect of the decrease in price, and the move from point *s* to point *d* is the income effect of the decrease in price.

Income and Substitution Effects of a Decrease in Price

We've seen that a decrease in price increases the quantity of movies demanded. We can break down the increase in the quantity demanded into two separate effects. The first is the substitution effect.

- **Substitution effect.** A decrease in the price of movies decreases the price of movies relative to the price of books, causing the consumer to substitute movies for books.

We can show the substitution effect with a simple thought experiment. Suppose that when price of movies decreases from $3 to $2, we decrease the consumer's nominal income from $27 to $21. In other words, the consumer's nominal income drops by $6, leaving just enough money to afford the original bundle of 6 movies (a cost of $12) and 9 books (a cost of $9). The price reduction is exactly offset by the $6 decrease in nominal income, meaning that the consumer's real income hasn't changed.

If the original bundle of movies and books is just affordable at the lower price, will the consumer choose it? As shown by points *c* and *b* in Figure 22.6, the still-affordable original bundle of 6 movies and 9 books violates the equimarginal rule: the marginal bang per buck of movies is 18 utils, compared to 12 utils for books. The consumer will reallocate the $21 budget in favor of movies. The new movie price is twice the book price, so for each additional movie, the consumer sacrifices 2 books. In Figure 22.6, the consumer moves downward along the movie curve, starting from point *c*, and moves upward along the book curve, starting from point *b*.

The consumer will continue to shift money toward movies at a 2:1 rate until the equimarginal rule is satisfied. In Figure 22.6, this happens at point *s* for movies and point *t* for books, with a marginal utility per dollar of 16 utils for both movies and books. In the movie panel, the move from point *c* to point *s* is the substitution effect of the decrease in price. Holding the consumer's real income constant (by cutting the nominal income to make the original bundle just affordable), movie consumption increases from 6 to 8 movies.

The substitution effect is not the end of the consumer response to a decrease in price. The second response is the income effect.

- **Income effect.** A decrease in the price of movies increases the consumer's real income (purchasing power), and the consumer will buy more of all "normal" goods, including movies.

Recall that our thought experiment for the substitution effect cut nominal income by $6 to keep real income constant. To show the income effect of a decrease in price, we simply undo the $6 cut in nominal income. In other words, we give back the $6 and see how the consumer responds to the additional income.

The consumer will use the equimarginal rule to allocate the additional income. For each additional dollar, the consumer will spend the dollar on the good with the larger marginal utility per dollar. When the additional income is all spent, the marginal utility per dollar on movies will equal the marginal utility per dollar on books. In Figure 22.6, the consumer moves downward along the movie curve starting from point *s*, and moves downward along the book curve starting from point *t*. The movement downward along the curves continues until all the additional $6 is spent. In Figure 22.6, this happens at points *d* for movies and e for books.

- **Movies:** The quantity increases from 8 to 10, meaning that the consumer spends $4 of the additional $6 on movies. The income effect is the increase in movies from 8 to 10.
- **Books.** The quantity increases from 7 to 9, meaning that the consumer spends $2 of the additional $6 on books.

At points *d* and *e*, the equimarginal rule is satisfied: for both goods, the marginal utility per dollar is 14 utils.

We can summarize the two effects of a decrease in the price of movies. The substitution effect causes the move from point *c* to point *s*, an increase in movie consumption from 6 to 8 movies. The income effect causes the move from point *s* to point *d*, an increase in movie consumption from 8 to 10 movies. In this simple example, the substitution effect is equal to the income effect. In general, the substitution effect will not be the same as the income effect. But for normal goods, the two effects operate in the same direction. A decrease in price increases the relative attractiveness of the good, causing substitution in favor of the good (the substitution effect). In addition, a decrease in price increases the consumer's purchasing power (real income), increasing the quantity demanded of all normal goods (the income effect).

The Individual Demand Curve

Figure 22.7 shows the individual demand curve for our hypothetical consumer. At the initial price of $3, the consumer maximizes utility with 6 movies (point *i*). A decrease in price to $2 increases the quantity demanded to 10 movies (point *j*). The move from point *i* to point *j* reflects both the substitution effect and the income effect of a decrease in price. The consumer observes the law of demand, consuming a larger quantity of movies because (a) movies are less costly relative to books and other goods (the substitution

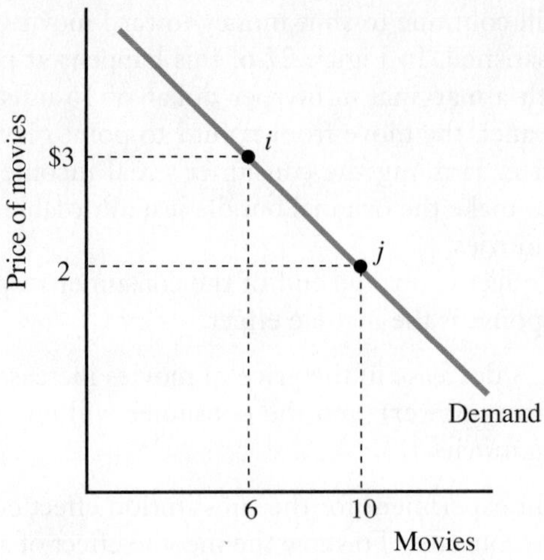

▲ **FIGURE 22.7**
The Individual Demand Curve
When the price of a movie is \$3, the consumer maximizes utility at point *i*, with 6 movies. At a price of \$2, utility is maximized at point *j*, with 10 movies.

application 2

A REVENUE-NEUTRAL GASOLINE TAX

APPLYING THE CONCEPTS #2: How would a simultaneous increase in the gasoline tax and a decrease in the income tax affect gasoline consumption?

Suppose the national government imposes a new tax of \$3 per gallon gasoline, which will bring gasoline taxation in the U.S. closer to the levels experienced in European countries. And suppose the gasoline tax is combined with a cut in income taxes to ensure that total tax revenue doesn't change. In other words, the gasoline tax is revenue neutral. How will such a tax policy affect total gasoline consumption?

It may be tempting to conclude that the change in tax policy will not change gasoline consumption. After all, the policy doesn't change the tax liability of the typical taxpayer: the increase in gasoline taxes is offset by a decrease in income taxes. This was the logic of Ronald Reagan in his campaign for president against John Anderson, who proposed a revenue-neutral increase in the gasoline tax. Reagan said that the idea was silly because it simply took money from one of the taxpayer's pockets and put it back into the other pocket.

This logic is faulty because it ignores the substitution effect of a price change. For example, consider the typical taxpayer Mr. Evgeny Slutsky, who buys 300 gallons of gasoline per year. He will pay \$900 in gasoline taxes per year, while his income taxes will be cut by \$900 per year. So Evgeny can still afford to do what he did before the change in taxes: his original bundle of gasoline and other goods is still affordable. Although Evgeny can still afford his original choice, that's not the best choice. As we've seen in our discussion of the substitution effect, the gas tax decreases the marginal utility per dollar spent on gasoline, which is now less than the marginal utility per dollar spent on other goods. Gasoline now generates a lower marginal bang per buck, and the rational response for Evgeny is to buy less gasoline and more of the other goods, which now have a larger marginal bang per buck. This is the substitution effect in action, and we know for sure that a revenue-neutral increase in the gasoline tax will decrease gasoline consumption. **(Related to Exercise 2.8.)**

effect) and (b) the decrease in price increases the consumer's real income, increasing the quantity of all "normal" goods, including movies (the income effect).

We could use the same process to derive other points on the individual demand curve. For example, an increase in price would generate substitution and income effects that decrease the quantity of movies demanded.

- **Substitution effect.** An increase in the price of movies increases the price of movies relative to the price of books, causing the consumer to substitute books for movies.
- **Income effect.** An increase in the price of movies decreases the consumer's real income (purchasing power), and the consumer will buy less of all "normal" goods, including movies.

The key lesson is that each point on a demand curve shows the utility-maximizing choice for a particular price.

22.3 The Neuroscience of Consumer Choice

In this part of the chapter we explore the mental processes involved in consumer decision-making. Neuroscientists have developed techniques to map and measure the brain activity involved in the valuation of the benefits and costs of various actions, including a consumer's product choice. By integrating the insights from neuroscience into our economic model of consumer choice, we can gain a deeper understanding of how consumers make decisions and why consumers sometimes make choices that appear to be irrational.

The Neuroscience of Benefit Valuation

Recent work in neuroscience shows that different regions of the brain are involved in the valuation of the benefits and costs of possible actions. Starting on the benefit side, the key region for the valuation of benefits is the Nucleus Accumbens (NAcc), the main part of the ventral striatum. When a person considers taking an action, the NAcc is activated, and the greater the anticipated benefit from the action, the stronger the NAcc activity. For example, if you think about buying an apple, your NAcc will be activated, and the more you expect to enjoy an apple, the stronger the brain activity. The strength of the NAcc activity associated with a particular product is determined by past experience. If you've had good apple experiences in the past, the NAcc activity generated by thinking about eating an apple will be relatively strong.

The calibration of the regions of the brain involved in benefit valuation comes from the brain's dopamine system. Dopamine is the reward chemical of the brain—when it flows over receptors in your brain, you feel good. When you consider buying a product such as an apple, your brain uses its past experience to form a conjecture about the likely pleasure and satisfaction from eating the apple. The greater the conjectured satisfaction, the greater the flow of dopamine to the receptors in your brain. It's important to note that the dopamine flow starts before you eat the apple. When you actually eat the apple, your brain will check its reward systems to see if its conjecture about the pleasure from the apple is realized. If the conjectures are realized—if the brain correctly predicted the pleasure—the (correct) dopamine flow continues.

Learning happens when a consumer's conjectures about the pleasure of consuming a product are wrong. For example, suppose you anticipate a sweet apple and thus have a large dopamine flow, but the first bite generates a sour taste. The invalidation of the brain's conjecture causes an abrupt decrease in the dopamine flow, causing an abrupt reduction of the good feelings produced by dopamine. The brain is especially sensitive to a decrease in the flow of dopamine, so the sour apple provides a memorable lesson: Some apples are sour. The next time you consider eating an apple, your conjectured pleasure—and dopamine flow—will be lower. In the other direction, if you are pleasantly surprised by the wonderful taste of an apple, you will update and upgrade your conjectures for the next time you consider eating an apple. Over years or decades of consumption, errors in benefit conjectures allow the brain to fine-tune its valuation of the benefits of different products. In effect, the dopamine system allows us to learn from our mistakes, honing our valuation of the benefit of all sorts of products.

How does your brain assess the benefit of a product you've never consumed? For a new product, the brain uses the notion of association, basing its benefit valuation on past experiences with similar products. For example, the first time you consider eating a pear, your brain may associate the pear with a look-alike fruit such as an apple, triggering NAcc activity of a similar strength. Over decades of choices, the NAcc uses the dopamine system to learn the benefits of a wide variety of products, providing an inventory of benefit valuations that can be used directly for repeat purchases and used indirectly for new products.

It's important to note that these benefit valuations are gut feelings that occur without any thinking or reflection. When you see an apple, the NAcc benefit valuation is instantaneous, without any conscious thought of the taste and the rewards from reducing your hunger. These gut feelings are calibrated by the dopamine trial and error system. Given the discomfort of the penalty for an error (the interruption of the dopamine flow), the brain quickly hones its benefit conjectures to more closely match the actual benefits from consuming the product.

The Neuroscience of Cost Valuation

On the cost side, the key regions for cost valuation are the insular cortex (insula for short) and the amygdala. These interconnected regions express aversion to various actions. For example, activity in the insula increases when you see someone in pain or imagine a foul odor. Insula activity also increases when you consider losing something of value such as money. The aversion to spending money is consistent with the principle of opportunity cost.

PRINCIPLE OF OPPORTUNITY COST

The opportunity cost of something is what you sacrifice to get it.

The money spent on one product cannot be used on another product, so it is natural that the brain reacts in a negative way (in the region that expresses aversion) to the thought of spending money. The higher the price of a product, the greater the opportunity cost of the product, and thus the stronger the activity of the insula.

It is not yet clear to neuroscientists how the insula is calibrated to represent, in neuron activity, the cost of buying a product. The leading theory is that the value of money is learned from conditioned association. For example, suppose you lose $10 (by misplacing it, giving it away, or spending it on a product), and that means you can't buy a $10 book you really want. You will experience a gut-feeling sense of loss from not getting the book. This gut feeling comes from a certain level of neuron activity, which you then associate with the $10 loss. If you lose $20 and then cannot go to a $20 concert, the loss of the concert opportunity will generate neuron activity that you will associate with the $20 loss. Over time, you will learn from experience what it means, in terms of neuron activity, to lose different amounts of money. This learning process incorporates the cost of spending money into your gut feelings. When you imagine spending a particular dollar amount, you will have an instantaneous gut-feeling reaction, a result of neuron activity that is based on learning from past experience. This learning process essentially builds opportunity cost into your gut feelings and neuron activity.

To summarize, neuron activity in the insula represents the dollar cost of buying a product. Although the mechanism that calibrates the insula has so far been elusive, we do know that the higher the price of a product, the stronger the insula activity. It's important to note that these cost valuations are gut feelings that occur without any thinking or reflection. When you look at the price tag on apple, the cost valuation in your insula is instantaneous.

The Wisdom of Gut Feelings

Scientists use a classic experiment, the Iowa Gambling Task, to demonstrate the power and wisdom of gut feelings. The subjects in the experiment draw cards from four different decks, and each card triggers either a monetary reward or a penalty. Two of the decks have favorable cards (on average, a positive payoff), and two have unfavorable cards (on average, a negative payoff and relatively large penalties). The subjects don't have any prior knowledge of the features of the decks, but they learn as they draw cards. The key question is, How long will it take for the subjects to start drawing exclusively from the favorable decks?

Scientists use skin-conductivity sensors attached to the subjects' hands to track their gut feelings. When the brain senses that a person is about to take a harmful action, it sends an alarm in the form of increased sweat production that increases the electrical conductivity of a subject's skin. In this case, the harmful action is reaching for an unfavorable deck and the possibility of a relatively large penalty. By observing the conductivity of the subjects' hands, scientists observe the timing of the gut-feeling alarm. On average, the alarm for the unfavorable decks starts after a subject has drawn only 10 cards. Based on only 10 trials, the dopamine learning system has seen enough: when the subject reaches for an unfavorable deck, the brain activates the sweat glands as a warning of an imminent harmful action.

Most subjects don't immediately heed the gut-feeling warning. On average, it takes a subject about 50 cards to respond to the warning and stop drawing from the unfavorable decks. At this point, the typical subject cannot explain why he or she started avoiding the unfavorable decks. Although the subjects' choices are affected by their gut feelings, they cannot articulate the reasons. After about 60 cards, the typical subject can finally explain their avoidance of the unfavorable decks.

The Iowa Gambling Task reminds us that the brain quickly processes lots of information without our knowledge. The dopamine learning system is unconscious, and generates gut feelings that are useful in assessing the benefits and costs of actions. Although the expression of the gut feelings is instantaneous, the feelings are based on experiences that go back hours or years. The brain is continuously monitoring our actions, using its dopamine learning system to hone its valuation of benefits and costs. Although we may not be able to articulate our gut feelings, these feelings reflect the wisdom of experience.

Scientists have used the Iowa Gambling Task to study the brain's learning system. They observed the choices of subjects whose amygdala (part of the cost-valuation system) was disabled. These subjects never learned to draw exclusively from the favorable deck. The data from skin conductivity tests explained their choices: the alarm system that warned normal subjects to avoid the unfavorable decks did not work in the disabled subjects. The disabling of the amygdala prevented the brain from learning which decks were unfavorable, so there were no gut-feeling alarms.

Cognition and Choice

To decide whether to take an action, a person compares the anticipated benefit of the action to its anticipated cost. The principal decision-making region of the brain is the prefrontal cortex (PFC). The PFC observes the benefit-valuation activity in various regions of the brain, and uses these activity levels as inputs into the decision-making process. In other words, the PFC uses gut feelings as inputs into the decision-making process.

Scientists have used variations on the Iowa Gambling Task to demonstrate the role of the PFC in decision-making. Scientists gave the task to people whose PFCs were disabled in the regions responsible for comparing gut-feeling benefits to gut-feeling costs. The subjects with disabled PFCs never learned to avoid the unfavorable decks, despite the fact that the regions of their brains responsible for valuing gut-feeling benefits and costs (NAcc and insula) functioned normally. This experiment shows the role of the PFC in processing benefit and cost information that originates in other regions of the brain.

The PFC is not a simple calculator of gut-feeling benefits and costs, but incorporates other factors into the decision-making process. The PFC uses cognition (conscious thought) to consider a broad set of possible consequences of an action. For example, suppose you have decided to buy either a donut or an apple, each of which costs $1. At the gut-feeling level, the consideration of each product will trigger activity in your NAcc in anticipation of the benefit of consumption, and this gut-feeling benefit will be transmitted to the PFC. Suppose the donut generates a stronger gut-feeling benefit, reflecting its delightful sugar and fat content. If you rely exclusively on your gut feeling, you will choose the donut. But you could use your PFC to incorporate other considerations into the decision. For example, you could stop to think about the health consequences of the high-fat donut. If the unfavorable health consequences of the donut seem large enough, you will ignore your gut feelings and choose the apple instead.

The dorsal-lateral portion of the PFC (DLPFC) is responsible for introducing other factors into the decision-making process. In particular, the DLPFC incorporates the possible future consequence of an action. Neuroscientists use transcranial magnetic stimulation (TMS) to down-regulate (partially disable) the DLPFC of subjects, and then observe their choices. The subjects with disabled DLPFCs make impulsive choices based on gut feelings rather than thoughtful choices based on cognition. For example, the subjects grab a small immediate reward rather than waiting a relatively short time for a larger reward. The general effect of disabling the DLPFC is to make the subjects more selfish and impulsive. In our example of the apple versus the donut, a person with a disabled DLPFC is more likely to choose the donut because he or she will ignore the long-term health consequences.

Why do people make different choices? People differ in two ways that are relevant to consumer decisions.

- **Strength of their gut feelings.** On the benefit side, consumers differ in the gut-feeling benefit of consuming a product, as represented by the strength of activity in the NAcc. On the cost side, consumers differ in the gut-feeling cost of spending money, as represented by the strength of activity in the insula. Consumers with relatively active insulas are tightwads (reluctant to spend money), while consumers with relatively quiet insulas are looser with their money.
- **Cognitive weighting.** Consumers who are relatively inactive in a cognitive sense tend to make impulsive purchases (the donut). In contrast, cognitively active consumers tend to exercise more self-control and make more thoughtful purchases (the apple). In one experiment, scientists were able to divide subjects into two groups: the self-controllers had relatively active DLPFCs, indicating lively cognition that generated non-impulsive behavior; the non-self-controllers had less active DLPFCs, indicating cognitive passivity that generated impulsive behavior.

Predicting Consumer Choice

We've seen that neuroscientists map and measure the brain activity associated with consumer decisions. After observing a consumer's brain activity while he or she considers different options, scientists can actually predict the consumer's choice. In the SHOP experiment (save holdings or purchase), scientists showed a consumer different products and prices, and observed the levels of activity in the NAcc (for benefit valuation), insula (for cost valuation), and PFC (benefit-cost analysis). The scientists used the observed activity levels to predict which product the consumer actually purchased. Although the scientists' predictions were not perfect, they were much better than would occur by chance.

Fuel for Cognition

As we've seen, the decision-making process that occurs in the PFC is complex. As a result, the cognitive process consumes a large amount of energy in supporting neurons as they perform their various tasks. The brain gets most of its energy from glucose (aka blood sugar), and operates effectively only when it has a plentiful supply of glucose.

To demonstrate the importance of glucose as brain fuel, scientists perform the following experiment. A subject is forced to make a series of decisions, each of which engages the cognitive process (considering benefits and costs and then making a choice). This engagement of the cognitive process burns glucose. After a long series of challenging decisions, the subject is asked to perform a task that requires cognition, for example solving a difficult puzzle. Compared to a control group (people who had not depleted their glucose by making decisions), the subjects were less persistent in trying to solve the puzzle. The simple lesson is that the depletion of cognitive fuel makes people less inclined to engage their cognitive systems.

The fuel requirements of cognition have important implications for consumer decision making. As we've seen, cognition can replace impulsive decisions (simply go with your gut) with thoughtful decisions that consider both gut feelings and other factors. A person with a low level of glucose is more likely to skip the energy-consuming cognitive process and make an impulsive decision. It doesn't take much energy to go with your gut feelings, and if you're low on fuel, that is the natural response.

Cognitive processing is particularly important in making consumer decisions that involve many options. To illustrate, consider the process of buying a new car, which typically involves a series of choices about style (color), performance (acceleration, fuel economy), and features (seats, sound systems). As a customer goes through a long series of decisions about style, performance, and features, each decision engages the cognitive process and consumes brain fuel. Eventually, the depletion of cognitive fuel causes decision fatigue, and the consumer is more likely to rely exclusively on gut feelings, making impulsive rather than thoughtful decisions.

The same logic applies when a consumer faces a large number of options for a single product. For example, consider a consumer who faces a display with 50 different types of toothbrushes. The consumer will naturally engage the cognitive process, assessing the benefits and costs of each toothbrush and weighing the trade-offs. Given the large number of options, the deliberative process will burn a lot of brain fuel and reduce the consumer's ability to effectively engage the cognitive process. A consumer may respond to the depletion of brain fuel in one of three ways: (a) simplify matters by focusing on a single dimension of the product (price, color, shine), (b) abandon cognition and make an impulse buy, or (c) abandon the decision-making process altogether and refrain from buying a toothbrush.

application 3

STORES VS. ONLINE RETAILERS

APPLYING THE CONCEPTS #3: How do the sales strategies of conventional stores and online retailers differ?

Conventional stores encourage shoppers to buy products by boosting the neural activity in the NAcc, the region of the brain responsible for the valuation of the benefit of a product. Some of the benefit boosting comes from tactile stimulation—feeling the softness of a cashmere sweater or the bounce of an athletic shoe. Conventional stores also down-regulate the insula, the region of the brain responsible for the valuation of the cost of a product. The suppression of insula activity comes from price reductions and low-price guarantees. On-line retailers can work with the insula by offering discounted prices and low-price guarantees, but they are at a disadvantage in boosting the neural activity in the NAcc. There is currently no substitute for the tactile sensations available in physical stores, so online retailers have an incentive to focus on products for which the stimulation of the NAcc is less critical to making a sale. **Related to Application 3.7.**

SOURCE: Based on Jonah Lehrer, "The Neuroscience of Groupon," *Wired*, September 8, 2011.

The problems caused by having too many options are illustrated by the famous jam experiment. Researchers ran the experiment in a fancy food store in Menlo Park, California. They set up a table with samples of jam, sometimes offering 6 different flavors, and other times offering 24 flavors. Although shoppers were more likely to stop by the table with more flavors, they were less likely to actually buy jam. After the taste test, only 3 percent of the shoppers at the 24-flavor table bought jam, compared to 30 percent at the 6-flavor table. The simple lesson is that sometimes having too many options makes it difficult to choose.

22.4 Consumer Decisions: Insights from Neuroscience

In this part of the chapter, we incorporate the key insights from neuroscience into our model of consumer choice. Specifically, we apply the equimarginal rule to several consumer decisions in which the engagement of the cognitive process—the forward-looking DLPFC—may change behavior as consumers switch from impulsive choices to more thoughtful choices. Some scientists speculate that the evolutionary development of the DLPFC in humans increased our fitness (likelihood of survival) because it gave us the ability to incorporate long-term considerations into the decision-making process.

Dietary Choice: Donut versus Apple

Consider the decision between healthy and unhealthy food. Suppose a consumer has a fixed budget of $10 to spend on apples and donuts, each of which has a price of $1. The gut-feeling benefit of the high-fat donut is relatively high: neuroscientists have shown that the subjective pleasantness of the oral texture of fat generates a high level of neural activity in the NAcc. In the left panel of Figure 22.8, the upper curve shows the gut-feeling marginal utility per dollar of donuts.

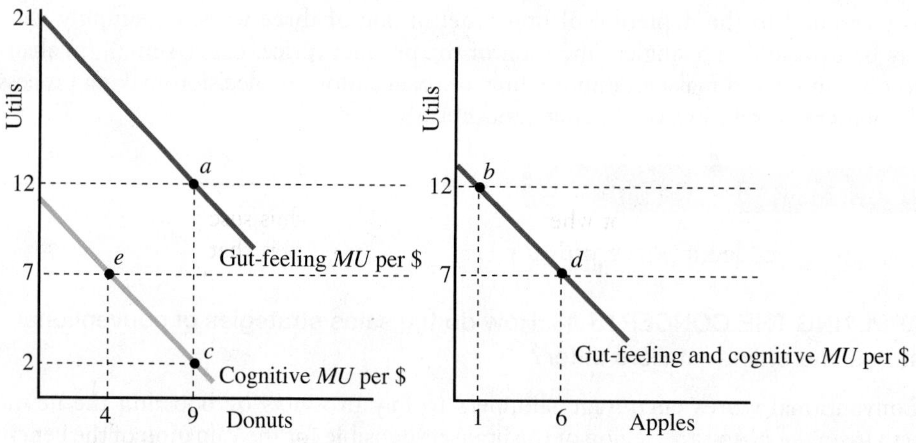

▲ FIGURE 22.8
Gut Feelings versus Cognition: Donuts versus Apples

For a decision based exclusively on gut feelings, a consumer using the equimarginal rule chooses points *a* and *b* (9 donuts and 1 apple). The engagement of the cognitive process decreases the perceived MU per $ of donuts, so at the original bundle (9 donuts, 1 apple), the MU per $ is 2 utils for donuts (point *c*), compared to 12 utils for apples (point *b*). The new utility-maximizing choice is shown by points *e* and *d*: cognitive engagement decreases donut consumption from 9 to 4 and increases apple consumption from 1 to 6.

Consider first the outcome for a consumer who relies exclusively on gut feelings. In this case, utility is maximized with point *a* (9 donuts) and point *b* (1 apple). This bundle satisfies the two conditions for utility maximization.

1 *Equimarginal rule.* For each good, the marginal utility per dollar is 12 utils.
2 *Affordability.* The consumer spends $9 on donuts and $1 on apples, for a total of $10.

In this case, a consumer who simply goes with his or her gut feelings eats a lot of donuts.

How does cognition affect the consumer's choice? Recent experiments by neuroscientists have shown that the more a person thinks about the health consequences of an unhealthy food like a donut, the lower the perceived benefit of the unhealthy food. In terms of neural activity, the DLPFC modulates (in this case reduces) the neural activity that signals the benefit of the donut. In the left panel of Figure 22.8, the lower curve shows the cognitive marginal utility per dollar: the incorporation of health concerns shifts the benefit curve downward. For the 9th donut, the marginal utility per dollar decreases from 12 utils (point *a*) to 2 utils (point *c*). The marginal utility per dollar of donuts (2 utils) is now less than the marginal utility per dollar of apples (12 utils, as shown by point *b*). The consumer's rational response is to buy more apples and fewer donuts. In other words, cognition that incorporates long-term health concerns decreases donut consumption and increases apple consumption.

How far will the consumer go in substituting apples for donuts? Since the price of each good is $1, the consumer trades off one donut for each additional apple, moving upward along the donut benefit curve (starting at point *c*) and downward along the apple curve (starting from point *b*). The consumer will continue substituting apples for donuts until the two products generate the same marginal utility per dollar (the same marginal bang per buck). This occurs at point *e* (4 donuts) and point *d* (6 apples), with a common marginal utility per dollar of 7 utils. The switch from impulsive choice (based on gut feelings) to thoughtful choice (based on cognition that incorporates health consequences) increases apple consumption at the expense of donuts.

What are the implications of brain fueling for dietary choices? Our gut feelings for food and nutrition are biased toward high-fat and high-calorie foods, meaning that impulsive choices generally lead to unhealthy choices. Although the cognitive process can counteract this bias by introducing health concerns, this requires cognitive fuel. So the best way to make healthy food choices is to shop when your brain is fully fueled and ready for impulse control, not when you are hungry and thus susceptible to impulsive decisions. An added problem with shopping while hungry is that a glucose-depleted brain seeks immediate refueling, and the quickest refueling comes from sugary food.

Present Bias: Spending versus Saving

Consider the broad consumer decision about how much income to spend now, and how much to save for the future. Since any money saved will eventually be spent, this is essentially a decision about the timing of consumption, now versus later. We can use the utilitarian framework to explore decisions about spending and saving.

Gut feelings are visceral, in-the-moment sensations, and humans are myopic with respect to gut feelings. In other words, humans do a poor job imagining the strength of future gut feelings, including the gut-feeling benefits of future consumption. Experiments by psychologists and neuroscientists have consistently shown that people systematically underestimate the strength of future gut feelings, both positive (benefits of consumption) and negative (monetary cost). Our underestimation of future consequences means that humans are subject to present bias: we accurately incorporate the present consequences of an action, but either ignore or underestimate the future consequences. This present bias can lead to misguided decisions, but the bias can be counteracted by cognitive processing.

Figure 22.9 illustrates utility maximization with respect to spending versus saving. In the left panel, the benefit curve shows the marginal utility per dollar spent in the present. For current consumption, gut feelings accurately represent the benefit of consumption. In the right panel, the lower curve shows the benefit of saving (the benefit of future consumption) for a consumer subject to present bias: the consumer systematically underestimates the future benefit of consumption. In the case of a consumer subject to present bias, utility is maximized with point *a* (spend $19 now) and point *b* (save $1 for the future). This bundle satisfies the two conditions for utility maximization.

1 *Equimarginal rule.* For both spending and saving, the marginal utility per dollar is 14 utils.

2 *Affordability.* The consumer spends $19 now and saves $1, for a total of $20.

In this case, a consumer who goes with his or her gut feelings doesn't save much.

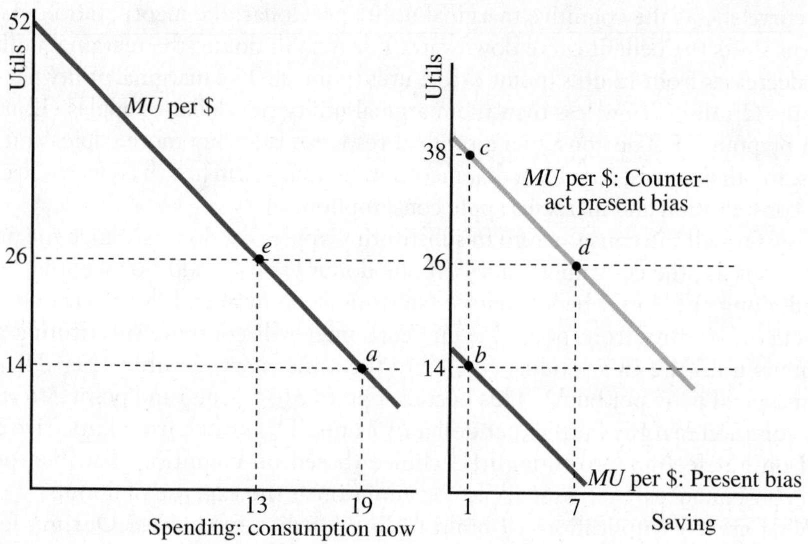

▲ **FIGURE 22.9**
Present Bias and Spending versus Saving
A consumer subject to present bias chooses points *a* and *b* (spend $19 and save $1). Cognition that reduces present bias increases the perceived MU per $ of saving, so at the original bundle (spend $19, save $1), the MU per dollar is higher for saving (point *c* versus point *a*). The new utility-maximizing choice shown by points *e* and *d*: cognitive engagement increases saving from $1 to $7 and decreases spending (consumption now) from $19 to $13.

Consider next a consumer who uses cognition to offset present bias. In the right panel of Figure 22.9, the upper curve shows the benefit curve for a consumer who engages the DLPFC and thus increases the perceived benefit of future consumption: cognition offsets present bias and shifts the benefit curve upward. For example, for the first dollar saved, the marginal utility per dollar increases from 14 utils (point *b*) to 38 utils (point *c*). The marginal utility per dollar of saving (38 utils) now exceeds the marginal utility per dollar of spending (14 utils). The consumer's rational response is to save more and thus have more to spend on future consumption. As in the case of the apple versus the donut, the engagement of the DLPFC incorporates the future consequences of a present action, and thus reduces impulsive behavior (spend most of the money now).

How much more will the consumer save? As current spending decreases and saving increases, the consumer moves upward along the spending benefit curve (starting at point *a*) and downward along the saving curve (starting from point *c*). The consumer will continue to increase saving until the marginal utility per dollar of saving equals the marginal utility per dollar of spending. This occurs at point *e* ($13 spent now) and point *d* ($7 saved), with a common marginal utility per dollar of 26 utils. The switch from impulsive choice (based on gut feelings) to thoughtful choice (based on cognition) increases saving and future consumption at the expense of current consumption.

Consumers use a number of strategies to counteract present bias and increase saving. Some workers pre-commit to regular saving programs, directing their employers to take out a fixed amount of money from each paycheck. This approach eliminates the monthly decision of how much to save, reducing the cognitive effort required to overcome present bias. Another commitment strategy is to join savings clubs such as a Christmas saving club that saves a fixed amount each month leading up to Christmas. In micro-finance programs in the less developed world, participants band together in small groups to monitor each others' savings programs and enforce commitments to save. The basic strategy behind these programs is for the consumer/saver to pre-commit to a saving program, and then get someone else to enforce the rules. This approach economizes on cognitive effort and reduces impulsive spending.

Present bias occurs because there is a mismatch in the timing of benefits and costs. In the case of saving for retirement, the cost occurs in the present (lower current consumption), while the benefit occurs in the future. One approach to counteracting present bias is to shift the cost of contributing to retirement accounts from the present to the future. For example, some employers allow new employees to delay their investment in a retirement account for a year or two. This approach avoids the powerful gut-feeling cost of contributing now, and puts the costs and the benefits of saving for retirement on an equal temporal footing: they are both in the future. By simply shifting the cost into the near future (even if the cost occurs sooner than the benefit), the employer counteracts present bias, increasing investment in retirement accounts.

Present Bias and Credit Cards

Consider next the implications of present bias for a consumer who purchases a product with a credit card. Credit cards cause a different sort of temporal mismatch between benefits and costs. In this case, the benefit of a product will be experienced now, but the cost will be delayed until some future date. Neuroscientists have measured the brain activity associated with cash purchases (pay now) and credit-card purchases (pay later). Consistent with the notion of present bias, credit-card purchases generate much weaker activity than cash purchases: the insula, which indicates cost (the degree of aversion or disgust), is relatively quiet for credit-card purchases. In other words, using a credit card weakens our gut-feeling aversion to spending money.

We can use cognition to counteract the failure of our gut feelings to represent future costs. Once the PFC recognizes the under-representation of the future cost, we can upgrade the perceived cost of a credit-card purchase, perhaps by imagining how it would feel to pay with cash. Alternatively, we can remind ourselves that a credit-card charge will eventually require a cash payment. In one experiment, people making credit-card purchases were simply shown their credit-card statements. A quick look at the credit-card balance triggered activity in the insula that was similar to the activity associated with cash purchases, thus eliminating present bias. Some organizations have developed mobile apps that send reminders to consumers about their credit-card balances, thereby activating the insula and mitigating present bias.

Present Bias and Smoking

The decision to smoke cigarettes is subject to present bias because there is a temporal mismatch between the present benefit (the good feeling from nicotine) and a future cost (health problems). Some people continue to smoke even when smoking is not in their long-term interest. One response to this case of present bias is to use self-imposed penalties to move the cost of smoking to the present. This allows a direct comparison of present benefit and present cost. For example, a smoker could commit to contribute $50 to a charitable organization for each cigarette smoked, and get someone else to enforce the commitment. Under this approach, when someone considers lighting up a cigarette, he or she instantaneously experiences both a gut-feelings benefit and a gut-feeling cost of losing $50. The increase in the present cost of smoking increases the likelihood that a smoker will quit.

Experiments with self-imposed penalties demonstrate their effectiveness. In one experiment, each subject voluntarily deposited the money that he or she would normally spend on cigarettes into a bank account that paid no interest. After six months, any subject who tested positive for nicotine forfeited the money in the account. Compared to a control group that was offered an alternative stop-smoking program, the smokers in the bank-account program were about 40 percent more likely to be nonsmokers after a year (six months after the program ended).

Another approach to pre-commitment comes from stickK.com. You start by picking your goal (stop smoking, lose weight, exercise regularly), and then pick your penalty and choose a referee to monitor your progress and impose any penalties. The penalty could be as light as emails from stickK.com to your friends informing them you are falling short of your goal, or it could be a financial penalty such as $50 deducted from your bank account and paid to your favorite charity. For extra incentive, you can send your penalty money to an anti-charity, an organization whose goals you vehemently oppose. In late 2011, nearly $9 million in potential penalties was in play, with over 120,000 commitments and over 2 million cigarettes not smoked. For people who pre-commit to a monetary penalty, the reported success rate is 80%, compared to only 35% for people without a monetary penalty.

Gambling as a Consumer Good

Why do people gamble when the expected reward is negative? For example, the typical state-run lottery pays out roughly half of what it takes in, so on average a person who plays the lottery for $10 can expect a payoff of roughly $5. Neuroscientists have discovered a possible reason for this seemingly irrational behavior.

Consider a simple gambling game. You put on a blindfold and draw a single ball from an urn that has three balls, marked #1, #2, and #3. As shown in the first row of the table in Figure 22.10, you win $12 if you draw #3, but get nothing if you draw #1 or #2. In this case, the expected monetary payoff equals the probability of winning (1/3) times the $12 prize, or $4. Suppose the cost of the gamble is $6: Each time you draw a ball from the urn you pay $6. If you draw a ball repeatedly, on average the payoff will be $4 per draw, or two-thirds the $6 cost per draw. This doesn't sound like a very attractive gamble: why pay $6 for an average payoff of $4?

A near miss is defined as an outcome that seems to be close to a winning outcome (a better label might be "near win"). In the case of drawing a ball from the urn, a person might consider drawing ball #2 a near miss in the sense 2 is close to 3, the winning number. Neuroscientists have discovered that the brain's dopamine reward system treats a near miss almost the same as a real win: the flow of dopamine generated by a near miss is almost the same as the flow generated by an actual win. In the second row of numbers in Figure 22.10, the dopamine benefit for a near miss (drawing #2) is 9 utils, which is almost as large as the 12-util reward for an actual win.

	Draw #1	#2	#3	Expected benefit
Monetary benefit ($)	0	0	12	$4 = 1/3 × $12
Dopamine benefit (utils)	0	9	12	7 utils = 1/3 × 9 + 1/3 × 12

▲ **FIGURE 22.10**
Near-Miss Benefits and Gambling as a Consumer Good
If you draw ball #3, you win $12. The expected monetary value of drawing a ball from the urn is $4 = 1/3 × $12. Suppose the dopamine benefit of winning is 12 utils, while the dopamine benefit for a near win (drawing ball #2) is 9 utils. The expected dopamine value of drawing a ball is 7 utils = 1/3 × 9 + 1/3 × 12.

The consideration of the dopamine benefits of near misses makes the gamble more attractive. There is a two-thirds chance of drawing #2 or #3, meaning that there is a two-thirds chance of getting a dopamine reward of at least 9 utils. More precisely, the expected dopamine reward is 7 utils, computed as the sum of two components:

- 4 utils = 1/3 × 12: a one-in-three chance of getting 12 utils by drawing #3
- 3 utils = 1/3 × 9: a one-in-three chance of getting 9 utils by drawing #2

On average, the dopamine reward is 7 utils, compared to a cost of $6 per draw from the urn. The consumer will take the gamble if the average reward of 7 utils exceeds the cost—the utility loss associated with paying $6 to draw a ball.

Because the brain rewards near misses with pleasure-generating dopamine, gambling can be considered a consumer good. The expected monetary payoff of the gamble is negative: the consumer pays $6 for an average payoff of $4, so the "price" of the gamble is the $2 lost, on average, on each ball draw. The consumer can buy dopamine brain rewards, exchanging a monetary loss of $2 per ball draw for a dopamine reward that averages 7 utils per draw.

Although the dopamine reward for near misses seems puzzling, scientists suggest that there is evolutionary rationale for this feature of the learning system. The reward for a near miss encourages skill acquisition. Suppose you are a basketball novice, and you want to learn how to shoot the basketball successfully. As a beginner, you are unlikely to make many shots, but you might occasionally hit the rim. If there are rewards only for successful shots, you may get discouraged and give up after a few dozen shots. As a result, you may never acquire the skill. In contrast, if you are rewarded for your occasional near miss (a rim shot) the rewards will encourage you to keep trying. In addition, the reward for a near basket will provide important feedback on what it takes to get close, and you can use this feedback to adjust your actions and get even closer. The reward for near baskets encourages you to keep trying, making it more likely that you will develop your shooting skills. In other words, rewards for near misses promote the acquisition of skills.

The dopamine rewards for near misses are problematic in truly random environments like gambling. In the case of drawing balls from an urn, rolling dice, or playing a slot machine, there are no skills to master: no matter how much you practice, you cannot increase your probability of drawing ball #3, rolling snake eyes, or getting a triple on the slot machine. But if the brain reward for a near miss is almost the same as a reward for an actual win, you have an incentive to keep playing (and losing money) despite the lack of skill acquisition. In a sense, you are buying the brain reward (pleasurable dopamine flow) with the money you leave behind.

application 4

TAXING CIGARETTES TO OFFSET PRESENT BIAS

APPLYING THE CONCEPTS #4: What is the appropriate cigarette tax?

The present bias that leads some people to smoke cigarettes raises an important policy question: Can we use taxes on cigarettes to offset present bias and actually make people better off in the process? A recent study concludes that to fully offset the present bias that underlies the decision to smoke, the appropriate tax is roughly $11 per pack of cigarettes.

The authors of the study focused on the effects of smoking on premature death. Smoking cuts the lifespan of the typical smoker by roughly 6 years, and given the economic value of one year of life, we can translate the cost associated with premature death into a cost of roughly $36 per pack of cigarettes. If smokers did not suffer from present bias, their present choices would fully reflect this future cost, meaning that they would compare the benefit of smoking (the nicotine experience) to the full cost of a pack of cigarettes (the purchase price plus the $36 cost associated with premature death). But present bias is sufficiently strong that a tax of roughly $11 per pack is required to ensure that the typical smoker considers the full cost associated with premature death. This tax put the benefits and costs of smoking on an equal temporal footing: a tax of $11 moves the neglected future cost to the present, allowing a person to make choices that consider the full benefits and costs of smoking.

How would the cigarette tax affect low-income households? Because smoking is more prevalent among the poor, a cigarette tax imposes a relatively large tax burden on low-income households: lower-income households spend a much larger fraction of their income on cigarettes and cigarette taxes. The authors of the study suggest that the cigarette tax would actually be beneficial for low-income households. The reason is that low-income households are relatively responsive to changes in the price of cigarettes, so they would experience a relatively large reduction in smoking, and a relatively large increase in lifespan. Of course, the whole idea of the tax is to reduce smoking, and anyone who quits gets the benefit of a longer lifespan and avoids paying the $11 tax too. **Related to Exercise 4.7.**

SOURCE: Based on Jonathan Gruber, Botond Koszegi, "A Modern Economic View of Tobacco Taxation," (Paris: International Union against Tuberculosis and Lung Disease, 2008).

SUMMARY

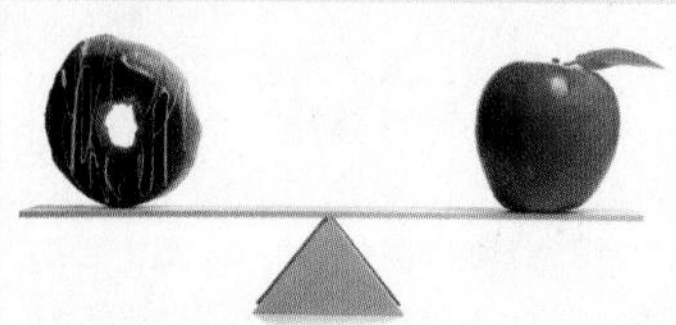

This chapter uses traditional utility theory, which originated with the utilitarians of the eighteenth century, to explain the economic logic behind the law of demand. We also use the insights of modern neuroscience to explore the distinction between impulsive and thoughtful consumer decisions. Here are the main points of the chapter.

1 The law of diminishing marginal utility: As the consumption of a product increases, utility increases at a decreasing rate.

2 The equimarginal rule: To maximize utility, choose the affordable bundle of goods such that the marginal utility per dollar spent on one good equals the marginal utility per dollar spent on a second good.

3 The individual demand curve is negatively sloped because a decrease in price (a) decreases the relative price of the good, causing consumers to substitute the good for other goods (the substitution effect) and (b) increases the consumer's real income, increasing the consumption of all normal goods (the income effect).

4 For some goods, thoughtful decisions (based on cognition) differ from impulsive decisions (based on gut feelings). Some examples are food choices (donut vs. apple) and saving decisions (consume now vs. later).

5 One explanation for consumers taking gambles that have a negative expected monetary payoff is that there are brain rewards (dopamine) for near misses as well as actual wins.

EXERCISES

All problems are assignable in MyEconLab.

22.1 Traditional Consumer Choice: Utility Theory

1.1 Based on Figure 22.1, fill the blanks in the following table to identify different points on the consumer's budget line.

Quantity of movies	2	4	6	8
Quantity of books	___	___	___	___

1.2 In Figure 22.1, suppose the price of movies increases to $9. Draw a new budget line. The horizontal intercept of the budget line is __________ and the slope of the budget line is __________.

1.3 In Figure 22.2, if the total utility from seven movies is 294 utils, the marginal utility of the seventh movie is __________ utils, which is __________ than the marginal utility of the sixth movie.

1.4 As the consumption of a product increases, utility __________ (increases/decreases) at a __________ (increasing/decreasing/constant) rate, so the marginal utility curve is __________ sloped. This illustrates the law of __________.

1.5 In Figure 22.3, suppose the price of movies decreases to $2. The marginal utility per dollar of the sixth movie is __________ utils.

1.6 Suppose the marginal utility of a video game is 48 utils and the marginal utility of an iTunes song is 2 utils. The price of a video game is $12 and the price of a song is $1. The opportunity cost of a video game is __________ songs and the marginal cost of a video game is __________ utils. The marginal benefit of a video game is __________ utils.

1.7 According to the equimarginal rule, a consumer chooses the combination of two goods that equalizes the __________ per __________ on each product consumed.

1.8 The conditions for utility maximization are

a. __________

b. __________

1.9 Suppose a consumer has a fixed amount to spend each week on iTunes songs ($1 each) and movies ($6 each). For the combination she chose this week, the marginal utility of movies is 30 and the marginal utility of songs is 3. For next week she should __________ (increase/decrease) the number of songs and __________ (increase/decrease) the number of movies.

1.10 Brain imaging provides evidence for the law of __________ utility. (Based on Application 1 on page 472.)

1.11 ***Change in Marginal Utility.*** In Table 22.1, suppose the marginal utility numbers for books change: for each quantity of books, the marginal utility is 6 utils higher. For example, for 24 books, the marginal utility is 8 utils instead of 2 utils, and for 21 books, the marginal utility is 10 utils instead of 4 utils. Determine the new utility-maximizing bundle.

1.12 ***Utility-Maximizing Rides and Games.*** Suppose the price of amusement rides is $2 and the price of a video arcade game is $1. The following table shows points on the budget line (given an income of $30) and the associated marginal utilities. Fill in the blanks in the table and find the utility-maximizing combination of rides and games. Illustrate with a figure like Figure 22.3.

Quantity		Marginal Utility		Marginal Utility per Dollar	
Rides	Games	Rides	Games	Rides: Price = $2	Games: Price = $1
1	28	50	10		
2	26	42	14		
3	24	36	18		
4	22	26	26		

1.13 ***Consumer Consultant.*** You have been hired to determine whether a consumer is maximizing his utility. He has a fixed budget of $2,500 per month to spend on food and housing. The price of food is $1 per pound, and the price of housing is $3 per square foot of living space. He currently lives in a 600-square foot apartment and spends $700 on food.

a. You can ask your client two questions—only two. What are your questions?

b. Your client's answers indicate that he is indeed maximizing utility. What are his answers?

22.2 The Law of Demand and the Individual Demand Curve

2.1 In Figure 22.5, suppose the price of movies increases from $3 to $6. The increase in price shifts the benefit curve (marginal utility per dollar) for movies __________ (upward/downward). For the initial quantity of 6 movies, the marginal utility per dollar becomes __________ utils, which is __________ (greater/less) than the marginal utility per dollar of books.

2.2 Suppose a consumer has a budget of $100 to spend on concerts (price = $6) and carnival rides (price = $2). For each of the following pairs of points in the figure below, indicate whether the pair (i) satisfies the budget constraint, (ii) satisfies the equimarginal rule, (iii) is the best affordable bundle.

a. Points *a* and *e*.

b. Points *b* and *h*.

c. Points *c* and *f*.

d. Points *d* and *g*.

e. Points *d* and *e*.

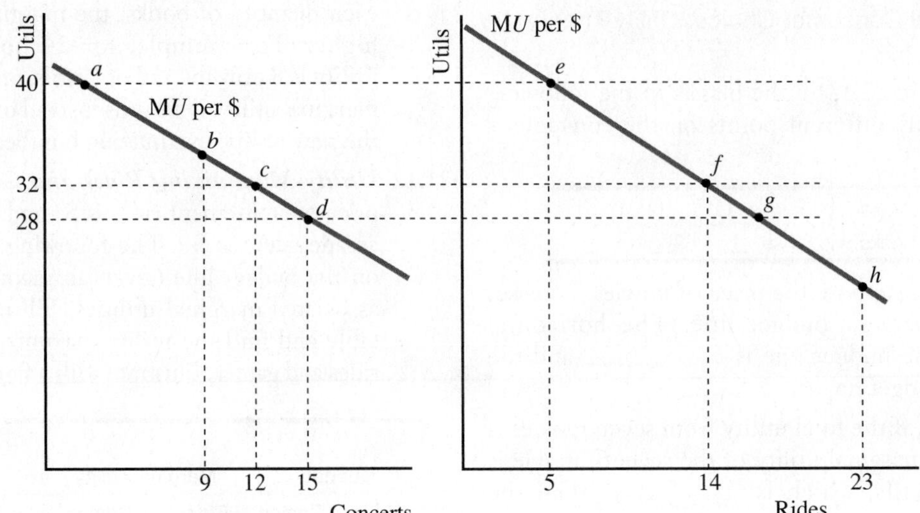

2.3 Arrow up or down: The income effect of a price change is that a decrease in price __________ a consumer's real income and __________ the consumption of a normal good.

2.4 Arrow up or down: The substitution effect is that a decrease in the price of movies __________ the relative price of movies and __________ the consumption of movies.

2.5 To show the substitution effect of a decrease in price, we __________ (increase/decrease) a consumer's nominal income so the consumer can just afford __________.

2.6 Suppose Maxine initially watches six movies at a price of $3 each and buys 9 books at a price of $1 each, and then the price of movies increases to $5. To make Maxine's original bundle just affordable, her income must __________ (increase/decrease) by __________. Her utility-maximizing consumption of movies will __________ (increase/decrease) because at the original bundle, __________ is now less than __________.

2.7 If the typical consumer buys 200 gallons of gasoline and the gasoline tax increases by $3, revenue neutrality requires that the consumer's income tax must __________ (increase/decrease) by __________. (Related to Application 1 on page 472.)

2.8 **Response to the Gas Tax.** Petrov initially pays $2,200 in income taxes and consumes 600 gallons of gasoline per year at a price of $3 per gallon. The price of the other good is $1. For Petrov's initial product bundle, the marginal utility of gas is 30 utils and the marginal utility of the other good is 10 utils. (Related to Application 2 on page 476.)

a. For his initial bundle, the marginal utility per dollar on gasoline is __________ utils.

b. Suppose the government imposes a new gasoline tax that increases the price of gas to $5. To make his initial consumer bundle just affordable, Petrov's income must __________ (increase/decrease) by __________.

c. Suppose the government cuts Petrov's income tax by the amount computed in (b). Given the new gas tax and the income tax cut, at his initial bundle, the marginal utility per dollar of gasoline is __________ utils, compared to __________ for the other good. To satisfy the marginal principle, Petrov will __________ (increase/decrease) his gasoline consumption.

2.9 ***Shipping the Good Apples Out?*** Suppose apples come in two quality levels, low and high. At a store in the apple-growing region, the price of low-quality apples is $1 per pound, and the price of high-quality apples is $4 per pound. Johnny lives in the apple-growing region and buys eight pounds of each type. His marginal utility of apples is 3 utils for low-quality apples and 12 utils for high-quality apples.

a. Is Johnny maximizing his utility?

b. Suppose Johnny moves to an area outside the apple-growing region. Shipping the apples to his new area adds $2 to the price of a pound of apples, for both low-quality and high-quality apples. To simplify matters, assume Johnny's income increases by an amount large enough to fully offset the higher prices of apples. In other words, he can still afford the original bundle of eight pounds of each type of apples. If he continues to buy eight pounds of apples of each type, is he maximizing his utility? If not, how should he change his mix of high- and low-quality apples?

c. What are the implications for the mix of high-quality and low-quality apples in apple-growing areas and other regions?

22.3 Neuroscience of Consumer Choice

3.1 The key region of the brain for the valuation of benefits is the __________.

3.2 In the dopamine learning system, learning happens when the __________ about the pleasure from a product are __________ (correct/wrong).

3.3 The key region of the brain for the valuation of costs is the __________.

3.4 In the Iowa Gambling Task, the brain sends an alarm to avoid drawing from the unfavorable decks after about __________ (3, 10, 25, 50, 75) cards, but the typical subject doesn't switch to the favorable decks until about __________ (3, 10, 25, 50, 75) cards.

3.5 The key region of the brain responsible for comparing benefits and costs is the __________.

3.6 The fuel for cognition is __________, and the depletion of this fuel increases the likelihood that a person will base a decision on __________.

3.7 Conventional stores encourage shoppers to buy products by boosting neural activity in __________ and reducing neural activity in the __________. (Related to Application 3 on page 481.)

22.4 Consumer Decisions

4.1 The introduction of cognition into a consumer's choice between healthy and unhealthy food shifts the __________ curve downward, causing the marginal utility per dollar of __________ to be less than the marginal utility per dollar of __________.

4.2 Consumers are subject to present bias in the sense that they systematically underestimate the strength of __________.

4.3 The introduction of cognition into a consumer's choice between consumption now and saving shifts the __________ curve upward, causing the marginal utility per dollar of __________ to exceed the the marginal utility per dollar of __________.

4.4 Compared to a cash purchase, a credit-card purchase generates __________ activity in the __________, which is responsible for valuation of the __________ (benefits/costs) of a product.

4.5 The organization stickK.com gives people the opportunity to exercise self-control by __________.

4.6 Neuroscientists have discovered that the brain's dopamine reward system of a gambler treats a __________ almost the same as a real __________. The evolutionary purpose is that the reward encourages __________.

4.7 To counteract the effects of present bias in smoking behavior, the tax per pack of cigarettes is roughly __________ ($1, $3, $11, $35) per pack. (Related to Application 4 on page 488.)

4.8 One possible reason for curse words is that they give us opportunities to exercise our __________.

4.9 ***How Many Donuts?*** Using Figure 22.8 as a starting point, suppose cognition shifts the MU per $ curve downward by a larger amount, as shown in the figure below. How many donuts and how many apples will the consumer choose?

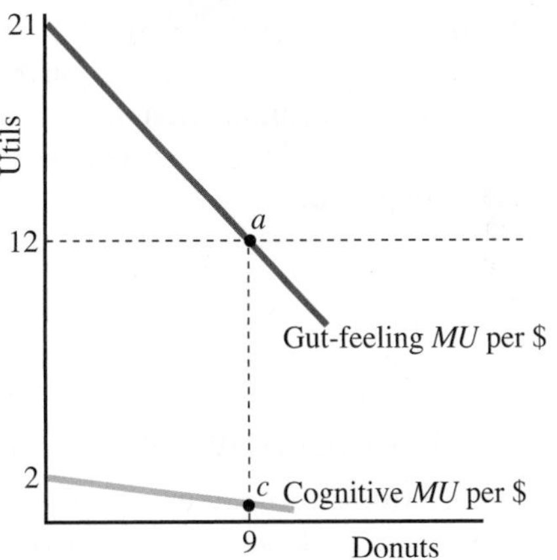

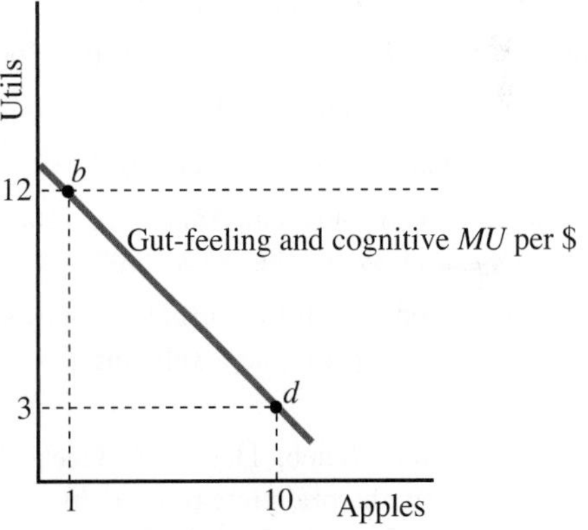

4.10 ***Effects of a Donut Tax.*** Using Figure 22.8 as a starting point, consider the effect of a donut tax equal to $2 per donut, which increases the price of a donut from $1 to $3. In the figure below, assume that the new (post-tax) equilibrium is shown by points *e* and *d*. Fill the blanks (shown by horizontal lines) with numbers. The marginal utility per dollar associated with point *c* is __________ utils. The number of apples associated with point *d* is __________.

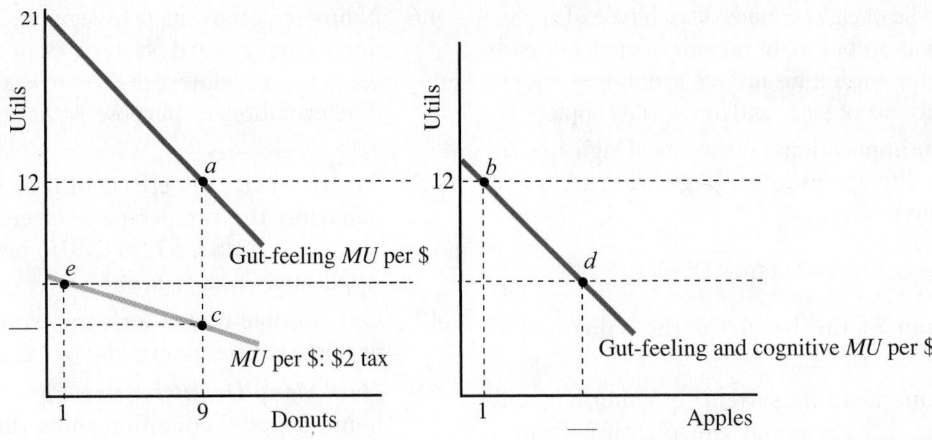

4.11 ***Effect of Consumption Tax.*** Using Figure 22.9 as a starting point, suppose the consumer chooses point *e* (spend $13 now) and point *d* (save $7). Suppose the government imposes a 20% tax on spending (consumption now), meaning that for every dollar spent now, $0.20 goes to the government, leaving only $0.80 to purchase products.

a. Use a graph to show the effect of the consumption tax on the relevant curves.

b. On your graph, show, for the initial bundle ($13, $7), the tax-induced gap between the marginal utility per dollar on spending and the marginal utility per dollar of saving.

c. Which direction will the consumer go—more spending or more saving?

NOTES

1. Baumeister, Ray, and John Tierney. Willpower (Penguin, 2011).

Our discussion of the neuroscience of consumer choice is based on a wide variety of material in books and scientific journals. In the following books, the authors explain many of the key insights from neuroscience in a non-technical fashion.

i. Lehrer, Jonas. *How We Decide* (Houghton Mifflin, 2009).

ii. Baumeister, Ray, and John Tierney. *Willpower* (Penguin, 2011).

iii. Ariely, Daniel. *Predictable Irrational* (Harper, 2008).

iv. Thaler, Richard, and Cass Sunstein. *Nudge: Improving Decisions about Health, Wealth, and Happiness* (Penguin, 2008).

The following articles from scientific journals present some key neuroscience research results that are relevant for consumer decision making.

i. Bastena, Ulrike, Guido Bieleb, Hauke R. Heekerenb, and Christian J. Fiebach. "How the brain integrates costs and benefits during decision making." *Proceedings of the National Academy of Science* 107 (50), pp. 21767–21772 (2010).

ii. Baumgartner, Thomas, Daria Knoch, Philine Hotz, Christoph Eisenegger & Ernst Fehr. "Dorsolateral and ventromedial prefrontal cortex orchestrate normative choice." *Nature Neuroscience* 14, pp. 1468–1474 (2011).

iii. Chasel, Henry and Luke Clark, Gambling Severity Predicts Midbrain Response to Near-Miss Outcomes, *Journal of Neuroscience* 30 (2010), pp. 6180–6187.

iv. Grabenhorst, Fabian, and Edmund T. Rolls. "Value, pleasure and choice in the ventral prefrontal cortex." *Trends in Cognitive Sciences* 15 (2011).

v. Hare, Todd, Colin Camerer, Antonio Rangel. "Self Control in Decision-Making Involves Modulation of the vmPFC Valuation System." *Science* 324, pp. 646–648 (2009).

vi. Hare, Todd, Jonathan Malmaud, Antonio Rangel, "Focusing attention on the health aspects of foods changes value signals in vmPFC and improves dietary choice." *Journal of Neuroscience* 31 (2011), pp. 11077–11087.

vii. Kable, Joseph and Paul W. Glimcher. "The Neurobiology of Decisions: Consensus and Controversy." *Neuron* 63 (2), pp. 733–745 (2009).

viii. Knoch, Daria and Ernst Fehr. "Resisting the Power of Temptations." *Annals of the New York Academy of Science* 1104, pp. 123–134 (2007).

ix. Knutson, Brian, Scott Rick, G. Elliott Wimmer, Drazen Prelec, and George Loewenstein. "Neural Predictors of Purchases." *Neuron* 53, pp. 147–156 (2007).

x. Pine, Alex, Ben Seymour, Jonathan P. Roiser, Peter Bossaerts, Karl J. Friston, H. Valerie Curran, and Raymond J. Dolan, "Encoding of Marginal Utility across Time in the Human Brain." *Journal of Neuroscience* 29 (2009), pp. 9575–9581.

xi. Winstanley, C., Dopamine modulates reward expectancy during performance of a slot machine task in rats: Evidence for a near-miss effect. *Neuropsychopharmacology* 36 (2011) pp. 913–925.

The following books contain collections of articles that relate recent advances in neuroscience to consumer choice.

i. Dolan, Raymond, and Tali Sharot (editors). *Neuroscience of Preference and Choice* (Academic Press, 2012).

ii. Glimcher, Paul, Colin Camerer, Ernst Fehr, Russell Poldrack (editors). *Neuroeconomics: Decision Making and the Brain* (Academic Press and Elsevier, 2009).

APPENDIX TO CHAPTER 22

MENTAL SHORTCUTS AND CONSUMER PUZZLES

Although the brain has billions of cells and trillions of synapses to process information and make decisions, the decision-making process is far from perfect. Mental processing takes time and energy, and the brain uses a number of time-saving shortcuts that sometimes lead to puzzling and misguided decisions. Economists and psychologists have identified several types of puzzling consumer behavior.

- Spending choices sometimes depends on the source of income.
- The willingness to pay for a product sometimes is affected by irrelevant information.
- Product choices are sometimes influenced by irrelevant alternatives.
- Decisions are sometimes based on percentage differences rather than absolute differences.

These are ongoing puzzles in the sense that we do not fully understand the mental processes behind what appears to be misguided consumer behavior.

One possible explanation for a consumer puzzle is that people sometimes base their decisions on heuristics. A heuristic is a simple rule for dealing with a complex situation, and provides a "fast and frugal" decision. A simple rule may work well in most circumstances, but in some cases may generate misguided choices. In the case of misguided choices generated by heuristics, a key question concerns the motivation for the heuristic: What are the advantages of using a heuristic rather than a more thoughtful and deliberative decision-making process?

22A.1 Mental Accounting and Bundling

One way to economize on decision making is to separate decisions into different type or accounts. For example, a consumer could establish separate accounts for food ($300 per month) and entertainment ($100 per month). If the price of a particular food increases, the consumer would reallocate its fixed food budget, but would not consider changing its entertainment budget. This shortcut—known as mental accounting—simplifies the decision-making process because it limits the calculation of tradeoffs.

An important application of mental accounting concerns the classification of money from different sources. Consider the treatment of income that comes unexpectedly, for example, a $50 birthday gift or $50 found on the street. For many people, unexpected income is "play money" that is frequently spent on fun or frivolous purchases. In contrast, people are more careful with regular income, allocating it to buying regular goods, paying bills, and saving. Who would blame you for spending birthday cash on a restaurant meal rather than paying down your credit card or putting the money into your savings account? Similarly, money picked up off the street is considered "fun money" and not spent in the same way as regular income.

Another mental shortcut is to monitor consumption by bundles rather than individual units. People tend to track consumption by the bundles in which a product is delivered rather than the actual consumption of the product. In a famous experiment, people had the opportunity to use a scoop to get free M&Ms from a bowl. When the experimenters switched to a larger scoop, people continued to get roughly the same number of scoops, but of course a lot more M&Ms. In other words, people monitor their consumption by scoops (bundles) of the product, not the actual quantity of the product. In another experiment, diners were provided a bottomless bowl of soup: using a secret tube, the experimenters refilled the bowl every time the diner consumed some soup. The result was consistent with the notion of consumer bundling: the subjects drank much more soup than people drawing from a normal bowl of soup.

22A.2 Anchoring

Another mental shortcut is called anchoring. Suppose the brain is asked to compute the numerical value of something, for example, the amount you are willing to pay for a car or a house. In computing a numerical value, the brain tends to latch onto numbers in a seemingly random way. In the classic experiment, each participant writes down the last two digits of his or her social security number, and then bids (expresses a willingness to pay) for a t-shirt. The bizarre result is the larger the participant's social-security number, the higher the bid on the t-shirt. In other words, the social-security number provides an anchor for an unrelated mental task.

There are some important implications of the anchoring effect. A person's expressed valuation of a product is affected by the numbers in his or her head. In a negotiation over the price of a product, the seller has an incentive to plant a relatively large number in the buyer's head, while the buyer has incentive to plant a low number in the seller's head. One way to plant an anchoring number is to be the first to state a price. In other words, there is a first-mover advantage in negotiations over price. This provides one reason for relatively high (and negotiable) sticker prices on new and used cars. Using a high price as an anchor, a buyer can negotiate a lower price and feel good about getting a bargain, while the seller can get less than the anchor price but more than his or her true willingness to accept.

The notion of anchoring helps explain the large effects of "sales" for retail goods. The regular price of a product provides an anchor for your underlying value of the product. When a product goes on sale at a 20% discount, it looks like a great deal, given your anchor, the regular price. So a store that has a 20% off sale is likely to experience a relatively large increase in the quantity sold.

22A.3 The Decoy Effect

One of the most puzzling quirks of consumer decision making is the decoy effect. Consider the options for an mp3 player represented in Figure 22A.1. In the left panel, there are two options: a low-price player with a capacity of 8 GB (option A), and a high-price player with a capacity of 16 GB (option B). Suppose that in a direct comparison of A versus B, a consumer chooses A: when the consumer considers the trade-offs between price and capacity, the extra 8GB of capacity is not worth the additional $100. In a direct comparison, A is superior to B.

► FIGURE 22A.1

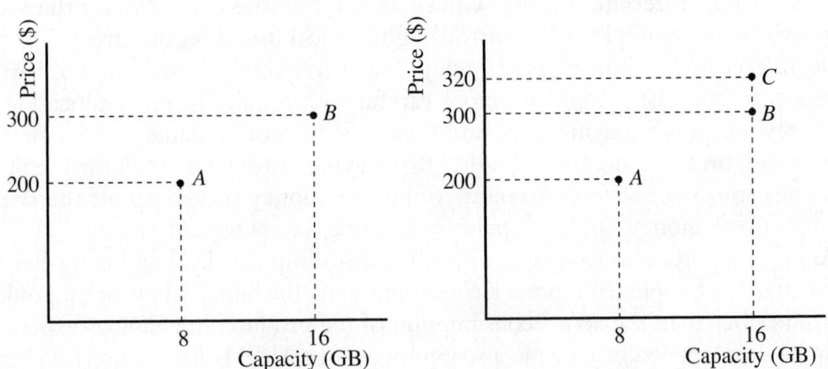

The right panel introduces a third option, a decoy. Option C has the same capacity as option B, but its price is $20 higher. The comparison of B versus C is quick and easy: the consumer doesn't have to think about any trade-offs, but simply recognizes that the extra $20 spent on C doesn't buy anything. The typical consumer will then choose option B over options A and C. The consumer focuses on the easy comparison of B versus C, and neglects the more difficult task of comparing B to A. The introduction of a clearly inferior option (the decoy C) changes the consumer's choice from A to B.

The decoy effect occurs for all sorts of preferences and decisions. In a standard decoy-effect experiment, each person in a control group is shown three faces (A, B, C) and asked to choose the most attractive face. Suppose the control group chooses A as the most attractive and C as the least attractive. For the treatment group, a fourth face (C–) is introduced, one that is similar to face C (the least attractive face) but just a bit less attractive. When the treatment group looks at four faces (A, B, C, C–) the participants tend to focus on the comparable faces C and C–, and ignore faces A and B. As a result, the treatment group picks C, not A, as the most attractive face. The decoy focuses attention on comparable faces and diverts attention from the most attractive face and thus changes the outcome.

The decoy effect has important implications for consumer decision-making. Marketers have an incentive to introduce products that are not designed to sell, but are designed to manipulate consumers into choosing a similar but superior product. A savvy consumer can use cognition to avoid being affected by the decoy effect. If you can identify a decoy and recognize the slightly better product, you could then continue evaluating the other options, rather than stopping your valuation prematurely. Assessing tradeoffs is cognitively challenging, but may be worthwhile.

22A.4 The Appeal of Percentage Changes

People use another mental shortcut to assess numerical changes, for example an increase in price. The natural inclination is to translate a numerical change into a percentage change. For example, a change in price from $1.00 to $0.90 is a 10 percent change, and so is a change from $200 to $180. The translation into percentages means that all 10% changes appear to be alike, despite the fact that 10% of $200 is much larger than 10% of $1.00.

The percentage shortcut can lead to misguided decisions. In the classic demonstration of percentage bias, we ask a consumer two questions.

1 Would you drive a dozen miles to save 10% on a quart of milk?

2 Would you drive a dozen miles to save 3% on a new chair?

The typical consumer responds "yes" to the first question, and "no" to the second question. In other words, the 10% saving on milk is worthwhile, but the 3% saving on a new chair is not. This is puzzling and illogical because a chair is much more expensive than milk. The numerical saving associated with 10% off a $1.00 quart of milk is only $0.10, but the numerical savings associated with 3% off a $200 chair is $6.00. If it is sensible to drive a dozen miles to save $0.10, why isn't it sensible to drive the same distance to save $6.00? In assessing numerical changes, the brain appears to be naturally inclined to work in percentage or relative terms rather than absolute terms, leading to misguided decisions.

As an application of the percentage shortcut, consider the provision of Internet service in hotels. A hotel can either include Internet service as part of its room charges, or have a separate charge. In general, low-price hotels include Internet service as part of the room charge, while high-price hotels have a separate charge. In a low-price hotel ($50 per night), a separate charge of $10 per day is a 20% surcharge, a relatively large surcharge in percentage term. Consumers subject to percentage bias are likely to react strongly to the seemingly large surcharge. In a hotel with a price $200 per night, a separate charge of $10 is only 5% of the price, a small enough percentage that the consumer response is likely to be relatively small.

SUMMARY

In this appendix to the chapter on consumer choice we've discussed some puzzling aspects of consumers' behavior. Here are the main points of the appendix.

1 Spending choices sometimes depend on the source of income.

2 The willingness to pay for a product sometimes is affected by irrelevant information.

3 Choices are sometimes influenced by irrelevant alternatives.

4 Decisions are sometimes based on percentage differences rather than absolute differences.

Production Technology and Cost

CHAPTER 23

Consider the challenge of providing safe water to rural families in less developed countries.

In India, the conventional approach is for each family to use an individual carbon-activated filter, at a monthly cost of $2 per month. The alternative approach developed by the Byrraju Foundation exploits economies of scale in water filtration. A community filtration plant with a capital cost of $15,000 can provide clean water to 1,500 families at a monthly cost of only $1 per family. An added advantage of the filtration plant is that villagers can pay for water on a daily basis rather than being required to come up with large amounts of cash to buy the individual filter and replacement cartridges.[1]

LEARNING OBJECTIVES

- Define economic cost and economic profit.
- Draw the short-run marginal-cost and average-cost curves.
- Draw the long-run marginal-cost and average cost curves.
- Provide examples of production costs.

MyEconLab

MyEconLab helps you master each objective and study more efficiently.

This chapter explores the relationship between the quantity of output produced and the cost of production. As we'll see, a firm's production cost is determined by its production technology—the way the firm combines capital, labor, and materials to produce output. After we explain the link between technology and costs, we'll look at the actual cost curves of several products, including aluminum, hospital services, wind power, truck freight, and airplanes.

Economists distinguish between the short run and the long run. The long run is a period long enough that a firm is perfectly flexible in its choice of all inputs, including its production facility. In contrast, when a firm cannot modify its facility, it is operating in the short run. In this chapter, we'll explore both short-run and long-run costs. In later chapters, we'll show how firms use short-run and long-run cost curves to make decisions about whether to enter a market and how much output to produce.

23.1 Economic Cost and Economic Profit

economic profit
Total revenue minus economic cost.

This is the first of several chapters on the decisions firms make. A firm's objective is to maximize its **economic profit**, which equals its total revenue minus its economic cost:

$$\text{economic profit} = \text{total revenue} - \text{economic cost}$$

As we saw earlier in the book, a firm's total revenue is the money it gets from selling its product. If a firm charges the same price to every consumer, its total revenue equals the price per unit of output times the quantity sold.

economic cost
The opportunity cost of the inputs used in the production process; equal to explicit cost plus implicit cost.

This chapter explores the firm's cost of production. A firm's **economic cost** equals the cost of all the inputs used in the production process; we measure it as the opportunity cost of the inputs. Recall the first key principle of economics.

PRINCIPLE OF OPPORTUNITY COST

The opportunity cost of something is what you sacrifice to get it.

To compute a firm's economic cost, we must determine what the firm sacrifices to use inputs in the production process. Economic cost is opportunity cost.

explicit cost
A monetary payment.

implicit cost
An opportunity cost that does not involve a monetary payment.

As shown in the first column of numbers in Table 23.1, a firm's economic cost can be divided into two types. A firm's **explicit cost** is its actual monetary payments for inputs. For example, if a firm spends a total of $10,000 per month on labor, capital, and materials, its explicit cost is $10,000. This is an opportunity cost because money spent on these inputs cannot be used to buy something else. A firm's **implicit cost** is the opportunity cost of the inputs that do not require a monetary payment. Here are two examples of inputs whose costs are implicit rather than explicit:

TABLE 23.1 Economic Cost versus Accounting Cost

	Economic Cost	Accounting Cost
Explicit: monetary payments for labor, capital, materials	$10,000	$10,000
Implicit: opportunity cost of entrepreneur's time	5,000	—
Implicit: opportunity cost of funds	2,000	—
Total	17,000	10,000

- ***Opportunity cost of the entrepreneur's time.*** If an entrepreneur could earn $5,000 per month in another job, the opportunity cost of the time spent running the firm is $5,000 per month.
- ***Opportunity cost of the entrepreneur's funds.*** Many entrepreneurs use their own funds to set up and run their businesses. If an entrepreneur starts a business with $200,000 withdrawn from a savings account, the opportunity cost is the interest income the funds could have earned in the bank, for example, $2,000 per month.

application 1

OPPORTUNITY COST AND ENTREPRENEURSHIP

APPLYING THE CONCEPTS #1: What is the opportunity cost of an entrepreneur?

For many entrepreneurs, starting a new business means leaving paid employment. A study of Canadian workers showed that the lower a worker's earnings in paid employment, the more likely the worker was to become an entrepreneur. In other words, businesses are started by people with relatively low wages. After controlling for gender, age, education, marital status, and region, the wage gap between workers who become entrepreneurs and workers who remain in paid employment was about 12 percent. This is sensible because the lower the wage in paid employment, the lower the opportunity cost of leaving a job and starting a business. **Related to Exercise 1.8.**

SOURCE: Based on Rafael Amit, Eitan Muller, Iain Cockburn, "Opportunity Costs and Entrepreneurial Activity," *Journal of Business Venturing* 10 (1995), pp. 95–106.

Economic cost equals explicit cost plus implicit cost:

$$\text{economic cost} = \text{explicit cost} + \text{implicit cost}$$

In the first column of Table 23.1, the firm's economic cost is $17,000, equal to $10,000 in explicit cost plus $7,000 in implicit cost.

Accountants have a different approach to computing costs. Their narrower definition of cost includes only the explicit cost of inputs:

$$\text{accounting cost} = \text{explicit cost}$$

In other words, **accounting cost** includes the monetary payments for inputs, but ignores the opportunity cost of inputs that do not require an explicit monetary payment. In the second column of Table 23.1, the accounting cost is the $10,000 in monetary payments for labor, capital, and materials. **Accounting profit** equals total revenue minus accounting cost:

accounting cost
The explicit costs of production.

accounting profit
Total revenue minus accounting cost.

$$\text{accounting profit} = \text{total revenue} - \text{accounting cost}$$

A firm's accounting cost is always lower than its economic cost, so its accounting profit is always *higher* than its economic profit. For the rest of this book, when we refer to cost and profit, we mean *economic* cost and *economic* profit.

23.2 A Firm with a Fixed Production Facility: Short-Run Costs

Consider first the case of a firm with a fixed production facility. Suppose you have decided to start a small firm to produce plastic paddles for rafts. The production of paddles requires a workshop where workers use molds to form plastic material into paddles. Before we can discuss the cost of production, we need information about the nature of the production process.

Production and Marginal Product

The table in Figure 23.1 shows how the quantity of paddles produced varies with the number of workers. A single worker in the workshop produces one paddle per day. Adding a second worker increases the quantity produced to five paddles per day. The **marginal product of labor** is the change in output from one additional unit of

marginal product of labor
The change in output from one additional unit of labor.

Labor	Quantity of Output Produced	Marginal Product of Labor
1	1	1
2	5	4
3	8	3
4	10	2
5	11	1
6	11.5	0.5

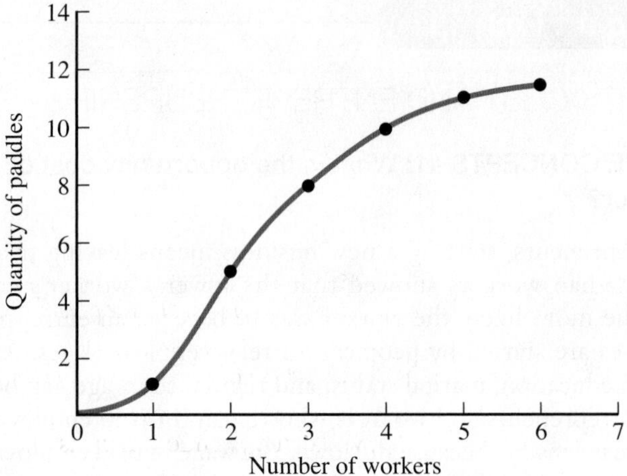

▲ **FIGURE 23.1**
Total-Product Curve
The total-product curve shows the relationship between the quantity of labor and the quantity of output, given a fixed production facility. For the first two workers, output increases at an increasing rate because of labor specialization. Diminishing returns occurs for three or more workers, so output increases at a decreasing rate.

labor. In the table, the marginal product of the first worker is one paddle, compared to a marginal product of four paddles for the second worker.

Why does the marginal product increase as output increases? As we saw earlier in the book, when a firm increases its workforce, workers can specialize in production tasks. Productivity increases because of the benefits of continuity—each worker spends less time switching between production tasks. In addition, there are benefits from repetition—each worker becomes more proficient at an assigned task. A two-worker operation produces more than twice as many paddles as a one-person operation because the two workers can specialize, one being responsible for preparing the plastic for the mold and the other for working the mold.

diminishing returns
As one input increases while the other inputs are held fixed, output increases at a decreasing rate.

Starting with the third worker, the production process is subject to **diminishing returns**, one of the key principles of economics.

PRINCIPLE OF DIMINISHING RETURNS

Suppose output is produced with two or more inputs and we increase one input while holding the other inputs fixed. Beyond some point—called the *point of diminishing returns*—output will increase at a decreasing rate.

The third worker adds three paddles to total output, down from four paddles for the second worker. As the firm continues to hire more workers, the marginal product drops to two paddles for the fourth worker and one paddle for the fifth worker. As we saw earlier in the book, diminishing returns occurs because each worker gets a smaller share of the production facility. In the paddle example, the workers share a mold; as the number of workers increases, they will spend more time waiting to use it.

total-product curve
A curve showing the relationship between the quantity of labor and the quantity of output produced, *ceteris paribus*.

Figure 23.1 shows the firm's **total-product curve**, which represents the relationship between the quantity of labor (on the horizontal axis) and output (on the vertical axis), *ceteris paribus*. The total-product curve shows the effects of labor specialization as well as diminishing returns. For the first two workers, output increases at an increasing rate because labor specialization increases the marginal product of labor. Starting with the third worker, however, total output increases at a decreasing rate because of diminishing returns.

Short-Run Total Cost

We've seen the production relationship between labor input and output, so we're ready to show the relationship between output and production cost. Suppose the opportunity cost of your time is \$50 per day, and you can hire workers for your workshop at the market wage of \$50 per day. You can purchase your workshop, including the building and the paddle mold, for \$365,000. If the interest rate you could have earned on that money is 10 percent per year, the opportunity cost of tying up your \$365,000 in the workshop is \$36,500 per year, or \$100 per day.

In the short-run analysis of costs, we divide production costs into two types, fixed cost and variable cost.

- **Fixed cost (*FC*)** is the cost that does not vary with the quantity produced. In our example, the fixed cost is the cost of the workshop, including the cost of the building and the mold. As shown in the third column of Table 23.2, the fixed cost is \$100 per day, regardless of how much output is produced.
- **Variable cost (*VC*)** is the cost that varies with the quantity produced. For example, to produce more paddles, you must hire more workers. If the cost per worker is \$50 per day, your daily variable cost is \$50 times the number of workers, including you. As shown in the fourth column of Table 23.2, variable cost is \$50 for one worker, \$100 for two workers, and so on.

fixed cost (*FC*)
Cost that does not vary with the quantity produced.

variable cost (*VC*)
Cost that varies with the quantity produced.

TABLE 23.2 Short-Run Costs

1 Labor	2 Output	3 Fixed Cost (*FC*)	4 Variable Cost (*VC*)	5 Total Cost (*TC*)	6 Average Fixed Cost (*AFC*)	7 Average Variable Cost (*AVC*)	8 Average Total Cost (*ATC*)	9 Marginal Cost (*MC*)
0	0	\$100	\$ 0	\$100	—	—	—	—
1	1	100	\$ 50	150	\$100.00	\$50.00	\$150.00	\$ 50.00
2	5	100	100	200	20.00	20.00	40.00	12.50
3	8	100	150	250	12.50	18.75	31.25	16.67
4	10	100	200	300	10.00	20.00	30.00	25.00
5	11	100	250	350	9.09	22.73	31.82	50.00
6	11.5	100	300	400	8.70	26.09	34.78	100.00

To compute the firm's total cost, we simply add the fixed and variable costs. The firm's **short-run total cost (*TC*)** equals the sum of fixed and variable costs:

$$TC = FC + VC$$

The fifth column in Table 23.2 shows the total cost for different quantities of output. For example, one worker produces one paddle at a total cost of \$150, equal to the fixed cost of \$100 plus a variable cost of \$50. Hiring a second worker increases output to five paddles and increases total cost to \$200, equal to \$100 in fixed cost and \$100 in variable cost. Moving down the fifth column, the total cost rises to \$250 for 8 units of output, \$300 for 10 units, and so on.

short-run total cost (*TC*)
The total cost of production when at least one input is fixed; equal to fixed cost plus variable cost.

Figure 23.2 shows the short-run cost curves corresponding to columns 3, 4, and 5 of Table 23.2. The horizontal line on the graph shows the fixed cost of \$100. The lower of the two positively sloped curves shows the variable cost (*VC*), and the

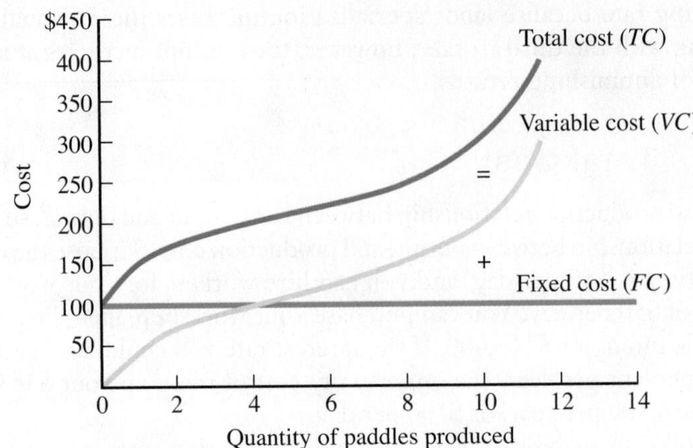

▶ FIGURE 23.2
Short-Run Costs: Fixed Cost, Variable Cost, and Total Cost
The short-run total-cost curve shows the relationship between the quantity of output and production costs, given a fixed production facility. Short-run total cost equals fixed cost (the cost that does not vary with the quantity produced) plus variable cost (the cost that varies with the quantity produced).

higher of the two positively sloped curves is total cost (*TC*). Total cost is the sum of fixed cost and variable cost, so the vertical distance between the *TC* curve and the *VC* curve equals the firm's fixed cost. Notice that this distance is the same at any level of output.

Short-Run Average Costs

average fixed cost *(AFC)*
Fixed cost divided by the quantity produced.

There are three types of average cost. **Average fixed cost *(AFC)*** equals the fixed cost divided by the quantity produced:

$$AFC = \frac{FC}{Q}$$

To compute *AFC* for our paddle company, we simply divide the fixed cost ($100) by the quantity of paddles produced. In Table 23.2, we divide the number in column 3 by the number in column 2. This calculation gives us the values for *AFC*, which are shown in column 6. For example, the output in the second row is one paddle, so the average fixed cost is $100 = $100/1. In the third row, output is five paddles, so the average fixed cost is $20 = $100/5. As output increases, the $100 fixed cost is spread over more units, so *AFC* decreases.

average variable cost *(AVC)*
Variable cost divided by the quantity produced.

A firm's **average variable cost *(AVC)*** incorporates the costs that vary with the quantity produced. Average variable cost equals the variable cost divided by the quantity produced:

$$AVC = \frac{VC}{Q}$$

To compute *AVC* for our paddle company, we simply divide the number in column 4 of Table 23.2 by the number in column 2. That calculation gives us the values for *AVC*, shown in column 7. For example, the output in the third row is five paddles and the variable cost is $100, so the average variable cost is $100/5 paddles, or $20 Notice that for small quantities of output, the *AVC* decreases as the quantity produced increases—from $50 for one paddle, $20 for two paddles, and so on. The *AVC* declines because of the benefits of labor specialization. Adding workers to a small workforce makes workers more productive on average, so the amount of labor required per unit of output drops, pushing down the average variable cost. In contrast, for large quantities of output, average variable cost increases as output increases because of diminishing returns. Adding workers to a large workforce makes workers less productive on average, pulling up the average variable cost. In Figure 23.3, the *AVC* curve is negatively sloped for small quantities, but positively sloped for large quantities.

A firm's total cost is the sum of its fixed cost and variable cost, so the **short-run average total cost (*ATC*)**, or what we'll simply call "average cost," is the sum of the average fixed cost and the average variable cost:

short-run average total cost (*ATC*) Short-run total cost divided by the quantity produced; equal to *AFC* plus *AVC*.

$$ATC = \frac{TC}{Q} = \frac{FC}{Q} + \frac{VC}{Q} = AFC + AVC$$

In Figure 23.3, we go from the *AVC* to *ATC* by adding the average fixed cost to *AVC*. For example, for 5 paddles *AFC* is \$20 and *AVC* is \$20, so *ATC* is equal to \$40, the sum of \$20 + \$20. For 10 paddles, the average fixed cost is lower—only \$10—while the average variable cost is \$20, so *ATC* is \$30, the sum of \$10 + \$20. In Figure 23.3, the gap between the *AVC* and *ATC* curves is the average fixed cost.

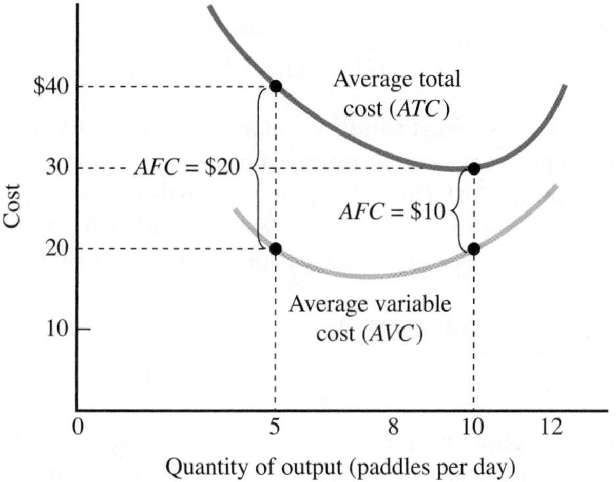

◀ FIGURE 23.3
Short-Run Average Costs
The short-run average-total-cost curve (*ATC*) is U-shaped. As the quantity produced increases, fixed costs are spread over more and more units, pushing down the average total cost. In contrast, as the quantity increases, diminishing returns eventually pulls up the average total cost. The gap between *ATC* and *AVC* is the average fixed cost (*AFC*).

The *ATC* curve in Figure 23.3 is negatively sloped at quantities less than 10 paddles. The negative slope results from two forces that work together to push average cost down as output increases:

- ***Spreading the fixed cost.*** For small quantities of output, a one-unit increase in output reduces *AFC* by a large amount because the fixed cost is pretty "thick," being spread over just a few units of output. For example, going from one paddle to five paddles decreases *AFC* from \$100 to \$20 per paddle.
- ***Labor specialization.*** For small quantities of output, *AVC* decreases as output increases because labor specialization increases worker productivity.

These two forces both push *ATC* downward as output increases, so the curve is negatively sloped for small quantities of output.

What happens once the firm reaches the point at which the benefits of labor specialization are exhausted? As the firm continues to increase output beyond that point, the average variable cost increases because of diminishing returns. There is a tug-of-war between two forces: The spreading of fixed cost continues to push *ATC* down, while diminishing returns and rising average variable cost pull *ATC* up. The outcome of the tug-of-war varies with the quantity produced, giving the *ATC* curve its U-shape:

- ***Intermediate quantities of output, such as output between 3 and 10 paddles.*** The tug-of-war is won by the spreading of fixed cost, because the fixed cost is still relatively "thick" and diminishing returns are not yet very strong. As a result, *ATC* decreases as output increases. For example, at 5 paddles *ATC* is \$40, but at 10 paddles *ATC* drops to only \$30.

- ***Large quantities of output, such as 11 or more paddles.*** The tug-of-war is won by diminishing returns and rising average variable cost. In this case, the reductions in *AFC* are relatively small because the fixed cost is already spread pretty thinly and diminishing returns are severe. As a result, *ATC* increases as output increases. For example, at 10 paddles *ATC* is $30, but at 11.5 paddles *ATC* jumps to $34.78.

Short-Run Marginal Cost

short-run marginal cost (*MC*) The change in short-run total cost resulting from a one-unit increase in output.

The **short-run marginal cost (*MC*)** is the change in short-run total cost per unit change in output. In other words, it is the increase in total cost resulting from a one-unit increase in output. Mathematically, marginal cost is calculated by dividing the change in total cost (*TC*) by the change in output (*Q*):

$$MC = \frac{\Delta TC}{\Delta Q} = \frac{\text{change in TC}}{\text{change in output}}$$

The marginal cost of the first paddle is the increase in cost when the firm produces the first paddle. To produce the first unit of output, the firm hires a single worker at $50. As shown in column 9 of Table 23.2, the marginal cost of the first paddle is $50. Moving down the ninth column, hiring the second worker for $50 increases output to five paddles. A $50 increase in total cost increases output by four paddles, so the marginal cost is $12.50:

$$MC = \frac{\Delta TC}{\Delta Q} = \frac{\text{change in TC}}{\text{change in output}} = \frac{\$50}{4} = \$12.50$$

In this case, marginal cost decreases as output increases because of labor specialization and rising worker productivity. The first worker produces just one paddle, but adding a second worker increases output by four paddles. The $50 expense of adding the second worker translates into a $12.50 expense for each of the four extra paddles produced. We saw earlier that specialization leads to increasing marginal productivity. Now we know that specialization also leads to decreasing marginal cost. In Figure 23.4, the short-run marginal-cost curve is negatively sloped for the first five paddles.

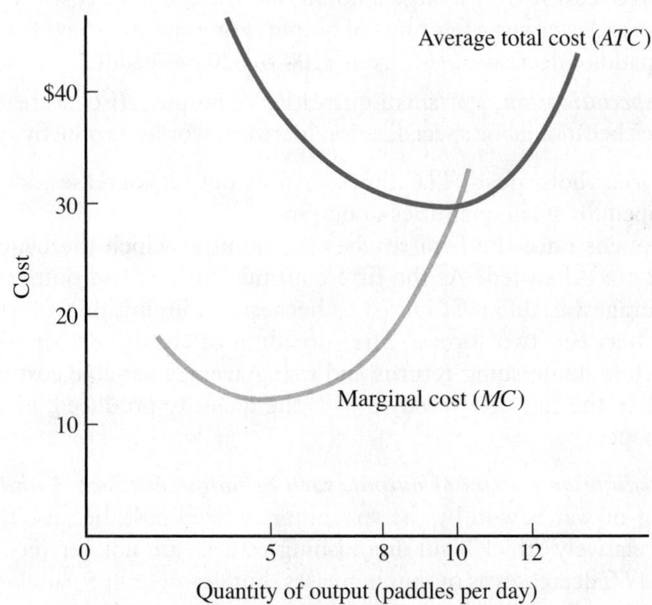

▶ **FIGURE 23.4**
Short-Run Marginal and Average Cost
The marginal-cost curve (*MC*) is negatively sloped for small quantities of output because of the benefits of labor specialization, and positively sloped for large quantities because of diminishing returns. The *MC* curve intersects the average-cost curve (*ATC*) at the minimum point of the average curve. At this point *ATC* is neither falling nor rising.

The positively sloped portion of the marginal-cost curve is a result of diminishing returns. Hiring the third worker increases output from 5 to 8, so the $50 expense translates into a $16.67 expense for each of the 3 extra paddles produced. Diminishing returns has set in, so marginal cost increases as output increases. The marginal cost increases to $25 for between 8 and 10 paddles ($50/2 paddles), then increases to $50 for between 10 and 11 paddles ($50/1 paddle), and so on. In general, diminishing returns decreases labor productivity and causes rising marginal cost.

The Relationship between Marginal Cost and Average Cost

Figure 23.4 shows the relationship between short-run marginal cost and short-run average total cost. Whenever the marginal cost is less than the average cost (for fewer than 10 paddles), the average cost is falling. In contrast, whenever the marginal cost exceeds the average cost (for more than 10 paddles), the average cost is rising. Finally, when the marginal cost equals the average cost, the average cost is neither rising nor falling. Therefore, the marginal-cost curve intersects the short-run average total cost curve at its minimum point.

We can use some simple logic to explain the relationship between average and marginal cost. Suppose that you start the semester with 9 completed courses and a cumulative grade-point average of 3.0. In the first row of Table 23.3, you have 27 grade points (4 points for each A, 3 points for each B, and so on), so your GPA is 3.0, which is 27 points divided by 9 courses. You enroll in a single course this semester—a history course. Your new GPA will depend on your grade in the history course, the marginal grade. There are three possibilities:

- ***Marginal grade less than the average grade.*** In the second row of Table 23.3, if you get a D in history, your grade point total increases from 27 points to 28 points. Dividing the new total by 10 courses, your new GPA is 2.80. It's lower because your marginal grade of 1.0 is less than the old average grade of 3.0.
- ***Marginal grade equal to the average grade.*** In the third row of Table 23.3, if you get a B in history, your grade point total increases from 27 points to 30 points. Dividing the new total by 10 courses, your new GPA is 3.0. It hasn't changed because your marginal grade of 3.0 equals the old average grade of 3.0.
- ***Marginal grade greater than the average grade.*** In the fourth row of Table 23.3, if you get an A in history, your grade point total increases from 27 points to 31 points, so your new GPA is 3.10. It's higher because your marginal grade of 4.0 is greater than the old average grade of 3.0.

To summarize, whenever the marginal grade is less than the average grade, the average will fall; whenever the marginal grade exceeds the average grade, the average will rise; and whenever the marginal grade equals the average grade, the average will not change.

TABLE 23.3 Marginal Grade and Average Grade

	Marginal Grade	Number of Courses	Grade Points	Grade Point Average
Starting point	—	9	27	3.0 = 27/9
Marginal grade < GPA	D	10	28 = 27 + 1	2.8 = 28/10
Marginal grade = GPA	B	10	30 = 27 + 3	3.0 = 30/10
Marginal grade > GPA	A	10	31 = 27 + 4	3.1 = 31/10

application 2

IDLE CAPITAL AND SHORT-RUN MARGINAL COST

APPLYING THE CONCEPTS #2: Why is the marginal-cost curve positively sloped?

Consider the following simple production process. A firm that simply digs holes has a fixed amount of capital (10 standard shovels) and can vary the number of workers. Armed with a standard shovel, a worker requires two hours to dig one hole. To produce one hole per day, the firm hires a worker and uses only one of its 10 shovels. If the wage is $12 per hour, the marginal cost of the first dug hole is $24. As the quantity of output increases, the firm adds workers and uses more of its shovels, and the marginal cost remains at $24 for the first 10 holes. In this case, marginal cost is constant for the first 10 units of output because the firm doesn't experience diminishing returns. Normally, diminishing returns occurs because an increase in the number of workers means that each worker gets a smaller share of the production facility. But in this case, each worker gets one shovel, so for the first 10 units of output, the firm does not experience diminishing returns. As a result, marginal cost is constant, not increasing. Of course, beyond 10 units of output, the firm will experience diminishing returns and rising marginal cost.

The same logic applies to other sorts of firms that can adjust their utilization of capital. For example, a firm can vary the run time of its factory, choosing one, two, or even three 8-hour shifts per day. Going from a single shift to two shifts, the firm doubles its workforce and utilizes its factory for twice as many hours, but does not experience diminishing returns because each worker gets the same share of the production facility. In general, for a production process that can tap idle capital, marginal cost is constant over some range of output. Of course, diminishing returns sets in as soon as the capital is fully utilized, for example, once a factory is running 24/7. **Related to Exercise 2.8.**

SOURCE: Based on Richard Miller, "Ten Cheaper Spades: Production Theory and Cost Curves in the Short Run, *Journal of Economic Education* (2000), pp. 119–130.

23.3 Production and Cost in the Long Run

Up to this point, we've been exploring short-run cost curves, which show the cost of producing different quantities of output in a given production facility. We turn next to long-run cost curves, which show production costs in facilities of different sizes. The *long run* is defined as the period of time over which a firm is perfectly flexible in its choice of all inputs. In the long run, a firm can build a new production facility such as a factory, store, office, or restaurant. Another option in the long run is to modify an existing facility.

The key difference between the short run and the long run is that there are no diminishing returns in the long run. Recall that diminishing returns occur because workers share a fixed production facility, so the larger the number of workers in the facility, the smaller the share of the facility available for each worker. In the long run, a firm can expand its production facility as its workforce grows, so there are no diminishing returns.

Expansion and Replication

Continuing the example of paddle production, suppose you have decided to replace your existing workshop with a new one. You have been producing 10 paddles per day at a total cost of $300 per day, or an average cost of $30 per paddle. Suppose a company that sponsors rafting adventures orders new paddles, and you decide to produce twice as much output in your new facility. What should you do?

One possibility is simply to double the original operation. You could build two workshops identical to the original shop and hire two workforces, each identical to the original workforce. In the table in Figure 23.5, your firm moves from the third row of numbers (four workers and $100 worth of capital produces 10 paddles per day) to the fourth row, with twice as much labor, capital, and output. A firm's **long-run total cost (*LTC*)** is the total cost of production when the firm is perfectly flexible in choosing its inputs, including its production facility. As shown in column 5 of the table in Figure 23.5, if your firm doubles its output from 10 paddles to 20 paddles, the long-run total cost doubles too, from $300 to $600.

long-run total cost (*LTC*) The total cost of production when a firm is perfectly flexible in choosing its inputs.

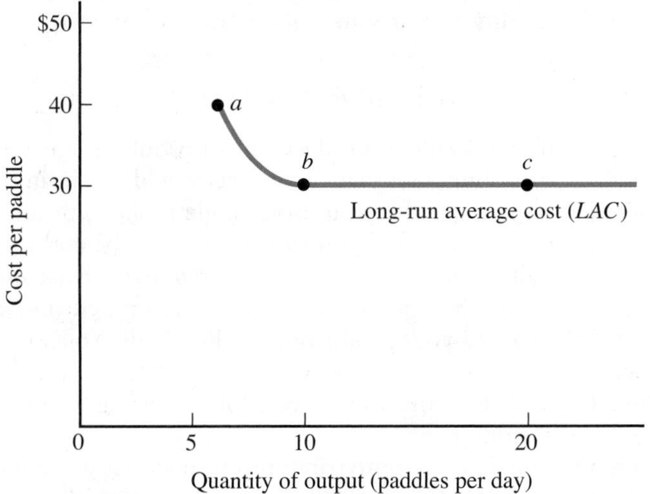

Labor	1 Capital	2 Output	3 Labor Cost	4 Long-Run Total Cost (*LTC*)	5 Long-Run Average Cost (*LAC*)
1	$100	1	$ 50	$150	$150
2	100	5	100	200	40
4	100	10	200	300	30
8	200	20	400	600	30
12	300	30	600	900	30

◄ FIGURE 23.5
The Long-Run Average-Cost Curve and Scale Economies
The long-run average-cost curve (*LAC*) is negatively sloped for up to 10 paddles per day, a result of indivisible inputs and the effects of labor specialization. If the firm replicates the operation that produces 10 paddles per day, the long-run average-cost curve will be horizontal beyond 10 paddles per day.

The firm's **long-run average cost (*LAC*)** equals the long-run cost divided by the quantity produced. As shown in column 6 of the table in Figure 23.5, doubling output from 10 to 20 paddles doesn't change the long-run average cost because doubling output by doubling both labor and capital increases costs proportionately. In the graph in Figure 23.5, point *b* shows the average cost with 10 paddles and point *c* shows the average cost with 20 paddles. As the quantity produced increases, the average cost doesn't change, so the average-cost curve is horizontal over this range of output. This is the case of **constant returns to scale**: As a firm scales up its operation, costs increase proportionately with output, so average cost is constant.

long-run average cost (*LAC*) The long-run cost divided by the quantity produced.

constant returns to scale A situation in which the long-run total cost increases proportionately with output, so average cost is constant.

The same logic applies to larger output levels. Your firm could build a third workshop identical to the first two workshops, and its production costs will increase proportionately, from \$600 to \$900. In the table in Figure 23.5, the average cost for 30 paddles is \$30, the same as for 10 and 20 paddles. In general, the replication process means the long-run total cost increases proportionately with the quantity produced, so the average cost is constant. In Figure 23.5, the long-run average-cost curve is horizontal for 10 or more paddles per day. In other words, there are constant returns to scale for output levels of 10 or more paddles.

We've seen that if a firm wants to double its output in the long run, replication is one option. By simply replicating an existing operation, a firm can double its output and its total costs, leaving average cost unchanged. Another possibility is to build a single larger workshop, one that can produce twice as much output at a lower cost than would be possible by simply replicating the original. If so, the long-run average cost of producing 20 or 30 paddles would be less than \$30 per paddle.

long-run marginal cost (*LMC*)
The change in long-run cost resulting from a one-unit increase in output.

A firm's **long-run marginal cost (*LMC*)** is the change in long-run cost resulting from producing one more unit of output. In the long run, the firm is perfectly flexible in choosing its inputs. Therefore, *LMC* is the increase in cost when the firm can change its production facility as well as its workforce.

Reducing Output with Indivisible Inputs

What would happen if you decide to produce only 5 paddles per day instead of 10? Although it's tempting to think that your total costs would be cut in half, that's not necessarily the case. Remember that you use a single mold to produce 10 paddles per day. If you cut your output in half, you would still need the mold, so your capital costs won't be cut in half. In addition, if each mold requires a fixed amount of floor space, you would still need the same floor space. Therefore, cutting output in half wouldn't decrease the cost of your production facility at all. You would still have a cost of \$100 per day for the mold and the workspace. Because cutting output in half doesn't cut capital costs in half, the average cost for producing 5 paddles will exceed the average cost for 10 paddles.

indivisible input
An input that cannot be scaled down to produce a smaller quantity of output.

The mold is an example of an **indivisible input**, one that we cannot scale down to produce a smaller quantity of output. When a production process requires the use of indivisible inputs, the average cost of production increases as output decreases, because the cost of the indivisible inputs is spread over a smaller quantity of output. Most production operations use some indivisible inputs, but the costs of these inputs vary. Here are some examples of firms and their indivisible inputs:

- A railroad company uses tracks to provide freight service between two cities. The company cannot scale down by laying a half set of tracks—a single rail.
- A shipping firm uses a large ship to carry TV sets from Japan to the United States. The company can't scale back by transporting TVs in rowboats.
- A steel producer uses a large blast furnace. The company can't scale back by producing steel in a toaster oven.
- A hospital uses imaging machines for X-rays, CAT scans, and MRIs. The hospital can't scale back by getting mini-MRI machines.

The second row of the table in Figure 23.5 shows labor and capital costs in the smaller operation. Suppose that to produce 5 paddles, you'll need two workers, including yourself. In this case, your labor cost will be \$100. Adding the \$100 cost of the indivisible input (the mold and shop space), the total cost of producing 5 paddles per day will be \$200, or \$40 per paddle. This cost exceeds the average cost of 10 paddles because in the smaller operation you still need the same amount of capital. In Figure 23.5, point *a* shows that the average cost of 5 paddles per day exceeds the average cost for larger quantities.

Scaling Down and Labor Specialization

A second possible reason for higher average long-run costs in a smaller operation is that labor will be less specialized in the small operation. As we saw earlier in the chapter, labor specialization—each worker specializing in an individual production task—makes workers more productive because of continuity and repetition. Reversing this process, when we reduce the workforce each worker will become less specialized, performing a wider variety of production tasks. The loss of specialization will decrease labor productivity, leading to higher average cost.

To see the role of labor specialization, consider the first row of numbers in the table in Figure 23.5. To produce one paddle per day, the firm needs a full day of work by one worker. The single worker performs all production tasks and is less productive than the specialized workers in larger operations. This is one reason for the relatively high average cost in a one-paddle operation ($150). The second reason is that the cost of the indivisible input is spread over fewer paddles.

Economies of Scale

A firm experiences **economies of scale** if the long-run average cost of production decreases as output increases, meaning that the long-run average-cost curve is negatively sloped. In Figure 23.5 on page 507, the paddle producer experiences economies of scale between points *a* and *b*. At point *a*, the long-run average cost is $40, compared to $30 at point *b* and beyond. An increase in output from 5 to 10 paddles decreases the long-run average cost of production because the firm spreads the cost of an indivisible input over a larger quantity, decreasing average cost. In other words, there are some economies—cost savings—associated with scaling up the firm's operation.

economies of scale
A situation in which the long-run average cost of production decreases as output increases.

One way to quantify the extent of scale economies in the production of a particular good is to determine the minimum efficient scale for producing the good. The **minimum efficient scale** is defined as the output at which scale economies are exhausted. In Figure 23.5, the long-run average-cost curve becomes horizontal at point *b*, so the minimum efficient scale is 10 paddles. If a firm starts out with a quantity of output below the minimum efficient scale, an increase in output will decrease the average cost. Once the minimum efficient scale has been reached, the average cost no longer decreases as output increases.

minimum efficient scale
The output at which scale economies are exhausted.

Diseconomies of Scale

A positively sloped long-run average-cost curve indicates the presence of **diseconomies of scale**. In this case, average cost increases as output increases. Diseconomies of scale can occur for two reasons:

diseconomies of scale
A situation in which the long-run average cost of production increases as output increases.

- ***Coordination problems.*** One of the problems of a large organization is that it requires several layers of management to coordinate the activities of the different parts of the organization. A large organization requires more meetings, reports, and administrative work, leading to higher unit cost. If an increase in the firm's output requires additional layers of management, the long-run average-cost curve may be positively sloped.
- ***Increasing input costs.*** When a firm increases its output, it will demand more of each of its inputs and *may* be forced to pay higher prices for some of these inputs.

For example, an expanding construction firm may be forced to pay higher wages to attract more workers. Alternatively, an expanding firm may be forced to hire workers who are less skilled than the original workers. An increase in wages or a decrease in productivity will increase the average cost of production, generating a positively sloped long-run average-cost curve.

Firms recognize the possibility of diseconomies of scale and adopt various strategies to avoid them. An example of a firm that adjusts its operations to avoid diseconomies of scale is 3M, a global technology company that produces products ranging from Post-it notes to pharmaceuticals and telecommunications systems. The company makes a conscious effort to keep its production units as small as possible to keep them flexible. When a production unit gets too large, the company breaks it apart.

Actual Long-Run Average-Cost Curves

Figure 23.6 shows the actual long-run average-cost curves for three products: aluminum production, truck freight, and hospital services.[2]

▶ **FIGURE 23.6**
Actual Long-Run Average-Cost Curves for Aluminum, Truck Freight, and Hospital Services

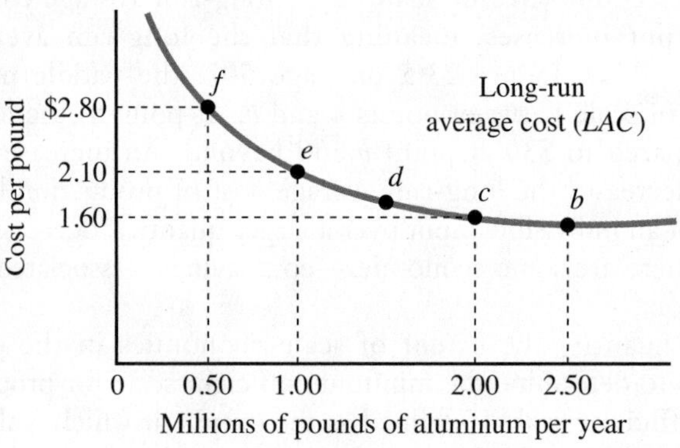

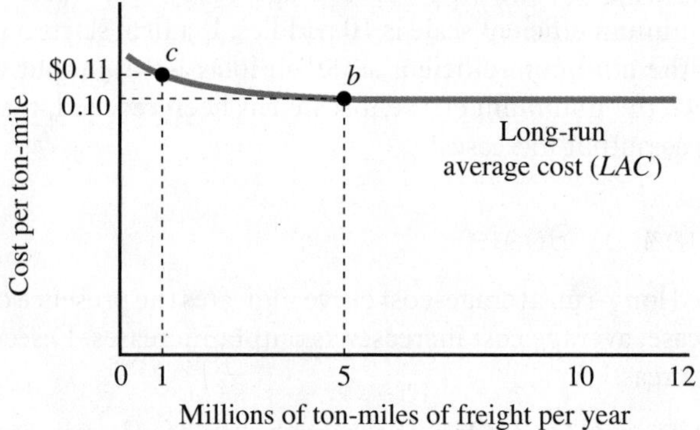

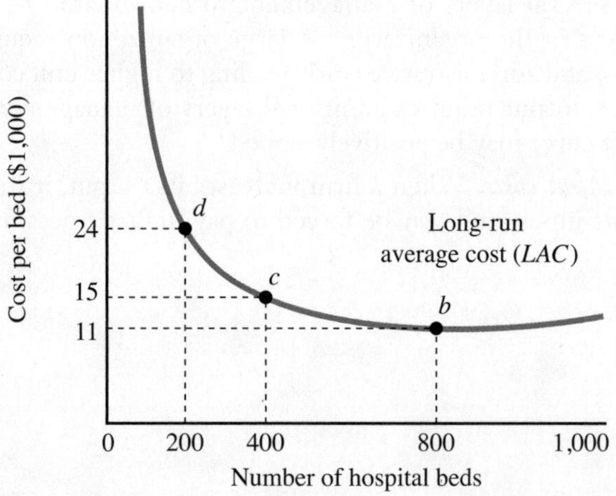

In each case, the long-run average cost curve is negatively sloped for small quantities of output and relatively flat—almost horizontal—over a large range of output. In other words, these curves are L-shaped. Other studies suggest that the long-run cost curves of a wide variety of goods and services have the same shape.

Why is the typical long-run average-cost curve L-shaped? The long-run average-cost curve is negatively sloped for small quantities of output because there are economies of scale resulting from indivisible inputs and labor specialization. As output increases, the average-cost curve eventually becomes horizontal and remains horizontal for a wide range of output. Over the horizontal portion of the cost curve, increases in inputs lead to proportionate increases in output, so the average cost doesn't change. In other words, the long-run average total cost (*LAC*) is constant and production is subject to constant returns to scale.

Short-Run versus Long-Run Average Cost

Why is the firm's short-run average-cost curve U-shaped, while the long-run average-cost curve is L-shaped? For large quantities of output, the short-run curve is positively sloped because of diminishing returns and the resulting decrease in labor productivity and increase in marginal cost. If a firm increases its output while at least one input is held fixed, diminishing returns eventually occur, pulling up the average cost of production.

The difference between the short run and long run is a firm's flexibility in choosing inputs. In the long run, a firm can increase all of its inputs, scaling up its operation by building a larger production facility. As a result, the firm will not suffer

application 3

INDIVISIBLE INPUTS AND THE COST OF FAKE KILLER WHALES

APPLYING THE CONCEPTS #2: How do indivisible inputs affect production costs?

Sea lions off the Washington coast eat steelhead and other fish, depleting some species threatened with extinction and decreasing the harvest of the commercial fishing industry. Rick Funk is a plastics manufacturer who has offered to build a life-sized fiberglass killer whale, mount it on a rail like a roller coaster, and send the whale diving through the water to scare off the sea lions, whales' natural prey. According to Funk, it would cost about $16,000 to make the first whale, including $11,000 for the mold and $5,000 for labor and materials. Once the mold is made, each additional whale would cost an additional $5,000. In other words, the cost of producing the first fake killer whale is more than three times the cost of producing the second. In terms of total cost, producing two whales would cost a total of $21,000, while three whales would cost a total of $26,000, and so on.

This little story illustrates the effects of indivisible inputs on the firm's cost curves. The mold is an indivisible input, because it cannot be scaled down and still produce whales. If Funk wants to cut his production from two whales per month down to one, he still needs the mold; he cannot simply produce half as many whales with half a mold or a mold that is half the size. The cost of producing the first whale, $16,000, includes the cost of the mold, the indivisible input. Once the firm has the mold, the marginal cost for each whale is only $5,000, so the average cost per whale decreases as the number of whales increases. **Related to Exercises 3.4 and 3.9.**

SOURCE: Based on Sandi Doughton, "Killer Whale Latest Idea on Sea Lions," *Oregonian*, January 7, 1995.

from diminishing returns. In most cases, the long-run average-cost curve will be negatively sloped or horizontal. In some cases, firms experience diseconomies of scale, so the long-run average-cost curve will be positively sloped for high output levels. Nonetheless, the long-run average cost will not be as steep as the short-run curve, which is relatively steep because of diminishing returns.

23.4 Examples of Production Cost

So far we've explored the links between production technology and the cost of production. We've seen the firm's short-run cost curves, which show how production costs vary with the quantity produced when at least one input is fixed. We've also seen the long-run average-cost curve, which shows how the average cost of production varies when the firm is perfectly flexible in choosing its inputs. In this part of the chapter, we look at actual production costs for several products.

Scale Economies in Wind Power

There are scale economies in the production of electricity from wind because electricity can be generated from turbines of different sizes. Although large wind turbines are more costly than small ones, the higher cost is more than offset by greater generating capacity. The scale economies occur because the cost of purchasing, installing, and maintaining a wind turbine increases less than proportionately with the turbine's generating capacity. Table 23.4 shows the costs of a small turbine (150-kilowatt capacity) and a large turbine (600-kilowatt capacity), each with an assumed lifetime of 20 years.

TABLE 23.4 Wind Turbines and the Average Cost of Electricity

	Small Turbine (150 kilowatt)	Large Turbine (600 kilowatt)
Purchase price of turbine	$150,000	$420,000
Installation cost	$100,000	$100,000
Operating and maintenance cost	$75,000	$126,000
Total cost	$325,000	$646,000
Electricity generated (kilowatt-hours)	5 million	20 million
Average cost (per kilowatt-hour)	$0.065	$0.032

SOURCE: Based on Danish Wind Turbine Manufacturers Association, "Guided Tour of Wind Energy" (2003), www.windpower.dk (accessed June 27, 2006).

The large turbine has four times the generation capacity of the small turbine—20 million kilowatt hours versus 5 million kilowatt hours—but its purchase price is less than three times as much. The two turbines have the same installation cost, and the operating and maintenance cost of the larger turbine is less than twice as large. Adding the various costs, the larger turbine, with four times the generating capacity, has less than twice the cost. As a result, the average cost per kilowatt-hour is only $0.032 for the large turbine, compared to $0.065 for the smaller turbine.

The Average Cost of a Music Video

A music video is an information good—a product that is essentially a bundle of information. Most of the cost of producing an information good results from collecting the information and making a first copy. Once the information is organized and digitized, the marginal cost of reproduction is tiny. In other words, an information good has large first-copy cost, and a tiny marginal cost.

For a music video, the first-copy cost is the cost of putting images and sounds into a digital format. The typical music video has a first-copy cost of $223,000—an amount that includes $28,000 for the people responsible for the script or "treatment," $81,000 for two days of filming, $81,000 for editing, and $33,000 for other costs. Once the images and sounds are digitized, the marginal cost of making additional copies is small, or in the case of a music video distributed online, actually zero.

The average cost of a music video depends on how many copies are distributed. Suppose the music video can be distributed online, at zero marginal cost. The average cost is $223 if 1,000 copies are distributed, and drops to $0.23 if one million copies are distributed. In Figure 23.7, the average-cost curve is negatively sloped and gets closer and closer to the horizontal axis as the quantity distributed increases. The gap decreases as the fixed production cost is spread over a larger number of copies. If consumers can download the music video at a price of $1, the break-even quantity is 223,000 copies distributed.

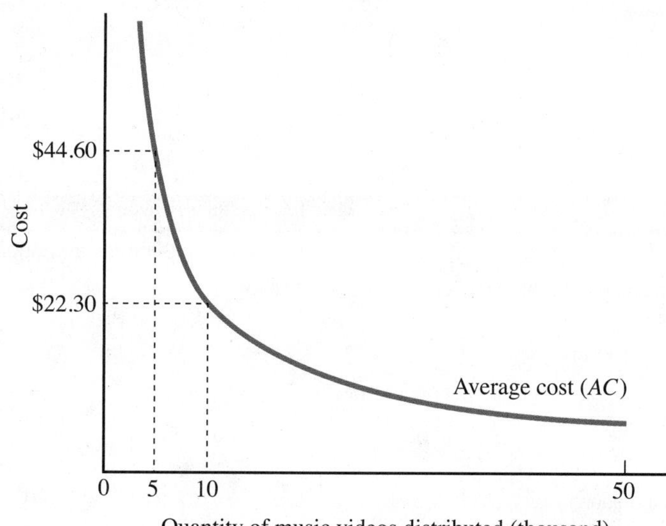

◄ **FIGURE 23.7**
Average-Cost Curve for an Information Good
For an information good such as a music video, the cost of producing the first copy is very high, but the marginal cost of reproduction is relatively low, and for products distributed online, the marginal cost is zero.

Solar versus Nuclear: The Crossover

In 1998, the cost of electricity produced with solar technology was $0.32 per kilowatt hour (Kwh), compared to $0.07 per Kwh for electricity produced with nuclear technology.[3] Recent innovations in photovoltaic technology have reduced the unit cost of solar power, to $0.21 per Kwh in 2005 and to $0.16 per Kwh in 2010. Over the same period, the unit cost of nuclear power increased, in large part because the capital cost of a nuclear reactor has increased, from $3 billion in 2002 to

$10 billion in 2010. For a new nuclear facility, the projected unit cost of electricity is about $0.16 per Kwh. In other words, the cost gap between solar and nuclear power has been eliminated: the cost of solar power is roughly the same as the unit cost of nuclear power.

SUMMARY

In this chapter, we explored the cost side of a firm, explaining the shapes of the firm's short-run and long-run cost curves. Table 23.6 summarizes the definitions of various types of costs. Here are the main points of the chapter:

1 The negatively sloped portion of the *short-run marginal-cost curve (MC)* results from input specialization that causes increasing marginal returns.

2 The positively sloped portion of the *MC* results from *diminishing returns*.

3 The *short-run average-total-cost curve (ATC)* is U-shaped because of the conflicting effects of (a) fixed costs being spread over a larger quantity of output and (b) diminishing returns.

4 The *long-run average-cost curve (LAC)* is horizontal over some range of output because replication is an option, so doubling output will no more than double long-run total cost.

5 The *LAC* is negatively sloped for small quantities of output because (a) there are indivisible inputs that cannot be scaled down and (b) a smaller operation has limited opportunities for labor specialization.

6 *Diseconomies of scale* arise if there are problems in coordinating a large operation or higher input costs in a larger organization.

TABLE 23.5 The Language and Mathematics of Costs

Type of Cost	Definition	Symbols and Equations
Economic cost	The opportunity cost of the inputs used in the production process; equal to explicit cost plus implicit cost	—
Explicit cost	The actual monetary payment for inputs	—
Implicit cost	The opportunity cost of inputs that do not involve a monetary payment	—
Accounting cost	Explicit cost	—
Short-Run Costs		
Fixed cost	Cost that does not vary with the quantity produced	FC
Variable cost	Cost that varies with the quantity produced	VC
Short-run total cost	The total cost of production when at least one input is fixed	$TC = FC + VC$
Short-run marginal cost		$MC = \Delta TC/\Delta Q$
Average fixed cost	Fixed cost divided by the quantity produced	$AFC = FC/Q$
Average variable cost	Variable cost divided by the quantity produced	$AVC = VC/Q$
Short-run average total cost	Short-run total cost divided by the quantity produced	$ATC = AFC + AVC$
Long-Run Costs		
Long-run total cost	The total cost of production when a firm is perfectly flexible in choosing its inputs	LTC
Long-run average cost	Long-run total cost divided by the quantity produced	$LAC = LTC/Q$
Long-run marginal cost	The change in long-run cost resulting from a one-unit increase in output	$LMC = \Delta LTC/\Delta Q$

KEY TERMS

accounting cost, p. 499
accounting profit, p. 499
average fixed cost (*AFC*), p. 502
average variable cost (*AVC*), p. 502
constant returns to scale, p. 507
diminishing returns, p. 500
diseconomies of scale, p. 509
economic cost, p. 498
economic profit, p. 498
economies of scale, p. 509
explicit cost, p. 498
fixed cost (*FC*), p. 501
implicit cost, p. 498
indivisible input, p. 508
long-run average cost (*LAC*), p. 507
long-run marginal cost (*LMC*), p. 508
long-run total cost (*LTC*), p. 507
marginal product of labor, p. 499
minimum efficient scale, p. 509
short-run average total cost (*ATC*), p. 503
short-run marginal cost (*MC*), p. 504
short-run total cost (*TC*), p. 501
total-product curve, p. 500
variable cost (*VC*), p. 501

EXERCISES

All problems are assignable in MyEconLab.

23.1 Economic Cost and Economic Profit

1.1 The computation of economic cost is based on the principle of ________.

1.2 A firm's implicit cost is defined as the ________ cost of nonpurchased inputs, such as the entrepreneur's ________ and ________.

1.3 Economic profit equals ________ minus ________.

1.4 Fill with "economic" or "accounting": Because ________ cost typically exceeds ________ cost, ________ profit typically exceeds ________ profit.

1.5 Suppose a person quits a job paying $40,000 per year and starts a business with $100,000 withdrawn from a money-market account earning 8 percent per year. The implicit cost of the business is ________ for the entrepreneur's time plus ________ for the entrepreneur's funds.

1.6 The ________ (long/short) run is defined as a period over which a firm cannot change its production facility.

1.7 When a firm is perfectly flexible in its choice of all inputs, the firm is operating in the ________ (long/short) run.

1.8 Workers who become entrepreneurs earn roughly ________ percent ________ (less, more) than workers who remain in paid employment. (Related to Application 1 on page 499.)

1.9 **Compute the Cost.** Edward the entrepreneur takes two hours to cut a lawn, and he cuts 1,000 lawns per year. He uses solar-powered equipment (truck and mower) that will last forever—and can be sold at any time for $20,000. Edward could earn $12 per hour as a pedicurist. The interest rate is 10 percent.

a. Given his current output level, compute his marginal cost and average cost of cutting lawns.

b. Suppose he decides to reduce the number of lawns cut by half, to 500 per year. Compute the new marginal cost and average cost.

23.2 A Firm with a Fixed Production Facility: Short-Run Costs

2.1 The short-run marginal cost curve is shaped like the letter ________ and the short-run average cost curve is shaped like the letter ________.

2.2 The negatively sloped portion of the short-run marginal-cost curve is explained by ________ and the positively sloped portion is explained by ________.

2.3 Over the positively sloped portion of the short-run average-cost curve, the effect of ________ dominates the effect of ________.

2.4 At the current level of output, the marginal cost of MP3 players exceeds the average cost. If you increase output, the average cost will ________ (increase/decrease).

2.5 If marginal cost equals average cost, we are at the minimum point of the ________ cost curve.

2.6 Arrows up or down. When marginal cost is less than average cost, an increase in output ________ average cost. When marginal cost exceeds average cost, an increase in output ________ average cost.

2.7 The short-run average cost of production is the same for two different quantities. ________ (True/False)

2.8 For a firm that doubles its workforce and adds a second shift at its factory, production ____ (is, is not) subject to diminishing returns, so marginal cost is ________. (Related to Application 2 on page 506.)

2.9 **Compute the Costs.** Consider a firm that has a fixed cost of $60. Complete the following table:

Output	Fixed Cost (FC)	Variable Cost (VC)	Total Cost (TC)	Marginal Cost (MC)	Average Fixed Cost (AFC)	Average Variable Cost (AVC)	Average Total Cost (ATC)
1		$10					
2		18					
3		30					
4		45					
5		65					

2.10 **Changing Costs.** Consider the paddle production example shown in Table 23.2 on page 501. Compute the short-run average cost for 10 paddles with the following changes.

a. Your opportunity cost of work time triples, from $50 to $150.

b. The interest rate for invested funds is cut in half, from 10 to 5 percent.

c. Labor productivity—the quantity produced by each workforce—doubles.

2.11 **Compute the Short-Run Costs.** Consider a firm with the following short-run costs:

a. What is the firm's fixed cost?

b. Compute short-run marginal cost (*MC*), short-run average variable cost (*AVC*), and short-run average total cost (*ATC*) for the different quantities of output.

c. Draw the three cost curves. Explain the relationship between the *MC* curve and the *ATC* curve and the relationship between the *AVC* curve and the *ATC* curve.

Quantity	Variable Cost (VC)	Total Cost (TC)	Marginal Cost (MC)	Average Variable Cost (AVC)	Average Total Cost (ATC)
1	$ 30	$ 90			
2	50	110			
3	90	150			
4	140	200			
5	200	260			

2.12 **Same Average Cost with Different Quantities?** Suppose there are two pencil producers with identical production facilities—identical factories and equipment. The firms pay the same wages and pay the same prices for materials. Sam has a small workforce and produces 1,000 pencils per minute; Marian has a medium-size workforce and produces 2,000 pencils per minute. The two firms have the same average total cost of 10 cents per pencil. Suppose you build a production facility identical to the ones used by the other firms and hire enough workers and buy enough materials to produce 2,500 pencils per minute. Would you expect your average cost to be 10 cents per pencil (like the other two firms), less than 10 cents, or more than 10 cents?

23.3 Production and Cost in the Long Run

3.1 The presence of ________ explains the negatively sloped portion of a long-run average-cost curve, and the notion of ________ explains the horizontal portion of the curve.

3.2 Consider the information provided in Figure 23.6 on page 510. Suppose the output of a large aluminum firm drops from two million pounds to one million pounds per year. The long-run average cost of producing aluminum will go from $________ to $________.

3.3 The typical *short-run* average-cost curve is shaped like the letter U, while the typical *long-run* average-cost curve is shaped like the letter L because __________ are not applicable in the __________ run.

3.4 The cost of producing the first fake killer whale is about three times the cost of producing the second because the firm uses __________ inputs. (Related to Application 3 on page 511.)

3.5 **Deregulation and the Cost of Trucking.** Suppose the government initially limits the number of trucking firms that can haul freight. The market for truck freight is served by a single firm that produces five million ton-miles of service per year, where one ton-mile is the hauling of one ton of freight one mile. The newly elected governor has proposed that other firms be allowed to enter the market. At a public hearing on the issue of eliminating the entry restrictions, the manager of the existing firm issued a grim warning: "If you allow entry into the market, four or five firms will enter, and the unit cost of truck freight will at least triple. There are big economies of scale in trucking services, so a single large firm is much more cost-efficient than several small firms would be." What's your reaction to this statement?

3.6 **Draw the Long-Run Cost Curve.** Consider the long-run production of shirts. The cost of the indivisible inputs used in the production of shirts is $400 per day. To produce 1 shirt per day, the firm must also spend a total of $5 on other inputs—labor, materials, and other capital. For each additional shirt, the firm incurs the same additional cost of $5.

a. Compute the average cost for 40 shirts, 100 shirts, 200 shirts, and 400 shirts.

b. Draw the long-run average-cost curve for 40 to 400 shirts per day.

3.7 **Diminishing Returns versus Diseconomies of Scale.** Explain the difference between diseconomies of scale and diminishing returns. Based on the cost curves you've seen in this chapter, which is more likely in firms?

3.8 **Constant Marginal Cost.** Consider a firm operating in the long run with an indivisible input that has a cost of $120. The marginal cost of production is constant at $3 per unit. Draw the firm's long-run average-cost curve for 1 to 12 units of output. The long-run average cost drops from $__________ for the first unit to $__________ for the twelfth unit.

3.9 **A Better Whale Mold?** Suppose a new mold is developed for producing fake killer whales. The new mold has twice the cost of the original mold, but cuts the marginal cost of whales to $1,000. (Related to Application 3 on page 511.)

a. How does the cost of the first whale produced with the new mold compare to the cost with the original mold?

b. At what quantity of whales will production with the new mold be less costly than production with the original mold?

23.4 Examples of Production Cost

4.1 The average cost of electricity __________ (increases/decreases) as the size of the wind turbine increases.

4.2 For information goods such as a music video distributed online, the cost of producing the first copy is very __________, but the marginal cost is __________.

4.3 **The Average Cost of a Super-Sized Turbine.** Suppose a new super-sized wind turbine is developed. Fill in the blanks in the following table.

	Super-Sized Turbine (1,000 kilowatt)
Purchase price of turbine	$500,000
Installation cost	$100,000
Operating and maintenance cost	$200,000
Total cost	
Electricity generated (kilowatt-hours)	40 million
Average cost (per kilowatt-hour)	

4.4 **The Average Cost of a Music Video.** In Figure 23.7 suppose a strike by wardrobe and makeup artists increases the cost of wardrobe and makeup by $17,000. Draw the average-cost curve for producing the video and distributing it online, with quantities up to 50,000.

4.5 **The Average Cost of Drama DVDs.** You have been hired to produce a DVD of a play put on by a high-school drama club. It will take you about 50 hours to make the master, which will be stored on a hard drive on your computer. The opportunity cost of your time is $20 per hour. The marginal cost of burning DVDs is constant at $2. Draw the average-cost curve for producing the DVD, with quantities up to 100 DVDs.

NOTES

1. Ashish Karamchandani, Michael Kubzansky, and Paul Franano, "Emerging Markets, Emerging Models: Market-Based Solutions to the Challenges of Global Poverty," Monitor Company Group L.P., 2009.

2. Laurits Christensen and William H. Greene, "Economies of Scale in U.S. Electric Power Generation," *Journal of Political Economy* 84 (1976): 655–676. Reprinted by permission of The University of Chicago Press; Joel P. Clark and Merton C. Flemings, "Advanced Materials and the Economy," *Scientific American* 255 (October 1986): 51–60. Copyright 1986 by Scientific American, Inc. All rights reserved; Roger Koenker, "Optimal Scale and the Size Distribution of American Trucking Firms," *Journal of Transport Economics and Policy* (January 1977): 62; Harold A. Cohen, "Hospital Cost Curves with Emphasis on Measuring Patient Care Output," in *Empirical Studies in Health Economics*, ed. Herbert E. Klarman (Baltimore, MD: Johns Hopkins University Press, 1970); John Johnson, *Statistical Cost Analysis* (New York: McGraw-Hill, 1960).

3. Diana Powers, Nuclear Energy Loses Cost Advantage, *The New York Times* July 26, 2010; John Blackburn and Sam Cunningham, "Solar and Nuclear Costs—The Historic Crossover" (July 2010).

Perfect Competition

CHAPTER

24

In the award-winning 2004 movie *Sideways*, the main character raved about pinot noir wine, noting that the pinot grape requires special care and attention, and can be grown only in a few places. The character said that the payoff from all the attention is a wine whose subtle and brilliant flavors make it one of the best wines on the planet.[1]

This rave review increased the demand for pinot noir wine grown in the Willamette Valley in Oregon. As a result, the price of wine soared, and for some brands the price tripled. A few years later, growers competed fiercely for consumers by cutting prices, in many cases back to pre-*Sideways* prices. As we'll see in this chapter, this is a common pattern in markets that experience increases in demand, even if the higher demand persists.

LEARNING OBJECTIVES

- Distinguish between four market structures.
- Explain the short-run output rule and the break-even price.
- Explain the shut-down rule.
- Explain why the short-run supply curve is positively sloped.
- Explain why the long-run industry supply curve may be positively sloped.
- Describe the short-run and long-run effects of changes in demand for an increasing-cost industry.
- Describe the short-run and long-run effects of changes in demand for a constant-cost industry.

MyEconLab
MyEconLab helps you master each objective and study more efficiently.

This is the first of four chapters exploring the decisions firms make in different types of markets. Markets differ in the number of firms that compete against one another for customers. In this chapter, we'll look at a perfectly competitive market. In a **perfectly competitive market**, hundreds, or even thousands, of firms sell a homogeneous product. Each firm is such a small part of the market that it takes the market price as given: Each firm is a **price taker**. For example, each soybean farmer takes the market price as given. There is no reason to cut the price to sell more soybeans, because the farmer can sell as much as he wants at the market price. There is no reason to increase the price, because the farmer would lose all his customers to other farmers selling at the market price.

perfectly competitive market
A market with many sellers and buyers of a homogeneous product and no barriers to entry.

price taker
A buyer or seller that takes the market price as given.

A perfectly competitive market has two other features. First, on the demand side of the market there are hundreds, or even thousands, of buyers, each of whom takes the market price as given. Second, there are no barriers to market entry, so firms can easily enter or exit the market. To summarize, here are the five features of a perfectly competitive market:

1. There are many sellers.
2. There are many buyers.
3. The product is homogeneous.
4. There are no barriers to market entry.
5. Both buyers and sellers are price takers.

If you're thinking that the model of perfect competition is unrealistic, you're right. Most firms actually have some flexibility over their prices. For example, when Target increases its price of DVDs, it will certainly sell fewer DVDs, but the quantity sold will probably not drop to zero. Although perfect competition is rare, it's a good starting point for analyzing a firm's decisions, because a price-taking firm's decisions are easy to understand. The firm doesn't have to pick a price; it just decides how much to produce, given the market price. Once you understand this simple case, you will be ready to tackle the more complex decisions made by firms that are *price makers*—able to affect prices. We'll discuss that scenario in later chapters.

In this chapter, we'll see how price-taking firms use information on revenues and costs to decide how much output to produce. The output decisions of price-taking firms underlie the market supply curve and the law of supply. In other words, this chapter reveals the economic logic behind the market supply curve and the law of supply.

24.1 Preview of the Four Market Structures

Let's start by distinguishing between a market demand curve and the demand curve for an individual firm. As we saw earlier in the book, the market demand curve shows the relationship between the price and the quantity that suppliers can sell in the market, assuming all firms charge the same price. In contrast, the **firm-specific demand curve** shows the relationship between the price charged by a specific firm and the quantity that firm can sell. In a *monopoly*, a single firm serves the entire market, so the firm-specific demand curve is the same as the market demand curve. As shown in Panel A of Figure 24.1, the monopolist can choose any point on the market demand curve, recognizing that the higher the price, the smaller the quantity the firm will sell.

firm-specific demand curve
A curve showing the relationship between the price charged by a specific firm and the quantity the firm can sell.

As shown in Panel B of Figure 24.1, things are different for a perfectly competitive firm. The firm-specific demand curve is horizontal—perfectly elastic. A perfectly competitive firm can sell as much as it wants at the market price of $12, but if it raises its price even a penny, it will sell nothing.

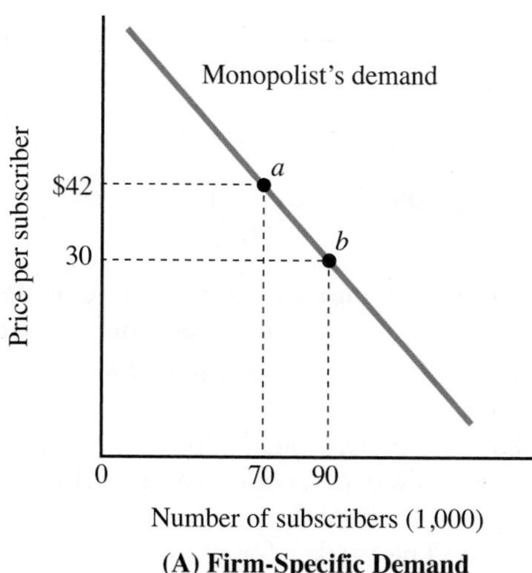

(A) Firm-Specific Demand Curve of Monopolist

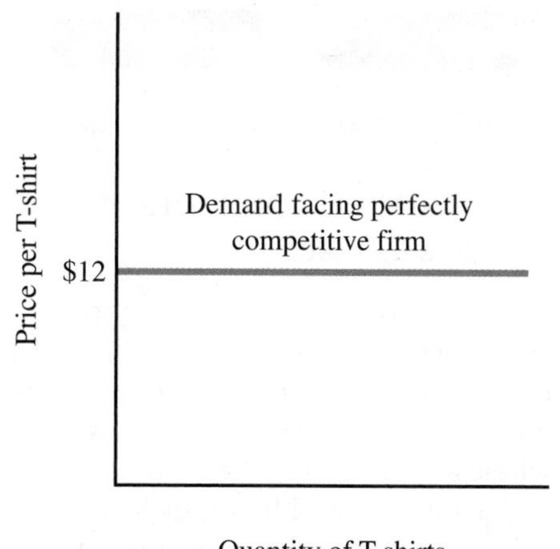

(B) Firm-Specific Demand Curve of Perfectly Competitive Firm

◀ FIGURE 24.1
Monopoly versus Perfect Competition
In Panel A, the demand curve facing a monopolist is the market demand curve. In Panel B, a perfectly competitive firm takes the market price as given, so the firm-specific demand curve is horizontal. The firm can sell all it wants at the market price, but would sell nothing if it charged a higher price.

Most markets lie between the extremes of monopoly and perfect competition. Table 24.1 compares perfectly competitive markets with three alternative market structures, which we'll discuss in the next three chapters:

- ***Monopoly.*** A single firm serves the entire market. A monopoly occurs when the barriers to market entry are very large. This can result from very large economies of scale or a government policy that limits the number of firms. Some examples of monopolies that result from large economies of scale are local phone service, cable TV, and electric power transmission. Some examples of monopolies established by government policy are drugs covered by patents, the selling of firewood in national parks, and the U.S. Postal Service.
- ***Monopolistic competition.*** There are no barriers to entering the market, so there are many firms, and each firm sells a slightly different product. For example, coffee shops in your city provide slightly different goods and compete for customers. Your local grocery store sells many brands of toothbrushes, with slight differences in size, shape, color, and style.
- ***Oligopoly.*** The market consists of just a few firms because economies of scale or government policies limit the number of firms. Some product examples are automobiles, computer processor chips, airline travel, and breakfast cereals. The large economies of scale in automobile production result from the large startup costs, with billions of dollars required to build a factory or assembly plant. Similarly, a fabrication plant for computer processor chips costs several billion dollars.

TABLE 24.1 Characteristics of the Four Market Structures

Characteristic	Perfect Competition	Monopolistic Competition	Oligopoly	Monopoly
Number of firms	Many	Many	Few	One
Type of product	Homogeneous	Differentiated	Homogeneous or differentiated	Unique
Firm-specific demand curve	Demand is perfectly elastic	Demand is elastic but not perfectly elastic	Demand is less elastic than demand facing monopolistically competitive firm	Firm faces market demand curve
Entry conditions	No barriers	No barriers	Large barriers from economies of scale or government policies	Large barriers from economies of scale or government policies
Examples	Corn, plain T-shirts	Toothbrushes, music stores, groceries	Air travel, automobiles, beverages, cigarettes, mobile phone service	Local phone service, patented drugs

application 1

WIRELESS WOMEN IN PAKISTAN

APPLYING THE CONCEPTS #2: How do entry costs affect the number of firms in a market?

For another example of a competitive market, consider phone service in the developing world, where many people relied on pay phones until the recent development of mobile phones generated a new competitive industry. In Pakistan, phone service is now provided by thousands of "wireless women," entrepreneurs who invest $310 in wireless phone equipment (transceiver, battery, charger), a signboard, a calculator, and a stopwatch. Then they sell phone service to their neighbors, charging by the minute and second. On average, their net income is about $2 per day, about three times the average per capita income in Pakistan. The market for phone service has the features of a perfectly competitive market, with easy entry, a standardized good, and a large enough number of suppliers that each takes the market price as given. In contrast, to enter the phone business in the United States, your initial investment would be millions, or perhaps billions, of dollars, so the market for phone service is not perfectly competitive. **Related to Exercise 1.4.**

SOURCE: Based on TeleCommons Development Group, "Grameen Telecom's Village Phone Programme: A Multi-Media Case Study," 2000, www.telecommons.com/villagephone (accessed June 27, 2006).

24.2 The Firm's Short-Run Output Decision

We'll start our discussion of perfect competition with an individual firm's decision about how much output to produce. The firm's objective is to maximize *economic profit*, which, as we saw in the previous chapter, equals total revenue minus economic cost. Recall that economic cost includes all the opportunity costs of production, both explicit costs (cash payments) and implicit costs (the entrepreneur's opportunity costs). In the preceding chapter, we saw that the cost of production varies with the quantity produced. In this chapter, we'll see how economic profit varies with the quantity produced and then show how a firm can pick the quantity that maximizes its economic profit.

Remember that economic profit differs from the conventional notion of profit. Accountants focus on the flow of money into and out of a firm, so they ignore costs that do not involve explicit transactions. *Accounting profit* equals total revenue minus explicit costs. Because accountants ignore implicit costs, accounting profit usually exceeds economic profit.

We will use the market for plain T-shirts to illustrate decision making in a perfectly competitive market. Some plain T-shirts are sold directly to consumers, and others are sold to firms that imprint words and images on the T-shirts and then sell the finished shirts to consumers. Plain T-shirts are produced in countries around the world by a large number of producers.

The Total Approach: Computing Total Revenue and Total Cost

One way for a firm to decide how much to produce is to compute the economic profit at different quantities and then pick the quantity that generates the highest profit. As we've seen, economic profit equals total revenue minus economic cost. We looked at the cost side of the profit equation in Chapter 23. The revenue side for a perfectly competitive market is straightforward. A firm's total revenue is the money it gets by selling its product. Total revenue is equal to the price of the product times the quantity sold. For example, if a firm sells eight T-shirts at $12 per shirt, total revenue is $96 (equal to 8 × $12). If our T-shirt producer has an economic cost of $63, the firm's profit is $33 (equal to $96 – $63).

Table 24.2 shows the total revenue and total costs of a hypothetical producer of plain cotton T-shirts. Follow the row for an output of eight shirts. As shown in the second and third columns, the fixed cost is $17, and the variable cost increases with the amount produced. The fourth column shows total cost, the sum of the fixed and variable costs. As shown in the fifth column, at a price of $12 per shirt, the firm's total revenue is $12 times the number of shirts produced. The sixth column shows economic profit, equal to total revenue minus total cost.

TABLE 24.2 Deciding How Much to Produce When the Price Is $12

1 Output: Shirts per Minute (*Q*)	2 Fixed Cost (*FC*)	3 Variable Cost (*VC*)	4 Total Cost (*TC*)	5 Total Revenue (*TR*)	6 Profit = *TR* – *TC*	7 Marginal Revenue = Price	8 Marginal Cost (*MC*)
0	$17	$0	$ 17	$ 0	–$17		
1	17	5	22	12	–10	$12	$ 5
2	17	6	23	24	1	12	1
3	17	9	26	36	10	12	3
4	17	13	30	48	18	12	4
5	17	18	35	60	25	12	5
6	17	25	42	72	30	12	7
7	17	34	51	84	33	12	9
8	17	46	63	96	33	12	12
9	17	62	79	108	29	12	16
10	17	83	100	120	20	12	21

Figure 24.2 shows one way to choose the quantity of output that maximizes profit. We're looking for the largest profit, shown by the biggest gap between total revenue and total cost. For example, for five shirts the gap is $25: Total revenue (*TR*) equals $60, and total cost (*TC*) equals $35. Moving down the table and across the figure, we see that profit increases to $30 for six shirts:

$$TR - TC = \$72 - \$42 = \$30$$

Profit is maximized at $33 when the firm produces either seven or eight shirts:

$$TR - TC = 84 - 51 = \$33$$

$$TR - TC = 96 - 63 = \$33$$

When profit reaches its highest level with two different quantities (seven and eight shirts in this example), we assume the firm produces the larger quantity. When the firm produces eight shirts, its total revenue is $96 and its total cost is $63, leaving a profit of $33.

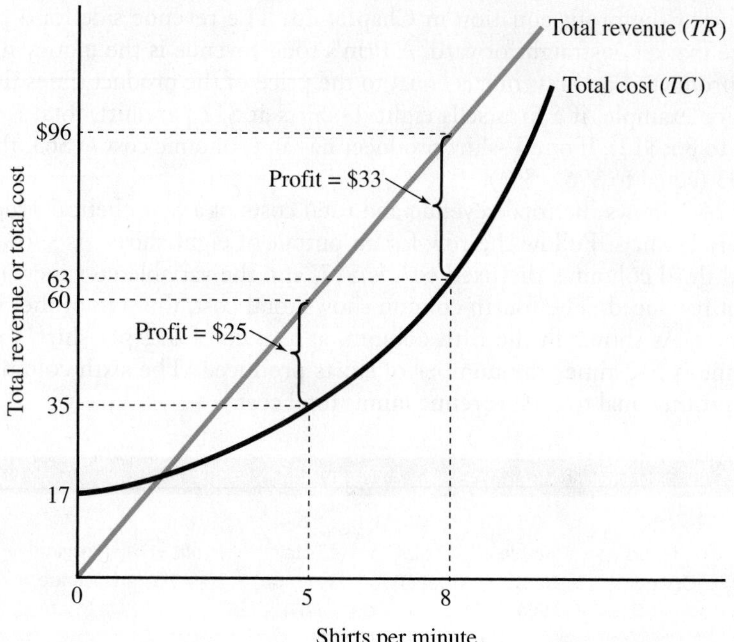

► FIGURE 24.2
Using the Total Approach to Choose an Output Level
Economic profit is shown by the vertical distance between the total-revenue curve and the total-cost curve. To maximize profit, the firm chooses the quantity of output that generates the largest vertical difference between the two curves.

The Marginal Approach

The other way for a firm to decide how much output to produce relies on the marginal principle, the general decision-making rule that is one of the key principles of economics.

MARGINAL PRINCIPLE

Increase the level of an activity as long as its marginal benefit exceeds its marginal cost. Choose the level at which the marginal benefit equals the marginal cost.

marginal revenue
The change in total revenue from selling one more unit of output.

Because our firm is in business to make money, the benefit it gets from producing shirts is revenue. The *marginal* benefit—or **marginal revenue**—of producing shirts is the change in total revenue that results from selling one more shirt. A perfectly competitive firm takes the market price as given, so the marginal revenue—the change in total revenue from one more shirt—is simply the price:

$$\text{marginal revenue} = \text{price}$$

The marginal principle tells us that the firm will maximize its profit by choosing the quantity at which price equals marginal cost:

To maximize profit, produce the quantity where price = marginal cost

In Figure 24.3, the horizontal line shows the market price for T-shirts, which our shirt producer takes as given. The price line intersects the marginal-cost curve at eight shirts per minute, so that's the quantity that satisfies the marginal principle and maximizes profit.

To see that an output of eight shirts per minute maximizes the firm's profit, imagine that the firm initially produced only five shirts per minute. Could the firm make more profit by producing more—that is, six shirts instead of five?

- From the seventh row of numbers in Table 24.2 on page 523 and point *c* in Figure 24.3, we know the marginal cost of the sixth shirt is $7.
- The price of shirts is $12, so the marginal revenue is $12.

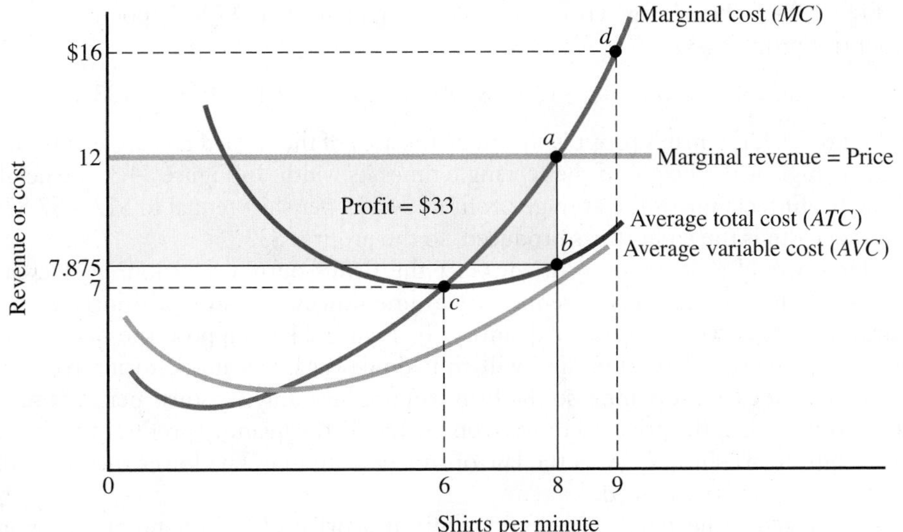

◄ **FIGURE 24.3**
The Marginal Approach to Picking an Output Level
A perfectly competitive firm takes the market price as given, so the marginal benefit, or marginal revenue, equals the price. Using the marginal principle, the typical firm will maximize profit at point **a**, where the $12 market price equals the marginal cost. Economic profit equals the difference between the price and the average cost ($4.125 = $12 – $7.875) times the quantity produced (eight shirts per minute), or $33 per minute.

Because the extra revenue from the sixth shirt (price = $12) exceeds the extra cost (marginal cost = $7), the production and sale of the sixth shirt increases the firm's total profit by $5 (equal to $12 – $7). Therefore, it is sensible to produce the sixth shirt. The same logic applies, with different numbers for marginal cost, for the seventh shirt. For the eighth shirt, marginal revenue equals marginal cost, so the firm's profit doesn't change. To be consistent with the marginal principle, we'll assume the firm produces to the point where marginal revenue equals marginal cost. In this case, the firm chooses point *a* and produces eight shirts.

If the firm produced more than eight shirts, it would earn less than the maximum profit. Imagine that the firm initially produced nine shirts. From Table 24.2 and the marginal-cost curve in Figure 24.3, we see that the marginal cost of the ninth shirt is $16 (point *d*), which exceeds the marginal revenue (the market price) of $12. The ninth shirt adds more to cost ($16) than it adds to revenue ($12), so producing the shirt decreases the firm's profit by $4. The marginal principle suggests that the firm should choose point *a*, with an output of eight shirts. The output decision is the same whether the firm uses the marginal approach or the total approach.

The advantage of the marginal approach is that it is easier to apply. To use the total approach, a firm needs information about the total revenue and total cost for all possible output levels. In contrast, a firm can apply the marginal principle by simply increasing its output by one unit and computing the marginal revenue (the price) and the marginal cost. Using the marginal principle, the firm should produce more output if the price exceeds the marginal cost, or produce less if the opposite is true. The firm can use the marginal principle to fine-tune its decision until the price equals the marginal cost.

Economic Profit and the Break-Even Price

We've seen that the perfectly competitive firm maximizes its profit by producing the quantity at which its marginal revenue (price) equals its marginal cost. How much profit does the firm earn? The firm's economic profit equals its total revenue minus its total cost. One way to compute a firm's total economic profit is to multiply the average profit per unit produced—the gap between the price and the average cost—by the quantity produced:

$$\text{economic profit} = (\text{price} - \text{average cost}) \times \text{quantity produced}$$

In Figure 24.3, the average cost of producing eight shirts is \$7.875 (point *b*), so the economic profit is \$33:

$$\text{economic profit} = (\$12 - \$7.875) \times 8 = \$4.125 \times 8 = \$33$$

In Figure 24.3, the firm's profit is shown by the area of the shaded rectangle. The area of a rectangle is the height of the rectangle times its width. In Figure 24.3, the height of the profit rectangle is the average profit of \$4.125 per shirt (equal to \$12 – \$7.875) and the width is the eight shirts produced, so the profit is \$33.

How would a decrease in price affect the firm's output decision? A decrease in price shifts the marginal-revenue (price) line downward, so it will intersect the marginal-cost curve at a smaller quantity. In Figure 24.3, suppose the price drops to \$7. The marginal-revenue line will shift downward, causing it to intersect the marginal-cost curve at point *c*, so the firm will produce only six shirts per minute. In other words, when the price decreases from \$12 to \$7 the quantity produced decreases from eight to six shirts. This is the law of supply in action: The lower the price, the smaller the quantity supplied.

break-even price
The price at which economic profit is zero; price equals average total cost.

What about the firm's economic profit at a price of \$7? At point *c*, average total cost is \$7, the same as the price. Therefore, economic profit is zero. We have discovered the **break-even price**, the price at which economic profit is zero. The

application 2

THE BREAK-EVEN PRICE FOR SWITCHGRASS, A FEEDSTOCK FOR BIOFUEL

APPLYING THE CONCEPTS #1: What is the break-even price?

In the search for alternatives to fossil fuels, a prominent contender is switchgrass, a perennial grass that is native to the U.S. plains states. The principal advantage of switchgrass and other cellulosic feedstocks for biofuels is their small carbon footprint. At what price will farmers convert their fields to switchgrass?

A recent study estimates the break-even price for growing switchgrass in North Dakota. The price per ton varies with the fertility of the land, from \$56 on the least fertile land to \$95 on the most fertile, or \$76 on average. To compute the break-even price, the researchers started by adding up the explicit costs of production, including the costs of capital (machinery and equipment), labor, and raw materials. Then they added the opportunity cost of using land for switchgrass rather than another crop, for example, alfalfa, wheat, or soybeans.

We can illustrate the calculations with a simple example. Suppose the most profitable alternative to switchgrass is alfalfa, and the implicit rent on land used to grow alfalfa is \$120 per acre—that's how much a farmer can earn in alfalfa production. If the switchgrass yield is 3 tons per acre, the opportunity cost of land per ton of switchgrass is \$40 per ton (equal to \$120/3). If the explicit cost of a ton of switchgrass (for capital, labor, and raw materials) is \$36, the break-even switchgrass price is \$76 = \$36 + \$40.

What are the implications for switchgrass biofuel? To get some North Dakota farmers to switch their crops to switchgrass, the price must be at least \$56 per ton. And the higher the price, the larger the acreage devoted to switchgrass. To get the most fertile land in North Dakota switched to switchgrass, the price must be \$95. **Related to Exercises 2.9 and 2.10.**

SOURCE: Based on Dean A. Bangsund, Eric A. DeVuyst, and F. Larry Leistritz, "Evaluation of Breakeven Farm-gate Switchgrass Prices in South Central North Dakota," *Agribusiness and Applied Economics Report* 632, North Dakota State University (2008).

break-even price is shown by the minimum point of the *ATC* curve, where marginal cost equals average total cost. Remember that zero economic profit means that the firm is making just enough money to cover all its costs, including the opportunity costs of the entrepreneur.

24.3 The Firm's Shut-Down Decision

Consider next the decisions faced by a firm that is losing money. Suppose the price of shirts drops to $4, which is so low that the firm's total revenue is less than its total cost. In Table 24.3, the marginal principle tells the firm to produce four shirts at this price, but the firm's total cost of $30 exceeds its total revenue of $16, so the firm will lose $14 per minute. Should the firm continue to operate at a loss or shut down?

TABLE 24.3 Deciding How Much to Produce When the Price Is $4

1 Output: Shirts per Minute (*Q*)	2 Fixed Cost (*FC*)	3 Variable Cost (*VC*)	4 Total Cost (*TC*)	5 Total Revenue (*TR*)	6 Profit = *TR* − *TC*	7 Marginal Revenue = Price	8 Marginal Cost (*MC*)
0	$17	$ 0	$17	$ 0	−$17		
1	17	5	22	4	−18	$4	$5
2	17	6	23	8	−15	4	1
3	17	9	26	12	−14	4	3
4	17	13	30	16	−14	4	4
5	17	18	35	20	−15	4	5
6	17	25	42	24	−18	4	7

Total Revenue, Variable Cost, and the Shut-Down Decision

The decision to operate or shut down is a short-run decision, a day-to-day decision to temporarily halt production in response to market conditions. Suppose our shirt factory hires workers by the day, so it makes the decision at the beginning of each day. The decision-making rule is

operate if total revenue > variable cost

shut down if total revenue < variable cost

As we saw in Chapter 23, a firm's variable cost includes all the costs that vary with the quantity produced. In the case of the shirt firm, it includes the costs of workers, raw materials such as cotton, and the cost of heating and powering the factory for the day. The variable cost does not include the $17 fixed cost of the production facility—for example, the cost of the machines or the factory itself—because these costs are not affected by the decision to operate or shut down.

Although the decision is made at the beginning of each day, we can use the revenue and costs per minute to compare total revenue to variable cost. From Table 24.3, when the price is $4, the best quantity is four shirts and the variable cost is $13. The total revenue from selling four shirts at $4 per shirt is $16, which exceeds the $13 variable cost. By operating the factory, the firm pays $13 in variable cost to generate $16 in revenue, so the firm is better off operating the facility. The benefit of operating the facility exceeds the variable cost, so it is sensible to produce four shirts per minute.

Figure 24.4 shows the firm's choice when the price of shirts is \$4. The marginal principle is satisfied at point *a*, where the price equals the marginal cost. As shown by point *b*, the average cost of producing four shirts is \$7.50, so the firm loses \$3.50 per shirt. The shaded rectangle shows the firm's loss of \$14. The height of the rectangle is the \$3.50 loss per shirt, and the width of the rectangle is the four shirts produced.

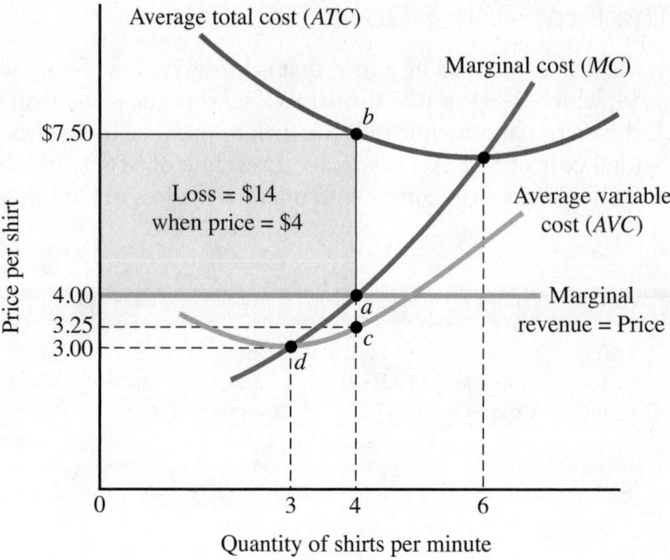

▶ **FIGURE 24.4**
The Shut-Down Decision and the Shut-Down Price
When the price is \$4, marginal revenue equals marginal cost at four shirts (point a). At this quantity, average cost is \$7.50, so the firm loses \$3.50 on each shirt, for a total loss of \$14. Total revenue is \$16 and the variable cost is only \$13, so the firm is better off operating at a loss rather than shutting down and losing its fixed cost of \$17. The shut-down price, shown by the minimum point of the *AVC* curve, is \$3.00.

Of course, if the price drops to a low enough level, the firm will shut down the factory. For example, if the price drops to \$1, the marginal principle is satisfied with two shirts per day. At this quantity, the variable cost is \$6, which exceeds \$2 revenue (\$1 per shirt times two shirts). With this low price, the firm's total revenue is not high enough to cover the firm's variable cost from operating the facility, so it is better to shut down for the day.

The Shut-Down Price

There is a shortcut for determining whether it is sensible to continue to operate—compare the price to the average variable cost. Total revenue equals the price times the quantity produced, and the variable cost equals the average variable cost times the quantity produced. Therefore, total revenue will exceed variable cost if the price exceeds the average variable cost. If that happens, the firm should continue to operate. Otherwise, the firm should shut down.

$$\text{operate if price} > \text{average variable cost}$$

$$\text{shut down if price} < \text{average variable cost}$$

In Figure 24.4, with a price of \$4, the marginal principle is satisfied at point *a*, and the average variable cost of producing four shirts is \$3.25 (point *c*). The price exceeds the average variable cost, so it is sensible to continue operating, even at a loss.

shut-down price
The price at which the firm is indifferent between operating and shutting down; equal to the minimum average variable cost.

The firm's **shut-down price** is the price at which the firm is indifferent between operating and shutting down. To find the shut-down price, we find the minimum point on the *AVC* curve. In Figure 24.4, *AVC* reaches its minimum of \$3 at a quantity of three shirts per minute, so the shut-down price is \$3 (shown by point *d*). The average variable cost never drops below \$3, so if the price drops below \$3 it would be impossible to generate enough revenue to cover the firm's variable cost. When the price equals the shut-down price, the firm is generating just enough revenue to cover its variable costs, so it is just as well off operating as shutting down.

How long will a firm continue to operate at a loss? Let's think about what happens when the firm must decide whether or not to build a new production facility. The firm will build a new facility—and stay in the market—only if the price of shirts exceeds the average total cost of production. In other words, the firm will stay in the market only if the market price is high enough for its total revenue to cover *all* the costs of production, including the cost of the new facility. In other words, the price must be greater than or equal to the firm's break-even price. Although a firm might make a short-run decision to operate an existing facility at a loss, it won't replace the facility unless a new facility will be profitable.

Fixed Costs and Sunk Costs

Note that the decision whether to operate or shut down does not incorporate the fixed costs of the production facility. If we assume the facility cannot be rented out to some other firm while the shirt firm isn't using it, the fixed cost is a **sunk cost**, a cost the firm has already paid or committed to pay, so it cannot be recovered even by shutting down the factory. Therefore, the firm should ignore the cost of the facility when deciding whether to operate or shut down.

sunk cost
A cost that a firm has already paid or committed to pay, so it cannot be recovered.

Rent is just one example of an irrelevant sunk cost. The marginal principle tells us that decisions are based on the costs that depend on what we do, not on costs that we can do nothing about. Suppose a dairy farmer spills two-thirds of a 300-gallon load of milk on the way to an ice-cream plant. Should the farmer return to the farm or deliver the remaining 100 gallons? As long as the marginal cost of delivering the milk—the opportunity cost of the farmer's time and the cost of fuel—is less than the amount the farmer will be paid for the remaining 100 gallons, it is sensible to deliver the milk. The spilt milk is a sunk cost that is irrelevant to the farmer's delivery decision. The farmer should not cry over spilt milk, but deliver the rest.

application 3

STRADDLING THE ZINC COST CURVE

APPLYING THE CONCEPTS: What is the shutdown price?

Zinc is a vital input to the production of steel. Because the cost of mining zinc varies from one mine to another, the shutdown price varies too. The world price of zinc decreased from roughly $2,300 per ton in 2010–2011 to $1,900 in early 2012. The lower price was below the shutdown prices of Alcoa's mines in Italy and Spain: at a price of $1,900, the total revenue from the mines was less than the variable cost of operating the mines. The shutdown of Alcoa's mines decreased mining output by 531,000 tons. Although mines with lower production costs continued mining at a price of $1,900, many mines have shutdown prices in the range $1,500 to $1,900, and will shut down if the price continues to drop. **Related to Exercise 3.5.**

SOURCE: Based on Metal Bulletin, "No widespread shutdowns in zinc unless LME prices fall below $1,900," January 10, 2012; London Metal Exchange, LME Price Graph (lme.com/zinc_graph; accessed February 23, 2012).

24.4 Short-Run Supply Curves

Now that we've explored the output decision of a price-taking firm, we're ready to show how a firm responds to changes in the market price of its product. We'll show the relationship between price and quantity supplied with two short-run supply curves, one for the individual firm and one for the entire market.

The Firm's Short-Run Supply Curve

short-run supply curve
A curve showing the relationship between the market price of a product and the quantity of output supplied by a firm in the short run.

The firm's **short-run supply curve** shows the relationship between the market price and the quantity supplied by the firm in the short run, over a period of time during which one input—the production facility—cannot be changed. In the case of shirt producers, the firm's supply curve answers the following question: At a given market price for shirts, how many shirts will the firm produce? In Figures 24.3 and 24.4, we used the marginal principle to answer this question for several different prices: At a price of $3, the quantity is 3 shirts; at a price of $7, the quantity is 6 shirts; at a price of $12, the quantity is 8 shirts.

The firm's short-run supply curve is the part of the firm's short-run marginal-cost curve above the shut-down price. The shut-down price for the shirt firm is $3, so, as shown by point *a* in Figure 24.5, the short-run supply curve is the marginal-cost curve starting at $3. For any price above the shut-down price, the firm will choose the quantity at which price equals marginal cost, so we can read the firm's quantity supplied directly from its marginal-cost curve. If the price is $7, the firm will supply 6 shirts per minute (point *b*). As the price increases, the firm responds by supplying more shirts: 8 shirts at a price of $12 (point *c*) and 10 shirts at a price of $21 (point *d*).

What about prices below the shut-down price? If the price drops below the shut-down price, the firm's total revenue will not be high enough to cover its variable cost, so the firm will shut down and produce no output. In Panel A of Figure 24.5, the firm's supply curve starts at point *a*, indicating that the quantity supplied is zero for any price less than $3.

The Short-Run Market Supply Curve

short-run market supply curve
A curve showing the relationship between the market price and quantity supplied in the short run.

The **short-run market supply curve** shows the relationship between the market price and the quantity supplied by firms as a whole in the short run. Panel B of Figure 24.5 shows the short-run market supply curve when there are 100 identical shirt firms. For

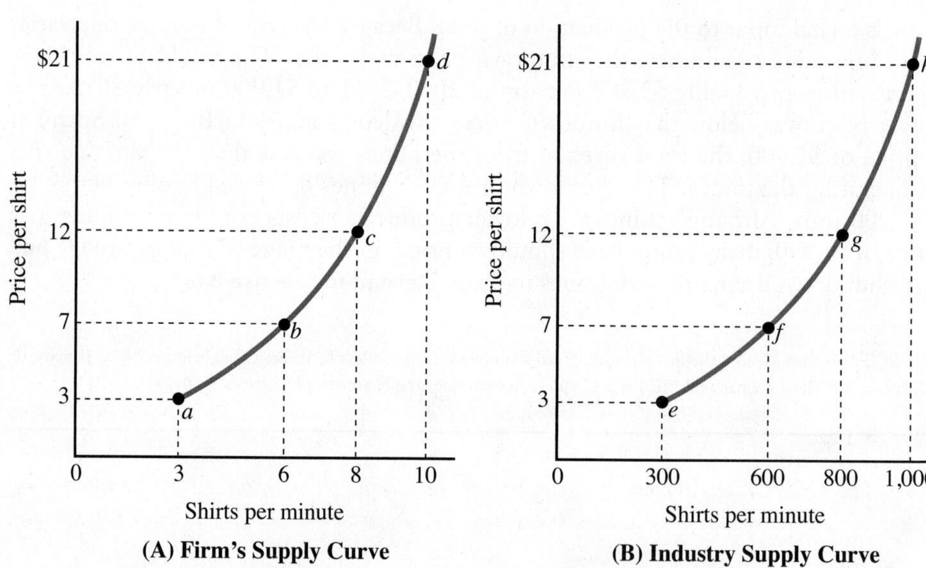

► FIGURE 24.5
Short-Run Supply Curves
In Panel A, the firm's short-run supply curve is the part of the marginal-cost curve above the shut-down price. In Panel B, there are 100 firms in the market, so the market supply at a given price is 100 times the quantity supplied by the typical firm. At a price of $7, each firm supplies 6 shirts per minute (point *b*), so the market supply is 600 shirts per minute (point *f*).

each price, we get the quantity supplied for the entire market by multiplying the quantity supplied by the typical firm (from the individual supply curve) by 100. At a price of $7, each firm produces 6 shirts (point *b* in Panel A), so the market supply is 600 shirts (point *f* in Panel B). If the price increases to $12, each firm increases production to 8 shirts (point *c* in Panel A), so the market supply is 800 shirts (point *g* in Panel B).

What happens if firms are not identical but instead have different individual supply curves? To compute the market supply in this case, we add the quantities supplied by the hundreds of firms in the market. The assumption that firms are identical is harmless: It makes it easier to derive the market supply curve from the supply curve of the typical firm, but it does not change the analysis.

Market Equilibrium

Figure 24.6 shows a perfectly competitive market in equilibrium. For a short-run equilibrium, two conditions are satisfied:

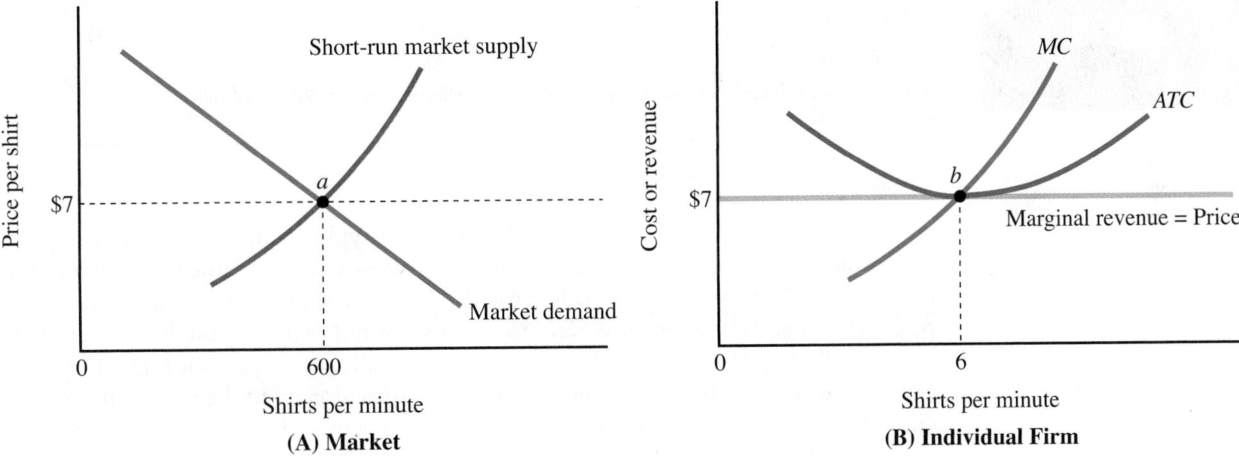

▲ FIGURE 24.6
Market Equilibrium
In Panel A, the market demand curve intersects the short-run market supply curve at a price of $7. In Panel B, given the market price of $7, the typical firm satisfies the marginal principle at point *b*, producing six shirts per minute. The $7 price equals the average cost at the equilibrium quantity, so economic profit is zero, and no other firms will enter the market.

1 At the market level, the quantity of the product supplied equals the quantity demanded. The demand curve intersects the short-run market supply curve at a price of $7 and a quantity of 600 shirts per minute (Panel A).
2 The typical firm in the market maximizes its profit, given the market price. Given the market price of $7, each of the 100 firms maximizes profit by producing 6 shirts per minute (Panel B).

In Figure 24.6, the market has reached a short-run equilibrium because the price of $7 generates a total of 600 shirts per minute, exactly the quantity demanded by consumers at this price.

In the long run, firms can enter or leave an industry, and existing firms can modify their facilities or build new facilities. The market reaches a long-run equilibrium when the two conditions for short-run equilibrium are met, and a third long-run condition holds as well:

3 Each firm in the market earns zero economic profit, so there is no incentive for existing firms to leave the market and no incentive for other firms to enter the market.

application 4

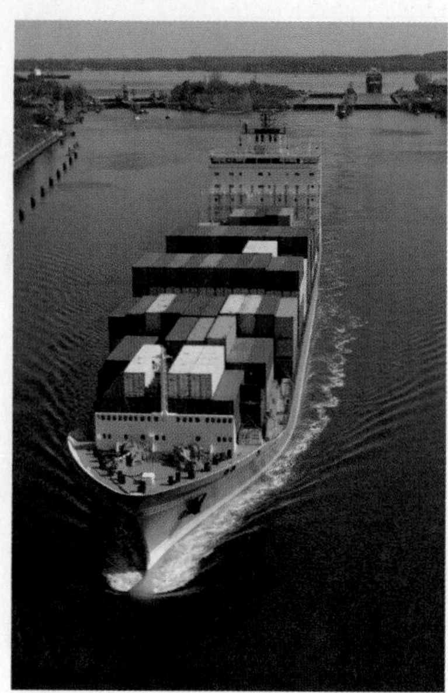

SHORT-RUN SUPPLY CURVE FOR CARGO

APPLYING THE CONCEPTS #4: Why is the short-run supply curve positively sloped?

Consider the supply of shipping services. The law of supply suggests that as the price of shipping increases, the quantity of shipping services will increase. At a relatively low freight rate of $2 per ton, only the most efficient ships operate, and they economize on fuel by traveling at a relatively low speed. As a result, the annual quantity of shipping services is only 70 units per year. At an intermediate freight price of $3 per ton, less efficient ships join the fleet. In addition, all the ships travel at a greater speed, using more fuel in the process. The combination of more ships and faster travel increases the quantity of shipping services provided to 85 units per year. At a high freight rate of $7 per ton, the least efficient ships join the fleet and all the ships run at full speed. As a result, the quantity of shipping services increases to 96 units per year. **Related to Exercise 4.6.**

SOURCE: Based on Martin Stopard, *Maritime Economics*, 3rd edition (New York: Routledge, 2007).

In Figure 24.6, at the quantity chosen by the typical firm (six shirts), the price ($7) equals the average total cost, so each firm makes zero economic profit, with total revenue equal to total cost. In other words, the market price equals the break-even price. When economic profit is zero, the firm's revenue is high enough to cover all its costs—including the opportunity costs of the entrepreneur—but not high enough to cause additional firms to enter the market. Each firm already in the market makes just enough money to stay in business, so there is no incentive for new firms to enter the market, and no incentive for existing firms to leave.

24.5 The Long-Run Supply Curve for an Increasing-Cost Industry

long-run market supply curve
A curve showing the relationship between the market price and quantity supplied in the long run.

Let's look at the **long-run market supply curve**, which shows the relationship between the market price and the quantity supplied by all firms in the long run, a period long enough that firms can enter or leave the market. Suppose the typical shirt firm produces six shirts per minute, using a standard set of inputs, including a factory, some workers, and raw materials of cotton and thread. In a perfectly competitive industry, there are no restrictions on entry, so anyone can use the standard set of inputs to produce six shirts per minute.

increasing-cost industry
An industry in which the average cost of production increases as the total output of the industry increases; the long-run supply curve is positively sloped.

We'll start with the case of an **increasing-cost industry**, in which the average cost of production increases as the total output increases, for two reasons:

- ***Increasing input price.*** As an industry grows, it competes with other industries for limited amounts of various inputs, and this competition drives up the prices of these inputs. For example, suppose the shirt industry competes against other industries for a limited amount of cotton. To get more cotton to produce more shirts, firms in the shirt industry must outbid other industries for the limited amount available, and this drives up the price of cotton.

- ***Less productive inputs.*** A small industry will use only the most productive inputs, but as the industry grows, firms may be forced to use less productive inputs. For example, a small shirt industry will use only the most skillful workers, but as the industry grows, it will hire workers with lower skills. As the average skill level of the industry's workforce decreases, the average cost of production increases: A firm will require more labor time—and pay more in labor costs—to produce each shirt.

Another example of progressively less productive inputs is the production of agricultural products such as sugar. Because of variation in climate and soil conditions, it is cheaper to grow sugar in some areas than in others. As the quantity of sugar produced increases, growers are forced to produce sugar in areas with less favorable climates and soil conditions, and this results in higher costs.

Production Cost and Industry Size

Table 24.4 shows hypothetical data on the cost of producing shirts. Let's start with the first row, which shows the firm's production costs in an industry with 100 firms and a total of 600 shirts produced per day (6 shirts per firm). To compute the total cost for the typical firm, we add the cost of the firm's production facility (the cost of the shirt factory), the cost of labor, and the cost of materials. In the first row, the total cost of the typical firm producing 6 shirts per minute is $42, and the average cost is $7 per shirt ($42 divided by 6 shirts). In the second row, if the number of firms doubles to 200 and each firm continues to produce 6 shirts per minute, the total output of the industry will double to 1,200 shirts per minute. For the two reasons listed earlier (higher input prices and less productive inputs), the total cost per firm increases to $60, so the average cost per shirt increases to $10. In the last row, when the total output of the industry increases to 1,800 shirts per minute, the average cost per shirt increases to $13.

TABLE 24.4 Industry Output and Average Production Cost

Number of Firms	Industry Output	Shirts per Firm	Total Cost for Typical Firm	Average Cost per Shirt
100	600	6	$42	$ 7
200	1,200	6	60	10
300	1,800	6	78	13

The shirt industry is an example of an increasing-cost industry. In the last column of Table 24.4, the average cost increases from $7 for an industry that produces 600 shirts, to $10 for an industry that produces 1,200 shirts, and so on. The average cost increases because firms in a larger industry pay higher input prices and use less productive inputs.

Drawing the Long-Run Market Supply Curve

The long-run supply curve tells us how much output will be produced at each price in the long run, when the number of firms in the market can change. Recall that in the long-run equilibrium, each firm makes zero economic profit, meaning that the price equals the average cost of production.

The data in Table 24.4 shows three points on the long-run supply curve. At a price of $7, a total of 100 firms will be in the market, with each producing 6 shirts per hour. This combination (price = $7 and quantity = 600 shirts) is on the long-run supply curve because the price equals the average cost. Each firm makes zero economic profit, so there is no incentive for firms to either enter or exit the market. This is shown by point *a* in Figure 24.7. Suppose the price of shirts increases. At the higher price, shirt making will be more profitable, and firms will enter the market, increasing total output. Firms will continue to enter the market until the economic profit becomes zero again, which happens when the average cost again equals the price. From Table 24.4, we see that entry will continue until the market reaches 200 firms producing 1,200 shirts at an average cost and price of $10. This is shown by point *b* in Figure 24.7. Point *c* shows another point on the long-run supply curve, with a price of $13 and a quantity of 1,800 shirts.

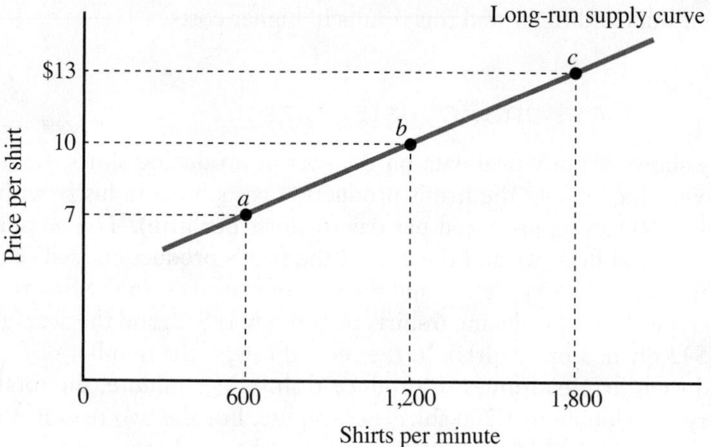

▶ **FIGURE 24.7**
Long-Run Market Supply Curve
The long-run market supply curve shows the relationship between the price and quantity supplied in the long run, when firms can enter or leave the industry. At each point on the supply curve, the market price equals the long-run average cost of production. Because this is an increasing-cost industry, the long-run market supply curve is positively sloped.

The long-run supply curve in Figure 24.7 is positively sloped, as it will be for any increasing-cost industry. This is another example of the law of supply. An increase in the price of shirts initially makes shirt production profitable, so firms enter the market and produce more shirts. As industry-wide output increases, the greater demand for cotton and labor increases input prices, which in turn increases the average cost of producing shirts. Firms will continue to enter the market until the average cost rises to the point where it equals the price of shirts. The positively sloped supply curve tells us the market won't produce a larger quantity of shirts unless the price rises to cover the higher average cost associated with the larger industry.

Examples of Increasing-Cost Industries: Sugar and Apartments

The sugar industry is an example of an increasing-cost industry. If the price of sugar is only 11 cents per pound, sugar production is profitable in areas with relatively low production costs, including the Caribbean, Latin America, Australia, and South Africa. At a price of 11 cents, the world supply of sugar equals the amount produced in these areas. As the price increases, sugar production becomes profitable in areas where production costs are higher, and as these areas enter the world market, the quantity of sugar supplied increases. For example, at a price of 14 cents per pound, sugar production is profitable in some countries in the European Union, too. At a price of 24 cents, production is profitable even in the United States.

application 5

CHINESE COFFEE GROWERS OBEY THE LAW OF SUPPLY

APPLYING THE CONCEPTS #5: How do producers respond to an increase in price?

Pu'er is a city in southern China that is famous for its tea, but is now getting a reputation for its coffee. Between 2009 and 2012, the world price of coffee beans nearly doubled. Farmers in Pu'er responded to the higher price by doubling the acreage of coffee, and cleared forested hillsides to grow more beans. At the relatively high world price, a hectare of coffee earns a family about $10,000 per year, which is three times the earnings from growing tea and five times the earnings from growing rice. The farmers' response illustrates the law of supply: an increase in price increases the quantity supplied. **Related to Exercise 5.7.**

SOURCE: Based on "For all the coffee in China," *The Economist*, January 28, 2012, pp. 44–45.

The market for apartments is another example of an increasing-cost industry with a positively sloped supply curve. Most communities use zoning laws to restrict the amount of land available for apartments. As the industry expands by building more apartments, firms compete fiercely for the small amount of land zoned for apartments. Housing firms bid up the price of land, increasing the cost of producing apartments. Producers can cover these higher production costs only by charging higher rents to tenants. In other words, the supply curve for apartments is positively sloped because land prices increase with the total output of the industry, pulling up average cost and necessitating a higher price for firms to make zero economic profit.

24.6 Short-Run and Long-Run Effects of Changes in Demand

We can use what we've learned about the short-run and long-run supply curves to get a deeper understanding of perfectly competitive markets. Let's use the two supply curves to explore the short-run and the long-run effects of a change in demand in a perfectly competitive market.

The Short-Run Response to an Increase in Demand

Figure 24.8 shows the short-run effects of an increase in the demand for shirts. Panel A shows what's happening at the market level. Let's start with the initial equilibrium shown by point *a*: The original demand curve intersects the short-run market supply curve at a price of $7 per shirt and a quantity of 600 shirts. When demand increases, the new demand curve intersects the supply curve at a price of $12 and a quantity of 800 shirts (point *b*). In Panel B, an increase in price from $7 to $12 increases the output per firm from 6 shirts to 8 shirts. At this quantity, the $12 price now exceeds the average total cost, so the typical firm makes an economic profit, as shown by the shaded rectangle.

Point *b* is not a long-run equilibrium because each firm is making a positive economic profit. Firms will enter the profitable market, and as they compete for customers the price of shirts will decrease. New firms will continue to enter the market until the price drops to the point at which economic profit is zero. How far will the price drop?

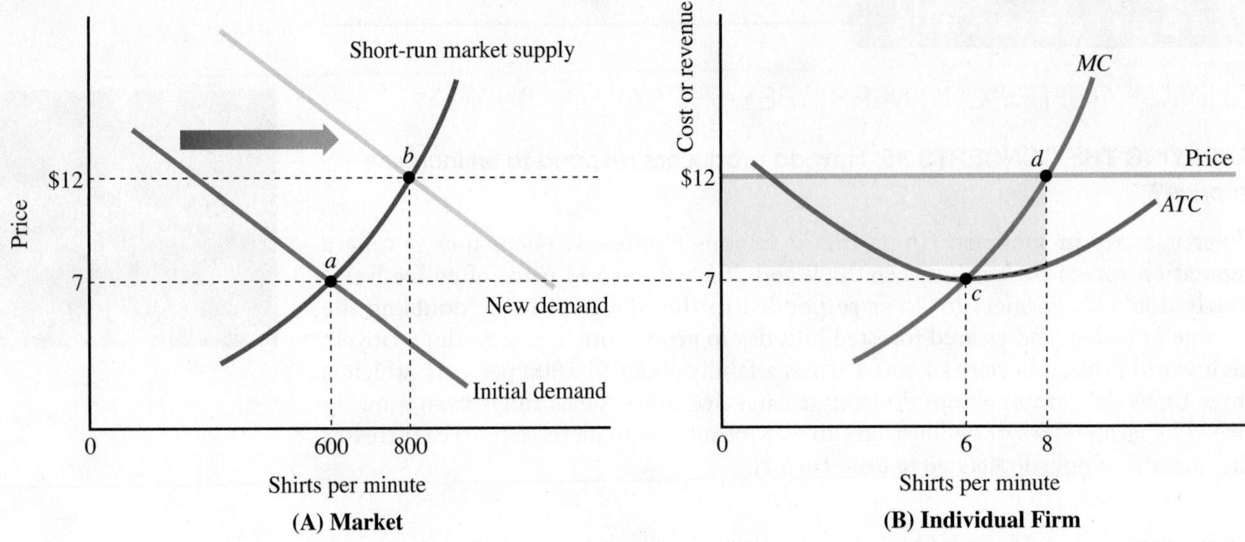

▲ FIGURE 24.8
Short-Run Effects of an Increase in Demand
An increase in demand for shirts increases the market price to $12, causing the typical firm to produce eight shirts instead of six. Price exceeds the average total cost at the eight-shirt quantity, so economic profit is positive. Firms will enter the profitable market.

The Long-Run Response to an Increase in Demand

We can use the long-run supply curve to determine the long-run price after an increase in demand. In Figure 24.9, the short-run effect of the increase in demand is shown by the move from point *a* to point *b*: The price increases from $7 to $12, and the quantity increases from 600 to 800. Economic profit is positive, so firms will enter the market. As shown by the long-run supply curve, entry will continue until

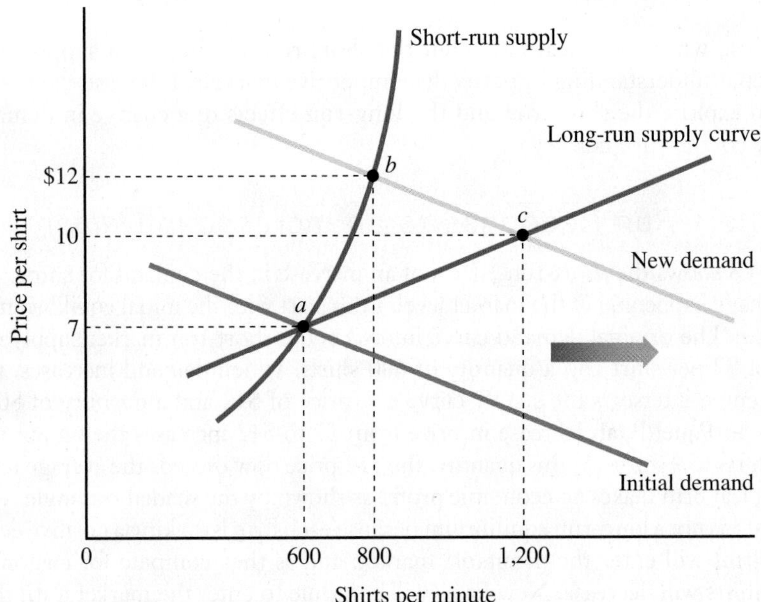

▶ FIGURE 24.9
Short-Run and Long-Run Effects of an Increase in Demand
The short-run supply curve is steeper than the long-run supply curve because of diminishing returns in the short run. In the short run, an increase in demand increases the price from $7 (point *a*) to $12 (point *b*). But in the long run, firms can enter the industry and build more production facilities, so the price eventually drops to $10 (point *c*). The large upward jump in price after the increase in demand is followed by a downward slide to the new long-run equilibrium price.

application 6

THE UPWARD JUMP AND DOWNWARD SLIDE OF WINE PRICES

APPLYING THE CONCEPTS #6: Why is the time path of market prices after an increase in demand?

As we saw in the chapter opener, the on-screen rave review of pinot noir wine increased the demand for pinot noir wine grown in the Willamette Valley in Oregon. In the short run, the supply of wine is inflexible, and eager consumers competed for the limited stock, causing prices to soar. For some brands, the price tripled. Producers responded to higher prices by expanding the vineyard acreage devoted to the pinot grape. A few years later, the new acreage came on line, increasing the quantity of wine produced. Eager growers competed for consumers by cutting prices, in many cases back to pre-*Sideways* prices. As we'll see in this chapter, when an increase in demand meets an inflexible short-run supply, prices rise in the short run. Eventually suppliers catch up with demand, and prices fall. **Related to Exercise 6.2.**

---

the price drops to $10 and the quantity is 1,200 shirts per minute. The new long-run equilibrium is shown by point *c*, where the new demand curve intersects the long-run supply curve. At this price and quantity, each of the 200 firms produces six shirts per minute and earns zero economic profit.

Figure 24.9 shows how the price of shirts changes over time. An increase in demand causes a large upward jump in the price from $7 to $12 in the short run, followed by a slide downward to the new long-run equilibrium price of $10. In the short run, firms respond to an increase in price by squeezing more output from their existing production facilities. Because of diminishing returns, it is very costly to increase output in the short run, so the price must increase by a large amount to cover these much higher production costs. The higher price causes new firms to enter the market and, as they enter, the price gradually drops to the point at which each firm makes zero economic profit. The long-run supply curve is relatively flat because firms enter the industry and build new factories, so there are no diminishing returns to increase production costs.

24.7 Long-Run Supply for a Constant-Cost Industry

So far we have examined products produced by increasing-cost industries, whose average cost increases as the industry expands. We turn next to a **constant-cost industry**, an industry whose average cost is constant—it doesn't change as the industry expands. That is, the prices of inputs such as labor and materials do not change as the total output of the industry increases. This happens when the industry uses a relatively small amount of the available labor and materials, meaning that events in the industry—increases or decreases in output—do not affect the price of the input. As a result, the average cost of production for the typical firm doesn't change as the industry grows. In Table 24.4, the shirt industry would be a constant-cost industry if the average cost of shirts was constant at $7 regardless of how many shirts were produced.

constant-cost industry
An industry in which the average cost of production is constant; the long-run supply curve is horizontal.

Long-Run Supply Curve for a Constant-Cost Industry

As an example of a constant-cost industry, consider the production of birthday cake candles. As the industry grows, it will use more workers, wicks, and wax, but because the industry is such a small part of the markets for labor and materials, the prices of these inputs won't change. As a result, the average cost of production won't change as the industry grows.

The long-run supply curve for a constant-cost industry is horizontal at the constant average cost of production. If the average cost of birthday cake candles is $0.05 per candle, the long-run supply curve for candles will be horizontal at $0.05, as shown by Figure 24.10. At any lower price, the quantity of candles supplied would be zero, because in the long run no rational firm would provide candles at a price lower than the average cost of production. At any higher price, firms would enter the candle industry in droves, and entry would continue until the price dropped to the constant average cost of $0.05 per candle.

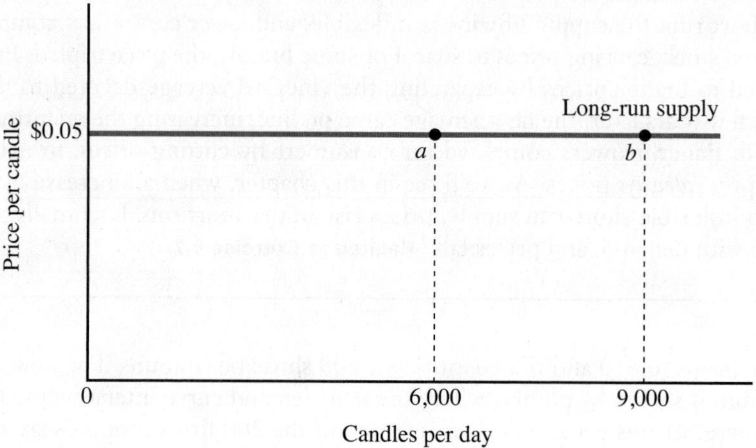

► FIGURE 24.10
Long-Run Supply Curve for a Constant-Cost Industry
In a constant-cost industry, input prices do not change as the industry grows. Therefore, the average production cost is constant and the long-run supply curve is horizontal. For the candle industry, the cost per candle is constant at $0.05, so the supply curve is horizontal at $0.05 per candle.

Hurricane Andrew and the Price of Ice

For an example of the effects of an increase in demand in a constant-cost industry, let's look at the short-run and long-run effects of a hurricane. In 1992, Hurricane Andrew struck the southeastern United States, leaving millions of people without electricity for several days. Figure 24.11 shows the short-run and long-run effects of the hurricane on the price of ice, which was used to cool and preserve food in areas without electricity. Before the hurricane, the market was at point *a*, with a price of $1 per bag of ice. The long-run supply curve is horizontal, indicating that the ice industry is a constant-cost industry.

In the short run (a day or two), the number of ice suppliers is fixed. The increase in demand caused by the hurricane moved the market from point *a* to point *b*, and the price rose to $5 per bag of ice. In the long run, firms responded to the higher price

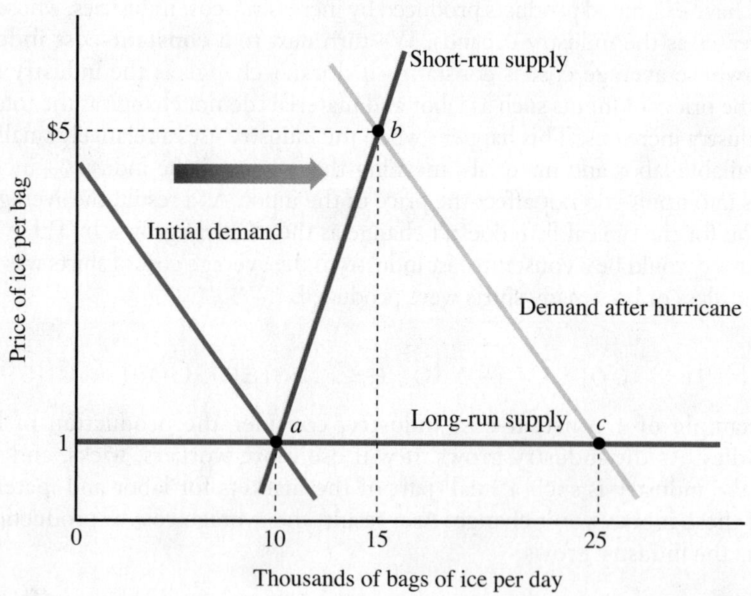

► FIGURE 24.11
Hurricane Andrew and the Price of Ice
A hurricane increases the demand for ice, shifting the demand curve to the right. In the short run, the supply curve is relatively steep, so the price rises by a large amount—from $1 to $5. In the long run, firms enter the industry, pulling the price back down. Because ice production is a constant-cost industry, the supply is horizontal, and the large upward jump in price is followed by a downward slide back to the original price.

application 7

ECONOMIC DETECTIVE AND THE CASE OF MARGARINE PRICES

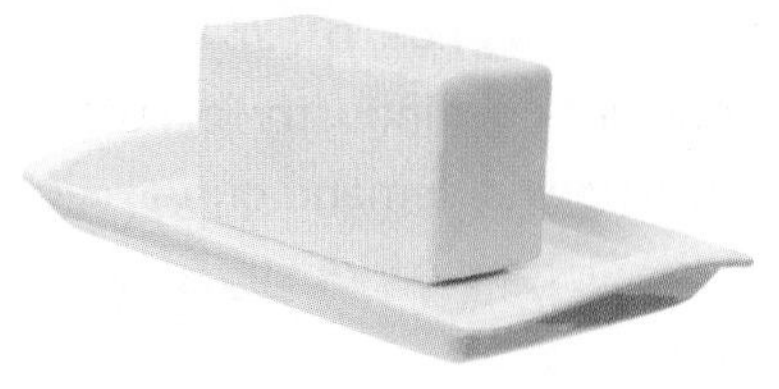

APPLYING THE CONCEPTS #7: How does a permanent decrease in demand affect the equilibrium price in a constant-cost industry?

Between 2000 and 2009, concerns about the health effects of trans-fatty acids decreased the demand for margarine. Although total consumption in the U.S. decreased by roughly half, the price of margarine in 2009 was roughly the same, in real terms, as the price in 2000. Why didn't the decrease in demand decrease the equilibrium price?

The margarine industry is an example of a constant-cost industry. As the total output of the industry changes, the prices of the key inputs to the production of margarine don't change, so the unit cost of production is unaffected by changes in total output. Of course a decrease in demand decreases the equilibrium price in the short run, but the exit of firms from the unprofitable industry causes the price to rise, and in the new long-run equilibrium, the original price—equal to the constant long-run marginal cost—will be restored. **Related to Exercises 7.3 and 7.5.**

SOURCE: Based on USDA/Economic Research Service, Food Availability Data Sets (http://www.ers.usda.gov/data/foodconsumption/FoodAvailDoc.htm). Accessed February 25, 2012.

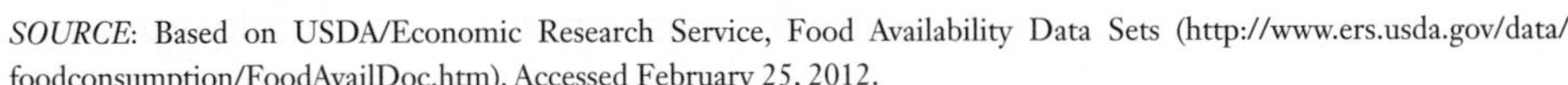

by entering the market. Many people trucked ice from distant locations and sold it from trucks parked on streets and highways. As these firms entered the ice market in the days after the hurricane, the price of ice gradually dropped, and the market eventually reached the intersection of the new demand curve and the long-run supply curve (point *c*), with a price equal to the pre-hurricane price. In the case of the retail ice industry, the long run is just a few days.

This pattern of price changes following the hurricane was observed in other markets. Immediately after the hurricane, $200 chain saws were sold for $900, but the price dropped steadily as new roadside firms entered the market. The same sort of price changes occurred for bottled water, tarpaper, and plywood. The basic pattern was a large upward jump in price followed by a downward slide to the long-run equilibrium price.

SUMMARY

In this chapter, we explored the decisions made by perfectly competitive firms and the implications of these decisions for the supply side of the market. In the short run, a firm uses the marginal principle to decide how much output to produce. In the long run, a firm will enter a market if the price exceeds the average cost of production. Here are the main points of this chapter:

1 A *price-taking* firm should produce the quantity of output at which the marginal revenue (the price) equals the marginal cost of production.

2 An unprofitable firm should continue to operate if its total revenue exceeds its total variable cost.

3 The long-run supply curve will be positively sloped if the average cost of production increases as the industry grows.

4 The long-run supply curve is flatter than the short-run supply curve because there are diminishing returns in the short run, but not in the long run.

5 An increase in demand causes a large upward jump in price, followed by a downward slide to the new long-run equilibrium price.

KEY TERMS

break-even price, p. 526
constant-cost industry, p. 537
firm-specific demand curve, p. 520
increasing-cost industry, p. 532
long-run market supply curve, p. 532
marginal revenue, p. 524
perfectly competitive market, p. 520
price taker, p. 520
short-run market supply curve, p. 530
short-run supply curve, p. 530
shut-down price, p. 528
sunk cost, p. 529

EXERCISES

All problems are assignable in MyEconLab.

24.1 Preview of the Four Market Structures

1.1 The firm-specific demand curve shows the relationship between the __________ charged by the firm and the __________ by the firm.

1.2 The firm-specific demand curve is __________ (horizontal/negatively) sloped for a perfectly competitive firm and __________ (horizontal/negatively) sloped for a monopolist.

1.3 For a monopolist, the firm-specific demand curve is the same as the __________ demand curve.

1.4 A perfectly competitive firm is a price __________, while a monopolist is a price __________.

1.5 In Pakistan, the market for phone service is perfectly __________, because a person can enter the market with a relatively small initial investment—only $310. (Related to Application 1 on page 522.)

24.2 The Firm's Short-Run Output Decision

2.1 Economic profit equals __________ minus __________.

2.2 Economic cost equals __________ cost plus __________ cost.

2.3 For a perfectly competitive firm, marginal revenue equals __________, and to maximize profit, the firm produces the quantity at which __________ equals __________.

2.4 The market price for wheat is $5. If a farmer's marginal cost is $7, the farmer should produce __________ (more/less) output.

2.5 At the current output level, a farmer's marginal cost of producing sugar is $0.30. If the price of sugar is $0.22 per pound, the farmer should __________ (increase/decrease) production. If the price of sugar is $0.32 per pound, the farmer should __________ (increase/decrease) production.

2.6 A firm produces 20 units of output at a market price of $5, a marginal cost of $5, and an average cost of $3. The firm's economic profit is $__________, and the firm __________ (is/is not) maximizing its economic profit.

2.7 If the market price equals a firm's break-even price, the firm earns __________ economic profit because __________ equals __________.

2.8 A decrease in price __________ (increases/decreases) a firm's marginal revenue, so it __________ (increases/decreases) the quantity supplied. This is the law of __________ in action.

2.9 The break-even price for switchgrass varies with __________, and on average is __________ per ton. (Related to Application 2 on page 526.)

2.10 **Changes in the Break-Even Price.** Consider a switchgrass farmer whose initial break-even price is $76 = $36 explicit cost + $40 opportunity cost for land. For each of the following changes, explain the effects on the farmer's production cost and break-even price. (Related to Application 2 on page 526.)

a. The cost of fertilizer increases.

b. The market price of alfalfa increases.

2.11 **More or Fewer Deliveries?** Consider a delivery firm that delivers packages by bicycle, charging $13 per package and paying each of its workers $12 per hour. One day, one of the workers was two hours late to work, and the number of packages delivered that day decreased by one package.

a. Did the tardiness of the worker increase or decrease the firm's profit?

b. Based on the new information provided by this experience, should the firm produce more deliveries by increasing its workforce, or produce fewer deliveries by reducing its workforce? Explain, using the marginal principle.

2.12 Advice for a Firm. You've been hired as an economic consultant by a price-taking firm that produces scarves. The firm already has a factory, so it is operating in the short run. The price of scarves is $9, the hourly wage is $24, and each scarf requires $1 worth of material. The following table shows the relationship between the number of workers and the output of scarves.

Workers	10	11	12	13	14	15
Output	5	29	41	47	50	52
Labor cost						
Material cost						
Fixed cost	$2	$2	$2	$2	$2	$2
Total cost						
Marginal cost						

a. Fill in the blanks in the table.

b. What is the profit-maximizing output?

24.3 The Firm's Shut-Down Decision

3.1 A firm will continue to operate an unprofitable business if __________ exceeds __________ cost.

3.2 Your firm has a total revenue of $500, a total cost of $700, and a variable cost of $600. You should __________ (operate/shut down) because __________ exceeds __________.

3.3 A firm that is losing money should continue to operate in the short run if the market price exceeds __________.

3.4 Your firm has a price of $5, an average total cost of $7, and an average variable cost of $4. In the short run, you should __________ (operate/shut down) because __________ exceeds __________. In the long run, you should __________ (stay in/exit) the market because __________ exceeds __________.

3.5 When the price of zinc dropped below $1,900, the price dropped below Alcoa's __________ price, the company __________. (Related to Application 3 on page 529.)

3.6 Advice for an Unprofitable Firm. You've been hired as an economic consultant by a price-taking firm that produces baseball caps. The firm already has a factory, so it is operating in the short run. The price of caps is $5, the hourly wage is $12, and each cap requires $1 worth of material. The firm has experimented with different workforces and the results are shown in the first two columns of the following table.

a. Fill in the blanks in the table.

b. Is it sensible to continue to operate at a loss with 14 workers?

c. Would it be better to operate with 15 workers? Explain, using the marginal principle.

Workers	Caps	Labor Cost	Material Cost	Variable Cost	Total Revenue	Marginal Cost of Caps
14	56					
15	60					

3.7 A Bluffing Farmer? Consider the following statement from a wheat farmer to his workers: "The price of wheat is very low this year, and the most I can get for the crop is $35,000. If I paid you the same amount as I paid you last year ($30,000), I'd lose money because I also have to worry about the $20,000 I paid three months ago for seed and fertilizer. I'd be crazy to pay a total of $50,000 to harvest a crop I can sell for only $35,000. If you are willing to work for half as much as last year ($15,000), my total cost will be $35,000, so I'll break even. If you don't take a pay cut, I won't harvest the wheat." Is the farmer bluffing, or will the farm workers really lose their jobs if they reject the proposed pay cut?

3.8 Operate or Shut Down? In Figure 24.4 on page 528, suppose the market price of shirts drops to $2. At this price, the marginal principle will be satisfied at a point below point __________ on the marginal-cost curve. Price is __________ (less/greater) than *AVC*, so the firm will be better off __________ (operating/shutting down).

24.4 Short-Run Supply Curves

4.1 A firm's short-run supply curve shows the relationship between __________ on the horizontal axis and __________ on the vertical axis.

4.2 To draw a firm's short-run supply curve, you need its __________ curve and its __________ price.

4.3 A perfectly competitive industry has 100 identical firms. At a price of $8, the typical firm supplies seven units of output, so the market quantity supplied is __________ units of output.

4.4 Figure 24.6 on page 531 shows a long-run equilibrium because (1) the quantity ________ equals the quantity ________; (2) the typical firm maximizes ________ by picking the quantity at which ________ equals ________; (3) each firm makes ________ economic profit because ________ equals ________.

4.5 A firm making zero economic profit stays in the market because total revenue is high enough to cover all the firm's costs, including the opportunity costs of the entrepreneur's ________ and ________.

4.6 As the price of shipping services increases, the quantity supplied ________ as firms deploy ________ ships and as each ship travels ________ (Related to Application 4 on page 532.)

4.7 **Soybeans versus Processor Chips.** Why is the market for soybeans perfectly competitive, with thousands of soybean farmers, while the market for computer processor chips is dominated by a few large firms? (Related to Application 2 on page 526.)

4.8 **Draw the Supply Curves.** The following table shows short-run marginal costs for a perfectly competitive firm:

Output	100	200	300	400	500
Marginal cost	$5	$10	$20	$40	$70

a. Use this information to draw the firm's marginal-cost curve.

b. Suppose the shut-down price is $10. Draw the firm's short-run supply curve.

c. Suppose there are 100 identical firms with the same marginal-cost curve. Draw the short-run industry supply curve.

4.9 **Equilibrium and Break-Even Price.** Explain why the equilibrium price in a perfectly competitive industry is sometimes below the break-even price, sometimes above it, and sometimes equal to it.

4.10 **Maximizing the Profit Margin?** According to the marginal principle, the firm should choose the quantity of output at which price equals marginal cost. A tempting alternative is to maximize the firm's profit margin, defined as the difference between price and short-run average total cost. Use the firm's short-run cost curves to evaluate this approach. Draw the firm's short-run supply curve and compare it to the supply curve of a firm that maximizes its profit.

4.11 **Expand If Profit Margin Is Positive?** Consider a firm that uses the following rule to decide how much output to produce: If the profit margin (price minus short-run average total cost) is positive, the firm will produce more output. Use the firm's short-run cost curves to evaluate this approach. Draw the firm's short-run supply curve and compare it to the short-run supply curve of a profit-maximizing firm.

24.5 The Long-Run Supply Curve for an Increasing-Cost Industry

5.1 The long-run supply curve shows the relationship between ________ on the horizontal axis and ________ on the vertical axis.

5.2 Arrows up or down: As the total output of an increasing-cost industry increases, the average cost of production ________ because input prices ________ and the productivity of inputs used by firms ________.

5.3 As the total output of an increasing-cost industry increases, the average cost of production ________ (increases/decreases), so the supply curve is ________ (horizontal/positively sloped/ negatively sloped).

5.4 In Table 24.4 on page 533, suppose the relationship between industry output and the total cost for the typical firm is linear, and each firm produces six shirts. If there are 400 firms in the industry, the total cost for the typical firm is $________, and the average cost per shirt is $________. Another point on the supply curve is a price of $________ and a quantity of ________ shirts.

5.5 An increase in the price of shirts will cause firms to ________ the industry, and as output increases the ________ cost of production increases. Entry will continue until ________ equals ________.

5.6 Land-use zoning that limits the amount of land for apartments generates a relatively ________ (flat/ steep) supply curve for housing, so an increase in the demand for apartments leads to a relatively ________ (large/small) increase in price.

5.7 An increase in the price of coffee increased the quantity supplied as land was converted from growing ________ to growing coffee. (Related to Application 5 on page 535.)

5.8 **Copper Price Elasticity of Supply.** Suppose the price of copper increases from $1,500 to $2,500 per ton and the quantity supplied increases from 9 million tons to 11 million tons. Use the midpoint formula to compute the price elasticity of supply for copper.

5.9 **Sugar Import Ban.** Suppose that initially there are no controls on sugar imported into the United States, so the price paid in the United States equals the prevailing world price.

a. If the world price is 13 cents per pound, what areas of the world supply sugar to the world market and the United States?

b. Suppose the United States bans sugar imports. The new price of sugar will be at least $__________.

5.10 **Long-Run Supply Curve of Lamps.** Suppose each lamp manufacturer produces 10 lamps per hour. Complete the following table. Then use the data in the table to draw the long-run supply curve for lamps.

Number of Firms	Industry Output	Total Cost for Typical Firm	Average Cost per Lamp
40		$300	
80		360	
120		420	

5.11 **How Steep a Supply Curve?** Consider two cities, one on a small island, and a second on a large plain.

a. Draw a long-run supply curve for housing for each city, and explain any differences between the two supply curves.

b. If demand for housing increases by the same amount in each city, which city will experience a larger increase in price?

24.6 Short-Run and Long-Run Effects of Changes in Demand

6.1 The short-run supply curve is steeper than the long-run supply curve because of the principle of __________.

6.2 Arrows up or down: Suppose the demand for shirts increases. In the short run, the price __________ by a relatively large amount. As firms enter the market, the price __________. In the new long-run equilibrium, there is a net __________ in price relative to the old equilibrium. (Related to Application 6 on page 537.)

6.3 An increase in demand causes a large initial upward (jump/slide) in price, followed by a downward (jump/slide) to the new long-run equilibrium price.

6.4 **Increase in Housing Demand in Britain versus the United States.** Suppose that in both Britain and the United States, the initial equilibrium price of housing is $200,000. Britain has more severe restrictions on residential development in the short run. Suppose the demand for housing increases by the same amount in the two countries.

a. Draw a set of supply and demand curves showing the effects on housing prices in the short run.

b. The price increase is larger in __________ because that country has a relatively __________ supply curve.

c. Suppose the long-run supply curves in the two countries have the same slope. Show the long-run effects of the increase in demand.

d. In the long run, Britain's price of housing is __________ (higher/lower/the same).

24.7 Long-Run Supply for a Constant-Cost Industry

7.1 As the total output of a constant-cost industry increases, the __________ cost does not change, so the long-run supply curve is __________ (horizontal/positively sloped/negatively sloped).

7.2 A constant-cost industry consumes a relatively __________ (small/large) amount of inputs such as labor and materials, so as industry output increases the prices of these inputs __________ (increase/ decrease/ don't change).

7.3 Arrow up, down, or horizontal: In a constant-cost industry, when demand increases the long-run equilibrium price __________ (Related to Application 7 on page 539.)

7.4 **The Price of Haircuts.** The haircutting industry in your city uses a tiny fraction of the electricity, scissors, and commercial space available on the market. In addition, the industry employs only about 100 of the 50,000 people who could cut hair.

a. Draw a long-run supply curve for haircutting in your city.

b. Suppose the initial equilibrium price of haircuts is $12. Draw demand and supply graphs to show the short-run and long-run effects of an increase in population. Does population growth affect the long-run equilibrium price of haircuts?

7.5 **Margarine Prices.** Several years ago, people became concerned about the undesirable health effects of eating margarine. The demand for margarine dropped, decreasing its price. Some time later, the price started rising steadily, although demand hadn't been changing. After several months of price hikes, the price of margarine reached the price observed before demand decreased. A blogger suggested that the rising price was evidence of a conspiracy on the part of margarine producers. Provide an alternative explanation for the rising price of and its eventual return to the original price. (Related to Application 7 on page 539.)

7.6 **The Price of Tattoos.** According to a market expert, tattooing in your city is a constant-cost industry. The initial equilibrium price is $24.

a. Arrows up or down: In the long run the wage of tattoo artists ________ as industry output increases.

b. If the demand for tattoos doubles and stays at the higher level for three years, the price of tattoos three years from now will be $________.

c. Show the change in (b) using a supply-demand graph.

NOTES

1. *Sideways*, 2004 Twentieth Century Fox; written by Alexander Payne and Jim Taylor. Based on the novel *Sideways* by Rex Pickett; New York, St. Martin's Press, 2004.

Monopoly and Price Discrimination

CHAPTER 25

On college campuses across the country, beverage companies like Coca-Cola and Pepsi pay cash in exchange for monopoly power—exclusive rights to sell beverages on campus.

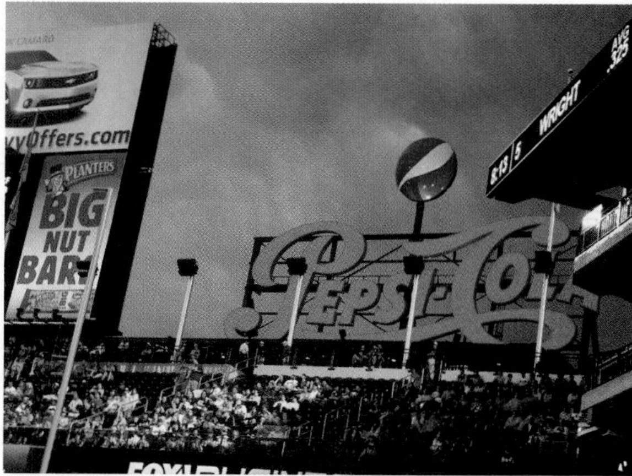

For example, under the Coca-Cola agreement with the University of California Berkeley that expired in 2011, the company paid an average of $615,000 per year to support recreational sports, intercollegiate athletic programs, and various student groups. The exclusive agreement bans competing products on campus, and directs the university to "maximize the sale and distribution of (Coca-Cola) Products, including hawking Products . . . at all sporting events." As we'll see in this chapter, a firm is willing to pay for the rights to monopoly because the exclusion of competing products allows the monopolist to charge higher prices.

In recent years, the battles over campus beverage monopolies have become heated and more lucrative. In 2011, UC Berkeley responded to student concerns about the business practices of Coca-Cola by signing an exclusive contract with Pepsi. Under the new agreement, Pepsi will pay the university $1.6 million per year.

LEARNING OBJECTIVES

- Describe and explain a monopolist's output decision.
- Explain why a monopoly is socially inefficient.
- Identify the trade-offs associated with a patent.
- Describe the practice of price discrimination.

MyEconLab

MyEconLab helps you master each objective and study more efficiently.

In the previous chapter we explored the decisions made by firms in a perfectly competitive market, a market in which there are many firms. This chapter deals with the opposite extreme: a **monopoly**, a market in which a single firm sells a product that does not have any close substitutes. In contrast with a perfectly competitive, or price-taking, firm, a monopolist controls the price of its product, so we can refer to a monopolist as a *price maker*. A monopolist has **market power**, the ability to affect the price of its product. Of course, consumers obey the law of demand, and the higher the monopolist's price, the smaller the quantity it will sell.

monopoly
A market in which a single firm sells a product that does not have any close substitutes.

market power
The ability of a firm to affect the price of its product.

A monopoly occurs when a **barrier to entry** prevents a second firm from entering a profitable market. Among the possible barriers to entry are patents, network externalities, government licensing, the ownership or control of a key resource, and large economies of scale in production:

barrier to entry
Something that prevents firms from entering a profitable market.

patent
The exclusive right to sell a new good for some period of time.

network externalities
The value of a product to a consumer increases with the number of other consumers who use it.

- A **patent** grants an inventor the exclusive right to sell a new product for some period of time, currently 20 years under international rules.
- When the value of a product to a consumer increases with the number of consumers who use it, **network externalities** are at work. For example, the larger the number of people on an online social network, the greater the opportunities for interaction. Similarly, the larger the number of people using a software application such as a word processor, the greater the opportunities to share files. Network externalities provide an advantage to existing firms and may inhibit the entry of new ones.
- Under a licensing policy, the government chooses a single firm to sell a particular product. Some examples are licensing for radio and television stations, off-street parking in cities, and vendors in national parks.
- If a firm owns or controls a key resource, the firm can prevent entry by refusing to sell the input to other firms. The classic example is DeBeers, the South African company that controls about 80 percent of the world's production of diamonds. Before the 1940s, the Aluminum Company of America—ALCOA—had long-term contracts to buy most of the world's available bauxite, a key input to the production of aluminum.
- A **natural monopoly** occurs when the scale economies in production are so large that only a single large firm can earn a profit. The market can support only one profitable firm, because if a second firm entered the market, both firms would lose money. Some examples are cable TV service, electricity transmission, and water systems.

natural monopoly
A market in which the economies of scale in production are so large that only a single large firm can earn a profit.

In this chapter, we will discuss "unnatural" monopolies, which result from artificial barriers to entry. Later in the book, we'll explore the reasons for natural monopolies and various public policies to control them.

This chapter examines the production and pricing decisions of a monopoly and explores the implications for society as a whole. As we'll see, monopoly is inefficient from society's perspective because it produces too little output. We'll also discuss the trade-offs with patents, which lead to monopoly and higher prices but also encourage innovation. We'll also explore the issue of price discrimination, which occurs when firms such as airlines and movie theaters charge different prices to different types of consumers. Although we discuss price discrimination in a monopoly, it also happens in markets with more firms, including oligopoly (a few firms) and monopolistic competition (many firms selling differentiated products).

25.1 The Monopolist's Output Decision

Like other firms, a monopolist must decide how much output to produce, given its objective of maximizing its profit. We learned about production costs in an earlier chapter, so we start our discussion of the monopolist's output decision with the revenue side of the profit picture. Then we show how a monopolist picks the profit-maximizing quantity.

Total Revenue and Marginal Revenue

A firm's total revenue—the money it gets by selling its product—equals the price times the quantity sold. In this part of the chapter, we'll assume that the monopolist charges the same price to each customer. The table in Figure 25.1 shows how to use a demand schedule (in columns 1 and 2) to compute a firm's total revenue (in column 3). At a price of $16, the firm doesn't sell anything, so its total revenue is zero. To sell the first unit, the firm must cut its price to $14, so its total revenue is $14. To get consumers to buy two units instead of just one, the firm must cut its price to $12, so the total revenue for selling two units is $24. As the price continues to drop and the quantity sold increases, total revenue increases for a while but then starts falling. To sell five units instead of four, the firm cuts its price from $8 to $6, and total revenue decreases from $32 to $30. The total revenue for selling six units is even lower, only $24.

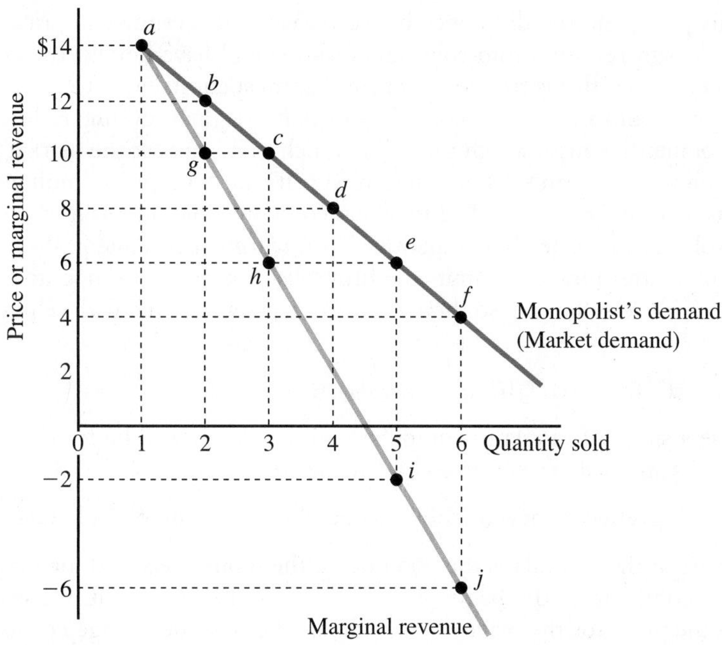

◄ **FIGURE 25.1**
The Demand Curve and the Marginal-Revenue Curve
Marginal revenue equals the price for the first unit sold, but is less than the price for additional units sold. To sell an additional unit, the firm cuts the price and receives less revenue on the units that could have been sold at the higher price. The marginal revenue is positive for the first four units, and negative for larger quantities.

(1) Price (*P*)	(2) Quantity Sold (*Q*)	(3) Total Revenue (*TR* = *P* × *Q*)	(4) Marginal Revenue *MR* = Δ*TR*/Δ*Q*
$16	0	0	—
14	1	$14	$14
12	2	24	10
10	3	30	6
8	4	32	2
6	5	30	-2
4	6	24	-6

The firm's marginal revenue is defined as the change in total revenue that results from selling one more unit of output. You can see this in column 4 of the table in Figure 25.1. For example, the marginal revenue for the third unit is $6, equal to the total revenue from selling three units ($30) minus the total revenue from selling only two units ($24). As shown in the table, marginal revenue is positive for the first four units sold. Beyond that point, selling an additional unit actually decreases total revenue, so marginal revenue is negative. For example, the marginal revenue for the fifth unit is –$2, and the marginal revenue for the sixth unit is –$6.

The table in Figure 25.1 illustrates the trade-offs faced by a monopolist in cutting the price to sell a larger quantity. When the firm cuts its price from \$12 to \$10, there is good news and bad news:

- **Good news:** The firm collects \$10 from the new customer (the third), so revenue increases by \$10.
- **Bad news:** The firm cuts the price for all its customers, so it gets less revenue from the customers who would have been willing to pay the higher price of \$12. Specifically, the firm collects \$2 less from each of the two original customers, so revenue from the original customers decreases by \$4.

The combination of good news and bad news leads to a net increase in total revenue of only \$6, equal to \$10 gained from the new customer minus \$4 lost on the first two customers.

Our discussion of good news and bad news has revealed a key feature of a monopoly: *Marginal revenue is less than price*. To sell one more unit, the monopolist must cut its price, and the difference between marginal revenue and price is the bad news—the loss in revenue from consumers who would have bought the good at the higher price. In fact, this is true for any firm that must cut its price to sell more.

You may recall from the previous chapter that marginal revenue is different for a perfectly competitive firm, which can sell as much as it wants at the market price. If a perfectly competitive firm sells one unit at \$12, it can sell a second unit at the same price, so its marginal revenue is \$12 for the second unit sold, just as it was \$12 for the first unit sold. For a perfectly competitive firm, marginal revenue is always equal to the price, no matter how many units the firm sells. A perfectly competitive firm does not cut the price to sell more, so there is no bad news associated with selling more.

A Formula for Marginal Revenue

We can use a simple formula to compute marginal revenue. The formula quantifies the good news and bad news from selling one more unit:

$$\text{marginal revenue} = \text{new price} + (\text{slope of demand curve} \times \text{old quantity})$$

The first part of the formula is the good news, the money received for the extra unit sold. The second part is the bad news from selling one more unit, the revenue lost by cutting the price for the original customers. The revenue change equals the price change required to sell one more unit—the slope of the demand curve, which is a negative number—times the number of original customers who get a price cut.

We can illustrate this formula with an example. Suppose the monopolist wants to increase the quantity sold from two to three, so it cuts the price from \$12 to \$10. The new price is \$10, the old quantity is two units, and the slope of the demand curve is –\$2, so marginal revenue is \$6:

$$\text{marginal revenue} = \$10 - (\$2 \text{ per unit} \times 2 \text{ units}) = \$6$$

Similarly, to sell the fifth unit, the firm would cut the price from \$8 to \$6, and marginal revenue is actually negative:

$$\text{marginal revenue} = \$6 - (\$2 \text{ per unit} \times 4 \text{ units}) = -\$2$$

Marginal revenue is negative because the \$8 revenue lost from the original customers exceeds the \$6 gain from the new customer. This happens because there are so many original customers who get a price cut. If a monopolist continues to cut its price, marginal revenue will eventually become negative because there will be so many consumers who get price cuts.

The graph in Figure 25.1 shows the demand curve and marginal-revenue curve for the data shown in the table. For the first unit sold, the marginal revenue equals the price. Because the firm must cut its price to sell more output, the marginal-revenue curve lies below the demand curve. For example, the demand curve shows that the firm will sell three units at a price of $10 (point *c*), but the marginal revenue for this quantity is only $6 (point *h*). The firm will sell five units at a price of $6 (point *e*), but the marginal revenue for this quantity is –$2 (point *i*). The marginal revenue is positive for the first four units and negative for larger quantities.

Using the Marginal Principle

A monopolist can use the marginal principle to decide how much output to produce. Suppose a firm called Curall holds a patent on a new drug that cures the common cold and must decide how much of the drug to produce.

MARGINAL PRINCIPLE

Increase the level of an activity as long as its marginal benefit exceeds its marginal cost. Choose the level at which the marginal benefit equals the marginal cost.

The firm's activity is producing the cold drug, and it will pick the quantity at which the marginal revenue from selling one more dose equals the marginal cost of production.

In Figure 25.2, the first two columns of the table show the relationship between the price of the cold drug and the quantity demanded. We can use these numbers to draw the market demand curve, as shown in the graph in Figure 25.2. Because the firm is a monopolist—the only seller of the drug—the market demand curve shows how much the firm will sell at each price. The demand curve is negatively sloped, consistent with

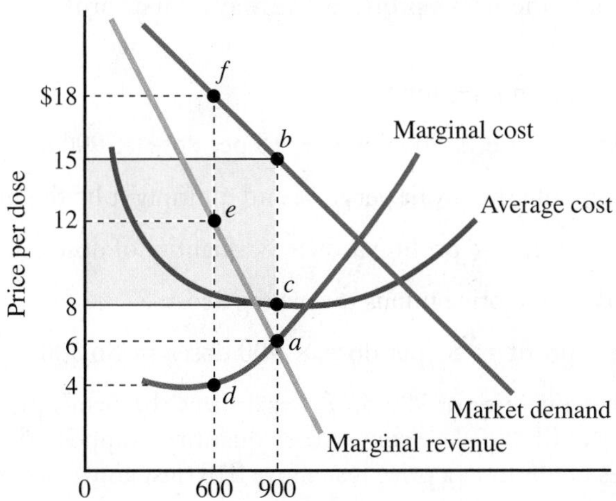

◄ **FIGURE 25.2**
The Monopolist Picks a Quantity and a Price
To maximize profit, the monopolist picks point *a*, where marginal revenue equals marginal cost. The monopolist produces 900 doses per hour at a price of $15 (point *b*). The average cost is $8 (point *c*), so the profit per dose is $7 (equal to the $15 price minus the $8 average cost) and the total profit is $6,300 (equal to $7 per dose times 900 doses). The profit is shown by the shaded rectangle.

(1) Price (*P*)	(2) Quantity Sold (*Q*)	(3) Marginal Revenue	(4) Marginal Cost	(5) Total Revenue (*TR* = *P* × *Q*)	(6) Total Cost (*TC*)	(7) Profit (*TR* – *TC*)
$18	600	$12	$4.00	$10,800	$5,710	$5,090
17	700	10	4.60	11,900	6,140	5,760
16	800	8	5.30	12,800	6,635	6,165
15	900	6	6.00	13,500	7,200	6,300
14	1,000	4	6.70	14,000	7,835	6,165
13	1,100	2	7.80	14,300	8,560	5,740
12	1,200	0	9.00	14,400	9,400	5,000

the law of demand. For example, at a price of $18 per dose, the quantity demanded is 600 doses per hour (point *f*), compared to 900 doses at a price of $15 (point *b*).

Like other monopolists, the firm must cut its price to sell a larger quantity, so marginal revenue is less than price. This is shown in the third column of the table as well as the graph. We can use the marginal-revenue formula explained earlier to compute marginal revenue for different quantities of output:

$$\text{marginal revenue} = \text{new price} + (\text{slope of demand curve} \times \text{old quantity})$$

The slope of the demand curve is –$0.01 per dose. To simplify the arithmetic, rather than using the "new" price and "old" quantity, we can use a matched pair of price and quantities from the demand curve to get an approximation of marginal revenue. When the change in price is relatively small (for example, $0.01) the difference between the new and old price is small enough to be ignored. For example, at a price of $18, the quantity sold is 600 doses, so marginal revenue is $12:

$$\text{marginal revenue} = \$18 - (\$0.01 \times 600 \text{ doses}) = \$12$$

Similarly, at a price of $15, the quantity is 900 doses and marginal revenue is $6:

$$\text{marginal revenue} = \$15 - (\$0.01 \times 900 \text{ doses}) = \$6$$

We're ready to show how a monopolist can use the marginal principle to pick a quantity to produce. To maximize its profit, the firm will produce the quantity at which the marginal revenue equals marginal cost. As shown in the fourth row in the table in Figure 25.2, this happens with a quantity of 900 doses. In the graph, the marginal-revenue curve intersects the marginal-cost curve at point *a*, with a quantity of 900 doses, so that's the quantity that maximizes profit. To get consumers to buy this quantity, the price must be $15 (point *b* on the demand curve). The average cost of production is $8 per dose (shown by point *c*).

We can compute the firm's profit in two ways. First, profit equals total revenue minus total cost:

$$\text{profit} = \text{total revenue} - \text{total cost}$$

$$\text{profit} = \$15 \text{ per dose} \times 900 \text{ doses} - \$8 \text{ per dose} \times 900 \text{ doses} = \$6{,}300$$

Second, we can compute the profit per dose and multiply it by the number of doses:

$$\text{profit} = \text{profit per dose} \times \text{quantity of doses}$$

The profit per dose is the price minus the average cost: $7 = $15–$8:

$$\text{profit} = \$7 \text{ per dose} \times 900 \text{ doses} = \$6{,}300$$

To show that a quantity of 900 doses maximizes the firm's profit, let's see what would happen if the firm picked some other quantity. Suppose the firm decided to produce 599 doses per hour at a price just above $18 (just above point *f* on the demand curve). Could the firm make more profit by cutting the price by enough to sell one more dose? The firm should answer two questions:

- What is the extra cost associated with producing dose number 600? As shown by point *d* on the marginal-cost curve, the marginal cost of the 600th dose is $4.
- What is the extra revenue associated with dose number 600? As shown by point *e* on the marginal-revenue curve, the marginal revenue is $12.

If the firm wants to maximize its profit, it should produce the 600th dose because the $12 extra revenue exceeds the $4 extra cost, meaning the firm's profit will increase by $8. The same argument applies, with different numbers for marginal revenue and marginal cost, for doses 601, 602, and so on, up to 900 doses. The firm should continue to increase the quantity produced as long as the marginal revenue exceeds the marginal cost. The marginal principle is satisfied at point *a*, with a total of 900 doses.

Why should the firm stop at 900 doses? Beyond 900 doses, the marginal revenue from an additional dose will be less than the marginal cost associated with producing it. Although the firm could cut its price and sell a larger quantity, an additional dose would add less to revenue than it adds to cost, so the firm's total profit would decrease. As shown in the fifth row in the table in Figure 25.2, the firm could sell 1,000 doses at a price of $14, but the marginal revenue at this quantity is only $4, while the marginal cost at this quantity is $6.70. Producing the 1,000th dose would decrease the firm's profit by $2.70. For any quantity exceeding 900 doses, the marginal revenue is less than the marginal cost. Therefore, the firm should produce exactly 900 doses.

Let's review what we've learned about how a monopolist picks a quantity and how to compute the monopoly profit. The three-step process is as follows:

1 Find the quantity that satisfies the marginal principle, that is, the quantity at which marginal revenue equals marginal cost. In the example shown in Figure 25.2, marginal revenue equals marginal cost at point *a*, so the monopolist produces 900 doses.
2 Using the demand curve, find the price associated with the monopolist's chosen quantity. In Figure 25.2, the price required to sell 900 doses is $15 (point *b*).
3 Compute the monopolist's profit. The profit per unit sold equals the price minus the average cost, and the total profit equals the profit per unit times the number of units sold. In Figure 25.2, the profit is shown by the shaded rectangle, with height equal to the profit per unit sold and width equal to the number of units sold.

application 1

MARGINAL REVENUE FROM A BASEBALL FAN

APPLYING THE CONCEPTS #1: How does a monopolist maximize profit?

We expect the owner of a MLB (major-league baseball) team to choose the quantity (the number of fans at the game) at which marginal revenue equals marginal cost (MR = MC). The marginal cost of an additional fan is close to zero, so the profit-maximization rule simplifies to MR = 0. And yet for the typical team, it appears that MR is actually negative: adding fans by selling more tickets actually decreases total revenue from tickets. What explains this puzzling behavior?

We can illustrate the puzzle with a simple example. Suppose that with a ticket price of $24, the team sells 20,000 tickets. If the slope of the demand curve is –0.002, marginal revenue is –$16:

$$\text{MR} = \$24 - 0.002 \times 20{,}000 = -\$16.$$

In this case, cutting the price to sell one more ticket generates good news ($24 collected from the new fan) that is less than the bad news (the $40 lost on the 20,000 fans who would have paid the higher price). The marginal revenue is negative, so the team could increase its total revenue from tickets by increasing the price and decreasing the quantity of tickets sold. Why don't MLB teams increase their ticket prices?

The solution to this puzzle is concessions. Suppose the average MLB fan spends $20 per game on merchandise that costs the owner about $4 to provide. In this case, each ticket sold generates an additional $16 in net concession revenue to the owner, just enough to offset the $16 revenue loss on ticket sales. Once we expand the definition of marginal revenue to include the net revenue from concessions, the owner's choice is consistent with profit-maximization. What appears to be too low a price could be just about right. **Related to Exercises 1.8 and 1.9.**

SOURCE: Based on Anthony Krautmann and David Berri, "Can we find it at the concession? Understanding price elasticity in professional sports," *Journal of Sports Economics* 8 (2007), pp. 183–191.

25.2 The Social Cost of Monopoly

Why should we as a society be concerned about monopoly? Most people are not surprised to hear that a monopolist uses its market power to charge a relatively high price. If this were the end of the story, a monopolist would simply gain at the expense of consumers. In other words, a monopoly would change how we slice the economic "pie," with a bigger slice for producers and a smaller slice for consumers. As we'll see in this part of the chapter, the social consequences of monopoly go beyond a different slicing of the pie: A monopoly causes inefficiency and actually reduces the size of the pie, so there is less to divide among consumers and producers.

Deadweight Loss from Monopoly

How does a monopoly differ from a perfectly competitive market? To show the difference, let's consider an example of an arthritis drug that could be produced by a monopoly or a perfectly competitive industry. Let's take the long-run perspective—a period of time long enough that a firm is perfectly flexible in its choice of inputs and can enter or leave the market.

Consider the monopoly outcome first. Let's assume the long-run average cost of producing the arthritis drug is constant at $8 per dose. As we saw in the chapter on production and cost, if average cost is constant, the marginal cost equals the average cost. In Panel A of Figure 25.3, the long-run marginal-cost curve is the same as the long-run average-cost curve. Given the demand and marginal-revenue curves in Panel A of Figure 25.3, the monopolist will maximize profit where marginal revenue equals marginal cost (point *a*), producing 200 doses per hour at a price of $18 per dose (point *b*). The monopolist's profit is $2,000 per hour—a $10 profit per dose ($18 – $8) times 200 doses.

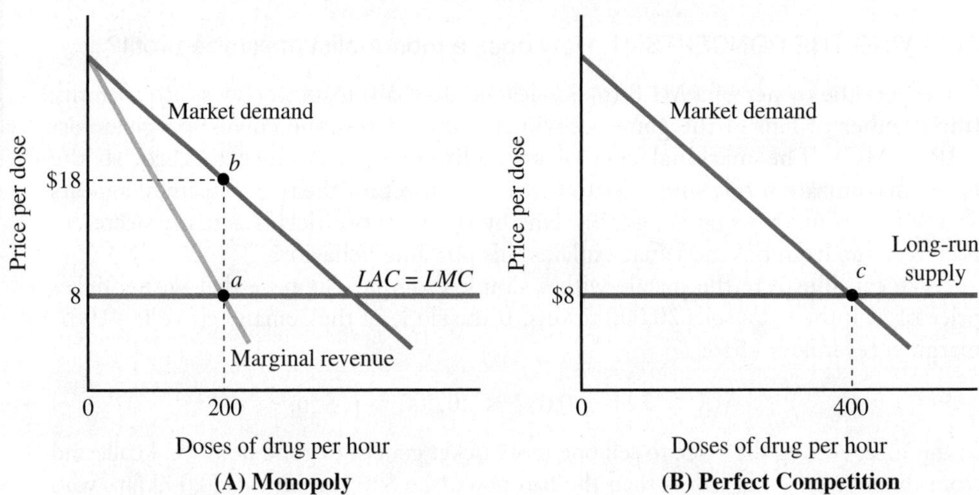

▲ **FIGURE 25.3**
Monopoly versus Perfect Competition: Its Effect on Price and Quantity
(A) The monopolist picks the quantity at which the long-run marginal cost equals marginal revenue—200 doses per hour, as shown by point *a*. As shown by point *b* on the demand curve, the price required to sell this quantity is $18 per dose. (B) The long-run supply curve of a perfectly competitive, constant-cost industry intersects the demand curve at point *c*. The equilibrium price is $8, and the equilibrium quantity is 400 doses.

Consider next the market for the arthritis drug under perfect competition. We're assuming the arthritis drug industry is a constant-cost industry: Input prices do not change as the industry grows, so the long-run market supply curve is horizontal at the long-run average cost of producing the drug, which is \$8 per dose. In Panel B of Figure 25.3, the horizontal long-run supply curve intersects the demand curve at point *c*, with an equilibrium price of \$8 and an equilibrium quantity of 400 doses per hour. Compared to a monopoly outcome, the perfectly competitive outcome has a lower price (\$8 instead of \$18 per dose) and a larger quantity (400 doses instead of 200).

To examine the social cost of monopoly power, let's imagine we start with a perfectly competitive market, and then switch to a monopoly. Consumers will be worse off under monopoly, and we can use the concept of consumer surplus to determine just how much worse off they will be. As we saw in the chapter on market efficiency, consumer surplus is shown by the area between the demand curve and the horizontal price line. In Figure 25.4, the monopoly price is \$18, so the consumer surplus with a monopoly is shown by triangle *A*. In contrast, the perfectly competitive price is \$8, so the consumer surplus with perfect competition is shown by the larger triangle consisting of triangle *A*, rectangle *B*, and triangle *D*. In other words, a switch from perfect competition to monopoly decreases consumer surplus by the areas *B* and *D*.

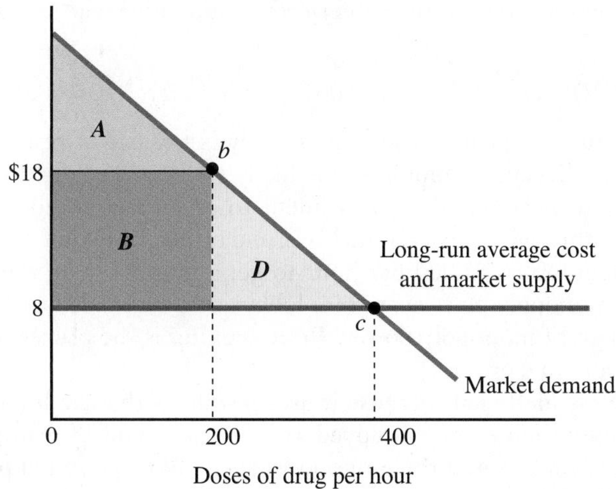

◄ **FIGURE 25.4**
The Deadweight Loss from a Monopoly
A switch from perfect competition to monopoly increases the price from \$8 to \$18 and decreases the quantity sold from 400 to 200 doses. Consumer surplus decreases by an amount shown by the areas *B* and *D*, while profit increases by the amount shown by rectangle *B*. The net loss to society is shown by triangle *D*, the deadweight loss from monopoly.

We can use some simple geometry to compute the reduction in consumer surplus. The formula for the area of a rectangle is

$$\text{area of rectangle} = \text{base} \times \text{height}$$

In Figure 25.4, the base of rectangle *B* is 200 and the height is \$10, so the area is \$2,000:

$$\text{area of rectangle } B = 200 \text{ doses} \times \$10 \text{ per dose} = \$2{,}000$$

The switch to monopoly increases the price by \$10 per dose, so consumers pay \$10 extra on the 200 doses they buy from the monopolist, resulting in a loss of \$2,000. The other part of the consumer loss is triangle *D*. The formula for the area of a triangle is

$$\text{area of triangle} = 1/2 \times \text{base} \times \text{height}$$

In Figure 25.4, the base of triangle *D* is 200 and the height is \$10, so the area is \$1,000:

$$\text{area of triangle } D = 1/2 \times 200 \text{ doses} \times \$10 \text{ per dose} = \$1{,}000$$

The switch to monopoly increases the price and decreases the quantity demanded because consumers obey the law of demand. Consumers lose consumer surplus on the doses they would have consumed at the lower price, and this \$1,000 loss is shown by triangle *D*. The total loss of consumers is the sum of the areas of rectangle *B* and triangle *D*, or \$3,000.

It's clear that consumers lose from monopoly, but what about the monopolist? Under perfect competition, each firm makes zero economic profit. In contrast, the monopolist earns positive economic profit, shown by rectangle *B* in Figure 25.4. The monopolist's profit per dose is $10, the $18 price minus the $8 average cost. The monopolist's profit is $2,000:

$$\text{profit} = \$10 \text{ per dose} \times 200 \text{ doses} = \$2{,}000$$

This $2,000 gain by the monopolist comes at the expense of consumers.

Because the monopolist recovers only part of the loss experienced by consumers, there is a net loss from switching to monopoly. Consumers lose rectangle *B* and triangle *D*, but the monopolist gains only rectangle *B*. That leaves triangle *D* as the net decrease in the market surplus, or the **deadweight loss from monopoly**. The word *deadweight* indicates this loss is not offset by a gain to anyone. Triangle *D* measures the consumer surplus lost because the monopoly produces less output than a perfectly competitive market. The monopolist prevents consumers from getting consumer surplus for the 201st through the 400th units of output, meaning it reduces the size of the economic pie and causes inefficiency. The lesson is that monopoly is inefficient because it generates less output than a perfectly competitive market.

deadweight loss from monopoly
A measure of the inefficiency from monopoly; equal to the decrease in the market surplus.

Rent Seeking: Using Resources to Get Monopoly Power

Another source of inefficiency from a monopoly is the use of resources to acquire monopoly power. Because a monopoly is likely to earn a profit, firms are willing to spend money to persuade the government to erect barriers to entry that grant monopoly power through licenses, franchises, and tariffs. In Figure 25.4, a firm would be willing to spend up to $2,000 per hour to get a monopoly on the arthritis drug. One way to get monopoly power is to hire lobbyists to persuade legislators and other policymakers to grant monopoly power. **Rent seeking** is the process of using public policy to gain economic profit.

rent seeking
The process of using public policy to gain economic profit.

Rent seeking is inefficient because it uses resources that could be used in other ways. For example, the people employed as lobbyists could instead produce goods and services. In Figure 25.4, if the monopolist spent all its potential profit of $2,000 per hour on rent-seeking activity, the net loss to society would be areas *B* and *D*, not just area *D*. A classic study of rent seeking by economist Richard Posner found that firms in some industries spent up to 30 percent of their total revenue to get monopoly power.[1]

application 2

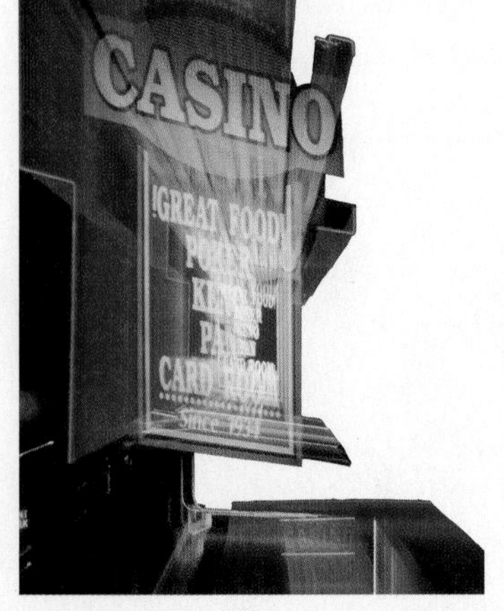

A CASINO MONOPOLY IN CRESWELL, OREGON?

APPLYING THE CONCEPTS #1: What is the value of a monopoly?

A developer interested in building a casino in Creswell, Oregon, placed a curious announcement in the local newspaper. If local voters approved the casino, the developer promised to give citizens a total of $2 million per year. With an adult population of about 1,600, each adult in Creswell would receive a cash payment of $1,250 per year. Why did the developers propose this deal? This is an example of rent seeking: The casino developer was seeking the profits that would come from having a monopoly in the casino market, and was willing to pay at least $2 million to get it. **Related to Exercises 2.5, 2.6, and 2.7.**

SOURCE: Based on Sherri Buri, "Creswell Casino Wins Few Friends," *Eugene Register Guard*, April 2, 1996, 1.

The chapter opener provides an example of rent seeking. Beverage companies pay millions of dollars to universities to get a monopoly on campus beverages. Like any monopolist, a beverage company will use its monopoly power to charge higher prices, so students pay, indirectly, for the programs supported by the beverage companies, for example recreational sports and intercollegiate athletic programs.

Monopoly and Public Policy

Given the social costs of monopoly, the government uses a number of policies to intervene in markets dominated by a single firm or likely to become a monopoly. We'll examine these policies later in the book. In the case of natural monopoly—a market that can support only a single firm—the government can intervene by regulating the price the natural monopolist charges. In other markets, the government uses antitrust policies to break monopolies into smaller companies and prevent corporate mergers that would lead to others. These policies are designed to promote competition, leading to lower prices and more production.

25.3 Patents and Monopoly Power

One source of monopoly power is a government patent that gives a firm the exclusive right to produce a product for 20 years. As we'll see, a patent encourages innovation because the innovators know they will earn monopoly profits on a new product over the period covered by the patent. If the monopoly profits are large enough to offset the substantial research and development costs of a new product, a firm will develop the product and become a monopolist. Granting monopoly power through a patent may be efficient from the social perspective because it may encourage the development of products that would otherwise not be developed.

Incentives for Innovation

Let's use the arthritis drug to show why a patent encourages innovation. Suppose a firm called Flexjoint hasn't yet developed the drug but believes the potential benefits and costs of doing so are as follows:

- The economic cost of research and development will be $14 million, including all the opportunity costs of the project.
- The estimated annual economic profit from a monopoly will be $2 million (in today's dollars).
- Flexjoint's competitors will need three years to develop and produce their own versions of the drug, so if Flexjoint isn't protected by a patent, its monopoly will last only three years.

Based on these numbers, Flexjoint won't develop the drug unless the firm receives a patent that lasts at least 7 years. That's the length of time the firm needs to recover the research and development costs of $14 million ($2 million per year times 7 years). If there is no patent and the firm loses its monopoly in 3 years, it will earn a profit of $6 million, which is less than the cost of research and development. In comparison, with a 20-year patent the firm will earn $40 million, which is more than enough to recover its $14 million cost.

Trade-Offs from Patents

Is the patent for Flexjoint's drug beneficial from the social perspective? The patent grants monopoly power to the firm, and the firm responds by charging a higher price and producing less than the quantity that would be produced in a perfectly competitive market. Looking back at Figure 25.4, a monopolist produces 200 doses per hour instead of 400. From society's perspective, 400 doses is better than 200 doses, but we don't have that choice. Flexjoint won't develop the drug unless a patent protects the firm from competition for at least seven years. Therefore, society's choice is between the monopoly outcome of 200 doses or 0 doses. Because a quantity of 200 doses is clearly better than none, the patent is beneficial from society's perspective.

What about a product a firm develops without the protection of a patent? Suppose we change the Flexjoint example by altering one number: The cost of research and development is only $5 million, not $14 million. Suppose it still takes Flexjoint's competitors three years to develop a substitute, and Flexjoint's profit per year is still $2 million. Without a patent, Flexjoint would earn an economic profit of $6 million during its three-year monopoly ($2 million per year times three years), which is more than the $5 million cost of research and development. Therefore, the firm would develop the new drug even without a patent. In this case, a patent would merely prolong a monopoly, and so it would be inefficient from society's perspective.

What are the general conclusions about the merits of the patent system? It is sensible for a government to grant a patent for a product that would otherwise not be developed, but it is not sensible for other products. Unfortunately, no one knows in advance whether a particular product would be developed without a patent, so the government can't be selective in granting patents. In some cases, patents lead to new products, although in other cases, they merely prolong monopoly power.

application 3

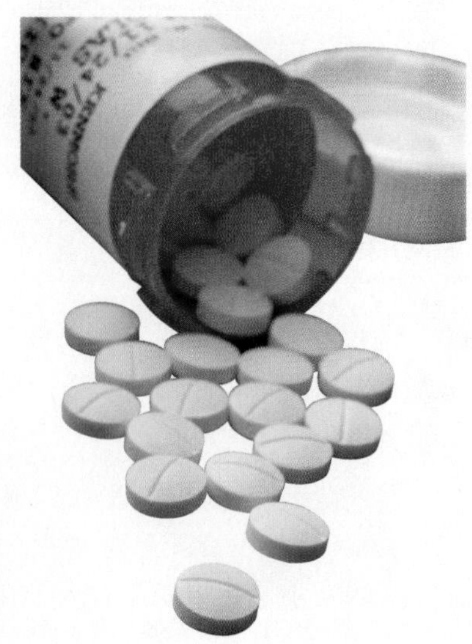

BRIBING THE MAKERS OF GENERIC DRUGS

APPLYING THE CONCEPTS #3: What happens when a patent expires and a monopoly ends?

When a patent expires, new firms enter the market, and the resulting competition for consumers decreases prices and increases quantities. In the pharmaceutical drug market, when the patent for a brand-name drug expires, other firms introduce generic versions of the drug. The generics are virtually identical to the original branded drug, but they sell at a much lower price. The producers of branded drugs have an incentive to delay the introduction of generic drugs and sometimes use illegal means to do so.

In recent years, the Federal Trade Commission (FTC) has investigated allegations that the makers of branded drugs made deals with generic suppliers to keep generics off the market. The alleged practices included cash payments and exclusive licenses for new versions of the branded drug. In 2003, the FTC ruled that two drug makers had entered into an illegal agreement when Schering-Plough paid Upsher-Smith Laboratories $60 million to delay the introduction of a low-price alternative to its prescription drug K-Dur 20, which is used to treat people with low potassium.

Another tactic is to claim that generics are not as good as the branded drug. DuPont has claimed that generic versions of its Coumadin (a blood thinner) are not equivalent to Coumadin and may pose risks to patients. Because generic versions are virtually identical to the branded drugs, such claims are not based on science. **Related to Exercises 3.4 and 3.5.**

SOURCE: Based on Federal Trade Commission, "Commission Rules Schering-Plough, Upsher, and AHP Illegally Delayed Entry of Lower-Cost Generic Drug," www.ftc.gov/opa/2003/12/schering.htm (accessed July 9, 2006).

25.4 Price Discrimination

Up to this point in the book, we've assumed a firm charges the same price to all its customers. As we'll see in this part of the chapter, however, a firm may be able to divide consumers into two or more groups and sell the good at a different price to each, a practice known as **price discrimination**. For example, airlines offer discount tickets to travelers who are flexible in their departure times, and movie theaters have lower prices for senior citizens. The only legal restriction on price discrimination is that a firm cannot use it to drive rival firms out of business.

price discrimination
The practice of selling a good at different prices to different consumers.

Although price discrimination is widespread, it is not always possible. A firm has an opportunity for price discrimination if three conditions are met:

1 **Market power.** The firm must have some control over its price, facing a negatively sloped demand curve for its product. Although we will discuss price discrimination by a monopolist, any firm that faces a negatively sloped demand curve can charge different prices to different consumers. In fact, the only type of firm that cannot engage in price discrimination is a perfectly competitive price-taking firm. Such a firm faces a horizontal demand curve, taking the market price as given. For all other types of markets—monopoly, oligopoly, and monopolistic competition—price discrimination is possible.
2 **Different consumer groups.** Consumers must differ in their willingness to pay for the product or in their responsiveness to changes in price, as measured by the price elasticity of demand. In addition, the firm must be able to identify different groups of consumers. For example, an airline must be able to distinguish between business travelers and tourists, and a movie theater must be able to distinguish between seniors and nonseniors.
3 **Resale is not possible.** It must be impractical for one consumer to resell the product to another consumer. Airlines prohibit consumers from buying and reselling tickets. If airlines allowed consumers to sell discount tickets to each other, you could go into business as a ticket broker, buying discount airline tickets one month ahead and then selling them to business travelers one week before the travel date. In general, the possibility of resale causes price discrimination to break down.

One approach to price discrimination is to identify consumers who are not willing to pay the regular price and offer them a discount. Here are some examples:

- **Discounts on airline tickets.** Airlines offer discount tickets to travelers who spend Saturday night away from home because they are likely to be tourists, not business travelers. The typical tourist is not willing to pay as much for air travel as the typical business traveler. Airlines also offer discount tickets to people who plan weeks ahead, because tourists plan further ahead than business travelers.
- **Discount coupons for groceries and restaurant food.** The typical coupon-clipper is not willing to pay as much as the typical consumer.
- **Manufacturers' rebates for appliances.** A person who takes the trouble to mail a rebate form to the manufacturer is not willing to pay as much as the typical consumer.
- **Senior-citizen discounts on airline tickets, restaurant food, drugs, and entertainment.** Some seniors have more time to shop for bargains, and are thus more sensitive to prices. Other seniors have relatively low income, and are willing to pay less than the typical consumer.
- **Student discounts on movies and concerts.** The typical student has less income than the typical consumer, and is thus willing to pay less for movies.

The challenge for a firm is to figure out which groups of consumers should get discounts. Firms can experiment with different prices and identify groups of consumers that are most sensitive to price. In September 2000, Amazon.com started charging different prices for different types of consumers. For example, consumers who used Netscape's browser paid $65 for the *Planet of the Apes* DVD, while Internet Explorer users paid $75 for the same DVD.[2] Prices also varied with the consumer's Internet service provider and the number of previous purchases from Amazon. An Amazon spokeswoman said the company varied prices in a random fashion, as part of ongoing tests to see how consumers respond to price changes. In other words, it appears that Amazon was assessing the willingness to pay of different types of consumers. In principle, Amazon could use the data collected to develop systems of price discrimination, giving discounts to the most price-sensitive consumers. After widespread protests of the Amazon pricing experiments, the company stopped the practice and issued refunds to about 7,000 consumers who had paid relatively high prices.

Senior Discounts in Restaurants

Consider a restaurant whose patrons fall into two groups, senior citizens and others. In Figure 25.5, the demand curve for senior citizens is lower than the demand curve for other groups, reflecting the assumption that the typical senior is willing to pay less than the typical nonsenior. Their lower willingness to pay could result from having lower income or more time to shop for low prices.

FIGURE 25.5
The Marginal Principle and Price Discrimination
To engage in price discrimination, the firm divides potential customers into two groups and applies the marginal principle twice—once for each group. Using the marginal principle, the profit-maximizing prices are $3 for seniors (point *b*) and $6 for nonseniors (point *d*).

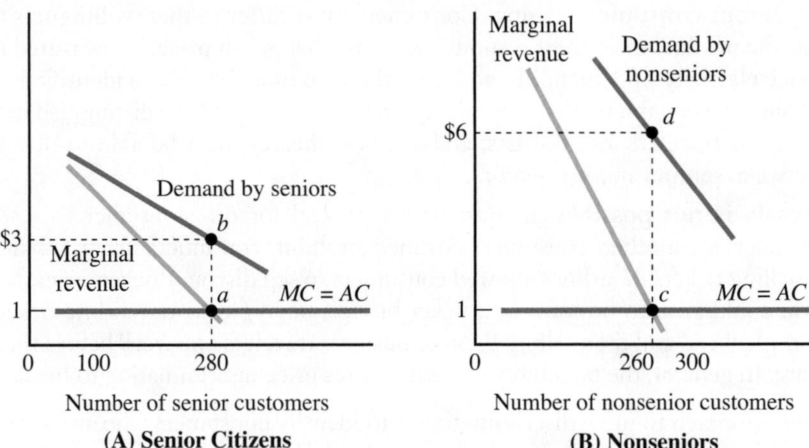

Under a price-discrimination plan, the restaurant will simply apply the marginal principle twice, once for seniors and a second time for nonseniors. This approach is sensible, because the two groups have different demands for restaurant meals, so the restaurant should treat them differently. Panel A of Figure 25.5 shows how to pick a price for senior citizens. The marginal principle—marginal revenue equals marginal cost—is satisfied at point *a*, with 280 senior meals per day. Therefore, the appropriate price for seniors is $3, as shown by point *b* on the senior demand curve. In Panel B of Figure 25.5, the marginal principle is satisfied at point *c* for nonseniors, with 260 meals per day and a price of $6 per meal.

We know the application of the marginal principle maximizes profit in each segment of the market. Therefore, price discrimination—with a price of $3 for seniors and $6 for everyone else—maximizes the restaurant's total profit. If the restaurant were instead to charge a single price of $5 for both groups, the profit from each group would be lower, so the restaurant's total profit would be lower, too.

Price Discrimination and the Elasticity of Demand

We can use the concept of price elasticity of demand to explain why price discrimination increases the restaurant's profit. From the chapter on elasticity, we know that when demand is elastic ($E_d > 1$), there is a negative relationship between price and total revenue: When the price decreases, total revenue (price times quantity sold) increases because the percentage increase in the quantity demanded exceeds the percentage decrease in price.

Suppose the restaurant initially has a single price of $5 for both seniors and nonseniors. Compared to other consumers, senior citizens have more elastic demand for restaurant meals, in part because they have lower income and more time to shop for low prices. A price cut for senior citizens brings good news and bad news for the restaurant:

- **Good news:** Demand is highly elastic, so total revenue increases by a large amount.
- **Bad news:** More meals are served, so total cost increases.

If the senior demand for meals is highly elastic, that is, E_d is well above 1.0, the good news will dominate the bad news: The increase in revenue will more than offset the increase in cost. Consequently, a price cut will increase the firm's profit.

For nonseniors, the firm will have an incentive to increase the price above the initial common price of $5. Suppose nonseniors have a mildly elastic demand for meals, with E_d just above 1.0. A price hike for nonseniors brings bad news on the revenue side and good news on the cost side:

- **Bad news:** Demand is mildly elastic, so total revenue decreases by a small amount.
- **Good news:** Fewer meals are served, so total cost decreases.

If the demand by nonseniors is mildly elastic, the good news will dominate the bad news: The savings in production costs will exceed the revenue loss. Consequently, the price hike for nonseniors will increase the firm's profit.

Examples: Movie Admission versus Popcorn, and Hardback versus Paperback Books

Why do senior citizens pay less than everyone else for admission to a movie, but the same as everyone else for popcorn? As we've seen, a senior discount is not an act of generosity by a firm, but an act of profit maximization. Senior citizens are typically willing to pay less than other citizens for movies, so a theater divides its consumers into two groups—seniors and others—and offers a discount to seniors. This price discrimination in favor of senior citizens increases the theater's profit. Why don't theaters offer a senior discount for popcorn? Unlike admission to the theater, popcorn can be easily transferred from one customer to another. If senior citizens could buy popcorn at half the regular price, many nonseniors would get seniors to buy popcorn for them, so the theater wouldn't sell as much popcorn at the regular price and its profit would decrease. In contrast, as long as ticket takers check consumers' admissions tickets, admission to the movie is not transferable.

Why are hardback books so much more expensive than paperback books? Most books are published in two forms—hardback and paperback. Although the cost of producing a hardback book is only about 20 percent higher than producing a paperback, the hardback price is typically three times the paperback price. The hardback edition comes first, and the paperback edition is published months, or even years, later. Booksellers use hardbacks and paperbacks to distinguish between two types of consumers: those who are willing to pay a lot and those who are willing to pay a little. Some people are eager to read a book when it first comes out, and publishers provide them with high-price hardbacks. The more casual readers are willing to wait for the lower-priced paperback. The pricing of hardback and paperback books is another example of price discrimination, under which consumers with less elastic demand pay a higher price.

application 4

WHY DOES MOVIE POPCORN COST SO MUCH?

APPLYING THE CONCEPTS #4: When do firms have an opportunity to charge different prices to different consumers?

That $4 bucket of popcorn you get in the movie theater costs less than $0.10 to produce. What explains the 4,000 percent markup? Economists have struggled with this question for years, and now we have an answer. Moviegoers vary in their willingness to pay for seeing a movie, and a movie theater has an incentive to identify the high demanders and charge them more, while keeping the price low for the low demanders. It turns out that a reliable predictor of the willingness to pay for a movie is the consumption of movie popcorn: The people who buy a lot of popcorn are the consumers who are willing to pay the most for a movie experience. So a convenient way for the theater to charge more to the consumers who are willing to pay more is to jack up the price of popcorn. As a result, the low demanders simply pay the admission price, while the high demanders pay the admission price plus the jacked-up price of a bucket of popcorn.

We can illustrate with a simple example. Suppose a low demander is willing to pay $11 for a movie, while a high demander is willing to pay $15 for a movie and popcorn. If the theater charges $10 for admission and $4 for popcorn, each consumer will get a consumer surplus of $1 (equal to $11 – $10 for the low demander and $15 – $14 for the high demander), so both consumers will see the movie. If instead the theater charged $12 for admission and $0.10 for popcorn, the high demander will see the movie, but the low demander won't. The theater's pricing strategy gets the low demander into the theater at a price of $10, and because the marginal cost of an additional consumer is close to zero, the theater's profit increases. **Related to Exercise 4.3.**

SOURCE: Based on Ricard Gil and Wesley Hartman, "Why Does Popcorn Cost So Much at the Movies? An Empirical Analysis of Metering Price Discrimination" (Research Paper 1983, Stanford Graduate School of Business, 2008).

SUMMARY

In this chapter, we've seen some of the subtleties of monopolies and their pricing policies. Compared to a perfectly competitive market, a monopoly charges a higher price, produces a smaller quantity, and wastes resources in the pursuit of monopoly power. On the positive side, some of the products we use today might never have been invented without the patent system and the monopoly power it grants. Firms with market power often use price discrimination to increase their profits. Here are the main points of the chapter:

1 Compared to a perfectly competitive market, a market served by a monopolist will charge a higher price, produce a smaller quantity of output, and generate a *deadweight loss* to society.

2 Some firms use resources to acquire monopoly power, a process known as *rent seeking*.

3 *Patents* protect innovators from competition, leading to higher prices for new products but greater incentives to develop new products.

4 To engage in *price discrimination*, a firm divides its customers into two or more groups and charges lower prices to groups with more elastic demand.

5 Price discrimination is not an act of generosity; it's an act of profit maximization.

KEY TERMS

barrier to entry, p. 546

deadweight loss from monopoly, p. 554

market power, p. 546

monopoly, p. 546

natural monopoly, p. 546

network externalities, p. 546

patent, p. 546

price discrimination, p. 557

rent seeking, p. 554

EXERCISES

All problems are assignable in MyEconLab.

25.1 The Monopolist's Output Decision

1.1 For a monopolist, marginal revenue is __________ (greater/less) than price.

1.2 A monopoly that cuts its price gains revenue from its __________ customers but loses revenue from its __________ customers.

1.3 At a price of $18 per CD, a firm sells 60 CDs. If the slope of the demand curve is –$0.10, marginal revenue for the 61st CD is $__________. The firm should cut the price to sell one more CD if the marginal cost is less than $__________.

1.4 Arrow up or down: As the quantity produced by a monopolist increases, the gap between the marginal-revenue curve and demand curve __________.

1.5 To maximize profit, a monopolist picks the quantity at which __________ equals __________.

1.6 Arrows up or down: At a price of $18 per CD, the marginal revenue of a CD seller is $12. If the marginal cost of CDs is $9, the firm should __________ its price to __________ the quantity.

1.7 You want to determine the profit-maximizing quantity for a monopolist. You can ask the firm's accountant to draw the firm's revenue and costs curves, but each curve will cost you $1,000. From the following list, indicate which curves you will request: average total cost, average fixed cost, average variable cost, marginal cost, demand, marginal revenue.

1.8 The marginal cost of an additional baseball fan is zero, so the profit-maximizing condition simplifies to __________. (Related to Application 1 on page 551.)

1.9 **Tickets and Merchandise.** Consider a baseball team that has a ticket price of $45 and sells 30,000 tickets at this price. The slope of the demand curve is –$0.002. The typical fan purchases $25 worth of merchandise that costs the owner $5 to provide.

a. The marginal revenue from ticket sales is __________.

b. Including both ticket sales and merchandise, the marginal fan contributes an additional __________ to the team's total revenue. (Related to Application 1 on page 551.)

1.10 **Book Pricing: Publishers versus Authors.** Consider the problem of setting a price for a book. The marginal cost of production is constant at $20 per book. The publisher knows from experience that the slope of the demand curve is –$0.20 per book: Starting with a price of $44, a price cut of $0.20 will increase the quantity demanded by one book. For example, here are some combinations of price and quantity:

Price per book	$44	$40	$36	$32	$30
Quantity of textbooks	80	100	120	140	150

a. What price will the publisher choose?

b. Suppose that the author receives a royalty payment equal to 10 percent of the total sales revenue from the book. If the author could choose a price, what would it be?

c. Why would the publisher and the author disagree about the price for the book?

d. Design an alternative author-compensation scheme under which the author and the publisher would choose the same price.

1.11 Restaurant Pricing. Consider a restaurant that charges $10 for all you can eat and has 30 customers at this price. The slope of the demand curve is –$0.10 per meal, and the marginal cost of providing a meal is $3. Compute the profit-maximizing price and quantity, and illustrate with a complete graph.

1.12 Empty Seats. Consider the Slappers, a hockey team that plays in an arena with 8,000 seats. The only cost associated with staging a hockey game is a fixed cost of $6,000: The team incurs this cost regardless of how many people attend a game. The demand curve for hockey tickets has a slope of –$0.001 per ticket ($1 divided by 1,000 tickets): Each $1 increase in price decreases the number of tickets sold by 1,000. For example, here are some combinations of price and quantity:

Price per ticket	$4	$5	$6	$7
Quantity of tickets	8,000	7,000	6,000	5,000

The owner's objective is to maximize the profit per hockey game (total revenue minus the $6,000 fixed cost).

a. What single price will maximize profit?

b. If the owner picks the price that maximizes profit, how many seats in the arena will be empty? Why is it rational to leave some seats empty?

c. Suppose the owner could engage in price discrimination. Would you expect the number of filled seats to increase or decrease? Explain.

1.13 Negative Marginal Revenue. The manager of your firm is puzzled because the larger the quantity of output sold, the lower its total revenue. The manager gets weekly data in a table with two columns of numbers: Quantity Sold and Total Revenue. After you do some computations and add a third and a fourth column of numbers, the manager looks at the new table and says, "Aha, now I see why selling more decreases total revenue."

a. The third column of numbers has data on __________, and the fourth column has data on __________.

b. How do the additional columns of numbers explain the negative relationship between quantity sold and total revenue?

25.2 The Social Cost of Monopoly

2.1 A monopoly is inefficient solely because the monopolist gets a profit at the expense of consumers. __________ (True/False)

2.2 To show the deadweight loss from monopoly, we compare the monopoly outcome to what would happen under __________.

2.3 The deadweight loss from monopoly is shown graphically by the area between the __________ curve and the __________ curve between the __________ quantity and the __________ quantity.

2.4 The average cost for providing off-street parking is $30 per space per day, and as a monopolist you could charge $35 per space per day for 200 spaces. The maximum amount that you are willing to pay for a monopoly is $__________.

2.5 The offer from casino developers to the citizens of Creswell, Oregon, is an example of __________. (Related to Application 2 on page 554.)

2.6 Ending a Casino Monopoly. Consider a state that initially has a single casino for gambling. Suppose the state allows a second casino to enter the market. How would you expect the entry of the second casino to affect (a) the variety of games offered in the casinos and (b) the payout (winnings) per dollar spent? (Related to Application 2 on page 554.)

2.7 Payoff for Casino Approval. Recall the Application on the casino developer's offer to pay citizens to approve a casino. Why aren't similar deals proposed for new clothing stores, music stores, or auto repair shops? (Related to Application 2 on page 554.)

2.8 Consumer Compensation. Consider the chapter opener about campus beverage monopolies. Your job is to fully compensate each student for the cost associated with a soft-drink monopoly. Suppose Coca-Cola increased the price of soft drinks by $0.20 per can and each student consumed 10 soft drinks before the monopoly was granted.

a. Kate continues to buy 10 soft drinks at the higher price. What is the appropriate compensation for her?

b. Elise buys only 4 soft drinks at the higher price. Her demand curve is linear. What is her appropriate compensation? Draw a graph that shows her change in consumer surplus.

2.9 Pricing with Zero Marginal Cost. Consider a natural spring that produces water with a unique taste. The monopolist who owns the spring has a fixed cost of installing plumbing to tap the water but no marginal cost. The demand curve for the spring water is linear. Draw a graph to show the monopolist's choice of a price and quantity. At the profit-maximizing quantity, what is the price elasticity of demand? If the spring were owned by a government that applied the marginal principle, what price would it charge?

2.10 Rules of Monopoly. In the board game Monopoly, a player who gets the third deed for a group of properties (for example, the third of three orange properties) doubles the rent charged to all other players who land on any property in the group. Similarly, a player who has a single railroad charges a rent of $25, while a player who has all four railroads charges a rent of $200 for each railroad.

a. Are these pricing rules consistent with the analysis of monopoly in this chapter?

b. In the game, is there a deadweight loss from monopoly? Why or why not?

2.11 The National Park Service Monopoly. The National Park service grants a single firm the right to sell food and other goods in Yosemite National Park.

a. What are the trade-offs associated with this policy? Who gains and who loses?

b. Does your answer to part (a) depend on whether the monopoly is granted as a political favor or auctioned to the highest bidder?

2.12 Deadweight Loss and Demand Elasticity. Using Figure 25.4 as a starting point, consider a similar product that has the same monopoly price and quantity ($18 and 200 doses), but a more elastic demand. The long-run marginal cost is the same ($8).

a. A more elastic demand generates a __________ (flatter/steeper) market demand curve.

b. Draw a graph like the one shown in Figure 25.4 and show the deadweight loss from the monopoly on the product.

c. The deadweight loss is __________ (larger/smaller) than the loss shown in Figure 25.4 because the change in is __________ (larger/smaller).

25.3 Patents and Monopoly Power

3.1 A patent increases the incentive to develop new products because it __________ the price of the product and thus generates profit to cover a firm's costs of __________.

3.2 In some cases, a patent is socially inefficient because it merely __________; in other cases, a patent is socially beneficial because it __________.

3.3 Consider the arthritis drug example on page 552. If the research and development costs are $20 million, Flexjoint will develop the drug if it gets a patent that lasts at least __________ years.

3.4 To prolong their monopoly power, the producers of branded drugs pay millions of dollars to __________. (Related to Application 3 on page 556.)

3.5 Paying to Keep a Generic Out. Suppose your firm produces a branded drug at an average cost of $2 per dose and a price of $5 per dose. You sell 1,000 doses per day. If a generic version of the drug were introduced, your daily sales would decrease to 400 doses. How much are you willing to pay each day to prevent the entry of the generic version? (Related to Application 3 on page 556.)

3.6 Patent for NoSmak. A potential new drug, NoSmak, could cure lip-smacking with one dose, but research and development would cost $80 million. The monopoly profit (earned while a single firm produces the product) will be $10 million per year. After a patent expires, the original developer of the drug will have sufficient brand loyalty to earn $3 million per year for another 10 years.

a. What is the shortest patent length required to induce a firm to develop the drug?

b. How would your answer to part (a) change if you ignore the profit earned after the patent expires?

25.4 Price Discrimination

4.1 A price-discriminating firm will charge a higher price to consumers with a relatively __________ (elastic/inelastic) demand and a lower price to consumers with a relatively __________ (elastic/inelastic) demand.

4.2 The aspirin sold in airports is more expensive than aspirin sold in grocery stores because the demand for aspirin in airports is relatively __________.

4.3 A reliable predictor of a consumer's willingness to pay for a movie is the consumption of __________. (Related to Application 4 on page 560.)

4.4 Senior citizens pay less than everyone else for admission to a movie, but the same as everyone else for beverages because beverages are __________, while admission is not.

4.5 The price of a hardback edition of a best-selling book is typically three times the price of the paperback edition because the demand from the eager consumers who buy hardbacks is relatively __________ (elastic, inelastic).

4.6 Senior Discounts for Movies. Your movie theater charges a single price of $6. The marginal cost of each patron is $1. A recent marketing survey revealed the following information about senior citizens and nonseniors.

	Price	Number of Patrons	Slope of Demand Curve
Seniors	$6	100	–$0.01 per patron
Nonseniors	6	80	–0.10 per patron

a. The marginal revenue for senior citizens is $________, while the marginal revenue for nonseniors is $________.

b. If your objective is to maximize profit, the marginal principle tells you to ________ the price for seniors and ________ the price for nonseniors.

4.7 **Book Pricing and Elasticity of Demand.** A publisher initially prices both hardback books and paperback books at $20 per book. The hardback version comes out first, followed two months later by the paperback version. The publisher initially sells the same number of hardbacks and paperbacks (100 each). Each book costs $2 to produce.

a. Complete the following table.

	Price	Quantity	Total Revenue	Total Cost	Profit
Hardback	$20	100			
Paperback	20	100			
Total		200			

b. The price elasticity of demand for hardback (eager) buyers is 0.50, and the price elasticity of demand for paperback (patient) buyers is 2.00. Suppose the publisher increases the price for hardbacks by 10 percent and decreases the price of paperbacks by 10 percent. Complete the following table.

	Price	Quantity	Total Revenue	Total Cost	Profit
Hardback	$22				
Paperback	18				
Total					

c. Does price discrimination increase or decrease the publisher's profit?

4.8 **Haircuts in Mulletville.** The town of Mulletville has a single hairstylist. The marginal cost of a haircut is the same for men and women ($10). The quantity of haircuts is 100 for men and 100 for women. The profit-maximizing price for women is $35, compared to $15 for men.

a. What explains the price difference?

b. Illustrate with a complete graph.

4.9 **Tax Cuts for Discounters?** Consider the following statement from a member of a city council: "Several of the merchants in our city offer discounts to our senior citizens. These discounts obviously decrease the merchants' profits, so we should decrease the merchants' taxes to offset their losses on senior-citizen discounts." Do you agree or disagree? Explain.

4.10 **Airline Pricing.** Consider an airline that initially has a single price of $300 for all consumers. At this price, it has 120 business travelers and 80 tourists. The airline's marginal cost is $100. The slope of the business demand curve is –$2 per traveler, and the slope of the tourist demand curve is –$1 per traveler. Does the single-price policy maximize the airline's profit? If not, how should it change its prices?

ECONOMIC EXPERIMENT

PRICE DISCRIMINATION

An experiment shows how a monopolist—a museum—picks different prices for different consumer groups. Here is how the experiment works:

- The instructor picks a group of three to five students to represent the museum.
- Of the remaining students—potential museum patrons—half represent senior citizens with senior-citizen cards. Each consumer receives a number indicating how much he or she is willing to pay for a trip to a museum.
- In each round of the experiment, the museum posts two prices: one for senior citizens and one for nonseniors. Each consumer then decides whether to buy a ticket at the relevant posted price.
- A consumer's score in a particular round equals the difference between his or her given willingness to pay and the amount he or she actually paid for admission.
- The museum's score in each round equals its profit, or its total revenue minus its total cost. The total cost equals $2 per patron (for ticket-takers, guides, cleanup, and other tasks) times the number of tickets sold.
- The experiment runs for five rounds. After the fifth round, each consumer computes his or her score by adding up the consumer surpluses. The museum's score equals the sum of its profits from the five rounds.

MyEconLab

For additional economic experiments, please visit ***www.myeconlab.com.***

NOTES

1. Richard A. Posner, "The Social Costs of Monopoly and Regulation," *Journal of Political Economy*, 83 (1975): 807–827.

2. Linda Rosencrance, "Amazon Charging Different Prices on Some DVDs," *Computerworld*, September 5, 2000, 23.

CHAPTER

26 Market Entry and Monopolistic Competition

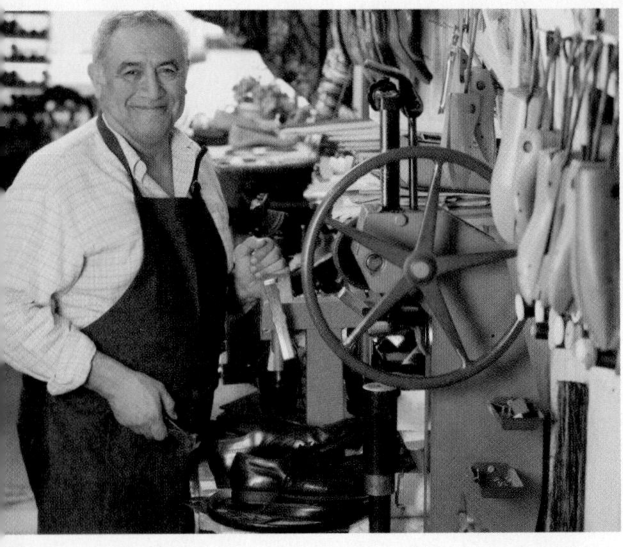

In the recession that started in 2008, some industries actually experienced increases in demand that caused market entry—new firms entered the markets.[1]

When total employment and income dropped, many consumers switched from buying new shoes to repairing old shoes, and the demand for shoe repair increased. In 2008 the sales of adult footwear decreased by about 3 percent, and the volume of shoe repairs increased dramatically; newspapers reported that in some shops sales increased by 40 to 50 percent. Some consumers purchased used shoes in thrift shops and brought them to cobblers for repairs and reconditioning. The surge in sales increased the profits of shoe-repair shops, and firms entered the market by opening new shops. The entry of new firms reversed—at least temporarily—a long decline of shoe-repair shops. The number of shops in the United States decreased from 120,000 during the Great Depression to 7,000 in 2008. As the economy comes out of the recession, the question is whether the long-term trend of disappearing cobblers will be restored, or whether a new consumer thriftiness will allow more cobblers to stay in business.

LEARNING OBJECTIVES

- Describe and explain the effects of market entry.
- List the conditions for equilibrium in monopolistic competition.
- Contrast monopolistic competition and perfect competition.
- Explain the role of advertising in monopolistic competition.

MyEconLab

MyEconLab helps you master each objective and study more efficiently.

In this chapter, we explore a firm's decision to enter a market and examine the consequences of entry on prices and the profits of other firms. Firms will enter a market as long as they can make an economic profit. As we'll see, the entry of firms squeezes profit in three ways: The price decreases, the average cost of production increases, and the quantity sold per firm decreases. Eventually the entry process stops, and we can count the number of firms serving the market. If entry stops at a single firm, we have a natural monopoly, a topic we cover later in the book. If many firms enter the market, we have monopolistic competition, the topic of this chapter.

Monopolistic competition is a hybrid market structure, with features of both monopoly and perfect competition. The term may seem like an oxymoron—a pair of contradictory words—similar to "virtual reality" and "books on tape." However, the term actually conveys the two key features of the market:

monopolistic competition
A market served by many firms that sell slightly different products.

- Each firm in the market produces a good that is slightly different from the goods of other firms, so each firm has a narrowly defined *monopoly*.
- The products sold by different firms in the market are close substitutes for one another, so there is intense *competition* between firms for consumers. For example, your local grocery store may stock several brands of toothbrushes with different design features. If the price of one brand increases, some loyal customers will continue to buy the brand, but others will switch to different brands that are close substitutes.

Some other examples of monopolistic competition are the markets for bread, clothing, restaurant meals, and gasoline. In each case, firms in the market sell products that are close, but not perfect, substitutes.

The analysis in this chapter is based on two assumptions. First, we assume there are no barriers to entry: There are no patents or government licensing programs to restrict the number of firms. Second, we assume that firms do not act strategically: Each firm acts on its own, taking the actions of other firms as given. This means that firms already in the market do not conspire to fix prices and do not try to prevent other firms from entering the market. In the next chapter, we'll explore several types of strategic behavior in an oligopoly, a market with just a few firms.

26.1 The Effects of Market Entry

Consider a market served by a single profitable firm, a monopolist. As we saw earlier in the book, a firm in any market can use the marginal principle to decide how much output to produce.

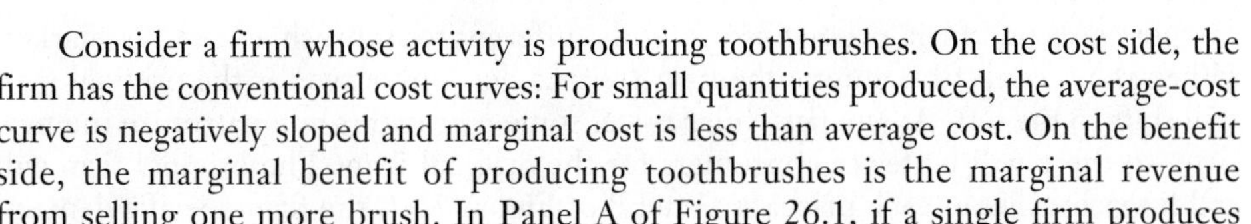

MARGINAL PRINCIPLE
Increase the level of an activity as long as its marginal benefit exceeds its marginal cost. Choose the level at which the marginal benefit equals the marginal cost.

Consider a firm whose activity is producing toothbrushes. On the cost side, the firm has the conventional cost curves: For small quantities produced, the average-cost curve is negatively sloped and marginal cost is less than average cost. On the benefit side, the marginal benefit of producing toothbrushes is the marginal revenue from selling one more brush. In Panel A of Figure 26.1, if a single firm produces toothbrushes, the firm-specific demand curve (the demand curve applicable to a

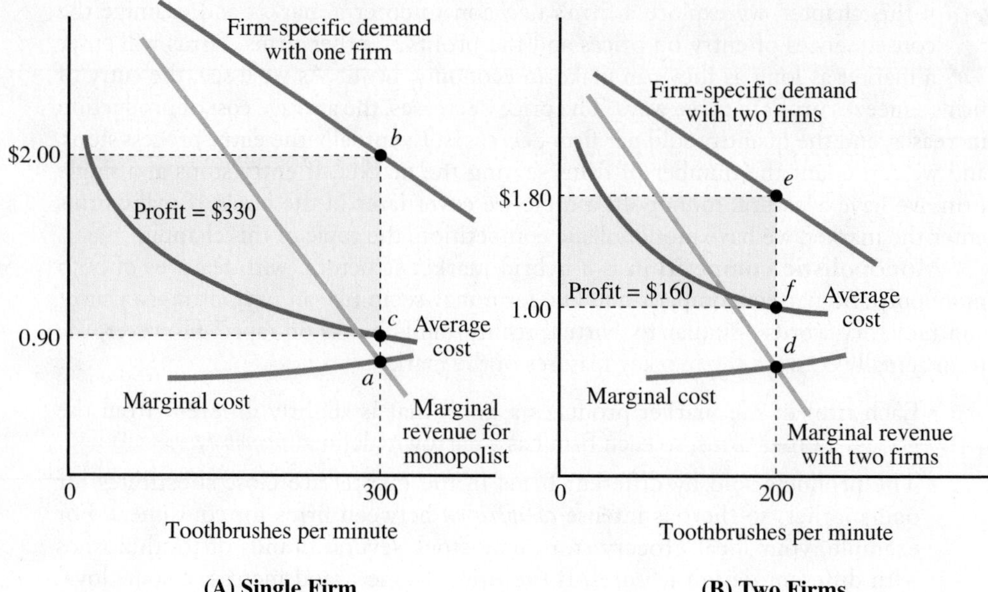

▲ FIGURE 26.1
Market Entry Decreases Price and Squeezes Profit
(A) A monopolist maximizes profit at point *a*, where marginal revenue equals marginal cost. The firm sells 300 toothbrushes at a price of $2.00 (point *b*) and an average cost of $0.90 (point *c*). The profit of $330 is shown by the shaded rectangle. (*B*) The entry of a second firm shifts the firm-specific demand curve for the original firm to the left. The firm produces only 200 toothbrushes (point *d*) at a lower price ($1.80, shown by point *e*) and a higher average cost ($1.00, shown by point *f*). The firm's profit, shown by the shaded rectangle, shrinks to $160.

specific firm) is the same as the market demand curve. As we saw in the chapter on monopoly, the firm's marginal-revenue curve lies below the demand curve because a monopolist must cut its price to sell more output.

As we saw in the previous chapter, a monopolist maximizes profit by picking the quantity at which marginal revenue equals marginal cost. In Figure 26.1, this happens at point *a*, with a quantity of 300 toothbrushes. From point *b* on the demand curve, the price associated with this quantity is $2.00. From point *c* on the average-cost curve, we see that the average cost of this quantity is $0.90. The firm's profit, shown by the shaded rectangle, is $330:

$$\text{profit} = (\text{price} - \text{average cost}) \times \text{quantity} = (\$2.00 - \$0.90) \times 300 = \$330$$

Given the large profits in the toothbrush market, will a second firm enter the market?

Entry Squeezes Profits from Three Sides

Suppose a second firm, producing a slightly different toothbrush, enters the market. When the second firm enters, the firm-specific demand curve for the original firm will shift to the left. At any particular price, some consumers will patronize the new firm, so there will be fewer consumers for the original firm: The original firm will sell fewer brushes at each price. In Panel B of Figure 26.1, the firm-specific demand curve for the original monopolist shifts to the left, and profit decreases for three reasons:

1 *The market price drops.* The marginal principle is satisfied at point *d*, so the original firm now produces 200 toothbrushes at a price of $1.80 (point *e*). The competition between the two firms causes the price to drop, from $2.00 to $1.80.
2 *The quantity produced by the first firm decreases.* The original firm produces only 200 toothbrushes, down from the 300 it produced as a monopolist.
3 *The first firm's average cost of production increases.* The decrease in the quantity produced causes the firm to move upward along its negatively sloped average-cost curve to a higher average cost per toothbrush, from $0.90 to $1.00 (point *f*).

The effects of entry are shown by comparing the profit rectangles in Panels A and B of Figure 26.1. Entry shrinks the firm's profit rectangle because it is squeezed from three directions. The top of the rectangle drops because the price decreases. The bottom of the rectangle rises because the average cost increases. The right side of the rectangle moves to the left because the quantity decreases. In this example, profit drops from $330 to $160:

$$\text{profit} = (\text{price} - \text{average cost}) \times \text{quantity} = (\$1.80 - 1.00) \times 200 = \$160$$

What about the second firm? If we assume the second firm has access to the same production technology as the first firm and pays the same prices for its inputs, the cost curves for the second firm will be the same as the cost curves for the first firm. If the product of the second firm is nearly identical to the product of the first firm, the firm-specific demand curve for the second firm will be nearly identical to the firm-specific demand curve of the first firm. As an approximation, we can use Panel B of Figure 26.1 to represent both firms. Each firm produces 200 toothbrushes at an average cost of $1.00 per toothbrush and sells them at a price of $1.80.

Examples of Entry: Car Stereos, Trucking, and Tires

To illustrate the effects of entry on price, cost, and profit, imagine that you just inherited enough money to start your own car-stereo business. Suppose that the existing monopolist sells 10 stereos per day at a price of $230 and an average cost of $200 per stereo, for a profit of $30 per stereo. If you enter the market, the increased competition will drop the price below $230, and if you sell fewer than 10 stereos (the monopoly quantity), your average will be greater than $200 because you will spread your fixed costs over fewer units. In other words, your entry squeezes profit per unit from both sides. For example, if the market price drops to $215 and the average cost increases to $205, your profit per stereo will be $10, significantly less than the monopolist's initial profit of $30 per stereo.

What happens when the government eliminates artificial barriers to entry? The Motor Carrier Act of 1980 eliminated the government's entry restrictions on the trucking industry, most of which had been in place since the 1930s. New firms entered the trucking market, and freight prices dropped by about 22 percent. The market value of a firm's trucking license indicates how much profit the firm can earn in the market. Deregulation increased competition and decreased prices and profits, and the average value of a trucking license dropped from $579,000 in 1977 to less than $15,000 in 1982.[2]

Empirical studies of other markets provide ample evidence that entry decreases market prices and firms' profits. In other words, consumers pay less for goods and services, and firms earn lower profits. In one study of the retail pricing of tires, a

application 1

SATELLITE v CABLE

APPLYING THE CONCEPTS #1: How does market entry affect prices?

Consider the market for television signals provided to residential consumers. How will an existing cable-TV provider respond to the entry of a firm that provides TV signals via satellite? In most cases, the entry of a satellite firm causes the cable firm to improve the quality of service and decrease its price, so consumer surplus increases. In some cases, the cable company improves the quality of service and *increases* price. Because the service improvement is typically large relative to the price hike, consumer surplus increases in this case too. On average, the entry of a satellite firm increases the monthly consumer surplus per consumer from $3.96 to $5.22, an increase of 32 percent. **Related to Exercises 1.6 and 1.8.**

SOURCE: Based on Chenghuan Chu, "The effect of satellite entry on cable television prices and product quality," *RAND Journal of Economics* 41 (2010), pp. 730–764.

market with only two tire stores had a price of $55 per tire, compared to a price of $53 in a market with three stores, $51 with four stores, and $50 with five stores. The larger the number of stores, the lower the price of tires.[3]

26.2 Monopolistic Competition

We've seen that the entry of a firm in a profitable market decreases the price and the profit per firm. Under a market structure called *monopolistic competition*, firms will continue to enter the market until economic profit is zero. Here are the features of monopolistic competition:

- *Many firms.* Because there are relatively small economies of scale, a small firm can produce its product at about the same average cost as a large firm. For example, a small donut shop can produce donuts and coffee at about the same average cost as a large shop. Because even a small firm can cover its costs, the market can support many firms.
- *A differentiated product.* Firms engage in **product differentiation**, the process used by firms to distinguish their products from the products of competing firms. A firm can distinguish its products from the products of other firms by offering a different performance level or appearance. For example, automobiles differ in horsepower and fuel efficiency, and toothpastes differ in flavor and their ability to clean teeth. Some products are differentiated by the services that come with them. For example, some stores provide informative and helpful salespeople, whereas others require consumers to make decisions on their own. Some pizza firms offer home delivery, and some software producers offer free technical assistance. As we'll see later in the chapter, some products are differentiated by where they are sold.

product differentiation
The process used by firms to distinguish their products from the products of competing firms.

- *No artificial barriers to entry.* There are no patents or regulations that could prevent firms from entering the market.

These characteristics explain the logic behind the label "monopolistic competition." Product differentiation means each firm is the sole seller of a narrowly defined good. For example, each firm in the toothbrush market has a unique design for its toothbrushes, so each is a monopolist in the narrowly defined market for that design. Because the products from different firms are close substitutes, there is keen competition for consumers. When one toothbrush maker increases its price, many of its consumers will switch to the similar toothbrushes produced by other firms. In other words, the demand for the product of a monopolistically competitive firm is very price elastic: An increase in price decreases the quantity demanded by a relatively large amount because consumers can easily switch to another firm selling a similar product.

When Entry Stops: Long-Run Equilibrium

We'll use the toothbrush example to illustrate the features of monopolistic competition. The producers of toothbrushes differentiate their products with respect to color, bristle design, handle size and shape, and durability. As we saw earlier, after a second firm enters the toothbrush market, both firms still make a profit. Will a third firm enter this lucrative market? The entry of a third firm will shift the firm-specific demand curve for each firm further to the left. As we saw earlier, a leftward shift of a firm's demand curve decreases the market price, decreases the quantity produced per firm, and increases the average cost per toothbrush. If after the third firm enters the market all three firms still earn positive profit, a fourth firm will enter.

Because there are no barriers to entering the toothbrush market, firms will continue to enter until each firm makes zero economic profit. Figure 26.2 shows the long-run equilibrium from the perspective of the typical firm. Suppose a total of six firms are in the toothbrush market. Given the firm-specific demand curve in a market with six firms, the typical firm satisfies the marginal principle

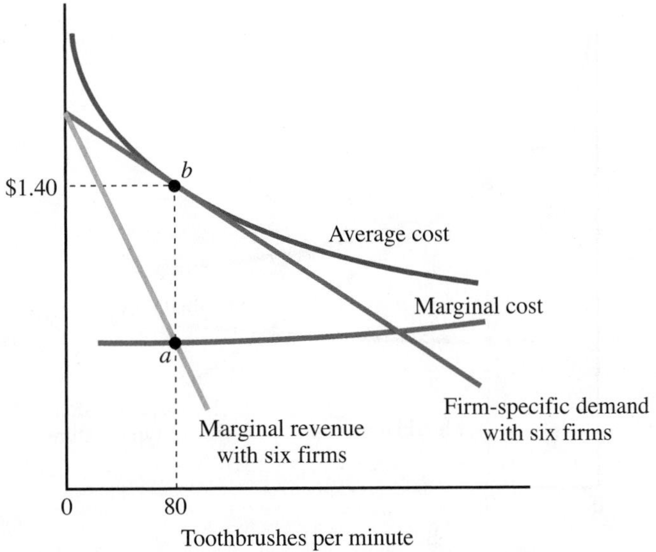

▲ FIGURE 26.2
Long-Run Equilibrium with Monopolistic Competition
Under monopolistic competition, firms continue to enter the market until economic profit is zero. Entry shifts the firm-specific demand curve to the left. The typical firm maximizes profit at point *a*, where marginal revenue equals marginal cost. At a quantity of 80 toothbrushes, price equals average cost (shown by point *b*), so economic profit is zero.

at point *a* by selling 80 brushes per minute at a price of $1.40 (point *b*) and an average cost of $1.40. Because the price equals the average cost, the typical firm makes zero economic profit. Each firm's revenue is high enough to cover all its costs—including the opportunity cost of all its inputs—but not enough to cause additional firms to enter the market. In other words, each firm makes just enough money to stay in business.

What are the implications of market entry for the market as a whole? In Figure 26.2, each of the six firms in the market produces 80 toothbrushes at a price of $1.40, so the total quantity produced is 480. In contrast, we started with a monopoly that had a price of $2.00 and a quantity of 300 toothbrushes. In other words, market entry decreased the price from $2.00 to $1.40 and increased the total quantity demanded from 300 to 480, consistent with the law of demand.

Differentiation by Location

In some monopolistically competitive markets, differentiation is simply a matter of location. Some examples are gas stations, music stores, bookstores, grocery stores, movie theaters, and ice-cream parlors. In each case, many firms sell the same product at different locations. Your city probably has several bookstores, each of which sells a particular book at about the same price. Everything else being equal, you are likely to purchase books from the most convenient store, but if a store across town offers lower prices, you might purchase your books there instead. In other words, each store has a monopoly in its own neighborhood, but competes with bookstores in the rest of the city.

Figure 26.3 shows the long-run equilibrium in the market for books. Because there are no barriers to entering the market, new bookstores will enter the market until each store makes zero economic profit. The typical bookstore satisfies the marginal principle at point *a*, selling 70 books per hour at a price of $14 per book

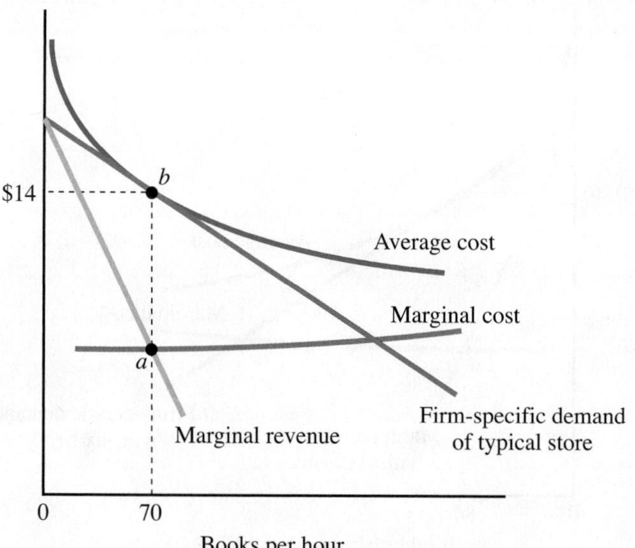

▲ **FIGURE 26.3**

Long-Run Equilibrium with Spatial Competition

Bookstores and other retailers differentiate their products by selling them at different locations. The typical bookstore chooses the quantity of books at which its marginal revenue equals its marginal cost (point *a*). Economic profit is zero because the price equals average cost (point *b*).

application 2

OPENING A DUNKIN' DONUTS SHOP

APPLYING THE CONCEPTS #2: Are monopolistically competitive firms profitable?

One way to get into a monopolistically competitive market is to get a franchise for a nationally advertised product. If you want to get into the donut market, you could pay a franchise fee of $40,000 to Allied Domecq, the parent company of Dunkin' Donuts. That gives you the right to sell donuts under the Dunkin' Donuts brand. You'll also get a few weeks of training at the corporate headquarters in Massachusetts and some help in organizing a grand opening. Once you start making money, you'll pay a royalty to the parent company equal to 5.9 percent of your sales.

How much money are you likely to make in your donut shop? You will compete for donut consumers with other donut shops, bakeries, grocery stores, and coffee shops. Given the small barriers to entering the donut business, you should expect keen competition for consumers. Although your brand-name donuts will give you an edge over your competitors, remember that you must pay the franchise fee and royalties. In the monopolistically competitive donut market, you should expect to make zero economic profit, with total revenue equal to total cost. Your total cost includes the franchise fee and royalties, as well as the opportunity cost of your time and the opportunity cost of any funds you invest in the business.

Table 26.1 shows the franchise fees and royalty rates for several franchising opportunities. The fees indicate how much entrepreneurs are willing to pay for the right to sell a brand-name product. **Related to Exercises 2.4 and 2.5.**

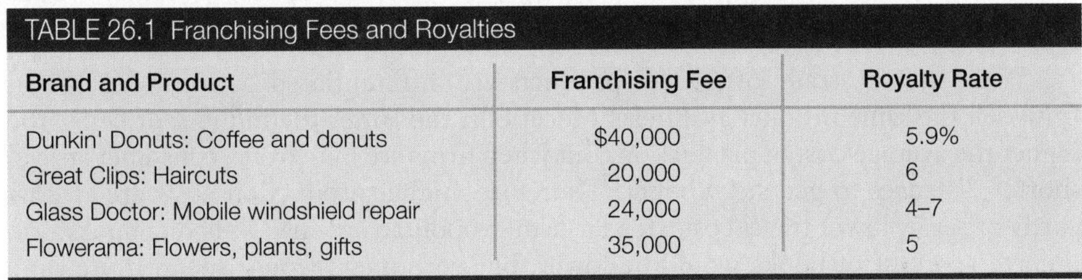

TABLE 26.1 Franchising Fees and Royalties

Brand and Product	Franchising Fee	Royalty Rate
Dunkin' Donuts: Coffee and donuts	$40,000	5.9%
Great Clips: Haircuts	20,000	6
Glass Doctor: Mobile windshield repair	24,000	4–7
Flowerama: Flowers, plants, gifts	35,000	5

SOURCE: Based on data from *www.entrepreneur.com* (accessed October 8, 2010).

(point *b*) and an average cost of $14 per book. The price equals the store's average cost, so the typical store makes zero economic profit. Each store's revenue is high enough to cover all its costs—including the opportunity cost of all its inputs—but not enough to cause additional stores to enter the market. In other words, the firm makes just enough money to stay in business.

26.3 Trade-Offs with Entry and Monopolistic Competition

We've seen that market entry leads to lower prices and a larger total quantity in the market. At the same time, entry decreases the output per firm and increases the average cost of production. As shown in Figure 26.2 and 26.3, monopolistically competitive firms operate on the negatively sloped portion of their average-cost curves, so average cost is higher than the minimum. In other words, the average cost of production would be lower if a single toothbrush firm served the entire market by providing a single type of toothbrush. What are the other consequences of entry and monopolistic competition?

Average Cost and Variety

There are some trade-offs associated with monopolistic competition. Although the average cost of production is higher than the minimum, there is also more product variety. In a market with many toothbrush firms, consumers can choose from a wide variety of designs, so the higher average cost is at least partly offset by greater product variety. Here are two other examples of the benefits of product variety:

- *Restaurant meals.* The typical large city has dozens of Italian restaurants, each of which has a different menu and prepares its food in different ways. Consumers can pick from restaurants offering a wide variety of menus and preparation techniques. Although a city with a single Italian restaurant would have a lower average cost of preparing Italian meals, consumers would get less variety.
- *Shoes and clothing.* Shoes are differentiated according to their style and performance. If we all wore the same type of shoes, the average cost of producing shoes would be lower, but consumers would be unable to match their shoe preferences with suitable shoes. Similarly, if we all wore uniforms, the average cost of clothing would be lower, but that would eliminate clothing choice.

What are the trade-offs when products are differentiated by location? When firms sell the same product at different locations, the larger the number of firms, the higher the average cost of production. But when firms are numerous, consumers travel shorter distances to get the product. Therefore, higher production costs are at least partly offset by lower travel costs. If a large metropolitan area had only one bookstore, the average cost of books would be lower, but consumers would spend more time traveling to get the books.

Monopolistic Competition versus Perfect Competition

Product differentiation is what makes monopolistic competition different from perfect competition. Perfectly competitive firms produce homogeneous products, while monopolistically competitive firms produce differentiated products. Panel A of Figure 26.4 shows the equilibrium for a perfectly competitive firm. Each price-taking firm has a horizontal demand curve. Point *a* shows the long-run equilibrium because the typical firm (1) satisfies the marginal principle, choosing the quantity where marginal revenue equals marginal cost, and (2) earns zero economic profit because price equals average cost:

$$\text{price} = \text{marginal cost} = \text{average cost}$$

The only place where price equals both marginal cost *and* average cost is the minimum point of the average-cost curve, shown by point *a*.

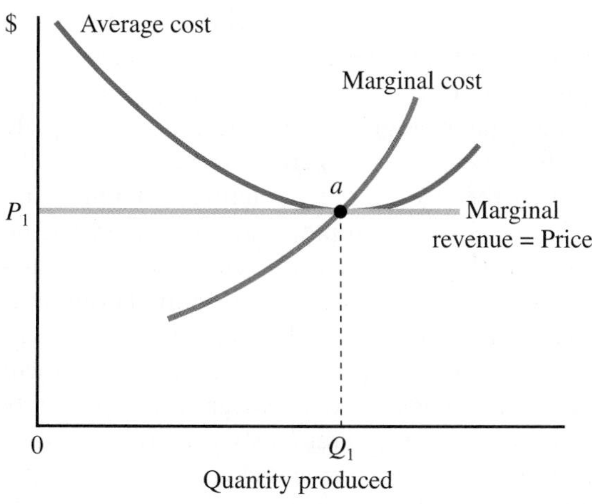

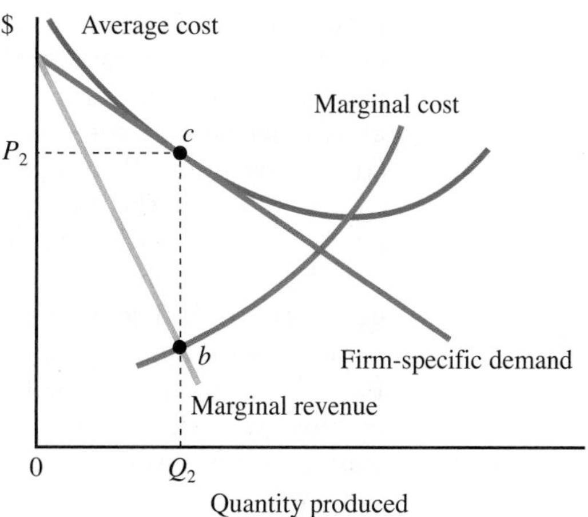

▲ FIGURE 26.4
Monopolistic Competition versus Perfect Competition
(A) In a perfectly competitive market, the firm-specific demand curve is horizontal at the market price, and marginal revenue equals price. In equilibrium, price = marginal cost = average cost. The equilibrium occurs at the minimum of the average-cost curve. (B) In a monopolistically competitive market, the firm-specific demand curve is negatively sloped and marginal revenue is less than price. In equilibrium, marginal revenue equals marginal cost (point *b*) and price equals average cost (point *c*).

Panel B shows the equilibrium for a monopolistically competitive firm. The firm has a differentiated product, so its demand curve is negatively sloped and marginal revenue is less than the price. With a negatively sloped demand curve, the zero-profit condition—price equals average cost—will be satisfied along the negatively sloped

application 3

HAPPY HOUR PRICING

APPLYING THE CONCEPTS #3: How does monopolistic competition compare to perfect competition?

Consider the phenomenon of "happy hour." Many bars and restaurants near workplaces face an increase in demand for food and drink around 5:00 p.m., and many cut their prices for an hour or two. According to the model of perfect competition, an increase in demand will lead to higher, not lower prices. What explains the happy-hour combination of higher demand and lower prices?

Bars are subject to monopolistic competition. Each bar has a local monopoly within its neighborhood, but faces competition from other bars outside its neighborhood. For an individual consumer, the higher the demand for food and drink, the greater the incentive to consider alternatives to the nearest bar. If you expect to purchase large quantities of bar food and drink, the savings achieved by finding a lower price at an alternative bar will be relatively large. In other words, when individual demand increases, each bar faces a more elastic demand for its products. In a market subject to monopolistic competition, the bar's rational response to more elastic demand (more sensitive consumers) is to decrease its price. In graphical terms, the demand curve facing each bar becomes flatter, and the demand curve will be tangent to the average-cost curve at a larger quantity and a lower price and average cost. **Related to Exercise 3.6.**

SOURCE: Based on Mark Fisher, "Happy Hour Economics, or How an Increase in Demand Can Produce a Decrease in Price," *Economic Review, Federal Reserve Bank of Atlanta* (Second Quarter 2005), pp. 25–34.

portion of the average-cost curve. In other words, the only place where a tangency can occur is along the negatively sloped portion of the average-cost curve. Compared to a perfectly competitive firm, a monopolistically competitive firm produces less output at a higher average cost. In Figure 26.4, the average cost for the monopolistically competitive firm is P_2, compared to P_1 for a perfectly competitive firm.

To illustrate the difference between the two market structures, imagine that product differentiation diminishes. Suppose, for example, that consumers decide that the distinguishing features of toothbrushes—color, shape, and bristle design—don't matter. As a result, the products of competing firms will become better substitutes, so the demand for a particular firm's product will become more elastic. In Panel B of Figure 26.4 the firm-specific demand curve will become flatter and will be tangent to the average-cost curve at a larger quantity, closer to the perfectly competitive quantity Q_1. As differentiation continues to diminish, the firm's demand curve will become flatter and flatter, and we will get closer and closer to the perfectly competitive outcome, where the average cost reaches its minimum.

26.4 Advertising for Product Differentiation

We've seen that product differentiation is a key feature of monopolistic competition. A firm can use advertising to inform consumers about the features of its product and thus distinguish its product from the products of other firms. In addition, advertisements can inform consumers about prices. A famous study of the eyeglass market found that advertising promoted price competition between firms and reduced eyeglass prices by about 20 percent.[4]

Some advertisements don't provide any real information about a product or its price. You've seen the advertisements featuring beer drinkers frolicking on the beach with attractive people, cigarette smokers riding horseback, drivers of sports cars impressing classmates at high-school reunions, and sports-drink

application 4

PICTURE OF MAN VERSUS PICTURE OF WOMAN

APPLYING THE CONCEPT #4: How does advertising affect consumer choices?

A South African consumer lender decided to use a mass mailing of 53,000 loan offers to test the sensitivity of consumers to variations in interest rates and other features of loan offers. The interest rates in the offer letters ranged from 3.75% to 11.75% *per month*. As expected, the uptake rate (the number of consumers who accepted a particular loan offer) was higher for offer letters with low interest rates. The elasticity of the uptake rate with respect to the interest rate was –0.34: a 10% decrease in the interest rate (from say an interest rate of 7.0% to 6.3%) increased the uptake rate by 3.4%.

More surprising was the finding that the uptake rate among men was much higher when the offer letter included a picture of a woman rather than a picture of a man. Replacing a male model with a female model was equivalent to cutting the interest rate by 25 percent, for example, from 7.0 percent to 5.25 percent. In contrast, the uptake rate for women consumers was unaffected by the gender of the model. **Related to Exercises 4.4 and 4.5.**

SOURCE: Based on Marianne Bertrand, Dean Karlan, Sendhil Mullainathan, Eddar Shafir, Jonathan Zinman, "What's Advertising Content Worth? Evidence from a Consumer Credit Marketing Field Experiment," *Quarterly Journal of Economics* 125 (2010), pp. 263–306.

consumers performing amazing athletic feats. These sorts of advertisements are designed to promote an image for a product, not to provide information about the product's features.

An advertisement that doesn't provide any product information may actually help consumers make decisions. Firms spend millions of dollars to get celebrities like Drew Brees and Kristen Stewart to endorse their products. When a famous athlete or actor appears in an advertisement for a product, everyone realizes the celebrity is doing the advertisement for money, not to share his or her enthusiasm for the advertised product. Nonetheless, these advertisements are effective in increasing sales. Why do they work?

By paying millions of dollars to run an advertisement featuring a celebrity, a firm sends a signal to consumers that the advertised product is appealing and likely to be popular. To illustrate this signaling effect, consider a firm that develops a new energy bar and picks a celebrity to endorse it. The purpose of a celebrity advertisement is to get people to try the product for the first time. After that, a consumer will base any repeat purchases on the taste and nutritional value of the energy bar. Suppose an advertisement with a cost of $10 million would cause 10 million consumers to try the energy bar. As shown in the first row of Table 26.2, energy bar A is an appealing product, and half the consumers who try it will become repeat consumers. If the firm makes a profit of $4 on each repeat customer, the firm's profit of $20 million exceeds the $10 million cost of the advertisement, so the firm will run the advertisement.

TABLE 26.2 Advertising Profitability and Signaling

Product	Number of Consumers Who Try the Product	Number of Repeat Customers	Profit per Repeat Customer	Profit from Repeat Customers	Cost of Advertisement
Energy bar A	10 million	5 million	$4	$20 million	$10 million
Energy bar B	10 million	1 million	4	4 million	10 million

What about a product that is less appealing? The second row of Table 26.2 shows the effects of an advertisement for energy bar B. Only 1 in 10 people who try energy bar B will become a repeat customer, so the firm's profit from an advertisement is only $4 million. That is not enough to cover the $10 million cost, so the firm won't advertise the less-appealing product. Notice that celebrity endorsements for the two products are equally effective in getting people to try the products, but what matters is repeat customers. The less-appealing product gets fewer repeat customers because it's an inferior product, and that's why it's not worthwhile to pay for an advertisement.

Celebrity endorsements and other expensive advertising send a signal to consumers that the producer expects many repeat customers. Firms undertake extensive marketing research to project the sales of their products and, when their research suggests the product will be popular, they have an incentive to spend money on advertising to send the signal to consumers. The signal tells consumers which new products are expected to have the greatest general appeal.

SUMMARY

This chapter is about market entry and monopolistic competition. In a monopolistically competitive market, entry continues until each firm in the market makes zero economic profit. Firms can differentiate their products by design, level of service, location, or product image. Here are the main points of the chapter:

1 The entry of a firm into a market decreases the market price, decreases output per firm, and increases the average cost of production.

2 In a *monopolistically competitive* market, firms compete for customers by producing *differentiated products*.

3 In the long-run equilibrium with monopolistic competition, marginal revenue equals marginal cost, price equals average cost, and economic profit is zero.

4 Under monopolistic competition, the average cost of production is higher than the minimum, but there is also more product variety.

5 A firm can use celebrity endorsements and other costly advertisements to signal its belief that a product will be appealing.

KEY TERMS

monopolistic competition, p. 567

product differentiation, p. 570

EXERCISES

All problems are assignable in MyEconLab.

26.1 The Effects of Market Entry

1.1 A profit-maximizing firm picks the quantity of output at which __________ equals __________.

1.2 Arrows up or down: At a firm's current level of output, marginal revenue exceeds the marginal cost. The firm should __________ its output and __________ its price.

1.3 The entry of a second firm shifts the firm-specific demand curve of the first firm to the __________ (left/right).

1.4 Arrows up or down: The entry of a third firm into a market with two original firms __________ the market price, __________ the average production cost, __________ the quantity produced per firm, and __________ profit of each original firm.

1.5 Arrows up or down: Changes in regulatory policy in the 1980s __________ the price of trucking services and __________ the profits of trucking firms.

1.6 Arrows up or down: The entry of a satellite TV firm __________ consumer surplus, in part because the cable company __________ the quality of service while either __________ price or __________ price by a relatively small amount. (Related to Application 1 on page 570.)

1.7 **Bidding for Bookstore Licenses.** Paige initially has the only license to operate a bookstore in Bookville. She charges a price of $9 per book, has an average cost of $4 per book, and sells 1,001 books per year. When Paige's license expires, the city decides to auction two bookstore licenses to the highest bidders. Suppose the relevant variables (price, average cost, and output per firm) take on only integer values—no fraction or decimals.

a. Suppose Paige is optimistic and imagines the best possible outcome with a two-firm market. What is the maximum amount she is willing to pay for one of the two licenses?

b. Suppose Paige is pessimistic and imagines the worst possible outcome with a two-firm market. What is the maximum amount she is willing to pay for one of the two licenses?

1.8 **Draw the Cable TV Graph.** Consider the "Satellite versus Cable" Application. Use a graph to show that the entry of satellite TV decreases the profit-maximizing price of a cable TV company from $40 to $35 (Related to Application 1 on page 570.)

1.9 **Beware the Too-Easy Answer.** Your city initially restricts the number of pizzerias to one. The existing monopolist sells 3,000 pizzas per day. A pizzeria reaches the horizontal portion of its long-run average cost curve at an output of about 1,000 pizzas per day. Suppose the city eliminates the entry restrictions. Predict the equilibrium number of pizzerias. Beware of the TEC (too easy to be correct) answer.

1.10 Equilibrium? In your city, there are currently three firms providing oil changes. For each firm, there is a fixed cost of $80 per day and a marginal cost of $12 per oil change. Each firm currently maximizes its profit by providing 10 oil changes per day.

a. For each firm, marginal revenue = $________.

b. This is a monopolistically competitive equilibrium if ________ equals $________.

26.2 Monopolistic Competition

2.1 *Monopolistic competition* refers to a market in which old boys act naturally as they transport tight slacks in the back of Dodge Ram pickup trucks. ________ (True/False)

2.2 Perfectly competitive firms sell a ________ product, while monopolistically competitive firms sell a ________ product.

2.3 There are two conditions for a long-run equilibrium in a monopolistically competitive market:
(1) ________ equals ________ and
(2) ________ equals ________.

2.4 To enter the donut market as a seller of Dunkin' Donuts, you'll pay a one-time franchise fee of $________ and then pay ________ percent of your sales. (Related to Application 2 on page 573.)

2.5 **Willingness to Pay for a Dunkin' Donuts Franchise.** You operate a Dunkin' Donuts shop under a franchise agreement. You pay a royalty of 6 percent of your sales revenue to the parent company. Your profit-maximizing quantity is 10,000 donuts per year, and at this quantity your price is $1.00 and your average cost per donut (including all the opportunity cost of production but not the 6 percent royalty) is $0.44. (Related to Application 2 on page 573.)

a. Draw a graph with revenue and costs curves to show your profit-maximizing choice.

b. What is the maximum amount you are willing to pay per year for the franchise?

2.6 **How Many Bookstores?** The city of Bookburg initially allows only one bookstore, which sells books at a price of $20 and an average cost of $11. Suppose the city eliminates its restrictions on bookstores, allowing additional stores to enter the market. According to an expert in the music market, "Each additional music store will decrease the price of books by $2 per book and increase the average cost of selling books by $1 per book." Predict the equilibrium number of bookstores.

2.7 **Lawn-Cutting Equilibrium.** Consider the market for cutting lawns. Each firm has a fixed daily cost of $18 for equipment, and the marginal cost of cutting a lawn is $4. Suppose each firm can cut up to three lawns per day. The market demand curve for lawn cuts is linear, with a vertical intercept of $70 and a slope of –$1 per lawn.

a. If each firm in the market cuts three lawns, what is the average cost per lawn?

b. What is the equilibrium price under monopolistic competition?

c. How many lawns will be cut in total, and how many firms will be in the market?

2.8 **Zero Price for a Permit.** Consider a city that initially issues five licenses to pet groomers and does not allow the licenses to be bought and sold. Shortly after an economist joins the city licensing authority, the city decides to allow the licenses to be bought and sold on the open market. Much to the surprise of the licensers, the price of the licenses was zero: No one was willing to pay a positive amount for a pet grooming license.

a. Explain why the price of grooming licenses was zero.

b. Illustrate your answer with a complete graph.

2.9 **Auctioning Business Licenses.** The following table shows the relationships between the number of firms in the market, the market price, the quantity per firm, and the average cost of production.

Number of Firms	Price	Quantity per Firm	Average Cost
1	$20	38	$ 9
2	18	35	10
3	16	32	11
4	14	29	12
5	12	26	13
6	10	23	14
7	8	20	15

A business license allows a firm to operate the business for one day. The city will auction up to seven business licenses to the highest bidders, and the auctioning of licenses will continue as long as someone bids a positive amount for one of the licenses. Assume that each firm can buy only one license. What is the maximum amount you would be willing to pay for a license?

26.3 Trade-Offs with Entry and Monopolistic Competition

3.1 The trade-off with entry is that an increase in the number of firms leads to higher ________ but greater ________.

3.2 When products are differentiated by location, the entry of firms generates benefits for consumers in the form of ________.

3.3 A perfectly competitive firm has a __________ demand curve, whereas a monopolistic competitive firm has a __________ demand curve.

3.4 In the long-run equilibrium in a perfectly competitive market, price is equal to both __________ and __________.

3.5 Arrows up or down: As product differentiation diminishes, the price elasticity of demand for the product of a monopolistically competitive firm __________ and the average cost of production __________.

3.6 The phenomenon of "happy hour" pricing (__________ prices when demand is relatively high) results from relatively __________ (elastic/inelastic) demand. (Related to Application 3 on page 575.)

3.7 **Uniform Trade-Offs.** A prominent feature of Mao's Communist China in the 1940s through the 1970s was the blue uniform worn by all citizens.

a. Explain the trade-offs associated with the use of uniforms. What were the benefits? What were the costs?

b. Suppose people had a choice among five uniform colors rather than being required to wear blue. Would you expect the benefits of requiring uniforms to decrease by a little or a lot?

26.4 Advertising for Product Differentiation

4.1 Advertising for eyeglasses __________ (increases/decreases) the price of eyeglasses because advertising promotes __________.

4.2 An advertisement that succeeds in getting consumers to try the product will be sensible only if the number of __________ customers is large.

4.3 In Table 26.2 on page 577, the profit from repeat customers will equal the cost of the advertisement if there are __________ repeat customers.

4.4 Arrows up or down. In the application on consumer loans in South Africa, the loan uptake rate __________ as the interest rate decreased and __________ when the model on the offer was switched from a man to a woman. (Related to Application 4 on page 576.)

4.5 **Advertising for Loans.** Consider the numbers provided in Application 4 on South African consumer loans. Suppose a lender initially charges an interest rate of 10 percent and uses male models in its advertisements. The firm wants to increase its uptake rate among male consumers. Suppose the firm switches to female models in its advertisements. The male uptake rate will increase by __________ (1, 3, 8, 25) percent. (Related to Application 4 on page 576.)

4.6 **The Cost of Celebrities.** Consider a firm that hires an expensive celebrity to advertise its products. Does the firm have an incentive to prevent its customers from discovering how much it pays the celebrity?

4.7 **Word-of-Mouth Book Sales.** Consider a publisher who earns a profit of $2 per book sold. An advertisement that costs $320,000 would sell 100,000 books directly. To make the advertisement worthwhile, how many of the original buyers must each persuade just one other person to buy the book?

ECONOMIC EXPERIMENT

FIXED COSTS AND ENTRY

Here is an experiment that shows the implications of entry for prices and profits. Students play the role of entrepreneurs who must decide whether to enter the market for lawn cutting. If they decide to enter the market, they must then decide how much to charge for cutting lawns.

- There are eight potential lawn-cutting firms, each represented by one to three students. The firms have two sorts of costs: a fixed cost per day and a marginal cost of cutting each lawn. Each firm can cut up to two lawns per day.
- There are 16 potential consumers. Each potential consumer is willing to pay a different amount to have his or her lawn cut.
- The experiment has two stages. In the first stage, each potential firm decides whether to enter the market. The entry decision is sequential: The instructor will go down the list of potential firms, one at a time, and give each firm the option of entering the market. The entry decisions are public knowledge. When a firm enters the market, it incurs a fixed cost of $14.
- Each firm in the market posts a price for lawn cutting, and consumers shop around and decide whether to purchase lawn care at the posted prices.
- Each trading period lasts several minutes, and each firm can change its posted price up to three times each period.
- A consumer's score in a trading period equals the difference between the amount that the consumer is willing to pay for lawn care and the price actually paid.
- A firm's score equals its profit, which is its total revenue minus its total cost (the fixed cost of $14 plus the variable cost, equal to $3 per lawn times the number of lawns cut).

MyEconLab

For additional economic experiments, please visit *www.myeconlab.com*.

NOTES

1. Sarah Needleman, "In a Sole Revival, the Recession Gives Beleaguered Cobblers New Traction," *New York Times*, February 2, 2009, 1; Franco Capaldo, "Timpson Enjoys Shoe Repair Boom," *Financial Mail*, October 2008; Eric Apalategui, "Cobblers Step Up to Fill Need for Repair, Reuse," *The Oregonian*, January 8, 2010, B1.

2. Theodore E. Relate, "Deregulation and Scale Economies in the U.S. Trucking Industry: An Econometric Extension of the Survivor Principle," *Journal of Law and Economics* 32 (October 1989): 229–253; Thomas Gale Moore, "Rail and Truck Reform—The Record So Far," *Regulation* (November– December 1988): 57–62; Leonard W. Weiss, ed., *Concentration and Price* (Cambridge, MA: MIT Press, 1989).

3. Timothy F. Bresnahan and Peter C. Reiss, "Entry and Competition in Concentrated Markets," *Journal of Political Economy* 99 (October 1991): 977–1009.

4. Lee Benham, "The Effect of Advertising on the Price of Glasses," *Journal of Law and Economics* 15, no. 2 (1972): 337–352.

CHAPTER

27 Oligopoly and Strategic Behavior

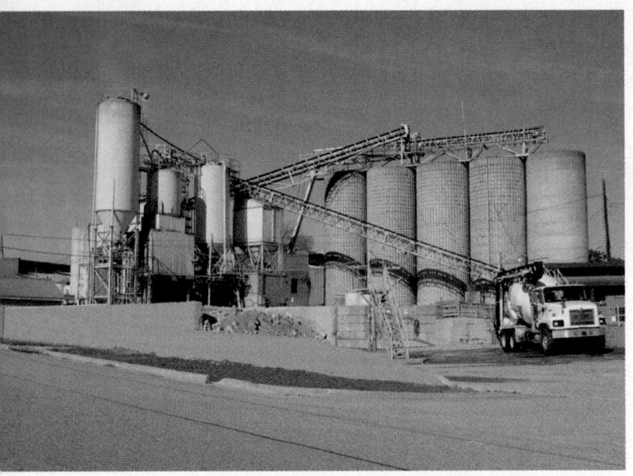

In an oligopoly, defined as a market with just a few firms, each firm has an incentive to act strategically, anticipating the possible actions and reactions of its fellow oligopolists.

In Brazil, a few firms dominate the market for cement, and the domestic cement producers are strategic oligopolists, with a twist.[1]

Although imported cement is just a tiny part of the market, it appears that importers are always poised to enter the market, and this constant threat of entry keeps prices lower than we would expect in an oligopoly. In a sense, the Brazilian cement firms are insecure oligopolists, keeping prices high enough to get a profit, but low enough to prevent importers from entering the market.

The prices of Brazilian firms depend on the degree of competition from importers. When imports become less costly and thus more competitive, the domestic firms cut their prices to protect their oligopoly power. On the other hand, when imports become more costly and thus less competitive, the domestic firms increase their prices and thus exploit their oligopoly power. For example, when an increase in the price of diesel fuel increases shipping costs and makes imports less competitive, domestic firms increase their prices. Domestic firms also charge relatively high prices in the interior area of Brazil, where the costs of importers are relatively high.

LEARNING OBJECTIVES

- Explain why a price-fixing cartel is difficult to maintain.
- Explain the effects of a low-price guarantee on the price.
- Describe the prisoners' dilemma.
- Explain the behavior of an insecure monopolist.
- Explain two advertisers' dilemmas.

MyEconLab
MyEconLab helps you master each objective and study more efficiently.

This is the fourth chapter on decision making by firms. In this chapter, we look at an **oligopoly**, a market with just a few firms. Given the small number of firms in an oligopoly, the actions of one firm have a large effect on the other firms. Therefore, firms in an oligopoly act strategically. Before a firm takes a particular action, it considers the possible reactions of its rivals. For example, before Southwest Airlines cuts its fares in an attempt to sell more tickets, it will consider the possible reactions by other airlines. If the rivals maintain their old fares, Southwest's fare cut will increase its sales and profit. But if the rivals match the lower fare, Southwest is likely to gain only a few customers, and its profit may actually decrease.

oligopoly
A market served by a few firms.

Game theory is the study of decision making in strategic situations. We can apply the theory to the game of chess as well as the decisions of oligopolists. A chess player develops a strategy to win the game, anticipating his or her opponent's reaction to each of his or her moves. Similarly, an oligopolist develops a strategy to maximize profit, anticipating the reactions of rival firms. We'll use game theory to discuss three business strategies: conspiring to fix prices, preventing another firm from entering the market, and advertising.

game theory
The study of decision making in strategic situations.

In an oligopoly, a few firms have market power—the power to control prices. Economists use **concentration ratios** to measure the degree of concentration in a market, computed as the percentage of the market output produced by the largest firms. For example, a four-firm concentration ratio is the percentage of total output in a market produced by the four largest firms. In Table 27.1, the four-firm concentration ratio for house slippers is 97 percent, indicating that the largest four firms produce 97 percent of house slippers in the United States.

concentration ratios
The percentage of the market output produced by the largest firms.

TABLE 27.1 Concentration Ratios in Selected Manufacturing Industries

Industry	Four-Firm Concentration Ratio (%)	Eight-Firm Concentration Ratio (%)
Primary copper smelting	99	Not available
House slippers	97	99
Guided missiles and space vehicles	96	99
Cigarettes	95	99
Soybean processing	95	99
Household laundry equipment	93	Not available
Breweries	91	94
Electric lamp bulbs	89	90
Military vehicles	88	93
Primary battery manufacturing	87	99
Beet sugar processing	85	98
Household refrigerators and freezers	85	95
Small arms (weapons)	84	90
Breakfast cereals	82	93
Motor vehicles and car bodies	81	91
Flavoring syrup	Not available	89

SOURCE: U.S. Bureau of the Census, 2002 Economic Census, Manufacturing, *Concentration Ratios: 2002* (Washington, D.C.: U.S. Government Printing Office, 2006).

An alternative measure of market concentration is the *Herfindahl–Hirschman Index (HHI)*. It is calculated by squaring the market share of each firm in the market and then summing the resulting numbers. For example, consider a market with two firms, one with a 60 percent market share and a second with a 40 percent share. The HHI for the market is 5,200:

$$\text{HHI} = 60^2 + 40^2 = 3{,}600 + 1{,}600 = 5{,}200$$

In contrast, for a market with 10 firms, each with a 10 percent market share, the HHI is 1,000:

$$\text{HHI} = 10^2 \times 10 = 100 \times 10 = 1{,}000$$

According to the guidelines established by the U.S. Department of Justice in 1992, a market is "unconcentrated" if the HHI is below 1,000 and "highly concentrated" if it is above 1,800. For example, a market with five firms, each with a 20 percent market share, has an HHI of 2,000 and would be considered highly concentrated:

$$\text{HHI} = 20^2 \times 5 = 400 \times 5 = 2{,}000$$

An oligopoly—a market with just a few firms—occurs for three reasons:

1 *Government barriers to entry.* As we saw in Chapters 21 and 25, the government may limit the number of firms in a market by issuing patents or controlling the number of business licenses.
2 *Economies of scale in production.* As we saw in Chapter 25, a natural monopoly occurs when there are relatively large economies of scale in production, so a single firm produces for the entire market. In some cases, scale economies are not large enough to generate a natural monopoly, but are large enough to generate a natural oligopoly, with a few firms serving the entire market.
3 *Advertising campaigns.* In some markets, a firm cannot enter a market without a substantial investment in an advertising campaign. For example, the breakfast-cereal oligopoly results from the huge advertising campaigns required to get a foothold in the market. As in the case of economies of scale in production, just a few firms will enter the market.

27.1 Cartel Pricing and the Duopolists' Dilemma

One of the virtues of a market economy is that firms compete with one another for customers, and this leads to lower prices and larger quantities. But in some markets, firms cooperate instead of competing with one another. Eighteenth-century economist Adam Smith recognized the possibility that firms would conspire to raise prices: "People of the same trade seldom meet together, even for merriment and diversion, but the conversation ends in a conspiracy against the public, or in some contrivance to raise prices."[2] We'll see that raising prices is not simply a matter of firms getting together and agreeing on higher prices. An agreement to raise prices is likely to break down unless the firms find some way to punish a firm that violates the agreement.

duopoly
A market with two firms.

We'll use a market with two firms—a **duopoly**—to explain the key features of an oligopoly. The basic insights from a duopoly apply to oligopolies with more than two firms. Consider a duopoly in the market for air travel between two hypothetical cities. The two airlines can use prices to compete for customers, or they can cooperate and conspire to raise prices. To simplify matters—and to keep the numbers manageable—let's assume that the average cost of providing air travel is constant at $100 per passenger. As shown in Figure 27.1, the average cost is constant, which means that marginal cost equals average cost.

cartel
A group of firms that act in unison, coordinating their price and quantity decisions.

A **cartel** is a group of firms that act in unison, coordinating their price and quantity decisions. In our airline example, the two airlines could form a cartel and choose the monopoly price. In Figure 27.1, the firm-specific demand curve for a monopolist is the market-demand curve, and the marginal-revenue curve intersects the marginal-cost curve at a quantity of 60 passengers per day (point *a*). If the two airlines act as one, they will pick the monopoly price of $400 and split the monopoly output, so each will have 30 passengers per day. The average cost per passenger is $100, so each airline earns a daily profit of $9,000:

$$\text{profit} = (\text{price} - \text{average cost}) \times \text{quantity per firm} = (\$400 - \$100) \times 30 = \$9{,}000$$

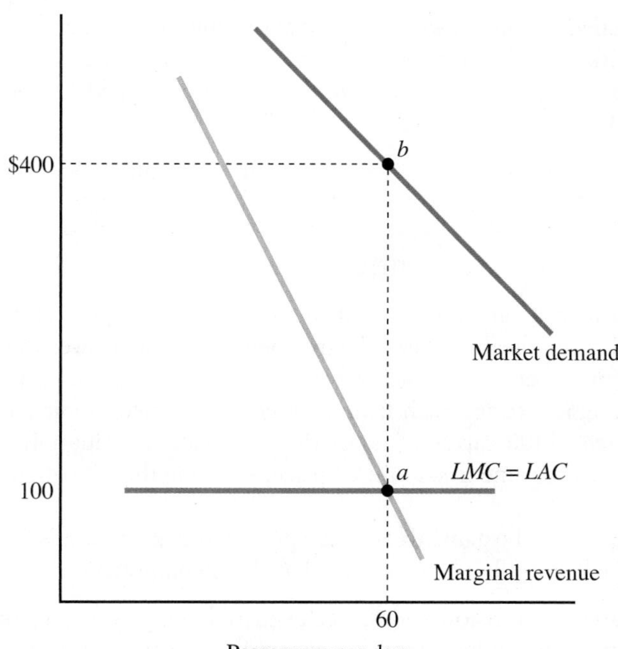

◄ FIGURE 27.1
A Cartel Picks the Monopoly Quantity and Price
The monopoly outcome is shown by point *a*, where marginal revenue equals marginal cost. The monopoly quantity is 60 passengers and the price is $400. If the firms form a cartel, the price is $400 and each firm has 30 passengers (half the monopoly quantity). The profit per passenger is $300 (equal to the $400 price minus the $100 average cost), so the profit per firm is $9,000.

This is an example of **price fixing**, an arrangement in which firms conspire to fix prices. As we'll see later in the chapter, cartels and price fixing are illegal under U.S. antitrust laws.

price fixing
An arrangement in which firms conspire to fix prices.

What would happen if the two firms competed rather than conspired to fix the price? If they competed, each firm would have its own demand curve. As we saw in the previous chapter, the firm-specific demand curve for the typical firm lies to the left of the market demand curve because consumers can choose from two firms. At a particular price, consumers will be divided between the two firms, so each firm will serve only part of the market. In Figure 27.2, the demand curve for the typical duopolist is below the market demand curve. For example, at a price of $300, point *d* shows that the market quantity is 80 passengers, while point *b* shows that each firm has 40 passengers.

Panel A in Figure 27.2 shows the quantity and price choice of an individual firm. Given the firm-specific demand curve and marginal-revenue curve, the marginal

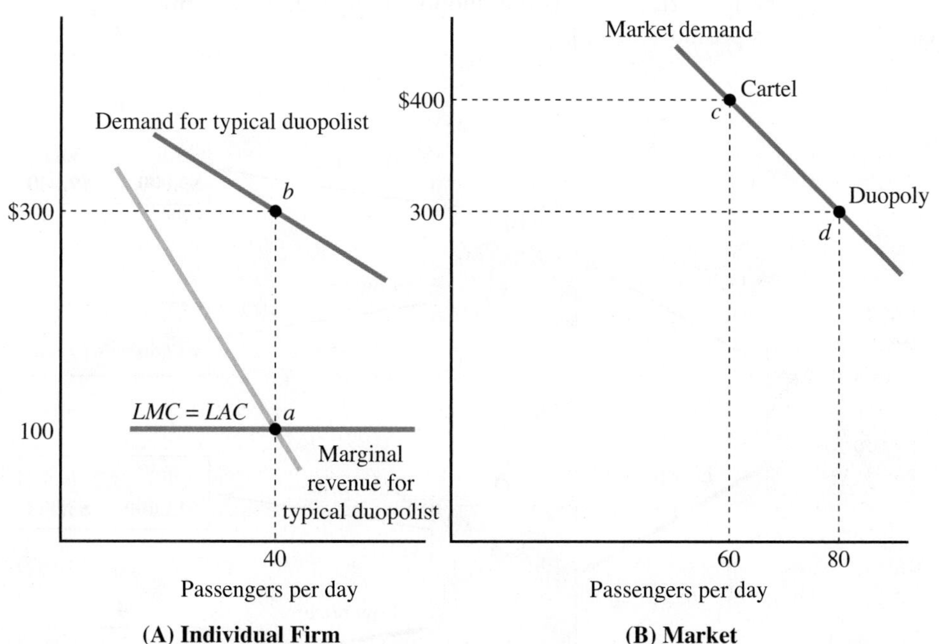

◄ FIGURE 27.2
Competing Duopolists Pick a Lower Price
(A) The typical firm maximizes profit at point *a*, where marginal revenue equals marginal cost. The firm has 40 passengers. (B) At the market level, the duopoly outcome is shown by point *d*, with a price of $300 and 80 passengers. The cartel outcome, shown by point *c*, has a higher price and a smaller total quantity.

principle is satisfied at point *a*, where marginal revenue equals marginal cost. The firm has 40 passengers at a price of \$300 (point *b*). The two firms are identical, so each has 40 passengers at a price of \$300. Given an average cost of \$100, each firm earns a profit of \$8,000:

profit = (price − average cost) × quantity per firm = (\$300 − \$100) × 40 = \$8,000

Price Fixing and the Game Tree

game tree
A graphical representation of the consequences of different actions in a strategic setting.

Clearly, each firm will earn more profit under a price-fixing cartel, but will a cartel succeed, or will firms cheat on a cartel agreement? We can answer this question with the help of a **game tree**, a graphical representation of the consequences of different actions in a strategic setting. Each firm must choose a price for airline tickets, either the high price (the \$400 cartel price) or the low price (the duopoly price of \$300). Each firm can use the game tree to pick a price, knowing that the other firm is picking a price too.

Figure 27.3 shows the game tree for the price-fixing game. Let's call the managers of the airlines Jack and Jill. The game tree has three components:

- The squares are decision nodes. Each square has a player (Jack or Jill) and a list of the player's possible actions. For example, the game starts at square *A*, where Jill has two options: high price or low price.
- The arrows show the possible paths of the game from left to right. Jill chooses her price first, so we move from square *A* to one of Jack's decision nodes, either square *B* or square *C*. If Jill chooses the high price, we move from square *A* to square *B*. Once we reach one of Jack's decision nodes, he chooses a price—high or low—and then we move to one of the rectangles. For example, if Jack chooses the high price too, we move from square *B* to rectangle 1.
- The rectangles show the profits for the two firms. When we reach a rectangle, the game is over, and the players receive the profits shown in the rectangle. There is a profit rectangle for each of the four possible outcomes of the price-fixing game.

We've already computed the profits for two payoff rectangles. Rectangle 1 shows what happens when each firm chooses the high price. This is the cartel or price-fixing outcome, with each firm earning \$9,000. Rectangle 4 shows what happens when each firm chooses the low price. This is the duopoly outcome, when firms compete and each firm earns a profit of \$8,000.

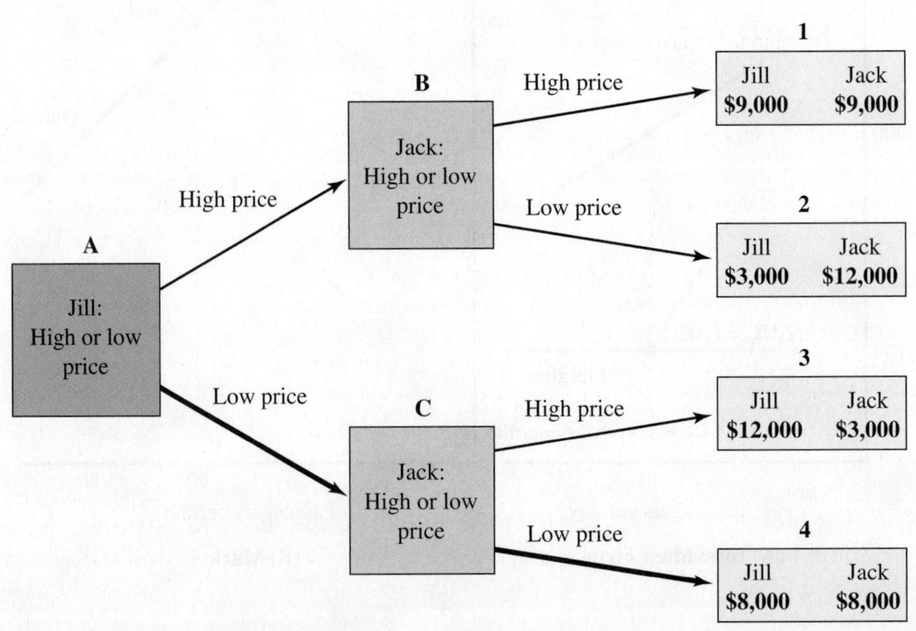

▶ FIGURE 27.3
Game Tree for the Price-Fixing Game
The equilibrium path of the game is square *A* to square *C* to rectangle *4*: Each firm picks the low price and earns a profit of \$8,000. The duopolists' dilemma is that each firm would make more profit if both picked the high price, but both firms pick the low price.

What would happen if the two firms chose different prices? If Jill chooses the high price and Jack chooses the low price, Jack will capture a large share of the market and gain at Jill's expense. In the first column of Table 27.2, Jill charges the high price and has only 10 passengers at a price of $400, so her profit is $3,000:

profit = (price − average cost) × quantity per firm = ($400 − $100) × 10 = $3,000

TABLE 27.2 Duopolists' Profits When They Choose Different Prices

	Jill: High Price	Jack: Low Price
Price	$ 400	$ 300
Average cost	$ 100	$ 100
Profit per passenger	$ 300	$ 200
Number of passengers	10	60
Profit	$3,000	$12,000

In the second column, Jack charges the low price and has 60 passengers at a price of $300, so his profit is $12,000:

profit = (price − average cost) × quantity per firm = ($300 − $100) × 60 = $12,000

This is shown by rectangle 2 in Figure 27.3: The path of the game is square *A* to square *B* to rectangle 2. The other underpricing outcome is shown by rectangle 3. In this case, Jill chooses the low price and Jack chooses the high price, so Jill gains at Jack's expense. The roles are reversed, and so are the numbers in the profit rectangle.

Equilibrium of the Price-Fixing Game

We can predict the equilibrium of the price-fixing game by a process of elimination. We'll eliminate the rectangles that would require one or both firms to act irrationally, leaving us with the rectangle showing the equilibrium of the game:

- If Jill chooses the high price, we'll move along the upper branches of the tree and eventually reach rectangle 1 or 2, depending on what Jack does. Although Jill would like Jack to choose the high price too, this would be irrational for Jack. He can earn $12,000 profit by choosing the low price, compared to $9,000 with the high price. Therefore, we can eliminate rectangle 1.
- If Jill chooses the low price, we'll move along the lower branches of the tree and eventually reach rectangle 3 or 4, depending on Jack's choice. Jack won't choose the high price because he can earn $8,000 with the low price, compared to $3,000 with the high price. Therefore, we can eliminate rectangle 3.

We've eliminated the two profit rectangles that represent a high price for Jack—rectangles 1 and 3. For Jack, the low price is a **dominant strategy**: Regardless of what Jill does, Jack's best choice is the low price.

dominant strategy
An action that is the best choice for a player, no matter what the other player does.

Two profit rectangles are left—2 and 4—and Jill's action will determine which rectangle is the equilibrium. Jill knows Jack will choose the low price regardless of what she does. She could choose the high price and allow Jack to capture most of the market, leaving her with a profit of only $3,000 in rectangle 2. A better choice is to pick the low price and get a profit of $8,000 in rectangle 4. In other words, it would be irrational for Jill to allow herself to be underpriced, so the outcome of the game is shown by profit rectangle 4: Each player chooses the low price. The thick arrows show the equilibrium path of the game, from square *A* to square *C* to rectangle 4.

Both firms will be unhappy with this equilibrium because each could earn a higher profit with rectangle 1. To get there, however, each firm must choose the high price. The **duopolists' dilemma** is that although both firms would be better off if they both chose the high price, each firm chooses the low price. The dilemma occurs because

duopolists' dilemma
A situation in which both firms in a market would be better off if both chose the high price, but each chooses the low price.

there is a big payoff from underpricing the other firm and a big penalty from being underpriced, so both firms pick the low price. As we'll see later in the chapter, to avoid the dilemma, the firms must find some way to prevent underpricing.

Nash Equilibrium

Nash equilibrium
An outcome of a game in which each player is doing the best he or she can, given the action of the other players.

We have used a game tree to find the equilibrium in a price-fixing game. It is an equilibrium in the sense that each player (firm) is doing the best he or she can, given the actions of another player. The label for such an equilibrium is **Nash equilibrium**. This concept is named after John Nash, the recipient of the 1994 Nobel Prize in economics, who developed his equilibrium concept as a 21-year-old graduate student at Princeton University. Nash's life story, which includes a 25-year bout with schizophrenia and a dramatic recovery, is chronicled in the book *A Beautiful Mind*, later made into a movie starring Russell Crowe as Nash.[3]

In the Nash equilibrium for the price-fixing game, both firms pick the low price. Each firm is doing the best it can, given the action of the other firm:

- If Jill picks the low price, Jack's best action is to pick the low price.
- If Jack picks the low price, Jill's best action is to pick the low price.

What about the other potential outcomes? Consider first the possibility that both firms pick the high price. This is not a Nash equilibrium because neither firm is doing the best it can, given the action of the other firm:

- If Jill picks the high price, Jack's best action is to pick the low price.
- If Jack picks the high price, Jill's best action is to pick the low price.

Consider next the possibility that Jill picks the low price and Jack picks the high price. This is not a Nash equilibrium because Jack is not doing the best he can, given Jill's choice:

- If Jill picks the low price, Jack's best action is to pick the low price.

The concept of the Nash equilibrium has been applied to a wide variety of decisions. Analysts have used it to study the nuclear arms race, terrorism, evolutionary biology, art auctions, environmental policy, and urban development. Later in the chapter, we will use it to predict the outcomes of games of entry deterrence and advertising.

application 1

FAILURE OF THE SALT CARTEL

APPLYING THE CONCEPTS #1: Why do cartels sometimes fail to keep prices high?

At the beginning of the nineteenth century, high overland transportation costs protected salt producers from competition with one another, generating local salt monopolies. Over the course of the nineteenth century, decreases in overland transportation costs increased competition between salt producers and decreased prices. In response to the increased competition, salt producers colluded by forming salt pools, enterprises that set a uniform price and distributed the salt of all participating producers. Some pools established output quotas or paid firms not to produce salt for a year, a practice known as "dead-renting" a salt furnace. Every salt pool eventually broke down, usually within a year or two of its formation. In some cases, individual firms cheated on the cartel by selling salt outside the cartel. In other cases the artificially high price caused new firms to enter the market and underprice the salt pool. **Related to Exercise 1.9.**

SOURCE: Based on Margaret Levenstein, "Mass Production Conquers the Pool: Firm Organization and the Nature of Competition in the Nineteenth Century," *The Journal of Economic History* 55 (1995), pp. 575–611.

27.2 Overcoming the Duopolists' Dilemma

The duopolists' dilemma occurs because the two firms are unable to coordinate their pricing decisions and act as one. Each firm has an incentive to underprice the other because the low-price firm will capture a larger share of the market and earn a larger profit. Firms can avoid the dilemma in two ways: low-price guarantees and repetition of the pricing game, with retaliation for underpricing.

Low-Price Guarantees

The duopolists' dilemma occurs because the payoff from underpricing the other firm is too lucrative to miss. To eliminate the possibility of underpricing, one firm can guarantee it will match a lower price of a competitor. Suppose Jill places the following advertisement in the local newspaper:

> If you buy an airline ticket from me and then discover that Jack offers the same trip at a lower price, I will pay you the price difference. If I charge you $400 and Jack's price is only $300, I will pay you $100.

Jill's **low-price guarantee** is a credible promise because she announces it in the newspaper.

low-price guarantee
A promise to match a lower price of a competitor.

Suppose Jack makes a similar commitment to match a lower price from Jill. Figure 27.4 shows the effect of low-price guarantees on the game tree. Jill now has two decision nodes. As before, she starts the game in square *A*. If Jill picks the high price and then Jack picks the high price, we end up at rectangle 1, as before. But if Jill picks the high price and Jack picks the low price, we get to square *D*. Jill will issue a refund of $100 to each of her consumers. In effect, she has retroactively chosen the low price, and payoff rectangle 2 is the duopoly outcome, with both firms picking the low price. For the lower half of the game tree, recall that Jack has committed to match a lower price by Jill, so the old payoff rectangle 3 disappears, leaving us with rectangle 4, where both firms choose the low price and get the duopoly profit.

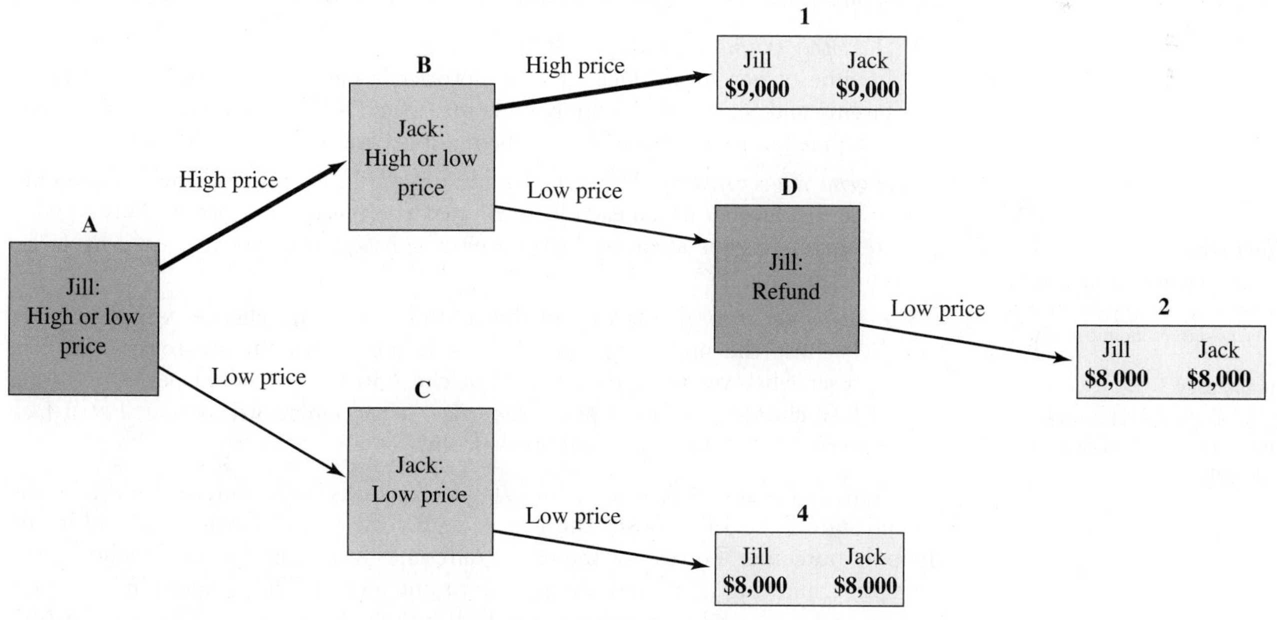

▲ FIGURE 27.4
Low-Price Guarantees Increase Prices
When both firms have a low-price guarantee, it is impossible for one firm to underprice the other. The only possible outcomes are a pair of high prices (rectangle 1) or a pair of low prices (rectangles 2 or 4). The equilibrium path of the game is square A to square B to rectangle 1. Each firm picks the high price and earns a profit of $9,000.

The thick arrows show the path of the game with low-price guarantees. Consider Jack's decision first:

- If Jill picks the high price, Jack chooses between payoff rectangles 1 and 2, a pair of high prices or a pair of low prices. His profit is higher at $9,000 with a pair of high prices (rectangle 1), so if Jill picks the high price, he will too.
- If Jill picks the low price, Jack is committed to the low price too.

Consider Jill's decision. She knows Jack will match her price—either high or low—meaning she chooses between profit rectangles 1 and 4. Profit is higher with rectangle 1, so she will pick the high price.

The low-price guarantee eliminates the possibility of underpricing, so it eliminates the duopolists' dilemma and promotes cartel pricing. The firms don't have to create a formal cartel to get the benefits from cartel pricing. The motto of a low-price guarantee is "Low for one means low for all," so both firms charge the high price. Once the possibility of underpricing has been eliminated, the duopoly will be replaced by an informal cartel, with each firm picking the price that a monopolist would pick.

To most people, the notion that a low-price guarantee leads to higher prices is surprising. After all, if Jill promises to give refunds if her price exceeds Jack's price, we might expect Jill to keep her price low to avoid handing out a lot of refunds. In fact, Jill doesn't have to worry about giving refunds because Jack will also choose the high price. In other words, the promise to issue refunds is an *empty* promise. Although consumers might think that a low-price guarantee will protect them from high prices, it means they are more likely to pay the high price.

Repeated Pricing Games with Retaliation for Underpricing

Up to this point, we've assumed the price-fixing game is played only once. Each firm chooses a price and keeps it for the lifetime of the firm. What happens when two firms play the game repeatedly, picking prices over an extended period of time? We'll see that repetition makes price fixing more likely because firms can punish a firm that cheats on a price-fixing agreement, whether it's formal or informal.

1 *A duopoly pricing strategy*. Jill chooses the lower duopoly price for the remaining lifetime of her firm. Once Jill is underpriced, she abandons the idea of cartel pricing and accepts the duopoly outcome, which is less profitable than the cartel outcome but more profitable than being underpriced by the other firm.

2 *A grim-trigger strategy*. When Jack underprices Jill, she responds by dropping her price to a level at which each firm will make zero economic profit. This is called the **grim-trigger strategy** because grim consequences are triggered by Jack's underpricing.

grim-trigger strategy
A strategy where a firm responds to underpricing by choosing a price so low that each firm makes zero economic profit.

3 *A tit-for-tat strategy*. Starting in the second month, Jill chooses whatever price Jack chose the preceding month. This is the **tit-for-tat strategy**—one firm chooses whatever price the other firm chose in the preceding period. As long as Jack chooses the cartel price, the cartel arrangement will persist. But if Jack underprices Jill, the cartel will break down.

tit-for-tat strategy
A strategy where one firm chooses whatever price the other firm chose in the preceding period.

Figure 27.5 shows how a tit-for-tat system works. Jack underprices Jill in the second month, so Jill chooses the low price for the third month, resulting in the duopoly outcome. To restore the cartel outcome, Jack must eventually choose the high price, allowing Jill to underprice him for one month. This happens in the fourth month, and the cartel is restored in the fifth month. Although Jack can gain at Jill's expense in the second month, if he wants to restore cartel pricing, he must allow her to gain at his expense during some other month. Under a tit-for-tat strategy, a duopolist does exactly what his or her rival did the last round. This encourages firms to cooperate rather than compete. Several studies have shown that a tit-for-tat strategy is the most effective strategy to promote cooperation.[4]

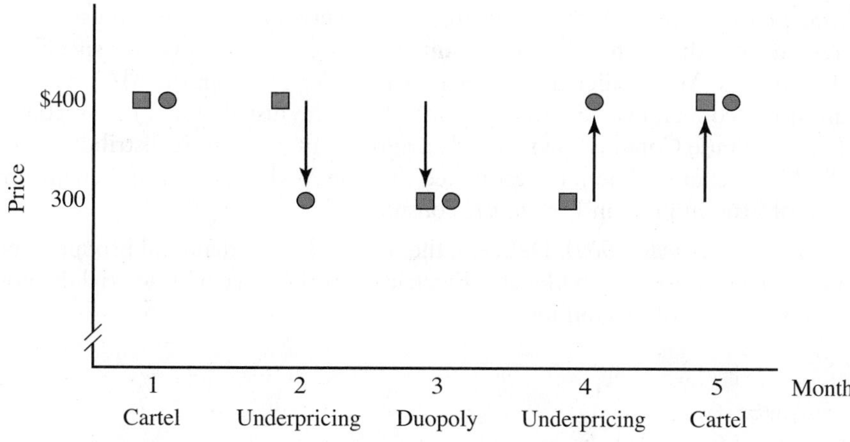

▲ FIGURE 27.5
A Tit-for-Tat Pricing Strategy
Under tit-for-tat retaliation, the first firm (Jill, the square) chooses whatever price the second firm (Jack, the circle) chose the preceding month.

These three pricing schemes promote cartel pricing by penalizing the firm that underprices the other firm. To decide whether to underprice Jill, Jack must weigh the short-term benefit against the long-term cost:

- The short-term benefit is the increase in profit in the current period. If Jack underprices Jill, he can increase his profit from the cartel profit of $9,000 to the $12,000 earned by a firm that underprices the other firm. Therefore, the short-term benefit of underpricing is $3,000.
- The long-term cost is the loss of profit in later periods. Jill will respond to Jack's underpricing by cutting her price, and this decreases Jack's profit. For example, if Jill retaliates with the duopoly price, Jack's future profit will be $8,000 per day instead of the $9,000 he could have earned by going along with the cartel price. The cost of underpricing is the daily loss of $1,000 in profit.

If the two firms expect to share the market for a long time, the long-term cost of underpricing will exceed the short-term benefit, so underpricing is less likely. The threat of punishment makes it easier to resist the temptation to cheat on the cartel.

Price Fixing and the Law

Under the Sherman Antitrust Act of 1890 and subsequent legislation, explicit price fixing is illegal. It is illegal for firms to discuss pricing strategies or methods of punishing a firm that underprices other firms. In one of the early price-fixing cases (*Addyston Pipe*, 1899), six manufacturers of cast-iron pipe met to fix prices. Several months after the Supreme Court ruled that their cartel pricing was illegal, the firms merged into a single firm, so instead of acting like a monopolist, they became a monopolist. Here are some other examples of price fixing:

1. *Electric generators (1961).* Executives from General Electric and Westinghouse were convicted of fixing prices for electrical generators, resulting in fines of over $2 million and imprisonment or probation for 30 corporate executives.
2. *Carton-board pricing in Europe (1994).* The European Union Commission fined 19 manufacturers of carton board a total of 132 million euros ($165 million) for operating a cartel that fixed prices at secret meetings in luxury Zurich hotels.
3. *Food additives (1996).* An employee of Archer Daniels Midland (ADM), a huge food company, provided audio and videotapes of ADM executives conspiring to fix prices. ADM pleaded guilty to the charges of price fixing and was fined $100 million.

4 *Music distribution (2000).* In exchange for advertising subsidies, music retailers agreed to adhere to the minimum advertised prices (MAP) specified by distributors. Any retailer that advertised a CD for less than the MAP would lose all of its "cooperative advertising" funds from the distributor. In May 2000, the Federal Trade Commission reached an agreement with music distributors to end the MAP scheme. The FTC estimated that the MAP scheme imposed an annual cost of $160 million on U.S. music consumers.[5]

5 *Industrial diamonds (2004).* DeBeers, the world's largest diamond producer, plead guilty to conspiring with General Electric to fix the price of industrial diamonds, and paid a fine of $10 million.

Price Leadership

price leadership
A system under which one firm in an oligopoly takes the lead in setting prices.

Because explicit price fixing is illegal, firms sometimes rely on implicit pricing agreements to fix prices at the monopoly level. Under the model of **price leadership**, one of the oligopolists plays the role of price leader. The leading firm picks a price, and other firms match the price. Such an agreement allows firms to cooperate without actually discussing their pricing strategies.

The problem with an implicit pricing agreement is that it relies on indirect signals that are often garbled and misinterpreted. Suppose two firms have cooperated for several years, both sticking to the cartel price. When one firm suddenly drops its price, the other firm could interpret the price cut in one of two ways:

- **A change in market conditions.** Perhaps the first firm observed a change in demand or production cost and decides that both firms would benefit from a lower price.
- **Underpricing.** Perhaps the first firm is trying to increase its market share and profit at the expense of the second firm.

The first interpretation would probably cause the second firm to match the lower price of the first firm, and price fixing would continue at the lower price. In contrast, the second interpretation could trigger a price war, undermining the price-fixing agreement.

application 2

LOW-PRICE GUARANTEE INCREASES TIRE PRICES

APPLYING THE CONCEPTS #2: Do low-price guarantees generate higher or lower prices?

In two successive months (November and December), a Florida tire retailer listed prices for 35 types of tires in newspaper advertisements. In November the average price was $45, and in December the average price was $55. The December advertisement was different in another way: it included a low-price guarantee under which the retailer agreed to match any lower advertised price (and also pay the customer some percentage of the price gap). In fact, for each of the 35 types of tires, the December price was the same or higher than the November price. In this case, a low-price guarantee generated higher prices.

Is the relationship between low-price guarantees and prices apparent or real? A careful study of the retail tire market suggests that prices are generally higher in markets where firms offer low-price guarantees. On average, the presence of a low-price guarantee increases prices by $4 per tire, or about 10 percent of the price. **Related to Exercise 2.5.**

SOURCE: Maria Arbatskaya, Morten Hviid, Greg Shaffer, "Promises to Match or Beat the Competition," *Advances in Applied Microeconomics* 8 (1999), pp. 123–138.

27.3 Simultaneous Decision Making and the Payoff Matrix

So far we have considered a game with sequential decisions. Jill chooses her price first, and then Jack observes her choice and then makes his own. An alternative scenario is that the two firms make their decisions simultaneously, so each firm picks its price without knowing the other firm's price. The analysis of a simultaneous game requires a different tool. A **payoff matrix** shows, for each possible outcome of a game, the consequences—or payoffs—for each player.

payoff matrix
A matrix or table that shows, for each possible outcome of a game, the consequences for each player.

Simultaneous Price-Fixing Game

Figure 27.6 shows the payoff matrix for the price-fixing game. Each cell in the matrix shows the payoffs from a potential outcome of the game. In the northwest corner of the matrix, if both firms pick the high price, each firm earns a profit of $9,000. In the southeast corner, if both firms pick the low price, each firm earns a profit of $8,000. If one firm picks the low price and the other picks the high price, the low-price firm earns $12,000 and the high-price firm earns only $3,000. For example, in the northeast corner, if Jill picks the high price and Jack picks the low price, Jill earns a profit of $3,000 and Jack earns a profit of $12,000.

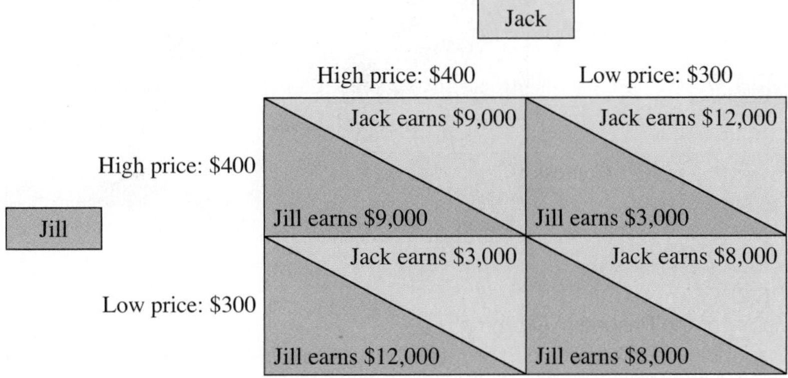

▲ FIGURE 27.6
Payoff Matrix for the Price-Fixing Game
Jill's profit is in red, and Jack's profit is in blue. If both firms pick the high price, each firm earns a profit of $9,000. Both firms will pick the low price, and each firm will earn a profit of only $8,000.

We can use the payoff matrix to predict the equilibrium of the price-fixing game. In a simultaneous-decision game, Jack doesn't know whether Jill will pick the low price or the high price. There are two possibilities:

- If Jill picks the high price, we will be in the upper half of the matrix, and Jack's best response is the low price. In the northeast corner of the matrix, he can earn $12,000 by picking the low price. This is better than the $9,000 he can earn by picking the high price in the northwest corner.
- If Jill picks the low price, we will be in the lower half of the matrix, and Jack's best response is the low price. In the southeast corner of the matrix, he can earn $8,000 by picking the low price. This is better than the $3,000 he can earn by picking the high price in the southwest corner.

In other words, the low price is the dominant strategy for Jack. Jill knows this, so she realizes that the equilibrium will be in the eastern half of the matrix. Her best response is the low price. In the southeast corner of the matrix, she can earn $8,000 by picking the low price. This is better than the $3,000 she can earn in the northeast corner by picking the high price. Therefore, the equilibrium is the same as with the game-tree approach: Both firms pick the low price.

The Prisoners' Dilemma

We can gain some insight into the duopolists' dilemma by examining the classic prisoners' dilemma. Consider two people, Bonnie and Clyde, who have been accused of committing a crime. The police give each person an opportunity to confess to the crime. The traditional version of the story is a simultaneous decision-making game: The two are put in separate rooms, and each makes a choice without knowing the other's choice.

The police confront Bonnie and Clyde with the payoff matrix in Figure 27.7. If both confess, each gets 5 years in prison, as shown in the southeast corner of the matrix. If neither confesses, the police can convict both of them on a lesser charge, and each gets 2 years, as shown in the northwest corner of the matrix. If only one confesses, he or she will implicate the other prisoner. The confessor is rewarded with a 1-year prison sentence, while the other prisoner gets 10 years. If Bonnie confesses and Clyde does not, we are in the southwest corner of the matrix. If the roles are reversed, we are in the northeast corner.

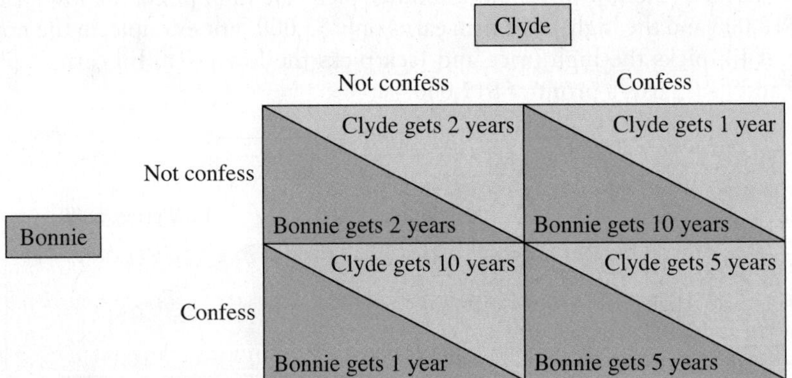

▲ **FIGURE 27.7**
Payoff Matrix for the Prisoners' Dilemma
The prisoners' dilemma is that each prisoner would be better off if neither confessed, but both people confess. The Nash equilibrium is shown in the southeast corner of the matrix. Each person gets five years of prison time.

We can use the payoff matrix to predict the equilibrium of the prisoner game. In a simultaneous-decision game, Clyde doesn't know whether Bonnie will confess or not:

- If Bonnie does not confess, we are in the upper half of the matrix, and Clyde's best response is to confess. In the northeast corner of the matrix, he gets one year in prison if he confesses. This is better than the two years he would get in the northwest corner by not confessing.
- If Bonnie confesses, we are in the lower half of the matrix, and Clyde's best response is to confess. In the southeast corner of the matrix, he gets 5 years in prison. This is better than the 10 years he would get in the southwest corner by not confessing.

In other words, confessing is the dominant strategy for Clyde. Bonnie knows this, so she realizes that the equilibrium will be in the eastern half of the matrix. Her best response is to confess. In the southeast corner of the matrix, she gets 5 years in prison. This is better than the 10 years she would get in the northeast by not confessing.

If both prisoners confess and each gets 5 years in prison, we have a Nash equilibrium because each prisoner is doing the best he or she can, given the actions of the other prisoner. Although both would be better off if they both kept quiet, they implicate each other because the police reward them for doing so. There is an incentive for squealing, just as there is an incentive for one duopolist to underprice the other.

application 3

CHEATING ON THE FINAL EXAM: THE CHEATERS' DILEMMA

APPLYING THE CONCEPTS #3: When does cooperation break down?

An economics professor discovered three students cheating on the final exam. Speaking to the students individually in his office, he gave each student two options:

1 If the student confessed, he or she would receive a zero on the final exam, but suffer no other consequences.

2 If the student did not confess, he or she would go before the Office of Student Judicial Affairs, and any confessions by the other two students would be used as evidence.

During the sessions in the professor's office, one of the accused said, "This feels like you put me in a prisoners' dilemma game." By the end of the day, the professor had three confessions. **Related to Exercise 3.3.**

27.4 The Insecure Monopolist and Entry Deterrence

We've seen what happens when two duopolists try to act as one, fixing the price at the monopoly level. Consider next how a monopolist might try to prevent a second firm from entering its market. We will use some of the numbers from our airline example, although we will look at a different city with a different cast of characters.

Suppose Mona initially has a secure monopoly in the market for air travel between two cities. When there is no threat of entry, Mona uses the marginal principle (marginal revenue equals marginal cost) to pick a quantity and a price. In Figure 27.8, we start at point *c* on the market demand curve, with a quantity of 60 passengers per day and a price of \$400 per passenger. Her profit is \$18,000:

$$\text{profit} = (\text{price} - \text{average cost}) \times \text{quantity per firm} = (\$400 - \$100) \times 60 = \$18,000$$

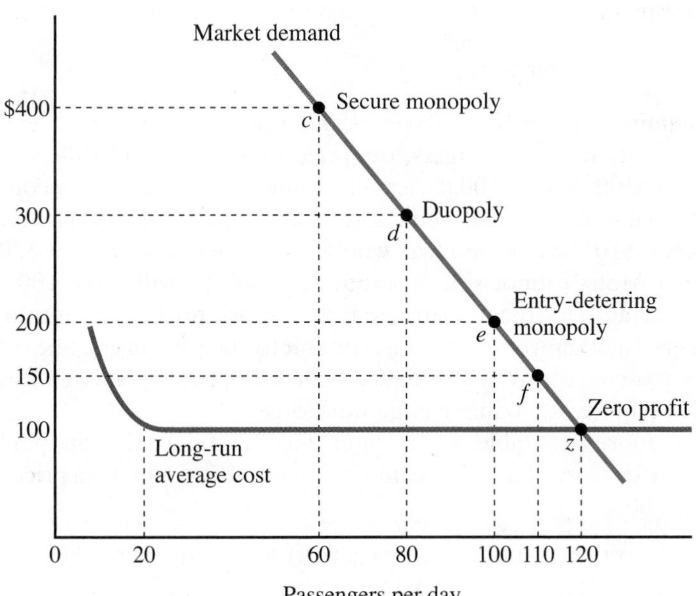

◀ **FIGURE 27.8**
Deterring Entry with Limit Pricing
Point *c* shows a secure monopoly, point *d* shows a duopoly, and point *z* shows the zero-profit outcome. The minimum entry quantity is 20 passengers, so the entry-deterring quantity is 100 (equal to 120 – 20), as shown by point *e*. The limit price is \$200.

If Mona discovers that a second airline is thinking about entering the market, what will she do? Now that her monopoly is insecure, she has two options: She can be passive and allow the second airline to enter the market, or she can try to prevent the other firm from entering the market.

The passive approach will lead to the duopoly outcome we saw earlier in the chapter. In Figure 27.8, if the second firm enters the market, we move downward along the market demand curve from point *c* to point *d*. In a duopoly, each firm charges a price of $300 and serves 40 passengers, half the total quantity demanded at a price of $300. For each duopolist, the daily profit is $8,000:

$$\text{profit} = (\text{price} - \text{average cost}) \times \text{quantity per firm} = (\$300 - \$100) \times 40 = \$8{,}000$$

Entry Deterrence and Limit Pricing

The second option is to take actions to prevent the second firm from entering the market. To decide whether to deter the entry of the other firm, Mona must answer two questions:

- What must she do to deter entry?
- Given what she must do to deter entry, is deterrence more profitable than being passive and sharing the market with the second firm?

To prevent the second firm from entering the market, Mona must commit herself to serving a large number of passengers. If she commits to a large passenger load, there won't be enough passengers left for a potential entrant to make a profit. Suppose there are economies of scale in providing air travel, and the minimum entry quantity is 20 passengers per day: That is, it would be impractical for a firm to serve fewer than 20 passengers. In Figure 27.8, the long-run average cost curve is negatively sloped for relatively low levels of output, and the average cost for the minimum entry quantity of 20 passengers is just over $100, say $101.

Mona must compute the quantity of output that is just large enough to prevent the second firm from entering the market. In Figure 27.8, point *z* shows the point of zero economic profit in the market: If the two firms serve a total of 120 passengers per day and split the market equally, with 60 passengers each, the price ($100) equals average cost, so each firm would earn zero economic profit. The quantity required to prevent the entry of the second firm is computed as follows:

$$\text{deterring quantity} = \text{zero profit quantity} - \text{minimum entry quantity}$$

$$100 = 120 - 20$$

If Mona commits to serve 100 passengers and a second firm were to enter with the minimum quantity of 20 passengers, the price would drop to $100. Mona, with an average cost of $100 to serve 100 passengers, would break even. The second firm, with an average cost just above $100, would lose money. Specifically, if the average cost of 20 passengers is $101, the second firm would lose $1 per passenger, or $20 in total.

Note that Mona cannot simply announce that she will serve 100 passengers. She must take actions that ensure that her most profitable output is in fact 100 passengers. In other words, she must commit to 100 passengers. She could commit to the larger passenger load by purchasing a large fleet of airplanes and signing labor contracts that require her to hire a large workforce.

Which is more profitable, entry deterrence or the passive duopoly outcome? The deterrence strategy, shown by point *e* in Figure 27.8, generates a price of $200 and a profit of $10,000:

$$\text{profit} = (\text{price} - \text{average cost}) \times \text{quantity per firm}$$

$$= (\$200 - \$100) \times 100 = \$10{,}000$$

This is larger than the $8,000 profit under the passive approach, so deterrence is the best strategy.

Figure 27.9 uses a game tree to represent the entry-deterrence game. Mona makes the first move, and she considers the consequences of her two options:

- If Mona is passive and commits to serve only 40 passengers, we reach the upper branch of the game tree. The best response for Doug, the manager of the second firm, is to enter to earn a profit of $8,000, as shown by rectangle 1.
- If Mona commits to serve 100 passengers, we reach the lower branch of the game tree. If Doug enters with the minimum entry quantity of 20 passengers, his average cost will be $101, which exceeds the market price of $100. Therefore, the best response is to stay out of the market and avoid losing money.

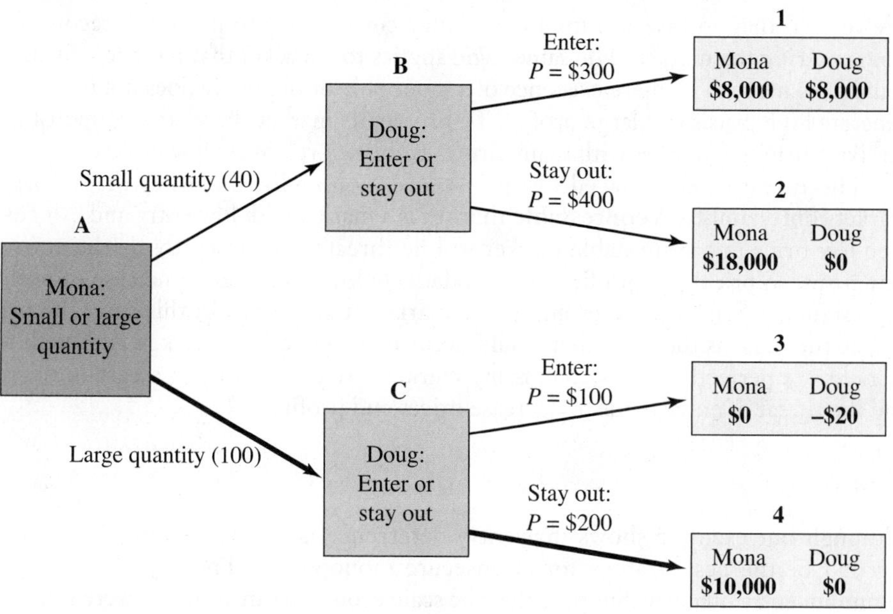

▲ FIGURE 27.9
Game Tree for the Entry-Deterrence Game
The path of the game is square *A* to square *C* to rectangle 4. Mona commits to the entry-deterring quantity of 100, so Doug stays out of the market. Mona's profit of $10,000 is less than the monopoly profit but more than the duopoly profit of $8,000.

Mona can choose between rectangles 1 and 4. Mona's profit is higher in rectangle 4, so that's the equilibrium. The equilibrium path of the game is square *A* to square *C* to rectangle 4.

Mona's entry-deterrence strategy generates a market price of $200, which is less than the $400 price charged by a secure monopolist and less than the $300 price with two competing firms. Mona can keep the second firm out of the market, but only by producing a large quantity and charging a relatively low price. This is known as **limit pricing**: To prevent a firm from entering the market, the firm reduces its price. The price that is just low enough to prevent entry is known as the **limit price**.

limit pricing
The strategy of reducing the price to deter entry.

limit price
The price that is just low enough to deter entry.

Examples: Aluminum and Campus Bookstores

For an example of limit pricing, consider the Aluminum Company of America (Alcoa). Between 1893 and 1940, Alcoa had a monopoly on aluminum production in the United States. During this period, Alcoa kept other firms out of the market by producing a large quantity and keeping its price relatively low. Although a higher price would have generated more profit in the short run, the entry of other firms would eventually have reduced Alcoa's profit.

We can apply the notion of entry deterrence to your favorite monopoly: your campus bookstore. On most college campuses, other organizations are prohibited, usually by the state government or the college, from selling textbooks on campus. Internet commerce has given students another option: Order textbooks online and have them shipped by mail, UPS, FedEx, or DHL. Several online booksellers charge less than the campus bookstore, and the growth of Internet book sales thus threatens the campus bookstore monopoly. If your campus bookstore suddenly feels insecure about its monopoly position, it could cut its prices to prevent online booksellers from capturing too many of its customers. If it does this, you will pay lower prices even if you don't patronize the Internet seller.

Entry Deterrence and Contestable Markets

We've seen that an insecure monopolist may cut its price to prevent a second firm from entering the market. The same logic applies to a market that has a few firms but could have many. The mere existence of a monopoly or oligopoly does not necessarily generate high prices and large profits. To protect its market share, an oligopolist may act like a firm in a market with many firms, leading to relatively low prices.

contestable market
A market with low entry and exit costs.

The threat of entry faced by an insecure monopolist underlies the theory of market contestability. A **contestable market** is a market with low entry and exit costs. The few firms in a contestable market will be threatened constantly by the entry of new firms, so prices and profits will be relatively low. In the extreme case of perfect contestability, firms can enter and exit a market at zero cost. In this case, the price will be the same as the price that would occur in a competitive market. Although few markets are perfectly contestable, many markets are contestable to a certain degree, and the threat of entry tends to decrease prices and profits.

When Is the Passive Approach Better?

Although our example shows that entry deterrence is the best strategy for Mona, it won't be the best strategy for all insecure monopolists. The key variable is the minimum entry quantity. Suppose that the scale economies in air travel were relatively small, so a second firm could enter the market with as few as 10 passengers. In this case, if Mona commits to serving only 100 passengers, that won't be enough to deter entry: A firm entering with 10 passengers will still make a profit. If the minimum entry quantity is 10 passengers, the entry-deterring quantity rises to 110 passengers:

$$\text{deterring quantity} = \text{zero profit quantity} - \text{minimum entry quantity}$$

$$110 = 120 - 10$$

Mona can commit to serving 110 passengers and thus prevent the second firm from entering the market, but is this the most profitable strategy? As shown by point *f* in Figure 27.8, the limit price associated with an entry-deterring quantity is \$150. Mona's profit from entry deterrence would be \$5,500:

$$\begin{aligned} \text{profit} &= (\text{price} - \text{average cost}) \times \text{quantity per firm} \\ &= (\$150 - \$100) \times 110 = \$5{,}500 \end{aligned}$$

This is less than the \$8,000 profit she could earn by being passive and letting the second firm enter the market. In this case, the minimum entry quantity is relatively small, so the entry-deterring quantity is large and the limit price is low. As a result, sharing a duopoly is more profitable than increasing output and cutting the price to keep the other firm out.

For another example of the passive response to market entry, consider the ballpoint pen, introduced in 1945 by Reynolds International Pen Corporation.[6] For three years Reynolds earned enormous profits producing this revolutionary product and selling it for \$12.50, about 16 times the average production cost of \$0.80.

application 4

MICROSOFT AS AN INSECURE MONOPOLIST

APPLYING THE CONCEPT #4: How does a monopolist respond to the threat of entry?

Microsoft has a virtual monopoly in the market for personal-computer operating systems and business software. But there is a constant threat that another firm will launch competing products, so Microsoft engages in limit pricing to deter entry into its key markets. A recent study revealed some of the numbers behind the insecure monopoly.

1 The pure monopoly price for a software bundle of the Windows operating system and the Office Suite of business tools is about $354, but the actual price (the limit price) is about $143. The estimated cost for a second firm to develop, maintain, and market an alternative software bundle is about $38 billion, and Microsoft's actual price is just low enough to make such an investment unprofitable.

2 The pure monopoly profit would be about $191 billion, while the profit under Microsoft's limit pricing is about $153 billion. Although the profit under the entry-deterrence strategy is less than the pure monopoly profit, it is greater than the profit Microsoft would earn if it allowed a second firm to enter the market ($148 billion). In other words, entry deterrence is the best strategy. **Related to Exercise 4.8.**

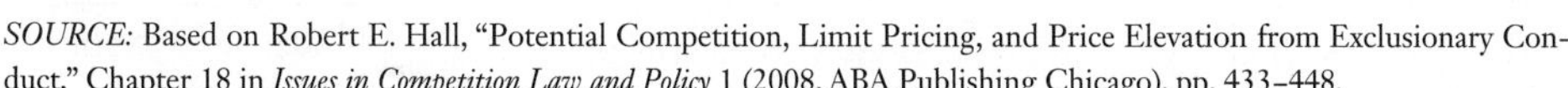

SOURCE: Based on Robert E. Hall, "Potential Competition, Limit Pricing, and Price Elevation from Exclusionary Conduct," Chapter 18 in *Issues in Competition Law and Policy* 1 (2008, ABA Publishing Chicago), pp. 433–448.

Then in 1948, Reynolds stopped producing pens, dropping out of the market entirely. Why? Other producers could easily copy the simple production technology of the ballpoint pen. The limit price was thus so low that it was better for Reynolds to charge a high price and squeeze out as much profit as possible from a short-lived monopoly while it lasted. By 1948, a total of 100 firms had entered the ballpoint market, and the price had fallen to the average cost of production, so each firm made zero economic profit.

27.5 The Advertisers' Dilemma

We have explored two sorts of strategic behavior of firms in an oligopoly—price fixing and entry deterrence. A third type of strategy concerns advertising. As we'll see, firms in an oligopoly may suffer from an advertisers' dilemma: Although both firms would be better off if neither spent money on advertising, each firm advertises.

Consider the producers of two brands of aspirin. Each firm must decide whether to spend $7 million on an advertising campaign for its product. In Table 27.3, the first two columns show what happens if neither firm advertises. Each firm earns $8 million in net

TABLE 27.3 Advertising and Profit

	Neither Advertises		Both Advertise		Adeline Advertises	
	Adeline	Vern	Adeline	Vern	Adeline	Vern
Net revenue from sales ($ million)	$8	$8	$13	$13	$17	$5
Cost of advertising ($ million)	0	0	7	7	7	0
Profit ($ million)	8	8	6	6	10	5

revenue (revenue minus production cost) and spends no money on advertising, so each firm earns $8 million in profits. The third and fourth columns show what happens if each firm spends $7 million on advertising. The net revenue for each firm increases by only $5 million, so the profit of each firm drops by $2 million, to $6 million.

What happens if one firm advertises and the other does not? As shown in the last two columns in Table 27.3, a firm can increase its profit by advertising. If Adeline spends $7 million on advertising and Vern spends nothing, Adeline's net revenue increases to $17 million and her profit increases to $10 million. Adeline's advertisements cause some of Vern's consumers to switch to Adeline, and Vern's profit drops to $5 million.

We can use the data in Table 27.3 to construct a game tree for the advertising game. In Figure 27.10, Adeline makes her decision first, followed by Vern:

- If neither firm advertises, we go from square *A* to square *C* to rectangle 4, and each firm gets a profit of $8 million.
- If both firms advertise, we go from square *A* to square *B* to rectangle 1, and each firm earns a profit of $6 million.
- If Adeline advertises and Vern does not, we go from square *A* to square *B* to rectangle 2. Adeline earns $10 million, while Vern earns $5 million. If the roles are reversed, we end up in rectangle 3, with Vern the advertiser earning $10 million and Adeline earning only $5 million.

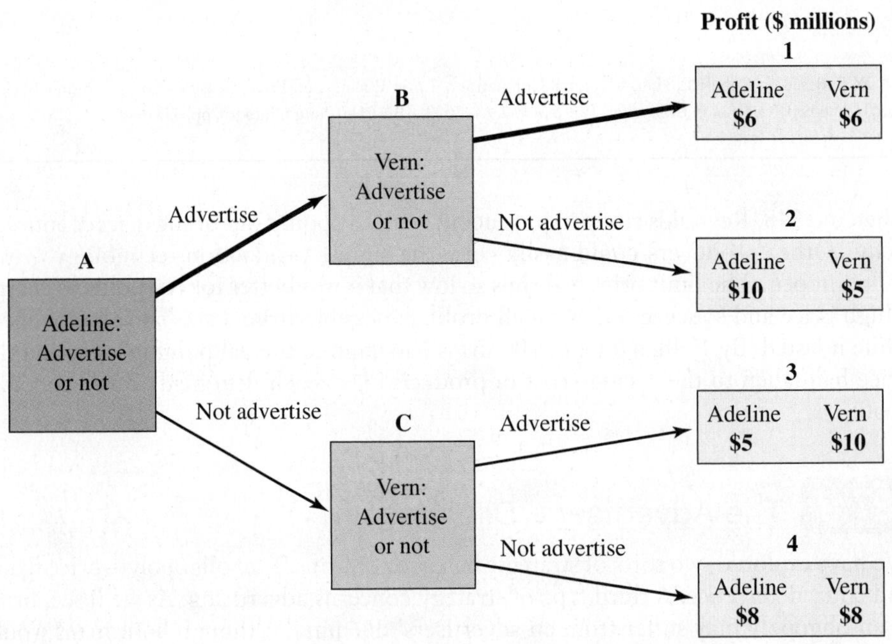

► **FIGURE 27.10**
Game Tree for the Advertisers' Dilemma
Adeline moves first, choosing to advertise or not. Vern's best response is to advertise no matter what Adeline does. Knowing this, Adeline realizes that the only possible outcomes are shown by rectangles 1 and 3. From Adeline's perspective, rectangle 1 ($6 million) is better than rectangle 3 ($5 million), so her best response is to advertise. Both Adeline and Vern advertise, and each earns a profit of $6 million.

To determine the outcome of this advertising game, let's start with Vern's possible actions:

- If Adeline advertises, we move along the upper branches of the game tree from square *A* to square *B*. Vern will earn $6 million if he advertises (rectangle 1), but only $5 million if he does not advertise (rectangle 2). Therefore, Vern's best response is to match Adeline's campaign.

- If Adeline does not advertise, we move along the lower branches from square *A* to square *C*. Vern will earn \$10 million if he advertises, but only \$8 million if he does not. Therefore, if Adeline does not advertise, Vern's best response is to advertise.

Advertising is Vern's dominant strategy because it is the best response no matter what Adeline does.

Consider next the options faced by Adeline. She will figure out that advertising is a dominant strategy for Vern, so she realizes that the only possible outcomes are shown by rectangles 1 and 3. To get to rectangle 1, she advertises and gets a profit of \$6 million. This is better than not advertising and going to rectangle 3, with a profit of \$5 million. So Adeline's best response is to advertise. The thick arrows show the equilibrium path of the game, from square *A* to square *B* to rectangle 1. In equilibrium, both firms advertise and each earns a profit of \$6 million.

What is the advertisers' dilemma? Both Adeline and Vern would be better off if neither advertised. Each would get a profit of \$8 million, compared to \$6 million when they both advertise. But each firm has an incentive to use advertising to increase its sales at the expense of the other. Stuck in the dilemma, each firm earns \$2 million less than it would if neither advertised.

Why does the advertisers' dilemma occur? In general, it happens when advertising causes a relatively small increase in the total sales of the industry but allows a firm that advertises to gain at the expense of firms that don't. In our example, a pair of advertising campaigns costing a total of \$14 million increases the net revenue of the entire industry by only \$10 million. The increase in revenue is less than the cost of advertising, so advertising decreases total profit. Nonetheless, each firm has an incentive to advertise to take sales away from the other firm. If the increase in industry-wide net revenue were larger, advertising could benefit both firms.

application 5

GOT MILK?

APPLYING THE CONCEPTS #5: What is the rationale for generic advertising?

The Got Milk? advertisement campaign is run by the National Fluid Milk Producers, an industry group that is funded by a tax of \$0.20 per hundredweight of processed milk. Milk producers pool their resources and run a generic (non-brand) advertising campaign. Why?

Milk is a standardized good, so advertising by one producer increases demand and benefits other producers. The Got Milk? campaign increases the demand for milk by about 6 percent, and the bang per buck (the increase in milk sales per dollar on advertising) is about \$5. No single firm has an incentive to incur the cost of an advertising campaign, because the firm bears all the cost but experiences only a fraction of the benefits. The result is an advertisers' dilemma: All firms would benefit from an advertising campaign, but no single firm has an incentive to pay for a campaign. The solution to this advertisers' dilemma is to share the cost of an advertising campaign, along with the benefits. **Related to Exercise 5.6.**

SOURCE: Based on Noel Blisard, "Advertising and What We Eat: The Case of Dairy Products," in *America's Eating Habits: Changes and Consequences*, ed. Elizabeth Frazao (U.S. Department of Agriculture, 1999), chap. 10.

SUMMARY

In this chapter, we've seen that when a few firms share a market they have an incentive to act strategically. Firms in an oligopoly try to use cartel pricing—price fixing—to avoid competition and keep prices high. A monopolist may commit to a large quantity and a low price in order to prevent a second firm from entering the market. Oligopolists may use advertising to increase their sales at the expense of competitors. Here are the main points of the chapter:

1 Each firm in an oligopoly has an incentive to underprice the other firms, so price fixing will be unsuccessful unless firms have some way of enforcing a price-fixing agreement.

2 One way to maintain price fixing is a low-price guarantee: One firm chooses the high price and promises to match any lower price of a competitor.

3 Price fixing is more likely to occur if firms choose prices repeatedly and can punish a firm that chooses a price below the cartel price.

4 To prevent a second firm from entering the market, an insecure monopolist may commit itself to producing a relatively large quantity and accepting a relatively low price.

5 The advertisers' dilemma is that both firms would be better off if neither firm advertised.

KEY TERMS

cartel, p. 584
concentration ratio, p. 583
contestable market, p. 598
dominant strategy, p. 587
duopolists' dilemma, p. 587
duopoly, p. 584
game theory, p. 583
game tree, p. 586
grim-trigger strategy, p. 590
low-price guarantee, p. 589
limit price, p. 597
limit pricing, p. 597
Nash equilibrium, p. 588
oligopoly, p. 583
payoff matrix, p. 593
price fixing, p. 585
price leadership, p. 592
tit-for-tat strategy, p. 590

EXERCISES

All problems are assignable in MyEconLab.

27.1 Cartel Pricing and the Duopolists' Dilemma

1.1 A market is considered "unconcentrated" if the Herfindahl–Hirschman Index (HHI) is below __________ and is "highly" concentrated if the HHI is at least __________.

1.2 For a market with four firms, each with a 25 percent market share, the Herfindahl–Hirschman Index (HHI) is equal to __________.

1.3. Arrows up or down: If we move from the cartel outcome to the duopoly outcome, the price __________, the quantity per firm __________, and the profit per firm __________.

1.4 A dominant strategy is the strategy that allows one firm to dominate the market. __________ (True/False)

1.5 The duopolists' dilemma is that each firm would make more profit if both picked the __________ price, but both firms pick the __________ price.

1.6 In a Nash equilibrium, each player is doing the best he or she can, given __________.

1.7 In Figure 27.3 on page 586, rectangle 3 is not a Nash equilibrium because if __________ picks a(n) __________ price, the best response of __________ is to pick the __________ price.

1.8 In Figure 27.3 on page 586, suppose Jack promises Jill that if she picks the high price, he will too. Is this promise credible? Explain.

1.9 The salt cartels of the nineteenth century were __________ (short/long) lived, in part because individual firms __________ on the cartel. (Related to Application 1 on page 588.)

1.10 Buzz and Moe are duopolists in the lawn-care market. The following game tree shows the possible pricing outcomes and their payoffs. The outcome of the pricing game is that Buzz will pick the __________ price and Moe will pick the __________ price.

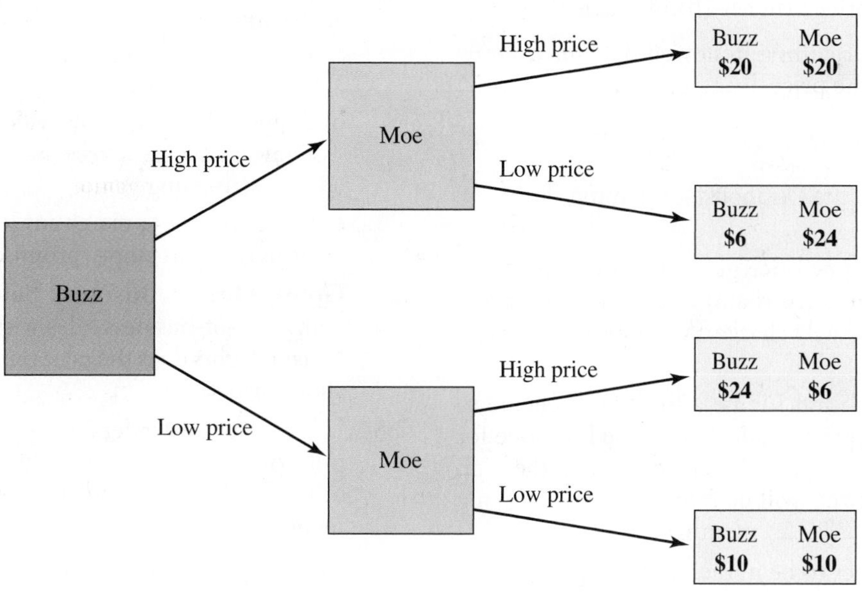

Use this figure to complete Exercise 1.10.

1.11 **Vitamin Market Areas.** Beta and Gamma produce vitamin A at a constant average cost of $5 per unit. Assume that low-price guarantees are illegal. Here are the possible outcomes:

- Price fixing (cartel). Each firm sells 30 units at a price of $20 per unit.
- Duopoly (no price fixing). Each firm sells 40 units at a price of $12 per unit.
- Underpricing (one firm charges $20 and the other charges $12). The low-price firm sells 70 units and the high-price firm sells 5 units.

a. Suppose Beta chooses a price first, followed by Gamma. Draw a game tree for the price-fixing game and predict the outcome.

b. Suppose the firms agree to pick the high price. Once Beta picks the high price, how much more could Gamma earn if it cheated on the price-fixing agreement?

c. Suppose the firms divide the market into two areas of equal size and assign each firm one of the areas. Each firm agrees to sell only in its assigned areas. Will this arrangement generate a successful cartel?

1.12 **Airporter Price Fixing?** Hustle and Speedy provide transportation service from downtown to the city airport. Assume that low-price guarantees are illegal. The average cost per passenger is constant at $10. Here are the possible outcomes:

- Price fixing (cartel). Each firm has 15 passengers at a price of $25.
- Duopoly (no price fixing). Each firm has 20 passengers at a price of $20.
- Underpricing (one firm charges $20 and the other charges $25). The low-price firm has 28 passengers and the high-price firm has 5 passengers.

Hustle chooses a price first, followed by Speedy. Draw a game tree for the price-fixing game and predict the outcome.

1.13 **Hotel Price Fixing?** Waikiki Beach has two hotels, one run by Juan and a second run by Tulah. The average cost of providing rooms is constant at $30 per day. Assume that low-price guarantees are illegal. Here are the possible outcomes:

- Price fixing (cartel). Each firm has 30 customers at a price of $40.
- Duopoly (no price fixing). Each firm has 40 customers per day at a price of $37.
- Underpricing (one firm charges $40 and the other charges $37). The low-price firm has 50 customers and the high-price firm has 10 customers.

Juan chooses a price first, followed by Tulah. Draw a game tree for the price-fixing game and predict the outcome.

27.2 Overcoming the Duopolists' Dilemma

2.1 For firms with a low-price guarantee, the promise of matching a lower price is a(n) __________ promise, because all firms will charge the same __________ price.

2.2 Suppose that Jack and Jill use a tit-for-tat scheme to encourage cartel pricing. Jill chooses the low price for two successive months, and then switches to the high price. The two firms will deviate from cartel pricing for a total of __________ months.

2.3 If two firms expect to be in the market together for a long time, the __________ (cost/benefit) of underpricing will be large relative to the __________ (cost/benefit).

2.4 If a seller promises to refund any difference between its price and the price of its competitors, this practice will lead to __________ (higher/lower) prices.

2.5 A careful study of the retail tire market suggests that low-price guarantees __________ (increase/decrease) prices by about __________ (1, 10, 25, 37) percent. (Related to Application 2 on page 592.)

2.6 **Low-Price Guarantees for a Canopy Tour.** Dip and Zip provide canopy tours in a rain forest. The average cost per rider is constant at $10. Here are the possible outcomes:

- Price fixing (cartel). Each firm has 6 passengers at a price of $20.
- Duopoly (no price fixing). Each firm has 8 passengers at a price of $15.
- Underpricing (one firm charges $20 and the other charges $15). The low-price firm has 13 passengers and the high-price firm has 2 passengers.

Dip chooses a price first, followed by Zip.

a. Assume that the firms do not provide low-price guarantees. Draw a game tree and predict the outcome of the price-fixing game.

b. Suppose both firms provide low-price guarantees. Draw a new game tree and predict the outcome of the price-fixing game.

c. Is the promise to match any lower price a substantive promise or an empty promise?

2.7 **Going Out of Business Sales?** Many firms have going-out-of-business sales with remarkable bargains. What insights does the material in this chapter provide about such sales?

2.8 Under a price-leadership model, a sudden drop in price by the leader is unlikely to trigger a price war if other firms believe that the price cut was caused by higher __________.

27.3 Simultaneous Decision Making and the Payoff Matrix

3.1 Consider a market with two firms managed by Harry and Vera. Under a cartel (both firms pick the high price), each firm earns a profit of $80. Under a duopoly (both firms pick the low price), each firm earns a profit of $60. If the two firms pick different prices, the high-price firm earns a profit of $20 and the low-price firm earns a profit of $90.

a. Fill in the following payoff matrix.

b. The outcome of the pricing game is that Harry picks the __________ price and Vera picks the __________ price.

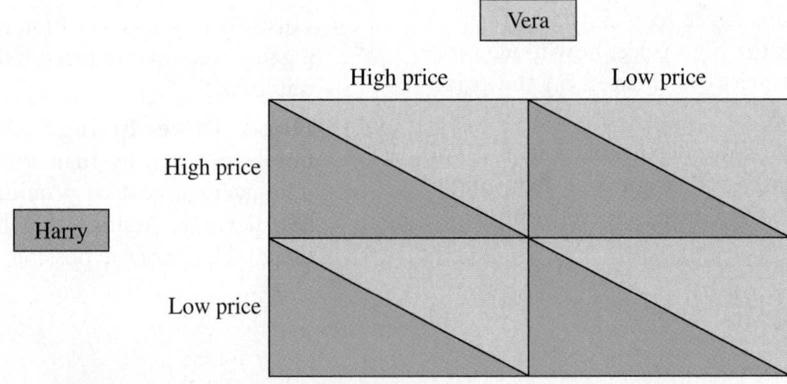

Use this figure to complete Exercise 3.1.

c. The outcome identified in part (b) is a Nash equilibrium because neither firm has an incentive to ________.

3.2 The prisoners' dilemma is that each prisoner would be better off if both prisoners ________, but both end up ________.

3.3 The cheaters' dilemma is that all three cheaters would be better off if each ________, but each cheater has an incentive to ________. (Related to Application 3 on page 595.)

27.4 The Insecure Monopolist and Entry Deterrence

4.1 Otto has a monopoly on limousine service, and Carla is thinking about entering the market. The outcome of the entry-deterrence game represented by the game tree on the following page is that Otto picks the ________ quantity and Carla ________ the market.

4.2 Use the game tree in the previous exercise as a starting point. If the minimum entry quantity increases, a single number in one of the profit rectangles changes from $________ to a smaller number. If the relevant number is reduced by half, the new outcome of the entry-deterrence game is that Otto picks the ________ quantity and Carla ________ the market.

4.3 Consider a market with an insecure monopolist. The zero-profit quantity is 60 units and the minimum entry quantity is 5 units. The entry-deterring quantity is ________ units. The zero-profit price is $80. The slope of the market demand curve is –$2 per unit of output. The limit price is ________.

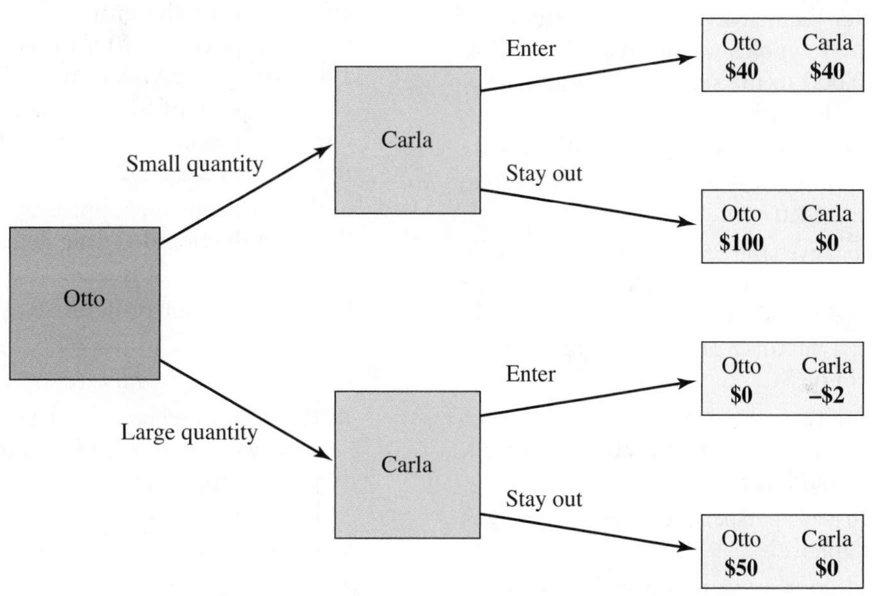

Use this figure to complete Exercise 4.1.

4.4 To deter entry, a monopolist can simply threaten that if a second firm enters, the monopolist will cut its price to the average cost. ________ (True/False)

4.5 Arrows up or down: As the minimum entry quantity decreases, the entry-deterring quantity ________, the limit price ________, and the profit from the entry-deterrence strategy ________.

4.6 In Figure 27.9 on page 597, rectangle 2 is not a Nash equilibrium because if ________ picks a small quantity, the best response for ________ is to ________.

4.7 A contestable market has relatively ________ (high, low) ________ costs.

4.8 Microsoft is a(n) ________ (secure/insecure) monopolist, and the limit price is roughly ________ (10, 20, 40, 60, 90, 100) percent of the pure monopoly price. (Related to Application 4 on page 599.)

4.9 **Ninja Turtles versus Tai Chi Frogs.** The demand for fantasy amphibians is linear, with a slope of –$0.01 per amphibian. The average cost of production is constant at $3. The demand curve intersects the horizontal average-cost curve at a quantity of 600 amphibians. A firm selling ninja turtles currently has a monopoly, selling 300 turtles at a price of $4. A second firm is considering entering the market with tai chi frogs, and the minimum entry quantity is 100 amphibians. If the turtle firm is passive and lets the frog firm enter, each firm will sell 200 amphibians at a price of $5.

a. Draw a graph like the one shown in Figure 27.8 on page 595 with all the relevant numbers.

b. Draw a game tree like the one shown in Figure 27.9 on page 597 and predict the outcome of the game. How will the turtle firm respond to the threat of entry? Will the frog firm enter the market?

c. How would your response to part (a) change if the minimum entry quantity dropped to 50 amphibians?

4.10 Take the Pen Money and Run? Consider the example of Reynolds International Pen and the ballpoint pen. Suppose the unit cost of a ballpoint pen is $1.00. Reynolds has two options:

1. *Passive.* Pick the monopoly price of $13. In the first year, Reynolds will sell 100,000 pens. Over time as other firms enter the market with lower prices, the quantity sold by Reynolds will decrease by 20,000 per year, to 80,000 in the second year and so on, down to zero in the sixth year.
2. *Deterrence.* Commit to produce one million pens per year, an amount large enough to deter entry. The limit price is $1.05.

a. Under the passive strategy, the profit per year is $__________ in the first year, $__________ in the second year, and so on, down to zero in the sixth year. The total profit over the 6-year period would be $__________.

b. Under the deterrence strategy, the profit per year is $__________. Over a 20-year period, total profit would be $__________.

c. Taking a 20-year perspective, which strategy is more profitable?

d. How would your answer to part (c) change if the limit price were $1.50 rather than $1.05?

4.11 Shuttle Deterrence? Consider the market for air travel between Boston and New York. The long-run average cost is constant at $100 per passenger, and the demand curve is linear, with a slope of –$2 per passenger. The demand curve intersects the horizontal average-cost curve at a quantity of 120 passengers. The minimum entry quantity is 20 passengers. FirstShuttle currently has a monopoly, with 60 passengers at a price of $220. Another firm, SecondShuttle, is considering the market, and the minimum entry quantity is 20 passengers. If FirstShuttle is passive and lets the other firm enter, each firm will have 40 passengers at a price of $180.

a. Draw a graph like the one shown in Figure 27.8 on page 595 with all the relevant numbers.

b. Draw a game tree like the one shown in Figure 27.9 on page 597 and predict the outcome of the game. How will FirstShuttle respond to the threat of entry? Will SecondShuttle enter the market?

c. How would your response to (a) change if the minimum entry quantity dropped to 10 passengers?

4.12 Going off Patent. Consider the producer of a branded drug that will soon go off patent and compete with generic versions of the drug. The average cost of production is constant at $8 per dose. The producer could prevent the entry of generics by committing to a limit price of $10. At this price, the firm will sell 100 doses per day. Alternatively, the producer could charge a price of $12 and passively allow generics to enter the market. The price elasticity of demand for the branded drug is 2.0.

a. Under the passive approach (price = $12), the quantity of the branded drug demanded is __________; the firm's profit is __________.

b. Under the entry-deterrence approach, the firm's profit is $__________.

c. The best approach is (entry deterrence, passive).

d. If the price elasticity of demand for the branded drug were 3.0 instead of 2.0, the profit under the passive approach would be $__________, so the best strategy is __________ (entry deterrence, passive).

27.5 The Advertisers' Dilemma

5.1 The advertisers' dilemma is that both firms would be better if __________ advertises, but each has an incentive to __________.

5.2 The advertisers' dilemma shown in Figure 27.10 on page 600 occurs when advertising causes a relatively __________ increase in the total sales of an industry.

5.3 Consider a duopoly with two firms managed by Huck and Stella. A standard advertising campaign has a cost of $5 million per firm. If both firms run a standard campaign, the net revenue from sales increases by $4 for each firm. If only one firm runs a campaign, the advertiser's net revenue from sales increases by $8 million, and the other firm's net revenue from sales decreases by $7 million. Fill in the blanks in the following table, draw a game tree, and predict the outcome of the advertising game.

	Neither Advertises		Both Advertise		Huck Advertises	
	Huck	Stella	Huck	Stella	Huck	Stella
Net revenue from sales ($ million)	$10	$10				
Cost of advertising ($ million)	0	0	5	5	5	0
Profit ($ million)						

5.4 In Figure 27.10 on page 600, rectangle 2 is not a Nash equilibrium because if __________ advertises, the best response of __________ is to __________.

5.5 **Automobile Advertising.** Consider two automobile companies that are considering advertising campaigns. If neither firm advertises, each will earn net revenue of $5 million. If each spends $10 million on advertising, each firm's net revenue will be $12 million. If one advertises and the other does not, the firm that advertises will earn $17 million in net revenue, while the firm that does not will earn $1 million. Draw a game tree and predict the outcome. From the industry perspective, do the benefits of advertising exceed the costs?

5.6 **Got Milk?** Bessie and George are milk producers, and each must decide whether to spend $7 million on an advertising campaign. If neither advertises, each will earn $10 million in net revenue from sales (net revenue). If both advertise, each will earn $20 million in net revenue and $13 million in profit ($20 million minus $7 million for advertising). If only one producer advertises, that firm will earn $16 million in net revenue, and the other firm will earn $15 million in net revenue. Prepare a game tree like Figure 27.10 on page 600. Assume that Bessie decides first. What is the outcome of this advertising game? If there is an advertisers' dilemma, how does it differ from the advertisers' dilemma discussed earlier in the chapter? How might the dairy industry solve this dilemma? (Related to Application 5 on page 601.)

ECONOMIC EXPERIMENT

PRICE-FIXING

Here is a price-fixing or cartel game for the classroom. You'll have an opportunity to conspire to fix prices in a hypothetical market with five firms. The instructor divides the class into five groups. Each group represents one of five firms that produce a particular good. Each group must develop a pricing strategy for its firm, recognizing that the other groups are choosing prices for their firms at the same time. Only two choices are possible: a high price (the cartel price) or a low price. The profit of a particular firm depends on the price chosen by the firm and the prices chosen by the four other firms. The profit matrix is shown below.

From the second row, if one of the five firms chooses the high price, and the other four firms choose the low price, the high-price firm earns a profit of $2, and each low-price firm

Number of High-Price Firms	Number of Low-Price Firms	Profit for Each High-Price Firm	Profit for Each Low-Price Firm
0	5	—	$5
1	4	$2	7
2	3	4	9
3	2	6	11
4	1	8	13
5	0	10	—

earns a profit of $7. The game is played for several rounds. In the first three rounds, the firms make their choices without talking to each other in advance. In the fourth and fifth rounds, the firms discuss their strategies, disperse, and then make their choices. The group's score equals the profit earned by the firm.

MyEconLab
For additional economic experiments, please visit ***www.myeconlab.com.***

NOTES

1. Alberto Salvo, "Inferring market power under the threat of entry: The case of the Brazilian cement industry," *RAND Journal of Economics* 41 (2010), pp. 326–360.

2. Adam Smith, *An Inquiry into the Nature and Causes of the Wealth of Nations* (1776); Book 1, Chapter 10.

3. Sylvia Nassar, *A Beautiful Mind* (New York: Simon & Schuster, 1998).

4. Robert Axelrod, *The Evolution of Cooperation* (New York: Basic Books, 1984).

5. Federal Trade Commission, "Record Companies Settle FTC Charges of Restraining Competition in CD Music Market," Press Release, May 10, 2000.

6. Thomas Whiteside, "Where Are They Now?" *New Yorker*, February 17, 1951, 39–58.

Controlling Market Power: Antitrust and Regulation

CHAPTER 28

In 1997, a U.S. court blocked the proposed merger of Staples and Office Depot, the nation's two largest office-supply retailers.

The judge in the case observed that the merger would eliminate Office Depot as a competitor and allow Staples to increase its prices by 13 percent. Where did the judge get that number?

When you buy groceries, hardware, or office supplies, a scanner at the checkout reads bar code information, recording the price you pay and the quantity you purchase. The scanner system helps retailers keep track of their stock and allows them to instantly change prices without putting new price tags on their products. The scanner data can also be used to observe the pricing patterns of firms such as Staples. Economists with the Federal Trade Commission (FTC) found an interesting pattern: The prices charged by Staples were lower in cities where Office Depot also had a store. The competition generated by Office Depot led to prices that were, on average, 13 percent lower.[1]

LEARNING OBJECTIVES

- Define a natural monopoly and explain the average-cost pricing policy.
- List three features of antitrust policy.

MyEconLab

MyEconLab helps you master each objective and study more efficiently.

This chapter looks at various public policies dealing with markets that are dominated by a small number of firms. We'll start with the case of natural monopoly, which occurs when the scale economies in production are so large that only a single large firm can survive. In this case, the government can intervene by regulating the price charged by the natural monopolist. Then we'll look at markets in which the government can affect the number of firms in the market by using various policies to promote competition.

The government uses antitrust policies to break monopolies into several smaller companies, prevent corporate mergers that would reduce competition, and regulate business practices that tend to reduce competition. Sometimes prior government regulations actually end up inhibiting competition, so the government later deregulates an industry to promote more competition. In the last part of the chapter, we'll look at the recent deregulation of three markets: air travel, telecommunications, and electricity. In these three markets, the government reversed a long history of regulation, deregulating the industries to promote competition.

28.1 Natural Monopoly

In an earlier chapter, we considered monopolies that resulted from artificial barriers to entry, such as patents and government licenses. In this chapter, we'll look at natural monopolies, which occur when the economies of scale for producing a product are so large that only a single firm can survive. Some examples of natural monopolies are water systems, natural gas distribution, electricity transmission, and cable TV service. It is efficient for a city to have a single supplier of water service because a second supplier would install a second set of water pipes when a single set of pipes would suffice. Similarly, it is efficient to have a single set of transmission lines for electricity and a single set of cables for TV service.

Picking an Output Level

Figure 28.1 shows the long-run average-cost curve for water service in a particular city. The curve is negatively sloped and steep, reflecting the large economies of scale that occur because water service requires a costly system of pipes, and the cost is the same whether the firm pipes 70 or 70 million cubic meters of water. As the quantity of water increases, the average cost per unit decreases because the cost of the pipe system is spread over a larger volume of water.

What about the long-run marginal cost—the cost of an additional cubic meter of water delivered to a customer—once the system is built? For each additional unit, a water company incurs a cost for the energy required to pump the unit from the water source to a customer. The pumping cost depends on the distance (horizontal and vertical) from the source to the customer. To simplify matters, we'll assume that the marginal cost is constant at $0.80 per cubic meter.

Figure 28.1 shows how to use the cost curves and revenue curves to pick the output level that maximizes profit. Like other firms, the provider of water can use the marginal principle.

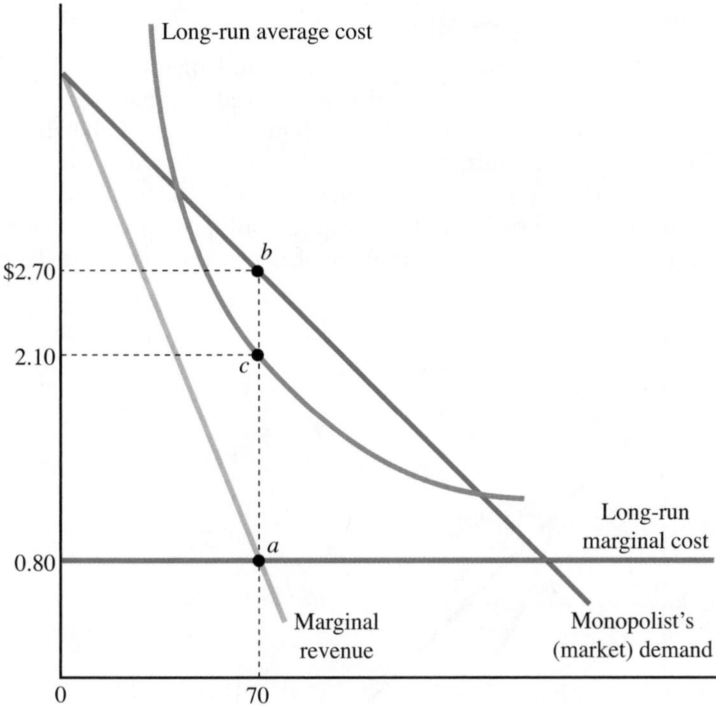

▲ FIGURE 28.1

A Natural Monopoly Uses the Marginal Principle to Pick Quantity and Price

Because of an indivisible input (the pipe system), the long-run average-cost curve is negatively sloped. The monopolist chooses point *a*, where marginal revenue equals marginal cost. The firm sells 70 million units of water at a price of \$2.70 (point *b*) and an average cost of \$2.10 (point *c*). The profit per unit of water is \$0.60 (equal to \$2.70 – \$2.10).

MARGINAL PRINCIPLE

Increase the level of an activity as long as its marginal benefit exceeds its marginal cost. Choose the level at which the marginal benefit equals the marginal cost.

If a single firm—a monopolist—provides water, the firm-specific demand curve is the same as the market demand curve: The market demand curve shows, for each price, the number of units sold by the monopolist. From the firm's perspective, the marginal benefit of a cubic meter of water is the increase in revenue—the marginal revenue. The marginal principle is satisfied at point *a*, with 70 million cubic meters. The price associated with this quantity is \$2.70 per unit (shown by point *b*), and the average cost is \$2.10 per unit (shown by point *c*), so the profit per unit is \$0.60. The price exceeds the average cost, so the water company will earn a profit.

Will a Second Firm Enter?

If there are no artificial barriers to entry, a second firm could enter the water market. What would happen if a second firm entered the market? In Figure 28.2, the entry of a second firm would shift the demand curve of the first firm—the former monopolist—to the left, from D_1 to D_2: At each price, the first firm will sell less water because it now shares the market with another firm. For example, at a price of \$2.70, a total of 70 million units are sold, or 35 million for each firm (point *d*). In general, the larger the number of firms, the lower the demand curve for the typical firm.

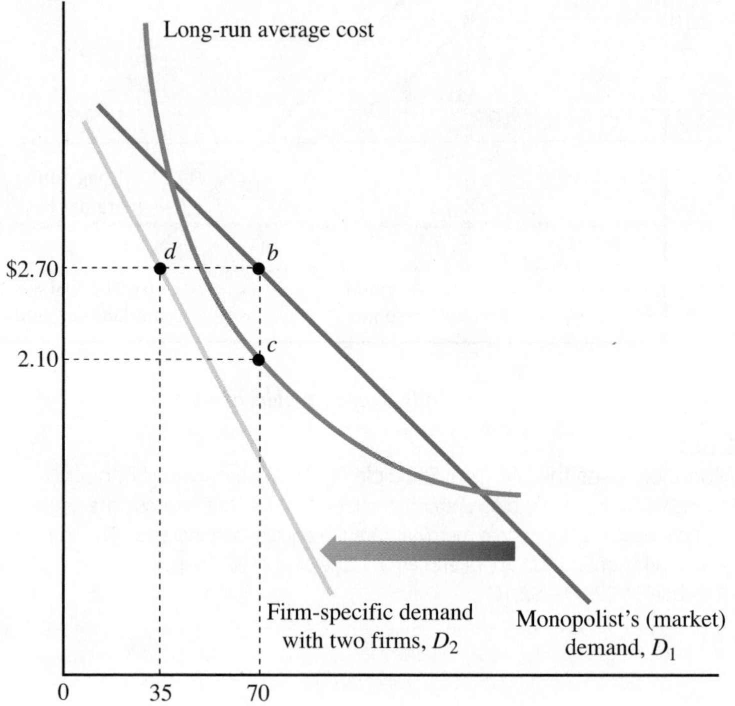

▲ FIGURE 28.2
Will a Second Firm Enter the Market?
The entry of a second firm would shift the demand curve of the typical firm to the left. After entry, the firm's demand curve lies entirely below the long-run average-cost curve. No matter what price the firm charges, it will lose money. Therefore, a second firm will not enter the market.

Will a second firm enter the market? Notice that the demand curve of the typical firm in a two-firm market lies entirely below the long-run average-cost curve, so there is no quantity at which the price exceeds the average cost of production. No matter what price the typical firm charges, it will lose money. The firm's demand curve lies below the average-cost curve because the average-cost curve is steep, reflecting the large economies of scale for water provision. A second firm—with half the market—would have a very high average cost and wouldn't be able to charge a price high enough to cover the cost of building the pipe system in the first place. Therefore, the second firm will not enter the market, so there will be a single firm, a natural monopoly.

Price Controls for a Natural Monopoly

When a natural monopoly is inevitable, the government often sets a maximum price that the monopolist can charge consumers. There are many examples of natural monopolies that are subject to maximum prices. Local governments regulate utilities and firms that provide water, electricity, cable service, and local telephone service. Many state governments use public utility commissions (PUCs) to regulate the electric power industry.

We can use the water market to explain the effects of government regulation on a natural monopoly. Suppose the government sets a maximum price for water and requires the water company to serve all consumers who are willing to pay the maximum price. In other words, the government—not the firm—picks a point on the market demand curve. Under an *average-cost pricing policy*, the government picks the price at which the market demand curve intersects the monopolist's long-run average-cost curve. In Figure 28.3, the average-cost curve intersects the demand curve at point *e*, with a price of $1.20 per cubic meter. This is much lower than the profit-maximizing price of $2.70. As a result, the total quantity of water demanded is much larger—150 million units compared to 70 million. The purpose of the

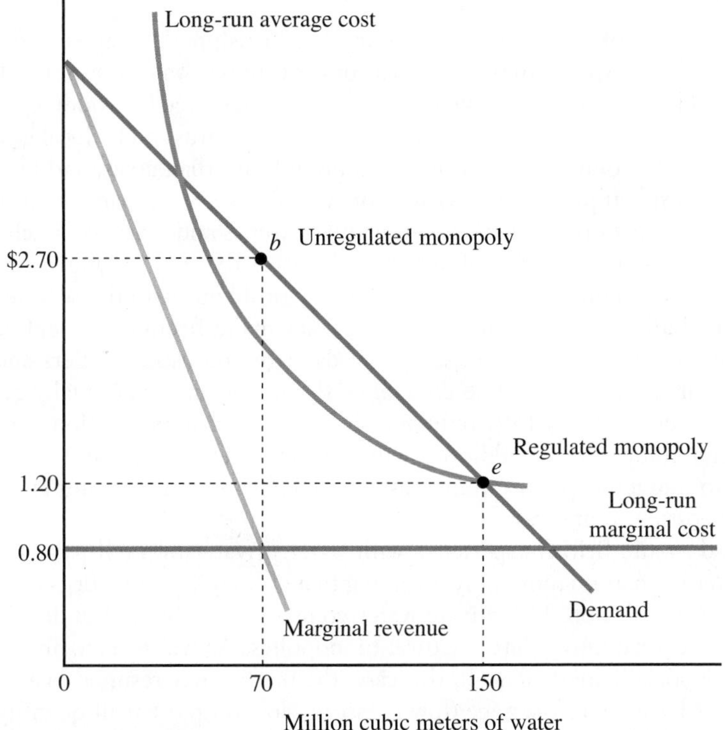

▲ FIGURE 28.3
Regulators Use Average-Cost Pricing to Pick a Monopoly's Quantity and Price
Under an average-cost pricing policy, the government chooses the price at which the demand curve intersects the long-run average-cost curve. Regulation decreases the price and increases the quantity.

average-cost pricing policy is to get the lowest feasible price. The water company would lose money at any price less than $1.20, so a lower price isn't feasible.

How will this regulatory policy affect the monopolist's production costs? Under average-cost pricing, a change in the monopolist's production cost will have little effect on its profit, because the government will soon adjust the regulated price to keep the price equal to the average cost. The government will increase the regulated price when the monopolist's cost increases and decrease the price when the monopolist's cost decreases. Because the monopolist has no incentive to cut costs and faces no penalty for higher costs, its costs are likely to creep upward. As average cost increases, the regulated price will too.

application 1

PUBLIC VERSUS PRIVATE WATERWORKS

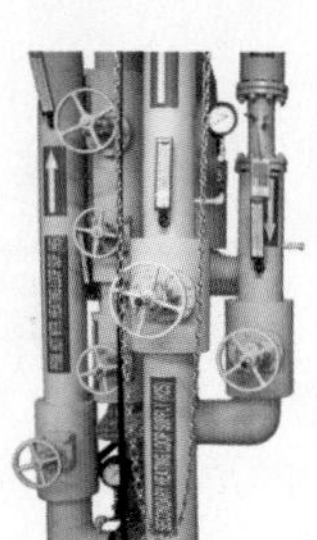

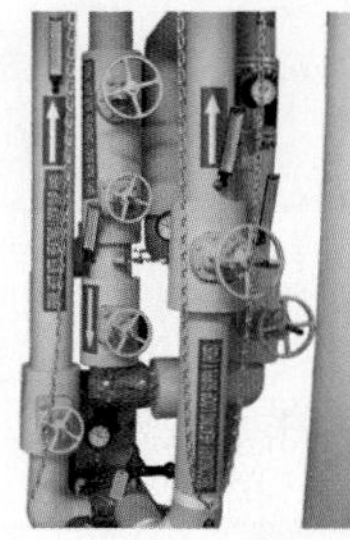

APPLYING THE CONCEPTS #1: What is the rationale for regulating a natural monopoly?

In the middle part of the nineteenth century, the British parliament staged an experiment in private enterprise. In the early part of the century, water was drawn from local rivers, stored in ponds on higher ground, and then distributed by wooden pipes to customers. In most urban areas, this primitive water system was run by local government. The Industrial Revolution caused the rapid growth of urban areas, and local governments lacked explicit powers to borrow money to finance the expansion of their water systems. The policies of Parliament caused many towns and cities to switch to private water companies, and by 1851 about three-fifths of the urban population got their water from private companies. There were many problems with the private provision of water, including low pressure that sometimes made firefighting ineffective, and water hardness (high mineral content) that damaged industrial boilers and reduced the quality of silk products. The control of the water supply gradually returned to local governments, and by 1891 only one-sixth of the urban population was served by private water companies. In addition to improving water pressure and water softness, the move to municipal provision increased total consumption of water and decreased the capital cost per unit of water.

What does the British experience with water privatization tell us? The distribution of water is a natural monopoly, meaning that although a single firm will be profitable, two firms will not. The private water companies established under the policies of Parliament were unregulated natural monopolies. As we've seen, an unregulated monopoly is socially inefficient. In this case, the inefficiency resulted in a low-quality product (hard water), low service (low pressure), low output (small quantity of water per capita), and high capital cost. If the water monopolies had been regulated in an efficient manner, the experience with privatization of the water supply might have been different. **Related to Exercises 1.5 and 1.9.**

SOURCE: J. S. Hassan, "The Growth and Impact of the British Water Industry in the Nineteenth Century," *The Economic History Review* 38 (1985): 531–547.

application 2

SATELLITE RADIO AS A NATURAL MONOPOLY

APPLYING THE CONCEPTS #2: When does a natural monopoly occur?

In 2008, the nation's only two satellite radio providers, Sirius Satellite Radio and XM Satellite Radio, merged into a single firm. Together the two firms had 14 million subscribers, each paying $13 per month for dozens of channels, most of which are free of advertisements. Both firms were losing money as they struggled to get enough subscribers to cover their substantial fixed costs. The cost of the infrastructure to set up a single system—satellites and ground stations—is about $2 billion. In addition, both firms added to their setup costs by signing contracts with radio personalities, news organizations, and sports information sources. One possible advantage of a merger was that the new firm could have a lower fixed cost per subscriber and thus could earn a profit. One possible disadvantage was that the new firm might charge higher prices.

Two years later, the new firm, Sirius XM, earned its first quarterly profit of $14.2 million, compared to a loss one year earlier of $245.8 million. The firm became profitable—just barely—by increasing the number of subscribers to 19 million and thus lowering its cost per subscriber. In other words, the merger transformed two unprofitable firms into a single profitable firm.

There was some concern that the merger would increase prices. Consumers choose from five packages of stations, including a limited set of stations for $10, the original Sirius stations for $13 (the same price as before the merger), a package that combines the original Sirius stations and a subset of the XM radio stations for $17, and a complete package for $19. In other words, the merger did not increase the price of the original Sirius package, but gave consumers more options for lower-priced and higher-priced packages. **Related to Exercises 1.6 and 1.10.**

SOURCES: Reuters, "Sirius XM Posts Profit, Its First Since Merger," *New York Times*, February 25, 2010; "They Cannot be Sirius," *Economist*, February 22, 2007.

28.2 Antitrust Policy

A **trust** is an arrangement under which the owners of several companies transfer their decision-making powers to a small group of trustees. The purpose of antitrust policy is to promote competition among firms, which leads to lower prices for consumers.

trust
An arrangement under which the owners of several companies transfer their decision-making powers to a small group of trustees.

Two government organizations, the Antitrust Division of the Department of Justice and the Federal Trade Commission, are responsible for initiating actions against individuals or firms that may be violating antitrust laws. The courts have the power to impose penalties on the executives found to be in violation of the laws, including fines and prison sentences. In some cases, the government seeks no penalties but directs the firm to discontinue illegal practices and take other measures to promote competition. We'll explore three types of antitrust policies: breaking up monopolies, blocking mergers, and regulating business practices.

Breaking Up Monopolies

One form of antitrust policy is to break up a monopoly into several smaller firms. The label "antitrust" comes from the names of the early conglomerates that the government broke up. The classic example is John D. Rockefeller's Standard Oil Trust, which was formed in 1882 when the owners of 40 oil companies empowered nine trustees to make the decisions for all 40 companies. The trust controlled over 90 percent of the market for refined petroleum products, and the trustees ran it like a monopoly. In 1911, the government ordered its breakup. The Supreme Court found that Rockefeller had used "unnatural methods" to maintain his monopoly power and drive his rivals out of business. In addition to forming the trust, he coerced railroads to give him special rates for shipping, and he spied on his competitors. The government broke up Standard Oil into 34 separate companies, including the corporate ancestors of Exxon, Mobil, Chevron, and Amoco.

The American Tobacco Company started in 1890 as a merger of several tobacco firms. By 1907, the company had acquired over 200 rival firms and controlled 95 percent of the U.S. cigarette market. The Supreme Court found that American Tobacco maintained its monopoly power by driving rivals out of business and agreeing to exclusive contracts with wholesalers that prevented them from purchasing cigarettes from other companies. The court-ordered breakup in 1911 led to new companies, including several of today's big cigarette companies: Reynolds, Liggett and Meyers, and P. Lorillard.

In 1982, the government broke up American Telephone and Telegraph (AT&T) into seven regional phone companies. AT&T had used its legal monopoly in local telephone service to prevent competition in the markets for long-distance service and communications equipment. After an eight-year legal battle, AT&T agreed to form seven Regional Bell Operating Companies, transforming "Ma Bell" into seven "Baby Bells." The new AT&T was allowed to compete in the market for long-distance service, where it faced competition from newcomers MCI and Sprint. AT&T was also allowed to operate in the market for communications equipment, where it faced competition from newcomers Mitel and Northern Telecom.

Blocking Mergers

merger
A process in which two or more firms combine their operations.

A **merger** occurs when two or more firms combine their operations. A *horizontal merger* involves two firms producing a similar product, for example, two producers of pet food. A *vertical merger* involves two firms at different stages of the production process, for example, a sugar refiner and a candy producer. A second type of antitrust policy is to block corporate mergers that would reduce competition and lead to higher prices. We saw in an earlier chapter that as the number of firms in a market increases, competition among firms drives down prices. Because a merger decreases the number of firms in a market, it is likely to lead to higher prices. In 1994, Microsoft tried to purchase Intuit, the maker of Quicken, a personal-finance software package that was a substitute for a similar Microsoft product. The merger would have reduced competition in the personal-finance software market, so the government blocked it.

Of course, the government does not oppose all corporate mergers. One possible benefit from a merger is that the new firm could combine production, marketing, and administrative operations, producing products at a lower average cost. Consumers might reap the rewards in the form of lower prices. In 1997, the Justice Department and the Federal Trade Commission (FTC) released new guidelines for proposed mergers. The new guidelines allow companies involved in a proposed merger to present evidence that the merger would reduce costs and lead to lower prices, better products, or better service. If the evidence for greater efficiency is convincing, the government might allow a merger that reduces the number of firms in a market. The chairman of the FTC assessed the effects of the new guidelines as follows:[2]

> There may be some deals that go through which otherwise would not have. But it won't change the result in a large number of cases [rather it will have] the greatest impact in a transaction where the potential anticompetitive problem is modest and efficiencies that would be created are great.

The new guidelines will bring the U.S. antitrust rules closer in line with those of Europe and Canada and could help U.S. companies compete in those markets.

In recent years, the analysis of proposed mergers has shifted from counting the number of firms in a market to predicting how a particular merger would affect prices. The data generated by retail checkout scanners provide an enormous amount of information about prices and quantities sold. Using these data, economists can determine how one firm's pricing policies affect the sales of that firm and its competitors. Economists can use this information to predict whether a merger would lead to higher prices.

As we saw in the chapter opener, the FTC used pricing data to support its decision to block a proposed merger between Staples and Office Depot. The data showed that Staples charged lower prices in cities where Office Depot also had stores. Figure 28.4 shows Staples' revenue and cost curves for one specific product: file folders. Panel A shows what happens when Staples faces no competition from an Office Depot, and Panel B shows what happens when it does. The demand curve of Staples is lower in the city where it faces competition with Office Depot because the two firms share the market. Using the marginal principle, Staples picks the quantity and price where its

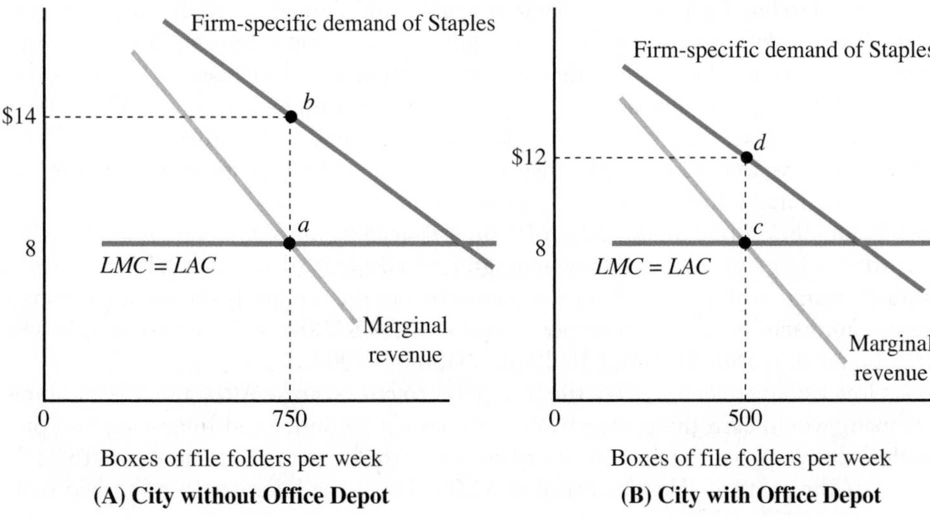

▲ FIGURE 28.4
Pricing by Staples in Cities with and without Competition
Using the marginal principle, Staples picks the quantity at which its marginal revenue equals its marginal cost. In a city without a competing firm, Staples picks the monopoly price of $14. In a city where Staples competes with Office Depot, the demand facing Staples is lower, so the profit-maximizing price is only $12.

TABLE 28.1 A Merger Increases Prices

	Wonder Brand		Interstate Brand		Total	
	1	2	3	4	5	6
	Before Merger	After Merger	Before Merger	After Merger	Before Merger	After Merger
>0	$1.50	$1.50	$1.50	$1.50		
Price	$2.00	$2.00	$2.00	$2.20		
Quantity	100	110	100	70	200	180
Profit	$ 50	$ 55	$ 50	$ 49	$100	$104

marginal revenue equals its marginal cost. The profit-maximizing price is $14 in a city without an Office Depot and $12 in a city with one.

The FTC used this logic to convince the court that the proposed merger of Staples and Office Depot would lead to higher prices. The judge in the case observed that,

> direct evidence shows that by eliminating Staples' most significant, and in many markets, only, rival, the merger would allow Staples to increase prices or otherwise maintain prices at an anticompetitive level.

Evidence from the companies' pricing data showed that the merger would have allowed Staples to increase its prices by about 13 percent. According to an FTC study, blocking the merger saved consumers an estimated $1.1 billion over five years.

Merger Remedy for Wonder Bread

In some cases, the government allows a merger to happen but imposes restrictions on the new company. In 1995, Interstate Bakeries, the nation's third-largest wholesale baker, tried to buy Continental Baking, the maker of Wonder bread. Based on grocery store scanner data, the government concluded that Wonder bread is a close substitute for Interstate's bread: The demand for Wonder bread increases when the price of Interstate's bread increases, and vice versa.[3] The scanner data showed that when Interstate increased its price, many consumers switched to Wonder bread, so their bread money went to Continental instead of Interstate. The substitutability of the two brands discouraged Interstate from increasing its prices.

Table 28.1 shows an example of a merger leading to higher prices and smaller quantities. Let's assume that the average cost per loaf of bread is $1.50, and this doesn't change with a merger. The situation before the merger is shown in columns 1 and 3: For each brand, the price per loaf of bread is $2.00, the quantity is 100 loaves, and the profit is $50 (the profit $0.50 per loaf times 100 loaves).

How would a merger affect the incentives to raise prices? After a merger, a single company would earn the profits from both brands (Wonder and Interstate) and pick both prices. Suppose the new company increased the price of Interstate bread to $2.20 but kept the price of Wonder bread at $2.00. The price hike would bring bad news and good news for the new company:

- Bad news: Less profit on Interstate Bread. As shown in columns 3 and 4, the price hike decreases the quantity of Interstate bread from 100 to 70 loaves. Although the profit per loaf increases to $0.70 (the new price of $2.20 minus the average cost of $1.50), only 70 loaves are sold, so the profit from the brand drops to $49, down from $50. The bad news is the $1 loss of profit on Interstate Bread.

- Good news: More profit on Wonder bread. As shown in columns 1 and 2, the increase in the price of Interstate Bread increases the quantity of Wonder bread sold from 100 to 110 loaves. The profit per loaf is still $0.50 per bread, so the profit on Wonder bread increases to $55, up from $50. The good news is the extra $5 of profit on Wonder bread.

In this case, the good news ($5 more profit from Wonder) exceeds the bad news ($1 less profit from Interstate), so the price hike increases the total profit of the merged company. This is shown in columns 5 and 6. Although the total quantity drops, total profit increases by $4. A merger means that the good news from a price hike stays within the larger firm, encouraging that firm to increase prices.

The lesson from this example is that a merger of two firms selling close substitutes may lead to higher prices. That's what the Department of Justice concluded in the case of Interstate Bakeries and Continental Bakery. The government allowed the merger between the two companies but forced Interstate to sell some of its brands and bakeries. For example, Interstate sold the rights to sell its Weber brand bread to Four-S Baking Company. The idea was to ensure that other companies would be able to compete with the newly merged company.

Regulating Business Practices

The third type of antitrust policy involves the regulation of business practices. As we saw in the previous chapter, price fixing—a cooperative agreement among firms to collude rather than compete—is illegal. Under the law, firms cannot discuss their pricing strategies with their competitors.

The government may intervene when a specific business practice increases market concentration in an already concentrated market. A **tie-in sale** occurs when a business forces the buyer of one product to purchase another product. The FTC recently charged a pharmaceutical company with tying the sale of clozapine, an antipsychotic drug, to a blood testing and monitoring system. Another illegal business practice is a cooperative agreement to limit advertising. The FTC recently charged a group of auto dealers with restricting comparative and discount advertising.

tie-in sale
A business practice under which a business requires a consumer of one product to purchase another product.

The Robinson–Patman Act prohibits the selling of products at "unreasonably low prices" with the intent of reducing competition, a practice known as **predatory pricing**. A firm engages in predatory pricing when it sells a product at a price below its production costs, with the objective of driving a rival out of business. Once the predator's rivals drop out of the market, the firm then charges a monopoly price, well above its production cost. This strategy will be profitable if the firm can charge the monopoly price for a long enough period to offset the losses it experienced while driving its rivals out of business.

predatory pricing
A firm sells a product at a price below its production cost to drive a rival out of business and then increases the price.

But is predatory pricing really practical? Consider a market with two firms, one of which is determined to have the market to itself. By cutting its price below its cost, the firm can drive its competitor out of business, losing perhaps $10 million in the process. If it increases its price next year, there may be nothing to prevent a new firm from entering the market. If so, it would have to cut its price below its cost again to drive the new firm out. The problem with predatory pricing is that it never ends. The firm must repeatedly lose money to drive out an endless series of competitors.

A Brief History of U.S. Antitrust Policy

Table 28.2 provides a brief summary of the history of antitrust policy. The first legislation was the Sherman Antitrust Act of 1890, which made it illegal to monopolize a market or to engage in practices that result in a restraint of trade. Because the act did not specify which practices were illegal, it led to conflicting court rulings.

TABLE 28.2 Key Antitrust Legislation

Law	Date Enacted	Regulation Enacted
Sherman Act	1890	Made it illegal to monopolize a market or to engage in practices that result in a restraint of trade.
Clayton Act	1914	Outlawed specific practices that discourage competition, including tie-in sales contracts, price discrimination for the purpose of reducing competition, and stock-purchase mergers that would substantially reduce competition.
Federal Trade Commission Act	1914	Created a mechanism to enforce antitrust laws.
Robinson–Patman Act	1936	Prohibited selling products at "unreasonably low prices" with the intent of reducing competition.
Celler–Kefauver Act	1950	Outlawed asset-purchase mergers that would substantially reduce competition.
Hart–Scott–Rodino Act	1980	Extended antitrust legislation to proprietorships and partnerships.

Many of the ambiguities of the Sherman Act were resolved by the Clayton Act of 1914. The Clayton Act outlawed specific practices that discourage competition, including tie-in sales contracts and price discrimination that reduces competition. The act also outlawed mergers resulting from the purchase of a competitor's stock when such a merger would substantially reduce competition.

Subsequent legislation clarified and extended antitrust laws. The Robinson–Patman Act of 1936 prohibited predatory pricing. The Celler–Kefauver Act of 1950 closed a loophole in the Clayton Act by prohibiting one firm from purchasing another firm's physical assets, such as buildings and equipment, when the acquisition would reduce competition substantially. The Hart–Scott–Rodino Act of 1980 extended antitrust legislation to proprietorships and partnerships. Before this act, antitrust legislation applied only to corporations.

application 3

MERGER OF PENNZOIL AND QUAKER STATE

APPLYING THE CONCEPTS #3: How does a merger affect prices?

In 1998, Pennzoil Motor Oils purchased Quaker State Motor oils in an acquisition valued at $1 billion. The merger brought together two of the five brands of premium motor oil, with a combined market share of 38% (29% for Pennzoil and 9% for Quaker State). The antitrust agencies approved the merger without any modifications. A recent study of the merger concludes that the new company increased the price of the Quaker State products by roughly 5%, but did not change the price of Pennzoil products. The market share of Pennzoil products increased, while the market shares of Quaker State products decreased.

The study also examines the price effects of four other mergers. In three of four cases, the merger increased prices, with price hikes between 3 and 7 percent. The modest price effects might be surprising to (1) people who expect relatively large positive price effects as firms exploit their greater market power and (2) people who expect negative price effects as the firms become more efficient. **Related to Exercise 2.5.**

SOURCE: Based on Orley Ashenfelter and Daniel Hosken, "The effects of mergers on consumer prices: Evidence from five selected case studies," NBER Working Paper (2008).

application 4

FAQ ABOUT PREDATORY PRICING FROM THE FTC

APPLYING THE CONCEPTS: What is predatory pricing?

The Federal Trade Commission (FTC) is responsible for enforcing laws against predatory pricing. Consider the following FAQ dialog from the FTC web site.

> Q: The gas station down the street offers a discount program that gives members cents off every gallon purchased. I can't match those prices because they are below my costs. If I try to compete at those prices, I will go out of business. Isn't this illegal?
>
> A: Pricing below a *competitor's* costs occurs in many competitive markets and generally does not violate the antitrust laws. Sometimes the low-pricing firm is simply more efficient. Pricing below your own costs is also not a violation of the law unless it is part of a strategy to eliminate competitors, and when that strategy has a dangerous probability of creating a monopoly for the discounting firm so that it can raise prices far into the future and recoup its losses. In markets with a large number of sellers, such as gasoline retailing, it is unlikely that one company could price below cost long enough to drive out a significant number of rivals and attain a dominant position. **Related to Exercise 2.6.**

SOURCE: Federal Trade Commission, *FTC Guide to the Antitrust Laws* (Washington DC, 2010).

SUMMARY

In this chapter, we've explored public policies for markets with a few dominant firms. In the case of natural monopoly, the government can regulate prices. In other industries, the government uses antitrust policies to affect the number of firms in the market, encouraging competition that leads to lower prices. Here are the main points of the chapter:

1 A natural monopoly occurs when there are large-scale economies in production, so the market can support only one firm.

2 Under an average-cost pricing policy, the regulated price for a natural monopoly is equal to the average cost of production.

3 The government uses antitrust policy to break up some dominant firms, prevent some corporate mergers, and regulate business practices that reduce competition.

4 The modern approach to merger policy uses price data to predict the effects of a merger.

5 In most circumstances, predatory pricing is unprofitable because the monopoly power is costly to acquire and hard to maintain.

6 The deregulation of the airline industry led to more competition and lower prices on average, but higher prices in some markets.

KEY TERMS

merger, p. 616

tie-in sales, p. 619

trust, p. 615

predatory pricing, p. 619

EXERCISES

All problems are assignable in MyEconLab.

28.1 Natural Monopoly

1.1 Arrows up or down: At a natural monopolist's current level of output, marginal cost exceeds marginal revenue. The firm should ________ its output and ________ its price.

1.2 The entry of a second firm shifts the demand curve of the original firm to the ________, so that at each price the original firm will sell a(n) ________ quantity.

1.3 A natural monopoly occurs when the long-run cost curve lies entirely ________ (above/below) the demand curve of the typical firm in a two-firm market.

1.4 Under an average-cost pricing policy, the maximum price is shown by the intersection of the ________ curve and the ________ curve.

1.5 When the British switched from private water supply to public supply, the quality of water, consumption per capita ________, and capital cost per unit of output ________. (Related to Application 1 on page 614.)

1.6 Sirius XM Radio became profitable—just barely—with about ________ subscribers. (Related to Application 2 on page 615.)

1.7 **Decrease in Cable Demand.** Consider a cable TV company that has a fixed cost of $48 million and a marginal cost of $5 per subscriber. The company is regulated with an average-cost pricing policy.

a. The first two columns of the following table show three points on the initial demand curve. For example, at a price of $15 the quantity demanded is six million subscribers. For each $2 reduction in price, the number of subscribers increases by one million. Fill in the blanks in the following table. The regulated price is ________.

Price	Subscribers (Millions)	Average Cost
$15	6	
13	7	
11	8	

b. Suppose the demand for the product decreases, with the demand curve shifting to the left by one million subscribers. Fill in the blanks in the following table. The new regulated price is $________.

Price	Subscribers (Millions)	Average Cost
$15		
13		
11		

1.8 **Environmental Costs for Regulated Monopoly.** The Bonneville Power Administration (BPA) is a regulated monopoly in the Northwest that uses dozens of hydroelectric dams to generate electricity. Unfortunately, the BPA's dams block the paths of migrating fish, contributing to the decline of several species. Suppose that BPA spends $100 million to make its hydroelectric dams less hazardous for migrating fish. Who will bear the cost of this program?

1.9 **From Private to Public Water Supply.** Consider the British experience with water provision. Suppose that an unregulated private monopoly has a price of

$3 per unit, a quantity of 10 million units, an average cost of $2 per unit, and a constant marginal cost of $1. (Related to Application 1 on page 614.)

a. Use a graph to show the price, quantity, and average cost as an outcome of profit maximization.

b. Use your graph to show the effects of average-cost regulation on the price, the average cost, and the quantity of output.

1.10 **Satellite Radio Merger.** Suppose each of the two satellite radio firms initially has 9.5 million subscribers and generates negative economic profit: Average cost exceeds the $13 price. Assume that the marginal cost is constant at $2 per subscriber. (Related to Application 2 on page 615.)

a. Use a graph to show the average-cost curve and firm-specific demand curve for one of the two satellite firms.

b. Suppose the two firms merge into a single firm. The profit-maximizing price is $13 and the average cost is $12. Illustrate with a graph.

28.2 Antitrust Policy

2.1 The purpose of antitrust policy is to promote __________, which leads to lower __________.

2.2 There are three types of antitrust policies: (1) __________, (2) __________, and (3) __________.

2.3 In the Staples case discussed in this chapter, the data showed that competition with Office Depot led to __________ prices, suggesting that a merger would harm __________.

2.4 In the Interstate Baking case discussed in this chapter, scanner data showed that the products of Interstate and Continental Baking were __________, so a merger would lead to higher __________.

2.5 Predatory pricing provides a practical and effective means of getting and keeping a monopoly. __________ (True/False)

2.6 The merger of companies with two of the top five brands of motor oil (Pennzoil and Quaker State) increased the price of one of the brands by roughly __________ percent (1, 5, 20, 50) percent. (Related to Application 3 on page 620.)

2.7 Pricing below a competitor's cost is __________ (legal/illegal). Pricing below your own cost is illegal if it is part of a strategy to __________ and then __________ prices. (Related to Application 4 on page 621.)

2.8 **Incentive to Raise Prices after a Merger.** Suppose the merger of two firms, Heinz and Beech-Nut, will reduce the price elasticity of demand for each firm's product from 3.0 to 1.50. For each firm, the average cost of production is constant at $5 per unit. Suppose Heinz initially has a price of $10 and is considering raising the price to $11.

a. Fill in the blanks in the following table, showing the payoffs from raising the price before the merger (elasticity = 3.0) and after the merger (elasticity = 1.50).

Price	Quantity	Total Revenue	Total Cost	Profit
Initial: $10	100	$1,000	$500	$500
New: $11 Before merger: Elasticity of demand = 3.0				
New: $11 After merger: Elasticity of demand = 1.50				

b. Before the merger, raising the price would __________ the firm's profit. After the merger, raising the price would __________ the firm's profit.

c. Why is it reasonable to assume that the merger will decrease the elasticity of demand for each firm's products?

2.9 **Recovering the Acquisition Cost.** The long-run average cost of production is constant at $6 per unit. Suppose firm X acquires Y at a cost of $24 million and increases the price to $14. At the new price, X sells 1.5 million units per year.

a. How does the acquisition affect X's annual profit?

b. How many years will it take for X to recover the cost of acquiring Y?

2.10 **Check YellowPages.com?** On Yellin's first day on the job as an economist with the FTC, she was put on a team examining a proposed merger between the country's second- and fourth-largest hardware store chains. Her job was to predict whether a merger would increase hardware prices. Her boss handed her some CDs with checkout scanner data from the second-largest chain. Each CD contained scanner data from one small town, listing the prices and quantities of hammers, wrenches, nuts, bolts, rakes, glue, drills, and hundreds of other hardware products. Her boss also gave her the Web address for YellowPages.com. How can she use the information in the disks and YellowPages.com to make a prediction?

2.11 Cost Savings from a Merger. Consider the following statement from a firm that has proposed a merger between two companies: "The two companies could save about $50 million per year by combining our production, marketing, and administrative operations. In other words, we could realize substantial economies of scale. Therefore, the government should allow the merger." In light of the new guidelines concerning mergers, how would you react to this statement?

2.12 Deadweight Loss from a Merger. Consider a market that is initially served by two firms, each of which charges a price of $10 and sells 100 units of the good. The long-run average cost of production is constant at $6 per unit. Suppose a merger increases the price to $14 and reduces the total quantity sold from 200 to 150. Compute the consumer loss associated with the merger. How does it compare to the increase in profit? What is the net loss from the merger?

NOTES

1. "The Economics of Antitrust: The Trustbuster's New Tools," *Economist*, May 2, 1998, 62–64; *Federal Trade Commission v. Staples, Inc.*, 970 F. Supp. 1066 (D.D.C. 1997, Hogan, J); U.S. Federal Trade Commission, *Promoting Competition, Protecting Consumers: A Plain English Guide to Antitrust Laws*, www.ftc.gov/bc/compguide/index.htm (accessed June 28, 2006).

2. John R. Wilke, "New Antitrust Rules May Ease Path to Mergers," *Wall Street Journal*, April 9, 1997.

3. "The Economics of Antitrust: The Trustbuster's New Tools," *Economist*, May 2, 1998, 62–64.

CHAPTER

29

Imperfect Information: Adverse Selection and Moral Hazard

"So, why are you selling this used car?"

The buyers of used cars ask this question frequently and then listen carefully to the answer. Assuming the car seller is honest, the answer the buyer hopes for is "Because I need a different car for my new job," or "I buy a new car every three years." The buyer wants to avoid sellers who are trying to get rid of a "lemon"—a car that breaks down frequently and generates large repair bills. People don't ask this sort of question in other markets. For example, no one ever asks, "So, why are you selling this pizza?"

"Does my insurance policy cover accidental death from bungee jumping?"

Life is risky, and people buy insurance to decrease their financial losses from events such as theft, sickness, injury, and death. The question from the potential bungee jumper reveals an important fact about insurance: It causes people to take greater risks because they know insurance will cover part of the cost of an accident.

LEARNING OBJECTIVES

- Explain the notion of adverse selection for buyers.
- Discuss the possible responses to adverse selection for buyers.
- Explain the notion of adverse selection for sellers.
- Explain the notion of moral hazard.
- Use the marginal principle to describe optimal search by consumers.

MyEconLab
MyEconLab helps you master each objective and study more efficiently.

This chapter explores the role of information in markets and what happens when one side of the market has better information than the other. In the market for used cars, sellers know more about the quality of the product than buyers do. In the market for life insurance, buyers know more about the risks they face than sellers do. As we saw earlier in the book, the model of supply and demand is based on several assumptions, one of which is that buyers and sellers have enough information to make informed choices. In a world of fully informed buyers and sellers, markets operate smoothly, generating an equilibrium price and an equilibrium quantity for each good. In a world with imperfect information, some goods will be sold in very small numbers or not sold at all. In addition, buyers and sellers will use resources to acquire information to help make better decisions. The 2001 Nobel Prize in economics was awarded to three economists—George Akerlof, Michael Spence, and Joseph Stiglitz—who studied the effects of imperfect information on all sorts of markets.

29.1 Adverse Selection for Buyers: The Lemons Problem

The classic example of a market with imperfect information is the market for used cars.[1] Suppose there are two types of cars, low quality and high quality. A low-quality car, also known as a "lemon," breaks down frequently and has relatively high repair costs. A high-quality car, also known as a "plum," is reliable and has relatively low repair costs. Suppose buyers cannot distinguish between lemons and plums. Although a buyer can get some information about a particular car by looking at the car and taking it for a test drive, the informati on gleaned from this kind of inspection is not enough to determine the quality of the car. In contrast, a person selling a car after owning it for a while knows from experience whether the car is a lemon or a plum. We say there is **asymmetric information** in a market if one side of the market—either buyers or sellers—has better information than the other side. Because buyers cannot distinguish between lemons and plums, there will be a single market for used automobiles: Both types of cars will be sold together in this **mixed market** for the same price.

asymmetric information
A situation in which one side of the market—either buyers or sellers—has better information than the other.

mixed market
A market in which goods of different qualities are sold for the same price.

Uninformed Buyers and Knowledgeable Sellers

How much is a consumer willing to pay for a used car that could be either a lemon or a plum? To determine a consumer's willingness to pay in a mixed market with both lemons and plums, we must answer three questions:

1. How much is the consumer willing to pay for a plum?
2. How much is the consumer willing to pay for a lemon?
3. What is the chance that a used car purchased in the mixed market will be of low quality?

Suppose the typical buyer is willing to pay $4,000 for a plum and $2,000 for a lemon. The buyer is willing to pay less for a lemon because it is less reliable and has higher repair costs. For someone willing to put up with the hassle and repair expense, a lemon is a reasonable car. That's why the typical buyer is willing to pay $2,000, not $0, for a low-quality car we tag with the label "lemon." Someone who pays $2,000 and gets a lemon is just as happy as someone who pays $4,000 and gets a plum.

Consumer expectations play a key role in determining the market outcome when there is imperfect information. Suppose half the used cars *on the road* are lemons, and consumers know this. A reasonable expectation for consumers is that half the cars *on the used-car market* will be lemons, too. In other words, buyers initially expect a 50–50 split between the two types of cars. A reasonable assumption is that a buyer in the mixed market is willing to pay the average value of the two types of cars, or $3,000. In other words, a buyer is willing to pay $3,000 for a 50–50 chance of getting either a plum or a lemon.

The current owner of a used car knows from everyday experience whether the car is a lemon or a plum. Given the single market price for all used cars, lemons and plums alike, the question for each owner is "Should I sell my car?" The answers to this question are shown by the two supply curves in Figure 29.1, one for lemons and one for plums:

- ***Lemon supply.*** As shown by the lower curve, the minimum supply price for lemons is $500: At any price less than $500, no lemons will be supplied. Lemons have a lower minimum price because they are worth less to their current owners. The number of lemons supplied increases with price. For example, 80 cars will be supplied at a price of $3,000 (point *b*).
- ***Plum supply.*** As shown by the upper curve, the minimum supply price for plums is $2,500: At any price less than $2,500, no plums will be supplied. Consistent with the law of supply, the higher the price of used cars, the larger the number of plums supplied. For example, 20 plums will be supplied at a price of $3,000 (point *a*).

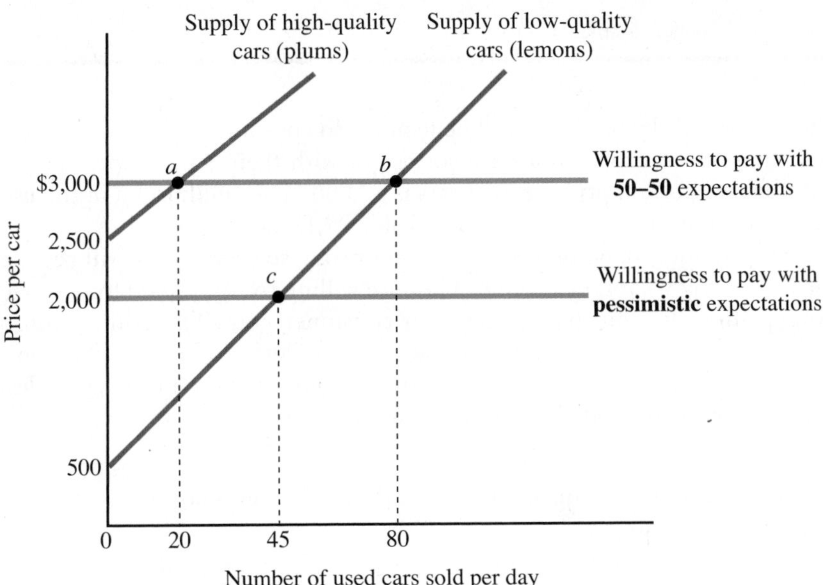

◄ **FIGURE 29.1**
All Used Cars on the Market Are Lemons
If buyers assume that there is a 50–50 chance of getting a lemon or a plum, they are willing to pay $3,000 for a used car. At this price, 20 plums are supplied (point *a*) along with 80 lemons (point *b*). This is not an equilibrium because consumers' expectations of a 50–50 split are not realized. If consumers become pessimistic and assume that all cars on the market will be lemons, they are willing to pay $2,000 for a used car. At this price, only lemons will be supplied (point *c*). Consumer expectations are realized, so the equilibrium is shown by point *c*, with an equilibrium price of $2,000.

Equilibrium with All Low-Quality Goods

Table 29.1 shows two scenarios for our hypothetical used-car market, based on the supply curves shown in Figure 29.1. In the first column, we assume buyers have 50–50 expectations about the quality of used cars. As we saw earlier, if buyers expect a 50–50 split between lemons and plums, the typical buyer will be willing to pay $3,000 for a used car. From the supply curves in Figure 29.1, we know that at this price 20 plums and 80 lemons will be supplied, so 80 percent of the used cars (80 of 100) will be lemons. In this case, consumers are too optimistic and underestimate the chance of getting a lemon.

The experiences of these 100 consumers show that the actual chance of getting a lemon is 80 percent, not 50 percent as initially assumed. Once future buyers realize this, they will of course become more pessimistic about the used-car market. Suppose they assume that all the used cars on the market will be lemons. Under this assumption, the typical buyer will be willing to pay only $2,000 (the value of a lemon) for a used car. As shown in Figure 29.1, this price is less than the $2,500 minimum price for supplying plums, so plums will disappear from the used-car market. At a price of $2,000, the quantity of plums supplied is zero, but the quantity of lemons supplied is 45 (point *c*).

TABLE 29.1 Equilibrium with All Low-Quality Goods

	Buyers Initially Have 50–50 Expectations	Equilibrium: Pessimistic Expectations
Demand Side of Market		
Amount buyer is willing to pay for a lemon	$2,000	$2,000
Amount buyer is willing to pay for a plum	$4,000	$4,000
Assumed chance of getting a lemon	50%	100%
Assumed chance of getting a plum	50%	0%
Amount buyer is willing to pay for a used car in mixed market	$3,000	$2,000
Supply Side of Market		
Number of lemons supplied	80	45
Number of plums supplied	20	0
Total number of used cars supplied	100	45
Actual chance of getting a lemon	80%	100%

In other words, all the used cars will be lemons, so consumers' pessimism is justified. Because consumers' expectations are consistent with their actual experiences in the market, the equilibrium price of used cars is $2,000. The equilibrium in the used-car market is shown in the second column of Table 29.1.

In this equilibrium, no plums are bought or sold, so every buyer will get a lemon. People get exactly what they pay for: They are willing to pay $2,000 for a serviceable but low-quality car, and that's what each consumer gets. The domination of the used-car market by lemons is an example of the **adverse-selection problem**. The uninformed side of the market (buyers in this case) must choose from an undesirable or adverse selection of used cars. The asymmetric information in the market generates a downward spiral of price and quality:

adverse-selection problem
A situation in which the uninformed side of the market must choose from an undesirable or adverse selection of goods.

- The presence of low-quality goods on the market pulls down the price consumers are willing to pay.
- The decrease in price decreases the number of high-quality goods supplied, decreasing the average quality of goods on the market.
- This decrease in the average quality of goods on the market pulls down the price consumers are willing to pay again.

In the extreme case, the downward spiral continues until all the cars on the market are lemons.

A Thin Market: Equilibrium with Some High-Quality Goods

The disappearance of plums from our hypothetical used-car market is an extreme case. The plums disappeared from the market because informed plum owners decided to keep their cars rather than sell them at a relatively low price in the used-car market. This outcome would change if the minimum supply price of plums were lower, specifically if it were below $2,000. In this case, most but not all the used cars on the market will be lemons, and some lucky buyers will get plums. In this case, we say asymmetric information generates a **thin market**: Some high-quality goods are sold, but fewer than would be sold in a market with perfect information.

thin market
A market in which some high-quality goods are sold but fewer than would be sold in a market with perfect information.

Figure 29.2 shows the situation that leads to a thin market. The minimum supply price for plums is $1,833, and the quantity of plums supplied increases with the price of used cars. Suppose consumers are initially pessimistic, assuming all cars for sale will be lemons. This means consumers are willing to pay only $2,000 for a used car. Because the minimum supply price for plums ($1,833) is now less than the willingness to pay for a lemon, some plums will be supplied at a price of $2,000. In Figure 29.2, 5 plums and 45 lemons are supplied at this price, so 1 of every 10 buyers will get a plum. In this case, pessimism is not an equilibrium, because some buyers will get plums when they expect lemons. This is also shown in the first column of Table 29.2.

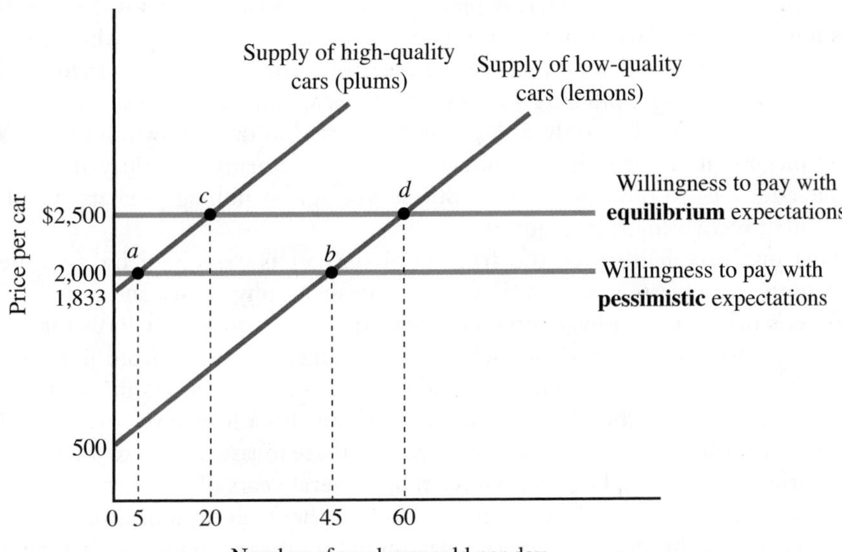

▲ **FIGURE 29.2**
The Market for High-Quality Cars (Plums) Is Thin
If buyers are pessimistic and assume that only lemons will be sold, they are willing to pay $2,000 for a used car. At this price, 5 plums are supplied (point *a*), along with 45 lemons (point *b*). This is not an equilibrium because 10 percent of consumers get plums, contrary to their expectations. If consumers assume that there is a 25 percent chance of getting a plum, they are willing to pay $2,500 for a used car. At this price, 20 plums are supplied (point *c*), along with 60 lemons (point *d*). This is an equilibrium because 25 percent of consumers get plums, consistent with their expectations. Consumer expectations are realized, so the equilibrium is shown by points *c* and *d*.

TABLE 29.2 A Thin Market for High-Quality Goods

	Initial Pessimistic Expectations	Equilibrium: 75–25 Expectations
Demand Side of Market		
Amount buyer is willing to pay for a lemon	$2,000	$2,000
Amount buyer is willing to pay for a plum	$4,000	$4,000
Assumed chance of getting a lemon	100%	75%
Assumed chance of getting a plum	0%	25%
Amount buyer is willing to pay for a used car in mixed market	$2,000	$2,500
Supply Side of Market		
Number of lemons supplied	45	60
Number of plums supplied	5	20
Total number of used cars supplied	50	80
Actual chance of getting a lemon	90%	75%

application 1

ARE BASEBALL PITCHERS LIKE USED CARS?

APPLYING THE CONCEPTS #1: What is adverse selection for buyers?

Professional baseball teams compete with each other for players. After six years of play in the major leagues, a player has the option of becoming a free agent and offering his services to the highest bidder. A player is likely to switch teams if the new team offers him a higher salary than his original team. A puzzling feature of the free-agent market is that pitchers who switch teams are more prone to injuries than pitchers who don't. On average, pitchers who switch teams spend 28 days per season on the disabled list, compared to only 5 days for pitchers who do not switch teams. This doesn't mean that all the switching pitchers are lemons; many are injury-free and are valuable additions to their new teams. But on average, switching pitchers spend five times longer recovering from injuries.

This puzzling feature of the free-agent market is explained by asymmetric information and adverse selection. Because the coaches, physicians, and trainers from the player's original team have interacted with the player on a daily basis for several years, they know from experience whether he is likely to suffer from injuries that prevent him from playing. In contrast, the new team has much less information. Its physicians can examine the pitcher, and the team can check league records to see how long the pitcher has spent on the disabled list, but these measures do not eliminate the asymmetric information. The original team has several years of daily experience with the pitcher and has better information about the pitcher's physical health.

Now consider the incentives for a team to outbid another team for a pitcher. Suppose the market price for pitchers is $1 million per year, and a pitcher who is currently with the Detroit Tigers is offered this salary by another team. If the Tigers think the pitcher is likely to spend a lot of time next season recovering from injuries, they won't try to outbid the other team for the pitcher: They will let the pitcher switch teams. But if the Tigers think the pitcher will be injury-free and productive, he will be worth more than $1 million to them, and they will outbid other teams and keep him. That's why an injury-prone pitcher is more likely to switch teams. As in the used-car market, there are many "lemons" on the used-pitcher market. The market for baseball players playing other positions does not suffer from adverse selection, perhaps because the injuries that affect their performance are easier for other teams to detect.

Although you may think it's bizarre to compare baseball pitchers to used cars, people in baseball don't think so. They recognize the similarity between the two markets. Jackie Moore, who managed a free-agent camp where teams looking for players can see free agents in action, sounded like a used-car salesman: "We want to get players off the lot. We want to cut a deal. How many camps can you go into where you can look at a player and take him home with you?" **Related to Exercises 1.7, 1.8, and 1.16.**

SOURCES: Based on Kenneth Lehn, "Information Asymmetries in Baseball's Free Agent Market," *Economic Inquiry* 22 (January 1984): 37–44; Associated Press, "Free Agents at End of Baseball's Earth," *Corvallis Gazette-Times*, April 15, 1995.

In equilibrium, consumer expectations about the chances of getting the two types of cars are realized. Suppose consumers expect one of every four cars to be a plum. Let's assume each consumer is willing to pay $2,500 for a used car under these circumstances. Consumers are willing to pay a bit more than the value of a lemon because there is a small chance of getting a plum. In Figure 29.2, at this price 20 plums are supplied (point *c*) and 60 lemons are supplied (point *d*), so in fact one in four consumers actually gets a plum. This is an equilibrium because 25 percent of the cars sold are plums and 75 percent are lemons, consistent with consumers' expectations. This is also shown in the second column of Table 29.2.

Evidence of the Lemons Problem

The lemons model makes two predictions about markets with asymmetric information. First, the presence of low-quality goods in a market will at least reduce the number of high-quality goods in the market and may even eliminate them. Second, buyers and sellers will respond to the lemons problem by investing in information and other means of distinguishing between low-quality and high-quality goods. What is the evidence for the lemons model?

Studies of the market for used pickup trucks have provided mixed results concerning the lemons problem.[2] It appears that for trucks less than 10 years old, those sold on the market are just as reliable, on average, as those that remain with their current owners. These studies provide support for the second implication of the theory of lemons, that people acquire information and develop effective means to deal with the problem of asymmetric information. In contrast, there does seem to be a lemons problem for trucks at least 10 years old, which represent about one-third of transactions. Compared to old trucks that remain with their current owners, old trucks that are sold have significantly higher repair costs, with a difference in cost of about 45 percent. Old trucks that are sold have a much higher probability of requiring engine and transmission repairs.

29.2 Responding to the Lemons Problem

In a market with asymmetric information, there are strong incentives for buyers and sellers to solve the lemons problem. In our example of a thin market, the price of a used car is $2,500, but consumers are willing to pay $4,000 for a plum. This $1,500 gap between the willingness to pay for a plum and the price in the mixed market provides an opportunity for mutually beneficial exchange. A person who owns a high-quality car may not be willing to sell it for $2,500, but might accept something closer to $4,000, an amount a buyer is willing to pay. The challenge is to identify a high-quality car in the mixed market.

Buyers Invest in Information

In our model of the thin market, one in four buyers pays $2,500 to get a plum worth $4,000. The more information a buyer has, the greater the chance of picking a plum from the cars in the mixed market. Suppose a buyer gets enough information to identify the plums in a market. The buyer could purchase a plum worth $4,000 at the prevailing price of $2,500, generating a gain of $1,500. A buyer can get information about individual cars by taking the car to a mechanic for a careful inspection. In addition, a buyer can get general information about the reliability of different models from magazines and the Internet. *Consumer Reports* publishes information on repair histories of different models and computes a "Trouble" index, scoring each model on a scale of 1 to 5. By consulting these information sources, a buyer improves the chances of getting a high-quality car. Another information source is Carfax.com, which provides information on individual cars, including their accident histories.

Consumer Satisfaction Scores from ValueStar and eBay

The problem of asymmetric information in consumer goods such as cars also occurs for some types of consumer services. Most consumers can't easily determine the quality of service they will receive from an auto repair shop, a landscaper, or a plumber. How can a high-quality service provider distinguish itself from low-quality providers?

Some organizations provide information about firms that provide consumers services such as landscaping, auto repair, and home improvement. ValueStar is a consumer guide and business directory that uses customer satisfaction surveys to determine how well a firm does relative to its competitors in providing quality service. To earn the right to display a Customer-Rated seal from ValueStar, a firm must prove that it has all the required licenses and insurance and must agree to pay for a survey of its past customers. ValueStar uses consumer surveys to compute a consumer-satisfaction score for each company. Any company receiving a score of at least 85 out of 100 has the right to display a Customer-Rated Gold seal for a one-year period. In New York City, servicemagic.com rates all kinds of contractors and household service providers, with scores based on reports from consumers.

Online consumers help each other by rating online sellers. On eBay, buyers must rely on sellers to honestly disclose the quality of the goods they are auctioning and to promptly ship them once a consumer pays. Buyers help other purchasers distinguish "good" from "bad" sellers on eBay by rating them online with "stars," indicating their satisfaction with their transactions. The same sort of information is provided by people who buy second-hand books.

Guarantees and Lemons Laws

Used-car sellers also have an incentive to solve the lemons problem. If a plum owner persuades a buyer that his or her car is a plum and then sells the car for $4,000 rather than $2,500, the seller's gain is $1,500. Sellers can identify a car as a plum in a sea of lemons by offering one of the following guarantees:

- ***Money-back guarantees.*** The seller could promise to refund the $4,000 price if the car turns out to be a lemon. Because the car is in fact a plum—a fact known by the seller—the buyer will not ask for a refund, so both the buyer and the seller will be happy with the transaction.
- ***Warranties and repair guarantees.*** The seller could promise to cover any extraordinary repair costs for one year. Because the car is a plum, there won't be any extraordinary costs, so both the buyer and the seller will be happy with the transaction.

Many states have laws that require automakers to buy back cars that experience frequent problems in the first year of use. For example, under California's Song-Beverly Consumer Warranty Act, also known as the "Lemons Law," auto dealers are required to repurchase vehicles that have been brought back for repair at least four times for the same problem or have been in the mechanic's shop for at least 30 calendar days in the first year following purchase. A vehicle repurchased under the lemons law must be fixed before it is sold to another customer and must be identified as a lemon with a stamp on the title and a sticker on the car that says "lemons law buyback." One problem with enforcing these laws is that lemons can cross state lines without a paper trail. The interstate commerce in lemons has led to new laws in some states requiring the branding of lemons on vehicle titles to follow the car when it crosses state lines.

application 2

REGULATION OF THE CALIFORNIA KIWIFRUIT MARKET

APPLYING THE CONCEPTS #2: How can government solve the adverse-selection problem?

Kiwifruit is subject to imperfect information because buyers cannot determine its sweetness—its quality level—by simple inspection. The sweetness level at the time of consumption is determined by the fruit's maturity—its sugar content at the time of harvest. Kiwifruit continues to convert starch into sugar after it is picked, but fruit that is picked early has a low sugar content at harvest time and never tastes sweet. There is asymmetric information because producers know the maturity of the fruit, but fruit wholesalers and grocery stores, who buy fruit at the time of harvest, cannot determine whether a piece of fruit will ultimately be sweet or sour.

Before 1987, kiwifruit from California suffered from the "lemons" problem. Maturity levels of the fruit varied across producers. On average, the sugar content at the time of harvest was below the industry standard, established by kiwifruit from New Zealand. Given the large number of "lemons" among California kiwifruit, grocery stores were not willing to pay as much for California fruit. In other words, the presence of low-quality (immature) fruit in the mixed market pulled down the price of California fruit. Mature kiwifruit is more costly to produce than immature fruit, and the low price decreased the production of mature fruit. This result is similar to the way low used-car prices decrease the number of high-quality used cars on the market. In general, adverse selection led to low prices and a relatively large volume of low-quality kiwifruit from California.

In 1987, California producers implemented a federal marketing order to address the lemon–kiwi problem. The federal order specified a minimum maturity standard, and as the average quality of California fruit increased, so did the price. Within a few years, the gap between California and New Zealand prices had decreased significantly. **Related to Exercises 2.3 and 2.6.**

SOURCE: Based on Christopher Ferguson and Hoy Carman, "Kiwifruit and the 'Lemon' Problem: Do Minimum Quality Standards Work?" (working paper, International Food and Agribusiness Management Association, 1999).

29.3 Adverse Selection for Sellers: Insurance

So far, we have explored the effects of asymmetric information when sellers are more knowledgeable than buyers. The same sort of problems occur when buyers are more knowledgeable than sellers. The best example of superior knowledge on the demand side of the market is insurance. A person who buys an insurance policy knows much more about his or her risks and needs for insurance than the insurance company knows. For example, when you buy an auto insurance policy, you know more than your insurance company about your driving habits and your chances of getting into an accident. We'll see that insurance markets suffer from the adverse-selection problem: Insurance companies get an adverse or undesirable selection of customers.

Health Insurance

To illustrate the information problems in the market for insurance, consider health insurance provided to individual consumers. Suppose there are two types of consumers: low-cost consumers with relatively low medical expenses of $2,000 per year and high-cost consumers with relatively high medical expenses of $6,000 per year. The amount a consumer is willing to pay for an insurance policy covering all medical expenses increases with the anticipated medical expenses, so high-cost people are willing to pay more for health insurance.

The insurance company cannot distinguish between high-cost and low-cost people, but it still must pick a price for its coverage. To simplify matters, let's assume there are no administrative costs, so the only cost for the insurance company is the medical bills it pays for its customers. Let's also assume the insurance company sets the price equal to its average cost per customer, equal to the total medical bills paid by the insurance company divided by the number of customers. These assumptions simplify the math without affecting the basic results.

What is the insurance company's average cost per customer? To determine the average cost in a mixed market, we must answer three questions:

- What is the cost of providing medical care to a high-cost person?
- What is the cost of providing medical care to a low-cost person?
- What fraction of the customers are low-cost people?

Suppose that half the population is high cost and the other half is low cost. Let's assume the insurance company is somewhat naive and initially assumes that the mix of insurance buyers will be the same as the population mix. In other words, the insurance company initially assumes that half its customers will be high cost and half will be low cost. In this case, the average cost per customer is $4,000, that is, the average of $2,000 for each low-cost customer and $6,000 for each high-cost customer.

There is asymmetric information in the insurance market because potential buyers know from everyday experience and family histories what type of customer they are, either low cost or high cost. For each person, the question is "Given the single market price for all insurance, for low-cost and high-cost people alike, should I buy insurance?" The answers to this question are shown in two demand curves in Figure 29.3. The demand curve for the high-cost people is higher than

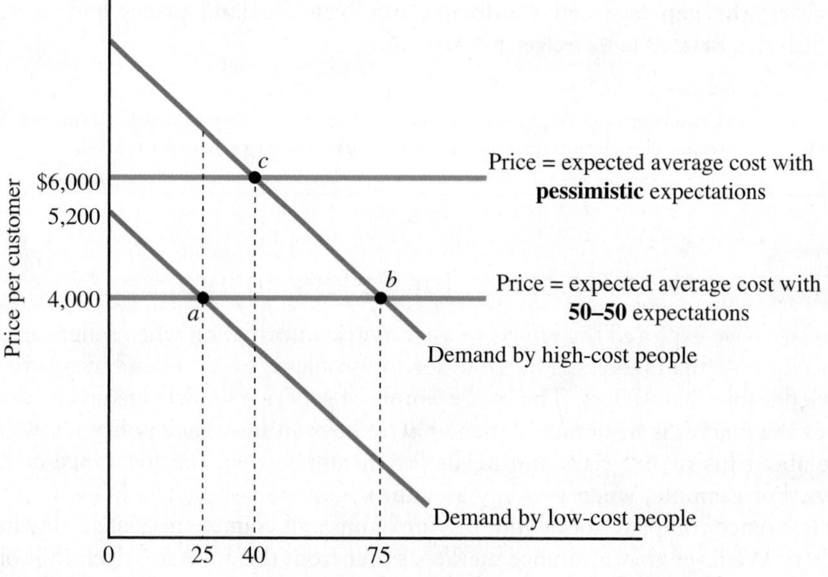

▲ **FIGURE 29.3**

All Insurance Customers Are High-Cost People

If insurance companies assume there will be a 50–50 split between high-cost and low-cost customers, the average cost of insurance and its price is $4,000. At this price, there are 25 low-cost customers (point *a*) and 75 high-cost customers (point *b*). This is not an equilibrium, because 75 percent of insurance buyers are high-cost customers, contrary to the expectations of a 50–50 split. If insurance companies become pessimistic and assume that all buyers will be high-cost consumers, the average cost and price is $6,000. The insurance company's expectations are realized, so the equilibrium is shown by point *c*.

the curve for the low-cost people, reflecting their larger benefits from having medical insurance.

Equilibrium with All High-Cost Consumers

Table 29.3 shows two scenarios for our hypothetical insurance market, with numbers based on the demand curves shown in Figure 29.3. In the first column, firms initially assume a 50–50 mix of customers. As we saw earlier, if sellers expect a 50–50 split between the two types, the average cost per customer is $4,000, and that's the price they charge for medical insurance. From the demand curves in Figure 29.3, we know that at this price 25 low-cost people will buy insurance (point *a*), along with 75 high-cost people (point *b*). In this case, insurance companies are too optimistic and underestimate the fraction of customers with large medical bills. The actual fraction of high-cost customers is 75 percent, and the actual average cost is $5,000 (equal to 0.25 times $2,000, plus 0.75 times $6,000). The company's average cost of $5,000 exceeds its price of $4,000, so the firm will lose money.

TABLE 29.3 Equilibrium with All High-Cost Customers

	50–50 Expectations	Equilibrium: Pessimistic Expectations
Supply Side of Market		
Cost of serving a high-cost customer	$6,000	$6,000
Cost of serving a low-cost customer	$2,000	$2,000
Assumed fraction of high-cost customers	50%	100%
Assumed chance of low-cost customers	50%	0%
Expected average cost per customer (price)	$4,000	$6,000
Demand Side of Market		
Number of high-cost customers	75	40
Number of low-cost customers	25	0
Total number of customers	100	40
Actual fraction of high-cost customers	75%	100%
Actual average cost per customer	$5,000	$6,000

Suppose that after observing the outcome in the first column, insurance companies become very pessimistic. They assume that all their customers will be high-cost people. Under this assumption, the average cost per customer is $6,000, the average cost per high-cost customer, and that's the pessimistic price. As shown in Figure 29.3, this price exceeds the maximum that low-cost people are willing to pay for insurance ($5,200), so none of the low-cost consumers will buy insurance at this price. But a total of 40 high-cost consumers will buy insurance at this price (point *c*). In other words, all the customers will be high-cost people, so the company's pessimism is justified. The price chosen by the insurance company equals the actual average cost of providing service, so the equilibrium is shown by point *c*, with an equilibrium price of $6,000. This equilibrium is shown in the second column of Table 29.3.

The domination of the insurance market by high-cost people is another example of the adverse-selection problem. The uninformed side of the market (sellers in this case) must choose from an undesirable or adverse selection of consumers. The asymmetric information in the market generates an upward spiral of price and average cost of service:

- The presence of high-cost consumers in the market pulls up the average cost of service, pulling up the price.
- The increase in price decreases the number of low-cost consumers who purchase insurance.
- This decrease in the number of low-cost consumers pulls up the average cost of insurance.
- In the extreme case, the upward spiral continues until all insurance customers are high-cost people.

Our example of health insurance indicates that only high-cost people buy insurance. A more realistic outcome is a thin market, with a relatively small number of low-cost people buying insurance. The adverse-selection problem could be less severe, but it will still be present as long as insurance companies cannot distinguish perfectly between low-cost and high-cost people.

Responding to Adverse Selection in Insurance: Group Insurance

Insurance companies use group insurance plans to diminish the adverse-selection problem. By enrolling all the employees of an organization in one or two insurance plans, they ensure that all workers, not just high-cost people, join the pool of consumers.

In our example, group insurance would generate a 50–50 mix of low-cost and high-cost customers, and the break-even price would be $6,000. In contrast, when a firm sells insurance to individuals, the low-cost people have an incentive to go without insurance, leading to the adverse-selection problem and higher prices.

experience rating
A situation in which insurance companies charge different prices for medical insurance to different firms depending on the past medical bills of a firm's employees.

Most insurance companies use **experience rating** to set their prices for group insurance. They charge different prices to different firms, depending on the past medical bills of the firm's employees. A firm whose employees have low medical bills pays a low price for its employees' health insurance. Experience rating gives firms an incentive to decrease the health costs of their workers by investing in safety and health programs for them. Firms also have an incentive to avoid hiring applicants with health problems. Under experience rating, a firm that hires a worker with above-average medical costs will ultimately pay a higher price for its group insurance.

The Uninsured

One implication of asymmetric information in the insurance market is that many low-cost consumers who are not eligible for a group plan will not carry insurance. Given the adverse-selection problem, the price for an individual insurance plan is relatively high, and many consumers go without insurance. This is a contributing factor to the problem of the uninsured. In 2008, about 47 million people (about 14 percent of the U.S. population) were not covered by health insurance. About 70 percent of working-age people have private insurance, and another 10 percent have some sort of government insurance, leaving 20 percent without health insurance. In general, the uninsured are the people and their families who do not receive insurance through their employers, are unemployed or between jobs, or are poor but do not qualify for Medicaid. The uninsured obtain care for medical emergencies but typically do not receive routine—and ultimately less costly—preventive care.

In 2010 the U.S. Congress approved legislation to regulate the nation's health insurance markets and reduce the number of uninsured people. The new law will prevent insurance companies from denying coverage based on preexisting conditions and outlaws lifetime caps on reimbursement. In addition, the law requires individuals to get health insurance, and imposes penalties on people who remain uncovered. Other provisions impose penalties on employers that do not provide insurance to their employees. For small businesses and low-income individuals, the law provides subsidies and tax credits to partly offset the cost of insurance. The law is expected to significantly reduce the number of uninsured citizens.

Other Types of Insurance

The same logic of adverse selection applies to the markets for other types of insurance, including life insurance, home insurance for theft and property damage, and automobile insurance. Buyers know more than sellers about their risks, so there is adverse selection, with high-risk individuals more likely to buy insurance. Life insurance companies provide group coverage to get a broader base of consumers and also try to distinguish between high-risk and low-risk people with physical exams. However, because the companies are unable to distinguish between high-risk and low-risk people with sufficient precision, the adverse-selection problem persists.

application 3

UNISEX AUTOMOBILE INSURANCE IN THE EUROPEAN UNION

APPLYING THE CONCEPTS #3: What is adverse selection for sellers?

Starting in 2012, the European Union prohibits gender discrimination (different prices for men and women) in automobile insurance. On average, women are much safer drivers: in Britain, the average insurance claim of an 18-year-old woman is about £2,700, compared to £4,400 for an 18-year-old man. Before the unisex pricing policy, women paid lower prices because they were less costly for insurance companies. The ban on gender discrimination is expected to increase prices for women by about 25 percent and decrease insurance prices for men by about 10 percent.

Unisex insurance pricing will promote adverse selection in the insurance market. Some women will respond to the higher price by dropping out of the insurance pool, while some men will respond to the lower price by entering the pool. The pool will have a more costly (more adverse) mix of customers, leading to a higher average cost for insurance companies and a higher price. Unisex pricing promotes adverse selection because it eliminates one way to control adverse selection—a lower price for lower-cost customers. **Related to Exercise 3.3.**

SOURCE: Based on BBC News, "Insurance and pension costs hit by ECJ gender ruling," March 1, 2011.

29.4 Insurance and Moral Hazard

Does insurance affect people's risk-taking behavior? The answer is yes. Insurance causes people to take greater risks because they know part of the cost of an undesirable outcome will be borne by their insurance companies. Here are some examples of people taking greater risks because they have insurance:

- Will Irma buy a fire extinguisher for her kitchen? If she had to pay for any property damage caused by a fire, she would definitely buy a fire extinguisher. But because her homeowner's insurance covers property damage from fires, she doesn't buy a fire extinguisher.
- Will Harry drive his car carefully? If he had to pay for all repairs resulting from a collision out of his own pocket, he would drive very carefully. But because his auto insurance covers some of the repair costs, he drives fast and recklessly.
- Will Flo fly on a commercial airline or hitch a ride with her pilot friend in a four-seat airplane? Traveling in small airplanes is much riskier. If Flo dies in an airplane crash, her family will lose the income she would otherwise earn. If she didn't have life insurance to offset these income losses, she would be less likely to risk harming her family by flying on the small plane instead of the commercial airline. But because she knows her family will collect $1 million in life insurance, she is willing to take the risk.

moral hazard
A situation in which one side of an economic relationship takes undesirable or costly actions that the other side of the relationship cannot observe.

The risky behavior triggered by insurance is an example of the moral-hazard problem. **Moral hazard** occurs when one side of an economic relationship takes undesirable or costly actions that the other side of the relationship cannot observe. For example, Irma's insurance company doesn't know whether she has a fire extinguisher. If there is a fire, Irma's hidden action—going without an extinguisher—is costly for the insurance company. Similarly, Harry's insurance company doesn't know how fast and recklessly he drives, and insurance encourages him to drive recklessly. His hidden action of reckless driving increases the likelihood of a costly accident. Just as collision insurance encourages risky driving, life insurance encourages risky activities such as flying small airplanes, parachuting, and bungee jumping. Similarly, health insurance encourages risky behavior such as smoking, drinking, and unhealthy diets.

Insurance Companies and Moral Hazard

Insurance companies use various measures to decrease the moral-hazard problem. Many insurance policies have a deductible—a dollar amount that a policy holder must pay before getting compensation from the insurance company. For example, if your car insurance policy has a $500 deductible and the damage from a collision is $900, the insurance company will pay you only $400. You pay the other $500 as your deductible. Deductibles reduce the moral-hazard problem because they shift to the policy holder part of the cost of a claim on the policy. Like a deductible, an insurance copayment shifts part of the cost of risky behavior to policy holders and thus reduces the moral-hazard problem.

Savvy insurance companies anticipate moral hazard. To illustrate, suppose 1 of 10 bicycles on your campus was stolen in 2008. If you decide to be the first to offer bicycle theft insurance, you might naively assume that the theft rate wouldn't change. But the moral-hazard problem tells us that people with insurance take greater risks, so we'd expect a higher theft rate on a campus where insurance is widespread. Students who buy theft insurance are likely to be less careful in protecting their bikes, perhaps using flimsy locks or no locks at all. Or they might start leaving their bikes on campus overnight. A savvy insurance company would assume a theft rate higher than 10 percent and set its price accordingly.

Deposit Insurance for Savings and Loans

For another example of moral hazard, consider the insurance provided for bank deposits. When you deposit money in a Savings and Loan (S&L), the money doesn't just sit in a vault. The S&L will invest the money, loaning it out and expecting to make a profit when loans are repaid with interest. Unfortunately, some loans are not repaid, and the S&L could lose money and be unable to return your money. To protect people who put their money in S&Ls and other banks, the Federal Deposit Insurance Corporation (FDIC) insures the first $250,000 of your deposit, so if the S&L goes bankrupt, you'll still get your money back. The government enacted the federal deposit insurance law in 1933 in response to the bank failures of the Great Depression.

How does deposit insurance affect you and the people who manage the S&L? If you know you'll get your money back no matter what happens to the S&L, you may deposit your money there without evaluating the performance of the S&L and the riskiness of its loans to borrowers and investments in the stock market. The manager of an S&L will also be more likely to make risky investments knowing that if it doesn't pay off and the S&L goes bankrupt, the federal government will reimburse depositors. Recognizing this moral hazard problem, the federal government has historically limited S&Ls to relatively safe investments.

In the 1980s, the federal government loosened some of the investment restrictions on S&Ls, and S&L managers began investing in volatile securities, including high-risk commercial mortgages and junk bonds. When these risky investments failed, many of the S&Ls went into bankruptcy. The government then bailed out the failed S&Ls, at a total cost to taxpayers of about $200 billion.

application 4

CAR INSURANCE AND RISKY DRIVING

APPLYING THE CONCEPTS #4: What is moral hazard in car insurance?

The theory of moral hazard suggests that an insured driver, who bears less than the full cost of a collision, will drive less carefully than an uninsured driver. A recent study suggests that the moral-hazard cost of automobile insurance is substantial. When a state makes car insurance compulsory and thus decreases the number of uninsured drivers, roads become more hazardous: The number of collisions and the number of traffic deaths increase. Roads become more dangerous because the newly insured drivers drive less cautiously. The study estimates that a one percentage point decrease in the share of uninsured drivers increases the number of traffic fatalities by 2 percent. Of course, there are benefits associated with compulsory insurance, but in the interests of efficiency, we must compare the benefits to the costs, including the increase in fatalities on more hazardous roads. **Related to Exercises 4.5 and 4.11.**

SOURCE: Based on Alma Cohen and Rajeev Dehejia, "The Effect of Automobile Insurance and Accident Liability Laws on Traffic Fatalities," *Journal of Law and Economics* XLVII (2004): 357–393.

29.5 The Economics of Consumer Search

Suppose the price of a particular television model varies from one store to another. If you don't know which store has the lowest price, should you keep shopping until you find it? The short answer is "No." Searching is costly because it takes time to visit a store, make a phone call, or visit a Web site. We can apply the marginal principle to the problem of searching for low prices. It will be sensible to continue searching if the marginal benefit of search (the expected savings from finding a lower price) exceeds the marginal cost (the time cost). In most cases, it will be rational to stop shopping before you find the lowest possible price.

Search and the Marginal Principle

We can illustrate the economics of search with a simple example. Suppose the price of a television ranges from $100 at the lowest price store to $180 at the highest price store. In addition, suppose that for a randomly selected store, any price from the low price to the high price is equally likely. Let's assume that the opportunity cost of the time required to visit a store—the marginal cost of search—is constant at $0.90 per visit.

discovered price
The lowest price observed so far in a search process.

The marginal benefit of search depends on your **discovered price**—the lowest price you have found so far in your search. The first column in Table 29.4 shows how to compute the marginal benefit of another visit when the discovered price is $140. A price of $140 is at the 50th percentile of the price range of the television (from $100 to $180). In other words, half the stores have lower prices (from $100 to $139), and half have higher prices (from $141 to $180). We compute the marginal benefit of an additional visit as follows:

- Row 2: If you visit one more store, the probability of finding a lower price is 0.50. You have a 50–50 chance of finding a lower price.
- Row 3: If you actually find a lower price, it will be between the low price of $100 and your discovered price of $140. The best guess for a lower price is the midpoint of this range, or $120.
- Row 4: The best guess for the savings from a lower price is the gap between the discovered price ($140) and the lower price ($120), or $20.
- Row 5: The probability of finding a lower price is 0.50, so your expected savings from visiting another store is $10 (equal to the anticipated $20 price gap times 0.50). You have a 50–50 chance of saving $20, so on average a visit to another store will generate a $10 savings.

To summarize, the marginal benefit of search is $10, which exceeds the $0.90 marginal cost. Therefore, if your discovered price is $140, it is sensible to visit one more store.

TABLE 29.4 Marginal Benefit of Searching for a Lower Price

Discovered price (lowest so far)	$140	$120	$110	$112
Probability of discovering lower price in next visit	0.500	0.250	0.125	0.150
Best guess of lower price	$120	$110	$105	$106
Best guess of savings from lower price	$ 20	$ 10	$ 5	$ 6
Marginal benefit: Expected savings	$ 10.00	$ 2.50	$ 0.625	$ 0.900

As shown in the second column of Table 29.4, if the discovered price is $120, the marginal benefit of another visit is only $2.50. This is lower than the marginal benefit shown in column 1 (discovered price = $140) for two reasons. First, a discovered price of $120 is in the 25th percentile of the price range of $100 to $180 (only one-fourth of stores have lower prices), so the probability of finding a lower price is only 0.25. Second, if you actually find a lower price, the savings will be smaller because you start with a lower discovered price. A lower price will be between $100 and $120, so your best guess of a lower price is $110 (the middle of the range) and your best guess of the savings from a lower price is only $10 (equal to $120 – $110). Multiplying the probability of finding a lower price (0.25) by the $10 price gap, the expected savings is $2.50. This marginal benefit still exceeds the $0.90 marginal cost, so it is sensible to visit an additional store to try to improve on your discovered price of $120.

As shown in the third column of Table 29.4, if the discovered price is only $110, visiting an additional store is not sensible. In this case, only one in eight stores has lower prices, meaning that the probability of finding a lower price at the store you visit is only 0.125. In addition, your best guess of a lower price is $105 (the middle of the range from $100 to $110), and your savings from a lower price is only $5. The expected savings from an additional visit is only $0.625 (equal to 0.125 times $5), which is less than the $0.90 marginal cost. In this case, the cost of an additional visit exceeds the expected benefit, so it is best to pay your discovered price of $110 rather than continuing to search for a lower price.

Figure 29.4 illustrates the application of the marginal principle to the search process. The horizontal axis shows the discovered price, and the vertical axis shows the marginal benefit and marginal cost. As we saw in Table 29.4, the higher

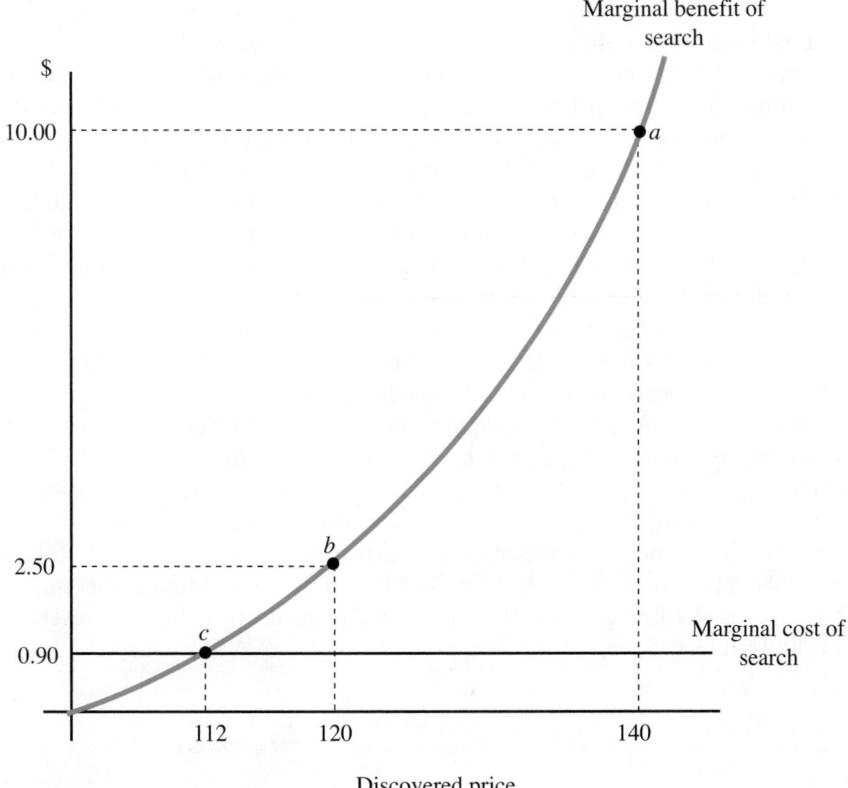

▲ FIGURE 29.4
Marginal Benefit and Marginal Cost of Search
The marginal benefit of search increases with the discovered price (the lowest price found so far), while the marginal cost of search is constant. If at a particular discovered price the marginal benefit exceeds the marginal cost, it is sensible to continue searching for a low price. The reservation price, defined as the price where the marginal benefit of search equals the marginal cost, is $112 (shown by point *c*).

the discovered price, the larger the marginal benefit of additional search, so the marginal-benefit curve is positively sloped. For example, the marginal benefit is $2.50 for a discovered price of $120 (point *b*), compared to $10 for a discovered price of $140 (point *a*). If the marginal cost is constant at $0.90 per visit (per unit of search), the marginal-cost curve is horizontal. If the discovered price is less than $112 (for example $110), the marginal benefit is less than the marginal cost, and it is not sensible to search for a lower price.

Reservation Prices and Searching Strategy

reservation price
The price at which a consumer is indifferent about additional search for a lower price.

A consumer's **reservation price** is defined as the discovered price at which the consumer is indifferent about additional search. If the discovered price exceeds the reservation price, additional searching is sensible, but if the discovered price is lower, additional searching is irrational. In Table 29.4, the reservation price is computed as $112.

- The probability of finding a lower price is 0.15 (a price of $112 is in the 15th percentile of the price range $100 to $180).
- The best guess of a lower price is $106 (the midpoint of the range $100 to $112).
- The marginal benefit (the expected savings over the discovered price) is $0.90, equal to 0.15 times $6.

The marginal benefit equals the marginal cost, so the consumer is indifferent about additional search. In Figure 29.4 the reservation price is shown by the intersection of the marginal-cost curve and the marginal-benefit curve at point *c*.

The reservation price provides consumers with a convenient rule for when to stop searching for a lower price. The consumer should continue to search until the discovered price (the lowest price found) is less than or equal to the reservation price. Some consumers will get lucky and discover a price below their reservation prices with just a little bit of searching, while others will take longer. But a consumer who knows the range of prices from lowest to highest can compute a reservation price before starting the search, and then search until the discovered price is less than or equal to the reservation price.

Figure 29.5 provides two examples of price searches that stop when the discovered price drops below the reservation price. The dots show one sequence of observed prices, starting at $174, followed by $175, then $165, and so on to $110 after 10 visits. The solid line connects the discovered prices—the lowest price observed over the course of the search. The dots above the line are the observed prices that, at the time they were observed, exceeded the discovered price. The discovered price finally drops below the reservation price in the 10th visit. The triangles show a second sequence of observed prices, starting with $151, followed by $152, then $162, then $130, and finally $107. The second (diamond) sequence is half as long as the first because the discovered price drops below the reservation price in the fifth visit.

The Effects of Opportunity Cost and Product Prices on Search Effort

Reservation prices and search efforts vary across consumers. A consumer with a relatively high opportunity cost of search time will have a higher marginal cost of search and will naturally spend less time searching for lower prices. In Figure 29.4 an increase in the marginal cost of search will shift the marginal-cost curve upward, increasing the reservation price. For example, if the cost per visit were $2.50 instead

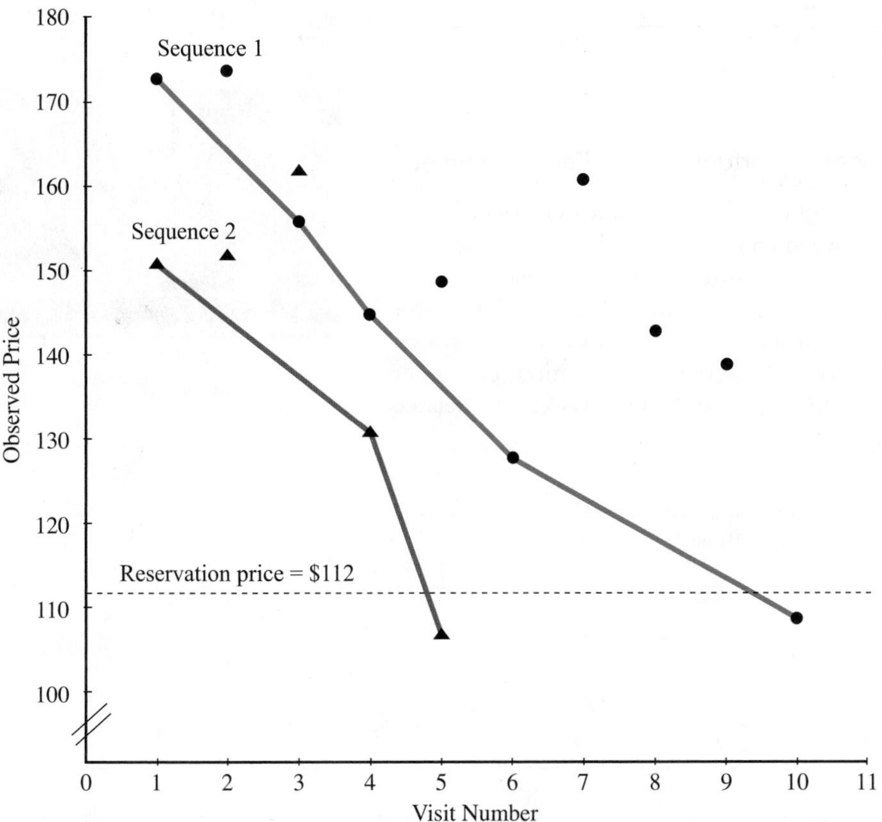

▲ FIGURE 29.5
Price Sequences and the Reservation Price
Each sequence (indicated by dots in #1 or triangles in #2) shows prices observed on visits to different stores. The lines connect the discovered prices (lowest price so far). A rational consumer stops shopping for lower prices when the discovered price is less than or equal to the reservation price ($112).

of $0.90, the reservation price would be $120 rather than $112. The higher the reservation price, the less time it will take, on average, to discover a price below the reservation price. Therefore, a consumer with a high opportunity cost of search won't spend as much time searching for low prices.

The amount of searching for low prices also depends on the price of the product. The higher the price, the bigger the payoff from discovering a price that is, say, 2 percent lower. For example, if an additional visit to a car dealer could save you 2 percent on a $10,000 car ($200), an additional visit will be sensible if your opportunity cost is less than $200. In contrast, if additional searching might save you 2 percent on a $10 pizza ($0.20), it is not sensible to continue searching unless your opportunity cost is less than $0.20. In general, the higher the price of a product, the greater the incentive to search for a lower price.

The amount of searching also depends on the range of prices, from lowest to highest. The smaller the gap between the low and high price, the smaller the possible savings from additional search. In our example, suppose the price range for the television is only $139 to $141, and suppose your discovered price is $140 (the average price). As before, there is a 50–50 chance that an additional visit will generate a lower price. But at most you'll save only $1, and your best guess for a lower price is $139.50 (the middle of the range $139 to $140). Given the relatively small anticipated savings, additional search will be rational only if your marginal cost is very low ($0.25). In general, the smaller the price range for a product, the less time consumers will spend searching for lower prices.

application 5

INCOME AND CONSUMER SEARCH

APPLYING THE CONCEPTS #5: How does opportunity cost affect consumer search?

A recent study explores the relationship between consumer search and income. The opportunity cost of search depends on income because one hour of search means one less hour available for earning income. The study examines search behavior for liquid detergents, and shows that a doubling of income increases the cost of search and decreases the amount of searching by about 14 percent. In addition, consumer search on workdays is more costly and thus less extensive than on weekends. **Related to Exercise 5.6.**

SOURCE: Based on Nitin Mehta, Surendra Rajiv, Kannan Srinivasan, "Price Uncertainty and Consumer Surplus: A Structural Model of Consideration Set Formation," *Marketing Science* 22 (2003), pp. 58–84.

SUMMARY

In this chapter, we've seen what happens when one of the assumptions underlying most supply and demand analysis—that people make informed decisions—is violated. If either buyers or sellers don't have reliable information about a particular good or service, the market will suffer from the adverse-selection problem. The uninformed side picks from an adverse selection of goods or customers. Here are the main points of the chapter:

1 The *adverse-selection problem* occurs when one side of the market cannot distinguish between high-quality and low-quality goods. The presence of low-quality goods pulls down the price that buyers are willing to pay, which decreases the quantity of high-quality goods supplied, which further decreases the average quality and the price. In the extreme case, only low-quality goods are sold.

2 A *thin* market occurs when the sellers of high-quality goods have a relatively low minimum supply price, so some high-quality goods are sold.

3 In a market subject to *asymmetric information*, buyers have an incentive to invest in information to help make better choices and sellers have an incentive to provide quality guarantees.

4 Insurance markets suffer from adverse selection because compared to insurance sellers, buyers have better information about the risks they face.

5 Insurance encourages risky behavior because part of the cost of an unfavorable outcome will be paid by an insurance company.

6 Searching for low prices is costly, and a rational consumer is likely to stop searching for low prices before finding the lowest possible price.

KEY TERMS

adverse-selection problem, p. 628
asymmetric information, p. 626
discovered price, p. 640
experience rating, p. 636
mixed market, p. 626
moral hazard, p. 638
reservation price, p. 642
thin market, p. 628

EXERCISES

All problems are assignable in MyEconLab.

29.1 Adverse Selection for Buyers: The Lemons Problem

1.1 There is asymmetric information in the used-car market because __________ (buyers/sellers) cannot distinguish between lemons and plums but __________ (buyers/sellers) can.

1.2 The supply curve for high-quality used cars lies __________ (above/below) the supply curve for low-quality used cars.

1.3 The following table shows the prices and quantities in three different used-car markets. Complete the table by filling in the last two rows.

	Market A	Market B	Market C
Assumed chance of getting a lemon	60%	80%	95%
Willingness to pay for a used car	$6,000	$5,000	$4,500
Number of lemons supplied	70	40	90
Number of plums supplied	30	10	10
Total number of used cars supplied	100	50	100
Equilibrium: Yes or No?			
If disequilibrium, will price then rise or drop?			

1.4 We will have a thin market for used cars if the minimum supply price for plums (high quality) is __________ (greater than/less than) the willingness to pay for a lemon.

1.5 Arrows up or down: A decrease in the minimum supply price for a plum (high quality) shifts the plum supply curve __________ and the likelihood of buying a plum __________.

1.6 Suppose you are willing to pay $1,000 for a low-quality used car and $5,000 for a high-quality used car. If there is an 80 percent chance of getting a low-quality car and a 20 percent chance of getting a high-quality car, you are willing to pay __________ for a used car.

1.7 Professional baseball pitchers are like used __________ because there is __________ information: A player's __________ has better information about the pitcher's health and likelihood of injury. (Related to Application 1 on page 630.)

1.8 Your favorite baseball team just announced that it signed a new pitcher from the free-agent market. We expect the new pitcher to be injured __________ (more/less) often than free-agent pitchers who returned to their old teams. (Related to Application 1 on page 630.)

1.9 ***Consumer Reports*.** You want to buy a used car, specifically a 1999 Zephyr. According to *Consumer Reports*, half the 1999 Zephyrs now on the road are lemons, meaning they break down frequently and generate large repair bills. Consumers are willing to pay $2,000 for a lemon, but $5,000 for a plum. According to Ms. Wizard, "The equilibrium price of used 1999 Zephyrs will be $2,000 in Sourland but $2,600 in Sweetland."

a. Illustrate with a complete graph for each market.

b. What is the fundamental difference between the two markets?

1.10 **Fashion and Prices.** You are in the market for a used car and have narrowed your options to two types of cars, type F and type P. According to *Consumer Reports*, the two types of cars have roughly the same frequency of lemons (50 percent). Like other consumers, you are willing to pay $1,000 for a lemon and $7,000 for a plum. The people who buy new F cars are fashion-conscious and purchase a new car every three years. The people who buy new P cars are insensitive to the whims of fashion. Predict the equilibrium prices of the two types of cars and defend your answer with two graphs, one for each type of car.

1.11 **Double Ignorance.** Suppose both buyers and sellers of used cars are ignorant: No one can distinguish between lemons and plums. Would you expect the market to be dominated by lemons? Illustrate with a completely labeled graph.

1.12 **Groucho Club.** Consider a classic quip from Groucho Marx: "I won't join any club that is willing to accept me as a member." Suppose Groucho wants to associate with high-income people (the higher the income the better) and everyone else has the same preferences as Groucho.

a. Use the notion of adverse selection to explain this quip.

b. Relate the quip to the adverse-selection problem.

1.13 **Purchasing a Fleet of Used Cars.** You are responsible for buying a fleet of 10 used cars for your employees and must pick either brand B or brand C. For your purposes, the two brands are identical except for one difference: Based on your experience with the two brands, you figure that 50 percent of B cars in the market are lemons and only 20 percent of C cars in the market are lemons. You are willing to pay $1,000 for a known lemon and $3,000 for a known plum. If the price of B cars is $1,800 and the price of C cars is $2,200, which brand of car should you pick?

1.14 **Adverse Selection of MP3 Players.** Consider the market for used MP3 players, with knowledgeable sellers and ignorant buyers. Half the MP3 players in existence are plums and half are lemons. Each buyer is willing to pay $50 for a plum or $20 for a lemon. The minimum supply price for a plum is $10 and the minimum supply price for a lemon is $2.

a. In equilibrium, will the market be "thin" or will all the used MP3 players in the market be lemons? Explain and illustrate your answer with a complete graph.

b. Suppose that at a price of $26, the quantity of plums is 20 and the quantity of lemons is 80. Is this an equilibrium? Explain and illustrate your answer with a complete graph.

1.15 **Mix of Lemons and Plums in the Week-Old Car Market.** Suppose the value of a high-quality week-old car (a plum) is $20,000 (the same as the purchase price of a new car), while the value of a low-quality week-old car (a lemon) is $10,000. Suppose that at a price of $16,000 per car, 6 of 10 cars on the used market are plums and 4 of 10 are lemons.

a. How much is the typical buyer willing to pay for a used car in the mixed market?

b. Is the $16,000 price an equilibrium price? Why or why not?

c. Suppose that for every 10 new cars sold by new-car dealers, 9 are plums and only 1 is a lemon. Why is the equilibrium mix in the used car market different from the mix of new cars sold?

1.16 **Willingness to Pay for Used Baseball Pitchers.** Suppose a healthy baseball pitcher is worth $5 million per year to his team, compared to only $1 million per year for an unhealthy pitcher. Suppose that half the pitchers in the league are healthy, and half are unhealthy. According to an executive of a baseball team, "If my assumptions are correct, our team is willing to pay a maximum of $3 million for a pitcher in the free-agent market." (Related to Application 1 on page 630.)

a. What are the executive's assumptions?

b. Are these assumptions realistic?

29.2 Responding to the Lemons Problem

2.1 Consider a thin used-car market. Someone just developed a device that can instantly identify the nearest plum in a used-car lot. The device works only once. The maximum amount that a consumer would be willing to pay for the device equals __________ minus __________.

2.2 A money-back guarantee will be provided by the owners of __________, but not by the owners of __________ (lemons/plums).

2.3 Arrows up or down: Government regulations for kiwifruit __________ the average quality and __________ the price of kiwifruit. (Related to Application 2 on page 633.)

2.4 **Paying for Information.** You are willing to pay $7,000 for a high-quality car—a plum. The current price of used cars is $4,000, and 4 of 5 cars in the market are lemons, meaning that 1 in 5 is a plum.

a. Suppose you could pay a finder's fee to a personal shopper/mechanic who will find you a plum at a price of $4,000. What is the maximum you are willing to pay as a finder's fee?

b. As you shop for a used car, you will bring each car you consider to your mechanic, who will thoroughly inspect the car and tell you for certain whether it is a plum or a lemon. If the price per inspection is $400, is it worth the money?

c. How would your answer to part (b) change if only 1 out of 10 used cars was a plum?

2.5 **Money-Back-Plus Guarantee.** The equilibrium price in the thin market is $2,600. Suppose car sellers provide a special money-back-plus guarantee: A dissatisfied buyer can return a car for a refund plus $100.

a. If a lemon owner sells his or her car for $5,000, the owner's gain from providing the guarantee is $__________.

b. If a plum owner sells his or her car for $5,000, the owner's gain from providing the guarantee is $__________.

2.6 **Equilibrium in the Kiwifruit Market.** Consumers are willing to pay 10 cents for a sour kiwifruit and 30 cents for a sweet kiwifruit. The minimum supply price for sour kiwifruit is 6 cents and the minimum supply price for sweet kiwifruit is 18 cents. The slope of each supply curve is 1 cent per thousand kiwifruit. (Related to Application 2 on page 633.)

a. Suppose consumers initially expect a 50–50 mix of sweet and sour kiwifruits. Is this an equilibrium? Illustrate with a graph.

b. Suppose consumers are pessimistic, expecting all sour kiwifruit. Is this an equilibrium? Illustrate with a graph. What is the price of kiwifruit?

c. Suppose the state outlaws sour kiwifruit, and they disappear from the market. What happens to the equilibrium price of kiwifruit? What is the equilibrium quantity of sweet kiwifruit?

29.3 Adverse Selection for Sellers: Insurance

3.1 Suppose the average annual malpractice cost is $40,000 for reckless doctors and $2,000 for careful doctors. If half of an insurance company's insured doctors are reckless, the company will earn zero economic profit if the price of insurance is $_________. If careful doctors are not willing to pay any more than $5,000 for insurance, the price required for zero economic profit is $_________.

3.2 Arrows up or down: In an insurance market, the presence of high-cost consumers _________ the average cost of providing insurance. The resulting _________ in the number of low-cost consumers _________ the average cost of providing insurance and _________ price.

3.3 Arrows up or down: The European Union ban on gender discrimination in automobile insurance will _________ insurance prices for women and _________ insurance prices for men. (Related to Application 3 on page 637.)

3.4 **Genetic Testing and Insurance Prices.** Suppose the likelihood that a person will get disease X is determined in large part (but not exclusively) by his or her genes. Initially, it is impossible to determine who carries the gene for the disease, and many people spend $500 on special health insurance to cover the costs of treatment for the disease. Suppose scientists uncover the gene responsible for the disease and develop a simple test for the gene.

a. Suppose the government passes a law that prevents insurance companies from getting the results of a customer's genetic test for X. Will the new price of X insurance be greater than or less than $500?

b. Suppose insurance companies have access to the results of genetic tests and they require all customers to get the test. How will the insurance company change its price of X insurance?

3.5 **Rising Insurance Rates.** Consider an insurance company that provides group medical coverage for university employees. The company discovered that some of its younger employees had switched to other insurance companies. The company responded to the loss of customers by increasing its price. This is puzzling because you might think the insurance company would drop its price to prevent other employees from switching to other companies.

a. What is the rationale for increasing the price?

b. If you change one word in the second sentence, it would be logical for the insurance company to decrease rather than increase its price. What is the word, and why is it decisive?

3.6 **State Auto Insurance Pool.** Consider a state in which automobile drivers are divided equally into two types of drivers: careful and reckless. The average annual auto insurance claim is $400 for a careful driver and $1,200 for a reckless driver. Suppose the state adopts an insurance system in which all drivers are placed in a common pool and allocated to insurance companies randomly. An insurance company cannot refuse coverage to any driver it is assigned, but a driver who is unhappy with the insurance company has the option of being randomly reassigned to another insurance company. By law, each insurance company must charge the same price to all its customers. Predict the price of auto insurance under the two alternative policy scenarios:

a. Under Policy M, auto insurance is mandatory.

b. Under Policy V, auto insurance is voluntary.

29.4 Insurance and Moral Hazard

4.1 In the market for insurance, the moral-hazard problem is that _________ encourages _________.

4.2 While shopping for office equipment, an office manager sees a display of fire extinguishers. After making a single phone call, the manager decides not to buy a fire extinguisher. The manager had called her _________ and asked, "_________?"

4.3 Many professional athletes purchase insurance against career-ending injuries. We expect the insured players to experience _________ (more/fewer) injuries than uninsured players.

4.4 If the single firm providing bicycle theft insurance on campus disappears and is not replaced, we would expect bicycle theft rates on campus to _________.

4.5 Car insurance increases traffic _________ because insured drivers _________. (Related to Application 4 on page 639.)

4.6 **Selling iPod Insurance.** On the campus of Klepto College, half the iPods are expensive (replacement value is $400) and half are cheap (replacement value is $100). There is a 20 percent chance that any particular iPod—expensive or cheap—will be stolen in the next year. Suppose a firm offers iPod-theft insurance for $50 per year: The firm will replace any insured iPod that is stolen. Suppose the firm sells 20 insurance policies.

a. Assume for the moment that the theft rate remains at 20 percent for both types of iPods. The firm's total revenue equals _________. The firm's cost—the money paid out to replace stolen iPods—will be $_________ to replace expensive iPods and $_________ to replace cheap iPods, for a total of $_________. The insurance firm will make zero economic profit with a price of $_________.

b. Is it realistic to assume that the introduction of insurance will not affect the theft rate? Which is a more plausible assumption, that the theft rate will decrease to 10 percent or that it will increase to 30 percent? For the more plausible theft rate, compute the zero-profit insurance price when insurance is purchased exclusively by the owners of expensive iPods.

4.7 **Skydiver Question.** Several of your friends have offered to take you on a tandem skydiving adventure: Strapped together with a single set of parachutes (main and emergency), you will all jump out of an airplane and then either float to earth or crash. All your skydiving friends are equally skillful, and none of them has the thrill-seeker gene. You can ask each of them a single question.

a. What's your question?

b. Provide the answer you're looking for in a skydiving mate.

4.8 **Insurance and Fire Prevention.** In a given year, there is a 10 percent chance that a fire in Ira's warehouse will cause $100,000 in property damage. If Ira spends $4,000 on a fire-prevention program, the probability of a fire would drop to zero.

a. If Ira doesn't have fire insurance, will he spend the money on the prevention program?

b. If Ira has an insurance policy that covers 80 percent of the property damage from a fire (covering $80,000 of the $100,000 worth of damage), will he spend the money on the prevention program?

4.9 **Mandatory Insurance.** Consider a city with 100 drivers and a perfectly competitive market for automobile insurance. The demand curve for auto insurance is linear and negatively sloped, with a slope of –$10 per customer. At the initial price of $1,500, half the city's drivers (50 drivers) buy insurance. The price is just high enough to cover all the costs of providing insurance, including a 50 percent premium to cover the costs associated with uninsured drivers. Suppose the city makes auto insurance mandatory. Predict the new equilibrium.

4.10 **Crop Insurance.** Consider a state in which farmers are divided equally into two types: high risk and low risk. The average annual crop loss (and possible insurance claim) is $200 for a low-risk farmer and $1,200 for a high-risk farmer.

a. If all farmers were to buy insurance, what is the break-even price for the insurance company?

b. Suppose a farmer will purchase insurance only if the price (the annual premium) is no more than 50 percent higher than his or her average crop loss. What is the equilibrium price?

4.11 **Safety Rebate from the Insurance Company.** In 2010 a leading insurance company started a policy that pays a policy holder a 5 percent rebate on his or her insurance premium in any year in which the driver does not file an insurance claim. For example, a household with an annual premium of $1,200 will get a $60 rebate check each year it does not file a claim. Explain the rationale for the rebate policy. What problem is the policy trying to solve? (Related to Application 4 on page 639.)

29.5 The Economics of Consumer Search

5.1 The reservation price is the price at which the consumer is __________ about additional search, meaning that the __________ of search equals the __________.

5.2 If a consumer knows that a product is available at some store at a price as low as $100, it is sensible to continue shopping until the consumer finds the lowest-price store. __________ (True/False)

5.3 Suppose the range of prices for a product is $10 to $20 and your discovered price (lowest price so far) is $16. If you visit one more store and discover a lower price, the best guess for a lower price is __________ and the savings if you discover this lower price is __________.

5.4 As the opportunity cost of search time increases, the reservation price __________ (increases, decreases) and the amount of search time __________ (increases, decreases).

5.5 A doubling of prices __________ (increases, decreases) the marginal benefit of search at a given __________ price, and the percentage gap between the reservation price and the lowest price __________ (increases, decreases).

5.6 A study of consumer search for liquid detergents estimated that a doubling of income decreased the amount of search by roughly __________ (1, 14, 50, 70) percent. (Related to Application 5 on page 644.)

5.7 **Compute the Reservation Price.** Suppose the range of prices for a consumer good is $20 to $60, and all prices in this range are equally likely.

a. Fill in the blanks in the table.

Discovered price (lowest so far)	$40	$30
Probability of discovering lower price in next visit	____	____
Best guess of lower price	____	____
Savings if lower price is discovered	____	____
Marginal benefit: Expected savings from additional visit	____	____

b. If the marginal cost of search is $1.25, the reservation price is __________.

5.8 **Internet and Reservation Prices.** Consider a country that initially has no Internet service or telephones, so consumers must travel to stores to get information about prices. Use a graph to show the effects of introducing Internet service on the reservation price for a consumer good.

ECONOMIC EXPERIMENT

ROLLING FOR LEMONS

In this experiment, students play the role of consumers purchasing used cars. Over half the used cars on the road (57%) are plums, and the remaining cars (43%) are lemons. Each consumer offers a price for a used car and then rolls a pair of dice to find out whether he or she gets a lemon or a plum. In general, rolling a big number is good news: To get a plum, you need to roll a big number. The higher the price you offer, the smaller the number you must roll to get a plum. Here is how the experiment works:

- Each consumer tells the instructor how much he or she is offering for a used car and then rolls the dice.
- The instructor tells the consumer whether the number rolled is large enough to get a plum. If the number is not large enough, the consumer gets a lemon.
- The consumers' scores equal the difference between the maximum amount they are willing to pay for the type of car they got ($1,200 for a plum and $400 for a lemon) and the price they actually paid. For example, if Otto offers $500 and gets a plum, his score is $700. If Carla offers $600 and gets a lemon, her score is –$200.
- The instructor announces the result of each transaction to the class.
- There are three to five buying periods. At the end of the last trading period, each consumer adds up his or her score.

MyEconLab
For additional economic experiments, please visit *www.myeconlab.com*.

ECONOMIC EXPERIMENT

BIKE INSURANCE

This experiment shows the effect of asymmetric information on the market for bicycle insurance. Consider a city with two types of bike owners: Some face a relatively high probability of bike theft, and others face a relatively low probability of bike theft. Bike owners know from experience whether they face a high probability or a low probability of theft, but the insurance company cannot distinguish between the two types of owners. For the city as a whole, 20 percent of bicycles are stolen every year. Here is how the experiment works:

- The class is divided into small groups. Each group represents an insurance company that must pick a price at which to offer bike-theft insurance. The insurance company must pay $100 for each insured bike that is stolen.
- The instructor has a table that shows for each price of bike insurance how many owners of each type (high probability and low probability) will purchase insurance. Using the numbers supplied by the instructor, each insurance company can compute its total revenue (the price per bike insured times the number of insured bikes), the number of bikes stolen, and the company's total replacement cost.
- The group's score for a trading period equals the company's profit, which is the total revenue less the total replacement cost for stolen bikes.
- The experiment runs for several trading periods, and a group's score equals the sum of its profits over these trading periods.

MyEconLab
For additional economic experiments, please visit *www.myeconlab.com*.

NOTES

1. George Akerlof, "The Market for 'Lemons': Quality Uncertainty and the Market Mechanism," *Quarterly Journal of Economics* (August 1970): 488–500.

2. Eric Bond, "A Direct Test of the Lemons' Model: The Market for Used Pickup Trucks," *American Economic Review* 72 (September 1982): 836–840; Michael Pratt and George Hoffer, "Test of the Lemons Model: Comment," *American Economic Review* 74 (September 1984): 798–800; Eric Bond, "Test of the Lemons' Model: A Reply," *American Economic Review* 74 (September 1984): 801–804.

Public Goods and Public Choice

CHAPTER

30

Meteors regularly enter the earth's atmosphere, and most burn up before they reach the earth's surface or are too small do much harm.

But the impact of the occasional large meteorite—at least 200 meters in diameter—would have catastrophic global effects. In 2012 the European Union initiated NEOShield, a project that will explore alternative responses to the threats posed by large near-earth objects (NEOs). The cooperative project draws support and expertise from Germany, France, Britain, Spain, Russia, and the U.S.

Scientists are exploring three options for preventing an NEO impact: nudge, tug, and blast.

Nudge: Launch a kinetic impactor to strike the NEO and change its velocity so that it arrives at the crossing point with the earth's orbit at an earlier or later time, thus avoiding an impact. A nudge replaces an impact with a near miss.

Tug: Position a spacecraft close to the NEO and use long-term thrusters to maintain a constant distance between the objects and use the gravitational force between the two objects to pull the NEO off course.

Blast: Detonate a nuclear device close enough to the NEO to change its course.

The purpose of the NEOShield project is to study each of the three options and recommend a course of action.

LEARNING OBJECTIVES

- Define a public good and the free rider problem.
- Define an external benefit from a private good.
- Describe the median-voter rule and its consequences for public policy.

MyEconLab

MyEconLab helps you master each objective and study more efficiently.

In this chapter, we'll see that if a particular good generates external benefits, government intervention can make beneficial transactions happen. For example, although everyone on Earth would benefit from a system to deal with NEOs, the cost is so high that no single person would provide it. We will never have such a program—even if its benefits exceed its costs—unless we make a collective decision about what sort of system to develop and how to pay for it. One purpose of government is to help make this kind of collective decision.

This chapter explores the challenges associated with providing goods that generate external benefits. After an overview of government spending programs and tax sources, we'll look at the differences between private goods, such as housing, and public goods, such as levees. We'll discuss various responses to the problem of free riders—people who benefit from public goods but don't pay for them. We'll also discuss the external benefits from education and other private goods. Then we'll show how the preferences of citizens affect elections and decisions in the public sector. Finally, we'll look at some alternative theories on government decision making.

Although it's convenient to talk about "the" government, there are thousands of governments in the United States, and each citizen deals with at least three different levels of government. Figure 30.1 shows the budget breakdown for the three levels of government. The United States has more than 80,000 local governments, including

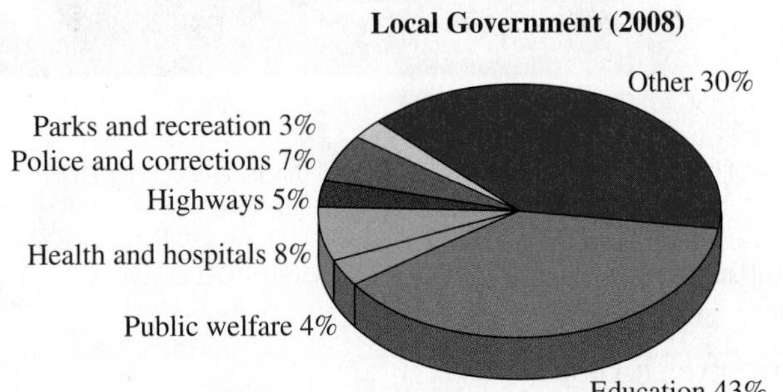

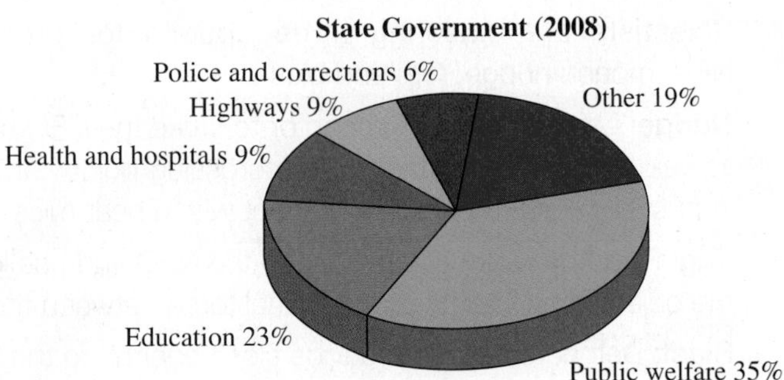

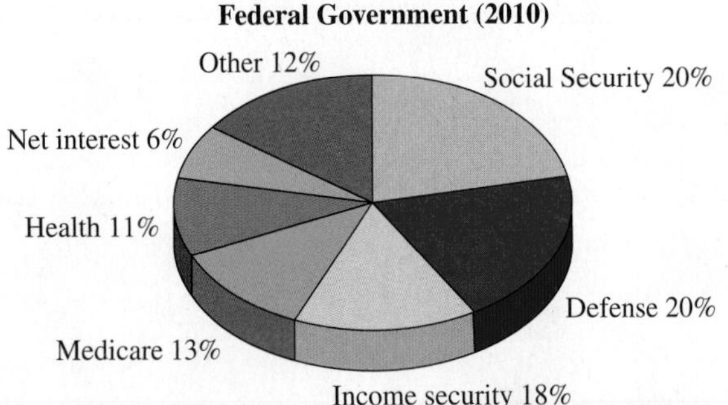

▲ FIGURE 30.1
Spending Programs for Local, State, and Federal Governments
SOURCE: Statistical Abstract of the United States, 2008.

municipalities (city governments), counties, school districts, and special districts responsible for providing services such as water, fire protection, and libraries. Local governments spend most of their money on education (kindergarten through high school), public welfare and health (payments to poor households and support for public hospitals), highways, fire protection, and police and corrections. For states, the biggest spending programs are education (including colleges and universities), public welfare, highways, health and hospitals, and corrections (state courts and prisons). For the federal government, the biggest spending programs are programs for the elderly (Social Security and Medicare), national defense, income security (payments to the poor), and interest on the national debt.

Figure 30.2 shows the revenue sources for local governments, states, and the federal government. About two-fifths of local government revenue comes from higher levels of government in the form of intergovernmental grants. The other major revenue source for local governments is the property tax, which is a fixed percentage of the value of residential, commercial, or industrial property. At the state level, the most important revenue sources are intergovernmental grants from the federal government, the sales tax, and the individual income tax. A person's state income tax liability is based on how much he or she earns, with tax rates that typically increase as income increases. At the federal level, the major revenue sources are individual income taxes and employment taxes, which include taxes collected to support Social Security and Medicare.

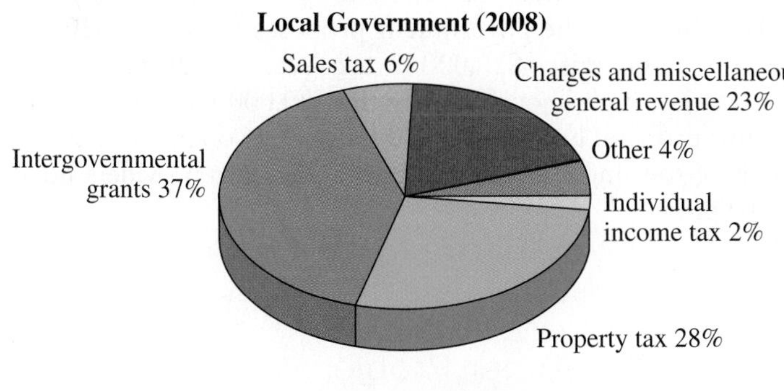

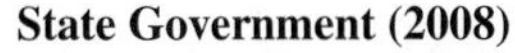

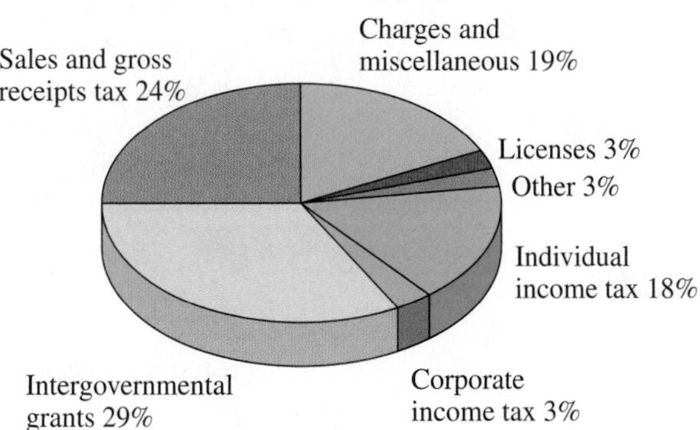

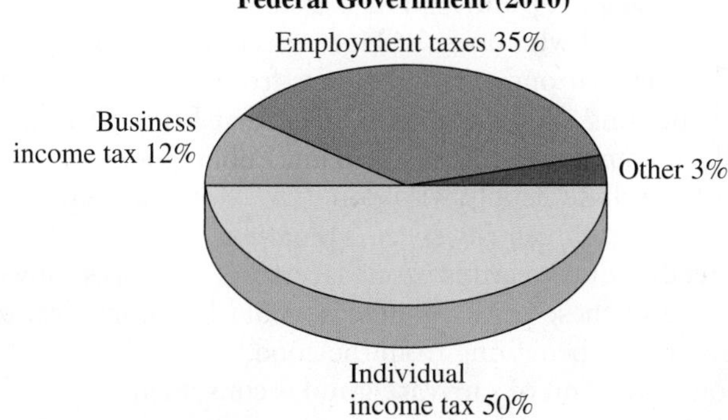

▲ FIGURE 30.2
Revenue Sources for Local, State, and Federal Governments
SOURCE: Statistical Abstract of the United States, 2008.

30.1 External Benefits and Public Goods

As we saw earlier in the chapter on market efficiency, when there are neither external benefits nor external costs, the market equilibrium is efficient. When a government intervenes in an efficient market, the result is inefficiency. In this chapter, we'll see that a market with external benefits is inefficient, so there is an opportunity for government to promote efficiency.

For most goods, the benefits of consumption are confined to the person who buys the good. The benefit experienced by a buyer is called a *private benefit*. In contrast, when someone else benefits from a good, the good generates an **external benefit**. To illustrate the idea of external benefits and inefficiency, consider a dam built for flood-control purposes. One thousand people would be protected by the dam, and each person would get a $50 benefit. If one person builds a dam, the private benefit is $50 and the external benefit is $49,950, or $50 for each of the 999 other people who benefit. If the cost of building the dam is $20,000, no single person will build it because the cost exceeds the $50 private benefit. In other words, if we rely on the forces of supply and demand, with each person considering only the private benefits and costs of the dam, it won't be built.

external benefit
A benefit from a good experienced by someone other than the person who buys the good.

When there are external benefits from a good, collective decision making generates more efficient choices. In the case of the dam, the total benefit of $50,000 exceeds the $20,000 cost, so the dam is efficient and society as a whole will be better off if it is built. The government can solve this problem by collecting enough tax revenue to pay for the dam. Suppose the government proposes to collect $20 per person to pay for the dam. The tax raises $20,000 in tax revenue ($20 per person times 1,000 people), which is just high enough to pay the $20,000 cost of the dam. Most people will support this proposal because the $20 tax per person is less than the $50 benefit per person. The government can use its taxing power to provide a good that would otherwise not be provided.

Public Goods and the Free-Rider Problem

The dam is an example of a *public good*. A **public good** is available for everyone to utilize, regardless of who pays for it and who doesn't. More precisely, a public good is *nonrival* in consumption: The fact that one person benefits from a good does not prevent another person from benefiting. For example, the fact that I benefit from a flood-control dam doesn't reduce your benefit from the dam. Public goods are also *nonexcludable*: It is impractical to exclude people who don't pay. Some examples of public goods are national defense, law enforcement, space exploration, the preservation of endangered species, the protection of the earth's ozone layer, and fireworks shows. If someone refuses to pay for one of these public goods, it would be impractical to prevent that person from consuming or benefiting from the good.

public good
A good that is available for everyone to consume, regardless of who pays and who doesn't; a good that is nonrival in consumption and nonexcludable.

In contrast with public goods, each unit of a **private good** is consumed by a single person or household. For example, only one person can eat a hot dog, so it is a private good. If a government hands out free cheese, is the free cheese a public good or a private good? Although anyone can get in line for the cheese, only one person can actually consume a particular piece of cheese, so the free cheese is a private good that happens to be available free of charge from the government. Similarly, an apartment in a public housing project can be occupied by a single household, so it is a private good provided by the government.

private good
A good that is consumed by a single person or household; a good that is rival in consumption and excludable.

Most public goods are supported by taxes. What would happen if we eliminated taxes and asked people to contribute money to pay for national defense, dams, city streets, and the police? Would people contribute enough money to support these programs at the efficient level? The problem with using voluntary contributions to support public goods is known as the *free-rider problem*. A **free rider** is a person who gets the benefit from a good but does not pay for it. Each person has a financial incentive to try to get the benefits of a public good without paying for it. That is, some people will try to get a "free ride" at the expense of others who do pay. Of course, if everyone tries to get a free ride there will be no money to support the public good, so it won't be provided.

free rider
A person who gets the benefit from a good but does not pay for it.

The flip side of the free-rider problem is the chump problem: No one wants to be the chump—the person who gives free rides to other people—so no one contributes any money. The free-rider problem suggests that if taxes were replaced with voluntary contributions, the government would be forced to cut back or eliminate many programs.

Overcoming the Free-Rider Problem

Many organizations, including public radio and television, religious organizations, and charitable organizations, raise money through voluntary contributions. So it appears that some people overcome their inclination to be free riders and contribute voluntarily to organizations that provide public goods. The successful organizations use a number of techniques to encourage people to contribute:

- ***Giving contributors private goods such as coffee mugs, books, musical recordings, and magazine subscriptions.*** People are more likely to contribute if they get something for it.
- ***Arranging matching contributions.*** You are more likely to contribute if you know your $30 contribution will be matched with a contribution from another person or your employer.
- ***Appealing to a person's sense of civic or moral responsibility.*** People are more likely to contribute when they are reminded that they benefit from the service.

Note, however, that these organizations are only partly successful in mitigating the free-rider problem. Public radio is one of the success stories, even though the typical public-radio station gets contributions from fewer than a quarter of its listeners.

application 1

FREE RIDERS AND THE THREE-CLOCK TOWER

APPLYING THE CONCEPTS #1: How can we respond to the free-rider problem?

In the days before inexpensive wristwatches, most people did not carry their own timepieces. Many towns built clock towers to help their citizens keep track of time. The towns paid for the clock towers with voluntary contributions from citizens. One town in the northeastern United States built a four-sided tower but put clock faces on only three sides of the tower. To most people, this seems bizarre. If you build a clock tower, why not put clock faces on all four sides? It turns out that one of the town's wealthy citizens refused to contribute money to help build the clock tower. The town officials decided not to put a clock face on the side of the tower facing this citizen's house. In other words, the citizen tried—unsuccessfully—to get a free ride. The problem is that other citizens on the same side of town also suffered from not having a clock. In this case, preventing a free ride by one citizen caused problems for other citizens. It also caused inefficiency because the cost of a fourth clock was presumably much less than the foregone benefits to the excluded citizens. **Related to Exercises 1.4 and 1.5.**

application 2

GLOBAL WEATHER OBSERVATION

APPLYING THE CONCEPTS #2: What happens when external benefits spill across international borders?

As another example of a public good, consider global weather observation. In this case, information gathered by one country generates external benefits when it is shared with other countries. Satellites, nomadic buoys, and weather stations monitor weather in different parts of the world, but no single organization gathers all the information to reveal the big weather picture. Another problem is that the uninhabited parts of the world, in particular the vast oceans of the Southern Hemisphere, receive little monitoring. This makes it difficult to observe the interactions between oceans and atmosphere, and difficult to measure any changes in sea level that might be caused by global warming.

In recent years, the United States has taken the lead in encouraging cooperation and the sharing of data collected by different organizations around the world. The experience of coordination in monitoring El Niño, the intermittent ocean current that affects weather in the western United States, is encouraging. According to the National Oceanic and Atmospheric Administration (NOAA), early warnings of a change in the current in 1997–98 reduced damage to the California economy by about $1.1 billion. **Related to Exercise 1.6.**

SOURCE: Based on "Flying Blind: Earth Observation," *Economist*, July 26, 2003.

30.2 Private Goods with External Benefits

In contrast to a public good, a private good can be utilized by only a single person or household. However, some private goods generate benefits for people who do not directly consume the good. For example, suppose I replace the peeling paint on my house with a fresh coat of paint. I benefit from the new paint because it protects my house from decay and my house will look better. My neighbors will also benefit from the improved appearance of the neighborhood. Similarly, if I buy a fire extinguisher and install fireproof roofing, my neighbors benefit because a fire is less likely to spread to their houses.

External Benefits from Education

Education is another private good that generates external benefits. Most of the benefits of education go to the student because education increases productivity and income, and presumably it makes everyday life easier and more interesting. Education generates three kinds of external benefits:

1 *Workplace externalities.* In most workplaces, people work in groups and teamwork is important. A well-educated person understands instructions readily and is more likely to suggest ways to improve the production process. As a result, when a well-educated person joins a work team, the productivity of everyone on the team increases. Higher productivity generally leads to higher profits for firms, and members of the team are likely to earn higher salaries.

2 *Civic externalities.* Citizens in a democratic society make collective decisions by voting in elections, and each citizen must live with these decisions. A well-educated person is more likely to vote intelligently, so there are external benefits for other citizens.

3 *Crime externalities.* Educated people earn higher legal incomes and thus commit less crime. High-school dropouts have relatively low wages and high crime rates, so increasing the high-school graduation rate generates large reductions in crime.

A recent study estimates the external benefits of education related to lower crime rates.[1] For every high-school student who graduates rather than dropping out after 11th grade, the cost of crime decreases by about $1,600 per year for the rest of the graduate's working life. The average cost of one year of high school is about $6,000, so for a one-time expense of $6,000 society gets a crime-reduction benefit of $1,600 per year for 30 or 40 years.

External Benefits and the Marginal Principle

Consider a parent's decision about how much time and money to spend on a child's education. Suppose the parent bases the decision on his or her cost and the child's private benefits—the child's increase in potential earnings as an adult. To be specific, consider the decision on how many books to buy for the child. In Figure 30.3, the marginal private benefit curve shows the extra benefit to the child from each additional book, measured as the increase in future income. Assume the marginal cost of books is constant at $8 per book. Applying the marginal principle, the parent will choose point *a*, where the marginal benefit equals the marginal cost, and buy nine books.

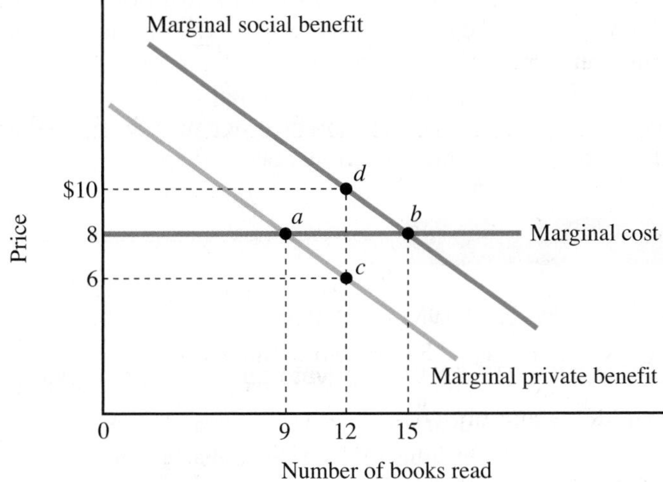

▲ FIGURE 30.3
External Benefits and the Marginal Principle
Education (represented here as the number of books read) generates external benefits, so the marginal social benefit exceeds the marginal private benefit. Using books as an example of education, an individual picks point *a*, where the marginal private benefit equals the marginal cost. Point *b* is the socially efficient point, where the marginal social benefit equals the marginal cost.

MARGINAL PRINCIPLE

Increase the level of an activity as long as its marginal benefit exceeds its marginal cost. Choose the level at which the marginal benefit equals the marginal cost.

The higher of the two negatively sloped curves is the marginal social benefit of education. The marginal social benefit equals the marginal private benefit plus the marginal external benefit. As we've seen, there are external benefits from education, so the social benefit exceeds the private benefit. From society's perspective, the best point is *b*, where the marginal social benefit equals the marginal cost. The socially efficient quantity is 15 books. As an illustration, consider the 12th book. The marginal private benefit is $6 (shown by point *c*) and the external benefit is $4, so the marginal social benefit is $6 plus $4, or $10 (shown by point *d*). The social benefit exceeds the $8 cost, so providing the book is efficient from the social perspective. The private benefit of $6 is less than the $8 cost, however, so the parent won't buy the 12th book, but instead will stop with 9 books. The lesson is that when there are external benefits, decisions based on private benefits will generate an inefficiently small quantity of the good.

Because of the external benefits from education, the government uses various policies to encourage people to become educated. Local governments provide free education through high school. States subsidize students at public colleges and universities, providing college education at a fraction of its actual cost. In addition, the federal government provides financial aid to students in both public and private schools.

Other Private Goods That Generate External Benefits

The government subsidizes other goods that generate external benefits. Subsidies for on-the-job training and education encourage workers and firms to invest in human capital and increase labor productivity. It is sensible for the government to subsidize training and education because some of the benefits are transferred to other firms when workers change employers. Another example of external benefits is research at universities and other nonprofit organizations. If a research project provides knowledge or technology that leads to the development of new products or the improvement of old ones, the benefits from the project spill over onto consumers and producers. When there are external benefits, the government can encourage people to take actions that benefit other people. By making beneficial transactions happen, the government can increase efficiency.

application 3

EXTERNAL BENEFITS FROM LOJACK

APPLYING THE CONCEPTS #3: What private goods generate external benefits?

LoJack, a system used to recover stolen vehicles, is a private good that generates external benefits. A small, silent transmitter hidden in a vehicle allows police to track a stolen car. The name is a play on words, meant to convey the idea that LoJack will recover vehicles that are hijacked or stolen. A thief who steals a LoJack-equipped car won't keep the car for long and is likely to get caught, so LoJack is an effective deterrent to car theft. Car thieves cannot distinguish between cars with and without LoJack, so the system decreases the payoff from car theft in general, and criminals steal fewer cars. People who install LoJack systems in their cars generate benefits for themselves and external benefits for other car owners who don't have LoJack.

A study by two economists estimated the private and external benefits from LoJack. The annual cost of a LoJack system is about $100. For a car owner who carries theft insurance, the benefit from a LoJack system is the discount offered by an insurance company, typically well below the $100 annual cost. For every three LoJack systems installed, the number of auto thefts decreases by one car per year. The external benefit from fewer vehicle thefts is about $1,300 per LoJack per year. The benefits are experienced by people who don't buy their own LoJack systems but who benefit because thieves can never be sure whether a particular car is protected by LoJack or not. **Related to Exercises 2.6 and 2.8.**

SOURCE: Based on Ian Ayres and Steven Levitt, "Measuring Positive Externalities from Unobservable Victim Precautions: An Empirical Analysis of Lojack," *Quarterly Journal of Economics* 113 (1998): 43–77.

application 4

THE PRIVATE AND EXTERNAL BENEFIT OF TREES

APPLYING THE CONCEPTS #4: What happens when neighbors benefit?

Mature trees in residential neighborhoods have private costs and both private and social benefits. The initial cost—to purchase a seedling and plant it is relatively low, but the owner's opportunity cost of upkeep (time and money spent watering, raking leaves, trimming) can be large. The benefits—from shade, improved air quality, and aesthetics—go to the property owner and the neighbors. A forest economist estimates that a mature tree adds about $7,000 to the value of the owner's house, and also increases the value of neighboring houses (within 100 feet) by a total of $13,000. Given the $13,000 external benefit, we anticipate that the equilibrium number of trees will be less than the socially efficient number. To address this problem, some cities subsidize the purchase of trees. For example, the city of Portland, Oregon, pays $50 for each new tree. In addition, some cities provide public services such as leaf pickup that reduce the cost of upkeep. **Related to Exercise 2.7.**

SOURCE: Based on Matthew Preusch, "The Money Trees," *The Oregonian*, February 12, 2010, E1.

30.3 Public Choice and the Median Voter

We have discussed the challenges associated with providing and paying for goods that generate external benefits. In this part of the chapter, we study **public-choice economics**, a field that uses models of rational choice to explore decision making in the public sector. We'll start with a model of government decisions based on voting and then look at some alternative models.

public-choice economics
A field of economics that uses models of rational choice to explore decision making in the public sector.

Voting and the Median-Voter Rule

As citizens in a democracy, we pick people to make public decisions. We vote for people to represent our viewpoints in legislative bodies (city council members, state legislators, and congressional representatives), and we vote for people in executive positions (mayors, governors, and presidents). The basic idea of a democracy is that the government will take actions that are approved by the majority of citizens. If governments are responsive to voters, the voting public ultimately makes all the important decisions, and the actions of the government will reflect their preferences.

One concept of public-choice economics is known as the **median-voter rule**. According to this rule, the choices made by the government will match the preferences of the median voter, defined as the voter whose preferences lie in the middle of the set of all voters' preferences: Half the voters want more of something (for example, a larger government budget) and half want less (a smaller government budget). As we'll see, this rule has some important implications for decision making and politics.

median-voter rule
The choices made by the government will match the preferences of the median voter.

To see the logic of the median-voter rule, consider a state where there are two candidates for governor—Penny and Buck—and the only issue in the election is how much the state should spend on education. Each citizen will vote for the candidate whose proposed education budget is closest to the citizen's preferred budget. Figure 30.4 shows citizens' preferences for education spending, with different preferred budgets on the horizontal axis and the number of voters on the vertical axis. For example, two citizens have a preferred budget of $1 billion, four have a preferred budget of $2 billion, and so on. The median budget, which splits the rest of the voters into two equal groups (20 voters on each side), is $5 billion.

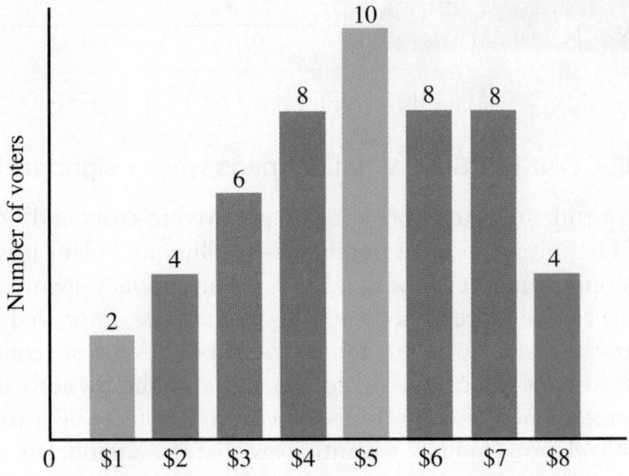

▲ **FIGURE 30.4**
The Median-Voter Rule
If Penny proposes a $3 billion budget and Buck proposes a $7 billion budget, the election will result in a tie. By moving toward the median budget, Penny can increase her chance of being elected. In equilibrium, both candidates will propose a budget close to the $5 billion preferred budget of the median voter.

Suppose the two candidates start out with very different proposed education budgets. Penny proposes a budget of $3 billion, and Buck proposes $7 billion. The 20 citizens with preferred budgets less than or equal to $4 billion will vote for Penny because her proposed budget is closest to their preferred budgets. Buck's supporters include the 20 citizens with preferred budgets greater than or equal to $6 billion. The two candidates will split the 10 voters with a preferred budget of $5 billion (halfway between the two proposed budgets), so each candidate will get a total of 25 votes, resulting in a tie.

Penny could increase her chance of being elected by increasing her proposed budget. Let's say she proposes $4 billion instead of $3 billion. All the voters with a preferred budget of $5 billion will vote for Penny because Penny's $4 billion proposal is now closer to their $5 billion preferred budget than Buck's $7 billion proposal. Penny won't lose any of her other votes either, so she will win the election by a vote of 30 (equal to 2 + 4 + 6 + 8 + 10) to 20 (equal to 8 + 8 + 4). If Buck is smart, he will realize that he could get more votes by moving toward the median budget. For example, if he decreases his proposed budget to $6 billion, the election would result in a tie vote again. Penny and Buck will continue to move their proposed budgets toward the median budget ($5 billion) until they both propose budgets that are very close to the median budget.

Powerful forces pull the two candidates toward the preferences of the median voter. As long as Penny proposes a smaller budget than Buck, the people with small preferred budgets will continue to vote for her. The benefit of moving toward the median is that she can take some votes from Buck. Similarly, Buck doesn't have to worry about people with large preferred budgets but can concentrate instead on the battle for voters in the middle. The result is that by election day the two candidates have adopted virtually the same position: The position of the median voter. Voters trying to choose between two candidates may feel they don't have much choice. In fact, the median-voter rule says the choices made by government will match the preferences of the median voter, regardless of who wins the election.

Although we usually think that people make political decisions by voting in elections, it is also possible to "vote with your feet." In 1956 economist Charles M. Tiebout suggested that a household's choice of which community to live in is based in part on the tax and spending policies of different communities.[2] Households express their preferences by moving to communities that offer the best package of services and taxes. A community with inefficient public services will experience a loss in population, perhaps causing the local officials to make public services more efficient to attract new residents.

It is clear that people vote with their ballots *and* with their feet. In both cases, citizens can express their preferences for public goods, taxes, and public policies. These two sources of citizen power limit the ability of governments to take actions that are inconsistent with the preferences of most voters.

The Median Voter and the Median Location

The logic of the median-voter result also applies to competition among some types of sellers. Imagine a one-mile stretch of beach with 120 swimmers and sunbathers distributed evenly along it. Suppose each person on the beach will purchase one ice-cream cone and is willing to travel up to a mile to get it. If there are two ice-cream vendors on the beach selling identical products, where will they locate?

The most efficient arrangement is to locate the two vendors a half mile apart. We could divide the beach into two half-mile territories and locate each vendor at the middle of a territory. As shown in Panel A of Figure 30.5, Lefty would be at the 1/4 mile mark, and Righty would be at the 3/4 mile mark. If beachgoers patronize the closer vendor, each vendor would sell 60 ice-cream cones. This arrangement will minimize the total travel costs of ice-cream patrons.

Is this an equilibrium arrangement? If Lefty were to move to the right—to the 1/2 mile mark, the median location that splits consumers into two equal halves—he would not lose any of his customers to his left but would capture part of Righty's market. As shown in Panel B of Figure 30.5, Lefty would then be the closer vendor for the people located between the 1/2 mile mark and the 5/8 mile mark. Therefore, Lefty would sell 75 cones (up from 60) and Righty would sell only 45 cones. To protect her market, Righty would move to the median location, too, locating right next to Lefty. By doing so, Righty can recover her 50 percent share of the market, again serving the consumers on the right half of the beach. At any other location, she would get less than half the market, given Lefty is at the median location. In equilibrium, shown in Panel C of Figure 30.5, both vendors pick the median location and each serves half the market.

The outcome of the ice-cream vendors' game is the same as for the politicians' game. Like politicians, the vendors have an incentive to move to the median location, so there is no real difference between the two vendors.

Alternative Models of Government: Self-Interest and Special Interests

Several economists, including Nobel Laureate James Buchanan, have suggested a model of government that focuses on the selfish behavior of government officials. According to this view, politicians and bureaucrats pursue their own narrow interests, which, of course, may differ from the public interest. For example, politicians or bureaucrats may gain prestige from starting a new spending program even if the cost of the program exceeds its social benefit. Because voters don't have much information about the costs and benefits of public services, they may not be in a position to evaluate the actions of politicians or bureaucrats and vote accordingly.

The *self-interest theory* of government explains why voters sometimes approve explicit limits on taxes and government spending. For example, many states have limits on property tax rates and total revenue, and many states also limit total government spending. According to the self-interest theory of government, limitations on taxes and spending are necessary safeguards against politicians and bureaucrats who benefit from larger budgets.

If the two sellers start at the 1/4 and 3/4 mile marks, each has a territory of 1/2 mile and sells 60 cones:

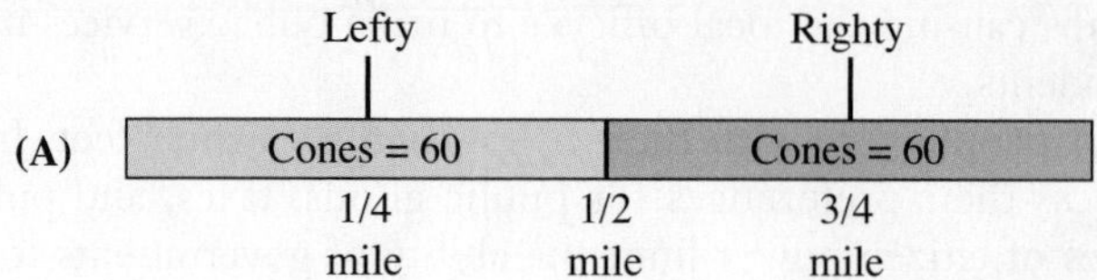

If Lefty moves to the median location, his territory increases to the 5/8 mile mark, and he sells 75 cones, compared to 45 for Righty:

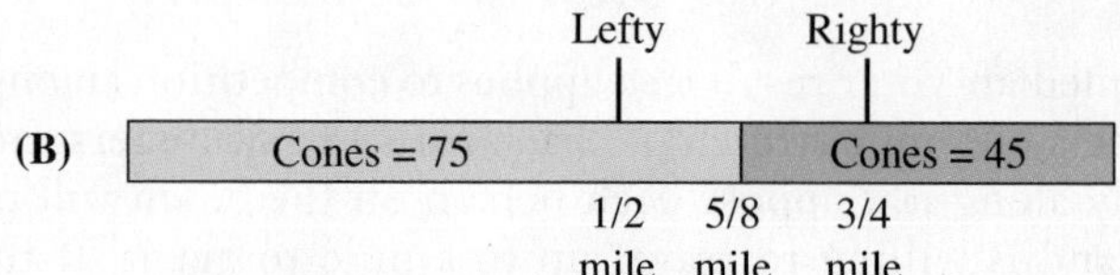

Righty can recover her lost territory by moving to the median location. In equilibrium, both sellers locate at the median location and each has half the market:

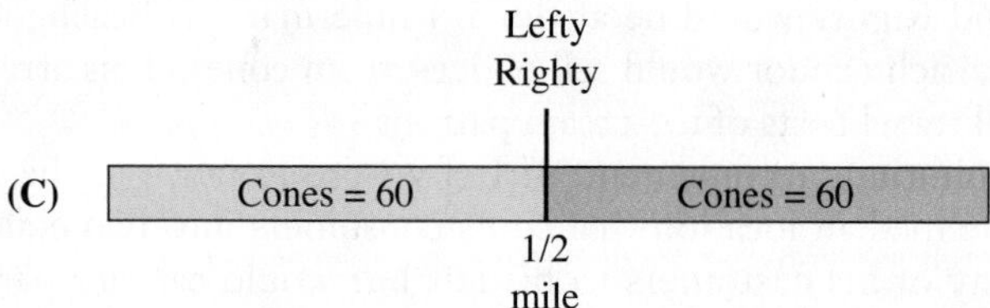

▲ **FIGURE 30.5**

Competition on a Beach Leads to a Median Location for Both Sellers

(A) If one seller starts at the 1/4 mile mark and the other starts at the 3/4 mile mark, each has a territory of 1/2 mile and sells 60 cones. (B) If Lefty moves to the median location, his territory increases to the 5/8 mile mark, and he sells 75 cones, compared to 45 for Righty. (C) Righty can recover her lost territory by moving to the median location. In equilibrium, both sellers locate at the median location and each has half the market.

Another model of government is based on the idea that small groups of people manipulate government for their own gain. Suppose the total benefit of a dam is less than its total cost, so the project is inefficient, but a few farmers reap large benefits from the dam, while the costs are spread over a million taxpayers. The farmers have a strong incentive to spend time and money convincing policymakers to build the dam. In contrast, if the tax is only $1 per person, few taxpayers will make their preferences known to policymakers because the marginal benefit (the $1 tax savings) is less than the marginal cost (the opportunity cost of their time). If politicians listen to people who express their preferences and contribute money to political campaigns, the inefficient project may be approved. This is an example of a special-interest group (farmers) manipulating the government at the expense of a larger group (all taxpayers). In general, when a few people share the benefit from a project and a large number of people share the cost, the government is more likely to approve inefficient projects.

Whenever benefits are concentrated on a few citizens but costs are spread out over many, we expect special-interest groups to form. Special-interest organizations often use lobbyists to express their views to government officials and policymakers.

application 5

THE MEDIAN VOTER IN THE NBA

APPLYING THE CONCEPTS #5: What is the median voter rule?

The National Basketball Association (NBA) uses labor agreements between players and owners to control player salaries. In the absence of a collective bargaining agreement regarding salaries, the market equilibrium would generate very high salaries for a small number of superstar players. Labor agreements are approved by majority rule, and as in other voting environments, the winning proposals reflect the preferences of the median voter, defined in this case as the player with the median salary. To predict the outcome of a vote between two competing labor agreements, we can ask, Which agreement does the median player prefer?

Recent NBA agreements use salary caps and other provisions to shift salary money away from the superstars in favor of less super players, including the median player. For the 1997 agreement, all players with salaries below the median salary gained from the agreement, and the largest gains went to players with salaries closest to the median salary. **Related to Exercise 3.5.**

SOURCE: Based on J. Richard Hill and Peter Groothuis, "The new NBA collective bargaining agreement, the median voter model, and a Robin Hood redistribution," *Journal of Sports Economics* 2 (2001), pp. 131–144.

Which Theory Is Correct?

Which of these theories or viewpoints best describes the actual practices of governments? This is a very difficult question. Economists and political scientists have studied many dimensions of the decision-making processes underlying tax policies and spending policies. There is evidence that people do vote with ballots and with their feet, and that these two forms of voting make a difference. There is also evidence that government officials sometimes pursue their own interests and those of special-interest groups. The field of public choice is a very active area of research for both economists and political scientists.

SUMMARY

In this chapter, we've seen why the government provides public goods. The free-rider problem means that we can't rely on voluntary contributions to support public goods and subsidies, so taxes are necessary to support public programs. We've also examined different views on how governments actually make decisions. Here are the main points of the chapter:

1 When a good generates *external benefits*, collective decision making generates more-efficient choices.

2 A *public good* is available for everyone to consume (nonrival in consumption), regardless of who pays and who doesn't (nonexcludable).

3 A system of voluntary contributions suffers from the *free-rider problem*: People do not have a financial incentive to support public goods.

4 Education generates external benefits in the workplace and in elections and reduces crime.

5 The *median-voter rule* suggests that government choices will match the preferences of the median voter, defined as the voter whose preferences lie in the middle of voter preferences.

KEY TERMS

external benefit, p. 654

free rider, p. 655

median-voter rule, p. 659

private good, p. 654

public-choice economics, p. 659

public good, p. 654

EXERCISES

All problems are assignable in MyEconLab.

30.1 External Benefits and Public Goods

1.1 Suppose 1,000 people would each get a benefit of $40 from a levee. Building the levee is socially efficient if its cost is less than $__________. If the cost is $30,000, a tax of $__________ per person would generate unanimous support for the levee.

1.2 An external benefit is experienced by __________.

1.3 A public good is __________ (rival/nonrival) in consumption and __________ (excludable/nonexcludable).

1.4 The three-clock tower—a response to the __________ problem—caused inefficiency because the __________ of a fourth clock was greater than its __________. (Related to Application 1 on page 655.)

1.5 **Paying for a Wi-Fi Network.** Consider a small town with 1,000 households. The town could install a wireless Wi-Fi network that would give everyone in town access to the Internet. Each household is willing to pay a maximum of $50 per year for the network, and the cost of the system is $20,000 per year. (Related to Application 1 on page 655.)

a. Is the Wi-Fi system efficient?

b. Suppose the town asks for voluntary contributions to support the network. Would you expect the total contributions to cover the $20,000 cost?

c. Suppose the town keeps track of the contributions and issues passwords to people who contributed at least $20. Would you expect the total contributions to cover the $20,000 cost?

1.6 **Cost Sharing for Monitoring El Niño.** Suppose the monitoring of El Niño's current costs a total of $12 billion per decade. Over a decade, early warning of the current's path would reduce its damages by $9 billion in the United States, $6 billion in Canada, and $3 billion in Mexico. (Related to Application 2 on page 656.)

a. Does any country, acting unilaterally, have an incentive to monitor El Niño?

b. Do the social benefits of monitoring exceed the costs?

c. Design a cost-sharing arrangement that will cause all three countries to support a monitoring system.

1.7 **Defenders of Wildlife.** Each of the 80,000 citizens in a particular county is willing to pay $0.10 to increase the number of wolf litters by one. Each litter of wolves imposes a cost of $5,000 in livestock losses to ranchers.

a. Is the provision of an additional litter of wolves efficient from the social perspective?

b. Visit the Web site of Defenders of Wildlife. Then design a system that will generate the socially efficient outcome.

1.8 **Class Participation.** Consider a course with 40 students, some of whom are confused after the professor explains a concept. The professor doesn't know whether students are confused but will clarify the concept if one student asks a question. A student who asks a question—and reveals his or her confusion—loses 10 utils. When the professor clarifies the concept in response to a question, each confused student gets a benefit of 2 utils.

a. At what level of confusion (measured by the number of confused students) is a question from a confused student socially efficient?

b. In the absence of participation incentives, will a confused student ask a question when it would be socially efficient to do so?

c. Design an incentive system to generate efficient questioning.

1.9 **Fireworks as Public Goods.** A three-person city is considering a fireworks display. Bertha is willing to pay $100 for the proposed fireworks display, Marian is willing to pay $30, and Sam is willing to pay $20. The cost of the fireworks display is $120.

a. Will any single citizen provide the display on his or her own?

b. If the cost of the fireworks display is divided equally among the citizens, will a majority vote be in favor of the display?

c. Describe a transaction that would benefit all three citizens.

1.10 **Stream Preservation.** Consider a trout stream that is threatened with destruction by a nearby logging operation. Each of the 10,000 local fishers would be willing to pay $5 to preserve the stream. The owner of the land would incur a cost of $20,000 to change the logging operation to protect the stream.

a. Is the preservation of the stream efficient from the social perspective?

b. If the landowner has the right to log the land any way he wants, will the stream be preserved?

c. Propose a solution to this problem. Describe a transaction that would benefit the fishers and the landowner.

30.2 Private Goods with External Benefits

2.1 A fire extinguisher is an example of a(n) ________ good with a(n) ________ benefit.

2.2 Education generates three types of external benefits: ________, ________, and ________.

2.3 The external benefit of transforming a high-school dropout into a graduate is about $________ per year.

2.4 A parent chooses the level of education at which the marginal ________ benefit equals marginal cost and chooses ________ (more/less) than the socially efficient level because the parent ignores the ________.

2.5 It is sensible for the government to subsidize worker training and education because some of the benefits from training go to ________.

2.6 The external benefit of a LoJack is about $ ________ per year, compared to an annual cost per LoJack of $ ________. (Related to Application 3 on page 658.)

2.7 The external benefit of a tree is measured by the change in ________, and is equal to about ________. (Related to Application 4 on page 659.)

2.8 **LoJack and Insurance Companies.** Consider the application "External Benefits from LoJack." Suppose all vehicles in a state carry theft insurance. The benefit from reduced vehicle theft goes to insurance companies because they replace fewer stolen vehicles. Insurance companies do not offer any discounts for customers who install LoJack. The cost of LoJack is $100 per vehicle per year. To simplify matters, assume that the private benefit of LoJack is zero, so the social benefit equals the external benefit. (Related to Application 3 on page 658.)

a. Suppose a single insurance company provides automobile insurance to all vehicles in the state. Will the insurance company provide free LoJacks to at least some of its customers? Explain.

b. Suppose that there are 20 companies in the state, each with a market share of 5 percent. Will the insurance company provide free LoJacks?

c. What is the threshold number of insurance companies—the number at which each insurance company will be indifferent about providing free LoJack systems?

2.9 **External Benefits from Education and Deadweight Loss.** Using Figure 30.3 on page 657 as a starting point, compute the deadweight loss associated with reaching the market equilibrium at point *a* rather than the socially efficient outcome at point *b*. Notice that the marginal external benefit is constant at $4 per book, so the gap between the marginal private benefit curve and the marginal social benefit curve is $4.

30.3 Public Choice and the Median Voter

3.1 According to the model of voting developed in the chapter, the choices made by the government match the preferences of the ________ voter.

3.2 The self-interest theory of government explains why many states have limits on ________ and ________.

3.3 The special-interest theory of government suggests a government will approve an inefficient project if the costs of the project are paid by a ________ (large/small) number of citizens and the benefits go to a ________ (large/small) number of citizens.

3.4 In the example of ice-cream vendors, the vendors choose the ________ location, and this is an ________ (efficient/inefficient) choice.

3.5 The labor agreements of the National Basketball Association favor players with close to the ________ (lowest/average/median/highest) salaries. (Based on Application 5 on page 663.)

3.6 Consider the application on the median voter and public education. (Based on Application 5 on page 663.)

a. Fill in the blanks in the following table.

	Income: Voter 1	Income: Voter 2	Income: Voter 3	Average income	Tax share of median (Voter 2)
A: Median Income < Average	10	30	80		
B: Median Income > Average	10	30	32		

b. Under what scenario is the median voter more likely to vote in favor of public schooling?

c. Consider the scenario that is least favorable to the median voter. Under what conditions will the median voter vote in favor of public schooling?

3.7 **Alienation and the Median-Voter Rule.** Consider the example of the ice-cream vendors on the beach. Suppose people are unwilling to walk more than 1/4 mile for an ice-cream cone. As a starting point, suppose both sellers locate at the median location, the 1/2 mile mark.

a. Fill in the blanks in the following table.

	Location Lefty	Location Righty	Quantity Lefty	Quantity Righty
Starting point: Median location	1/2	1/2		
Lefty moves to 1/4 mile mark	1/4	1/2		
Righty moves to 3/4 mile mark	1/4	3/4		

b. Does Lefty have an incentive to move to the left, to the 1/4 mile mark?

c. If Lefty moves to the 1/4 mile mark, does Righty have an incentive to move to the right, to the 3/4 mile mark?

d. What are the equilibrium locations for the two sellers? How does it differ from the equilibrium when everyone bought an ice-cream cone, regardless of the distance to the nearest seller?

e. Recall the discussion of the median-voter rule. Suppose voters are subject to alienation: A citizen will not vote in a budget election if the difference between the voter's preference and the politician's position is too large. Does the median-voter rule still hold?

3.8 **More Voters.** Consider the example of the gubernatorial election shown in Figure 30.4 on page 660. Suppose 18 new people move into the state and each newcomer has a desired education budget of $9 billion. Predict the proposed education budgets for the two candidates for governor.

3.9 **Change in Preferences and Proposed Budgets.** Consider the example of the election shown in Figure 30.4 on page 660. Suppose the preferences of the four voters who prefer a budget of $8 billion change, with each person preferring $15 billion instead. Will this change in preferences change the proposed budgets of the two candidates?

ECONOMIC EXPERIMENT

VOLUNTARY CONTRIBUTIONS

Do people really try to get free rides? Or would most people contribute at least some money to support a public good? Here is a classroom experiment that helps to answer this question:

- The instructor selects 10 students and gives each student 10 dimes.
- Each student can contribute money to support a public good by dropping 1, 2, or 3 dimes into a public-good pot. Each student has the option of keeping all the dimes and not contributing anything. The contributions are anonymous: No one knows how much a particular student contributes.
- For each dime in the pot, the instructor adds 2 dimes. For example, if the students contribute a total of 40 dimes, the instructor adds 80 dimes, for a total of 120 dimes in the pot. The two-for-one match represents the idea that the benefits of public goods exceed the costs. In this case, the benefit/cost ratio is three to one.
- The instructor divides the money in the public-good pot equally among the 10 students. For example, if there are 120 dimes in the pot, each student receives 12 dimes.
- Steps 2 through 4 can be repeated four or five times.

We can change the experiment to mimic the compulsory tax system. The instructor could require each student to contribute 3 dimes, the maximum amount. Would a switch to a compulsory tax system make the students better or worse off?

DEBRIEFING

After completing the experiment, do the following exercise: Consider the contribution incentives for Margie, one of the 10 students in the experiment. She thinks in marginal terms and asks herself, "If I contribute one more dime, how would that affect my payoff from the experiment?"

a. Answer Margie's question, assuming her contribution does not affect the contributions of other students.

b. If Margie uses the marginal principle to make all her decisions, will she contribute the extra dime?

MyEconLab

For additional economic experiments, please visit *www.myeconlab.com*.

NOTES

1. Lance Lochner and Enrico Moretti, "The Effect of Education on Crime: Evidence from Prison Inmates, Arrests, and Self Reports," *American Economic Review* 94 (2004): 155–189.

2. "A Pure Theory of Local Public Expenditures," *Journal of Political Economy* 64 (1956): 416–424.

CHAPTER 31 External Costs and Environmental Policy

Buildings account for about 40 percent of our consumption of raw materials and energy, and are responsible for about 30 percent of greenhouse gas emissions.

To encourage the construction of energy-efficient buildings, the U.S. Environmental Protection Agency (EPA) awards Energy-Star certificates to buildings that meet certain efficiency targets. In addition, a private organization awards LEED certificates (Leadership in Environmental and Energy Design) to buildings that meet energy-efficiency targets, among other "sustainability" goals. Many states and cities in the U.S. require LEED certification for new commercial buildings and renovations.

How do the market prices of Energy-Star and LEED buildings compare to the prices of less energy-efficient buildings? A recent study[1] shows that the typical building certified under one of the programs sells at a premium of about $5.7 million, or about 16 percent of the purchase price. A certified building sells at a premium because its greater energy efficiency means lower utility bills for its tenants. In addition, there are other unmeasured benefits such as higher worker productivity and a more favorable corporate image. The certified buildings vary in their energy efficiency, and the greater the energy efficiency, the larger the premium: a 10 percent decrease in the actual energy used in a building increases the market price by 1.2 percent.

LEARNING OBJECTIVES

- Use the marginal principle to describe the optimum level of pollution.
- Describe the role of taxation in promoting efficient environmental policy.
- Explain the superiority of taxation over traditional regulation.
- Describe the virtues of marketable pollution permits and the factors that determine their price.
- List three external costs associated with automobiles.

MyEconLab
MyEconLab helps you master each objective and study more efficiently.

As we saw earlier in the chapter on market efficiency, one condition for market efficiency is that there are no external costs in production. The cost of producing a product is confined to the person who sells it. In contrast, when production generates external costs such as air or water pollution, we say there is market failure: Markets fail to allocate resources efficiently. The role of public policy is to intervene in the market to make it more efficient. As we'll see in this chapter, the best response to market failure is not to abandon markets, but instead to use them to reduce pollution in the most efficient manner. We'll discuss two market-oriented policies: pollution taxes and auctions for pollution permits. The chapter's theme is that often the economic solution to market failure is to create markets where they do not currently exist.

One of our most challenging environmental problems concerns climate change. The mission of the Intergovernmental Panel on Climate Change (IPCC), an organization that reports to the United Nations, is to provide comprehensive scientific assessments of the causes and consequences of rising levels of atmospheric greenhouse gases (GHGs). In a recent report[2], the IPCC presents three key conclusions.

1 ***Observed changes in climate.*** The warming of the climate system is unequivocal, as shown by increases in average air and ocean temperatures, widespread melting of snow and ice, and rising sea levels.
2 ***Causes of change.*** The energy balance of the climate system has been altered by changes in (a) atmospheric concentrations of greenhouse gases (GHGs) and aerosols, (b) land cover, and (c) solar radiation. Between 1970 and 2004, the GHG emissions from human activities increased by 70%.
3 ***Projected climate change and its impacts.*** Under current practices (including current climate-change mitigation policies), there is much evidence that global GHG emissions will continue to increase over the next few decades.

To summarize, IPCC concludes that the climate is warming, that human activities contribute to warming, and that under current practices, warming will continue.

The IPCC reports the most reliable projections of changes in surface temperatures and sea levels for the rest of this century. The projected changes are large enough to cause significant changes in economies throughout the world. The anticipated increase in sea level will inundate coastal land., and the anticipated changes in the climate will alter the patterns of winds and rainfall, affecting the production of food and other agricultural products. As we'll see in this chapter, the economic approach to the problem of global warming is to impose a unit tax on greenhouse gases such as CO_2. This approach ensures that any reduction in CO_2 emissions will be achieved in the most efficient way.

31.1 The Optimal Level of Pollution

Should we eliminate all pollution? Although a pristine environment with pure water and air sounds appealing, there would be some very unappealing consequences. To reduce air pollution, we could eliminate trucks, but shipping goods by horse-drawn wagon would result in higher freight costs and higher prices for most products—and a different sort of pollution. We could reduce water pollution by shutting down all the paper mills, but reverting to parchment and slate boards would be unwieldy. Given the consequences of eliminating pollution, it is sensible to allow some pollution to occur. What's the optimal level of pollution?

Using the Marginal Principle

The most convenient way to discuss pollution policies is in terms of pollution abatement, that is, reductions in pollution from some starting level. We can use the marginal principle to determine the optimal level of pollution abatement.

MARGINAL PRINCIPLE

Increase the level of an activity as long as its marginal benefit exceeds its marginal cost. Choose the level at which the marginal benefit equals the marginal cost.

According to this principle, we should cut pollution to the level where the marginal benefit of abatement equals its marginal cost.

The marginal principle focuses our attention on the trade-offs from pollution—its costs and benefits. From society's perspective, there are many benefits from pollution abatement:

- ***Better health.*** Cleaner water means less sickness from waterborne pollutants, and cleaner air means fewer respiratory problems and thus lower health-care costs and fewer sick days taken by workers.
- ***Increased enjoyment of the natural environment.*** Improving the air quality increases visibility and improves the health of trees. Improving the water quality enhances recreational activities, such as swimming, boating, and fishing.
- ***Lower production costs.*** Some firms are dependent on clean water for survival: Farmers use water for irrigation, and some manufacturers use clean water as part of the production process. Cleaner water means lower production costs for these firms.

On the other hand, pollution abatement is costly because resources—labor, capital, and land—are used in the abatement process. Using the marginal principle, we look for the level of pollution abatement at which the marginal benefit equals the marginal cost.

Example: The Optimal Level of Water Pollution

To illustrate the determination of the optimum level of pollution, consider a lake shared by a steel mill and a fishing firm. The mill dumps waste into the lake, and pollution degrades the fish habitat and decreases the fish harvest. Figure 31.1 shows

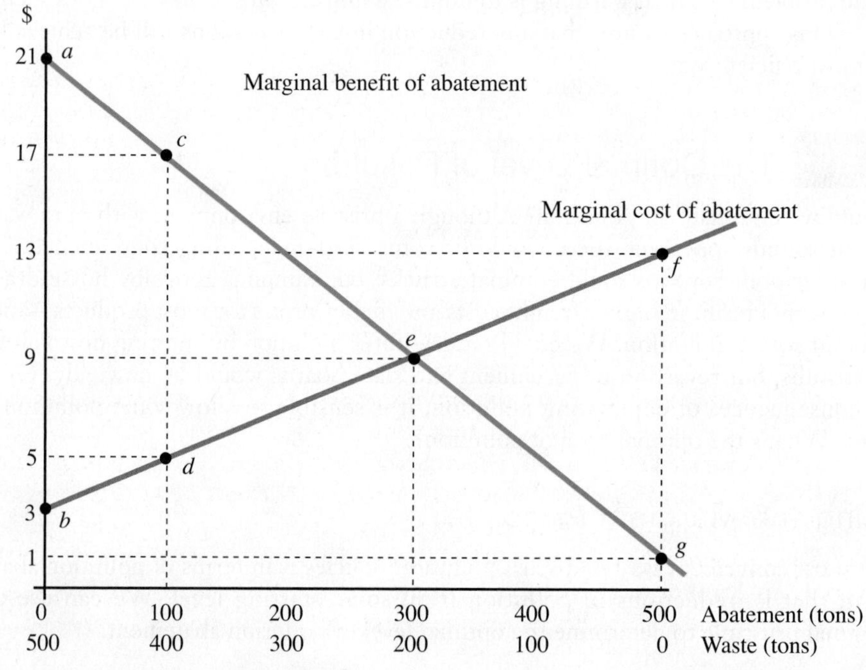

► **FIGURE 31.1**
Efficient Abatement and Coase Bargaining
The efficient level of pollution abatement, where the marginal benefit equals the marginal cost, is 300 tons (200 tons of waste). If the property rights are assigned to the polluter (steel mill), we start with zero abatement, and the other party (the fishing firm) pays to reach 300 tons of abatement. If the property rights are assigned to the other party, we start with zero pollution, and the polluter pays to increase pollution to 200 tons of waste.

the marginal benefits and marginal costs of pollution abatement. The firm can abate pollution, and the positively sloped curve is the marginal cost of abatement, which increases from $3 for the first unit abated (point *b*) to $13 for the last unit abated (point *f*). The negatively sloped curve is the marginal benefit of abatement, equal to the increase in the fish harvest from a one-ton decrease in pollution. The marginal benefit decreases as abatement increases, from $21 for the first ton of abatement (point *a*) to $1 for the last ton abated (point *g*).

We can apply the marginal principle to determine the socially efficient outcome. The efficient outcome is shown by point *e*, where the marginal benefit of abatement equals the marginal cost at 300 tons of abatement and 200 tons of waste. For any smaller quantity of abatement, the marginal benefit exceeds the marginal cost, so increasing abatement is more beneficial than costly. For example, if we start with 100 tons of abatement (400 tons of waste), the marginal benefit is $17, compared to a marginal cost of $5. Abating an additional ton increases the fish harvest by $17 but costs the steel firm only $5, so additional abatement is socially efficient. At the other extreme, we could have a pristine lake, with zero waste and 500 tons of abatement (points *f* and *g*). This is inefficient because the last unit of abatement (decreasing pollution from 1 ton to 0) has a cost of $13 (point *f*) and a benefit of only $1 (point *g*). Stated another way, the first unit of pollution is less costly to experience ($1) than it is to prevent ($13), so it is efficient to have some pollution. The same logic applies to the 301st through the 500th units of abatement: The marginal benefit of abatement is less than the marginal cost.

Coase Bargaining

Under some circumstances, an external-cost problem can be resolved through bargaining among the affected parties. The Coase bargaining solution, named after economist Ronald Coase, applies to a situation when there is a small number of affected parties, and the transactions costs of bargaining are relatively low.

We can illustrate the bargaining solution with our example of a lake shared by a steel mill and a fishing firm. If the steel mill has the property rights to the lake, it can dump waste into the lake. The fishing firm benefits from abatement, and would be willing to pay the mill to reduce pollution. For the first ton of abatement, the fishing firm is willing to pay $21, the cost of abating the first ton is only $3, and the two parties can cut a deal. If they split the difference between the benefit and the cost, the fishing firm will pay $12 to the mill for one ton of abatement, and both will be better off. The fishing firm pays $12 to get $21 in additional fish, while the mill gets $12 to incur an abatement cost of $3. The same logic applies to the second ton of abatement: The marginal benefit (just below $21) exceeds the marginal cost (just above $3), so the two parties can cut a deal. As shown by points *c* and *d*, the marginal benefit of the 100th ton of abatement exceeds the marginal cost by $12, so there is still an opportunity for an abatement deal. The deal making continues until we reach point *e*, where the marginal benefit to the fishing firm equals the marginal cost to the mill. Beyond this point, the marginal benefit of abatement is less than the marginal cost: The amount the fishing firm is willing to pay for one more ton of abatement is less than the cost of abatement.

How would things change if we assigned the property rights to the fishing firm rather than the steel mill? In this case, we would start with a pristine lake, with 0 tons of pollution and thus 500 tons of abatement. In Figure 31.1, we start at points *f* and *g*. As shown by point *g*, the marginal benefit of the last unit of abatement (going from 1 ton of pollution to 0), is a $1 increase in the fish harvest. As shown by point *f*, the marginal cost of the last unit of abatement is $13. In other words, going from 1 ton of pollution to 0 generates a cost to the steel mill of $13. Reversing direction, allowing 1 ton of pollution would save the steel firm $13. In other words, allowing the first ton of waste would harm the fishing firm by only $1 and save the mill $13, so there is room to bargain. Splitting the difference between the $1 harm and $13 cost savings, if the steel mill paid $7 for the right to dump 1 ton of waste, both firms would be better off: The fishing firm would receive $7 to tolerate a $1 loss in harvest, while the steel mill would pay $7 to avoid $13

application 1

REDUCING METHANE EMISSIONS

APPLYING THE CONCEPTS #1: How do we determine the optimum level of pollution?

Methane is one of the greenhouse gases that contribute to global warming. It is released into the atmosphere from landfills, natural gas systems, coal mining, and livestock management. In this case, abatement of emissions requires methane recovery—capturing the gas before it is released into the atmosphere and then using it to generate heat or electricity. The marginal cost of abatement is less than $10 per ton for the first 36 million metric tons, and increases at an increasing rate, reaching $150 per ton at 69 million metric tons. It is relatively cheap to recover moderate amounts of methane from landfills and coal mines and to reduce leaks in the distribution of natural gas. As the volume recovered increases, however, the abatement systems become progressively more expensive. For example, it is relatively cheap to reduce natural-gas leakage by maintaining surface facilities such as pipelines, but relatively expensive to reduce venting at production sites.

What is the optimal level of methane abatement? It depends on the marginal benefit of abatement. For example, if the marginal benefit is $10, the optimum level is about 36 million metric tons. But if the marginal benefit is $150, the optimum level of abatement is about 69 million metric tons. **Related to Exercises 1.3 and 1.4.**

SOURCE: Based on U.S. Environmental Protection Agency, "U.S. Methane Emissions 1990–2020: Inventories, Projections and Opportunities for Reductions," EPA 430-R-99-013 (September 1999).

in abatement cost. The same logic applies to the second ton of pollution: The harm to the fishing firm (just above $1) is less than the cost savings to the steel firm (just below $13), so the fishing firm can cut a deal to allow 2 tons of waste. The bargaining stops at the socially efficient point (200 tons of waste and 300 tons of abatement) because an additional ton of pollution harms the fishing firm by more than it saves the steel firm.

We've seen that assigning property rights to either the steel mill or the fishing firm generates the socially efficient outcome. Once property rights are assigned, bargaining and side payments allow the firms to adjust the level of pollution as long as the marginal benefit exceeds the marginal cost. For efficiency purposes, it doesn't matter who owns the lake as long as *someone* owns it. Of course, the assignment of property rights has important equity implications: Whoever owns the lake collects the side payments from the party that doesn't.

Under what circumstances can we rely on Coase bargaining to generate the socially efficient outcome? In our example, bargaining is plausible because there are only two parties. In contrast, if there were several polluting and fishing firms, bargaining among all the affected parties would probably be unwieldy. In general, Coase bargaining requires a small number of affected parties and small transactions costs (the costs of arranging side payments). When the number of affected parties is large, the bargaining process won't work, and the solution to a spillover problem requires a centralized policy such as pollution taxes, regulations, or marketable permits.

31.2 Taxing Pollution

private cost of production
The production cost borne by a producer, which typically includes the costs of labor, capital, and materials.

The economic approach to pollution is to get producers to pay for the waste they generate, just as they pay for labor, capital, and materials. The costs of labor, capital, and materials are the **private cost of production**, the cost borne by the producer of the product. The **external cost of production** is the cost incurred by someone other than the producer, for example, the cost associated with health problems and premature deaths from sulfur dioxide. The **social cost of production** is the sum of the private cost and the external cost. The idea of a **pollution tax** equal to the external cost per unit of pollution is to "internalize" the externality—to make the producer responsible for the external cost of production. When the tax equals the external cost imposed on others, the externality is internalized. In the example of sulfur dioxide pollution, the appropriate pollution tax is the external cost of $3,500 per ton.

external cost of production
A cost incurred by someone other than the producer.

social cost of production
Private cost plus external cost.

pollution tax
A tax or charge equal to the external cost per unit of pollution.

A Firm's Response to a Pollution Tax

A polluting firm will respond to a pollution tax in the same way it responds to the prices of labor and materials. The firm will use the marginal principle to decide how much waste to generate and how much to abate. The firm will increase the level of abatement as long as the marginal benefit exceeds the marginal cost and stop when the marginal benefit equals the marginal cost.

Figure 31.2 shows an electricity producer's marginal benefits and costs of abating SO_2. The marginal cost is $2,200 for the first ton abated (point *a*), and the marginal cost increases with the level of abatement to $3,500 for the sixth ton abated (point *c*) and $4,500 for the seventh ton (point *d*). The marginal cost increases with the amount abated because the firm must use progressively more costly means to cut emissions. From the firm's perspective, the benefit of abating pollution is that it can avoid paying the pollution tax. The marginal benefit of abatement is the $3,500 savings in pollution taxes from abating a ton of SO_2 rather than discharging it into the air.

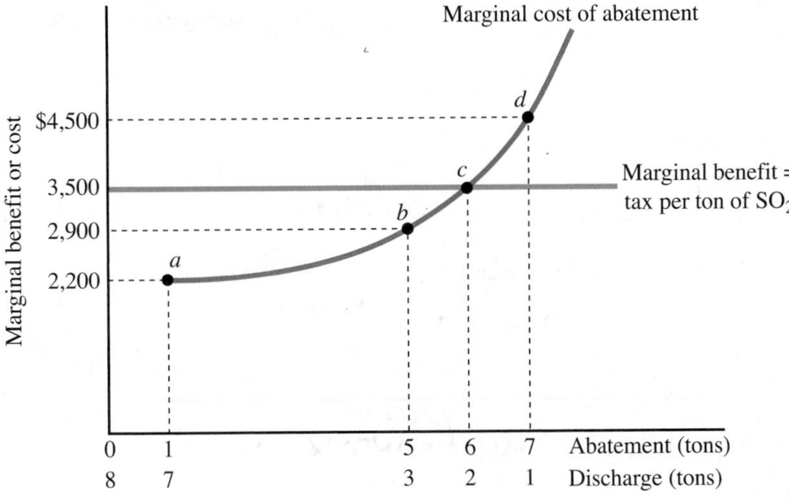

◄ FIGURE 31.2
The Firm's Response to an SO_2 Tax
From the perspective of a firm subject to a pollution tax, the marginal benefit of abatement is the $3,500 pollution tax that can be avoided by cutting pollution by one ton. The firm satisfies the marginal principle at point *c*, with six tons of abatement, leaving two tons of SO_2 discharged into the atmosphere.

The firm satisfies the marginal principle at point *c*, with six tons of abatement. For the first six tons abated, the marginal benefit of abatement—avoiding the $3,500 tax—is greater than or equal to the marginal cost. The firm stops at six tons because the marginal cost of abating a seventh ton ($4,500, as shown by point *d*), exceeds the marginal benefit (the $3,500 tax avoided). Instead of paying $4,500 to abate one more ton, the firm will instead pay the $3,500 tax.

The Market Effects of a Pollution Tax

Consider the effect of a pollution tax on the market for the product produced by polluting firms. For example, a tax on SO_2 increases the cost of producing electricity because firms pay for abatement and also pay pollution taxes on any remaining waste they generate. As we saw in an earlier chapter on market efficiency, a tax shifts the supply curve upward by the amount of the tax, decreasing the equilibrium quantity and increasing the equilibrium price.

Consider the effects of pollution taxes on the market for electricity. The production of electricity generates two major pollutants:

- ***Sulfur dioxide.*** Electric power plants are responsible for about two-thirds of SO_2 emissions. As we saw earlier in the chapter, the marginal damage from SO_2 is $3,500 per ton, so that's the appropriate pollution tax.
- ***Nitrogen oxides (NO_x).*** Power plants are also responsible for about one-quarter of the nation's NO_x emissions, a contributing factor in acid rain and the most important factor in urban smog. The study cited earlier in the chapter estimated that the appropriate tax for NO_x is about $1,100 per ton.

Figure 31.3 shows the effects of pollution taxes in the market for electricity. The taxes increase the cost of producing electricity, shifting the supply curve upward. The equilibrium moves from point *a* to point *b*, where the demand curve intersects the new supply curve. According to the electricity study, the pollution taxes would increase the price of electricity from $64.90 to $67.60 per megawatt-hour, an increase of 4 percent. The price elasticity of demand for electricity is 0.28, so the 4 percent increase in price decreases the quantity of electricity demanded by 1.1 percent, from 4,294 to 4,247 megawatt-hours. Like other taxes, the pollution tax is shifted forward to consumers in the form of a higher price, and they respond by consuming less of the polluting good. When consumers face the full cost of producing electricity, they buy less of it.

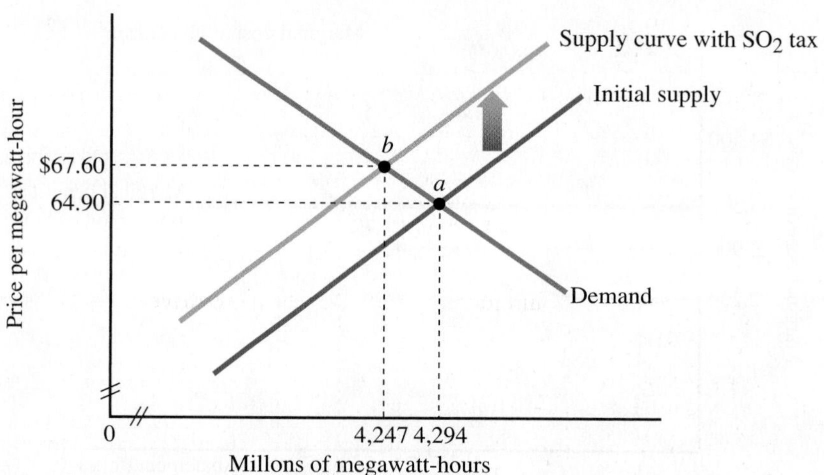

▶ FIGURE 31.3
The Effects of SO_2 and NO_x Taxes on the Electricity Market
The pollution tax increases the cost of producing electricity, shifting the market supply curve up. The equilibrium moves from point *a* to point *b*. The tax increases the equilibrium price from $64.90 to $67.60 per megawatt-hour and decreases the equilibrium quantity.

A pollution tax also changes the production process as firms switch to cleaner technology. Figure 31.4 shows the effects of pollution taxes on the energy sources used to generate electricity. Producers respond to the taxes by switching to low-sulfur coal, which is more expensive but reduces their SO_2 taxes. The share of power generated with low-sulfur coal increases from 0.43 to 0.53. The taxes increase the cost of using coal relative to the cost of using natural gas and nuclear power, so the share of electricity from these other sources increases while the share of power from coal decreases. As firms shift to cleaner energy sources, the amount of SO_2 and NO_x emissions per unit of electricity generated decreases.

These pollution taxes decrease the total amount of air pollution for two reasons. First, as shown in Figure 31.3, the increase in the price of electricity decreases the quantity of electricity demanded by 1 percent. Second, as shown in Figure 31.4,

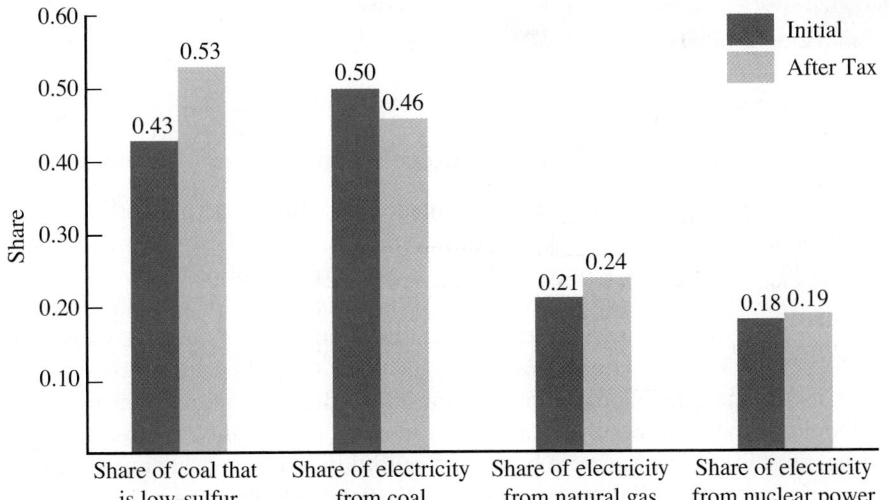

◄ **FIGURE 31.4**
Responses to SO_2 and NO_x Taxes on Electricity Generation
Taxes on SO_2 and NO_x cause electricity generators to switch to low-sulfur coal and to alternative energy sources that generate less SO_2 and NO_x.
SOURCE: Based on Spencer Banzhaf, Dallas Burtraw, and Karen Palmer, "Efficient Emission Fees in the U.S. Electricity Sector," *Resource and Energy Economics* 26 (2004): 317–341.

the shift to cleaner energy sources means that each unit of electricity generates less pollution. The combined effect of these two changes is a substantial reduction in pollution: SO_2 decreases to 11 percent of its initial volume, and NO_x decreases to 30 percent of its initial volume. An added bonus of the pollution tax is that the government could use the revenue from the tax to cut other taxes, for example, the payroll tax or the income tax.

Example: A Carbon Tax

An ongoing environmental issue is how to respond to the problem of global warming caused by greenhouse gases. One approach is to tax carbon-based fuels. A carbon tax of $100 per ton of carbon content would translate into taxes of $0.28 per gallon of gasoline, $12 per barrel of oil, and $70 per ton of coal. The tax on coal would be relatively high because of its higher carbon content.

A carbon tax would reduce greenhouse emissions in several ways:

- The price of gasoline would increase, causing people to drive less and buy more energy-efficient vehicles.
- The tax would increase the price of electricity, decreasing the quantity of electricity demanded and the quantity of fossil fuels burned.
- The higher price of home heating would cause people to turn down their thermostats and improve the heating efficiency of their homes, perhaps by installing energy-efficient windows or more insulation.
- Some electricity producers would switch from coal to natural gas, which has a lower carbon content, and thus a lower carbon tax. Others would switch to noncarbon energy sources such as wind power, solar power, and geothermal sources.

Carbon taxes have been imposed by governments around the world. In Canada, the province of British Columbia has a revenue-neutral carbon tax of $30 per ton of CO_2. The revenue raised from the carbon tax is returned to taxpayers through reductions in taxes on personal and business income. Since 2008, per-capita fuel consumption in the province has decreased by 4.5 percent, and citizens use less fuel—and pay lower income taxes—than elsewhere in Canada. According to local observers, the tax has been good for the environment and taxpayers, and hasn't harmed the economy.[3] In the U.S., the city of Boulder, Colorado has a tax on carbon emissions from electricity. In Europe, there are carbon taxes in Britain, Finland, and Sweden.

application 2

POLLUTION TAXES IN RURAL AND URBAN AREAS

APPLYING THE CONCEPTS #2: How do pollution taxes vary across space?

A recent study estimates the marginal damages (marginal external cost) for 10,000 sources of air pollution in the United States. The study reveals substantial spatial variation in the marginal damage from pollution, a result of differences in population densities around the pollution sources. For example, the marginal damage from SO_2 is \$220 per ton for an electricity-generating unit in rural Oregon, compared to \$10,860 per ton for a generator upwind of New York City. The appropriate pollution tax equals the marginal damage from pollution, so the tax on a polluter in an urban area would be much higher than the tax on a rural polluter. One response to a system of efficient pollution taxes would be to shift pollution to less densely populated areas, where damages from pollution are much lower. **Related to Exercise 2.6.**

SOURCE: Based on Nicholas Z. Muller and Robert Mendelsohn, "Efficient Pollution Regulation: Getting the Prices Right," *American Economic Review* 99, no. 5 (2009): 1714–1739.

31.3 Traditional Regulation

Although the economic approach to pollution is to get polluters to pay for the waste they generate, governments often take a different approach. Under a traditional regulation policy, the government tells each firm how much pollution to abate and what abatement techniques to use.

Uniform Abatement with Permits

To illustrate the effects of regulation, consider an area with two electricity generators, firm L (for low cost) and firm H (for high cost). Suppose that in the absence of pollution-abatement efforts, each firm would discharge two tons of pollution per hour. The government sets a target abatement level of two tons of SO_2 per hour, divided equally between the two firms. Under this *uniform abatement policy*, the government will issue four pollution permits to each firm, forcing each firm to cut pollution from two tons to one ton.

Table 31.1 shows the numbers behind the example. The marginal abatement cost of firm L is \$2,000 and the marginal abatement cost for firm H is \$5,000. Under the uniform-abatement policy, the total cost of abatement is \$2,000 for firm L and \$5,000 for firm H, for a total of \$7,000. Suppose instead the government imposes a pollution tax of \$3,000 per ton. Firm L will respond by abating two tons because the marginal cost of abatement (\$2,000) is less than the tax. In contrast, firm H will pay the tax because the marginal cost of abatement (\$5,000) exceeds the tax. When the low-cost firm does all the abating, the total cost of reducing pollution by two tons is only \$4,000.

TABLE 31.1 Uniform Reduction versus Pollution Tax

		Abatement Cost	
	Marginal Abatement Cost	Uniform Abatement Policy	Pollution Tax = \$3,000 per Ton
Low-Cost Firm	\$2,000	\$2,000	\$4,000
High-Cost Firm	\$5,000	\$5,000	\$ 0
Total		\$7,000	\$4,000

A policy of uniform abatement is inefficient because it does not take advantage of the differences in abatement costs between the two firms. In contrast, a pollution tax encourages abatement by the most efficient abaters. When we treat firms equally in terms of the consequences of their pollution (each pays the same tax per ton), we get an efficient response. The low-cost firm incurs abatement costs to avoid the tax, while the high-cost firm incurs tax costs to avoid costly abatement.

Command and Control

Traditional regulation policies have another dimension that contributes to higher compliance costs. Under a command-and-control policy, the government requires each firm to produce no more than a certain volume of pollution and requires the abatement be done with a particular technology. The problem with this approach is that the mandated abatement technology—the control part of the policy—is unlikely to be the most efficient technology for two reasons:

- The regulatory policy specifies a single abatement technology for all firms. Because the producers of a polluting good often use different materials and production techniques, an abatement technology that is efficient for one firm may be inefficient for others.
- The regulatory policy decreases the incentives to develop more efficient abatement technologies. The command part of the policy specifies a maximum volume of waste for each firm, so there is no incentive to cut the volume of waste below the maximum allowed. In other words, the benefit of developing new technologies is relatively small because there is no payoff from using them. In contrast, a pollution tax provides the right incentives: If the firm develops a new technology that cuts pollution, it will pay less in pollution taxes.

A command-and-control policy causes firms to use inefficient abatement technologies, so production costs will be higher than they would be under a pollution tax.

Market Effects of Pollution Regulations

How do the market effects of pollution regulation compare to the effects of a pollution tax? Recall that the uniform abatement policy achieves the same reduction in pollution at a higher cost because it doesn't exploit differences in abatement costs across firms. In addition, the control part of command and control may lead to relatively costly abatement techniques because there's no incentive to develop better ones. This will cause the supply curve for the polluting good to shift upward by a larger amount than it would with a tax. A larger supply shift causes a larger increase in the equilibrium price and a larger reduction in quantity. The inefficiency of regulations is passed on to consumers, who pay higher prices.

One advantage of the command-and-control policy is its predictability. The policy specifies how much waste each firm can produce, so we can predict the total volume of waste. In contrast, we don't know exactly how firms will respond to the pollution tax—they could pollute a little or a lot, depending on the tax and the cost of abating pollution—so it is difficult to predict the total volume of waste that will be emitted.

Lesson from Dear Abby: Options for Pollution Abatement

We've seen that one problem with traditional environmental policy is that it is inflexible. It doesn't allow firms to use the most efficient abatement methods available. An example of different abatement strategies comes from advice columnist Abigail Van Buren.[4] A person with the moniker "Dreading Winter" sought advice about how to deal with a pollution problem. Her neighbors heated their home with a wood-burning stove, and the smell and smoke from the wood fire gave Dreading Winter burning eyes, a stuffy nose, and painful sinuses. She offered the neighbors $500 to stop burning wood, but

application 3

OPTIONS FOR REDUCING CO2 EMISSIONS FROM INTERNATIONAL SHIPPING

APPLYING THE CONCEPTS #3: What is the most efficient way to reduce pollution?

International shipping is responsible for about 3% of global CO_2 emissions, and there are many ways to reduce (abate) CO_2 emissions. As a tool for comparing the cost of alternative reduction methods, policy analysts compute the marginal abatement cost (MAC) of each method, defined as the cost per ton of CO_2 abated. For low-cost methods such as propeller maintenance and weather-sensitive routing, the fuel savings cover the cost of the abatement method, so the MAC for these methods is close to zero. For other abatement methods, the MAC are higher:

- Switch from diesel to gas-powered engines: $20 per ton
- Reduce speed and increase fleet size: $90 per ton
- Install fixed sails and wings to tap wind power: $105 per ton

Related to Exercise 3.7.

SOURCE: Based on Magnus Eide, Tore Longva, Peter Hoffmann, Oyving Endresen, Stig Balssoren, "Future cost scenarios for reduction of ship CO_2," *Maritime Policy Management* 38 (2011), pp. 11–37.

they declined the offer. The readers of "Dear Abby" offered the following suggestions to Dreading Winter:

- Buy the neighbors a catalytic add-on for the wood stove or a wood-chip gasifier for an oil furnace. In either case, there would be much less air pollution from burning wood.
- Soak a towel in water, swish it around the room, and watch the smoke disappear.
- Leave a saucer of vinegar in each room to eliminate the smoke odor.
- Pay your neighbors to hire a chimney sweep to clean their flue.
- Seal and caulk your windows to keep the smoke outside at a cost of less than $500.
- Use the $500 to purchase an air purifier for your home.

These suggestions demonstrate a fundamental idea behind environmental economics: There is usually more than one way to deal with a pollution problem. The economic question is "What is the most efficient and least costly way to reduce the problem?" In some cases, it may be more efficient to prevent pollution (by modifying the stove or switching to an alternative fuel) than to let pollution happen and then clean up the environment (by using an air purifier). In other cases, cleanup will be more efficient than prevention.

31.4 Marketable Pollution Permits

marketable pollution permits
A system under which the government picks a target pollution level for a particular area, issues just enough pollution permits to meet the pollution target, and allows firms to buy and sell the permits; also known as a *cap-and-trade system*.

In recent years, policymakers have developed a new approach to environmental policy. The approach uses **marketable pollution permits**, sometimes called *pollution allowances*. Here is how a government runs a system of marketable pollution permits:

- Pick a target pollution level for a particular area.
- Issue just enough permits to meet the pollution target.
- Allow firms to buy and sell the permits.

In the policy world, this is known as a *cap-and-trade system*: The government "caps" the total emissions by issuing a fixed number of permits, and then allows firms to trade the permits.

Voluntary Exchange and Marketable Permits

Making pollution permits marketable is sensible because it allows mutually beneficial exchanges between firms with different abatement costs. This is another illustration of the principle of voluntary exchange.

THE PRINCIPLE OF VOLUNTARY EXCHANGE

A voluntary exchange between two people makes both people better off.

Firms will buy and sell pollution permits only when an exchange will make both firms better off. This happens when the firms have different abatement costs.

To illustrate the effects of marketable permits, let's return to the example of the two electricity generators with different abatement costs shown in Table 31.1. Suppose the government issues each firm one permit (one less than the initial level of pollution). In other words, the government will reduce pollution by two tons. Can the two firms make a deal for a permit?

- Firm H is willing to pay a maximum of $5,000 for a permit because that's how much it costs to abate a ton of pollution.
- Firm L is willing to accept a minimum of $2,000 for a permit because that's how much it costs to abate a ton of pollution.

Firm H is willing to pay up to $5,000 and firm L is willing to accept as little as $2,000, so there is an opportunity for mutually beneficial exchange. If the two firms split the difference, the price of a permit is $3,500, and each firm gains $1,500 from the transaction. Firm H pays $3,500 to save $5,000 on abatement cost, for a savings of $1,500. Firm L gets $3,500 but pays an additional $2,000 in abatement cost, for a benefit of $1,500.

How does the marketability of permits affect the total cost of abatement? In our example, the total cost with nonmarketable permits is $7,000, including $2,000 for firm L and $5,000 for firm H. In contrast, when a single firm does all the abating, the cost for two tons of abatement is $4,000 (two tons times $2,000 per ton). The savings of $3,000 equals the gap between the abatement cost of the high-cost and low-cost firm. Making the permits marketable exploits differences in abatement costs across firms, so we get the same level of abatement at a lower total cost.

The first program of marketable pollution permits, started in 1976 by the U.S. Environmental Protection Agency, allowed limited trading of permits for several airborne pollutants. Trading was later extended to lead in gasoline (in 1985) and to the chemicals responsible for the depletion of the ozone layer (in 1988).

The Clean Air Act of 1990 established a system of marketable pollution permits (also known as *allowances*) for SO_2. Under the cap-and-trade program, in 1990 the government issued permits for SO_2 emissions based on a firm's emission levels 10 years earlier. Each company initially received enough permits to discharge between 50 and 70 percent of the volume it had discharged a decade earlier, and over time the number of permits will decrease. Firms can also trade the permits. For example, if one firm has an abatement cost of $140 and a second firm has an abatement cost of $180, the low-cost firm could sell a permit to the high-cost firm at a price of $160, giving each firm a benefit of $20: The low-cost firm gets $160 for a permit and incurs an abatement cost of $140; the high-cost firm pays $160 for a permit but saves $180 in abatement cost. A report from the National Acid Precipitation Assessment Program (NAPAP) showed that being able to buy and sell permits lowered firms' total cost of abatement by 15 to 20 percent.

Each year the Environmental Protection Agency issues permits to existing SO_2 sources but withholds some for auction on the Chicago Board of Trade. In 2008, a total of 125,000 permits were auctioned at an average price of $390 per ton. Individuals and environmental groups are allowed to buy the permits and, if they wish, reduce pollution by withdrawing them from the market. In 2001 a total of 31 permits went to schools and environmental groups.

Supply, Demand, and the Price of Marketable Permits

We can use a model of supply and demand to represent the market for pollution permits. Figure 31.5 depicts a trading system introduced in the Los Angeles basin for smog pollutants such as NO_x. The supply curve for permits is vertical at the fixed number of permits provided by the government. The demand for permits comes from firms that can use a permit to avoid paying for pollution abatement, and the willingness to pay for a permit equals the savings in abatement costs. In Figure 31.5 the demand curve for permits is negatively sloped, meaning that the larger the number of permits available, the lower the willingness to pay for a permit. This is sensible because with more permits and pollution, the marginal cost of abatement will be relatively low. With a fixed supply of 100 permits in 1994, the equilibrium price, shown by the intersection of the demand curve and the 1994 supply curve at point *a*, is $7.

Under Los Angeles's smog program, the number of NO_x permits decreased each year, and in 2003 reached its goal of cutting NO_x discharges to 30 percent of the level attained nine years earlier.[5] In Figure 31.5, the decrease in the number of permits from 100 to 30 shifts the supply curve to the left, increasing the equilibrium price of permits from $7 at point *a* to $21 at point *b*. Polluters in Los Angeles responded to the higher permit prices by abating more. The Los Angeles Department of Water and Power installed abatement equipment—at a cost of $40 million—because abatement was cheaper than buying pollution permits. Libbey Glass Company installed low-pollution burners in its plant, dropping its emissions below the volume allowed

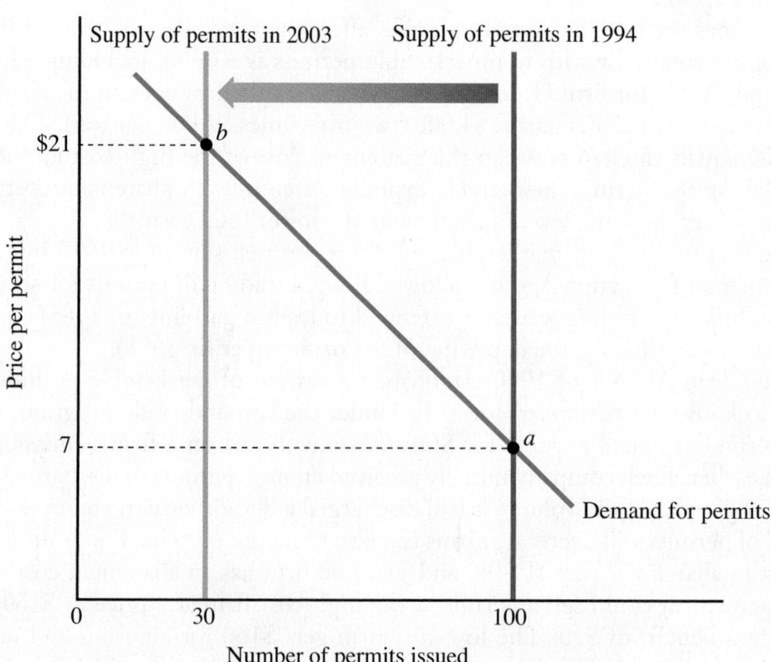

▸ **FIGURE 31.5**
The Market for Pollution Permits
The equilibrium price of permits is shown by the intersection of the demand curve and the vertical supply curve. The supply curve is vertical because each year the government specifies a fixed number of permits. A decrease in the number of permits shifts the supply curve to the left, increasing the equilibrium price.

application 4

WEATHER AND THE PRICE OF POLLUTION PERMITS

APPLYING THE CONCEPTS #4: How is the price of pollution permits determined?

The European Climate exchange is a market for the CO_2 allowances issued to European Union (EU) countries under the EU cap-and-trade system. The equilibrium price of an allowance is determined by the interplay of supply and demand. The EU determines the total quantity of allowances issued, and distributes the allowances to organizations in the energy-intensive industries, including iron and steel production, building materials, pulp and paper, electricity generators, and heat generators. The demand for the allowances is determined by a number of factors, including the level of economic activity, fuel prices, and the weather.

The Nordic countries rely heavily on hydroelectric power to generate electricity. In a dry year, the amount of power generated by hydroelectric plants is relatively low, and the Nordic countries shift to coal-fired plants. For example, in the exceptionally dry year of 1996, the emissions from power and heat generation in Denmark were roughly 70 percent higher than the emissions in 1990, a relatively wet year. A dry year will generate a relatively high demand for CO_2 emissions and thus increase the equilibrium price of the allowances. **Related to Exercises 4.5 and 4.10.**

SOURCE: Based on European Climate Exchange (www.ecx.eu).

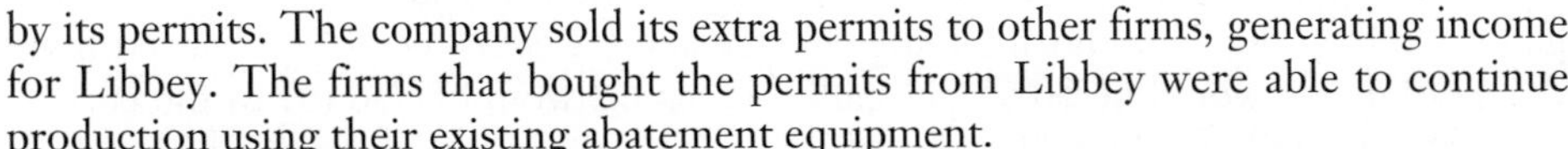

by its permits. The company sold its extra permits to other firms, generating income for Libbey. The firms that bought the permits from Libbey were able to continue production using their existing abatement equipment.

How do technological advances in abatement technology affect the price of pollution permits? A pollution permit allows a firm to avoid paying for abatement, and the higher the abatement cost that can be avoided, the larger the amount a firm is willing to pay for a permit. A technological innovation that decreases abatement costs will encourage firms to use the new technology to abate pollution rather than buying permits that allow pollution. As a result, the demand curve for permits shifts downward and to the left, and the equilibrium price of permits decreases.

31.5 External Costs from Automobiles

The use of automobiles generates three types of external costs. First, as we saw in Chapter 1, a person who uses a congested highway slows down other travelers, imposing time costs on other people. Second, automobiles generate air pollution, so drivers impose external costs on people sensitive to air pollutants. The third externality is motor-vehicle accidents—collisions with other vehicles, bicycles, and pedestrians. In this part of the chapter, we'll explore various policy responses to these externalities.

External Costs from Pollution

Ozone pollution, more commonly known as smog, is one of our most persistent environmental problems. Smog results from the mixing of several pollutants, including nitrogen oxides, sulfur dioxide, and volatile organic compounds. Smog causes health problems, triggering asthma attacks in the 15 million people in the United States who suffer from asthma and causing other respiratory problems, leading to premature deaths. Smog also retards plant growth and decreases agricultural productivity.

Because of health and other problems created by smog, the EPA has established standards for smog concentrations in urban areas. Nonetheless, in many cities ozone pollution levels rise above these healthful levels.

The Breathmobile provides a visible reminder of the health effects of smog. Started in Los Angeles in 2000, the mobile asthma clinic, housed in a 34-foot recreational vehicle, provides free diagnosis and treatment for asthmatic schoolchildren. The clinic identifies and treats children who experience aggravated asthma symptoms on smoggy days. The Breathmobile program started in low-income neighborhoods and has since spread to other cities.[6]

The automobile is by far the biggest source of smog-causing pollutants. We currently use a command-and-control approach to regulate automobile pollution: The EPA tells automakers what abatement equipment to install in cars. The equipment does not control the total emissions of the car, just the pollution per mile driven. If people buy cleaner cars but then drive more miles, total emissions can actually increase.

The economic approach to air pollution is to internalize the external cost with a pollution tax. Under such a tax, a car owner would have the car tested at the end of the year to determine how much pollution it generated per mile and then pay a tax equal to the miles driven times the external cost per mile. For example, if the external cost for a particular car is $0.02 per mile and the mileage for the year is 10,000 miles, the pollution tax for the year would be $200. The pollution tax would encourage people to buy cleaner cars, maintain their emissions equipment, drive less, and use alternative modes of transportation. The tax is consistent with the idea that people should pay the full cost of driving their automobiles, including the external costs.

One alternative to a direct pollution tax on automobile travel is a gasoline tax. According to a recent study, smog-related damages from automobiles average about $0.02 per mile driven, which translates to an average of $0.40 per gallon of gasoline.[7] Burning gasoline also contributes to global warming, and if the appropriate carbon tax is $100 per ton of carbon, the associated gasoline tax would be about $0.28 per gallon. Adding the $0.40 tax for smog damage and the $0.28 tax for global warming, the gasoline tax would be $0.68 per gallon. This tax would be added to the current gasoline taxes (a federal tax of $0.18 and state taxes that average about $0.22), which pay for highway construction and maintenance. A gasoline tax would be inferior to a real pollution tax because a driver's gasoline tax bill would not depend directly on pollution, so there would be less incentive to drive cleaner cars.

Figure 31.6 shows the market effects of a gasoline tax equal to $0.68 per gallon. The tax shifts the supply curve upward by the amount of the tax, as shown by points *a* and *b*. The new equilibrium is shown by point *c*, with an equilibrium price of $2.00 (up from $1.60) and an equilibrium quantity of 80 million gallons (down from 100 million

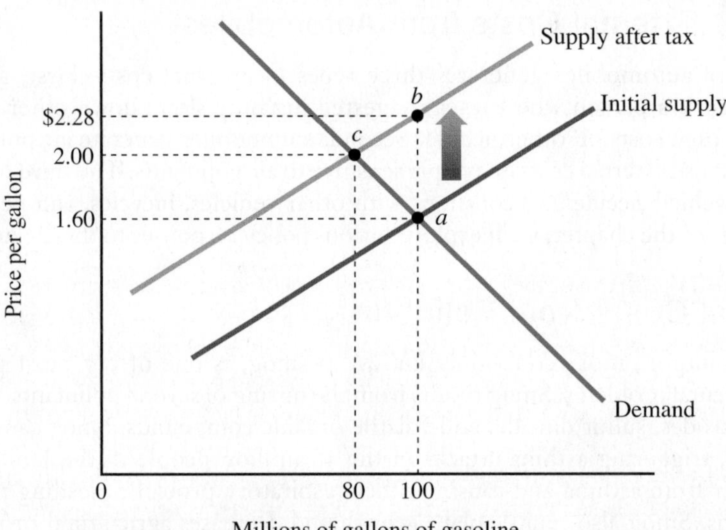

▸ **FIGURE 31.6**
The Market Effects of a Gasoline Tax
A gasoline tax of $0.68 per gallon shifts the supply curve upward by the amount of the tax and increases the equilibrium price by $0.40. The tax is shifted forward onto consumers, who pay $0.40 more per gallon, and backward onto input suppliers, who receive lower prices for crude oil.

gallons). The increase in price decreases the quantity demanded as consumers drive fewer miles, switch to alternative travel modes—bus, train, bicycle, walking—and switch to more fuel-efficient cars.

The equilibrium price rises by $0.40, which is less than the $0.68 tax. As we saw earlier in the book, a tax is shifted forward to consumers in the form of a price hike ($0.40 in this example) and backward onto input suppliers in the form of lower prices for inputs. The decrease in the quantity of gasoline produced will decrease the demand for crude oil, decreasing its price. In other words, part of the gasoline tax will be borne by the people and governments who own crude oil.

External Costs from Congestion

As we saw in Chapter 1, the typical urban commuter wastes about 47 hours per year in slow traffic and wastes $84 worth of fuel. The economic approach to congestion is to internalize the external cost by imposing a tax on drivers equal to the external costs they impose on others. To compute the appropriate tax per mile driven, we compute the change in total travel time caused by one additional car on the highway and multiply the change in travel time by the opportunity cost of travel time. For peak travel in the typical large metropolitan areas, the external cost is about $0.21 per mile traveled, so a commuter who makes a 10-mile trip during peak travel times would pay a congestion tax of $2.10. During off-peak periods when highways are less crowded, the external cost is much lower, around $0.04 per mile driven. When traffic volume is low enough that everyone can travel at the legal speed limit, the external cost is zero, so there would be no congestion tax.

Modern technology allows the efficient collection of congestion taxes. Under a vehicle identification system (VIS), each car is equipped with a transponder—an electronic device that allows sensors along the road to identify a car as it passes. The system records the number of times a vehicle uses a congested highway and sends a congestion bill to the driver at the end of the month. For example, a driver who travels 10 miles along a congested highway 20 times per month would pay a monthly congestion bill of $42.00 (20 times $2.10). The alternative approach is to use anonymous debit cards to charge for driving on congested roads.

The use of congestion taxes and other time-sensitive pricing of highways is spreading. Singapore uses Electronic Road Pricing (ERP), a debit-card system with charges that increase with the level of congestion. In Toronto, users of the Express Toll Road pay fees that depend on the distance traveled and time of day. The per-kilometer toll is $0.10 (Canadian) during peak periods, $0.07 during other weekday times, and $0.04 on the weekend. Along some highways in Southern California, drivers can pay a fee to use lanes normally reserved for carpools. The toll varies in "real time" from $0.50 to $4.00, depending on the level of congestion, and is highest from 7 A.M. to 8 A.M. and 4 P.M. to 5 P.M.

External Costs from Collisions

A third externality from the use of the automobile comes from motor-vehicle accidents—collisions with other vehicles, bicycles, and pedestrians. In the United States, the annual cost of property damage, injuries, and deaths from traffic collisions is about $300 billion per year. On average, the driver who causes an accident incurs about two-thirds of the costs, leaving one-third as an external cost imposed on others. On average, the collision-related external cost of travel is about 4.4 cents per mile driven. By way of comparison, the fuel cost per mile is about 10 to 15 cents. The direct approach to internalize this externality would be to impose a tax of 4.4 cents per vehicle-mile traveled, a VMT tax. Such a tax would improve traffic safety by reducing the number of miles driven.

Consider two alternatives to the VMT tax. First, the premium for automobile insurance could be based on miles driven rather than being a fixed amount per year. A person who drove less would pay less for insurance, which is sensible because he or she would be less likely to have an accident and impose an external cost on someone else.

Second, a gasoline tax could be imposed. The basic problem is that a person's gas-tax bill depends on the amount of gasoline consumed, not the number of miles driven and the external cost of collisions. Gas mileage varies across vehicles, and a person in a car with better gas mileage would pay less than the external cost of collisions.

application 5

YOUNG DRIVERS AND COLLISIONS

APPLYING THE CONCEPTS #5: What is the external cost of young drivers?

A VMT tax of 4.4 cents per mile would internalize the external cost from collisions on average, but the external cost varies with the age of the driver. The external cost per mile is 11 cents for young drivers (age less than 25 years), 3.4 cents for middle-aged drivers (age 25 to 70), and 5.4 cents for older drivers. A precise VMT tax would involve a higher tax rate for young drivers and generate a relatively large decrease in the miles driven by drivers with the highest collision rates and external costs. **Related to Exercises 5.6 and 5.7.**

SOURCE: Based on Ian W.H. Parry, "Comparing Alternative Policies to Reduce Traffic Accidents," *Journal of Urban Economics* 56 (2004): 346–368.

TABLE 31.2 The External Accident Costs for Different Vehicles and Driver Ages

	Younger Than Age 25	Between the Ages of 25 and 70	Over Age 70
Cents per mile	11	3.4	5.4

SUMMARY

The theme of this chapter is that the best way to control pollution and other external costs is to rely on the exchange principle and markets. A *pollution tax* internalizes the external cost of pollution, causing firms to cut the pollution per unit of output and consumers to buy less of a polluting product. A *cap-and-trade system* for emissions achieves a pollution target at the lowest possible cost because the firms with the lowest cost do most of the abatement. The external costs from automobiles could be internalized with taxes on pollution, congestion, and miles driven. Here are the main points of the chapter:

1 The optimum level of pollution abatement is where the marginal benefit equals the marginal cost.

2 A tax on the emissions of electricity generators decreases total emissions as firms switch to cleaner fuels and consumers buy less electricity at the higher price.

3 Compared to a pollution tax, traditional pollution regulations lead to higher production costs and higher product prices.

4 Allowing firms to buy and sell pollution permits reduces the cost of abatement because low-cost firms do more of the abatement.

5 Urban smog is a continuing problem, in part because the traditional command-and-control policies are less effective than an annual automobile pollution tax.

6 The external cost from traffic congestion could be internalized with a tax that varies with the level of traffic congestion.

7 The external cost from traffic collisions could be internalized with a tax that varies with the likelihood of causing a collision.

KEY TERMS

external cost of production, p. 673
marketable pollution permits, p. 678
pollution tax, p. 673
private cost of production, p. 672
social cost of production, p. 673

EXERCISES

All problems are assignable in MyEconLab.

31.1 The Optimal Level of Pollution

1.1 The optimal level of pollution abatement is the level at which the __________ of abatement equals the __________ of abatement.

1.2 The marginal cost of abatement typically __________ (increases/decreases) with the level of abatement.

1.3 The marginal cost of abating methane __________ at a(n) __________ rate. If the marginal benefit of methane abatement is $150 per metric ton, the optimal level of abatement is about __________ million metric tons. (Related to Application 1 on page 672.)

1.4 Optimal Pollution Abatement. Suppose the marginal benefit of pollution abatement is constant at $12 per unit. The marginal cost of abatement is $2 for the first unit abated and increases by $2 for each additional unit, to $4 for the second unit, $6 for the third unit, and so on. Draw the marginal-benefit and marginal-cost curves and show the optimum level of pollution abatement. (Related to Application 1 on page 672.)

1.5 Coase and Noise Pollution. Vivian is trying to learn to play the violin, much to the dismay of her housemates. Vivian and her roommates are willing to bargain over her practice time, and will split the difference between the willingness to pay for noise reduction and the willingness to accept it. The following table shows her marginal benefits from playing for one to five hours as well as the marginal external cost incurred by her housemates (constant at $5 per hour).

Hour	1	2	3	4	5
Marginal benefit to Vivian	$10	$8	$6	$4	$2
Marginal external cost	$ 5	$5	$5	$5	$5

a. Suppose Vivian has the property rights to make as much noise as she likes. How many hours will Vivian practice? Who gets how much money?

b. Suppose the housemates have the property rights to a quiet house. How many hours will Vivian practice? Who gets how much money?

31.2 Taxing Pollution

2.1 The private cost of production includes the amount a firm pays for __________, __________, and __________.

2.2 The external cost of production is the cost incurred by __________.

2.3 The social cost of production equals the __________ cost plus the __________ cost.

2.4 A pollution tax will decrease the amount of pollution a firm generates if the tax exceeds the __________ of abatement.

2.5 A pollution tax decreases the volume of pollution in two ways, by decreasing __________ and decreasing __________.

2.6 The marginal damage from pollution varies with __________, so they are higher in __________ areas than in __________ areas. (Related to Application 2 on page 676.)

2.7 Arrows up or down: A carbon tax will shift the supply curve for home heating oil __________, causing the equilibrium price to __________ and the equilibrium quantity to __________.

2.8 The Market Effects of a Carbon Tax. Consider the market for gasoline. In the initial equilibrium, the price is $2.00 per gallon and the quantity is 100 million gallons. The price elasticity of demand is 0.70, and the price elasticity of supply is 1.0. Suppose a carbon tax shifts the supply curve upward by $0.34 and to the left by 17 percent.

a. Use a graph to show the effects of the tax on the equilibrium price and quantity of gasoline.

b. After reviewing the price-change formula in the earlier chapter on elasticity, compute the new price and quantity. The new price is $__________ per gallon and the new quantity is million __________ gallons.

c. Consumers pay $__________ of the $0.34 tax and producers pay the remaining $__________ of the tax.

2.9 Shifting a Tax on Home Heating Oil. You are an economic consultant to a member of Congress. Someone just introduced a bill that would impose a carbon tax of $100 per ton, which would shift the supply curve for heating oil upward by $0.30 per gallon and to the left by 15 percent. The initial (pretax) price of heating oil is $2.00.

a. Use a graph to show the effects of the tax on the price and quantity of heating oil. Will the entire tax be paid by consumers? If not, who else will bear part of the tax?

b. Suppose the price elasticity of the supply of heating oil is 1.0 and the price elasticity of demand is 0.50. Use the price-change formula developed in the chapter on elasticity to predict the new equilibrium price. What fraction of the tax is passed forward to consumers?

31.3 Traditional Regulation

3.1 Compared to a pollution tax, a uniform-abatement policy is __________ (more/less) efficient because it does not exploit differences in __________ across firms.

3.2 The "command" part of a command-and-control pollution policy specifies a __________ for each firm.

3.3 A command-and-control policy is likely to be inefficient because it requires firms to use __________.

3.4 A pollution tax encourages firms to develop more efficient abatement technology. __________ (True/False)

3.5 Arrows up or down: A switch from a pollution-tax policy to a uniform-reduction policy will shift the supply curve of the polluting product __________ and __________ the equilibrium price.

3.6 The lesson from the Dear Abby column is that sometimes __________ is more efficient than __________, and sometimes the reverse is true.

3.7 Arrange the following CO_2 abatement techniques for international shipping in order of increasing MAC (marginal abatement cost): reduce speed, switch to gas-powered engines, propeller maintenance, tap wind-power with sails and wings. (Related to Application 3 on page 678.)

3.8 Options for Abating Noise Pollution. Janis enjoys loud music and is willing to pay $9 for the first song and $1 less for each succeeding song ($8 for the second, $7 for the third, and so on). For her dormmates, the external cost from the noise pollution is $4 per song. (Related to Application 3 on page 678.)

a. Suppose initially the price of songs is $0. How many songs will Janis play? Illustrate with a graph.

b. Suppose the government imposes a pollution tax of $4 per song. How many songs will Janis play? Compute the loss in consumer surplus from the tax, which increases the price of songs from $0 to $4.

c. Janis could soundproof her room, eliminating the noise pollution and her responsibility to pay the pollution tax. If the soundproofing costs $30, is it worthwhile?

d. Janis could compensate her dormmates for each unit of noise pollution—each song played. How much compensation would be required? From her perspective, is paying compensation better than paying the tax, worse, or the same?

3.9 Regulations Eliminate a Market? Consider a market in which the initial equilibrium quantity of a polluting good is 20 tons.

a. Use a graph to show the effects of a pollution tax that decreases the equilibrium quantity to 12 tons.

b. Consider a command-and-control policy that generates the same volume of pollution as the pollution tax but decreases the equilibrium quantity of the polluting good to zero. Use a graph to show the effects of the command-and-control policy.

31.4 Marketable Pollution Permits

4.1 Under a system of marketable pollution permits, a firm with __________ (low/high) abatement costs will buy permits from a firm with __________ (low/high) abatement costs.

4.2 Arrow up or down: A switch from regular pollution permits to marketable permits __________ the total cost of abatement.

4.3 A decrease in the supply of marketable pollution permits will shift the supply curve for permits to the __________ and the __________ equilibrium price of permits.

4.4 Arrows up or down: A technological advance that decreases abatement costs will __________ the demand for marketable pollution permits and __________ the equilibrium price.

4.5 Dry weather in the Nordic countries will __________ the demand for CO_2 allowances and __________ the equilibrium price. (Related to Application 4 on page 681.)

4.6 Split the Difference for a Pollution Permit. Consider two firms, each of which is issued three marketable pollution permits. For firm H, the marginal cost of abatement is $190. For firm L, the marginal cost of abatement is $130.

a. Is there room for a mutually beneficial exchange of one permit? If so, which firm will buy a permit and which firm will sell a permit?

b. If the two firms split the difference, what's the price of a permit?

c. Suppose that after the exchange of one permit, the marginal cost of abatement for the firm that sold the permit is $170 and the marginal cost of the firm that bought the permit is $150. Will the firms exchange another permit, or are they done trading?

d. What is the savings in abatement cost from allowing firms to buy and sell a permit?

4.7 **Reforestation versus Abatement.** Suppose your firm commits to reducing greenhouse gases by 11 tons per year. You can pay for a reforestation project that offsets your emissions at a cost of $7 per ton of carbon offset. Or you can modify your production cost to abate pollution. Your marginal cost of abating the first ton is $3; the marginal cost increases by $1 for each additional ton, to $4 for the second ton, $5 for the third ton, and so on.

a. What's the best combination of reforestation offsets and abatement?

b. How much money does your firm save by using the offsets?

4.8 **No Permits Exchanged?** A state issued marketable permits for sulfur dioxide emissions to several electricity generators. Most of the permits were given to the utilities with the oldest generating facilities. One year later, none of the permits had been bought or sold. What could explain the absence of permit exchanges?

4.9 **Lower Abatement Cost and Permit Prices.** Suppose new technology decreases the cost of abating pollution by half. Depict graphically the implications of the decrease in abatement cost on the equilibrium price of marketable permits. Use Figure 31.5 on page 680 as a starting point, with an initial permit price of $21 (point *b*). What's the new equilibrium price?

4.10 Consider the demand for CO_2 allowances in the European Union. The supply of allowances is fixed, and the initial price is $20 per ton. Suppose that dry weather in the Nordic countries increases the demand for allowances by 6 percent, and the price elasticity of demand for permits is 2.0. Predict the new equilibrium price, and illustrate with a graph. (Related to Application 4 on page 681.)

31.5 External Costs from Automobiles

5.1 A pollution tax on automobiles provides an incentive to buy ________, maintain ________, drive ________, and use alternative ________.

5.2 Arrows up or down: A gasoline tax will shift the supply curve for gasoline ________, causing the equilibrium price to ________ and the equilibrium quantity to ________.

5.3 A gasoline tax will be shifted forward to ________ and backward to ________, such as the suppliers of ________.

5.4 To internalize the external cost associated with automobile emissions that cause urban smog, the appropriate gasoline tax is about ________ ($0.20/$0.40/$0.80/$1.00) per gallon.

5.5 To internalize the external cost associated with traffic collisions, the appropriate VMT tax is about ________ ($0.01/$0.02/$0.04/$0.20) per mile.

5.6 The external accident cost per mile for the typical young driver is about ________ (1/3/6/11/15) cents, compared to ________ (1/3/6/11/15) cents for a driver between the ages of 25 and 70. (Related to Application 5 on page 684.)

5.7 **Youngsters Pay to Drive.** The demand for automobile travel by the typical young driver (age less than 25 years) is linear, with a vertical intercept of $1.00 per mile and a horizontal intercept of 200 miles per week. Initially, the cost of automobile insurance is a fixed weekly sum, independent of mileage. The average cost of driving—for gasoline, oil, maintenance, and repair—is constant at $0.20 per mile. (Related to Application 5 on page 684.)

a. Use a graph to show the driver's choice of how many miles to drive, labeled as point *a*.

b. Use the data in Table 31.2 on page 684 in the application "Young Drivers and Collisions" to show the socially efficient outcome, labeled as point *b*.

ECONOMIC EXPERIMENT

POLLUTION PERMITS

In this pollution-permit experiment, students play the role of paper firms that buy or sell pollution permits. The class is divided into groups of three to five students, with each group representing a firm that produces one ton of paper per period. The instructor provides each firm with data about its cost of production. The cost depends on how much waste the firm generates: The smaller the volume of waste, the higher the production cost. Here is an example:

Each firm receives three pollution permits for each of the five trading periods. A firm that does not sell any of its permits to other firms has the right to generate three gallons of waste in that period. A firm that sells one of its three permits can generate only two gallons of waste, and a firm that buys a permit from another firm can generate four gallons of waste.

Gallons of waste generated	2	3	4
Production cost per ton	$36	$26	$20

At the beginning of each of the five trading periods, firms meet in the trading area to buy or sell pollution permits for that day. Each firm can buy or sell one permit per day. Once a transaction has been arranged, the buyer and the seller inform the instructor of the transaction, record the transaction on their report cards, and then leave the trading area. The firm's objective is to maximize profit, and in each trading period we compute the firm's profit with the following equation:

$$\text{profit} = \text{price of paper} - \text{production cost}$$
$$+ \text{revenue from permit sold} - \text{cost of permit purchased}$$

In each period, a firm will either buy or sell a permit, so we compute the firm's profit with just three numbers. For example, using the production cost numbers shown in the table, if the price of paper is $50 per ton and a firm buys a permit for $5 and generates four gallons of waste, the firm's profit is

$$\text{profit} = \$50 - \$20 + \$0 - \$5 = \$25$$

If another firm sells a permit for $5 and generates two gallons of waste, the firm's profit is

$$\text{profit} = \$50 - \$36 + \$5 - 0 = \$19$$

For the fourth and fifth trading periods, several environmental groups have the option of buying pollution permits. Each environmental group is given a fixed sum of money to spend on permits, and its objective is to get as many permits as possible, reducing the total volume of pollution in the process.

MyEconLab

For additional economic experiments, please visit ***www.myeconlab.com*****.**

NOTES

1. Piet Eichholtz, Nils Kok, John Quigley, "Doing Well by Doing Good? Green Office Buildings," *American Economic Review* 100 (2010), pp. 2492–2509.

2. Intergovernmental Panel on Climate Change, *Climate Change 2007: Synthesis Report and Summary for Policymakers* (2007).

3. Economist, "Greenery in Canada: We have a winner; British Columbia's carbon tax woos skeptics July 21st 2011, p. 33.

4. Abigail Van Buren, "Aid for Reader's Winter Woe," *Sacramento Bee*, February 15, 1984, http://www.epa.gov/airmarkets/auctions/ (accessed July 9, 2006).

5. Gary Polaroid, "Cost of Clean Air Credits Soars in Southland," *Los Angeles Times*, September 5, 2000.

6. South Coast Air Quality Management District, "New Mobile Asthma Clinic to Serve L.A. County Children," May 12, 2000.

7. Kenneth Small and Camilla Kazimi, "On the Costs of Air Pollution from Motor Vehicles," *Journal of Transport Economics and Policy* 29 (1995): 7–32.

The Labor Market and the Distribution of Income

CHAPTER 32

A key factor in a worker's earnings is educational attainment.

In 2009, the median annual earnings of high-school graduates were $32,600, compared to $56,700 for college graduates.[1] In other words, the college premium—the increase in earnings from earning a college degree rather than stopping with a high school education—was 74 percent. Over a lifetime, the payoff from a college degree was $964,000. Over the last several decades, the college premium has almost doubled.

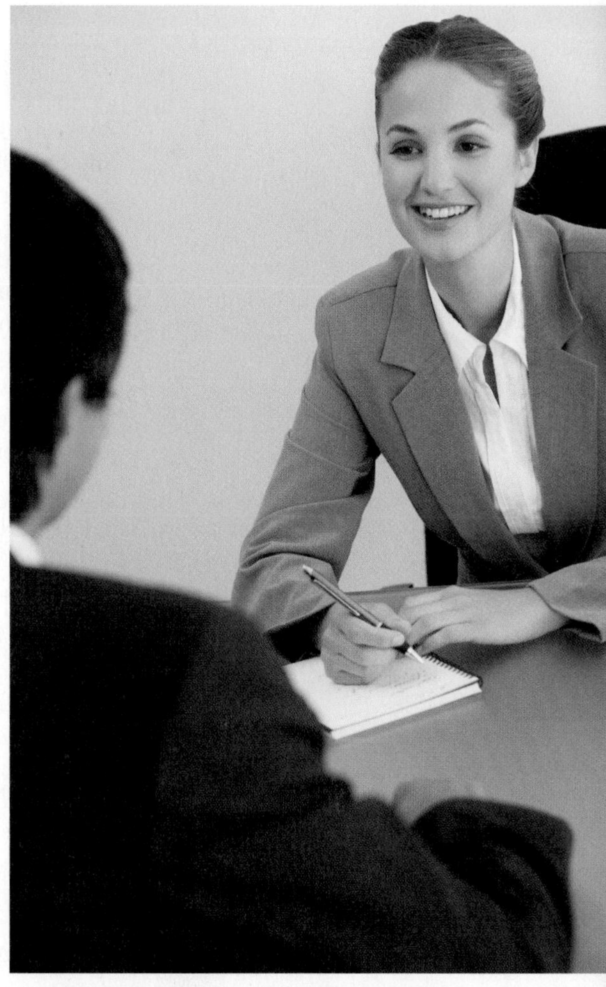

LEARNING OBJECTIVES

- Explain why competition generates wages equal to marginal revenue product.
- Explain why an increase in the wage could increase, decrease, or not change hours worked.
- Explain why wages differ across occupations and levels of human capital.
- Describe recent changes in the distribution of income.
- Describe the effects of government policies on poverty and the distribution of income.

MyEconLab
MyEconLab helps you master each objective and study more efficiently.

Up to this point in the book, we have discussed the markets for final goods and services. In this chapter, we switch to the market for one of the factors of production—labor. Labor costs are responsible for about three-fourths of production costs, and for most people labor income is by far the most important source of income. We'll use a model of demand and supply to see how wages are determined and why wages differ between college graduates and high-school graduates, men and women, and people in different occupations. We'll also take a look at recent changes in the distribution of income and the effects of government tax and transfer policies on poverty and the distribution of income.

32.1 The Demand for Labor

We can use demand and supply curves to show how wages are determined and examine how changes in the labor market affect wages and employment. We'll start with the demand side of the labor market, looking first at how an individual firm can use the key principles of economics to decide how many workers to hire.

The demand for labor and other productive inputs is different from the demand for consumer products such as iPods, books, haircuts, and pizza. Firms use workers to produce the products demanded by consumers, and so economists say that labor demand is a "derived demand." That is, it is determined by, or derived from, the demand for the products that workers produce. As we'll see in this chapter, the demand for labor is determined by the demand for consumer products and the price of those products.

Labor Demand by an Individual Firm in the Short Run

Consider a perfectly competitive firm that produces rubber balls. Because this firm is perfectly competitive, it takes the price of its output and the prices of its inputs as given. Because it hires a tiny fraction of the workers in the labor market, it takes the market wage as given and can hire as many workers as it wants at that wage. In addition, the firm produces a tiny fraction of the rubber balls sold in the market, so it takes the price of its output as given. Let's say the price of rubber balls is $0.50.

Consider the firm's hiring decision in the short run, defined as the period during which at least one input—for example, its factory—cannot be changed. We can use two of the key principles of economics to explain the firm's hiring decision. Recall the marginal principle.

MARGINAL PRINCIPLE

Increase the level of an activity as long as its marginal benefit exceeds its marginal cost. Choose the level at which the marginal benefit equals the marginal cost.

The firm will pick the quantity of labor at which the marginal benefit of labor equals the marginal cost of labor. It can hire as many workers as it wants at the market wage, so the marginal cost of labor equals the hourly wage. If the wage is $8 per hour, the extra cost associated with one more hour of labor—the marginal cost—is $8, regardless of how many workers the firm hires.

What is the marginal benefit of labor? The firm hires labor to produce balls, so the marginal benefit equals the monetary value of the balls produced with an additional hour of labor. Table 32.1 shows how to compute the marginal benefit associated with different quantities of labor. The first two columns show the relationship between the number of workers and the quantity of balls produced. Recall the principle of diminishing returns.

TABLE 32.1 Using the Marginal Principle to Make a Labor Decision

(1) Workers	(2) Balls	(3) Marginal Product of Labor	(4) Price	(5) Marginal Revenue Product of Labor (*MRP*)	(6) Marginal Cost When Wage = $8
1	26	26	$0.50	$13	$8
2	50	24	0.50	12	8
3	72	22	0.50	11	8
4	92	20	0.50	10	8
5	108	16	0.50	8	8
6	120	12	0.50	6	8
7	128	8	0.50	4	8
8	130	2	0.50	1	8

PRINCIPLE OF DIMINISHING RETURNS

Suppose that output is produced with two or more inputs and we increase one input while holding the other inputs fixed. Beyond some point—called the *point of diminishing returns*—output will increase at a decreasing rate.

As we saw earlier in the book, the **marginal product of labor**, the change in output from one additional unit of labor, typically rises for the first few workers and then eventually decreases. To simplify matters, we'll assume diminishing returns start to occur with the second worker. As shown in the third column of Table 32.1, the marginal product of labor decreases as the number of workers increases, from 26 for the first worker, to 24 for the second worker, and so on.

marginal product of labor
The change in output from one additional unit of labor.

The marginal benefit of labor equals the **marginal-revenue product of labor (*MRP*)**, which is defined as the extra revenue generated by one additional unit of labor. To compute the *MRP*, we multiply the marginal product of labor by the price of output ($0.50 per ball in this example):

marginal-revenue product of labor (*MRP*)
The extra revenue generated from one additional unit of labor; *MRP* is equal to the price of output times the marginal product of labor.

$$MRP = \text{marginal product} \times \text{price of output}$$

Figure 32.1 shows the marginal-revenue product curve. Because the marginal product drops as the number of workers increases, the *MRP* curve is negatively sloped, falling from $11 for the third worker (point *a*) to $8 for the fifth worker (point *b*), and so on.

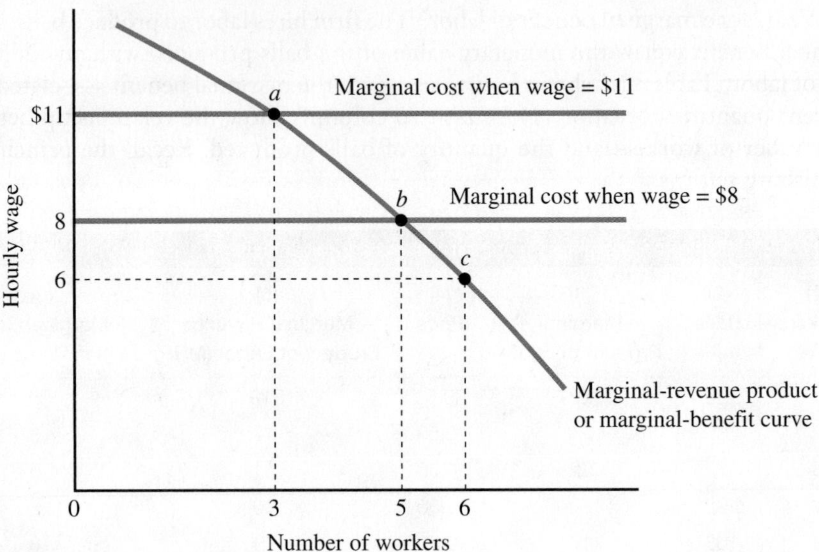

▲ FIGURE 32.1
The Marginal Principle and the Firm's Demand for Labor
Using the marginal principle, the firm picks the quantity of workers at which the marginal benefit (the marginal-revenue product of labor) equals the marginal cost (the wage). The firm's short-run demand curve for labor is the marginal-revenue product curve.

A firm can use its *MRP* curve to decide how much labor to hire at a particular wage. In Figure 32.1, the marginal-cost curve is horizontal at the market wage ($8). The perfectly competitive firm takes the wage as given, so the marginal-cost curve is also the labor-supply curve faced by the firm. The marginal principle is satisfied at point *b*, where the marginal cost equals the marginal-revenue product. The firm will hire five workers because for the first five workers, the marginal benefit (the *MRP*) is greater than or equal to the marginal cost (the $8 wage). It would not be sensible to hire another worker, because the additional revenue from the sixth worker ($6) would be less than the $8 additional cost of that worker. If the wage increases to $11, the firm will satisfy the marginal principle at point *a*, hiring only three workers.

short-run demand curve for labor
A curve showing the relationship between the wage and the quantity of labor demanded over the short run, when the firm cannot change its production facility.

The *MRP* curve is also the firm's **short-run demand curve for labor**, which shows the relationship between the wage and the quantity of labor demanded in the short run, when the firm cannot change its production facility. The demand curve answers the following question: At each wage, how many workers does the firm want to hire? We've already used the *MRP* curve to answer this question for two different wages ($11 and $8), and we can do the same for any other wage. Because the *MRP* curve is a marginal-benefit curve, and the firm uses the marginal principle to decide how much labor to hire, the *MRP* curve is the same as the firm's demand curve for labor. If you pick a wage, the *MRP* curve tells you exactly how much labor the firm will demand at that wage.

What sorts of changes would cause the demand curve to shift? To draw the labor-demand curve, we fix the price of the output and the productivity of workers. Therefore, an increase in the price of the output will increase the *MRP* of workers, shifting the entire demand curve for labor to the right: At each wage, the firm will hire more workers. This is shown in Figure 32.2. An increase in the price of balls shifts the labor-demand curve to the right. At a wage of $8, the firm hires seven workers instead of five. Similarly, if workers become more productive, the increase in the marginal product of labor will increase the *MRP* and shift the demand curve to the right. Conversely, a decrease in price or labor productivity will shift the demand curve to the left.

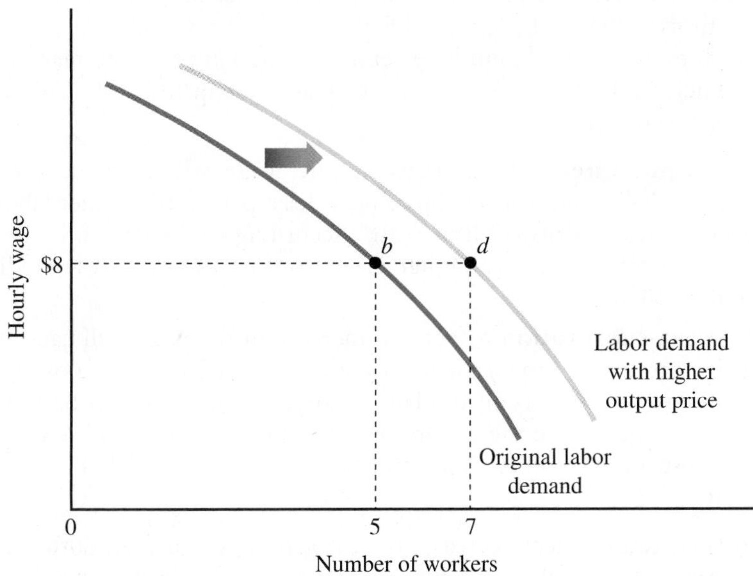

▲ FIGURE 32.2
An Increase in the Price of Output Shifts the Labor-Demand Curve
An increase in the price of the good produced by workers increases the marginal revenue product at each quantity of workers, shifting the demand curve to the right. At each wage, the firm will demand more workers. For example, at a wage of $8, the demand for labor increases from five workers (point *b*) to seven workers (point *d*).

Market Demand for Labor in the Short Run

To draw the short-run market demand curve for labor, we add the labor demands of all the firms that use a particular type of labor. In the simplest case, all firms are identical, and we simply multiply the number of firms by the quantity of labor demanded by the typical firm. If there were 100 firms and each hired 5 workers at a wage of $8, the market demand for labor would be 500 workers. Similarly, if the typical firm hired 3 workers at a wage of $11, the market demand would be 300 workers. In the more realistic case of non-identical firms, we use the same technique used for the market demand for a consumer good. We draw the individual demand curves and then sum them horizontally to get the market demand curve. In other words, for each wage we add up the labor demands of all the firms to get the aggregate or market demand.

Labor Demand in the Long Run

long-run demand curve for labor
A curve showing the relationship between the wage and the quantity of labor demanded over the long run, when the number of firms in the market can change and firms can modify their production facilities.

Recall that in the long run, firms can enter or leave the market and firms already in the market can change all their inputs, including their production facilities. The **long-run demand curve for labor** shows the relationship between the wage and the quantity of labor demanded over the long run, when the number of firms in the market can change and firms in the market can modify their production facilities.

Although there are no diminishing returns in the long run, the market demand curve is still negatively sloped. As the wage increases, the quantity of labor demanded decreases for two reasons:

output effect
The change in the quantity of labor demanded resulting from a change in the quantity of output produced.

input-substitution effect
The change in the quantity of labor demanded resulting from an increase in the price of labor relative to the price of other inputs.

- The **output effect**. An increase in the wage will increase the cost of producing balls, and firms will pass on at least part of the higher labor cost to their consumers: Prices will increase. According to the law of demand, firms will sell fewer balls at the higher price, so they will need less of all inputs, including labor.
- The **input-substitution effect**. An increase in the wage will cause the firm to substitute other inputs for labor. At a wage of $4, it may not be sensible to use much machinery in the ball factory, but at a wage of $20, it may be sensible to mechanize the factory, using more machinery and fewer workers. This substitution of other inputs for labor decreases the labor input per unit of output.

The input-substitution effect decreases the labor input per unit of output while the output effect decreases total output. The two effects operate in the same direction, so the market demand curve is negatively sloped.

The notion of input substitution applies to other labor markets as well. For the most graphic examples of factor substitution, we can travel from a developed country, such as the United States, Canada, France, Germany, or Japan, to a less-developed country in South America, Africa, or Asia. Wages are much lower in the less-developed countries, so production tends to be more labor intensive. In other words, labor is less costly relative to machinery and equipment, so labor is substituted for these other inputs. Here are some examples:

- ***Mining.*** U.S. firms use huge earthmoving equipment to mine for minerals; firms in some less-developed countries use thousands of workers digging by hand.
- ***Furniture.*** Firms in developed countries manufacture furniture with sophisticated machinery and equipment; firms in some less-developed countries make furniture by hand.
- ***Accounting.*** Accountants in developed countries use computers and sophisticated software programs; some accountants in less-developed countries use simple calculators and ledger paper.

application 1

MARGINAL REVENUE PRODUCT IN MAJOR LEAGUE BASEBALL

APPLYING THE CONCEPTS #1: Are workers paid their marginal revenue product (MRP)?

In 2011, the average salary in Major League Baseball (MLB) was $3.3 million. Are players really worth that much? A team will pay $3.3 million for a player only if the player's marginal revenue product (MRP) is at least $3.3 million. The MRP of a player equals his contribution to the firm's total revenue from ticket sales and television contracts. People are willing to pay for winners, and a player whose performance increases the team's winning percentage increases its revenue from tickets and TV. For example, a player with a relatively high slugging percentage increases the team's winning percentage, increasing the revenue from ticket sales and TV.

A recent study shows that for some types of players, the salary is less than the player's MRP. Some MLB players are free agents, meaning that they are free to negotiate a contract with any MLB team. Given the competition between teams for the services of free agents, their salaries are close to their MRPs. In contrast, two types of players are not allowed to change teams, and the limited competition for their services means that they earn relatively low salaries.

1 Journeymen (3–6 years in the league) are restricted to a single team, but can enter salary arbitration to change their salaries.
2 Apprentices (up to 3 years in the league) are restricted to a single team and cannot change their salaries.

Given the immobility of journeymen and apprentices, we expect them to be paid less than their MRPs. According to a recent study, the average MRP of journeymen is about $1.08 million, which is about 17 percent higher than the average journeyman salary. For apprentices, the average MRP is about $810,000, which is about 3.6 times the average apprentice salary. **Related to Exercise 1.7.**

SOURCE: Based on Anthony Krautmann, "What's Wrong with Scully-Estimates of a Player's Marginal Revenue Product," *Economic Inquiry* 37 (1999), pp. 369–381.

Short-Run versus Long-Run Demand

How does the short-run demand curve for labor compare to the long-run demand curve? There is less flexibility in the short run because firms cannot enter or leave the market and they cannot modify their production facilities. As a result, the demand for labor is less elastic in the short run. That means the short-run demand curve is steeper than the long-run demand curve. In the chapter on perfect competition we used the same logic to explain why the short-run supply curve for a product (plain cotton T-shirts) was steeper than the long-run supply curve for the product.

32.2 The Supply of Labor

The labor-supply curve answers the following question: How many hours of labor will be supplied at each wage? When we speak of a labor market, we are referring to the market for a specific occupation in a specific geographical area. Consider the supply for nurses in the hypothetical city of Florence. The supply question is "How many hours of nursing services will be supplied at each wage?" To answer that question, we must think about how many nurses are in the city and how many hours each nurse works.

The Individual Labor-Supply Decision: How Many Hours?

Let's start with an individual's decision about how many hours to work. The decision to work is a decision to sacrifice some leisure time for money: Each hour of work reduces leisure time by one hour. Therefore, the demand for leisure is the flip side of the supply of labor. The price of leisure time is the income sacrificed for each hour of leisure, that is, the hourly wage. We know from earlier chapters that an increase in the price of a good has two effects: a substitution effect and an income effect. An increase in the wage—the price of leisure—has two effects on the demand for leisure.

substitution effect for leisure demand
The change in leisure time resulting from a change in the wage (the price of leisure) relative to the price of other goods.

Consider first the **substitution effect for leisure demand**. The worker faces a trade-off between leisure time and consumer goods such as music, books, food, and entertainment. For each hour of leisure time Leah takes, she loses one hour of work time, and her income drops by an amount equal to the wage. Therefore, she has less money to spend on consumer goods. For example, if the wage is $8 per hour, each hour of leisure decreases the amount of income available to spend on consumer goods by $8. When the wage increases to, say, $10, Leah will sacrifice more income—and consumer goods—for each hour of leisure she takes. Given the larger sacrifice of consumer goods per hour of leisure time, she will demand less leisure. That means she will work more hours and earn more money for consumer goods. In other words, as the wage increases, she will substitute income—and the consumer goods it buys—for leisure time.

income effect for leisure demand
The change in leisure time resulting from a change in real income caused by a change in the wage.

Consider next the **income effect for leisure demand**. For most people, leisure is a normal good in the sense that the demand for leisure increases as real income increases. An increase in the wage increases Leah's real income in the sense that she can afford more of all goods, including leisure time. Suppose Leah has a total of 100 hours per week to divide between leisure and work. At a wage of $10, she works 36 hours and has 64 hours of leisure. She also earns $360 ($10 per hour times 36 hours of work) and spends that amount on consumer goods. If her wage increases to $15, her real income increases because she can have more consumer goods and more leisure time. For example, if she worked only 30 hours, she could buy $450 worth of consumer goods ($15 per hour times 30 hours) and have 70 hours of leisure (100 hours per week minus 30 hours of work). The increase in real income causes Leah to consume more of all normal goods, including leisure time. The increase in real income causes her to demand more leisure and supply less labor.

In the labor market, the income and substitution effects of an increase in wages operate in opposite directions. The substitution effect decreases the desired leisure time, while the income effect increases the desired leisure time. Therefore, we can't predict whether an increase in the wage will cause a worker to demand more leisure time (supply less labor) or less leisure (supply more labor).

An Example of Income and Substitution Effects

A simple example will show why we can't predict a worker's response to an increase in the wage. Suppose each nurse in Florence initially works 36 hours per week at an hourly wage of $10 and the wage increases to $12. The following are three reasonable responses to the higher wage:

1 *Lester works fewer hours.* If Lester works 30 hours instead of 36 hours, he gets 6 hours of extra leisure time and still earns the same income per week ($360 = 30 hours × $12 per hour).

2 *Sam works the same number of hours.* If Sam continues to work 36 hours per week, he gets an additional $72 of income ($2 per hour × 36 hours) and the same amount of leisure time.

3 *Maureen works more hours.* If Maureen works 43 hours instead of 36 hours, she sacrifices 7 hours of leisure time but earns a total of $516, compared to only $360 at a wage of $10 per hour.

Empirical studies of the labor market confirm that each of these responses is reasonable. When the wage increases, some people work more, others work less, and others work about the same amount. At the market level, the aggregate response to an increase in the wage varies across markets.

The Market Supply Curve for Labor

Now that we know how individual workers respond to changes in wages, we're ready to consider the supply side of the labor market. The **market supply curve for labor** shows the relationship between the wage and the quantity of labor supplied. In Figure 32.3, the market supply curve for labor is positively sloped, consistent with the law of supply: There is a positive relationship between the wage (the price of labor) and the quantity of labor supplied, *ceteris paribus*. An increase in the wage affects the quantity of nursing supplied in three ways:

market supply curve for labor
A curve showing the relationship between the wage and the quantity of labor supplied.

1 ***Hours worked per employee.*** When the wage increases, some nurses will work more hours, some will work fewer hours, and some will work the same number of hours. We don't know for certain whether the average number of work hours will increase, decrease, or stay the same, but the change in the average number of hours worked is likely to be relatively small.

2 ***Occupational choice.*** An increase in the nursing wage will cause some workers to switch from other occupations to nursing and motivate more new workers to pick nursing over other occupations.

3 ***Migration.*** Some nurses in other cities will move to Florence to earn the higher wages offered there.

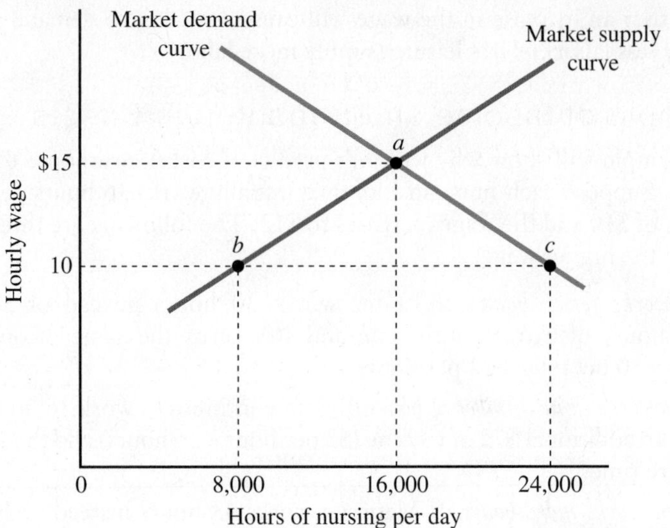

▲ FIGURE 32.3
Supply, Demand, and Labor Market Equilibrium
At the market equilibrium shown by point *a*, the wage is $15 per hour and the quantity of labor is 16,000 hours. The quantity supplied equals the quantity demanded, so there is neither excess demand for labor nor excess supply of labor.

application 2

CABBIES RESPOND TO AN INCREASE IN THE WAGE

APPLYING THE CONCEPTS #2: When the wage increases, will the typical person work more hours or fewer hours?

Taxi drivers have a lot of flexibility in choosing their work hours, and we can readily observe their response to an increase in the wage. An increase in the taxi fare, which is regulated by cities, represents an increase in the wage earned by taxi drivers. A recent study of the taxi market in New York City shows that an increase in the regulated fare (an increase in the wage) actually decreases the quantity of labor supplied. In 2004 a 19 percent increase in the regulated fare decreased the miles driven per cabbie by 5.6 percent. Overall, the elasticity of miles driven (quantity of labor supplied) with respect to the fare per mile (the wage) is –0.22. In other words, a 10 percent increase in the wage decreases the quantity of labor supplied by 2.2 percent. **Related to Exercises 2.6 and 2.11.**

SOURCE: Based on Orley Ashenfelter, Kork Doran, Bruce Schaller," A Shred of Credible Evidence on the Long Run Elasticity of Labor Supply" (working Paper 551, Industrial Relations Section, Princeton University, 2009).

The second and third effects reinforce one another, so an increase in the wage causes movement upward along the market supply curve. If the wage of Florence nurses increases from $10 to $15 per hour, the quantity of nurses supplied increases from 8,000 hours per day (point *b*) to 16,000 hours per day (point *a*). Although individual workers may not work more hours as the wage increases, the supply curve is positively sloped because an increase in the wage changes workers' occupational choices and causes migration.

32.3 Labor Market Equilibrium

We're ready to put demand and supply together to think about equilibrium in the labor market. A market equilibrium is a situation in which there is no pressure to change the price of a good or service. Figure 32.3 shows the equilibrium in the market for nurses. The supply curve intersects the demand curve at point *a*, so the equilibrium wage is $15 per hour and the equilibrium quantity is 16,000 hours of nursing per day. At this wage, there is neither an excess demand for labor nor an excess supply of labor, so the market has reached an equilibrium.

Changes in Demand and Supply

How would a change in the demand for nurses affect the equilibrium wage of nurses? We know from Chapter 4 that a change in demand causes the equilibrium price and the equilibrium quantity to move in the same direction: An increase in demand increases the equilibrium price and quantity, whereas a decrease in demand decreases the equilibrium price and quantity. For example, suppose the demand for medical care increases. Nurses help to provide medical care, so an increase in the quantity of medical care demanded will shift the demand curve for nurses to the right: At each wage, firms will demand more hours of nursing services. As shown in Figure 32.4, an increase in demand increases the equilibrium wage and the equilibrium quantity of nursing services.

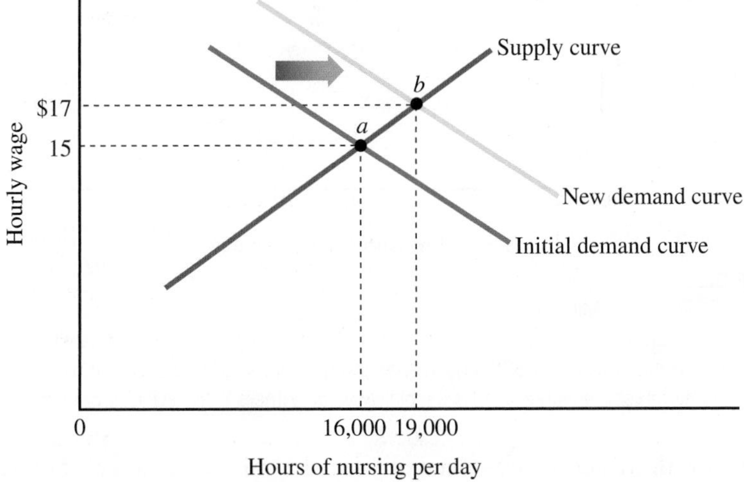

▲ FIGURE 32.4
The Market Effect of an Increase in Demand for Labor
An increase in the demand for nursing services shifts the demand curve to the right, moving the equilibrium from point *a* to point *b*. The equilibrium wage increases from $15 to $17 per hour, and the equilibrium quantity increases from 16,000 hours to 19,000 hours.

How would a change in supply of nurses affect the equilibrium wage of nurses? We know from Chapter 4 that a change in supply causes price and quantity to move in opposite directions: An increase in supply decreases the equilibrium price but increases the equilibrium quantity, whereas a decrease in supply increases the equilibrium price but decreases the equilibrium quantity. Suppose a new television program makes nursing look like an attractive occupation, causing a large number of young people to become nurses rather than accountants, lawyers, or doctors. The supply curve for nurses will shift to the right: At each wage, more nursing hours will be supplied. The equilibrium wage will decrease, and the equilibrium quantity will increase.

The Market Effects of the Minimum Wage

We can use the model of the labor market to show how various public policies, such as the federally mandated minimum wage, affect total employment. In 2012 the federal minimum wage was $7.25 per hour. Figure 32.5 shows the effects of a minimum wage on the market for restaurant workers. The market equilibrium is shown by point *a*: The supply of restaurant workers equals demand at a wage of $6.05 and a quantity of 50,000 worker hours per day. Suppose a minimum wage is established at $7.25 per hour. At this wage, the quantity of labor demanded is only 49,000 hours (point *b* on the demand curve). In other words, the minimum wage decreases the quantity of labor restaurants use by 1,000 hours per day.

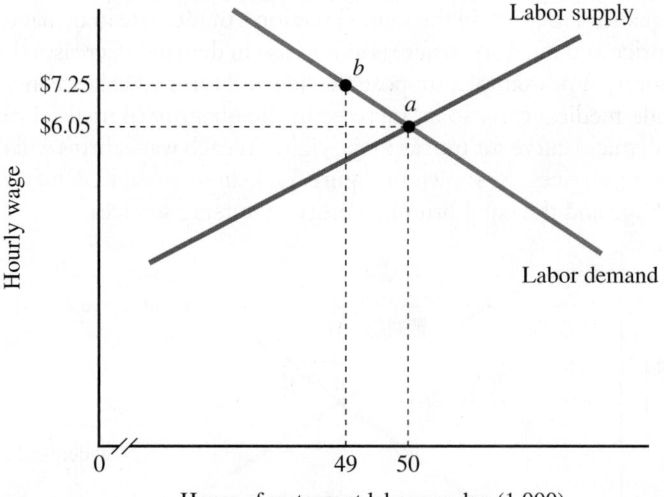

▲ **FIGURE 32.5**
The Market Effects of a Minimum Wage
The market equilibrium is shown by point *a*: The wage is $6.05 per hour, and the quantity of labor is 50,000 hours. A minimum wage of $7.25 decreases the quantity of labor demanded to 49,000 hours per day (point *b*). Although some workers receive a higher wage, others lose their jobs or work fewer hours.

What are the trade-offs associated with the minimum wage? For restaurant workers and restaurant diners, there is good news and bad news:

- ***Good news for some restaurant workers.*** Some workers keep their jobs and receive a higher wage ($7.25 per hour instead of $6.05 per hour).

- ***Bad news for some restaurant workers.*** Some workers lose their jobs. If the typical workday for restaurant workers is 5 hours, the loss of 1,000 hours of restaurant work per day translates into a loss of 200 jobs.
- ***Bad news for diners.*** The increase in the wage increases the cost of producing restaurant meals, increasing the price of meals.

There are winners and losers from the minimum wage. Workers who keep their jobs gain at the expense of other workers and at the expense of diners. A recent study suggests that a 10 percent increase in the minimum wage decreases the number of minimum wage jobs by about 1 percent.[2]

Why Do Wages Differ across Occupations?

There is substantial variation in wages across occupations. Most professional athletes earn more than medical doctors, who earn more than college professors, who earn more than janitors. We'll see that the wage for a particular occupation will be high if the supply of workers in that occupation is small relative to the demand for those workers. This is shown in Figure 32.6, where the supply curve intersects the demand curve at a high wage. The supply of workers in a particular occupation could be small for four reasons:

1 ***Few people with the required skills.*** To play professional baseball, people must be able to hit balls thrown at them at about 90 miles per hour. The few people who have this skill are paid a lot of money, because baseball owners compete with one

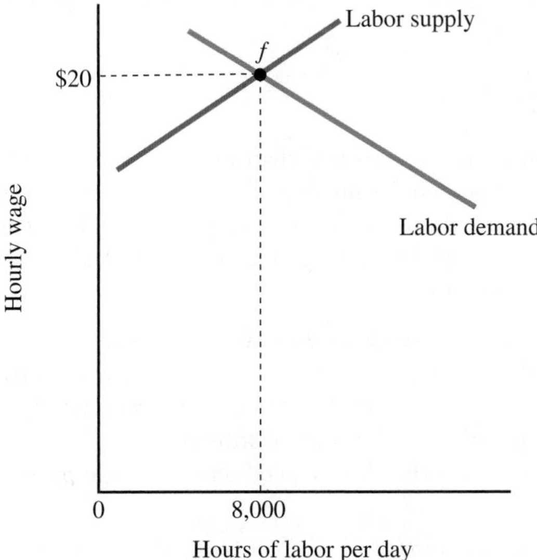

▲ FIGURE 32.6
The Equilibrium Wage When Labor Supply Is Low Relative to Demand
If supply is low relative to demand—because few people have the skills, training costs are high, or the job is undesirable—the equilibrium wage will be high.

another for skillful players, bidding up the wage. The same logic applies to other professional athletes, musicians, and actors. The few people who have the skills required for these occupations are paid high wages.

2 ***High training costs.*** The skills required for some occupations can be acquired only through education and training. For example, the skills required of a medical doctor call for medical school training, and legal skills must be acquired in law school. If it is costly to acquire these skills, a relatively small number of people will become skilled, and they will receive high wages. The higher wage compensates workers for their training costs.

3 ***Undesirable working conditions.*** Some occupations have undesirable working conditions, and workers demand higher wages as compensation. Wages are higher for jobs that are dirty or stressful or require people to work at odd hours.

4 ***Danger.*** Some jobs are dangerous, and wages are higher to compensate for the risk of injury or death. The workers with the greatest risk of losing their lives on the job are lumberjacks, boilermakers, taxicab drivers, and mine workers. To compensate for the higher risk of getting killed on the job, steelworkers receive a wage premium of 3.7 percent. In the United States, the average job fatality rate is 1 in 25,000 workers per year. For a worker who faces twice the average fatality rate, the wage is about 1 percent higher. The wage premium for jobs with an annual injury rate of 2 percent is 1.15 percent for men and 3.68 percent for women.[3]

5 ***Artificial barriers to entry.*** As we'll see in the next chapter, government and professional licensing boards restrict the number of people in certain occupations, and labor unions restrict their membership. These supply restrictions increase wages.

The Gender Pay Gap

Why do women, on average, earn less than men? In the United States, the typical woman earns about 80 percent as much as the typical man.[4] A recent study explored several factors that contribute to the gender pay gap.[5] The study observed a gap of about 20 percent among workers aged 26 to 34, and identified four factors that contribute to the gender gap:

- ***Difference in worker skills and productivity.*** On average, women have less education and work experience, so they are less productive and thus receive lower wages. An important factor in the lower level of work experience among women is that many women interrupt their careers to raise children. The study concluded that lower productivity is the most important factor in the gender gap.
- ***Differences in occupational preferences.*** Wages vary across occupations: Clerical and service occupations receive lower wages than craft and professional occupations. Compared to men, women express stronger preferences for low-wage occupations, such as clerical and service occupations, and weaker

preferences for some high-wage occupations, such as craft and operator occupations. In contrast, men have slightly stronger preferences for high-wage professional and technical occupations. On balance, the general orientation of women toward low-wage occupations contributes to the gender gap.

- ***Occupational discrimination.*** Given the variation in wages across occupations, if employers have a bias against hiring women for high-paying occupations, women will receive lower wages. The study shows that on average, women are less successful than men in attaining their desired occupations, and this occupational discrimination by employers explains between 7 and 25 percent of the gender gap.
- ***Wage discrimination.*** If employers pay women less than their equally productive male counterparts, women's wages will be lower. The results of the study on this issue are mixed, with some evidence that wage discrimination is a significant factor in the gender pay gap.

The general conclusion of the study is that differences in productivity and occupational status are the most important factors in the gender pay gap. It appears that the relatively large number of women in low-paying occupations results both from the occupational preferences of women and employer discrimination that inhibits occupational attainment for women.

Racial Discrimination

What about differences in earnings by race? African-American males who work full-time earn 73 percent as m as their white counterparts, while African-American females earn 85 percent as much as their white counterparts. Hispanic males earn 65 percent as much as white males, while Hispanic females earn 78 percent as much as white females.[6] For both males and females, part of the earnings gap is caused by differences in productivity: On average, whites have more education and work experience, so they are paid higher wages. However, part of the wage gap is caused by racial discrimination. Some African-American and Hispanic workers are paid lower wages for similar jobs, and others are denied opportunities to work in some high-paying jobs.

How much of the earnings gap is caused by discrimination? Recent studies suggest that racial discrimination decreases the wages of African-American men by about 13 percent and that these earnings differences have decreased over the last few decades and are now small enough that "most of the disparity in earnings between blacks and whites in the labor market of the 1990s is due to the differences in skills they bring to the market, and not to discrimination within the labor market."[7] The differences in skills brought to the labor market are caused by a number of factors, including past discrimination that has inhibited the acquisition of job skills and differences in educational opportunities. For example, in urban areas about one-third of African-American high-school students have above-average scores on reading and math exams, compared to about two-thirds of white students.

Why Do College Graduates Earn Higher Wages?

In 2009, the college premium—the increase in earnings from a college degree—was 74 percent. A college education provides the skills necessary to enter certain occupations, so a college graduate has more job options than a high-school graduate. Both high-school grads and college grads can fill jobs that require only a high-school education, so the supply of workers for these low-skill jobs is plentiful, and the equilibrium wage for these jobs is low. In contrast, there is a smaller supply of workers for jobs that require a college education, so the wages in these high-skill jobs are higher than the wages for low-skill jobs. This is the **learning effect** of a college education: College students learn the skills required for certain occupations, increasing their human capital.

learning effect
The increase in a person's wage resulting from the learning of skills required for certain occupations.

A second explanation of the college premium requires a different perspective on college and its role in the labor market. Suppose certain skills are required for a particular job, but an employer cannot determine whether a prospective employee has these skills. For example, most managerial jobs require the employee to manage time efficiently, but it is impossible for an employer to determine whether a prospective employee is a good manager of time. Suppose that these skills are also required to complete a college degree. For example, to get passing grades in all your classes, you must be able to use your time efficiently. When you get a college degree, firms will conclude that you have some of the skills they require, so they may hire you instead of a high-school graduate. This is the **signaling effect** of a college education: People who complete college provide a signal to employers about their skills. This second explanation suggests that colleges simply provide a testing ground where students can reveal their skills to potential employers.

signaling effect
The information about a person's work skills conveyed by completing college.

The most important factor in the doubling of the college premium over the last few decades is technological change. Changes in technology have increased the demand for college graduates relative to the demand for other workers. In all sectors of the economy, firms are switching to sophisticated machinery and equipment that require highly skilled workers. Consequently, the share of jobs that require a college education has increased steadily, increasing the demand for college graduates. Of course, the supply of college graduates has increased too, but not by as much as demand. Because the increase in demand is large relative to the increase in supply, the wages of college graduates have increased. Another factor in the growing college premium is the pace of technological change. Workers with more education can more easily learn new skills and new jobs, so firms are willing to pay more for college graduates.

Labor Unions and Wages

labor union
A group of workers organized to increase job security, improve working conditions, and increase wages and fringe benefits.

A **labor union** is a group of workers organized to increase job security, improve working conditions, and increase wages and fringe benefits.[9] Acting as a group, union members have some control over the wages and fringe benefits they receive. In the U.S., about one in eight workers in the United States belongs to a union, down from about one in three workers in the 1950s. The unionization rate is 8.2 percent for private-sector workers, compared to 39.8 percent for public-sector workers. In the rest of the world, unionization rates vary widely, from 2 percent in India to 78 percent in Sweden.

There is evidence that unions raise the wages of union workers. For the United States, the consensus is that union workers earn 10 to 20 percent more than nonunion workers doing the same work. As we saw earlier in the chapter, an increase in the wage decreases the quantity of labor demanded because of the output effect and the input-substitution effect. Given the trade-off between wages and employment, an increase in the union wage increases the income of the workers who keep their jobs, but also decreases the number of union jobs.

One response to the trade-off between wages and jobs is to impose work rules that increase the amount of labor required to produce a given quantity of output.

application 3

THE BEAUTY PREMIUM

APPLYING THE CONCEPTS #3: What explains differences in wages?

How does physical attractiveness affect earnings? Studies of the U.S. labor market show that beautiful people earn more than people of average looks, and unattractive people earn less. The beauty premium is 5 percent for the 33 percent of workers who are considered beautiful or handsome, and the beauty premium is larger for men than for women. The penalty for bad looks is about 8 percent for the 10 percent of workers who are considered plain or unattractive. The beauty premium and the plain penalty have been observed in other countries and within specific occupations such as lawyers.

Why do beautiful people earn more income? According to biologists, beauty is a marker for underlying characteristics such as health and intelligence, and beautiful people start with a slight edge in the labor market. Beautiful people get more opportunities to learn through experience, and they also acquire better professional contacts. Because of these wider opportunities, a small difference in innate characteristics can be amplified into a large difference in earnings. Another factor in the beauty premium is that some workers and consumers simply like dealing with attractive people, so there is a higher demand for beautiful workers, resulting in higher wages. **Related to Exercises 3.10 and 3.11.**

SOURCES: Based on Daniel Hamermesh and Jeff Biddle, "Beauty and the Labor Market," *American Economic Review* 84 (2001): 1174–1194; "To Those That Have, Shall Be Given," *Economist*, December 22, 2007, 53–54.

featherbedding
Work rules that increase the amount of labor required to produce a given quantity of output. Featherbedding may actually decrease the demand for labor.

This is called **featherbedding**. One example of featherbedding is requiring a minimum crew size, which forces a firm to hire more workers than it needs to perform a particular task. For example, the typical unionized airline hires three workers to guide an airplane into the gate, while nonunion airlines use only two workers. In the past, railroad unions forced railroads to use firemen (whose job was to shovel coal) on diesel-powered engines, which don't use coal.

Although featherbedding forces the firm to use more labor per unit of output, it also decreases the quantity of output produced. A firm that hires workers it doesn't need will have higher production costs, resulting in a higher price for its product. Consumers respond to a higher price by purchasing less output, so although the firm may use more labor per unit of output, it sells less output. If output falls by a large amount, the quantity of labor demanded by the firm will actually decrease.

We've seen that unions lead to higher wages and may impose work rules that reduce productivity. In other words, unions increase production costs. What are the possible benefits of unions? First, unions may increase worker productivity by facilitating communication between workers and managers. A second possible benefit of unions is lower turnover among workers. If a worker is unhappy with a job, one option is to quit. From the firm's perspective, this is costly because the firm loses an experienced worker and must train a new one. A dissatisfied worker who belongs to a union has a second option: The worker can use the union as an intermediary to discuss job issues with managers. This sort of communication can solve problems before they become so severe that the worker quits. There is evidence that firms whose workers are in unions have lower turnover rates, in part because they facilitate communication between workers and managers. These lower turnover rates lead to lower training costs and a more experienced workforce. The savings from less turnover is equivalent to a 1 to 2 percent reduction in costs.

32.4 The Distribution of Income

In 2009 the median household income in the United States was $49,777. In other words, half of households earned more than $49,777, and half earned less. There is substantial variation in household income, with some households earning much more and others earning much less. In this part of the chapter, we'll discuss the extent of income inequality in the United States and recent trends in the distribution of income. We'll also explore the effects of several government policies on the distribution of income.

Income Distribution in 2007

Market income is defined as all earnings received from labor and capital markets. It includes wages and salaries, as well as earnings from bonds, stocks, and real estate. Market income does not account for the effects of government tax and transfer payments. We'll discuss the effects of government tax and transfer programs in the next section of the chapter.

Table 32.2 shows the distribution of market income in 1979 and 2007. Both years were peak economic years, when the nation's economy was thriving. To compute the numbers in a column of the table, we take four steps:

1. Rank the nation's households according to market income: The household with the highest income is at the top of the list, and the household with the lowest income is at the bottom of the list.
2. Divide the households into five groups, or "quintiles": The lowest fifth includes the poorest 20 percent of households (the lowest 20% of the list); the second fifth is the next poorest 20 percent, and so on.
3. Compute each group's income by adding up the income received by all the households in the group.
4. Compute each group's share of market income (the numbers in the second and third columns of the table) by dividing the group's income by the nation's total income.

In the case of perfect income equality, each quintile would earn 20 percent of income.

TABLE 32.2 Distribution of Market Income, 1979–2007

Group	Share of Market Income, 1979	Share of Market Income, 2007	Percentage growth in income, 1979–2007
Quintile 1 (percentiles 0–20)	2.9	2.5	18.3
Quintile 2 (percentiles 20–40)	10.1	7.3	27.5
Quintile 3 (percentiles 40–60)	15.3	12.2	35.2
Quintile 4 (percentiles 60–80)	22.4	19.0	43.3
Quintile 5 (percentiles 80–100)	49.6	59.9	75.6
Percentiles 80–99	39.1	38.6	65.0
Top 1 percent	10.5	21.3	277.5

SOURCE: Congressional Budget Office, Trends in the Distribution of Household Income between 1979 and 2007 (Washington, DC, 2011).

The third column of Table 32.2 shows the distribution of market income in 2007. As shown near the top of the table, the lowest fifth earned only 2.5 percent of the total income. If we combine the first two quintiles, the lowest 40 percent of households earned 9.8 percent of total income. In contrast, the top quintile (percentiles 80–100) earned about 60 percent of total income. At the very top, households in the top 1 percent earned 21.3 percent of market income. In other words, the one percenters earn over 20 times the income they would earn in the case of perfect income equality. In contrast, households in the first quintile earn one-eighth of the income they would earn in the case of perfect equality.

What explains the substantial differences in market income? There are three key reasons for income inequality in a market-based economy.

1. ***Differences in labor skills and effort.*** Some people have better labor skills—more human capital—than others, so they earn higher wages. Labor skills are determined by innate ability, education, and work experience. In addition, some people work longer hours or at more demanding jobs, so they earn more income.
2. ***Luck and misfortune.*** Some people are luckier than others in investing their money, starting a business, or picking an occupation. Among the unlucky people are those who develop health problems that make it difficult to earn income. Among the lucky people are those who inherit wealth and earn income by investing their inheritance.
3. ***Discrimination.*** Some people are paid lower wages or have limited opportunities for education and work because of their race or gender.

Recent Changes in the Distribution of Income

Table 32.2 shows changes in market income between 1979 and 2007. The last column shows the percent growth in income over the 28-year period for different groups of households. As we move down through the column to progressively higher income, the growth rate of market income increases. For example, the growth rate for the poorest quintile was 18.3 percent, compared to 43.3 for the fourth quintile and 75.6 percent for the top quintile. For the one percenters, the growth rate was 277.5 percent.

The second and third columns in the table show the changes in the income shares over the 28-year period. The shares of the bottom 99 percent of households (quintiles 1 through 4 and percentiles 80–99) decreased, while the share of the top one percent increased. Although the income share of the top quintile increased (from about 50 percent to about 60 percent), the increase in income was concentrated among the top one percent of households.

Over the period 1979–2007, all major sources of income became less evenly distributed. Consider the income share of the bottom 80 percent of households. As shown in Table 32.2, the share of *overall* income earned by the 80 percenters decreased from 51.4 percent to 41.1 percent. This group's share of *labor* income decreased from 60 percent to 50 percent, while its share of income from capital, business, and capital gains decreased from 41 percent to 25 percent. Another factor in the increased concentration of income is that the share of income from capital gains (the most concentrated source of income) increased.

Why has labor income become less evenly distributed? It appears that the most important reason for growing inequality is what labor economists call an "increase in the demand for skill."[8] In the labor market, the demand for highly skilled (highly educated) workers has increased relative to the demand for less-skilled (less-educated) workers. As a result, the wage gap between the two groups has widened. Over the last few decades, the college premium doubled, and the advanced-degree premium—the increase in earnings from getting post-graduate degrees—has increased as well. At

application 4

TRADE-OFFS FROM IMMIGRATION

APPLYING THE CONCEPTS #2: Who benefits from the immigration of low-skilled workers?

Since about 1850, international migration has played an important role in labor markets. In the first wave of immigration, from 1850 to 1913, over a million people migrated to the Americas each year. Most were from European countries. After several decades of war and economic depressions, massive immigration resumed in 1945, and most of the immigrants were from less-developed countries. The most recent wave of immigration started in 1990 and has increased the supply of labor to the U.S. economy by about 10 percent per decade.

Immigration creates winners and losers within the economy. The increase in the supply of labor decreases wages for the native workers who have the same skill level as the immigrants. Because the average U.S. immigrant has less education and earns less income than the average native, immigrants compete with low-skill natives, decreasing their wages. On the benefit side, the decrease in the wages of low-skill labor decreases production costs and product prices, so consumers benefit. In general, we expect low-skill workers to lose as a result of immigration because the lower wages will dominate the benefits of lower consumer prices. In contrast, we expect high-skill workers to benefit from lower prices.

Economists have estimated the net effect of immigration on the U.S. economy. George Borjas shows that immigration to the United States has a small positive effect, with the losses in wages of low-skilled workers more than offset by gains to consumers and firms. This conclusion is consistent with the idea that exchange increases efficiency and the size of the overall economic pie. Studies of the most recent wave of immigration suggest that immigration decreases the wages of high-school dropouts and other low-skilled workers. **Related to Exercises 4.5, 4.6, and 4.7.**

SOURCES: Based on George Borjas, "The Economics of Immigration," *Journal of Economic Literature* 32 (1994): 1667–1717; George Borjas, "The Labor Demand Curve Is Downward Sloping: Reexamining the Impact of Immigration on the Labor Market," *Quarterly Journal of Economics* 108 (2003): 1335–1374; Gianmarco Ottaviano and Giovanni Peri, "Rethinking the Gains from Immigration: Theory and Evidence from the U.S." (working paper 11672, NBER, 2005).

the low end of educational attainment, the dropout penalty—the income loss from dropping out of high school, rather than simply graduating from high school—has nearly doubled.

Why did the demand for skill increase over the last three decades? Economists have explored this issue, and provide evidence for two key factors.

- ***Technological change.*** Advances in technology have simultaneously decreased the demand for less-educated workers and increased the demand for college graduates and people with advanced degrees. While the new technology has made it possible to replace many low-skilled workers with "smart" machines and computers, it has also increased the demand for workers who have the education and skills required to produce the new technology and use it.
- ***Increased international trade.*** An increase in international trade means more exports and imports. Trade allows developed countries like the United States to easily export goods produced with high-skilled labor and import goods produced with low-skilled labor. As a result, the expansion of international trade in the last three decades has increased the demand for high-skilled workers and decreased the demand for low-skilled workers in the United States.

Economists have not yet reached a consensus on the relative importance of these two factors.

32.5 Public Policy and the Distribution of Income

Government policies affect the distribution of income through taxes and transfer policies. In this part of the chapter, we explore the broad effects of federal tax and transfer policies on the distribution of income. We also discuss specific policies designed to boost the income and economic prospects of the poor.

Effects of Tax and Transfer Policies on the Distribution of Income

Table 32.3 shows the shares of income for the five quintiles before and after accounting for federal taxes and transfers. The federal policies redistribute income from the top fifth, whose income share decreases by about 7 percentage points (from 59.9 percent to 52.7 percent) to the lowest four-fifths, which collectively gain about 7 percentage points. The largest gain occurs for the lowest fifth (2.6 percentage points), and the other three quintiles gain between 0.9 and 1.9 percentage points.

In the last few decades, the redistributional effects of federal tax and transfer policies have diminished. Between 1979 and 2007, the government took less from high-income households and gave less to low-income households for two reasons.

1 Although the total amount of transfer payments was roughly constant over the period, a decreasing share of payments were for means-tested programs (eligibility is determined by income) such as Temporary Assistance to Needy Families

TABLE 32.3 Government Policies and the Distribution of Income

Group	Share of Market Income, 2007	Share of Income After Federal Tax and Transfers, 2007	Change in Share from Federal Tax and Transfers
Quintile 1 (percentiles 0–20)	2.5	5.1	+2.6
Quintile 2 (percentiles 20–40)	7.3	9.2	+1.9
Quintile 3 (percentiles 40–60)	12.2	14.0	+1.8
Quintile 4 (percentiles 60–80)	19.0	19.9	+0.9
Quintile 5 (percentiles 80–100)	59.9	52.7	−7.2
Percentiles 80–99	38.6	35.6	−3.0
Top 1 percent	21.3	17.1	−4.2

SOURCE: Congressional Budget Office, Trends in the Distribution of Household Income between 1979 and 2007 (Washington, DC, 2011).

(TANF). In contrast, an increasing share was spent on Medicare, a program that is not means-tested. Households in the lowest quintile received only 36 percent of all federal transfer payments in 2007, down from 54 percent in 1979.

2 The overall average federal tax rate decreased from 22 percent in 1979 to 20 percent in 2007. The average rate for the individual income tax, which is responsible for bulk of the redistributional effects of federal taxes, decreased from over 11 percent in 1979 to less than 10 percent in 2007.

Poverty and Public Policy

The U.S. government defines a poor household as one with a total income less than the amount required to satisfy the "minimum needs" of the household. The government estimates a minimum food budget for each type of household and multiplies the food budget by three to get the official poverty budget. A household with income lower than the official poverty budget is considered poor. In 2010 the poverty budget was $22,113 for a two-adult, two-child household, which is less than half of the median household income. In 2010, almost 47 million people were below the poverty line, or 15.2 percent of the population.

Table 32.4 shows the incidence of poverty among different groups of people. For each group, the poverty rate equals the percentage of people in that group who live in households with incomes lower than the official poverty budget.

TABLE 32.4 Poverty Rates for Different Groups, 2010

Characteristic	Poverty Rate in 2010
All Races	15.2%
White	13.1
Black	27.5
Hispanic	26.7
Asian	12.1
Type of Family	
Married couple	7.6
Female-headed household	28.7
Age	
Under 18 years	22.5
65 years and older	9.0

SOURCE: U.S. Census Bureau, Current Population Reports:. Report P60-241 (November 2011).

1 ***Race.*** The poverty rates for both Blacks and Hispanics are more than twice the poverty rates for whites.
2 ***Type of family.*** The poverty rate for female-headed households is about five times the poverty rate for households headed by a married couple.
3 ***Age.*** The poverty rate is relatively low for the aged, and relatively high for children.

Education is a key factor in determining wages, and poverty rates are lower for more-educated workers. As we saw earlier in the chapter, college graduates earn 74 percent more than high-school graduates. The poverty rate for college graduates is 3 percent, compared to 9 percent for high-school graduates. For high-school dropouts, the poverty rate is 22 percent.

The government uses a number of programs to provide assistance to the poor. In decreasing order of spending, they include medical care (about half of spending), cash assistance (about one-fifth of spending), food assistance, and housing assistance. These programs, broadly defined as "welfare programs," are **means-tested programs**, meaning that only people whose incomes fall below a certain level receive assistance. These programs reduce the poverty rate by a substantial margin. The poverty rates shown in Table 32.4 account for cash transfers to poor households. Cash transfers decrease the overall poverty rate by about one-third. The poverty rates listed in Table 32.4 do not account for the value of noncash programs such as food stamps, which decrease poverty rates by roughly two percentage points.

means-tested programs
A government spending program that provides assistance to those whose income falls below a certain level.

In 1996, the overhaul of federal antipoverty programs ended decades of policy based on the notion that poor families are entitled to cash and in-kind assistance. The Personal Responsibility and Work Opportunity Reconciliation Act of 1996 eliminated the entitlement of poor families to receive cash assistance. The federal government now provides block grants to states to provide Temporary Aid to Needy Families (TANF), with restrictions on what recipients must do to qualify for assistance and limits on how long they can receive assistance:

- A recipient must participate in work activities, defined as employment, on-the-job training, work experience, community service, or vocational training.
- After a total of 60 months of cash assistance (consecutive or nonconsecutive), assistance stops. States can allow exceptions to the 60-month rule for up to 20 percent of recipients.

The general thrust of welfare reform was to change an entitlement program into a program that requires work in exchange for time-limited assistance. Since the implementation of welfare reform, the number of people receiving assistance has decreased dramatically.

How does cash assistance to the poor affect their incentives to work? Two features of an assistance program affect work incentives.

- **Base cash payment.** The larger the amount provided as a base—the payment to someone who earns no market income—the lower the incentive to work to supplement the base income.
- **Benefit reduction rate.** When a recipient earns market income, the welfare payment decreases by a rate that varies from state to state. The reduction rate is 100 percent in about one-third of states ($1 of market income decreases the welfare payment by $1), and less than 50 percent in about one-third of states ($1 of market income decreases the welfare payment by less than $0.50). The lower the reduction rate, the larger the payoff for each hour of market income, and the greater the incentive for the recipient to earn additional income.

The Earned Income Tax Credit

The government also provides assistance to low-income households through the tax system. In 2010, federal spending on the earned income tax credit (EITC) was $55 billion, which was more than twice the spending on TANF. EITC is an earnings subsidy for low-income households that is determined by the number of children in the household. Here is how the EITC works for a household with two children (roughly two-fifths of EITC recipients).

- Phase in: For the first $12,590 of earnings, the subsidy rate is 0.40: for each $1 of earnings, the government provides a subsidy of $0.40.
- Flat spot: The credit reaches its maximum of $5,036, when household earnings reach $12,590. For the next $2,410 of income, the credit remains at the maximum.
- Phase out. For income above $15,000, the phase-out rate is 0.21: for each additional dollar of earnings, the credit decreases by $0.21. The earnings subsidy reaches zero at an income of $40,363.

The subsidy rate and the phase-out rate are lower for households with fewer children.

The EITC is a successful anti-poverty policy on two counts.[10] First, the policy encourages participation in the workforce. For a $1,000 increase in the maximum credit, the employment rate of single mothers increases by about 3.6 percentage points. Between 1992 and 1999, the employment rate for single mothers increased

application 5

STATE LOTTERIES AND THE DISTRIBUTION OF INCOME

APPLYING THE CONCEPTS #5: How do government policies affect the distribution of income?

A total of 41 states use lotteries to raise money for government programs. In 2003, lottery ticket sales totaled over $40 billion. Roughly half of lottery revenue is paid out as prizes, leaving 20 percent for administrative costs and 30 percent as net revenue to the state. On average, every dollar spent on a lottery ticket pays out only $0.50, so buying a $1 lottery ticket is equivalent to a voluntary contribution of $0.50 to the state. How is this lottery contribution distributed across income groups?

According to a recent study, the average annual spending on lotteries ($212 per adult in lottery states) is roughly constant across income groups. On average, a low-income household spends about the same amount per year on lotteries as a medium-income household and a high-income household. In other words, the lottery contribution is regressive in the sense that a low-income household contributes a larger percentage of its income. **Related to Exercise 5.5.**

SOURCE: Based on Melissa Kearney, "The Economic Winners and Losers of Legalized Gambling," *National Tax Journal* 58 (2005), pp. 281–302.

from 71 percent to 86 percent, and increases in the maximum credit over this period were responsible for a large share of the increase in the employment rate. Second, the EITC reduces poverty. In 2003, the program lifted 4.4 million people in low-income working families out of poverty. For the period 2002–2004, the EITC decreased the poverty rate among participants from 57 percent to 49 percent. For households below the poverty line, the EITC filled 31 percent of the gap between income and the poverty line.

SUMMARY

In this chapter, we've seen how wages are determined in perfectly competitive labor markets and why wages differ from one occupation to another. We've also looked at the distribution of income in the United States and explored possible reasons for growing inequality. Here are the main points of the chapter:

1 The *long-run demand curve for labor* is negatively sloped because the output and input-substitution effects operate in the same direction: An increase in the wage decreases labor per unit of output and decreases the total output produced.

2 An increase in the wage triggers *income* and *substitution effects* that operate in opposite directions, so an increase in the wage has an ambiguous effect on the quantity of labor supplied.

3 The wage in a particular occupation will be relatively high if supply is small relative to demand. This will occur if (1) few people have the skills required for the occupation, (2) training costs are high, or (3) the job is dangerous or stressful.

4 College graduates earn more than high-school graduates because a college education provides new skills and allows people to reveal their skills to employers.

5 The trade-off with a minimum wage is that some workers earn higher income, but others lose their jobs.

6 In the last few decades, the distribution of income has become more unequal. Federal tax and transfer policies diminish income inequality, but the redistributional effect has diminished in recent decades.

7 Poverty rates are relatively high among Blacks, Hispanics, high-school dropouts, and female-headed households.

KEY TERMS

featherbedding, p. 706

income effect for leisure demand, p. 696

input-substitution effect, p. 694

labor union, p. 705

learning effect, p. 704

long-run demand curve for labor, p. 694

marginal product of labor, p. 691

marginal-revenue product of labor (*MRP*), p. 691

market supply curve for labor, p. 697

means-tested programs, p. 713

output effect, p. 694

short-run demand curve for labor, p. 692

signaling effect, p. 704

substitution effect for leisure demand, p. 696

EXERCISES

All problems are assignable in MyEconLab.

32.1 The Demand for Labor

1.1 The marginal revenue product of labor equals __________ times __________.

1.2 A profit-maximizing firm will hire the number of workers where __________ equals __________.

1.3 Your favorite professional team is considering hiring a new player for $3 million per year. It will be sensible (profitable) to hire the player if his __________ is greater than the $3 million cost.

1.4 Arrows up or down: The logic of the output effect is that a decrease in the wage will __________ production costs, so the price of output will __________ and the quantity of output demanded will __________. As a result, the quantity of labor demanded will __________.

1.5 The input-substitution effect is that a decrease in the wage __________ (increases/decreases) the quantity of labor per unit of __________, so the quantity of labor demanded __________ (increases/decreases).

1.6 The short-run market demand curve for labor is __________ (steeper/flatter) than the long-run demand because __________ occur(s) in the short run.

1.7 Fill the blanks with 75, 100, 117, 200, or 360. In major league baseball, the marginal revenue product of the typical free agent is roughly __________ percent of his salary, compared to __________ percent for a journeyman and __________ percent for an apprentice. (Related to Application 1 on page 695.)

1.8 Demand for News Kids. Consider the market for newspaper delivery kids in Kidsville. Each news kid receives a piece rate of $2 per subscriber per month and has a fixed territory that initially has 100 subscribers. The price elasticity of demand for subscriptions is 2.0. Suppose the new city council of Kidsville passes a law that establishes a minimum piece rate of $3 per subscriber per month. As a result, the publisher increases the monthly price of a subscription by 20 percent. How will the new law affect the monthly income of the typical news kid?

1.9 **Demand for Airline Pilots.** Comment on the following: "There is no substitute for an airline pilot: Someone has to fly the plane. Therefore, an increase in the wage of airline pilots will not change the number of pilots used by the airlines."

32.2 The Supply of Labor

2.1 Arrows up or down: An increase in the wage __________ the opportunity cost of leisure time, which tends to __________ leisure time and __________ labor time.

2.2 Arrows up or down: An increase in the wage __________ real income, and if leisure is a normal good this tends to __________ leisure time and __________ labor time.

2.3 We __________ (can/cannot) predict a worker's response to an increase in the wage because the __________ effect and the __________ effect work in __________ (the same/opposite) direction(s).

2.4 Your objective is to earn exactly $120 per week. If your wage decreases from $6 to $4 per hour, you respond by working __________ hours instead of __________ hours. In other words, your labor-supply curve is __________ sloped.

2.5 If every worker in a particular occupation works exactly 40 hours per week, regardless of the wage, the individual supply curve is vertical. __________ (True/False)

2.6 For cabbies in New York City, the elasticity of supply of labor is __________ (positive/negative/zero). (Related to Application 2 on page 698.)

2.7 Income and Substitution Effects. Sabrina works for a workers' cooperative that initially pays her a lump sum of $200 per week (as long as she works at least 15 hours per week) and a wage of $20 per hour of work. She initially works 40 hours per week. Suppose the cooperative changes its pay plan by increasing the lump-sum payment to $280 and decreasing the hourly wage to $18.

a. If Sabrina continues to work 40 hours per week, how does the change in the pay plan affect her total income?

b. Use the concepts of the income and substitution effects to predict whether Sabrina will work more hours, fewer hours, or the same number of hours. (*Hint:* Is there an income effect to consider?)

2.8 City versus National Carpenter Supply. Draw two supply curves for carpenters: one for the market in the city of Portland and one for the market in the United States. In which market would you expect a more elastic supply of carpenters?

2.9 Tax Rate and Tax Revenue. Critically appraise the following statement: "The law of supply says that an increase in price increases the quantity supplied. A decrease in the income tax rate will increase the worker's net wage, so each worker will work more hours. As a result, the revenue from the income tax will increase."

2.10 Personal Labor Supply. We discussed the responses of Lester, Sam, and Maureen to a wage increase. Which person's response is closest to your own? If your wage increased, would you work more hours, fewer hours, or about the same number of hours?

2.11 Cabbie Wages and Income. Suppose New York City increases the taxi fare by 20 percent. (Related to Application 2 on page 698.)

a. For the typical cabbie, daily income will increase by __________ (more than/less than/exactly) 20 percent. Explain.

b. Suppose the initial fare per mile is $0.60 and the initial miles per day is 100. Compute the percentage change in daily income.

32.3 Labor Market Equilibrium

3.1 Arrows up or down: A decrease in the supply of nurses will __________ the equilibrium wage and __________ the equilibrium quantity of nursing services.

3.2 Arrows up or down: An increase in the demand for nursing services will __________ the equilibrium wage and __________ the equilibrium quantity of nursing services.

3.3 Arrows up or down: A minimum wage __________ the quantity of labor demanded and __________ the quantity of labor supplied.

3.4 A minimum wage for restaurant workers brings good news to __________, but bad news to __________ and __________.

3.5 In Figure 32.5 on page 700, an increase in the wage decreases the quantity of labor demanded. Using the simple approach to computing percentage changes (see the Appendix to Chapter 1), the implied elasticity of demand for labor is __________.

3.6 The wage for a particular occupation will be relatively low if labor __________ (demand/supply) is small relative to labor __________ (demand/supply).

3.7 If a city has a relatively high crime rate, we would expect the wage for taxi drivers to be relatively __________ (high/low).

3.8 In some countries, it is customary to tip restaurant waiters. We would expect the wages paid to waiters to be __________ (higher/lower/the same) in countries where tips are customary.

3.9 If a worker switches from a relatively safe factory job to a job in a steel mill, the wage will increase by roughly __________ (2/4/10/30) percent.

3.10 The wage premium for beautiful people is about __________ percent, while the wage penalty for unattractive people is about __________ percent. (Related to Application 3 on page 705.)

3.11 Beautiful workers get wider opportunities to __________, so a small difference in innate characteristics can lead to a large difference in __________. (Related to Application 3 on page 705.)

3.12 Living Wage and Labor Income. Consider a university that has sweatshirts bearing its logo produced overseas by a contractor who initially pays a wage of $8 per sweatshirt and has other costs of $12 per sweatshirt, resulting in a price of $20 per sweatshirt. At this price, the university sells 100 sweatshirts per week. Suppose a student group succeeds in getting the contractor to increase the wage to $10 per shirt and the other costs of production don't change.

a. The price per sweatshirt will increase from __________ to __________, an increase of __________ percent.

b. Suppose the price elasticity of demand for the university's sweatshirts is 3.0. At the higher price, a total of ________ sweatshirts will be purchased and the total spending on sweatshirt labor (total labor income) will change from $__________ to $__________.

c. Suppose consumers are willing to pay a higher price for sweatshirts made by workers receiving a higher wage. How would this change the numbers in part (b)? Provide an example in which the higher wage actually increases the total spending on sweatshirt labor.

3.13 Payroll Tax. You are an economic consultant to a city that just imposed a payroll tax of $1 per hour of work. This payroll tax is paid by workers through a payroll deduction: For each hour of work, the employer deducts $1 and sends the money to the city government. The initial wage (before the tax) is $10, and total employment is 20,000 hours per day. Use a graph to show the effect of the tax on the equilibrium wage and employment.

3.14 Higher Teacher Salaries. Advocates of higher salaries for teachers point out that most teachers have college degrees and that teaching children is an important job.

a. Why aren't teachers' salaries higher, given the importance of the job and the education required?

b. Suppose a new law establishes a minimum teacher salary that is 20 percent higher than the prevailing salary. How would you expect this law to affect the average quality of teachers and the taxes paid by the typical household?

3.15 Improved Safety and Wages. Consider an occupation that initially has a relatively high rate of nonfatal injuries. The equilibrium wage is $20 per hour, and the equilibrium quantity is 100,000 hours. Suppose a new safety device cuts the injury rate in half, and the supply of labor increases by 12 percent: The labor supply curve shifts to the right by 12 percent.

a. Use a graph to show the effects of the safety device on the equilibrium wage and employment.

b. Suppose the elasticity of supply of labor is 3.0 and the elasticity of demand is 1.0. Use the price change formula discussed in an earlier chapter on elasticity to compute the change in the equilibrium wage.

c. Suppose the demand curve you've drawn is a long-run demand curve. Explain the roles of the output effect and substitution effect on the change in the quantity of labor demanded.

3.16 Waiter Tips and Income. Consider a city where the typical waiter has a five-hour shift and daily "sales" (total bills presented to customers) of $400. The customary tip is 15 percent, so tips add up to $60 per day (15% of $400). The initial wage is $10 per hour, so the typical waiter initially earns $50 in wages paid directly by the restaurant. Suppose a local waiter association runs a successful campaign to get the city's restaurant patrons to increase the average tip from 15 to 20 percent.

a. Use a supply and demand graph with wage (excluding tips) on the vertical axis to show the effects of the new tip rate on the labor market.

b. How will the new tip rate affect the daily income (wages plus tips) of the typical waiter?

32.4 The Distribution of Income

4.1 Government transfer and tax policies increase the income share of the lowest quintile of the income distribution from about __________ percent to about __________ percent.

4.2 The college premium is defined as the percentage difference between the incomes of __________ and __________. It is currently about __________ percent.

4.3 Arrows up or down: Since 1970, the income share of the top fifth of the income distribution has __________, while the shares of the lowest and middle fifths have __________.

4.4 Arrows up or down: An important factor in growing inequality over the last 30 years is technological change that has __________ the demand for college graduates and __________ the demand for less-educated workers.

4.5 The average immigrant has __________ (less/more) education than the average native, so immigration __________ (increases/decreases) the wages of __________ (low/high) skill natives. (Related to Application 4 on page 709.)

4.6 The immigration of low-skill workers generates net benefits for __________ workers because they benefit from lower __________ without bearing the cost associated with lower __________. (Related to Application 4 on page 709.)

4.7 Wage and Price Effects of Immigration. In the initial equilibrium in the market for farm workers, the wage is $10 per hour. The elasticity of supply of farm workers is 2.0, and the elasticity of demand for farm workers is 1.0. Suppose that immigration increases the supply of farm workers by 12 percent: The supply curve shifts to the right by 12 percent. (Related to Application 4 on page 709.)

a. Use the price-change formula discussed in an earlier chapter on elasticity to compute the change in the equilibrium wage.

b. Suppose that farm workers are responsible for one-fourth of the production cost of food. What are the implications of immigration for the cost of producing food and its price?

32.5 Public Policy and the Distribution of Income

5.1 For each of the following pairs of population groups, indicate which group has a higher poverty rate:

a. __________ White vs. __________ Hispanic

b. __________ White vs. __________ Asian

c. __________ Married couple vs. __________ Female-headed household

d. __________ Under 18 years vs. __________ 65 years and older

5.2 Government spending and tax policies reduce the overall poverty rate from roughly __________ (25/20/15/10) percent to roughly __________ (15/10/5/2) percent.

5.3 Cash aid to the poor makes up roughly __________ (90/50/30/20) percent of the total spending on means-tested programs.

5.4 A low-income person receiving cash aid under TANF receives a fixed sum per month for an unlimited length of time. __________ (True/False)

5.5 On average, a low-income household spends __________ (more, less, the same) on lotteries as a high-income household. (Related to Application 5 on page 714.)

NOTES

1. Anthony Carnevale, Stephen, Rose, Ban Cheah, *The College Payoff: Education, Occupations, and Lifetime Earnings* (2009: Georgetown University Center on Education and the Workforce)

2. Victor R. Fuchs, Alan B. Krueger, and James M. Poterba, "Why Do Economists Disagree about Policy? The Role of Beliefs about Parameters and Values," *Journal of Economic Literature* 36, no. 3 (1998): 1387–1426.

3. Craig Olson, "An Analysis of Wage Differentials Received by Workers on Dangerous Jobs," *Journal of Human Resources* 16 (Spring 1981): 167–185; John Leeth and John Ruser, "Compensating Wage Differentials for Fatal and Nonfatal Injury Risk by Gender and Race," *Journal of Risk and Uncertainty* 27 (2003): 257–277; Michael French and Laura Dunlap, "Compensating Wage Differentials for Job Stress," *Applied Economics* 30 (1998): 1067–1075; Ronald Ehrenberg and Robert Smith, *Modern Labor Economics* (Boston: Pearson Addison Wesley, 2005).

4. U.S. Department of Labor, Bureau of Labor Statistics, www.bls.govdata/ (accessed August 5, 2008).

5. Eric J. Solberg, "Occupational Assignment, Hiring Discrimination, and the Gender Pay Gap," *Atlantic Economic Journal* 32 (2004): 11–27.

6. U.S. Department of Labor, Bureau of Labor Statistics, www.bls.govdata/ (accessed August 5, 2008).

7. William Darity and Patrick Mason, "Evidence on Discrimination in Employment: Codes of Color, Codes of Gender," *Journal of Economic Perspectives* 12, no. 2 (1998): 63–90; James Heckman, "Detecting Discrimination," *Journal of Economic Perspectives* 12, no. 2 (1998): 101–116.

8. Finis Welch, "In Defense of Inequality," *American Economic Review* 89, no. 2 (1999): 1–17.

9. Ronald Ehrenberg and Robert Smith, *Modern Labor Economics: Theory and Public Policy* (Boston: Pearson Addison Wesley, 2006); Richard B. Freeman and James Medoff, *What Do Unions Do?* (New York: Basic Books, 1985).

10. Nicole Simpson, Jill Tiefenthaler, Jameson Hyde, "The Impact of the Earned Income Tax Credit on Economic Well-Being: A Comparison Across Household Types," *Population Research Policy Review* 29 (2010), pp. 84–864; Nada Eissa, Hilary Hoynes, "Redistribution and Tax Expenditures: The Earned Income Tax Credit," *National Tax Journal* 64 (2011), pp. 689–730; Jeffrey Grogger, "The Effects of Time Limits, the EITC, and Other Policy Changes on Welfare Use, Work, and Income among Female-Headed Families," *Review of Economics and Statistics* 85 (2003), pp. 394–408.

Glossary

absolute advantage The ability of one person or nation to produce a product at a lower resource cost than another person or nation.

accelerator theory The theory of investment that says that current investment spending depends positively on the expected future growth of real GDP.

accounting cost The explicit costs of production.

accounting profit Total revenue minus accounting cost.

adverse-selection problem A situation in which the uninformed side of the market must choose from an undesirable or adverse selection of goods.

aggregate demand curve A curve that shows the relationship between the level of prices and the quantity of real GDP demanded.

aggregate supply curve (AS) A curve that shows the relationship between the level of prices and the quantity of output supplied.

anticipated inflation Inflation that is expected.

appreciation of a currency An increase in the value of a currency.

assets The uses of the funds of a bank, including loans and reserves.

asymmetric information A situation in which one side of the market—either buyers or sellers—has better information than the other.

automatic stabilizers Taxes and transfer payments that stabilize GDP without requiring policymakers to take explicit action.

autonomous consumption The part of consumption that does not depend on income.

autonomous consumption spending The part of consumption spending that does not depend on income.

average fixed cost *(AFC)* Fixed cost divided by the quantity produced.

average variable cost (*AVC*) Variable cost divided by the quantity produced.

balance of payments A system of accounts that measures transactions of goods, services, income, and financial assets between domestic households, businesses, and governments and residents of the rest of the world during a specific time period.

balance of payments deficit Under a fixed exchange rate system, a situation in which the supply of a country's currency exceeds the demand for the currency at the current exchange rate.

balance of payments surplus Under a fixed exchange rate system, a situation in which the demand of a country's currency exceeds the supply for the currency at the current exchange rate.

balance sheet An account statement for a bank that shows the sources of its funds (liabilities) as well as the uses of its funds (assets).

bank run Panicky investors simultaneously trying to withdraw their funds from a bank they believe may fail.

barrier to entry Something that prevents firms from entering a profitable market.

barter The exchange of one good or service for another.

Board of Governors of the Federal Reserve The seven-person governing body of the Federal Reserve System in Washington, D.C.

break-even price The price at which economic profit is zero; price equals average total cost.

budget deficit The amount by which government spending exceeds revenues in a given year.

budget surplus The amount by which government revenues exceed government expenditures in a given year.

capital account The value of capital transfer and transaction in nonproduced, nonfinancial assets in the international accounts.

capital deepening Increases in the stock of capital per worker.

capital gains Profits investors earn when they sell stocks, bonds, real estate, or other assets.

cartel A group of firms that act in unison, coordinating their price and quantity decisions.

central bank A banker's bank: an official bank that controls the supply of money in a country.

centrally planned economy An economy in which a government bureaucracy decides how much of each good to produce, how to produce the good, and who gets the good.

ceteris paribus The Latin expression meaning that other variables are held fixed.

chain-weighted index A method for calculating changes in prices that uses an average of base years from neighboring years.

change in demand A shift of the demand curve caused by a change in a variable other than the price of the product.

change in quantity demanded A change in the quantity consumers are willing and able to buy when the price changes; represented graphically by movement along the demand curve.

change in quantity supplied A change in the quantity firms are willing and able to sell when the price changes; represented graphically by movement along the supply curve.

change in supply A shift of the supply curve caused by a change in a variable other than the price of the product.

classical models Economic models that assume wages and prices adjust freely to changes in demand and supply.

closed economy An economy without international trade.

commodity money A monetary system in which the actual money is a commodity, such as gold or silver.

comparative advantage The ability of one person or nation to produce a good at a lower opportunity cost than another person or nation.

complements Two goods for which a decrease in the price of one good increases the demand for the other good.

concentration ratios The percentage of the market output produced by the largest firms.

constant-cost industry An industry in which the average cost of production is constant; the long-run supply curve is horizontal.

constant returns to scale A situation in which the long-run total cost increases proportionately with output, so average cost is constant.

Consumer Price Index A price index that measures the cost of a fixed basket of goods chosen to represent the consumption pattern of a typical consumer.

consumer surplus The amount a consumer is willing to pay for a product minus the price the consumer actually pays.

consumption expenditures Purchases of newly produced goods and services by households.

consumption function The relationship between consumption spending and the level of income.

consumption possibilities curve A curve showing the combinations of two goods that can be consumed when a nation specializes in a particular good and trades with another nation.

consumption taxes Taxes based on the consumption, not the income, of individuals.

contestable market A market with low entry and exit costs.

contractionary policies Government policy actions that lead to decreases in aggregate demand.

convergence The process by which poorer countries close the gap with richer countries in terms of real GDP per capita.

corporate bond A bond sold by a corporation to the public in order to borrow money.

cost-of-living adjustments (COLAs) Automatic increases in wages or other payments that are tied to the CPI.

creative destruction The view that a firm will try to come up with new products and more efficient ways to produce products to earn monopoly profits.

cross-price elasticity of demand A measure of the responsiveness of demand to changes in the price of another good; equal to the percentage change in the quantity demanded of one good (*X*) divided by the percentage change in the price of another good (*Y*).

crowding in The increase of investment (or other component of GDP) caused by a decrease in government spending.

crowding out The reduction in investment (or other component of GDP) caused by an increase in government spending.

current account The sum of net exports (exports minus imports) plus net income received from abroad plus net transfers from abroad.

cyclical unemployment Unemployment that occurs during fluctuations in real GDP.

deadweight loss The decrease in the total surplus of the market that results from a policy such as rent control.

deadweight loss from monopoly A measure of the inefficiency from monopoly; equal to the decrease in the market surplus.

deadweight loss from taxation The difference between the total burden of a tax and the amount of revenue collected by the government.

deflation Negative inflation or falling prices of goods and services.

demand schedule A table that shows the relationship between the price of a product and the quantity demanded, *ceteris paribus*.

deposit insurance Federal government insurance on deposits in banks and savings and loans.

depreciation Reduction in the value of capital goods over a one-year period due to physical wear and tear and also to obsolescence; also called *capital consumption allowance*.

depreciation of a currency A decrease in the value of a currency.

depression The common name for a severe recession.

devaluation A decrease in the exchange rate to which a currency is pegged under a fixed exchange rate system.

diminishing returns As one input increases while the other inputs are held fixed, output increases at a decreasing rate.

discount rate The interest rate at which banks can borrow from the Fed.

discouraged workers Workers who left the labor force because they could not find jobs.

discovered price The lowest price observed so far in a search process.

discretionary spending The spending programs that Congress authorizes on an annual basis.

diseconomies of scale A situation in which the long-run average cost of production increases as output increases.

dominant strategy An action that is the best choice for a player, no matter what the other player does.

double coincidence of wants The problem in a system of barter that one person may not have what the other desires.

dumping A situation in which the price a firm charges in a foreign market is lower than either the price it charges in its home markets or the production cost.

duopolists' dilemma A situation in which both firms in a market would be better off if both chose the high price, but each chooses the low price.

duopoly A market with two firms.

economic cost The opportunity cost of the inputs used in the production process; equal to explicit cost plus implicit cost.

economic growth Sustained increases in the real GDP of an economy over a long period of time.

economic model A simplified representation of an economic environment, often employing a graph.

economic profit Total revenue minus economic cost.

economics The study of choices when there is scarcity.

economies of scale A situation in which the long-run average cost of production decreases as output increases.

efficiency A situation in which people do the best they can, given their limited resources.

elastic demand The price elasticity of demand is greater than one, so the percentage change in quantity exceeds the percentage change in price.

entitlement and mandatory spending Spending that Congress has authorized by prior law, primarily providing support for individuals.

entrepreneurship The effort used to coordinate the factors of production—natural resources, labor, physical capital, and human capital—to produce and sell products.

equilibrium output The level of GDP at which planned expenditure equals the amount that is produced.

euro The common currency in Europe.

excess burden of a tax Another name for deadweight loss.

excess demand A situation in which, at the prevailing price, the quantity demanded exceeds the quantity supplied.

excess reserves Any additional reserves that a bank holds above required reserves.

excess supply A situation in which the quantity supplied exceeds the quantity demanded at the prevailing price.

exchange rate The price at which currencies trade for one another in the market.

expansion The period after a trough in the business cycle during which the economy recovers.

expansionary policies Government policy actions that lead to increases in aggregate demand.

expectations of inflation The beliefs held by the public about the likely path of inflation in the future.

expectations Phillips curve The relationship between unemployment and inflation when taking into account expectations of inflation.

expected real interest rate The nominal interest rate minus the expected inflation rate.

experience rating A situation in which insurance companies charge different prices for medical insurance to different firms depending on the past medical bills of a firm's employees.

explicit cost A monetary payment.

export A good or service produced in the home country (for example, the United States) and sold in another country.

external benefit A benefit from a good experienced by someone other than the person who buys the good.

external cost of production A cost incurred by someone other than the producer.

factors of production The resources used to produce goods and services; also known as *production inputs* or *resources*.

featherbedding Work rules that increase the amount of labor required to produce a given quantity of output. Featherbedding may actually decrease the demand for labor.

federal funds market The market in which banks borrow and lend reserves to and from one another.

federal funds rate The interest rate on reserves that banks lend each other.

Federal Open Market Committee (FOMC) The group that decides on monetary policy: It consists of the 7 members of the Board of Governors plus 5 of 12 regional bank presidents on a rotating basis.

Federal Reserve Bank One of 12 regional banks that are an official part of the Federal Reserve System.

fiat money A monetary system in which money has no intrinsic value but is backed by the government.

financial account The value of a country's net sales (sales minus purchases) of assets.

financial intermediaries Organizations that receive funds from savers and channel them to investors.

firm-specific demand curve A curve showing the relationship between the price charged by a specific firm and the quantity the firm can sell.

fiscal policy Changes in government taxes and spending that affect the level of GDP.

fixed cost (*FC*) Cost that does not vary with the quantity produced.

fixed exchange rate system A system in which governments peg exchange rates to prevent their currencies from fluctuating.

flexible exchange rate system A currency system in which exchange rates are determined by free markets.

foreign exchange market intervention The purchase or sale of currencies by the government to influence the market exchange rate.

free rider A person who gets the benefit from a good but does not pay for it.

frictional unemployment Unemployment that occurs with the normal workings of the economy, such as workers taking time to search for suitable jobs and firms taking time to search for qualified employees.

full employment The level of unemployment that occurs when the unemployment rate is at the natural rate.

full-employment output The level of output that results when the labor market is in equilibrium and the economy is producing at full employment.

game theory The study of decision making in strategic situations.

game tree A graphical representation of the consequences of different actions in a strategic setting.

GDP deflator An index that measures how the prices of goods and services included in GDP change over time.

General Agreement on Tariffs and Trade (GATT) An international agreement established in 1947 that has lowered trade barriers between the United States and other nations.

gold standard A monetary system in which gold backs up paper money.

government purchases Purchases of newly produced goods and services by local, state, and federal governments.

grim-trigger strategy A strategy where a firm responds to underpricing by choosing a price so low that each firm makes zero economic profit.

gross domestic product (GDP) The total market value of final goods and services produced within an economy in a given year.

gross investment Total new investment expenditures.

gross national product GDP plus net income earned abroad.

growth accounting A method to determine the contribution to economic growth from increased capital, labor, and technological progress.

growth rate The percentage rate of change of a variable from one period to another.

growth version of the quantity equation An equation that links the growth rates of money, velocity, prices, and real output.

human capital The knowledge and skills acquired by a worker through education and experience and used to produce goods and services.

hyperinflation An inflation rate exceeding 50 percent per month.

illiquid Not easily transferable to money.

implicit cost An opportunity cost that does not involve a monetary payment.

import A good or service produced in a foreign country and purchased by residents of the home country (for example, the United States).

import licenses Rights, issued by a government, to import goods.

import quota A government-imposed limit on the quantity of a good that can be imported.

income effect for leisure demand The change in leisure time resulting from a change in real income caused by a change in the wage.

income elasticity of demand A measure of the responsiveness of demand to changes in consumer income; equal to the percentage change in the quantity demanded divided by the percentage change in income.

increasing-cost industry An industry in which the average cost of production increases as the total output of the industry increases; the long-run supply curve is positively sloped.

individual demand curve A curve that shows the relationship between the price of a good and quantity demanded by an individual consumer, *ceteris paribus*.

individual supply curve A curve showing the relationship between price and quantity supplied by a single firm, *ceteris paribus*.

indivisible input An input that cannot be scaled down to produce a smaller quantity of output.

inelastic demand The price elasticity of demand is less than one, so the percentage change in quantity is less than the percentage change in price.

infant industries Industries that are at an early stage of development.

inferior good A good for which an increase in income decreases demand.

inflation Sustained increases in the average prices of all goods and services.

inflation rate The percentage rate of change in the price level.

input-substitution effect The change in the quantity of labor demanded resulting from an increase in the price of labor relative to the price of other inputs.

inside lags The time it takes to formulate a policy.

intermediate goods Goods used in the production process that are not final goods and services.

labor Human effort, including both physical and mental effort, used to produce goods and services.

labor force The total number of workers, both the employed and the unemployed.

labor force participation rate The percentage of the population over 16 years of age that is in the labor force.

labor productivity Output produced per hour of work.

labor union A group of workers organized to increase job security, improve working conditions, and increase wages and fringe benefits.

Laffer curve A relationship between the tax rates and tax revenues that illustrates that high tax rates could lead to lower tax revenues if economic activity is severely discouraged.

law of demand There is a negative relationship between price and quantity demanded, *ceteris paribus*.

law of one price The theory that goods easily tradable across countries should sell at the same price expressed in a common currency.

law of supply There is a positive relationship between price and quantity supplied, *ceteris paribus*.

learning by doing Knowledge and skills workers gain during production that increase productivity and lower cost.

learning effect The increase in a person's wage resulting from the learning of skills required for certain occupations.

lender of last resort A central bank is the lender of last resort, the last place, all others having failed, from which banks in emergency situations can obtain loans.

leverage Using borrowed funds to purchase assets.

liabilities The sources of funds for a bank, including deposits and owners' equity.

limit price The price that is just low enough to deter entry.

limit pricing The strategy of reducing the price to deter entry.

liquid Easily convertible into money on short notice.

liquidity demand for money The demand for money that represents the needs and desires individuals and firms have to make transactions on short notice without incurring excessive costs.

liquidity trap A situation in which nominal interest rates are so low, they can no longer fall.

long run in macroeconomics The period of time in which prices have fully adjusted to any economic changes.

long-run aggregate supply curve A vertical aggregate supply curve that reflects the idea that in the long run, output is determined solely by the factors of production and technology.

long-run average cost (*LAC*) The long-run cost divided by the quantity produced.

long-run demand curve for labor A curve showing the relationship between the wage and the quantity of labor demanded over the long run, when the number of firms in the market can change and firms can modify their production facilities.

long-run marginal cost (*LMC*) The change in long-run cost resulting from a one-unit increase in output.

long-run market supply curve A curve showing the relationship between the market price and quantity supplied in the long run.

long-run neutrality of money A change in the supply of money has no effect on real interest rates, investment, or output in the long run.

long-run total cost (*LTC*) The total cost of production when a firm is perfectly flexible in choosing its inputs.

low-price guarantee A promise to match a lower price of a competitor.

M1 The sum of currency in the hands of the public, demand deposits, other checkable deposits, and traveler's checks.

M2 M1 plus other assets, including deposits in savings and loans accounts and money market mutual funds.

macroeconomics The study of the nation's economy as a whole; focuses on the issues of inflation, unemployment, and economic growth.

marginal benefit The additional benefit resulting from a small increase in some activity.

marginal change A small, one-unit change in value.

marginal cost The additional cost resulting from a small increase in some activity.

marginal product of labor The change in output from one additional unit of labor.

marginal propensity to consume (MPC) The fraction of additional income that is spent.

marginal propensity to import The fraction of additional income that is spent on imports.

marginal propensity to save (MPS) The fraction of additional income that is saved.

marginal revenue The change in total revenue from selling one more unit of output.

marginal-revenue product of labor (*MRP*) The extra revenue generated from one additional unit of labor; *MRP* is equal to the price of output times the marginal product of labor.

market demand curve A curve showing the relationship between price and quantity demanded by all consumers, *ceteris paribus*.

market economy An economy in which people specialize and exchange goods and services in markets.

market equilibrium A situation in which the quantity demanded equals the quantity supplied at the prevailing market price.

market power The ability of a firm to affect the price of its product.

market supply curve A curve showing the relationship between the market price and quantity supplied by all firms, *ceteris paribus*.

market supply curve for labor A curve showing the relationship between the wage and the quantity of labor supplied.

marketable pollution permits A system under which the government picks a target pollution level for a particular area, issues just enough pollution permits to meet the pollution target, and allows firms to buy and sell the permits; also known as a *cap-and-trade system*.

means-tested programs A government spending program that provides assistance to those whose income falls below a certain level.

median-voter rule The choices made by the government will match the preferences of the median voter.

Medicaid A federal and state government health program for the poor.

Medicare A federal government health program for the elderly.

medium of exchange Any item that buyers give to sellers when they purchase goods and services.

menu costs The costs associated with changing prices and printing new price lists when there is inflation.

merger A process in which two or more firms combine their operations.

microeconomics The study of the choices made by households, firms, and government and how these choices affect the markets for goods and services.

minimum efficient scale The output at which scale economies are exhausted.

minimum supply price The lowest price at which a product will be supplied.

mixed market A market in which goods of different qualities are sold for the same price.

monetarists Economists who emphasize the role that the supply of money plays in determining nominal income and inflation.

monetary policy The range of actions taken by the Federal Reserve to influence the level of GDP or inflation.

monetizing the deficit Purchases by a central bank of newly issued government bonds.

money Any items that are regularly used in economic transactions or exchanges and accepted by buyers and sellers.

money illusion Confusion of real and nominal magnitudes.

money market The market for money in which the amount supplied and the amount demanded meet to determine the nominal interest rate.

money multiplier The ratio of the increase in total checking account deposits to an initial cash deposit.

monopolistic competition A market served by many firms that sell slightly different products.

monopoly A market in which a single firm sells a product that does not have any close substitutes.

moral hazard A situation in which one side of an economic relationship takes undesirable or costly actions that the other side of the relationship cannot observe.

multiplier The ratio of the total shift in aggregate demand to the initial shift in aggregate demand.

multiplier-accelerator model A model in which a downturn in real GDP leads to a sharp fall in investment, which triggers further reductions in GDP through the multiplier.

Nash equilibrium An outcome of a game in which each player is doing the best he or she can, given the action of the other players.

national income The total income earned by a nation's residents both domestically and abroad in the production of goods and services.

natural monopoly A market in which the economies of scale in production are so large that only a single large firm can earn a profit.

natural rate of unemployment The level of unemployment at which there is no cyclical unemployment. It consists of only frictional and structural unemployment.

natural resources Resources provided by nature and used to produce goods and services.

negative relationship A relationship in which two variables move in opposite directions.

neoclassical theory of investment A theory of investment that says both real interest rates and taxes are important determinants of investment.

net exports Exports minus imports.

net international investment position Domestic holding of foreign assets minus foreign holdings of domestic assets.

net investment Gross investment minus depreciation.

network externalities The value of a product to a consumer increases with the number of other consumers who use it.

new growth theory Modern theories of growth that try to explain the origins of technological progress.

nominal GDP The value of GDP in current dollars.

nominal interest rate Interest rate quoted in the market.

nominal value The face value of an amount of money.

nominal wages Wages expressed in current dollars.

normal good A good for which an increase in income increases demand.

normative analysis Answers the question "What *ought to be*?"

oligopoly A market served by a few firms.

open economy An economy with international trade.

open market operations The purchase or sale of U.S. government securities by the Fed.

open market purchases The Fed's purchase of government bonds from the private sector.

open market sales The Fed's sale of government bonds to the private sector.

opportunity cost What you sacrifice to get something.

output effect The change in the quantity of labor demanded resulting from a change in the quantity of output produced.

outside lags The time it takes for the policy to actually work.

outsourcing Firms producing components of their goods and services in other countries.

owners' equity The funds provided to a bank by its owners.

patent The exclusive right to sell a new good for some period of time.

payoff matrix A matrix or table that shows, for each possible outcome of a game, the consequences for each player.

peak The date at which a recession starts.

perfectly competitive market A market with many sellers and buyers of a homogeneous product and no barriers to entry.

perfectly elastic demand The price elasticity of demand is infinite.

perfectly elastic supply The price elasticity of supply is equal to infinity.

perfectly inelastic demand The price elasticity of demand is zero.

perfectly inelastic supply The price elasticity of supply equals zero.

permanent income An estimate of a household's long-run average level of income.

personal disposable income Personal income that households retain after paying income taxes.

personal income Income, including transfer payments, received by households.

physical capital The stock of equipment, machines, structures, and infrastructure that is used to produce goods and services.

planned expenditures Another term for total demand for goods and services.

political business cycle The effects on the economy of using monetary or fiscal policy to stimulate the economy before an election to improve reelection prospects.

pollution tax A tax or charge equal to the external cost per unit of pollution.

positive analysis Answers the question "What *is*?" or "What *will be*?"

positive relationship A relationship in which two variables move in the same direction.

predatory pricing A firm sells a product at a price below its production cost to drive a rival out of business and then increases the price.

present value The maximum amount a person is willing to pay today to receive a payment in the future.

price ceiling A maximum price set by the government.

price discrimination The practice of selling a good at different prices to different consumers.

price elasticity of demand (E_d) A measure of the responsiveness of the quantity demanded to changes in price; equal to the absolute value of the percentage change in quantity demanded divided by the percentage change in price.

price elasticity of supply A measure of the responsiveness of the quantity supplied to changes in price; equal to the percentage change in quantity supplied divided by the percentage change in price.

price fixing An arrangement in which firms conspire to fix prices.

price floor A minimum price set by the government.

price leadership A system under which one firm in an oligopoly takes the lead in setting prices.

price taker A buyer or seller that takes the market price as given.

private cost of production The production cost borne by a producer, which typically includes the costs of labor, capital, and materials.

private good A good that is consumed by a single person or household; a good that is rival in consumption and excludable.

private investment expenditures Purchases of newly produced goods and services by firms.

procyclical Moving in the same direction as real GDP.

producer surplus The price a producer receives for a product minus the marginal cost of production.

product differentiation The process used by firms to distinguish their products from the products of competing firms.

production function The relationship between the level of output of a good and the factors of production that are inputs to production.

production possibilities curve A curve that shows the possible combinations of products that an economy can produce, given that its productive resources are fully employed and efficiently used.

public good A good that is available for everyone to consume, regardless of who pays and who doesn't; a good that is nonrival in consumption and nonexcludable.

public-choice economics A field of economics that uses models of rational choice to explore decision making in the public sector.

purchasing power parity A theory of exchange rates whereby a unit of any given currency should be able to buy the same quantity of goods in all countries.

Q-theory of investment The theory of investment that links investment spending to stock prices.

quantity demanded The amount of a product that consumers are willing and able to buy.

quantity equation The equation that links money, velocity, prices, and real output. In symbols, we have $M \times V = P \times y$.

quantity supplied The amount of a product that firms are willing and able to sell.

rational expectations The economic theory that analyzes how the public forms expectations in such a manner that, on average, it forecasts the future correctly.

real business cycle theory The economic theory that emphasizes how shocks to technology can cause fluctuations in economic activity.

real exchange rate The price of U.S. goods and services relative to foreign goods and services, expressed in a common currency.

real GDP per capita Gross domestic product per person adjusted for changes in prices. It is the usual measure of living standards across time and among countries.

real GDP A measure of GDP that controls for changes in prices.

real interest rate The nominal interest rate minus the inflation rate.

real value The value of an amount of money in terms of what it can buy.

real wage The wage rate paid to employees adjusted for changes in the price level.

recession Commonly defined as six consecutive months of declining real GDP.

rent seeking The process of using public policy to gain economic profit.

required reserves The specific fraction of their deposits that banks are required by law to hold as reserves.

reservation price The price at which a consumer is indifferent about additional search for a lower price.

reserve ratio The ratio of reserves to deposits.

reserves The portion of banks' deposits set aside in either vault cash or as deposits at the Federal Reserve.

retained earnings Corporate earnings that are not paid out as dividends to their owners.

revaluation An increase in the exchange rate to which a currency is pegged under a fixed exchange rate system.

Ricardian equivalence The proposition that it does not matter whether government expenditure is financed by taxes or debt.

rule of 70 A rule of thumb that says output will double in $70/x$ years, where x is the percentage rate of growth.

saving Income that is not consumed.

savings function The relationship between the level of saving and the level of income.

scarcity The resources we use to produce goods and services are limited.

seasonal unemployment The component of unemployment attributed to seasonal factors.

securitization The practice of purchasing loans, re-packaging them, and selling them to the financial markets.

seignorage Revenue raised from money creation.

shoe-leather costs Costs of inflation that arise from trying to reduce holdings of cash.

short run in macroeconomics The period of time in which prices do not change or do not change very much.

short-run aggregate supply curve A relatively flat aggregate supply curve that represents the idea that prices do not change very much in the short run and that firms adjust production to meet demand.

short-run average total cost (*ATC*) Short-run total cost divided by the quantity produced; equal to *AFC* plus *AVC*.

short-run demand curve for labor A curve showing the relationship between the wage and the quantity of labor demanded over the short run, when the firm cannot change its production facility.

short-run marginal cost (*MC*) The change in short-run total cost resulting from a one-unit increase in output.

short-run market supply curve A curve showing the relationship between the market price and quantity supplied in the short run.

short-run supply curve A curve showing the relationship between the market price of a product and the quantity of output supplied by a firm in the short run.

short-run total cost (*TC*) The total cost of production when at least one input is fixed; equal to fixed cost plus variable cost.

shut-down price The price at which the firm is indifferent between operating and shutting down; equal to the minimum average variable cost.

signaling effect The information about a person's work skills conveyed by completing college.

slope of a curve The vertical difference between two points (the *rise*) divided by the horizontal difference (the *run*).

social cost of production Private cost plus external cost.

Social Security A federal government program to provide retirement support and a host of other benefits.

sovereign investment fund Assets accumulated by foreign governments that are invested abroad.

speculative demand for money The demand for money that arises because holding money over short periods is less risky than holding stocks or bonds.

stabilization policies Policy actions taken to move the economy closer to full employment or potential output.

stagflation A decrease in real output with increasing prices.

stock of capital The total of all machines, equipment, and buildings in an entire economy.

store of value The property of money that holds that money preserves value until it is used in an exchange.

structural unemployment Unemployment that occurs when there is a mismatch of skills and jobs.

substitutes Two goods for which an increase in the price of one good increases the demand for the other good.

substitution effect for leisure demand The change in leisure time resulting from a change in the wage (the price of leisure) relative to the price of other goods.

sunk cost A cost that a firm has already paid or committed to pay, so it cannot be recovered.

supply schedule A table that shows the relationship between the price of a product and quantity supplied, *ceteris paribus*.

supply shocks External events that shift the aggregate supply curve.

supply-side economics A school of thought that emphasizes the role that taxes play in the supply of output in the economy.

tariff A tax on imported goods.

technological progress More efficient ways of organizing economic affairs that allow an economy to increase output without increasing inputs.

terms of trade The rate at which units of one product can be exchanged for units of another product.

thin market A market in which some high-quality goods are sold but fewer than would be sold in a market with perfect information.

tie-in sale A business practice under which a business requires a consumer of one product to purchase another product.

tit-for-tat strategy A strategy where one firm chooses whatever price the other firm chose in the preceding period.

total revenue The money a firm generates from selling its product.

total surplus The sum of consumer surplus and producer surplus.

total-product curve A curve showing the relationship between the quantity of labor and the quantity of output produced, *ceteris paribus*.

trade deficit The excess of imports over exports.

trade surplus The excess of exports over imports.

transaction demand for money The demand for money based on the desire to facilitate transactions.

transfer payments Payments from governments to individuals that do not correspond to the production of goods and services.

trough The date at which output stops falling in a recession.

trust An arrangement under which the owners of several companies transfer their decision-making powers to a small group of trustees.

unanticipated inflation Inflation that is not expected.

unemployment insurance Payments unemployed people receive from the government.

unemployment rate The percentage of the labor force that is unemployed.

unit elastic demand The price elasticity of demand is one, so the percentage change in quantity equals the percentage change in price.

unit of account A standard unit in which prices can be stated and the value of goods and services can be compared.

value added The sum of all the income—wages, interest, profits, and rent—generated by an organization. For a firm, we can measure value added by the dollar value of the firm's sales minus the dollar value of the goods and services purchased from other firms.

variable A measure of something that can take on different values.

variable cost (*VC*) Cost that varies with the quantity produced.

velocity of money The rate at which money turns over during the year. It is calculated as nominal GDP divided by the money supply.

voluntary export restraint (VER) A scheme under which an exporting country voluntarily decreases its exports.

wage–price spiral The process by which changes in wages and prices cause further changes in wages and prices.

wealth effect The increase in spending that occurs because the real value of money increases when the price level falls.

willingness to accept The minimum amount a producer is willing to accept as payment for a product; equal to the marginal cost of production.

willingness to pay The maximum amount a consumer is willing to pay for a product.

World Trade Organization (WTO) An organization established in 1995 that oversees GATT and other international trade agreements, resolves trade disputes, and holds forums for further rounds of trade negotiations.

Photo Credits

CHAPTER 01: Pages 1 and 13, Ulrich Niehoff/Alamy; Page 9, Alamy; Page 10, Photos.com; Page 24, Stefan Witas/iStockphoto.

CHAPTER 02: Pages 28 and 43, Puwanai/Shutterstock, Page 33, Fotolia, Page 36, Shutterstock; Page 38, Alamy; Page 40, Navarone/Dreamstime.

CHAPTER 03: Pages 49 and 62 (bottom), Bill Bachman/Alamy; Page 55, Fotolia; Page 59, Joyce/Photo Researchers, Inc.; Page 62, Charles Sturge/Alamy (top).

CHAPTER 04: Pages 67 and 91, Steshkin Yevgeniy/Shutterstock; Page 71, Michal Bednarek/Shutterstock; Page 76, Diether Endlicher/AP Images; Page 78, Hemis/Alamy; Page 82, J JAVA/Fotolia; Page 89, Shutterstock.

CHAPTER 05: Pages 97 and 115, Andresr/Shutterstock; Page 100, Kathy deWitt/Alamy; Page 106, Tobik/Shutterstock; Page 109, Tom Grill/Corbis.

CHAPTER 06: Pages 120 and 136, Enrique Garcia Medina/Reuters; Page 125, Robert Daly/Alamy; Page 127, Bob Daemmrich/The Image Works; Page 129, Luba V Nel/Shutterstock; Page 132, Yuriy Zhuravov/Shutterstock.

CHAPTER 07: Pages 139 and 155, Stuart Dee/Getty Images; Page 145, Interfoto/Alamy; Page 150, Manu Fernandez/AP Images; Page 151, SuperStock.

CHAPTER 08: Pages 159 and 177 (bottom), Getty Images; Page 164, SuperStock; Page 165, Ivan Nesterov/Alamy; Page 170, Lain Masterton/Alamy; Page 171, Andrey Burmakin/Shutterstock; Page 174, Hulton Archive/Getty Images; Page 175, Library of Congress Division of Prints and Photographs [LC-USZ62-103992]; Page 177 (top), Jeffrey Bosdet/Alamy.

CHAPTER 09: Pages 185 and 202, M. Spencer Green/AP Images; Page 188, p. Elisheva Monasevich/Fotolia; Page 195, Paul Fleet/Alamy; Page 199, Spencer Platt/Getty Images.

CHAPTER 10: Pages 205 and 220, Bill Fitz-Patrick/CNP/Newscom; Page 210, Don Hammond/Corbis; Page 216, Compdrw/Getty Images; Page 219, Gerald Herbert/AP Images.

CHAPTER 11: Pages 223 and 245, AGE Fotostock; Page 229, David Duprey/AP Images; Page 233, Getty Images; Page 238, Fotolia; Page 243, An Xin/AP Images.

CHAPTER 12: Pages 253 and 268, Mikeledray/Shutterstock; Page 255, Ric Feld/AP Images; Page 259, Yuri Arcurs/Shutterstock; Page 263, Shutterstock; Page 267, Richard Drew/AP Images.

CHAPTER 13: Pages 272 and 286, Bjarki Reyr FCR/Alamy; Page 276, Alamy; Page 284, Bebeto Matthews/AP Images; Page 285, Getty Images.

CHAPTER 14: Pages 291 and 307, Mandal Ngan/AFP/Getty Images; Page 294, Feng Yu/Alamy; Page 297, Anneka/Shutterstock; Page 301, Joe Pavel/Reuters.

CHAPTER 15: Pages 311 and 325, Rich Pedroncelli/AP Images; Page 313, Britt Leckman/Federal Reserve Board/AP Images; Page 318, Saul Loeb/AFP/Getty Images; Page 323, Corbis.

CHAPTER 16: Pages 329 and 344, Shutterstock; Page 332, Thinkstock; Page 337, R. Nagy/Shutterstock; Page 339, Alamy.

CHAPTER 17: Pages 347 and 361, Alex Wong/Bloomberg/Getty Images; Page 354, National Archives and Records Administration; Page 357, David Papazian/Alamy; Page 360, Stephen Barnes/Alamy.

CHAPTER 18: Pages 364 and 381, Stephen Barnes/Alamy; Page 372, Dior Azcuy/AP Images; Page 374, Arkadiusz Komski/Shutterstock; Page 376, Lawrence Manning/Alamy; Page 379, Jason Turner/AP Images.

CHAPTER 19: Pages 385 and 405, Alamy; Page 396, Yoshikazu Tsuno/AFP/Getty Images; Page 402, Patryk Kosmider/Shutterstock; Page 404, Raul Ferrari/AP Images.

CHAPTER 20: Pages 409 and 432 (bottom), Oleg - F/Shutterstock; Page 415, Justin Sullivan/Getty Images; Page 419, Mike Kahn/Alamy; Page 422, Fotolia; Page 424, Economic Research Service; Page 428, Dennis Donohue/Shutterstock; Page 432 (top), Shutterstock.

CHAPTER 21: Pages 439 and 458, Andy Kropa/Redux; Page 443, Shutterstock; Page 446, Owe Andersson/Alamy; Page 449, Coprid/fotolia; Page 452, Shutterstock; Page 457, Oleg Golovnev/Shutterstock.

CHAPTER 22: Pages 464 and 488 (bottom), Mike Kemp/AGE Fotostock; Page 472, Stephanie Pilick/Newscom; Page 476, Martin Shields/Alamy; Page 481, Tim Pannell/Alamy; Page 488 (top), Shutterstock.

CHAPTER 23: Pages 497 and 514, Appujee/Fotolia; Page 499, Anthony Lee/AGE Fotostock; Page 506, Alamy; Page 511, Juniors Bildarchiv/Alamy.

CHAPTER 24: Pages 519 and 539 (bottom), David Espin/Fotolia; Page 522, Getty Images; Page 526, Jim Parkin/Alamy; Page 529, Timothy Epp/Shutterstock; Page 532, Dedi/Fotolia; Page 535, Joachim E Röttgers/AGE Fotostock; Page 537, Alamy; Page 539 (top), Fotolia.

CHAPTER 25: Pages 545 and 560 (bottom), Doug Schneider/Alamy; Page 551, Rhona Wise/Newscom; Page 554, John Reddy/Alamy; Page 556, John Reddy/Alamy; Page 560 (top), Larry Mulvehill/The Image Works.

CHAPTER 26: Pages 566 and 578, Ariel Skelley/Alamy; Page 570, Lexaarts/Fotolia; Page 573, Judith Collins/Alamy; Page 575, Dutourdumonde/Shutterstock; Page 576, Kurhan/Shutterstock.

CHAPTER 27: Pages 582 and 602, SeanPavonePhoto/Shutterstock; Page 588, LianeM/Fotolia; Page 592, Tony Freeman/PhotoEdit, Inc.; Page 595, Lisa F. Young/Shutterstock; Page 599, Lightworks Media/Alamy; Page 601, Michael Siluk/The Image Works.

CHAPTER 28: Pages 609 and 621 (bottom), Sheila Halsall/Alamy; Page 614, Samuel Wheeler/Alamy; Page 615, Earth Observing System/NASA; Page 620, Joe Belanger/Shutterstock; Page 621 (top), Glow Images.

CHAPTER 29: Pages 625 and 644 (bottom), Vitalii Nesterchuk/Shutterstock; Page 630, Duane Burleson/AP Images; Page 633, Ron Redfern/Dorling Kindersley, Ltd.; Page 637, Andrey Kekyalyaynen/Alamy; Page 639, Nick Lylak/Alamy; Page 644 (top), Iofoto/Shutterstock.

CHAPTER 30: Pages 651 and 663 (bottom), Detlev van Ravenswaay/Photo Researchers, Inc.; Page 655, Duncan Smith/Getty Images; Page 656, National Oceanic and Atmospheric Administration; Page 658, Mitch Kezar/Getty Images; Page 659, Frank Tozier/Alamy; Page 663 (top), Action Plus/Alamy.

CHAPTER 31: Pages 668 and 684 (bottom), Elxeneize/Shutterstock; Page 672, Repina Valeriya/Shutterstock; Page 676, Anne Kitzman/Shutterstock; Page 678, Chris Cheadle/Alamy; Page 681, FB-Rose/Alamy; Page 684 (top), Lisa F. Young/Shutterstock.

CHAPTER 32: Pages 689 and 715, WavebreakmediaMicro/Fotolia; Page 695, Cstyle/Fotolia; Page 698, Shutterstock; Page 705, Stephen Coburn/Shutterstock; Page 709, Michael Newman/PhotoEdit, Inc.; Page 714, Gabe Hernandez/AP Images.

Index

A

Absolute advantage, 52, 55
Accelerator theory, 254
Accounting, growth, 169–171
Accounting rules, 56
Acemoglu, Daron, 174
Adjustment process
  economics of, 319–324
  speed of, 316–317
Adverse technological shocks, 149–150
Afghanistan War, 349
Africa
  economic growth in, 159, 164
  poverty in, 5–6, 159
African Americans, unemployment and, 123–124
Aggregate demand, 188–195
  components of, 189
  fiscal policy and, 206–207
  long-run aggregate supply and, 196–197
  money supply and, 302–303
  multiplier and, 192–195
  short-run aggregate supply and, 198–199
Aggregate demand curve (AD), 188–189, 314
  deriving, 243–244
  downward slope of, 189–190
  income-expenditure model and, 243–245
  shifts in, 190–192, 244
Aggregate supply, 196–200
Aggregate supply curve (AS), 196
  long-run, 196–197
  short-run, 197–199
  supply shocks and, 199–200
Aghion, Phillipe, 175
Aging populations, entitlement programs and, 210
Agriculture policy, 78
Airbus, 374
American International Group (AIG), 267, 285
American Recovery and Reinvestment Act, 219
Annuities, 259
Anticipated inflation, 134–135
Antitrust policy, 61
Apple iPod, 360–361
Appreciation of a currency, 304, 386–387
Argentina
  financial crisis in, 404
  hyperinflation in, 342, 404
  inflation statistics in, 120
Asian financial crisis, 403
Asian Pacific Economic Cooperation (APEC), 375
Assets, 277
Assumptions, use of, for simplification, 7, 9
Auction prices, 186
Authoritarian institutions, 174
Automatic stabilizers, 214–215, 237–240, 353, 356
Automobile emissions standards, marginal principle and, 35–36
Autonomous consumption, 227–228
Autonomous consumption spending, 192
Autor, David, 127

B

Baby boomers, 125
Balanced budget, debate over, 348–354
Balanced-budget amendment, 353–354
Balanced-budget multiplier, 235, 251
Balance of payments, 393, 395–397
Balance of payments deficit, 400
Balance of payments surplus, 400
Balance sheet, 277–278
Ball, Larry, 313
Bank failures, 266, 272
Bank of England, 282
Bank runs, 266
Banks. *See also* Central banks; Federal Reserve
  balance sheet for, 277–278
  creation of money by, 277–281
  excess reserves held by, 280
  reserve ratio of, 278, 279
  reserve requirements for, 296
Bar graphs, 15
Barro, Robert, 233, 353
Barter, 273
Base year, 130
Basket of goods, 130, 131
Bear Stearns, 266, 285
Becker, Gary, 173
Beef, hormone-treated, 378
Beg, Andrew, 165
Bernake, Ben S., 291, 313, 356, 385
Big Mac, exchange rates and price of, 392
Bils, Mark, 188
Black Death, living standards and, 145
Blanchflower, David, 109
Blinder, Alan, 301
Board of Governors of the Federal Reserve, 283
Boeing, 374
Bolivia, hyperinflation in, 342
Bond prices
  economy and, 300
  interest, 299–300
  open market operations and, 300
Bonds
  corporate, 259–260, 261–262
  interest rates on long-term, 306–307
Boom economy, 200–201
  returning to full employment after, 315–316
Bosworth, Barry, 170
Brazil
  currency devaluation in, 404
  local currency in, 276
Bretton Woods system, 399, 401
Broda, Christian, 379
Broken Windows fallacy, 238
Brown, E. Cary, 216
Brown, Gordon, 337
Bubonic plague, 145
Buchholz, Todd, 54
Budget deficit, 214–216
  1996–2011, 220
  as burden on future generations, 350–351
  debates over, 350–354
  as good for economy, 353
  hyperinflation and, 343

inflation and, 350
recent history of, 348–350
size of government and, 352–353
Budget surplus, 214, 348–349
Bureau of Labor Statistics (BLS), 123
Bush, George H. W., 98, 335
Bush, George W., 218–219, 236, 349, 372
Bush administration, fiscal policy during, 218–219
Business cycles, 112–113, 186
political, 318
real business cycle theory, 148–150
Business decisions, using macroeconomics to make, 11

C

Cagan, Philip, 341, 343
Capital
diminishing returns to, 180–181
human, 2, 160, 173–174
increase in supply of, 165–166
intangible, 171
physical, 2
stock of, 141, 142–143
Capital account, 394–395
Capital consumption allowance, 103
Capital deepening, 160, 165–168
crowding out and, 324
economic growth and, 170
influences on, 167–168
model of, 180–184
Capital gains, 359–360
Capivaris, 276
Cargo ships, speeds, marginal principle and, 36
Carter, Jimmy, 98, 335
Cell phones, bias in CPI and, 132
Central banks, 281, 282, 284. *See also* Federal Reserve
credibility of, and inflation, 337–339
independence of, 337, 339
inflation targeting by, 357–358
Centrally planned economy, 56
Ceteris paribus, 8, 10, 69–70, 72, 73, 78, 83
Chain-weighted index, 111, 130–131
Chairman of the Federal Reserve, 283
Change in demand, 79
vs. change in quantity demanded, 78–79
market effects of, 90
Change in quantity demanded, 70
vs. change in demand, 78–79
Change in quantity supplied, 73
vs. change in supply, 83–84
Change in supply, 83
vs. change in quantity supplied, 83–84
effects of, across markets, 89
Changes
marginal, 8, 10
using microeconomics to predict, 12
Checkable deposits, 275
Check collection and clearing system, 281, 284
Checking accounts, 275, 276, 279
Childcare, GDP and, 114
Child labor, 163
China
demand for pecans in, 82
economic growth in, 164, 174, 243
exchange rate of, 392
fiscal policy in, 236
global recession and, 223
government investment in, 152
imports from, 374
sources of growth in, 170
trade sanctions on, 364
trade with, 379
Cigarette prices, law of demand and, 62
Circular flow of production and income, 99–100, 108–109
Civil liberties, 62
Clark, Andrew E., 129
Clark, Gregory, 145, 175
Classical economics, 324–325
Classical models, 140
Climate change, economic growth and, 164
Clinton, Bill, 98, 209, 218, 236
Clinton administration, fiscal policy during, 218
Closed economy, 153
crowding out in, 152–153
Cole, Harold L., 151
College degree
benefits of, 173
opportunity cost of, 29–30
College facilities rental, marginal principle and, 35–36
Collins, Susan, 170
Colony collapse disorder (CCD), 89
Commerce Department, 376
Committees, effectiveness of, 301
Commodity money, 274
Commodity prices, Fed policy and, 297
Common Agricultural Policy (CAP), 78
Comparative advantage, 52
vs. absolute advantage, 52
exchange and, 50–55
international trade and, 53–54
in Latvia, 55
terms of trade and, 367
Competition
imperfect, 60
in market economy, 61
unfair, 373–374
Complements, 70, 80, 81
Computer software, pirated, 172–173
Concorde, 374
Congressional Budget Office, 211, 219, 349
Conservation, of rainforests, 28
Constrained discretion, 356
Consumer confidence, autonomous consumption and, 228
Consumer markets, measuring price stickiness in, 188
Consumer preferences, shifts in, 80, 82
Consumer Price Index (CPI), 129–130
bias in, 132
vs. chain index for GDP, 130–131
components of, 131
cost-of-living adjustments and, 131
Consumer products, information about, 60–61
Consumer spending
falling home prices and, 229
income and, 227, 240
Consumer wealth, autonomous consumption and, 228
Consumption
autonomous, 227
consumer, 240
inequality, trade, and, 379
Consumption expenditures, 102, 103, 152
Consumption function, 192, 227–228
changes in, 227–228
equilibrium output and, 229–233
tax rate and, 239–240

Consumption possibilities curve, 367–368
Consumption taxes, 358–361
Continental Congress, 354
Continuity, 53
Contractionary policies, 207, 317
Contracts, 56
Convergence, 163
Corporate bonds, 259–260, 261–262
Corporate taxes, 213
Corrado, Carol, 171
Costa Rica, GNI per capita, 162–163
Cost of living, 129–130
Cost-of-living adjustments (COLAs), 131
Costs
  marginal, 33
  menu, 134
  opportunity. *See* Opportunity cost
  shoe-leather, 134
Cost savings, from outsourcing, 54
Creative destruction, 172
Credit cards, 276–277
Credit systems, economic growth and, 177
Crop yields, fertilizer and, 40
Crowding in, 154–155, 324
Crowding out, 153
  in closed economy, 152–153
  government spending and, 238
  increasing health-care expenditures and, 323
  in long run, 322–324
  in open economy, 154
Culture, economic growth and, 175
Currency
  appreciation, 304, 386–387
  demand and supply of, 387–390
  depreciation, 304, 386–387
  devaluation, 400
  Federal Reserve and supply of, 281
  revaluation, 400
Currency markets, 386–387
Current account, 393, 394–395
Current account deficit, 396–397
Curves. *See also* Demand curve; Production possibilities curve; Supply curve
  consumption possibilities, 367–368
  expectations Phillips, 333–336
  Laffer, 213–214
  moving along vs. shifting, 20–21
  nonlinear, 22–23
  slope of, 19
  supply, 71–76
Custom duties, 213
Custom prices, 186
Cyclical unemployment, 126, 140, 146

D

Debit cards, 277
Decision making
  by committees, 301
  in market economy, 57
  using microeconomics for, 12
Deflation, 42, 133–134
Dell, Melissa, 164
DeLong, Brad, 165
Demand, 68. *See also* Aggregate demand
  aggregate, 188–195
  change in, 78–79
  changes in, and aggregate demand curve, 191–192
  currency, 387–390
  excess, 76–77
  increases in, 79–81
  labor, wages and, 143–145
  law of, 68–70
  market effects of changes in, 78–82
  for money, 292–295
  short-run determination of output by, 187–188
  simultaneous changes in supply and, 87–89
Demand and supply model, 78–89
Demand curve, 68–71. *See also* Aggregate demand curve (AD)
  decreases in, 81–82
  individual, 68–70
  labor, 143, 147–148
  law of demand and, 68–70
  market, 70–71
  movement along, 70
  shifts in, 79–81
Demand deposits, 275
Demand policies, 317
Demand schedule, 68–69
Demographics, 336, 347
Denison, Edward, 169
Deposit accounts, 275
Deposit creation formula, 290
Deposit insurance, 266
Depreciation, 103
  as function of stock of capital, 181–182
  saving, capital deepening and, 180–184
Depreciation of a currency, 304, 386–387
Depression, 113, 224
DeSoto, Hernando, 177
Devaluation, 400
Developing countries
  economic growth in, 163–165
  knowledge accumulation in, 174
  lack of incentives for growth in, 176
  price structures in, 162
  property rights in, 176–177
Dickens, William, 332
Diminishing marginal returns, 142
Diminishing returns, 39
Diminishing returns principle, 39, 142, 167, 180–181
Disability insurance, unemployment and, 127
Discount rate, 296
Discouraged workers, 123
Discretionary spending, 211
Division of labor, exchange and, 53
Doha trade negotiations, 375
Dollars. *See* U.S. dollar
Dolphins, tuna fishing and, 377–378
Domestic industries, helping, with protectionist policies, 373–374
Dominican Republic-Central America Free Trade Agreement (DR-CAFTA), 375
Double coincidence of wants, 273
Draghi, Mario, 385
Driving speed, marginal principle and, 36
Drug prices, 90
Duggan, Mark, 127
Dumping, 376–377

E

Earnings, retained, 261
Easterly, William, 176
Econometric models, 210
Economic analysis, problem solving and, 5–7
Economic boom, returning to full employment after, 315–316
Economic fluctuations, 186
  lags and, 208–210
  technology and, 149–150
  using macroeconomics to understand, 11

Economic growth, 102
in Africa, 159
capital deepening and, 165–168
culture, evolution, and, 175
in developing countries, 163–165
global warming and, 164
inequality and, 165
international comparisons of, 162–163
measuring, 161–162
new growth theory and, 174–175
vs. per capita income, 163–164
property rights and, 176–177
rates, 160–165
role of government in, 176
role of political factors in, 174
sources of, 170
technological progress and, 168–171, 180–184
using macroeconomics to understand, 11
Economic models, 4–5
classical models, 140
to determine causes of recessions, 195
econometric, 210
Economic policy
debates over, 347–361
speed of adjustment and, 316–317
using, to fight recession, 317
Economic principles, 30. *See also* Diminishing returns principle; Marginal principle; Opportunity cost; Real-nominal principle; Voluntary exchange principle
Economic questions, 4
Economic rate of return, civil liberties and, 62
Economic recovery, after recession, 314–315
Economics, 1, 2
classical, 324–325
supply-side, 205, 213–214, 218
Economic stability, 240
Economic uncertainty, 61, 210–211, 255
Economic way of thinking
elements of, 7–9
example, 9–10
Economic well-being, 97
Economy
boom, 200–201, 315–316
centrally planned, 56
in short run, 200–201, 224

Edison, Thomas, 1
Education, 173–174
Efficiency, 1
Elections, 318
Email, spam, 10
Employment
free trade and, 368–369
part-time, 123
Employment taxes, labor demand and supply and, 147–148
Energy prices, investment spending and, 255
Entitlement and mandatory spending, 212
Entitlement programs, 210, 212
Entrepreneurs, role of, 58
Entrepreneurship, 2, 6
Environment, GDP and, 114–115
Environmental protection, trade laws and, 377–378
Equality, economic growth and, 165
Equations, using, to compute missing values, 25
Equilibrium
labor market, 144, 146–147
long-run, 201
in money market, 297–299
short-run, 201
Equilibrium output, 224–226
adjusting to, 226–227
consumption function and, 229–233
determining, 225
formulas for, 249–252
in open economy, 241–242
saving and investment and, 230–231
Equilibrium price
consequences of price above, 78
decrease in demand and, 81–82
decrease in supply and, 87
increase in demand and, 80–81
increase in supply and, 85–86
simultaneous changes in demand and supply and, 87–89
Equilibrium quantity, simultaneous changes in demand and supply and, 87–89
Estate taxes, 213
Euro, 386, 387–390, 402
Europe, taxes differences in, 150
European Central Bank, 385
European Community (EC), 49, 55
European Union (EU), 375

Evolution, economic growth and, 175
Excess demand, 76–77
Excess reserves, 278, 280
Excess supply, 77–78
Exchange
comparative advantage and, 50–55
division of labor and, 53
Exchange rate, 304, 386
appreciation, 397
current systems of, 401
depreciation, 397–398
determination of, 386–390
fixed, 397–401
flexible, 399–401
net exports and, 391
real, 390–393
Excise taxes, 213
Expansion, 112
Expansionary policies, 207, 317
Expectations of inflation, 330
Expectations Phillips curve, 333–336
Expected real interest rate, 258
Expenditures, planned, 225
Exports, 54, 104
in income-expenditure model, 241–242
net, 102, 104–105, 152
Externalities, negative, 59–60

F

Fackler, Jack, 195
Factors of production, 2
Fannie Mae, 265, 266, 267
Federal budget, 211–216. *See also* Budget deficit
debate over balancing, 348–354
recent history of, 348–350
Federal deficit, 214–216
Federal funds market, 296
Federal funds rate, 296, 306–307, 317
Federal government. *See also* Government
states and, 354
Federal Open Market Committee (FOMC), 283
Federal Reserve
commodity prices and, 297
functions of, 281–282
housing boom and, 357
independence of, 283–284
inflation and, 337–339

inflation targeting by, 355–358
interest rates and, 297–299, 300, 301
market expectations and, 306–307
monetary policy and, 282, 283, 291–307
money supply and, 295–297
open market operations of, 295–296, 300
quantitative easing by, 297
response by, in financial crisis, 284–285, 294
structure of, 282–283
tools of, 295–297
Federal Reserve Banks, 282–283
Federal Reserve float, 284
Federal Reserve System, 281–284
Federal revenues, 212–214
Federal spending, 211–212, 220
Feldstein, Martin, 148
Fertilizer, crop yields and, 40
Fiat money, 274–275
Final goods and services, 101
Finance, investment and, 253
Financial account, 394–396
Financial crises
of 2008-2009, 266–267, 272, 285, 311, 329, 402
economic view of, 6–7
management of, 402–404
response of Federal Reserve to, 284–285, 294
Financial intermediaries, 263–268
Financial panics, 281
Fiscal multipliers, 207–208, 234–237
Fiscal policy, 206
aggregate demand and, 206–207
automatic stabilizers, 214–215, 237–240
contractionary policies, 207
expansionary policies, 207
federal deficit and, 214–216
Keynesian, 234, 236–237, 238
lags and, 208–210
role of, 206–211
stabilization policies, 208–210
in U.S. history, 216–220
Fiscal stimulus, 218–219, 237
Fiscal-year basis, 211
Fischer, Stanley, 164, 385
Fitoussi, Jean-Paul, 97
Fixed exchange rates, 397–401
Fixed exchange rate system, 399
Flat tax, 360–361
Flexible exchange rate system, 399–401
Flexible prices, 186–187
Forecasting, economic uncertainties, 210–211
Foreign competition, workers and, 373
Foreign demand, affect on output of, 243
Foreign exchange market intervention, 398–399
Foreign producers, dumping by, 376–377
45° line, 224–225
France
GDP per capita in, 139
GNI per capita, 162
government consumption in, 152
Freddie Mac, 265, 266, 267
Freedom House, 62
Free trade, 173, 364, 365
dumping and, 376–377
employment and, 368–369
reasons for protests against, 380
Frictional unemployment, 126, 140
Friedman, Milton, 311, 317, 333, 343
Full employment, 127, 140, 186
dividing output among competing demands for GDP at, 151–155
labor market equilibrium and, 146–147
opportunity cost of increased government spending at, 153
returning to, after recession, 314–315
returning to, from a boom, 315–316
wage and price changes and, 314–318
Full-employment model, 140, 147–151
Full-employment output, 146–147

G

Galor, Oded, 175
GATT. *See* General Agreement on Tariffs and Trade (GATT)
GDP. *See* Gross domestic product
GDP deflator, 110–111
General Agreement on Tariffs and Trade (GATT), 375
The General Theory of Employment, Interest, and Money (Keynes), 237
Genetically modified crops, 378
Germany
central bank of, 338
government investment in, 152
U.S. dollar and, 400–401
Gift taxes, 213
Global economy, 53–54
Globalization, 150
Global recession, 97, 223, 272
Global warming. *See* Climate change
GNP. *See* Gross national product
Gold prices, inflation and, 329
Gold standard, 274
Goods
basket of, 130
complement, 80
complementary, 81
inferior, 80, 81
intermediate, 101
new, and bias in CPI, 132
nondurable, 379
normal, 79, 81
public, 60
smuggled, 372
substitute, 80, 81
Google, 171
Government
capital deepening and, 167–168
enforcement of rules of exchange by, 60–61
role of, in market economy, 59–62, 176
size of, 352–353
Government bonds, 214
Government debt, 212, 329, 348. *See also* Budget deficit
as burden on future generations, 350–351
international comparisons of, 352
as percentage of GDP, 349–350, 352
Government investment, 152, 167–168
Government purchases, 102, 104, 152, 153–154
Government spending
aggregate demand and, 206
Broken Windows fallacy and, 238
capital deepening and, 167–168
changes in, and aggregate demand curve, 191

crowding in and, 154–155, 324
crowding out and, 322–323
decreases in, 324
federal budget and, 211–212
GDP and, 233–234
income-expenditure model and, 233–240
multiplier, 234–235, 251
U.S. consumption and, during WWII, 154
U.S. investment and, during WWII, 154
Graphs
of negative relationships, 21–22
of nonlinear relationships, 22–23
of single variable, 15–17
of two variables, 17–19
using, 15–23
Great Depression, 113, 186, 197
bank failures during, 266
deflation during, 134
fiscal policy during, 216
inside lag during, 209
labor market policies and, 151
unemployment during, 127, 140, 185
Greece, hyperinflation in, 3, 341–342
Greenspan, Alan, 263, 291, 305, 338–339
Gross domestic product (GDP), 100
affect of imports and exports on, 243
chain-weighted index for, 130–131
components of, 102–105
contributions to growth of real, 169
debt as percent of, 349–350, 352
dividing output among competing demands for, 151–155
fluctuations in, 112–113
GDP equation, 105
vs. GNP, 106–107
government spending and, 233–234
growth in, 160
growth rates of U.S., 1871-2011, 238
happiness and, 109
historical U.S. price index for, 133
interest rates and, 301–303
investment spending as share of U.S., 255
as measure of welfare, 113–115
measuring macroeconomic activity using, 100–105
measuring real vs. nominal, 109–110
money demand and, 292–293
nominal, 101–102, 109–111
per capita, 139
real, 101, 102, 109–111
real, per capita, 161
real exchange rates and net exports as percentage of, 391
research and development as percentage of, 172
shortcomings in, 114–115
Gross investment, 103–104
Gross national income, international comparisons of, 162–163
Gross national product (GNP), 106–107
real, 162
Group think, 313
Growth accounting, 169–171
Growth rate, 161
international comparisons of, 162–163
vs. per capita income, 163–164
Growth version of the quantity equation, 340–341

H

Hall, Robert E., 323, 360
Hamilton, Alexander, 354
Hanseatic League, 49
Happiness
GDP and, 109
unemployment, social norms, and, 129
Hausman, Jerry, 132
Hayek, Friedrich, 56
Hazlitt, Henry, 238
Health-care expenditures, crowding out and, 323
Heller, Walter, 217
Heston, Alan, 162
Home prices, 229
Homes, underwater, 263
Honeybees, price of ice cream and, 89
Hong Kong
economic growth in, 176
financial crisis in, 403
government consumption in, 152
Hoover, Herbert, 151, 216
Hormone-treated beef, 378
Housework, GDP and, 114
Housing boom, 357
Housing market, 253, 267
Housing prices
fall in, 253, 266, 291
increase in, 67
in Japan, 162
Howitt, Peter, 175
Hulten, Charles, 171
Humana index, 62
Human capital, 2, 160, 173–174
Human capital theory, 173–174
Hungary, hyperinflation in, 341–342, 343
Hybrid vehicles, incentives to buy, 9
Hyperinflation, 135, 339, 341–343, 404

I

Ice cream prices, honeybee population and, 89
Iceland, bank failures in, 272
Illiquid, 295
Imperfect competition, 60
Imperfect information, 60
Import bans, 369–370
Import licenses, 370–371
Import quotas, 370
Imports, 54, 104, 241–242, 374
Incentives, 8–9, 176
Income, 98–99
circular flow of, 99–100
consumer spending and, 227, 240
decrease in, 80, 81
increase in, 79, 81
national, 106–109
per capita, 162–164
permanent, 218
personal, 107
personal disposable, 107
relationship between hours worked and, 17–18
Income-expenditure model, 224–227
aggregate demand curve and, 243–245
automatic stabilizers in, 237–240
consumption function in, 227–233
equilibrium output in, 229–233
exports and imports in, 241–242
government spending and taxation in, 233–240
multiplier in, 232–233

Income inequality, outsourcing and trade and, 379–380
Income tax, 212–213, 239–240
India
  central bank of, 282
  economic growth in, 164, 243
  GNI per capita, 162
  per capita output in, 167
  price structures in, 162
  sources of growth in, 170
Individual demand curve, 68–70
Individual supply curve, 72–73
Indonesia, 403
Induced innovation, 173
Industrial Revolution, 174, 175
Inefficiencies, 1
Inequality
  economic growth and, 165
  international trade and, 379
Infant industries, 373
Inferior good, 80, 81
Inflation, 98, 132–134, 261, 401
  anticipated, 134–135
  Argentinian statistics on, 120
  budget deficits and, 350
  costs of, 134–135
  credibility of central bank and, 337–339
  effect on real minimum wage, 41–42
  expectations of, 330
  gold prices and, 329
  hyperinflation, 339, 341–343, 404
  public expectations about, 334
  repayment of student loans and, 42
  in steady state, 330–331
  unanticipated, 134, 135, 333
  unemployment and, 333–336
  U.S., and unemployment in 1980s, 334–335
  velocity of money and, 340–341
Inflation expectations
  central banks and, 337–339
  interest rates and, 330–331
  money demand and, 331
Inflation rate, 132–134
Inflation targeting, by Fed, 355–358
Information
  about consumer products, 60–61
  imperfect, 60
Innovation, 53
  induced, 173
  monopolies and, 172–173
Input prices, 187, 197–198
Inside lags, 208–210, 305–306
Insourcing, 54
Institutional changes, 336
Institutions, economic growth and, 176
Insurance, 56, 61
  deposit, 266
  disability, 127
  risk and, 264–265
  unemployment, 128–129, 237
Intangible capital, growth accounting and, 171
Intellectual property rights, 172–173
Interest, net, 212
Interest rate effect, 190
Interest rates
  approaching zero, 320
  bond prices and, 299–300
  on corporate and government investment, 2002-2022, 259
  crowding out and, 324
  determination of, 297–301
  GDP and, 301–303
  inflation and, 330–331
  investment and, 260–261, 301–303
  on long-term bonds, 306–307
  monetary policy and, 302
  money demand and, 292–293
  nominal, 258–260, 261, 320, 331
  present value and, 256–257
  real, 258–260, 261
Intermediate goods, 101
International comparisons
  of government debt, 352
  of growth rate, 162–163
International Financial Statistics, 152
International Monetary Fund, 152, 162, 403, 404
International trade, 365. *See also* Free trade; Trade
  comparative advantage and, 53–54
  income-expenditure model and, 241–242
  inequality and, 379
  monetary policy and, 303–305
International trade effect, 190
Inventions, patents on, 56
Inventory cycle, 240
Inventory management, 240
Investment, 152, 240, 254–256
  finance and, 253
  financial intermediaries and, 263–268
  government, 152
  gross, 103–104
  interest rates and, 260–261, 301–303
  multiplier and, 232–233
  neoclassical theory, 261
  net, 103–104, 167
  present value and, 260
  private, 103–104
  Q-theory of, 262
  saving and, 166–167, 230–231
  stock market and, 261–263
Investment decisions, 260–263
Investment spending
  accelerator theory of, 254
  energy prices and, 255
  money market and, 301–302
  multiple-accelerator model, 256
  procyclical, 254
  real interest rates and, 261
  as share of U.S. GDP, 255
Investors, 254, 264
Invisible hand, 57
iPod, 360–361
iPod Shuffle, 1
Iraq
  invasion of Kuwait by, 305
  war in, 349
Italy, GNI per capita, 162

J

Japan
  economic growth in, 163
  financial crisis in, 266
  GNI per capita, 162, 163
  government spending in, 237
  housing prices in, 162
  protectionist policies, 372
  recession in, 236
Job loss, from outsourcing, 54
Johnson, Lyndon, 217
Jones, Benjamin, 164
Jones, Charles I., 323
Jorgenson, Dale, 261
Juo, Yu, 216

K

Kashyap, Anil, 188
Kennedy, John F., 205, 217
Kennedy administration, fiscal policy during, 217

Keynes, John Maynard, 186, 192, 197, 224, 237, 311
 classical economics and, 324–325
 on economic stabilization, 317
 on investment spending, 254
Keynesian cross, 224
Keynesian fiscal policy, 234, 236–237, 238
Kilian, Lutz, 199
Kirchner, Cristina, 120
Klenow, Peter, 188
Kleven, Henrik Jacobsen, 150
Knowledge accumulation, 173
Koppel, Ted, 90
Kuwait, Iraqi invasion of, 305

L

Labor, 2, 141
 child, 163
 division of, and exchange, 53
 relationship between output and, 141–142
 skilled, 380
 taxes and demand and supply for, 147–148
 unskilled, 380
 wages and demand and supply for, 143–145
Labor demand curve, 143, 147–148
Labor force, 121, 122, 123
Labor force participation rate, 121, 125
Labor market, 2
Labor market equilibrium, 144
 full employment and, 146–147
Labor market policies, Great Depression and, 151
Labor productivity, 171, 336
Labor supply curve, 144, 147–148
Laffer, Arthur, 213–214
Laffer curve, 213–214
Lags, 208–210, 305–306
Landais, Camille, 150
Latvia, 49, 55
Law of demand, 69–70
 cigarettes and, 71
Law of one price, 393
Law of supply, 73, 76
Learning by doing, 373
Lebergott, Stanley, 148
LEED certification, 668
Lehman Brothers, 266–267, 285
Leisure, GDP and, 114
Lender of last resort, 281, 282
Leverage, 265
Liabilities, 277
Liberty ships, 373
Life expectancy, entitlement programs and, 210
Lincoln, Abraham, 54
Liquid, 263
Liquidity demand for money, 295
Liquidity traps, 313, 317, 319
Living standards, 1, 130
 Black Death and, 145
 differences in, 160
 growth in GDP and, 160
 trade and, 379
Loan repayment, effect of inflation and deflation on, 42
Locomotive effect, 243
Long run
 crowding out in, 322–324
 neutrality of money in, 320–322
Long-run aggregate supply curve, 196–197, 314
Long-run equilibrium, 201
Long run in macroeconomics, 312
Long-run neutrality of money, 320–322
Lucas, Robert E., 174, 334
Luxembourg, 162

M

M1, 275, 279
M2, 275–276, 340
Macroeconomic activity
 measuring using gross domestic product, 100–105
 measuring using national income, 106–109
Macroeconomic policy, debates over, 347–361
Macroeconomics, 10, 98
 linking the short and long run in, 200–201, 312–314
 short run in, 187–188
 use of, 11
Malaysia, 403
Malthus, Thomas, 145, 324
Mandatory spending, 212
Manufacturing firms, inventory management by, 240
Marginal benefit, 33
Marginal change, 8, 10
Marginal cost, 33
Marginally attached workers, 123
Marginal principle, 33–36, 73, 144
 automobile emissions standards and, 35–36
 driving speed and, 36
 movie sequels and, 34–35
 of renting facility, 35–36
Marginal propensity to consume (MPC), 192, 227, 232–234, 239–240
Marginal propensity to import, 241
Marginal propensity to save (MPS), 192, 231
Market changes, predicting and explaining, 90–91
Market demand curve, 70–71
Market economy, 55–56
 risk in, 61
 role of government in, 59–62, 176
Market effects
 of changes in demand, 78–82
 of changes in supply, 83–89
 of simultaneous changes in demand and supply, 87–89
Market equilibrium, 76–78
Market-equilibrium price. *See* Equilibrium price
Market expectations, 306–307
Market failure, role of government and, 59–61
Markets, 2, 50, 55–59. *See also* Labor market
 development of, 58–59
 emergence of, in POW camps, 58
 perfectly competitive, 68, 75
 role of entrepreneurs in, 58
 scale of, 173
 using microeconomics to understand, 12
 virtues of, 56–58
 voluntary exchange and, 37–38
Market supply curve, 74–75
 slope of, 75
McMillin, Douglas, 195
Medicaid, 210, 212
Medicare, 210, 212, 213
Medium of exchange, 273–274

Menu costs, 134
Merrill Lynch, 266
Meteorite market, 59
Mexico
  financial crisis in, 402–403, 404
  GNI per capita, 162–163
Microeconomics, 12–13
Military spending, opportunity cost of, 30–31
Mill, John Stuart, 324
Minimum supply price, 73
Minimum wage, 187
  value of the, 41–42
Mining industry, 67
Minorities, unemployment and, 123–124
Moav, Omer, 175
Modigliani, Franco, 325, 385
Monetarists, 343
Monetary policy, 281, 283
  challenges, 305–307
  contractionary, 317
  expansionary, 317
  Fed and, 291–307
  housing boom and, 357
  interest rates and, 302
  international trade and, 303–305
  lags in, 305–306
  in long run, 322
  in short run, 322
Monetary systems, types of, 274–275
Monetizing the deficit, 350
Money, 273
  changes in growth rate of, and steady state, 331–332
  commodity, 274
  creation of, by banks, 277–281
  demand for, 292–295
  fiat, 274–275
  long-run neutrality of, 320–322
  M1, 275, 279
  M2, 275–276
  measuring, in U.S. economy, 275–277
  as medium of exchange, 273–274
  nominal value of, 41
  properties of, 273–274
  real-nominal principle and, 40–42
  real value of, 41
  as store of value, 274
  velocity of, 340–341
Money demand
  GDP and, 293–294
  inflation and, 331
  interest rates and, 292–293, 297–301
  other components of, 295
  price level and, 293–294
  transaction, 292
Money illusion, 330
Money market, 292–295
  equilibrium in, 297–299
  investment spending and, 301–302
Money multiplier, 279–281
Money supply
  aggregate demand and, 302–303
  changes in, 190
  Federal Reserve and supply of, 295–297
  interest rates and, 297–301
Monopolies
  antitrust policies and, 61
  helping domestic firms establish, in world markets, 373–374
  innovation and, 172–173
Mortgages, subprime, 266, 267, 285, 291, 357
Movie sequels, marginal principle and, 34–35
Mozambique, 6
Multilateral real exchange rate, 391
Multiple-accelerator model, 256
Multiplier effect, 243
Multiplier(s), 192–195, 207–208
  balanced-budget, 235, 251
  fiscal, 207–208, 234–237
  formulas for, 249–252
  government spending, 234–235, 251
  in income-expenditure model, 232–233
  money, 279–281
  tax, 234–235, 236, 251
  using, 235–237
  using long-term macro data to measure, 233
Music piracy, 172–173

N

National Bureau of Economics Research (NBER), 113
National debt. *See* Budget deficit; Government debt
National income, 106
  measuring, 106–108
  value added and, 107–108
National Industrial Recovery Act, 151
Natural disasters, 149
Natural rate of unemployment, 126–128, 146–147, 332, 336
Natural resources, 2
Negative externalities, 59–60
Negative relationship, 19
  graphing, 21–22
Neoclassical theory of investment, 261
Net exports, 102, 104–105, 152, 391
Net interest, 212
Net international investment position, 396
Net investment, 103–104, 167
Net national product (NNP), 107
New Deal, 151
New growth theory, 174–175
New York Federal Reserve, 283
New Zealand, central bank of, 338, 358
Nicaragua, hyperinflation in, 342
Nigeria, GNI per capita, 162
NNP. *See* Net national product (NNP)
Nominal GDP, 101–102, 109–111
Nominal interest rate, 258–260, 320, 331
Nominal value, 41
Nominal wages, 330
Nondurable goods, 379
Nonlinear relationships, graphing, 22–23
Normal good, 79, 81
Normative analysis, 3–4
North American Free Trade Agreement (NAFTA), 364, 375
Norway, 162

O

Obama, Barack, 219
Obama administration, fiscal stimulus of, 218–219, 237, 349
Obstfeld, Maurice, 163
Offshoring, 54
Ohanian, Lee E., 151
Oil industry, 67
Oil prices, 148–149, 297
Oil supply disruptions, 199
Okun, Arthur, 186
Olken, Benjamin, 164

Online games, market exchange and, 38
Open economy, 154
crowding out in, 154
equilibrium output in, 241–242
Open market operations, 295–296, 300
Open market purchases, 295
Open market sales, 295
Opportunity cost, 29, 50
of college degree, 29–30
crowding out and, 152–153
of holding money, 292–293
of military spending, 30–31
production possibilities curve and, 31–33
productivity and, 50, 55
of running a business, 33
Opportunity cost principle, 153, 215, 237, 256, 292, 351, 365
Ostry, Jonathan, 165
Oswald, Andrew, 109
Output
determining long-run, 196–197
dividing among competing demands for GDP, at full employment, 151–155
equilibrium, 224–227
full-employment, 146–148
interest rates and, 301–303
potential, 146–148
relationship between labor and, 141–142
short-run determination of, 187–188
taxes and, 147–148
Outside lags, 208–210, 305–306
Outsourcing, 54, 379–380
Owner's equity, 277

P

Pakistan
economic growth in, 164
GNI per capita, 162, 163
price structures in, 162
Participatory institutions, 174
Part-time employment, 123
Patents, 56, 172
Patinkin, Don, 325
Peak, 112
Pecan prices, 82
Per capita incomes, 162–164
Percentage changes, computing, 23–25
Perfectly competitive markets, 68, 75
Permanent income, 218
Personal disposable income, 107
Personal income, 107
Peru, lack of property rights in, 177
Phelps, Edmund, 333
Phillips, A.W., 333
Physical capital, 2
Pie graphs, 15
Pinkovskiy, Maxis, 159
Piracy, 172–173
Planned expenditures, 225
Point of diminishing return, 39, 167
Political business cycles, 318
Political institutions, affect on economic growth of, 174
Political parties, 318
Pollution, 59–60
GDP and, 114–115
Poor, impact of tariffs on, 372
Poor countries. *See* Developing countries
Population, decreases in, 82
Population growth, capital deepening and, 167
Population increases, 80
Positive analysis, 3–4
Positive relationship, 19
Potential output, 146
taxes and, 147–148
Poverty, 1
in Africa, 5–6, 159
Present value, 256–257
interest rates and, 256–257
Presidential elections, 318
Presidential popularity, economic conditions and, 98
Price ceiling, 77
Price discrimination, 377
Price flexibility, full employment and, 140
Price floor, 78
Price level
determining long-run, 196–197
money demand and, 292–293
Price-level targeting, 357
Prices
adjustment over time in, 312–314
auction, 186
changes in demand and, 90
of complementary goods, 80
custom, 186
decreases in, 90
demand schedule and, 68–69
equilibrium, 80–82, 85–89
excess demand and, 76–77
excess supply and, 77–78
expectations of higher, 80
expectations of lower, 82
flexible, 186–187
full employment and, 314–318
inflation and, 132–134
input, 187, 197–198
in market economy, 57
minimum supply price, 73
problems in measuring changes in, 131
retail, 188
scarcity and, 57
sticky, 186–187, 188
of substitutes, 80
supply schedule and, 72
trade and, 379
wages and, 312–314
Prisoner of war (POW) camps, emergence of markets in, 58
Private investment expenditures, 102, 103–104
Problem solving, economic analysis and, 5–7
Procyclical, 254
Production, 98–99
circular flow of, 99–100
factors of, 2, 140–141
Production facilities, sharing, and diminishing returns, 39
Production function, 140–143, 146
Production possibilities curve, 31, 160–161, 365–367
opportunity cost and, 31–33
scarcity and, 31
shifting the, 32
Productivity
increased, from specialization, 53
labor, 171
opportunity cost and, 50, 55
Property rights, 176–177
Prosperity, 1
Protectionist policies, 369–374
import bans, 369–370
quotas, 370–371
artionales for, 372–374
responses to, 371–372
tariffs, 371
voluntary export restraints, 370–371

Protestantism, 175
Protests, against free trade, 380
Public goods, 60
Public policies, using microeconomics to evaluate, 12–13
Purchasing power parity, 393

Q

Q-theory of investment, 262
Quantitative easing, 297
Quantity demanded, 68, 78–79
Quantity equation, 340
Quantity supplied, 71–72
Quotas
 import, 370
 vs. tariffs, 371

R

Rabushka, Alvin, 360
Rainforest conservation, 28
Rational expectations, 334, 338
Reagan, Ronald, 98, 205, 218, 335
Reagan administration, fiscal policy during, 218
Real business cycle theory, 148–150
Real exchange rates, 390–393
Real GDP, 101, 102, 109–111
 contributions to growth of, 169
 fluctuations in growth of, 186
Real GDP per capita, 161
Real GNP, 162
Real interest rate, 258–260
Real-nominal principle, 40–42, 101, 129, 189, 258, 292, 313, 319, 331, 390
Real value, 41
Real wages, 41, 143, 330
Recessions, 112
 2007-2009, 112–113, 223
 budget deficits and, 353
 causes of, 195
 economic view of current, 6–7
 reasons for, 185, 186
 returning to full employment after, 314–315
 since WWII, 113
 using economic policy to fight, 317
Redlick, Charles, 233
Repetition, 53
Required reserves, 278
Research and development
 as percentage of GDP, 172
 technological progress and, 172
Reserve Bank of India, 282
Reserve ratio, 278, 279
Reserve requirements, 296
Reserves, 278, 282
Resources, scarcity of, 2
Retail prices, 188
Retained earnings, 261
Revaluation, 400
Revolutionary War debt, 354
Ricardian equivalence, 351–352
Ricardo, David, 324
Risk
 financial intermediaries and, 263–265
 insurance and, 56, 61
 in market economy, 61
Rogoff, Kenneth, 163
Romalis, John, 379
Romer, Paul, 174
Ronaldo, Cristiano, 150
Roosevelt, Franklin, 216, 274
Rule of 70, 161–162
Rules of thumb approach, to predicting inflation, 334
Russia, hyperinflation in, 341–342

S

Saez, Emmanuel, 150
Safety, driving speed and, 36
Sales taxes, 358–361
Sali-i-Martin, Xavier, 159
Samuelson, Paul, 333
Sargent, Thomas J., 339, 354
Savers, 264
Saving, 166–167
 consumption taxes and, 359
 depreciation, capital deepening and, 180–184
 as function of stock of capital, 181–182
 increase in, 182–184
 investment and, 230–231
Savings accounts, 276
Savings and loan crisis, 266
Savings function, 231
Say, Jean-Baptiste, 324
Say's law, 324
Scale of the market, 173
Scarcity, 2
 prices and, 57
 production possibilities curve and, 31
 trade-offs and, 2–3
Schumpeter, Joseph, 172
Seasonal unemployment, 125
Seat belts, marginal principle and, 36
Securitization, 265, 266, 267
Seignorage, 343
Self-interest, 37, 57–58
Self-sufficiency, 37, 50, 51
Sen, Amartya, 97
September 11, 2001, 218, 236, 284
Shoe-leather costs, 134
Shortage, 76–77
Short-run aggregate supply curve, 197–199, 314
Short-run equilibrium, 201
Short run in macroeconomics, 187–188, 224, 312
Simon, Herbert, 334
Six-month treasuries, 259–260
Skilled labor, 380
Slope, of aggregate demand curve, 189–190
Slope of a curve, 19, 73, 75
Smith, Adam, 8–9, 37, 53, 57, 173
Smoot-Hawley Tariff Act, 372
Smoot-Hawley tariffs, 374–375
Smuggling, 372
Soccer players, taxes on, 150
Social insurance taxes, 213
Social safety net, 61
Social Security, 210, 212, 213
 cost-of-living adjustments, 131
 real-nominal principle and, 41
Solow, Robert, 169, 180, 333, 385
South Korea, 403
Sovereign investment fund, 397
Spam, 10
Specialization
 benefits of, 365–369
 gains from trade and, 50–52
 increased productivity and, 53
 rationale for, 55
 voluntary exchange and, 37, 38
Speculation, in oil markets, 199
Speculative demand for money, 295
Speed, marginal principle and, 36
Spigel, Mark, 337
Stabilization policies, 208–210, 317, 356
Stagflation, 199–200
Standard of living. *See* Living standards
State government, federal government and, 354

Steady state
  growth rate of money and, 331–332
  inflation in, 330–331
Steel tariffs, 372
Sticky prices, 186–187, 188
Stiglitz, Joseph, 97, 403
Stockman, David, 348
Stock market, investment and, 261–263
Stock of capital, 141, 142–143, 180–184, 254
Store of value, 274
Structural unemployment, 126, 140
Student loans, inflation and cost of repaying, 42
Subprime mortgage crisis, 267
Subprime mortgages, 266, 285, 291, 357
Sub-Saharan Africa, 1, 5–6, 176
Subsidized firms, 374
Substitutes, 70, 80, 81
Summers, Robert, 162
Supply
  aggregate, 196–200
  of capital, 165–166
  currency, 387–390
  decrease in, and equilibrium price, 87
  excess, 77–78
  increase in, and equilibrium price, 85–86
  labor, wages and, 143–145
  law of, 73, 76
  market effects of changes in, 83–89
  of money, 190
  simultaneous changes in demand and, 87–89
Supply curve, 71–76
  aggregate, 314
  decreases in supply and shifts in, 86
  downward shift in, 83
  increase in supply and shifts in, 83–85
  individual, 72–73
  labor, 144, 147–148
  market, 74–75
  movement along, 73
  rightward shift, 83
  slope of, 73, 75
Supply schedule, 72
Supply shocks, 199–200
Supply-side economics, 205, 213–214, 218
Surplus, 77–78
Switzerland, central bank of, 338

T

Tariffs, 364, 371
  history of, 374–375
  impact of, on poor, 372
Tax cuts
  during Bush administration, 218–219, 349
  as economic stimulus, 205
  during Kennedy administration, 205, 217
  in long run, 323–324
  during Reagan administration, 205, 218
Taxes
  1996-2011, 220
  aggregate demand and, 206
  changes in, and aggregate demand curve, 191
  consumption, 358–361
  corporate, 213
  estate, 213
  excise, 213
  flat, 360–361
  gift, 213
  government investment and, 167–168
  income, 212–213, 239–240
  income-expenditure model and, 233–240
  increases in, 324
  potential output and, 147–148
  revenues from, 212–213
  sales, 358–361
  on soccer stars, 150
  social insurance, 213
  value-added, 360–361
  withholding, 213
Tax multiplier, 234–235, 236, 251
Tax rates, 213–214, 239–240, 353
Tax revenues
  economy and, 214
  tax rates and, 214
Tax system, 135
Taylor, John, 219, 356–357
Technological progress, 160
  causes of, 172–175
  economic growth and, 168–171, 180–184
  measuring, 169–170
  new growth theory and, 174–175
Technology, economic fluctuations and, 149–150
Teenagers, unemployment and, 123–124
Temin, Peter, 195
Terms of trade, 367
Thailand, 403
Time-series graph, 16–17
Tobin, James, 262
Total market value, 100
Trade. *See also* Free trade; International trade
  benefits of, 365–369
  capital deepening and, 168
  comparative advantage and terms of, 367
  gains from, and specialization, 50–52
  income inequality and, 379–380
  inequality and, 379
  international, comparative advantage and, 53–54
  policy debates, 376–380
  protectionist policies and, 369–374
  rationale for, 55
Trade agreements, history of, 374–375
Trade balance, 105
Trade deficit, 105, 168, 396–397
Trade laws, environmental protection and, 377–378
Trade sanctions, 364
Trade surplus, 105
  capital deepening and, 168
Traffic congestion
  economic view of, 5
  economic way of thinking about, 9–10
Transaction demand for money, 292–293
Transfer payments, 104, 237
Traveler's checks, 275
Treasury Department, 398
Treasury securities, 294
Troubled Asset Relief Program (TARP), 267
Trough, 112
Truman, Harry S., 3
Tuna fishing, dolphins and, 377–378
Two-variable graphs, 17–19

U

Unanticipated inflation, 134, 135, 333
Underground economy, GDP and, 114
Underwater homes, 263
Unemployed, 121
Unemployed individuals, 123–125
Unemployment, 98, 121–229
  in 2011, 311
  alternative measures of, 122–123

categories of, 125–126
costs of, 128–129
cyclical, 126, 140, 146
disability insurance and, 127
duration of, 128
frictional, 126, 140
during Great Depression, 140, 185
inflation and, 333–336
measurement of, 121–122
natural rate of, 126–128, 146–147, 332, 336
prolonged, 311
seasonal, 125
social norms, happiness, and, 129
statistics on, 123–124
structural, 126, 140
Unemployment insurance, 61, 128–129, 237
Unemployment rate, 121
in 2012, 121–122, 124
in developed countries, 122
Unfair competition, 373–374
United Kingdom
central bank of, 282, 284, 338
GNI per capita, 162
inflation targeting in, 357
United States
annual productivity growth, 1947-2011, 171
consumption and government spending during WWII in, 153–154
consumption of GDP in, 152
exchange rates in, 400–401
fiscal policy in, 216–220
GDP per capita in, 139
GNI per capita, 162
growth rates of GDP, 1871-2011, 238
inflation and unemployment in 1980s, 334–335
investment and government spending during WWII in, 154
investment spending as share of GDP, 255
net international investment position, 396
prosperity in, 1
real GNP, 162
research and development funding in, 172
trade deficit of, 396–397
world trade and, 242–243
Unit of account, 274
Unskilled labor, 380
U.S.-China currency tensions, 392
U.S. dollar
demand and supply of, 387–390
depreciation, 297, 304
government intervention with price of, 398–399
U.S. economy
oil supply disruptions and, 199
world economy and, 242–243
U.S. Treasury bonds, 212, 259–260

V

Value added, 100, 107–108
Value-added tax (VAT), 360–361
Variables, 7
graphs of single, 15–17
graphs of two, 17–19
isolation of, 7–8, 10
negative relationships between, 21–22
nonlinear relationships between, 22–23
VAT. *See* Value-added tax (VAT)
Velocity of money, 340–341
Vertical intercept, 18
Vietnam War era, fiscal policy during, 217–218
Volcker, Paul, 291, 335
Voluntary exchange principle, 37–38, 52, 274
markets and, 37–38
online games and, 38
specialization and, 38
Voluntary export restraint (VER), 370
Voter expectations, 318

W

Wachovia Bank, 266
Wage flexibility, full employment and, 140
Wage-price spiral, 313, 317
Wages
adjustment over time in, 312–314
demand and supply for labor and, 143–145
full employment and, 314–318
inequalities, and outsourcing, 379–380
minimum, 187
nominal, 330
prices and, 312–314
real, 143, 330
real-nominal principle and, 41
sticky, 187
taxes and, 147–148
Wal-Mart, 100, 379
War on terror, 349
Wars, 149
Wealth, autonomous consumption and, 228
Wealth effect, 190, 229
Wealth of Nations (Smith), 53
Weber, Max, 175
Welfare, GDP as measure of, 113–115
Withholding taxes, 213
Women, in labor force, 122
Wool industry, 76
Worker productivity, 55
Workers
discouraged, 123
foreign competition and, 373
marginally attached, 123
skilled, 380
unskilled, 380
Work hours, relationship between income and, 17–18
World Bank, 62, 162, 176
World savings, 396
World Trade Organization (WTO), 375

Y

Yellen, Janet, 297

Z

Zambia, economic growth in, 164
Zambia, GNI per capita, 162
Zimbabwe, hyperinflation in, 343

Applying the Concepts #4: How do you measure the technological revolution?
Application 4: *Growth Accounting and Intangible Capital*
Applying the Concepts #5: How do varying political institutions affect economic growth?
Application 5: *The Role of Political Factors in Economic Growth*
Applying the Concepts #6: Did culture or evolution spark the Industrial Revolution?
Application 6: *Culture, Evolution, and Economic Growth*
Applying the Concepts #7: Why are clear property rights important for economic growth in developing countries?
Application 7: *Lack of Property Rights Hinders Growth in Peru*

Chapter 9 Aggregate Demand and Aggregate Supply

Applying the Concepts #1: What does the behavior of prices in consumer markets demonstrate about how quickly prices adjust in the U.S. economy?
Application 1: *Measuring Price Stickiness in Consumer Markets*
Applying the Concepts #2: How can we determine what factors cause recessions?
Application 2: *Two Approaches to Determining the Causes of Recessions*
Applying the Concepts #3: Are oil price increases caused by true shocks to supply?
Application 3: *Oil Supply Disruptions, Speculation and Supply Shocks*

Chapter 10 Fiscal Policy

Applying the Concepts #1: Why are the United States and many other countries facing dramatically increasing costs for their government programs?
Application 1: *Increasing Life Expectancy and Aging Populations Spur Costs of Entitlement Programs*
Applying the Concepts #2: How are tax rates and tax revenues related?
Application 2: *The Confucius Curve?*
Applying the Concepts #3: Was the fiscal stimulus in 2009 successful?
Application 3: *A Closer Look at the 2009 Stimulus Package*

Chapter 11 The Income-Expenditure Model

Applying the Concepts #1: How do changes in the value of homes affect consumer spending?
Application 1: *Falling Home Prices, the Wealth Effect, and Decreased Consumer Spending*
Applying the Concepts #2: What evidence does the long historical record provide about multipliers?
Application 2: *Using Long-Term Macro Data to Measure Multipliers*
Applying the Concepts #3: How does Keynesian economics change our normal ideas of economic scarcity?
Application 3: *The Broken Window Fallacy and Keynesian Economics*
Applying the Concepts #4: How do countries benefit from growth in their trading partners?
Application 4: *The Locomotive Effect: How Foreign Demand Affects a Country's Output*

Chapter 12 Investment and Financial Markets

Applying the Concepts #1: How Do Fluctuations in Energy Prices Affect Investment Decisions by Firms?
Application 1: *Energy Price Uncertainty Reduces Investment Spending*
Applying the Concepts #2: How can understanding the concept of present value help us evaluate an annuity?
Application 2: *The Value of an Annuity*
Applying the Concepts #3: Is reducing the debt owed on home mortgages a good policy to deal with an ailing housing market?
Application 3: *Debt Forgiveness?*
Applying the Concepts #4: How have recent financial innovations created new risks for the economy?
Application 4: *Securitization: The Good, the Bad, and the Ugly*

Chapter 13 Money and the Banking System

Applying the Concepts #1: How do small Brazilian towns use currency to encourage local commerce?
Application 1: *Money with the Face of Rodents*
Applying the Concepts #2: Why have banks recently started to hold vast amounts of excess reserves?
Application 2: *The Growth in Excess Reserves*
Applying the Concepts #3: How did the Fed manage to keep the financial system in operation immediately following the attacks on September 11, 2001?
Application 3: *The Financial System under Stress: September 11, 2001*
Applying the Concepts #4: How did the Fed successfully respond to the collapse of major financial institutions in 2008?
Application 4: *Coping with the Financial Chaos Caused by the Mortgage Crisis*

Chapter 14 The Federal Reserve and Monetary Policy

Applying the Concepts #1: How has the Fed recently expanded its role in financial markets?
Application 1: *Beyond Purchasing Treasury Securities*
Applying the Concepts #2: What is the link between a dollar depreciation and increases in commodity prices?
Application 2: *Did Fed Policy Cause the Commodity Boom?*
Applying the Concepts #3: Is it better for decisions about monetary policy to be made by a single individual or by a committee?
Application 3: *The Effectiveness of Committees*

Chapter 15 Modern Macroeconomics: From the Short Run to the Long Run

Applying the Concepts #1: Why did Chairman Bernanke change his views on how to fight a liquidity trap?
Application 1: *How to Fight a Liquidity Trap*
Applying the Concepts #2: What are the links between presidential elections and macroeconomic performance?
Application 2: *Elections, Political Parties, and Voter Expectations*
Applying the Concepts #3: Will increases in health-care expenditures crowd out consumption or investment spending?
Application 3: *Increasing Health-Care Expenditures and Crowding Out*

Chapter 16 The Dynamics of Inflation and Unemployment

Applying the Concepts #1: How can data on vacancies and unemployment be used to measure shifts in the natural rate?
Application 1: *Shifts in the Natural Rate of Unemployment*
Applying the Concepts #2: Can changes in the way central banks are governed affect inflation expectations?
Application 2: *Increased Political Independence for the Bank of England Lowered Inflation Expectations*
Applying the Concepts #3: Why do hyperinflations end suddenly?
Application 3: *The Ends of Hyperinflations*

Chapter 17 Macroeconomic Policy Debates

Applying the Concepts #1: Why did the early U.S. federal government take over the debts of the thirteen colonies?
Application 1: *Creating the U.S. Federal Fiscal System through Debt Policy*

Applying the Concepts #2: Did the Federal Reserve cause the housing boom through excessively loose monetary policy?
Application 2: *Would a Policy Rule Have Prevented the Housing Boom?*

Applying the Concepts #3: Can the United States adopt a European-style value-added tax?
Application 3: *Is a VAT in Our Future?*

Chapter 18 International Trade and Public Policy

Applying the Concepts #1: Do tariffs (taxes) on imported goods hurt the poor disproportionately?
Application 1: *The Impact of Tariffs on the Poor*

Applying the Concepts #2: What have been the local effects of Chinese imports?
Application 2: *Chinese Imports and Local Economies*

Applying the Concepts #3: How does the Commerce Department try to determine whether countries are dumping their products?
Application 3: *Are They Really Dumping?*

Applying the Concepts #4: Why might international trade reduce measured inequality in the United States?
Application 4: *Trade, Consumption, and Inequality*

Chapter 19 The World of International Finance

Applying the Concepts #1: How can the price of a Big Mac in China shed light on the U.S.–Chinese currency tensions?
Application 1: *The Chinese Yuan and Big Macs*

Applying the Concepts #2: What factors may allow the United States to continue running large trade deficits with the rest of the world?
Application 2: *World Savings and U.S. Current Account Deficits*

Applying the Concepts #3: What are the fundamental causes for the problems with the euro?
Application 3: *A Troubled Euro*

Applying the Concepts #4: What are the causes of financial collapses that occur throughout the globe?
Application 4: *The Argentine Financial Crisis*

Chapter 20 Elasticity: A Measure of Responsiveness

Applying the Concepts #1: How does the price elasticity of demand vary over time?
Application 1: *A Closer Look at the Elasticity of Demand for Gasoline*

Applying the Concepts #2: How does an increase in price affect total expenditures?
Application 2: *Vanity Plates and the Elasticity of Demand*

Applying the Concepts #3: Will a firm choose a point on the lower half of a linear demand curve?
Application 3: *Trampolines and the Lower Half of a Linear Demand Curve*

Applying the Concepts #4: Where do I find estimates of elasticities of demand?
Application 4: *I Can Find that Elasticity in Four Clicks!*

Applying the Concepts #5: Why is supply more price-elastic in the long run?
Application 5: *The Short-Run and Long-Run Elasticity of Supply of Milk*

Applying the Concepts #6: How does a decrease in supply affect the equilibrium price?
Application 6: *A Broken Pipeline and the Price of Gasoline*

Chapter 21 Market Efficiency and Government Intervention

Applying the Concepts #1: How do we compute consumer surplus?
Application 1: *Consumer Surplus of Internet Service*

Applying the Concepts #2: Why does the market equilibrium maximize the value of a market?
Application 2: *Rent Control and Mismatches*

Applying the Concepts #3: How do price controls affect the market?
Application 3: *Price Controls and the Shrinking Candy Bar*

Applying the Concepts #4: What are the effects of import restrictions?
Application 4: *The Cost of Protecting a Luggage Job*

Applying the Concepts #5: How does a tax cut affect prices?
Application 5: *Response to Lower Taxes in French Restaurants*

Chapter 22 Consumer Choice: Utility Theory and Insights from Neuroscience

Applying the Concepts #1: How does marginal utility change with the quantity consumed?
Application 1: *Measuring Diminishing Marginal Utility*

Applying the Concepts #2: How would a simultaneous increase in the gasoline tax and a decrease in the income tax affect gasoline consumption?
Application 2: *A Revenue-Neutral Gasoline Tax*

Applying the Concepts #3: How do the sales strategies of conventional stores and online retailers differ?
Application 3: *Stores vs. Online Retailers*

Applying the Concepts #4: What is the appropriate cigarette tax?
Application 4: *Taxing Cigarettes to Offset Present Bias*

Chapter 23 Production Technology and Cost

Applying the Concepts #1: What is the opportunity cost of an entrepreneur?
Application 1: *Opportunity Cost and Entrepreneurship*

Applying the Concepts #2: Why is the marginal-cost curve positively sloped?
Application 2: *Idle Capital and Short-Run Marginal Cost*

Applying the Concepts #3: How do indivisible inputs affect production costs?
Application 3: *Indivisible Inputs and the Cost of Fake Killer Whales*

Chapter 24 Perfect Competition

Applying the Concepts #1: How do entry costs affect the number of firms in a market?
Application 1: *Wireless Women in Pakistan*

Applying the Concepts #2: What is the break-even price?
Application 2: *The Break-Even Price for Switchgrass, a Feedstock for Biofuel*

Applying the Concepts #3: What is the shutdown price?
Application 3: *Straddling the Zinc Cost Curve*

Applying the Concepts #4: Why is the short-run supply curve positively sloped?
Application 4: *Short-Run Supply Curve for Cargo*

Applying the Concepts #5: How do producers respond to an increase in price?
Application 5: *Chinese Coffee Growers Obey the Law of Supply*

Applying the Concepts #6: Why is the time path of market prices after an increase in demand?
Application 6: *The Upward Jump and Downward Slide of Wine Prices*